READER'S ENCYCLOPEDIA® OF EASTERN EUROPEAN LITERATURE

READER'S ENCYCLOPEDIA® OF EASTERN EUROPEAN LITERATURE

Edited by
Robert B. Pynsent

With the Assistance of
S.I. Kanikova

HarperCollins*Publishers*

Library of Congress Cataloging-in-Publication Data

Reader's encyclopedia of Eastern European literature / edited by Robert Pynsent & S.I. Kanikova.
    — 1st ed.
        p.   cm.
    Includes index.
    ISBN 0-06-270007-3
    1. East European literature—Encyclopedias. I. Pynsent, Robert B. II. Kanikova, S. I. (Sonia I.), 1954– .
    PN849.E9R38 1993
    809'.8947'03—dc20   93-2953

93 94 95 96 97 RRD 10 9 8 7 6 5 4 3 2 1

Contents

Preface and Notes for users

The term Eastern Europe is not simply geographical. This Companion covers East European literature, and that is a political designation, for writers of the 'imperial' languages, e.g. Brod, Canetti, Kafka, Werfel, let alone Dostoevski, Pushkin or Tolstoy, are not included. Nor are writers who chose English (Conrad) or French (Moréas, Apollinaire) as their language of literary expression. Eastern Europe indicates those linguistic areas or nation-states which were or considered themselves oppressed by (or, in a 19th-century cliché, under the yoke of) one of the four great European continental empires (Austrian, Prussian, Ottoman and Russian) for anything from fifty to a thousand years. Essentially these cultures were Christian: here Albania is an anomaly, like Bosnia; Yiddish literature is an exception of a different kind: the authors were Jewish, but what they wrote was composed on 'Christian' territory. The 'intellectuals' (producers of literature) of these linguistic areas once felt politically or socially oppressed, usually by Germans, Turks or Russians, but it is more complicated than that. For example, Slovaks felt oppressed by Hungarians and Hungarians by Vienna; or Roumanians felt they were oppressed by Greeks and Greeks by Turks. Whatever one may as an historian think about degrees of oppression, the literature represented in this volume was produced by intellectuals who, at best, felt like the Welsh under the English, at worst, like the Jews under the Nazis or the Armenians under the Turks. The reader will not normally find here E European writers of non-fiction, literary theorists, political writers, historiographers. This volume concentrates on composers of verbal art.

No entry was normally permitted to have more than three works in its registration of translations. This will seem unfair to lovers of particular writers. The advice on further reading was also limited by the editors to three items on a given author or work (in English, French, German or Italian). Some contributors have chosen longer articles on fewer writers, some briefer articles on more writers. The number of entries does not indicate any scale of literary importance. On the other hand, contributors assigned the literature on a linguistic group which has a continuous original literature since the Middle Ages were given more space than those whose linguistic group produced a literature only in the 19th or 20th century. No doubt some apparent unfairness has crept in, but that was not the editors' intention.

The editors have attempted to give some stylistic unity to the volume, without altering individual contributors' expressions of enthusiasm or approaches to literary criticism and history. Contributors were encouraged to express original views as far as it was possible in such limited space. The choice of authors to be included was left entirely up to the contributors, with two provisos. First, any author who, whatever his literary value to a late 20th-century critic, significantly contributed to the development of a given literature should be included. Secondly, any author who has or had an international reputation, however meagre his contribution actually was or is, should be included.

The editors have tried to make the Companion as easy to use as possible. Except in the case of the titles of some periodicals and anthologies (see Abbreviations), all abbreviations used are such as any 'general reader' will recognise. References to literary movements will be explained by consulting Index C. Cross-references are indicated by the fact that a writer's name appearing in an article on another writer or in the brief historical essays is printed in SMALL CAPITALS.

To find all mentions of authors in SMALL CAPITALS, or authors who have no entry of their own, and of authors outside East European literature, all references to movements, groups, trends, periodicals, the user should turn to Index C.

Likewise, any user desiring some comparative view of, say, Romanticism in Eastern Europe should turn first to Index C. By consulting Index A a user may establish which authors were writing in the same or a comparable period.

Index B concerns anonymous and collective works, and adaptations which were important for the development of an individual literature. Two things have to be borne in mind. First, if, say, the Apollonius of Tyre romance does not appear, that indicates only that none of the contributors considered the version of that romance sufficiently important in the assigned literature to merit an entry. Secondly, if for only one literature, say, the Troy Book is entered, that does not mean that other literary traditions do not have a version of the Troy Book. The oral tradition and popular literature have entries for only very few literatures, which does not signify that other literatures had no such traditions. The one unifying aspect to Index B lies in the fact that all contributors were asked to provide a brief account of the history of Bible translation in the linguistic area about which they were writing.

The editors have done everything they could to make the Companion enjoyable as well as informative reading. Reading just the lives, particularly of Yiddish and Balkan writers, provides themes for novels. On the other hand, the reader will find accounts of writers, particularly in the West of E Europe, who appeared to have had stolidly peaceful noble or bourgeois lives. The editors hope that this volume will give some insight into the culture of those Europeans who at some time over the last few hundred years felt themselves cut off from the luckier (??) W Europeans.

Many E Europeans hate being called E Europeans. Two things, however, do unite all the literatures contained in this volume. Whether Finnish or Greek, Armenian or Hungarian, writers thought of 'Europe' as something outside them, at least for some period, in some cases only during the years since Communist take-over – hence the post-1989 'back to Europe' slogan. Secondly, in most of the cultures studied in this volume some sense of a period of suffering or some 'national trauma' lies at the centre of Xness. Some of the 'national cultures' described in this volume did not seriously come into being much before Herder and the Romantics' invention of the notion of nation. One only has to think of what those writers from E Europe who adopted a W language have contributed, especially in the 20th century, to W European literature to see how little it matters in what language one writes: Conrad, Moréas, Tzara, Ionesco . . . let alone Canetti or Kafka.

The editors hope that users will learn as much about 'less-known' literature as they have from putting together this volume. The idea of the Companion came from Mr Malcolm Gerratt at Dent's some time before the collapse of socialism. Most of the tiresome typing and sorting work has been done by Nicola Mooney, Radojka Miljević and Sarah Safraz. Without all of these, even with modern computer technology, the editors would not have been able to compile this volume.

The contributors

ABMcM   Arnold McMillin, Professor of Russian Literature, School of Slavonic and East European Studies, University of London

CFR   Christopher Robinson, Fellow of Christ Church, Oxford

DJD   Dennis Deletant, Senior Lecturer in Roumanian Studies, School of Slavonic and East European Studies, University of London

DR   Donald Rayfield, Professor of Russian and Georgian, Queen Mary and Westfield College, University of London

EB   Endre Bojtár, Research Fellow, Literature Institute, Hungarian Academy of Sciences, Budapest

ECH   Celia Hawkesworth, Senior Lecturer in Serbo-Croat Language and Literature, School of Slavonic and East European Studies, University of London

GCS   Gerald Stone, Fellow of Hertford College, Oxford

GFC   George Cushing, Emeritus Professor of Hungarian Language and Literature in the University of London

GSNL   George Luckyj, Professor Emeritus of Slavic Languages and Literatures at the University of Toronto

HD   Hugh Denman, Lecturer in the Department of Hebrew and Jewish Studies, University College, London

HL   Harry Leeming, Emeritus Reader in Slavonic Philology at the University of London

KB   Karel Brušák, Visiting Lecturer in Czech with Slovak, University of Cambridge

MAB   Michael Branch, Professor of Finnish, School of Slavonic and East European Studies, University of London

MR   Martyn Rady, Lecturer in Central European History, School of Slavonic and East European Studies, University of London

MSz-M   Mihály Szegedy-Maszák, Professor of Comparative Literature, Indiana University, Bloomington

RBP   Robert Pynsent, Professor of Czech and Slovak Literature, School of Slavonic and East European Studies, University of London

RŠ   Rimvydas Šilbajoris, Professor Emeritus of Slavic and East European Languages and Literatures, the Ohio State University

SE   Stanislaw Eile, Senior Lecturer in Polish Language and Literature, School of Slavonic and East European Studies, University of London

ShM   Shpëtim Mema, Senior Librarian, Albanian National Library, Tirana, and Lector of Albanian at the School of Slavonic and East European Studies, University of London

SIK   Sonia Kanikova, Lecturer in Bulgarian Literature, School of Slavonic and East European Studies, University of London

StB   Stanisław Barańczak, Alfred Jurzykowski Professor of Polish Language and Literature, Harvard University

VDM   Vasa Mihailovich, Professor of Slavic Literature, University of North Carolina, Chapel Hill

VM   Vladimír Macura, Deputy Director, Literary Institute, Czechoslovak Academy of Sciences, Prague

VN   Vrej Nersessian, Curator Christian Middle East, the British Library, London

Abbreviations

AMSL	*Anthology of Modern Slavonic Literature in Prose and Verse*, trans. by P. Selver (London, New York, 1919)
AMYL	*An Anthology of Modern Yiddish Literature*, ed. J. Leftwich (The Hague, 1974)
AMYP	*An Anthology of Modern Yugoslav Poetry in English*, trans. and ed. with an introd. by J. Lavrin (London, Ljubljana, 1962)
AOH	*Ashes out of Hope, Fiction by Soviet-Yiddish Writers*, ed. I. Howe & E. Greenberg (New York, 1977)
AYP	*American Yiddish Poetry, a Bilingual Anthology*, ed. B. and B. Harshav (Berkeley, Los Angeles, London 1986)
GWJF	*Yenne Velt, The Great Works of Jewish Fantasy & Occult*, 2 vols, ed. J. Neugroschel (New York, 1976)
GYP	*The Dybbuk and Other Great Yiddish Plays*, trans. and ed. J. C. Landis (New York, Toronto, London, 1976)
IYL	*Introduction to Yugoslav Literature*, ed. B. Mikasinovich *et al.* (New York, 1973)
Liptzin (1963)	S. Liptzin, *The Flowering of Yiddish Literature* (New York, London, 1963)
Liptzin (1970)	S. Liptzin, *The Maturing of Yiddish Literature* (New York, 1970)
Liptzin (1972)	S. Liptzin, *A History of Yiddish Literature* (Middle Village, NY, 1972)
LS	*Le Livre slovène* (Ljubljana, 1963)
Madison	A. Madison, *Yiddish Literature, Its Scope and Major Writers* (New York, 1968)
Miron	D. Miron, *A Traveler Disguised: A Study on the Rise of Modern Yiddish Fiction in the Nineteenth Century* (New York, 1973)

MPT	*Modern Poetry in Translation*, No. 8: *Slovenia*, ed. T. Hughes and D. Weissbort (London, 1970)
NWY	*New Writing in Yugoslavia*, ed. B. Johnson (Harmondsworth, 1970)
Parnassus, 1957	*The Parnassus of a Small Nation*, ed. W. K. Matthews and A. Slodnjak (London, 1957)
Parnassus, 1965	*The Parnassus of a Small Nation*, 2nd enl. ed., arranged and introd. by J. Lavrin and A. Slodnjak (Ljubljana, 1965)
PBMYV	*The Penguin Book of Modern Yiddish Verse*, ed. I. Howe, R. Wisse and K. Shmeruk (New York, 1987)
SEEJ	*Slavic and East European Journal*
SEER	*Slavonic and East European Review*
SOYN	*A Shtetl and Other Yiddish Novellas*, ed. R. Wisse (New York, 1973)
SPT	*Slovene Poets of Today*, trans. A. Mackinnon (Ljubljana, 1965)
TYP	*A Treasury of Yiddish Poetry*, ed. I. Howe and E. Greenberg (New York, 1969)
TYS	*A Treasury of Yiddish Stories*, ed. I. Howe and E. Greenberg (New York, 1953, 1973)
VFY	*Voices from the Yiddish*, ed. I. Howe and E. Greenberg (Ann Arbor, 1972; New York, 1975)
WdSl	*Die Welt der Slaven*
Wiener	L. Wiener, *The History of Yiddish Literature in the Nineteenth Century* (New York, 1975)
WWT	*The Way We Think, Anthology of Essays*, 2 vols, ed. J. Leftwich (South Brunswick, NY, London, 1969)
ZfS	*Zeitschrift für Slawistik*

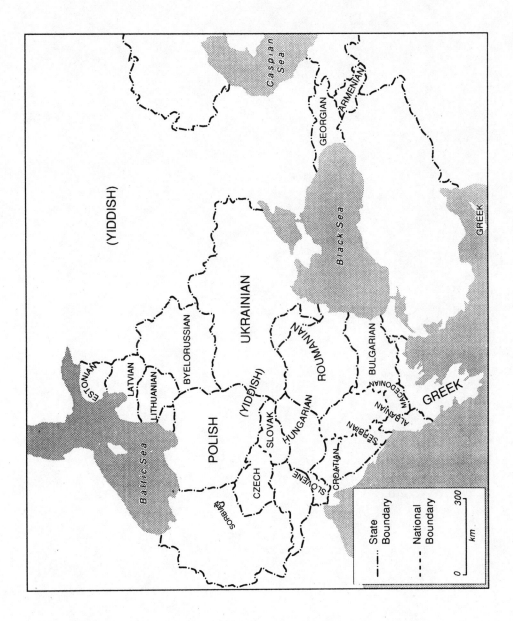

(YIDDISH)

ESTONIAN

LATVIAN

LITHUANIAN

BYELORUSSIAN

UKRAINIAN

POLISH

(YIDDISH)

CZECH

SLOVAK

SORBIAN

HUNGARIAN

SLOVENE

CROATIAN

SERBIAN

ROUMANIAN

BULGARIAN

MACEDONIAN

ALBANIAN

GREEK

GREEK

GEORGIAN

ARMENIAN

Baltic Sea

Caspian Sea

Black Sea

— · — · —	State Boundary
– – – – –	National Boundary

300

km

0

Historical introduction

The history of E Europe rests on its geography. The region lies between the Russian steppeland and the more clement climes of continental Europe, and it has long acted as a corridor through which invaders have passed. In the 5th and 6th centuries, E Europe was overrun by the nomadic Huns and Avars. Despite the havoc caused by their irruption, neither tribe left an enduring mark on the region: 'They have vanished like the Avars' was a saying among the Franks.

Other newcomers left a more permanent trace. During the 6th and 7th centuries, Slav tribes established petty principalities in the lands of present-day Poland, eastern Germany, Bohemia, Croatia and Serbia. The home of the Slavs remains to this day uncertain, but most probably it was in an area to the north of the Carpathians. Between the 7th and 9th centuries Turkic warriors belonging to the Asiatic Bulgar and Onogur tribes founded the Bulgarian and Hungarian khanates in E Europe. Both groups were rapidly assimilated by the larger nations of Slavs and Magyars over which they ruled. The Magyars, whose early home was in central Siberia, had previously migrated to the west of the Urals, where they had fallen under Onogur rule. The Magyars speak a language distantly related to that of the Finns, Lapps and Estonians.

The conversion of E Europe, which took place in the last two centuries of the millennium, was accomplished by emissaries of the Pope in Rome and of the Patriarch in Constantinople. The most notable evangelists were the Byzantine monks, Cyril and Methodius, who traversed E Europe in the late 9th century. Cyril and Methodius are reputed to have brought Christianity not only to the Bulgarians but also to the Slavs living in the Great Moravian Empire (which included a part of present-day Bohemia). They devised the Glagolitic script, the forerunner of Cyrillic. The Orthodox Slavonic liturgy was composed in Cyrillic characters and so this alphabet came to predominate in a large part of E Europe. For political reasons, however, the rulers of the Great Moravian Empire, Hungary, Croatia and Poland embraced the Roman Catholic faith. The Balkans remained for the most part Orthodox, owing a loose spiritual allegiance to the Patriarch in Constantinople, head of the Byzantine Greek Church.

Farther to the east, the Armenian and Georgian Churches had their own alphabets and liturgies. The Armenian Church adhered, however, to a mild version of Monophysitism, which was a Christological heresy condemned in the 5th century. Armenia was also the home of Paulicianism, which taught that the material world was created by Satan. This heresy spread to the Balkans, where it strongly influenced the formation of Bogomilism, and later affected communities in southern France, Italy, Hungary and Bohemia.

With the Mongol invasion of the mid-13th century, E Europe experienced a fresh onslaught from the steppeland. The depredations of the Mongols may well have claimed the lives of half the population of Hungary. The Mongols also invaded Georgia on several occasions and their irruption fatally weakened the kingdom, leaving it an easy prey for the Ottoman Turks. Throughout the late medieval and early modern period, the Tatar descendants of the Mongols practised continual warfare against Armenia, Poland, Hungary and the Roumanian principalities. They were frequently assisted in their campaigns by the warrior communities of Cossacks established on the steppeland of the Ukraine.

During the 13th and 14th centuries, the first Gipsies crossed into the Balkans from Anatolia. As former subjects of the E Roman or Byzantine emperor, the Gipsies called themselves 'Roma', but their real place of origin was the Punjab. The pagan beliefs and rituals of the Gipsies, as well as their dark complexion, singled them out for persecution. In Asia Minor, the double pressure exerted by the Byzantine emperors and the Seljüki Turks (or Saracens) resulted in the movement of Armenians from the Anatolian interior to the Mediterranean coast and in the subsequent formation of the Cilician Armenian kingdom.

The pattern of migration was not just from east to west. The passage of the crusaders through Germany was attended by an unprecedented series of pogroms and massacres, which sent a flood of Jewish refugees into the lands of present-day Poland and the Ukraine. These Ashkenazi Jews were speakers of form of Middle High-German, Yiddish, which is written in Hebrew characters. The Ashkenazi are to be distinguished from the Ladino-speaking Sephardic Jews, who entered the region later having been driven out of the Iberian peninsula by the Inquisition.

In the 12th and 13th centuries, the pressure of population in W Europe resulted in a new movement of peoples to the still sparsely inhabited lands of E Europe. Although accompanied by Frenchmen and Italians, the majority of the newcomers were of German stock. In time, the Germans would forget the circumstances of their migration into E Europe and would believe themselves to be descended either from an ancient Germanic tribe or, in Transylvania, from the children kidnapped in legend by the Pied Piper.

The majority of German settlers were free peasants, organised into their own villages. They were later joined by German merchants and craftsmen, who became citizens in the region's nascent urban communities. Along the Baltic shore, however, the eastward movement of Germans assumed a more violent course. The Teutonic Knights, a crusading order transplanted into E Europe during the 13th century, set about the forcible conversion of the pagan Prussians and Lithuanians. Service with the Teutonic Order was considered a valuable training for warriors from across Europe, including both Chaucer's knight and the future Henry IV of England. While the Prussians perished at the hands of the Order, the Lithuanians found safety in baptism and in the union of their own state with the Polish kingdom.

The pattern of migration and settlement resulted both in the fragmentation of peoples and in the creation of a large number of small and medium-sized kingdoms. Dynastic intermarriage often created the illusion that large blocks of territory owed allegiance to a single ruler. Biological failure within the royal house and domestic conflict frequently led to the disintegration of an inheritance into its smaller components. Throughout the medieval period, the fluctuating fortune of the Bagratid dynasty in Georgia led to a relentless pattern of territorial dissolution and reconsolidation. In continental Europe, the Angevin union of Hungary and Poland fell apart in the 1380s, the Luxemburg inheritance in Bohemia and Hungary perished in the 1430s, and the hegemony of the Polish Jagellons over Poland and Bohemia ended in the early 16th century. Four centuries later, the same process of disintegration would attend the fall of the Habsburg dynasty.

Frequent changes of dynasty contributed to an overall weakening of central authority. The nobility of E Europe exploited the *interregna* to extract political concessions and to curtail the power of the ruler. Noblemen dominated the parliaments (diets or estates) of Poland, Bohemia and Hungary and treated with the king as an equal. By 1500, the representatives of the Bohemian nobility had taken over all the most important government offices and they forced the king to agree never to reduce their rights. In Poland, the nobles retained the right to elect their king. Although the influence of the boyars in the Balkan kingdoms was never so express, their powers were as real and as sharply exercised.

The growth of the political power of the nobility was reflected in social and economic institutions. During the later Middle Ages, the nobility began to increase their power over the peasantry and to compel them into a condition of bondage. The peasantry were gradually tied to the soil and obliged to work four or five days a week on their lord's private land. Whereas the period of the 14th and 15th centuries saw the emergence in W Europe of a largely free peasantry, in much of E Europe the very reverse occurred. The institution of serfdom, which lasted until the 19th century, hindered the prosperity of the region and condemned the economy of E Europe to lag behind the West.

Peasant dissatisfaction frequently spilled over into outbreaks of revolt, all of which were savagely suppressed. It also contributed to the efflorescence of heretical movements, for countryfolk frequently interpreted their plight by reference to their religious beliefs. During the 15th century, the Bohemian Hussite movement, a forerunner of Protestantism, attracted widespread popular support. Hussitism also affected Hungary and parts of the Balkans, and was infused with older heresies which had previously taken root in the region. During the 16th century, the E European lands of Catholic Christendom provided a fertile ground for the Protestant movement, which captured a substantial popular following in Bohemia, Moravia, Poland and Hungary.

The fragmentation of political power left the region exposed to foreign conquest. In the 14th century, the Ottoman Turks began to occupy parts of E Europe. Bulgaria, Bosnia, Serbia and the territories belonging to the Byzantine Empire rapidly fell to the Ottoman advance. The Roumanian principalities of Moldavia and Wallachia were converted into tributary states of the Sultan. Owing to Persian intervention, Georgia and Armenia were occupied only partly.

In 1453, the Turks took Constantinople, which by this time was almost all that was left of the Byzantine Empire. Part of the Greek population of the city fled and joined older Greek communities settled on the Mediterranean coast and in Asia Minor. Others established new centres of the Greek diaspora in London, Venice, Marseilles, Vienna and Odessa. Among those Greeks who remained behind in Constantinople, one small group known as the Phanariots (so named because they dwelled in the *phanar* or lighthouse district of the city) acquired significant wealth and power in the service of the Sultan.

In 1526 Sultan Suleiman the Magnificent defeated the Hungarian army at the Battle of Mohács and killed the King of Bohemia and Hungary. The Turks subsequently occupied the central portion of the Hungarian kingdom. The Turkish conquest of Hungary coincided with the expansion of the Austrian Habsburg dynasty into Eastern Europe. Following the Battle of Mohács, the Austrian archduke, Ferdinand, was appointed King of Hungary and Bohemia. His descendants ruled the region in an unbroken line for four centuries. The principal concerns of Ferdinand and of his immediate successors were to defend their new acquisitions from the Turks and to ensure religious conformity among their subjects.

The Habsburgs were a Roman Catholic dynasty, committed to the promotion of the faith. In this regard, their most signal achievement was the defeat of Protestantism in Bohemia and Moravia, which they accomplished at the Battle of the White Mountain (1620). Following their victory, the Habsburgs trimmed the powers of the Czech nobility and confiscated the properties of all those who would not embrace Catholicism. In Hungary, however, the Habsburgs were unable to achieve the same triumph. The Protestant principality of Transylvania, established in the mid-16th century, provided a counterweight to Habsburg power and impeded the progress of the Counter-Reformation in Hungary.

Habsburg support of the Counter-Reformation made itself felt as much in literature and learning as in warfare. The courts of E Europe had participated in the rediscovery of Classical knowledge during the Renaissance. One of the earliest schools of Humanist learning had been established in Prague during the reign of Charles IV (1346–78), and one of the finest libraries had been founded at Buda under King Matthias Corvinus of Hungary (1458–90). The Habsburg rulers exploited these traditions in the service of the Church. During the 16th and 17th centuries, eminent scholars were employed to refute the central tenets of Protestant belief and to produce a new corpus of Roman Catholic devotional literature. Universities and seminaries were established as springboards for the propagation of belief, and the art and architecture of the Baroque set out to glorify the faith.

The countries bordering the Baltic Sea were less troubled by Habsburg and Turkish expansion than by Swedish and Russian. During the reign of Ivan III (1462–1505), the tsardom of Muscovy had extended its sway into Byelorussia (previously a part of Lithuania) and had obtained an outlet to the Baltic Sea. With the decline of the Teutonic Order in the 16th century, the lands of Livonia (modern-day Latvia and Estonia) were partitioned between Russia and Sweden, which was at that time the premier power in the Baltic. The eventual defeat of Sweden by the armies of Peter the Great in the Northern War (1700–21) resulted in Russia capturing all the lands on the E Baltic shore. Finland, a Swedish possession, was subsequently also incorporated in the Russian Empire.

During the 18th century, Russian influence over Poland grew substantially and the elected kings of Poland were frequently the nominees of the tsar and tsarina. Between 1772 and 1795, Poland was partitioned by her neighbours. Russia obtained the largest share of the spoils and now took possession of the entirety of the Ukraine. The advent of Russian rule led to a period of considerable suffering for the Jews of Poland.

By the close of the 18th century, no more independent states were left in E Europe. Poland had been divided up by its neighbours; the Bohemian Lands and Hungary had been incorporated in the Habsburg Monarchy; and the Balkan peninsula was under Ottoman suzerainty. For their part, Georgia and Armenia still lay under Turkish and Persian rule. Russian interest in these two countries led, however, to their incorporation in the Tsarist Empire during the reign of Nicholas I (1825–55).

During the late 18th and 19th centuries, a belief in the principle of nationhood arose. In E Europe, national identity was closely identified with language. Because so many different dialects prevailed, the standardisation of the language was considered a precondition of nationhood. In Greece and Armenia, standardisation involved replacing the old literary language with the vernacular as the vehicle of the written word. In Armenia, this process was pioneered by an Armenian scholar working in the University of Dorpat (Tartu) in Estonia. In Croatia and Serbia and among the Slovenes and Slovaks, standardisation was achieved by promoting a single dialect to the status of a national language. Among the Sorbs of Saxony, however, full standardisation came about only after World War II.

The newly codified languages were broadcast through educational institutions and the press. A similar sense of common identity was inculcated by the teaching of national mythologies and by the publication of folk-tales (most notably, the dubious Finnish *Kalevala*). During the course of the 19th century, the idea of nationhood gained common currency and became infused with demands for political rights resting on the principle of popular sovereignty.

Unsurprisingly, the empires which ruled E Europe refused concessions to the idea of nationhood, for they saw in this idea their own destruction. As a consequence, the imperial powers experienced a succession of national rebellions and uprisings. During the course of the century, Greece, Serbia, the Roumanian principalities and Bulgaria wrested independence from the Turkish sultan. In 1848, there were unsuccessful national uprisings in Bohemia, Hungary and among the Armenian community in Constantinople. The Habsburg Monarchy was sufficiently tolerant, however, to permit various experiments in home rule. The benign and accommodating character of Habsburg government in the late 19th century helped make Vienna and Prague important centres of fin-de-siècle culture, but did not spare the Monarchy its final ruin.

The defeat of the Russian, German, Turkish and Habsburg empires in World War I was followed by the establishment of nation-states in E Europe. Most of these were entirely new creations with only a tenuous link to the past; most also contained large and disaffected minority populations. All proved highly vulnerable to the ambitions of their larger neighbours. In the early 1920s, Soviet Russia reestablished its hold over the Ukraine, Georgia and Armenia. In the next decade, Germany re-emerged as a powerful aggressor in E Europe. Eventually in 1939 the two powers partitioned the region between them and unleashed World War II.

Following the defeat of Nazi Germany, the boundaries of E Europe were largely restored. But the Soviet Union annexed not only the Baltic states, eastern

Poland and parts of Czechoslovakia, Germany and Roumania but also the ideological complexion of the whole region. Although introduced by Soviet tanks, Communism was not perceived at this time as a failed and false creed. Throughout the interwar period the population in most of E Europe had endured poverty, land-hunger and exploitation. Soviet Communism strongly stressed the benefits of rapid industrialisation and the collectivisation of agriculture in the interest of greater efficiency. It promised, therefore, not just a fairer society but a speedy way out of the condition of backwardness present in many E European societies. In the event, Soviet Communism achieved neither; thus it too has shared the Avars' fate.

MR

Authors:
alphabetical entries

A

ABOVYAN, Khatchatour (1809–?48), the founder of Armenian pedagogy and the first to introduce Western principles of education, wrote the first Armenian novel and created the E Armenian literary language. He was born in Kʻanakʻeṙ, a large village N of Yerevan, received his elementary education at the monastery school at Etchmiadzin under the direct supervision of the Catholicos Ephraim (1809–31). After matriculating, 1824, he was sent to the Nersisyan Academy in Tiflis (Tbilisi), which since 1801 had been the centre of Tsarist rule in Caucasia and the focal point of Armenian cultural life in the Russian Empire. He graduated in 1829 and returned to Etchmiadzin as secretary to the Catholicos and was ordained deacon. Here he met Friedrich Parrot of the University of Dorpat (Tartu) who had come to Armenia in search of Noah's Ark, and Abovyan was Parrot's guide and interpreter. Encouraged by Parrot, Abovyan embarked on a 6-year course of study in pedagogy and literature at Dorpat. He returned to Armenia impatient to impart to his countrymen the riches of Western civilisation. But the opposition, and conservative elements in the Armenian community, inside and outside the Church, frustrated his efforts. 1839 he settled in Tiflis where he opened a school. 1845 he returned to Armenia and was appointed the director of a government school in Yerevan. His novel *Verkʻ Hayastani* (The wounds of Armenia: the lamentations of a patriot) written 1841–2 and published in 1858, narrates events that take place in Armenia on the eve of the last Russian war with Persia. Written in the form of a popular epic, its fundamental theme is the triumph of patriotism and of the Armenian sense of national honour over the tyranny of foreign rule. The novel is written in a curious mixture of Realist and Romantic styles, adorned with decorative passages and Oriental elaborations; the action is interrupted by lyrical interpolations and by tiresome didactic sermons. Abovyan's collected works, Yerevan, 1947–61, fill 10 volumes. His earliest works consisted of poems in classical Armenian based on patriotic themes. Later he wrote short stories, essays, plays and fables. On 14 April 1848 Abovyan left home, supposedly on a brief errand, and was never seen or heard of again.

•H. Adjemian, *Khatchadour Abovian et la Renaissance littéraire en Arménie orientale* (Antelias, 1986).   VN

ADY, Endre (1877–1919), Hungarian poet, short-story writer and publicist, was born to a family of almost no property, although his father was descended from a noble family. Ady attended the Piarist grammar school in Nagykároly before he went to the College of the Reformed Church in Zilah, where he started a periodical for which he wrote poems. 1896 he began law studies in the College of the Reformed Church in Debrecen. For four months he was a junior clerk in Temesvár, then returned to Debecen to resume law studies. Soon he left the College and joined the staff of various newspapers. 1900 he accepted a post with a newspaper in Nagyvárad, where he became acquainted with Adél Brüll, a married woman who belonged to the rising Jewish bourgeoisie. 1904 he joined *Budapesti Napló* (Budapest daily). This newspaper sent him to Paris several times during subsequent years. In 1906 his third volume of verse, *Új versek* (New poems), brought him recognition. He became one of the most important contributors of *Nyugat* (West). 1912 he severed his relationship with Adél Brüll. Suffering from syphilis, he was forced to spend much time in hospitals. In April 1914 he went to Csucsa to visit Berta Boncza, who had first written to him at age 16, and the following year they were married. Since he was fatally ill by the time the revolution broke out in October 1918, it would be idle to speculate about his attitude towards the political changes that occurred after WWI. Modernity in Hungarian literature started with Ady's activity. His political radicalism and his outspoken love poetry shocked the contemporary public. He harshly criticised the remnants of feudalism, regarded Dózsa, the leader of a 16th-century peasant uprising, as an exemplary hero, and identified himself with those who rebelled against the Habsburgs. His criticism was also directed against capitalism, and in some poems he went as far as associating himself with the working class. His political message was free of any nationalism; he emphasised the common fate of Hungarians, Slavs and Roumanians. Still, it would be misleading to simplify the political aspects of his poetry. His article *A duk-duk affér* (The Duk-duk affair) is a devastating attack on the superficiality of the liberals associated with *Nyugat*. He became a friend of Oszkár Jászi (1875–1957), the leader of the bourgeois Radicals and the editor of the journal *Huszadik század* (20th century), but he disagreed with him in two respects: he was a pacifist from the beginning of the war and had no naive illusions about the aspirations of some Roumanian leaders. Realising that the poet and publicist Octavian Goga's interest was not in human rights but in the Roumanian occupation of Transylvania, he distanced himself from him. Self-contradictions bound up with a sense of the tragic characterise the best of Ady's poems. The volumes *Vér és arany* (Blood and gold, 1907), *Az Illés szekerén* (On the chariot of Elijah, 1908), *Szeretném, ha szeretnének* (I would love to be loved, 1909), *A Minden-Titkok versei* (The verse of all mysteries, 1909), *A menekülő Élet* (This fugitive life, 1912), *A magunk szerelme* (Love of ourselves, 1913), *Ki látott engem?* (Who has seen me?, 1914) and *A halottak élén* (Leading the dead, 1918) consist of close-knit cycles which make the whole of his poetry much more than the sum of its parts. The highly artificial, *Secession* language of the love poems centred on 'Leda' (Adél Brüll), the prophetic pathos of *A magyar messiások* (The Hungarian messiahs, 1907) and the intentional obscurity of *A fekete zongora* (The black piano, 1907) were replaced by a more Expressionist style in the 1910s. While the political message is quite explicit in the earlier poems, the later stage is characterised by a less subjective tone and greater complexity. *Az eltévedt lovas* (The lost horseman, 1914) concerns both Hungarian history and Europe entering a war. One of his last poems, *Krónikás ének 1918-ból* (A chronicle sung in 1918, 1918) even anticipates the Neoclassicism which dominated European culture in the following period.

●*Poems* (Budapest, 1941); *Poems of Endre Ady* (Buffalo, NY, 1969).
A. Balakian (Ed.), *The Symbolist Movement in the Literature of European Languages* (Budapest, 1982); G. Stade (Ed.), *European Writers: The Twentieth Century*, vol. 9 (New York, 1989), pp. 859–80.   MSz-M

AGAT'ANGEŁOS (5th century ?) was an Armenian historian, and of all the historical works written in classical Armenian, that attributed to Agat'angełos (i.e. Gk, 'the good messenger') is the most complicated. The complication is of two kinds: an attempt to bring order to a group of documents dealing with the Conversion of Armenia by St Gregory the Illuminator (239–325/6 AD), and the political events of the 3rd century. But the text as we have it is not the first witness to these traditions. An earlier Armenian text, now lost, lies behind versions in Greek, Syriac and Arabic. Other versions in Greek,

Arabic and other languages derive from the extant Armenian. No other Armenian literary work was so well known in other Christian literatures. The History begins with the establishment of Sasanian power in Iran in AD 224. The Armenian King Khosrov, who was related to the rival Parthian dynasty, was deposed. Khosrov's death provides the opportunity for the emergence of Trdat, who is later to become the first Christian king of Armenia, and of Gregory the Illuminator. The political events from the Sasanian revolution (224) to the conversion of Trdat (287–330) is the primary theme of this work. Although the 'History of the Armenians' has diverse origins, a certain unity of style rather than composition reflects the literary interests of 5th-century Armenian scholars. The influence of biblical terminology and imagery is all-pervasive. The wide theological learning of the author is also evident from the complex document known as the 'Teaching of St Gregory' as well as the 'Catecheses' of Cyril of Jerusalem, the 'Hexaemeron' of Basil of Caesarea, the biblical commentaries of John Chrysostom and the homilies of Ephrem the Syrian. Over thirty manuscripts have survived, the earliest of which dates from the 12th century, but several earlier fragments have been found. The longest is a palimpsest in the Mekhitarist Library at Vienna, which was edited and published by G. Galemk'èarian in *Hushardjan* (Vienna, 1911). The first printing of Agat'angełos was 1709, Constantinople.

●*Agat'angelay Patmut'iwn Hayots* (History of Armenia by Agathangelos), ed. G. T. Mkrtchyan and S. Kanayants (Tiflis, 1909); facsimile reproduction of the 1909 Tiflis ed. with an introduction by R. W. Thomson (New York, 1980); *History of the Armenians*, trans. and commentary by R. W. Thomson (New York, 1976); R. W. Thomson, *The Teaching of Saint Gregory: An Early Armenian Catechism* (Cambridge, Mass. 1970).   VN

AGOLLI, Dritëro (b. 1931), Albanian poet and prose writer, born into a peasant family in Mekulas in the Devoll region, 1952 went to the Faculty of Arts at Leningrad. Agolli worked for fifteen years as a journalist and 1973 became president of the Albanian Union of Writers and Artists. His first work was the collection of verse *Në rrugë dolla* (I went out on the street, 1958), followed by, e.g., *Shtigje malesh dhe trotuare* (Mountain paths and pavements, 1965) or the narrative poem *Devoll, Devoll* (1964). His best-known long poem is perhaps *Nënë Shqipëri* (Mother Albania, 1974), written for the 30th anniversary of the liberation which had a print-run of over 100,000 copies. It was followed by the collections *Të pagjumët* (The insomniacs, 1980) and *Udhëtoj i menduar* (I travel pensively, 1985). A bard of the soil, Agolli is the most popular contemporary Albanian poet. His verse manifests his love for his homeland, affection for the ordinary people and respect for their struggle for a better life. Among Agolli's novels are *Komisari Memo* (Commissar M., 1970), episodes from the War of Liberation, *Shkëlqimi dhe rënia e shokut Zylo* (The splendour and fall of comrade Z., 1973), a powerful satire on conformism, servility and vanity, evident in the everyday life of contemporary Albania, and *Njeriu me top* (The man with a gun, 1975), again depicting episodes from the War of Liberation.   ShM

AHO, Juhani (i.e. Johannes Brofeldt, 1861–1921), Finnish novelist, essayist and journalist, was throughout his life an influential supporter of the Finnish national cause. The son of a well-to-do pastor, he grew up in Savo, attended Helsinki University and later studied in Paris. In the 1880s he turned to fiction and journalism. In the 1890s as a founder of the *Päivälehti* (Daily paper) newspaper, he was active in the liberal Young Finland movement. During the russification period at the turn of the century he criticised both the Russian and the Finnish authorities in a series of allegorical essays and stories. Aho is one of the outstanding Finnish portrayers of social change. A recurrent theme in his writing is the effect of the new and unfamiliar, be it a mechanical invention, religious beliefs, moral and social values, or political aims. In his early writings his attention focuses on ordinary Finnish country people. Exploring their response, for example, to the introduction of the oil lamp in *Siihen aikaan kun isä lampun osti* (When father bought the lamp, 1883) or the steam locomotive in *Rautatie* (The railway, 1884), Aho encapsulates the encroaching modernisation of Finland. At this time he also began to write his *Lastuja* (Shavings, 1891–1921), brief sketches of social types from all classes. Society's attitudes to women, particularly those of the middle classes and their education, are the subject of a two-part *Bildungsroman*, *Papin tytär* (The pastor's daughter, 1885), and *Papin rouva* (The pastor's wife, 1893). The second novel shifts from a Realism influenced by Ibsen and Bjørnson to the style of Daudet and the Decadent aspect of Maupassant as the female protagonist responds to the ideas and moral values introduced into a remote country parsonage from Europe by her husband's one-time student colleague. Set in Paris, *Yksin* (Alone, 1890) was excoriated by the Finnish critics for its exploration of male sexuality which includes a visit to a brothel. At the height of the neo-Romantic period Aho turned to the historical novel. *Panu* (1897), set in 17th-century Savo, examines the struggle between shamanism and Christianity. *Kevät ja takatalvi* (Spring and the return of winter, 1906) takes place in the mid-19th century, in the same location and with the main characters descendants of those in *Panu*. This powerful allegorical novel is concerned with the crisis of national identity brought about on the one hand by the struggle between the established liberal Church and the new intolerant anti-intellectual pietism, and on the other between those who are seeking a new national culture, symbolised by folklore collection, and those resistant to any social and political change. Aho's last major novel returns to one of his earlier plots, the triangle of husband-wife-outsider. *Juha* (1912), superficially typical of the Karelian 'romanticism' popular in early 20th-century Finland, can be read as a critical study of the conflict between Finnish and Karelian culture.

●*Squire Hellman and Other Stories* (London, 1893); I. Väänänen-Jensen and K. B. Vähämäki (Eds), *Finnish Short Stories* (New York Mills, 1982), pp. 14–34.   MAB

AISTIS, Jonas (i.e. J. Aleksandravičius, 1904–73), Lithuanian poet, essayist and critic, educated at the universities of Kaunas and Grenoble, spent most of his life abroad, in France, working in the archives of the Paris National Library, and in the United States, teaching at secondary school, then working with the Free Europe Committee and the Library of Congress. Aistis's first collection, *Eilėraščiai* (Poems, 1932), broke with the then prevalent traditions of rhetorical patriotism and of soul-searching, at times rather obscure, Symbolism. Instead Aistis offered new imagery based on unfamiliar, sometimes even jarring, poetic associations, as in the lines describing the colours of sunset: 'wax and blood spread through the sky, through the scabs and wounds'. Such, and similar, imagery produced a highly personal and idiosyncratic poetic world, even though the topics themselves were for the most part conventional enough: love, the fatherland, and the art of poetry. Each of these, while passing through Aistis's imagination, acquired an air of ambiguity, sometimes of self-mockery or hidden despondence. Love might appear to be a mere game, a theatrical performance where pretended suffering could suddenly become real and pierce the heart with fatal pain. Love for one's country often became a form of melancholy, a mournful devotion to her poverty, bleak landscapes and her long, depressive history of subjugation to alien rulers. Finally, poetry might become a mere record of the impossibility of articulating the endless, haunting beauty of one's internal visions. 'The word', wrote Aistis, 'is a blossom wilted in the bud that perishes in transit to the world.' Nevertheless, Aistis's poetic idiom has a fierce intensity that seizes the reader's emotions and remains in the mind. Idiosyncratic personal lyrics began to give way to poems expressing historical and political concerns with Lithuania's fate in the years after 1944, when it became clear that Lithuania had been engulfed by the

Soviet empire. Aistis, however, did not merely lament the tragic destiny of his country – he also scrutinised the nation's own traditions and character, looking for flaws contributing to its fall from the heights it had occupied in medieval history. What he found were petty but fatal vices: envy, backbiting, pugnacity and a certain taste for self-destruction. RŠ

ALECSANDRI, Vasile (1821–90), Roumanian poet and dramatist, son of a rich Moldavian boyar, was sent 1834 to continue his education in Paris where he passed his baccalaureate in 1835. He failed to complete a university education and 1839 returned to Moldavia and was appointed an official in the Ministry of Finance. A year later he became one of three directors of the newly created National Theatre and was induced to create a Roumanian repertory. He began with an adaptation of a French farce and his work as a playwright extended over the next forty years. He moved from farce to comedy, and then on to historical drama. In the 1840s he took a close interest in the oral tradition and travelled throughout Moldavia collecting ballads which he published at his own expense and in 'corrected form' in Paris in 1852. His collection not only gave a 'national' image to Roumanian verse but also, through translation, introduced it to a European audience. His own most accomplished poems are grouped in *Pasteluri* (Pastels, 1875) and portray the Moldavian landscape throughout the seasons. As bard of the union of Moldavia and Wallachia (1859) and of the War of Independence (1877–8) he acquired the status of poet laureate during his lifetime but since then his literary reputation has suffered a continuous depreciation, unable to withstand charges of banality and superficiality.
●A. Cioranescu, *Vasile Alecsandri* (New York, 1973). DJD

ALEXIOU, Elli (1894–1986), Greek prose writer and dramatist, sister of novelist Galateia Kazantzaki (1881–1962, first wife of KAZANTZAKIS), went to Athens (1911), where she got to know the socially progressive writers of the day (including KARKAVITSAS, THEOTOKIS and VARNALIS). She qualified as a teacher (1913) and was sent to the Third Christian Girls' School in Herakleion, where her experiences furnished the material for her first collection of stories (1931) and for her eponymous novel (1934). She joined the Communist Party (1928), and during WWII worked for the left-wing resistance movement EAM (National Liberation Front). 1945 she went to Paris on a French government scholarship to study at the Sorbonne. There she met the leading French Communist intellectuals. 1950 she was deprived of her citizenship and moved to Budapest, which became her base for the next fifteen years. She returned to Greece in 1962 (though her citizenship was restored only in 1965). During the junta she continued her literary and journalistic activities unmolested, but in 1972 the Ministry of the Press and Information refused permission for a production of her play Μιά Μέρα στο Γυμνάο – (A day in the secondary school, publ. 1973). The bulk of her work has been prose fiction. From the socially concerned realism of her early works she moved to a psychological analytical novel, Λούμπεν (Luben, 1940), with a strong feminist element. The fiction of her Bucharest period took a more overtly committed stance, with constant recourse to themes of exile, rootlessness and the struggle for freedom, as in Παραπόταμοι (Tributaries, 1956) and Και ούτω καθεξής (And so on, 1965). The inherent idealism of her writing is at its most evident in Δεσποζουσα (The dominant, 1972), which breaks with standard narrative form, presenting what is in essence a debate between a multiplicity of young middle-class characters faced with the changed values of contemporary Athenian society.   CFR

ALUNĀNS, Juris (1832–64), Latvian poet, journalist, translator, son of a rich tenant-farmer, 1856–61 studied at Tartu and St Petersburg. From 1862 he was editor of *Pētersburgas avīzes*, organ of the New Latvia movement, the first nationalist Latvian paper. He was one of the creators of the Latvian literary language and the first authoritative Latvian poet. As a language reformer, he invented many new words and cleansed Latvian of germanisms. The merit of his only book of poetry, *Dziesminas* (Songs, 1856), in which translations and adaptations are in the majority, is not so much aesthetic as in its being innovative in language. His three-volume *Sēta, daba, pasaule* (Around our house, Nature and the cosmos, 1859–60) is an encyclopaedic work containing verse, folk poetry and translations.   EB

ALVER, Betti (1906–89), Estonian poet and prose writer, daughter of a railway worker, who, after her matriculation (1924), began to read Estonian at Tartu, left her studies in 1927 to devote herself entirely to writing. 1937 she married the poet Heiti Talvik (1904–47). After his arrest by the Soviet security services and his death in exile, and as a result of the campaign against 'decadence and cosmopolitanism', Alver was unable to contribute to literary life until the mid-1960s, and even then she kept away from the Writers' Union and refused to compromise in her poetry. Her death during the Estonian 'Singing Revolution' stimulated a demonstration of Estonian national unity. Her first work was the novel *Tuulearmuke* (The wind's darling, 1927), which she wrote while still a schoolgirl, but in the 1930s she decided to devote herself to verse and became a member of the group of poets who were represented in the 1938 programmatic anthology *Arbujad* (Logomancers). Within this programme, Alver saw art as a counterbalance to the social and political uncertainties of life just before WWII and evolved a dramatic conception of art as a romantic, rebellious gesture which combined pathos with parody. The vehicle for this paradox was a lyric heroine whose approach swayed between expression of the Absolute and ostentatious epicurism, Symbolist pose and self-irony. This type of literary mask had already been evident in her Oneginesque verse novel *Lugu valgest varesest* (Story of a rare bird, 1931) and was fully formed by the collection of lyric verse *Tolm ja tuli* (Powder and fire, 1936). A selection of her verse, *Luuletused ja poeemid* (Lyric and narrative poems, 1956), was brought out in Stockholm. When she began publishing in Estonia again her verse manifested a diminishment of neo-Romantic stylisation, an emphasis on the moral aspect of the poet's role in society, the close connection between literary expression and an uncompromising statement of human values. That is to be seen in her collections, *Tähetund* (Star hour, 1966), *Eluhelbed* (Flakes of life, 1971), *Tuju* (Mood, 1976), *Lendav* linn (Flying city, 1979) and *Korallid Emajões* (Corals in the River Emajõgi, 1986).

●Selections in E. H. Harris, *Literature in Estonia* (London, 1943) and W. K. Matthews (Ed.), *An Anthology of Modern Estonian Poetry* (Gainesville, 1953).
I. Ivask, *Books Abroad*, 41 (1967), 4, pp. 493–4; I. Ivask, *World Literature Today*, 54 (1980), 4, pp. 670–1; A. Aspel, *Books Abroad*, 43 (1969), 1, pp. 46–50.   VM

AMADE, László (1704–64), Hungarian poet, enjoyed all the privileges of a rich and aristocratic youth and graduated from the University of Graz in 1727. Thereafter he led a chaotic life. His flirtatious escapades as an army officer gave way to quarrels with his parents and endless lawsuits as he struggled with his mounting debts. Very little of this emerges from his verse, which he began to write in his youth. He was both musical and a good dancer, and his knowledge of Italian and German light verse led him to introduce new rhythms into his own work. This consists mainly of love poems of dazzling virtuosity but little depth. A handful of poems in Latin and German reveal the same lightness of touch. Like BALASSI, with whose religious verse he was familiar, he had moments of remorse and wrote penitential poems and a few attractive hymns which became popular in his lifetime. Amade's poetry quickly escaped from the aristocratic salon to the wayside inn, where peasants danced to his rhythms and adapted his words, just as they did a century later with PETŐFI. Many examples of so-called folk poetry collected in the following century can be traced to him.

●Excerpts in W. Kirkconnell (Ed.), *Hungarian Helicon* (Calgary, 1985). GFC

AMIREJIBI, Ch'abua [Mzech'a-buk'] (b. 1921), Georgian novelist, began late with the short stories of *Gza* (The road, 1962). He achieved fame with one substantial novel, *Data Tutashkhia* (1973–5). Like many Georgian novels it is the story of an outlaw and folk hero, Data Tutashkhia, but it achieves narrative tension and interesting ambiguities by having a gendarme for a narrator. It is a thriller and a spy novel, with justified Dostoevskian pretensions to dealing with the fate of an individual and national soul. The hero is modelled on the pagan god Tutashkha, one of several Promethean prototypes in the Georgian pantheon. Despite writing an historical novel ending with the 1917 Revolution and paying lip service to Soviet affirmative canons, Amirejibi won popularity by combining national mythology with a covert defence of free spirit. Since 1978 he has been writing a second novel based on his experiences as an escaped prisoner in Siberia.

●*Data Tutashkhia* (Moscow, 1985).
G. Blankoff-Scarr, 'Deux écrivains géorgiens' in *Quatre écrivains de la littérature soviétique multinationale* (Brussels, 1987); Giuli Lezhava, 'Mythological Aspects in . . . Chabua Amiradjibi's [*sic*] Data Tutashkia' in R. B. Pynsent (Ed.), *Modern Slovak Prose Fiction since 1954* (London, 1990), pp. 143–51.   DR

ANAGNOSTAKIS, Manolis (b. 1925), Greek poet whose Communist sympathies manifested themselves early, during the Occupation enrolled in a youth movement which was a branch of EAM (the left-wing resistance movement). Then, while studying medicine at Thessaloniki, he became involved in the running of Ξεκίνημα, a publication of the University Cultural Society which expressed pro-left-wing views. Eventually he took part in the Civil War on the Communist side, and was sentenced to death in 1948. The sentence was commuted to three years' imprisonment, and he was duly released in 1951. He then completed his medical studies, and his subsequent medical career has given him opportunities for foreign travel. For a long time he was an overt sympathiser with Communist social views but remained outside the Party, criticising the political apparatus and intellectually repressive policies of Soviet Communism. However, in 1974, and again in 1977, he ran for parliament as a representative of the Greek Communist Party of the Interior, feeling that there had been a sufficient evolution in its attitudes for its policies to coincide with his own beliefs. Over a long period he has interested himself in the problems of social realism, of the relationship of the poet to the ordinary person, and of how to reconcile the need for 'progressive' writing with the need for artistic freedom. His first three collections of poetry, Εποχές I–III (Epochs I–III), appeared during his most intensive period of political activism and subsequent imprisonment (1945–51). Three further collections, Συνέχεια I–III (Continuation I–III), followed in the next decade. Τα Ποιήματα 1941–71 (Poems 1941–1971, 1971) contains the six collections previously published, plus Ο Στοχός (The target), and in 1979 appeared Γο Περιθώρισ '68–'69 (The margin '68–'69). Anagnostakis has also published two retrospective collections of critical articles, Υπέρ και κατά (For and against, 1965) and Αντιδογματικά (Antidogmatically, 1978). The style of his poetry is spare and elliptical,

recalling the verbal manner of CA-VAFY. Unexpected though a comparison of a socially committed poet with an aesthete may be, it is substantiated by the references within Anagnostakis's writing to specific poems of CAVAFY, e.g. 'Νέοll της Σίδωνος 1970' ('Young men of Sidon 1970', in *The Target*).
●*The Target: Selected Poems* (New York, 1980).   CFR

ANDRIĆ, Ivo (1892–1975), Serbian fiction writer, was a native of Bosnia. During WWI he was imprisoned for his participation in the struggle against Austro-Hungarian rule. He studied literature and history in Zagreb, Vienna, Cracow and Graz. Between the wars he was in the diplomatic service in various European capitals; he was the ambassador in Berlin when Germany attacked Yugoslavia. He spent WWII in Belgrade writing his novels. After the war he was recognised as the leading Yugoslav writer, and in 1961 he received the Nobel Prize. Andrić built his reputation for excellence in the 1920s and 1930s by writing short stories about the past and present life of the Bosnians. In the stories he established the basic themes of his entire oeuvre: man's yearning for happiness and his inability to achieve it; love and passion as the main driving forces of human behaviour; and the need for understanding and tolerance between the various ethnic groups living together in Bosnia but often feuding with each other. He would enlarge on these and other themes in his main works, the novels *Na Drini ćuprija* (The bridge on the Drina, 1945), *Travnička hronika* (The chronicle of Travnik, 1945). *Gospodjica* (Miss, 1945) and *Prokleta avlija* (The accursed yard, 1954). In his best work, *Na Drini ćuprija*, he draws a panoramic picture of the history of the bridge that, in its beauty and permanence, reflects the character and destinies of the people living around it. Andrić uses the bridge as a metaphor for the link between races, religions and nationalities, and as a constant reminder of their common roots. *Travnička hronika* is equally epic in proportions and significance, depicting the constant struggle of the Bosnians for survival amid the perfidious play of foreign interests vying for supremacy over the Balkans. And in *Prokleta avlija* he strikes at the insidious practice of totalitarianism. It is through such universal themes, presented in a remarkable artistic fashion, that Andrić has become one of the best writers in contemporary world literature.

●*The Bridge on the Drina* (London and New York, 1959); *Devil's Yard* (New York, 1962; London, 1964); *The Vizier's Elephant* (New York, 1962); *Pasha's Concubine, and Other Tales* (New York, 1968; London, 1969).
E. C. Hawkesworth, *Ivo Andrić: Bridge between East and West* (London, 1984); E. C. Hawkesworth (Ed.), *Ivo Andrić* (London, 1984); R. Minde, *Ivo Andrić. Studien über seine Kunst* (Munich, 1962).   VDM

ANDRZEJEWSKI, Jerzy (1909–83), Polish novelist, based for most of his life in Warsaw where he was active in cultural and political life, a R. Catholic writer before WWII, joined and supported the Communist Party during the postwar years. However, from the mid-1950s he gradually became one of the most outspoken dissidents. His first novel, *Ład serca* (Inner peace, 1938), reflected the style of Georges Bernanos's fiction. His literary career after 1945, initiated by the collection of war stories

Noc (Night, 1945), gained momentum with the publication of *Popiół i diament* (Ashes and diamonds, 1948), filmed by A. Wajda (b. 1927). Its biased picture of the non-Communist Home Army and staunch support for the Party line secured official recognition and over twenty-five editions were printed. Andrzejewski's denunciation of Stalinism was reflected above all in the historical allegory *Ciemności kryją ziemię* (Darkness covers the Earth, 1957) and in the novella *Apelacja* (The appeal, 1968), originally published in Paris. His experiments with modern narrative techniques achieved their best results in *Bramy raju* (The gates of Paradise, 1960), composed of monologue-confessions. *Idzie skacząc po górach* (He cometh leaping on the mountains, 1963), set in France, is a harsh condemnation of Western civilisation. *Miazga* (Pulp, 1979) undermines the novel form and exposes the author's growing doubts about all things, including his own artistic mission. Andrzejewski's novels are not flawless, but their challenging content and skilful narration guarantee them a prominent place in modern Polish fiction.

●*Ashes and Diamonds* (London, 1962); *The Gates of Paradise* (London, 1963); *The Appeal* (London, 1971).   SE

AN-SKI(i.e. Shloyme Zaynvl Rapoport, 1863–1920), Yiddish folklorist, ethnographer and playwright, born in Chashniki in the Vitebsk guberniya, Byelorussia. At an early age he became active in the Narodnaya Volya (People's will) movement and received formative impressions while 'going to the people' in Latvia, Central Russia and the Ukraine. 1902 he composed 'Di shvue' (The oath) which became the anthem of the

Bund. Disillusioned by the collapse of the 1905 Revolution and the ensuing pogroms he turned from radical politics to Jewish folklore. He was a member of the Jewish Ethnographic Society in St Petersburg and from 1912 till WWI led an expedition to Podolia during the course of which he collected material which served as the basis for *Der dibek* (The Dybbuk, 1919), a powerful neo-Romantic drama of crossed love and spirit-possession seen against the background of a Ḥasidic *shtetl*. In translation it has been more frequently performed than any other Yiddish play. An outstanding Yiddish-language film version of *Der dibek* was shot in Poland in 1938.

●*The Dybbuk* (London, New York, 1926); 'The Dybbuk' in *GYP*, pp. 15–68; 'I Enlighten a Shtetl' in L. S. Dawidowicz (Ed.), *The Golden Tradition* (New York, 1967), pp. 306–11.

E. Mlotek (Ed.), *S. Ansky (1863–1920), His Life and Works*, catalogue of an exhibition (New York, 1980); D. G. Roskies, 'The Maskil as Folk Hero', *Prooftexts* 10:2 (1990), pp. 219–35.   HD

ARAGVISP'IRELI, Shio (i.e. S. Dedabrishvili, 1867–1926), Georgian prose writer, the sixth son of a priest, was educated in the Tbilisi seminary and a Warsaw veterinary college, where he formed the League for Georgia's Freedom. After imprisonment, he worked as a veterinary inspector in the Tbilisi slaughter-house and used his observations in a series of short stories from 1895. They won popularity for their hyperbolically grim contrasts of oppressed underlings and decadent overlords. Typical is *Mits'aa* (It's earth, 1901), in which a consumptive Georgian convict is sent to Siberia and thrashed to death for refusing to throw away a bag of Georgian earth he has kept for his grave. Though Aragvisp'ireli was a Europeanised writer, over-indebted to Maupassant and the demonic PRZYBYSZEWSKI, his origins, his idealisation of the primitive and his pessimism had much in common with 'mountain' writers such as Q'AZBEGI. A Maeterlinckian drama *Shio Tavadi* (Prince S., 1905), which took a Symbolist view of Georgian history, failed, but his one novel, a sentimental fairy tale, idealising the love of a princess and goldsmith, *Gabzaruli guli* (A fractured heart, 1920), pleased Soviet critics who abhorred his earlier gruesome Expressionism.

DR

ARALICA, Ivan (b. 1930), Croatian novelist, graduated in Slavonic studies in Zadar, where he worked as a teacher. His style is somewhat traditional compared with the Modernist and Postmodernist modes dominating the literary scene. His first works treated contemporary ethical and moral conflicts: *Ima netko siv i zelen* (There is someone grey and green, 1977); but most of his works set such themes in historical contexts: *Psi u trgovištu* (Dogs in the market-place, 1979), widely considered his best work; *Put bez sna* (Journey without sleep, 1982); *Duše robova* (The souls of slaves, 1984); *Okvir za mržnju* (Framework for hatred, 1987). Aralica uses historical settings, abounding in informative detail, to treat both perennial and topical themes. His style combines features of medieval chronicles, the oral tradition, devotional works and the contemporary language. Aralica's novels focus on a section of Croatian society rarely treated in literature before him: the peasantry of the hinterland, the ancient 'Morlachs'. In his recent novels,

Aralica has been turning increasingly to contemporary life.   ECH

ARANY, János (1817–82), Hungarian poet, essayist, translator, and short-story writer, was born in a small town on the outskirts of the Great Hungarian Plain. His parents came from families of noble origin, but were rather poor. 1833 he entered the College of the Reformed Church in Debrecen but had to leave for lack of funds. 1834 he became a schoolmaster in Kisújszállás. 1835 he returned to Debrecen but left in the second term and became an actor in a travelling company. Returning to his native Nagyszalonta, he again became a teacher. 1839 he was appointed assistant notary, and 1840 married. Having read *Toldi* (see below), PETŐFI recognised him as a poet of great talent. They became friends, although their personalities were very different. During the revolution of 1848–9 Arany became co-editor of the popular newspaper *A nép barátja* (Friend of the people). 1850 he was a tutor in a noble family. The following year he moved to a town in central Hungary, where he taught at a grammar school. 1858 he was elected member of the Hungarian Academy. Two years later he became director of the Kisfaludy Association. This made it possible for him to move to Pest. The two literary journals he edited, *Szépirodalmi Figyelő* (Literary observer, 1860–2) and *Koszorú* (Wreath, 1863–5), proved to be too sophisticated for the general public. His later years were spent in retirement because of poor health. Arany was the finest Hungarian poet of the period between Romanticism and the 20th century. Viewing himself as a late-comer, he made irony and elegy the most important elements of his works. Although he was an excellent story-teller, even his narrative poems are dominated by lyricism and self-irony. Of the three verse tales he wrote about the legendary character Miklós Toldi, (*Toldi* [1846], *Toldi szerelme* [T.'s love, 1879] and *Toldi estéje* [T.'s eve, 1847–8]), *Toldi estéje*, centred on the tension between progress and nationalism, is the most significant. The mock-heroic *A nagyidai cigányok* (The Gipsies of Nagyida, 1852) is a grotesque portrayal of 1848–9. His third most important epic poem, *Buda halála* (The death of Buda, 1863), is the only finished part of a trilogy he planned to write about the Huns. Its title hero is too weak to rule his country. He is killed by his younger brother, Etele (Attila), who will lose his strength as a result of his deed. The poem concerns the self-destructive nature of power. Fate and freedom of will are at the centre of the ballads representing Arany's desire to combine story-telling with dramatic tension and lyric tone. The peasant woman in *Ágnes asszony* (Mistress A., 1853) believes that she had no choice but to help murder her husband; the heroine of *Zách Klára* (K.Z., 1855), a medieval lady-in-waiting, is raped by the younger brother of the queen. Both *Szondi két apródja* (The two pageboys of Szondi, 1856) and *A walesi bárdok* (The bards of Wales, 1857) have political undertones; they concern singers who refuse to praise their oppressors. Arany himself refused to pay homage to the Emperor Francis Joseph when he visited Hungary. These ballads indicate that Arany's main interest lay in experimenting with different structures. His late ballads, such as *Tengerihántás* (Corn-husking, 1877) or *Vörös Rébék* (Red R., 1877), in which polyphonic arrangement and fragmentation play a major role, manifest even greater complexity. As a lyric poet, he revived Classicist models and anticipated Symbolism. Seeing the rise of capitalism, he was afraid of the consequences of alienation. *A rab gólya* (The captive stork, 1847) is a portrait of psychological captivity, and the vision expressed in *Kertben* (In the garden, 1851) is of a world in which people ignore each other. Tormented by a sense of decay, Arany has doubts about any teleology. Life is viewed from the perspective of death both in the short lyric 'A lejtőn' (Down the hill, 1852–7) and in the ironic, self-reflective meditation 'Mindvégig' (Until the very end, 1877), and existence is compared to endless circularity in the dramatic monologue *As örök zsidó* (The eternal Jew, 1860). His essay *A magyar nemzeti versidomról* (On Hungarian versification, 1856) is a highly original attempt at creating a generative study of prosody, and *Zrínyi és Tasso* (Z. and T., 1859) is an early example of comparative literature. He also made a lasting contribution to criticism and literary history.

•*The Death of King Buda* (Cleveland, 1936).

J. Reményi, *Hungarian Writers and Literature* (New Brunswick, 1964); F. Garber (Ed.), *Romantic Irony* (Budapest, 1988).   MSz-M

ARAPI, Fatos (b. 1930), Albanian poet and literary critic, born in Vlorë, studied economics at the Karl Marx Institute in Sofia, worked as journalist and lecturer in economics and Albanian literature at Tirana. Arapi has written a novel, several short stories, literary criticism and folklore studies but he is known mainly for his impulsive poetry reflecting the reciprocity of bonds between the inner life of the individual and the profound social changes of the postwar period. Among his verse collections are *Shtigje poetike* (Poetic paths, 1962), *Poema dhe vjersha* (Ballads and lyrics, 1966), *Kaltërsia* (Blues, 1971) and *Fatet* (The Fates, 1979). His prose is gathered in *Patat e egra* (The wild geese, 1969), *Dhjetori i shoetësuar* (Uneasy December, 1970) and *Dikush më buzëqeshte* (Someone smiled at me, 1972).   ShM

ARBES, Jakub (1840–1914), Czech prose writer and publicist, son of a Prague cobbler, was a pupil of NERUDA at grammar school, became a liberal journalist, spent a year in prison for indictments of the police and the government and, after dismissal from his journalist post, went freelance. Arbes conceived his own type of tale, reminiscent of Poe, which he called 'romanetto' at NERUDA's suggestion. His 'romanetti' are usually short novels with thrilling plots evolving around a mystery; at the end, the seemingly insoluble mystery is explained in a rational way, either by science, as in *Zázračná madona* (The miraculous madonna, 1874), in which the startling transformation of an ugly wife into a beauty resembling Murillo's madonna is brought about by drugs, or by psychology as in *Ukřižovaná* (The girl crucified, 1876) where the recurring mental fits of the main character result from a trauma caused by his discovery of the Jewish girl whom he loves crucified by peasants. Some of the 'romanetti', e.g. *Newtonův mozek* (Newton's brain, 1877), which uses the ideas of time travel and brain transplants, point towards science fiction. The determinist, materialist outlook of the 'romanetti' is combined with socialism in novels such as *Kandidáti existence* (Candi-

dates for existence, 1878) which ironically describes the attempts of two
young men to put socialist principles
into practice; one of them ends up a
capitalist; the other dies in poverty.
Arbes also wrote a great number of
studies on Czech and foreign writers,
musicians and artists; he was especially interested in MÁCHA and de-
ciphered the encoded passages in his
diaries.   KB

ARCHIL (1647–1712), Georgian
writer, King of Imeretia 1664–75 and
for a few months at a time in the
1690s, died near Moscow. His exile
was devoted to setting up Georgian
printing presses; he worked on the
Georgian Bible that was to be printed
in 1742 (see BIBLE), compiled chronicles, translated Russian and Greek
texts. He versified earlier prose texts,
e.g. *Visramiani* (see ROMANCE), in
Rustavelian metre, wrote didactic
poems, such as *Gabaaseba k'atsisa da
soplisa* (Dispute between man and the
world, 1684) and *Sakartvelos
zneobani* (Georgia's morality, 1684),
and a few euologies. His *Samijnuro
leksebi* (Love verses, c. 1703) imitate
the *Majama* of King TEIMURAZ I.
Archil's masterpiece, however, is
Teimuraziani (The life of Teimuraz I,
before 1663); written as a *gabaaseba*
(Dispute, or: Comparison), it shows
empathy with the conflicts of poetry
and power and with the mind of
RUSTAVELI, who is made to tell
TEIMURAZ, his rival after four centuries: 'I am the root of poetry, poets
build on me. I said what was unsaid
before me and afterwards is not to be
invented.' Sections (*p'asukhebi*)
15–18 evoke the hell of TEIMURAZ I'S
times in contrast with the glory of
Queen Tamar's.

•D. M. Lang, *The Last Years of the
Georgian Monarchy* (New York, 1957).
                                            DR

ARGHEZI, Tudor (i.e. Ion
Theodorescu, 1880–1967), Roumanian poet, novelist and pamphleteer,
who after the publication of his first
poems in 1896 turned to the Orthodox Church and became a monk in
1899. His disillusion with monastic
life, reflected in the novel *Icoane de
lemn* (Wooden icons, 1930), led him
to renounce his orders in 1904. To
make a complete break with the seclusion of his recent past, he jour-
neyed in Switzerland and France,
paying his way first as a commercial
traveller and then as a factory
worker. He returned to Roumania in
1910 and acquired a name as a fiery
polemicist and, after Roumania's entry into WWI in 1916, as a pacifist.
He was sent to prison for a year in
1918 for writing for a pro-German
newspaper published during the German occupation of Bucharest. He
was almost fifty before he achieved
recognition as a major poet with the
publication of *Cuvinte potrivite* (Fitting words, 1927), his first volume of
collected poems from the previous
thirty years. It caused consternation
in literary circles by breaking with
conventions of prosody and language; among the poet's innovations
was the use of lurid and abrasive
metaphor to express a bitterness often bordering on the blasphemous.
Many of the poems reflect the anguish of a soul in search of God and the
poet's identification with the land
and the peasant. *Flori de mucegai*
(Mildewed flowers, 1931) is based on
life in prison and has hallucinatory
qualities which suggest that the poet
was close to mental breakdown; a
third collection, *Cărticică de seară*
(Little book for evening, 1935), manifests child-like wonder at acutely
observed phenomena of Nature.
Wartime pamphleteering again

brought him into conflict with the authorities in 1943 when he was interned for attacking the German minister to Roumania. After the war his poetry was the subject of an attack in the Communist Party daily *Scînteia* (The spark) for 'representing the standard goods of decadent bourgeois art' and he was condemned to silence 1948–54. He emerged with two cycles of verse in harmony with the cultural dictates of the period: *1907* (1955), devoted to the peasant uprisings of that year, and *Cîntare omului* (Hymn to mankind, 1956), depicting man's gradual evolution towards self-discovery and his self-realisation in the Communist order. Both lack the imaginative fire of his earlier verse, although in *1907* the vitriol is still there. His alignment with the régime led to his official elevation to the status of a living classic and officially sponsored candidacy for the Nobel Prize and the price he paid was loss of independence.

•*Selected poems of Tudor Arghezi* (Princeton, 1976). DJD

ASATIANI, Lado (1917–43), Georgian poet, emerged like a bolt from the blue at the end of the 1937 purges with lyrics that show no constraints or ideology. Song-like celebrations of everyday pleasures, believable tributes to friends, to Georgia and its classic poets, they use a lively colloquial Georgian and gentle irony. The innocent hedonism is infectious: 'Though my wife is beautiful, I want one more beautiful, Exploding like a peach tree, waving her wings like a merlin' (*Salaghobo* [A joke, 1940]); but Asatiani has intimations of his mortality: 'Before death wraps me in a dark gown. . . . For the last time lay me down in my wooden cottage, . . . For the last time with-out grumbling leave me thus. Before death stiffens my restless soul' (*Vidre sik'vdili* . . . ['Before death . . .', 1941]). In the war years, Soviet poets were commissioned to celebrate heroic battles of the past: Asatiani evoked the 18th-century Battle of Aspindza with incomparable dramatic verve, but official disapproval of Georgian nationalism cut the print-run to ten copies. Nothing to match Asatiani's poetry had been – or was to be – written in Georgian for a decade. DR

ASDRENI (i.e. Aleks Stavri Drenova, 1872–1947), Albanian poet, was born of a poor peasant family in the village of Drenovë near Korçë. After elementary schooling in his native village, he went to the Greek secondary school in Korçë until his father's death when he emigrated to Roumania. He briefly continued his studies at Bucharest, where he came into contact with the national movement in exile. The dominant themes in his poetry are ardent patriotism and the beauties of Nature. His main works are *Rreze dielli* (Sunbeams, 1904); *Ëndrra dhe lotë* (Dreams and tears, 1912), and *Psallme murgu* (Psalms of a monk, 1930). ShM

ASH, Sholem/Asch, Scholom (1880–1957), Yiddish novelist and playwright, was born in Kutno, Congress Poland. Early in his career, like many writers of his generation, he received help and encouragement from PERETS. He established his reputation with *Dos shtetl* (The small town, 1905) and was the first Yiddish writer to achieve widespread international fame. Even his early play *Meshiekhs tsaytn* (In the days of the Messiah, 1906) was soon translated into German, Polish and Russian and performed in St Petersburg. Ash's writing was prolific and uneven, but he gave new scope to Yiddish fiction.

His *Kidesh hashem* (Sanctification of the Name, 1919), for example, set against the background of the Khmel'nitski massacres of 1648–9, was one of the earliest Yiddish historical novels. However, such was Ash's belief in his mission to reconcile Jews and Christians by seeking common factors in their respective traditions and by emphasising the Jewishness of NT figures that he eventually alienated his Yiddish readership to such an extent that his later novels became the object of a Yiddish publishers' boycott orchestrated by Abe Cahan's (1860–1951) influential New York daily, *Forverts* (Forward), and were published only in translation. Thus the original Yiddish version of *The Nazarene* (1939) did not appear till 1943 (*Der man fun natsres*), while the remaining two volumes of this 'Christian' trilogy, *The Apostle* (1943) and *Mary* (1949), have never been published in the original Yiddish. Ash was a constant traveller. He died in London.

●*GYP*, pp. 69–113; *TYS*, pp. 255–75, 519–23; *AMYL*, pp. 27–41, 155–61, 189–98.

B. Siegel, *The Controversial Sholem Asch, An Introduction to his Fiction* (Bowling Green, Ohio, 1976).   HD

AŠKERC, Anton (1856–1912), Slovene poet, after ordination served as priest in various Styrian parishes, 1881–98. Coming into conflict with the Church authorities, he resigned from the ministry and settled in Ljubljana (Laibach) as municipal archivist. Mainly a narrative poet, he took themes for his 'ballads' and 'romances' from episodes in Slovene history such as the 16th-century peasants' revolt, the activities of the Protestant reformers, the smuggling of DALMATIN's Bible translation into Slovenia. He also dealt with social problems, believing that eventually human intelligence would prevail against prejudice. His collections include: *Balade in romance* (Ballads and romances, 1890); *Lirske in epske poezije* (Lyric and epic poems, 1896), describing the suffering of workers, not from the socialist viewpoint but as a sympathetic observer, with some satirical rejoinders to his critics; *Nove poezije* (New poems, 1900), where he manifests himself as a free-thinking satirist; *Četrti zbornik poezij* (Fourth collection of poems, 1904), with Homer's death and the siege of Vienna among the themes; *Primož Trubar* (1905); *Jadranski biseri* (Adriatic pearls, 1908), stories of the lives of Slovene fishermen; *Akropolis in piramide* (The Acropolis and the pyramids, 1909), sketches from travels in the Levant; *Atila v Emoni* (A. in Emona, publ. posth.).

●Translations in: *AMSL*, 1919; *Parnassus*, 1957; *The Slav Anthology* (Portland, Maine, 1931); *Slovene Poetry* (Cleveland, Ohio, 1928).   HL

ASPAZIJA (i.e. Elza Rozenberg, 1868–1943), Latvian poet, playwright, daughter of a landowner, 1887 interrupted her studies to get married. Between 1893 and 1903 she was editor of the liberal paper, *Dienas Lapa* (Daily gazette). She divorced her first husband 1897 and married the poet RAINIS. They emigrated and 1905–20 lived in Switzerland. Returning to her country, she became an MP. In her early works, especially the dramas *Zaudētas tiesības* (Lost rights, 1891), *Vaidelote* (The priestess, 1892) and *Neaizsniegts mērķis* (Unreached goal, 1895) and journalistic writings, she showed herself a passionate fighter for women's emancipation. She joined the independence movements of the so-called New Current. Her, in tone,

Symbolist volume of verse, *Sarkanās puķes* (Red flowers, 1897), gives voice to her romantic rebellion against social injustice and the world of the bourgeoisie as well as her insistence on national independence. Following the official liquidation of New Current, her work was given new impetus by the Revolution of 1905, as is indicated by the play *Sidraba šķidrauts* (Silver blanket, 1905). In exile Aspazija lost some of her élan in turning to 'eternal human questions'; her Symbolism blended with modern trends she encountered abroad, especially with Expressionism: *Saulainis stūrītis* (Sunny corners, 1910) and *Ziedu klēpis* (A pile of flowers, 1912). After her husband's death (1929) she retired from public and literary activities.   EB

AVYŽIUS, Jonas (b. 1922), Lithuanian novelist and short-story writer, graduated from the Joniškis grammar school, was a member of the editorial boards of *Jaunimo gretos* (Ranks of youth), a Young Communist League paper, and *Tiesa* (The truth), the Lithuanian equivalent of the Russian *Pravda*. Avyžius devoted his talent to depictions of the Lithuanian countryside during the decades of the, sometimes bloody, radical changes introduced into the quiet agrarian settings by the Soviet régime. In his earlier works, before the death of Stalin and Khrushchev's Thaw, Avyžius worked from a Communist Party mould, praising all change, indifferent to personal feelings, or to the characterisation of his heroes as full human beings. Beginning with the novel *Kaimas kryžkelėj* (Village at the crossroads, 1964), he developed a daring approach, pointing out clearly what misconceived ideological principles, and the human greed that exploits them, can do in a war-torn countryside. The earlier optimistic Communist heroes who dealt with all problems without a moment's doubt were now shown as people often descending into blackest despair in their efforts to continue believing in a system that was clearly destroying the country. This critical, accusatory, voice grew stronger in Avyžius's next novel, *Sodybų tuštėjimo metai* (When the homesteads were emptying, 1970), dealing with the WWII German occupation of Lithuania, when the ruthless German régime and its Lithuanian supporters came into conflict with the subdued, but omnipresent, Soviet power that was spreading the tentacles of its guerrilla movement across the country. *Degimai* (Forest clearings, 1982) showed the other side of the coin – the depredations of the Soviet régime once it regained its foothold in Lithuania, particularly in the countryside, where it destroyed the entire traditional fabric of life in order to assert and fulfil an abstract totalitarian conception of society. The novel *Chameleono spalvos* (Colours of the chameleon, 1979) turned its attention to the Soviet Lithuanian bourgeoisie – intellectuals, artists, Communist Party bosses – and exposed their lack of conscience, of any system of beliefs, their callous selfishness and nihilism.   RŠ

AXIOTI, Melpo (1905–73), Greek poet and prose writer, was brought up by her father after her mother deserted them, and the figure of a frightened girl growing up in an unloving upper-class household is a frequent theme in her works. 1918–22 she was educated in a convent on the Aegean island of Tinos, acquiring a fluent command of French and an interest in French literature. After four years of unsuccessful marriage to one of her teachers she settled in Athens in 1930, and began writing. She established herself in the public eye in 1938 with her prize-winning experimental novel, Δύσκολες Νύχτες (Difficult nights), followed by the long poem Σύμπτωση (Coincidence, 1939) and a second experimental novel, Θέλετε να χορέψομε, Μαρία (Shall we dance, Maria, 1940). 1940 Axioti joined the Communist Party, and during the Occupation and the Civil War she worked for the left-wing resistance movement. Her political commitment is reflected in her non-fictional Χρονικά (Chronicles, 1945), a set of ten short stories based on her wartime experiences, and the novel Είκοστός αιώνας (Twen-

tieth century), a tribute to the part played in resistance to Fascism by the women of Greece. From 1947 Axioti was in exile, first in France, then (because of diplomatic pressures on the French government by the Greeks) in East Germany. 1958–64 she taught Modern Greek language and literature in the Classics Institute of the Humboldt University. The publication of her second long poem Κοντραμπάντο (Contraband, 1959) brought her into contact with RITSOS, who oversaw the publication of her works from 1959 to 1964, when she was finally allowed to return to Greece. Her last work of fiction, the novella Η Καδμώ (Cadmo), came out in 1972.   CFR

B

BABITS, Mihály (1883–1941), Hungarian poet, essayist, prose writer and translator, was the son of a judge who later served at the Court of Appeals in Budapest and Pécs. On both sides, Babits was a descendant of the lesser nobility. He studied at the Cistercian grammar school in Pécs and later, 1901–5, at the University of Budapest, where he specialised in Latin and Hungarian and became a close friend of KOSZTOLÁNYI. Later he studied Greek, French, German, English and Italian, and translated works by authors such as Sophocles, Baudelaire, Kant, Shakespeare and Dante. Having completed his studies, he worked as a teacher in Baja, 1905–6, and Szeged, 1906–8. When ADY's *Új versek* was published, both Babits and KOSZTOLÁNYI were rather critical of Ady's style, but soon all three became important contributors to *Nyugat* (West), the journal which became the centre of literary modernity in Hungary. In 1908 Babits moved to Fogaras, in S Transylvania, where he became aware of the ethnic tension between Hungarians and Roumanians. Three years later, he got a job in a suburb of Budapest. This made it easier for him to participate in literary life. He continued to work as a teacher until 1915, when he lost his post because of a pacifist poem. Although he agreed with the goals of the 1918 revolution, he became alienated from the Commune of 1919. In 1921 he married Ilona Tanner (1895–1955), who later published her own poetry, fiction and essays under the pen-name Sophie Török. 1927 he became the curator of the Baumgarten Foundation and 1929 the editor of *Nyugat*. Diagnosed as having cancer in 1937, he spent his last years mostly in hospitals. In contrast to ADY, Babits aimed as a lyric poet at objectivity. In his early years he planned to become both a philosopher and a poet, and his interest in William James's concept of stream of consciousness, Bergson's interpretation of time, and Nietzsche's idea of eternal recurrence helped him create a poetry with philosophical implications. In the first half of his career, he experimented with various forms. In *Fekete ország* (Black country, 1906–7) the repetition of the word 'black' and the absence of verbs are meant to suggest an autonomous and static world. The visual Symbolism of this poem is a far cry from the *Secession* style of *A Danaidák* (The Danaids, 1909), in which a labyrinthine syntax is used to create an image of death, and the auditory effect of Greek words creates the impression of a highly artificial style. During WWI his writing became more Expressionist: *Húsvét előtt* (Before Easter, 1916), his most powerful pacifist poem, is built around a series of verbs culminating in a shriek. His ambition was to bring the culture of his nation into harmony with European standards, and his long essay *Magyar irodalom* (Hungarian literature, 1913) is a drastic re-evaluation of the intellectual legacy of his country; his short novel *A gólyakalifa* (The stork caliph, 1913) is a serious attempt to portray the disintegration of personality in the spirit of Freud. The Communist dictatorship of 1919 and the Peace Treaty of Trianon of 1920, the loss of more than two thirds of the territory of Hungary, made him reassess his goals. He became more conservative politically and aesthetically. Having reached the conclusion that the poet acts as a medium rather than as a charismatic personality, he was inclined to view art as re-creation rather than creation. *Az európai irodalom története* (The history of European literature, 1934–6), his most sustained effort as an essayist, epitomises Neoclassical ideals and constitutes an outline of European literary traditions, with a heavy emphasis on Classical Antiquity and the Latin Middle Ages. *Jónás könyve* (The Book of Jonah, 1939) is a subjective adaptation of the OT book.

•*The Nightmare* [*A gólyakalifa*] (Budapest, 1966).

M. Szegedy-Maszák, 'Symbolism and Poetry in the Austro-Hungarian Monarchy', *Neohelicon*, XI/2 (1984), pp. 135–45; G. F. Cushing, 'Mihály Babits: "All Great Poets are Decadent"' in L. Péter and R. B. Pynsent (Eds), *Intellectuals and the Future in the Habsburg Monarchy, 1890–1914* (Basingstoke, 1988).

MSz-M

BACOVIA, George (i.e. G. Vasiliu, 1881–1957), Roumanian poet, the son of a shopkeeper in the Moldavian town of Bacău, read law at Iaşi (degree 1911). Afflicted by neurosis, he was unable to settle down to a career at the bar and spent his professional life in a series of clerical jobs until ill-health forced him into retirement in 1932. He took his pseudonym from his birthplace whose monotonous provincial life provided the setting for much of his poetry. His volumes *Plumb* (Lead, 1916) and *Scîntei galbene* (Yellow sparks, 1926) are infused with melancholy pessimism. The poet is haunted by damp, decay, rain and snow and these elements constitute Bacovia's universe of putrefaction and gloom. Recurrent dusk and night, autumn and winter, grey, black and violet characterise his neurasthenic verse. Grotesque faces and bodies, screaming and howling, add an Expressionist note. His limited vocabulary and Symbolist exploration of association give his verse richness.

•*Plumb: lead* (Bucharest, 1980).   DJD

BACZYŃSKI, Krzysztof Kamil (1921–44), Polish poet, the most legendary figure of the decimated 'War Generation', precocious son of a literary critic, during the German occupation studied literature at a clandestine university while writing at a hectic speed. Only two slim collections of his poems, however, had come out underground before he died fighting in the Warsaw Uprising. A powerful talent, he made use of an ambiguous, symbolic vision which drew from the Romantic and catastrophist traditions while remaining highly original in dealing with his major themes: the spiritual devastation caused by the inhumanity of war and the refuge to be found in love.

StB

BAGRYANA, Elisaveta (i.e. E. Belcheva, 1893–1991), Bulgarian poet, began publishing 1915, and soon became one of the leading figures of the Zlatorog (Golden horn, 1920–43) circle. She studied Slavonic philology at Sofia, then worked in the provinces as a teacher. Her marriage with an army officer was unhappy; 1924 she met her former teacher, Boyan Penev (1882–1927); they experienced three years' clandestine love and when the possibility of marriage was nigh, Penev died. Bagryana published her first collection just after his death, *Vechnata i Svyatata* (The eternal and the sacred, 1927), which was to become one of the most celebrated collections of Bulgarian poetry. She treats standard lyric themes like love, youth, the yearning for liberty and self-fulfilment, but she creates an image of woman unusual for Bulgarian literature: woman whose desire for freedom is elemental, and who represents a new perception of 'das ewig Weibliche'. Woman is identified with forces of Nature (e.g. wind, fire) or with folklore feminine archetypes (e.g. wood-nymphs); her love is an extension of her individuality and freedom; maternal love is sacred, self-sacrificing and related to the tribal. In 'Kukuvitsa' (Cuckoo) Bagryana's wanderer-woman is compared to the cuckoo, who in the folk tradition connotes a selfish and carefree style of life; Bagryana regards the cuckoo as an emblem of individual liberty, of the overcoming of the biological collective's imperatives. She believes, however, that submission to the beloved is not a sacrifice of individual liberty, but its ultimate expression ('Lyubov' [Love]). The immense variety of her metres and rhymes produces the characteristic rhapsodic tone of her

verse. In *Zvezda na moryaka* (Sailor's star, 1932), she introduces the motifs of sea and wandering (as attraction to the unknown), and uses free verse for the first time. The dominant mood of her later verse is contemplative; she returns to the motifs of her early collections and blends them with meditations on the past, memory, body and spirit, sin and benediction.   SIK

BAHDANOVIČ, Maksim (1891–1917), Byelorussian poet, prose writer, translator and critic, did more than any other to raise his native literature from its ethnographically based past to a new, European, level of sophistication. Born in Minsk, the son of a teacher and folklorist, he moved to Nizhnii Novgorod at the age of five and was educated in Russia, visiting Byelorussia again for the first time only in 1911. A second visit came in 1916, but tuberculosis took him to the Crimea where his premature death robbed Byelorussia of one of its brightest lights. Well grounded in Byelorussian, Russian, Polish, W European and Classical culture, Bahdanovič reflected this education in everything he wrote, from his use of epigraphs, to translations, to the revival of such forms as the sonnet, octet, triolet, *terza rima* and rondeau, democratising them, as it were, in the presentation of such themes as the national renascence, the peasants' lot, Nature, love, art, and the 'tragedy' of war and exile. His translations from many Classical and W European as well as Slav poets, particularly Verlaine and Heine, were important for Byelorussian cultural development, as was his whimsical, imaginative reworking of national folk material including the creation of a new form of Byelorussian verse (*vieršy bietaruskaha* *składu*). Strophic and metrical virtuosity combined with a poignancy in poems like 'Słuckija tkačychi' (The weaver-women of Słuck, 1912), 'Emihrackaja pieśnia' (Emigrants' song, 1914), the triolet on the suicide of a fellow-poet, 'S. Pałujanu' (To S. Pałujan', 1913), and the emotive *Madonny* (Madonnas, 1912) cycle produce memorable poetry. His sole collection, *Vianok* (A garland), published in Vilna in 1913, marked a milestone in Byelorussian cultural history. Bahdanovič's thoughtful historico-critical essays also did much to raise the quality of literary criticism in Byelorussia. The most imaginative examples of his prose are two experiments in stylisation: *Apokryf* (Apocryphon, 1913), a reflection on the purpose of poetry, and *Apaviadańnie ab ikońniku i załataru* (The story of the icon-painter and the gilder, 1914), an imaginary manuscript written in the chancery language of the Grand Duchy of Lithuania. In these, as in his poetry, he showed himself ahead of his time and a catalyst for future developments.

●A. B. McMillin (Ed.), *The Images Swarm Free: A Bi-lingual Selection of Poetry by Maksim Bahdanovič, Aleś Harun and Żmitrok Biadula* (London, 1982). ABMcM

BAHUŠEVIČ, Frańcišak (1840–1900), Byelorussian poet and prose writer, the most colourful writer of his century, was born into the minor gentry and came, through publicistic and creative writing, to embody many of his country's social and national aspirations. It is as an eloquent nationalist and poet that Bahuševič will be best remembered; most of his work was collected in *Dudka biełaruskaja* (The Byelorussian pipe, 1891) and *Smyk biełaruski*

(The Byelorussian bow, 1894), both published illegally in Cracow. A true democrat, he writes from a peasant viewpoint about village life, customs and beliefs, mixing didacticism with humour and lyricism. His prose is competent but less significant. Bahuševič's achievement in Byelorussian poetry was to broaden the range of genres, enrich the literary vocabulary and to develop away from syllabic and syllabo-tonic towards tonic verse. ABMcM

BAJZA, Jozef Ignác (1755–1836), Slovak writer, a R. Catholic priest, was author of the first novel in Slovak, a language he tried to codify, but his system differed from that of BERNOLÁK and his followers and was rejected by them. The first volume of Bajza's *René mlád'enca príhodi a skúsenosti* (Young René's adventures and experiences, 1783) combines the narrative of the adventures of the hero in the Arabic world and Italy with sentimental eroticism and is primarily didactic in a somewhat Voltairean manner. The second volume (1785), a more openly critical work, where Bajza condemns aspects of the feudal and monastic systems in contemporary Hungary and criticises the non-existence of Slovak literature, was confiscated on publication by the Church authorities. KB

BAKOUNTS, Ak'sel (1899–1936), Armenian journalist and writer, born in Goris, the capital of the province of Zangezour, received his primary education in Goris (1905–10) and his secondary at the Etchmiadzin College (1910–17). He was engaged in public life and journalism for a while, then spent a period at the Tiflis (Tbilisi) Polytechnic. 1920–3 he studied at the Agricultural Institute in Kharkov. Thereafter, he lived and worked exclusively in Armenia; he occupied positions as an agricultural expert, at the same time playing a prominent role in the creation of Soviet Armenian literature until his arrest and death in July 1936. Bakounts's literary career began in 1924 with his regular column 'Letters from the Provinces'. Thereafter appeared *Hovnatan* (March, 1927), *Patmuatsk'ner* (Tales, 1928), *Spitak Djin* (The white horse, 1929), *Sev Tseleri Sermnatsanê* (The sower on black soil, 1933), *Andjrev* (Rain, 1935), *Eghbayroutian Enkouzeninere* (The walnut trees of brotherhood, 1936). His unfinished novel *Kamrak'ar* was published in 1929 in the monthly *Nor Oughi*, and his historical novel *Khatchatour Abovyan*, also unfinished, was published in the literary magazine *Khorhrdayin Grakanut'yun* in 1935. Bakounts's works are mainly devoted to Armenian life, and reflect the everyday activities and the emotions of the people. He was especially interested in rural life, and in depicting pre-Soviet and Soviet Armenian reality; he never allowed himself to be influenced by Communist slogans. His favourite themes were connected with the reconstruction of Armenian towns and villages and revealed the fundamental characteristic of his outlook, a profound love for his people and country. Bakounts's works attained a high artistic level, which is reflected in the purity of his language, his style and in his authentic and vivid illustrations of the national atmosphere. They are remarkable for their rhythmic construction, and for the harmony between form and subject. His narrative moods are both lyrical and satirical.

●L. Mkrtitchian, 'Aksel Bakounts as Champion of the True Concept of the Popular Basis of Literature in Soviet Armenia', *The Caucasian Review*, VII (1958), pp. 66–91. VN

BALANTIČ, France (1921–43), Slovene R. Catholic poet, started reading Slavonic studies in Ljubljana, 1941, spent six months in Italian internment, 1942, and on return joined the right-wing White Guard and fell in battle against the partisans. His chief themes were earth, love, death and man's relation to God. One of the best Slovene sonneteers, he wrote his first garland of sonnets in 1940, while still a schoolboy; he even projected a garland of garlands. A collection of his poems was published posthumously by Tine Debeljak (b. 1903) under the title *V ognju groze plapolam* (I blaze in the fire of terror, 1944). HL

BALASSI, Bálint (1554–94), Hungarian lyric poet and translator, was tutored by BORNEMISZA. He led a turbulent life, fighting the Turks who learnt to fear his name, quarrelling with relations and neighbours to improve his finances and relentlessly pursuing rich women for the same purpose. His verse reflects his life: the exhilaration of battle and the tortures of unrequited love are intermingled with sudden attacks of remorse. These themes he explores in verse of dazzling virtuosity, most of it intended for singing. Balassi's musical sources range from Italian to Turkish popular melodies. His verse forms are equally varied; one of them, a three-line stanza with internal rhymes adapted from the Geneva Psalter, became popular in Hungary and bears his name. Before 1879 only his intensely personal penitential verse was known. Then the discovery of his amorous verse, based on the courtly-love tradition but inflamed with genuine passion, together with his Nature and battle poems, revealed him as the first dynamic personality and original lyric poet in Hungarian literature. Modern research demonstrates that he intended to arrange his verse in three cycles, each of 33 poems preceded by a hymn to the Trinity. Balassi also adapted an Italian comedy and translated religious works from Latin and German. His lively correspondence continues to come to light.

•Balassi's metrical ingenuity is difficult to reproduce in English, but specimens occur in T. Klaniczay (Ed.), *Old Hungarian Literary Reader* (Budapest, 1985) and W. Kirkconnell (Ed.), *Hungarian Helicon* (Calgary, 1985). G. Gömöri, 'Baroque Elements in the Poetry of M. S. Szarzyński and B. Balassi', *SEER*, 46 (1968), pp. 383–96.

GFC

BALLEK, Ladislav (b. 1941), Slovak novelist, after teachers' training college and military service, spent only one year as a schoolmaster, and 1968–77 held various editorial posts; 1977 he joined the Communist bureaucracy, but became ever more disillusioned and, as Secretary to the Writers' Association, he had left the Party before the events of November 1989. He became an MP in 1992. He is a writer of lyrical irony and unconventional political commentary. The background to his chief works is Palánk (i.e. his native Šahy, near the Hungarian border) and the multiracial origins of modern Slovaks is a recurrent theme of his writing. The first Palánk work is the series of loosely linked episodes, *Južná pošta* (Southern post, 1974), which provides many themes of the later novels. The first of these, *Pomocník* (The assistant, 1977), covering 1945–6, describes a period of chaos and hope; a sense of insecurity prevails in all but the petty criminals,

aspiring women, and the police. The luxuriant, but war-scarred, countryside forms an evocative background to dominant selfishness and materialism. The optimistic Ballek's sensualism emerges most strongly in his minute descriptions here and in *Agáty* (Acacias, 1981), whose action runs from 1946 to the Communist take-over in 1948. Nostalgia is more in evidence here than in *Pomocník*, and Ballek's sensualism lusher. Much of it is narrated in monologues and soliloquies which allows the author to present a variety of views on events. If the novel has a message, it is that political 'progress' is part of Nature's grand design. Although the main character of *Lesné divadlo* (Theatre in the forest, 1987) comes from Palánk and many flashback episodes occur there, the setting is the 1960s in SW Bohemia, a training camp for frontier guards. Ballek's optimism has gone; the *vita activa* fails and proves unjust; the *vita contemplativa* is a dead end. The sexual drive, which had been celebrated in the earlier novels, is now largely destructive. *Čudný spáč zo Slovenského raja* (Strange sleeper from the Slovak Paradise region, 1990) leaves Palánk almost completely; it depicts a Slovak society (1968–85) disintegrating, morally, spiritually, economically and politically. It lacks the linguistic grace and skill in the transmission of atmosphere which marked the earlier novels. Even as a condemnation of socialist society it fails.

•R. B. Pynsent (Ed.), *Modern Slovak Prose: Fiction Since 1954* (London, 1990). RBP

BARANAUSKAS, Antanas (1835–1902) was the Bishop of E Lithuania and a writer best known for a single poem, *Anykščių šilelis*

(The pine grove of Anykščiai, 1858–9). The poem begins as a lamentation for the lost beauty of a pine grove that has become a wasteland of forlorn stumps and dead branches. The deeper the poet's memory retreats into the grove's former beauty, the richer does that world become in its varied visual, olfactory, auditory and tactile delights; these blend into a stream of consciousness running through the mind like an endless river of life. When the narration moves on to past events that led to the destruction, rebirth and repeated destruction of the grove, it becomes clear that the history of this corner of Nature represents an allegory of the former glories and, later, tribulations of the Lithuanian nation through the centuries. As was the case with DONELAITIS's *Metai* (The seasons), Baranauskas's poem stands alone against the background of a minimal literary tradition. While still very popular with Lithuanian readers today, in its time it did not stimulate any imitations or start any literary movement basically because other literary trends and influences appeared on the scene before *Anykščių šilelis* could reach all strata of the reading public. Among other works by Baranauskas, the anti-Russian *Kelionė Petaburkan* (Journal to St Petersburg, c. 1858) has achieved wide recognition. It is a travel journal depicting the miserable state of the Russian domains as compared with the simple but orderly life in Lithuania.   RŠ

BARAŃCZAK, Stanisław (b. 1946), Polish poet and critic, born and educated in Poznań where he worked as a university teacher, was among the most active and outspoken dissident writers of the 1970s, which resulted in his victimisation by the authorities. Since 1981 he has been Professor of Polish Language and Literature at Harvard. Barańczak's critical essays (*Nieufni i zadufani* [The mistrustful and the presumptuous, 1971]) and poems (*Jednym tchem* [In a single breath, 1970]), committed to contemporary problems and distrustful of linguistic clichés, paved the way for the development of the 'New Wave' in Polish poetry. His American poems (e.g. *Widokówka z tego świata* [A postcard from this world, 1988]) demonstrate the influence of the Metaphysical Poets. As a literary critic, Barańczak has published a number of books, particularly about modern Polish poetry. He also translates English, American and Russian poets into Polish.

● *The Weight of the Body* (Chicago, 1989).   SE

BARATASHVILI, Mamuk'a (before 1700–after 1750) was a Georgian poet of royal blood, and a protégé of VAKHT'ANG VI, but his identity is obscure. He is first heard of in Astrakhan with VAKHT'ANG as Prince Matvei Baratov. He may have been influenced by GURAMISHVILI. He versified a chapter of the prose romance *Rusudaniani* (see ROMANCE). His lyrics were new for the Georgian renascence in exile: they celebrate earthly, not heavenly love. He was in effect a court poet for VAKHT'ANG VI and the heir, Bakar, and slavishly eulogised and mourned them, as he did Peter the Great. His main achievement was *Ch'asknik'i anu leksis sts'avlis ts'igni* (The sample of wine, or Book of studying verse, 1731), the first modern 'Poetics' in Georgian – though Baratashvili still felt the main purpose of poetry to be divine (only his first poem,

Ts'amebuli [Of belief, 1725] was religious, however). His European orientation (breaking free of medieval Georgian metres and themes), his linguistic range and theoretical knowledge made Baratashvili influential on later, more inspired, poets. DR

BARATASHVILI, Nik'oloz (1817–45), despite a tiny oeuvre, fewer than forty lyrics, is the greatest of the Georgian Romantic poets. Born to an impoverished nobleman working for the Russian Army, on his mother's side he was an Orbeliani – a family rich in royal and literary history. He was one of the first Georgians to be fired with modern nationalism and European Romanticism. The tragic quality of his poetry was determined by early physical injury and by the catastrophic failure of the Georgian nationalist conspiracy in 1832. He was forced to become a civil servant in Ganja; the love of his life, K'aterine Ch'avch'avadze (Griboedov's sister-in-law), married Prince Davit Dadiani. Poetry became his sole outlet, but he died of malaria, unmourned and unpublished. Posthumously, as his lyrics were published between 1861 and 1876, he came to be idolised: his longest poem, the historical *Bedi Kartlisa* (The fate of Kartli, 1839), which he wrote at the age of 22, became famous as one of the most inspiring and articulate laments for his or any other crushed country, while *Merani* (Pegasus, 1842) has been crucially influential on later Georgian poets as a mystical, apocalyptic vision of the future. Baratashvili could write odes as powerfully as Shelley and could contemplate death with the sensuousness of Keats. He evolved a language all his own, obscure, but sonorous, that combined modern laconicism with medieval grandeur. The Georgian fusion of Persian and European works well with Baratashvili, who could give the sensibility of Lamartine a Sufi mystique, and who anticipated Symbolism with his cult of the azure and his sense of the apocalyptic. Baratashvili has resisted translation, though Pasternak's free Russian versions work as poems.

•L. Magarotto, 'Die romantische Revolte: Barataschwili und Leopardi', *Georgica* (Jena) 6 (1983), pp. 27–32. DR

BARBU, Ion (i.e. Dan Barbilian, 1895–1964), Roumanian poet and mathematician, the only son of a magistrate, showed a rare talent for mathematics at an early age and studied the subject at Bucharest before interrupting his course to join the army during WWI. On graduation in 1925 he received a bursary to continue his studies in Germany and returned to become a lecturer in mathematics at Bucharest in 1929. 1942 he was appointed Professor of Algebra at the same university. He made his début as a poet in 1918, his first collection *După melci* (After the snails, 1921) being largely cast in the Parnassist mould. His compositions 1920–5 are marked by their Turkish flavour, offering charming cameos of life inspired by the former Ottoman-ruled province of Dobrogea (Dobrudza), on the Black Sea coast. After 1925 his poems are cryptic, hermetic, reflect a mathematical vision of the world. His collected verse was gathered in *Joc secund* (Second play, 1930) upon which his reputation rests, for afterwards he devoted himself entirely to mathematics. His preoccupation with the analogies between poetry and mathematics inspired work distinguished by mathematical metaphor, by the symmetrical regularity of stanzas, but also by striking musicality. To the geometry of his form the poet added rich associations of ideas and references to persons or facts which are sometimes the product of his imagination, thereby transforming his poetry into a cryptic message, one made more private by the metonymous use of scientific terms.

● A. Cioranescu, *Ion Barbu* (New York, 1981). DJD

BARDHI, Frang (1606–43), author of the first Albanian dictionary, was born in Kallmet in N Albania into a high clerical family. He studied theology at the Loreto College near Ancona and 1635 was appointed Bishop of Sapë, N Albania. 1641 he went to Rome to submit a report on his diocese to the Pope. Bardhi's *Dictionarium latino-epiroticum* (Latin-Albanian dictionary) has c. 5,000 entries supplemented by a list of phrases and proverbs. 1636 Bardhi published his second Latin work, *Georgius Castriottus Epirensis vulgo Scanderbeg. Epirotarum Princeps . . .*, in which he refuted the assertion by the 17th-century Bosnian Bishop Tomeus Marnavitius that the Albanian national hero was of Bosnian origin.

● M. Roques, *Le Dictionnaire albanais de 1635* (Paris, 1932). ShM

BARLETI, Marin (i.e. Marinus Barletius, c. 1450–c. 1512), Albanian Humanist and historian, the earliest known and one of the greatest authors of early Albanian literature, was born and lived in Shkodër where he participated in the defence of the city against the Turks in 1478. After the fall of Shkodër, he fled to Italy, where he came into contact with the culture and the ideas of the Italian Renaissance. Although writing in Latin, Barleti is considered the father of Albanian historiography. In his first work on the siege of Shkodër, *De obsidione Scodrensi* (1504), he describes the events he experienced during the year before Shkodër fell to the Ottomans. His major work is his history of Scanderbeg, *Historia de vita et gestis Scanderbegi, Epirotarum Princeps* (1508–10), which was widely read and translated. It constitutes a basic source of our knowledge of 15th-century Albania. His last work on the lives of the popes and Roman emperors, *Compendium vitarum summorum pontificium*, was published posthumously in 1555.

● F. Pall, *Marino Barlezio, uno storico umanista* (Bucharest, 1938). ShM

BARNOVI, Vasil (1856–1934), was despite the Russian form of his name a Georgian novelist, very popular in the first twenty years of the 20th century. He produced a stream of historical novels, for which he plundered medieval chronicles. They are informative, but vitiated by heavy-handed Romantic interest and naive dialogue, patriotism and psychology. Best known are *Isnis tsisk'ari* (The dawn of Isani, 1901), *Mimkrali sharavandedi* (The faded crown, 1913) and *Didmouravi Giorgi Saak'adze* ([the patriotic 17th-century rebel, 'The Great Governor'], 1925). Barnovi also tried his hand, with less success, at village novels and the Zola and Korolenko genre of contemporary sociological reportage. His rich vocabulary and rhythmic prose style, however, influenced the next generation of prose writers. DR

BARONS, Krišjānis (1835–1923), Latvian writer and collector of folksongs, known as the 'father of the Latvian folksong', born the son of an estate manager, studied at Tartu. From 1863 he was editor of *Péterburgas avīzes*, the first 'progressive'

Latvian newspaper. 1865–93 he lived in Moscow, and from 1894 in Riga, where he collected folk songs. He joined the New Latvia movement and was an eminent language-reformer. His short stories, poetry and *feuilletons*, attacking the clergy and landowners, look minor in importance beside his main work, the six-volume *Latviju daīnas* (Latvian folksongs, 1894–1915). Barons published under the auspices of the Russian Imperial Academy of Sciences. When he took upon himself the task of collecting these folk-songs, the response was so great from all corners of the country that he collected about 35,000 original songs. His work was later, during Latvian independence, continued by the Archives of Latvian Folklore. The Archives collected about 775,000 additional variants of songs and increased the number of original songs to 60,000. Barons arranged the songs in the sequence in which they would be sung throughout a man's life, beginning with songs about pregnancy and those sung at baptisms, passing on through childhood, and eventually coming to old age, death and the funeral wake. Mythological songs, war songs, and songs dealing with seasonal work were grouped separately.

●O. Krātiņš, 'An Unsung Hero: Krišjānis Barons and his Lifework in Latvian Folk Songs', *Western Folklore*, XX (1961), 4, pp. 239–55   EB

BART-ĆIŠINSKI, Jakub (BART, Jakub, 1856–1909), Upper Sorbian poet, born into the family of a smallholder in the R. Catholic village of Kukow (Kukau), attended school locally and in Bautzen until 1871, when he joined the Wendish Seminary in Prague; he studied theology at Prague University 1878–81, edited the Sorbian students' literary journal *Lipa Serbska* (The Sorbian lime) from 1877. While still a student, he wrote *Nawoženja* (The bridegroom, 1877), a bucolic poem of over 3,000 hexameters, *Narodowc a wotrodźenc* (The patriot and the renegade, 1879), a novella, and *Na hrodźišću* (On the rampart, 1880), a drama in five acts. It was, however, as a lyric poet that he was to achieve eminence. Fourteen volumes of his collected poems appeared 1884–1914 (the last two posthumously). He served as a R. Catholic priest in Ralbicy (Ralbitz), Radwor (Radibor), Schirgiswalde, Dresden, Chemnitz and Radeberg. A distinctly turbulent priest, he was regularly in conflict with the hierarchy and eventually in 1903 he was forced into retirement at the early age of 46. He settled first in his native village and then in the neighbouring village of Pančicy (Panschwitz). His retirement was fruitful. Possibly as much as half of his lyric output dates from these years. In contrast to his predecessors and contemporaries, Bart-Ćišinski was little influenced by folk poetry. His work thus achieved a new level of sophistication. The influence of the Classics, the Bible and German literature may be discerned, as well as that of other Slavonic poets. To an unprecedented degree Bart-Ćišinski concentrated on the technical side of versification. Nature, the destiny of the poet and his nation, religion and morality figure prominently. The tone is predominantly contemplative and intellectual.

●Selected poems in R. Elsie (Ed.), *An Anthology of Sorbian Poetry from the Sixteenth Century to the Present Day* (London, Boston, 1990), pp. 25–31. G. Stone, *The Smallest Slavonic Nation. The Sorbs of Lusatia* (London, 1972), pp. 72–7.   GCS

BARTOL,   Vladimir   (1903–67),

Slovene novelist, short-story writer and essayist, born in Trieste, studied biology and philosophy in Ljubljana and Paris, 1921–7. His works include a collection of short stories and essays, *Al Araf* (1935), amply demonstrating his interest in psycho-analysis; a novel, *Alamut* (1938), set in 11th-century Iran, with the city of Alamut a centre of absolutist ideology demanding blind obedience to the ruler, which clearly alludes to contemporary European dictator-ships; *Tržaške humoreske* (Triestan humoresques, 1957) consists in fan-tastic and satirical scenes from the life of the port, peopled with black-marketeers, swindlers, charming temptresses and political charlatans.

HL

BASHEVIS(-ZINGER), Yitskhok (i.e. Isaac Bashevis Singer, 1904–91), Yiddish novelist and short-story writer, the brother of Ester Kraytman (1891–1954) and of Yisroel-Yeshue ZINGER, born in Leoncin near War-saw, grew up in the Jewish quarter of Warsaw and in the Galician *shtetl* Bi/lgoraj. His father, grandfather and uncle were Ḥasidic rabbis and an atmosphere of traditional piety permeates his semi-autobiographical *Mayn tatns beys-din-shtub* (In my father's court, New York, 1956), which invites comparison with ZINGER's *Fun a velt vos iz nishto mer* and Kraytman's lightly fictionalised account, *Der sheydim-tants* (Dance of the demons, Warsaw, 1936). Other quasi-autobiographical works were serialised in the New York daily *Forverts* (Forward) and appeared in English in book form as *Shosha* (New York, 1978), *A Little Boy in Search of God* (New York, 1976) and *Lost in America* (New York, 1979). Much of his work has appeared in book form only in English versions which often differ substantially from the Yiddish text. A major unifying factor in his prolific career was his search for identity both as a Jew and as writer. He won recognition in 1935 with his *Der sotn in Goray* (Satan in Goraj, in *Globus*, Warsaw, 1933), which de-picts a 17th-century Galician *shtetl* under the spell of the Sabbatean heresy. A preoccupation with the praeternatural and the uneasy rela-tionship between piety and sensuality are the main themes. Later the same year he joined ZINGER in New York. Bashevis's work falls loosely into three categories defined by their lo-cales. In his historical novels like *Der kuntsnmakher fun Lublin* (The magi-cian of L., Tel Aviv, 1971), *Der knekht* (The slave, New York, 1962) and *Kenig fun di felder* (King of the fields, New York, 1988) his pro-tagonists seek a balance between in-stinct and intellect in a world gover-ned by Cabala and superstition. Another group of novels deals with Jewish life in Poland from the late 19th century to the 'Holocaust': *Der hoyf* (The estate, in *Forverts*, 1952–5) and *Di familye mushkat* (The Musz-kat family, New York, 1950). These novels present an ambivalent view of the loss of cultural cohesion. *Sonim, di geshikhte fun a libe* (Enemies, a love story, in *Forverts*, 1966) deals with deracination and moral dis-orientation in the New World, while in *Der bal-tshuve* (The penitent, Tel Aviv, 1974), set mostly in Israel, Bashevis probes his recurrent themes of the sensualist's yearning for female innocence and the envy of the culti-vated free-thinker for the moral cer-tainties of the pious philistine. Bashevis develops his virtuosity to the full in his short stories, often employing monologue techniques to produce a rich variety of narrative voices in a manner which places him in direct line of descent from MENDELE MOYKHER SFORIM and SHOLEM ALEYKHEM. His first story appeared in 1925 and subsequently a large number of stories were written for a variety of Yiddish periodicals. A small selection was collected as *Der sotn in goray un andere dertseylungen* (Satan in Goraj and other stories, New York, 1943), *Gimpl tam un andere dertseylungen* (Gimpl the fool and other stories, New York, 1963) and *Mayses fun hintern oyvn* (Stories from behind the stove, Tel Aviv, 1971). Many of his Yiddish works remain uncollected. A much larger selection of stories has appeared in English. All translations into other languages including Hebrew have been made, at the author's insistence, from the English versions. In 1978 Bashevis was awarded the Nobel Prize for Literature.

● *In My Father's Court* (New York, 1962); *The Magician of Lublin* (New York, 1960); *Gimpel the Fool and Other Stories* (New York, 1953). I. H. Buchen, *Isaac Bashevis Singer and the Eternal Past* (New York, London, 1968); K. Shmeruk, in *The Jewish Quarterly* 29:4 (1981–2), pp. 28–36; Clive Sinclair, *The Brothers Singer* (London, New York, 1983).   HD

BAZHAN, Mykola (1904–83), Ukrainian poet, started out as a Futurist. He was the author of the collections *Rizblena tin* (The sculpted shadow, 1927), *Budivli* (Buildings, 1929) and *Doroha* (The road, 1930). His 'Expressionism gave him the taste for a passionate consciousness ... the Ukrainian Baroque offered the totality of detail and the Romanticism of Hoffmann and Gogol gave him the expansive world of fantasy' (Iurii Lavrynenko, 1959). Bazhan's poems often deal with historical and philosophical themes. One such long poem, *Sliptsi* (The blind men), begun in 1930, was interrupted and remained unfinished. Soon afterwards, under official pressure, he converted to Socialist Realism. His *Anhliiski vrazhennia* (English impressions, 1949) abounds in Soviet propaganda. In the 1960s Bazhan sometimes returned to his earlier intellectual stance – *Chotyry opovidannia pro nadiiu, variatsii na temu R. M. Rilke* (Four tales about hope; variations on a theme by R. M. R., 1966). His fine earlier poems, banned 1930–80, have now been republished. Bazhan also translated RUSTAVELI.

● 'Nights of Hoffmann', *Kenyon Review*, no. 3, 1980; Z. Honcharuk (Ed.), *Anthology of Soviet Ukrainian Poetry* (Kiev, 1982). G. Mihaychuk, 'The Dual World of Bazhan's "Sliptsi" ', *Harvard Ukrainian Studies*, December 1990, pp. 461–82.

GSNL

BEĆKOVIĆ, Matija (b. 1939), Serbian poet and dramatist, was born in Senta, Vojvodina, of Montenegrin parents. He studied literature in Belgrade, where he has been a freelance writer ever since. In 1988 he was elected the president of the Serbian Writers' Association. Bećković has published several volumes of poetry, mostly long narrative poems of unusual originality, sharp wit and topical satire. He combines a keen awareness of his people's 'tragic' experiences with a masterful control of the language and the high rhetoric of a Montenegrin dialect. He also writes for stage and television.

● (A play written with Dušan Radović) *Che, a Permanent Tragedy* (New York, 1970).   VDM

BEDNÁR, Alfonz (1914–89), Slovak novelist, read Latin, Czech and

Slovak at Prague and Bratislava, started as a schoolmaster but then worked for various cultural institutions and translated from English. His first novel *Sklený vrch* (Glass mountain, 1954), marks the beginning of the Thaw in Slovak literature; the effectiveness of socialism is questioned but the novel is not anti-Communist. His next work, however, the stylistically sophisticated *Hodiny a minúty* (The hours and minutes, 1956), compares Communism with Fascism, and manifests Bednár's abiding interest in the psychology of violence. *Hromový zub* (The thunderbolt, 1964), set 1913–23, depicts the Slovak village in flux; the old order, emblemised by the mythology of the thunderbolt, is gradually whittled away. The linking theme of the monumental novel is land and land-reforms and man's permanent urge to move forwards, acquire more. The greed, violence and inconstancy of modern society form the subject of the trilogy *Za hrst' drobných* (For a handful of change, 1970–81); here Bednár exhibits a wry irony which he often embodies in grotesque scenes and images. As in the trilogy, Bednár depicts the disintegration of society in the pessimistic satirical *Ako sme sušili bielizeň* (How we dried the washing, 1985); the main character is a blind painter, a victim of physical violence, who anyway sees civilisation as violence: the very naming of living things deprives them of life. *Výpoved'* (The testimony, 1986), whose plot mainly concerns the arrangements for a divorce, satirises modern materialism, but also considers, largely by means of parody, the degeneration of language. The latter is also a theme of the complex novel concerning the nature of identity, *Ad revidendum, Gemini* (1988).

●L. Richter, *Slowakische Literatur. Entwicklungstrends vom Vormärz bis zur Gegenwart* (Berlin, 1979); R. B. Pynsent (Ed.), *Modern Slovak Prose: Fiction Since 1954* (London, 1990). RBP

BEDNÁŘ, Kamil (1912–72), Czech poet, studied law and philosophy, after the closure of the Czech universities in 1939 worked in various publishing houses and eventually devoted himself entirely to literature. In his first collection, *Kámen v dlažbě* (A stone in the paving, 1937), he expressed, in both cold reflective and sensitive intimate verse, the mood of a generation coming to maturity in a period of disillusion, uncertainty and alienation, and seeking an escape from hopelessness and self-torment. After the intimate lyrical verse of *Milenka modř* (Blue, my beloved, 1939), Bednář overcame his anxiety by turning to sensuous experience; metaphysical terror prevails in his verse on the mystery of life and death in *Veliký mrtvý* (The great dead man, 1940), inspired by the death of his father. Bednář summarised the anxieties and hopes of his generation in his programmatic essay *Slovo k mladým* (A word to the young, 1940) in which he rejected the dissolution of the individual in the collective and the adoption of ideology, and proclaimed the return to a 'naked man' who would concentrate on timeless values and problems of personality. His postwar poetry revealed a search for faith, and in his collection *Jim hostinou bylo* (It was their feast, 1948), which treats concentration camps and mass murders and expresses visionary reflections on the majesty of dying, Bednář approached the problem in a 'Christian way'; a man can be saved only by suffering. KB

BELŠEVICA, Vizma (b. 1931), Latvian poet, worked as a printer. 1961 she graduated in literary studies at the Gorky Institute, Moscow. By her fourth collection of verse, *Gadu gredzeni* (Annual rings, 1969), Belševica had achieved prominence not only in her native country but also beyond. In many of Belševica's structurally complex, individual, at times even idiosyncratic, poems, which represent perhaps the most important achievement in contemporary Latvian poetry, she generalises in allegorical form about the human condition. The formal structure as well as the contents of Belševica's masterful poem *Indriķa Latviesa piezīmes uz Livonijas hronikas malām* (The annotations of Henricus de Lettis in the margins of the Livonian Chronicle, 1969) struck most readers and critics as truly exceptional, even sensational in the best sense of the word. (The *Livonian Chronicle*, known in its original Latin as *Heinrici Chronicon Livoniae*, is judged to have been written 1225–27 and describes mainly the progress of the German conquest of Livonia 1180 – 1227.) At the same time, the poet accuses not only the many invaders who 'with blazing iron' have done everything to 'torture and extirpate' her people, but also those of her countrymen who naively and submissively carried out the orders of the foreign oppressors, and those who did nothing but turn the other way. The Henricus of Belševica's poem curses his people as a 'treacherous' and 'cur-like' and 'servile and slavish' nation. Although never expelled from the (Soviet) Latvian Writers' Union, Belševica was repeatedly excluded from the list of officially recognised Latvian writers.   EB

BENEŠOVÁ, Božena (1873–1936), Czech prose writer, came from an upper-middle-class family, had little formal education, and married a railway official (1896); she published her first story in 1900, and continued to write under her maiden name, B. Zapletalová, until 1905. Her main characters tend to be female outsiders. The three stories, *Nedobytá vítězství* (Incomplete triumphs, 1910), are anti-sentimental psychological studies of small-town life: in youth people revolt against the oppressive rules of that life, but soon they surrender. The picture of woman's disappointment in love and marriage constitutes a contribution to the contemporaneous discussion of the 'woman question' in Czech literature. The overwrought novel set in the first year of WWI, *Úder* (The blow, 1926), has a mentally powerful, and rather priggish, educated heroine who sets off in disguise to work for the defeat of the Austrians from abroad after her sweetheart has been executed. Benešová's best-known work is *Don Pablo, don Pedro a Věra Lukášová* (D.P., D.P. and V.L., 1936), a gently ironic depiction of an eleven-year-old girl's achievement of emotional maturity through an encounter with a child-molester.

•J. Rozendorfský, 'A. M. Tilschová e Božena Benešová', *L'Europe orientale*, 17 (Rome, 1937).   RBP

BERENT, Wacław, (1873–1940), Polish novelist, came from a middle-class background and spent most of his rather uneventful life in Warsaw. He took a PhD in natural sciences, having studied in Switzerland and Germany. Although never popular, Berent ranks among the best novelists of Polish early Modernism. His main literary output includes four novels and three volumes of biographical essays, typically concerned with decay and regeneration, art and society, and the role of outstanding individuals. Berent developed his own lyrical style, remote from the Realist tradition, and composed Symbolist fiction with a strong universal message. *Próchno* (Rotten wood, 1903) is located in an unnamed German city, and in its almost plotless structure represents the then innovative condensation of story in time and space. Events, arranged in a subtle network of analogies and contrasts illuminated by symbolic imagery and an atmospheric background, present the problem of the incompatibility of art with a hostile, commercialised urban environment. *Ozimina* (Winter wheat, 1911) transforms a description of a social gathering at one of Warsaw's aristocratic houses into a nightmare, reflecting the author's disapproval of the inertia of the Polish Establishment. The tone becomes more optimistic towards the end with the introduction of symbols of regeneration patterned on the Eleusinian Mysteries. *Żywe kamienie* (Living stones, 1918), set in a medieval city in the N Alps, is stylised as a minstrel's tale and contains strongly lyrical language and imagery. The author found in Arthurian legend and Gothic art the everlasting search for the Spiritual Kingdom, overtly opposed to the materialistic culture of the middle classes.

•J. T. Baer, *Wacław Berent* (London, 1974).   SE

BERGADIS (fl. 15th century), Greek author – otherwise unknown – of a poem of 558 15-syllable verses, Απόκοπος (Apokopos), written in Crete in the late 15th century and first published in Venice in 1519. The poem describes a dream in which the narrator, while out hunting, is tempted to climb a tree in pursuit of honey, but is plunged by a series of suitably surreal contingencies into Hades. The dead come to him to ask anxiously about the world above. The genre leads one to expect a highly moralising allegory, but in practice the focus of the poem is quite different. Two young noblemen relate the story of a journey, of the shipwreck in which they had been drowned and of their re-uniting with their sister, who had died at the same hour. The poem concentrates on the joys of life far more than on the evils of death. Hades is here simply characterised by the absence of light, time, movement and beauty, as is the case in Greek folksongs. At the same time the didactic, admonitory tradition is residually present.   CFR

BERGLSON,   **Dovid**/David Bergelson (1884–1952), Yiddish prose fiction writer and playwright, regarded as possibly the most brilliant of modern stylists, was born in Okhrimovo, a village near Umań in the Kiev guberniya. Orphaned young, he lived in Kiev, Odessa and Warsaw. His literary career began with *Arum vokzal* (At the railway station, 1909) which was published partly at his own expense, but received enthusiastic critical acclaim. Other early works were the story *Der toyber* (The deaf man, 1910, dramatised, 1929), the major novel *Nokh alemen* (When all is said and done, 1913), whose heroine, Mirl Hurvits, is the first female protagonist in Yiddish fiction to be portrayed as a real individual, and *In a fargrebter shtot* (At the back of beyond, 1919). All are set in disintegrating provincial towns of the Pale of Settlement. An atmosphere of alienation and fatalistic stagnation is evoked not only by the use of impressionistic detail but also by means of disconcertingly in-direct narrative techniques. During the Civil War Berglson moved to Berlin and lived in voluntary exile for most of the next thirteen years. Together with DER NISTER he edited the leading avant-garde journals *Eygns* (Our own, Kiev, 1918, 1920) and *Milgroym* (Pomegranate, Berlin, London, 1922, 1924). Though his work had already been severely criti-cised by such Communist Party es-tablishment figures as Moyshe Litva-kov (1875–?1938) for its alleged Jew-ish nationalism and its lack of 'prog-ressive' commitment, Berglson hesi-tantly moved closer to the cultural politics of the USSR which he felt to be the only major Jewish centre hold-ing out the promise of a bright future for Yiddish literature. In Berlin he coedited a pro-Soviet journal, *In shpan* (In harness, 1926), to enable non-Party émigrés to align themsel-ves with what many of them felt to be the march of history. From this point on the ostensible content of Berg-lson's fiction adheres more closely to the required optimistic view of Soviet society. This is the case, e.g., in *Mides hadin* (The quality of justice, 1929, extracts from which had al-ready appeared in *In shpan*), the stories in the collections *Shturemteg* (Stormy days, 1927) and *Tsugvintn* (Gusting winds, 1930), and especially in the long *Bildungsroman*, *Baym dnyeper* (On the banks of the Dnepr, 1932–40), but the superficial confor-mity of the plots is subverted, whether consciously or uncon-sciously, by Berglson's unchanging style with its impressionistic narra-tive strategies and the rich Jewish cultural allusions that continue to convey a profoundly perplexing world-view. During the atmosphere of greater cultural freedom which

prevailed in the USSR during WWII Berglson, like a number of his con-temporaries, turned to national ques-tions with historical settings and in 1941 his play *Prints reuveni* (Prince of the Reubenites, 1946) was perfor-med by the Moscow Yiddish State Theatre under the direction of Shloyme Mikhoels (1890–1948). Berglson was active in the Jewish Anti-Fascist Committee soliciting solidarity with the USSR from world Jewry. The Committee was also in-strumental in saving works from sup-pression by sending them abroad for publication, as in the case of *Prints reuveni* which was published in New York. Scarcely a year after the allied victory the repression recommenced and the Yiddish writers were once again accused of 'Jewish national-ism'. Berglson was able to publish one further volume in Moscow, *Naye dertseylungen* (New stories, 1947), before being arrested in the spring of 1949 together with all the leading Yiddish intellectuals. He was shot on 12 August 1952 together with Hof-Shteyn, Markish, Kvitko and many others. 1961 he was 'rehabili-tated' and a volume of his selected writings was published.

•*AMYL*, pp. 55–64; *AOH*, pp. 29–123; 'At the Depot' [*Arum vokzal*] in *SOYN*, pp. 79–139.

Madison, pp. 426–48.   HD

BERNOLÁK, Anton (1762–1813), Slovak philologist and R. Catholic priest, attempted the first codifica-tion of the Slovak language, based on the W Slovak dialect, which is fairly close to Czech. Bernolák published a Slovak grammar and several philolo-gical works in Latin, a six-vol-ume Slovak-Czech-Latin-German-Hungarian dictionary (1825–7) as well as some homilies in Slovak. Although his version of literary Slovak survived sporadically until the late 1880s, it was not adopted by Lutheran writers and their followers, who continued to use Czech until the codification of Slovak by ŠTÚR and his followers.   KB

BERZSENYI, Dániel (1776–1836), Hungarian poet and essayist, born into the middle ranks of the nobility, entered the Sopron Lyceum c. 1790, where he studied Latin and German. He left in 1795, was a soldier for one month in Keszthely, then visited relations in Nikla, where he spent four months learning the art of agriculture, and returned home to farm. In 1799 he married and moved to Sömjén, later returning to Nikla. He indulged in literary activity for some time before 1803, and was discovered by KAZINCZY, who asked him to make changes in his poems and urged him to prepare an edition. 1817 KÖLCSEY published a largely unfavourable review of the second edition of his poems in a scholarly journal. When Berzsenyi's reply was rejected by the editors, he started working on *Poétai harmonistika* (Poetic harmony, 1832), a lengthy essay on poetics. In his later life he wrote few poems and became an active supporter of the political reform programme of SZÉCHENYI. 1830 he became a member of the Hungarian Academy, and 1833 he finished his prose work *A magyarországi mezei szorgalom némely akadályairul* (On the difficulties of agriculture in Hungary). He was a late neo-Classicist who anticipated Romanticism. His elegiac odes have more artistic value than the epistles in which he popularised the ideas of the Enlightenment in his later years. At his best he combined the use of Greek and Latin verse forms with originality of diction. Whereas earlier poets used language, he cre-

ated it. In his early verse – for example 'A tizennyolcadik század' (The eighteenth century) – he praised the stability of the 18th century. The second version of his ode 'A magyarokhoz' (To the Hungarians) and other poems lamented the decay of the nation and thus paved the way for political reforms. Although he was a landowner, he became alienated from the traditional way of life of his class. His finest poems, 'Életfilozófia' (A philosophy of life), 'Levéltöredék barátnémhoz' (Fragmentary epistle to a lady friend) and 'A közelítő tél' (Winter approaching), are elegiac expressions of his sense of decay. After 1808, however, he made an effort to participate in social life and composed poems which either were didactic or served as self-commentary. He blamed Buonaparte for being disloyal to the cause of liberty in the epigram 'Napoleonhoz' (To Napoleon, 1814). In *Vitkovics Mihályhoz* (To Mihály V., 1815), an epistle addressed to a poet who published verse in both Hungarian and Serbian, he wrote about his nostalgia for urban life. In *Dukai Takács Judithoz* (To Judit D.T., 1815), composed for an interesting woman poet (1795–1836), he writes of *ut musica poesis* and the use of symbols as the characteristic features of his own work.   MSz-M

BESIK'I (i.e. Besarion Gabashvili 1750–91), Georgian poet, born in Tblisi, died suddenly at Iassy (Iaşi), Bessarabia, was the most gifted poet of his time in Georgia, adulated for sheer musicality and spontaneity, and he was the first to adopt a predominantly Voltairean stance. The Gabashvilis were a proud, but impoverished, family at the centre of intrigues both at the court of the Kings of Kartli (VAKHT'ANG VI,

TEIMURAZ II and Erek'le II) and in the patriarchate of Ant'on I. Besik'i's father was anathematised and fled to Russia. Quarrels with the Church made it impossible for Besik'i to receive an education at Catholicos Ant'on I's model grammar school, but his poetry demonstrates that he studied Greek poetry and philosophy, Oriental languages and French. Besik'i's favourite pseudonym was Velizariani, from Bélisaire, the freethinking hero of the eponymous *conte* by the French *encyclopédiste* Marmontel. (The *Encylopédie* was one of King Erek'le II's chief weapons in his campaign to modernise Georgian culture.) At the age of 27, Besik'i aroused the wrath of King Erek'le II and had to flee to Russia first as the emissary of Solomon I of Imeretia, then as attaché to Potemkin, in whose service he died. His passionate poem *Dedopals Anazed* (On Queen Ana) and tradition credit him with an illicit love affair with a Queen Ana: who Ana was – whether TEIMURAZ II's widowed daughter (Erek'le's sister), then in her fifties, or a mere child, Ana Orbeliani, the future wife of Solomon I – is unknown, but the scandalous and improbable were the essence of Besik'i's reputation. His personal poetry, however intoxicating in its assonance, its rhythms and erotic passion, is sometimes obscure – who, for instance, are the two women in the lyric 'Shavni shashvni' (Blackbirds)? Much of Besik'i's life and Georgia's history in those unsettled times is conjectural. No precise dates can be given for his work. Nevertheless, hypnotic and moving lyrics such as 'Sevdis baghs shevel' (I entered the garden of sadness) manifest the depth of Besik'i's feelings and the culture of an apocalyptic

Georgia. Besik'i died unpublished, but hundreds of manuscript copies circulated for decades after his death; the titles and notes to many poems may be inventions of amateur copyists. His early style is florid and shares some similes with the polyglot Armenian *ashugh* (minstrel) SAYAT-NOVA, but Besik'i soon learnt to be direct in his imagery. His energy was developed in exchanges of satire with his many enemies at court and abroad: his scurrilous attacks on Catholicos Ant'on are such ingenious anagrammatical word-play that they might almost have been a pleasure to receive. The same élan makes his bitter historical ode *Aspindzisatvis* (On the Battle of Aspindza) a graphic denunciation of Russia's policy of leaving the Georgians in the lurch after urging them to take on the Turks: 'Alas, how can I who mention this day slander anyone? The Russians misled the King: there was nothing good there for us. The Count turned back with his army – and it does his name no good – He gave the same answer to all: "Whence I came, there I shall go!" ' Besik'i's verse and his heritage to later poets are impulsiveness and pulse: a Byronic prototype, he provided the standard and the genre that the next generations of Georgian poets struggled to match.

●Edition: A. Baramidze and V. Topuria (Eds.), *B. Gabashvilis tkhzulebata sruli k'rebuli* (Tbilisi, 1932).   DR

BETHLEN, Kata (1700–59), Transylvanian writer, was a fanatical Protestant who at the age of 17 was forced to marry a R. Catholic; widowed after three years, she remarried only to be widowed once again in 1732. She was rich and well educated, had a good knowledge of medicine and botany and was an expert needlewoman. She also collected a large library and promoted better education for girls. She published two religious works in her lifetime; the first, *Bujdosásnak emlékezetköve* (Memorial of exile, 1733), was frequently reprinted and sold over 26,000 copies, while the second, *Védekező erős pais* (Strong shield and defence, 1759), also had a measure of success. But her literary reputation depends on her autobiographical *Életének maga által való rövid leírása* (A brief account of her own life, 1740s–59). a revelation of her spiritual stress and agony that foreshadows psychoanalysis. Her style is crisp and succinct; the recently discovered final chapters end in mid-sentence, describing her last illness – a poignant ending to an unusually powerful memoir.

●Excerpt in T. Klaniczay (Ed.), *Old Hungarian Literary Reader* (Budapest, 1985).   GFC

BETHLEN, Miklós (1642–1716), Transylvanian (Hungarian) prose writer, statesman, was educated in Calvinist colleges in his homeland before attending the universities of Heidelberg, Utrecht and Leyden. After a brief tour of England and France he returned to become one of the leading Transylvanian politicians. He was arrested in 1704 for the publication of a pamphlet advocating Transylvanian independence and addressed among others to Queen Anne (*Olajágat viselő Noe galambja* [Noah's dove bearing an olive branch] The Hague, 1704). He was imprisoned in Nagyszeben (Sibiu), Eszék (Osijek) and finally Vienna, where he died shortly after regaining his freedom. While in prison, Bethlen worked on his impressive *Önéletírás* (Autobiography, written 1708–10, published, 1858–60). Circulated in manuscript, it is an apologia which ranges over the political and social concerns of his age as well as his personal problems. Its structure shows his debt to St Augustine's *Confessions*; the narrative is interrupted by meditations, and the autobiography proper is followed by a book of prayers which reveal his political views as well as his religious beliefs. Bethlen also wrote several tracts and maintained an extensive correspondence. His literary reputation depends on his autobiography, which is a masterpiece of late Baroque prose. Bethlen excels in vivid description and characterisation and has a fine sense of drama, as evidenced, for example, by his account of the death of ZRÍNYI.

●Excerpts in T. Klaniczay (Ed.), *Old Hungarian Literary Reader* (Budapest, 1985).   GFC

BEVK, France (1890–1970), Slovene novelist, short-story writer, playwright and author of travelogues and memoirs, completed teacher training at Gorica, 1913, and worked as a schoolmaster, though this was interrupted by service on the Eastern Front, 1917. After the war he worked briefly as a journalist in Ljubljana, then returned to Gorica as editor and publisher until the Italian authorities banned the Slovene press. Released from confinement after the collapse of Fascist Italy in 1943, he joined the partisans; after WWII he held important political posts. His historical novels include *Kresna noč* (Midsummer night, 1927), a tale of murder and jealousy set in the 15th century; *Človek proti človeku* (Man against man, 1930), about the 14th-century struggle between the patriarch of Aquilea and rebellious nobles. Rural novels with a modern background include: *Krivda* (Guilt, 1929), a tale of marital infidelity and a son's vengeance, *Bridka ljubezen* (Bitter love, 1927) and *Veliki Tomaž* (Big T., 1932). One of his finest works was *Kaplan Martin Čedermac* (Fr. M.Č., 1938) concerning the persecution of a Venetian-Slovene priest and his struggle against Fascist oppression; the author disguised his identity with the pseudonym Pavle Sedmak.

•The play, 'In the depths' (*SEER*, 1936). HL

BEZRUČ, Petr (i.e. Vladimír Vašek, 1867–1958), Czech poet, was born the son of a patriotic Silesian schoolmaster; he started to read Classics at Prague, but after three years left to become a minor civil servant (1888). 1915–16 he was imprisoned for two anti-Austrian poems wrongly attributed to him. Half of his one major collection, *Slezské písně* (Silesian songs, 1909), had previously appeared as *Slezské číslo* (Silesian number, 1903). He was a social visionary poet who had little time for anyone but the outcast Czech Silesian poor: he was anti-Prague Czech, anti-German, anti-Polish and anti-Jewish (unless the Jew is poor). In his verse he stylises himself as a coarse, ill-endowed miner who stands up for those Czechs who were exploited by the landlords, mine-owners and local-government officials and were ignored by Prague, as they were gradually becoming polonised and germanised. The angry poems express gloom and disillusion, almost nihilism. Their artistic originality and emotive force derive from Bezruč's stark, dour sincerity and rugged monumentality.

•*Silesian Songs* (Prague, 1966).
A. Cronia, *Petr Bezruč* (Rome, 1932); O. F. Babler, 'Rudolf Fuchs als Bezruč-Übersetzer' in the conference proceedings, *Weltfreunde* (Berlin and Neuwied, 1967). RBP

BIADULA, Žmitrok (i.e. Samuił Płaŭnik, 1886–1941), Byelorussian prose writer and poet, showed equal talent in both genres. Born into the family of a literate Jewish forester in the Łahojsk region, he studied in Talmudic schools before being expelled for writing poetry. The period of National Revival before WWI was both happy and productive, but the War and ensuing Revolution brought despair and silence. He recovered, however, and produced several major works before Stalin ended all original creativity. He died fleeing the invading Germans. Biadula's lyric poetry, like his earliest stories, is emotionally vivid, quirky and poignantly romantic with persistent social and patriotic notes. Nature is often linked with art and, especially after the Revolution, embellished with fanciful mythology. As with the poetry, Biadula began his story-writing in 1912 when he published *Abrazki* (Images), a collection of lyrical prose miniatures, melancholy in content, complex and ambitiously experimental in form. Later a tragic strain enters stories like *Aščaślivita* (Happiness, 1913), but more often than not it is mingled with comedy, and always Biadula's psychological acuity is matched by stylistic sophistication. After the Revolution Biadula continued to use short forms but also turned to novels: *Sałaviej* (The nightingale, 1927) is a romantic work about a harsh 18th-century lord and his musically talented but rebellious serf; the language is dense, hyperbolic and highly lyrical; the plot, though never dull, is episodic and historically unconvincing, but receives an added dimension from the possibility that the book is an allegory of contemporary Soviet reality. The other major work was *Jazep Krušynski* (1929), a gripping canvas of life in the 1920s focusing on the rise of a wilful and unscrupulous swindler, with a wide and vivid range of other characters; the second part (1932) is ruined by the already compulsory idealisation of the positive characters. His last works, written shortly before his death, were for children: a narrative poem and a fable. Biadula's rich legacy in prose and verse makes him one of the best-loved of Byelorussian classics.

●A. B. McMillin (Ed.), *The Images Swarm Free: A Bilingual Selection of Poetry by Maksim Bahdanovič, Aleś Harun and Žmitrok Biadula* (London, 1982).   ABMcM

BIAŁOSZEWSKI,   Miron (1922–83), Polish poet, playwright and author of autobiographical prose, the most innovative of all writers living in Poland after WWII, was born in Warsaw and spent virtually all his life there. During the German occupation, he had only begun his studies at an underground university when the Warsaw Uprising broke out in 1944. In postwar Poland Białoszewski never completed his education; he made his living doing odd jobs until he lost the last of those in 1952. He had been writing since the war years but published only a few poems in periodicals in the late 1940s; in subsequent years, unable to conform with the norms of Socialist Realism, he wrote 'for his desk drawer'. While living in destitution under Stalinism, he adopted his characteristic way of life of a modern-day hermit confined by choice to his shabby Warsaw apartment and aloof from any public activity. A decisive turn in his life occurred 1955–6, when political relaxation made it possible for him to resume publishing. 1956 his first collection, *Obroty rzeczy* (The revolution of

things), was a major sensation of the rapid 'Thaw' in culture. Another sensation was the miniature theatre operating in a private apartment, where Białoszewski and a few of his friends staged and acted his plays from 1955 until 1963. Meanwhile, critical reaction became polarised after the publication of his next three collections. Before 1970, even his admirers considered him a difficult and largely solipsistic experimenter. This opinion underwent a reversal with the publication of his *Pamiętnik z powstania warszawskiego* (Memoir of the Warsaw Uprising, 1970), a best-seller where the controversial historical event was shown from the perspective of a non-heroic civilian and described in a narrative style which combined elements of intimate diary, lyric, reportage and oral tale. After *Pamiętnik*, Białoszewski published other works in the same style, and focused on his immediate everyday experiences. The last of these books was the posthumous collection *Oho* (1985), in which the grim reality of martial law in 1981–2 was presented in a grotesque yet ultra-realistic way. Białoszewski's singular contribution to Polish literature can be defined as an act of opening literary discourse to the areas of reality – be they realms of material objects, words or human interrelations – that had traditionally been considered too trivial to attract the attention of a 'serious' writer.

●*The Revolution of Things: Selected Poems* (Washington, DC, 1974); *Memoir of the Warsaw Uprising* (Ann Arbor, 1977).

M. G. Levine, *Contemporary Polish Poetry, 1925–1975* (Boston, 1981).   StB

BIERNAT OF LUBLIN(?–after 1529), the first Polish author writing solely in the vernacular whose name we know, was the author of one of the first books printed in Polish (a prayerbook, *Raj duszny* [Paradise of the soul, 1513]). Not much is known of his life except that he was a well-educated clergyman of humble origins, who served as a secretary and chaplain at magnates' courts. His chief work is *Żywot Ezopa* (The life of Aesop, 1522), a fictitious 'biography' in verse of the legendary slave, including a collection of fables purported to be Aesop's. While still a thoroughly medieval poet in form and style, Biernat expresses ideas and beliefs heralding the arrival of Humanism.

•Poems in B. Carpenter (Ed.), *Monumenta Polonica* (Ann Arbor, 1989).   StB

BLAGA, Lucian (1895–1961), Roumanian poet, dramatist and philosopher, son of an Orthodox priest from central Transylvania, attended a German-language primary school in Sebeş and a Roumanian lycée in Braşov. At the outbreak of WWI he enrolled in the Orthodox Seminary in Sibiu to avoid being called up into the Austro-Hungarian army. He studied philosophy at Vienna 1917–20 and two years later was awarded his doctorate there for a thesis *Kultur und Erkenntnis* (Culture and cognition). He helped found the influential cultural journal *Gîndirea* (Thought) in 1921. 1926 he joined the diplomatic service and held positions as press attaché and cultural counsellor in Warsaw, Prague, Berne and Vienna, and was minister in Lisbon. 1937 he was appointed to the chair of the Philosophy of Culture at Cluj University. He was dismissed from the chair in 1948 for failing to give his support to the new educational reforms introduced by the Communist government and spent the rest of his

life as an archivist. He is preoccupied with 'light' as a natural agent of the universe and its mysterious character is explored, often against the background of myth, in *Poemele luminii* (The poems of light, 1919). For the poet, man lives aspiring to the revelation of mysteries and his existence is a genetic transition towards death: *În marea trecere* (In the great transition, 1924). As a dramatist he adapted national myths in *Zamolxe* (1921), *Meşterul Manole* (Master M., 1927) as well as universal myths in *Arca lui Noe* (Noah's Ark, 1944). His principal work on the philosophy of culture, *Trilogia culturii* (The trilogy of culture, 1944), formulates the concept of the 'stylistic matrix', the impression of which is given by the unconscious to everything created by man.

•*Poems of Light* (Bucharest, 1975). DJD

BLANDIANA, Ana (b. 1942), Roumanian poet, is widely admired by Roumanians as a champion of moral integrity as a result of her courageous stand against the opportunism and sycophancy which characterised much of literary expression during the 1970s and 1980s. Born in Timişoara, she spent her childhood and youth in Transylvania, attending school in Oradea and university at Cluj, where she took a degree in Romance languages. After graduating she moved to Bucharest to work as editor of the students' review *Amfiteatru* and in 1964 her first collection, *Persoana întiia plural* (First person plural), received widespread acclaim. She then took up full-time writing and was a regular weekly columnist for *România literară*, the Writers' Union journal, 1974–88, with occasional interruptions caused by her clashes with the authorities. Following the publication in December 1984 of four poems critical of the brutalising impact of Ceauşescu's rule on the daily lives of his people, Blandiana was placed under house arrest for one month. In spring 1988 a satirical poem about a cat was adjudged by the authorities to be an allegory of Ceauşescu and her column for *România literară* was suspended for several months. In opinion polls taken in Roumania since the overthrow of Ceauşescu her name has been among those heading the list of nominations for the office of president. In September 1990 she played a leading role in setting up the Civic Alliance, a voluntary association with no political affiliation, of student, professional and trade-union organisations which has proved remarkably successful in mobilising anti-government street protests. Her early cycles *A treia taină* (The third sacrament, 1970) and *Octombrie, noiembrie, decembrie* (October, November, December, 1972) are infused by a powerful religious drive inherited from her father, who was a priest, and this has led to her work being called 'a poetry of epiphanies'. She seeks in Nature and in the cycles of life a harmony with the world and with herself. In her preoccupation with purity, expressed by angels, butterflies and crystalline waters, there is a vulnerability which she converts in later collections, e.g. *Ora de nisip* (The hour of sand, 1983), *Stea de pradă* (Star of prey, 1985) and *Poezii* (Poems, 1989), into a forceful weapon with which to confront a corrupt age. Yet, unlike a number of her contemporaries, she is not cynical, but writes as a wounded romantic who is concerned that civilised human values have been perverted. That concern stems from a Transylvanian sense of probity and dedication which has been virtually drowned in contemporary public life by the 'Levantine' values of Bucharest.

●*The Hour of Sand. Selected Poems 1969–89* (London, 1990).   DJD

BLATNÝ, Ivan (1919–90), Czech poet, son of L. BLATNÝ, studied philosophy at Brno and, after the Germans closed Czech universities in 1939, worked in his grandmother's opticians shop, went to London in 1948 with a writer's delegation, and defected; he developed schizophrenia in the 1950s and spent the rest of his life in care. His intimate lyric verse, mixing the sensuous enjoyment of conventional beauty with a sense of foreboding at the enigma of things perceived, is suffused with a nostalgia which is defined as 'a desire to return where we have never been'. His verse in *Melancholické procházky* (Melancholy walks, 1941), *Tento večer* (This evening, 1945) and *Hledání přítomného času* (Remembrance of things present, 1947), melodious, mostly rhymed and using playful metaphors – 'the dawn was crunching the wet cauliflower of the sky' – is sometimes reminiscent of that of SEIFERT, NEZVAL and his friend ORTEN.   KB

BLATNÝ, Lev (1894–1930), Czech dramatist and short-story writer, once a railway clerk, later dramaturg at the Brno National Theatre, was one of the first Czech dramatists to adopt Expressionism. In his play *Tři* (Three, 1920), he treats an erotic triangle, while *Ko-Ko-Ko dák* (Cluck-cluck, 1922) is a vicious satire on the petty bourgeois, who are likened to stupid and frightened chickens. The borderline between comedy and tragedy is erased in his *Smrt na prodej* (Death for sale, 1929), a grotesque story of a mother and daughter who try to make money by selling the rope on which the alcoholic father had hanged himself. The characters of his stories *Vítr v ohradě* (Storm in the pen, 1923) are people whose sheltered lives have been physically and mentally shattered by some malevolent external force. With Vladimír Raffel (1898–1967) and LANGER he introduced Expressionism into Czech prose. KB

BLAUMANIS, Rudolfs (1863–1908), Latvian writer, the son of a cook, graduated from the Commercial Academy in Riga, worked as a journalist in Riga and St Petersburg, and acted as editor of *Dienas Lapa*, a paper of the so-called New Current. Blaumanis, a classic Realist, has left works in all branches of literature, except the novel. The patriarchal Latvian homestead, the generation conflict and the life of fishermen and people working on the Baltic German baronial estates furnished the themes for most of his short stories: *Salna pavasarī* (Hoar-frost in the spring, 1898) and *Purva bridējs* (The wader in the marsh, 1898). His plays, which till this day have remained the backbone of the Latvian theatrical repertoire, stress the 'tragedy' of human life, e.g., *Sestdienas vakars* (Saturday night, 1907), a one-acter of almost mystical character. EB

BOGDANI, Pjetër (c. 1625–89), the author of the first original Albanian prose work, was born in Guri i Hasit near Kukës, N Albania, studied in Rome, where he took a doctorate of philosophy and theology. He became Bishop of Shkodër and then Archbishop of Skopje. Bogdani took an active part in the contemporary anti-Turkish movement in N Albania. For this reason the Turkish authorities forced him into exile in Italy; towards the end of his life he returned to Albania; he died in Prishtinë. Bogdani's work *Çeta e pro-fetëve* (Lat. *Cuneus prophetarum*, The wedge of the prophets, 1685), written in Albanian and Italian, was published in Padua and republished, in 1691 and 1702 in Venice, under different titles. It is mainly a theological and philosophical work, but it also handles problems of history, geography and astronomy and includes Albanian poetry, written by Bogdani himself and by other minor contemporary authors. This poetry reveals the presence of a literary tradition in N Albania. Bogdani is considered the father of Albanian prose. He enriched the Albanian language with words for abstract concepts.

●M. Sciambra, *Bogdanica, studi di Pietro Bogdani e l'opera sua* (Bologna, 1965). ShM

BOHORIČ, Adam (c. 1520–c.1600), Slovene Protestant reformer, author of the first Slovene grammar, studied at Wittenberg with Melanchthon and later became director of the Protestant school in Ljubljana. His greatest achievement was his Slovene grammar in Latin modelled on Melanchthon's Latin primer, with the charming title *Arcticae horulae succisivae* (Spare winter hours, 1584); his introduction emphasised the geographical and historical importance of the Slavonic nations. The orthography he introduced was named after him the *bohoričica*; it remained in use until the 1840s.

●Reprint with (modern) Slovene version ed. by J. Toporišič (Maribor, 1987). HL

BOR, Matej (i.e. Vladimir Pavšič, b. 1913), Slovene poet, playwright, novelist, critic, essayist and translator, read Slavonic studies at Ljubljana University (degree 1937), and worked for a time as a journalist and then as a teacher before WWII. During the war he joined the partisans, publishing illegally a defiant set of verse in 1942, entitled *Previharimo viharje* (We shall weather the storms), and writing for the partisan stage. His first postwar collection of poems, *Pesmi* (Poems, 1946), added to his violent partisan verse a cycle of love poetry, 'Ljubezen v viharju' (Love in the storm), including the moving ballad 'Srečanje' (The encounter) on the identification and burial of the remains of his wife, shot two years earlier. His next collection, intimate and reflective, *Bršljan nad jezom* (Ivy over the dam, 1951), showed greater care for language, melody and form. *Sled naših senc* (The track of our shadows, 1958) included a cycle of love poetry, 'Med tamariskimi' (Among the tamarisks), and a despairing protest against the nuclear arms race, 'Šel je popotnik skozi atomski vek' (A wanderer went through the atomic age). His first novel, *Daljave* (Distant parts, 1961), dealt in a fresh way with life among the partisans. His dramatic works are partly concerned with social problems: *Vrnitev Blažonovih* (The return of the Blažonovs, 1954) on the conflict between 'progressive' and reactionary elements in postwar rural Primorje and *Kolesa teme* (The wheels of darkness, 1954) on negative aspects of modern society.

●In *AMYP* 1962, 1961; *Parnassus*, 1957, 1965; *SPT*, 1965.   HL

BORNEMISZA, Péter (1535–84), Hungarian poet, playwright and preacher, was a turbulent priest in a turbulent age. Educated in Padua, Wittenberg and Vienna, he became chaplain to the powerful Balassi family and tutor to the poet Bálint BALASSI. Embracing Lutheranism, he became engaged in a constant battle with the R. Catholic hierarchy, resulting in continual harassment and a personal reprimand from the Emperor. He acquired his own press and eventually settled in Sempte (Šintava) where he published his monumental series of sermons (5 volumes, 1573–9). The fourth of these included a separate work, *Ördögi kísértetek* (Temptations of the Devil, 1578), in which he attacked contemporary authorities, both ecclesiastical and political, so fiercely that he was imprisoned. He escaped and sought refuge in the isolated castle of Detrekő (Plavecké Podhradie), where he published a verse anthology, *Énekek három rendbe* (Triple hymnal, 1582), and a further volume of sermons (1584). Bornemisza excelled in the writing of scholarly polemical prose; his style indicates the shift from oral to written polemics that marked the Counter-Reformation. His verse, as lyrical as his prose is robust, includes a lullaby reminiscent of Blake and the haunting *Cantio optima* of 1556. But it is his adaptation for contemporary conditions of Sophocles' *Electra*, *Tragoedia magyar nyelven* (Tragedy in the Hungarian language, 1558) that reveals the touch of a master. The moral problem of tyrannicide remains central, but Bornemisza's subtle changes in both characterisation and presentation make it a remarkable achievement.

●*Cantio optima* and *Temptations of the Devil* (excerpts) in T. Klaniczay (Ed.), *Old Hungarian Literary Reader* (Budapest, 1985).   GFC

BOROWSKI, Tadeusz (1922–51), Polish short-story writer, during the German occupation took part in clandestine cultural activities. Arrested in 1943, he spent the rest of the war in concentration camps. After 1945 he joined the Communist Party and contributed numerous articles to Party newspapers. His prison-camp experiences are reflected in two collections of short stories: *Pożegnanie z Marią* (Farewell to Mary, 1948) and *Kamienny Świat* (World of stone, 1948). In contrast to the prevailing martyr tone of conventional concentration-camp fiction, Borowski gives impassive, behaviouristic descriptions of the camps and stresses the ruthless, often brutal, struggle for survival, where heroism and compassion were in short supply. Regarded by some as a nihilist, he has nevertheless been widely recognised as one of the most objective chroniclers of German atrocities.

●*This Way for the Gas, Ladies and Gentlemen and Other Stories* (New York, 1967). SE

BOTEV, Hristo (1848–76), Bulgarian poet, was the son of a schoolmaster who was educated in Russia and used to translate and write himself; Botev was sent to Odessa (1863) to finish his secondary education but showed little interest in his school work, read the works of socialists and anarchists like Charles Fourier, Saint-Simon, Proudhon, Bakunin and Marx and developed radical socialist views. Because of his outbursts of revolutionary enthusiasm (on one occasion he had beaten up a representative of the authorities), he was expelled from school and from Odessa and then worked as a teacher in a small Russian village, but had to leave because of his speeches criticing social injustice. He returned to his native Kalofer and sometimes used to take over his father's classes; his expression of his political views made it impossible for him to remain and he left for Russia to continue his education, but instead of going there, he went to Roumania and made contacts with the Bulgarian exiles. Here he established several periodicals, e.g. *Duma na balgarskite emigranti* (Word of the Bulgarian exiles, 1871), the satirical *Budilnik* (Alarm-clock, 1873) or *Zname* (Banner, 1874–5); he also wrote for KARAVELOV's papers. His journalistic work concerns only the national cause and revolution, which Botev imagined as both national and social. During his time in Roumania he was involved in the activities of the Bulgarian Revolutionary Committee who planned to liberate Bulgaria through an uprising in the country supported by armed groups trained abroad. 1876, after the April Uprising, about which the Committee had not had adequate information, Botev crossed the Danube with a group of 200 men, but after only a few days, the group was traced and destroyed by the Turks and Botev was killed. His poetic work, published in various journals, 1867–75, consists of only twenty-two poems; these made him, however, the most celebrated poet of Bulgarian literature. The ideology of the National Revival culminates in Botev's verse; the national idea is sublimated in poetic archetypes such as 'hero' and the 'mother-country' (who have a 'mother-son' relationship), where historical, geographical and human realities are modified into an ideal Romantic super-reality. Death in the fight for the ideal is anticipated with exaltation and is equated with immortality; Nature is perceived as an aspect of the 'mourning widowed mother-country' and her sorrow for the death of the hero (e.g. 'Hadzhi Dimităr', 1873) attains almost cosmic dimensions. Botev was the first to convert the folk motifs and imagery which dominated patriotic verse before him into lyrical metaphors, thus creating a poetic language which became a model for generations of Bulgarian poets.

●*Poems* (Sofia, 1955). SIK

BOTTO, Ján (1829–81), Slovak Romantic poet, who started writing while still a pupil at the Levoča Lyceum, studied engineering in Pest and earned his living as a land surveyor in various parts of Upper Hungary. His chief work is *Smrt' Jánošíkova* (Jánošík's death, 1862; expanded ed. 1880). Taking his inspiration from oral-tradition songs concerning the Slovak bandit Juraj Jánošík, from the verse of P. J. Šafařík (1795–1861), MÁCHA and MICKIEWICZ, Botto tells the story of Jánošík's betrayal by a fellow bandit and an old Slovak woman, his torture, his execution and his ascent to a fairy paradise where his terrestrial beloved is now queen. Botto's picture of a titanic Slovak bandit in communion with a grand, patriotic Slovak Nature, of bandits standing for the irrepressible freedom which will come to Slovaks, and of Slovak humour and vitality overcoming Magyar and German 'blackness' is vividly rhapsodic; its tone varies from the folksy to the metaphysically symbolic.
● *The Death of Jánošík* (Pittsburgh, 1944).
W. Giusti, '"La morte di Janosik" di Ján Botto', *Rivista delle Letterature slave*, I, 1926, pp. 329–40; L. Richter, *Slowakische Literatur. Entwicklungstrends vom Vormärz bis zur Gegenwart* (Berlin, 1979).
                                                    RBP

BOZDĚCH, Emanuel (1841– ? 90), Czech dramatist, studied law, languages and history at Prague and Paris; he worked as a private tutor and later as the dramaturg of the Provisional Theatre in Prague. His comedies *Z doby kotilionův* (From the age of cotillions, 1872), *Zkouška státníkova* (A statesman's trial, 1874) and *Světa pán v županu* (The master of the world in a dressing-gown, 1876), set at the time of the Marquise de Pompadour, Empress Maria Theresa and Napoleon, although reminiscent of those by Eugène Scribe in their construction, were significant in the Czech context by their turning away from Romantic pathos to a witty, ironical natural conversational dialogue. Bozděch was not interested in ideas and his plays are not dramatic; instead they concentrate on depicting the far-reaching consequences of trifling events and on debunking great personalities and their lives. His early tragedy *Baron Goertz* (1868), whose plot concerns the assassination of the Swedish Charles XII, concentrates on the psychology of the regicide Kundson, but Bozděch's talent was more suited to conversational comedy.
● *A Trial in Statesmanship* (Prague, 1874).
                                                    KB

BRAZDŽIONIS, Bernardas (b. 1907), Lithuanian poet and critic, educated at Kaunas, taught at grammar school and later worked as an editor in the main Lithuanian publishing house. 1940–4 Brazdžionis was director of the Maironis Literary Museum in Kaunas; then he fled to Germany and went to the USA in 1949, where he worked in a printing shop and later as an editor of a Lithuanian journal. 1989 he returned to Lithuania for a visit. It was a triumphant tour for a poet who had long symbolised the endurance of the nation under Soviet oppression and the undying longing for their lost home of the Lithuanian diaspora. This he had achieved by the sonorous rhetorical cadences of his patriotic verse, written abroad, in which love for his nation and the pain of the exile's dispossession were conveyed with emotional intensity and with the noble grandeur of the born orator. This strident patriotism is one of the main motifs of Brazdžionis's poetry.

Some readers feel it has less artistic merit than his poetry written between the wars in Lithuania, e.g. *Ženklai ir stebuklai* (Omens and miracles, 1936), *Kunigaikščių miestas* (The city of princes, 1939) and *Šaukiu aš tautą* (I call the nation, 1941). These collections are dominated by religious themes conveyed in terms of longing for the exotic places and times of the Bible, or for the Gothic thrust of medieval piety, or, finally, for the distant gates of Heaven as the ultimate, comforting home for the soul. In all this, Brazdžionis remained a master of poetic language, skilfully blending conventional Romantic imagery with bold new metaphors that strained the bounds of conventional logic. Brazdžionis has also written verse for children and literary criticism. RŠ

BRĚZAN, Jurij (b. 1916), Sorbian prose writer, a leading exponent of Socialist Realism in the GDR, born in Worklecy (Räckelwitz), SE of Kamenz, the son of a quarryman and smallholder, attended the Bautzen grammar school 1927–36, when he was expelled for 'political immaturity'. He continued his studies in Prague and Toruń. 1938, after returning home, he was arrested and imprisoned for a few weeks, then released but expelled from Lusatia. Nevertheless, he returned in 1941. He served as a conscript in the Wehrmacht 1942–6. 1946–8 he was active in the Sorbian youth movement. Later he became a professional writer in German as well as Sorbian. Brězan began his literary career as a poet and achieved fame in the 1950s for his poem 'Kak wótčinu namakach' (How I found my fatherland). His story *Kak stara Jančowa z wyšnosću wojowaše* (How old Mrs Janč fought with the authorities, 1952) marks the beginning of Socialist Realism in Sorbian literature. Hereafter he concentrated on prose and produced a partly autobiographical trilogy of novels under the general title of *Feliks Hanuš*, consisting of *Šuler* (The schoolboy, 1958), *Wučbne lěta* (Years of study, 1961), and *Zrałe lěta* (Years of maturity, 1969). The hero is a representative of Brězan's generation whose experience in the Third Reich leads him to participate cheerfully in building a socialist homeland. Krabat, a figure from Sorbian folklore, is the hero of Brězan's novel *Krabat* (1976), in which both topical and timeless questions of the human predicament are explored. Brězan's collected works in Sorbian were published in ten volumes in 1965–82. His latest novel, *Stary nan* (Old father, 1982), is based largely on the life of Brězan's own father and revolves around ideas of human dignity.

●*The Fallow Years* (Berlin, 1963).

J. Keil (Comp.), *Betrachtungen zum Werk Brězans* (Bautzen, 1976). GCS

BŘEZINA, Otokar (i.e. Ignác Jebavý, 1868–1929), Czech poet, a schoolmaster, lived the life of a recluse and, even when acknowledged as a great poet and thinker, refused a university chair. Březina published five books of poetry and several philosophical essays but gave up writing when 35 years old. His ambition was to evolve a philosophical and artistic system, and the sequence of his works reveals an intentional progression of spiritual life from individual despair to salvation in the brotherhood of all creation. After vainly seeking refuge in art in *Tajemné dálky* (Mysterious distances, 1895), inspired by Baudelaire, the French Symbolists and Schopenhauer, in his subsequent collection, *Svítání na západě* (Dawn in the West, 1896), he envisages liberation from sensual perception by acquiring occult powers to penetrate the mysteries of the universe. Following Plato, the medieval mystics and Indian philosophy, he adheres to monism; he expresses love for all organic and inorganic creation and a belief in cosmic evolution towards a mysterious will in *Větry od pólů* (Winds from the poles, 1897), to some extent foreshadowing Teilhard de Chardin. But in *Stavitelé chrámu* (The temple builders, 1898), Březina returns to Earth and celebrates individual redemption restricted to the initiated – martyrs, prophets, impulsive builders of the temple – through suffering and work. Březina's last completed volume of poetry, *Ruce* (Hands, 1901), is an apotheosis of life; not only the chosen but all humanity will be saved by forging a magic chain of hands resulting in the arrival of 'the luminous, mysterious Man'. Březina gradually freed himself from poetic convention, rejected his early liturgical imagery and strict metre and elaborated a free-verse style with carefully contrived metaphors, mostly oxymora.

●P. Selver, *Otokar Březina* (Oxford, 1921).   KB

BRIDEL, Bedřich (Bridelius, 1619–80), Czech poet, Jesuit priest, teacher of rhetoric and poetics at Jesuit colleges and administrator of the Jesuit printing house in Prague, was primarily a preacher and missionary. He died caring for the sick during an outbreak of pestilence. Bridel is the most important poet of the Czech Counter-Reformation; he fully exploited Baroque ideas and style. Apart from various works in verse and prose, he published many translations of hagiographic works from Latin and German. In his *Život svatého Ivana, poustevníka a vyznavače* (The life of St Ivan, hermit and confessor of the Faith, 1657), the story of the legendary Croat prince who became the hermit in Bohemia during the 9th century, the prose alternates with verse deploring the deceptiveness of the world, celebrating the loveliness of the Bohemian mountains and forests and hallowing Nature as a reflection of the metaphysical beauty of God. *Jesličky: Staré nové písničky* (The manger. Songs old and new, 1658) contains, apart from traditional Christmas carols, several of his own compositions, in particular a meditative poem of 532 lines describing a vision of cosmic harmony brought about by the sounds of planets circling through space. Bridel's key work is the poem *Co Bůh? Člověk?* (What is God? What man?, 1658), an interior dialogue of 576 lines contemplating the antithesis between God as being and the human I as non-being in an existentialist manner devoid of moralising. Bridel concentrates on the foregrounding of expressive language and pushes the possibilities of Baroque poetics to the extreme, using devices like oxymoron (garmentless vesture) and mystical paradox (three-sided sphere and threefold roundness). Bridel's forceful dismissal of the hollowness of earthly existence found an echo in the poetry of MÁCHA and HALAS.   KB

BRLIĆ-MAŽURANIĆ, Ivana (1874–1938), Croatian poet and prose writer, was the first woman member of the Yugoslav Academy of Science and Arts, and granddaughter of MAŽURANIĆ. Her writing for children, noteworthy for its wit and liveliness, and its mixture of fantasy and reality, Slav mythology and the oral tradition, continues to have a significant influence today. She has been called the 'Croatian Andersen'. Her main works are the verse *Slike* (Pictures, 1912); *Čudnovate zgode šegrta Hlapića* (The strange adventures of Hlapić the apprentice, 1913), a miniature picaresque novel about a bright, hard-working boy who overcomes many obstacles before becoming a responsible member of society; *Priče iz davnine* (Stories of long ago, 1916), a virtuoso collection of fairy tales; *Jaša Dalmatin, potkralj Gudžerata* (JD, Viceroy of Gujarat, 1937), an historical novel portraying similar qualities of determination and energy to those of the young hero Hlapić; *Srce od licitara* (The gingerbread heart, 1938), poems and stories.

•F. Copeland (Ed.), *Croatian Tales of Long Ago* (London, 1924); *The Brave Adventures of Lapitch* (New York, 1972); 'Thin Little Dwarf', 'Strange Medicine Box', *The Bridge*, 50 (1976), pp. 45–6.   ECH

BRONIEWSKI,   Władysław (1897–1962), Polish poet and translator, raised in a traditionally patriotic family, fought bravely in the Polish-Soviet war of 1920–1, and yet fairly soon he was subscribing to Communist ideology; never a Party member, since his début in 1925 he was considered a leading representative of 'revolutionary' poetry; despite that, he was arrested by Stalin's secret police in 1940 in Soviet-occupied Lwów; released a year later, he left with the newly formed Polish Army for the Middle East and W Europe, yet all his disappointments did not dissuade him from returning in 1945 to Poland where he became an official cult figure. His authentic popular appeal over the years has, ironically, had almost nothing to do with his Communism; he owes it to his rebel

pose, stylistic propinquity to the Polish Romantic tradition, and his skilful fusing of intense emotion with colloquial language and self-deprecating humour.   StB

BRYL, Janka (b. 1917), Byelorussian prose writer, born in Odessa, whence his family moved to Byelorussia when he was five, served in the Polish Navy, was captured by the Germans in 1939, escaped and returned to Byelorussia where he fought with the partisans. These experiences, together with impressions of childhood, form the basis of most of his elevated, highly lyrical short stories and prose miniatures, many of which are virtually poems in prose. Subjective and emotional in tone, they are also notable for psychological subtlety, lively, picturesque language and appealing humour. Similar features mark his lyrical polyphonic novel *Ptuški i hniozdy* (Birds and nests, 1963), which traces the hero's life through childhood and the war. Bryl's first story appeared in 1938, but he has flourished particularly after the death of Stalin and is now the doyen of Byelorussian short-story writers.

•*Short Stories* (Moscow, 1955); *First Snow: Short Stories* (Moscow, 1982).

ABMcM

BRZOZOWSKI,   Stanisław (1878–1911), Polish literary critic and philosopher, had for most of his life to fight TB contracted in a Russian prison. An industrious and prolific writer, he rapidly became influential through his original ideas and uncompromising attacks against established national failings and literary celebrities. 1907 he settled in Florence. His final years were marred by unproved allegations of his serving the Russian police. Brzozowski has left dozens of essays on literature, philosophy and aesthetics. His works include dramas and novels; the latter (particularly *Sam wśród ludzi* [Alone among men, 1911]) have won him critical recognition. He was a conscientious critic zealously committed to his cause which he argued with a rhetoric verging on the predicatory. He believed that criticism formed the highest level of understanding, serving readers and writers in their search for spiritual guidance. For Brzozowski moral assessment in art also involved its form, whose faults stemmed from inconsistencies of thought. He introduced his own philosophy of culture inspired by thinkers as various as Marx and Nietzsche. Starting from a 'philosophy of action' (*Kultura i życie* [Culture and life, 1907]), he eventually developed an influential 'philosophy of labour' which determined his revisionist evaluation of Polish culture, particularly Romanticism and its impact. Following studies of the modern Polish novel (1906) and modern criticism (1907), he published his best-received book, on contemporary culture, *Legenda Młodej Polski* (The legend of 'Young Poland', 1910). During the last stage of his life Brzozowski's ideas approached those of Bergsonian irrationalism. He became fascinated by English literature (essays in *Głosy wśród nocy* [Voices in the night, 1912]) and found his final solutions in the works of Cardinal Newman whose *Grammar of Assent* he translated into Polish. Brzozowski's works have exerted a powerful influence on the modern Polish mind.

SE

BUDI, Pjetër (1566–1623), Albanian religious writer, was born in Guri i Bardhë in the Mati region of north-central Albania. He served as a priest in Kosovo, then was appointed vicar general of the Serbian Church, and 1621 became Bishop of Zadrimë. He was drowned, probably by accident, while crossing the River Drin. Budi wrote works in Albanian to facilitate missionary activity and to help strengthen the faith of the Albanian people: *Doktrina e Krështenë* (Christian doctrine, 1618); *Rituali Roman* (Roman ritual, 1621), containing Latin prayers and rites with commentary in Albanian; and *Pasëqyra e t'rrëfyemit* (The mirror of confession, 1621), which includes several religious poems. Budi composed more than 3,000 lines of religious verse, which constitute the earliest poetry in Albanian, while his original prose is particularly important for the study of the language of N Albania at the beginning of the 17th century.   ShM

BULATOVIĆ, Miodrag (1930–91), Serbian fiction writer, was born in a Montenegrin village and spent his adult life in Belgrade as a freelance writer. 1990 he was elected to the Serbian parliament. Bulatović gained early fame with his first works, the short stories *Djavoli dolaze* (The devils are coming, 1956), and the novels *Crveni petao leti prema nebu* (The red cock flies to heaven, 1959), *Heroj na magarcu* (A hero on a donkey, 1964) and *Rat je bio bolji* (The war was better, 1968). Later he wrote several novels about Yugoslav émigrés. He is attracted by the unusual and the bizarre, and by the plight of insulted, injured, demented, drifting and alienated members of the lowest reaches of society.

●*The Red Cockerel* (London, 1962; as *The Red Cock Flies to Heaven*, New York, 1962); *A Hero on a Donkey* (London, 1966; New York, 1969); *The War Was Better* (New York, 1972. VDM

BULKA, Nonda (1906–72), Albanian

essayist and satirist, together with MIGJENI, is one of the main figures of 1930s Albanian literature. He was born in Permet, S Albania, and studied at the French lycée in Korçë, from where he went to study law in Paris. He worked as barber, photographer and spirits retailer before becoming a journalist and a writer. After the war, he taught French at the University of Tirana. His humorous and at times bitter sketches published under the pseudonym of Chri-Chri in periodicals such as *Bota e re* (New world) and *Rilindja* (Rebirth) were known for their criticism of social and political conditions under King Zog's régime. Many of them were collected in the volume *Kur qan e qesh bilbili* (When the nightingale cries and laughs, 1934). Among other works are *Skica dhe tregime* (Sketches and tales, 1950), *Maska të çierra* (Torn masks, 1960) and *Tregime të zgjedhura* (Selected short stories, 1972).   ShM

BUNIĆ-VUČIĆ,   Ivan   (c. 1591–1658), Croatian poet, born into a patrician family, elected Rector (Governor) of Dubrovnik on five occasions, wrote lyric verse, whose themes ranged from love to religion, but favoured pastoral settings for somewhat unconventional characters. He has become established as 'the finest Dubrovnik lyric poet of the 17th century'. His verse represents the last flowering of Petrarchism in early Croatian literature, a mode which dominates even his three-part devotional epic *Mandaljena pokornica* (Magdalene the penitent, 1630), where the same feminine features in which the poet delights in his love poetry are attributed to Mary Magdalene, and in which the account of the sin rings truer than that of the penitence. Bunić's collection of love poems, *Plandovanja* (Idle moments), part of which was not published until 1849, is widely considered among the best Marinist collections in any language. Despite the long-established conventional nature of the subgenre, Bunić succeeds in bringing his verse to life through his fresh evocations of mood.

●Selected poems in *Yugoslavia*, 4 (1951), p. 21; H. B. Segel (Ed.), *The Baroque Poem. A Comparative Survey* (New York, 1974), pp. 239, 308–10; T. Butler (Ed.), *Monumenta Serbocroatica* (Ann Arbor, 1980), pp. 218–19.   ECH

BÚTORA, Martin (b. 1944), Slovak prose writer, read sociology and philosophy at Bratislava and while a student was on the editorial board of several journals; 1977, while employed in academic research, he refused to sign the anti-Charter 77 document and so spent the next eleven years working in an alcoholics' counselling service; 1990 he became President HAVEL's adviser on human rights. His two collections of short stories, *L'ahkým perom* (With an easy pen, 1987) and the more openly political *Posolené v Ázii* (Salted in Asia, 1990), reveal a writer of human warmth (sometimes expressed as melancholy), profound humour (ranging from word-play to parody, satire and affectionately wry irony) and an exceptionally rich lexis. In the second collection he tends to experiment in form and to discuss the art of writing, either from a psychological or a satirical literary-critical point of view. Bútora's somewhat verbose fictionalised memoir of the 1960s and the beginnings of 'Normalisation', *Skok a kuk* (Leap and look, 1990), suggests that he is a writer who should not treat directly his own experiences. Here he has lost his irony and is inclined towards the banal.   RBP

BUZUKU, Gjon (16th century), is the author of the first Albanian book, known as the *Meshari* (Missal, 1555). Very little is known of his life, except that he was a R. Catholic priest from N Albania. There is only one copy of this book, which is to be found in the Vatican Library, where it was discovered in 1740. The title and the first 16 pages are missing. According to the author, the book was begun on 29 March 1554 and finished on 5 January 1555. Buzuku's work, a liturgical translation, provides us also with a record of 16th-century Albanian, at a stage when the dialectal differences were not as obvious as in the works of later writers such as BUDI, BARDHI and BOGDANI. Buzuku's work shows that there was in N Albania already a tradition of writing the Albanian language.

•N. Resuli, *Il 'Messale' di Giovanni Buzuku* (Vatican City, 1958); M. Camaj, *Il 'Messale' di Gjon Buzuku* (Rome, 1960).   ShM

BUZURA, Augustin (b. 1938), Roumanian novelist, who was one of the few writers to challenge the cultural dictates of Nicolae Ceauşescu, born in northern Transylvania to industrial workers, completed his secondary education at Baia Mare and then took a degree in medicine at Cluj in 1964. His first collection of essays, *Capul Bunei Speranţe* (Cape of Good Hope), appeared in 1963 and on graduation he began work as an editorial assistant for the Cluj review *Tribuna*. His first novel, *Absenţii* (The absent, 1970) was withdrawn from circulation within a year because of the critique it offered of contemporary Roumanian society. His repeated attacks on the compliance of Roumanian society in later novels, and two thinly veiled parodies of Ceauşescu in *Tribuna* in January 1985, led to his brief suspension from the review and anonymous threats to his person. After Ceauşescu's overthrow he accepted the post of director of the newly founded government-sponsored cultural foundation România. The main themes of Buzura's novels are the corruption of Roumanian society by the psychosis of opportunism, its degradation by brutalisation, and its passivity. *Absenţii* examines the spiritual crisis of a young doctor which is provoked by the corruption and opportunism around him. By overcoming the burden on his conscience the doctor represents the survival of the individual and the triumph of positive, one might say, Transylvanian values, in a society deformed by 'Levantine' practices. *Feţele tăcerii* (The faces of silence, 1974) allows the reader to compare two 'faces' or 'versions' of rural collectivisation given by a Communist Party activist and a political opponent. *Orgolii* (Forms of pride, 1977) is also an exploration of the past although here the parallel narrative of the previous novel gives way to a mesh of three interwoven personal histories covering the period from WWII to the late 1950s. All three characters display forms of pride, in the author's interpretation moral integrity and unflinching adherence to a belief. The absence of such qualities explains that Roumanian passivity castigated in *Refugii* (Places of refuge, 1984). Passivity, often elevated to a virtue by Roumanians, is interpreted by the author as cowardice. In the postures of conformity and compliance lies an explanation for the moral despoliation of Roumanian society under Ceauşescu. How desperate that situation had become for the writer is revealed in *Drumul cenuşii* (The road to ash, 1989), where the central character, a journalist, is overwhelmed by a sense of futility in his search for an engineer who disappeared after trying to defend miners' rights during the strike of 1977. Writing itself becomes a 'strange and absurd exercise of survival, an antidote for suicide'. DJD

BYKAŬ, Vasil (in Russian Bykov, b. 1924), Byelorussian novelist, is a major figure in his country's cultural and political rebirth. Born into a peasant family, Bykaŭ served as a young officer in WWII and this is the theme of nearly all his works. In recent years he has been instrumental in setting up such democratic organisations as Renaissance and the Byelorussian National Front for Restructuring (BNFP), in restoring to the canon previously banned authors like HARUN and in publicising Stalin's crimes such as the mass graves at Kurapaty near Minsk. His moral prestige in Byelorussia is second to none. Many of Bykaŭ's stories depict young soldiers facing situations of moral crisis and extreme physical danger. Works like the largely autobiographical *Miortvym nie balić* (The dead feel no pain, 1965), *Abielisk* (The obelisk, 1971) and *Kar'er* (The quarry, 1986) relate the problems of wartime to those of the present day, in particular the residue of Stalinist attitudes and behaviour. In *Znak biady* (The sign of misfortune, 1982), on the other hand, the bitter harvest of Stalin's collectivisation of agriculture is linked to the wartime collaboration and treachery of some of its

victims. Long before it was fashionable, Bykaŭ had adopted a strongly moral stance (he has been more than once compared to Solzhenitsyn) and it is for this as much as for his muscular prose (after early bowdlerisation by professional translators he now puts his own works from Byelorussian into Russian) that he is one of the most respected figures both in his native country and throughout the former Soviet Union. Rejecting the panoramic, glorifying trends of much Soviet war literature, Bykaŭ chooses narrow settings for his psychodramas, with little or no broad overview or comment. Confronted by extreme moral choices, his predominantly young heroes often find themselves in a trap with, on the one hand, the ruthlessness of the German enemy and, on the other, the cynical, rigidly doctrinaire and not infrequently self-serving Soviet commanders. The focus of his stories and novels, be they about soldiers or partisans, is narrow, but clear, and the author's psychological perceptiveness ensures that Bykaŭ's reputation as a writer will remain high long after the topical elements in his works have become history.

●*The Third Flare* (Moscow, 1964); *Alpine Ballad* (Moscow, 1966); *The Ordeal* (London, 1972); *His Battalion. Live Until Dawn* (St Lucia, 1982); *The Sign of Misfortune* (New York, 1990). A. B. McMillin, 'War and Peace in the Prose of Vasil Bykaŭ', *Die Welt der Slaven*, XXVIII, 1 (1983), pp. 110–21.

ABMcM

C

ÇAJUPI, Andon Zako (i.e. A. Çako, 1866–1930), Albanian poet and playwright, was born in Sheper, Zagorie. He completed his secondary education in a French lycée in Egypt, where he lived until his death. 1887, after visiting his native village for the last time, he went to Switzerland where he took a doctorate in law. 1893 he returned to Cairo. Çajupi was active in organising the Albanian community in Egypt as part of the struggle against Turkish rule in Albania and was in close contact with Albanian activists in Asia Minor, Bulgaria and Roumania. 1902 he published his collection of verse *Baba T.* (Father Tomorri), named after Mt Tomorr, the Parnassus of Albanian mythology, in which he gave expression to his patriotic sentiments. The book ends with a pleasant comedy, *Katërmbëdhjet vjeç dhëndër!* (A fourteen-year-old bridegroom!), in which the poet ridicules the backward custom of marrying off adolescents. His pamphlet *Klubi i Selanikut* (The Salonica Club, 1909) defended the Albanian alphabet. *Burri i dheut* (The hero, 1937) was a drama in verse about Scanderbeg; he also wrote the one-act comedy *Pas vdekjes* (After death, 1937). These plays earned him wide acclaim. Çajupi also wrote verse for children, and translated La Fontaine's fables (1921) and a selection of Sanscrit verse (1922). Although inspired by Naim FRASHËRI in his patriotic verse (his meeting with Naim, in 1889, greatly influenced him), Çajupi found his own poetic voice.   ShM

ČAKLAIS, Māris (b. 1940), Latvian poet and essayist, took a PhD at Riga in 1964. Čaklais is an intellectual poet whose usually analytical and reflective, and often difficult, esoteric poetry is thought out to the smallest detail; it repeatedly asserts that 'man without the past is man without the future'. Therefore, it must be the poet's duty to teach 'man to man'. His literary essays and collections of verse are almost always characterised by an organic unity of theme and form: *Sastrēgumstunda* (Rush hour, 1974), *Cilvēks, uzarta zeme* (Man is ploughed earth, 1976), *Pulkstenu ezers* (Lake of hours, 1979). Čaklais turns to Auseklis (1850–79), PUMPURS and other leaders of the Latvian National Awakening, as well as to writers like RAINIS, PORUKS, Fricis Barda (1880–1919) and ČAKS in order to achieve self-awareness and a 'place in history'. Often he envisions these men as addressing the nation, 'their voice wise, slow, bitter, and sad'. EB

ČAKS, Aleksandrs (i.e. A. Čadarainis, 1902–50), Latvian poet, son of a tailor, began his medical studies in 1918 at Moscow, later switched to the University of Riga but never graduated. For a while he worked as a schoolmaster, then, from the end of the 1920s, was active in literary life as editor of various periodicals. In the first Soviet annexation the liberal public was perplexed by Čaks's new posture: he joined the Writers' Union in 1941 and wrote a few ephemeral poems lauding the new régime. His vital Modernism played an important part in shaping the style of the Soviet Latvian poets of the 1960s, as well as the generation who began to publish in exile in the 1950s and 1960s. During the last years of his life Party hacks invented various ways of abusing Čaks; most of his best works were banned and a great many were 'ideologically improved' by the censors who sometimes rewrote entire stanzas. Čaks suffered immensely and drank himself to death. In his early volumes, *Sirds uz trotuāra* (Heart on the pavement, 1928) and *Es un šis laiks* (I and this age, 1928), Čaks was strongly influenced by Yesenin and, especially, Mayakovsky, adopting the latter's poster-like expressive, broken rhythms. Čaks wrote poems mainly about his birthplace, the old Hanseatic city of Riga, and sang of its outskirts as his paradise (*Pasaules krogs* [In the world's inn, 1929]; *Mana paradīze* [My paradise, 1932]). His poetry reflects modern city life and its flavours and the feverish, tormented, harsh broken voice of the lonely man. In *Iedomu spoguli* (In the mirror of imagination, 1938) the 'catastrophist' mood of the 1930s is evident. His talent found its most forceful expression in his two-volume collection *Mūžibas skartie* (Touched by eternity, 1937–9), devoted to the battles of the Latvian riflemen in WWI. His poetry written under the Soviet régime indicates that Čaks, out of necessity or perhaps merely for personal safety, was trying to change his style and subject matter but could not succeed without first effecting a corresponding change in his own personality.　　EB

CANKAR, Ivan (1876–1918), Slovene novelist, playwright, essayist and poet, the outstanding master of Slovene prose, who developed his own rich, poetic style, was born eighth of twelve children into a poverty-stricken tailor's family; after a harsh life as a penniless student, he managed to support himself by his writing. After the publication of his collected early verse in *Erotika* (1st edition 1899, whose unsold copies were bought up and destroyed by the Bishop of Ljubljana; 2nd, enlarged edition, 1902) he decided to devote himself to prose, realising that he could not rival the poetic gifts of his Modernist contemporaries. *Vinjete* (Vignettes, 1899) revealed his inclination for satire and social protest. *Na klancu* (On the slope, 1902) is a story of dedication, self-sacrifice, yearning, resignation and despair, based on the life of the author's mother. *Hiša Marije Pomocniče* (The ward of Our Lady of Mercy, 1904) depicts the lives of terminally ill children awaiting death as a release from pain. *Hlapec Jernej in njegova pravica* (Yerney and his rights, 1907) is a classic parable of a man's search for justice. Among his seven plays should be mentioned *Kralj na Batajnovi* (The king of Betajnova, 1902) and *Hlapci* (The flunkeys, 1910). Towards the end of his life he produced some cycles of short reflective sketches: *Moje življenje* (My life, 1920) and *Podobe iz sanj* (Dream visions, 1917).

●*The Ward of Our Lady of Mercy* (1976); *The Bailiff Yerney and his Rights* (1968); *Dream Visions and Other Selected Stories* (1982).

A. Slodnjak, 'Ivan Cankar in Slovene and World Literature', *SEER*, 59 (1981), pp. 186–96.   HL

CANTEMIR, Dimitrie (1673–1723), Roumanian historian and philosopher, as the son of Constantin Cantemir, Prince of Moldavia 1685–93, enjoyed a privileged education, first at the court, from Jeremiah Cacavelas, a philosophy teacher from Crete, and later in Constantinople at the Academy of the Patriarchate. He remained there for 22 years, learning several languages, including Persian, Arabic and Turkish. Appointed Prince of Moldavia in 1710 with the consent of the Turks, he turned against them by joining Peter the Great in his anti-Ottoman campaign. After his defeat in 1711 he fled to Russia where he died and where he wrote most of his works, whose subjects range from astronomy to philosophy. Cantemir was a polymath and deserved his reputation as one of the most erudite men of his time. He wrote the first geographical and economic study of Moldavia (*Descriptio Moldaviae*, 1715) and a history of the Ottoman Empire, the first of its kind, which was translated from the Latin original into a number of languages. The manuscript was taken to London by his son Antioch Cantemir (1708–44) who went there as Russian minister to Britain in 1731.
● *The History of the Growth and Decay of the Othman Empire* (London, 1734).
                                                      DJD

CANTH, Minna (1844–97), Finnish novelist, short-story writer and playwright, was the first major Realist writer in Finland. Widowed while still young and left in poverty to raise a large family, she opened a draper's shop. Despite social opposition she proved to be so astute a businesswoman that by the age of 40 she was able to devote herself wholly to writing and various social causes. An outsider, usually a woman, who resists the attitudes of her family, class or society for the sake of a principle is the main theme of her work. At first Canth was determinedly programmatic, drawing directly on her own experience of poverty. In the play *Työmiehen vaimo* (The labourer's wife, 1885) she highlights the injustice of laws relating to women's rights through the melodramatic life and death of a diligent working wife married to a drunkard. In her short stories *Köyhää kansaa* (The poor, 1886), her play *Kovan onnen lapsia* (Children of misfortune, 1888) and the short story 'Kauppa-Lopo' (1889), Canth turns to wider questions of social hardship brought about by industrialisation, showing how poverty can drive people into crime, illness or madness. With its prophecy of revolution if conditions do not improve, *Kovan onnen lapsia* was one of the first plays in Scandinavia to dispute the legality of unjust laws. Women and their families dominate Canth's other major works. *Hanna* (1886), a *Bildungsroman*, questions the values of a society that educates women but does not let them make proper use of that education. The question of different sexual codes for men and women is developed further in two novelle, *Salakari* (The reef, 1887) and *Agnes* (1892), which illustrate how social attitudes condone infidelity by men, while condemning it in women. The psychological analytical play *Papin perhe* (The pastor's family, 1891) is a refreshing treatment of the generation conflict. The obvious struggle between father and son is overshadowed by the more intense conflict between the conservative pastor and daughter determined to become an actress. Reconciliation is brought about only through a melodramatic catharsis experienced by both father and daughter. Throughout her life Canth had seen the Church and religion as her archenemies. Towards the end of her life, influenced by Tolstoy, she evolved a personal Christian belief which finds expression in her play *Anna Liisa* (1895). Just before her wedding the eponymous main character is rejected by her well-to-do family and community after confessing to the murder of her illegitimate child which she had borne in secret. Condemned in the eyes of the law and society, the pastor declares her the only true Christian present because of the peace she has achieved within herself (see PREISSOVÁ).

●I. Väänänen-Jensen and K. B. Vähämäki (Eds), *Finnish Short Stories* (New York Mills, 1982), pp. 6–15. MAB

ČAPEK, Karel (1890–1938), Czech dramatist, prose writer and columnist, read philosophy, aesthetics and history of art at Prague (1909–15); a seminar paper on Jamesian Pragmatism (rev. version publ. 1918) points towards Čapek's conception of human behaviour. With his brother, Josef Č. (1887–1945), he wrote the lively satirical revue-drama *Ze života hmyzu* (From insect life, 1921); among the most popular of the plays he wrote alone are the science-fiction dramas *RUR* (1920), *Věc Makropulos* (The M. Affair, 1922) and, most imaginative and interpretable of all, *Bílá nemoc* (The white disease, 1930). In prose he is most popular for his science fiction and his short stories (often detective tales), though his least superficial is one of his studies of identity, *Hordubal* (1933). His travel writing (for example, on the UK and Spain) constitutes condescendingly comic concatenations of prejudice. *Hovory s T.G.M.* (Conversations with T. G. Masaryk, 1928–35) is a useful source for the study of the first Czechoslovak president's attitudes and contributed to the cult of Masaryk, especially after WWII. Čapek's main concern is humanity threatened by its own endeavours to master the world (for example, in the misuse of technological progress or big business). Under the influence of William James, he sees man as made up of many potential selves, and conceives of a sound man as one dominated by the moderate self. Čapek questions all absolutes and, thus, frequently displays moral relativism. Until the mid-1930s Čapek's writing mostly glorified the ordinary man, expressed a dislike of anything 'romantic' and nostalgia for a quiet life of petty bourgeois orderliness; 'ordinary' down-to-earthness avoids the potential 'inhumanity' of daring, self-sacrifice or self-conscious sexuality. For the last years of his life, however, he saw the need for dangerous disorderliness to protect mankind from Nazism.

●*The Power and the Glory* [*Bílá nemoc*] (London, 1938); *Hordubal* (London, 1934); *President Masaryk Tells His Story* (London, 1934). A. Matuška, *Karel Čapek. An Essay* (Prague and London, 1965); W. E. Harkins, *Karel Čapek* (New York, 1962); O. Elton, *Essays and Addresses* (London, 1939), pp. 151–90.   RBP

ČAPEK CHOD, Karel Matěj (1860–1927), Czech prose writer, art critic and minor dramatist, started reading law at Prague, but soon left his studies to become a journalist. He was a great polemicist and wit. Up to 1915 he wrote simply as K. M. Čapek. His first work, *Povídky*

(Tales, 1892, rev. ed. 1922), manifests the chief elements of his writing, a gift for the reproduction of dialect and colloquial speech, profound irony, compassion, determinism and a delight in the grotesque. His second book, *Nejzápadnější Slovan* (The westernmost Slav, 1893), demonstrates his gifts as an analytical parodist and self-ironist; its experimental literary-critical nature foreshadows *Větrník* (The windmill, 1923). The stories of *Dar svatého Floriana* (St Florian's gift, 1902) show him as a master of Sternean whimsy and of slapstick. Čapek Chod was unjustly ignored by critics of all generations until the publication of the satirical study of obsession, *Kašpar Lén mstitel* (K.L., the avenger, 1908), whose bricklayer eponymous hero constitutes the strongest representation so far of the author's conception of man as a puppet. The most popular of his novels is his satire on the haute bourgeoisie and on modernisation in industry and social manners, *Turbina* (The turbine, 1916). His masterpiece is, however, *Antonín Vondrejc* (1917–18), a complex satire on the cultural trends of the Fin de siècle, on sentimental love, scholarship, religion, the Czech versions of Austrian institutions as a whole. Čapek Chod's irony here has intensified into compassionate mockery. The most generally respected of his postwar novels, *Jindrové* (The Jindras, 1921), reflects his desire to be more 'constructive' about human relationships; he still manifests his gift for comic observation, though his irony is somewhat feeble; his determinism is still blatant, but then the potentially optimistic ending, which suited the atmosphere of the times, jars.
●R. B. Pynsent (Ed.), *Karel Matěj Čapek Chod* (London, 1985).   RBP

CARAGIALE, Ion Luca (1852–1912), Roumanian writer of plays and short stories, born into a family of actors, followed in their footsteps by attending a school for mime and declamation run by his uncle in Bucharest. 1870 he became a prompter at the National Theatre and 1878 joined the editorial staff of the newspaper *Timpul* (The time) where he met EMINESCU who introduced him to the literary circle Junimea (Youth). His first play was *O noapte furtunoasă* (A stormy night, 1879), a comedy of lower middle-class life in Bucharest, and his best play was *O scrisoare pierdută* (A lost letter, 1884), a satire of political intrigue in a provincial town. These comedies show the playwright as a master of comic dialogue. His last play, *Năpasta* (Injustice, 1890), is an unconvincing drama of a peasant woman's revenge prompted by psychological aberration. A preoccupation with the macabre pervades a number of his short stories, notably *O făclie de Paşte* (An Easter torch, 1890), and the supernatural is handled subtly in *La Hanul lui Mînjoală* (At M.'s inn, 1898). In 1904 Caragiale inherited money and moved with his family to Berlin. The novella *Kir Ianulea* (1909), adapted from Machiavelli's *Belfagor* and set in 18th-century Wallachia, is the highlight of his final years. His collections of sketches, publ. 1892, 1896, 1897 and 1910, present scenes of contemporary life in Bucharest and the provinces and sparkle with vivid dialogue and humour. A keen observer of human types, Caragiale applied this talent to his journalism which often offers what have proved to be uncannily accurate observations of perennial Roumanian attitudes.
●*The Lost Letter and Other Plays*

(London, 1956); *Sketches and Stories* (Cluj, 1979).

E. D. Tappe, *Ion Luca Caragiale* (New York, 1974).   DJD

CARAGIALE, Matei (1885–1936), Roumanian novelist whose reputation rests on a single novel and one short story, the illegitimate son of I. L. CARAGIALE, attended secondary school in Bucharest and then followed his father to Berlin where he failed to complete his university studies. On his father's death he settled in Bucharest and took a series of administrative posts in ministries before lapsing into depression in 1934 and retiring to a country estate. His short story *Remember* (1924) is one of the most memorable creations of Roumanian literature. Set in the Berlin of the 1900s it is the story of the author's encounter with an English gentleman, Aubrey de Vere. Both subject and setting are enveloped in an air of mystery which leaves the reader hovering on the boundary between dream and reality. The description of Berlin's art galleries and parks produces a hypnotic atmosphere reminiscent of Nerval's hallucinatory tales. With its suggestion of depravity and mystery *Remember* is the curtain-raiser for the novel *Craii de Curtea Veche* (The profligates of the Old Court, 1929), which portrays in an unprecedented flamboyant style a society of aristocratic degenerates who frequented a seedy quarter of Bucharest.   DJD

CARPELAN, Bo (b. 1926), Finland-Swedish poet, novelist and playwright, combines a career as librarian with literary criticism and writing. For Carpelan life is a mystery. He wanders spatially and temporally in his search to reproduce an experience that conveys meaning. What may appear as burlesque in his work has as its serious counterpoint the need to distinguish between dream and reality. In this process language is crucial. 'Poor language means poor experience ... It is a tragedy for a human being when he cannot use language.' *Som en dunkel värme* (Like a dark warmth, 1946) quickly established his reputation as a skilled poet in the style of the Swedish 1940s. The lurking optimism of this work soon gave way to hopelessness. *Landskapets förvandlingar* (Changes in the landscape, 1957) marked a move to more reflective writing; the poet turns to town and country in his open-minded search for inspiration and a comprehension of life. In *Gården* (The yard, 1969) the symbolisation of minor incidents gives a sense of perspective and meaning to his own past. His play *Rösterna in den sena timmen* (Voices at the late hour, 1971) examines individuals' possible responses to the news of the outbreak of nuclear war. *Axel* (1986) is a fictional re-creation of his great-uncle's diary (1868–1919), conveying in its exploration of the centrality of art, a powerful account of the years when the Finns were creating the cultural and political strengths that were to culminate in independence.

•*The Courtyard* (Gothenburg, 1982); *Room without Walls. Selected Poems* (London, Boston, 1987); *Axel* (London, 1991).

K. Laitinen, 'An introduction to the writing of Bo Carpelan', *Books from Finland* (1977), pp. 189–91.   MAB

CASSIAN, Nina (b. 1924), Roumanian poet and composer, was born in Galaţi, a town at the mouth of the Danube. When she was eleven her parents moved to Bucharest but her father was unable to find employment and the family lived a hand-to-mouth existence. Music and drawing were her main passions at secondary school and she showed little enthusiasm for other studies. At the age of 18, she married Vladimir Colin (1921–91), a young Jewish Communist poet, and herself became a convinced Communist. Five years later she divorced and married Alexandru Ştefănescu (1915–83), a Christian ten years her senior. Her first poem appeared in the Communist Party daily, *România liberă*, in 1945. Her first volume of poetry, *La Scara 1/1* (On the scale of one to one, 1947), was attacked for failing to reflect Marxist-Leninist principles and on pain of being barred from publication she published a 'self-criticism'. Sincere in her Communist beliefs, she wrote four verse collections in the spirit of Socialist Realism which she now rejects on aesthetic grounds: *Sufletul nostru* (Our spirit, 1949), *An viu – nouă sute şi şaptesprezece* (Vital year – nine hundred and seventeen, 1949), *Tinereţe* (Youth, 1953) and *Florile patriei* (The flowers of the fatherland, 1954). During this same period she composed a symphonic poem, *Griviţa roşie* (Red G., 1953), and a suite of songs, *Cîntece pentru Republică* (Songs for the republic, 1956), and a number of illustrated tales for children, *Nică fără frică* (Fearless N., 1950) and *Ce-a văzut Oana* (What O. saw, 1952). In the early 1960s Cassian took advantage of the dilution of the Stalinist dogma that had pervaded Roumanian cultural life throughout the previous decade to produce a string of verse collections remarkable for their sensuality and vigour. In 1985, during a visit to the USA, she learned that a long-standing friend, Gheorghe Ursu (1938–85), had been denounced for

keeping a political diary and arrested. The diary contained unpublished verses written by Cassian lampooning the Ceauşescus and the authorities; as a result Ursu was brutally interrogated and died from his injuries. Realising that it would be unsafe for her to return to Roumania Cassian requested political asylum in the USA and since 1985 she has been living and teaching in New York. Exuberant love of life, of freedom and of sexual passion characterise her poetry written since the late 1960s. Her fascination with the body as the source of the erotic is a striking feature of *Sîngele* (Blood, 1966), *Destine paralele* (Parallel destinies, 1967), *Marea Conjugare* (The great conjugation, 1971) and *Numărătoarea inversă* (Countdown, 1983). In the last collection she is preoccupied with the physical process of aging which is viewed at times with despair. Her most recent poems express the pain of exile, but she remains heroic, 'with one foot in the grave and the other on a tiger skin, defeated and triumphant' ('Tapestry', 1986).

•*Call Yourself Alive? The Love Poems of Nina Cassian* (London, 1988); *Life Sentence. Selected poems* (London, 1990).   DJD

CAVAFY, Constantine (i.e. Konstandinos Kavafis, 1863–1933), Greek poet, was born in Alexandria of a prosperous merchant family (Greek by blood but naturalised British subjects) trading in England and Egypt. His father having died in 1870, his mother moved to England with her five sons and settled in Liverpool, where the younger boys probably went to school. This laid the foundation of Cavafy's fluency in English and of his fondness for English literature. 1877, after the collapse of the family company and the loss of their fortune, the mother and the three youngest boys returned to Alexandria. During the riots of 1882 the family was evacuated to Constantinople, where Cavafy's maternal grandmother lived. It was here that for the first time Constantine was able to explore his homosexuality, initiated (directly or indirectly) by his cousin George. After the family's return to Alexandria in 1885 Cavafy was more or less permanently settled there until his death. (He left the city on trips to Paris and London in 1897 and to Athens in 1901 and 1903.) By his own account his first job was in some sort of journalism. He then worked as a broker for his brother Aristides. By 1889 he had taken an unpaid job in the Irrigation Office in the hope of getting a salaried post. He finally obtained official employment and remained in it for thirty years. Cavafy seems to have started publishing verse in 1886, writing in *katharevousa* on conventional Romantic themes. His first characteristically 'Cavafean' poem was 'Τείχη' (Walls, 1896). The corpus of his acknowledged poems totals 154. The curious phrase 'acknowledged poems' is designed to cover, first, the fact that Cavafy left a large body of unpublished poetry and, secondly, that his poetry was not published in the conventional sense during his lifetime. Initially he privately issued six poems on broadsheets between 1891 and 1904. He then had two pamphlets printed for private distribution: that of 1904 contained fourteen poems, the enlarged version of 1910 twenty-one poems. During 1910 he devised a method which made it easier for him to make alterations to poems already printed and to discard such poems. Henceforth,

when a poem appeared in a periodical, he would mount offprints of it on separate broadsheets which were clipped together in folders, available for circulation to friends. Eventually earlier poems were sewn into booklets, to take the weight out of the ever-expanding folders. Thus Cavafy's poetry was focused on a very private 'public' – the group of friends with access to his folders – and could be reworked in a way which formally printed collections of poems could not have been. Since most of his major work belongs to the post-1911 period, he seems to have found a means of distributing his poetry which satisfied him at just the moment when he had found his artistic identity. The themes of Cavafy's poetry have traditionally been divided into three categories: philosophical, historical and erotic. Such divisions are plainly misleading if taken literally. Many of the poems are both historical and erotic; few are overtly 'philosophical' but many have philosophical implications. Similarly Cavafy's historical poetry rarely reveals an historian's interest in cause and effect. His fascination with the past is a fascination with individual personal moments, and with the recurrence of experiences and types of experience across time. Themes like memory, art and the act of creation, and beauty cut across the other sorts of division. None the less, it is significant that both ancient and modern Alexandria, and the civilisation of Hellenistic Greece and the Greek diaspora play an enormous part in the settings and events around which his poems are written. Using this material the poet produces a series of artistic variations on the problems of the instability of human values and judgements. The poetry is not primarily trying to convey pictures, emotions or physical sensations, let alone ideas. By filtering a poem through a voice or voices, very often a speaking character (as in a Browning monologue), the poet offers us a vision of reality which is discreetly and ironically at odds with, for example, historical material implied by the title of the poem or known to the reader from outside. A comparable effect is achieved by manipulating internal clashes between different voices. The structure of the poems metrically, phonetically and dramatically is used to point up the ironies still further and to create other possible contrasts. The result is some of the most subtle and disturbing poetry in any European language.

•*The Complete Poems of C. P. Cavafy* (London, 1961); *C. P. Cavafy: Collected Poems* (Princeton and London, 1975).

C. Robinson, *C. P. Cavafy* (Bristol, 1989).   CFR

ČECH, Svatopluk (1846–1908), Czech writer, son of a land agent, studied law but gave up a legal career, became editor of the monthly *Lumír* (1873–7), which supported cosmopolitanism, and founded and edited *Květy* (Flowers, 1879–99). He shunned public life and spent his last years in seclusion. Čech represents a new trend in Czech nationalism, combining Panslavism with liberalism and social concern. His allegorical epic poems reflect contemporaneous ethical and social problems but his attitude towards these problems is indeterminate and his works are overrhetorical. In *Evropa* (Europe, 1878), the story of a ship carrying the condemned Paris communards to a desert island, the conflict of ideas in society is represented by a poet, an idealist communist, and an anarchist.

The narrator appears to side with the communist but the conflict remains unresolved as the ship is blown up by the anarchist. In *Slavie* (1884), also set on a ship, the discord between the Russian, Polish and Czech passengers is resolved by KOLLÁRian Slav idealism; when the crew mutinies, the ship is saved by the Russian and the Pole whose political difficulties end with the Russian's marrying the Polish girl. *Lešetínský kovář* (The Lešetín blacksmith, 1883), the story of a Czech who is shot by the military when resisting eviction by a German industrialist, is a protest poem against national and social oppression. His liveliest satire is *Hanuman* (1884) concerning a war between the progressive apes who try to introduce a pseudo-human civilisation and the nationalist apes with their slogan 'Back to the ape!' *Písně otroka* (Songs of a slave, 1895) castigates Czech subservience to Vienna and urges heroism. Two of Čech's anti-bourgeois satirical novels about Mr Brouček were used by Janáček for an opera. Čech and VRCHLICKÝ were generally considered the leading poets of the Fin de siècle but, although outstanding both in his lyrical and descriptive passages and in his command of metre and rhyme, Čech lacks spontaneity, imagination, the empathy and linguistic inventiveness of VRCHLICKÝ.

•*Hanuman* (London, 1894, republ. in W. W. Strickland, *Poems*, New York, 1929).   KB

ČELAKOVSKÝ, František Ladislav (1799–1852), Czech poet, the son of a carpenter, studied at Prague and Linz, worked as a private tutor, later as a lecturer in Czech language and literature at Prague University and editor of two Czech newspapers but was dismissed in 1835 because of his criticism of the Tsar; later he worked as a librarian and finally as Professor of Slavonic Philology at the universities of Breslau and Prague. Following the views of Herder and Goethe on folk-poetry, he wanted to contribute to the mutual understanding of Slavs by publishing their folk-songs, but in his *Slovanské národní písně* (Songs of the Slav peoples, 3 vols, 1822–7) he was rather selective, rejecting those of which he did not approve either morally or aesthetically. His main original works are *Ohlas písní ruských* (Echoes of Russian songs, 1829) and *Ohlas písní českých* (Echoes of Czech songs, 1839). The first contains adaptations of Russian heroic *byliny*, historic songs, erotic lyrics, animal fables and military songs. Čelakovský suppresses the crude hyperboles of his models, invents new plots and heroes, supplies psychology, imbues his versions with compassion and religious feeling and provides poetic evocations of Nature, but in spite of this reworking he captures the Russian character of his models. While in his Russian 'echoes' the narrative poems prevail, his Czech 'echoes' are mainly lyrical, humorous and often satirical. He manages to imitate the language and melodiousness of Czech folk poetry and re-creates, in his own fashion, the joys and troubles of the contemporary Czech peasant's social and private life. KB

CHASHULE, Kole (b. 1921), Macedonian playwright and prose writer, was born in Prilep, 1938 started to read medicine at Belgrade, but left when WWII began; after the war he became director of the National Theatre, of the State Film Company, and of Radio Skopje; in the meantime he edited various literary journals; 1962–5 he was a diplomat in Bolivia, and 1972 went as a diplomat to Peru. Chashule published several collections of short stories in the 1940s and 1950s before he began writing plays, the first of which appeared in 1951 (*Zadruga* [The clan]). His best-known plays are *Veyka na vetrot* (Twig in the wind, 1956), *Gradskiyot saat* (The clocktower, 1965) and *Crnila* (Black things, 1960). *Veyka* and *Gradskiyot saat* are concerned with social problems; *Crnila* examines the Macedonian 'national' character as part (and to some extent the cause) of the country's fate. It is concerned with the split in the Internal Macedonian Liberation Organisation at the beginning of the 20th century and with the murders of its leaders by fellow Macedonian hired killers. The action in *Crnila* takes place in Sofia where most of Macedonian political émigrés lived at the time. The story of the murder of one of the leaders attempts to reveal the motives and the psychology of the killers. There are three groups of people behind such a murder: the organisers, who are easily affected by manipulation from outside the organisation (they are people who tend to solve problems by physical violence and who doubt the ideals of the organisation since they lack ideals of their own); the waverers, who might be suspected by the organisation, are killed and thus provide the external 'motivation' for the planned murder; and, thirdly, the naive, ignorant type who are not able to see behind such political plotting, are persuaded of the 'just' cause and finally execute the murder. Chashule is concerned with the figure of the innocent victim and the similarity of the fates of Macedonia and such victims. He is generally a pessimist in his work and motifs such as the 'vicious circle of Macedonian life' recur in his social dramas. He wrote several family-chronicle novels, where his characters, preoccupied with the idea of 'change', 'moral resurrection' and 'beginning a new, second life', are in the end defeated. Man's failure to achieve what is best in him is the main concern of Chashule's writing.   SIK

CH'AVCH'AVADZE, Aleksandre (1786–1846), Georgian Romantic poet, began as a political fighter: aged 18, he joined Prince Parnaoz in a hopeless attempt at restoring the Georgian throne. After prison, he joined the Russian Army, and fought Napoleon all the way to Paris. He became a Romantic poet with the rank of lieutenant-general, a polymath who spoke the major European and Asiatic languages. In middle age he failed once more at political conspiracy: the real disaster was the burning of almost everything he had written before 1832, lest it be used as evidence against him. The Tsar forgave him once more, and he died outside his home, a youthful general, his skull crushed by bolting horses. His surviving, mature poetry is less Romantic than his life, some of it contrived neo-Persian, some sentimental in style, with melody and symmetry ousting originality. One of his best lyrics, an elegy, *Gogcha* (Lake Gokcha, 1841), shows a retrogressive assimilation of Lamartine's 'Le Lac' to Epicurean lament, half Hafiz, half *grand siècle*. Like his son-in-law, the Russian poet-playwright Griboedov, he applied Byronic principles more to action than to literature. His translations from French poetry and drama (the classics as well as the Romantics) widened the resources of Georgian verse and made a European theatre possible in Tbilisi.   DR

CH'AVCH'AVADZE,   Ilia (1837–1907) is the most revered of Georgian writers and civic leaders – so much so that he is known just as Ilia. He was born in Q'vareli, E Georgia, assassinated in 1907 and canonised in 1987. As a poet, he was soon convinced, in his words, 'Not only for sweet sounds, Did heaven send me to earth, Heaven assigns me and the people bring me up: Earthly for heavenly, I speak to God so as to move my people nearer Him.' After grammar school in Tbilisi where earlier poets, BARATASHVILI and Grigol ORBELIANI, had been pupils, he studied law in St Petersburg (1857–61); thus, as a *tergdaleuli*, 'one who has drunk from, i.e. crossed, the river Terek', Ilia became the archetype of the new Russian-educated Georgian intellectual. He made a precocious and stunning entry into literature with the first intellectually and aesthetically satisfying Georgian novella, *K'atsia-adamiani?* (Is he human? 1861–3): a portrait of tyrannical, degenerate stupefaction among the rural Georgian gentry, it rivals Saltykov-Shchedrin, for it combines loving detail, black humour and savage indignation with narrative skill. Other prose pieces, e.g. *Otaraant kvrivi* (The widow of Otar's family, 1888), mine the same vein. His narrative poetry exalts self-immolation, whether for the nation as in *Mepe Dimit'ri tavdadebuli* (King Dimitri's self-sacrifice, 1878) or for religious redemption as in *Gandegili* (The hermit, 1883). A rather unorthodox, ecstatic Christianity informs Ilia Ch'avch'avadze's national liberalism. His lyric talent is lower than his idealistic aspirations, but his devotion to public causes, expressed through his journals (*Sakartvelos moambe* [The messenger of Georgia,

1863]) and newspapers (e.g. *Iveria* from the 1880s), made him at first a rebel against the previous generation of Georgians who had integrated with Russian society and by the 1870s, together with Ak'ak'i TS'ERETELI, the unofficial national leader. His *Mgzavris ts'erilebi* (A traveller's essays, 1861–71) set out a programme of national revival. He led activities in every direction: the Propagation of Literacy, the Agricultural Bank of Georgia. After 1905 he allied himself with the liberals in the Russian Duma and State Council and fought for causes such as the abolition of capital punishment (the subject of a story *Sakhrchobelaze* [On the gallows, 1879]). His murder at Ts'its'amuri as he rode home to Saguramo is still unsolved. The left blamed the Tsarist *okhranka*, the right blamed Social Democrat bands: possibly the killers were working for both sides. The killing of Ch'avch'avadze is still a burning issue in Georgia; his writings are regarded as above ordinary literary criticism. Ilia can be credited, as can A.TS'ERETELI, with creating a language of intellectual debate, polemic and reporting, as well as a standard style for narrative prose.

● *The Hermit* (London, 1895).

L. Magarotto, 'La poetica dello sguardo nel poemetto "L'eremita" ' in *Annali di Cà Foscari* (Venice, 1987), 3, pp. 265–9.

DR

CHELČICKÝ, Petr (c. 1390–c. 1460), Czech lay theologian and essayist, was either a rich farmer or a petty nobleman in Chelčice (S Bohemia), where he gathered a group of disciples. He had met and spoken with HUS in Prague, was again in Prague 1419–20, appears to have once been called before a commission for heresy, but otherwise remained at home. He had little training in Latin and, although the influence of Wyclif, ŠTÍTNÝ and HUS is evident in his writings, he was largely an independent thinker. His chief works were *O boji duchovním* (The spiritual struggle, 1419–21), *O trojiem lidu řeč* (Words on the three classes of men, 1424), *Postilla* (Postil, late 1430s, first printed 1522) and *Siet' viery* (The net of faith, early 1440s, first printed 1521). His thought certainly develops, becomes more precise and inconsistencies are ironed out, but his essential ideas remain the same. He is a Christian anarchist: Christ or God is the only authority; all terrestrial authority is violence. Since the 'Donation of Constantine' (he believed in that forgery as he did in the other great medieval forged document, concerning the woman pope), since the clergy have owned property, Christianity has increasingly failed to be Christianity. Christian society is ruled by love, not kings and nobles, popes and bishops. Even the Jews had not had a king until their faith had become weak. The worst human beings are so-called Christians, for they profess to believe in Christ, but deny him in thought and deed. The Jews were a little better, for they had simply refused Christ from the beginning. The heathens were the best, since they are ignorant of Christ. Having kings is necessary in heathen society. Heathen society is probably the best organised and fairest. Chelčický shows no sign of medieval anti-feminism; for him both sexes are equal. People who acknowledge no terrestrial authority and behave thus, who 'live in faith', could be true Christians. Others are blasphemers and exploiters. He preaches total pacifism, rejects capital punishment and taxes. His thought, which sometimes approaches the Waldensians', even the Cathars', formed the basis for the thinking of the Unitas Fratrum (Bohemian Brethren).

•C. Vogl (Ed. and Trans.), Peter Cheltschitzki, *Das Netz des Glaubens* (Dachau, 1923).
P. Brock, *The Political and Social Doctrines of the Unity of Czech Brethren* (The Hague, 1957); M. L. Wagner, *Petr Chelčický. A Radical Separatist in Hussite Bohemia* (Scottdale, Penn., 1983); P. Brock, *Freedom from Violence. Sectarian Nonresistance from the Middle Ages to the Great War* (Toronto, 1991).   RBP

CHIKOVANI, Simon (1902/3–66), was the most important 'Futurist' poet in Georgia. Though there is little proletarian about him, he allied himself to the rising 'left' poets and became their star and most articulate spokesman. 1924 he was an editor of the notorious Futurist journal H_2SO_4. 1924–29 he produced a brilliant series of poems, published as *Mkholod leksebi* (Only poems, 1930). Most are energetic and provocative Whitmanesque heckling and satirising of the older generation of poets: Chikovani sported Mayakovsky's mantle. The last section of his book, however, 'Ork'est'riuli leksaoba' (Orchestrated versification), contains thirteen of the most innovative poems in the language. Chikovani combines onomatopoeia, elaborate assonance, invented words and Mingrelian, Georgian's sonorous sister-language, to create a half-intelligible, quite untranslatable, truly musical set of hypnotic incantations: they realise a stage beyond the metalogy (*zaum*) of Khlebnikov or the whimsy of Edward Lear. Poems such as 'Tsira: bade baidebs, bude baidebs' (untranslatable) were to become mantras for his readers. The defeat of

the 'left' in 1932 by a Stalinist literary monopoly put an end to Chikovani's innovations. In Beria's purges his brother was liquidated: he saw no alternative to becoming a subservient apparatchik in literature. His later verse is technically competent, but of interest only when he tries to make sense of the tragic fate of earlier poets, such as GURAMISHVILI, (*Simghera Davit Guramishvilze* [A song about Davit Guramishvili, 1944]) or BARATASHVILI. He became a member of the Party and the Supreme Soviet and reached his nadir in 1958 when, hounding his friend and translator, he declared at a meeting of the Union of Writers, 'I am proud that Georgia has no writer like Pasternak.'   DR

CH'ILADZE, Otar (b. 1933), Georgian novelist and poet, was the brother of Tamaz Ch'iladze (b. 1931), a more facile writer. In the late 1950s his poetry asserted total alienation from Soviet themes: it was obsessed with Orphic and other myths. His first novel (over 500 pages), *Gzaze erti k'atsi midioda* (A man went down the road, 1972–3), likewise goes back to myth, imagining the ancient Georgian site of Vani in prehistory, at the meeting of Jason and Medea. Later novels have the same pattern of ill-starred Orphic redemption: *Q'ovelman chemman mp'ovnelman* (Everyone that findeth me, 1976) covers the whole of the 19th century in the village of Uruki, but beneath a family saga and a catalogue of dementia explores, despite a superficially upbeat ending, the same hell of relationships, this time through the legend of Cain and Abel. *Rk'inis teat'ri* (The iron theatre, 1981) moves to the 1900s and shows a conflict of life and art comparable with Thomas Mann. His latest somewhat autobiographical novel, *Mart'is mamali* (The March cockerel, 1987), explores perennial predicaments in a contemporary setting: the trauma afflicting Nik'o, a boy who accidentally witnesses a tragedy. Otar Ch'iladze's novels have genius, although his lax sententiousness cries out for editing. He still writes the best modern Georgian lyrical and narrative verse; despite fatal fluency, it attains the originality and mythopoeia of his best prose.

●D. Rayfield, 'Use and Abuse of History in Recent Slovak and Georgian Fiction' in R. B. Pynsent (Ed.), *Modern Slovak Prose. Fiction Since 1954* (London, 1990), pp. 114–24.   DR

CHINGO, Zhivko (1935–87), Macedonian prose writer, was born in a village on Lake Ohrid near Struga, studied at Skopje, then worked as a schoolmaster, journalist and also at the Macedonian Folklore Institute; he became artistic director of the National Theatre. In his collection of short stories, *Paskvelia* (1962), Chingo creates an imaginary land, somewhere in a lake district south of Macedonia; the revolution comes to the land where old beliefs in the supernatural survive; collectivisation begins, and that is like the Great Flood for the Paskvelians; the spread of revolution is perceived in a manner similar to perception of the Plague in the Middle Ages. The past (represented by the Paskvelians' mythic consciousness) meets the present day (represented by the revolution) only to clash. On the one hand, this clash reveals the human emptiness of revolution and shows that only the Paskvelians' old patriarchal morality can contain some humanity but, on the other, Chingo parodies the idealistic depiction of rural life both in traditional rustic literature and in Socialist Realism. In his second work on Paskvelia, *Nova Paskvelia* (New P., 1965), the conflict becomes more complicated, because the two sides are no longer so polarised; both the old and the new values contain some beauty, though Chingo here ironises human thinking. Human instinct, he demonstrates, can prevail over all principles, however noble. His lyrical novel *Golemata voda* (The great water, 1971), set in an orphanage immediately after WWI, compares and contrasts the beauty of childhood dreams with the existential anguish which childhood involves. The narrator himself is a great dreamer, as is his friend Isak: together they look forward to the land one will never arrive in. His last works, the unfinished novel, *Al* (1989, and *Bunilo* (Tempestuous times, 1989), were found among his papers after his death; *Al* again concerns an imaginary land and deals with the principles of human morality; *Bunilo* is a vision of the late 1960s and the effects of socialist 'reconstruction' on life; Chingo depicts people living as if afflicted by mad dreams, nightmares and hallucinations. His style reminds one of Isaak Babel's in *Red Cavalry*; he shared a similar vision of the 'revolution', as something which causes monstrous ecstasy, but he also goes further in his depiction of a nightmarish, claustrophobic existence engendered by the revolution where the only way out is into dreamworlds.   SIK

CHRISTOPOULOS, Athanasios (1772–1847), Greek poet, son of a poor priest who emigrated to the Danubian provinces, had the advantage of being raised in Bucharest, in what was culturally and intellectually the most progressive part of the Greek-speaking world at the period.

He was probably taught by Grigorios Kostandas (1758–1844), known for his forward-looking ideas on linguistic issues. After general schooling in Bucharest, he went further west for higher education, studying philosophy, medicine and Latin literature at Buda, then law and medicine at Padua. 1797 he returned to Bucharest, and 1799 was appointed to the household of Alexandros Mourouzis, currently ruler of Wallachia for the second time. He followed him to Moldavia when he took the throne of that principality in 1802, and thence to Constantinople when Mourouzis fell from power in 1806. During this period he acted as tutor to Mourouzis's two sons, as legal adviser and court poet. Christopoulos's important work of this period is his Γραμματική της Αιολοδωρικής ήτοι της ομιλουμένης των Ελλήνων Γλώσσας (Grammar of Aeolo-Doric or of the spoken Greek language, Vienna, 1806), a somewhat eccentric defence of the virtues of the spoken language, accompanied by an 'heroic verse drama' on the wrath of Achilles. The first edition of his poems, Λυρικά (Lyrics), came out in Vienna in 1811: ten more editions appeared during his lifetime. Christopoulos next attached himself to Dimitrakis Mourouzis, younger brother of his patron, who held the rank of Grand Interpreter from 1808 until his murder by the Turks in Adrianopole (Edirne) in 1812. Christopoulos narrowly escaped the slaughter and was invited by the current ruler of Wallachia, Ioannis Karatzas, to return to the judiciary as *megalos logothetis*. 1816 he was charged with drawing up a modernised legal code for Wallachia, although the extent of his contribution to the final version of the code is questionable. 1818 Karatzas, forewarned of the Sultan's intentions towards him, fled to the West. Christopoulos, suddenly without a protector, withdrew to Sibiu (Hermannstadt) in Transylvania, where there was a large Greek community, and devoted himself to philosophical studies and translations. His study of sceptical relativism had a profound effect on his views on many issues – political, social and linguistic. Hence, perhaps, his energetic contribution to the Philiki Etaireia (Friendly society, 1819). His whereabouts during the early stages of the Greek War of Independence are unknown, though he was in Corfu in 1823. Only in 1836 did he visit the now long-independent Kingdom of Greece but found himself out of sympathy with the cultural climate and returned to Transylvania, where he died. It is easy to dismiss Christopoulos as an intellectual lightweight and court versifier. His political ideology certainly wavered according to the circumstances in which he found himself, and his scientific and philosophical ideas reveal the same superficiality of learning as his literary and linguistic judgements. But these are the faults of his milieu and his epoch. His Λυρικά were undoubtedly an important positive influence on the poets of the Ionian Islands and mark the beginning of the 19th-century Revival. With their themes of lovesickness and intoxication, and their allegorical personifications and references to Classical mythology, they bear the hallmark of the light classicising lyric traditions of 18th-century French and Italian poetry, but they also reveal a distinctly Romantic sensibility to Nature.

CFR

CHROBÁK, Dobroslav (1907–51),

was one of the leading writers of the Slovak Lyrical Prose school, and heavily dependent on Western literature, particularly Jean Giono. He went to technical college in Bratislava and then read electrical engineering at Prague. From 1934 onwards he worked in broadcasting, and from 1947 till his death he was director-general of the Slovak section of Czechoslovak Radio. The collection of short stories, *Kamarát Jašek* (My friend, J., 1937), tells of a humanity that usually fails to live up to the beauty and intensity of the natural world and is all too easily depraved by urban life. The author combines determinism with Unanimism; man's salvation lies in a conscious belonging to the collective into which he is born, but this belonging is inevitable anyway; attempts to contravene 'natural' conventions lead to alienation and disaster. The eponymous hero of *Drak sa vracia* (The Dragon [nickname] returns, 1943) is a titanic child of Nature who, like Nature herself, may be scarred by man, but always survives. He is a loner and, like Nature with her forest-fires, can also be self-destructive; he represents the stable strength of Nature as his foil, Šimon, represents human lability.

RBP

CÍGER HRONSKÝ, Jozef (1896–1960), Slovak novelist, son of a carpenter, teacher by profession, fought on the Italian Front in WWI, a secretary of the central Slovak cultural institution Matica slovenská, in 1945 emigrated to Argentina where he died. Although his works on Slovak village life such as *Chlieb* (Bread, 1931) are written in a neo-Realist manner also used by URBAN and JESENSKÝ, his prose has some affinities with the Lyrical Prose of ŠVANTNER on account of his preoccupation

with the close bond between man and Nature and his concept of natural man. The eponymous anti-hero of his *Jozef Mak* (1933), a peasant transformed from a self-willed man into a passive weakling by military service, the greed of his brother, and the betrayal of his love, may be seen as an allegory of the passive side of the Slovak character. While Mak accepts his servitude and suffering, *Pisár Gráč* (Gráč the writer, 1940), whose war experience was similar, becomes a cantankerous cynic. Hronský's last novel, *Svet na Trasovisku* (The world of Trasovisko, publ. in USA, 1960), contains a realistic description of the disastrous impact of the WWII Slovak National Uprising on village life. Hronský was the first to give a true picture of these events.

•*Jozef Mak* (Columbus, Ohio, 1985). KB

ČOP, Matija (1797–1835), Slovene literary historian, critic, classicist, polyglot and aesthete, after grammar school and higher education, with three years in Vienna, 1814–17, and three as a theology student in Ljubljana, taught in Rijeka (Fiume), 1820 and at Lwów (Lemberg) University, 1822–7, before returning to Ljubljana, to work first as teacher and later librarian at the Lyceum. His most notable contributions to Slovene literature are as champion of the poetic 'almanac' *Krajnska čbelica* (Carniolan bee), as mentor to his friend PREŠEREN and as successful opponent of Franc Metelko's (1789–1860) alphabet, which used Cyrillic and other characters to supplement its Latin basis. HL

ČORNY, Kuźma (i.e. Mikałaj Ramanoŭski, 1900–44), Byelorussian novelist, was a master of technique who profited greatly from the European heritage and virtually created the Byelorussian socio-political and psychological analytical novel. Born into a farm labourer's family, he trained as a teacher before devoting himself to literature. A first story appeared in 1923 and he soon developed a reputation for stylistic polish and realistic characterisation. Dostoevski was a clear influence, and Čorny's most important work is in longer forms which allow space for polyphonic structures. His first novel, *Siastra* (The sister, 1927–8), describes the lucubrations of a group of intellectuals in the NEP period, but is most interesting as a *roman à clef*. *Ziamla* (Land, 1928), technically more accomplished, depicts, rather poetically, a village on the eve of collectivisation. *Lavon Bušmar* (1929) is a splendid epic portrait of a ruthless exploiter, but several novels in the 1930s were less successful, though none an outright failure; the melodramatic novella *Luba Łutk'anskaja* (1936), for instance, is a masterful character study of a downtrodden orphan girl. There is a strong cyclical element in Čorny's works, but his last novel, *Mlečny šlach* (The Milky Way, 1944), stands apart: in this strange but compelling work a group of mysterious strangers gradually discover each other's identity. His strength in psychological characterisation and narrative technique make Čorny one of the best Byelorussian novelists of the interwar period.   ABMcM

ĆOSIĆ, Dobrica (b. 1921), Serbian novelist, was born in Velika Drenova, central Serbia. After finishing agricultural college, he took part in WWII as a political commissar with the partisans. After the war he occupied many senior posts, was a member of the Central Committee of the Communist Party and of parliament, but because of his opposition to official policies he was relieved of all his duties. 1992 he was elected President of residual Yugoslavia. He is respected as the best living Serbian author. Ćosić has written only novels so far. His first, *Daleko je sunce* (Far away is the sun, 1951), was universally received as the best fictional treatment of the events of WWII in Yugoslavia. His subsequent novels, *Koreni* (Roots, 1954), *Deobe* (Divisions, 1961), *Bajka* (A fable, 1966), *Vreme smrti* (A time of death, 1972–7) and *Vreme zla* (A time of evil, 1985–90), have two themes in common: the role of the Serbian peasants as the most vital social force over the last hundred years and the effect the policies have had on their destiny. This is especially evident in the last two novels, a multi-volume account of Serbian heroism in WWI (*Vreme smrti*) and the emergence of the Communist Party as a force in Yugoslav politics on the eve of and during the first months of WWII (*Vreme zla*). Though not narrated strictly chronologically, the novels make up a well-ordered, vast panorama of the historical and social developments of the Serbian people in the 20th century. While Ćosić has always been a *homo politicus*, he has shown that he is also a *homo litterarum* by endowing his politically and historically orientated novels with credible characters and dramatic plots of epic proportions. He champions the 'little man' and, by following his destiny, he arrives at general conclusions, showing in a Tolstoyan fashion that great events are often made great by seemingly insignificant participants. In addition, *Vreme zla* traces the development of leftist intellectuals, their *engagement* in the Communist Party's struggle for power, and their disillusion and fall from grace; thus they parallel the author's own pre-1992 lot.

•*A Time of Death* (New York, 1978); *Into the Battle* (New York, 1983); *South to Destiny* (New York, 1983).   VDM

CRNJANSKI, Miloš (1893–1977), Serbian poet, novelist and playwright, was born in Csongrád, Hungary. He fought in the Austro-Hungarian Army in WWI and later entered the Yugoslav diplomatic service, which took him to London. After WWII, he remained in London, declining to return home for political reasons until 1965. He spent his last years in Belgrade, revered as a great writer. Crnjanski began with a book of verse, *Lirika Itake* (The lyrics of Ithaca, 1919), and a short lyrical novel, *Dnevnik o Čarnojeviću* (Diary about Čarnojević, 1921), in which he depicted the horrors of war in an Expressionist fashion. His best work, a two-volume novel *Seobe* (Migrations, 1929 and 1962), concerns the fate of the Serbs in the Vojvodina in the second half of the 18th century and their dream of migrating to Russia. He wrote little verse after 1924, but one of his later poems, *Lament nad Beogradom* (Lament over Belgrade, 1962), is among his best. From his émigré experiences stems also the novel *Roman o Londonu* (Novel about London, 1971), depicting the 'tragic' fate of a Russian émigré. He also wrote plays and memoirs. Crnjanski began as a Modernist and as such was instrumental in shaping Serbian poetry after WWI. He remained in the literary vanguard throughout his career. Relying more on emotions than on thought, he helped give Serbian literature a modern and cosmopolitan outlook. His vitality and masterful use of the language made him influential among younger Serbian poets.

•D. A. Norris, *The Novels of Miloš Crnjanski: An Approach through Time* (Nottingham, 1990).   VDM

CSOKONAI VITÉZ, Mihály (1773–1805), Hungarian poet, playwright and prose writer, whose father was a surgeon and grandfather was a Protestant clergyman, studied philosophy and theology in the most important college of the Hungarian Reformed Church. Having learned Italian, he drew inspiration from the works of Metastasio. His first poems were published in the periodical *Uránia* in 1793. He became a teacher in the college in Debrecen, but was barred from classes in 1795 because of his behaviour. The following year he moved to Pressburg, where he began *Diétai Magyar Múzsa* (The Hungarian muse at the Diet, 1796), a verse periodical. 1797 he visited Komárom and met Juliánna Vajda, whom he called 'Lilla' in his poems; her father, a well-to-do merchant, prevented marriage, upon which Csokonai went to Somogy County and worked as a substitute teacher. Poverty worsened his health, and while delivering a funeral oration he caught cold and died of pneumonia. Influenced by the French Enlightenment in general and by the works of Rousseau in particular, he became the first major lyric poet in Hungary since the Baroque. Combining elements of the *ut pictura poesis* of the neo-Classicists with the traditions of popular culture, he created an individual style. His comic epic *Dorottya* (1804) is full of grotesque humour and stylistic innovation. The legacy of the late Baroque, neo-Classicist didacticism and description, and the cult of sensibility are combined in his two collections of lyrics, *Lilla* (1805) and *Odák* (Odes, 1805).

●A. B. Katona, *Mihály Vitéz Csokonai* (Boston, 1980).   MSz-M

CZECHOWICZ, Józef (1903–39), Polish poet, born in Lublin, made his living as a teacher there, before he moved to Warsaw in 1933 to work as an editor. Both in Lublin (where he co-founded the poetry group Reflektor) and in Warsaw he was a central figure within avant-garde movements of young poets. He was killed in the first German bombing of Lublin, where he found himself while fleeing east from the advancing German troops. Seven volumes published by Czechowicz in 1927–39 put him alongside MIŁOSZ as the most outstanding young poet of the 1930s. Highly conscious of his craft, he created a model of modern lyricism in which free verse and metaphorical concision did not preclude a special musicality and emotional spontaneity. Initially a poet of serene provincial landscapes, in the late 1930s he became a catastrophist observer of the modern world.

●B. Carpenter, *The Poetic Avant-garde in Poland, 1918–1939* (Seattle, 1983).
                                                                    StB

CZERNIAWSKI, Adam (b. 1934), Polish poet and translator, born in Warsaw, 1947 found himself in England, where he has lived ever since. He co-founded the group of young Polish émigré poets Kontynenty and edited its journal *Kontynenty*. Alongside collections of his original poetry he has published numerous translations of English verse into Polish and Polish verse and drama into English (in particular, works by NORWID, SZYMBORSKA and RÓŻEWICZ, and the anthology of modern Polish poetry *The Burning Forest*, 1988).   StB

D

DĄBROWSKA, Maria (1889–1965), Polish novelist, read philosophy and sociology at Lausanne and Brussels. During WWI and after, she was linked to peasant and cooperative movements. In Communist Poland she was the recipient of many honours and awards. Dąbrowska is one of the foremost representatives of Realist fiction in Polish literature. Realism and a commitment to social causes place her in close proximity to the 19th-century traditions of the Polish Positivists. Like the latter, she believed that individuals should never overshadow their surroundings and that their life should be guided by a sense of duty towards society. Meticulously accurate in the portrayal of everyday details, her works carry the universal message that human life will always go on. Dąbrowska's literary position was established by the cycle of short stories about farmhands, *Ludzie stamtąd* (Folk from there, 1926). Her main literary achievement is a long family-saga novel, *Noce i dnie* (Nights and days, 1932–4), where she relates a history of the Polish gentry in the years preceding WWI and portrays their transformation into the urban intelligentsia.

●*A Village Wedding and Other Stories* (Warsaw, 1957).

Z. Folejewski, *Maria Dąbrowska* (New York, 1957).   SE

DAČICKÝ z HESLOVA, Mikuláš (1555–1629), Czech poet and auto-biographer, a member of the rich lower nobility, was renowned as a reveller, womaniser and gambler; after killing one of his peers in a fight he spent nearly three years in prison and thirty-three years in litigation with the man's widow. Dačický's poems, which he collected in *Prostopravda* (The naked truth, 1620), but which for two centuries remained unpublished, are comments on the national and political situation and reflections on life written in an unaffected style, witty, indecent and often obscene. As a patriot and a staunch defender of Protestantism, Dačický despises the Germans and the Roman Church and he satirises priests, women, physicians and lawyers. His main prose work is *Paměti* (Memoirs), in which he summarises the memoirs of his ancestors from 1470 onwards and writes a sequel covering his own life to the year of his death. He does not remain an indifferent witness and never conceals his opinions, whether writing about the affairs of the kingdom or his native Kutná Hora (Kuttenberg) or about the comedies and dramas of ordinary people. It is the mixture of indignation and dry humour which elevates his work far above the average.   KB

DALCHEV, Atanas (1904–77), Bulgarian poet and literary critic, was born in Salonica, son of a lawyer and a Turkish-language teacher who was also a member of the Turkish parliament; until 1914 his family lived in Constantinople and then moved to Bulgaria, where Dalchev read philosophy at Sofia (degree, 1927). His interest in art took him to Italy, France and England (1927–9); later he returned to France once more and lived in Toulouse (1936–7); he taught Bulgarian in Istanbul (1938–9) and after that lived in Bulgaria where he worked as a headmaster, in the Ministry of Information, and as an editor of a journal for children's literature. He also translated and wrote literary criticism. His *Fragmenti* (Fragments, 1967) consist of brief, witty essays mainly on literature. Dalchev began publishing in 1923; he became involved with the Strelets (Sagittarius, 1926–7) literary circle, a group of writers whose 'new aesthetics' involved a rejection of 'individualist' art (mainly Symbolism), the restoration of the ties between literature and society and the adoption of the best of 'Western cultural values' in order to 'heal' Bulgarian literature. Dalchev's articles make the case for a literature which would be an extension but also a 'liberation' of reality. The title of his first collection, *Prozorets* (Window, 1926), emblematically suggests the end of the alienation of the poet and of established visionary perception; the 'window' was open for the observation of the prosaic 'materiality' of the world. His poetic world is a space filled by objects. Dalchev's verse is highly graphic and that is effected by a careful selection of words; for Dalchev, words are more important for their connotations than for their denotations. With his concentration on the object, he laid the foundations of a new poetics. Recurrent motifs ('window', 'balcony', 'wall', 'door') suggest the ever-present alienation of the poet from the 'desert of the world' which he observed while remaining 'inside' his own world. His collections *Paris* (1930) and *Angelăt na Shartăr* (The angel of Chartres, 1943) are concerned with time and memory, and express solitude, but also unity with some universal destiny; the introduction of characters from the lowest classes of society to represent the human condition adds to the severity of his poetic vision.   SIK

'DALIMIL' (?–soon after 1314): Since the 16th century the anonymous petty-noble author of the first vernacular chronicle of the Bohemian Lands, the 106-chapter Boleslav Chronicle (c. 1314), has been known as Dalimil. It survives in a large number of manuscripts, the oldest of which is in the Wren Library at Trinity, Cambridge. It remained a work of patriotic inspiration well into the 19th century; it was printed in 1620, at the time of the Estates' rebellion against the Habsburgs, then banned, until it appeared again in 1786, then banned again until 1849. It is written in low style because 'Dalimil' was concerned with his message not form; the octosyllabic couplets are so irregular that the work often approaches prose, but the convention was that secular works be written in verse. 'Dalimil' used Latin and German sources, particularly the *Chronica Boëmorum* by Cosmas Pragensis (1045?–1125). 'Dalimil' traces the history of the Czechs from the Tower of Babel to the accession of John of Luxemburg (1314). In the early mythical chapters he recounts a long, hitherto unrecorded, episode, a Czech Amazon's seduction and delivery to death of a leading anti-woman warrior. Dalimil lays down his own ideas of how Bohemia should be governed in speeches attributed to various past rulers: look after the petty nobility, take them into your council rather than Germans and burghers; class is less important than nationality; citizens should settle their disputes among themselves and not rush off to the king. Otherwise he instructs that it is safest to abide by old customs; new-fangled foreign fashions like jousting and hunting to hounds have depraved the Czech nobility and brought hard times on the lower classes. His xenophobia is directed mainly against the Germans, although he mocks the foppish Italians and Jews are good only when they cut off German noses. 'Dalimil' is a passionate writer. Recently (1992) it has been suggested that 'Dalimil' was the Bohemian magnate Petr z Rožmberka.

•J. Jireček (Ed.), *Rýmovaná kronika česká tak řečeného Dalimila* – edition with c. 1345 German translation (Prague, 1882); B. Havránek and J. Daňhelka, *Nejstarší česká rýmovaná kronika tak řečeného Dalimila* (Prague, 1957).

R. B. Pynsent, *Conceptions of Enemy* (Cambridge, 1988). RBP

DALMATIN, Jurij (c. 1547–89), Slovene Protestant reformer and BIBLE translator, educated at BOHORIČ's school, Krško, and later at Tübingen, 1566–9, was awarded a master's degree for his thesis *De catholica et catholicis disputatio*. After ordination he returned to Ljubljana. His first printed work was *Ena srčna molitva zuper Turka* (A heartfelt prayer against the Turks, 1574). 1575–80 he published in Slovenia *Jesus Sirach* (1575), *Pasijon* (Christ's Passion, 1576), *Ta celi Katehismus* (The complete Catechism, 1579), *Salomonove pripuvisti* (The Proverbs of Solomon, 1580). Although he had completed his translation of the whole BIBLE by 1578 he had to wait for the imprimatur of a revisory commission, 1581. By the time he was ready to publish, his printer, Janez Mandelec (d. after 1605), had gone into exile, with the result that the Bible was printed in Germany: *Biblija, tu je, vse svetu pismu* (Bible, that is, the Holy Scriptures, complete, Wittenberg, 1584). HL

ĐALSKI, Ksaver Šandor (i.e. Ljubo Babić, 1854–1935), Croatian prose writer, received his earliest education from a private tutor, before attending secondary school in Varaždin and studying law at Zagreb and Vienna. He entered government service in 1878, but came into conflict with the régime of Ban Khuen-Hédeváry and, in 1891, retired to the family estate where he occupied himself with literature. He returned to public life in 1906, as a deputy to both the Croatian and the Hungarian Diets, but he was soon dissatisfied with the new post-1918 state and returned definitively to the country in 1919. Well read, and drawn particularly to Russian and French literature, Đalski has been called 'the Croatian Turgenev' and his most characteristic work contains much of the melancholy, gentle nostalgia of the Russian. While understanding the inevitability of the social transformation around him, Đalski writes with profound sympathy of the displaced aristocracy and the disappearance of the world of his childhood. This was the theme of his first and perhaps best-known story, 'Illustrissimus Battorych' (1884) and of the whole collection of stories *Pod starimi krovovi* (Under old roofs, 1886), regarded not only as

Đalski's best work but one of the finest achievements of Croatian Realism altogether. It offers a chronicle of Croatian society from the National Revival in the 1840s to the creation of the first Yugoslav state. Đalski has been described as the 'moral historian' of Croatian society.

● Two short stories in B. H. Clark (Ed.), *Great Short Novels of the World* (New York, 1927).
C. Schwarz, *Die Bedeutung Turgenevs für das Schaffen von L. Lazarević, J. Kozarac und K. Š. Đalski* (Vienna, 1949). ECH

DAPONTIS, Konstandinos (known as Kesarios, 1713/14–84), Greek poet, was initially educated in Skopelos in a school set up by his father; 1731 he studied in Constantinople and Bucharest, then went to Jassy (Iaşi). Constantine Mavrogordato, then ruler of Wallachia, became his patron and set him to writing a history of the Russo-Turkish War of 1736–9. He served as Mavrogordato's undersecretary and accompanied him to Moldavia in 1741. Failing to receive the preferment he sought, he abandoned his protector in 1743, and went to Constantinople, where he joined the service of John Mavrogordato, who shortly succeeded in taking the throne of Moldavia from Constantine. However, he clearly made enemies easily, and eventually (1753), worn out by a further series of political adventures, he became a monk, under the name Kesarios. 1757 he went to Athos, only to be dispatched to the Danubian provinces as a fund-raiser. 1765 he returned after a successful trip, which he then described in his Κῆπος χαρίτων (Garden of the Graces). He died on Athos. He is primarily remembered as a poet, influenced by the ideas of the Enlightenment but preseving much of Byzantine tradition. His works, which include Καθρέφτης γωναικών (The mirror of women, 1766) and Υμνος εις την Θεοτόκον (Hymn to the Virgin, Venice, 1770), display a range of historical, geographical, theological and devotional material. But the most important, 'The garden of the Graces' and his great history, remained in manuscript until the 19th century. CFR

DARA, Gavrill, the Younger (1826–85), Arbëresh (Italo-Albanian) poet and man of letters, son of Andrea Dara (1796–1872) and grandson of Gavril Dara the Elder (1766–1832), well-known figures of Arbëresh history and culture, was born in Palazzo Adriano in Sicily of an old Arbëresh family, one of the first to have left Albania after the death of Scanderbeg (1468). He studied at the Arbëresh seminar in Palermo and later received a degree in law. Dara became ever more active in the turbulent political life of Italy during Garibaldi's liberation movement and was appointed by Garibaldi to high office. 1867–9 he was governor of the city of Trapani; 1871–4 editor-in-chief of the periodical *La Riforma* in Rome. Dara's literary interests were wide-ranging, but he is primarily remembered for his Romantic epic *Kënka e Sprapsme e Balës* (The last song of Bala, 1906), first published in instalments in the periodical *Arbri i ri* (New Albanian, 1887). The ballad describes the resistance of the Albanians led by Scanderbeg against the Turks and recounts the adventures of the Albanian national heroes Nik Peta and Pal Golemi.

● G. Petrotta, *Poeti siculo-albanesi* (Palermo, 1950). ShM

DAVIT Aghmashenebeli (i.e. King Davit IV the Builder, 1073–1125), acceded to the throne of Georgia 1089. He rebuilt the Georgian state by recovering provinces lost to the Seljük Turks and by dominating tribesmen, nobility and Church. He created a tolerant flourishing culture, founding a university-monastery (*ak'ademia*) at Gelati. Davit himself composed eight *Galobani sinanulisani* (Hymns of repentance, c. 1120), a powerful sequence of highly emotional free-verse psalms: for all their Christianity and cult of the Virgin, the king clearly sees himself as reincarnating the Biblical David, with a similar relationship to God and to his people. Each hymn in this finely wrought cycle has its own intricate and subtle stanza form. The hymns share the idealistic zeal of the European crusaders to whom Davit was for a time allied.

●M. Lortkipanidse, 'Die Politik Dawit des Erbauers und seine "Reuegesänge"', *Georgica* (Jena) 3 (1980), pp. 46–51. DR

DEBELYANOV, Dimcho (1887–1916), Bulgarian poet, lost his father at the age of 9 and for years experienced hardship. The memory of these years often embitters his verse. 1904 he went to Sofia to complete his secondary education; 1906 he began to publish. He read law, then literature, at Sofia, but left university because of lack of money. He supported himself with odd jobs; he became involved with the editing of the journal *Zveno* (Link) and with the literary circle around it who supported 'pure art' and propagated W European Symbolism; 1912–14 he was conscripted; 1916 he volunteered for the Army since he considered living in safety while others were dying immoral; he fell in Greece. Debelyanov published no collection during his lifetime; his verse (c. 115 poems) was later collected and some of it was published in *Stihotvoreniya* (Poems, 1920). When at the Front, he wrote six poems which differ from his previous Symbolist and neo-Romantic work in their Realist manner. Debelyanov was influenced by SLAVEIKOV and YAVOROV's verse but also by the French Symbolists (mainly Albert Samain), although that influence means simply that in his verse appear motifs typical of them (e.g. SLAVEIKOV and YAVOROV's solitude, memory, French Symbolists' 'sorrowful sunsets', fading flowers, mysterious or 'dead' waters), but then, these are Symbolist 'archimages', transformed by Debelyanov's own sensitivity. The loss of faith and 'light' is the main source of his melancholy, the sense of guilt, bitter memories, and his anticipation of a future in which dream and the desire for happiness are blended with an overwhelming sense of inevitable loss. Every image of a happy past (e.g. home, childhood) is soured by an awareness of predetermined misfortune; the 'happy' past is simply one of the dreams of a tormented soul. He is existentially alien; the white quietness of childhood implies innocence and the 'golden dreams' of an 'ideal', but the ideal is only dreamt, and then destroyed in frustration. His conception of love is marked by the same knowledge of the inevitability of loss. For the most part, Debelyanov's verse contains Symbolist formal elements, but his only long poem, 'Legenda za razbludnata tsarkinya' (Legend of the prodigal princess), is one of the most hermetic Bulgarian Symbolist works; it is a complicated play with the 'archimages' and 'archmotifs' of Symbolism within Debelyanov's own concepts of the 'iron prison', 'shame' and the 'fragrant dream'.SIK

DELLAPORTAS, Leonardos (c.1350–1419/20), Greek poet, fought in Crete as a young man, became a lawyer there, then served on various Venetian embassies. He was imprisoned, possibly wrongly, some time after 1403 and released before 1414. While in prison he wrote four didactic poems in unrhymed 15-syllable lines, of which the most substantial (over 3,000 lines) is couched as a dialogue between the poet and Truth (personified as a beautiful girl). The poem is both a 'complaint' and a 'consolation', and gives an opportunity for the narration of various stories from Antiquity and the Bible, as well as of contemporary and autobiographical matters. The themes and rhetorical conventions have points in common with the poetry of SAHLIKIS. The other poems contain a version of Christ's Passion, a set of prayers and hymns to Christ and the Virgin, and an invitation to his soul to repent.   CFR

DEML, Jakub (1878–1961), Czech poet and publicist, born into a family of Moravian peasants of German ancestry, became a R. Catholic priest, but only seven years after ordination was suspended for his attacks on the religious indifference of the Church hierarchy and for his defence of Catholic orthodoxy. Deml combined in his personality the simple faith and humility of St Francis with the militancy and intolerance of Léon Bloy. Some of his early verse in *Notantur Lumina* (1907, republ. in 1917 as *Nová světla* [New lights]) shows the influence of BŘEZINA but also heralds the arrival of an outsider on the Czech literary scene. Having for a time used a somewhat Expressionist mode, Deml found a highly personal style in his prose poems *Moji přátelé* (My friends, 1913) in which he ad-

dresses plants in free-flowing associations: 'Sunflower, your face drinks in my soul with your curiosity. Sister mine, beware of sparrows! Keep quiet – look, the hangman of Reading Gaol!' In his *Miriam* (1917), where humility merges with ecstasy and spiritual with sensual love, the virginal soul of his deceased sister lifts him to God, whilst his *Hrad smrti* (The castle of death, 1912) and *Tanec smrti* (The dance of death, 1914) evoke sombre, almost medieval, visions and break the divide between waking and dreaming. To Deml external reality was only a symbol of mysterious manifestations of the soul, whose dramas are reminiscent of the contests between the grace of God and the temptations of the Devil in mystery plays. 1917–41 Deml was engaged in the publication at his own expense of irregular issues of *Šlépěje* (Footprints, 26 vols) consisting of his own invective comments on national and religious life, his correspondence and his poems. NEZVAL saw in him a precursor of Surrealism.   KB

DE RADA, Jeronim (i.e. Girolamo De Rada, 1814–1903), Arbëresh (Italo-Albanian) poet and writer, founding father of Arbëresh literature and culture, leading figure of the Albanian national movement, was born in Macchia Albanese, Cosenza. After attending the College of Sant'Adriano in San Demetrio Corone, he registered at the Faculty of Law at Naples, but studied literature and began writing. At an early age he started to collect Albanian folklore. His first and best-known work in Albanian is under the Italian title *Poesie albanesi del secolo XV. Canti di Milosao, figlio del despota di Scutari* (1836), a long Romantic epic of highly original rhapsodic structure, portraying the love of a noble youth from 15th-century Shkodër for a poor shepherd's daughter, Rina. His second poem is *Canti storici albanesi di Serafina Thopia* (1839), which was later republished by the author under the title *Canti di Serafina Thopia, principessa di Zadrima nel secolo XV* (1843). He is also the author of *Skanderbeku i pafan* (The unlucky Scanderbeg, 1843) and *Rrëfime të Arbërisë* (Stories of Albania, 1848). 1848 he founded the newspaper *L'Albanese d'Italia*, which included articles in Albanian. By the end of 1848 he had left Naples and returned to San Demetrio Corone to teach. There he managed to have Albanian included in the curriculum but was dismissed in 1853 for his liberal political views. 1868–78 he was director of the secondary school in Corigliano Calabro. He published the bilingual monthly periodical *Fiamuri i Arbërit – La bandiera dell'Albania* (The Albanian flag, 1883–8) which was widely read by the Albanians despite Turkish and Greek censorship. 1892 he was appointed to teach Albanian language and literature at the college in San Demetrio Corone and 1895 organised the first Albanian Studies congress in Corigliano Calabro. Through his works and publications De Rada was the first to put before the European powers the 'Albanian question', calling for a 'solution in justice and liberty'. He was a Romantic poet whose verse, usually written in Longfellowesque octosyllabic metre, was highly regarded by Hugo and Lamartine. His journalistic activity was instrumental in reinforcing Albanian patriotism and fostering national awareness in the Arbëresh minority.

●N. Douglas, *Old Calabria* (London, 1923); G. Gualtieri, *Girolamo de Rada, poeta albanese* (Palermo, 1930).   ShM

DER NISTER (i.e. Pinkhes Kahanovitsh, 1884–1950), Yiddish prose writer and poet, was born in Berdichev and moved in 1905 to Zhitomir where he lived under an assumed name, a fact which is reflected in his pseudonym, 'the hidden one', and became a Hebrew teacher. His first collection of poetry, *Gedanken un motivn* (Thoughts and motifs, 1907), met with a mixed reception, but he was befriended by BERGLSON and the critic Nakhmen Mayzl (1887–1966). During the turbulent years 1918–20 Der Nister lived in Kiev and helped Berglson to edit the epoch-making journal *Eygns* (Our own, 1918, 1920) which published the Kiev group of writers including Hofshteyn, Kvitko, MARKISH and Molodovski. After Bolsheviks regained control of the Ukraine for the second time, Yiddish culture in Kiev lost its short-lived autonomy and all the important figures emigrated, including Der Nister, who joined BERGLSON in Berlin where together they edited *Milgroym* (Pomegranate, 1922, 1924) and Der Nister published two volumes of polished Symbolist stories, *Gedakht* (Imagined, 1922–3). Following the 1925 Party decree specifically licensing literary activity on the part of the 'Fellow-Travellers', Der Nister returned to the USSR and settled in Kharkov contributing to various NEP journals such as *Di royte velt* (Red world) in which he published his *Unter a ployt* (Under a fence, 1929), a complex allegorical dream sequence which expresses in highly encoded form the remorse he suffered for having betrayed his own spiritual authenticity. This led to renewed vilification from the Proletarian critics, once more in the ascendant, and for a number of years Der Nister supported himself by translation and writing 'fartseykhenungen', the Yiddish equivalent of the Russian *ocherki* or 'sketches', at that time regarded as a 'progressive' genre. However, in his novel *Di mishpokhe mashber* (The family Mashber, 1939–48) Der Nister found a medium that evaded ideological pitfalls and yet enabled him to create a masterpiece of Yiddish fiction by setting his family saga in the relatively uncontroversial 1870s. Nevertheless, the second volume could appear only in New York. During the war years Der Nister worked for the Jewish Anti-Fascist Committee and in 1947 on its behalf he accompanied refugees to Birobidzhan where his wish to encourage the founding of Yiddish schools exposed him to the accusation of 'nationalism'. He shared the fate of his colleagues, being arrested probably early in 1949, tried on fabricated charges and imprisoned in a Gulag, where he died.

●*The Family Mashber* (London, 1987); in: *AMYL*, pp. 65–84; in *GWJF* 1, pp. 44–59, 123–7, 246–64.

D. Bechtel, *Der Nister's Work 1907–1929, A Study of a Yiddish Symbolist* (Berne, Frankfurt on Main, 1990); L. Bodoff, 'Der Nister's "Under a Fence, A Review" ', *Yiddish*, 8:1 (1991), pp. 75–80; K. Shmeruk, 'Der Nister's "Under a Fence": Tribulations of a Soviet Yiddish Symbolist', *The Field of Yiddish*, 2 (The Hague, 1965), pp. 263–87.   HD

DESNICA, Vladan (1905–67), Croatian prose writer, born in Zadar, studied law, but early devoted himself to writing. His best works were written after WWII: several volumes of short stories, 1951–7, introduce an individual voice and an original blend of realism and fantasy. His novel *Zimsko ljetovanje* (A winter summer holiday, 1951) describes the effect of WWII on the inhabitants of a Dalmatian village. Social relations are turned upside down: the villagers see the bombing as revenge for the way they feel they have been exploited by the townspeople. Desnica does not take sides: he regards all his characters with calm scepticism, aware of the complexities behind individual behaviour. The novel *Proljeća Ivana Galeba* (The springs of Ivan Galeb, 1957) is Desnica's finest work, an original blend of observation and lyrical meditation. It takes the form of a monologue, composed in hospital where the narrator is cut off – from other people and from the violin which defined his working life – and able to take a balanced look back over all the expectations that constituted his 'springs', and the actual direction of his life. Its measured wisdom gives it a special place in Croatian literature.

●Selected stories in B. Lenski (Ed.), *Death of a Simple Giant* (New York, Toronto, 1965), pp. 271–8, 283–90; A. Stipčević (Ed.), *An Anthology of Yugoslav Short Stories* (New Delhi, 1969), pp. 149–55; B. Johnson (Ed.), *New Writing in Yugoslavia* (Baltimore, Harmondsworth, 1970), pp. 83–6.

M. Banjanin, 'The Short Stories of Vladan Desnica', *Florida State University Slavic Papers*, 2 (1967), pp. 74–80; N. Pribić, 'The Motif of Death in Vladan Desnica's Prose', *American Contributions to the Eighth International Congress of Slavists* (Columbus, 1978), pp. 644–56.   ECH

DESTOVNIK, Karel (pseudonym: Kajuh; 1922–44), Slovene poet, was expelled from grammar school in Celje for spreading Communist ideas, continued his education in Maribor, was deported to Serbia in 1941; he joined the partisans in 1943, died in battle against the Germans, and was proclaimed a national hero in 1953. He published his partisan poems in autumn 1943, since when they have been reprinted several times: *Pesmi* (Poems, 1943).

•Translations of individual poems in *AMYP*; *Parnassus*, 1957, 1965.   HL

DIK, Yitskhok Meyer/Isaac Meir Dick (1814–93), Yiddish novelist, was born in Vilna (Vilnius) and was soon absorbed into the Jewish Enlightenment movement or Haskalah. In his early Hebrew writings he manifested a characteristic disdain towards the Yiddish language. However, he came to appreciate that the divulgation of enlightened values could best be achieved through the medium of entertaining Yiddish fiction. In the 1850s he introduced sentimental, quasi-realistic adventure stories to a readership alienated by the satire of his more radically anti-Ḥasidic predecessors, such as Yisroel Aksnfeld (1787–1866) and ETINGER and even MENDELE. As a consequence Dik was the first Yiddish fiction writer to achieve widespread popularity. He wrote with astonishing facility, often freely adapting his works from other literatures, and at one time he was under contract to his publisher to write a novelette a week. As in the case of the more sensational and even more prolific Shomer (1849–1905) who followed in his footsteps, his work had the virtue of creating for Yiddish literature a wide public whose taste could later be developed by more demanding authors.

•Miron, pp. 253–6 and passim; D. G. Roskies, *Ayzik Meyer Dik and the Rise of Yiddish Popular Literature* (Ann Arbor, 1983).   HD

DIMITROVA, Blaga (b. 1922), Bulgarian poet and novelist, studied Slavonic philology at Sofia and, as a postgraduate, in Moscow. Later she earned her living as an editor at various publishing houses. Dimitrova began as a somewhat left-wing writer before WWII; during the 1950s she became a typical Stalinist poet but, since the 1960s, has gradually drifted away from her Communist beliefs. After her novel *Litse* (Face, abridg. 1981, complete ed. 1991) was banned she was considered a dissident, but she continued publishing. 1989 she joined the newly founded 'Club for *glasnost* and *perestroika*' which demanded change in the spirit of Gorbachev. After the fall of Zhivkov's régime she became one of the leading figures of the Democratic movement, was elected MP (1990) and vice-president (1992). Dimitrova's work reflects her political self-questioning and her concern about the role of the intellectual in a society which denies its members freedom of choice and replaces human values with ideology. In her later verse (*Glas* [Voice, 1985]) she attempts to give these questions a transcendental dimension, but her views are unconvincing because her negative sense of unfreedom tends to obliterate any positive statement. In her anti-war verse concerning Vietnam (*Osadeni na lyubov* [Condemned to love, 1967]) she tries to solve the problem of unfreedom through generalising meditation on the human condition. She did, however, succeed in expressing her intimate relationship with ordinary people. Her prose work is ideationally more accomplished. It reveals the deformation of humanity produced by living under Communism and demonstrates her horror at the disappearance of idealism, honesty, social and personal responsibility and culture and their replacement by a vulgar 'survivor' mentality. *Litse*, in which she indulges in a great deal of linguistic experimentation, is in its full version somewhat more bombastic than its censored version in its exposure of the failings of socialist 'morality' and the stultifying results of the doctrine of class conflict.

•*Journey to Oneself* [*Pătuvane kăm sebe si*, 1965] (London, 1969); *The Last Imperial Eagle* [selection of verse] (London, 1992).
S. I. Kanikova, 'Blaga Dimitrova' in C. Hawkesworth (Ed.), *Writers from Eastern Europe* (London, 1991), pp. 12–13.   SIK

DINESCU, Mircea (b. 1950), Roumanian poet who became one of the most outspoken critics of Nicolae Ceauşescu, was born in Slobozia, a provincial town E of Bucharest, and completed his secondary education there. His first poem was published in 1967 by the journal *Luceafărul* (Lucifer/Venus), whose editor helped him to find a post on the staff of the Union of Writers. 1981 he joined the editorial staff of the Writers' Union weekly, *România literară*, and in the same year caused a stir with the publication of his *Democraţia naturii* (Nature's democracy, 1981) which contained thinly veiled attacks on totalitarian rule. In September 1988 he visited the USSR as a guest of the Soviet Union of Writers and publicly expressed his support for *glasnost*. On his return he was placed under surveillance and the manuscript of his latest volume of poems, *Moartea citeşte ziarul* (Death reads the newspaper), was refused an imprimatur. On 13 March 1989 he wrote an open letter to the president of the Writers' Union criticising censorship and the inactivity of the Union. Shortly before, he gave an interview to the Parisian daily *Libération* in which he attacked the régime's degrading treatment of its subjects. On the day of its publication, 17 March, he was placed under house arrest. For nine months he received orchestrated death threats through the post. On 22 December, the day of Ceauşescu's flight, Dinescu's police guards ran off and he was carried in triumph by demonstrators to the TV station where he pronounced the overthrow of the dictatorship and became a national celebrity. In spring 1990 he was elected president of the Writers' Union. Dinescu is the 'angry young man' of contemporary Roumanian poetry, a moralist of the modern age. He admits to being born with anger and his verse is conceived and delivered with violence. His revolt is against what we do to ourselves in the name of progress, and at what is done to us under the banner of utopianism. The inconsistencies of progress are underlined stridently and uncompromisingly in his collections *Invocaţie nimănui* (Invocation to no one, 1971), *Elegii de cînd eram mai tînăr* (Elegies from a time when I was younger, 1973), *Proprietarul de poduri* (The proprietor of bridges, 1976), *La dispoziţia dumneavoastră* (At your disposal, 1979) and *Exil pe o boabă de piper* (Exile on a peppercorn, 1983).
•*Exile on a Peppercorn: The Poetry of Mircea Dinescu* (London, 1985).   DJD

DOINAŞ, Ştefan Augustin (i.e. Ştefan Popa, b. 1922), Roumanian poet, born into a family of peasants near Arad in W Transylvania, read literature and philosophy at Cluj, where he studied under BLAGA, and graduated in 1948. A year earlier he won a prestigious poetry prize for a manuscript volume of verse which remained unpublished, like all his poetry of the following decade, because of his refusal to conform to the literary dictates of the Communist régime. He spent a year in prison 1957–8 for political reasons and subsequently worked on the editorial staff of the periodicals *Teatru* and *Lumea* (The world). His first published collection, *Cartea mareelor* (The book of the tides), appeared in 1964 in the wake of the relaxation of rigid ideological control, and has been followed by more than fifteen others. Doinaş's courageous and uncompromising stand on the right of the writer to independence of expression was marked by his poem 'Habeas Corpus Poeticum' which was published in the Writers' Union journal *România literară* in June 1978. In April 1985 he was a signatory, alongside such as the philosophers Constantin Noica (1908–87) and Alexandru Paleologu, of a memorandum sent to the mayor of Bucharest, protesting about the planned demolition of a monastery, and in April 1989 he joined six other writers condemning the placing under house arrest of the poet DINESCU. In *Lampa lui Diogene* (The lamp of Diogenes, 1970) the poet gave his own definition of his work: 'In each of us the spirit borders on all those chasms which humanity has explored for aeons. Pain, joy; despair, ecstasy; resolution, impotence; solitude, companionship; language, silence – all these are our responses to impassable thresholds. Usually they have a merely personal meaning. It takes a poet to present them with the dignity of a message for humanity itself. There is only one constant message: acknowledgement of the attempt to break out of the human condition.'

●*Alibi and other poems* (London, 1975).

DJD

DONELAITIS, Kristijonas (1714–80), author of the first Lithuanian epic poem *Metai* (The seasons, c. 1765–75, first printed, 1818), was the pastor of Tolminkiemis (Tolmingkehmen), a small village in E Prussia, now called Čistye Prudy (Russia). Educated in Classics and theology at Königsberg, he was equally fluent in German and Lithuanian, and showed an early interest in poetry and music. His life was uneventful, a succession of Sundays preaching to the people. Out of these sermons and homilies an idea grew to write in Greek hexameters, but in the language of the rural Lithuanians around him, a compendious and emotionally effective picture of country life as a daily encounter with God. Thus Donelaitis created the first extended artistic text in Lithuanian, a language which had no literary tradition; moreover, he did it in a masterly way – there is no comparable lyrical epic in Lithuanian literature. The poem describes various incidents in the life of a peasant community during the four seasons, each confronting the farmers with different tasks. The seasons, as cyclical changes in Nature, form a background to the joys and sorrows that visit the people throughout their lives. The poem has no central plot, nor central human force, like Achilles' anger, that would drive the action along. It is held together as an epic whole by other devices. One of these is the hexameter, sustained throughout the some 3,000 lines of the poem, which gives it an 'epic flow'. Another is the course of the seasons, shaping the affairs of individual human beings into a recurrently emphasised overall design. The third device consists of the use of the image of the sun, advancing and

retreating with the seasons, a dominant presence to which Donelaitis
gives human qualities. A fourth device is dialogue: we learn of events as
the main speakers relate them to each
other; they are impersonations of the
author's voice, morally upright
peasants who add to their tales comments promoting the virtues of the
meek. The ultimate unity of the work
comes from its religious spirit, per-
vading everything as the breath of
God.
•R. Šilbajoris, 'Kristijonas Donelaitis, a
Lithuanian Classic', *Slavic Review*, 41
(1982), 2, pp. 251–65.   RŠ

DRACH, Ivan (b. 1936), Ukrainian
poet and political activist, published a
long philosophical poem, *Nizh u
sontsi* (Knife in the sun, 1961), a
meditation on Ukrainian history. His
power lies in his daring use of association. His first collection of verse
was *Soniashnyk* (Sunflower, 1962).
Drach was one of the leaders of a
group of young poets (the Sixtiesers)
in the 1960s. In the era of *glasnost* he
wrote less and devoted himself to
political activity. 1989 he published a
long poem, *Chornobylska Madonna*
(The Chernobyl Madonna). 1989–92
he served as the president of the
Ukrainian national movement for independence – RUKH.
•*Orchard Lamps* (New York, 1978); M.
Maslov (Ed.), 'Le Couteau dans le
soleil', *La nouvelle Vague littéraire en
Ukraine* (Paris, 1967).   GSNL

DRAGOJEVIĆ, Danijel (b. 1934),
Croatian poet and essay writer, born
on the island of Korčula, was educated there, then in Dubrovnik and
Zagreb, where he works in broadcasting. His first volume of verse,
Kornjača (Tortoise, 1961), introduced an original voice into contemporary Croatian poetry. Dragojević's
central theme is paradox, and a search

for 'the essential words'. He has been
particularly successful in developing
the prose poem and an expressly
intellectual, complex style, abounding in intertextual references.
•Translations of selected poems in
NWY, pp. 78–82; *The Bridge*, 19–20
(1970), pp. 79–82; V. D. Mihailovich
(Ed.), *Contemporary Yugoslav Poetry*
(Iowa City, 1977), pp. 194–7.   ECH

DRDA, Jan (1915–70), Czech novelist, studied philology, worked as a
journalist, after 1948 became an MP
and later a member of the Central
Committee of the Communist Party.
In his novel *Městečko na dlani* (A
small town in my palm, 1940), he
recounts the fortunes of the simple
craftsmen and miners of his native
Příbram, mixing reality with fairy-
tale fiction in a narration lightened
with whimsy and optimism. He uses
the same style in the novel *Putování
Petra Sedmilháře* (The wanderings of
Peter the liar, 1943) about a boy who
invents fantastic stories about himself
and his unknown father. His short
stories in *Němá barikáda* (The silent
barricade, 1946), a tribute to the
Czechs facing German occupation,
are marred by false idealisation and
sentimentality.   KB

DROSINIS, Yiorgos (1859–1951),
Greek poet, under the influence of
his father registered to study law at
Athens, but swiftly changed to literature. 1885–8 he studied modern
European languages in Germany on
the advice of Nikolaos Politis
(1852–1921), the specialist in folk
studies. On his return to Greece,
Drosinis took up the editorship of the
literary periodical *Estia* (Hearth and
home), and 1894 turned it into an
evening newspaper, continuing to
edit it until 1898. Throughout his
career he took an interest in educational and literary ventures, usually

of a nationalist colouring. His contributions were rewarded, on the founding of the Athens Academy in 1926, by election as one of its founder members. In his student days he started publishing demotic poetry in periodicals, mostly on folk themes, with some personal lyrics. His first collection, Ιστοί αράχνης (Spider's webs, 1880), showing the influence of Coppée, Musset and Heine as well as of folk material, helped to launch the so-called 'New School of Athens'. He used the same material for idealised stories of village life, but the fragile and stylised themes were overwhelmed by the didactic intention. Other collections of poetry in the same vein followed. Γαλήνη (Calm, 1902) shows a greater degree of technical perfection matched by greater profundity in the treatment of the themes. With Φωτερά σκοτάδια (Bright darkness, 1914) Drosinis moved to a more symbolic, often allegorical style. The collection is marked by a nationalist fervour which reflects the poet's response to the Balkan Wars. He continued publishing verse until 1947, but his sources of inspiration and his technique were never renewed.   CFR

DRŽIĆ, Marin (1508?–67), Croatian playwright, born in Dubrovnik, was one of the few non-nobles to achieve prominence in the literary life of the republic. His life had as much colour and drama as his plays. He held various positions as a cleric and played the organ in the cathedral to augment his income. He studied canon law in Siena, 1538–44. For part of that time he was deputy vice-chancellor of the university. He was more attracted to Renaissance comedy than to canon law, and so he did not complete his studies. He was given various appointments by the Dubrovnik government, but these tended to end in official inquiries. Finally frustration with his social situation and conflict with the ruling class of Dubrovnik drove him to seek to overthrow the nobility and establish a government of which half would be ordinary citizens. 1566 he was in Florence where he tried to secure from the Tuscan Prince Cosimo financial and military support for an armed revolt. He received no reply and died in Venice the following year. Držić had a wide knowledge of both Classical and Renaissance literature, particularly drama. While in Siena, he had spent much of his time watching popular street theatre. On his return to Dubrovnik he was able to exploit his knowledge of this and its Classical models in a series of pastoral plays and plays modelled more or less closely on Plautus (e.g. *Dundo Maroje* [Uncle M., 1556], *Novela od Stanca* [The dream of S., 1551], *Skup* [The miser]). Držić exploited the pastoral convention to his own advantage: the characters of the aristocratic 'shepherds' and 'nymphs' tend to be one-dimensional, conventional figures, but he introduces also memorable peasant characters, giving them fresh, lively dialogue. His best-known work is *Dundo Maroje*, with its intricate plot of coincidence and intrigue, its vivid characters (some the stock figures of Plautine comedy) and imaginative exploitation of the Dubrovnik Croatian-Italian bilingualism. Much has been made of the implicit criticism of contemporary Dubrovnik society, expressed mainly through Pomet, the wily servant who manipulates the entire plot and outwits all his 'superiors', and in the Aesopian language of the lengthy Prologue, spoken by a 'necromancer' recounting the loss of the Golden

Age and the presence in contemporary society of monstrous beings – these are given attributes which identify them as individuals in Dubrovnik society who would have been known to the audience. Držić intended his play for all ranks of society, but it is clear that some of its message is aimed specifically at non-nobles like himself.

●*Grižula, Uncle Maroje* (Dubrovnik, 1967); selected poems in *The Bridge*, 25 (1971), pp. 68–9; The Dream of Stanac', *BC Review*, 17 (1980); pp. 3–17.
V. Javarek, 'Marin Držić: A Ragusan Playwright', *SEER*, 37 (1958), pp. 141–59; E. Stankiewicz, 'The Legend of Opulent India, Marin Držić, and South Slavic Folk Poetry', *Zeitschrift für Balkanologie* (1967), 5, pp. 120–8; J. Torbarina, 'A Croat Forerunner of Shakespeare: In Commemoration of the 400th Anniversary of the Death of Marin Držić (1508–1567)', *Studia romanica et anglica Zagrebiensia*, 24 (1967), pp. 5–21.   ECH

DUBOŬKA, Uładzimir (1900–76), Byelorussian writer, was one of the most technically gifted poets and outspoken nationalists of the 1920s. Born into a peasant family, he worked as a teacher before becoming a founding member of the literary group Uzvyšša (Excelsior) in 1926 but was arrested four years later and exiled to the Urals and subsequently Siberia. After rehabilitation in 1958 he continued to write, but with far less fire. Duboŭka's best narrative poems are *Kruhi* (Circles, 1925), *I purpurovych vetriaziaŭ uživy* (And the purple sails unfurled, 1929) and *Šturmujcie budučyni avanposty* (Storm the outposts of the future, 1930). Psychologically subtle, they explore with cleverly ambiguous irony the relationship between, on the one hand, the individual and society in the Soviet Union, and, on the other, the problems of a small nation in a supposedly federal system. His lyric verse is exceptionally rich, combining refined diction with fresh imagery, rhythmic verve with lofty imagination. The main collections of his best period include *Stroma* (Rapids, 1923), *Tryście* (The reed, 1925), *Credo* (1926), *Nala* (1925–6) and *Piaresty bukiet* (A many-coloured bouquet, 1929), the last containing many recklessly satiric barbs against proletarianisation and political repression. Duboŭka's two-volume collected works, *Vybranyja tvory* (Minsk, 1965), omit most of the works that reflect his major achievement.

●A. Adamovich, *Opposition to Sovietization in Belorussian Literature (1917–1957)* (New York, 1958).

                                        ABMcM

DUČIĆ, Jovan (1871–1943), Serbian poet and essayist, was a native of Trebinje, Herzegovina. He went to school in the Vojvodina, later studied in Geneva and Paris, entered the diplomatic corps, and served as a diplomat for the rest of his life. When Yugoslavia was attacked by the Germans, he was in Madrid and in 1941 he went to the USA. He died in Gary, Indiana. During WWII he supported the nationalist side in the civil war in Yugoslavia and for that reason was proscribed until 1991, when his remains were allowed to be returned to Trebinje. During his studies in Paris Dučić came under the influence of the Parnassians and Symbolists and he wrote his early poetry in a similar vein. Together with RAKIĆ, he was instrumental in transforming and modernising Serbian poetry at the beginning of the 20th century. After publishing two collections in 1901 and 1908, he wrote less and less verse and turned to prose poems, essays, travel journals and historical writing. It is in verse, however, that he left his mark. He was attracted to the esoteric and self-elevating themes of the Decadent poets. Eschewing the Romantic and Realist orientation of his predecessors, he gave expression to his egocentric, sensitive inner life in poems suffused with melancholy pessimism. He was an advocate of art for art's sake, a strict formalist whose poems excel in clarity, precision, elegance, musicality, and picturesque images. His influence on Serbian poetry was considerable in his own time and still persists.

•*Plave legende–Blue Legends* (Columbus, Ohio, 1983).   VDM

DUNIN-MARCINKIEVIČ, Vikienci (1807–84), Byelorussian playwright, poet and translator, born into the polonised minor gentry, overcame official persecution successfully to lay the foundations of modern Byelorussian drama. His early macaronic libretto *Sialanka* (An idyll, 1846) combined 18th-century traditions with the sentimental bucolic idyll. His best play, banned until 1917, was *Pinskaia šlachta* (The gentry of Pinsk, 1866), a satire on social pretensions and legal corruption. *Zaloty* (Flirtation, 1870), though old-fashioned, includes an unusually realistically characterised main figure. The best of the narrative poems are *Hapon* (1855) and *Chalimon na karanacyi* (Ch. at the coronation, 1857), rich in ethnographic detail, with lively descriptions and humour. Also significant was the earliest Slav translation of MICKIEWICZ's *Pan Tadeusz*, confiscated in 1859 and largely destroyed. Writing when the literary language was in its infancy and, moreover, banned, Dunin-Marcinkievič was important as the first professional Byelorussian writer.   ABMcM

ĐURĐEVIĆ-ĐORĐIĆ, Ignjat (1675–1737), Croatian poet and historian, born into a noble Dubrovnik family, studied at the Jesuit college there. He joined the Jesuit Order in Rome 1698, studied philosophy and worked as a teacher. On his return to Dubrovnik 1706, he became a Benedictine monk, but was subsequently driven out of Dubrovnik for political reasons, lived in Rome and Naples 1710–12, and was abbot on the island of Mljet (1725–8) before returning to Dubrovnik in 1731. The last significant Croatian Baroque poet, Đurđević was one of the most varied and prolific of all Dubrovnik writers. He began to write early, compiling a large manuscript collection of poems – lyric and religious verse, eclogues, ballads and imitations of oral traditional songs – as early as 1716. He wrote erotic verse, *Ljuvene pjesni* (Love songs, 1716); a devout meditation, *Uzdasi Mandalijene pokornice* (The sighs of penitent Magdalene, 1728), displaying flexibility in his use of metre, and an unfinished play, *Judita* (Judith, c. 1736). One of his most original works is a humorous narrative poem, described even as 'lascivious', *Suze Marunkove* (The tears of Marunko, 1724), in which he parodies the Petrarchan conventions of love poetry in the figure of a shepherd, unhappily in love.

•J. Torbarina, 'The English Version of a Poem by Ignjat Đjurđjević', *Zbornik Filozofskog Fakulteta*, 1 (1951), pp. 651–706.
R. Lachmann-Schmohl, *Ignjat Đorđić. Eine Untersuchung zum slavischen Barock* (Cologne, Graz, 1964); I. Pudić, 'Ignjat Đjurdjević (Ignatio Giorgi), Eighteenth-

Century Scholar from Dubrovnik',
Balkan Studies, 7 (1966), pp. 123–34;
A. Kadić, 'Ignjat Djurdjević,
Croatian Baroque Writer', *Journal of
Croatian Studies*, 18–19 (1977–8),
pp. 92–7.   ECH

DURYCH, Jaroslav (1886–1962),
Czech writer, read medicine at Prague, where he qualified 1913, served
as an MO on the Eastern and Southern Fronts in WWI; he was then in
the Czechoslovak Army until 1939.
As a strict R. Catholic, he was particularly interested in the Baroque, the
Counter-Reformation in Bohemia,
which is witnessed by his two most
accomplished works. *Rekviem* (Requiem, 1927–30) contains three pictures of the atmosphere in Bohemia
after the assassination of Wallenstein
(1634). This atmosphere is evoked by
a brittle, rhapsodic style which
reflects the dark, violent forces dominating the period and which supports
a psychological characterisation that
depends almost entirely on characters' physical behaviour. The monumental *Bloudění* (Wandering,
1929–30), set against the background
of Wallenstein's rise and fall, presents
a panoramic view of the world in
flux. The novel incorporates Baroque
polarity, is a contorted embellishment surrounding a beautiful picture,
hideous earthly existence surrounding 'the beautiful Catholic soul'.
Bloudění depicts a violent, deceitful,
depraved, cynical age where,
however, smiles (sometimes grimaces) constantly strive to overcome
the despair and frustration of the
times. Another 'Baroque' work is
essentially an ironic comedy of misunderstanding, *Masopust* (Carnival,
1938). One of the strengths of this
balladic novel about superstition and
love is that Durych condemns or
praises nothing. *Píseň o růži* (Song of

a rose, 1934) is an ironic psychological case-study of three beautiful
seamstresses. It is a sensitive, intricate, sensualist tale where human lots
are ruled by a Fate comprising Nature, chance and some unexplained
guiding force. His first verse work,
the lengthy ballad *Cikánčina smrt*
(Death of a Gipsy woman, 1916),
runs completely contrary to the
Czech ballad tradition (see ERBEN) in
that it presents death as the only true
sensual happiness on earth; furthermore, although divine salvation may
come through woman, earthly sensuality is violent and verges on the
diabolical. His collection *Beskydy*
(The Beskyd Mountains, 1926) presents earthly existence as a prison in
which we are constantly subjected by
passion and filth. Here he also expresses his sense of exclusion from
Czechoslovak   life.   Durych's
travel-writing may be exemplified by
Plížení   Německem   (Creeping
through Germany, 1926), an ironic
essay on anonymous people, mainly
women, and on the spirit of nations;
the spirit of Germany is embodied in
the summoning of the madame of a
Baltic brothel.
●*The Descent of the Idol* [*Bloudění*]
(London, 1935).
H. Jílek 'Jaroslav Durychs "Wallenstein" ', *Jahrbücher für Kultur und
Geschichte der Slaven*, New Series, 9
(1933), pp. 596–609.   RBP

DUŠEK, Václav (b. 1944), Czech
novelist, after elementary schooling,
a rough childhood in the Karlín slums
of Prague, 1979 finished an external
degree at the Prague Academy of
Film and then worked mainly as a
screenwriter. Dušek introduced the
underworld and the coarse life of
slum children of the 1950s and 1960s
into Czech literature; more than anyone else since WWII he also used

underworld slang in his writing. His novels and stories of violence, criminality, love and friendship among Prague working-class and has-been youth (*Panna nebo orel* [Heads or tails, 1974], *Tuláci* [Vagabonds, 1978] or *Dny pro kočku* [Dog days, 1979]) have as their narrator Tadeáš Falk, a rough-hewn, sensitive equivalent to ŠKVORECKÝ's Danny Smiřický. The picture they paint is far from that of the ideal socialist working class, but Dušek tends to have optimistic endings, and for all the pictures of alienation, is not overtly anti-socialist. His long, somewhat clumsy semi-autobiographical novel *Skleněný Golem* (Glass G., 1989) constitutes one of the keenest evocations of the 1950s police state in Czech literature; it is new in that it presents a working-class picture of Stalinism. In his most accomplished work, *Lovec štěstí* (The happiness hunter, 1980), Dušek writes in a neat blend of argot and literary Czech. This novel about a newly released criminal, who had been unjustly imprisoned, and who tries and fails to stop drinking and having any contact with his criminal friends, is a powerful determinist indictment of socialist consumer society, and shows that society crushing anyone who has a sense of honour. It is the first Czech novel to describe large-scale organised crime under socialism.

●R. B. Pynsent, 'Social Criticism in Czech Literature of 1970s and 1980s Czechoslovakia', *Bohemia*, I (1986), pp. 1–36.   RBP

DYK, Viktor (1877–1931), Czech writer, was taught at school by JIRÁSEK; after school he read law at Prague (1896–1900). From his schooldays to his death he was involved in politics, first, as a canvasser for the Social Democrats and finally, as a right-wing National Democrat Senator. 1916–17 he was in prison as a Czech patriot. His first collection of verse, *A porta inferi* (1897), is the work of a self-ironic rebellious Decadent, but by his third collection, *Marnosti* (Futilities, 1900), he has more in common with MACHAR than the Decadents. The ironic epic *Milá sedmi loupežníků* (Sweetheart of seven robbers, 1906) mixes literary and social satire with a study of passion, particularly in the titular heroine, who combines the character of a tomboy *femme fatale* with that of a nymphomaniac. Works like *Prohrané kampaně* (Lost campaigns, 1914) or *Pan poslanec* (MP, 1921) constitute political pamphleteering. After WWI his lyric verse gained in elegance and dignity. In prose, although he had previously shown himself adept at analysis of character and emotion, Dyk came into his own in his political novels, particularly *Konec Hkackkenschmidův* (Hackenschmid's end, 1904) and *Prosinec* (December, 1906), satirical novels on Czech political and literary circles in the 1890s; though permeated by an abundance of contemporary allusions, these novels express with irony and wit existing as a 'small nation' and remain readable. Despair, combined with old-fashioned nationalism, takes over from irony in later political novels like *Děs z prázdna* (Horror vacui, 1932). His most read novel, *Krysař* (The Pied Piper, 1915), however, is not political; it constitutes a reluctant lyrical statement that it is time to cease chasing chimeras and to look to practical life, however reprehensible the mobility of contemporary society may be. Dyk was an innovative and many-sided dramatist. He began with experimental drama like the dialogue of two burnt-out souls, *Zcela vážný rozhovor* (An entirely serious conversation, 1898) or *Kouzelník* (The magician, 1897–9), where the magician is searching for a cure for human pain, much to the distress of God, witches and local inhabitants. He attained dramatic maturity with *Posel* (The messenger, 1907); set in 1620, its characters represent standard Czech world-views and the action consists of conflict between these views. Dyk uses a similar technique in his play in admiration of the idea, but contempt for the methods, of the French Revolution, *Revoluční trilogie* (Revolutionary trilogy, 1921). His greatest dramatic achievement, *Zmoudření dona Quijota* (Don Quixote achieves wisdom, publ. 1913, perf. 1938), is a sensitive, ironic picture of Cervantes's hero as a dreamy, tragic figure who is killed by attaining his chimera.

RBP

DYRLICH, Benedikt (b. 1950), Sorbian poet, born in Nowa Wjeska (Neudörfel), east of Kamenz, into the family of a carpenter and wood-carver, attended school in Worklecy (Räckelwitz) 1956–64, and in Schöneiche 1964–8. 1968 he became a student of R. Catholic theology in Erfurt, but did not complete the course and worked for a time (1971–2) as a medical attendant in Chemnitz. He studied drama in Leipzig 1975–80, then worked in the German-Sorbian People's Theatre in Bautzen. 1990 he was elected an SPD deputy of the Saxon Landtag in Dresden. Dyrlich's poems have appeared in four volumes: *Zelene hubki* (Green kisses, 1975), *Třeće wóčko* (The third eye, 1978), *Nocakowanje* (Nocturne, 1980) and *W paslach* (In the trap, 1986). A pupil of Kito LORENC, he has long since developed a distinct style of his own. In *W paslach*, apart from verse, he sometimes uses poetic prose in brief lyrical essays, including one on his father, 'Rězbarstwo mojeho nana' (My father's wood-carving). Dyrlich frequently reflects on the social and ethical questions of his generation. He occasionally responds to perceived links between his native environment and events of world history. His love poems are collected in *Nocakowanje*.

GCS

DZERENTS (i.e. Hovsepʻ Shishmanian, 1822–88), W Armenian novelist, was born in Constantinople; at the age of 10 he was sent to the Mekhitharist school on the island of San Lazaro, in Venice, but a few years later he was back in his birthplace and spent some time teaching at the Illuminator's School of Ortakoy. Although he aspired to become a physician, lack of funds prevented him from embarking upon the career immediately. 1843, after teaching and working as a pharmacist for a number of years, he undertook an eight-month journey into W Armenia and the Caucasus. During this trip, he gathered material for his novels. 1848 he left for Paris to study medicine (degree 1853) and then returned to Constantinople, where he plunged himself into the feverish social, political and educational activity of the Armenian community. 1862 he co-founded the Charitable Association, one of whose principal aims was economic improvement through education in Turkish Armenia. It was with the purpose of acquiring land and establishing agricultural schools that he went to Cilicia in 1863. Unfortunately, the enmity that he had created during bitter religious disputes caused him to be recalled by the Turkish government and posted to

Cyprus as a physician in the public service in 1875. This was in reality exile. His first novel, *T'oros Levoni* (Thoros Levon, 1877), is the story of the reconquest of the barony of Cilicia by T'oros, the son of Levon I. An adventure story based on historical reality, it has more unity than Dzerents's other novels, although in essence it simply describes a series of military campaigns with a brief love story of T'oros and Yevp'ime. There is neither character development nor psychological analysis. The author's primary purpose is to present his readers with a picture of a past in which their ancestors had fought successfully for their rights. He soon embarked on his second novel, *Erkunk' 9 daru* (Labours of the ninth century, 1879), which attempts to present a picture of Armenia between 851 and 861, when Arab and Byzantine persecution of the Armenians had reached almost unprecedented severity and the Armenians revolted under the leadership of Hovnan Khut'etsi; this had resulted in victory by the recognition of the Ashod Bagraduni as the 'Prince of Princes' by the khalif of Baghdad and the eventual restoration of the Armenian monarchy. His next novel, *T'eodoros Rshtuni* (1881), deals with the 7th-century incursions of the Arabs and the ultimate conquest of Armenia by the Arabs. The eponymous hero was the nominal commander-in-chief of the Armenian Army who, with varying degrees of success, hastened from one end of the country to the other fighting the invading armies. Dzerents is the creator of the Armenian historical novel. Despite his failure to reach the artistic excellence of RAFFI in E Armenian literature, his literary labours gave birth to the genre and put it on a respectable basis. VN

E

EGHISHE, Vardapet (c. 410–70/75), Armenian chronicler, the author of *Patmut'iwn Vardanants Paterazmin* (History of the Vardanians), is said to have been born between 410 and 420. He was among those students sent abroad to study with a group of young men destined later to be called the Junior Translators c. 434. He returned to Armenia in 441/2 following the death of their patron, St Sahak (348–438) and Mesrop (355–439). 442–9 he was in Persia, a soldier and later secretary to the *sparapet*. He was a participant at the Council of Shahapivan (444) and it is possible that he also represented the bishopric of Bagrevand at the Council of Artashat (449). He composed his 'History of the Vardanians' c. 458–60. Considerable doubt is expressed about this dating of Eghishe's History. Some place it in the 7th century, others in the 6th and still others in the 5th. Those who with Nerses Akinian would see in him an author not of the 5th, but of the 7th century must face the difficulty of explaining how, in view of the religious development of Armenia, he could after 555 refer to the 'holy clergy' of Constantinople, and, after 505–6, to the 'holy bishop of Rome' when following the Council of Chalcedon (451) Armenia had officially adopted an anti-Chalcedonian stance and broken with R. Catholicism. The cause of the Armenian revolt was the Persian decree attempting to impose Zoroastrianism on Armenia. Armenians took up arms to defend their faith. Some *nakharars*, under the leadership of Vasak Suni, apostatised and joined the Persians, and in the Battle of Avarayr, Vardan Mamikonian, the commander-in-chief, fell with eight of his generals and 1,027 soldiers. Those who survived were taken captive and some eventually returned home 464–5. The story is told in seven chapters, ending with Vasak's disgrace and death; a martyrological chapter was added later. Eghishe's History is not a work in the category of P'AWSTOS BUZAND or Ghazar P'arp'etsi's (437–500) but rather in the genre of the life of Mashtots by KORIWN. It is not an historical account of an event in the ordinary sense of the word. The author calls his work a *Yishatakaran*, 'Memorial' or 'Recollection', of an event in history with the intention to 'reprove his sins [i.e. Vasak Suni's], so that everyone who hears and knows, may cast curses on him and not lust after his deeds'. Eghishe immortalises the 'heavenly valour' of his main character with the aim of providing 'comfort to friends, hope to the hopeful, and encouragement to the brave'. In short it is a glorification of Christianity, for Christianity provides the faithful with the moral and physical strength to endure all and to wage battle with the defiant call: 'No one can shake our faith, neither angels nor men, neither sword nor fire, neither water nor any other horrible tortures. . . . Yours the sword, ours the neck.' In a more restricted sense, this is a war waged for the preservation of the Armenian ethnic identity with internal independence. This 'Golden Book' of classical Armenian literature has captured the minds and the imagination of writers and artists alike. Among the historians and religious writers who have felt Eghishe's impact, one might mention T'omva Ardsruni (840–906), Aristakes Lastivertsi (100–73), and NERSĒS SHNORHALI. Among the modern authors both secular and religious, some of the best known are ABOVYAN, Ghewond Alishan (1820–1901), Derenik Demirdjyan (1877–1956).

•*Eghishei Vasn Vardanay ew Hayots paterazmin* (The History of Vardan and the War of the Armenians), critical ed. by E. Ter Minasyan (Yerevan, 1957); *Elish History of Vardan and the Armenian War*, translation and commentary by R. W. Thomson (Cambridge, Mass. 1982) reviewed by V. Nersessian in *Haigazian Armenological Review*, 10 (1984), pp. 309–15.   VN

ELIADE, Mircea (1907–86), Roumanian novelist and historian of religion, is better known in his latter capacity to most English-speaking readers and yet he was also an accomplished author of novels and short stories. The son of an army officer, he grew up in Bucharest in very modest surroundings. At secondary school he showed a talent for writing tales of the fantastic, the first of which was published when he was 14. He coupled his creative writing with a prodigious number of articles on entomology and by the age of 18 had more than fifty published pieces to his name. After graduating in philosophy at Bucharest in 1928 Eliade received an offer of a bursary to study in India from the Maharajah of Kassimbazar in reply to a letter Eliade had written to him. Thus began a three-year study of Indian philosophy under the tutelage of Surrendranath Dasgupta, Professor of Philosophy at Calcutta University. On his return to Roumania he was appointed associate professor at Bucharest University. 1940 he became Roumanian cultural attaché in London and 1941 took up the same post in Lisbon. After the war he remained in the West, holding positions at various European universities before becoming (1956) Professor of the History of Religions at Chicago. Eliade's early fiction is marked by its autobiographical character and draws heavily on his journal, conceived as he admitted as a repository of recollections, observations and intimate experiences. Thus *Maitreyi* (1933) is a semi-autobiographical love story about a young European and a teenage Indian girl. In *Domnişoara Christina* (Miss C., 1936) Eliade explored by means of a horror story the manner in which the supernatural reveals itself in everyday life. *Noaptea de Snziene* (The night of St John the Baptist), first published in French in 1955 as *La Forêt interdite*, follows its hero's search to distinguish the sacred and profane in everyday life in terms of fundamental time as opposed to historical time. These concepts are expounded in Eliade's philosophy of myth, expressed in *Le Mythe de l'éternel retour* (1949). The themes of *Pe Strada Mântuleasa* (On M. Street,

1968) are the conflicts between suspicion and trust, fantasy and fact, myth and history, articulated by the fabricated denunciations made to the Roumanian security police by a retired schoolteacher about his former pupils. A preoccupation with the supernatural dominates the three novelle, written 1975–9, which make up the collection *Youth without Youth* (*Tinreţe fără de tinereţe*). His fiction serves the same function as myth by creating fresh meanings. In Eliade's own words these stories employ the supernatural to reveal 'various and sometimes dramatic irruptions of the sacred into the world'.

●*Two Tales of the Occult* (New York, 1970); *The Forbidden Forest* (Notre Dame, Indiana, 1978); *The Old Man and the Bureaucrats* (Notre Dame, Indiana, 1979); *Youth without Youth and other Novellas* (London, 1989). *Autobiography*, (San Francisco, 1981–8).

N. J. Girardot and M. L. Ricketts (Eds), *Imagination and Meaning: The Scholarly and Literary Worlds of Mircea Eliade* (New York, 1982); M. L. Ricketts, *Mircea Eliade* (Boulder, Colorado, 1989).   DJD

ELIN PELIN (i.e. Dimităr Stoyanov, 1878–1949), Bulgarian prose writer, came from a peasant background, and became a teacher; his attempt to study at the Academy of Art failed and he gradually committed himself entirely to literature. From 1899 Elin Pelin lived in Sofia and worked for newspapers and at the University Library; he spent a year in France (1906–7); during WWI he was a war correspondent; 1926–44 he worked at the VAZOV Museum and then on various literary journals. After the Communist take-over he supported the new establishment but criticised the literature of Socialist Realism for its neglect of the individual. Elin Pelin is best known for his short stories gathered in two collections (1904 and 1911), and in the uncompleted *Pod manastirskata loza* (Beneath the monastery vineyard, 1936); he also attempted longer prose but with little success; he wrote sketches, *feuilletons*, comic tales in Shop (from Shopsko, near Sofia) dialect, and books for children. On account of his short stories, which concern rural life, Elin Pelin was called a 'singer of rural misery'; his characters, however, evince remarkable conservativism and lively pertinacity in the face of hardship. The importance of his work, apart from his skill as a story-teller, lies in his modification of the concept of Bulgarian village life characteristic for earlier literature. In contrast to the patriotic perception of Nature and the use of rural life as historical-patriotic subject matter or as an object of sentimental idealisation, for Elin Pelin 'rural' no longer means 'Bulgaria'. For his characters the new 'Bulgaria' has no patriotic attraction. It is merely the name of a hostile state and the villagers feel no loyalty to it. The two typical villager reactions to the state are, first, to mock it and, secondly, to commit even murder out of despair, for they do not trust the justice system of the state. Nature is their state and their morality is derived from her laws. 'Sin' takes on a political meaning; it is a sin to deprive people of their property but not to drink in church or to desire women. The Church represents authority, i.e. the state; desiring women is a product of Nature. In *Pod manastirskata loza* the villagers express their mythoclastic approach to saints and organised religion. In this Elin Pelin manifests his anti-fanaticism and his disapproval of dogmatic conceptions of good and evil.

•*Short Stories* (Sofia, 1965).
M. Kuseff, 'Elin Pelin (Dimiter Ivanov)', *SEER*, 34 (1956), pp. 355–77; V. Pinto, 'Elin Pelin (1878–1949): Humanist of Shopsko', *SEER*, 41 (1962), pp. 158–82. SIK

ELYE BOKHER/ Elye ben Asher ha-Levi Ashkenazi (known in Christian sources as Elias/ Elijah Levita, 1468–1549), Yiddish poet and Hebrew grammarian, though born in Neustadt near Nuremberg, spent most of his life in Italy, 1514–27 in the house of Cardinal Egidio of Viterbo to whom he taught Hebrew. Elye Bokher's popular translation of the Psalms was the first Yiddish version to be printed. Two slight Yiddish lampoons of his have also survived, but he is chiefly remembered as the author of the *Bove-bukh* or *Bove dantone*, as it was entitled in the earliest extant edition (Isny, Württemberg, 1541). It is an abridgement and skilful adaptation of an Italian version of an Anglo-Norman *chanson de geste* on the adventures and star-crossed love of Sir Bevis of Hampton. The moulding of the Italian *ottava rima* stanza to the Yiddish language is evidence of exceptional literary talent. Over the centuries the *Bove-bukh* has gone through almost forty editions. His *Shmoys dvorim* (Names of things, Venice, 1542) is the earliest example of a Hebrew-Yiddish dictionary. He would be accounted the most accomplished Yiddish writer of his day, were the elegant *Pariz un viene* (Paris and Vienna, Verona, 1594), long thought to be his, not now be attributed to another, unidentified hand.
•Liptzin (1972), pp. 5–8; Jacob Shatzky, *WWT*, 2, pp. 689–96; W.

Weinberg, *Jewish Book Annual*, 27 (New York, 1969–70), pp. 106–10; I. Zinberg, *History of Jewish Literature*, vol. 7, pp. 66–86. HD

ELYTIS, Odysseus (i.e. Odysseas Alepoudelis, b. 1911), Greek poet, was educated in Athens 1917–28, and studied law at the university there 1930–5, without taking his degree. As early as 1929 he came in contact with Surrealism via a collection of the poems by Paul Eluard. 1935, hearing EMBEIRIKOS lecture on Surrealism, he was inspired to experiment with automatic writing and to make fantastical collages, two of which he exhibited, in the same year, at the first International Surrealist Exhibition in Athens, whilst a group of the poems, under the title 'First poems', appeared in the influential Modernist periodical *Ta Nea Grammata* (New writing). 1936–9 he issued further groups of poems in another avantgarde periodical, *Makedonikes Imeres* (Macedonian days), and published an article on Eluard together with a selection of translations in *Ta Nea Grammata* (1938). Elytis's Surrealism seems to have focused on two major elements: the attempt to attain an ideal alternative perception of reality via the experience of the world of the senses, and the view that poetry is a revelatory medium rather than simply a literary form. His first collection, Προσανατολισμοί (Orientations, 1939), is an expression of identification with the beauty and exuberance of the Greek landscape, a statement of vitality and joy both personal and cosmic. The second collection, Ηλιος ο πρώτος (The sovereign sun, 1943), intensifies the surreal exploration of the world around him, extending it into a psychological and spiritual affirmation of joy. 1940 Elytis was called up and served on the Albanian Front. His experiences inspired the long poem Ασμα ηρωικό και πένθιμο για τον χαμένο ανθυπολοχαγό της Αλβανίας (Heroic song of grief for the lieutenant dead in Albania, 1945). The 'Heroic song' contains fourteen poems or subsections, each reflecting a moment in the life and death of the protagonist. There is no narrative as such, but there is an underlying structure – a forbidding Greek-Albanian landscape which hints at death, the fact of the death of the protagonist, the consequences of that death, the effect on his mother, the diminishing effect of that death on the world, the punishment of those responsible for it, and the transfiguration and resurrection of the fallen hero. The whole is told in the startling metaphoric language of the early poems, where the juxtaposition in a single phrase of elements with no rational connection lends a dream-like quality to the text. After 'Heroic song' Elytis published no collection of poems for over twelve years. 1948–52 he settled in Paris, studying literature at the Sorbonne, broadening his experience as an art critic, and associating with the major Surrealist writers (Breton, Char, Eluard) and painters. In the same period he travelled to England, Switzerland, Italy and Spain. 1953 he returned to Greece and for a year resumed the senior post in the National Broadcasting Institute which he had held 1945–6. 1955–6 he was on the Board of Karolos Koun's (b. 1908) Art Thatre, and 1956–8 he was president of the governors of the Greek Ballet. Then in 1959 he published his major work, Το Αξιον εστί (The Axion Esti – the title refers to part of the Orthodox liturgy). This difficult work has a severe structure:

its three parts, Genesis, Passion and Gloria, are themselves built around elements of the form and language of the liturgy. Into this religious context the poet works a blend of personal and national experience, synthesising past and present, subjective and objective, physical and metaphysical. The collections which follow Το Αξιον εστί are less innovatory, though their blending of text and original illustrations is often striking. The most important is Μαρία Νεφέλη (Maria Cloud, 1978). In the same period Elytis continued his work as painter and art critic, and produced a significant collection of critical essays, Ανοιχτά χαρτιά (Open book, 1974). He was awarded the Nobel Prize for Literature in 1976.

•*The Sovereign Sun: Selected Poems*(Philadelphia, 1974); *The Axion Esti* (bilingual edition) (Pittsburgh, 1974).

I. Ivask (Ed.), *Odysseus Elytis: Analogies of Light* (Norman, Oklahoma, 1981).   CFR

EMBEIRIKOS, Andreas (1901–75), Greek poet and novelist, born in Braila, Roumania, into a family of international shipping magnates, was brought up in Athens, worked in his father's London office 1921–5, then went to France to study psychoanalysis (1925–31). There he became a member of the Surrealist group headed by Breton. 1932 he returned to Greece to set up a group of psychoanalysts. His first collection of Surrealist poetry, Υψικάμινος (Blast furnace, 1935), contains a series of 'prose' pieces of a type characteristic of automatic writing, apart from the disconcerting fact that their language is heavily laced with *katharevousa*. His second collection, Σνδοχώρα (Interior, 1945), while quintessentially Surrealist in its belief in the erotic as the saving force of the world and in its uninhibited exploration of the erotic, shows a degree of conscious poetic control in its expression. 1960 he produced a volume of prose pieces under the title Γραπτά η προσωπική μυθολογία (Written texts or personal mythology), with a revealing preface entitled 'Amour-amour'. A 'novel', Αργώ η πλους αεροστάτσυ (Argo or a journey by balloon), though written much earlier, came out in 1965: it had previously been thought too daring to print.

●K. Friar (Ed.), *Modern Greek Poetry* (Athens, 1982), pp. 128–35. *Amour Amour, Writing or Personal Mythology* (London, 1966).   CFR

EMINESCU, Mihai (1850–89), Roumanian poet and prose writer who continues to shape the cultural awareness of his people, the seventh of eleven children born to a petty boyar and his peasant wife in N Moldavia, attended spasmodically German-language elementary and secondary schools across the border in the Austro-Hungarian town of Czernowitz where he was profoundly influenced by his Roumanian nationalist schoolteacher Aron Pumnul (1818–66). The latter's death in 1866 led Eminescu to abandon his studies and for a time he was prompter to a travelling troupe of actors until his father sent him to Vienna to continue his education. 1869–72 he attended the philosophy classes of Richard Zimmermann at the university and read extensively, filling scores of notebooks with information on every conceivable subject. 1872 he was awarded a bursary by a Roumanian literary society to study in Berlin where he also followed courses in philosophy and his-tory. 1874 he returned to Moldavia and worked as a librarian at Iaşi University. Three years later he became a journalist and editor for a conservative newspaper in Bucharest where he displayed an excessively xenophobic nationalism. Six years of intense work brought on a mental breakdown and up to his death he suffered periods of madness. Only one volume of his verse, *Poesii* (Poems, 1883), was published during his lifetime but his allegorical, pessimistic and patriotic verse, exquisitely crafted in a literary language which he himself created, made him popular with the reading public. The influence of Schopenhauer can be detected in several of his poems, but his greatness lies in his ability to weave his motifs of national history, of folk myth and of erotic disenchantment into a grand design, and to express the commonplace in a language of crystalline simplicity and striking musicality. His legacy is the most influential of any Roumanian writer and is symptomatic of a culture still struggling to reconcile the impact of Western-inspired modernity with a veneration of indigenous tradition based largely on folk myth. His verse made him easy prey for those who sought credibility for their attempts to diminish the influence of the West at various periods during the 20th century and his obsession with a pristine paradise and anxiety in the face of reality strike a sympathetic chord in those facing the uncertainty of radical change.

●*The Last Romantic: Mihail Eminescu* (Iowa City, 1972); *In Celebration of Mihai Eminescu* (London, 1989); *Poems* (Bucharest, 1990).   DJD

ENGONOPOULOS, Nikos (b. 1910), Greek poet and critic, studied painting and Byzantine art history at the School of Fine Art in Athens, and pursued the artistic career which has remained central to his life, becoming a lecturer in drawing at the Polytechnic. In the late 1930s he was the enfant terrible of Greek Surrealism, promoting the importance of revolution and the flouting of conventional values as essential to the renewal of the arts. His first two collections of poetry, Μην ομιλείτε εις τον οδηγόν (Don't speak to the driver, 1938) and Τα κλειδοκύμβαλα της σιωπής (The pianos of silence, 1939), show, none the less, how rooted his work is in aspects of Greek landscape and tradition. His language moves in and out of *katharevousa* for more provoking effect than that of EMBEIRIKOS. 1944 he published Μπολιβάρ (Bolivar), a long poem taking as its central figure the eponymous S American revolutionary, signifying symbolically the quest for national freedom. Around the central figure are worked Greek settings and heroes from the War of Independence to the Albanian campaign. The poem uses the 'non-logicality' and linguistic 'freedom' of Surrealism to great effect within its more ordered context. His postwar collections, returning to a more conventionally Surrealist style while retaining his characteristic use of sharp pictorial detail and swift changes of tone, include Η επιστροφή των πουλιών (Return of the birds, 1946) and Ανθήρω Ελληνι λόγω (In the florid Greek style, 1957). In the 1960s and 1970s he also published literary and art criticism.

●K. Friar (Ed.), *Modern Greek Poetry* (Athens, 1982), pp. 239–47.   CFR

EÖTVÖS, Baron József (1813–71), Hungarian publicist, novelist, short-story writer, poet and playwright, was the son of a conservative aristocrat and a German baroness. He was an outstanding student and could enter the University of Pest as early as 1826. 1832 he attended the parliamentary session in Pressburg, where he became acquainted with KÖLCSEY. Having visited Switzerland, England, France and Germany 1836–7, he formed a group of liberals later nicknamed the 'Centralists'. Although he accepted the post of Minister of Religion and Public Education in the revolutionary government of April 1848, his disagreement with Kossuth's idea that the counties and the lesser nobility could serve as a basis for social modernisation and that Hungary should be independent of Austria made him resign and leave the country in September. He returned in 1851, but did not participate in political life until 1867, when he again became Minister of Religion and Public Education. The new acts of parliament based on his suggestion granted full emancipation to the Jews, proclaimed the equality of all nationalities living in Hungary, and introduced a liberal education system. His fame rests chiefly on his novels and discursive prose. *A karthausi* (The Carthusian, 1842) is a Romantic novel written in the form of a confession. His essay *Szegénység Irlandban* (Poverty in Ireland, 1830) and his book *Die Emancipation der Juden* (The emancipation of the Jews, 1840) testify to the universality of his liberalism. His later fiction is somewhat didactic. *A falu jegyzője* (The village notary, 1845) is a satire on the corruption among local authorities in Hungary, whereas *Magyarország 1514-ben* (Hungary in 1514, 1847) is an historical novel about a peasant uprising. His most lasting achievement is *Der Einfluss der herrschenden Ideen des 19. Jahrhunderts auf den*

Staat (The influence of the dominant ideas of the 19th century on the State, 1851–4), a sophisticated analysis of the ways in which the ideals of equality, liberty and nationality mutually contradict each other.

●*The Village Notary* (London, 1850).
S. B. Vardy, *Baron J. Eötvös* (Bloomington, Indiana, 1969); P. Bödy, *Joseph Eötvös and the Modernization of Hungary* (Philadelphia, 1972). MSz-M

ERBEN, Karel Jaromír (1811–70), Czech writer and scholar, was taught by KLICPERA at school, where he started writing verse; he read philosophy and law at Prague, and then became a court official and part-time piano teacher. Subsequently he became actuary to the Royal Bohemian Learned Society and secretary of the Bohemian Museum; now he could begin his collecting of folk-songs and folk-tales in earnest. He tried, but did not entirely succeed, to avoid politics in 1848–9. 1850 he was archivist of the Bohemian Museum, 1851 became archivist of the City of Prague. He edited and published important medieval and Renaissance Czech texts, brought out an immensely popular collection of 100 Slav folk-tales (1865) and did a monumental edition of Bohemian children's rhymes, folk-songs and marriage rituals (1862–4), which were carefully bowdlerised in keeping with his patriotic view of Czechness. From a literary point of view he is most important for his cycle of narrative poems, *Kytice z pověstí národních* (Garland of national legends, 1853, exp. ed. 1861). One poem here, 'Záhořovo lože' (Záhoř's bed), Baroque in tone, is a true R. Catholic's response to MÁCHA's nihilism. Otherwise the poems are expressions of personal pessimism, based on folk and fairy tales. The most usual subject matter is young women punished for disobedience, to mothers or the laws of God. Men usually represent law and order, women disorder. Erben uses European folk motifs to express his own fatalism. One poem, 'Vodník' (The waterman), is often interpreted politically: even if one ceases one's dealings with political evil and returns to a life of goodness, one will always be punished for one's past weakness.

●*Panslavonic folk-lore, in four books. Translated from Karel Jaromír Erben's 'A hundred genuine popular Slavonic fairy stories . . .'* (New York, 1930).
M. Součková, *The Czech Romantics* (The Hague, 1958); N. G. Nagarajan, *Karel Jaromír Erben's Book of Ballads Kytice (The Garland). A Thematic Study* (Berkeley, 1973). RBP

ERISTAVI, Giorgi (1813–64), Georgian playwright, was the first writer to provide original drama for the new Georgian theatre. He had a brief education in Moscow, befriended the Russian dramatist Griboedov and translated parts of his *Gore ot uma* (Woe from wit). Involved with the Orbelianis and Bagratids in the 1832 anti-Russian conspiracy, betrayed by Iase Palavandishvili, Eristavi spent a year in prison and four years in exile in Poland. There MICKIEWICZ's Romanticism gave his poetry a nationalist pathos. On return to Georgia he married and became assistant to the Russian viceroy. In the 1850s he took charge of the Georgian theatre in Tbilisi, founded and edited the 24 issues of *Tsisk'ari* (Dawn). He left a bewildered account of a journey to London in 1862 to inspect machinery. Eristavi's first published verse, *Osuri motkhroba, anu Zare da Q'animat* (An Ossetian tale, or Zare and Q'animat, 1832) on the 'Romeo and Juliet' structure, has a dynamism missing from even his comedies and certainly his later lyrics. He sets his ill-starred lovers against the background of the desperate fight of the Georgian and Ossetian mountain tribes against Shah Abbas; the relevance to the conspiracy he was engaged in is obvious. His early lyrics echo the gentle Romanticism of Grigol ORBELIANI, but unlike other aristocrats who capitulated to Russian rule, Eristavi expressed his indignation in a series of short comedies. While the plotting is perfunctory, the characterisation is sharp and the dialogue witty: this is the first record of the Georgian spoken in the streets of Tbilisi. The best plays are *Dava, anu t'ochk'a da zap'etaia* (The lawsuit, or semicolon, 1840) and *Gaq'ra* (The family settlement, 1849): they show a degenerate nobility, abandoning, like the Russian gentry after their failed revolt of 1825, all ideals, exploiting their serfs, feeling nothing but envy and anger. Eristavi balances them with a younger generation with a European education, but in his bitter comedies they too are corrupt or idle. The third force of his plays is the Armenian moneylenders and Russian civil servants who exploit the feuding landowners (*Dava*) or the quarrelling brothers (*Gaq'ra*). These comedies had popular success and the viceroy's encouragement. (*Gaq'ra* anticipates a Russian play of the same title [*Razdel*] and theme by Pisemsky.) Eristavi's reputation rests on his comedies; they have something of the denunciatory power of the Russian Realists, even though they make the crude moral impact of eighteenth-century comedy. Younger Georgians rejected Eristavi for his very strengths: Giorgi TS'ERETELI, for instance, in an article, *Vnakhe da mets'q'ina* (I saw and disliked, 1873), wrote ' "The Lawsuit" as a comedy isn't worth mentioning as literature. It is just scenes collected from the street, linked together God knows how. . . . G. Eristavi has . . . spent his life within four walls and when he hears the sound of talking in the street, looks out of the window.' Not until Davit K'LDIASHVILI appeared did the Georgian theatre find a second playwright so original.   DR

ERISTAVI, Rapiel (1824–1901), Georgian poet and journalist, belonged to one of the oldest families, the Aragvi Dukes (*eristavebi*): he was linked by marriage and education to the Georgian intellectual aristocracy, the *tergdaleulebi* (those that drank from the River Terek', i.e. crossed to Russia for education) – I. CH'AVCH'AVADZE, Aleksandre Q'AZBEGI. His outlook was affected by the mountain landscapes of Kist'auri in Kakhetia, the village where he was born and died. 1847–70, a high flyer in the reformist viceroy's civil service, he helped set up the Georgian Museum, contributed articles in Russian to the journal *Kavkaz* (The Caucasus) and published a story in Russian, *Oborvanets* (A man in rags, 1855): they attracted the Russian public by their fluent Russian and by the anthropological and historical material Eristavi retrieved from his travels all over Georgia. Despite his official status – he resigned in 1870 – Eristavi in articles on serfdom in Mingrelia *inter alia* 'was the first among us to bear witness for the unjustly oppressed' (I. CH'AVCH'AVADZE). Like his sister Barbare Jorjadze (1811–95), Rapiel Eristavi tried vaudeville, e.g. his play *Dedak'atsma tu gaits'ia, tskhra ugheli kharis umdzlavresia* (If a woman moves, she is stronger than nine yoke of oxen, 1870). Unrequited love inspired lyrics, e.g. *Ristvis miq'varkhar?* (Why do I love you?, 1858), until he married a Gurian princess in 1863. Advocacy, journalism, scholarship, the Georgian theatre, lexicography absorbed his energies: 1895 his jubilee was fêted by poets, among them the young JUGHASHVILI (Stalin): 'When the laments of the toiling peasants / Moved you to tears of pity . . . / Then, O Bard, a Georgian / Would listen to you as to a heavenly testament.' His ethnographic work is valuable, but his best is a handful of lyrics. The death from typhus in 1878 of his sister Ana, while nursing Russian casualties in Turkey, only strengthened his stoic positivism. His most affirmative lyric, *Samshoblo Khevsurisa* (The Khevsur's homeland, 1881), which influenced VAZHA PSHAVELA, has the refrain, 'I would not change the bare rocks for the tree of immortality. I would not change my homeland for another land's paradise.' Eristavi vainly strove to reconcile Georgians' virtues and vices – e.g. his poem *Ghvino* (Wine, 1868): 'Wine, the source of evil, Wine the medicine for impotence . . . The remitter of our sins, The cross of life, of both worlds.' Nevertheless his writings are felt to have finally established a national identity.   DR

ERISTAV-KHOSHT'ARIA, Anast'asia (1868–1951), Georgian

novelist, began as a teacher. In the 1890s Ak'ak'i TS'ERETELI encouraged her to write: her first novel, the 400-page *Molip'ul gzaze* (On the slippery path, 1897), followed by the compact *Bedis t'riali* (The wheel of Fate, 1901), had success. Her novels and stories follow a pattern: they trace the career of a Georgian noblewoman, thrown into turmoil by the collapse of the old economic and moral orders in the mid-19th century, defending her ideals of free work and truthful love against a corrupt background and clay-footed heroes. *Molip'ul gzaze* focuses on Ketino, an artist, who escapes marriage to Okro, finds her vocation abroad but returns mortally ill to her true love P'alik'o. In *Bedis t'riali* the idealistic Sidonia endures disillusion as her husband Geno bullies peasants and seduces servants. Here too death intervenes: maddened peasants lynch Geno. Eristav-Khosht'aria's novels end with the bereaved rejecting suicide in order to raise their child for a better world. There are few references to any identifiable place or time; characters are referred to largely by their pet-names; clichés recur: 'he went white as mistletoe', 'his joy knew no bounds'. Nevertheless, she had narrative drive, noble aims and could suspend disbelief. After the Soviet invasion, she became a 'living classic' and wrote little, except ideologically corrective introductions to reprints of her work. She remains the one woman novelist of note in Georgian, which says more about the female condition in Georgia than all her volumes.   DR

ESTERHÁZY, Péter (b. 1950),

Hungarian novelist, short-story writer, and essayist, was born into the most famous aristocratic family of his country. He spent most of his childhood in a small village because his family had been deported to the countryside by the Communist authorities in 1951. After the October 1956 Uprising, the Soviet-type dictatorship became somewhat more tolerant, allowing the family to move to Budapest, where Esterházy went to school. At Budapest University he read mathematics. 1974 he got a job

as a computer scientist. Four years later he became a freelance writer. He is regarded by some critics as the most significant Hungarian prose writer of his generation. He has succeeded in changing reading habits by rejecting many of the conventions of narrative prose. On the basis of the combination of the structural devices of the Avant-garde with the techniques of earlier periods, the mixing of visual effects and texts, his works have been associated with Postmodern writing by some critics. The general reader did not recognise him as a major writer until the publication of his third book, *Termelési-regény* (Production novel, 1979). His most significant achievement to date is, however, *Bevezetés a szépirodalomba* (Introduction to literature, 1986), whose various sections set out to explore different possibilities of prose writing. For example, 'Fuharosok' (The transporters), a short text full of quotations from Pascal, is the story of a rape that can be read as an allegory of the Soviet occupation of Hungary, whereas 'A szív segédigéi' (Helping words of the heart) is a sublime, even religious testimony to the memory of the author's mother.
●*The Transporters* (Budapest, 1985); *Helping Verbs of the Heart* (New York, 1991).
M. Calinescu and D. Fokkema (Eds), *Exploring Postmodernism* (Amsterdam, 1987).   MSz-M

ETINGER, Shloyme/ Solomon Etinger (1803–56), Yiddish author, born in Warsaw, absorbed the spirit of the Jewish Enlightenment movement while studying medicine in Lemberg (Lwów), but none the less took a remarkably positive attitude towards Yiddish. Influenced by Menakhem-Mendl Lefin (1749–1826), the first writer to employ modern E

Yiddish, Etinger pioneered the use of the contemporary colloquial language for poetry and drama. During the 1820s he wrote *Serkele* (Johannisburg, E Prussia, 1861), an extraordinary five-act *comédie larmoyante* or *bürgerliches Trauerspiel* in the style of Lessing, in which enlightened attitudes are rewarded and snobbery and greed discomfited. *Serkele* became the first modern Yiddish play to be actually performed when in 1862 it was put on at the Zhitomir rabbinical seminary by GOLDFADN, on whose career it exerted a decisive influence.
●J. Leftwich (Ed.), *The Golden Peacock, A Worldwide Treasury of Yiddish Poetry* (New York, 1961), pp. 693ff.
Miron, pp. 101–3, 257–8; Wiener, pp. 101–3, 136–40.   HD

EVTIMII OF **TĂRNOVO** (c. 1325/30–c. 1401/12), Bulgarian author, was born into a rich family and educated most probably in the Tărnovo monasteries. He took orders as a monk at the newly founded Kilifarevo Monastery (c. 1350), where he became acquainted with the mystical Hesychast teaching to which he remained true for the rest of his life. 1369 he went with his teacher Teodosii of Tărnovo (c. 1300–63) to Constantinople, then spent several years on Mount Athos, the centre of Orthodox culture and of Hesychast teachings. On his return to Bulgaria (1371), he settled in the Holy Trinity Monastery near Tărnovo, where he later established the 'Tărnovo literary school'. Evtimii became the patriarch of Bulgaria (1375) and one of the leaders of the Bulgarian independence movement. When the Turks took Tărnovo (1393), he was exiled to the Bachkovo Monastery where he died. Apart from his translations of liturgical texts, his original oeuvre comprises numerous *vitae* of Bulgarian saints, liturgical texts, panegyrics and theological treatises. His Lives of such as St John of Rila or Petka Tărnovska created norms which profoundly influenced Old Russian and Old Bulgarian culture. His new 'high style', based on his Hesychast beliefs, included lyrical introductions describing heavenly joy and the spiritual blessing obtained through meditation on a saint's life, established a new aesthetics founded on descriptions of contemplative living, asceticism and mystical revelations in visions; in the depiction of temptations a new demonology was invented. Linguistically, Evtimii archaised vocabulary, which demonstrates the Hesychast influence, since Hesychasts believed that the divine nature is reflected in the Word; thus the Word is a manifestation of absolute Nature and the eternal. The world, presented in an exclusive idealisation, could be described only in archaic, complex words, or neologisms. Evtimii's orthographical reform, which attempted to regularise the norms of the literary language on the basis of the archaic Cyrillo-Methodian norms, exemplifies the same beliefs. The 'Tărnovo literary school' of Evtimii started revising the translations of liturgical texts by comparing them with the Greek originals and changing the orthography; the revision of meaning brought these texts closer to Orthodox dogma.

●E. Kaluzniacki (Ed.), *Werke des Patriarchen von Bulgarien Euthimios* (Vienna, 1901); English trans. (London, 1971).   SIK

EZNIK KOGHBATSI (c. 390–455) is one of the most brilliant Armenian minds, as well as one of the most rigorous thinkers, of the 5th century. He occupies a central position in the defence of the accepted tenets of Christianity at a critical period. Eznik was born in the village of Koghb in the province of Ayrarat. He was among the students sent by SS Sahak and Mashtots to Edessa (427) and Constantinople (430) to bring back translations of patristic literature. After the Council of Ephesus, Eznik and his friends returned to Armenia (434), bringing with them new texts, particularly critical texts of the Holy Scriptures, on the bases of which the revised translation of the BIBLE was done (434–8). Eznik was appointed Bishop of Bagrevand (450–5), and his name is listed among the bishops who participated in the Council of Artashat in 449. Eznik's masterpiece, the only work we have from his pen, is *Eghds Aghandots* (Refutation of sects). There is no precise information about the date of its composition, although it is generally placed 441–9 or 443–8, at the climax of the Armenian crisis precipitated by Hazkert's edict demanding the Armenians renounce Christianity and adopt Zoroastrianism. The 'Refutation of sects' consists of four books: 'Against pagan sects', 'Against the Persian K'esh' (Zoroastrianism), 'Against the religion of the Greek philosophers' and 'Against Marcion's heresy'. The common denominator among these systems of 'sects' is their dualistic approach to the problem of good and evil, the antithesis of the monotheistic trinitarianism of Christianity. Marcion's heresy, with its docetic approach to the nature of Christ, unique to his heresy, is singled out for attack from among all the Christian sects. The work has survived in a single MS, copied in 1280. It was first printed in Smyrna in 1762.

•*Eznekay vardapeti Koghbatswoy Eghds Aghandots* (Tiflis, 1914); Eznik Koghbatsi, *Eghds Aghandots*, trans., introduction and annotations by A. A. Abrahamyan (Yerevan, 1970); *Eznik de Kolb De Deo*, traduction, notes et tables par Louis Maries et Ch. Mercier (Paris, 1959) [*Patrologia Orientalis*; vol. XXVIII; fasc. 3–4]. VN

F

FÁBRY, Rudolf (b. 1915), Slovak poet, short-story writer and graphic artist, introduced Surrealism into Slovak poetry, emulating NEZVAL, Apollinaire, Breton and Rimbaud in mental automatism, the evocation of the unconscious and the collision of disparate signs. His early collections, such as *Uťaté ruky* (Severed arms, 1935) and *Vodné hodiny piesočné* (Water-clock hourglass, 1938), illustrated with his collages in the manner of Max Ernst, show great originality in the use of imagery, e.g. 'the sun, the blood-soaked fly, buzzes'. He was less successful in accommodating his method to reflections on society and the meaning of life in *Na štít ruže kraváca* (The rose bleeds onto the shield, 1977) and in his mediocre ironical dystopian stories, *Takým zvony nezvonia* (The bell does not toll for these, 1978). KB

FALIEROS, Marinos (i.e. Marin Falier, c. 1395–c. 1474), Greek poet, probably the second son of Marco Falier di Michiel, a Veneto-Cretan aristocrat, was born in Crete. Little is known of his life and activities. He was a prominent landowner, his estates being devoted to viticulture. As a member of the 'concilium pheudatorum' he will also have served as a member of the Senate. 1436 he was appointed as a 'provisor', i.e. a member of a board of experts in Cretan affairs. Towards the end of his life, after the siege and capture of Negroponte, Falier was one of the members of a committee set up to fix special taxes to raise money for the fortification of Crete. He wrote two moralising poems (akin to those of SAHLIKIS) 1420–30. His other works, which are not easily datable, are a short dramatised version of the Crucifixion and two erotic poems, which involve a combination of dreams (with a strong sensual element) and allegory.

●G. Zoras (Ed.), Ὁ ποιητής Μαρίνος Φαλιέρος' Χρητικά Χρονικά 2 (1948) contains an edition of three poems. CFR

FALUDI, Ferenc (1704–79), Hungarian poet and translator, entered the Jesuit Order at the age of 16. After studying and teaching in Austria he was appointed Hungarian confessor in Rome, where he developed an interest in French and Italian literature and began to translate and write verse. He returned to Hungary and eventually became director of the Jesuit library in Pressburg, a post he held for sixteen years till the Jesuits were disbanded in 1773. He then found refuge with the Batthyány family in Rechnitz. During Faludi's lifetime only his translations of moralising works by fellow-Jesuits and his textbooks were published. In his forewords to these he declares himself to be a stylist, and this is borne out by the polished elegance of his prose. In his retirement he translated a book with no other purpose than to amuse: *Téli éjszakák* (Winter nights) is a collection of tales, mainly from Antonio de Eslava's *Noches de Invierno* (1609), adapted and translated from a German version. These stories, with their crisp dialogue and choice vocabulary, may be regarded as the forerunners of the modern Hungarian short story. Faludi's lyric poetry, published in 1787 with *Téli éjszakák* by Révai, who had a high opinion of his literary merits, successfully blends Rococo elements with rustic simplicity. He experiments with foreign forms, e.g. the sonnet 'A pipáról' (On the pipe), and uses strict rhyme rather than assonance. Although he had no explicit programme for literature like KAZINCZY, he pointed the way from the old, inward-looking traditions of Hungarian verse to the new, urbane tone demanded by the enlightened intelligentsia.

•Selected poems in J. Bowring, *Poetry of the Magyars* (London, 1830) and W. Kirkconnell (Ed.), *Hungarian Helicon* (Calgary, 1985).   GFC

FIGULI, Margita (b. 1909), Slovak novelist, born in a mountain village, studied at commercial academy and worked in a bank. Together with CHROBÁK and ŠVANTNER, she represents the Lyrical Prose school. Her novel *Tri gaštanové kone* (Three chestnut horses, 1940) was innovatory in its narrative mode, exploiting the potential of the lyrical to evoke Nature and its portraits of characters and their relationships. A proud girl wooed by two men, a gentle commercial traveller Peter, and a rich farmer, promises Peter she will marry him if he returns with three chestnut horses, but while he is trying to get rich, she breaks her pledge and marries the farmer; eventually Peter and the girl are brought together when her husband is killed by one of his horses. In her *Babylon* (1946), a detailed description of the rise and fall of the Chaldean empire, Figuli shows a preoccupation with ethical issues; she finds these issues in the OT and puts her own interpretation on them. Less accomplished are her *Zuzana* (1949), a sketch of two lovers against the social background of a city between the wars, and *Vichor v nás* (Storm within us, 1974), set in a Slovak village. Here she traces the fate of the traumatised victims of violence during WWII, whose psychological wounds are healed by work and love.

KB

FINŽGAR, Fran Saleški (1871–1962), Slovene novelist and playwright, after grammar school and seminary in Ljubljana, served as priest in various locations. He portrayed in vivid, pithy language the life of the peasantry and the working class. His historical novel, *Pod svobodnim soncem* (Under a free sun, 1912), modelled on the work of SIENKIEWICZ, describing the conflicts between Slovenes, Antes, Huns and Byzantines, was intended to strengthen Slovene national awareness; it gained great popularity. *Strici* (Uncles, 1927) is a stylised eulogistic account of peasant life, combining a love story with the countryman's devotion to the land. His plays include *Divji lovec* (The poacher, 1902), a tragic love story against the background of the events of 1848, *Naša kri* (Our blood, 1912), set in the final days of the French occupation of Slovenia, 1813, and *Razvalina življenja* (A life ruined, 1921), depicting the misfortunes brought about by an unhappy forced marriage and the evils of drink.   HL

FISHTA, Gjergj (1871–1940), Franciscan friar, poet and one of the leading literary figures of the Albania of his time, born in the village of Fishtë, studied theology and philosophy in Bosnia and 1894 was ordained. Fishta founded in Shkodër the first Albanian secondary school to teach all subjects in Albanian. 1899 he cofounded the *Bashkimi* (Union) literary society; he participated in the 1908 Congress of Monastir, which accepted his proposal for an Albanian alphabet; he published the periodical *Hylli i Dritës* (The day-star, 1913–44), was a delegate in 1919 to the Paris Peace Conference and Shkodër MP in the first Albanian parliament, 1921. *Lahuta e Malcís* (The highland lute, 1905–6), a long historical ballad, is Fishta's major literary work, an epic portrayal of 19th-century Albanian encounters with Montenegrins trying to seize Albanian territories after the Congress of Berlin. Fishta also published religious verse and is the author of more than thirty plays, translations and political tracts.   ShM

FLAŠKA z PARDUBIC A RYCH-MBURKU, Smil (1340s–1403), Czech writer, son of a rich nobleman, nephew of the Archbishop of Prague, studied and took a BA at Prague. On his father's death (1389/90), he inherited large estates, but in the end let or sold most of them. He was a leader of a baronial league against Wenceslas IV and fell in battle in the barons' campaign against the royal city of Kuttenberg (Kutná Hora). His chief work is the didactic *Nová rada* (New council, 1394), parts of which were written 1378–84 (one assumes a first complete version called *Rada*), when the author was or intended to be on good terms with Wenceslas. It is a 2,126-line council of animals in which 22 quadrupeds and 22 birds give their counsel to the lion-king. Some counsel is serious (there birds prevail) and some sarcastic. The first counsellor is the Eagle, the last the Swan; their counsels, which emphasise the duties of a Christian, provide the moral framework. The other creatures' counsels may be divided into those that advise on how any ruler should comport himself (these often clearly from *Rada*) and those that reflect Flaška's personal grievances (escheatage, the ignoring of barons' advice) or Wenceslas's weaknesses (indulgence in alcohol and public baths). Flaška's approach varies from the witty to the censorious. The 658-line *Rada otce synovi* (A father's advice to his son, 1380s) is a humourless manual of chivalry which does, however, reveal Flaška as a thoughtful, even wise, man, e.g. in the psychologically observant passage on the need for moderation. It is unlikely that the collection of 238 Czech proverbs attributed to Flaška, *Proverbia Flasskonis, generosi domini et baccalarii Pragensis* (c. 1400), was compiled by him; he certainly uses proverbs and sententiae in *Nová rada*, but entirely conventionally; he shows no delight in them.

●J. Daňhelka (Ed.), Smil F. z P., *Nová rada* (Prague, 1950); H. Kunstmann (Ed.), *Denkmäler der alttschechischen Literatur von ihren Anfängen bis zur Hussitenbewegung* (Berlin, 1955); J. Jungmann (Ed.), *Výbor z literatury české*, I (Prague, 1845), pp. 839–47. J. B. Čapek, 'Die Ironie des Smil Flaška', *Slavische Rundschau* 10 (1936), 6, pp. 68–79.   RBP

FRAKULLA, Nezim (c. 1680–1760), Albanian Muslim poet,

also known as Nazim Berati and Ibrahim Nezimi, was born in the village of Frakulla near Fier and lived for many years in Berat, a flourishing centre of Islamic culture in the 18th century. He studied in Constantinople where he wrote his early verse in Turkish and Persian. c. 1731 he returned to Berat where, inspired by Oriental literature, he started to compose verse in Albanian. After some years he went again to Constantinople, from where, for unknown reasons, he was sent into exile in Bessarabia and, after his release from prison, returned to Albania, living for a time in Elbasan and afterwards in Berat. But he was again exiled, this time to Constantinople, where he died in prison. Frakulla's first *Divan* in Albanian (written 1731–47) contains the first secular poetry in the Albanian language. Apart from traditional religious themes, it includes Nature poetry and interesting details on city life in 18th-century Albania. He also wrote love lyrics.

●E. Rossi, 'Notizie su un manoscritto del canzoniere Nezim (sec XVII–XVIII) in caratteri arabi', *Rivista degli studi orientali*, 21 (1945–6), pp. 219–46. ShM

FRANKO, Ivan (1856–1916), Ukrainian writer, scholar and journalist, born in W Ukraine, the son of a village blacksmith, was educated at L'viv (Lemberg), Chernivtsi (Czernowitz) and Vienna universities. He received his doctorate from Vienna, but failed to obtain a position at the University of Lemberg. Active in radical student circles, he was frequently arrested. At first a populist, he later co-founded with Mykhailo Drahomanov (1841–95) the Ukrainian Radical Party. A lifelong socialist, Franko firmly believed in national independence for Ukraine. He was a prolific writer; his collected works (with some omissions) run to 50 vols. He was a Realist as a prose writer, often under the influence of Zola, and wrote the novels *Zakhar Berkut* (1883), *Perekhresni stezhky* (Crossed paths, 1900) and *Velyky shum* (The great noise, 1907) in this mode. He was a refined lyric poet: *Z vershyn i nyzyn* (From the heights and the depths, 1887), *Ziviale lystia* (Withered leaves, 1896). Though he publicly attacked Ukrainian Modernists, his poems show some Modernist traits. Many of his works deal with the social conditions of the working class. His greatest poetic achievement is his long poem *Moisei* (Moses, 1905), discussing the problems of leadership and service to the people. Franko was a leading member of the Shevchenko Scholarly Society and made important contributions to Ukrainian scholarship, especially in his edition of old apocrypha and legends from Old Ukrainian manuscripts. A brilliant literary critic, he was also a distinguished journalist, writing in Ukrainian, Polish and German. Despite poor health after 1905, he continued his efforts to build bridges between Ukrainian and Western literature.

●*Moses and Other Poems* (New York, 1973); *Zakhar Berkut* (New York, 1944); *Selected Poems* (New York, 1948).

E. Fedorenko (Ed.), *Ivan Franko: The Artist and the Thinker* (New York, 1981).   GSNL

FRASHËRI, Naim (1846–1900), Albanian poet and prose-writer, the 'national poet' of Albania, was born in the village of Frashër, in S Albania. In his native village he was taught Turkish, Persian and Arabic as well as Islamic (Bektashi) theology. He was educated in Classics and modern

European civilisation, and was influenced by the French Enlightenment; he was particularly interested in classical Persian authors; he was equally at home in Oriental and Occidental culture. After finishing secondary school and spending some time in Constantinople, he worked as a civil servant in Berat and 1874–7 as a customs officer in Sarandë. He also spent some time at the Austrian spa of Baden. 1881–2 he returned to Constantinople and began organising the national movement with his brothers Abdyl (1839–92) and Sami FRASHËRI. Naim is the author of 22 works: fifteen in Albanian, four in Turkish, two in Greek and one in Persian. His prose writing in Albanian was of decisive influence in the creation of a literary language. Among his major Albanian works are *Istori e përgjithshme* (General history, 1886) and *Dituritë për mësonjëtoret e para* (Knowledge for elementary schools, 1888), both of which were used as textbooks in the first Albanian schools. Then followed *Bagëti e bujqësi* (Herds and crops, 1886), a collection of bucolic verse and georgics, depicting the beauties of the Albanian countryside; *Lulet e verës* (The flowers of spring, 1890), a selection of lyric poetry. *Istoria e Skënderbeut* (History of Scanderbeg, 1898) is an epic based on BARLETI's history of the Albanian national hero and one of the most widely read books of Albanian literature. Naim has also written several fables and has translated a good number of foreign works, including the first book of the Iliad, *Iliadë e Omirit* (The Iliad of Homer, 1896). Together with his brother S. FRASHËRI, he published the influential periodical *Drita* (The light, 1884) and also helped found the first Albanian school, in Korçë in 1884.   ShM

FRASHËRI, Sami (1850–1904), Albanian man of letters, publicist and ideologist of the Albanian national movement, known in Turkish as Samseddin Sami, younger brother of Abdyl and Naim FRASHËRI, born in the village of Frashër, S Albania, studied, with his brother Naim, at the Zosimea secondary school in Yoannina, N Greece. He received education in Turkish, Persian and Arabic from private tutors. He spent most of his life in Constantinople, where he made a name for himself as an Albanian and Turkish writer. Frashëri is the author of about fifty major works and articles. Among his early works in Albanian are his school textbooks and his grammar, the first Albanian school grammar. His major work in Albanian is his political manifesto *Shipëria – Ç'ka genë, ç'është dhe ç'do të bëhetë* (Albania – what she was, what she is and what will become of her, 1899), subtitled 'Thoughts about the salvation of the motherland from the dangers it faces', in which he presents his views on Albania's past and his visions of her future. This work, together with N. FRASHËRI's history of Scanderbeg, was one of the most widely read and translated Albanian books. S. Frashëri's publications in Turkish are no less significant than his Albanian, for example his Turkish-French and French-Turkish dictionaries, the *Kamus-u Türki* (Turkish dictionary, 1901), which was used by the Turkish Philological Society in 1932 as a guideline for the creation of the modern Turkish literary language; and his monumental six-volume Turkish encyclopaedia of history and geography, *Kamus al-a'lam* (Universal dictionary, 1889–99).   ShM

FREDRO, Aleksander (1793–1876),

Polish comic dramatist, was born near Lemberg into a rich gentry family. He joined the army of the Duchy of Warsaw and participated in the Napoleonic campaign of 1812–14. The experience is described with humour in his memoirs, *Trzy po trzy* (Gibberish, 1877). After the war he settled in Lemberg, taking part in Galician politics and cultural life. Silenced by hostile critics in 1835, he resumed writing c. 1853, but his later comedies were neither published nor staged in his lifetime. Regarded as the greatest writer of comedy in Polish literature, Fredro demonstrates a masterly touch in the construction of traditional plot and comic situations patterned on Molière and his followers. The classical rules of comedy and its stock characters, sometimes going back to the Roman tradition (e.g. *miles gloriosus*), are adjusted to realistic observation of the Polish nobility. His largely sympathetic portrayal of this group, despite its satirical undertones, was later disapproved of by liberal critics. Although Fredro often provokes laughter with slapstick and farce, he has above all mastered the representation of social types through vivid characters who are among the most popular on the Polish stage. The late plays (after 1855) reflect the influence of contemporary French theatre in their interest in the impact of money on relationships. The plot of *Pan Jowialski* (Mr J., 1832) follows the traditional motif of disguise followed by discovery. Its eponymous hero has provoked much controversy. While some regard the character as simply jovial, in accordance with his suggestive name, others either condemn his alleged senile idiocy or attempt to find a deeper meaning behind the apparent joker and story-teller. *Śluby panieńskie*

(Maiden vows, 1833) is a lyrical comedy concentrating on the development of feelings between two young couples. *Zemsta* (Vengeance, 1834), Fredro's most popular play, is based on a family feud involving a quick-tempered bully and a secretive hypocrite. Even the forced optimism of the happy ending fails to solve the conflict of temperaments. *Dożywocie* (The annuity, 1835), ridiculing a greedy usurer, has established itself as one of the funniest of Fredro's comedies.

●*The Major Comedies of A. Fredro* (Princeton, 1969).   SE

FRIED, Jiří (b. 1923), Czech novelist, went straight into the film industry after his matriculation (1942), where he remained, mainly as a screenwriter, until 1959, and whither he returned after the Soviet occupation of Czechoslovakia. 1954 he published a collection of appalling 'socialist' verse, *Rozsvícená okna* (Lit windows), but then he became one of the most original Czech prose writers of the 1960s. The central character of the first three of his works is essentially the same man. *Časová tíseň* (Time pressure, 1961) analyses the mental crisis of a Communist intellectual. It describes the process of becoming self-aware and, thus, of social disaffection. His sense of guilt looks forward to the mental state of the eponymous hero of *Abel* (1966). This brief novel about the futile waiting for love or satisfaction of an artist who had compromised himself in the 1950s, describes, much in the manner of a *nouveau roman*, the mechanical or despairing actions of one vacuous morning. It also concerns the insecurity felt by Czechoslovak intellectuals in the early 1960s. *Pověst* (The rumour, 1966) also concerns insecurity, though here the subject is the fear and curiosity of children. The author draws a skilful picture of his child narrator, an average boy of average brain, average brawn and average courage. *Pověst* contains elements of the grotesque, which figures strongly in his last brief novel, *Hobby* (1969). This work is a study in obsession, obsession with calligraphy as an escape from insecurity. Through his obsession the main character gains independence, because he has no need to communicate with society, except where a member of that society can serve his obsession.

●R. B. Pynsent, 'Uncertainty and Jiří Fried', *Cambridge Review*, 89A (1968), pp. 402–5. RBP

FUKS, Ladislav (b. 1923), Czech novelist, read philosophy and psychology at Prague. After his doctorate (1949) he worked in the paper industry, 1956–9 in the Office for National Movements, and then, until 1962, when he went freelance, in the National Gallery. Most of his novels have Jewish themes. *Pan Theodor Mundstock* (Mr T.M., 1963) considers the nature of identity and man's foolishness in training himself to bear suffering, plan his fate, in the example of a Jew waiting to be transported to an extermination camp. In *Mí černovlasí bratři* (My black-haired brethren, 1964) Fuks studies the confrontation of innocence with persecution; the purveyor of persecution, the manic geography master, represents the eternal dark forces in humanity and, simultaneously, knowledge of transcendental 'truths'. The forces of light (mainly represented by artists) and darkness, and the threat of *chiaroscuro*, are rather too schematically treated in *Variace pro temnou strunu* (Variation for a dark string, 1966). That schematicality is lacking in

Fuks's masterpiece, *Spalovač mrtvol* (The cremator, 1967), a powerful, grotesque horror-tale, whose unctuous main character reveals his unfeelingness in his sentimentality, and whose occultism finds its spiritual home in Nazism; it is also a study in the evil of messianism. The comic element of *Spalovač* is continued with far less intensity in the short stories of *Smrt morčete* (Death of a guinea pig, 1969), but the occultist element, combined with Jewish mysticism, is pursued more intensely in the picture of total destruction, *Oslovení z tmy* (Address from the darkness, 1972). As in *Variace*, fear and WWII dominate *Obraz Martina Blaskowitze* (The picture of Martin Blaskowitz, 1980), a novel concerned with the Fuks theme of human brutality, but also with the idealisation of memory and the responsibility of the individual. *Vévodkyně a kuchařka* (The duchess and the cook, 1983), set in and around fin-de-siècle Vienna, is an effete work of central European snobbery which tries and fails to ironise such snobbery. It is didactic and parodies didacticism; unlike in *Theodor Mundstock*, the factual errors in the text appear unintentional. Fuks displays here more clearly than anywhere else his condescension towards his readers.

●*Mr Theodor Mundstock* (London, 1969); *The Cremator* (London, 1984). T. G. Winner, 'Mythic and Modern Elements in the Art of Ladislav Fuks: *Natalia Mooshaber's Mice*' in H. Birnbaum and T. Eekman (Eds), *Fiction and Drama in Eastern and Southeastern Europe* (Columbus, Ohio, 1980), pp. 443–61; S. I. Kanikova, 'The Jews in the Works of Ladislav Fuks' in E. Maxwell *et al.* (Eds), *Remembering for the Future* (Oxford, 1989), vol. III, pp. 2,946–57. RBP

FURNADZHIEV,   **Nikola** (1903–68), Bulgarian poet, studied medicine at Sofia but, because of his involvement with Communists, had to go into hiding; he was arrested and lived under police surveillance in the provinces. He then read philosophy at Sofia, taught in Sofia and Istanbul, worked as a librarian and edited various literary periodicals. Furnadzhiev's most original work is the collection *Proleten vyatăr* (Spring wind, 1925). The poems are written under the influence of the suppression of the 1923 September Uprising against the right-wing government. The brutality of the internecine persecution that followed resulted in ka cultural trauma. The Expressionist-Imaginist fictional world in *Proleten vyatăr* reflects that traumatic reality in metaphors based on primal elements in man's mythological thinking, e.g. blood, fire, sun, death, fear, rain, wind, and in a paradoxical perception of violence (e.g. as wedding). The ultimate horror of this world where 'blood is shining and singing', 'death chants', 'the river shines like death', 'the field is chanting and dying', lies in the complete lack of frontier between physical and psychological states. The image of the 'tormented mother-country' which had occupied a vital place in Bulgarian literary mythopoeia since BOTEV is oxymoronically displayed in depictions of carnivalesque horrors; the work marks the end of mythopoeic National Revival perceptions. After this, Furnadzhiev was never able to achieve the emotional power of *Proleten vyatăr* or even to create a similar poetic world.   SIK

FÜST, Milán (1888–1967), Hungarian poet, prose writer, playwright and essayist, was originally named Fürst and his parents were Jewish. His father was a civil servant and the young Füst lived in a sheltered middle-class atmosphere. After obtaining a degree in jurisprudence, he taught in a commercial academy in Budapest. The beginning of his literary career coincided with the founding of the periodical *Nyugat* (West). His first collection of verse was published in 1914. Because of his involvement in the 1918 revolution, he was retired after the end of the 1919 Commune, and he travelled extensively. 1947 he became associate professor of aesthetics at Budapest. He is one of the creators of free verse in Hungarian, and his best poems, e.g. 'Tél' (Winter, 1934) or *Öregség* (Old age, 1947), abound in intentional archaisms, biblical and Classical echoes. The poet often speaks from behind a mask, and a similar stylisation is evident in his most stylish work in prose, *A feleségem története* (The story of my wife, 1942), in which a Dutch captain tries to find out the truth about his coquettish French wife. The novel has epistemological implications: the jealous husband's search is so inconclusive that the very existence of facts is undermined by his narrative.

•*The Story of My Wife* (New York, 1987).   MSz-M

G

GAILIT, August (1891–1960), Estonian prose-writer, the son of a building contractor of Latvian extraction, educated in state and private schools in Valga and Tartu, worked as a journalist in Riga, then as a war correspondent, and, from 1916, again as a journalist in Tallinn and Tartu. 1920–2 he was press attaché in Latvia; then he lived for two years in France, Italy and Germany, and from 1924 was a freelance writer in Tartu (managing director of the Vanemuine Theatre, 1932–4) until his defection to Sweden in 1944; he died in Örebro. He entered the literary scene with the Siuru group as an author mainly of short prose pieces which, in the 1920s, developed into a highly individual form, a grotesque combination of accurate observation and unrestrained imagination, hyperbole, a sense of the exceptional and a longing for the unattainable, e.g. *Saatana karussell* (Satan's roundabout, 1917) and *August Gailiti surm* (The death of A. Gailit, 1919). With this form Gailit was consciously going against the domestic literary tradition, particularly in his picturesque depiction of the countryside (the customary domain of Estonian prose) in his masterpiece, *Toomas Nipernaadi* (1928), and in *Karge meri* (Rough seas, 1938). In spite of his attempt at an artistic representation of the Estonian war of liberation against Soviet Russia in the novel *Isade maa* (Land of our fathers, 1935), Gailit retained his exclusive position as a literary eccentric, whom contemporary critics tended to link with the Scandinavian novel of the Hamsun brand. His inclination to the neo-Romantic and his tendency to use novella-like plots remained in his extensive work written in exile, the 'Estonian Decameron' *Kas mäletad, mu arm?* (Do you remember, my love?, 1951–9). VM

GAŁCZYŃSKI, Konstanty Ildefons (1905–53), Polish poet, between the wars the most popular, albeit controversial, member of the Kwadryga group and a frequent contributor to the radical right-wing weekly *Prosto z mostu* (Straight from the shoulder), spent the war in a German POW camp, and 1946 returned to Poland to become, despite his past and his penchant for the grotesque and absurd, one of the celebrities of 'official' literature. Gałczyński's uniqueness lies not in his political cynicism but in that he was a great poet of the absurd who happened to live in a politicised age. He deliberately adopted the pose of the man in the street who, faced with the impossible demands of ideologies, fakes cooperation while in fact seeking refuge either in simple, authentic 'private' emotions or in a jester-like mockery. As a result, Gałczyński earned his enormous popularity with personal, direct lyrics, such as the sequence *Pieśni* (Songs, 1953), as well as wildly nonsensical, hilarious pieces like his miniature 'plays' from *Teatrzyk 'Zielona Gęś'* (The Green Goose Theatre, 1946–50).

●Plays in D. Gerould (Ed.), *Twentieth-Century Polish Avant-garde Drama* (Ithaca, London, 1977).   StB

GAMSAKHURDIA, K'onst'ant'ine, (1893–1975), Georgian novelist, born in Abasha, Mingrelia, studied in St Petersburg, where he quarrelled with Nicolas Marr. He spent WWI mostly in Germany, France and Switzerland, taking his PhD in Munich. He was briefly interned in Trauenstein, where Thomas Mann sent him chocolate. He wrote a number of short stories which owe much to German Expressionism and French post-Symbolist prose. On finally returning to Tbilisi, he edited literary journals and formed his own élite group, Aripioni, quite out of joint with the times. A typically Georgian theme of the hero-seer undone by alien captivity is realised in his first extended work, *Dionisos ghimili* (The smile of Dionysos, 1925), nine years in the writing – the manuscript was lost once in Geneva and once in Tbilisi. It is an elaborate chain of incidents around the semi-autobiographical persona of K'onst'ant'ine Savarsamidze, a Georgian abroad, a modern 'superfluous man' and, though Gamsakhurdia denied it, an alienated *alter ego* of the author. (Savarsamidze is the name of the Promethean Amiran's follower in the Georgian medieval romance *Amiran-Darejaniani*, and the novel is, like the romance, divided into 'gates'.) The refined elegance of the style and arrogance of the narrative voice rival Montherlant; the detached, existen-tialist sensibility of a stranger in Paris recalls Rilke's Malte Laurids Brigge. Gamsakhurdia brought such unprecedented subtlety of phrasing to Georgian prose that this work alone has sufficed grammarians for models of every syntactic construction in modern Georgian. The work ends with the opening phrase of Dante's *Inferno* and led Gamsakhurdia to become the Georgian translator of Dante. Gamsakhurdia protested to Lenin on the crushing of Georgian independence and was deported in the repressions of 1926 and hounded out of literature until the early 1930s by leftists: suicide threatened. When Beria (another Mingrelian) came to power and redressed the balance, understandably, Gamsakhurdia felt glimmers of gratitude. This was expressed in his first 'socialist' novel, the bad, very long and finely written *Mtvaris mot'atseba* (Stealing the moon, 1935–6), a story of love and collectivisation in Abkhazia. A flamboyant novella of this period is *Khogais Mindia* (Mindia, son of Khogay, 1937), a psychological exploration of the Khevsur myth of Mindia so crucial to VAZHA PSHAVELA and Grigol ROBAKIDZE. This was not the 180-degree turn that Beria had demanded: Gamsakhurdia was arrested for an affair with Lida Gasviani (a 'Trotskyist'), but interrogated and released by Beria who slapped him on the back and told him that sexual relations with enemies of the people were permitted. Thereafter Gamsakhurdia was feared as a favourite of Beria, but the archives prove that in the terrible year 1937 he fearlessly refused to denounce others and spoke of the purges with irony, even disgust, reporting Orjonikidze's promise not to imitate Hitler by repressing intellectuals. His relations with tyranny resembled Bulgakov's with Stalin, a mutual balance of respect and detestation. Like many Georgian survivors of the purges, he was constrained to write on the childhood of Stalin. *Beladi* (The leader, 1939) is by no means the worst at handling this impossible remit. The novel's first part ends with the young Soso remarking how wonderful the world is after a thunderstorm; Stalin disliked his Christ-like personification: the novel was abandoned. Gamsakhurdia then published what he called his *art poétique*, his second 'Constantine' novel, *Didost'at'is marjvena* (The right hand of the Grand Master, 1939), set in the 1010s around King Giorgi I's mutilation and killing of the architect, K'onst'ant'ine Arsak'idze, who built the cathedral of the living pillar (*svet'i tskhoveli*) at Mtskheta. The novel works a typically Georgian clash of illicit love and duty to the nation and a universal tragedy of eros, art and necessity: it suffers from the Georgian's duty to magnify his nation's past glories and from a paucity of real information. Gamsakhurdia's contrast of an ideal Arsak'idze and an antithetical cosmopolitan sophist Parsman, like his justification of Giorgi I's ruthlessness, is uncomfortably close to Stalinist propaganda; refuge in history was only too transparent a device for harassed Soviet novelists. Yet the novel remains a personal testament. His postwar work *Vazis q'vaviloba* (The flowering of the vine, 1955) and magnum opus *Davit Aghmashenebeli* (David the Builder, 1942–62) cover no new ground. Publication of his superb memoirs (*Landebtan latsitsi*, [Flirting with ghosts, Mnatobi, 1963, 8,9]) and of his testament (Mnatobi, pulped 1959 issue) was aborted; he died

with unquestioned moral and artistic authority.

●*The Hand of a Great Master* (Moscow, 1959); *Mindia, the Son of Hogay (and other stories)* (Moscow, 1961).

D. Rayfield, 'Beria and the Policing of Poetry', *Scottish Slavonic Review*, Spring 1992.   DR

GAPRINDASHVILI, Valerian (1890–1941), Georgian poet, studied in Moscow. In 1915/16 he was one of the founder members of the Symbolist *tsisperq'ants'lebi* (Blue horns) group of poets in Kutaisi. His first and best book, *Daisebi* (Sundowns, 1919), at a time he called 'the Dionysian night' of Georgia, enthusiastically introduced into Georgian the aesthetics of Baudelaire and clarity of Paul Valéry, as well as the mannerisms of the Russian Symbolists (Bryusov, Balmont). (He also wrote Russian verse and translated Nik'oloz BARATASHVILI into Russian.) Until 1923 he edited the Blue horns journal *meotsnebe niamorebi* (Dreaming gazelles), and was their most articulate manifesto-writer: his articles, such as 'The Elysium of the Lyric' (9, 1923), asserted the solitude of the poet in the twilight, hallucinatory world, which became the theme of his hauntingly absurd poems, e.g. *Napt'alinis dedopali* (The queen of mothballs, 1923): 'She loves my chest of drawers and searches in it for winter's sweets. She has convinced me that she exists, But manages to hide again When I decide to capture her.' By 1925 Soviet literary policies forced Gaprindashvili to follow the other 'Blue horns' and recant his cult of the irreal and mystical: he announced, in an article 'Dabruneba mits'astan' (Return to the Earth), the interment of his individuality.   DR

GEORGIEVSKI, Tashko (b. 1935),

Macedonian prose writer, was born in a village in 'Aegean Macedonia' (N Greece) which, until 1945, had had a predominantly Slav population; 1946 he moved with his family to Yugoslavia; 1952 he settled in Skopje where he attended secondary school and studied at the Arts Faculty. Since then he has worked for Macedonian radio and television. Georgievski is best known for his novels, *Zidovi* (Walls, 1962), *Crno seme* (Black seed, 1966), *Crveniyot kon* (The red horse, 1966) and *Zmiski veter* (Wind of the serpent, 1969); his main theme is the fate of Macedonians in Aegean Macedonia. His preoccupations are history, home (*Heimat*), identity, the survival of humanity, and the harm violence does to man. He depicts the polarisation of values produced by the pressure of horror and violence, but also the face of a new human integrity. In his picture of the Macedonians in history, he paints humanity as the victim of historical events. *Crno seme* is his most accomplished work: it is set in the Greek Civil War; a group of mainly Macedonian soldiers from the Royal Greek Army are suspected of Communist activities and sent to an island because they refuse to sign a document renouncing both the CP and their nationality. They are submitted to psychological and physical torture. In this novel violence constitutes an encylopaedia of torture. Violence, which is not even bestial because it is so refined, is put across as an ordeal which 'humaneness' must undergo to remain intact. For Georgievski, the individual's deprivation of his national identity is the worst brutality a human being can be submitted to. He believes that, if one's national identity is expunged, one is condemned to vacuity, loses one's

humanity, becomes the 'black seed' which can never bring fruit.

SIK

GERGEI, Albert (16th century), Hungarian poet, was the author of *Historia egy Argirus nevű királyfiról és egy tündér szűzleányról* (Story of a prince named Argirus and a fairy maiden, n.d.). Nothing is known of Gergei, whose *széphistória* (see ROMANCE) is one of the finest of the genre and also the most popular. Unlike other narrative poets, Gergei makes no attempt to disguise his tale as historical. The mortal prince who pursues the vision of the once-glimpsed fairy princess through a series of blood-curdling adventures remains mythical. Gergei declares his source to be Italian, but none has been discovered. There are Classical and Hellenistic Greek elements in the tale, together with folklore motifs still to be found in Hungary. Gergei's technical skill and evocative vocabulary compensate for his inability to hold the complicated plot together. Countless variations on it exist. The 19th-century poet VÖRÖSMARTY used themes from it in his fairy play *Csongor és Tünde* (1831).

●Excerpt in T. Klaniczay (Ed.), *Old Hungarian Literary Reader* (Budapest, 1985). GFC

GJATA, Fatmir (1922–90), Albanian prose writer, poet and dramatist, was born in Korçë where he studied at the French secondary school before becoming a partisan in WWII. After the war, he studied at the Gorki Institute in Moscow and later became journalist and editor of various periodicals. Gjata is mainly known as a prose writer. Most of his work deals with the liberation struggle in WWII, e.g. the novel *Përmbysia* (The overthrow, 1954), and with the early years of the postwar period, e.g. the novel *Brezat*

(The generations, 1968). But his best
novel is *Këneta* (The marsh, 1959), a
moving description of the draining of
the marsh of Maliq on the Korçë
Plain. Among his short stories are
'Pika giaku' (Blood drops, 1954);
'Tana' (1955); and 'Në pragun e jetës'
(On the threshold of life, 1960). His
volume of verse *Këngët e maleve*
(The songs of the mountains, 1954)
includes his popular 'folk' ballad
'Kënga e partizanit Benko' (The song
of partisan Benko).   ShM

GLATSHTEYN, Yankev/ Jacob
Glatstein/Gladstone (1896–1971),
Yiddish poet, novelist and critic, was
born in Lublin, emigrated to the
USA a few months before the outbreak of WWI and 1918 began studying law at New York University.
Soon, however, he made the acquaintance of Nokhem-Borekh
Minkov (1893–1958) and LEYELES
with whom he collaborated in laun-
ching the Inzikh or Introspectivist
movement named after the anthology
which they published under the title
In zikh (In oneself, 1920). Glatshteyn was one of the most cosmopolitan and intellectual of Yiddish poets
and dominated a whole generation of
Yiddish cultural life. He had a passion for linguistic experimentation
and created highly original imagery
which he combined with popular
speech rhythms to form a unique
voice. His *Yankev glatshteyn* (1921)
was the first collection of Yiddish
poems entirely in free verse and immediately established him as one of
the foremost Modernist Yiddish
poets. The impressions made on him
by a journey to Poland undertaken in
1934 to visit his dying mother provided the material for two autobiographical novels, *Ven yash iz geforn*
(When Yash set out, 1938) and *Ven
yash iz gekumen* (When Yash ar-

rived, 1940). The two volumes of
essays collected as *In tokh genumen*
(The heart of the matter, 1947–56)
exemplify his balanced judgement
and honest agnosticism both in literary and ideological questions. As
with LEYELES, Glatshteyn's verse
moved in later years from Modernist
innovation to more overtly Jewish
themes. Under the impact of the
'Holocaust' he turned to more conservative and prosaic structures to
mourn the destruction of Jewish life
in E Europe, though still finding
startling linguistic means with which
to express his horror in the face of the
catastrophe. 1956 he published a
selection from his earlier poetic
works entitled *Fun mayn gantser mi*
(From my whole toil). With his death
the history of Yiddish poetry in
America virtually came to an end.

•*Homecoming at Twilight* [*Ven yash iz
gekumen*] (New York, 1962); *Poems*
(Tel Aviv, 1970); *The Selected Poems of
Jacob Glatstein* (New York, 1972); 'The
Return' in *TYS*, pp. 555–67.
J. Hadda, *Yankev Glatshteyn* (Boston,
1980); Abraham Novershtern, 'The
Young Glatstein and the Structure of his
First Book of Poems', *Prooftexts* 6:2
(Baltimore, 1986), pp. 131–46.   HD

GLIKL HAML / Glückel von
Hameln (1646–1724), Yiddish memoir-writer born in Hamburg,
whose name is derived from her first
husband's place of birth, Hamelin.
Her *Zikhroynes* (Memoirs, Frankfurt
on Main, 1896), which she wrote
1689–99 and 1715–19, were not intended for publication, but represented a spiritual legacy for her twelve
widely scattered children. The writing is for the most part artless and
unassuming, but when she narrates
dramatic incident the influence of the
Mayse-bukh (Story book, Basle,
1602) is occasionally evident. The

varied matters on which she touches represent a highly informative source for the contemporary social, cultural and economic circumstances of Jewish life in central Europe.

•*The Life of Glückel of Hameln* (London, 1962).

Liptzin, pp. 14–15; N. B. Minkov, in *WWT* 2, pp. 697–713.   HD

GLYKAS, Michael (12th century), Greek historian and theologian, born on Corfu, was a well-known learned writer of the period who produced a Universal Chronicle and various theological works. On his imprisonment at the Emperor's instruction 1158/9, he wrote a poem of 581 verses, in a form of language containing demotic elements, and illustrated with many popular proverbs, under the title Στίχοι οὓς ἔγραψε καθ' ὅν κατεσχέθη καιρόν (Verses which he wrote during the time of his imprisonment). The poem is a recital of his sufferings and a plea for clemency. The didactic element is strong, and references to the Bible are plentiful. The Emperor was apparently unmoved, and Glykas was condemned to blinding. The punishment must in practice have been lighter, as he appeared to have continued his writing career.

                                        CFR

GOLAR, Cvetko (1879–1965), Slovene poet, after secondary education worked as writer, journalist and translator. His expressive Vitalist verse celebrates rural life and Nature in *Pisano polje* (The brightly coloured field, 1910), *Rožni grm* (The rose bush, 1919), *Poletno klasje* (Summer shoots, 1923), *Njiva zori* (The crop ripens, 1927).   HL

GOLDFADN, Avrom/ Abraham Goldfaden (1840–1908), poet, journalist and creator of modern Yiddish theatre, together with fellow students at the state rabbinical seminary of Zhitomir helped produce and played the leading role in ETINGER's *Serkele* in 1862. This was the first time a modern Yiddish play had ever been performed. GOTLOBER, at that time a teacher at the seminary, had an important influence on his development. 1875 Goldfadn attempted to edit a humorous weekly journal together with his friend and former fellow student, LINETSKI, but the distribution of the journal in Russia was banned and Goldfadn moved to Iaşi in Roumania. There in 1877 he formed the first professional Yiddish theatre company and successfully produced his *Shmendrik* (Kiev, 1940). This was followed later the same year by *Di bobe mitn eynikl* (Grandmother and granddaughter, Warsaw, 1888). His early plays were sentimental farces with a didactic undertone which light-heartedly mocked traditional Jewish life, in particular arranged marriages. In response to the wave of pogroms which followed the assassination of Alexander II Goldfadn's plays became more nationalist in tone. The première of *Dokter almasado* (Dr Almasado, Warsaw, 1887) took place in St Petersburg in 1882. Set for the benefit of the censor in 14th-century Palermo, it takes the form of an impassioned denunciation of anti-Semitism. In 1883 the government banned Yiddish theatre altogether. Goldfadn turned to poetry and then to producing his plays in German in Warsaw. 1887 he went to New York where he found the market for Yiddish theatre already saturated by Shomer (i.e. Nokhem Meyer Shaykevitsh, 1849–1905) and by his former associates Yoysef Latayner (1853–1935) and Moyshe Hurvits (1844–1910). Disappointed by

America, Goldfadn returned to Europe and in 1891 directed his *Meshiekhs tsaytn* (In the days of the Messiah, Cracow, 1899) in Lemberg (Lwów) where he could express himself more directly. This unwieldy, but shrewdly observed drama satirises in like measure misplaced confidence in tsarist reform and assimilationist materialism in the New World. Only tilling the soil of Palestine holds out some hope of a meaningful existence. Goldfadn was increasingly drawn to Zionism which is the inspiration of his last play, *Ben-ami* (Son of my people), loosely based on George Eliot's *Daniel Deronda* and first performed in New York in 1907. Despite repeated reverses he wrote over sixty plays, many of which achieved enduring success. His plots were often derivative, but he was a skilled adaptor whose humane spirit had a profound impact on Yiddish life and letters.

●Liptzin (1963), pp. 33–51; D. I. Silberbusch, 'Visiting Goldfaden, Father of the Yiddish Stage' in L. S. Dawidowicz (Ed.), *The Golden Tradition* (New York, 1967), pp. 321–6.

HD

GOLIA, Pavel (1887–1959), Slovene playwright and poet, after completing military academy, served as an officer in the Austrian Army in Trieste and Ljubljana. In 1915 on the Eastern Front he went over to the Russians with his unit and fought on the Russian side in Dobrudzha. Returning to Ljubljana after the war, he worked as playwright and theatre director. After WWII he became director of the Slovene National Theatre. His verse is polished, witty and melodious, rich in unusual imagery. His first collection, *Pesmi o zlatolaskah* (Poems about goldilocks, 1921), concerning prostitutes, was a challenge to false moralists: thereafter defiance, irony and satire came naturally. Other collections: *Večerna pesmarica* (Evening songbook, 1921); *Pesmi* (Poems, 1936); *Gospod Baroda in druge ljudske pesmi* (Mr B. and other folk poems, 1966), a reworking of oral-tradition works. His later poems dealt with themes from WWII and the struggle for national independence. He wrote many plays, some of the best of these for children: *Petrčkove poslednje sanje* (Pete's last dream, 1923); *Triglavska bajka* (The story of Triglav, 1927); *Princezka in pastirček* (The princess and the shepherd-boy, 1932); *Sneguljčica* (Snow White, 1950).

HL

GOMA, Paul (b. 1935), Roumanian prose writer, was the most defiant of a handful of Roumanian dissidents who expressed themselves publicly during the 1970s. Born in Bessarabia to parents who were both school-teachers, he had a childhood punctuated by the upheavals of war and migration. His father was arrested by the Soviet authorities after the annexation of Bessarabia in 1940 and on his release two years later the family made their way to Roumania and settled in Bucharest. He was arrested in 1951 on suspicion of wanting to join anti-Communist guerrillas based in the Carpathian foothills but was released after eleven days and joined the Communist Youth Movement. In 1953 and 1954 he acted as a group leader at a Pioneers' camp at Rupea near Braşov and in the latter year was admitted to the School of Literature and Literary Criticism in Bucharest. During a seminar in 1956 he read out part of his novel *Durerile facerii* (The pains of conception) in which the hero sets out to establish a students' movement similar to that in Hungary. He was promptly arrested on the charge of attempting to organise a strike at Bucharest University, convicted and sentenced to two years' imprisonment. On release he was exiled to a village E of Bucharest where he spent four years without being permitted to leave the village. As an ex-political prisoner unable to resume his studies, he took a number of manual jobs in various towns in S Transylvania until a decree of 1965 reopened the doors of universities to former detainees. He enrolled in the Arts Faculty at Bucharest but left within a year. 1966 his first short story was published in the journal *Luceafărul* (Lucifer/Venus) and his first volume of stories *In camera de alături* (In the room next door, 1968) appeared shortly before Goma joined the CP. The manuscript of his first novel, *Ostinato*, based on his experiences at the hands of the security police, was submitted for publication in the winter of 1967 but the reader claimed to recognise the dictator's wife, Elena Ceauşescu, in one of the characters and further publication of Goma's writings was prohibited. All his subsequent novels were published in the West. *Ostinato* appeared in German translation 1971 and as a result Goma was dismissed from the Party. During the summer of 1972 he was allowed to visit France where he wrote *Gherla* which was published in Paris in French translation in 1976. In April 1977 he was arrested after making public the contents of a letter addressed to KOHOUT and sending two letters to Ceauşescu denouncing the *securitate*. Released following an international outcry, Goma was allowed to leave Roumania with his wife and child in November 1977 and settled in Paris where he wrote a succession of novels drawing on his life in Roumania, which were pub-

lished in French. The principal theme of Goma's writing is the ambiguity of living in a totalitarian state. His novels portray the ever-present duplicity of existence in a society in which the citizen must daily strike a balance between the demands of 'official' life and the attempt to lead an 'unofficial' one. The double game played with the régime, relations, friends and the opposite sex is powerfully represented in *Bonifacia* (1986). His experience in the prison of Gherla in Transylvania provides the subject of *Gherla* (1976) and *Les Chiens de mort* (1981). The fear, uncertain loyalties and apathy of those whose aid Goma solicited when attempting to overcome the ban placed on his writing is chronicled in detail in *Le Tremblement des hommes* (1979). *Le Calidor* (1987) centres on Goma's childhood experiences in his native Bessarabia. 'The Gate of Unrest' of the English translation is the stoop of his parents' house, the hub of Goma's universe, the point where the paths for play, the roads for invading armies, and the tracks used by the villagers to move their flocks of sheep all intersect. The background of war in this disputed territory presents an epitome of the Balkan history of pillage and violence. Despite his father's arrest by the Soviet authorities on a contrived charge of 'hooliganism' and his absence for two years, Goma never dwells on this separation. His childhood memory fixes on his games in smoking stubble-fields, on his attempts to pick apricots with poles, and on his light-hearted adventures with girls. His exploits are described with the engaging innocence of a child.

●*My Childhood at the Gate of Unrest* [*Le Calidor*] (London, 1990).   DJD

GOMBROWICZ, Witold (1904–69), Polish novelist and playwright, came from a prosperous landowning family. Educated in Warsaw (law) and Paris (philosophy and economics), Gombrowicz eventually turned to writing in the mid-1930s. Finding himself on a short trip to Argentina at the outbreak of WWII, he settled there until 1963. He spent his final years in France. Gombrowicz holds a key place among modern Polish writers, having frequently anticipated later developments such as Existentialism and Postmodernism. His literary world consciously lacks stability and uniformity. A grotesque blend of high and low styles is accompanied by a sophisticated play on authenticity and fiction in the conception of first-person narration. Through the latter the author constructs his ironic *alter ego* set against a fully or partly imaginary background. Intellectually entertaining, the stories illustrate the philosophical principles always present in Gombrowicz's works: his interest in human 'roles' and 'masks' and the consequent want of authenticity. His idea that mutual relations generate 'forms' which control behaviour recalls contemporary French theories of 'ready-formed dictionaries' (Barthes), 'language games' (Lyotard) and 'discourses' (Foucault). Gombrowicz secured recognition with the publication of *Ferdydurke* (1937), still his most popular novel. The adventures of a thirty-year-old transformed into a schoolboy by a patronising teacher are set against a background of different social attitudes (traditional and 'progressive') treated with ironic distance. The hero's search for authenticity eventually leads to the conclusion that there is no escape from 'form' other than another 'form'. In *Trans-Atlantyk* (1953), set in Buenos Aires, everything is questioned and relativised. The grotesque portrayal of the Polish community and native Argentinians ridicules national clichés and undermines the idea of a 'fatherland' with its more sensual counterpart – 'sonland'. *Pornografia* (1960), set in a Polish country house during WWII, unmasks traditional approaches to love, conspiracy and moral standards. *Kosmos* (1965), the grimmest of Gombrowicz's novels, investigates the dark side of human eroticism. In *Dziennik* (Diary, 1957–66) Gombrowicz blurs the distinction between autobiography and fiction, teases the reader, constructs and deconstructs his own image and its surrounding reality, thus maintaining a process of perpetual reincarnation. Gombrowicz's plays blend tragedy with farce in their grotesque forms. *Ślub* (The marriage ceremony, 1953) is a key work for understanding the author's views on interpersonal relations and parodies the style of Shakespearian tragedy. *Operetka* (Operetta, 1966) combines the frivolity of the operetta with a bleak vision of 20th-century social upheavals.

●*Ferdydurke* (London, 1961); *Pornografia* (London, 1966); *Diary* (2 vols, London, 1988–9); *Operetta* (London, 1971).

F. M. Thompson, *Witold Gombrowicz* (Boston, 1979); A. Kurczba, *Gombrowicz and Frisch. Aspects of the Literary Diary* (Bonn, 1980); R. Gombrowicz, *Gombrowicz en Europe. Témoignages et documents 1963–69* (Paris, 1988). SE

GORDIN, Yankev (1853–1909), Yiddish dramatist, was born in Mirgorod in the Ukraine. As a young man he had been attracted by the ideals of the Narodniki, had written for the Russian liberal press and had set up an agricultural commune on Tolstoyan principles. 1891 the colony was suppressed and Gordin fled to America where he made the Yiddish stage his profession. At that time the New York Yiddish theatre was still dominated by the meretricious vaudeville of Yoysef Latayner (1853–1935), Moyshe Hurvits (1844–1910) and Shomer (i.e. Nokhem Meyer Shaykevitsh, 1849–1905). Gordin introduced higher artistic standards and more serious issues by adapting freely from world drama. His *Der yidisher kenig lir* (The Jewish King Lear, Warsaw, 1892) was successfully performed in New York in 1892. Perhaps the most powerful of all his dramas was *Mirele efros* (New York, 1911) which was first staged in 1898 and reworked the Lear-theme with a female protagonist. *Medea* (New York, 1897) is loosely based on Grillparzer's *Die Argonauten*. *Got, mentsh un tayvl* (God, man and the devil, New York, 1903), adapted from Goethe's *Faust*, was first staged in 1900. *Di shvue* (The oath, Warsaw, 1911) was derived from Gerhart Hauptmann's *Fuhrmann Henschel* and was also produced in New York in 1900, while Gordin's *Der umbakanter* (The stranger) premièred in New York in 1905, owed much to PRZYBYSZEWSKI's *Złote runo* (Golden fleece). He usually felt obliged to provide his works with happy endings and his characters were at times somewhat stereotyped, but he nevertheless attracted a more discriminating audience to Yiddish theatre. During the two decades of Gordin's dominance of the New York theatre he wrote and staged some seventy plays many of which were successfully adapted for the cinema after his

death, most notably Roman Rebush's 1939 version of *Mirele efros*.

●'Mirele Efros', *Jüdisches Theater*, vol. 1, Munich, 1919.

Liptzin (1963), pp. 149–56; Leonard Prager, 'Jacob Gordin's "The Jewish King Lear" ', *American Quarterly* 18:3 (Fall 1966), pp. 506–16.   HD

GÓRNICKI, Łukasz (1527–1603), Polish writer of middle-class background, acquired a comprehensive Humanist education in Italy. His chief work is a free adaptation of Castiglione's *Courtier*, published as *Dworzanin Polski* (The Polish courtier, 1566). The setting is polonised; women have been removed from the company of discussants, and the text expurgated of all ribald or excessively sophisticated content. Górnicki added some remarks of his own, chiefly about the Polish language, and some local anecdotes. The elegance of his style made a significant contribution to the development of Polish artistic prose.   SE

GOTLOBER, Avrom-Ber/ Abraham-Baer Gottlober (1811–99), Yiddish writer, was born in Starokonstantinov, Volhynia. Early in life he travelled to Tarnopol and came into contact with Yoysef Perl (1773–1839) and the Galician Haskalah movement. He is remembered primarily on account of his play *Der dektukh* (The marriage veil, Warsaw, 1876) which he wrote in 1838, not intending it for performance, and which represents an early example of the Maskilic satire on the supposed degeneracy of Ḥasidic life. 1865 he joined the staff of the Zhitomir rabbinical seminary at which GOLDFADN was already a student and he encouraged his interest in Yiddish literature. Superior to *Der dektukh* was his 'Der gilgl' (The metamorphosis, in: *Kol mevaser* [The herald], Warsaw,

1871), a satirical story narrating the comic avatars of a credulous Ḥasid, adapted from Yitskhok Erter's (1791–1851) Hebrew *Gilgul nefeš* (Metamorphosis of the soul, 1858) (itself based on Wieland's rendering of one of Lucian's dialogues). In this story Gotlober adopts the technique of the *faux-naïf* narrator recently developed by MENDELE MOYKHER SFORIM and LINETSKI.

●'The Gilgul or the Transmigration' in *GWJF* 2, pp. 40–80.

M. Waxman, *History of Jewish Literature*, vol. 3 (New York, 1960²), pp. 255–8; Wiener, pp. 101–3, 145–52.

HD

GOVEKAR, Fran (1871–1949), Slovene novelist and playwright, studied medicine in Vienna, but did not complete the course. He worked as a journalist, then as a civil servant, contributing to various periodicals including *Slovan* (Slav), which he edited 1902–10. He drew his material from the darker side of middle-class life, including sexual aberrations, without displaying any real social-critical or satirical intent. *V krvi* (In the blood, 1896), the first Slovene Naturalist novel, is largely concerned with the influence of heredity and environment on character *à la* Taine. He adapted stories from the oral tradition for the stage: *Rikovnjači* (The bandits, 1899); *Deseti brat* (The tenth brother, 1901); *Martin Krpan* (1905).

HL

GRADNIK, Alojz (1882–1987), Slovene poet, a gifted translator, was not influenced by Slovene Modernism. He retained an intuitive understanding of peasant mentality and love of the land. His first collection, *Padajoče zvezde* (Falling stars, 1916), deals with love and death, happiness and unhappiness (his recurrent themes) against the background of his native region. Other collections are *Pot bolesti* (The way of pain, 1922), *De profundis* (1926), *Večni studenci* (Eternal springs, 1938), *Bog in umetnik* (God and the artist, 1943).

●Selected translations in: *AMYP* and *Parnassus*; *Selected Poems* (London, 1964).

HL

GRAMENO, Mihal (1872–1931), Albanian politician, writer and journalist, was born into a merchant family in Korçë, where he studied at the Greek secondary school before emigrating 1885 to Roumania. In Bucharest he was involved in the national movement, and 1889 he became secretary of the *Drita* (Light) society. 1907 he joined the Çeçiz Topulli guerrilla unit fighting against the Turkish forces in S Albania. He was later the editor of the Korçë periodical *Lidhja Orthodokse* (The orthodox league, 1909–10), of *Koha* (Time), also published in Korçë, but later in America, where he lived 1915–19. He returned to Europe to represent American Albanians at the Paris Conference in 1919 and 1920 went back to Albania. In the 1920s he carried on his journalistic and literary activities until the Zog régime forced him to retire from public life. Grameno's principal works are the patriotic poem, *Vdekja* (Death, 1903), the comedy *Mallkimi i gjuhës shqipe* (The curse of the Albanian language, 1905), the historical tragedy (*Vdekja e Pirros* (The death of Pyrrhus, 1906) and his short stories, among the first in Albanian literature, e.g. *Oxhaku* (The hearth), *E puthura* (The kiss) and *Varr'i pagëzimit* (The font), all 1909; a volume of verse, *Plagët* (Wounds, 1912), and *Kryengritja shqiptare* (The Albanian uprising, 1925), an account of his experience as a guerrilla commander.

ShM

GREGORČIČ, Simon (1844–1906), Slovene lyric poet, attended grammar school in Gorica and in spite of his own doubts entered a seminary to study for the priesthood. His subsequent *Weltschmerz* arose from the conflict between his priestly mission and his personal emotions. His first years as a chaplain in Kobarid were happy and fruitful as he worked to improve the lot of the people. 1870 he began to publish his poems in various periodicals, and benefited from the advice of STRITAR. Poor health, depression and nostalgia for his native mountains following a transfer to other parts caused a three-year block. 1882 he published his first collection of poems, which was severely criticised by Anton Mahnič (1850–1920), a professor of theology, as dangerous to young people because of its sickly sensitivity and pessimistic outlook. His second collection came out in 1888 and again met with a hostile reception, this time because love and patriotism were themes unworthy of his calling. In spite of these criticisms he became revered as 'the nightingale of Gorica', a worthy successor to PREŠEREN and JENKO. Among his poems we may note 'V pepelnični noči' (Ash Wednesday eve), 'Soči' (To the Soča river), expressions of his patriotism; 'Nazaj v planinski raj' (Back to the mountain paradise) and 'Oj zbogom, ti planinski svet' (Goodbye, my mountain land), songs of nostalgia; 'Pastir' (The shepherd) and 'Veseli pastir' (The happy shepherd), invocations of an idyllic life; his pessimism is best expressed in 'Človeka nikar' (Never a man again!), a prayer to the Almighty not to re-create from the poet's ashes another human being doomed to suffer the same unhappiness, in 'Moj črni plašč' (My black coat), a song of mourning for buried ideals, hopes and dreams, and in 'Ujetega ptiča tožba' (Complaint of a caged bird).
●*Alone* (Ljubljana, 1919); 'O Nevermore, Ash Wednesday Eve' (*Parnassus*, 1957, 1965); *The Slav Anthology*, 1931; *Slovene Poetry*, 1928.   HL

GRIGOR NAREKATSI (i.e. Grigor of Narek, 951–?1003), Armenian writer, was born in a village in Vaspurakan to the S of Lake Van (now E Turkey), son of Khosrov Anjewatsi (900–63), bishop of the nearby province of Anjewatsik' in the kingdom of Vaspurakan. He was the author of *Meknut'iwn zhamakargut'ean* (Commentary on the holy hours, first printed, Constantinople, 1840) and *Meknut'iwn Pataragi* (Commentary on the holy liturgy, first printed, Venice, 1869). Both works exist in a manuscript of 950 copied by Grigor's son Sahak to which Grigor later added a colophon stating that he was unworthy to be son of Khosrov. Grigor together with his brother Hovhannes was sent to be educated by his mother's paternal first cousin Anania Narekatsi, abbot of the monastery of Narek, in the province of Rshtunik. The period between the middle of the 10th century and the middle of the 11th was relatively peaceful in Armenia, which was enjoying a cultural and spiritual renascence. Ani, where the capital of Armenia was located by King Ashot III Bagraduni (953–78), became an economic, political and cultural centre. In a manuscript of 977 Grigor refers to himself as a *k'ahanay* (married priest), and around this time he composed his first work *Meknut'iwn Ergots Ergoyn* (Commentary on the Songs of Songs) at the request of Prince Gourgen Artsruni (968–1003). Around this time Grigor also wrote his hymns devoted to the dominical feast days, saints and martyrs of the Armenian Church. Grigor is the inventor of the *gandj* ('treasure') literary form, and nine of these lengthy spiritual poems are attributed to him. However, it is for his allegorical liturgical chants (*taghs* and *meghedies*), of which over a score are preserved, that Grigor is justly famed. Their vivid, joyous imagery binds man, Nature and the wonder of God in delightful, alliterative cadences. Narekatsi's masterpiece is *Matean Oghbergut'ean* (The book of lamentations/Elegies), completed c. 1002. It was first printed in Marseilles (incomplete, 1673) and Constantinople (1700). This collection of 95 *ban* (colloquies with God), meditative prayers, has survived in more MSS and has more printed editions than any other work in Armenian except the Bible. It is sometimes known simply as *Narek*. A colophon of 1266 sums up the author's intentions: 'it is the gate and entry to the vestibules of God, which, with penitence and through the prayers of the holy father Grigor, recited in tearful, imploring petition, renews men who consist in sin, and they become of spirit, even as the angels'. The book is meant to guide one through three stages of contemplative prayer, purifying the repentant, earthly man and transforming the soul into spirit. Although each meditation is concerned with the mystic's separation from God and is therefore a lamentation, some chapters are suffused with hope in God's grace and his healing power. The first chapter begins with the confession: 'I offer up unto you, who seest hidden things, the voice of the heart's moan of distress and the clamour of lamentation', after which Grigor compares his soul to an offer-

ing to be wholly consumed in the fire of the altar. The final chapter is a plea that 'the ardent fire be consumed'. Grigor declares that 'strengthened in you, by you I shall be renewed'. The progress up the mountain from the initial gesture of total surrender to the Lord to the pilgrim's final confidence in eternal life through Christ is neither steady, nor always sure, nor calm. The chapters of the *Matean Oghbergut'ean* are a record of this struggle, each both a prayer to God and an exercise in the scrutiny of one's own soul.

●Grigor Narekatsi, *Matean Oghbergut'ean* (Book of lamentations, critical text, introduction, and annotations by P. M. Khatchatryan and A. A. Ghazinyan (Yerevan, 1985); *Grégoire de Narek, Le Livre de prières*, introduction, translation and notes by Isaac Kechichian (Paris, 1961); *Lamentations of Narek*, trans. from the classical Armenian by Mischa Kudian (London, 1977) (twenty-five elegies only). *Grégoire de Narek et l'ancienne poésie arménienne*, trans. and notes. L. -A. Marcel (Paris, 1953).   VN

GRIPARIS, Ioannis (1870–1942), Greek poet, born in Syphnos, but taken to Constantinople, where his father was a teacher, the profession in which Griparis himself was to start, went to school in Constantinople, then (1888) enrolled in the Philosophical School of Athens University. His family circumstances declined and he had to support himself as a drawing-master – a skill which has some relevance to the element of visual precision in his poetry. His first collection of poems, Δειλινά (Of the evening, written 1890–2), and essays on translation and literary criticism belong to his student period. 1893 he returned to Constantinople to teach and contributed to the literary periodical Φιλολογική Ηχώ (Literary echo), through which he paved the way for the aesthetic and linguistic practice which characterised his first major collection of poetry, the twelve sonnets entitled 'Σκαραβαίοι' (Scarabs), published 1895 in the periodical εστιά (Hearth and home). In December 1895 he gave up teaching to devote himself to the editorship of Φιλολογική Ηχώ, turning it into the first periodical devoted to the demoticist cause. 1896 he moved permanently to Athens (with the exception of 1912–14, when he went abroad to France, Germany and Italy to undertake literary studies). In Athens he found a new teaching post and stayed in the profession, eventually obtaining a position in the Ministry of Education (1922), where he remained until sacked under the dictatorship of Metaxas (1936). 1930 he was made director of the National Theatre. Griparis was instrumental in bringing together the influences of French Parnassism and Symbolism. His 'Scarabs', sonnets of 15-syllable lines, was a collection marked by a rich and apt lexis and by technical skill. The 11-syllable sonnets Τερρακότες (Terracottas) which eventually accompanied the 'Scarabs' when they appeared in book form (1919) were similar in themes and styles, but the Ιντερμέδια (Intermezzi, written 1899–1901), as their title suggests, manifest the French Symbolist concern with musicality: the poet is seeking ways to evoke and suggest rather than describe. The three Ελεγεία (Elegies, 1902–9) with their atmosphere of melancholy, decline and failure and their fluid symbolism, designed to cover both personal and universal forces, represent the peak of his writing. There-

after his major contributions to Modern Greek literature consisted of his translations of Ancient Greek plays and his wide-ranging literary criticism.   CFR

GRISHASHVILI, Ioseb (i.e. Mamulaishvili, 1889–1965), the most popular of 20th-century Georgian poets, was a mason's son and his roots were among the shopkeepers and tradesmen of old Tbilisi: he worked first as a theatre prompter, then as a compositor. While he translated from Armenian and Azeri Turkish (and even learnt French), he claimed that he knew no Russian. He was thus a purely 'native' *ashugh* (popular or court minstrel), unlike the 18th-century polyglot Armenian SAYAT-NOVA whose biography he wrote and emulated. Grishashvili's lyrics intentionally followed the tradition of the folk *q'arachoghlebi*, the 'black-tunics' – street traders renowned for their hedonism: he canonised their love songs. Nevertheless Grishashvili associated with Ilia CH'AVCH'AVADZE and Ak'ak'i TS'ERETELI in intellectual radicalism and scholarship. 1918, when Tbilisi University began tuition in Georgian, Grishashvili followed courses in history and literature, and proved himself as erudite as overtly literary poets. His poetry was frequently published under more than 100 pseudonyms. 1916 his eroticism became Decadent: he associated briefly with the Kutaisi *tsisper-q'ants'lebi* (Blue horns) poets ROBAKIDZE and T'itsian T'ABIDZE, but soon lost interest in their cosmopolitan aestheticism. Despite earlier radical fervour he was shocked into silence by the Soviet invasion of 1921. He published only a handful of poems before 1939 (although archives now reveal that he risked his life writing satirical, anti-Soviet verse – for instance, 'When I mentioned Lenin and Makharadze, Even the dogs began to howl', 1937). For a while Grishashvili belonged to the *ak'ademia* group of prose writers who refused to dismiss past literary standards; he relied for protection on his enormous popularity (comparable only to Galak't'ion T'ABIDZE's) and turned to memoirs, translation, bibliography and monographs. His slim but fascinating *Dzveli Tbilisis lit'erat'uruli Bohema* (Literary bohemia of old Tbilisi, 1927) is for the USSR an amazing exercise in literary nostalgia. Over his fallow years Grishashvili amassed the best private library in Georgia: its catalogue is an important Georgian bibliography. 1939 he capitulated and wrote the required Stalin panegyrics: but his real inspiration was in the catchy (and untranslatable) inventiveness of about two hundred love lyrics (to women and to Georgia) written 1907–20: 'I cannot give you real poems. And if I were to, Know that then, my beloved, you would die, I swear it.'   DR

GRITSI-MILLIEX, Tatiana (i.e. T. Gritsi, b. 1920), Greek prose writer, principally educated by a private tutor, and after false starts at a university degree and dance training, completed courses in singing and French During the latter she met Roger Milliex, whom she married 1939. 1941 she joined EAM (the left-wing resistance movement). After a year in Paris after the war, she and her husband returned to Athens, where Milliex was director of studies at the Institut Français until 1959, and she worked in the Centre for Asia Minor Studies (1952–9). 1959–71 the couple were in Cyprus, during which time the Junta deprived her of her Greek citizenship and confiscated her personal papers (including the MSS of 4 finished novels). 1971 her husband was transferred to Genoa, and she divided her time between there and the Greek community in Paris. They returned to Athens in 1974, since when she has concentrated on her writing and journalism. Her early fiction, from Πλατεία Θησείου (Thesion Square, 1947) up to Ημερολόγιο (Diary, 1952), while drawing on autobiographical elements in the exploration of the problematic relationships of individuals (specifically girls) to their family environment, already shows an awareness of the importance of form – interior monologue, narrative point of view, manipulation of chronology – in determining the meaning of a text. Her novels, Αλλάζουμε (We are changing, 1957) and Ιδού ίππος χλωρός (Behold a pale horse, 1963), extend the experiment: the former explores the evolution of a girl across a sequence of stories; the second explores the same sort of evolution in the context of the Occupation, allowing a complex interplay of the internal with the external and political. It is plain in all Gritsi-Milliex's work that she is aware of developments in French writing. This has helped her to develop ways of expressing her political and feminist 'instincts' which are not so fully explored in other Greek writers. Her novel Σπαράγματα (Distress, 1973), salvaged from the remains of confiscated papers, and the collection of stories Αναδρομές (Going back, 1982) are good examples of this.

CFR

GROCHOWIAK,   Stanisław, (1934–76), Polish poet, playwright, and fiction writer, one of the young poets who made their débuts in 1956, contributed arguably more than any other to the 'liberation of the imagination' in Polish poetry after Socialist Realism. In his first four collections, 1956–63, he emerged as the most accomplished representative of the anti-aestheticist tendency, dubbed 'turpism' or 'cult of ugliness' by its chief opponent, PRZYBOŚ. Beginning with the volume *Kanon* (Canon, 1965), his neo-Baroque aesthetics turned into a more Neoclassical approach.

• Selected poems in C. Milosz (Ed.), *Postwar Polish Poetry* (Berkeley, 1983). M. G. Levine, *Contemporary Polish Poetry, 1925–1975* (Boston, 1981).   StB

GRUDEN, Igo (1893–1948), Slovene poet with strong connections to the Maritime region (Primorje), studied law in Vienna, 1912–14, graduated after army service in 1918, and was awarded his doctorate in Prague, 1921. His legal career in Ljubljana was interrupted by internment and then imprisonment during WWII. On return to Yugoslavia, he worked first for Radio Belgrade, and from 1945 for the Ministry of Education in Ljubljana. He left five collections of poetry: *Narcis* (Narcissus, 1920); *Primorske pesmi* (Songs from Primorje, 1920); *Dvanajsta ura* (The twelfth hour, 1939); *V pregnanstvo* (Into exile, 1945); *Pesnikovo srce* (The poet's heart, 1946).

• Translated poems in *Parnassus*, 1957, 1965.   HL

GRUM, Slavko (1901–49), Slovene playwright and short-story writer, showed an interest in amateur drama and began to write while still a grammar-school pupil in Novo Mesto. As a student of medicine in Vienna, 1919–26, he became acquainted with Freud's psychoanalysis. Medical practice, partly in a mental hospital, gave him material for his short sketches of the unfortunate. His main work is the two-act play *Dogodek v mestu Gogi* (Happening in the town of Goga, written 1927, publ. 1930), with its echoes of Strindberg and German Expressionism. The stage presents a psychopathic menagerie with the victims trapped in their cages, attracting the spotlight for their individual episodes.   HL

GRUŠAS, Juozas (1901–86), Lithuanian playwright and prose writer, studied jurisprudence, philosophy and German at Kaunas and taught Lithuanian language and literature in various grammar schools. Later Grušas worked in theatre and publishing, and held important posts in the Lithuanian Writers' Union. In his works Grušas is first of all a 'humanist'; he believes in individual freedom, in conscience, in the pursuit of the sciences and arts, in the premise that life is or may be meaningful; he propagates human decency even in violent and 'tragic' situations. During the relatively stable years of Lithuanian independence, such beliefs could be held without involving drastic moral confrontations with reality, and Grušas's novel *Karjeristai* (The careerists, 1935) as well as his collection of stories *Sunki ranka* (The heavy hand, 1937) criticised human foibles without subjecting the characters to any great crises of conscience. Things changed with the advent of war and particularly of the Soviet occupation with its ruthless insistence on blind submission to Communist ideology and genocidal practices. Situations of moral ambiguity were now replaced by crucible-like circumstances which Grušas portrayed by altering his prose mode from the conventional Realist to something like the Surrealist, where things of genuine moral value stood close to dependable reality while falsehood acquired an aspect of the phantasmal and monstrous. From c. 1955, Grušas increasingly turned from prose to drama, and from contemporary scenes in such plays as *Professorius Markas Vidinas* (Professor M.V., 1962) and the tragicomic *Meilė, džiazas ir velnias* (Love, jazz and the Devil, 1967) that dealt with generation conflicts in new Soviet-ruled society, to historical plays. In the best-known of these, *Herkus Mantas* (1957) dealing with an uprising in medieval Prussia against German military rule, and the verse play *Barbora Radvilaitė* (1971) concerning a turbulent period in 16th-century Lithuanian history, modern problems gain perspective and definition in their transposition into a remote historical setting.   RŠ

GUNDULIĆ, Ivan (1589–1638), Croatian poet, born into a noble family, attended school in Dubrovnik. It is likely that his family came into contact with the Jesuits who were active in Dubrovnik from c. 1620. He held several high functions in the Dubrovnik Republic and devoted his life to writing. The outstanding Croatian poet of the 17th century and one of the finest poets in Serbo-Croatian, his works include neo-Classical mythological and pastoral plays, religious and epic verse. Of the ten plays he is known to have written, only four have been preserved, all translations or re-workings of Latin or Italian works. Gundulić is best known for his three original works: the devotional lament *Suze sina razmetnoga* (The tears of the prodigal son, 1622), the allegorical pastoral *Dubravka* (1628), and the epic *Osman* (unfinished, the earliest extant copy dates from 1651). *Suze sina razmetnoga* may be seen as fol-

lowing closely the instructions for meditation in Ignatius Loyola's *Exercitia spiritualia*. The poem is in three canti (or 'laments'), corresponding to the 'three movements of the soul'. *Dubravka* contains elements of mythological drama, Classical pastoral and details from contemporary life. The title represents a complex of associations: the name Dubrovnik, the pagan connotations of an oak grove ('dubrava') and the name 'Dubravka', a nymph who symbolises freedom. It is seen as typical of the patriotic tone which distinguishes Croatian literature composed in Dalmatia and Dubrovnik in the 16th and 17th centuries from its Italian models. The patriotism in this case, however, is narrower in scope: it is a hymn of praise to the freedom ensured Dubrovnik by its skilful nobility, a plea in favour of privilege and the preservation of the status quo. *Osman* is a lengthy epic, in 20 canti, closely modelled on Tasso's *Gerusalemme Liberata*, which Gundulić had intended to translate. Following the Battle of Hoćim (1621) and the death of Osman (1622), however, he decided instead to write his complex work, celebrating the ultimate triumph of the Christian Slavs over the Turks. The epic contains an abundance of episodes – women warriors, devils, nymphs and shepherds – while focusing on the historical figure of Osman. Like the strongest section of *Suze sina razmetnoga*, it is imbued with a melancholy Baroque preoccupation with transience and Fortune. Substitute canti were supplied for those missing (14 and 15) by MAŽURANIĆ, who had thoroughly absorbed Gundulić's idiom, thus ensuring the 17th-century poet an important role in the Croatian National Revival.

●'Dubravka', *BC Review* 9 (1976), pp. 1–24; *The Tears of the Prodigal Son* (London, Zagreb, 1990); *Osman* (Zagreb, 1991).

A. Jensen, *Gundulić und sein 'Osman'* (Göteborg, 1990); V. Lozovina, 'Gundulić, the Poet of the Ragusan Republic', *SEER* 17 (1939), pp. 668–76; C. Hawkesworth, 'Gundulić's *Suze sina razmetnoga* as a Meditative Poem', *SEER*, 40 (1982), pp. 172–88.   ECH

GURAKUQI, Luigj (1879–1925), Albanian publicist and writer, was born in Shkodër, where, after having studied at the Saverian college, he began writing poetry in Italian, Latin and Albanian. 1897 he left for Italy to study at the college of San Demetrio Corone under DE RADA. He also studied medicine in Naples where he met Arbëresh (Italo-Albanian) literary and political figures. 1908 Gurakuqi returned to Albania and soon became involved in the movement which led to independence, 1912. He was Minister of Education in the first Albanian government, Minister of the Interior in 1921, and Minister of Finance in 1924 in the democratic government of NOLI. In the same year, however, the rise of the Zog dictatorship made him flee to Italy, where he was murdered by a Zog agent. Gurakuqi wrote mainly didactic works. His poetry was published in *Vjersha* (Verses, 1941).   ShM

GURAMISHVILI, Davit (1705–92), Georgian poet, made his life into one great cycle of autobiographical poetry, the *Davitiani*. In 1727/8 he was kidnapped by tribesmen from Daghestan who then prowled Tbilisi for hostages and slaves; he escaped and made his way on foot to Russia, following King VAKHT'ANG VI into exile. Serving as a Russian hussar, he was held by the Prussians in 1758 in Magdeburg; the rest of his life he spent as a landowner near Myrhorod, the sleepy Ukrainian town Gogol´ was to make famous, on the estate granted him by the Tsaritsa (like all the exiled Georgian nobles). Here he wrote poetry to lament, repent and console himself for the destruction of the Georgian state and his life. Some of his poems are psalm-like prayers (not for nothing was he called David); others are accounts of his captivity, such as *Davit Guramishvilis lek'tagan dat'q'oeba* (Davit Guramishvili's imprisonment by the Lezgi). His most substantial poems are chronicles in the section of the *Davitiani* called *Kartlis ch'iri* (Kartli's afflictions). They are historically valuable for the sparsely documented 1720s and 1730s, when VAKHT'ANG VI was forced to choose Russian patronage as an alternative to Persian genocide and endure exile and death in Astrakhan. The most attractive of Guramishvili's work is the end of the *Davitiani*, where he develops the pastoral and pseudo-folk modes of 18th-century France and Russia into witty, delicate interludes, many designed to be set to Russian music. *Zubovka* (the name of his village) is a classic song of dalliance with a reluctant peasant girl, while the cycle of poems *Katsvia-mts'q'emsi* (Katsvia the shepherd) forms a dream-like idyll, full of invented family life, wisdom and playful pathos, though undone by moralising bathos. Guramishvili's historical and autobiographical verses emulate the medieval RUSTAVELI *shairi* stanzas of 4 rhyming 16-syllable lines along the lines of King ARCHIL and Mamuk'a BARATASHVILI; once he explores the varying metres and dramatic plasticity of the fable form used by French and Russian pastoral poets, he develops a subtle colloquial flexibility which makes him the pioneer of modern Georgian poetry.   DR

GURRA, Milto Sotir (1884–1972), Albanian short-story writer and journalist, born in Opari in the Korçë region, S Albania, lived most of his life abroad, in Russia, Bulgaria and Roumania. There he contributed to the literary and patriotic Albanian press in exile, becoming the editor of several journals. Gurra is one of the first Albanian short-story writers. Among his early works are *Rrëfenja* (Tales, 1911) and *Goca e malcis* (The highland girl, 1912). His next volume, *Plagët e kurbetit* (The torments of exile, 1938), deals with emigration as a social evil and the sufferings of Albanian émigrés. Gurra is also among the first Albanian authors of translations from Russian literature.

ShM

GVADÁNYI, József (1725–1801), Hungarian poet and translator, pursued an unspectacular army career after a Jesuit education. Retiring as cavalier-general in 1783, he led the life of a scholarly country gentleman, reading widely and corresponding in fluent verse with friends. This idyll was wrecked by the reforms of Joseph II which prompted him to write his best-known narrative poem, *Egy falusi nótáriusnak budai utazása* (A village notary's journey to Buda, 1790). He directed his patriotic indignation against all foreign influences that threatened Hungarian life and institutions – though he excluded food and dancing. His eye for detail, satirical humour, simple style and forceful language combined to catch the mood of the age. The poem remained popular despite KAZIN-CZY's strictures and won the admiration of both PETŐFI and ARANY. Gvadányi's other works include *Pöstényi förödés . . .* (Bathing at Piešt'any,

1787), whose humour savours more of the barrack-room than the salon, and *Rontó Pálnak . . . és Gróf Benyovszki Móritznak életek* (The lives of Pál R. and Count Móritz B., 1793), the first Hungarian verse with a swashbuckling serf as its hero. Gvadányi was not unaffected by the foreign influences he deplored. He translated Voltaire's biography of Charles XII of Sweden (*Tizenkettődik Károly . . . élete* 1792), omitting passages of which he disapproved, and had translated six volumes of Millot's History of the World (1796–1814) by the time of his death.

●Excerpt from *Egy falusi nótárius* in W. Kirkconnell, *The Magyar Muse* (Winnipeg, 1933).   GFC

GYÖNGYÖSI, István (1629–1704), Hungarian poet, rich and well educated, spent his life in private or public legal service. Totally uncommitted in a turbulent age, he led a Vicar-of-Bray-like existence, rising to the heights of local administration while changing his faith and politics as required. As a poet he represents the height of Baroque elegance. He excels in narrative and occasional verse, of which the most popular was *Márssal társalkodó murányi Vénus* (The Venus of Murány in conversation with Mars, 1664). This relates the romantic yet true story of his patron, Ferenc Wesselényi (1601–67), and Mária Széchy, the beautiful commander of the fortress of Murány that he was besieging. The triumph of Venus over Mars was admirably suited to Baroque treatment. *Porábul megéledett Phoenix* (The Phoenix revived from its ashes, 1693) concerns the capture of János Kemény, later Prince of Transylvania, by the Tatars, while *Palinodia Prosopopoeia Hungariae* (1695) pictures the nymph of Hungary beseeching the Esterházy family for protection. Gyöngyösi also wrote a deeply devotional poem, *Rózsakoszorú* (Rosary, 1690), and is probably the author of *Csalárd Cupidó* (Deceptive Cupid, 1695), a warning against the excesses of love whose erotic visions excited generations of schoolboys as it circulated in manuscript for over two centuries. Gyöngyösi wrote for pleasure and succeeded; his verse is light, dynamic and abounds in closely observed detail. His technique is exquisite, with never a doubtful rhyme, false stress or misplaced caesura. He set standards for narrative poetry that ıwere recognised by the finest 19th-century epic poet ARANY. Moreover he was the first Hungarian poet to achieve popularity among the higher nobility.

●Excerpts from *The Venus of Murány* in T. Klaniczay (Ed.), *Old Hungarian Literary Reader* (Budapest, 1985) and in W. Kirkconnell (Ed.), *Hungarian Helicon* (Calgary, 1985) which also includes part of *The Phoenix Revived from its Ashes*. Definitive edition: F. Badics (Ed.), *Gyöngyösi István összes költeményei*, 4 vols, Budapest, 1914–37.

GFC

H

HAAVIKKO, Paavo (b. 1931), Finnish poet, novelist and playwright, is one of the most versatile and prolific poets of postwar Finland. The son of a Helsinki businessman, he went from secondary school in 1951 straight into business as an estate agent, later joining a Helsinki publishing house from which he retired 1983 as literary director. He continues to work in publishing as manager of his own company. The central themes of Haavikko's writing are power, inevitability and ephemerality, seen through the prism of ironical, questioning self-consciousness. His context is the past and present vicissitudes of Finland and its neighbours, concentrating mainly on recent history, but sometimes stretching back to the Middle Ages as in *Ratsumies* (The horseman, 1974) or *Harald pitkäikäinen* (H. the long-lived, 1974). His early works such as *Tuulöinä* (On windy nights, 1953) or *Synnyinmaa* (The land of birth, 1955) have often been compared to Eliot for their imagery and unexpected juxtapositions. The preoccupation with power, particularly in Finland's relationship with the USSR, recurs in numerous works either through allusion or allegory as in, for example, *Lasi Claudius Civiliksen salaliittolaisten pöydällä* (A glass on the table of Claudius Civilis's conspirators, 1964) or *Puut,* *kaikki heidän vihreytensä* (Trees, all their greenery, 1966). More recently he has focused on various conceptions of Finnish identity. In *Kansakunnan linja* (The nation's line, 1977), he writes of recent history, while his *Rauta-aika* (Age of iron, 1982) presents a new interpretation of themes from LÖNNROT's *Kalevala*. Yet Haavikko remains quintessentially universal in his approach. He 'has no consolations or solutions to offer, only problems and confusing clarifications: the unresolved problems and confusions. . . . Yet the enigma is not an unfamiliar one; it is the "fate" of the intellectual who is unable to think his society out of its delusions and into integrated experience.' (Lomas)

●*Selected Poems* (Manchester, 1991); *The Superintendent* (New York, 1973); *The Horseman* (Lahti, 1974).
R. Dauenhauer, 'The view from the aspen grove: Paavo Haavikko in national and international context' in R. Dauenhauer and P. Binham (Eds), *Snow in May. An Anthology of Finnish Writing 1945–1972* (London, 1978), pp. 67–97; P. Binham, 'The writer's dilemma', *Books from Finland* (1984), pp. 49–53; H. Lomas, 'Introduction' to Lomas (Ed.), *Contemporary Finnish Poetry* (Newcastle, 1991), pp. 31–6.

MAB

HÁJEK z LIBOČAN, Václav (d. 1553), Czech chronicler, a Utraquist priest, converted to R. Catholicism, became a preacher in Prague; thanks to the patronage of the R. Catholic nobility he was appointed dean but later deposed; his greed caused him many conflicts with the ecclesiastical and secular authorities. He was commissioned by his patrons to write a chronicle siding with the interests of the nobility against those of the towns. He was given full support from the state archives but his *Kronika česká* (Bohemian chronicle, 1541) is not reliable. In order to record events happening at a certain time and to glorify the aristocracy, he often invented documents, names and dates and, although fair to HUS, he distorted the history of the Hussite Wars. Nevertheless, in his account of Bohemian history from the arrival of the fabulous forefather Čech (which he fancifully dates as AD 644) down to his own time, Hájek mentions many important facts derived from literary sources now lost and from legends in the oral tradition. His chronicle, republished as late as 1819, was popular with the public at large. Hájek relates events in an absorbing way and his work served as a model and source for the Romantic historical prose of TYL and MÁCHA.   KB

HALAS, František (1901–49), Czech poet, son of a textile worker, had little formal education, worked in a bookshop, later in a publishing house and after WWII in the Ministry of Information. He was ostracised after the Communist take-over (1948) and died a broken man. The themes of his early poetry, collected in *Sepie* (Sepia/Squid, 1927), were according to him 'the world, my love, and revolution' and combined the inspiration of MÁCHA, VRCHLICKÝ, HLAVÁČEK, and NEZVAL's Poetism with 'revolu-

tionary ideas'. Such crude politics, however, conflicted with Halas's sensitivity and contemplative mind; he felt himself a passive observer of a process he was unable to influence. The scale of his feelings is marked out by a sense of futility, grief, death and nothingness, which are expressed, together with the desire to return to some lost paradise, in *Kohout plaší smrt* (The cockerel frightens death, 1930) and *Tvář* (The face, 1931). But like Baroque poets Halas does not reject reality; he is possessed by the desire to uncover what lies beyond and below it. He alternately believes and rejects in despair the idea that reality can be liberated by poetry, by the word dug out from the deepest strata of language. He arrives at a private mythology, cruel and desperate because devoid of religious faith and the possibility of divine mercy. After the Munich Agreement (1938) Halas endeavoured to express the collective soul of an undaunted nation in *Torso naděje* (A torso of hope, 1938) but as the title itself suggests, his faith in its strength was incomplete. In his last completed collection, *V řadě* (In line, 1948), his terror of nothingness crystallises into an apocalyptic vision of the end of the world, but one also notices a glint of reconciliation with the cosmic order.
● *Old Women* [*Staré ženy*, 1935] (London, 1947).   KB

HALPERN, Moyshe-Leyb (1886–1932), Yiddish poet, was born in Zolochev, E Galicia. After studying in Vienna, where he wrote German poetry, and participating in the Czernowitz Yiddish language conference, he emigrated to the USA 1908 and soon became associated with the group of poets known as Di Yunge (The Young Ones) who were challenging what they saw as the tendentious rhymestering of their predecessors. His first collection of poems, *In nyu york* (In New York, New York, 1919), was written very much under the aegis of the movement and brought him recognition as a major poet. 1923 he published in the Communist daily, *Di frayhayt* (Freedom), to which he was a regular contributor, what is perhaps his best-known poem, 'Zlotshev, mayn heym' (My home-town, Zolochev), which is contemptuous of misplaced nostalgia for the *shtetl*. It was later reprinted in his *Di goldene pave* (The golden peacock, Cleveland, Ohio, 1924). From the 1920s onwards he turned away from the Impressionist poetics of Di Yunge and gave increasingly original and abrasive expression to his inner conflicts. 1929 he became an editor of the *Di vokh* (The week), founded by a group of writers disillusioned by the party-line of *Di frayhayt*. His loosely structured late poems in the collection *Moyshe-leyb halpern* (New York, 1934) employ free association in an almost conversational tone to convey a mood of intense anguish.

•*TYP*, pp. 102–14; *AYP*, pp. 388–505; *PBMYV*, pp. 165–215.

Kathryn Hellerstein, in *Prooftexts* 7:3 (Baltimore, 1987), pp. 225–48; Ruth Wisse, *A Little Love in Big Manhattan* (Cambridge, Mass., 1988).   HD

HARECKI, Maksim (1893–1939), Byelorussian writer and author of the first serious history of Byelorussian literature (1920), played a key role in his country's cultural development. Born into a peasant family he became a university lecturer, but was exiled to Siberia in 1931 and, after a second arrest in 1937, died in unknown circumstances. His highly lyrical early collection of stories, *Ruń* (Spring shoots, 1914), displays mastery in a variety of genres from diaries and letters to folk-tales retold, innovative impressionistic miniatures and psychological studies. Many of them treat relations between the new intelligentsia and the backward, mistrustful, often hostile, peasantry whom they seek to help. Ambitious Dostoevskian 'psychologism', particularly in the use of dreams, marks the longer stories 'Anton' (1914) and 'Cichaja płyń' (A quiet current, 1918). Harecki's horror at the destruction of WWI, in which he was seriously wounded, is reflected in several powerful anti-war stories, of which 'Na impieryjalistyčnaj vajnie' (In the imperialist war, 1914–19) is the best known. A pivotal work, long suppressed for its overt nationalism, was the short novel *Dźvie dušy* (Two souls, 1919), showing the confused political situation in Byelorussia through a series of changing scenes, rich in atmosphere and local colour, combining great beauty with descriptions of brutality, epic breadth of vision and a concise almost lapidary style, as the indecisive central character meets representatives of different strata and factions in society. Amongst other post-revolutionary works, a collection of historical stories, *Dośvitki* (Before dawn, 1926) contains depictions of appalling cruelty that preclude Harecki's earlier lyricism. The semi-documentary *Vilenskie kamunary* (The Vilna communards, written 1930–31, publ. 1963) is far less wooden than most tales of revolutionaries, and *Kamaroŭskaja chronika* (The Kamaroŭka chronicle, written 1930–32, 1937, publ. 1966) depicts the lot of the peasantry over two centuries, somewhat in the manner of the old Byelorussian chronicles. Bridging the National Revival and the post-revolutionary era, Harecki was too individual a figure to escape persecution. His strong yet unfanatical beliefs, philosophical breadth, erudition, psychological insight, profound lyricism, and sophisticated mastery of language and form ensure his permanent place in Byelorussian literature. ABMcM

HARTWIG, Julia (b. 1921), Polish poet, essayist and translator, based in Warsaw and married to MIĘDZYRZECKI, has been widely recognised as, beside SZYMBORSKA, one of the leading woman poets of recent decades. She published her first collection in 1956 but it was not until *Wolne ręce* (Unconstrained hands, 1969) that she emerged as a strong, individual voice. In particular, her latest collection, *Obcowanie* (Relations, 1987), shows her as a poet fascinated by the inevitable imperfection of human being.

•Selected poems in S. Barańczak and C. Cavanagh (Eds), *Polish Poetry of the Last Two Decades of Communist Rule: Spoiling the Cannibals' Fun* (Evanston, Ill., 1991). StB

HARUN, Aleś (i.e. Alaksandr Prušynski, 1887–1920), Byelorussian poet, story writer and dramatist, was exiled under the Tsars and his work was for many years banned by the Soviets. Born in Minsk into an impoverished but culturally aware branch of the minor nobility, he was sent to Siberia for socialist activity in 1908, returning only in 1917 when he chose Poland rather than Russia as the more likely defender of Byelorussian independence. In 1914, still in Siberia, he sent his only collection of verse, *Matčyn dar* (A mother's gift), to the *Naša niva* newspaper in Vilna, where it finally appeared in 1918 during the brief period of the Byelorussian National Republic. This slim volume, which was first reprinted in Byelorussia only in 1988, shows Harun to be a major lyric poet. Largely self-taught, he writes with an instinctive grasp of the richness of the Byelorussian lexicon and of the possibilities of metrical and strophic variation, at times handled with great virtuosity, e.g. in 'Zaviarucha' (Snowstorm). *Matčyn dar* contains many poems idealising (from afar) the beauties of the Byelorussian countryside, and emphasising the independence of the language and its users; some other poems are tinged with gloom, but Harun's faith in Byelorussia's future is constant. Highly lyrical, he rarely writes only about personal feeling, and he transmits his search for social and national justice often in the form of apostrophe, questions, dialogues and monologues. Folk imagery is widespread, and several poems are folk stylisations. The language of Harun's poems is exuberantly flexible and musical; rhyme and rhythm alike are used with bold and subtle freshness. Harun's unperformed drama comprises a number of delicately written children's plays. His prose (written under the pen-name of I. Žyvica), though exiguous, is of fine quality, both in traditional subjects such as *P'ero i Kałambina* (Pierrot and Colombine, 1918) and in wry yet socially acerbic contemporary stories like *Pan Šabunievič* (Mr Š., c. 1918). Harun is important mainly for the spontaneity, originality and dynamism of his untutored poetry, whose richness and variety were to influence contemporary and subsequent writers.

•A. B. McMillin (Ed.), *The Images Swarm Free: A Bilingual Selection of Poetry by Maksim Bahdanovič, Aleś Harun and Žmitrok Biadula* (London, 1982).

A. B. McMillin, *A History of Byelorussian Literature from Its Origins to the Present Day* (Giessen, 1977), pp. 161–74. ABMcM

HAŠEK, Jaroslav (1883–1923), Czech writer, author of some 1,500 short stories and *feuilletons*, after a short period as a bank clerk, was 1903 an established member of Prague anarchist circles. 1915 he was called up, promoted, won a medal, and became a Russian POW. He fought with the Czecho-Slovak Legion, won another medal, and eventually became teetotal and joined the Red Army. He returned to Prague and hard drinking in December 1920. His pre-1915 short stories and *feuilletons* are superior in skill and discipline to almost anything he wrote later. His best-known work, *Osudy dobrého vojáka Švejka za světové války* (The fortunes of the good soldier Švejk in the Great War, 1921–23), has a dull narrative framework, but vivid comic dialogue and skilfully manipulated anecdotes. The character, Švejk, has three versions. In *Dobrý voják Švejk a jiné podivné historky* (The good soldier Š. and other strange tales, 1911) he is a benign fellow of indestructible optimism; in the somewhat vicious, contemptuous novel *Dobrý voják Švejk v zajetí* (The good soldier Š. in captivity, 1917) he is more of a holy fool; in the picaresque *Osudy* Švejk is an inconsistent character, so inconsistent that he is hardly human, but he is probably unhuman rather than inhuman. He is a bully, a cunning fool and verges on amorality. He is a new mythic type in European literature. The vulgarity of *Osudy* lies not in the language of the narrative or the dialogue, but in the author's utter materialism; nevertheless Hašek's dehumanisation of humanity is so persuasively prosecuted that it beguiles.

•*The Good Soldier Švejk and His Fortunes in the World War* (London, 1973); *The Red Commissar, Including Further Adventures of the Good Soldier Švejk and Other Stories* (London, 1981); *The Bachura Scandal and Other Stories and Sketches* (London, 1991). C. Parrott, *The Bad Bohemian. The Life of Jaroslav Hašek* (London 1978); C. Parrott, *Jaroslav Hašek. A Study of Švejk and the Short Stories* (London, 1982); R. B. Pynsent, 'Jaroslav Hašek (1883–1923)' in G. Stade (Ed.), *European Writers. The Twentieth Century*, vol. 9 (New York, 1989), pp. 1091–1118. RBP

HATZOPOULOS, Konstandinos (1868–1920), Greek poet and prose writer, was the youngest of five in a poor family. The deprivation of his early life turned him into a nervous and reclusive child, so his parents, to get him the chance in life which his temperament and gifts warranted, allowed a rich childless couple to adopt him. Thus he was able to complete his education, and to qualify as a lawyer. 1898 he brought out his first two collections of poetry, Τραγούδια της ερημίας (Songs of solitude) and Τα ελεγεία και τα ειδύλλια (Elegies and idylls), under the pseudonym Petros Vasilikos. Already the main themes of his mature writing dominate: pain, sorrow, loss and isolation, motifs of night, dark, winter, tears, shadows and dreams. He also revealed here a preference for short lines, carefully crafted stanzas, great attention to musical effect, and an overall sense of the intangible and imprecise. 1900 he went to Germany, where he came under the influence of a wide range of German and Scandinavian ideas, not least those of the Socialist movement which he wished to promote in Greece in connection with the linguistic renewal of demoticism. Hence his founding (Munich, 1909) of the Socialist Demoticist Union, his translation of the Communist Manifesto into Greek (1909) and his numerous articles and essays on social issues of the period 1909–15. His early novelle, Αγάπη στο χωριό (Love in the village, 1910) and Ο Πύργος του Ακροποτάμου (The tower of Akropotamos, 1915), are ethographical works with a strong element of social ideology. Ο Υπεράνθρωπος (The superman, 1916) satirises the blind, egotistical absorption of fashionable Western ideas. His most original novel is his last, Φθινόπωρο (Autumn, 1917), a psychological study of an emotional relationship which transfers the motifs of his poetry into prose, exploring the emptiness of aimless lives through a pattern of symbols which creates a mood and suggests slight shifts of feeling. 1920 he published his final collections of poetry, Απλοί τρόποι (Simple ways) and Βραδυνοί θρύλοι (Evening legends), works which echo the mental world of the characters of 'Autumn' and represent an intensification, rather than a development, of his earlier poetic style.   CFR

HAVEL, Václav (b. 1936), Czech essayist and playwright, born into a rich entrepreneurial family and brought up under socialism, has always (until c. 1991) felt an outsider. Because of his background, he had to do both his school-leaving certificate and his degree externally. He entered Prague theatre life as a stage-hand in 1959; by the mid-1960s he was literary adviser of the main avant-garde theatre. From March 1969 to October 1989, he was the subject of secret-police persecution and was frequently imprisoned for periods be-

tween two days and nearly four years. By the mid-1970s he had become the leading Czech dissident. At the end of 1976 he co-founded the Czechoslovak civil rights movement, Charter 77. His imprisonment in January 1989 sparked off the first mass reaction against Communism in Czechoslovakia. After Prague students had forced dissidence into overt opposition in November 1989, he became the main spokesman for the ad hoc political assembly, Civil Forum, and December 1989 he became president of Czechoslovakia; he resigned July 1992. The main theme of his writing is humankind's subjugation to technology and ideology; man's spiritual and emotional worlds are being smothered by socialism and consumerism. He looks for a society whose goal is the transcendental, not the material. From his beginnings he is concerned with the power of the word, with (contaminated) language as a force of manipulation and alienation, language as something that conceals personal identity. That identity is coterminous with responsibility. Socialism and consumerism strive to prevent the transcendence of the self. Eastern 'socialism' and Western 'capitalism' are equally arid, devoid of the spiritual. His first plays, *Zahradní slavnost* (The garden party, 1964) and *Vyrozumění* (The memorandum, 1966), concern linguistic manipulation; his 'Faustus' *Pokoušení* (Temptation, 1986) concerns the danger of coming to any compromise with evil forces, spiritual or political. The most popular of his plays, the one-act *Audience* (1977), and *Ztížená možnost soustředění* (The increased difficulty of concentration, 1969), discuss the loss of identity or the interchangeability of personalities. In his essays he demonstrates an ability for precise political thinking. A great deal of perceptive irony is evident in *O lidskou identitu* (Towards human identity, 1984), where Havel's main ideas, responsibility, God, the devastation of consumer society, are first fully developed. In the essayistic prison-letters, *Dopisy Olze* (Letters to Olga, 1985), his conception of human identity is based on responsibility, on the essentiality of the spiritual and of the danger of indifference or resignation. His autobiographical 'conversation', based by his interviewer on the first Czechoslovak president's conversations with K. ČAPEK, *Dálkový výslech* (Long-distance interrogation, 1986), combine a certain self-importance with self-irony, but by his 1980s essays, *Do různých stran* (In various directions, 1989), one hears mainly the politician speaking, but still a politician in search of the spiritual. His essays, *Letní přemítání* (Summer musings, 1991), display a mind diminished into tediousness by state responsibility.

•*The Garden Party* (London, 1969); *Sorry . . . Two Plays* (London, 1978); *Temptation* (London, 1988); *The Power of the Powerless* (London, 1985).
P. I. Trensky, *Czech Drama since World War II* (White Plains, NY, 1978); M. Goetz-Stankiewicz, *The Silenced Theatre* (Toronto, 1979); J. Vladislav, *Václav Havel, or: Living in Truth. Twenty-two Essays . . .* [by and on Havel] (London, 1987).   RBP

HAVLÍČEK BOROVSKÝ, Karel (1821–56), Czech poet and publicist, became enthusiastic about KOLLÁR's ideas before he started studying at a seminary, from which he was expelled for 'Panslavism' (1841). His Slav interests took him, first, on a journey to Slovakia and Galicia and then

1843 he arrived in Russia. By the time he left (1844), he was cured of Panslav ideas. 1846 he became editor of the main Prague newspaper; 1848 he founded his own *Národní noviny* (National news); when that was banned (1850), he founded the weekly *Slovan* (The Slav, banned 1851). He was arrested and sent into internal exile in Brixen (Bressanone), from which he was released in 1855. A R. Catholic liberal, he demonstrated an incisive analytical mind in his anti-clerical, anti-Communist, anti-Panslavist journalism, where he supported social, religious and national tolerance, constitutional monarchy, federalism (Austro-Slavism), the use of the vernacular in the liturgy, the Irish struggle against the British. He bewails modern civilisation's tendency to alienate individuals and nations, the Czechs' servility and lack of national pride, Slovak linguistic separatism, clerical celibacy, and the size of the bureaucracy. His satirical epic poems, *Křest svatého Vladimíra* (The baptism of St Vladimir, 1876), *Tyrolské elegie* (Tyrolean elegies, 1861) and *Král Lávra* (King L., 1870), combine factual accuracy with grotesque deformation, mordant humour with compassionate warmth, mockery with empathy. Havlíček's influence on Czech political thinking is still alive today.

•*The Conversion of St Vladimir* (Cleveland, Ohio, 1930); 'The Danger of pan-Slavism' in H. Kohn, *Nationalism, its Meaning and History* (Princeton, 1955).
M. H. Heim, *The Russian Journey of Karel Havlíček* (Munich, 1979); B. K. Reinfeld, *Karel Havlíček (1821–1856). A National Liberation Leader of the Czech Renascence* (Boulder, Col., 1982); J. Herben, 'Karel Havlíček', *Slavonic Review* (1924–5), pp. 285–303.
                                                       RBP

HEČKO, František (1905–60), Slovak novelist, studied viticulture and fruit growing, worked in the head office of the Agricultural Cooperatives in Bratislava and as a publicist. In his novel *Červené víno* (Red wine, 1948), a chronicle of three generations in a village in W Slovakia during WWI and the Slump in the First Republic, he proves himself an able story-teller and psychologist and manifests an ironic sense of humour. *Drevená dedina* (The wooden village, 1951) describes from the Communist standpoint life in a poor village during collectivisation and the introduction of Socialism. His *Svätá tma* (Holy darkness, 1958), a semi-documentary novel dealing with the 1939–45 puppet Slovak State, was written in a similar Socialist Realist vein.   KB

HEKTOROVIĆ, Petar (1487–1572), Croatian poet, from the island of Hvar, born into a noble family, experienced two peasant uprisings (1510 and 1514) and two incursions of the Turks on to the island (1539, when his family took refuge in Italy, and 1571). Like many other poets of his time, Hektorović wrote love poetry in his youth which he later spurned and probably himself destroyed, turning to more spiritual themes. His first extant work is a free translation of Ovid's *Remedium amoris* (1528). Several verse epistles to established writers remain, suggesting that writers in different centres on the Dalmatian coast maintained active contact with one another. Hektorović's most important work also takes the form of an epistle: *Ribanje i ribarsko prigovaranje* (Fishing and fishermen's conversation, 1568) is a narrative poem, describing a three-day fishing trip which the poet made in the company of two fishermen from Starigrad. At one level, the poem is loosely based on the eclogue convention, to the extent that the fishermen entertain the poet with witty conversation, riddles and song. Growing out of Hektorović's personal experience of civil strife, it is a plea for his fellow nobles to recognise the worth of the common people both with the public purpose of urging all Christian peoples to unite against the Turks, and with the deeper personal, religious, aim of asserting the value of each individual regardless of birth in the eyes of God. The narrative reveals Hektorović's capacity to delight in new knowledge: he describes the fishing expedition in detail, evidently taking particular pleasure in the paraphernalia of the fishing itself, and listing the names of the different breeds of fish. When the fishermen entertain him with songs sung 'in the Serbian style', Hektorović is at pains to note down words and melody accurately, thus providing the earliest faithful record of traditional epic songs.

●'Fishing and Fishermen's Conversation', *BC Review*, 15 (1979), 13–46.
R. Bogišić, 'Marin Držić', *The Bridge*, 11 (1968), pp. 99–104; J. Teutschmann, *Petar Hektorović (1487–1572) und sein 'Ribanje i ribarsko prigovaranje'* (Vienna, 1971).   ECH

HELTAI, Gáspár (?–1574), Transylvanian Protestant pastor, writer and publisher, was born Caspar Helth. Of Transylvanian German stock, he learnt Hungarian only in 1536 and from 1551 wrote exclusively in that language. He became a leading figure in the Reformation, embracing the Lutheran, Calvinist and Unitarian creeds in turn. 1550 he established a successful press with his partner Georg Hoffgreff (dates unknown) in

Kolozsvár(Cluj); from 1555 he managed it alone and also set up a paper-mill to supply it. Heltai's works and his press were intended chiefly to serve the cause of the Reformation. He translated from Latin and German and began to publish a complete BIBLE, of which he was the editor. His *Száz fabula* (One hundred fables, 1566), though based on Aesop, are adapted to the morals of his time and include a fable of his own. *Háló* (The net, 1570) reveals the torments to which Protestants are subject in R. Catholic lands. Heltai also freely adapted and published *Die sieben wiesen Meister* (Frankfurt on Main, 1565) as *Ponciánus császár históriája* (The story of the Emperor Poncianus, 1572?); this is the earliest collection of short stories in Hungarian. His Hungarian version of Antonio Bonfini's Latin history, *Krónika az magyaroknak dolgairól* (Chronicle of the deeds of the Hungarians, 1575), was published by his widow. Heltai was no slavish translator. He discarded whatever did not suit his purpose and added anecdotes of his own. So Bonfini's staid Latin work becomes a lively and often humorous novelistic account of the Hungarians. His elegant style and lightness of touch brought him popularity and his press profitability. With BORNE-MISZA he represents the best of 16th-century prose in Hungary.

•Translation: his original fable in T. Klaniczay (Ed.), *Old Hungarian Literary Reader* (Budapest, 1985). GFC

HERBERT, Zbigniew (b. 1924), Polish poet, playwright and essayist, born in Lwów, during the Soviet and subsequently the German occupation of that city studied at a clandestine university and took part in Home Army resistance. Lwów having become part of the USSR with the end of war, he moved to Cracow, and in 1950 to Warsaw. At the universities of Cracow, Toruń and Warsaw he attended courses on philosophy and art history, but his main subjects were law and economics. In the late 1940s he published several poems but in the early 1950s, unable to conform to the dictates of Socialist Realism, wrote 'for his desk drawer' while having ill-paid jobs and living in straitened circumstances. His situation changed dramatically with the beginning of the Thaw in politics and culture. 1956 marks the publication of his first collection, *Struna światła* (Chord of light). His next volumes, *Hermes, pies i gwiazda* (Hermes, a dog, and a star, 1957) and *Studium przedmiotu* (Study of the object, 1961), brought him international recognition. 1960 he visited Italy and France; this first trip abroad resulted in the publication 1962 of a collection of essays on Mediterranean history and culture, *Barbarzyńca w ogrodzie* (Barbarian in the garden). 1969 his poems, *Napis* (Inscription), appeared, and 1970 a collection of short plays (mostly written for radio). A new phase in his development was ushered in by the volume *Pan Cogito* (Mr C., 1974) introducing Herbert's persona, Mr Cogito, who was to play an increasingly important role in his subsequent work. In the 1970s Herbert lived mostly in the West but he returned to Warsaw after the 1980 triumph of Solidarity and in December 1981 witnessed the imposition of martial law. His reflections on the latter are the matter of *Raport z oblężonego miasta* (Report from the besieged city, 1983), the first book he issued in an émigré press. His latest poems have appeared as *Elegia na odejście* (Elegy for the departure, 1990). Though Herbert is often interpreted as a stoical Neoclassicist, he is in fact a profoundly tragic poet torn between two sets of contradictory values: between the past and the present, the Western heritage and Poland's specific ordeal, myth and history, culture and tangible experience. The first of these sets of values is the heritage from which we have been dispossessed but to which we lay claim; the second is the lot which has befallen us regardless of our will but which cannot be simply dismissed or rejected. Therefore Herbert's Mr Cogito is always split, suspended between opposing values – but he finds a solution in the irony that helps him preserve a distance from his own misery. Irony, however, does not preclude in Herbert a moralistic stance, the call to maintain an 'upright attitude', to remain faithful to imponderable principles. An apparently hopeless defence of the 'besieged city' of human values is for him a mission that must not be abandoned under any circumstances.

•*Selected Poems* (New York, 1986); *Report from the Besieged City and other poems* (New York, 1985); *Barbarian in the Garden* (essays; Manchester, 1985). S. Barańczak, *A Fugitive from Utopia* (Cambridge, Mass., 1987).   StB

HERLING-GRUDZIŃSKI, Gustaw (b. 1919), Polish writer, after two years in Soviet prisons and labour camps joined the Polish Army of Gen. Anders and subsequently distinguished himself in the Battle of Monte Cassino. Grudziński eventually settled in Naples, collaborating with the Paris-based Polish émigré periodical *Kultura*. Grudziński's most distinguished work is the description of the Soviet Gulag, *Inny świat* (Another world, 1953), which first appeared in English translation, with an introduction by Bertrand Russell. Penetrating psychology, a moralistic approach and the humanitarian attitude towards the prisoners, irrespective of their nationality, make this book comparable to Solzhenitsyn's gulag works. Grudziński has also published allegorical short stories, essays and literary criticism.

•*A World Apart* (London, 1951).   SE

HERRMANN, Ignát (1854–1935), Czech novelist, started his working life as a shopkeeper's apprentice (1871), published his first comic short story 1873, but remained in clerical jobs, even when in his first minor literary post, until 1885, when he joined the editorial board of the leading newspaper, *Národní listy* (National mail). From then on he supported himself entirely by writing. His first novel, *U sněděného krámu* (Eaten out of shop and home, 1890), though marred by the over-detailed social topography of the first quarter, is a masterpiece of Realism. An ironic tragedy, it constitutes the aetiology of a suicide: the gullible, ambitious little shopkeeper kills himself, not because his shop fails, but because he has failed as a man. By far the most popular of Herrmann's novels are his affectionate satires on petty bourgeois life, *Otec Kondelík a ženich Vejvara* (Father K. and V. betrothed, 1898) and the slightly more superficial *Tchán Kondelík a zet' Vejvara* (Father-in-law K. and son-in-law V., 1906). Some of Herrmann's cleverest comic writing and keenest social satire is to be found in short-story collections like *Foxl-Voříšek a jiné historky kratochvilné* (The fox-terrier and other entertaining tales, 1912).

•'Childless' in B. H. Clark (Ed.), *Great Short Novels of the World* (New York, 1927).   RBP

HILBERT, Jaroslav (1871–1936),

Czech dramatist, after studying mechanical engineering worked in industry but later devoted himself entirely to literature. His chief model was Ibsen whom he visited as a young man to discuss the mission of the dramatist in the contemporary world. All his dramas are concerned with principles of justice and moral responsibility, and reject relativism and Positivism. The characters of his early dramas are women in conflict with convention, be it social or religious. The sensitive Mína in *Vina* (Guilt, 1896), who has been seduced in adolescence, cannot liberate herself from guilt and responsibility, and commits suicide. The drama *O Boha* (Of God and men, 1897), which was banned as blasphemous and not performed until 1905 under the title *Pěst* (The fist), depicts the torments of a religious and bigoted mother who, after the death of her young son, bargains in vain with God for the life of her small daughter, and finally rejects and curses Him. The dramas of Hilbert's middle period portray strong, Nietzschean individuals fighting against incomprehension and hatred. In *Falkenštejn* (1903) the eponymous hero, regent of Bohemia in the 13th century, is thwarted in his dream of making Bohemia strong, and in *Kolumbus* (1915) the hero, whose ship is for him a symbol of freedom and manliness, dies in prison when he realises that he has been robbed of greatness. Moral and religious problems predominate in Hilbert's trilogy, *Druhý břeh* (The other side, 1924), *Prapor lidstva* (The flag of mankind, 1926) and *Job* (1928). Hilbert was neither an original thinker nor a psychologist but his usually well-constructed plays sustain dramatic tension and use succint dialogue in somewhat stylised language.   KB

HLAVÁČEK, Karel (1874–98), Czech poet, graphic artist and essayist, began (1891) reading modern languages at Prague but never finished. After military service in Trent (1895–6) he returned to Prague with consumption. From his schooldays on he was keenly involved in the nationalist gymnastic movement, Sokol, and his interest in the Sokol never waned. Indeed his first collection of verse (1895) was primarily concerned with the Sokol and he continued to write manuals and essays on the joys of physical jerks almost till his death. At the same time he was the most imaginative Czech Decadent poet; his life thus embodied that ironic tension between vitalism and a delight in the macabre which characterises Decadence. Hlaváček's impressionist art criticism constitutes some of the most colourful prose of the period. His second collection of verse, *Pozdě k ránu* (The small hours, 1896), consists in a series of moods, autostylisations, depictions of intermediate states, but the poet is still not sure where he stands; in style he varies from the traditional to the 'new' (here Verlaine's influence is strongest), from the almost folksy to a delicately contrived rococo. His last, uncompleted, collection, *Žalmy* (Psalms, 1934), presents a dying man's self-ironic striving for mystical union with God, of whose existence he is uncertain. Hlaváček's masterpiece is the cycle, *Mstivá kantilena* (Cantilena of revenge, 1898), where he uses the histories of the Gueux's rebellion against the Spanish and of the Anabaptist state of Münster, and the figure of Manon Lescaut, to recount in a series of usually ironic pictures the fate of a rebellion doomed to fail from the beginning. He exploits the acoustic qualities of Czech like no one since MÁCHA, and creates an artefact of great aesthetic effectiveness to describe mostly ugliness and frustration. The only satisfied figure is the rat merchant who uses the Gueux's symbolic fox-tail hat to tie up his gaunt, sweaty nag as he buys his nudicaudate goods.

•R. B. Pynsent (Ed.), *Decadence and Innovation* (London, 1989).   RBP

HODROVÁ, Daniela (b. 1946), Czech novelist and literary critic, read French, Russian and comparative literature at Prague, worked as a publisher's editor, and then in the Institute of Literature at the Academy of Sciences. Her grossly abbreviated or censored work of literary theory, *Hledání románu* (The search for the novel, 1989), produces a persuasive taxonomy of the novel from the chivalrous romance and epic to the present. (A critic has suggested that *Hledání* is a conscious anagram of 'Daniela H.') Her main interest lies in novels of initiation and the novel as labyrinth, and her own first novel, the second part of an as yet incompletely published trilogy, *Kukly (Živé obrazy)* (polysemic title: Pupae/Masks. Tableaux vivants/Vivid pictures, 1991), is a labyrinthine work concerning initiation into being. Composed with cerebral precision, it constitutes a long prose poem on man's helplessness before Fate, on violence, death and love. Emotional, but never sentimentalised, analytical, but never cold, its verbal and factual associative technique makes for a statement on the associativeness of all our emotional or sensuous life. The main pair of eyes or sense of being that guides the reader through the labyrinths of Prague and of human perception is Sofie Syslová whose name embodies mystical wisdom (Sophia) and earthly, even earthy, knowledge (the suslik, ground-squirrel). *Kukly* is an erudite, ironic experiment in literary metempsychosis. The first part of the trilogy, *Podobojí* (In both kinds), was published at the end of 1991. As labyrinthine as *Kukly*, it introduces some of the characters in the latter, and sets the mood, since here the living coexist with the dead, and some characters appear first as living beings and then as souls. Violence and death play an ironic role in this work which studies maturation and 'Czechness', national mythopoeia and political opportunism. It is also a ludic spiritual analysis of oppression, particularly during the first years of the Soviet occupation of Czechoslovakia. She has also published a guidebook-cum-autobiography in French, *Visite privée – Prague* (Paris, 1991), published 1992 in a fuller version as *Město vidím . . .* (I see a city) in a Slovak peridical.   RBP

HOLAN, Vladimír (1905–80), Czech poet, publicist and translator, worked for seven years as a clerk at the State Pensions Office and then became a freelance writer. His first collection, *Blouznivý vějíř* (Delirious fanning, 1926), was influenced by Poetism, but in *Triumf smrti* (The triumph of Death, 1936), inspired by Mallarmé, Rilke and Valéry, he began a quest for 'pure poetry', intensified in *Vanutí* (Wafting, 1932) and *Kameni, přicházíš . . .* (Stone, you are coming . . ., 1937), where he endeavours to reproduce spiritual reality in artificial verbal constructs. In order to record the inner, non-material essence of being, he suppresses sensual perception and chooses a method of poetic expression which disregards the spontaneous flow of associations as well as rhythm and melody. His striving for a cold, cerebral statement encoded in a highly personal system of signs resulted in the violation of both linguistic and poetic norms. Holan uses neologisms, obsolete, recondite and deformed expressions; he distorts syntax and introduces cryptic metaphors. Just before WWII Holan turned to more conventional poetics in *Září 1938* (September 1938, 1938), an impassioned protest against the dismemberment of Czechoslovakia, and later wrote two lyrico-epic poems, *Terezka Planetová* (1943) and *Cesta mraku* (The journey of a cloud, 1945), stories of simple village characters. After WWII he paid homage to the Red Army in *Rudoarmějci* (Red Army soldiers, 1947), and his *Tobě* (To you, 1947) is an incongruous collection of poems remembering his dead friends, portraying people involved in the 1945 Prague Uprising and protesting against the injustice of the imperialists and the Naziphilia of Pope Pius XII. Holan turned to reflective verse in his *Noc s Hamletem* (Night with Hamlet, 1964), trying to reconcile the conflicts in the drama of human existence.

•*Selected Poems* (Harmondsworth, 1971); *A Night with Hamlet*, (London, 1980); *Mirroring: selected poems* (Middletown, Conn., 1985).   KB

HOLLÝ, Ján (1785–1849), Slovak poet, R. Catholic priest, translated a wide range of Greek and Latin poetry into the Slovak evolved by BERNOLÁK and, inspired by Homer's *Iliad*, composed epics on themes from the 9th-century Great Moravian Empire. These extol the assumed virtues of the Slavs and mythologise their scantily documented history in a KOLLÁR manner. In *Svatopluk* (1833), the historical figure of the ruler of Great Moravia (c. 870–94) is presented as sovereign of a powerful empire and propagator of Christianity. A strong Graeco-Roman influence is apparent both in the narration of the strife between the gods and people and in the form which eschews rhyme and uses Classical syllabic metre. Hollý's more sober and less mythopoeic *Cyrilo-Methodiada* (Legend of Cyril and Methodius, 1835) relates the missionary work of these two brothers. In the journal *Zora* (1835–40) Hollý published *Selanky* (Idylls), inspired by Virgil and painting an idealised picture of Slovak life, and *Žalospevy a Ódy* (Elegies and odes) express the grief of Slovak submission and Slav discord.   KB

HOLUB, Miroslav (b. 1923), Czech poet and essayist, an immunologist, writes cool, intellectual poems, inspired by everyday practical experience, ethical reflections on contemporary civilisation and those who sustain it by their work. His attitude to reality with its conflicts and paradoxes is benevolent but in many volumes of verse, such as *Achilles a želva* (Achilles and the tortoise, 1960) and *Naopak* (On the contrary, 1981), optimism alternates with irony and scepticism. His verse is unique in its rapprochement of poetry with science and he has analysed their relationship in several essays.

•*On the Contrary and Other Poems* (London, 1984); *The Fly* (London, 1984); *The Dimension of the Present Moment and Other Essays* (London, 1990).

E. Morgan (Ed.), *East European Poets* (Milton Keynes, 1976).   KB

HONCHAR, Oles (b. 1918), Ukrainian novelist, 1946–8 published *Praporonostsi* (Standard-bearers), dealing with WWII. His *Liudyna i zbroia*

(Man and arms, 1959) devoted to war is, in the words of an official critic, 'a portrayal in which the horror and evil of war are contrasted with the invincible force of humanity, encouraged by the socialist way of life'. 1968, in a different atmosphere, Honchar published his novel *Sobor* (The cathedral) concerning the historical awareness among some Soviet citizens whose small town is dominated by an ancient Cossack church. Honchar was vehemently criticised and the novel was banned. During the era of *glasnost* Honchar was in the forefront of the struggle for cultural and human rights.

●*Short Stories* (Moscow, 1960); *Standard-Bearers* (Moscow, 1948–50); *The Cathedral* (Washington, 1989). Ie. Sverstiuk, 'A Cathedral in Scaffolding' in *Clandestine Essays* (Littleton, 1976).   GSNL

HORA, Josef (1891–1945), Czech poet and novelist, born in a peasant family, studied law but became a journalist. Inspired by Vitalism, Hora reveals his love for life and its creative fire in his *Strom v květu* (A tree in blossom, 1920), but his enchantment was marred by the awareness of social injustice. Associating himself with the younger WOLKER generation, he joined the Communist Party and with *Pracující den* (Working day, 1920) turned to Proletarian Poetry because he longed for a fuller life, not because he wanted the end of capitalism; he greeted revolution as a necessary evil, the realisation of an ethical ideal. However, the conflict between his Unanimism and the constraints of tendentious verse led him to retreat to his former Vitalist lyricism in *Itálie* (Italy, 1925) and *Struny ve větru* (Strings in the wind, 1927) and 1929 he was expelled from the Party. These collections contain mo-

tifs which he treated right up to his death – memory, dreams, silence, solitude and above all a concept of time, half metaphysical and half material, which became 'the brother of the poet's heart'. In his lyrico-epic poems written just before or during WWII, *Jan Houslista* (The violinist J., 1939), the story of a musician returning from America to his spiritual roots in Bohemia, and *Zahrada Popelčina* (Cinderella's garden, 1940), Hora has liberated himself from his earlier emotionalism and meditating and, in a simple, melodious language, approaches transcendental verse. In his last collection *Zápisky z nemoci* (Notes from the sickbed, 1945) he speaks simply of his sickness in the midst of the suffering of mankind and expresses humble devotion to life.   KB

HORÁK, Jozef (1907–74), Slovak novelist, who spent most of his life as a village schoolmaster, is best known for his historical novels, of which *Zlaté mesto* (City of gold, 1942, rev. ed. 1967) is typical. It describes the life of German settler families, *Waldbürger*, mainly in the 16th century; a family whose mining fortune had been gradually building up since 1268 now declines and is ruined, largely thanks to the Turkish threat and to the manipulation of upstarts and corrupt businessmen. The nationalist suggestion is, however, that the representative family, the Rössels, have to be ruined because they are not Slovaks; their hereditary blood disease results from their being parted from their *Heimat* in Germany. Horák's most accomplished work, *Hory mlčia* (The mountain forests are silent, 1947), describes apolitically the impact of war after the German occupation (1944) on a hill-farming community which had never heard of

partisans or the Slovak National Uprising. The novel's title refers to Nature's silence to anti-natural German
brutality and to the violence it calls
forth in Nature's own people, the
hill-farmers. The main character,
Bartko, represents the stable, honourable life and institutions now destroyed by the Germans.   RBP

HORÁK, Karol (b. 1943), Slovak
prose writer and dramatist, read Slovak and Russian at Prešov, and then
taught Slovak literature at the same
university. The action of his lyrical
novel *Cukor* (Sugar, 1977), set just
after WWII, lies more in its language
and style than in the episodes it
relates. It is a novel in pursuit of
historical veracity, a pursuit represented by a woman's toilsome journey on foot to find sugar for her
pregnant daughter. *Súpis dravcov*
(List of predators, 1979) consists of
two pieces of comic, often satirical,
experimental prose concerning language, the extent to which language
can create reality and reality dispense
with language. The play *Medzi-
vojnový muž* (Interwar man, 1985),
is a grotesque satire on the military,
on the misuse of chemicals, on Slovak
culture, on nationalism and national
feeling altogether.
●R. B. Pynsent (Ed.), *Modern Slovak
Prose: Fiction Since 1954* (London,
1990).   RBP

HORTATSIS, Yorgos (late 16th and
early 17th centuries), Cretan playwright from Rethimnon, was probably a bilingual member of the upper
bourgeoisie: the fact that he obtained
the patronage of distinguished Venetian landowners for his plays indicates that he moved in high society.
He might possibly be identified with
one Yiorgos Yianni Hortatsis (c.
1545–1610), secretary to the influential soldier and diplomat Matteo

Calergi 1565–71. He wrote a tragedy, Ερωφίλη (Erofili, completed
after 1590), an urban comedy,
Κατζούρμπος (Katzourbos, possibly alternatively entitled Katzar-
opos, apparently completed between
1594 and 1601), and a pastoral comedy, Πανώρια (Panoria, formerly
known as Yiparis, also completed
after 1590). The dating of the plays
depends on internal evidence. Hortatsis has also been credited with the
anonymous Cretan comedy Στάθης
(Stathis) and is considered by some as
the possible author of the dozen
Cretan interludes found with early
texts of his plays. *Erofili* is a classical
tragedy influenced by Giraldi's *Or-
becche*, and its plot is marked by the
bizarre bloodthirstiness characteristic of the period. Erofili, daughter of
King Filogonos, is secretly married
to a brave young general, Panaretos.
Her cruel father, on learning of the
marriage, kills Panaretos and sends
severed parts of the body to the
princess under the guise of a marriage
gift. She commits suicide but her
death is revenged by the chorus of
maidens, who kill the king. The play
contains effective dramatic confrontations and is remarkable for the
quality of its lyrical writing, notably
in the choruses and in the final lament
of Erofili. *Katzourbos* combines
characteristics of Italian *commedia
erudita* and *commedia dell'arte*: its
plot, dependent on the final recognition of a long-lost daughter, is stock,
as are the comic types who sustain it,
including a bragging soldier, whores
and their madames, a pedantic
schoolmaster, a thief and a buffoon.
Within the limitations of the genre it
is fast-moving, bawdy and linguistically inventive. The hardest of the
three plays for the modern reader to
appreciate is undoubtedly *Panoria*. It

conforms to the typical pattern of Italian pastoral tragicomedy (it derives from Luigi Groto's *La Calisto*). Two pairs of shepherds fruitlessly woo two unwilling shepherdesses. Two elderly comic characters attempt to help persuade the girls to change their minds, but it takes the intervention of the goddess Aphrodite and her son Eros to bring about a happy ending. The originality of the Greek treatment of the theme depends on the playwright's exchanging the stylised Arcadian characters and conventions of his models for settings and manners much closer to the experience of his Cretan contemporaries. The extensive, elaborate and highly conventional love-rhetoric in which long sections are couched is tedious, a fact only underlined by the vigour of the comic interventions.   CFR

HOSTOVSKÝ, Egon (1908–73), Czech novelist, born into a Jewish family owning a small provincial factory, after studying philosophy worked in the Ministry of Foreign Affairs, and during WWII lived in Paris and the USA; after the war he was a diplomat in the Oslo embassy, and when the Communists came to power, he emigrated to the USA where he died. The anti-heroes of his analytical novels are defenceless, despondent intellectuals, neurotics burdened with a sense of inferiority, guilt, persecution mania and anxiety; they live in private worlds of their imaginations, desiring to prove themselves, to influence others and to acquire power. Unlike the men, the women in his novels are less complicated, well balanced and strong; this parallel with Kafka might have its roots in the Jewish tradition. He is interested more in the inner experience of his characters than in social

problems and his concern lies in psychological and even spiritual truths. In this he follows Alfred Adler in particular. At the same time, however, he is preoccupied by ethical problems and in this respect Dostoevski's work has had a catalytic effect. In Hostovský's early novels, *Ghetto v nich* (Ghetto within them, 1928), *Případ profesora Körnera* (The Körner case, 1932) and *Dům bez pána* (A house without a master, 1937), the outsiders are Jews who reject their Jewishness and vainly try to belong to what seems to them a community, while his later works, e.g. *Úkryt* (The hideout, 1943) *Půlnoční pacient* (The midnight patient, Eng. 1954, Cz. 1958), *Dobročinný večírek* (The charity ball, 1958) and *Všeobecné spiknutí* (General plot, 1969) dissect, in a self-ironising narration, the fantasy worlds of refugees from Nazism and Communism. Hostovský's novels, in which he combines a vivid presentation of breathless plots with meticulous scrutiny of the characters' personalities, can be interpreted as allegories of the fate of the 20th-century individual who has become a passive witness to a course of events he is unable to understand.

●*The Midnight Patient* (New York, 1954); *The Charity Ball* (London, 1957); *The Plot* (New York, 1961). KB

HOXHA, Enver (1908–85), leader of the Communist régime in Albania for more than four decades, a prolific political writer and essayist, was born in Gjirokastër, where he finished his elementary school. After having graduated at the French lycée in Korçë, he pursued, for several years, university studies in France. However foul a politician, he was a brilliant essayist. Apart from his prolific political output, more than seventy volumes, Hoxha is also the author of a number of memoirs, essays and articles in which his literary talent and merit are apparent. His impact on contemporary Albanian literature has had little to do with his intellectual ability. ShM

HOXHI, Koto (1824–95), poet of the Albanian National Revival from Qestorat in the Gjirokastër district, met in Constantinople the FRASHËRI brothers and other leaders of the movement. Later he served as a teacher at the Greek school in his native village, where he also secretly taught Albanian. He died there while preparing to open an Albanian school in Yoannina for which he had obtained authorisation from the Turkish government. Hoxhi is one of the founders of the Albanian theatre and has also written popular patriotic verse, which was published posthumously in the collections of Albanian folklore, *Mjalt' e mbletësë* (The bee's honey, 1898) and *Valët e detit* (The waves of the sea, 1908).

ShM

HRABAL, Bohumil (b. 1914), Czech prose writer and essayist, after studying law worked in a provincial notary public's office, as a platelayer, a travelling salesman, steelworker, packer of waste paper and scene shifter. In his highly individual narration Hrabal exploits the oral forms of the language and combines elements of crude vulgarity with Surrealism and lyricism. Hrabal's early texts such as *Perlička na dně* (The little pearl at the bottom, 1963) and *Pábitelé* (The bletherers, 1964) are plotless narratives, recollections of insignificant events, series of anecdotes, observations and arbitrary comments presented in associative continuity. The slightly mad or eccentric characters include the narra-

tor, who often talks to himself with an ironic blurring and distorting of reality reminiscent of chatter in a public bar. Hrabal's *Taneční hodiny pro starší a pokročilé* (Dancing lessons for older and advanced pupils, 1964) consists of a single sentence over ninety pages in length and represents the prattle of an old man who talks to a woman, probably young, and mixes reminiscences with anything which comes to his mind. More conventional in its plot and narration is the novel *Ostře sledované vlaky* (Closely watched trains, 1965) in which an adolescent talks about his sexual problem, his attempt at suicide and his attack on a German train during which he was killed. The style of Hrabal's early works but with an attenuated associative technique is revived in the novel *Obsluhoval jsem anglického krále* (I waited on the King of England, 1977) in which a crooked waiter obsessed by catering and money recounts his rise and fall before WWII, during the German occupation and under Communism. Hrabal's later, mainly autobiographical, prose follows, in his own words, 'Zola in its disregard for peripeteias and solutions' and is intended to present 'adventures of life' in a world turned upside down.

●*A Close Watch on the Trains* (London, 1968); *I Served the King of England* (New York, 1989); *Too Loud a Solitude* [*Příliš hlučná samota*] (London, 1991). S. Roth, *Laute Einsamkeit und bitteres Glück*, (Berne, 1986.) KB

HUS, Jan (c. 1370–1415), Czech religious reformer, theologian and philologist, professor and 'rector' of Prague University and popular preacher, was convicted of heresy by the Council of Constance and burnt at the stake. The subsequent reform movement and religious wars took their name from him (Hussite). In his Latin and Czech works he follows John Wyclif although he is not as radical as the English reformer. Amongst Hus's Czech works his *Postila* (Postil, 1413, publ. 1563) is the most important; unlike earlier prose writers Hus writes in a deliberately flat style, based on the contemporary spoken language, designed to influence ordinary people. His letters from prison sent to his friends and followers are more emotional; he recounts his physical suffering and interrogations and adjures all faithful Czechs to love one another, not to allow the good to be oppressed by violence, and to grant truth unto all. Disregarding Church prohibition, Hus introduced Czech hymns into divine service and composed some himself. As a philologist he was a purist; by abandoning obsolete forms such as the aorist and imperfect he contributed to the modernisation of the literary language and introduced a new orthography, which, in its fundamentals, has been retained to this day.

●*The Letters of John Huss* (Manchester, 1972); *John Hus Letters* (London, 1904).

F. Lützow, *The Life and Time of Master Jan Hus* (London, 1909); M. Spinka, *John Hus and the Czech Reform* (Hamden, Conn., 1966); P. Roubiczek and J. Kalmer, *Warrior of God* (London, 1947).   KB

HVIEZDOSLAV (i.e. Pál Országh, 1849–1921), Slovak poet and dramatist, a lawyer, began writing in Hungarian but turned to Slovak and adopted the national cause as one of the main advocates of Czech-Slovak cooperation. His efforts to raise Slovak literature from provincialism resemble those carried out in the Czech context by VRCHLICKÝ, who had a considerable influence on his verse. Hviezdoslav's poetry, initially inspired by SLÁDKOVIČ, is marked by patriotism, the principles of his Protestant faith and a strong belief in democracy and social justice. His verse novels depict the antagonism between the magyarised rich gentry and the Slovak people whom he idealises. *Hájnikova žena* (The gamekeeper's wife, 1884–6) tells the dramatic story of the consequences of the attempt of a lustful squire to rape the virtuous wife of his gamekeeper, while *Ežo Vlkolinský* (1890) and *Gábor Vlkolinský* (1897–9) set in the 1860s are chronicles of the decline of the impoverished gentry whose members, however, can regenerate themselves by marrying worthy peasants. Hviezdoslav also wrote epics and dramas with biblical themes and was a prolific translator. In lyric verse he was both intimate and reflective; for example in *Sonety* (Sonnets, 1882–6), after meditating about the universe, Nature and society he lauds the struggle of the Slovak people, and in *Krvavé sonety* (Sonnets written in blood, written 1914, publ. 1919) he protests against the madness of war. Although basically a Parnassist, Hviezdoslav is original in his unaffected, sensitive evocation of the Slovak countryside and in his endeavour to enrich the Slovak poetic language with dialect expressions and neologisms even if that means the impairment of comprehensibility.

●*A Song of Blood* (Bratislava, 1972).

S. Šmatlák, *Hviezdoslav* (Bratislava, 1969).   KB

I

IASHVILI, P'aolo (i.e. P'avle I., 1895–1937), a Georgian Symbolist, was born in Kutaisi. His poetry fell under the spell first of French Symbolism (Mallarmé and Verlaine), then, when he studied in Russia, of Russian Modernists, such as Andrei Bely, with whom he maintained life-long ties of friendship. Before he was 20 he was an accomplished pasticheur and improviser with a gift for elegant, musical verse, sonnets especially. In 1915, imitating Max Voloshin, he used a woman's pseudonym, Elene Dariani, for accomplished intimate missives to Anna Akhmatova, lamenting the life of a betrayed wife. The formation of the 'Blue horns' (*tsisperq'ants'lebi*) movement in 1915–16 under ROBAKIDZE turned him, with T'itsian T'ABIDZE, into a leader of this half-Futurist, half-Symbolist group, based on the magazine 'Dreaming gazelles' (*meotsnebe niamorebi*). In homage to Italian Futurists, Iashvili, like other 'Blue horns', italianised his Christian name to P'aolo. In 1918 Russian poets, such as Terentiev and Kruchonykh, fled to Tbilisi: the 'Blue horns' also moved to the newly independent capital, and Iashvili's poetry shifted to experimental, Surrealist modes. The entry of the Red Army in 1921 altered Iashvili's stance: seated on a white horse, he greeted the invaders at the city boundaries. His poetry abandoned Symbolism; old ties of friendship to the new régime survived the overthrow of one set of Communists by another and kept Iashvili influential, right until the coming of Lavrent´i Beria. Beria protected Iashvili from the 'Trotskyist' left and made him a Central Committee member; in return, Iashvili sacrificed his lyricism and became a propagandist. Like nearly all the 'Blue horns', he was marked by Beria in a speech of May 1937 for destruction. Kangaroo courts in the Union of Writers accused Iashvili of links with spies. On 22 July, he shot himself with his hunting gun in the Union building during a praesidium session, a suicide condemned by the secretariat as a 'provocative act arousing loathing in every gathering of decent Soviet writers'. Iashvili had been brutally hoist with his own petard: he had little of his own to say and was fatally vulnerable to cults of the day. Iashvili's feminine persona (despite his masculine beauty) brought fine verse: his translations of Pushkin (1930s) are most sensitive and compare with his best 'decadent' Symbolist *tombeau* poetry of pre-revolutionary years. Iashvili's poses (but not his support for the purges) captivated Pasternak, who made him famous in Russia.

●D. Rayfield, 'The Death of Paolo Iashvili', *SEER*, 68 (1990), 3, pp. 631–64.   DR

ILIĆ, Vojislav (1860–94), Serbian poet, was born in Belgrade, where he spent his whole brief life. By his death he had published two collections, 1888 and 1892, and established himself as the leading poet of his generation. Ilić wrote elegiac, descriptive, erotic and patriotic verse, as well as poems on Classical motifs. His poetry brought significant changes to the Romantic mode dominant in Serbian literature before him. He introduced formal innovations and achieved a harmony between content and form; he was intimate and direct and emphasised sensory perception. Many of his poems are models of structural perfection.

●R. Felber, *Vojislav Ilić. Leben und Werk* (Munich, 1965).   VDM

ILLYÉS, Gyula (1902–83), Hungarian prose writer, poet, translator and playwright, whose father was a manorial machine-minder, travelled to Vienna, Berlin and France in 1920. Having studied literature and psychology at the Sorbonne, he returned to Hungary in 1926. His writing began to appear in *Nyugat* (West) in 1928. 1934 he attended a writers' conference in Moscow; his last work *Szellem és erőszak* (Spirit and violence, 1978), a collection of essays about the life of the Hungarian minorities in Roumania and Czechoslovakia, was banned. Illyés was one of the leaders of the Populist movement in Hungary. In the 1930s he wrote penetrating sociographic works on the life of the peasantry. Much of his verse, directly or indirectly, concerns political issues. His plays and fiction are less significant, but his translations from French are of lasting value. His most important prose work, *Puszták népe* (People of the Puszta, 1936), is a successful combination of sociographic non-fiction and autobiography. Its political message was effective at the time of its first publication; the portrayal of the misery of the poorest section of the peasantry shocked the Hungarian public; Illyés showed himself to be a fine prose stylist. Among his poems the most important is *Egy mondat a zsarnokságról* (One sentence on tyranny), an effective criticism of totalitarianism, which was published during the Uprising of 1956, although it was written in 1950.

●*People of the Puszta* (Budapest, 1967). T. Kabdebo and P. Tabori (Eds), *A Tribute to Gyula Illyés* (Washington, D.C., 1968).   MSz-M

ILOSVAI (SELYMES), Péter (16th century), Hungarian poet, was a peripatetic tutor in E Hungary. Little is known of his life apart from the few hints of poverty that he includes in his verse. His main works were published in Debrecen in 1574 and include a verse version of the ALEX-ANDER ROMANCE (1548), a verse biography of St Paul based on the Acts of the Apostles and the story of King Ptolemy and the origin of the Septuagint. A strong moralising tone characterises these poems and becomes even more evident in his *Sokféle nevek magyarázata* (Explanation of various names, 1578), with its fierce condemnation of R. Catholic superstition. But his most popular work was *Az híres neves Tholdi Miklósnak jeles cselekedetiről és bajnokságáról való historia* (The story of the extraordinary acts and heroic deeds of the far-famed Miklós Toldi, 1574). In it the hero displays his incredible strength but also becomes a figure of fun: he is duped, becomes drunk and indulges in grave-robbing and murder. It is the first comic narrative verse in Hungarian and has remained immensely popular. Ilosvai was more of a story-teller than a poet. His verse is pedestrian, his rhymes often primitive. But like his contemporary TINÓDI he sang his poetry and like a good entertainer varied the mood and scenes to suit his audience. Ilosvai's *Tholdi* was used in the 19th century by ARANY as a source for his own highly refined *Toldi* trilogy.

●A. Szilády (Ed.), *Régi magyar költők tára, vol* IV (Budapest, 1883), pp. 81–263.   GFC

IOANE BAGRAT'IONI / BAT'ONISHVILI

([bat'onishvili = prince royal] 1768–1830), like all the Georgian royal blood, was compelled to live in Russia after the annexation of Georgia and, like many, filled his time with compilatory and encyclopaedic literature. Grandson of the statesmanlike Erek'le II, the penultimate King of Kartli and Kakhetia, Ioane was proud to be traumatised by his kingdom's desperate struggle to survive. His masterpiece of wit, rancour, recall and instruction is *K'almasoba - Khumarsts'avla* (Alms-gathering – Instruction by jokes, 1828). (*K'almasoba* refers to the travels of a mendicant monk to collect money for his monastery.) Ioane used real friends, his teacher, the monk and writer Iona Khelashvili (1772–1837), and a merchant, Zurab, as characters for a prolonged dialogue, as they travel Georgia together, the collection of alms being a pretext for innumerable discussions of the politics and culture of their dying country. This eccentric novel-cum-play displays much comic invention, as well as a determination to inform the reader of everything the Enlightenment and royal prerogatives had taught the author. There has been discussion about Ioane's entitlement to be called the last major writer of the Georgian renascence: Khelash-

vili may be part author, as well as protagonist and raisonneur, of *K'almasoba*, which remains regardless one of the most original creative prose narratives in Georgian.   DR

IOANNOU, Yorgos (1927–85), Greek prose writer and poet, was born into a family of refugees from E Thrace financially ruined by the Asia Minor Disaster (1922). After a materially difficult childhood he managed to complete his studies at Salonica, and for a while became a lecturer in the Ancient History department. 1960 he became a secondary-school teacher in various schools in the north, was transferred to Athens (1971) and eventually posted to the Ministry of Education. Although his first published works were collections of verse, it is as a prose writer that he is remembered. He regarded himself as representative of the group of writers known as the School of Thessaloniki (Salonica), though most, like Stelios Xefloudas (1901–84), Alkiviadis Yiannopoulos (1896–1981) and Nikos Pendzikis (b. 1908), are a generation older than he. The sufferings of the city under the Germans (e.g. the destruction of the Jewish community) and the events of the Civil War dominated his childhood and adolescence. The tendency of the other writers of the group to concentrate on inner life and psychological atmosphere is modified by younger writers like Ioannou into a method for coping with the horrors of outer reality. Ioannou's writings, which are difficult to classify generically, are dominated aesthetically by the use of changing narratorial points-of-view, multiple chronological levels and single thematic (rather than narrative) focuses. He excels at short, powerfully realistic prose pieces, sometimes overtly fictional such as Για ενα φιλότιμο (For honour, 1964) and Η Σαρκοφάγος (The sarcophagus, 1971), sometimes more documentary or essay-like, as Το δικό μας αίμα (Our blood, 1978), sometimes fragments of autobiographical chronicle as Εφηβών και μή (Of adolescents and those who aren't, 1982). The homosexual sensibility which colours some of his work was revealed more openly by his translation of Strato's *Musa puerilis* from the Palatine Anthology in 1980.   CFR

IRZYKOWSKI, Karol (1873–1944), Polish literary critic and writer, studied German at Lwów (Lemberg) but had to earn his living as a stenographer for most of his life whilst collaborating with various periodicals and newspapers. His first major work, the novel *Pałuba* (The hag, 1903), went largely unnoticed by contemporaries but was later hailed as an outstanding experiment in modern fiction. Its insight into self-deception verges on psychoanalysis, although this is achieved by non-literary means (e.g. commentaries, footnotes). Irzykowski's distinguished career as a critic, inaugurated by *Czyn i słowo* (Actions and words, 1913), reached its peak between the wars when he played a leading role in numerous literary debates. His principal collections of essays, e.g. *Walka o treść* (The struggle for content, 1929) and *Słoń wśród porcelany* (Elephant in a china shop, 1934), contain polemics with various artistic tendencies including WITKIEWICZ's theory of 'pure form'. Irzykowski believed in the creativity of literary criticism, elevating it to supremacy in the process of cognition initiated by works of art. He did not advocate specific ideas or aesthetic principles, but his personal preferences crept in; he sought consistency and precision in all literary works and trends. His trenchant criticism and intellectual coherence have exerted a powerful influence on modern Polish literary culture.   SE

IWASZKIEWICZ, Jarosław (1894–1980), Polish writer, descendant of a landowning family, friend of the composer Karol Szymanowski (1882–1937), traveller and diplomat, retained his cultivated artistic interests and countrified lifestyle even in Communist Poland where he cooperated with the government as the long-serving chairman of the Writers' Union and received many state awards. Iwaszkiewicz belonged to the Skamander group and launched his poetic career with highly sophisticated, irrational sensuality which later developed into a fascination with W European culture and universal problems. Although his prolific literary output also includes novels, plays and essays, his finest achievement lies in the short stories he published throughout his life. In them Iwaszkiewicz mastered a subtle representation of diverse states of the mind, particularly of death bordering upon vitality (*Brzezina* [The birch wood, 1932]), the interrelationship of past and present (*Panny z Wilka* [The maids of Wilko, 1932]), and unexpected decisions undermining the logic of events (*Słońce w kuchni* [The sun in the kitchen, 1938]). He also gave expression to the fatalistic conviction that life proceeds unaffected by human efforts to shape it (*Bitwa na równine Sedgemoor* [The Battle of S., 1942]).   SE

J

JAKOVA, Kolë (b. 1916), Albanian playwright, poet and prose writer, was born in Shkodër the son of a silversmith and began writing before WWII in which he fought as a partisan. Jakova's works deal with Albanian history, from the 17th century to the postwar period. His play *Halili dhe Hajria* (1950) portrays Albanian resistance to the Turks in the 18th century. Better known is his drama *Toka jonë* (Our land, 1955) about the efforts of the Albanian peasants to implement agrarian reform in the countryside after WWII. His long poem *Herojt e Vigut* (The heroes of Vig, 1953) deals with WWII partisans. His novel *Kulla buzë liqenit* (The lakeside fortress, 1984) describes the breakdown of traditional patriarchal society in the mountains of the Mirdita region in the 1950s.   ShM

JAKŠIĆ, Djura (1832–78), Serbian poet, prose writer and playwright, was born in Srpska Crnja, Vojvodina. He studied painting, but when the revolution of 1848 led him to move to Serbia, he took various occupations including schoolmastering, though he was mostly unemployed. As a liberal, he was persecuted by the authorities. Having taken part in the 1878 uprising against the Turks in Bosnia, he died in despair and ravaged by illness. Jakšić wrote stories and plays, but his best works are his poems, several of which are among the best in Serbian poetry. A Romantic spirit underlies most of his writings, and his hard life suffused them with profound pessimism.
●S. Škorić and G. V. Tomashevich, *Celebration of the 150th Birth Anniversary of Djura Jakšić* (Toronto, 1985).   VDM

JANUS PANNONIUS (1434–72), Hungarian Humanist poet, was educated in Ferrara and Padua. After graduating in 1458, he returned to the court of the newly crowned King Matthias Corvinus. After serving in the chancellery, he rose rapidly to become Bishop of Pécs, Governor of Slavonia and the king's personal envoy to Venice and Rome. He became involved in a plot against his master and fled before his wrath, but died near Zagreb of the TB that had dogged his life. His brilliance as a poet emerged during his school years under the tutelage of the Humanist Guarino da Verona. His verse, all in Latin, consists of erudite panegyrics on various Italian patrons, including Guarino, elegies of rare beauty and power revealing his personal conflicts and concerns, and waspish epigrams often interlaced with juvenile smut. His debt to the Classics is plain, but his deft craftsmanship and elegance of expression give his verse a freshness and clarity that made him one of the foremost Humanist poets. His fame

spread rapidly through Europe after
the publication of his panegyric on
Guarino (Vienna, 1512).

●*Epigrams* (Bilingual edition, ed.
Anthony Barrett) (Budapest, 1985); Ian
Thomson, *Humanist Pietas, The
Panegyric of Janus Pannonius on
Guarinus Veronensis* (Bloomington,
1988); selections in W. Kirkconnell
(Ed.), *Hungarian Helicon* (Calgary,
1985) and T. Klaniczay (Ed.), *Old
Hungarian Literary Reader* (Budapest,
1985).
T. Kardos, 'Janus Pannonius, Poet of
the Hungarian Renaissance', *New
Hungarian Quarterly*, Budapest, 1973;
Anthony Barrett and Ian Thomson (see
above).   GFC

JARC, Miran (1900–42), Slovene
poet, novelist, short-story writer and
essayist, after grammar school in
Novo Mesto, studied Slavonic and
Romance languages, 1918–22, without completing the course; he
worked as a bank clerk in Ljubljana.
Interned by the Italians in summer
1942, he was released with others by a
partisan assault on their train; he
joined the partisans and was killed
two months later. He wrote in an
Expressionist style of his own experiences and of man's helplessness in the
face of mysterious cosmic forces.
Collections of poems: *Človek in noč*
(Man and night, 1927); *Novembrske
pesmi* (November songs, 1936); *Lirika* (Lyric verse, 1940). His novel
Novo Mesto (1932) is based on his
schooldays in a provincial town before WWI.

●Translated poems in: *Parnassus*, 1957,
1965.   HL

JAŠÍK, Rudolf (1919–60), Slovak
novelist, brought up in poverty,
was imprisoned for political activities
in 1940; 1941 he joined a Slovak
artillery regiment and saw action in
Ukraine and the Caucasus, but soon

he was in military prison for his
politics and, after demobilisation, he
joined the partisans, and 1945 the
Communist-Party bureaucracy. *Na
brehu priezračnej rieky* (On the bank
of the translucent river, 1956)
attempts to combine Lyrical Prose
with Socialist Realism to describe the
poverty and growth of political
awareness in a 1930s village.
Námestie svätej Alžbety (St Elizabeth
Square, 1958) is a stylistically sophisticated and emotionally profound
depiction of the fate of the Jews when
the Germans enter a Slovak town.
The unfinished lyrical trilogy, *Mŕtvi
nespievajú* (The dead do not sing,
1961), depicts the lot of a Slovak
lieutenant fighting the USSR.

●*St Elizabeth's Square* (Prague, 1964);
Dead Soldiers Don't Sing (Prague,
1963).
L. Richter, 'Das Ringen um ästhetischen
Standard und revolutionäre Bewusstheit
in der Slowakischen Literaturentwicklung
1944/45–1963' in L. Richter, H.
Oschowsky, J. W. Bogdanov and S. A.
Scherlaimova, *Literatur im Wandel*
(Berlin, 1986); R. B. Pynsent (Ed.),
Modern Slovak Prose: Fiction Since 1954
(London, 1990).   RBP

JAVAKHISHVILI, Mikeil (real surnames: Tok'lik'ishvili, Adamashvili,
1880–1937), Georgian novelist, was
born, for all his aristocratic temperament, into a farmer's family. He went
to horticultural college in Yalta and
travelled in France and N America
before returning to Georgia, joining a
nationalist group, Eri (The People).
He was then exiled. Back in Georgia
in 1921, he turned to fiction (he
had made occasional forays with
short stories of dramatically love-
lorn women, such as *Ek'a*, 1905).
1923, when the Russians cracked
down on the first Georgian Communist government's 'nationalism',

Javakhishvili was sentenced to death: he was saved from Orjonikidze's firing squads by the Union of Writers. Javakhishvili headed Ak'ademia, a writers' group which put artistic excellence above political correctness. His release brought a torrent of prose from 1924 and 1930. His stories and novels contrast country and city life, Tsarist and Soviet times, but are too subtle to make a merely black and white contrast. Javakhishvili had a fondness for rogues and outlaws, which overrode Soviet canons: while the gentry whom the outlaw exploits were the enemy, the bandit was no ideal for the new proletarian. Primitive energy, whether the Khevsur tribesmen in *Tetri saq'elo* (The white collar, 1926) or swindlers such as Kvach'i Kvach'ant'iradze in the eponymous novel (1924), captivates an autobiographical, pliant narrator or dominates a once powerful civilised hero. Javakhishvili's most influential novella was *Jaq'os khiznebi* (Jaq'o's refugee serfs, 1924), in which, thanks to the Revolution, Teimuraz, the former squire, loses not just lands and power, but his much-loved wife to the avatar and opportunist Jaq'o. Although the story ends with the desolate Teimuraz hoping above hope and serving the village cooperative, an underlying pessimism and anarchy belie any superficial conciliation with the new world. *Kvach'a Kvach'ant'iradze* was dramatised in 1927 for Akhmet'eli's Rustaveli theatre – a tribute to the novelist – but the project was scrapped when a leading 'left' critic, Kikodze, denounced Javakhishvili's novel as pornography. (The play has since been lost.) Javakhishvili's masterpiece *Arsena Marabdeli* (A. of Marabda,

1933–6) reworks the life of a real bandit, Arsena, a hero of Georgian folklore. Javakhishvili stresses the tragic necessity that makes Arsena an outlaw – the historical connection between the medieval knight and the 19th-century bandit. Arsena embodies many of the author's ideas: 'Russia is galloping after Europe and the bleeding body it is dragging after it on a rope is Georgia' was an utterance that would cost him dear when Stalin (see JUGHASHVILI) re-evalued the role of the Russian empire. 1930 Javakhishvili clashed with the 'Trotskyist' president of the Union of Writers and commissar for education, Malakia T'oroshelidze (1880–1937), over the latter's wholesale ban on classics; when Beria came to power, Javakhishvili gained favour and medals: *Arsena* went into several editions. But the novelist could not bend low enough, despite attempts at a Socialist Realist novel *Kalis t'virti* (A woman's burden). Javakhishvili was suspected of warning the poet ROBAKIDZE of impending arrest; 1935 he was trapped into praising André Gide on the latter's visit to Georgia: when Gide's *Retour de l'URSS* reclassified him as hostile, Beria accused Javakhishvili of links with enemies of the people. In secret Union of Writers 'courts' Javakhishvili protested that he was a 'sacrificial lamb'; when P'aolo IASHVILI shot himself in the Union building, the novelist was the sole person present to praise the poet's courage. On 26 July 1937, the praesidium of the Union voted: 'Mikheil Javakhishvili, as an enemy of the people, a spy and diversionist, is to be expelled from the Union of Writers and physically annihilated.' He was tortured and shot by the NKVD. Twenty years later, rehabilitated and reprinted, he had an unassailable reputation: his vivid story-telling and moral courage merit comparison with Maupassant and Zola. In modern Georgian prose, only GAMSAKHURDIA can be put on the same international level.

• 'Too late' [*Q'bacham daigviana*] in *Mindia, son of Hogay and other stories* (Moscow, 1961).

S. Chotiwari-Jünger, ' "Arsena aus Marabda" und "Stepan Rasin" ', *Georgica* (Jena), 8 (1985), pp. 30–3; D. Rayfield, 'Beria and the Policing of Poetry', *Scottish Slavonic Review* (1992).   DR

JELÍNEK, Ivan (b. 1909), Czech poet, son of a judge, read law, worked as a journalist, 1939 escaped to France and later to UK, spent the last year of the war on the Eastern Front, worked in the Ministry of Information but emigrated in 1947 just before the Communist take-over, lived in Canada, USA, Rome and eventually settled in London. In his early collections *Perleté* (Shells, 1933) and *Nedělní procházka* (Sunday walk, 1936), Jelínek confesses to a purely personal enchantment with the dynamism of life, its sensuality and eroticism, in vigorous language, burdened with strained metaphors; in his *Kudy* (Which way, 1938), without forsaking Vitalism, he turns to contemporary reality, viewed from the position of the political left. His later verse, although not free from residues of Vitalism, marks a turn to a more serious contemplative approach. Material and spiritual reality are inseparable and unattainable; but, convinced of the independent existence of language signs, Jelínek believes that only the word can open their mystery and finally reveal the substance of God. He stubbornly follows this quest in his *V sobě letohrad* (The bower within,

1968), *Skutečna* (Realities, 1963), *Posel* (Messenger, 1975), *Slovozpěv* (The word-song, 1984), *Světlo a tma* (Light and darkness, 1991). 'I describe the stormy immateriality of my nature / in sentences of stone, plant, water and air / in sentences from the non-language of beasts and angels / in protestations of the fire's laughter.' On account of this quest which leads finally to a vision of the pansexuality of the indivisible universe, Jelínek is one of the few Czech metaphysical poets.   KB

JENKO, Simon (1835–69), Slovene poet and novelist, born the illegitimate son of a crofter, was cared for by his uncle, a Franciscan friar, during his grammar-school days in Novo Mesto. He completed his secondary education in Ljubljana, where he proved one of the most gifted of the 'Vajevci', i.e. contributors to a students' manuscript journal called *Vaje* (Exercises). Unable to afford studies at Vienna University, he first entered a seminary at Klagenfurt but moved to Vienna a year later. His first interests were Classical philology and history but ultimately he took up the law and somehow managed to qualify in spite of years of hardship and unhappiness which brought him to the verge of suicide. Assisted by LEVSTIK he was able to publish his collected verse, *Pesmi* (Poems, 1864), although the opposition of the clergy forced their publication in Graz, not Ljubljana. His poetry is a direct and sincere expression of his thoughts and feelings about his homeland, about man's dependence on Nature, about the history of Slovenia and the future of Slavdom. Particularly moving is his 'Trojno gorje' (Threefold grief), the despairing cry of a homeless, loveless stranger. His novel *Spomini* (Memories, 1858) is the romantic tale of two peasant families; *Tilka* (1858) and *Jeprški učitelj* (The schoolmaster of Jeprce, 1858), are tragicomic pictures of village life.

•Translations in *Parnassus*, 1957, 1965; *Slovene Poetry*, 1928.   HL

JESENSKÝ, Janko (1874–1945), Slovak poet and novelist, son of a petty-noble nationalist politician, was educated in Hungarian and German schools and colleges; he took his law degree in 1901 and worked as a lawyer until his call-up in 1914. He fought on the Eastern Front and went over to the Russians 1915; in Russia as a Czecho-Slovak legionary he was one of the leaders of Slovak cultural activity. 1919–35 he had senior government positions in Slovakia. His intimate verse in *Verše I–II* (1905, 1923) is refreshingly simple, sometimes self-ironic, but too prone to cliché; his sonnets attacking modern money-mindedness remind one of ADY; in the early verse his patriotism is particularly evident in occasional poems. That patriotism is more militant in *Zo zajatia* (From captivity, 1917, rev. ed. 1919), where the most lasting pieces satirise army life, particularly the behaviour of generals. The poems of *Čierne dni* (Black days, 1945) are of little artistic value; they condemn the Great Powers for the Munich Agreement and the Slovaks for their Fascist puppet state. Jesenský is best known for his mischievous, sometimes sentimental, social satirical novel *Demokrati* (Democrats, 1934–7). It depicts the politicking, petty corruption and prejudices of civil servants and the bourgeoisie in Bratislava and the provinces, and satirises the whole conception of 'democracy' in Slovakia. Jesenský manifests great affection for the society he is mocking and avoids moralisation. Society has to be hy-

pocritical because it is based on a hypocritical set of rules.

•*The Democrats* (Prague, 1961).   RBP

JIRÁSEK, Alois (1851–1930), Czech novelist and dramatist, created much of the modern Czechs' interpretation of 'national' history from the 15th to the 18th century. Having read history at Prague, he was a schoolmaster for most of his life. He is credited with being the moving force behind the 1917 manifesto of writers supporting Czechoslovak independence. He was, so to speak, a reincarnation of the Romantic historical novelist, and somewhat sentimentalised novels like *Psohlavci* (Dogheads, 1886), *Proti všem* (Against all, 1894), *Temno* (The dark age, 1915) and his artistically most accomplished novel, *Bratrstvo* (The brethren, 1898–1907) are compelling in their mythopoeia. The contrast between the old-fashioned nationalism of his novels and his 'modern' social dramas is glaring. His dialect drama, *Vojnarka* (Mrs Vojnarová, 1891), about the failed revival of an old love, about mental and physical violence in a village of 1860, reveals him as a dramatist of impeccable psychological observation. The same can be said of his determinist, pessimistic play about peasant greed and wilfulness, *Otec* (The father, 1895), which is a landmark in Czech Naturalist drama.

•*Gaudeamus igitur* (Westport, Conn., 1977); *Legends of Old Bohemia* (London, 1963).

Z. Nejedlý, *Alois Jirásek* (Prague, 1952 [in English]).   RBP

JOHANIDES, Ján (b. 1934), Slovak prose writer, started reading aesthetics and the history of art at Bratislava in 1954, but never finished his studies. He has had jobs varying from factory psychologist to minor official in the Writers' Union, but since 1969

he has been a freelance writer, although he could publish nothing, even in periodicals, 1969–76. At the beginning of his career he was under the influence of French Existentialism, but, especially since the early 1980s, the strongest external influence on him has been esoteric thought. In the short stories, *Súkromie* (Privacy, 1963), the individual is depicted as essentially alone and unable to communicate with his fellows; as in most of his works Johanides here examines personal responsibility, guilt, shame and the extent of free will. Guilt and the fact that 'everything is enigmatic when you look at it accurately' are the main themes of the densely packed novel *Nie* (No, 1966). The author's interest in the relationship between biological determinism and fatalism is first expressed in *Balada o vkladnej knižke* (Savings-book ballad, 1979), whose main subjects are greed and selfishness. Fatalism, guilt and purification form the leitmotive of Johanides's masterpiece, *Marek koniar a uhorský pápež* (Marek master of horse and the Hungarian pope, 1983), where he evokes the psychology of the 16th century – and Johanides considers the Renaissance the age when humanity began replacing mysticism with chewing-gum. *Najsmutnejšia oravská balada* (The saddest ballad of the Orava region, 1988) considers inherited guilt and genetic memory, and the nature of melancholy and laughter. The last plays a significant role in *Previest' cez most* (Taking across the bridge, 1991), a novel concerning different states of consciousness, particularly that state of non-being created by severe mental illness. Johanides, with his stylistic precision, his lively story-telling, his compassion (one notes the number of physically or mentally deformed characters in his works), his gift for representing the bizarre, and his concern for essential values and transcendental truths, is the most complex and versatile writer Slovakia has produced.

●R. B. Pynsent (Ed.), *Modern Slovak Prose: Fiction Since 1954* (London, 1990).   RBP

JOHN THE EXARCH (c. 860–c.930), Bulgarian author, was educated in Constantinople (c. 878–85/6), where he gained a for his times exceptional knowledge of literature, theology and the natural sciences. His first work, *Za pravoslavnata vyara* (On the Orthodox faith, c. 893), is a translation of the work of the Byzantine theologian St John of Damascus (c. 675–749), *De orthodoxa fide*. It became known as *Nebesa* (Heaven), after the title of the chapter designating heaven as a fifth element. *Nebesa* is among the first non-liturgical Slavonic books and introduces exegesis into Slav literature. It contains information about, e.g., man and Nature (the human body and psyche), the form of the Earth (spherical or flat), the planets. John's translation provides Bulgarian for the first time with literary and philosophical terminology. John's major work is his original cosmogony, *Shestodnev* (Hexaemeron), a polemical account of the six days of Creation. As models (and sources of information) John used the Hexaemerons of Basil the Great (330–79) and John Chrysostom (354–407). *Shestodnev* served as an encyclopaedia of natural history and philosophy. It contains a Prologue concerning King Simeon (reigned 893–927) and his cultural politics and an informative description of the medieval splendour of Preslav architecture. In an attempt to demonstrate the truthfulness of the biblical version of the Creation, he uses arguments based on his observation of man and Nature. For the first time in written form he introduces to the Slavs the views of non-Christian philosophers. His lively style contributed to the popularity of the book.

●A. Leskien, 'Die Übersetzungskunst des Exarchen Johannes', *Archiv für slavische Philologie*, 25 (1903), pp. 48–66; A. Leskien, 'Zum "Sestodnev" des Exarchen Johannes', *Archiv für slavische Philologie*, 26 (1904), pp. 1–10; H. Jaksche, 'Das "Weltbild" im "Sestodnev" des Exarchen Johannes', *Welt der Slawen*, 4 (1959), pp. 259–301; A. Lagreid, *Der rhetorische Stil im 'Sestodnev' des Johannes Exarchen* (Wiesbaden, 1965).   SIK

JÓKAI, Mór (1825–1904), Hungarian prose writer, publicist, poet and playwright, whose father was a lawyer from the lesser nobility, attended grammar school in Komárom until the age of 10, after which he was sent to study German in Pressburg. 1841 he began his studies in the college of the Reformed Church in Pápa, where he became a friend of PETŐFI. Having studied law in Kecskemét 1842–4, he passed his degree in 1846. The success of his first novel in 1846 caused him to abandon a law career. The following year he undertook the editorship of *Életképek* (Genre pictures). 1848 he became an active member of the radical 'March Youth' and married an actress. By 1849 he had moved closer to the political moderates. When the revolution was crushed, he hid for some time in the mountains. In the 1850s and 1860s he was active as a journalist, and 1865–96 was a member of the Hungarian parliament. 1886 his wife died, and 1899 he married another

young actress. Jókai was one of the most prolific writers in Hungary. His popularity was enormous not only in his lifetime but also in the decades following his death, despite the fact that serious critics held strong reservations about the aesthetic qualities of his works from the very beginning. Among his shorter works the best are the visionary short stories published in *Forradalmi és csataképek 1848 és 1849-ból* (Revolutionary and battle sketches from 1848–9, 1850) and *Egy bujdosó naplója* (The diary of a fugitive, 1851), inspired by the defeat of the Hungarian revolution. Most of his adventure novels abound in Romantic clichés. *Egy magyar nábob* (A Hungarian nabob, 1853–4) has a loose structure, but some of the anecdotes are well written and show psychological insight. His best work is *Az arany ember* (The man with the golden touch, 1872), which expresses a nostalgia for a complete withdrawal from the commercialism of contemporary civilisation, and is written in the tradition of Rousseau. In this novel genre painting is in harmony with visionary description and there is an attempt to portray a split personality.

●*A Hungarian Nabob* (New York, 1899); *The Poor Plutocrats* (London, 1900); *The Strange Story of Rab Ráby* (London, 1909); *The Man with the Golden Touch* (Budapest, 1963). MSz-M

JOVANOVIĆ ZMAJ, Jovan (1833–1904), Serbian poet, was born in Novi Sad. He studied law and medicine at Budapest, Prague and Vienna, and practised medicine all his life. He was also active as a theatre administrator and a journal editor. The loss of his wife and all his children, instead of breaking his spirit, deepened his love for children, making him the best-loved Serbian writer for young people. A prolific poet, Zmaj wrote mostly erotic, patriotic and political verse. He is best known for his collections *Djulići* (Rosebuds, 1864) and *Djulići uveoci* (Rosebuds withered, 1888). His poems are simple, direct, highly lyrical and express profound emotion.   VDM

JÓZSEF, Attila (1905–37), Hungarian poet, essayist, and translator, was 3 years old when his father, a soapmaker of partly Roumanian origin, left his wife and children. The poet's mother was then forced to board her son and younger daughter with a peasant family. József was 7 when his mother became able to support her family herself with earnings from domestic work. The three children, however, continued to live under difficult circumstances. József was sent to a boarding school in Makó, where he proved an outstanding pupil. *A szépség koldusa* (The beggar of beauty, 1922), his first volume of verse, was published with an introduction by Gyula Juhász (1883–1937), an older poet. József entered the University of Szeged to study French and Hungarian, but had to leave when Antal Horger (1872–1946), a distinguished professor of linguistics, objected to the anarchist attitude expressed in his poem *Tiszta szívvel* (With a pure heart, 1925). 1925 he went to Vienna with the help of his brother-in-law to study at the university, and the following year he studied at the Sorbonne. In Paris he read Hegel, Marx and Lenin, and after his return to Budapest joined the illegal CP in 1930. Soon, however, the Hungarian Communists became critical of his attempt to combine Marxism with the ideas of Freud and Croce, and he severed his connections with the Party in 1935. The next year he founded *Szép Szó* (Beautiful word), a periodical of urban Radicals who were opposed to the Populists. When Thomas Mann visited Hungary in 1937, József addressed him as the true representative of European traditions in the poem 'Thomas Mann üdvözlése' (Welcome to T.M., 1937). After he lost his faith in Communism, he grew increasingly despondent. Unhappy love affairs increased his loneliness, and he ended his life by throwing himself under a train. József's poetry as a whole is uneven, but at his best he is unquestionably a major writer. Such explicitly political pieces as *Munkások* (Workers, 1931) are of no great aesthetic value. At the time he joined the Communist Party, his vision of the Hungarian cultural legacy was based on a misleading dichotomy: he praised ADY for his revolutionary attitude in *Ady emlékezete* (The memory of A., 1930), but dismissed BABITS for his scepticism in *Egy költőre* (On a poet, 1930). During the next few years, however, he developed a style of great complexity. In an age dominated by Neoclassicism, he was one of the few who continued to experiment and focused on the general problems of human existence. In *Külvárosi éj* (Night in the suburbs, 1932) and *A város peremén* (On the outskirts of the city, 1933) the description of an industrial environment is a starting-point for existential meditation. *Eszmélet* (Consciousness, 1934) represents a successful attempt to write a poetry of philosophical implications. His last poems and short texts such as 'Talán eltűnök hirtelen . . .' (I may disappear all of a sudden . . ., 1937) or the self-addressing 'Karóval jöttél' (You have come with a stick . . ., 1937), are less complex but testify to the poet's ambition to understand nothingness and to write with great economy.

●*Poems* (London, 1966); *Selected Poems and Texts* (Cheadle, 1973); *Perched on Nothing's Branch* (Tallahassee, Florida, 1987).

J. Lotz, *The Structure of the Sonetti a corona of Attila József* (Stockholm, 1965).   MSz-M

JUBANI, Zef (1818–80), Albanian folklorist and writer from Shkodër, one of the first ideologists of the Albanian national movement, spent most of his life in his native town. He studied in Malta and worked for several years at the British and French missions in Shkodër. He took an active part in the Mirdita anti-Turkish movement of 1862. Jubani published a number of works in Italian. 1871 he brought out in Trieste his *Raccolta di canti popolari e rapsodie di poemi albanesi* (Collection of Albanian folk-songs and rhapsodies), after having lost, in Shkodër, in the 1866 flood, his first collection of folklore. This work constitutes the first collection of N Albanian folklore. It comprises also two studies on the political, economic and cultural situation in Albania, especially in the N part of the country. Jubani has left, in manuscript, in Albanian, a history of George Castrioti Scanderbeg. Of his verse, only two poems have survived, one of which is dedicated to Scanderbeg.   ShM

JUGHASHVILI, Ioseb (*nom de guerre* STALIN, 1879–1953), published six lyrics (two called *feuilletons*) at the age of 15 and 16 under the name of Soso or Soselo. Five were accepted by Ilia CH'AVCH'AVADZE for his paper, *Iveria*; one was honoured by the pedagogue Iak'ob Gogebashvili (1840–1912), who included it in the posthumous (1916) edition of his children's primer *Deda Ena* (Mother tongue). Romantically moonstruck, Jughashvili showed real talent in expressing depression and suspicion, though his Oriental imagery and patriotism, in a tribute to the aristocrat Rapiel ERISTAVI, are clichés. His last known poem, *Mokhutsi Ninik'a* ('Old Ninik'a' 28 vii 1896) is an evocation of frustrated strength, powerful enough to make Jughashvili's desertion of poetry for revolutionary politics regrettable, especially in view of the detrimental interest he took in the poets of the Soviet Union.

●D. Rayfield, 'Stalin as Poet', *Poetry & Nation Review* (Manchester), XLI (1984), pp. 44-7.   DR

JUNGMANN, Josef (1773–1847), writer and scholar, was the spiritual centre of the second stage in the Czech National Revival. After reading philosophy and law, he spent all his working life as a grammar-school master. He was a cumbersome poet, but his translations, particularly of Chateaubriand's *Atala* (1805) and Milton's *Paradise Lost* (1811), were linguistic masterpieces which influenced three generations of Czech poets. Many of the words he imported from Polish and Russian in his Milton became part of Czech vocabulary. His *Slovesnost* (Literature, 1820, rev. ed. 1845), intended as a grammar-school textbook, constituted the first piece of modern literary theory (mostly theory of genre) in Czech, though the anthology part was biased towards his own neo-Classical inclinations. His Czech-German dictionary (1835–9), which he started working on c. 1800, remains an invaluable tool for scholars; his definitions are remarkable for their political objectivity, but occasional moral subjectivity. His history of Czech literature is essentially a bibliography and his assessments largely derived from Josef Dobrovský (1753–1829). His notebooks (*Zápisky*), not published in full until 1973, reveal a liberal anti-egalitarian, a keen observer of human psychology and a man who was too prone to falling in love for his own liking.

•P. Brock and H. G. Skilling (Eds), *The Czech Renascence of the Nineteenth Century* (Toronto, 1970). RBP

JURCA, Branka (b. 1914), Slovene prose writer, particularly for young people, was born near Sežana and after the Italian occupation of the region was educated in Maribor, where she attended teachers' training college and worked for some time as a teacher. During WWII she was active in the resistance until internment in Gonars and Ravensbruck. After the war she worked for some time as teacher and later as editor and freelance writer. *Rodiš se samo enkrat* (You're only born once, 1972) is an autobiographical account of a politically disturbed childhood, told without rancour with the ironic clarity of a child's objective vision. Her most successful novel is *Ko zorijo jagode* (When the berries bloom, 1974), a sensitive account of adolescence. HL

JURČIČ, Josip (1844–81), Slovene novelist, educated in Ljubljana, studied Slavonic languages and Classics in Vienna but was unable to complete; he wrote for and worked as editor of various journals. Inspired in childhood by his grandfather's stories of the Turkish wars, and later by LEVSTIK's literary programme and by Walter Scott, he began to write historical novels and produced the first Slovene example of the genre in *Jurij Kozjak, slovenski janičar* (J.K., Slovene janissary, 1864). Other notable works of his early period are *Domen* (1864), the tragic tale of an illegitimate son's desire for revenge, and *Deseti brat* (The tenth brother, 1866), the first full-length Slovene novel. Realist trends appear in his later works describing peasant and provincial life: *Sosedov sin* (The neighbour's son, 1868), *Doktor Zober* (1876), *Med dvema stoloma* (Between two stools, 1876), *Lepa Vida* (The fair V., 1877).

•*George Koziak, a Slovenian Janissary* (Montreal, 1953). HL

K

KABÁTNÍK, Martin (d. 1503), an illiterate Czech artisan who dictated his one literary work, was sent 1491 to the Holy Land by the Unitas Fratrum (Bohemian Brethren) to find true primitive Christianity there. The result of his journey is the *Cesta z Čech do Jeruzalema a Egipta* (Journey from Bohemia to Jerusalem and Egypt, dictated c. 1500, publ. 1539). The author engages his reader with his modesty, sincerity and love of simple, unadorned things. With very few exceptions, when he reports another's words, he sticks to what he has actually seen and restricts that to what he considers might be useful to the Brethren. Much of his information is practical (costs, types of crop, local regulations). At the time Holy Land Jews were considered to be a noble version of European Jews, and so Kabátník has to inform his readers that they are the 'worst Jews' of all. On the other hand, he remarks on Muslim persecution of the Jews.

RBP

KAČIĆ-MIOŠIĆ, Andrija (1704–60), Croatian poet and prose writer, born in Dalmatia, joined the Franciscan order and worked as a teacher of philosophy and theology and later as Guardian of the Franciscan monastery on the island of Brač. He travelled widely along the Dalmatian coast and into Bosnia and Herzegovina. Wherever he went he recorded oral-tradition songs and legends, which he used as the core of his main work, *Razgovor ugodni naroda slovinskoga* (A pleasant conversation of the Slav people, 1756, exp. 1759). It is a chronicle largely in verse, containing some 200 decasyllabic poems, aiming to give as full as possible an account of the history of the S Slavs from the earliest known records to Kačić's day. Aware that the traditional songs were not accurate, he took his material from whatever sources he could find: the Croatian writer Pavao Ritter Vitezović (1652–1713), the Italian historian Mauro Orbini and the Venetian archives. Aiming to give a 'true' picture of history, he altered and adapted the traditional songs to suit his purpose, filling out the narrative with prose passages. The work enjoyed great popularity, both among the educated and the common people, who adopted some of the songs into their own tradition. His other works are *Elementa peripathetica*, (1752), a handbook of scholastic philosophy, and *Korabljica* (Coracle, 1760), a chronicle of the known history of the S Slavs.

●R. Burton, 'A Visit to Lissa and Pelagosa', *Journal of the Royal Geographical Society*, 39 (1879), pp. 151–90; 'A Ballad', *Monumenta Serbocroatica*, ed. Thomas Butler (Ann Arbor, 1980).

A. Kadić, 'The Importance of Kačić-Miošić', *SEEJ*, 16 (1958), pp. 109–14; J. Miletich, 'Elaborate Style in South Slavic Oral Narrative and in Kačić-Miošić's "Razgovor" ', in H. Birnbaum (Ed.), *American Contributions*, (Columbus, 1978), pp. 522–31.   ECH

KADARE, Ismail (b. 1936), Albanian prose writer and poet, was born in Gjirokastër, where he received his secondary education. 1958 he finished his studies at Tirana and then continued at the Gorki Institute in Moscow, until 1960. Kadare began as a poet, and became known with *Shekulli im* (My century, 1961), followed by collections like *Përse mendohen këto male* (What these mountains are thinking about, 1964), his best-known poetic work; *Motive me diell* (Themes with sun, 1968); and *Buzëqeshje mbi botë* (Smiles on the world, 1980). The titles of some of his poems demonstrate the wish of their author to be a topical writer. His international reputation rests primarily on his prose works like *Gjenerali i ushtrisë së vdekur* (The general of the dead army, 1964), a vision of postwar Albania through the eyes of an Italian general, accompanied by a priest, on a mission to Albania to find and repatriate the remains of Italian soldiers fallen in WWII; *Kështjella* (The castle, 1970); *Kronikë në gur* (Chronicle in stone, 1971); *Dimri i vetmisë së madhe* (The winter of great solitude, 1973) which became one of his most read novels under the new title *Dimr i madh* (The great winter, 1977), a panoramic work describing the events leading to the Soviet-Albanian rift. Among Kadare's other prose works are *Ura me tri harqe* (The bridge with three arches, 1978), *Gjakftohtësia* (Cold-bloodedness, 1980), *Pashallëqet e mëdha* (The great pashalics, 1980), *Koncert në fund të dimrit* (Concert by the end of winter, 1988), *Dosja H* (The H file, 1990), *Eskili ky humbës i madh* (Aeschylos this great loser, 1990) and *Nga një dhjetor në tjetrin* (From December to December, 1991), which show beyond any doubt that Kadare is the greatest contemporary Albanian prose writer.

•J. Byron, 'Albanian Nationalism and Socialism in the Fiction of Ismail Kadare', in *World Literature Today*, 53, 3 (Summer 1979), pp. 614–16; J. Byron, 'Albanian Folklore and History in the fiction of Ismail Kadare' in *World Literature Today*, 58, 1 (Winter 1984), pp. 40–2.   ShM

KADEN-BANDROWSKI, Juliusz (1885–1944), Polish novelist, a soldier in Marshal Piłsudski's legions during WWI, remained a staunch supporter of Piłsudski after the war. Bandrowski's fiction blends Naturalist factuality with Expressionist intensity of description and figurative language. His finest achievement is a cycle of political novels describing the ruthless and often brutal struggles for leadership at the inception of Poland's interwar independence. *Generał Barcz* (General Barcz, 1923) concerns Piłsudski's first bid for power. *Czarne skrzydła* (Black wings, 1928–9) describes political conflicts within the coal industry. *Mateusz Bigda* (1933) denounces the corruption and underhand deals in the Sejm (parliament).   SE

K'ALANDADZE, Ana (b. 1924), Georgian poet, made an instant impression in 1945 with her short lyrics. Rarely more than eight lines, they portray intimate moods, without obvious autobiographical source, but with delicate impressionism. Over forty years her poetry has changed a little: the yearning has become more affirmative, contemplation of others' lives now ousts her former solipsism. She asserted the right of a Georgian poet not to celebrate Soviet socialism and to revert to private feeling and musicality; the example of her verse has been as important as its filigree technique. A typical early poem, 'Tuta' (Mulberry tree, 1945), exemplifies her Oriental stylisation of Western emotionalism: 'I wish the mulberry would burst into the house, I wish it would lay its hand on my head. . . . The tall tree, the emerald green tree Will always call me, strike my eye. . . . What whispering my ears can hear! What whispering! Tormenting, burning. . . . I wish the mulberry would come in the house, I wish it would put its arm round my waist . . .'

●K. L. Osborne, 'Ana K'alandadze and Lia St'urua', *The Literary Review: Contemporary Writing* (Fall 1986), vol. 30 (1), pp. 5–16.   DR

KALEB, Vjekoslav (b. 1905), Croatian novelist and short-story writer whose particular strength lies in his short stories – terse understated sketches of life in Dalmatia – published his first volume, *Na kamenju* (On stony ground), in 1940, then *Izvan stvari* (Outside things, 1942). Much of Kaleb's work has been concerned with WWII: two volumes of stories, *Brigade* (Brigades, 1947) and *Ponižene ulice* (Humiliated streets, 1950), which do not rise above banal tendentiousness; and two novels, *Bijeli kamen* (White rock, 1957), which was well received, and *Divota prašine* (The wonder of dust, 1954), a spare, highly stylised work, generally regarded as his masterpiece. Employing a Modernist narrative technique, it avoids the monumentalism and pathos of many Yugoslav novels about WWII.

●'The Window', A. Kadić (Ed.),

Modern Yugoslav Literature, (Berkeley, 1956); *Glorious Dust* (London, 1960); 'The Guest', *BC Review*, 8 (London, 1976), pp. 5–9.
A. Kadić, 'Vjekoslav Kaleb', *Journal of Croatian Studies*, 20 (1979), pp. 102–10.
                                        ECH

KALINČIAK, Ján (1822–72), Slovak poet, essayist and novelist, who started writing Czech verse while at the Pressburg Lyceum, was at the February 1843 meeting with ŠTÚR and other patriots which decided on the codification of Slovak as a literary language. 1843–5 he studied at Halle; 1846–58 he was headmaster of Modra grammar school and then, until he was prematurely retired, ran a German grammar school in Teschen (Těšín). None of his works appeared in book form during his life. Most of his *Básne* (Poems, 1889) is intimate lyric verse, often of great emotional intensity; he also wrote passionate patriotic verse, and lively ballads. Best known of his works is the *feuilleton*-novel, *Reštavrácia* (Electing the deputy sheriff, periodical form 1860), an experimental comic novel, which combines a conventional love story with an affectionate socio-political study of the petty nobility and with an anthology of genuine and invented proverbs and idioms. The accomplished Romantic novel, *Orava* (1873), concerns the effects of the Thirty Years' War on two Lutheran families. The author attempts to analyse the special characteristics of natives of the Orava region (cf. JOHANIDES), especially its petty nobles. In his essays, Kalinčiak shows himself to be a balanced, sometimes severe, critic of Slovak culture.   RBP

KALVOS, Andreas (1792–1869), was a Greek poet of a Corfiot village family. His father, a junior officer in the Venetian merchant navy, deserted his wife and took his two sons to Leghorn towards the end of 1801. The family was in difficult circumstances, and the children's education was left to their own initiative. Such regular schooling as they got would have been in Italian, but Kalvos may also have attended the Greek school established in Leghorn in 1805, which would explain his knowledge of Classical Greek and Greek history and the nature of his patriotism. 1812, after the loss of their father, the Kalvos brothers left Leghorn for Florence. There Kalvos met a fellow native of Zakynthos, the Italian poet and intellectual Ugo Foscolo, who was to have a decisive influence on his life. Foscolo befriended him, had him appointed as tutor to his young cousin, and gradually began to use him as his secretary. At this period Kalvos seems to have been influenced by Italian neo-Classicism. His study of the works of Foscolo and of the Ancient Greeks led him to produce two tragedies in Italian, *Theramenes* and *The Daughters of Danae*. When Foscolo, because of his revolutionary political ideas, had to go into exile, he took Kalvos with him, first to Switzerland, then to London. Eventually, 1820, the two quarrelled and parted. 1824 Kalvos published a collection of ten patriotic Greek odes in Geneva under the title Λύρα (Lyre) and a further ten in 1826. In the preface to the second collection he declared his intention of settling in Greece, now in the throes of the War of Independence, but in practice he remained there only very briefly, then set up residence in Corfu. Little is known of his twenty-five-year stay there. He wrote no more poetry but seems to have taken some part in intellectual debate. 1852

he went to Louth, Lincolnshire, where he taught in a school until his death. The subject-matter of the twenty odes is largely drawn from the events of the War of Independence (e.g. the odes on Chios and Parga, on the destruction of the Turkish fleet by Canaris, and on the death of Byron). The language is a curious blend of Classical and Modern Greek, the metre equally unexpected (each stanza is made up of four heptasyllabic lines and one pentasyllable), the overall effect striving to be 'Classical'. The trappings of Classical poetry and its rhetoric are much in evidence: numerous references to gods and goddesses, the Graces, Muses and Furies. But the treatment of Nature and of the emotions is reminiscent of early English Romanticism, e.g. the lyrical invocation to Zakynthos in 'Ο φιλοπάτρας' (The patriot). There is even, in 'Εις θάνατον' (To death), a touch of the Gothic in the portrayal of the graveyard at night. Kalvos has always had an ambiguous status in the eyes of posterity, but since his critical rehabilitation by PALAMAS he has not lacked admirers among practising Greek poets.   CFR

KAMBERI, Hasan Zyko (18th–19th century), one of the best-known poets of Albanian literature, written at that time in Arabic script, was born in the second half of the 18th century in Starje, a village in Kolonja district, in S Albania. As a young man he took part 1789 in the battle of the Austrians against the Turks in Semender (Serbia) from where he returned financially ruined. He died at the beginning of 19th century. After his death, his tomb in Starje was turned into a shrine (the *turbeh* of Baba Hasani). Religious themes have an important place in Kamberi's work, but his poetry is also closely linked with Albanian reality. In a number of his poems he reflects aspects of Albanian town and country life, describing the grim conditions of the common people. Such poems are *Paraja* (Money), *Bahti im* (My luck) and *Gratë e va* (Widows), noted for their powerful satire. He is the author of a *mevlud*, a religious epic on the life of the Prophet, one of the first to be composed in Albanian, a number of hymns *(Ilahi)* and about fifty secular poems.   ShM

KANDREVA, Karmel (i.e. Carmelo Candreva, 1931–82), Arbëresh (Italo-Albanian) poet from San Giacomo di Cerzeto, Cosenza, took an active part in the fight against illiteracy in Calabria and encouraged, through his writings, the use of Albanian among the Arbëresh. Kandreva's verse has been published in Italy, Kosovo and Albania. Among his collections are *Shpirti i Arbërit rron* (The Albanian spirit lives, 1976), *Shpirti i Arbërit rron, arbëreshi tregon II* (The Albanian spirit lives; the Arbëresh recites, II, 1977), *Shpirti i arbërit rron, vuan dega e hershme III* (The Albanian spirit lives; the ancient branch suffers, III, 1979) and *Degë e hershme* (Ancient branch, 1983).   ShM

KANGRO, Bernard (b. 1910), Estonian writer and literary historian, took a degree at the Arts Faculty at Tartu in 1938, and then briefly worked there as a junior lecturer. 1943–4 he was literary adviser at the Vanemuine Theatre. 1944 he emigrated via Finland to Sweden, where he worked as an archivist. He is an important organiser of Estonian literature in exile (director of the publishing house Eesti Kirjanike Kooperatiiv and editor-in-chief of the journal *Tulimuld*). In his early verse, which was linked with the activities

of the Arbujad (Logomancers) group (whose name he had suggested), Kangro symbolically represents natural occurrences in programmatically anti-idyllic scenes. Behind conventional village scenery he uncovers dark signs of ancient magic forces and the discord in these forces. In his exile period he finds in them symbols of the émigré's sense of uprootedness and his depression, but also defiance at his nation's miserable lot. Drama and, particularly, prose gave Kangro the opportunity to broaden this theme and make it more concrete. Here Kangro achieved a modern, dynamic form which combines autobiographical facts and the melancholy of remembrance with the oneiric and the fantastic. He brought together his first thirteen collections of verse, from *Sonetid* (Sonnets, 1935) to *Puud kõnnivad kaugemale* (The trees progress, 1969), in one volume as *Minu nägu* (My face, 1970). After that he continued to write verse, e.g. *Merevalgus. Tuuletund* (The light of the sea. The hour of the wind, 1977) or *Hingetuisk jääminek* (Tempest in the soul. The ice is shifting, 1988). Although he wrote plays (published together as *Merre vajunud saar* [Sunken island, 1968]), Kangro's prose is of far greater literary significance, particularly the cycle of novels concerned with his native Tartu, *Jäälätted* (Icy fountains, 1958), *Emajõgi* (The River E., 1961), *Tartu* (1962), *Kivisild* (The stone bridge, 1963) and *Must raamat* (The black book, 1965). Kangro is also the author of a history of the Estonian sonnet (1938) and two volumes of essays on the poets of his generation (1981–3).

•*Earthbound* (Lund, 1951); *The Face of Estonia* (Lund, 1961); with A. Oras,

Estonian Literature in Exile (Lund, 1967).   VM

KAPLINSKI, Jaan (b. 1941), Estonian poet and essayist, was the son of a Polish university teacher who died in a concentration camp after the Soviet annexation of Estonia. He read Romance languages at Tartu (first degree, 1964), where he developed specialisations in structural linguistics, Oriental languages, sociology and ecology. 1973–9 he worked in the Tallinn Botanical Gardens, 1979–82 was literary adviser at the Ugala Theatre in Viljandi and since 1983 he has been academic adviser to the literary translation section at Tartu University. Kaplinski is one of the leading poets whose first works appeared in the 1960s, and the basic features of his poetics crystallised in his second collection of verse, *Tolmust ja värvidest* (Out of colour and dust, 1967). In his theme of the mutability of the material world of which man is a mere component, he draws on Oriental thought, particularly Buddhism – and the collection *Valge joon Võrumaa kohale* (White stripe above the region V., 1972) even contains direct references to Japanese and Chinese lyric verse. Kaplinski's search for harmony between the finite human individual and infinite Nature is fundamentally environmentalist. From this point of view his essays form an impressive parallel to his collections of verse, e.g. *Ma vaatasin päikese aknasse* (I looked into the sun's window, 1976), *Uute kivide kasvamine* (The growth of new stones, 1977), *Raske on kergeks saada* (It is laborious to be light, 1982) or *Õhtu toob tagasi kõik* (Evening will bring everything back, 1985).

•*The Same Sea in Us all* (Portland, Oregon, 1985).

I. Ivask, *Books Abroad*, 42 (1968), I, pp. 159–60; K. Vogelberg, 'Jaan Kaplinski' in C. Hawkesworth, *Writers from Eastern Europe* (London, 1991), pp. 34–5.   VM

KARADŽIĆ, Vuk Stefanović (1787–1864), Serbian literary scholar, was born in Tršić. Because he took part in the uprising against the Turks (1804–13), he had to flee Serbia. He was unable to attend school regularly, and so educated himself. In Vienna he came into contact with scholars who encouraged him to continue work on a collection of folk literature, the compilation of a dictionary, the formulation of Serbian grammar, the reform of the Serbian literary language, and the translation of the BIBLE. With their encouragement he was able to accomplish and publish much of this while abroad. On the liberation of Serbia, he travelled there on several occasions, although he was not always welcome on account of his foreign connections. In addition, his reform of the written language was opposed by the Church authorities, who wanted to retain Church Slavonic as the official language. Despite these difficulties, Karadžić succeeded in his efforts at modernising the literary language, basing his reform on oral tradition and on the principle 'Write as you speak'. 1868 his orthography was officially accepted. He also received recognition from the academies of many nations. Today he is revered as the father of modern Serbian literature and the language reformer who enabled Serbian literature to flourish. His most important works are *Pismenica serbskoga jezika* (Grammar of Serbian language, 1814), *Narodna srbska pesnarica* (Serbian folk-songs, 1814 and 1891–1902), *Srpski rječnik* (Serbian dictionary, 1818) and his translation,

Novi zavjet (New Testament, 1847).
●D. Wilson, *The Life and Times of Vuk Stefanòvić Karadžić, 1787–1864* (Oxford, 1970).   VDM

KARÁSEK ze LVOVIC, Jiří (i.e. Josef Antonín Karásek, 1871–1951), Czech writer, began reading theology at Prague (1889), but after two years left his studies to become a clerk in the postal service. He was a book and art collector, edited periodicals and wrote in all genres. As the leading Decadent he wrote poems on homosexual love, the beauty of passionate living, the consciousness of primal memory in man, the delight of organic and inorganic decay, e.g. *Zazděná okna* (Bricked-up windows, 1894), *Sodoma* (1895) and *Sexus necans* (1897). Later his verse turned to finely worked Parnassian picture-poems (*Endymion*, 1909). His prose fiction moved from something like Realism (*Bezcestí* [No exit, 1893]), to an Impressionist study of decay (*Stojaté vody* [Stagnant waters, 1895]), to dandyesque gloom (*Legenda o melancholickém princi* [Legend of the melancholy prince, 1897]), to a study of the fin-de-siècle psyche (*Gothická duše* [Gothic soul, 1900]), to studies of spiritual ecstasy (*Posvátné ohně* [Sacred fires, 1911]), to occultist novels like *Scarabaeus* (1908) and *Ganymedes* (1925) and decorative Christian mysticism as in *Barokové oltáře* (Baroque altars, 1922). His dramas range from Naturalist to uninventive historical; his most original are those which describe indecision or a sense of failure leading to a loss of power and beauty (*Apollonius z Tyany* [A. of Tyana, 1905]) and *Sen o říši Krásy* (Dream of the empire of Beauty, 1907). Karásek's volumes of literary and art criticism are gems of impressionist criticism (the influence of Pater and Baudelaire on his ideas and approach is evident) and he was, with HLAVÁČEK, the main theorist of Czech Decadence. Karásek was a true aristocrat of the soul.
●R. B. Pynsent, 'The Decadent Nation: The Politics of Arnošt Procházka and Jiří Karásek ze Lvovic' in L. Péter and R. B. Pynsent (Eds), *Intellectuals and the Future in the Habsburg Monarchy* (London, 1988); R. B. Pynsent (Ed.), *Decadence and Innovation* (London, 1989).   RBP

KARATKIEVIČ, Uładzimir (1930–84), Byelorussian poet, playwright and novelist, began writing in 1955. Most of his work, including the romantic lyric poetry, treats historical themes, like the highly imaginative novels for which he is best known. They include *Dzikaje palavańnie karala Stacha* (The wild hunting of King Stach, 1964), a fantastic first-person historical detective story, and the even more fanciful *Chrystos pryziamliŭsia ŭ Horadni* (Christ came to earth in Hrodna, 1966). His most successful work, however, is an epic novel about the 19th-century Byelorussian rebel leader, Kastuś Kalinoŭski, *Siarpy pad kałasom tvaim* (Ears of corn beneath your sickle, 1968). With a strong sense of period, impressionistic but convincing portraits of a wide range of characters, and rich lyrical impulse in both language and imagery, this is one of the best historical novels in Byelorussian. Karatkievič's special gift was to mix realism and fantasy in novels that, whatever else, never bore.   ABMcM

KARAVELOV, Lyuben (1834–79), Bulgarian poet, prose writer, publicist and scholar, attended school in Plovdiv (where he became aware of the humiliating situation of the Bulgarians and had his first patriotic outbursts), and attempted to study at military academies in Constantinople and Odessa (because of his dreams of the liberation of Bulgaria); then he went to Moscow and failed to pass his university entrance exams but, 1859, enrolled as an external student at the History and Philology Faculty. He obtained education through his own effort, had an extensive knowledge of literature, history and philosophy, and knew several languages (he wrote some of his works in Russian and Serbian, then translated them into Bulgarian). In Russia he came into contact with Slavophiles like Ivan Aksakov and Mikhail Pogodin who supported the publication of his *Pamyatniki narodnogo byta bolgar* (Monuments of the folk culture of Bulgars, 1861); Karavelov also came under the influence of contemporary Russian radical socialist thinking and knew the anarchist Bakunin. He wrote in Russian *Stranici iz knigi stradanii bolgarskogo plemeni* (Pages from the book of tribulations of the Bulgarian race, 1868), which includes the long story *Balgari ot staro vreme* (Bulgarians of the old days, 1867), influenced by Gogol´ mainly in its ironic characterisation. After his move to Serbia (1867), he established his own revolutionary newspaper, *Svoboda* (Liberty, 1869). He left Serbia for Roumania (1870), joined the Bulgarian exiles there and became involved (together with BOTEV) in the newly founded Bulgarian Revolutionary Committee. After 1874, however, Karavelov ceased to support the 'revolutionaries', joined the group of 'enlighteners' and founded his newspaper *Znanie* (Knowledge, 1875). His newspapers contributed to the development of Bulgarian journalism, its style and forms. After the Russo-Turkish War of 1877–8 he moved to Bulgaria where he died. Karavelov's verse is mostly patriotic, praises the beauty of his country and declares his devotion to its liberation. His prose works document a great deal about Bulgarian society under the Turks; his short stories concern Turkish violence and Bulgarian martyrdom ('Măchenik' [The martyr, 1879]), the Bulgarians' courage in defending themselves ('Voyvoda' [Bandit leader, 1871]) or the moral greatness of Bulgarian women ('Turski pasha: zapiski na edna bălgarka' [Turkish pasha: notes of a Bulgarian woman, 1866]). These characteristic motifs of National Revival literature greatly contributed to the growth of national awareness and the creation of nationalist ideology and mythology. Another group of Karavelov's works deals with social injustice and criticises rich Bulgarians (often collaborators with the Turks or Greeks): the novelle *Bogatiyat siromakh* (The rich poor man, 1872–3), *Khadzhi Nicho* (1870) and *Maminoto detentse* (Mummy's little child, 1867) depict the rich as immoral, sinister and animal-like; these works are among the earliest examples of social criticism in Bulgarian literature. When in Serbia, Karavelov wrote (in Serbian) a novel influenced by Chernyshevsky's *What to do?*, *Kriva li e sadbata?* (Is Fate to blame?, 1869), in which he rejects all forms of passivity.

●N. P. Semenov, *Ljuben Karavelov* (Freiburg im Breisgau, 1897); L. D. Andreychin, *La Langue et le style de Liouben Karavelov* (Sofia, 1950).   SIK

KARELLI, Zoi (i.e. Hrisoula Aryiriadou, née Pendziki, b. 1901), Greek poet and dramatist, sister of the novelist and poet Nikos Pendzikis (b. 1908), privately educated, becoming proficient in English,

French, German and Italian, and later studying music and drama, married at seventeen, read literature at Salonica. Although her writing was attracting attention as early as 1934, her first collection of poems, Πορεία (Route), did not appear until 1940. Since then a further nine collections have been published. Her impetus to write seems to have been strengthened by the death of her husband in 1953. Her poems are intellectual to the point of obscurity, largely as a result of her interest in contemporary philosophical dilemmas and her belief that new ideas require new poetic language and focus to express them. In her attempt to link her perception of man's alienation in a meaningless universe with her own intellectual and moral crises, she found her work becoming progressively more hermetic. Her response to this was to move into theatre, feeling that the creation of character in action would both help her to escape from excessive inwardness and make her abstract ideas more tangible. She has written three poetic dramas strongly influenced by Ancient Greek theatre and modern Symbolist drama, not least by T. S. Eliot, two of whose plays she has translated.

●K. Friar (Ed.), *Modern Greek Poetry* (Athens, 1982), pp. 120–7. CFR

KARIOTAKIS, Konstandinos (1896–1928), Greek poet, spent a rather rootless childhood in different parts of Greece as a result of his father's occupation (county engineer). After schooling in Athens and Hania (Crete) he read law at Athens (degree 1917). He started publishing poetry in periodicals in his late teens, and his first collection, Ο πόνος του ανθρώπου και των πραγμάτων (The pain of man and things), appeared 1919. He was given a civil-service appointment in Salonica in the same year, transferred to Arta 1920, and to Athens 1921, when his second collection, Νηπένθη (Nepenthe), was published. In order to stay in Athens he changed ministries 1923. 1927 he published what was to be his last collection, Ελεγεία και Σατίρες (Elegies and satires). Personal difficulties with his superiors led to his being sent to the provinces again in 1928, which may have been a factor in his suicide later that year. Other psychological factors, however, played a greater part. He had always been of a depressive, melancholic temperament, and the complexities of his emotional life had intensified his depression. 1913 he had fallen in love with Anna Skordili, who married in 1915. Kariotakis continued his erotic relationship with her at least until 1922, by which time he had also started a liaison with the poet Maria Polidouri, who wanted to marry him and was herself emotionally unstable. The poetry of Kariotakis is built on tensions – between a desire for life and an overwhelming sense of loss and futility, between emotional sensibility and ironic distance, between precision of form and language and dissolution and imprecision in the experiences conveyed. He conveys, through his anti-heroic and anti-idealistic stance, a classic post-Romantic nostalgia for ideals which he cannot locate in the modern world. The idiom in which he writes, while building on conventional poetics, is highly individual both in its mixture of formal and informal elements and in the unexpected uses to which patterning and musical effects are put.

●K. Friar (Ed.), *Modern Greek Poetry* (Athens, 1982), pp. 94–9. CFR

KARKAVITSAS, Andreas (1866–1922), Greek prose writer, studied medicine at Athens University (degree 1888). His first collection of short stories appeared in 1892, containing material published in periodicals since 1884. His first job was as ship's doctor for a domestic shipping line, hence his familiarity with the sea and life at sea, a frequent subject of his work, e.g. his best collection of stories, Θό Ξ (Tales of the prow, 1897). His first novella, Θ (Liyeri, 1896), describes realistically, but with characteristic touches of Romantic idealism and satirical perception, life in his native Lehaina. In the same year he was recruited into the army medical corps, consequently spending much time in the provinces. His careers as doctor and writer and his activity in the nationalist cause are closely interrelated. 1896 he became a member of the Ethniki Etaireia, supporting the principle of the Megali Idea, and went as a volunteer to fight in the abortive Cretan uprising. He was badly shaken and embittered by the humbling of the Greek Army in Thessaly in 1897, but continued as an army doctor until retirement in 1922 at the head of the service. His best novella, O Žo (The beggar, 1897), both records and criticises the conditions of village life in N Greece, and satirically attacks the political and military policies which make such conditions inevitable. His last novella, O Αόοο (The archaeologist, 1903), is an allegorical attack on the fashionable Greek idolatry of the Classical past, emphasising the importance of the youthfulness and freshness of the 'new' nation. Though his work is central to the ethographic movement, it is not Naturalist in the French sense, let alone merely documentary. His talents lie closer to Balzac than to Zola. He was associated with all the linguistically liberal movements of the first two decades of the 20th century, notably the founding of the Ekpedeftikos Omilos (an influential group promoting educational reform) in 1910. 1918–20 he contributed in practical terms to the movement by writing school 'readers'.

●R. Beaton (Ed.), *The Greek Novel. A.D. 1–1985* (London, 1988), pp. 31–41.

                                                    CFR

KARPIŃSKI, Franciszek (1741–1825), Polish poet, born into a destitute noble family, tried unsuccessfully to find steady employment in the service of numerous aristocrats and sought advancement at the royal court until 1793 when, disappointed, he withdrew from public life to settle down for the rest of his life as a provincial farmer. The seven volumes of his *Zabawki wierszem i prozą* (Entertainments in verse and in prose, 1782–7) demonstrate his achievement as the most characteristic representative of pre-Romantic Sentimentalism in Polish literature; he proffers stylistic simplicity, an emotional rather than cerebral approach, and directness rather than rhetoric as an alternative to prevailing rationalistic Classicism.

●Selected poems in B. Carpenter (Ed.), *Monumenta Polonica* (Ann Arbor, 1989).   StB

KARVAŠ, Peter (i.e. J. R. Lipka, b. 1920), Slovak dramatist, novelist and critic, son of a doctor, studied philosophy at Bratislava, worked as dramaturg of the Slovak National Theatre, at the embassy in Bucharest, and as lecturer at the Bratislava Academy of Drama. After recording the impact of WWII on Slovak society in short-story collections, for example, *Niet priestavov* (There are no harbours, 1946) and *S námi a proti nám* (With us and against us, 1950), he tried to paint a picture of the period from the last years of the First Republic to the Slovak National Uprising, *Toto pokolenie* (This generation, 1949) and *Pokolenie v útoku* (The attacking generation, 1952). He adopted a terse style necessitating a close involvement of the reader, but after unfavourable criticism he rewrote the novels in the style of descriptive Realism. In his plays *Jazva* (The scar, 1963), *Vel'ká parochňa* (The great wig, 1965) and *Absolútny zákaz* (Strictly prohibited, 1970) he ironically criticises some of the shortcomings and conflicts in postwar Slovak society.   KB

KASPROWICZ, Jan (1860–1926), Polish poet, playwright and translator, born into an illiterate peasant family in the Prussian-occupied part of Poland, received a good education and went on to become Professor of Comparative Literature at Lwów (Lemberg). In his youth he was a socialist, but in the end he espoused the National Democrats' politics. Kasprowicz's prolific work mirrors all the characteristic, often inconsistent, tendencies within the turn-of-the-century Young Poland movement. He started out as a Naturalist, producing several sequences of narrative and descriptive verse dealing with the harshness of peasant life. 1891 he turned to Modernism, initially in its Symbolist variant (e.g. the collection *Krzak dzikiej róży* [Briar bush, 1898]), then increasingly the Expressionist trend (in particular, the collection of 'hymns', *Ginącemu światu*, [To the perishing world, 1901]). In the last two decades of his career he turned from Promethean rebellion to a Franciscan acceptance

of being and from Expressionism to deliberate primitivism based on stylistic references to folklore (the collections *Księga ubogich* [The book of the poor, 1916] and *Mój świat* [My world, 1926]).

●Selected poems in J. Peterkiewicz and B. Singer, *Five Centuries of Polish Poetry* (London, 1960).   StB

KASSÁK, Lajos (1887–1967), Hungarian poet, prose writer, and visual artist, was the son of a technician in a pharmaceutical laboratory. Kassák left school at the age of 12 and became apprenticed to a locksmith. 1903 he moved from his native town to Győr and then, at the age of 17, to Angyalföld, an industrial suburb of Budapest. He was accompanied by his mother and two sisters. In Angyalföld he became interested in the working-class movement. His first poem was published in 1908. The following year he took a boat to Vienna, then walked to Paris via Germany and Belgium; he was expelled from Paris as a vagrant. 1913 he joined the Social Democratic Party, and two years later founded *A Tett* (Action), the first avant-garde journal in Hungary. When it was banned because of its pacifism in 1916, he started a new periodical called *Ma* (Today). Although he was a socialist, he never joined the Communist Party. When Béla Kun, the leader of the Hungarian Commune of 1919, called *Ma* 'a product of bourgeois decadence', Kassák protested in an open letter entitled *Levél Kun Bélához a Művészet nevében* (Letter to B. Kun in the name of art). As a result, in July 1919 *Ma* was banned by the Communist authorities. After the fall of the Commune, Kassák spent some time in prison and then emigrated to Vienna. Realising that internationalism was a spent force, he returned to Hungary in 1926. Although his ideas were not in harmony with the conservative political establishment of interwar Hungary, only the Stalinist period made it impossible for him to publish. Kassák played an important role in the international Avant-garde not only as a poet but also as a visual artist. His prose fiction has less aesthetic value than his best poetry, written in the 1910s and 1920s and at the end of his life. His early verse, published posthumously, imitated the style of the previous generation of Hungarian poets. *Mesteremberek* (Craftsmen, 1914), a free-verse poem, is an attempt to undermine the Romantic conception of the 'poetic'. Its message is prophetic and international. His greatest work, *A ló meghal a madarak kirepülnek* (The horse dies the birds fly out, 1922), concerns his trip to Paris and the Russian Revolution. It has structural similarities with Apollinaire's 'Zone' and with the autobiographical poems of Blaise Cendrars; it also contains inarticulate utterances reminiscent of Dadaist writing. His prose autobiography, *Egy ember élete* (The life of a man, 1928–39), originally published in eight volumes, is an important social document. His best novel, *Angyalföld* (1929), is a Naturalist portrayal of this suburb of Budapest.

●T. Straus, *Kassák: A Hungarian Contribution to Constructivism* (Cologne, 1975).   MSz-M

KATONA, József (1791–1830), Hungarian playwright, poet and essayist, whose father was a well-educated and very successful weaver, completed his studies in Piarist schools in Pest, Kecskemét and Szeged, passing his law exams at the University of Pest in 1813. From 1812 he engaged in theatrical activity as an actor, translator and adapter of foreign plays for Hungarian compa-

nies. His infatuation with the noted actress Róza Széppataki (1793–1872), later the wife of Déry, was unrequited. In 1815 the editor of *Erdélyi Muzeum* (The Transylvanian museum) organised a competition calling for an historical drama to mark the opening of the National Theatre of Kolozsvár (Cluj). He submitted his five-act play *Bánk bán* (Ban B.), written 1813–14, based on Antonio Bonfini's *Hungaricarum rerum decades IV et dimidia* (1496). Katona's work was not even listed among those deserving praise, but he rewrote the text and published it in 1819, although the play was not performed until the 1830s. Discouraged, he stopped writing and continued to work as a lawyer until his death. *Bánk bán* is the most important historical tragedy written in Hungarian in the 19th century. It concerns a conflict between foreigners and natives, as well as between central power and feudal 'anarchy'. A wide range of mental states is represented. Each of the characters speaks a highly idiosyncratic language, and tension is often heightened by clashes between individual styles.

●M. Szegedy-Maszák, 'Romantic Drama in Hungary', *Hungarian Studies* 4/2 (1988), pp. 195–212.   MSz-M

KAUDZĪTE, Reinis (1839–1920), Latvian prose writer and journalist, son of a serf, never attended school, learned to be a weaver, and later taught geography and religion. Privately he studied the German language, European literature and philosophy. He paid for the studies of his younger brother, Matīss (1848–1926), who became a teacher. During his holidays they travelled all over Russia and W Europe and wrote about their journeys in colourful sketches. He started publishing in

1871, and continued the anti-German and anticlerical struggle of the Young Latvians with his satirical articles and aphorisms, some of which have become Latvian sayings. His most outstanding work is *Mērnieku laiki* (The times of the land surveyors, 1879), written together with his brother Matīss. This was the first Realist novel in Latvian. It presents on a broad canvas, showing Gogol's influence, the Latvian village of the 1870s, folk customs, national types, and the penetration of capitalism. EB

KAZANTZAKIS, Nikos (1883–1957), Greek novelist, poet and essayist, was led by the 1896 uprising to spending two years at a R. Catholic school on Naxos. 1902–6 he studied law in Athens, 1907–9 in Paris, where he acquired a taste for philosophy. Although subsequently based in Athens, he spent much of 1914–39 travelling in Europe. His visits to Berlin (1922) and Russia (three times 1925–9) gave him some sympathy with Communist views, and his time in Spain (1932–3) and as war correspondent for a Greek paper during the Spanish Civil War (1936) strengthened his left-wing inclinations. He spent the war on Aegina, but left Greece in 1946, settling permanently in Antibes in 1948. Kazantzakis's intellectual development was influenced by a series of thinkers and emblematic figures. Initially shaped by the thought of Bergson and Nietzsche, his world-view expanded to embrace Christ, Buddha and Lenin. The volume in which the metaphysical aspect of his thought was most fully articulated, Ασκητική (Asceticism), came out in 1927 under the title *Salvatores Dei*. Although temporarily replaced by materialist nihilism after his Russian visits, the metaphysics of the Ασκητική forms

a basis for the ideologies of his later works. He himself considered his major literary and intellectual achievement to be his Οδυσσεία (The Odyssey, 1938), a continuation of Homer in which Odysseus embodies the modern hero, asserting the value of freedom for its own sake, despite the sense that nothing can be achieved through it. The work is in 24 books (like Homer's epic), totals 33,333 lines (a mystic number) and its metre (17-syllable lines) and its wildly exuberant neologistic language make it obscure. The rest of his pre-WWII writing in Greek consists of plays, from Ο Πρωτομάστορας (The master builder, 1910) to Ιουλιάνος ο Παραβάτης (Julian the Apostate, 1939), although he wrote a number of novels in French in the same period. At the centre of these plays stands the same figure, a solitary anti-hero, understanding (as the rest of the world does not) that the struggle at the heart of the play's action justifies itself but is inevitably fruitless. Only after the war did Kazantzakis turn to writing novels in Greek, both as a relaxation and as a way of gaining access to a wider public. His best-known work is his first, Βιός και Πολιτεία του Αλέξη Ζορμπα (Zorba the Greek, 1946), in which two philosophies of life are juxtaposed: action and hedonism as against reason and meditation. His second novel, Ο Χριστός ξανασταυρώνεται (Christ recrucified, 1948), looks at religious morality and social justice through the symbolism of the re-enactment of Christ's Passion in a Greek village in Asia Minor. The third of his major novels, Ο Καπετάν Μιχάλης (Freedom and death, 1950), returns to the obsessions of his plays. It looks at the theme of freedom bought at the price of death, in the context of the Cretan struggle against the Turks. Of his other prose works, which include several colourfully individual sets of travel impressions, the most important is his posthumously published lyrical autobiography, Αναφορά στο Γκρέκο (Report to Greco, 1961).

● *The Odyssey: A Modern Sequel* (London, 1959); *Zorba the Greek* (London, 1961); *Christ Recrucified* (London, 1954).

P. Bien, *Nikos Kazantzakis, Novelist* (Bristol, 1989).   CFR

KAZINCZY, Ferenc (1759–1831), Hungarian prose writer, poet and translator, descended from Protestant landed gentry, was educated at home before being sent to study German in Késmárk. 1769 he entered the Protestant College of Sárospatak, where he learned French. 1777–8 he studied drawing in Vienna, and 1781–2 law in Eperjes (Prešov). 1784 he joined the Freemasons. The same year he became vice-notary, and two years later district superintendent of elementary schools. He was one of the editors of *Magyar Museum* (Hungarian museum) in Kassa (Košice) in 1788, before starting his own periodical, *Orpheus*, in 1790. Arrested for Jacobin activity in 1794, he spent seven years in various prisons. After his release he married, 1804. Two years later he settled on his estate in NE Hungary, in a small village which he renamed Széphalom where he remained until his death from cholera. Kazinczy is chiefly remembered today as the organiser of the Hungarian language reform and of Revival literary life. His translations of Gessner, Shakespeare, Wieland, Herder, Goethe, Marmontel, La Rochefoucauld, Sterne, Macpherson, Lessing, Molière, Sallust and Cicero enlarged the scope of Hungarian culture. Since he had no lyric talent, he cultivated such didactic genres as the epistle and the epigram. His best prose works are autobiographical: *Pályám emlékezete* (Memories of my career) contains a moving portrait of Joseph II, whose enlightened policy Kazinczy and other intellectuals supported, and *Fogságom naplója* (Journal of my captivity) tells the story of his years in prison. The former was written in the 1810s, the latter at the end of his life. Neither was published in its entirety during his lifetime.

● J. Reményi, *Hungarian Writers and Literature* (New Brunswick, NJ, 1964).

MSz-M

KELMENDI, Ramiz (b. 1930), Albanian prose writer from Kosovo, born in Pejë, where he attended elementary school, studied agriculture in Prishtinë and later taught at the agricultural college. He studied at Belgrade, worked as a journalist and editor, and taught Albanian literature at Prishtinë. Among his major publications are *Vija e vragë* (The rut, 1958); *Letra prej Ulqini* (Letters from Ulcinj, 1966); *Heshtja e armëve* (The silence of weapons, 1971); *Abrakadabra* (Abracadabra, 1974); *Shtatë persona ndjekin autorin* (Seven personae following the author, 1975); *Njerëzit dhe kërmijtë* (People and snails, 1978); and *Shtegtimet e mia* (My wanderings, 1982).   ShM

KEMÉNY, Baron Zsigmond (1812–75), Hungarian novelist, short-story writer, and essayist, born into one of the most distinguished Transylvanian families, entered the R. Catholic grammar school in Zalatna 1820 and the prestigious College of the Reformed Church in Nagyenyed in 1823. 1834 he attended the Transylvanian Diet in Kolozsvár (Cluj); 1837 he started working as an articled clerk in Marosvásárhely, and in 1838 became a clerk in the governor-general's office in Kolozsvár. 1839 he went to Vienna to study medicine. His first article appeared in 1839. 1842–5 he was the leading publicist of *Erdélyi Hiradó* (Transylvania herald); when the liberals were defeated in Transylvania, he started publishing in *Pesti Hírlap* (Pest news), and the next year he moved to the Hungarian capital. His interest in the visual arts led him to visit Italy in 1847. Although he disapproved of Kossuth's plan to separate Hungary from Austria, he served as adviser to the Ministry of the Interior 1848–9. 1855–6, 1857–9, and 1860–7 he was editor of *Pesti Napló* (Pest daily), a paper which played an important role in the preparation of the Austro-Hungarian *Ausgleich* (1867). In the 1850s and 1860s he travelled extensively, with the purpose of seeing the masterpieces of European art in Germany, Greece and Italy. Kemény was unquestionably the most serious Hungarian novelist of the 19th century. Influenced by the German Romantics, in his earlier phase he was a tireless experimenter, whereas in the second half of his career he focused on the psychology of his characters. As an essayist his main interest was the philosophy of history and the theory of literary genres. *Gyulai Pál* (P.G., 1847) is an attempt to realise Friedrich Schlegel's ideal of the novel as a synthetic genre, a dialogue of very different discourses. *Alhikmet, a vén törpe* (A., the old dwarf, 1853) is a *Traumnovelle* inspired by Hoffmann's tales, and his romance *Ködképek a kedély láthatárán* (Phantom visions on the soul's horizon, 1853) displays consistent Romantic irony and employs the *Doppelgänger* motif. The structure of this work is complex. Since the chronology of the events is very different from the order in which they are narrated, and the different parts of the story are told by different narrators, the reader is forced into interpretation. *Özvegy és leánya* (A widow and her daughter, 1855–7), Kemény's first novel to combine Romanticism with Realism, is a psychological study of a self-destructive elderly woman. *A rajongók* (The fanatics, 1858–9) is a large-scale presentation of irrationalism in history, and *Zord idő* (Stormy times, 1862), a novel about the Turkish occupation of Hungary, suggests that the goal of the oppressor is to convince the oppressed that he has been raised to a higher level by the occupation. His most significant pamphlets, *A forradalom után* (After the revolution, 1850) and *Még egy szó a forradalom után* (One more word after the revolution, 1851), like the Czech Franz Palacký's (1798–1876) open letter to the Frankfurt parliament, call for a strong central Europe which could resist the attacks of Germany and Russia, the two great powers threatening the region. Among his long essays, *Élet és irodalom* (Life and literature, 1852–3) is an early example of the sociological analysis of culture, and *Eszmék a regény és dráma körül* (Ideas on drama and the novel, 1853) is a theoretical investigation of the relations between narrative fiction and dramatic presentation.

●F. Garber (Ed.), *Romantic Irony* (Budapest, 1988).   MSz-M

KERSNIK, Janko (1852–97), Slovene novelist, short-story writer and essayist, born to a bourgeois family with noble connections, was encouraged by his private tutor, the critic and literary historian Fran Levec (1846–1916) to write in Slovene rather than German. After law studies in Vienna and Graz, he became a notary public in 1880 and an MP in 1883. His notarial duties gave him an insight into the problems of peasant life. As a student he wrote without much success lyric poetry with his homeland and Nature as its themes, and JENKO and Heine as his models. After university he began to write light-hearted *feuilletons* but after 1876 his main interest was narrative prose. Here his influences were Turgenev and Bjørnson. Tales and novels devoted to the life of the provincial middle class are *Ciklamen* (Cyclamen, 1883), *Agitator* (1885), *Rošlin in Vranko* (R. and V., 1889), *Jara gospoda* (The upstarts, 1893). His sketches and short stories from peasant life, originally published in *Ljubljanski zvon* (The Ljubljana bell, 1882–91), of which he was one of the founders, and later collected as *Kmetske slike* (Peasant pictures, 1937), show him as the most notable Slovene Realist of the late 19th century.   HL

KETTE, Dragotin (1876–99), Slovene poet, with CANKAR, MURN and ŽUPANČIČ one of the chief representatives of Slovene Modernism, son of a teacher, orphaned and poverty-stricken during his schooldays, eventually matriculated in 1898, after which he went to Trieste for military service and there contracted TB. Fatally ill, he returned to Ljubljana and died in the one-time sugar factory where after the earthquake of 1895 his friend, the poet MURN's, landlady had found refuge and given sanctuary to other young poets. His love poems and reflective verse show an independent mind with a sense of humour. His pan-

theistic leanings are expressed in the cycle of sonnets *Moj Bog* (My God, 1898), where the influence of Maeterlinck is admitted in an epigraph. His poems were published by AŠKERC posthumously as *Poezije* (1900).
•Translations in *AMYP*; *Parnassus*; *IYL*.   HL

KHVYL'OVYI, Mykola (i.e. M. Fitilov, 1893–1933), Ukrainian prose writer and literary personality, leader of the Vaplite group (Free Academy of Proletarian Literature, 1925–8), combined his Communist and romantic ideology with nationalism. His literary reputation was achieved with his collections of lyrical, impressionist short stories, *Syni etiudy* (Blue studies, 1923) and *Osin* (Autumn, 1924). In the novel *Valdshnepy* (The woodcocks, only the first part of which appeared in 1927) as well as in his late 1920s short stories 'Revizor' (The inspector general) and 'Ivan Ivanovych' he satirised life under the Communist régime. During the 'Literary Discussion' (1925–8) he published a series of brilliant pamphlets, *Kamo hriadeshy?* (Where are you going?, 1925), *Dumky proty techii* (Thoughts against the current, 1926) and *Apolohety pysaryzmu* (The apologists of scribbling, 1927). In them he boldly criticised Communist 'graphomaniacs' and called on Ukrainian writers to turn away from Russia, pointing instead to W Europe as the source of true culture, and invoking the coming of the 'Asiatic renaissance'. His slogan 'away from Moscow' prompted a rebuff from Stalin in an unpublished letter to L. Kaganovich. In the eyes of the Party Khvyl'ovyi's literary policy amounted to a serious political deviation. He was hounded by officials, but he founded a new avant-garde journal *Literaturnyi yarmarok* (Literary fair,

1929). In the end, as a gesture of protest, he committed suicide. His works and ideas were banned until 1988, but in 1990 a two-volume edition of his stories was published. Both as a writer of great originality and as a charismatic leader Khvyl'ovyi remains the most striking figure of modern Ukrainian literature.

•*Stories from the Ukraine* (New York, 1960); trans. of *The Woodcocks* (part I) appeared in G. Luckyj (Ed.), *Before the Storm* (Ann Arbor, 1986); M. Shkandrij (Ed.), *The Cultural Renaissance in Ukraine: Polemic Pamphlets 1925–26* (Edmonton, 1986).

G. Luckyj, *Literary Politics in the Soviet Ukraine, 1917–34* (New York, 1956).

GSNL

KIŠ, Danilo (1935–89), Serbian fiction writer, was born in Subotica of a Jewish father and Montenegrin mother. In WWII he was subjected to the anti-Semitic persecution which most of his family did not survive. After the war he studied literature at Belgrade and lectured at French universities. He spent the rest of his life in Belgrade and France; he died in Paris. Kiš burst onto the literary scene with a group of talented young writers in the mid-1960s and was in the forefront of new trends in Serbian literature from then on. In his first novel, *Mansarda* (The attic, 1962), Kiš depicts the pains of adolescence. His subsequent novels deal, in one form or another, with the wartime persecution of the innocent, mostly Jews, for racial or political reasons. His novels *Bašta, pepeo* (Garden, ashes, 1965) and *Peščanik* (Hourglass, 1972) are, as it were, monuments to the fate of his father who perished in a pogrom after having left an indelible stamp on the memory of his young son. The death of his father contributed to Kiš's peculiar perception of reality as a cross between the real and the fantastic, between the comprehensible and the bizarre. His collection of short stories, *Grobnica za Borisa Davidovića* (A tomb for Boris Davidović, 1976), again concentrates on the victims of terror, this time spread over centuries. Kiš focuses here on the Communist brand of terror.

•*Garden, Ashes* (New York, 1975; London, 1985); *A Tomb for Boris Davidovich* (New York, 1978); *The Encyclopedia of the Dead* (New York, 1989); *Hourglass* (New York, 1990).

VDM

KITZBERG, August (1855–1927), Estonian prose writer and dramatist, self-taught son of a landless peasant, worked as a supply teacher and clerk in various locations in S Estonia; 1904–20 he was an office-worker in Tartu and from 1920 onwards a freelance writer. He began his literary career with the historical novella *Maimu* (1892) and short stories with rural themes later gathered under the title *Külajutud I–V* (Village tales I–V, 1915–21). Kitzberg is, however, most important for his drama. His play *Tuulte pöörises* (Caught in the whirlwind, 1906) was the first to be performed at the Estonian National Theatre, the Vanemuine. He was a prolific dramatist, but the zenith of his works is the tragedy *Libahunt* (The werewolf, 1912), which, in a blend of the Romantic and the Realist, describes the conflict of its independent-minded heroine with the servile spirit of village society.

•*Stories for Children* (Tallinn, 1984). VM

KIVI, Aleksis (i.e. A. Stenvall, 1834–72), Finnish novelist, poet and playwright, was the first Finnish writer to devote himself wholly to literature; in his work he essentially codified the Finnish literary language. The son of a country tailor, he studied at Helsinki University. His talents were quickly recognised and through prizes, occasional fees and individual charity he managed to eke out a living. Poverty, ill-health and the criticism of uncomprehending nationalists contributed to his insanity and early death. With the exception of his last major work, *Seitsemän veljestä* (Seven brothers, 1871), a novel, Kivi's literary output consists mainly of plays. Most of them, typical of contemporary European popular theatre, were written on commission. Two have a more lasting quality. Common to each of them is the theme of reconciliation. Cast in the form of a Greek tragedy and much influenced by Shakespeare, *Kullervo* (1860), set in prehistoric Finland, is the story of a tragic character from LÖNNROT's *Kalevala*. Kullervo becomes the unwitting seducer of his long-lost sister. Her suicide drives Kullervo to seek revenge on those responsible for her fate and finally to his own suicide. In the play *Nummisuutarit* (Village cobblers, 1864), superficially a comedy, and *Seitsemän veljestä*, the reconciliation theme is set in a contemporary social context. Falstaffian in his humour, inspired by a play by Ludvig Holberg (1684–1754), *Nummisuutarit* is a rumbustious comedy about overweening pride. Ignorance and arrogance lead to the downfall of the main characters and force them to recognise the needs and rights of others. In *Seitsemän veljestä* this theme is elevated to an allegory of the transformation of Finland into a modern society. For years the seven brothers reject the norms of their village, fleeing into the forest and living off the land, until a series of misadventures demonstrates the impossibility of continuing the old way of life and forces the brothers to seek reconciliation with the villagers and to take their proper place in society.

●*Seven Brothers* (Helsinki, 1973).

K. Laitinen, 'Aleksis Kivi: the Man and his work', P. Lounela, 'The Stages of Aleksis Kivi', *Books from Finland* (1984), pp. 100–4, 107–12.   MAB

K'LDIASHVILI, Davit (1862–1931), Georgian novelist and dramatist, served in the Russian Army until forced to resign in the 1905 Revolution. His prose, such as *Solomon Morbeladze* (1894), revolves around the degeneration of the country gentry and the miseries of the peasantry. His plays, e.g. *Irines bedniereba* (Irine's happiness, 1897) and *Darisp'anis gasach'iri* (The misfortunes of Darisp'an, 1903) are set in Imeretian villages, but the social comment is tempered with enough satirical good humour to make them theatrically viable to this day.   DR

K'LDIASHVILI, Sergo (1893–1986), son of the Georgian novelist D. K'LDIASHVILI, set out to be a very different writer (though in 1945 he wrote a book about his father). Before studying law in Moscow, he attended the Kutaisi grammar school which produced so many of Georgia's 20th-century intellectuals: he joined ROBAKIDZE's *tsisperq'ants'lebi* (Blue horns) poets and wrote mildly shocking Decadent verse. Under Soviet rule he converted quickly to conventional realist prose, of which *P'erp'li* (Ash, 1932) and *Mq'udro savane* (A cosy country retreat, 1958) are typical. His anticlerical satire met the demands of the time (*Abesalom nakhutsara* [Absalom the ex-priest, 1933]), but *Aznauri Lakhundarelis tavgadasavali*

(The adventures of Squire Lakhundareli, 1927) has unbridled fantasy. His drama (*Gmirta taoba* [A generation of heroes, 1937], *Irmis khevi* [Deer's gorge, 1944]) is patriotic, socialist and ineffectual. Despite his conformism, he was harassed in 1937, but released when his (and NADIRADZE's) interrogator was arrested.   DR

KLICPERA, Václav Kliment (1792–1859), Czech dramatist and novelist, after tailor's then butcher's apprenticeship, did a foundation course and became a grammar-school master but was suspended 1852 because his pupils published an unauthorised Czech literary magazine. Klicpera developed a passion for theatre and began writing popular Romantic plays in the manner of the *Ritterdrama*. The personae of his first play, *Blaník* (Blaník rock, 1813), based on a legend of knights in a cave who will one day wake up and liberate the nation, include the knights, robbers, a Gipsy and ghosts. The most accomplished of his historical plays is *Soběslav* (1824), the story of an 12th-century Czech ruler; in the play's revised form (1853–8), he is presented as a democrat whose humanist ideas are too advanced for backward Bohemia. Klicpera is most skilful as a writer of comedies in which he ridicules fashionable intellectuals, narrow-minded burghers and dull or cunning peasants, and he uses eccentrics and boisterous students as vehicles of his satire. His comedy *Hadrián z Římsů* (H. of Rheum, 1824), set in the 14th century, whose eponymous hero represents the opposite of chivalrous virtues, became, almost accidentally, a parody of the Austrian aristocracy. Klicpera was not interested in contemporary problems and his characterisation is primitive; his plays are not very dramatic but they abound in wit, and are written in lively language well differentiated for each character. Several of his 56 plays are still performed.   KB

KLÍMA, Ladislav (1878–1928), Czech writer and thinker, perhaps the only philosopher produced by the European Decadence, was banished from all grammar schools in Austria for an anti-Habsburg essay (1895) and so was sent to Zagreb to finish his schooling, but left after six months. At 21, with an inheritance from his mother, he went travelling in Austria and Switzerland. His works of eccentrically composed, deliberately inconsistent, witty, kind, vicious, life-affirming, world-scorning philosophy, *Svět jako vědomí a nic* (The world as consciousness and nothingness, 1904), *Traktáty a diktáty* (Tracts and diktats, 1922) and *Vteřina a věčnost* (The second and eternity, 1927), show the inspiration of Berkeley, Stirner, Schopenhauer and Nietzsche, but are essentially original. By 1904 the cornerstones of his thought are in place, absolute egoism and absolute voluntarism. That egoism becomes egodeism and ludibrionism (a version of the notion that life is a game). The two most valuable and most beautiful characteristics of the human being are not having to reproduce and to be able to die by his/her Will. The main ethical force is indifference, spiritual anarchism; '*Everything is only My toy*'; 'anyone who is not an absolute sceptic is an absolute swine'. Klíma's anti-novel, *Utrpení knížete Sternenhocha* (The sorrows of Prince Sternenhoch, 1928), is an elegant farrago of sex and violence, wit, caricature and philosophy. The mad, degenerate, hero-narrator, Kaiser Bill's minion, marries the hideous, violent superwoman, Helga *alias* Daemonka who kills her father and eventually kills her and Sternenhoch's child. The novel is a grotesque rampage of seriously slapstick nihilism. The title novel of the collection, *Slavná Nemesis* (Glorious N., 1932), is slightly more earnest and less inventive; its prime concern lies in the boundaries between life, dream and death. This time, the hero, Sider (*sic*), realises only when he is dying that the woman he had been attracted to and repelled by, and had been pursuing for fifteen years, is actually his wife, Orea, or a spectre of her in a previous incarnation. Of his four plays, one Klíma wrote while dying of tuberculosis, *Dios* (1990), is thematically linked with *Slavná Nemesis*: reincarnation, repellent attraction, spiritual aristocratism, but it also suggests some sense of personal failure in the author. The theme of *Dios* is the Will, and the extent to which the world of the spirit is actually on earth or not. Klíma is the most original Czech thinker since CHELČICKÝ.

●M. Nápravník, 'Auf der abgewandten Seite. Über Ladislav Klíma', *Akzente*, 5 (Oct. 1971), pp. 435–44; P. Wilson, 'A Note on Klíma', *London Magazine*, New Series, 16 (1976), 2, pp. 35–6. RBP

KLIMENT OF **OHRID** (i.e. St Clement of Ochrida, c. 840–c. 916), Bulgarian author, worked for about 20 years in Great Moravia as one of the pupils of Cyril and Methodius; after the death of Methodius (885), he went to Bulgaria where King Boris (reigned 852–89) sent him to Kutmichevitsa (SW Macedonia) where Kliment lived for about 30 years and established the so-called Ohrid School. He became the first Slav bishop (893), and his activities played an important role in the process of the consolidation of the country after its Christianisation (869). In Great Moravia Kliment helped Methodius in the translation of liturgical books, the *vitae* of Cyril and Methodius, the first historical sources on their lives, are ascribed to him. He is the author of about 75 homilies and eulogies, which not only contributed to the spread of Church culture, but also became the foundation of Bulgarian original literature. His most important contribution was the Ohrid School which educated numerous priests and translators (the author of Kliment's life cites 3,500) and was one of the centres where Bulgarian literature first developed. Kliment's *Pohvalno slovo za Kiril* (Eulogy of St Cyril), apostrophises the parts of a saint's body.

●D. Obolensky, *Six Byzantine Portraits* (Oxford, 1988), pp. 8–33; M. Kussef, 'St Clement of Ochrida', *SEER*, 27 (1948), pp. 193–216.   SIK

KNIAŹNIN, Franciszek Dionizy (1749?–1807), Polish poet, initially a Jesuit teacher, after the dissolution of the Order in Poland in 1773 was employed as a private tutor, secretary and court poet by Prince Adam Kazimierz Czartoryski (1734–1823), in whose service he remained for the next 20 years. The final years of his life were marked by the rapid progress of insanity, which rendered him incapable of communication around 1795. Within the Polish Age of Enlightenment, Kniaźnin represents a hybrid of Rococo and Sentimentalism. In his poetry, thematically ranging from the erotic to the patriotic, he increasingly prefers simple emotion to elaborate rhetoric and local specificity to universal setting, thus heralding the arrival of pre-Romantic tendencies in Polish literature.

●Selected translations: Poems in B.

Carpenter, *Monumenta Polonica* (Ann Arbor, 1989).   StB

KOCBEK, Edvard (1904–81), Slovene poet, essayist, diarist, short-story writer, after two years as a theology student in Maribor studied Romance languages in Ljubljana, Berlin, Lyons and Paris, and then worked as a grammar-school teacher. 1941 he was one of the founders of the Liberation Front and from 1942 played a major role in the partisan movement; during this time he kept a diary which he later published: *Tovarišija* (Comrades, 1949), *Slovensko poslanstvo* (Slovene mission, 1964), *Listina* (Document, 1967), *Pred viharjam* (Before the storm, 1980). He held ministerial office in the postwar government but withdrew from politics in 1952 after the hostile reception of his collection of short stories, *Strah in pogum* (Fear and courage, 1951), examining in an Existentialist manner episodes from the partisan war. His verse collection, *Zemlja* (The earth, 1934), concerns peasant life and the metaphysical powers that lie beyond it, and in *Groza* (Horror, 1963) he seeks a purified poetic language, insistent on the authenticity of impression and experience.

•Translations in: *AMYP*; *Parnassus*. HL

KOCH, Jurij (b. 1936), Sorbian prose writer, born in Hórki (Horka), east of Kamenz, the son of a quarryman, attended schools (1942–54) in Chróścicy (Crostwitz), Varnsdorf (Czechoslovakia), Bautzen and Cottbus. He studied journalism at the University of Leipzig 1956–60, then worked as a journalist for sixteen years, mainly in the Sorbian section of Radio GDR in Cottbus. Since 1976 he has been a freelance writer. Koch's first book, *Židowka Hana* (H. the Jewess, 1963), was based on the true story of Hana Šěrcec, a Jewish child adopted by a Sorbian family, but taken by the authorities in 1942 to a concentration camp where she died. It was followed in 1968 by *Mjez sydom mostami* (Between seven bridges), which centres on the problems of Wilhelm Kosak, a new administrator in a Sorbian village. Kosak appears again in Koch's first novel, *Róžamarja* (Rosemary, 1975). The administrator's efforts to change the village introduce a rudimentary ecological theme to Koch's work, a theme that is developed further in the story *Kotjatkowa dźiwna lubosć* (Kotjatko's strange love, 1976) and the novella *Wišnina* (The cherry tree, 1984). Koch sees the erosion of the Sorbian national substance as part of the general impoverishment of the environment resulting from technical progress. The novel *Nawrót sónow* (The return of dreams, 1983), the story of three friends' plan to form a pact of friendship for life, is partly autobiographical. Questions of truth and honesty form the basis of the novel *Wšitko, štož ja widźu* (Everything I see, 1989).

•P. Barker, 'Interview with Jurij Koch', *GDR Monitor*, no. 21 (Summer 1989), pp. 49–58.   GCS

KOCHANOWSKI, Jan (1530–84), Polish poet, born into a noble family of average means, 1544 entered Cracow Academy. He continued his studies abroad, first in Königsberg, then in Padua, where he stayed for more than four years and won acclaim as a Latin poet. His return to Poland via Paris in 1559 ushers in the second phase of his life, spent at the court of King Sigismund II August (reigned 1548–72); Kochanowski served as the King's secretary, while also writing, chiefly to entertain his courtier friends. Polish Renaissance culture was then rapidly entering its 'Golden Age'. A few years after the King's death, however (probably 1574), Kochanowski severed his ties with the royal court to retire to his family estate in Czarnolas. There he spent the third and last phase of his life continuing to write and preparing his collected works for publication. Kochanowski's work soars above the production of contemporary writers of the 'Golden Age', not to mention his medieval and early Renaissance predecessors, in every respect. He was the greatest poet in Polish literature before the beginning of the 19th century and is to be credited with two seemingly incompatible achievements: he opened Polish literature to Classical and W European influences while also endowing it with a particularly Polish experience and expression. An accomplished Latin poet, he wrote almost all his mature work in the vernacular, and it is thanks to his individual genius and to a deliberate effort that Polish was elevated, in the course of only a few decades, to the level of a fully effective literary language. Kochanowski's Polish output consists of the collections *Fraszki* (Trifles/Epigrams, 1584), *Pieśni* (Songs, 1586) and *Treny* (Threnodies, 1580); a lyrical adaptation of the Psalms, *Psałterz Dawidów* (The Psalter of David, 1578); several epic poems; and a Classical tragedy in verse, *Odprawa posłów greckich* (The dismissal of the Greek envoys, 1578). The largely Anacreontic *Fraszki* and Horatian *Pieśni* offer glimpses of his personality as a Humanist seeking equilibrium among the vicissitudes of life by favouring moderation and a stoical acceptance of whatever Fate might bring; in contrast to that, *Treny* adopts a dramatically different perspective and tone. This sequence of laments on the death of his little daughter covers a wide range of emotions and attitudes, from utter despair and religious doubt to final reconciliation with his Maker's decrees. Kochanowski's usually lucid and sedate style here acquires almost pre-Baroque complexity and dynamism. An uncontested authority, Kochanowski exerted an incomparable and manifold influence on the subsequent evolution of Polish poetry. He established a timeless norm of craftsmanship that virtually every Polish poet after him had to be aware of, if not overtly emulate. His most obvious achievement was his contribution to the development of Polish prosody. The revolution he single-handedly carried out consisted of replacing the remnants of a medieval approximate-syllabic verse system with a strictly syllabic system, made even more rigorous by exact rhyme, stabilised caesura, and paroxytonic cadence. This rigour enabled him to create an interplay between syntax and verse structure. Kochanowski's syllabism has endured in a virtually unchanged shape to this day as one of the basic verse systems in Polish poetry.

●*Poems* (Berkeley, 1928).

D. Welsh, *J. Kochanowski* (New York, 1974); D. Pirie (Ed.), *Kochanowski in Glasgow* (Glasgow, 1985).   StB

KOCHOWSKI,   Wespazjan (1633–1700), Polish poet, a country squire who distinguished himself in military service, was granted the honorary position of 'privileged historiographer' by King John III Sobieski (reigned 1674–96). As a poet, Kochowski was the last prominent representative of the 'Sarmatian' variety of Polish Baroque. His collection of lyrics and epigrams *Niepróżnujące próżnowanie* (Unleisurely leisure,

1674) stands out by virtue of its technical finesse, while his long poem in biblical prose, *Psalmodia polska* (Polish Psalmody, 1695), is an early manifestation of the messianic Polish philosophy of history.

●Selected poems in B. Carpenter (Ed.), *Monumenta Polonica* (Ann Arbor, 1989). StB

KOHOUT, Pavel (b. 1928), Czech poet, novelist and dramatist, read literature and philosophy at Prague (degree 1952), and during his studies worked for Czechoslovak Radio, was the Czechoslovak cultural attaché in Moscow (1949–50) and throughout the 1950s was on the editorial board of various periodicals. From the late 1950s to the Soviet occupation he worked mainly in theatre. Though a *nomenklatura* man he was blacklisted in the 1970s, co-created Charter 77, and 1978 was allowed to travel to Austria. 1979 he was deprived of his Czechoslovak citizenship. He is best known, first, for his collection of verse on the 'struggle for peace' and in mourning for the death of the Stalinist President Gottwald, *Čas lásky a boje* (A time of love and struggle, 1954), and, second, for his classic Socialist Realist drama, *Dobrá píseň* (The good song, 1952). This well-constructed piece of sentimental Komsomol propaganda inspired KUNDERA; it declares that anyone who betrays their beloved can betray their country and that the show trials are eminently just. Of his many subsequent dramas in quite a different style representative of his skill in adaptations is the satirical comedy *Cesta kolem světa za 80 dní* (Around the world in 80 days, 1962). His gimmicky novel *Katyně* (The hangwoman, 1980) is a sarcastic, salacious, ghoulish novel, a facile parody of *Trivialliteratur* which be-

comes itself *Trivialliteratur*. In *Hodina tance a lásky* (Lesson in dance and love, 1989) the author apparently seeks to whitewash Stalinism and, probably, Nazism; the main idea is that, whether we become extremist brutes or not depends on the star we are born under.

●*Poor Murderer. A Play* [*Ubohý vrah*, 1973] (Harmondsworth, 1977); *White Book* [*Bílá kniha*, 1978] (New York, 1977); *The Hangwoman* (New York, 1981).

P. I. Trensky, *Czech Drama Since World War II* (White Plains, NY, 1978); R. B. Pynsent, 'Kohout and the Banalisation of Brutality', *Bohemia*, 1, 31 (1990), pp. 130–6. RBP

KOIDULA, Lydia (i.e. L. Jannsen, 1843–86), Estonian poet and dramatist, daughter of the national-movement leader, J. V. Jannsen (1819–90), attended German secondary school in Pärnu and, from childhood, helped her father in the editing of his weekly, *Perno Postimees* (The Pärnu courier, later in Tartu, *Eesti Postimees*, The Estonian C.). She was the first Estonian woman journalist and writer. She came into close contact with KREUTZWALD and the younger generation of patriots, particularly Carl R. Jakobson (1841–82), who also gave her her *nom de plume* (*koit* = dawning). She was an active participant in the Vanemuine amateur dramatic society, the germ of the future National Theatre. 1873 she married a germanised Latvian, Eduard Michelson, and settled in Kronstadt (Russia). Her remains were brought to Tallinn in 1946. Koidula's verse constitutes one of the high-points of the poetry of the Estonian National Awakening. She took as her starting-point conventional 19th-century German verse, particularly as transmitted by Elise Polko's anthology, *Dichtergrüsse*. That involved her solving various problems of language, style and versification for a language which was literarily inchoate. She created prototypical forms for the intimate, Nature and, primarily, patriotic lyric modes, the last containing aggrandisement of the mother-country theme. Her prototypes served as models throughout the 19th century and, still now, constitute a component of the national cultural consciousness. Many of Koidula's poems have become part of the oral tradition, and her poem 'My country is my love' has become an unofficial Estonian national anthem. The two collections of verse published during her lifetime, *Vainulilled* (Wild flowers, 1866) and *Emajïe ööbik* (Nightingale of the River Emajõgi, 1867), which also include translations and adaptations from the German, constitute only a part of Koidula's writing. In all, 311 complete poems have survived and been posthumously published; a critical edition, *Luuletused* (Poems), appeared in 1969. Koidula's prose works were important for their time of writing, e.g. *Ojamölder ja tema minia* (The miller, the one by the brook and his daughter-in-law, 1863), as were her plays, particularly her comedy based on a Theodor Körner farce, *Saaremaa onupoeg* (The S. cousin, 1870), and the more original *Säärane Mulk* (Such a hayseed, 1872), which laid the foundations of Estonian drama.

●Selections in E. H. Harris, *A Glimpse of Estonian Literature* (Manchester, 1933) and E. H. Harris, *Literature in Estonia* (London, 1943).   VM

KOŁAKOWSKI, Leszek (b. 1927), Polish philosopher and writer, was among the most outspoken and influential Marxist revisionists of the late 1950s and 1960s. Expelled from the CP and deprived of the Chair in the History of Philosophy at Warsaw University, he settled in the W in 1968. A Fellow of All Souls (since 1970), he collaborates with various American universities. Apart from Polish, he writes in English, French and German. Kołakowski's academic output covers various periods of philosophical thought, from the medieval to the contemporary. He is best known as a critic of Marxism (*Główne nurty marksizmu* [The main currents of Marxism, 1976–8]), which he initially sought to reform. More recently he has written about the role of religion (*Religion. If there is no God . . .*, 1982). His numerous essays concern aspects of modern culture, morality and politics. Kołakowski's philosophical propensity and wit have been reflected in his one-act plays and collections of short stories. The latter are written in the form of fables (*13 bajek z królestwa Lailonii* [13 fables from the kingdom of Lailonia, 1963]), biblical parables (*Klucz niebieski* [The key to Heaven, 1964]), sermons, prayers, monologues and interviews (*Rozmowy z diabłem* [Conversations with the Devil, 1965]).

●*The Devil and Scripture* (London, 1973); *Main Currents of Marxism* (London, 1978).

G. Schwann, *L. Kołakowski – Eine marxistische Philosophie der Freiheit* (Stuttgart, 1971).   SE

KOŁAS, Jakub (i.e. Kanstancin Mickievič, 1882–1956), Byelorussian poet, dramatist and writer, created the two finest epic poems in Byelorussian and the first important novel. Born into a literate peasant family, he studied at Niaśviž teachers' training college and became a schoolmaster before being imprisoned 1908–11 for his socialist views. Kołas's earliest poems all concern peasant life, but from early days he showed surprising technical maturity and fine balance and concision of diction. Like many contemporaneous writers, he linked social and national issues; this is also evident in his prison poetry, where satire alternates with self-pity, and which also includes some fine Nature poems; the best of his early verse was published by the editors of the newspaper *Naša niva* (Our field) as a collection *Pieśni žalby* (Songs of lament, 1910). At this time Kołas began experimenting with narrative poems, in themselves mainly important as practice for his later novels and epic masterpieces. Of the latter, *Novaja ziamla* (The new land, 1911–23) describes the struggles of a peasant family to acquire some land; the poem's Nature descriptions, though lyrical, are without romanticising or idealisation, the picture of family life elevated and joyous, and the entire work, seen exclusively from a peasant perspective, an encyclopaedia of pre-revolutionary Byelorussian life. The other major poem, *Symon-muzyka* (S. the musician, 1911–25), demonstrates the widest imaginable range of metrical techniques in its symbolic description of the quest for knowledge and self-fulfilment of a brilliant violinist in an uncomprehending world. No other work by Kołas is so lyrical and emotional: if *Novaja ziamla* epitomises the fate of Byelorussia, *Symon-muzyka* reflects the individual poet's lot. As epic poems they have not been surpassed in Byelorussian. Kołas began writing prose at the same time as poetry, and within a few years he had attained considerable mastery in the short story. His particular strength was lifelike dialogue, and in the years immediately before WWI he became the first Byelorussian to portray rounded characters in psychological depth. Allegories were popular at this time and Kołas began a series, *Kazki žyćcia* (Tales of life), which was published as a collection in 1921 but to which he added in later years. He came to terms with the 1917 Revolution better than most Byelorussian writers, though some poems of 1921 show apprehension at developments. Kołas's main work in prose is a trilogy, *Na rostaniach* (At the crossroads): the first part, *U paleskaj hłušy* (In the backwoods of Polessia, 1923), was followed by *U hłyby Palessia* (In the depths of Polessia, 1927), but the last part, which gave the trilogy its name, did not appear until 1954. The novels trace the tribulations of an educated Polessian returning to his roots in the hope of enlightening the natives. Kołas was a born story-teller with fine psychological understanding, an eye for local colour and a lyrical narrative style that at times recalls his verse epics. Kołas's decline in the 1930s was less catastrophic than that of many of his fellow writers, and his narrative skill overcame endemic political schematism in several stories, e.g. *Adščapieniec* (The renegade, 1931) and *Dryhva* (The quagmire, 1933). His last major poem, *Rybakova chata* (The fisherman's hut, 1939–47), contains some fine quasi-autobiographical passages, but is weak in construction and overall conception. Three plays, all written after the Revolution, are undistinguished. Kołas never despaired, and throughout his life did much to encourage younger writers.

•*On Life's Expanses* (Moscow, 1982); *The Voice of the Land* (Moscow, 1982).

ABMcM

KÖLCSEY, Ferenc (1790–1838),

Hungarian poet, essayist and short-story writer, born into a landed-gentry family, entered the College of the Reformed Church in Debrecen in 1796, where he learned Latin and French, then German and Greek. 1808 he started corresponding with KAZINCZY. Having completed his studies in Debrecen in 1809, the following year he went to Pest to continue his study of law. But soon he returned to his estates in E Hungary. From the mid-1810s he gradually became independent of KAZINCZY, realising that the latter preferred translations to original works. As more and more periodicals appeared in Hungary, he started publishing essays which made him the most important critic of the next few decades. After 1825 he took part in the political life of Hungary: representing Szatmár County, he was one of the leaders of the liberal opposition in the Lower House when the Diet opened at the end of 1832, until he was recalled by his constituency in 1835, to the regret of all liberals. In his last years, he was preparing the legal defence of his friend Baron Miklós Wesselényi, the Transylvanian liberal who was charged with treason by the conservatives of the Viennese court. In his youth he was influenced by the French materialists of the Enlightenment, and under the influence of KAZINCZY he became a poet of Sensibility. Impressed by the ideas of Herder, he rejected his earlier cosmopolitanism and became interested in the concept of national character. At his best he was a fine lyric poet, but most of his verse has no great originality. In essay-writing, however, he was superior to all his contemporaries in Hungary. His essay on CSOKONAI, written in 1814 but not published until 1817, and his review of the second edition of the poems of BERZSENYI proved him a serious critic. They also revealed his intention to distance himself from the ideals of the previous generation. His main interest became history. One of his poems about the Hungarian past, 'Hymnus' (Hymn, 1823), was to become the text of the national anthem, after it was set to music by Ferenc Erkel in 1844. Obsessed by the idea of predestination, he was inclined to pessimism. His best poem, 'Vanitatum vanitas' (1823), gives a nihilistic view of history, and the vision of the death of the Hungarian nation is presented in 'Zrínyi dala' (The song of Zrínyi, 1830) and 'Zrínyi második éneke' (Zrínyi's second song, 1838). His most important essay, *Nemzeti hagyományok* (National traditions, 1826), served as a starting-point for Hungarian Romanticism. Inspired by Herder and Friedrich von Schlegel, he compared organic Greek and inorganic, imitative Roman culture, and urged Hungarians to develop their own organic culture, drawing inspiration from the songs of the peasantry. *Országgyűlési napló* (A diary kept during a Diet, 1832–5), is one of the most important documents of Hungarian liberalism. *Parainesis* (1837), addressed to his nephew, is the moral testament of a stoic whose intention was to fight even under hopeless circumstances.

●R. Porter and M. Teich (Eds), *Romanticism in National Context* (Cambridge, 1988).   MSz-M

KOLIQI, Ernest (1903–75), Albanian poet, prose writer, one of the leading literary figures of the 1930s and 1940s, was born in Shkodër, and educated at a Jesuit college in Brescia, where he first became acquainted with Italian literature. He returned to

Albania 1921, where he worked as a teacher and journalist. 1924 he had to leave Albania for political reasons and spent five years in Yugoslavia. 1937, after having finished a thesis on the Albanian popular epic, he was appointed to the chair of Albanian Language and Literature at the University of Rome. During the Italian occupation of Albania he served as Minister of Education. 1945 he fled to Italy where he lived for the rest of his life. Among Koliqi's best works are the dramatic poem *Kushtrimi i Skanderbeut* (Scanderbeg's warcry, 1924); the short-story collections *Hija e maleve* (Mountain shades, 1929) and *Tregtar flamujsh* (Flag merchant, 1935). His verse appeared as *Gjurmat e stinave* (The tracks of seasons, 1933) and *Symfonia e shqipevet* (The symphony of eagles, 1941). He has also written a novel, *Shija e bukës së mbrume* (The taste of homemade bread, 1960), as well as numerous studies on Albanian folklore and literary criticism.   ShM

KOLLÁR, Jan (1793–1852), Slovak-born Czech poet and prose writer, read theology at Jena (1817–19), where he came into contact with German nationalism and met a parson's daughter who became his muse but whom he did not marry until 1835. He spent most of his life as a Lutheran priest in Pest. His most influential work, where the intimate verse excels the historical, political and narrative, is the cycle *Slávy dcera* (Daughter of Sláva: first published as *Básně* [Poems], 1821, 86 sonnets; as *Slávy dcera*, 1824, 151 sonnets; 1832, 615 and 1852, 645 sonnets). In it he wanders from one Slav, or formerly Slav, land to another, bewails the present lot of the Slavs and glorifies their past. At the same time he besings his German parson's daughter in whom he incorporates the beautiful spirit of Slavness. Simultaneously, in a series of books and sermons, he elaborated his notion of cultural panslavism: the main Slav dialects, Russian, Polish, Czech and Illyrian, should be known by all good Slavs; libraries and other cultural institutes should be set up in all Slav areas where a panslav education could be attained. Being a Slovak, a group with no independent literary culture, he saw salvation in a unified Slav nationalism to match German nationalism: Russians and Czechs belonged to the same nation as much as Bavarians and Hamburgers. The older Kollár grew, the more of a fanatic he became. In his travel diaries (1841–63), his autobiography (1862) and *Staroitalia slavjanská* (Ancient Slav Italy, 1853), he found Slavonic roots wherever he went, and where he did not find or see them, people had an unpleasant appearance and even the weather was bad. Some of his apparently wild theories had some truth in them, e.g. the Slavonic origins of the Reformation in the Bogomils-Cathars as well as the later Hussites. At the same time he was a great admirer of the liberal principles he saw at work in industrialised Saxony.

●41 of Kollár's sonnets in J. Bowring, *Cheskian Anthology* (London, 1832). P. R. Black, *Kollár and Štúr. Romantic and Post-Romantic Visions of a Slavic Future* (New York, 1975); P. Brock, *The Slovak National Awakening* (Toronto, 1976); A. Pražák, 'The Slavonic Sources of Kollár's Pan-Slavism', *SEER*, VI (1927–8), pp. 579–92.   RBP

KOMENSKÝ, Jan Amos (J. A. Comenius, 1592–1670), Czech educationist, theologian and writer given to hermetic thought, the last bishop of the Bohemian Brethren (Unitas

Fratrum), had to leave Bohemia in 1628 when, after the Battle of the White Mountain (1620), Protestant-ism was forbidden in the country, and lived and worked in Poland, England, Sweden, Hungary, Prussia and, finally, Holland. His writings on didactics and his new methods in language teaching had a lasting influ-ence on the development of educa-tion theory and practice in Europe and America. The project he pursued all his life was the reform of society by unifying all knowledge on the basis of Christian faith. He went to England in 1641 at the invitation of Parliament which considered establ-ishing a learned college based on his ideas but the plan was thwarted by the outbreak of the Civil War. Komenský's most important Czech work is *Labyrint světa a ráj srdce* (The labyrinth of the world and the paradise of the heart, written 1623, publ. 1631). Inspired by the works of the German Johann Valentin An-dreae, in particular *Peregrini in Pat-ria Errores Utopiae* (1618), Komenský wrote an allegory of a pilgrim being conducted through a city, i.e. contemporary society, by dishonest guides who try to convince him of its perfection. They put over his eyes deceitful spectacles but these are askew and he sees everything as it really is. With shrewdness and irony he observes and comments on various estates and professions and, finding no justice, he nearly despairs. But finally the pilgrim turns to Christ as present in his own heart, the only firm point and haven of security in the universe. The first part of the book expresses a merciless criticism of society; it rejects all its institu-tions, as well as science and art; it is one of the most pessimistic works in world literature. Komenský is a mas-terly narrator; dramatic scenes pre-sented in vivid, often coarse, lan-guage alternate with descriptions of great poetic effect. Komenský's de-votional verse written in Classical metre had a considerable impact on the poetics of the Czech National Revival.

●*The Labyrinth of the World and the Paradise of the Heart* (London, 1971). M. Spinka, *John Amos Comenius* (Chicago, 1943); M. Blekastad, *Comenius* (Oslo, Prague, 1969); J. Needham (Ed.), *The Teacher of Nations* (London, 1942).   KB

KONDILAKIS, Ioannis (1862–1920), Greek prose writer, was born into a famous family of fighters: some of his male relations were involved in the 1866 uprising; hence both the heroic climate and the nostalgia which mark his work. He was edu-cated in Crete and Athens. After the next uprising (1877) his family's financial difficulties prevented him from continuing his education: he spent three years as a court clerk. 1884 he managed to finish his school-ing and enrolled to read literature at Athens. But 1885 he went as a teacher to a village in W Crete, his experi-ences furnishing the material for his later series of prose vignettes, Οταν ήμουν δάσκαλος (When I was a schoolmaster, 1916). He later became a journalist and settled in Athens. 1896–1918 he had his own column in *Embros* (Forward), under the pseudonym 'Wayfarer', and is regar-ded as 'father' of the *feuilleton* in Greece. Until late in life he was an opponent of demoticism. Ο Πατούχας (Patouhas, 1916), with its portrait of the first love of a naive Cretan shepherd boy, is an effective blend of ethographic and psychologi-cal fiction.   CFR

KONESKI, Blazhe (b. 1921),

Macedonian poet and prose writer, studied at Belgrade and Sofia and worked for the journals *Nov den* (New day) and *Makedonski yazik* (Macedonian language); he became one of the architects of the Macedonian literary language and wrote its first grammar (1952–4) and history (1966); he also wrote the first histories of Macedonian literature (two in 1945, one in 1950). 1957 he was given a chair in literature in the Arts Faculty at Skopje; he was president of the Macedonian Academy of Arts and Sciences. Koneski's verse in the long poem *Mostot* (The bridge, 1945) and in the collection *Zemyata i lyubovta* (Love and the soil, 1948) is dominated by somewhat bitter reminiscences of the Slav past of the Macedonian people, and their fight for freedom; the joy of victory and liberation is mixed with an even more joyous anticipation of the rejuvenation of the liberated land. The prevailing mood of his verse is patriotic. His second collection, *Pesni* (Poems, 1953), besides patriotic poems, contains verse based on the oral tradition and some impressionistic Nature poems. The verse in *Vezilka* (Embroidery, 1955) is focused on such perennial themes as love, future disappointment hidden in moments of joy, or the inevitability of death. Myth, legend and present times mingle in Koneski's work; the individual is perceived in his historical continuity and linked to the collective and mythological. Individualist themes (e.g. man and Fate) receive treatment on the basis of the emblematic figures of oral-tradition heroes (e.g. the warrior Krali Marko) and create a domestic version of the Prometheus myth. Koneski's poetic expression is based on rich associativeness, and he has a gift for inventive imagery. His only collection of short stories, *Lozye* (Vineyard, 1955), marks, technically, a new stage in the development of Macedonian prose; it treats themes linked with the everyday life of ordinary people behind whose 'ordinariness' he discovers profound emotions and drama.

●*Poems* (London, 1979).   SIK

KONICA, Faik (1875–1942), Albanian publicist, literary critic and publisher, was born in the village of Konica, N Greece; after elementary schooling in Turkish in his native village, he studied at the Jesuit college in Shkodër and at the Gallata French school in Constantinople. 1890 he went to France and graduated in Romance philology at Dijon. Thenceforth he lived only abroad. Konica is the founder of the periodical *Albania*, one of the most important organs of the Albanian National Revival, published first in Brussels (1897), moving to London 1902 and published there until 1910. Through *Albania* Konica helped make the Albanian cause known in W Europe and supported the national movement. Writers like ÇAJUPI, FISHTA, MITKO and KRISTOFORIDHI first became known there. Konica is the first to propagate the idea of editing older Albanian literature and to state the necessity of creating a unified literary language. Apart from his numerous articles on politics, language, literature and history, he has written a satirical novel, *Dr Gjëlpëra* (Dr Needle, 1924), and *Albania the Rock Garden of Southeastern Europe and Other Essays* (Boston, 1957). Konica virtually created a unified S Albanian language dialect.   ShM

KONOPNICKA, Maria (i.e. M. Wasiłkowska, 1842–1910), Polish poet and short-story writer, an emancipated woman, moved to Warsaw leaving behind her unloved husband and thereafter earned her living independently. Throughout her life she remained passionately committed to social issues. As a result, her work tends to suffer from overbearing ideological messages about the fates of the poor and the dispossessed. Konopnicka is most successful in those of her poems which emulate the simplicity of Polish folklore (*Na fujarce* [Pipe music, 1883]) or record her impressions of Italy and France (1901–3). Her short stories, as didactic as her poetry, occasionally achieve an appealing directness and simplicity of style (*Miłosierdzie gminy* [The community's compassion, 1891]). SE

KONSTANTIN OF **PRESLAV** (i.e. Constantine of P., c. 830–c. 907), Bulgarian author, was a disciple of Cyril and Methodius who was sold as a slave in Venice, sent to Constantinople and later went to Bulgaria. Konstantin worked at the Preslav School, one of the two early centres of Bulgarian culture (SEE KLIMENT OF OHRID). His most important work is *Uchitelno evangelie* (Didactic Gospel, completed c. 893–4), which contains the *Azbuchna molitva* (Alphabet prayer, often considered to be the first Slav poem), 51 sermons, *Skazanie cherkovnoe* (Ecclesiastical legend, a compilation from the work of the Constantinople patriarch German [715–30]) and *Istorikii* (Histories, a chronicle covering events from the beginning of Creation until 894; the first Slav chronicle). Konstantin translated the *Four Sermons against the Arians* of Athanasius of Alexandria (297–373), which marks the beginning of Bulgarian anti-heretical literature; here he introduced new theological terminology; *Sluzhba na Metodii* (Service in honour of

Methodius) is also attributed to Konstantin. His work laid the foundations of sermon and hymn writing in Bulgaria.

●P. Dinekov, 'Über die Anfänge der bulgarischen Literatur', *International Journal of Slavic Linguistics and Poetics*, 3 (1960), pp. 109–21; A. Vaillant, *Discours contre les Ariens du saint Athanase, version slave et traduction en français* (Sofia, 1954); J. Dujčev, *Übersicht über die bulgarische Geschichtsschreibung, Antike und Mittelalter in Bulgarien* (Berlin, 1960).

SIK

KONSTANTINOV, Aleko (1863–97), Bulgarian prose writer, so popular that he is known by his Christian name and also by his self-ironical pseudonym 'Shtastlivetsa' (The Happy One), came from a cultured family and was educated at grammar school in Russia, then read law at Odessa (1881–5). In Bulgaria he worked as a judge but came into conflict with the authorities after his refusal to accept the political corruption of the courts. Within five years he lost all his family and was unable to find a job; he turned to Nature to forget society. He travelled to the World Fairs in Paris (1889), Prague (1891) and Chicago (1893), and worked as a lawyer but still experienced financial hardship all his life. 1894 he began writing *feuilletons* in which he attacked King Ferdinand and the prime minister for Bulgaria's political corruption. He made many enemies through his writings and was assassinated. His best-known work is *Bay Ganyo* (1895), a collection of 'incredible' adventures of a modern Bulgarian abroad (*Bay Ganyo trăgva po Evropa* [B.G. goes to Europe]), and also at home (*Bay Ganyo pravi izbori* [B.G. involved in elections]). Konstantinov was involved with the

Vesela Bălgariya (Merry Bulgaria) bohemian circle, which tried to conquer the ugliness of society by laughter, and apparently constructed his figure Bay Ganyo in this circle. Each of Bay Ganyo's stories is told by someone (usually a Bulgarian student abroad), who had witnessed it. Bay Ganyo himself embodies the worst aspects of the Bulgarian character: he is vulgar, and vulgarly materialistic, insensitive and calculating; he is sexually aggressive, primitive and cruel; he is an authentic parvenu. Aleko's *homo balcanicus* is ridiculous when in Europe, but at home he is dangerous, even terrifying. Critics disagree on whether Bay Ganyo represents 'Bulgarianness'. In his character, typical 'national' features are combined with those of any upstart; thus he can also be interpreted as representative of human shamefulness. Konstantinov is also the author of one of the earliest Bulgarian travel books, *Do Chikago i nazad* (To Chicago and back, 1894), where he regards the American way of life as anti-human and foresees some of the disastrous effects of technological progress and civilisation.

●G. Gesemann, 'Der problematische Bulgare', *Slavische Rundschau*, 3, 1931, pp. 404–9.   SIK

KONWICKI, Tadeusz (b. 1926), Polish novelist and film director, born near Vilnius, whose native country, transformed into a paradisiac valley, haunts all his works, endorsed the postwar Communist régime and Socialist Realism for some time, but eventually became an outspoken dissident. He directed and wrote scripts for several films, beginning with *Ostatni dzień lata* (The last day of summer, 1958). Konwicki's fiction represents a lyrical blend of differing styles and levels of reality. In *Zwierzoczłekoupiór* (The bestio-

humanospectre, 1969) the plurality of coexisting worlds includes romantic adventure, science fiction and a realistic portrayal of contemporary Warsaw. Numerous flashbacks in *Kompleks polski* (The Polish complex, 1977) serve to juxtapose an heroic past with a trivial present. *Mała apokalipsa* (A little apocalypse, 1979), ostensibly set in an indefinite future, conveys a terrifying image of the total annihilation of moral values in contemporary Poland, reaching a point where even genuine tragedy becomes impossible. *Bohiń* (1987) confuses a mass of prose techniques in order to establish the impossibility of genuine representation. In addition to his novels, Konwicki has also published four books which lie on the borderline between fiction and autobiographical essay (e.g. *Wschody i zachody księżyca* [Risings and settings, 1981]).

●*The Anthropos-Spectre-Beast* (New York, 1977); *The Polish Complex* (New York, 1982); *A Minor Apocalypse* (London, 1983); *Bohin Manor* (New York, 1990).

H. Wlodarczyk (Ed.), *T. Konwicki, écrivain et cinéaste polonais d'aujourd'hui* (Paris, 1986).   SE

KORAËS, Adamandios (1748–1833), Greek scholar and publicist, son of a wealthy Chiot merchant family, was educated in his native Smyrna but wished to study further in the West, whereas his father wanted him to become a merchant. The compromise was that he should go to Amsterdam (1771), both a trading centre and a focus of intellectual liberalism. 1777, having failed in his commercial enterprise, he travelled back to Smyrna via Leipzig, Vienna, Trieste and Venice. 1782 he finally managed to escape again, to study medicine in Montpellier, and 1788, now a qualified doctor, settled in Paris, where he took up the cult of Antiquity in the new form practised by French liberals in the pre-revolutionary and revolutionary periods. Believing that a good education engendered the love of liberty, he decided that his contribution to the liberation of the Greek nation should be intellectual. He began by producing conventional editions of works by Ancient and Renaissance authors. 1798–1805 he diverted his energies to a series of anonymous political pamphlets, designed to support the short-lived French initiatives to foment revolution in Greece. Then, 1805 he started publishing his major work, the Ελληνική Βιβλιοθήκη (Greek library) – editions of the Classics with the text explained and accompanied by long introductions in which the editor sets out his linguistic, educational and political theories. The enterprise continued even after the outbreak of the War of Independence, with texts especially chosen for their moral values, e.g. Aristotle's *Politics* and *Ethics* (in the preface to the former he recommended that the new state should have a constitution modelled on the American). Unfortunately, Koraës's cautious linguistic views had the greatest influence on posterity. His belief in the Classical tradition as the embodiment of liberty led him to insist that only a classicising form of the language will express and preserve eternal values. In certain respects he was quite liberal. He believed in the necessity of the systematic study of linguistic principles and comparative linguistics; he proposed the compilation of a new dictionary to record vocabulary in current spoken use, and he rejected the revival of dead linguistic forms. But the purification process by which he wanted to make the spoken language a viable written form was entirely eclectic, and as such a recipe for just the macaronics which the 'purified language' adopted by the post-Independence constitution duly bred. Koraës was disillusioned with the political and intellectual direction taken by the newly independent Greek state, and died a disappointed man.   CFR

KORIWN, Vardapet (4th–5th century), Armenian writer, whose *Vark' Mashtotsi* (Life of Mashtots) is perhaps the earliest original writing in Armenian. It is the biography of the man who invented the Armenian alphabet in 406(?) and is the major source for the cultural history of early 5th-century Armenia. Little is known about the life and work of Koriwn. The main sources on his biography are the 'Life of Mashtots' and the 'History of Armenia' by the late 5th-century historian Ghazar P'arp'etsi (437–500). The latter knows of Koriwn, mentions him as Mashtots's pupil and biographer, and declares that the 'Life' is the authentic source of the events of the early decades of the century. Ghazar P'arp'etsi's testimony is important, since he was a pupil of Aghan Artsruni, who was a contemporary and schoolmate of Koriwn. Koriwn belonged to the group of students gathered soon after the invention of the alphabet at Vagharshapat and sent (c. 407) to teach in the Armenian provinces, and to translate the Scriptures into Armenian. In the 420s Koriwn was sent to Constantinople to join EZNIK to help him translate the works of the Greek Fathers. Koriwn's name does not appear in the lists of bishops or priests present at the councils of Shahapivan (444) and Artashat (449). The last datable reference in the Life seems to be the year 443, when Vahan Amatuni erected a shrine as a 'resting place' for Mashtots. Medieval writers and modern scholars attribute to Koriwn several works, including the 'List of Rituals' and probably the 'Catecheses' of Cyril of Jerusalem, translated into Armenian in the first half of the 5th century. The historian Kirakos Ganjaketsi (1203–72) attributes to Koriwn a 'History of Armenia'. Norayr Buzandatsi (1844–1916) proposed that Koriwn was the translator of the Histories of AGAT'ANGEŁOS, P'AWSTOS BUZAND and the Book of Maccabees. Recently Archbishop Norayr Pogharian has demonstrated that the 'Teachings of St Gregory' in AGAT'ANGEŁOS is also his work. These attributions are seriously challenged by various scholars. Unlike the works discussed above, the authorship of the 'Life of Mashtots' is attested by several early and medieval Armenian historians, who used it as an authentic source for the invention of the Armenian alphabet and the life of Sahak Catholicos of Armenia (348–438). There are two medieval editions of Koriwn's 'Life of Mashtots', one considerably longer than the other. The consensus among modern scholars is that the longer version is the original. The 'Life of Mashtots' is written with feeling and admiration. Religious sentiment is present throughout. Its style is uneven, its language at times bombastic and ornate. It tends to exaggerate and repeat to enhance the reputation of the biographee. The author is presenting St Mashtots as an example of a holy man, who should be emulated by contemporaries and future generations. Koriwn's 'Life', probably written in the mid 440s, is the most reliable source for the political, cultural and religious history of 5th-century Armenia.

• *Vark' Mashtotsi*, a photoreproduction of the 1941 edition with a modern Armenian translation, concordance and new introduction in English by K. Maksoudian (New York, 1985), includes an English translation by B. Norehad (New York, 1964).   VN

KORNAROS, Vitsentos (fl. 16th century), Cretan poet, was author of the verse romance Ερωτόκριτος (Erotokritos) and possibly of the single religious play produced by the Cretan Renaissance, Η Θυσία του Αβραάμ (The sacrifice of Abraham). The commonly accepted view now is that Kornaros belonged to the noble Veneto-Cretan family of Corner. He has often been identified with a Vitsentos Cornaro born near Siteia in 1553, married in Herakleion in the period 1587–90, who was a member of the Council of Nobles and occupied various administrative positions. This Vitsentos was a member of a literary society, the Academy of the Stravaganti, founded by his brother Andrea, and poems written by him in Italian have survived. He died in 1613 or 1614. If 'The sacrifice of Abraham' is by him, it is the earlier of his works. It derives from an Italian play by Luigi Groto on the same theme. The Greek author has reworked his model to emphasise the psychological aspects of the drama, creating rounded and emotionally convincing characters, particularly in the case of the boy Isaac. The *Erotokritos* is also a reworking, this time of an Italian prose version of the 15th-century French romance *Paris et Vienne*, by Pierre de la Cypède. But the model is of even less importance in this case. Though Kornaros has reset the tale in a nebulous pagan Athens, the situations, characters and values of the poem are firmly rooted in contemporary Crete. A princess falls in love with a young man of inferior birth, who proves himself worthy of her by victory in a tournament. The king has rejected the young man's suit, and on discovering that the couple are secretly meeting, he imprisons his daughter and sends her suitor into exile. When war breaks out between the Athenians and the Vlachs, the hero, in disguise, saves the day. The king gives the hand of the princess to his unrecognised benefactor, the truth is revealed and the couple are united. The themes of the poem are drawn from the same stock as those of the Byzantine romances: war, love, exile and the effect of chance upon human relations. But despite the stylised nature of the plot, the emotions and changes of attitude experienced by the princess Aretousa and her suitor Rotokritos, son of a palace adviser, are analysed in a manner more Renaissance than medieval. Stylistically, too, the work is typical of its period. The five-book structure reflects the five-act structure of the favourite Cretan literary form, the drama, and there is a high proportion of dialogue. The love rhetoric and plentiful supply of images drawn from Nature can be paralleled in contemporary pastoral plays. After the fall of Crete (1669) the *Erotokritos* circulated widely in oral form, giving rise to folk-songs based on episodes from it. The first surviving printed edition appeared in Venice in 1713. The work was to have a significant influence on the language and poetic technique of SOLOMOS and the poets of the Ionian Islands.

●*Erotocritos* (Athens, 1984).

D. Holton, *Erotokritos* (Bristol, 1991).

CFR

KORNIYCHUK, Oleksander (1905–72), Ukrainian playwright, an exponent of Socialist Realism, received official acclaim with the production of his plays *Zahybel eskadry* (Death of a squadron, 1934) and *Platon Krechet* (1934). The surgeon, Platon Krechet, is the embodiment of the new Soviet superman, the apogee of 'sunny optimism, humanism and patriotism'. Korniychuk's play *Bohdan Khmelnytsky* (1938) abounds in purple passages and praise for the Pereyaslav Council (1654) which proclaimed the re-unification of Ukraine with Russia. For his propagandist works Korniychuk received several Stalin Prizes and became a high state official. He wrote a topical propaganda play, *Front* (1942), excerpts of which appeared in *Pravda*. 1945 he published his 'American' play, *Missiia mistera Perkinsa v krainu bilshovykiv* (The mission of Mr Perkins into the land of the Bolsheviks). The first signs of the post-Stalin Thaw can be clearly seen in Korniychuk's *Kryla* (Wings, 1954). As secretary of the Ukrainian branch of the Writers' Union, Korniychuk dominated literary life in his country for almost two decades.

●*Wings* (Moscow, 1954).   GSNL

KORYTKO, Emil (1813–39), Polish ethnographer, collector of Slovene folk poetry, as a student in Lwów (Lemberg) fell under suspicion for seditious activities and was exiled to Ljubljana for complicity in the distribution of banned literature (including MICKIEWICZ's *Księgi narodu polskiego i pielgrzymstwa polskiego*). The last two years of his life were devoted to collecting and publishing Slovene folk poems. His insistence on stressing the independence of Slovene from Croat-Illyrian literature helped to establish Slovene linguistic and cultural autonomy. His correspondence reveals close ties with the Galician Romantics (August Bielowski, Jozef Dunin-Borkowski, Dominik Magnuszewski). His premature death thwarted plans for a comparative encyclopaedia of Slavonic ethnography. His collections of oral-tradition songs are in *Slovenske pesmi krajnskiga naroda* (Slovene songs of the Carniolan people, 5 vols, 1839–44).   HL

KOSMAČ, Ciril (1910–80), Slovene prose writer, was imprisoned for nationalist activities by the Italians in Koper, Gorica, Rome and Trieste, went after release to Ljubljana, where he was a freelance writer. 1938–44 he was in France and London; he then joined the partisans in Bari. After the war he worked as editor and screenwriter. His collection *Sreča in kruh* (Happiness and bread, 1946) contained six social-realist stories published in the periodical *Sodobnosti* (Today) before the war; among these notable is 'Gosenica' (The caterpillar), where the writer in a prison cell of the Regina Coeli gaol watches helplessly the assault of insect on vegetable life. His most interesting postwar experiment is the short novel *Balada o trobenti in oblaku* (The ballad of the trumpet and the cloud, 1968), where the action is reported by three narrators.

●B. Levski (Ed.), *Death of a Simple Giant and other Modern Yugoslav stories* (Toronto, 1965); *A Day in Spring* (London, 1959).   HL

KOSOVEL, Srečko (1904–26), Slovene poet, while studying Slavonic and Romance languages at Ljubljana university began to write verse, contributing to the student periodical *Lepa Vida* (Beautiful V.) and the left-wing *Mladina* (Youth). Shortly before his death he prepared a collec-

tion of poems entitled *Zlati čoln* (The golden boat), eventually published in 1954. Themes of importance in his poetry are love of his native Kras with its villages, woods, stone houses, storms, juniper bushes and fieldfares, awareness of his poor health and apprehension of an early death, an apocalyptic vision of catastrophe engulfing the old world, seen notably in 'Ekstaza smrti' (Death's ecstasy) and 'Tragedija na oceanu' (Tragedy on the ocean). Towards the end of his life he began to experiment with a verse form corresponding to the collage in visual art; to such poems he gave the name 'Kons' (construct or construction).

●Translations in: *AMYP*, 1962; *Parnassus*, 1957, 1962; *Introduction to Yugoslav Literature*, 1973, *LS* 1984. HL

KOSTENECHKI, Konstantin (i.e. Constantine of Kostenets, c. 1380-after 1431), Bulgarian author, who worked in Serbia, was a pupil of one of Patriarch EVTIMII's disciples, with whom he stayed at the Bachkovo Monastery until 1410, when the Turks invaded the Rhodopes; then he escaped to Serbia where King Stefan Lazarević (reigned 1389–1427) received him. Konstantin settled in Belgrade and devoted himself to literary and educational activities; he might have travelled to Palestine and probably participated in Lazarević's diplomatic mission to Timur (Tamerlane) and to the Turks. All trace of him disappeared after 1431. He wrote three works, the grammatical tract *Razyasnenie za bukvite* (Treatise on letters, c. 1418), *Zhitie na Stefan Lazarevich* (The life of S.L., c. 1431) and *Pătuvane do Palestina* (Journey to Palestine, date unknown), which may be a compilation. Konstantin's *Razyasnenie* comprises four parts concerning the problems of Serbian orthography, the education of children, the language of Cyril and Methodius and Serbian morals. At the time Konstantin went to Serbia, Serbian books differed in orthography and he, a zealous follower of EVTIMII's orthographic reform, proposes a solution in the spirit of that reform; moreover, he condemns the 'incorrect' orthography in liturgical books as 'blasphemy' or 'heresy'. The orthographical system proposed by him is, however, too complicated and artificial. On the education of children he suggests a 'phonetic method' in learning letters: pupils should first learn to form syllables then whole words. According to Konstantin, the language of Cyril and Methodius was a mixture of seven Slavonic languages, and the Cyrillic alphabet was created under Cyril's instruction by a group of scholars representing several Slav tribes. His condemnation of the morals of Serbia (e.g. drunkenness, cheating, the habit of sealing 'brotherhood' by drinking blood, the belief in and practice of magic, the corruption of churchmen) is linked with his dislike of the 'corrupt' orthography of sacred books; that orthography is seen as the root of all evil. His *Zhitie na Stefan Lazarevich* is the first Bulgarian 'biography'; it differs greatly from medieval hagiography in its descriptions of the history and geography of Serbia and in its introducing the ruler through his genealogy and the deeds of his predecessors. The *Zhitie* contains the first account of the topography of the Serbian lands, and the first description of their inhabitants. It also contains a great deal about Balkan history between the end of the 14th century and 1431. Only some fragments from the 16th century are

extant of his *Pătuvane do Palestina*, which is the first travel book in Bulgarian literature; it abounds in geographical and ethnographical facts and contains examples of a purely aesthetic perception of the beauty of Nature.

•V. Jagic (Ed.), 'Konstantin Filosof i nyegov zhivot Stefana Lazarevicha, despota srpskoga' in *Glasnik srpskog uchenog drustva*, 42 (1875), pp. 223–328.   SIK

KOSTENKO, Lina (b. 1930), Ukrainian poet, composed the collections *Prominnia zemli* (Earthly rays, 1957), *Vitryla* (Sails, 1958), *Mandrivka sertsia* (The wandering heart, 1961), *Nad berehamy vichnoi riky* (On the shores of the eternal river, 1971), *Nepovtornist´* (Not to be repeated, 1980) and *Sad netanuchykh skulptur* (Garden of unthawed scultures, 1987). The gaps between the publication dates of this prolific writer indicate the difficulties she encountered having her work published. Her historical novel in verse, *Marusia Churai*, appeared in 1979, but it was not until 1987 that it was recognised. A confessional poet and a master of the laconic phrase, Kostenko often explores recollected emotion. Her best work, *Marusia Churai*, deals with Ukrainian history of the Khmelnytsky era with many flashbacks into the past. Marusia Churai was an historical figure, through whom the poet assesses history and its meaning for the present. It is interesting that the vaunted event of the Khmelnytsky era – the Pereyaslav Union with Russia of 1654 – is mentioned only briefly as a 'cursed treaty'. 1987–8 there were three stagings of this work in Ukraine, which helped to restore the historical memory of the nation. Today, Kostenko is the undisputed 'ruling poet' of Ukraine.

●*Selected Poetry: Wandering of the Heart* (New York, London, 1990). 'Lina Kostenko' issue, *Canadian Slavonic Papers*, 2 (1991).   GSNL

KOSTIĆ, Laza (1841–1910), Serbian poet, dramatist and critic, was a native of the Vojvodina. He attended law school in Budapest and occupied posts in Novi Sad, Belgrade and Montenegro, where he was active in cultural and political life. He was one of the leaders of the United Serbian Youth and a Serbian representative in the Hungarian parliament, but he was also persecuted for his liberalism and patriotism. His first books of verse, *Pesme* (Poems, 1873 and 1874), reveal his basic traits: ebullience, inventiveness, a quest for new expression and forms, and a predominantly Romantic spirit based on folk poetry and emotionalism. At the same time, he brings into his works a cosmopolitan spirit acquired through his broad erudition. By treating universal concerns, such as man's relationship to God, society and his fellow men, he raised his poetry above the localised Romanticism of his predecessors. Yet his exuberance often left his Romanticism unchecked. His contribution to the development of a Serbian lyric style was significant. His plays are as Romantic as his poetry. Kostić also translated, especially Shakespeare.   VDM

KOSYK, Mato (i.e. Kossick, Matthias/Matthäus, 1853–1940), Lower Sorbian poet, born in the village of Wjerbno (Werben), eight miles NW of Cottbus, the son of a smallholder, began to learn German at the age of 9, attended schools in Wjerbno and Cottbus, then worked in Leipzig as a telegraphist on the Leipzig-Dresden railway (1873–7). He returned to Wjerbno in 1877 to concentrate on his literary activities,

which included revision of the Lower Sorbian hymnal and (1880–3) editing the weekly *Bramborske Nowiny* (Brandenburg news), but concentrated on the production of his pastoral narrative in 1,955 blank-verse hexameters, *Serbska swajźba w Błotach* (A Sorbian wedding in the Spree Forest, 1880), and a national epic of 100 stanzas (*ottava rima*), *Pśerada markgroby Gera* (The treachery of Margrave Gero, 1882). 1883 he emigrated to the USA, studied theology at Springfield, Illinois, and Chicago, and was appointed pastor of the German-speaking Lutheran parish of Wellsburg, Iowa, in 1885. Following an eight-month visit to Wjerbno he returned to the USA for good in May 1887. He was pastor of German-speaking parishes at Ridgeley, Princeton, Stamford and Ohiowa (all Nebraska), then (from 1907) at El Reno, Oklahoma, in Indian territory which had been first opened for European settlement in 1889. He became a naturalised US citizen in 1894; 1890 married Anna Wehr (died 1929). They had one child, Georg Ludwig (1891–1915). 1908 Kosyk bought a farm at Albion, Oklahoma, and lived there in retirement from 1913 to his death. From America Kosyk remained in contact by letter with his homeland and continued to write poems in Sorbian. They appeared in literary journals, but were also collected as *Zběrka dolnoserbskich pěsnjow* (A collection of Lower Sorbian poems, Hoyerswerda, 1893), *Pěsni I* (Poems I, Bautzen, 1929) and *Pěsni II* (Poems II, Bautzen, 1930). The national bucolic themes of his early work were modified in America not only by nostalgia and the psychology of the exile, but also by a positive response to his American environment, including an interest in the American Indians.

●R. Dalitz and G. Stone, 'Mato Kosyk in America', *Lětopis Instituta za serbski ludospyt*, Series A, 24 (Bautzen, 1977), pp. 42–79.   GCS

KOSZTOLÁNYI, Dezső (1885–1936), Hungarian poet, novelist, short-story writer, essayist, translator and playwright, was the son of the headmaster of the grammar school in Szabadka (Subotica), a small town in S Hungary. The Kosztolányis could trace their history back to the late 9th century, when Hungarians settled in the Danube Basin. Kosztolányi was a precocious child; his first poem was published in 1901. 1903–4 he studied German and Hungarian at Budapest, where he became a close friend of BABITS. Unlike his friend, he never finished his studies. Having given up the idea of becoming a teacher, he wrote articles for provincial newspapers, and 1904 went to Vienna to study philosophy. It was probably during this stay that he heard about Freud for the first time. 1906 ADY was sent to Paris by *Budapesti Napló* (Budapest daily), and the same newspaper asked Kosztolányi to replace his colleague as permanent contributor. Poems by ADY and Kosztolányi appeared in *Budapesti Napló* on alternate Sundays, and a rivalry that divided both writers and readers developed between the two poets. When Kosztolányi's first collection of poems, *Négy fal között* (Inside four walls, 1907), was published, ADY reviewed it in a condescending tone. It took the younger poet more than twenty years to answer the attack, which he did in the pamphlet *Az irástudatlanok árulása* (The treason of the illiterate, 1929). During the 1920s linguistics gradually replaced psychology as Kosztolányi's chief interest. 1933 he discovered a tumour in his mouth, which he immediately associated with cancer. Three times he visited specialists in Stockholm; eleven times he had blood transfusions; and he survived nine operations. While ADY was influenced by Baudelaire and Verlaine and while BABITS became infatuated with Swinburne, Kosztolányi's chief source of inspiration was Rilke. In later years he moved from *Secession* to Expressionism, and his focus on the unconscious was replaced by an interest in the philosophy of language and a post-Nietzschean, antihistorical view of existence. His position is unique in Hungarian literature: he is the only author in the language who has succeeded in writing first-rate works in both lyric verse and narrative prose. *A szegény kisgyermek panaszai* (The laments of a small child, 1910), Kosztolányi's second volume of verse, presents a boy's vision of a world of plenitude, in contrast to adults' alienation and materialism. This work is a masterpiece of the Hungarian *Secession* and is superior to Kosztolányi's early prose works. Although he published short stories from the very beginning, it was not till the 1920s that he emerged as a major writer of fiction. In *A véres költő* (The bloody poet, 1922), a novel based on a close reading of what Suetonius and Tacitus had written about Nero, tyranny is treated as a crisis in public mentality and insusceptible of rational analysis. The question asked is whether man can live without the idea of a higher form of existence. A similar problem is raised in *Pacsirta* (Skylark, 1924), a novel about a spinster living in a small town called Sárszeg (Muddy nook). The Sárszeg of 1899 is described as representing the Habsburg Monarchy on the eve of the 19th century, an epitome of the posthistorical state, of a loss of purpose that the whole world must face sooner or later. Love conceals hatred; what seems to be provinciality may in fact be wisdom. Values are no less ambiguous in *Aranysárkány* (The golden kite/dragon, 1925). This second novel about Sárszeg shows how strongly Kosztolányi reacted against Positivism. The suicide of the hero, a grammar-school teacher, is motivated by the humiliation he must undergo – he is beaten by his former pupils, who could not pass their final examinations, and his only child, Hilda, runs away from home – which makes it clear to him that his conception of the world has been unduly rationalistic. The 20th century is radically different from the previous century. The message is similar in *Édes Anna* (A.E., 1926), in which a peasant girl who seems to be the perfect maidservant murders her employers. The intimacy of domestic life and the optimism based on a belief in the victory of science have been replaced by unresolved tensions. The relation between the oppressor and the oppressed is portrayed as damaging to both sides. As an essayist, Kosztolányi aimed at verbal analysis. *Tanulmány egy versről* (The close reading of a poem, 1920) is a full-scale examination of Goethe's 'Wanderers Nachtlied'. His insights into the relation between language and thought are also reflected in the stories about Kornél Esti (Cornelius Nightly), written between 1925 and his death. Together they compose a work that has none of the conventional continuity of novels and is based on the idea that 'language speaks us'. While working on these stories, Kosztolányi also tried to find new modes of expression for lyric verse. *Számadás* (A summing up, 1935), his last collection of verse, contains 96 poems; in some the emphasis is on economy. 'Októberi táj' (October landscape), for example, is a three-line text inspired by the haiku form. In longer poems like 'Marcus Aurelius' and 'Halotti beszéd' (Funeral oration) life is viewed from the perspective of death. The last two lines of 'Hajnali részegség' (Daybreak drunkenness), the penultimate poem in *Számadás*, express a vague admission of some distant transcendental power. With supreme irony, the last poem, 'Ének a semmiről' (A song about nothing), denies any kind of certainty. The last book Kosztolányi published in his lifetime was *Tengerszem* (Tarn, 1936), a lengthy collection of prose containing many fine stories. One of these, 'Caligula', anticipates the play by Camus. In Kosztolányi's interpretation, the Roman emperor is obsessed by the idea of absolute freedom. Convinced of the absurdity of existence, his ambition is to turn violence into art. What his fate suggests is that irrationality is an inalienable characteristic of existence.

●*Darker Muses: The Poet Nero* (Budapest, 1990); *The Golden Kite* (Vienna, n.d.); *Anna Édes* (London, 1991); *Nero* (London, 1947).

D. Hunyadi Brunauer and S. Brunauer, *Dezső Kosztolányi* (Munich, 1983); G. Stade (Ed.), *European Writers: The Twentieth Century*, vol. 10 (New York, 1990), pp. 1,231–49.

MSz-M

KOTLIAREVSKYI, Ivan (1769–1838), the 'father of modern Ukrainian literature', is the author of one major work, *Eneida*, his comic travesty of Virgil's *Aeneid*. The first sections of this long poem appeared in 1798 but it was published in full in 1842. With great virtuosity Kotliarevskyi transformed the life of the Trojans into the adventures of Ukrainian Cossacks. His humour is matched by his patriotism and love of the common people. He used a modern syllabotonic metre and his language, close to the vernacular, has a Baroque quality. The poem contains a wealth of ethnographic detail. Kotliarevskyi also wrote a sentimental play, *Natalka Poltavka* (N. from Poltava, 1819) which has survived in the Ukrainian repertoire to this day. It attempted to correct the caricatured portrayal of Ukrainian life found in some contemporary Russian plays. His *Eneida* led to a great many imitations, known in the history of literature as Kotliarevism. Although a loyal subject of the Tsar, Kotliarevskyi the literary Classicist is regarded as an inspirer of the Ukrainian national spirit.

•Selection in G. Andrusyhen, W. Kirkconnell (Eds), *The Ukrainian Poets: 1189–1962* (Toronto, 1963).

Ch. X in D. Čyževskyj, *A History of Ukrainian Literature* (Littleton, 1975); Ye. Sverstiuk, 'Ivan Kotliarevskyi is Laughing', in *Clandestine Essays* (Littleton, 1976); M. Pavlyshyn, 'The Rhetoric and Politics of Kotliarevskyi's *Eneida*', *Journal of Ukrainian Studies* (Summer 1985), pp. 9–24.   GSNL

KOTSIUBYN´SKYI,   Mykhailo (1864–1913), Ukrainian prose writer of the Modernist era, began writing in the Realist manner but became known as an Impressionist, especially in his short stories *Intermezzo* (1909) and *Tsvit iabluni* (Apple blossom, 1902). With keen psychological insight he pursued his goal of harmony with Nature and social equilibrium. He is best known for two novels, *Fata Morgana* (1903–10) and

Tini zabutykh predkiv (Shadows of forgotten ancestors, 1912). The first offers a Modernist treatment of a social theme – a peasant rebellion, arising out of the 1905 Revolution. The second deals with the legends and ways of life of the Hutsuls (Ruthenians) in the Carpathians.

•*Fata Morgana and Other Stories* (Kiev, 1980); *Shadows of Forgotten Ancestors* (Littleton, 1981); *Chrysalis and Other Stories* (Moscow, n.d.).

B. Rubchak, 'The Music of Satan and the Bedevilled World', an introduction to *Shadows of Forgotten Ancestors*.   GSNL

KOTT, Jan (b. 1914), Polish literary critic and scholar, professor of literature at Warsaw and Wrocław (Breslau), subsequently lectured at the State University of New York, 1969–83. Linked with the left, in the postwar years Kott championed 'grand realism' in the Communist Party-sponsored literary magazine *Kuźnica* (The forge, 1945–50) and elsewhere. His initial hostility towards Modernism was reversed in the mid-1950s when Kott, who was chiefly interested in theatre, embarked on his modern reinterpretations of classics. His *Szekspir współczesny* (Shakespeare our contemporary, 1965) related the power struggles of Elizabethan times to the 20th century. *The Eating of the Gods* (1973) offered a modern perspective on Greek tragedy. He also translates modern French writers into Polish.

•*Shakespeare Our Contemporary* (New York, 1964).   SE

KOVAČIĆ, Ante (1854–89), Croatian prose writer, born into a poor peasant family, helped by the local priest to pursue his education in Zagreb, lived in great poverty, barely earning enough to keep his large family, but obtained a doctorate and wrote a large number of verse, prose and polemical works. He died in a mental hospital. Actively involved in politics, he wrote *feuilletons* and humorous sketches about Croatian statehood and social justice. He engaged in polemics with leading contemporary writers, including ŠENOA and MAŽURANIĆ. His first novel, *Barunčina ljubav* (The love of the baroness, 1877), was well received by critics, and he turned his attention to literature. The focal point of his work is the relationship between town and country, a dominant theme of Croatian prose writing in the last quarter of the 19th century. He had little literary culture, but his writing is lively, with a fine sense of satire. His novel *Fiškal* (The advocate, 1882) describes the dilemmas of the Croatian intelligentsia in the middle of the 19th century. His best-known work, *U registraturi* (In the registry, 1888), is regarded as the most important Croatian novel of the 19th century. The novel, in diary form, falls into two halves: the first, to a large extent autobiographical, describes the happy childhood and early education of a young peasant boy taken by a benefactor to pursue his schooling in Zagreb. It offers a vivid picture of village life and a convincing account of the common experience of young boys uprooted from their villages, exposed to poverty and the often cruel mockery of their city-dwelling contemporaries. The novel abounds in lively characters. The second part, describing the narrator's mature life, is less realistic. The narrator's great love, Laura, goes off to join the *hajduks* (bandits); she invites Ivica, the protagonist, to accompany her and when he refuses she systematically destroys his life. Isolated, he steadily loses control and finally kills himself, after taking all the papers in

their files from the shelves in the registry where he works and hurling them into the air, in a violent act of revolt against bureaucracy. ECH

KOVAČIĆ, Ivan Goran (1913–43), Croatian poet, short-story writer, and critic, born in the Croatian countryside which figures prominently in his work, studied Slavonic literature in Zagreb, where he worked as a journalist. 1942 he went with NAZOR to join the partisans in the liberated territories, from where he was abducted and killed. A notable feature of Kovačić's early work is his kajkavian dialect poetry, but he is best known for the long poem based on his direct experience of the Ustashe atrocities in WWII, *Jama* (The pit, 1944). Of all the many works to have been written about WWII in Yugoslavia, this is perhaps the hardest to read: a sustained shriek of agony which does not spare the reader from exposure to extremes of suffering and cruelty, it is also an example of the power of art to transform despair into triumph through the dignity and faith of the human spirit.

●*The Pit* (Zagreb, 1962).
M. Ristić, 'Ivan Goran Kovačić', *Yugoslavia*, 3 (1950), pp. 43–6. ECH

KOVIČ, Kajetan (b. 1931), Slovene poet and novelist, after completing studies in literature, Ljubljana, 1956, worked as journalist and editor. He was one of the contributors to *Pesmi štirih* (Poems of the four, 1953) which inaugurated a new personal lyric poetry into Slovene literature. Among his verse collections are *Prezgodnji dan* (Premature day, 1956), *Ogenjvoda* (Firewater, 1965), *Labrador* (1976) and *Dežele* (Lands, 1988). His two novels are *Ne bog ne žival* (Neither god nor animal, 1965) and *Tekma ali kako je arhitekt Nikolaj preživel konec tedna* (The match or How the architect N. survived the weekend, 1970).

•Translated verse in: *MPT*; *AMYP*; *SPT*; *NWY*; *Parnassus*.   HL

KRAIGHER, Lojz (1877–1959), Slovene prose writer and playwright, by profession a doctor and dentist, after publishing short stories and sketches in literary periodicals, wrote a successful drama, *Školjka* (The shell, 1911), dissecting emotional and sexual relations in middle-class society, condemning double standards of morality and upholding women's right to free and independent choice, the shell with a pearl being a symbol of the yearning for harmonious love, the only ethical basis for married life. His novel *Kontrolor Škrobar* (Š., the auditor, 1914) presents a picture of opportunism, compromise and defection among the Styrian middle class against a background of growing German dominance and exploitation. *Mlada ljubezen* (Young love, 1923) is a picture of the middle-class youth of Ljubljana. His play *Umetnikova trilogija* (An artist's trilogy, 1921) was an attempt to present the life and work of his friend and fellow writer CANKAR as a poet's quest for pure spiritual love.   HL

KRÁL', Janko (1822–76), the most imaginative and wide-ranging Slovak Romantic poet, began writing Czech verse while at the Pressburg (Bratislava) Lyceum in 1842. By 1843 he was writing in Slovak and published eight poems in the second book in ŠTÚR Slovak (the anthology, *Ňitra II*, 1844). 1845–8 he wandered around E and SE Europe. In March 1848 he started urging peasants to rebellion, was captured and imprisoned until January 1849; by March he was leading a band of anti-Hungarian insurgents. By December, however, he had begun his inauspicious career as a minor county clerk; 1867 he was dismissed and till his death he eked out a living as a lawyer; his place of burial is unknown. No collection of his mainly narrative and contemplative verse was published in his lifetime and some of his texts were not published until the 1950s. Irony, often self-irony, permeates his works which usually concern outsiders, situations of psychological tension, social injustice, personal betrayal, and alienated children. He is at once a Slav messianist and a questioner of all messianism. He combines echoes of oral-tradition verse with formal and verbal experimentation, including *poèmes en prose*. Intensely pessimistic fatalism, often expressed in complex symbols, fuses with a desire to believe in the individual's capacity to change society, and wry compassion blends with despair at the apathy of the Slovaks.

•M. Rúfus (introduction) and J. Vajda (translator), *Janko Král' 1822–1876* (Bratislava, 1972).

R. Auty, 'Janko Král' ', *SEER*, XXXIV, (1955–6). D. Chyzhevskyi, 'Mickiewicz, Štúr and Král' ' in W. Ledrucki (Ed.), *Adam Mickiewicz in World Literature* (Berkeley, 1956). RBP

KRANJČEVIĆ, Silvije Strahimir (1865–1908), Croatian poet, born in N Dalmatia, attended secondary school in Senj, before being sent to study theology at the Collegium Germanico-Hungaricum in Rome in 1883. Kranjčević came from a devout R. Catholic family, but was always a rebellious spirit, and left Rome after only six months. He worked as a schoolmaster in several towns in Bosnia before settling in Sarajevo in 1893, where he died. An original voice of exceptional vigour, Kranjčević began to write verse while still at school. He introduced two new elements into

Croatian poetry, personal meditative themes and the figure of 'the worker'. He was passionately interested in the philosophy of a range of different cultures; his most characteristic poems offer a panorama of human spirit and intellectual experience from Ancient Egypt to the revolutionary movements of the late 19th and early 20th centuries. Most of his best-known poems, however, are a blend of Christianity and socialism, with Christianity reduced to the symbol of Christ himself, as opposed to the corruption and distortions of the Church. The strength of these poems lies in their scope: they are poems which could be described as 'composed for full orchestra' as opposed to the more familiar 'chamber music' of most of Croatian 19th-century poetry. At times melodramatic, as for instance in the depiction of the innocent child in rags who climbs on a mountain made of all the steel implements and weapons in the world to reach God's Truth, these poems communicate indomitable strength through their focus on archetypal emblems.

•Translations of 3 poems in *AMYPECH*

KRANJEC, Miško (1908–83), Slovene prose writer, abandoned Slavonic studies in 1934 to take up journalism and politics. He was a member of the underground in WWII and from 1944 with the partisans. The most prolific of the Slovene social realists, he wrote chiefly about the life of the people of his native Prekmurje, a region in the hands of the Hungarians till 1919. In his best works he is an original and straightforward interpreter of human aspirations. *Os življenja* (Life's axletree, 1935) is a realistic novel of country folk and the failed hopes of a village carpenter whose children go their

own way instead of supporting him on the farm he has acquired by an agrarian reform; the novel *Povest o dobrih ljudeh* (A tale of good people, 1940) presents an idyllic picture among the pleasures of Nature on an island in the River Mur.

•'The Old Apple-tree' in *Yugoslav Short Stories* (Oxford, 1966).   HL

KRASICKI, Ignacy (1735–1801), Polish poet, fiction writer, playwright and essayist, the most outstanding literary figure of the Polish Age of Enlightenment, was born into a noble family whose impoverishment turned him towards the priesthood. Soon after the election of King Stanisław II August (reigned 1764–95), he became part of the inner circle of literati who collaborated with the monarch on his projects to reform Polish culture. Krasicki, among other things, created and served as editor of the influential periodical *Monitor*. 1766 he was consecrated bishop of the province of Warmia; from then on, his personal contacts with the royal court and Warsaw literary circles were sporadic. However, it is precisely the decade 1775–86 that marks the period of his literary success. He stirred up controversy in 1778 by publishing his anonymous *Monachomachia*, a mock epic in *ottava rima* ridiculing the ignorance and indulgence of monks. As a satirical poet, he reached his apogee in *Satyry* (Satires, 1779–84), a sequence of ironic observations on contemporary morals; thanks to his skilful use of dialogue and dramatic monologue, *Satyry* succeeded in being didactic without intrusive rhetoric. Another of his masterpieces was the collection *Bajki i przypowieści* (Fables and parables, 1779): here, the old genre of the fable took on a new shape, close to the epigram and marked by clarity and concision. The vision of humanity's erratic ways presented in the fables shows him, his wit and humour notwithstanding, as a bitter and disillusioned, if not overtly cynical, observer of reality. Krasicki also wrote the first original Polish novel, *Mikołaja Doświadczyńskiego przypadki* (The adventures of Mikołaj Doświadczyński, 1776), a didactic but vividly narrated tale of an individual attaining wisdom through experience. Krasicki's more general significance for Polish literature lies in the fact that his work set high standards of clarity, precision, intelligence and subtlety in the use of sarcasm, mockery and irony.

●Selected poems in B. Carpenter (Ed.), *Monumenta Polonica* (Ann Arbor, 1989).
P. Cazin, *Le Prince-Evêque de Varmie Ignacy Krasicki* (Paris, 1940).   StB

KRASIŃSKI, Zygmunt (1812–59), Polish poet, playwright, fiction writer, and epistolographer, cast for a long time alongside MICKIEWICZ and SŁOWACKI as one of the three national 'bards' of the 19th century, is today admired not so much for his poetry as his two plays and thousands of fascinating letters. He was the only son of Count Wincenty Krasiński, a former Napoleonic general who after the Emperor's defeat offered his services to the Russian Tsar. His father's loyalist conservative politics resulted in the young Krasiński's being ostracised by fellow students at the University of Warsaw. He discontinued his studies in 1829 and left for W Europe where he was to remain, with only brief interruptions, for the rest of his life. He began to write as a child and by 1829 had published a Gothic novel. Other novels were to follow, but while in Switzerland in 1830, Krasiński underwent a decisive turn in his evolution: under the influence of MICKIEWICZ, whom he met, and of a young Englishman, Henry Reeve, with whom he corresponded, and of his own extensive reading, he abandoned the superficial Romantic pose of his early fiction and started exploring the moral, social and transcendental problems brought about by the course of modern history. Inspired by Vico and Herder, Krasiński created the notion of 'historical Providence' whose manifestations form what appears to us as history's logic while still leaving the individual enough room to contribute to history's progress in the spirit of Christian love. These ideas provided the background for two of Krasiński's greatest achievements, his plays *Nie-Boska komedia* (The un-divine comedy, publ. anonymously in 1835), a chilling vision of the worldwide revolution of the future, and *Irydion* (1836), a drama of individual action opposing the course of history, set in the decaying Roman empire. After these two works, his increasingly conservative outlook found its expression in numerous treatises and essays and long visionary poems (in particular, *Przedświt* [Dawning, 1843] and *Psalmy przyszłości* [Psalms of the future, 1845]). In them he appeared as a vociferous advocate of Romantic 'organicism', i.e. revolutionary violence rejected in favour of peaceful cooperation between the nation's social strata. During the 1830s and 1840s he resided mostly in French and Italian spas, fighting against the disease which eventually led to his premature death. His lifelong habit of writing several letters a day (to his father, who continued to influence him all his life, and to his lovers and friends) ultimately produced a splendid epistolographic *oeuvre*, called by one of today's critics 'the greatest novel in Polish Romantic literature'.

●'Un-Divine Comedy', in H. Segel (Ed.), *Polish Romantic Drama* (Ithaca and London, 1977); *Irydion* (London, 1927).

W. Lednicki (Ed.), *Z. Krasiński – Romantic Universalist: An International Tribute* (New York, 1964).   StB

KRASKO, Ivan (i.e. Ján Botto, 1876–1958), the poet who inspired the so-called Slovak *Moderne*, went to German, Hungarian and Roumanian grammar schools and, after three years as a building-site overseer in Hungary and a year's military service in S Tyrol, read chemical engineering at Prague. From 1905 to his call-up, 1914, he worked in a sugar refinery and a chemicals plant in N Bohemia; he served on the Eastern Front and after the war joined the civil service; later he became an MP, then Senator for the Agrarian Party. He published only two collections, *Nox et solitudo* (1909) and *Verše* (1912, rev. ed. 1936). Especially the first manifests his reading of French Symbolists in Czech and of the Czech Decadent, HLAVÁČEK, but Krasko was no imitator. His often deceptively simple writing consists mainly in intimate lyric verse expressing loneliness and lyrical nationalist and social lyrical invocations. *Nox et solitudo* presents a series of shades of mood against a background of cemeteries, wayside crosses, dark mountains and forests, mist and rain which function as polysemic signs. Loneliness is dominated by visions of the white hands and dark eyes of a lost beloved, and thus the poet dissects and emblemises his own general pain. *Verše* is less unified; here pessimism is often expressed in macabre imagery and pictures of desolate landscapes. In *Nox*

Krasko's Christian feeling was ambiguous; in *Verše* he appears to have accepted the utter failure of religion; he condemns the Slovaks for their national and cultural indolence and in 'Baníci' (The miners) even expresses revolutionary messianism.   RBP

KRASNIQI, Mark (b. 1920), Albanian poet and folklorist from Kosovo, born in the village of Gllavaçicë near Pejë, went to school in Prizren. He studied literature at Padua. 1950–60 he worked for the Ethnographic Institute of the Academy of Sciences in Belgrade. He finished his doctorate in Ljubljana and taught at the University of Prishtinë. Krasniqi is known as an expert in folk culture of the Albanians of Kosovo and other Albanian regions in Yugoslavia. He has written the collections of verse *Jehona e kohës* (The echo of time, 1972) and *Postieri i maleve* (The mountain postman, 1984). He is the author of a number of works on ethnography and geography.   ShM

KRASZEWSKI, Józef Ignacy (1812–87), the most prolific Polish novelist, son of a noble family, studied literature at the University of Vilnius. Apart from writing novels Kraszewski was a journalist, publisher and historian, and also participated in politics. His novels focused on the social decline of the gentry and their message contained encouragement to hard work and professional training (*Morituri*, 1874). His novels about peasants paved the way for the fair, but not idealised, portrayal of this social group in Polish literature. In *Ulana* (1843) a simple peasant woman becomes a true Romantic heroine. Historical fiction makes up the bulk of Kraszewski's work. Rejecting the then dominant tradition of Scott, he restricted the role of fictional characters and conferred on his novels a quasi-documentary make-up. His most widely appreciated works include novels on the Saxon period (18th century) in Poland, such as *Hrabina Cosel* (The Countess C., 1874) and *Brühl* (1875), and the country's prehistory: *Stara Baśń* (An ancient tale, 1876). Kraszewski exerted a major influence on the development of Polish fiction. His lengthy, rambling narratives still find many admirers.

●*The Countess Cosel* (London, 1901); *Count Brühl* (London, 1911).

S. Bohdanowicz, *J. I. Kraszewski, in seinem Wirken und seinen Werken* (Leipzig, 1879).   SE

KREUTZWALD, Friedrich Reinhold (1803–82), Estonian poet and prose writer, 1826–33 read medicine at Tartu, 1833–77 was a general practitioner in Võru, and from 1877 to the end of his days lived in Tartu. Kreutzwald was moved to join the Estonian Learned Society by his interest in the meaning of 'Estonianness' and his faith in the potential development of national culture. He indulged in a programmatic endeavour to expand the basis of a 'national literature'. He began with entirely German-inspired didactic and light literature, works like *Viina katk* (The scourge of drink, 1840), based on Zschokke, *Reinuvader Rebane* (Reynard the fox, 1850), based on Goethe, or *Maailm ja mõnda, mis seal sees leida on* (The world and something of what it comprises, 1848–9). As a collector and propagator of the oral tradition of long standing, Kreutzwald, at the instigation of F. R. Faehlmann (1798–1850) and under the auspices of the Learned Society, made an attempt at creating a national epos, the *Kalevipoeg* (Son of Kalev, 1857–61). The work was presented as an artistic reconstruction of

an ancient composition (in 1860 Kreutzwald received the Russian Academy of Sciences' Demidov Prize for the work); it was, however, based on threadbare oral-tradition material, mostly fragmentary and mutually unconnected prose lays and was, also, stylistically dependent on the Finnish *Kalevala* (see LÖNNROT), from which it took over the basic octosyllabic 'runa' alliterative verse form. As a whole and in detail, it constitutes an original work expressing the contemporary demands and dreams of the patriotic intelligentsia. Not even in his collection *Eesti rahva ennemuistsed jutud* (Fairytales of the Estonian people, 1866) did Kreutzwald attempt to reflect the spirit of oral-tradition prose; instead he tried to establish an aesthetically effective form which might co-create a contemporaneously acceptable prototype of prose *belles lettres*. Both these works, in which Kreutzwald played the role of an organiser and collector rather than of a creator, were of greater significance than the rest of his literary production, including his volume of poetry, *Viru lauliku laulud* (Songs of a Viru bard, 1865), the long narrative poem *Sõda* (War, 1854) and the poem 'Lembitu' (posth., 1885).

●*The Secrets of the Night and Other Estonian Tales* (London, 1899); *Kalevipoeg* (Moorestown, NJ, 1982); *A Wise Man in the Pocket* (Tallinn, 1985). E. Nirk, *Kreutzwald ja eesti rahvuslik kirijanduse algus* [with an extensive résumé in German] Tallinn, 1978); W. F. Kirby (Ed.), *The Hero of Estonia and Other Studies in the Romantic Literature of that Country* (London, 1895).   VM

KREVE-MICKEVIČIUS, Vincas (1881–1954), Lithuanian author of novels, plays and short stories, was both a witness and an important driving force in the many complex and at times turbulent developments that shaped Lithuanian literary life from its beginnings at the turn of the century, through the independence period (1918–40), and almost to the new era initiated by the 1956 'Thaw' in the culture and politics of the Soviet Union. Krėvė briefly attended the Theological Seminary in Vilnius, then studied history and philology at Kiev and Lemberg (Lwów), where he took his degree. After a period spent on Oriental studies in Baku, he returned to Lithuania in 1929 and became Professor of Slavonic Literatures at the universities of Kaunas and, later, Vilnius. During the Soviet annexation of 1940, Krėvė became Acting Prime Minister of Lithuania, but resigned soon after he learned that Moscow intended to make his country a Soviet republic. Returning to scholarly life, Krėvė worked as director of the Institute of Lithuanian Studies until he emigrated in 1944. In the USA from 1949, Krėvė worked as Professor of Slavonic Languages and Literatures at the University of Pennsylvania. The main sources of Krėvė's inspiration were two imaginary lands wrapped in myth and poetic memory: the world of Oriental legends (Near East, the Caucasus, India) and the dimly perceived warlike Lithuania of the Middle Ages, which Krėvė exalted and lyricised in *Dainavos šalies senu žmoniu padavimai* (Tales of the old folk of Dainava, 1912) in almost ritual speech cadences depicting a highly stylised world of superhuman heroes. This old world was also the scene of Krėvė's much more realistic historical plays focused upon outstanding historical (*Skirgaila*, 1925) or legendary (*Šarūnas*, 1911) figures who undertook the

tasks of forging and defending the nation. The third source of his works was his native district in Lithuania – a land of rolling hills and humble, patient people who accepted the suffering Jesus Christ as one of their own, but also retained the memory of a basically pagan, animistic worldview that filled their daily speech with an unconscious potential for poetry and myth.   RŠ

KRISTOFORIDHI, Konstandin Nelko (1827–95), Albanian translator and linguist, born in Elbasan where he went to school and later attended the Zosimea secondary school in Yoannina, collaborated there with the Austrian vice-consul Johann Georg von Hahn on *Albanesische Studien* (Albanian studies, 1853). The following year took him to Athens, Durrës, perhaps to London, Izmir, Constantinople, Malta and Tunis, where he taught at a Greek school. It was during the 1860s that he began working for the British and Foreign Bible Society for whom he translated into Albanian the NT, in both the N (1872) and S (1879) dialects. These translations served as a basis for the creation of the modern literary language in its two dialect variants. He also wrote a grammar of the Albanian language in Greek, *Grammatiki tis alvanikis glosses* (1882), and compiled an Albanian-Greek dictionary, *Lexicon tis avaikis glossis* (1904, rev. ed. in modern orthography, 1961). Kristoforidhi is the author of children's books in Albanian, among which the tale *Gjahu i malësorëvet* (The hunt of the mountaineers, 1884) is one of the first works of modern Albanian literary prose.   ShM

KRLE, Risto (1900–75), Macedonian playwright, was a manual worker, civil servant, then worked in the tobacco industry and was a bank clerk in Belgrade; after WWII he became an official at the Macedonian Ministry of Education and the Writers' Union. His first play, *Parite se otepuvachka* (Money the killer), was completed in 1937, but not published until 1958; it treats the theme of the power of money which destroys moral barriers in man and, here, eventually leads to murder. Fatal coincidence plays an important role in the play but the true evil lies in man (his greed). The tragedy (because of money, a father kills his son, for whom he had waited for years) is interpreted as a result both of the power of destiny and of imperfect human nature. In the folksy love-drama *Antitsa* (1950) greed lies behind rich Macedonians' submission to Hellenisation; the morally pure young lovers are depicted as victims and have to fight for their love. *Milioni machenitsi* (A million martyrs, 1940) examines the collision of 'old' and 'new' thinking in a little town; the motif of greed appears here as the impetus for industrialisation, which makes people even crueller than before; the 'old' times are regarded with a certain nostalgia because they were more humane. *Graf Milivoj* (Count M., 1940) concerns the corrupt Serbian régime in Macedonia. Krle introduces here another sort of greed: his Count Milivoj is a little man, feels inferior and thus he easily becomes morally degenerate. If in his other plays Krle's depiction is black and white and there is almost no psychology, in *Graf Milivoj* he attempts an analysis of the count's psychology. Krle is the first Macedonian playwright, whose theme of greed and moral fall is later taken over by other writers and examined in different contexts (see Bozhin PAVLOVSKI).   SIK

KRLEŽA, Miroslav (1893–1981), Croatian playwright, novelist, essayist and poet, was the most important figure in Croatian literature in the 20th century. Born in Zagreb where he attended elementary school, he was sent to the military academy in Budapest. During WWI he fought in Galicia. Between the wars he spent some time in Belgrade in 1933 and 1934, when he founded the literary journal *Danas* (Today) with a group of Belgrade intellectuals. But he lived most of his life in Zagreb, where he edited a series of literary journals, often providing much of their contents himself. His writings were frequently censored or banned for their radical views, and always generated discussion. He refused to publish under the Ustasha government in the Independent State of Croatia during WWII. After the liberation, he returned to intensive literary activity. From 1950 until his death he was director of the Yugoslav Lexicographical Institute in Zagreb and editor of the Encyclopaedia of Yugoslavia. He began by writing poetry, and his most significant verse work, considered by some his most important work altogether, is *Balade Petrice Kerempuha* (The ballads of Petrica Kerempuh, 1936). Written in the 'kajkavian' dialect of Zagreb and its surroundings, enriched with archaisms, and characterised by gallows humour, the ballads express the history of the Croatian people through the voice of a peasant, victim through the centuries of poverty and persecution. This voice recurs in some of Krleža's stories about WWI, where its authenticity contrasts markedly with the caricatures of officers in the Austro-Hungarian Army. Krleža is chiefly known as a playwright. His first, Expressionist, plays deal with some of the basic myths of Western civilisation. Krleža's 'classic' work is the cycle of plays relating to the Glembaj family, *Gospoda Glembajevi* (The Glembajs, 1928), *U agoniji* (Death-throes, 1928) and *Leda* (1958). Krleža uses the family to express his vision of the rise and fall of the bourgeoisie in central Europe, its origins in violence and exploitation, its hypocrisy and corruption. The plays, particularly the first, are powerful statements, depending on the conflict of ideas. He wrote two other influential plays, *Vučjak* (The village of V., 1923) and *Aretej* (Aretheus, 1959), in which he takes a broader view of the destructive effects of human stupidity through the ages. Krleža published two volumes of stories, *Hrvatski bog Mars* (The Croatian god M., 1922), concerned with WWI, and *Novele* (Short stories, 1924) in which he explores some of the main themes of his novels: the fate of the intellectual in 20th-century European, particularly provincial, society. The best known of Krleža's four novels is *Povratak Filipa Latinovicza* (The return of Filip Latinovicz, 1932), his most developed account of the alienation of the artist. The others are *Na rubu pameti* (On the edge of reason, 1938), concerned with human stupidity and the individual's impotence to take a stand in the face of corruption and hypocrisy; *Banket u Blitvi* (Banquet in Blitva, 1938–9), a satirical picture of central European society; and *Zastave* (Banners, 1962–77), a vast panorama of modern Croatian history. One of the essential characteristics of Krleža's work is the dramatic clash of ideas and this drama is reflected in the numerous volumes of essays, diaries and polemical writings which represent an important contribution to the history of the cultural and political life of Croatia between the wars.

●*The Return of Philip Latinovicz* (London, 1969); *The Cricket Beneath the Waterfall and Other Stories* (New York, 1972); *On The Edge of Reason* (New York, 1976).

A. Ferguson, 'A Critical Approach to Miroslav Krleža's *The Return of Filip Latinovicz*', *Journal of Croatian Studies*, 14–15 (1973–4), pp. 134–44; S. Lukić, 'Miroslav Krleža's Place in Progressive World Literature Between the Two Wars', *The Bridge*, 56–8 (1980), pp. 35–41; R. Bogert, *The Writer as Naysayer* (Columbus, Ohio, 1990).   ECH

KROSS, Jaan (b. 1920), Estonian poet and prose writer, having (1938–45) read law at Tartu, taught in the Department of Constitutional and International Law until 1946. 1946–50 he was interned in the Komi and Krasnojarsk regions, but from 1954 onwards he was a freelance writer. Kross began his literary career with the collection of verse, *Söerikastaja* (The enricher of coal, 1958), which presages a new generation of Estonian poets. Since the 1970s he has devoted himself entirely to historical prose, either brief, concentrated novels concerning compromised morality like the cycle *Klio silma all* (Under the eyes of Clio, 1972), or in full-fledged novels. By the use of a richly differentiated *Ich-Form* stylising various contemporary idioms, Kross gives a colourful panoramic view of various figures in the distant and recent past of Estonia – e.g., of the painter, Johann Köler, in *Kolmandad mäed* (The third range, 1975), of the poet, Kristjan Jaak Peterson (1801–22) in *Taevakivi* (The stone from the sky, 1975), of Balthasar Russow (1542?–1600), in

Kolme katku vahel (Among three plagues, I–IV, 1970–80), of the aristocratic Timotheus von Bock (1787–1836) in *Keisri hull* (The Emperor's fool, 1978), the diplomat, Friedrich von Martens (1845–1909), in *Professor Martensi ärasôit* (Prof. Martens's departure, 1984), of Bernhard Schmidt (1879–1935), in *Vastutuulelaev* (Windward ship, 1987). Later, as the political situation improved, the autobiographical element in Kross's work increased with his turning to the 1930s, 1940s and later when his generation was forming its political opinions, e.g. in the novel of school-life *Wikmani poisid* (The Wikmans' lads, 1988), the short stories *Silmade avamise päev* (The day eyes opened, 1988) and the novel *Väljakaevamised* (Finds, 1990).

●*The Rock from the Sky* (Moscow, 1983); selection in the anthology of Estonian short stories, *The Love that Was . . .* (Moscow, 1982).   VM

KRÚDY, Gyula (1878–1933), Hungarian novelist, short-story writer and journalist, was the child of a successful lawyer from a gentry family. He attended school in Szatmár, Nyíregyháza and Podolin. His first writing was published when he was 14. From 1896 he lived in Budapest, spending most of his time in restaurants, inns and cafés. His two marriages were unsuccessful, and he had serious financial difficulties, especially in the last fifteen years of his life. It took him several years to develop an original style. His first book was published in 1897, but his maturity started only with the collection *Szindbád ifjúsága* (The youth of Sindbad, 1911). In the first half of his career the heavy emphasis on similes seemed to be a characteristic of a *Secession* style. From the 1910s,

however, the same stylistic device served as a starting-point for his highly original experimentation with narrative time and space. His short stories and novels about Sindbad constitute a whole by virtue of style rather than plot or character. The hero has no identity and the narrator no reliability; at some point Sindbad decides to leave his tomb and return to the world. Both character and plot become fragmented in *Napraforgó* (Sunflower, 1918), one of the most original Hungarian novels. *Boldogult úrfikoromban* (The age in which I was a young gentleman, 1930) has an extremely slow rhythm: action is more than delayed; it is also denied. The stories *Utolsó szivar az Arabs szürkénél* (The last cigar at the Grey Arab, 1928) and *A hírlapíró és a halál* (The journalist and death, 1928) are two versions of the same incident. The credibility of the narrator is questioned and fictionality is stressed: the colonel whose task is to have a duel with a poor journalist drinks from the glass his opponent has just broken.

●*The Crimson Coach* (Budapest, 1967).
                                                      MSz-M

KRYNICKI, Ryszard (b. 1943), Polish poet and translator, recognised, after the publication of his *Akt urodzenia* (Act of birth/Birth certificate, 1969) and *Organizm zbiorowy* (Collective organism, 1975), as one of the most original voices among the so-called 'Generation of '68' or 'New Wave', was blacklisted in 1976 in retaliation for his participation in political protest; his subsequent books up to 1989 were issued by underground or émigré presses. During the 1980s, his poetry of 'linguistic' exploration and social concern has evolved into a new model of lyricism based on extreme, gnomic concision and a metaphysical or moralistic perspective.

●*Citizen R.K. Does Not Live: Poems* (Forest Grove, Oregon, 1985).   StB

KUKUČÍN, Martin (i.e. Matej Bencúr, 1860–1928), Slovak novelist, studied medicine at Prague, practised as a doctor in Dalmatia and Chile, after WWI lived briefly in Slovakia, but returned to Yugoslavia where he died. Kukučín, the chief representative of early Slovak Realism, took his themes from Slovak, and later Croatian, village life and presented them with gentle humour and compassion. In his early brief novels such as *Neprebudený* (Unawakened, 1886) he analyses the mentality of simple characters in conflict with the society on whose fringes they live, whilst in his *Dies irae* (1893) he draws a broader, ironical picture of the narrow-mindedness and greed of that society. Kukučín's partly autobiographical novel *Mladé léta* (Young years, 1894) focuses on the emotional life of young students and throws light on the relationship between the young Slovak intelligentsia and the common people. The novel *Dom v stráni* (A house on the hillside, 1903–4), set in Dalmatia, is basically the story of two lovers who have to part because they come from different social backgrounds but it also provides an acutely observed picture of Croatian village and urban society. His novel *Mat' volá* (The mother calls, 5 vols, 1926–7) sets out to chronicle the life of Croat immigrants in Chile at the turn of the century and more than his other works comments from the Christian standpoint on the materialism and egoism of contemporary society, the problems of freedom and happiness of the nation and the individual.

●*Seven Slovak Stories* (Cleveland, Ohio, 1980).   KB

KULISH, Mykola (1892–1937), the most prominent modern Ukrainian playwright, of peasant origin, began by publishing a propagandist play, *Devianosto sim* (Ninety-seven, 1924). Soon he turned to more serious, Expressionist drama and produced four masterpieces: *Narodny Malakhii* (The people's M., 1928), *Myna Mazailo* (1929), *Patetychna sonata* (Sonata pathétique, 1930) and *Maklena Grasa* (1933). Some of these plays were performed by the Berezil Theatre, directed by Les Kurbas (1887–1942). 'The theme of Kulish's creativity is how man becomes human' (George Shevelov, 1956). Kulish was arrested in 1934 and died in the gulag. Today he has been rehabilitated and his plays are being staged.

●*Sonata Pathétique* (Littleton, 1975).

V. Revutsky, 'Mykola Kulish in the Modern Ukrainian Theater', *SEER*, 49 (1971), pp. 355–64.   GSNL

KULISH, Panteleimon (1819–97), Ukrainian prose writer, poet and translator, close friend of SHEVCHENKO, whom he criticised on one occasion, member of the Brotherhood of SS Cyril and Methodius (1845–7), was arrested 1847 for membership of the Brotherhood and exiled to Tula. He was allowed to return to St Petersburg in 1850 where he continued his literary activity. He wrote a long poem, *Ukraina* (1843), and the first Ukrainian novel, *Chorna rada* (The Black Council, 1857), written in the 1840s in the manner of Scott, many collections of lyric verse as well as historical poems. He was editor of *Zapiski o yuzhnoi Rusi* (Notes on S Rus', 1856–7) and co-editor of the journal *Osnova* (Foundation, 1860–2). He maintained connections with

Ukrainians in Galicia. An able translator of several plays of Shakespeare and of the BIBLE (completed by others after his death), Kulish also wrote extensive historical studies on Ukraine's relations with Russia and Poland. He was the first biographer of Gogol′. In life and in death, Kulish was a controversial figure. He advocated the political union of Ukraine with Russia while pleading for the development of an indigenous Ukrainian high culture. He was also critical of the Cossacks. Remaining aloof from any organised Ukrainian community life, long before his death he retreated to a smallholding in Motronivka. Throughout his life his egocentric personality made it difficult for him to collaborate with others. During the 1920s much useful research on his work was done in Soviet Ukraine. Afterwards he was vilified and banned as a 'bourgeois nationalist'. Today he has been restored to his full stature.

●*The Black Council* (Littleton, 1973).

G. Luckyj, *Panteleimon Kulish: A Sketch of His Life and Times* (New York, 1983).   GSNL

KULLURIOTI, Anastas (1822–87), Greek-Albanian publisher and writer, born in the Plaka district of Athens, inhabited by Albanians, in the years of the Albanian League of Prizren, published the weekly newspaper *I foni tis Alvanias* (The voice of Albania, 1878–80). He is the author of *Alvanikon alfavitarion* (Albanian primer, 1882) and the reader *Klumësht për foshnja* (Milk for babies, 1882). He also wrote a didactic poem, published in the folklorist Spiro Dine's collection of Albanian folklore *Valët e detit* (The waves of the sea, 1908). The goals of

his patriotic activities were the founding of an Albanian political party in Greece, the opening of Albanian-language schools, and the liberation of Albania from the Turks. This brought him into conflict with both Turkish and Greek authorities. He died in prison in Athens.   ShM

KUNDERA, Milan (b. 1929), Czech writer, began studying at the Arts Faculty of Prague University in 1948, but had to leave, and so studied film at the Academy of Performing Arts (degree 1958), where he then taught 'world literature'. He was banned after the Soviet occupation, but was allowed to take up a post as lector at the University of Rennes. 1979 he was deprived of his Czechoslovak citizenship; he then moved to Paris. His best-known verse work is the narrative *Poslední máj* (The last May, 1955) which, slightly inspired by a song in KOHOUT's first play, mawkishly compared the Communist hero Julius Fučík (1903–43) with Christ, and his Gestapo interrogator with the Devil. It is a work of 'agitpathos'. Kundera's gently sad *Monology* (Monologues, 1957, altered ed. 1965) is a series of simply expressed intimate lyric poems, usually with a first-person narrator, describing moods or episodes of finite love. His first play, *Majitelé klíčů* (The owners of the keys, 1962), is Socialist Realist in its plot and characterisation, a young man's choice: fight against the Germans or remain in the cosy security of his petty bourgeois in-laws' flat, but its realisation approaches the 'Absurdist'. The tension between theme and form, and the author's compassion for the victims, makes it one of the most original Czech post-war dramas. *Ptákovina* (Cock-up,

1969) combines black comedy with erotic farce and concerns power politics and the necessity of retaining two selves, the public and the intimate. His first prose work was his collection concerning failed or defiled or acted love, *Směšné lásky* (Laughable loves, vol. I, 1963, II, 1965, III, 1969). The most sophisticated of these stories are compact situation studies suffused with wistful irony. Kundera comes closest to profundity in the powerfully written 'Falešný autostop' (Trick hitchhiking, vol. II) where a girl starts playing a game with her lover, he joins in, but when she wants to stop play-acting, he continues, and she loses her identity. The boy humiliates the girl; and humiliation is the central theme of Kundera's first novel, *Žert* (The joke, 1967). The main character in intending to avenge the humiliation perpetrated on him by the socialist system uses humiliation as his weapon. The pompous young socialist poet of Kundera's next novel, *Život je jinde* (Life is elsewhere, 1979), dies of pneumonia after a year of socialism and after moral and sexual humiliation. The figure of the oppressive mother is significant here, since Kundera's fiction usually does not depict mothers, just as, except in *Směšné lásky*, the author has so far no convincing depiction of complete love, however riddled his novels are with eroticism. The sparingly narrated *Valčík na rozloučenou* (Farewell waltz, 1979) introduces the ironic conception of plot and character which marks the rest of his novels. Here, however, the narrator's philosophising does not interfere excessively. That contrasts with *Kniha smíchu a zapomnění* (Book of laughter and forgetting, 1981) where trendy intellectualism is expressed in pretty truisms and a sarcastic vision of sex and political systems. The central idea may be mawkish, but, put analytically, it would be acceptable: 'Man's fight against might is the fight of memory against forgetting'. *Nesnesitelná lehkost bytí* (The unbearable lightness of being, 1985) shows the apex of Kundera's technique: characters are ciphers, pegs on which he can hang his narrator's interminable philosophising.

●*Laughable Loves* (New York, 1974); *Life to Elsewhere* (Harmondsworth, 1986); *Immortality* [not published in Czech at the time of going to print] (London, 1991).
L. Doležel, *Narrative Modes in Czech Literature* (Toronto, 1973); R. C. Porter, *Milan Kundera. A Voice from Central Europe* (Aarhus, 1981); M. Němcová Banerjee, *Terminal Paradox. The Novels of Milan Kundera* (London, 1991).   RBP

KUPAŁA, Janka (i.e. Ivan Łucevič, 1882–1942), Byelorussian poet and playwright, enjoyed great authority in his lifetime and is regarded as the 'national poet'. Born into a family of tenant farmers at Viazanka in central Byelorussia, he had a sketchy formal education, but read voraciously and produced his earliest poem 'Mužyk' (The peasant) in 1905. His first cycle, *Žalejka* (The reed-pipe, 1908), was devoted to peasant life, with folk poetics a strong influence throughout. Various benefactors helped Kupała to study in Vilna and St Petersburg where his acquaintance with other writers widened his literary horizons. *Huślar* (The minstrel, 1910), his second cycle, is, however, in the same mould as *Žalejka*, barely touched by

Symbolism, though stylistically more assured, but by 1913 the *Šlacham žyćcia* (On the road of life) cycle showed Kupała's lyric verse at its best: dynamic, musical, simple yet memorable and, above all, showing maximum suppleness in rhythm. In this period he also wrote a number of neo-Romantic narrative poems of which *Bandarоŭna* (1913) is the most imaginative, treating national folk legends with great skill. Now Kupała was general editor of the *Naša niva* newspaper and by that token one of the most influential men in Byelorussia. His plays were important: *Paŭlinka* (1912) is an accomplished comedy on the genera-tion clash in a peasant family; less successful was a second revue-comedy, *Prymaki* (First-footers, written 1913, publ. 1920), but the socio-political drama *Raskidanaje hniazdo* (A scattered nest, written 1913, publ. 1919) is a masterpiece portraying the ruthless destruction of a peasant family which symbolises, perhaps, the fate of Byelorussia. His last play, *Tutejšyja* (The natives, 1922), reflects Kupała's despair and disillusion after the Revolution, like several poems of the *Spadčyna* (Heritage, 1922) cycle; it was banned after its first performance in 1926. Kupała had suffered depression throughout WWI but began writing again when the short-lived Byelo-russian National Republic was set up in 1918, and many poems of this time express hope mixed with apprehen-sion. Also depressing to the poet was the split of his country into W Byelorussia (E Poland) and Soviet Byelorussia, and he produced little original poetry in the 1920s; what he did was often ambiguous, as in the poems linked by the title *Bieznazoŭnaje* (Nameless, 1925) or the very ambivalent verse on the collectivisation of agriculture, 'Sychodziš, vioska, z jasnaj javy . . .' ('Thou passest, village, from bright story . . .', 1929). Simultaneously acclaimed and repressed, like many another prominent Soviet writer, Kupała was arrested in 1930 and attempted suicide in police custody. His original work in the 1930s was both exiguous and wooden, almost entirely lacking his earlier rhythmic dynamism; again like many others, he turned to translations, mainly from Russian and Ukrainian. Kupała died in what are still mysterious circumstances, falling down the stair-well of a Moscow hotel. Despite the sharp decline in the standard of his poetry after the Revolution, and although in his last years he was little more than a figure-head, Kupała continued and con-tinues to be revered by Byelorussians for his vigorously vital, accessible, musical and affecting earlier verse which very much answered the needs of his time and is widely known to this day.

●*Only by Song* (Moscow, 1982).

ABMcM

KUŚNIEWICZ, Andrzej (b. 1904), Polish novelist, turned to writing in his fifties following a long career abroad, firstly as an automobile industry representative and later as a diplomat. A successful début in poetry was rapidly followed by fiction, his principal field of activity since 1961. Kuśniewicz is one of the most sophisticated Polish novelists of the postwar period. He sets his characters against a background of European culture which deeply

influences their attitudes. His interests embrace the Austro-Hungarian Monarchy (*Król obojga Sycylii* [The King of the Two Sicilies, 1970]), Germany (*Trzecie królestwo* [The third kingdom, 1975]) and France (*Witraż* [Stained glass, 1980]). The intriguing temporal structures of Kuśniewicz's novels include a sophisticated use of recollection and flashback (*Eroica*, 1963; *Nawrócenie* [The conversion, 1987]), and an audacious imaginary journey through the centuries (*Stan nieważkości* [Weightlessness, 1973]).
●H. P. Hoelscher-Obermaier, *A. Kuśniewicz' synkretische Romanpoetik* (Munich, 1988). SE

KUTELI, Mitrush (i.e. Dhimitër Pasko, 1907–67), Albanian short-story writer, critic and poet from Pogradec, studied in Greece and Roumania. Returning to Albania in 1934, he worked first as an economist and then began writing and translating. Kuteli's collections of short stories include *Netë shqiptare* (Albanian nights, 1938), *Ago Jakupi* (1943), *Dashuria e barbarit Artan* (The barbarian Artan's love, 1946), *Tregime të moçme shqiptare* (Ancient Albanian tales, 1965), *Baltë nga kjo tokë* (Mud from this land, 1973) and *Në një cep të Ilirisë së poshtme* (In a corner of Lower Illyria, 1984). ShM

KVEDROVA, Zofka (1878–1926), Slovene feminist writer, escaped from unhappy family life (father an alcoholic, mother over-pious) and began to collaborate with the liberal and feminist press while working as a clerk in Ljubljana and Trieste. She travelled to Switzerland and Germany, always seeking to improve her education. She worked as a journalist in Prague, where she contracted the first of two unhappy marriages. Her first book, *Misterij žene* (The mystery of a woman, 1900), was a collection of sketches based on her own experiences and influenced by the Swedish writers Laure Marholm and Ellen Key, showing woman as an unhappy creature, whose misfortunes are aggravated by male hard-heartedness and capitalist society. Her best work, the novel *Njeno življenje* (Her life, 1914), describes the bitter disappointment of a loving loyal woman who is let down both by her husband and the son who inherits his moral weaknesses of drunkenness and dishonesty. Her play *Amerikanci* (The Americans, 1908) was the first Slovene drama to deal with the problems of mass emigration. HL

KYÇYKU, Muhamet (1784–1844), Albanian Muslim poet, also known as Muhamet Çami, born in Konispol in S Albania, studied theology in Cairo and returned to his native village as *hodja*, where he lived for the rest of his life. Kyçyku's poetry marks a transition between the classical Muslim verse and the Revivalist Albanian poetry of the second half of the 19th century. Among his works, most of which were discovered after WWII, are a poem written in 1824 condemning the drinking of wine and spirits; an historical poem dated 1826 dealing with the liberation of Missolonghi from the Turks; *Jusufi e Zelihaja*, a long verse tale on a biblical subject; and *Erveheja* (1820), his best-known work, based on a Turkish original. It was published in 1888 by VRETO, who transliterated it and purged it of its Turkish and Arabic words.
●E. Rossi, 'La fonte turca della novella poetica albanese "Erveheja" di

Muhamet Çami (sec. XVIII–XX), e il tema di "Florence de Rome" e di "Crescentia" ', *Oriente Moderno*, 28 (1948), pp. 143–53.

ShM

L

LAKO, Natasha (b. 1948), Albanian poet and novelist, one of the most prominent woman writers, was born in Korçë and studied journalism at Tirana. Lako's verse manifests a particular interest in the role of the Albanian woman in society. She has published several volumes of verse, e.g. *Marsi brenda nesh* (March within us, 1972), *E para fjalë e botës* (The world's first word, 1979), *Këmisha e pranverës* (The spring shirt, 1984), and the novel *Stinët e jetës* (The seasons of life, 1977). ShM

LALIĆ, Ivan V. (b. 1931), Serbian poet, was born in Belgrade. He studied law in Zagreb and worked in several publishing houses. He now lives in Belgrade. Lalić has been publishing collections of poetry since 1955, the most notable of which are *Melisa* (1959), *Argonauti i druge pesme* (The Argonauts and other poems, 1961), *Vreme, vatre, vrtovi* (Time, fires, gardens, 1961) and *Strasna mera* (Passionate measure, 1984). Lalić's poems, often centred on the Ancient civilisations of the Balkans and the Mediterranean, are written with a classical balance and technical brilliance that have earned him a reputation as one of the most accomplished poets of his generation.
● *Fire Gardens* (New York, 1970); *The Works of Love* (London, 1981); *Last Quarter* (London, 1987). VDM

LALIĆ, Mihajlo (b. 1914), Serbian fiction writer, is a native of Montenegro. He studied law in Belgrade and, because of his Communist ties, was imprisoned. He took part in WWII as a partisan. Afterwards he occupied many editorial positions and now works as a professional writer. Lalić started with short stories and later wrote a number of novels, the most important of which are *Svadba* (Wedding, 1950), *Zlo proljeće* (Evil spring, 1953), *Hajka* (The chase, 1960), and *Lelejska gora* (Leleja Mountain, 1962), his best work. His latest series of novels depict the life of the Montenegrins in the last half century. The central theme in almost all of his works is the struggle between the partisans and their opponents in the war, but he uses this setting to expound on the search for a meaning of existence and for moral values, and on his understanding of how his fellow men work.
● *The Wailing Mountain* [*Lelejska gora*] (New York, 1965). VDM

LANGER, František (1888–1965), Czech dramatist and prose writer, a physician by profession, served in the Austro-Hungarian Army and, after being captured, joined the Czecho-Slovak Legion in Russia; on his return he remained an officer; during WWII he was the Chief MO in the Czecho-Slovak Army in Britain and returned to Prague in 1945. Before

WWI he associated with writers tending to anarchism, ŠRÁMEK, NEUMANN and HAŠEK, but between the wars he became, together with ČAPEK, a supporter of the establishment as personified by President Masaryk. His first short stories, *Zlatá Venuše* (The golden Venus, 1910), shun psychology and lyricism and express bluntly, with a tendency to sadomasochism and even necrophilia, the insatiable desire of alienated men, a condottiere, a disposer of corpses, a ratcatcher and others, to possess a female body. In his later stories Langer turned to Neoclassicism and after the war recounted his experiences in a more realistic mode in *Železný vlk* (The iron wolf, 1920). His comedies *Velbloud uchem jehly* (The camel through the eye of the needle, 1923), about a poor girl's rise up the capitalist ladder, and *Obrácení Ferdyše Pištory* (Conversion of Ferdyš Pištora, 1929), a story of a safebreaker unwittingly changed into a hero, observed ordinary people with a sentimental, yet ironic humour, but his serious plays dealt with moral problems. Such was his Dostoevskian drama on crime and redemption, *Periferie* (On the periphery, 1925), analysing the conscience of a pimp who killed a client of his mistress. The relativity of justice is discussed in *Andělé mezi námi* (Angels amongst us, 1931) about a man-angel practising euthanasia, and in *Dvaasedmdesátka* (Number seventy-two, 1937), a play within a play which concerns an innocent woman condemned to death for murder. *Jízdní hlídka* (Mounted patrol, 1935) deals in a detached, relativist way with the moral and political problems of a group of Czech soldiers and the Bolshevik partisans beleaguering their hideout. In his memoirs, *Byli a bylo* (How they were and how it was, 1963), Langer writes about his friendship with ČAPEK and HAŠEK.

●*The Camel through the Needle's Eye* (New York, 1929).

B. R. Bradbrook, 'František Langer: An Appreciation', *SEER* 44 (1966), pp. 486–91.   KB

LAZAREVIĆ, Lazar (1851–91), Serbian short-story writer, was born in Šabac. He studied medicine at Berlin and practised in Serbia. As a young man he was attracted to liberal ideas but later became conservative, believing that the patriarchal life of Serbia should be preserved. Lazarević wrote exclusively short stories but completed only nine, leaving several incomplete. He was a founder of psychological realism in Serbian literature and one of the best representatives of the so-called 'village short story'. His characters are usually small-town or village inhabitants expounding traditional morality and endeavouring to preserve the centuries-old *zadruga* (cooperatives) that are under attack from new ideas and wilful individualism. The educated among his characters are equally threatened by the outside world. At the same time, Lazarević is not unaware of the shortcomings of the traditional way of life. Because of his social concerns, he is often linked with Turgenev. Lazarević's careful plot construction, attention to detail, and compactness contribute to his stature as one of the best prose writers in Serbian literature.

●A. Cronia, *Lazar K. Lazarević* (Rome, 1932).   VDM

LEC, Stanisław Jerzy (1909–66), Polish poet, aphorist and translator, he made his début in 1929 and throughout the 1930s contributed to periodicals of the radical left in Warsaw and Lwów. Imprisoned in a

German concentration camp in 1941, he escaped two years later and spent the rest of the war fighting in Communist guerrilla units. After 1945 he served as a diplomat in Vienna until 1950 when he defected to Israel. In 1952, however, he returned to Warsaw to live there until his death; meanwhile, his epigrams and aphorisms, the latter published systematically in periodicals under the heading 'Myśli nieuczesane' (Unkempt thoughts), won him a large following in Poland and abroad. Always favouring epigrammatic concision in his poetry, he took it to its furthest extreme in his miniature gnomic pieces (some only two words long), in which skilfully released ambiguities serve a wide range of purposes, from political satire to existential reflection.

•*Unkempt Thoughts* (New York, 1990).
StB

LECHOŃ, Jan (1899–1956), Polish poet, one of the five founders of the Skamander group (1920), earned his living as an editor until 1930, when he left for Paris as cultural attaché. With the fall of France in 1940, he escaped to the USA and settled in New York. Tormented all his life by bouts of severe depression, he jumped to his death from a window of a hotel in Manhattan. Lechoń's career started under the best of auspices: his collection of poems dealing with the burden of the Polish past, *Karmazynowy poemat* (A crimson poem, 1920), propelled him instantly to fame. His next volume, a collection of largely metaphysical lyrics, *Srebrne i czarne* (Silver and black, 1924), was also a success. This early fame paralysed Lechoń's creativity: only WWII led him to resume writing. His next two books, containing mostly poetry of patriotic lamentation, came out in London and New York in 1942 and 1945, when his elevated and rhetorical style sounded obsolete. The most romantic, artistically conservative, and history-obsessed among the Skamander poets, Lechoń chose to be a walking anachronism rather than to adjust to changing circumstances. His three-volume *Dziennik* (Diary, 1967–73) remains an illuminating document of both his personal misery and the fate of his generation.   StB

LEHTONEN, Joel (1881–1934), Finnish poet and prose writer, brought a scholarly precision to his attempt to understand the social upheavals of the 1910s and 1920s, particularly in the wake of the 1918 Civil War. The illegitimate son of a simple country woman, he was raised by a pastor's widow. After leaving school he travelled widely and quickly made a successful career for himself as journalist, translator, critic and writer. The trauma of his early years, disillusion and horror at the senselessness of life led to his suicide. Lehtonen rejected the 19th-century romanticisation of the rural Finn. By presenting a Naturalist picture of countryfolk ('people who have nothing but their hymnbooks and cockroaches'), he attacked the motives of those who had created and of those who had helped maintain the old Romantic idea. His early works from the neo-Romantic period hint at a Nietzsche-like personal tragedy. With its parody of RUNEBERG's *Elgskyttarne* (The elk hunters, 1832), *Markkinoilta* (From the market, 1912) signals the direction that culminates in his works of the years 1917–20: *Kerran Kesällä* (Once in summer, 1917), *Kuolleet omenapuut* (The dead apple trees, 1918) and *Putkinotko* (The weed patch, 1919–20). The central character of these works, a self-made man who had become rich as a bookseller dealing in trash, spends his summers on his country estate leading what he imagines to be the life of a man of letters. For reasons of conscience he employs a labourer and his huge family to look after his estate. In its description of twenty-four hours in the lives of the two households, *Putkinotko* lays bare the gulf of incomprehension between the two social groups. Set in idyllic summer surroundings, it contrasts apparent altruism with natural egotism, exposing the fear, hate and greed that motivate the actions of the main characters. In his later work Lehtonen continues to examine similar questions, turning his attention to the city. Towards the end of his life his disillusion reached new, even greater, depths. In *Henkien taistelu* (Struggle of the spirits, 1933), a Finnish Mephistopheles takes an innocent forester on a tour of his country, acquainting him with the corruption of the new urban middle classes, the poverty of the ordinary people and the looming threats of Communism and Fascism.

•I. Väänänen-Jensen, K. B. Vähämäki (Eds), *Finnish Short Stories* (New York Mills, 1982), pp. 50–67.

P. Tarkka, 'Joel Lehtonen and his alter ego', *Books from Finland* (1981), pp. 140–7.   MAB

LEINO, Eino (i.e. A. E. L. Lönnbohm, 1878–1926), Finnish poet, playwright and novelist, was the major Finnish poet of the fin-de-siècle neo-Romantic movement. The child of a surveyor's family in NE Finland, Leino grew up in an area closely associated with the ORAL POETRY tradition. Recognised as outstandingly talented while still at school, he was quickly lionised by Helsinki intellectual circles after arriving to begin his studies. He soon left university to devote himself wholly to journalism, criticism, translation and his own writing. He was active politically in the liberal Young Finland Party. Though he was prolific throughout his life, his best work belongs to the turn of the century. His importance lies principally in his contribution to the form and aesthetics of Finnish poetry. More than anyone else, Leino used themes, motifs and poetic forms of the Finnish 'little tradition' as the medium to adapt contemporary European philosophical and artistic ideas, particularly Nietzscheanism and Symbolism. Leino's main ideas concern immortality and the mystery of death, good and evil, and the poet's role in society. The influence of Nietzsche on his thinking and the coincidence of Russification invested these ideas with powerful political meaning. His early works draw heavily on cosmogenous themes from LÖNNROT's *Kalevala* and Finnish ORAL POETRY, as in *Tarina suuresta tammesta* (Tale of the great oak, 1896) and *Tuonelan joutsen* (Swan of Tuonela, 1898). Leino's best work, the masterpiece *Helkavirsiä* (Whitsongs, 1903), illuminates his own anxious preoccupation with death and reveals his understanding of his own role in society as akin to that of the traditional shaman. The distinction between senseless defiance, noble self-sacrifice and base treachery becomes blurred as Leino explores these subjects through the actions of well-known traditional characters. Leino never again reached the perfection of *Helkavirsiä*. Similar themes recur in much of his poetry and prose, often with political overtones, but they lack the intensity and vitality of his earlier work.

•*Whitsongs* (London, 1978); E. Tompuri (Ed.), *Voices from Finland. An Anthology of Finland's Verse and Prose* (Helsinki, 1947), pp. 108–13, 150–2. M. A. Branch, 'Introduction' to *Whitsongs*; A. Sarajas, 'Eino Leino 1878–1926', *Books from Finland* (1978), pp. 40–6.   MAB

LEM, Stanisław (b. 1921), Polish novelist and essayist, left his native Lwów after WWII and settled in Cracow. He studied medicine (1940–8), but also developed interests in mathematics and the sciences. Lem's early novels were close to traditional science fiction, with their optimistic account of technical innovations and utopian societies ruled by experts and scientists (*Astronauci* [Astronauts, 1951]; *Obłok Magellana* [Magellan's cloud, 1955]). In the 1960s he attained a fully individual style and philosophy, becoming one of the most ambitious of science-fiction writers. His novels and short stories, such as *Solaris* (1961), *Pamiętnik znaleziony w wannie* (Memoirs found in a bath, 1961) and *Cyberiada* (The Cyberiad, 1965), stress the gap between technology and the human ability to use it beneficially. His characters are cruel and power-hungry, incapable of promoting their true interests. Encounters with alien worlds eventually result in misunder-standing and useless combat (*Fiasko*, 1987). In his later works Lem diversi-fies his narratives by emulating dif-ferent styles (heroic epic, fairy tales, allegoric parables, memoirs) and de-ploying grotesque imagery. Lem's wide-ranging interests have mani-fested themselves in a variety of ways. *Śledztwo* (The investigation, 1959) undermines the plot structure of the detective story; *Doskonała próżnia* (A perfect vacuum, 1971) enters the realm of metafiction. His non-fiction works concern the influ-ence of technology on the human mind (*Summa technologiae*, 1964), the theory of literature (*Filozofia przypadku* [Philosophy of chance, 1968]) and science fiction (*Fantastyka i futurologia* [Fantasy and futurol-ogy, 1970]).

•*The Cosmic Carnival of S. Lem: An Anthology of Entertaining Stories . . .* (New York, 1981); *Solaris* (New York, 1970); *A Perfect Vacuum* (New York, 1978).

R. E. Ziegfeld, *Stanisław Lem* (New York, 1985); Lem issue of *Science Fiction Studies* (Montreal, 1986, XIII, 3); W. Berthel (Ed.), *Über Stanisław Lem* (Frankfurt on Main, 1981).   SE

LEONIDZE, Giorgi (1899–1966), Georgian poet, studied in a seminary. Despite his loyalty to his birthplace in Kakhetia (E Georgia), he began as the youngest member of the Kutaisi *tsisperq'ants'lebi* (Blue horns) poets (see IASHVILI, ROBAKIDZE, T'itsian t'abidze). He soon found an indi-vidual voice: his real talent emerged in 1925 with a flow of Nature lyrics, responding to powerful forces with Romantic vitality, to oak trees (e.g. *Mukha da mekhi* [The oak and the thunderbolt, 1926]) or to birds of prey ('Is this snow, or has the hawk Smashed the doves?' in *Simghera p'irveli tovlisa* [Song of the first snow, 1926]). He extended this genre into odes like *Ole* (Solitary tree, 1931): 'You stand like gallows – the moun-tains strangle you; You are like a hanging eagle With destroyed wings.' Leonidze was drawn to tragic, Prom-ethean figures, thunderstruck mar-tyrs or trees. *Nino ts'mindis ghame* ('St Nino's night', 1926) turns the tortured saint into a 'panther made woman', her breasts as 'golden trout'. Driving rhythms, inexhaustibly inventive metaphors and the cult of Kakhetia's landscapes and forefathers brought great popularity. Fluency and hero-worship were Leonidze's salvation and undoing. In the purges of 1937 initial incoherent terror of Beria led to panegyrics, such as his unfinished 150-page epic, remarkable for a total absence of biography, factual or invented, *St'alini – bavshvoba da q'rmoba* (Stalin – Childhood and youth, 1939). Leonidze was to write interestingly about earlier Georgian poets: his 'Baratashvili' (1945), apart from the enforced optimism of the end, is a convincing evocation of yet another solitary natural giant. In Leonidze's last years he directed his wealth to the benefit of his native village; he produced agreeable childhood memoirs, evocative prose – *Nat'vris khe* (The tree of yearning, 1956) was filmed by Tengiz Abuladze – and very fine literary scholarship: his study of BE-SIK'I is scrupulous.   DR

LERA, Nasi (b. 1944), Albanian prose writer from Korçë, took his degree at Tirana in history and philology in 1968 and has worked as a teacher and journalist in broadcasting and for various periodicals. He has published short stories, e.g. *Bora e fundit* (The last snow, 1972), *Era e pishave* (The scent of the pines, 1976), *Nisemi djema* (Let's go, boys, 1977), *Sytë e dashurisë* (The eyes of love, 1982) and a number of novels, among which *Gjaku i prillit* (The blood of April, 1981) concerns the April 1939 invasion of Albania. ShM

LEŚMIAN, Bolesław (1877–1937), Polish poet and essayist, transcends the historical constraints of the two epochs with which his life happened to coincide: the turn-of-the-century period of Young Poland and the interwar years. He grew up in the Ukraine and studied law at Kiev. After graduation in 1901 he moved to Warsaw, where in 1911 he co-founded the innovative Teatr Artystyczny (Arts Theatre). His first collection, *Sad rozstajny* (A crossroads orchard), was published only in 1912 and followed by just three more: in 1920 (*Łąka* [Meadow]), 1936 (*Napóje cienisty* [Shadowy drink]), and, posthumously, 1938 (*Dziejba leśna* [Woodland events]). 1918 he settled in the provincial town of Hrubieszów, and 1922 moved to Zamość: in both towns he worked as a notary public. Considered an outdated, if not bizarre, poet by most of his contemporaries, he was nevertheless elected member of the Polish Academy of Literature in 1933. In 1935 he moved back to Warsaw where he spent the rest of his life. Leśmian's original style and inimitable poetic language are direct consequences of his philosophical outlook. A follower of Henri Bergson, he viewed all reality as a field of incessant conflict between inert Matter and the creative force of Spirit; since this conflict can never be resolved, reality remains for ever *in statu nascendi*, in the continuous process of 'becoming'. Poetry's task is to grasp this 'becoming' and to reflect it in language or, rather, to structure the poem so that its stylistic arrangement 'fixes the reflection' of the world's dynamic instability. The poem's rhythm should express the world's *élan vital*, and its imagery should serve as an equivalent of reality's constant metamorphoses. The poet himself should adopt the cognitive perspective of a 'primeval man', whose act of perception creates rather than reproduces the world perceived. As a consequence of all these assumptions, Leśmian's poetry is distinguished by an astonishing variety of complex rhythms, figures of speech that emphasise the transformations of elements of reality into one another, frequent references to myth and folklore, and the constant invention of new words and derivates to capture the flux of experience.

●R. Stone, *B. Leśmian* (Berkeley, 1976); V. M. Pankowski, *Leśmian. La Révolte d'un poète contre les limites* (Brussels, 1967).   StB

LEVSTIK, Fran (1831–87), Slovene poet, literary critic and language reformer, was expelled from a seminary for publishing a collection of poems (*Pesmi* [Poems, 1854]) denounced by the Church authorities as scandalous and blasphemous, he spent some months in Vienna, where he met Fran Miklosich (1813–91) and KARADŽIĆ. Penniless, he returned home on foot, then worked for some time as a tutor in a noble household. After a spell in Trieste as secretary of the new reading room he moved to Ljubljana, becoming editor of the political journal *Naprej* (Forward, 1863), whose programme envisaged a greater role for the Slovene language, the opening of Slovene schools and the union of all Slovenes. But the proprietor, Miroslav Vilhar (1818–71), was imprisoned and Levstik himself was lucky to escape imprisonment. 1864 he became the secretary of Slovenska Matica but was eased out a year later by his opponents. From April 1866 to the end of 1868 he worked on Anton Alojzij Wolf's (1782–1859) Slovene-German dictionary, which eventually saw the light of day in 1894–5. In spite of his enemies, his lack of a permanent post and his penury, he was able to write and eager to help others. In 1866 he published a new edition of PREŠEREN's poems, pruning the language

of some archaisms. He helped the poet JENKO; JURČIČ's drama *Tugomer* (1876) is largely his work. He was invited by STRITAR to Vienna to help edit *Zvon* (The Bell). There he began to publish his own satirical paper, *Pavliha* (Punch, April–July 1870). His slanderers forced him to cease publication. 1872 he returned to Ljubljana to find a post in the grammar-school library, which he occupied for the rest of his life. His greatest contribution is found in the essays *Popotovanje iz Litije do Čateža* (A journey from Litija to Čatež, 1858) in which he set out a programme for the further development of Slovene literature, *Napake slovenskega pisanja* (Defects of Slovene writing, 1858), which recommended the use of rural Slovene as a remedy for German thought patterns, and in his tale of a salt-smuggling Slovene Hercules, *Martin Krpan* (1858), where he put his own theories into practice.

●*Martin Krpan* (1960).   HL

LEYELES, Arn/A. Glants-Leyeles (i.e. Aaron Glanz, 1889–1966), Yiddish poet, dramatist and essayist, was one of the founders of Introspectivism and its chief theoretician. Glants was born in Włocławek on the lower Vistula and received his schooling in Łódź. After four years in London, during which he attended lectures at the university, he emigrated to New York in 1909 where he became acquainted with American literature in the course of further study at Columbia. He began publishing poems in 1914 under the name A. Leyeles in the *Fraye arbeter-shtime* (The free workers' voice), while continuing to sign his journalism with his real name. In his first collection of poems, *Labirint* (Labyrinth, New York, 1918), he can be seen moving away from the neo-Romantic style of his predecessors towards the innovations that were to become characteristic of the Introspectivists. *In zikh, a zamlung introspektive lider* (In oneself, an anthology of Introspective poems, New York, 1920) contained the manifesto of the new movement. It called for poetry to express the internal associations evoked by external reality in rhythms that reflect the uniqueness of the experience. Nokhem-Borekh Minkov (1893–1958) and GLATSHTEYN also signed, but the manifesto was largely the work of Leyeles. He celebrated the multifarious life of the metropolis in *Rondos un andere lider* (Rondeaux and other songs, New York, 1926) which included the free-verse 'In sobvey' poems that gave kaleidoscopic expression to the powerful synaesthetic sensations of rush-hour travel. As in the case of GLATSHTEYN, the 'Holocaust' led him in the direction of greater conservatism and a return to more Jewish themes.

●*TYP*, pp. 257–9; *WWT* 2, pp. 605–14, 722–4; *AYP*, pp. 70–203; *PBMYV*, pp. 247–57.   HD

LEYVIK, H./ H. Leivick, (i.e. Leyvik Halpern, 1886–1962), Yiddish poet and playwright, was born in White Russia, attended a yeshivah in Minsk and in 1905 became involved in illegal Bundist activities. After completing a sentence of four years' hard labour in Minsk he was exiled to Siberia for life. 1913 he succeeded in escaping and making his way to the USA. He had started to write poetry in prison, and in New York he became an associate of Di Yunge, though he subsequently went his own way. He adopted the pen-name H. Leyvik in order to avoid confusion with the already established

Moyshe-Leyb HALPERN. His poetry ranges widely over the hardships of Siberia, the tenements of Manhattan's Lower East Side and the isolation of the TB-sanatorium to which he was confined 1932–5. Leyvik's ethical stance and the visionary quality of his work won him widespread acclaim. The poems of his first collection, *Hintern shlos* (Behind bars, New York, 1918), seek transcendent values in the suffering of imprisonment and transportation. In his play, *Der goylem* (The golem, New York, 1921), Leyvik suffuses the legendary material with contemporary, political significance. His prewar works were brought together in *Ale verk* (Complete works, New York, 1940). 1945 Leyvik visited Dachau and Jewish survivors in Germany. *In treblinke bin ikh nit geven* (I was not in Treblinka, New York, 1945) and *Khasene in fernvald* (Wedding in Fernwald, New York, 1949) attempt to articulate his feelings of rage and guilt in the face of the ineffable horror.

●*The Golem*, Boston, 1928; 'The Golem' in *GYP*, pp. 223–356; *TYP*, pp. 118–45; *WWT*, 2, pp. 596–604; *AMYL*, pp. 132–7, 215–20; *AYP*, pp. 674–769; *PBMYV*, pp. 227–45.

Liptzin (1972), pp. 299–311.   HD

LIBERAKI, Margarita (b. 1919), Greek prose writer and dramatist, brought up by her maternal grandfather, a publisher, after her parents were separated, was educated in Athens, specialising in French and drawing, and then read law at Athens (degree 1943). Her first novel, Τα Δέντρα (The trees), appeared in 1945 under her married name (M. Karapanou); it was followed by two further psychological analytical novels, each more experimental than the previous, Τα Ψαθινά Καπέλλα (The straw

hats, 1946) and O Αλλος Αλέξανδρος. (The other Alexander, 1950). After the success of the former she separated from her husband and took her daughter to Paris. Since then she has divided her time between the two countries. In Paris she became familiar with the intellectual fashions of the time, a factor partly responsible for the greater intellectual depth of 'The other Alexander', where the problems of individual identity and of the social and political identity of Greece as a whole are explored through a single set of symbols. After 1952 Liberaki turned her attention to theatre. 1954–70 she wrote six plays, most of them in both Greek and French. These are collected under the title Μυθικό Θέατρο (Mythical theatre, 1980). Since 1970 a further four plays have appeared. The themes of her work are historical or mythical, and they play on the parallels of sexual and political divisions, and patterns of decline and renewal. At the same time she has gone back to ancient ritual for the form of her texts, e.g. O Σπαραγμός (Rending, 1970). Her most original text, which synthesises aspects of her work as novelist and playwright, is To Μυστήριο (The mystery, 1976), a symbolic political text based on the student occupation of the Athens Polytechnic in November 1973 and its violent repression by the military government. The title refers to the Eleusinian mysteries, with their myth of ritual destruction and rebirth. Over the text presides the goddess Anetha – the reversal of the name Athena indicating the need to turn the world on its head to put it to rights.
●R. Beaton (Ed.), *The Greek Novel A.D.1 – 1985* (London, 1988), pp. 103–9.   CFR

LIIV, Juhan (1846–1913), Estonian poet and prose-writer, son of a smallholder, after schooling in Kodavere, worked as a journalist for *Virulane* in Tallinn (1885), for *Sakala* in Viljandi (1888–9) and *Olevik* in Tartu (1890–2). In 1893 it became clear that he was schizophrenic and he had long treatment sessions at the Tartu Clinic for Nervous Diseases (1894 and 1905). Up to 1902 he lived mainly on 'income support'. 1902–10 he constantly changed domicile, and those who manifested interest in his work were usually members of Young Estonia (e.g. SUITS and TUGLAS). Obsessed by the notion that he was a son of Tsar Alexander II, he tried, penniless, to get to Poland in 1913 in order to assume the Polish throne. Somewhere between Tartu and Valga he was thrown out of the train. Broken in health, he returned to his brother's estate in 1910, where he eventually died of TB. In his prose works, *Käkimäe kägu* (The K. cuckoo, 1893), *Vari* (The shadow, 1894) and *Nõia tütar* (The warlock's daughter, 1895), Liiv sets out to confront the contemporary 'romantic' tale, undermines its aesthetic conventionality with his down-to-earth approach to reality; that is particularly true of the short-story collection *Kümme lugu* (Ten tales, 1893). He rebelled against local literary convention. The sophisticated, ostentatious naivety of his lyric verse, which avoided complex metaphoricality and euphony and was based on a somewhat loud popular lexis, removed him from the eclecticism of contemporaneous patriotic verse and brought him close to the Modernist generation of Young Estonia. *Luuletused* (Poems, 1909) was an historic event in the development of Estonian literature. Liiv's sensitivity to the misery felt by his fellow Estonians, both nationally and socially, was suffused in Liiv's verse with his personal lot, the drastic experience of his own psychological disintegration – which almost became a representation of a generally felt depression resulting from the failure of national ideals.

●Two poems in E. H. Harris, *Literature in Estonia* (London, 1943); selection in W. K. Matthews (Ed.), *Anthology of Modern Estonian Poetry* (Gainesville, 1953).   VM

LILIEV, Nikolai (i.e. N. Popivanov, 1885–1960), Bulgarian poet, read literature at Lausanne (1905–6), and economics in Paris (1909–12); he fought in WWI, and, 1921, went to Vienna and Munich to write up a bibliography on the Bulgarian economy; he became literary adviser in the National Theatre (1924–8), taught French (1932–4), in 1934 again became literary adviser in the National Theatre. Liliev was a cultivated man and both his literary work and personality had a profound influence on Bulgarian cultural life. He published the Symbolist collections *Ptitsi v noshtta* (Birds in the night, 1913), *Lunni petna* (Moon spots, 1922) and *Stihotvoreniya* (Poems, 1932); the exquisiteness of his poetic language influenced generations of Bulgarian poets. His main themes are transcendental loneliness, the liberation of the soul from its terrestrial fetters (expressed e.g. through images like 'fading', 'dying', 'extinguishing' [of colours, sounds, emotion], 'resignation' and 'submission' [to 'dream', 'secret', 'infinity', 'eternal sun', 'imperishable beauty']), the poet's remoteness from the material world and his gradual path into the light produced by his Platonic dreamworld. Related to his negative metaphysics, which rejects everything terrestrial, is his motif of

yearning for absolute spiritual purity, equable with 'nothingness'; virginity (of body and soul) designates depersonalisation through rejection of the flesh and union with the very soul of the angelic world of spirituality. Liliev creates landscapes, all white and silver, lit by a 'white moon', which lack any solidity and epitomise the virginal world of the spiritual absolute. The melody of Liliev's verse supports the immaculate purity of feeling left by his dreamy 'prayers' to an otherworldly light. Liliev also wrote literary criticism and translated.

●R. Poggioli, 'Il poeta bulgaro Nikolaj Liliev', *Revista di letterature slave*, III, iii (June 1928), pp. 221–30.   SIK

LINETSKI, Yitskhok Yoel/ Isaac Joel Linetzky (1839–1915), Yiddish novelist and publicist, was born in Vinnitsa, Podolia. In his early youth he rebelled against his Ḥasidic background and became a spokesman for the radical wing of the Haskalah. He studied together with GOLDFADN at the Zhitomir rabbinical seminary where he came under the influence of GOTLOBER. His popular *Dos poylishe yingl* (The Polish lad, Odessa, 1869) was serialised from 1867 onwards in *Kol mevaser*. It is presented as the autobiography of a benighted Ḥasid, but in fact reflects much of the author's own experience of Ḥasidic fanaticism and in particular his arranged marriage. Linetski benefits from advances in narrative technique made by MENDELE MOYKHER SFORIM and adopts his device of the *faux-naïf* narrator. The tone, however, is less subtle and the humour is at times spoiled by the author's impassioned invective. In Lemberg (Lwów) in 1875, he and GOLDFADN attempted to produce a humorous weekly for the Russian market, but the tsarist government banned its distribution after the first few issues. *Linetskis ksovim* (Linetski's writings, Odessa, 1876) is a collection of *feuilletons* in which *inter alia* he expresses his positive attitude towards Yiddish and satirical narratives including 'Di khsidishe damf-mashin' (The Ḥasidic steam-engine) which is given a mock-mystical exegesis. His lifelong commitment to the Haskalah is reflected in his publication of a Yiddish translation of Lessing's *Nathan der Weise* (1884).

●*The Polish Lad* (Philadelphia, 1975).
Miron, pp. 241–8 and passim.   HD

LINNA, Väinö (1920–92), Finnish novelist, is Finland's most important post-war writer on social questions. Born into a working-class family, he worked in manual jobs until called up to serve in the Finnish Army during the 1941–4 war against the USSR. He returned to factory work after the war but left in 1955 to become a freelance writer. Linna is an enthralling story-teller. His eye for detail, his vivid use of dialect and his straightforward narrative style give his writing a photographic quality. His output is small and his reputation rests on two works, which both deal with traumatic periods in Finnish history. His episodic novel *Tuntematon sotilas* (The unknown soldier, 1954), reminiscent of Remarque's *All Quiet on the Western Front*, challenged conventional attitudes to Finland's role in the 1941–4 war. Through the experiences of a machine-gun platoon Linna conveys a picture of ordinary soldiers as reluctant heroes, loyal to their country but without sympathy for the aspirations of the officers or politicians. Thus the novel signals the futility of the expansionist nationalism and of-

fers in its place the undemanding patriotism of the ordinary people. Through the experiences of a poor tenant-farmer family, *Täällä Pohjantähden alla* (Here beneath the Pole Star, 1959–62) chronicles the social history of Finland from the 1880s until the mid-20th century. Linna's account of social conditions and of the hardships suffered by the family underlines the inevitability of the 1918 Civil War. Both works have had a powerful influence on how Finns understand these two critical periods in their history and have been catalytic in the process of coming to terms with their consequences.

●*The Unknown Soldier* (London, New York, 1957; Porvoo, 1975).
Y. Varpio, 'Väinö Linna. A Classic in his own Time' in *Books from Finland* (1977), pp. 192–7; H. Sihvo, 'Zum Romanbegriff Väinö Linnas', *Jahrbuch für finnisch-deutsche Literaturbeziehungen* (1980), pp. 21–30.   MAB

LINNANKOSKI, Johannes (i.e. J. V. Peltonen, 1869–1913), Finnish playwright, novelist and journalist, led a double life. Both Peltonen the journalist and Linnankoski the writer were moralists, committed to popular enlightenment. Born into a farming family Linnankoski worked as a lumberjack before entering teacher training college. Expelled, he embarked on a successful career in journalism, giving up his post as newspaper editor at the age of 30 to concentrate wholly on his own writing. Peltonen's work urges the ordinary people to educate themselves as thoroughly as possible for the greater good of their country. His writings range from moral treatises to advice on hygiene and works on science. The same aims lurk in Linnankoski's work (it was long before the two writers' common identity came to light). They find expression in a series of plays and novels about conscience and the need for the individual to suppress his own will for the sake of spiritual and social stability. The allegory of the emerging Finnish state, oppressed from the outside and riven by internal language, social and political conflicts, permeates the work of both Linnankoski and his alter ego. The recurrent theme in Linnankoski's work is a conflict of will. His dénouements comprise a tense triangle of proud, well-meaning husband/lover, quiet but determined wife/lover, and their child (symbolising the future). To ensure happiness for the child, the man and woman achieve a *modus vivendi* but only through the suppression of individual will. The female characters are especially powerful. As wives they force men to change their behaviour; as mothers their influence over the future is decisive. For Linnankoski's contemporaries the author's underlying moral messages were obscured by the settings and action, 'immoral' by the Finnish standards of the time, and a horror and violence reminiscent of Edgar Allan Poe. His first major play, *Ikuinen taistelu* (The eternal struggle, 1903), explored his theme of individual will through the story of Cain and Abel. *Laulu tulipunaisesta kukasta* (Song of the blood-red flower, 1905), an episodic *Bildungsroman*, is set against an Art Nouveau backdrop, in which a romanticised lumberjack progresses from one erotic affair to another until a crisis in a brothel forces him to take stock and leads to turbulent marriage and parenthood. The allegorically named *Pakolaiset* (The fugitives, 1908), the most Realist of Linnankoski's works, concerns two families brought together by a marriage of conveni-

ence. Each attempts unsuccessfully to escape the consequences of character, will and conscience.

●*Song of the Blood-red Flower* (London, 1920).
J. J. Meyer, 'A Modern Finnish Cain', *Modern Philology* (1909–10), pp. 221–43.   MAB

LOMNICKÝ z BUDČE, Šimon (1552–?1623), Czech poet and moralist, was educated by the Jesuits, was first a schoolmaster, later a clerk at the court of a nobleman, then a rich farmer and inkeeper-brewer. He was awarded a coat of arms for his literary work after fawning on the nobility, but because he took sides with the Estates in their fatal revolt of 1618 he was rejected by the victors and died in penury. Lomnický was a prolific writer both of devotional poems and occasional verse for his noble patrons and followed the medieval tradition in his verse dramas. Amongst his several moralising prose works condemning avarice, pride, luxury, slander and other vices, the most popular was *Kupidova střela* (Cupid's dart, 1590), castigating all manner of fornication. Lomnický alternates straight narration with direct addresses to the reader, thereby composing an amusing work perhaps partly because, as he admits, he is himself a great sinner and wooer of Venus. This qualifies him to discuss all species of lechers, rapists, adulterers, committers of incest and sodomites. Like many hypocritical moralists Lomnický produced a near-obscene treatise, passages of which were censored in the following century. Its main interest lies in some fifty illustrative racy anecdotes mostly taken from the Bible, medieval *exempla* and Renaissance *facetiae*. Several of those invented by Lomnický give a curious picture of the sexual mores of his time.   KB

LÖNNROT, Elias (1802–84), Finnish collector and editor of oral poetry, published a series of compilations – notably the *Kalevala* – which were central to the shaping of a Finnish national identity. Born the son of a country tailor, Lönnrot learned Swedish as a boy and attended university in Turku and Helsinki at a time of growing interest in collecting traditional ORAL POETRY and compiling from it a national epic. After qualifying as a physician he was commissioned by the Finnish Literature Society (Helsinki) to undertake the work of collection and compilation. He subsequently returned to the practice of medicine, and in 1853 was appointed to the chair of Finnish at Helsinki University. Lönnrot was educated in the Classical tradition. His interest in oral poetry was influenced by the philosophical ideas of Herder, as they were interpreted by early 19th-century Finnish nationalists. Lönnrot's oral-poetry material came partly from earlier collectors but mostly from what he collected himself on eleven expeditions 1828–44 to the E regions of Finland and to Karelia and Ingria in Russia. From this material he compiled collections of lyric poetry, *Kanteletar taikka Suomen Kansan Wanhoja Lauluja ja Wirsiä* (The spirit of the *kantele* or old songs and traditional poems of the Finnish people, 1840–1), proverbs, *Suomen Kansan Sananlaskuja* (Proverbs of the Finnish people, 1842) and riddles, *Suomen Kansan Arvoituksia* (Riddles of the Finnish people, 1844). His most important works, *Kalewalah taikka Wanhoja Karjulan Runoja Suomen Muinosista Ajoista* (Kalevala or Karelian old poems from the ancient times of Finland, 1835), appeared in two editions: the first, known as the *Old Kalevala*, and the definitive edition of 1849, *Kalevala*, comprising 22,795 trochaic tetrameters arranged in 50 canti. Most of the lines contained in the *Kalevala* were collected from living singers (about 600 were composed by Lönnrot), but were arranged and edited to elaborate those themes that Lönnrot felt were needed for his purposes. The outcome was a mythical history of the Finns from the time of the Creation of the world, under the leadership of the god/culture hero/shaman/chieftain/viking Väinämöinen, until the arrival of Christianity. The *Kalevala* provided the Finnish national movement with an epic that associated indigenous Finnish culture with the aesthetic criteria and achievements of the Classical tradition (and, important, won in its numerous translations the approval of outsiders) and that gave historical depth to the notion of a national history. Subsequently, *Kalevala* was to provide a continuing source of inspiration to the arts in Finland, particularly at the turn of the century. At the same time it set in train further collection of ORAL POETRY which in turn led to the development of international folklore scholarship.

●K. Bosley (Ed.), *The Kalevala. An epic poem after oral tradition by Elias Lönnrot* (Oxford, 1989); K. Bosley (Ed.), *The Kanteletar*, (Oxford, 1992). H. Fromm, *Kalevala: Kommentar* (Munich, 1967); K. Laitinen (Ed.), *Kalevala 1835–1985* (Helsinki, 1985); J. Pentikäinen, *Kalevala Mythology* (Bloomington, 1989).　　MAB

LORENC, Kito (or **LORENZ, Christoph**, b. 1938), Sorbian poet, essayist and translator, born at the saw-mill in Slepo (Schleife) established by his grandfather, the Sorbian prose writer Jakub Lorenc-Zalěski

(1874–1939), has always been conscious of his literary ancestry. 1952–6 he was a boarder at the Sorbian grammar school in Cottbus. He then read Sorbian and Russian at Leipzig. His first volume of poems, *Nowe časy – nowe kwasy* (New times – new weddings, 1961), was the fruit of his years as a student. 1961–72 he was employed as a research-worker in the Sorbian Ethnological Institute in Bautzen. His *Struga. Wobrazy našeje krajiny* (The Struga. Pictures of our landscape, 1967), a cycle in which the poems are printed in parallel Sorbian and German versions, was followed by *Kluče a puće* (Keys and ways, 1971), a collection of Sorbian poems originally written 1962–7. He worked as a dramatist with the State Ensemble for Sorbian Folk-Culture 1973–9, since when he has been a freelance writer. *Wortland* (Wordland, 1984) is a collection of his German and Sorbian poems to which a number of his German translations from other Sorbian poets have been added. He has a renowned propensity for paronomasia which is best demonstrated in *Rymarej a dyrdomdej* (Hey-ho and hey nonino, 1985). In his latest collection, *Ty porno mi* (You beside me, 1988), erotic themes predominate. Much of Lorenc's poetry springs from a search for his own cultural roots, involving exploration of the Sorbian landscape, scenes from the poet's childhood, from folklore and other traditions. He is intensely conscious of his Sorbian literary legacy, but has also been influenced by representatives of other Slavonic literatures and by the German Johannes Bobrowski. In Lorenc's work present-day concerns are regularly juxtaposed with echoes from folklore and the national literary heritage.

●Six poems in E. Mackinnon (Ed.), *East is East: Six Poets from the German Democratic Republic* (Paisley, 1984), pp. 49–60.
Marieluise de Wajier-Wilke, 'Fünf Fragen an Kito Lorenc' in Kito Lorenc, *Wortland. Gedichte* (Leipzig, 1984), pp. 155–67.   GCS

LORTKIPANIDZE,   Nik'o (1880–1944), Georgian novelist and playwright, born near Kutaisi, studied mining in Kharkov and Austria, returning in 1907 to teach German in Tbilisi and Kutaisi schools. He entered literature with grotesque stories from village life in Imeretia, *Mriskhane bat'oni* (The furious master, 1912), and progressed to historical novels, *Zhamta siave* (Bad times, 1920). His talent lay in graphic, almost cinematic scenes, condensed into powerful short pieces such as *Tavsapriani dedak'atsi* (The woman in a headscarf, 1926). Lortkipanidze adapted quickly to Soviet canons, celebrating industrialisation with predictable offerings, such as a treatment of the 1905 Revolution, *Bilik'-ebidan liandagze* (From paths to rails, 1928). His brisk stylistic flourishes have strongly influenced modern Georgian prose and cinema. He also wrote drama, original and adapted: *Keto* of 1914 is an agreeable comedy.

●*The Woman in Black* [*Tavsapriani dedak'atsi*] in *Mindia, the Son of Hogay (and other stories)* (Moscow, 1961). DR

LUCIĆ, Hanibal (c. 1485–1553), Croatian poet, born into a noble family on the island of Hvar, was given a Humanist education and served as a judge in the city of Hvar. He wrote love poems in the Petrarchan mode and translated Petrarch, Bembo and Ariosto, as well as Ovid. In 1519 he destroyed all but 22 of his early love poems. Those that survive include some of the most elegant 16th-century Croatian lyric poems. Poetic epistles to friends also survive, together with a lengthy poem 'In honour of the city of Dubrovnik', celebrating the strong aristocratic system of rule there. His main work is *Robinja* (The slave, 1638), which could be described as the first original Croatian secular drama, although it is more a lyrical than a dramatic work. Based on an historical incident, it is a blend of a theme typical of the oral tradition – the daughter of a Croatian governor being sold as a slave by the Turks – and the Petrarchan style.

•'No other nymph upon this earth', *The Bridge*, 25 (1971), pp. 62–4; The Captive' (extract) in T. Butler (Ed.), *Monumenta Serbocroatica* (Ann Arbor, 1980).   ECH

LUIK, Viivi (b. 1946), Estonian poet and prose writer, wife of the author Jaak Jõerüüt (b. 1947), after doing her matriculation in her free time and after a brief period as a librarian and archivist, became a freelance writer. The sentimentalised, almost infantile, tone of Luik's early verse, as represented by *Pilvede püha* (A feast-day of clouds, 1965), gradually gave way to a naivist mode which revealed a concern with the ineffable, e.g. *Pildi sisse minek* (Entering a picture, 1973) and *Põliskevad* (Perpetual spring, 1975). Since the end of the 1970s an interest in the lifestyle of the urban everyday has grown in her verse, in *Maapäälsed asjad* (Secular matters, 1978) and *Rängast rõõmust* (From harsh happiness, 1982). Luik's ever-increasing interest in prose corresponds with this development. Thus far, the zenith of her achievement in prose is the autobiographical novel, *Seitsmes rahukevad* (The

seventh spring of peace, 1985), which, from a child's-eye view, reconstructs the postwar experience of the 'sovietisation' of the Estonian countryside, and *Ajaloo ilu* (The charm of history, 1991), which evokes the atmosphere of the end of the 1960s and the psychological trauma of the Soviet occupation of Czechoslovakia.   VM

LUKÁČ, Emil Boleslav (1900–79), Slovak poet, after studying theology and philosophy, became a Lutheran pastor and general secretary of the Slovak Churches and later deputy in the Slovak parliament. His early verse was inspired by ADY, whose poems he translated, the French Symbolists and KRASKO, but the themes and their treatment in his later lyrics, both intimate and reflexive, tended rather to neo-Romanticism. Lukáč's *Dunaj a Seina* (The Danube and the Seine, 1925) testified to his attempts to overcome his disillusion, scepticism and pessimism by seeking peace of mind in the soothing charm of his homeland. But pessimism prevailed again in his collection of erotic verse *O láske neláskavej* (Of love unkind, 1928), and in particular in *Križovatky* (Crossroads, 1929) where grief drove him into an impasse. He eventually found a solution by abandoning his self-analysis and self-torment and turning to social and political problems, thus forcing himself to accept life in *Elixír* (1934). He ended as an almost didactic poet commenting on topical themes such as Fascism or chauvinism and extolling humaneness, democracy and international understanding in *Parížská romance* (The Paris romance, 1969) and *Srdce pod Kaukazom* (Heart under the Caucasus, 1978).   KB

M

MÁCHA, Karel Hynek (1810–36), Czech writer, read law at Prague, was a great walker (he once walked from Prague to Venice), amateur actor, and was fascinated by executions; a month after starting his first job, he died of cholera. His historical dramas and novels have survived only in fragments, but they reveal an author of an unusual capacity for psychological observation and creating tense atmospheres. The sentimental tale, *Marinka* (1834), a garret-poet's dream, is tinged by an ironic fatalism and may be interpreted as parody. The short story, *Pout' krkonošská* (Wayfarer in the Giant Mountains, 1835?), is a metaphysical study of the threshold between life and death, man and Nature, of existential disillusion and anxiety. Mácha's lyric verse ranges from intense expressions of fear and victimhood to *Kunstlieder* and patriotic jingles. His chief work is the contemplative epic *Máj* (May, 1836), which inspired Czech and Slovak writers throughout the 19th, but whose strongest impact has been on Czechs during the 20th, century. A simple story, based on the life of an Italian bandit (hero thrown out by father, brought up by bandits, becomes leader, falls in love with woman who has been seduced by older man whom hero kills; man turns out to be his father; hero imprisoned; woman drowns herself; hero executed), stimulates meditation on the nature of life, the nothingness out of which one is born and into which one returns after death, love as a trick played on man to make him aware that all existence is suffering, a notion that all action is culpable and that one's role on earth is to commit a crime to avenge another's crime and then to die. Nature is narcissistic, indifferent, often aggressive to man; woman often fuses with Nature, though may destroy the beauty of Nature (her tears kill flowers, do not create them like the BVM's or Narcissus's). Everything is narrated with profound irony, and simple, intricately euphonic language pretends to disguise cacophonic ideas.

●Several translations of *Máj*, the fullest being the inept, inaccurate one by H. H. McGoverne (London, 1949); the most elegant so far, only Canto II, by S. Spender and K. Brušák in A. French (Ed.), *Anthology of Czech Poetry* (Ann Arbor, 1973).

R. Wellek, *Essays on Czech Literature* (The Hague, 1963); R. B. Pynsent, 'Characterisation in Mácha's *Máj*' in M. Grygar (Ed.), *Czech Studies. Language, Literature, Culture* (Amsterdam and Atlanta, 1990); H. Granjar, *Mácha et la Renaissance nationale en Bohême* (Paris, 1957).   RBP

MACHAIRAS, Leontios (fl. first half 15th century), Greek chronicler,

had a post at the court of the Lusig-
nan kings of Cyprus and wrote a
chronicle   entitled   É
˴   ˴   Ḱo   in   Cypriot dialect. His choice of prose was
probably affected by the tradition of
the French chroniclers, whose work
would have been known at court. His
account begins with the death of King
Janus (1432) after the Turkish invasion, but the bulk of it focuses on the
reigns of Peter I and Peter II. It is a
colourful work, mixing documented
fact with lively anecdote, and marked
by the views of its narrator.

•R. M. Dawkins (Ed.), *Recital
Concerning the Sweet Land of Cyprus
entitled 'Chronicle'* (Oxford, 1932).CFR

MACHAR, Josef Svatopluk
(1864–1942), Czech poet and essayist, son of a mill worker, after
considering an army career became a
bank clerk in Vienna, was imprisoned
by the Austrian authorities during
WWI, 1919 was appointed Inspector
General of the Czechoslovak Army,
but resigned after four years, dissatisfied with the policy of the new
state. With T. G. Masaryk
(1850–1937) he was the instigator of
the 'Realist' political movement, advocating action instead of shallow
nationalism. As a Voltairean and rationalist Machar rejected the didactic
conception of Czech poetry in his
first collection, *Confiteor* (1887), defined his verse as a mirror of the times
and of his conscience, and set himself
up as judge of his nation, contemporary society and the whole of humanity throughout history. His *Tristium
Vindobona* (1897) and *Golgatha*
(1901) criticised the Czech national
character for its smugness, illusions
and vacillating between East and
West, whilst his *Tristium Praga*
(1926) condemned the corruption
and cynicism in the new state. His

verse stories *Zde by měly kvést růže
. . .* (Where roses should bloom . . .,
1894), portraits of women crushed by
society, were innovative for their
feminism while the verse novel *Mag-
dalena* (1894), about a woman who
became a prostitute to save her father
and who vainly struggled to rehabili-
tate herself in society, was an incul-
pation of Czech political and cultural
life. The nine volumes of his *Svědo-
mím věků* (The conscience of the
ages, 1906–26), an epic of humanity,
contradicting rather than emulating
VRCHLICKÝ's similar attempt, expressed a view opposite to that of
Hugo. Machar considered Greece
and Rome to be the ideal debased by
Christianity, had no sympathy for
the Middle Ages, Renaissance or
mysticism and viewed the Earth as
revolving with its damned humanity
in an unending spiral without sense
or goal. Machar's dismissing of the
conventional norm made him more a
social and political commentator than
a poet; his best verse were intimate
lyrics in which he deviated from his
'verse Realism'. In defiance of Parnassism, Symbolism and Decadence,
however, he brought a new tone into
Czech poetry.

•*Magdalene* (New York, 1916); *The Jail
Experience in 1916* (Oxford, 1921).   KB

MAČIULIS-MAIRONIS, Jonas
(1862–1932), the most important
Lithuanian poet from the end of the
19th and early 20th centuries, was
born into a well-to-do farming family. Maironis became a clergyman
and spent his life writing poetry,
celebrating Mass, teaching at the R.
Catholic Theological Academy in St
Petersburg, and at the Kaunas
Theological Seminary, where he was
Principal from 1909 to his death. One
of Maironis's most significant contributions to Lithuanian poetry was the

perfection of syllabo-tonic verse. By this he brought the Lithuanian poetic language closer to the rhythm of natural speech than was possible in the old, syllabic versification; he turned the poetic language into a flexible, creative tool capable of reflecting the nuances of relationships between emotion, rhythm and idea. Maironis's first collection of verse, *Pavasario balsai* (The voices of spring, 1895), immediately established him as an exciting new voice in Lithuanian poetry, one that could give full range to strong personal feelings, but at the same time, most important, could articulate in striking images and fine rhetorical cadences the feelings of a people emerging from centuries of foreign rule to become free. Maironis painted emotional views of the medieval Lithuanian past; he wept at the ruins of old castles and spoke with deep love of the Lithuanian soil, garnishing reality with the imagery of Romanticism. For all this he earned the reputation of being 'the bard of the Lithuanian National Awakening'. Many of his patriotic poems became popular songs that have lingered in the memory of every generation since. In intimate lyrics Maironis reveals a troubled mind, yearning for love and concerned with the passing of all things, including his own thirst for life. In addition to short lyrics, Maironis wrote narrative poems, among which the best known are the semi-autobiographical *Tarp skausmų garbè* (Through grief to glory, 1895), the satire *Raseinių Magdè* (M. of Raseiniai, 1909) and the historical ballad *Čičinskas* (1920). As a playwright, Maironis wrote an historical trilogy on medieval Lithuanian history.   RŠ

MACKIEWICZ, Józef (1902–85), Polish novelist, worked as a journalist in Vilnius. 1943 he visited the site of the Katyń Massacre and as a result voiced anti-Soviet opinions, initially in the German-controlled Polish press and later in the book *The Katyń Wood Murders* (London, 1951). After the war he settled in the West, representing an uncompromising attitude towards Communism. This is reflected in his political writings and various journalistic novels about the Soviet occupation of Vilnius, among them *Droga donikąd* (Road to nowhere, 1955) and *Nie trzeba głośno mówić* (No need to say it out loud, 1969). His controversial views on the Polish-Soviet war of 1920 shaped *Lewa wolna* (Open to the left, 1965).

●*Road to Nowhere* (London, 1963).   SE

MADÁCH, Imre (1823–64), Hungarian playwright, poet and essayist, came from the nobility, from an old and prosperous family of Upper Hungary. He first studied under private tutors, then attended the Piarist grammar school in Vác. 1837 he started reading law at Pest. After graduating, he became deputy clerk to the sub-prefect of Nógrád County; later he was appointed clerk, then high commissioner. Because of illness, he could not participate in the revolution of 1848–9. In 1852, however, he was imprisoned for helping Kossuth's secretary. Although he wrote plays and verse from an early age, recognition came to him only after he sent the manuscript of *Az ember tragédiája* (The tragedy of man), written 1859–60, to ARANY, who recognised the major poet in him. 1861 he became MP for a district in Nógrád County, and 1853 he was elected to the Hungarian Academy. Most of his early plays are tragedies based on Hungarian history. Both *Mária királynő* (Queen Mary) and

Csák végnapjai (The last days of Cs.), originally written in 1843, have later versions, from 1855 and 1861, respectively. 1859 he composed a comedy, *A civilizátor* (The civiliser), a sarcastic portrayal of Austrian oppression. His masterpiece, *Az ember tragédiája*, is a lyrical drama inspired by Milton, Goethe and Byron. The beginning of the work portrays the Creation and the Fall. In Scene 3 Adam is presented in a godless universe. The main body of the text offers samples from human history. Adam is anxious to know the fate of his race, and Lucifer gives him a chance to have a vision of the future through a long dream consisting of eleven episodes. Adam's values are those of a Romantic liberal, whereas Lucifer's mistrust of generalisations, value-judgements and teleology may remind one of Positivist reasoning. Egyptian tyranny, Greek democracy, nihilistic Rome, theChristian Middle Ages, the scholarly Renaissance, the French Revolution, free-market capitalism, and centralised socialism are presented as complete failures. At the end of the work there is a return to the landscape of the third scene. Adam cannot forget his dream and decides to save mankind from its future sufferings by committing suicide, but Eve tells him that she is expecting a baby. This incident has symbolic meaning: Adam's conclusion is refuted by Eve's suprahistorical wisdom. The open ending of the work has something in common with Nietzsche's reflections on the disadvantages of history for life. Adam's obsession with history has led to a paralysis of personality and a loss of self-respect. Madách's last drama, *Mózes* (Moses, 1861), has a less pessimistic conclusion.

●Various translations of *The Tragedy of*

Man from New York, 1909 to Budapest, 1989.

D. P. Lotze, *Imre Madách* (Boston, 1981).   MSz-M

MAHARI, Gourgen (i.e. G. Adjemian, 1903–69), Armenian poet and novelist, was born in Van (W Armenia). His father belonged to the Armenakan Party. 1907 his mother's brother, commissioned by the Dashnak party, shot his father dead in his house. His childhood began with his mother's tears, 'later with the smile of my grandmother, her stories, legends and prayers', he writes in his autobiography. He received his elementary education in Van, but his schooling was cut short by the 1915 Genocide, during which, with thousands of other refugees, Mahari fled to the Caucasus. He took refuge in orphanages in Igdir, Etchmiadzin, Dilijan and Yerevan, and, 1923, became one of the first students of the newly established State University of Yerevan, where he graduated in Armenian History. Mahari entered Armenian poetry under the influence of Vahan Teryan (1885–1920). His first poem was published 1917 and his first book 1923. His most accomplished collection, *Mrgahas* (Fruition, 1923), was regarded by TCHARENTS as a cornerstone of Soviet Armenian lyric verse. In the 1920s Mahari began to publish prose and the first two volumes of his autobiographical trilogy, which had an enormous impact on Soviet Armenian literature, could be published, *Mankut'yun* (Childhood, 1929) and *Patanekut'yun* (Adolescence, 1930), but the third volume, *Eritasardut'yan semin* (On the threshold of youth), was published only in 1955 because, as he states, 'On 9 August, 1936, I was arrested and exiled to Siberia . . . but was set free after eleven years. . . . The reason? The typist had typed 1947 instead of 1946. . . . I came to Yerevan on 20 August 1947. Where could I go? My mother had been dead since 1944; my wife was remarried.' In November 1948 he was rearrested and sent back to Siberia for life-exile. Mahari's account of that experience appeared in the literary weekly, *Grakan T'ert'*, in April 1964, under the title 'Gisher' (Night), long before Solzhenitsyn's *Gulag Archipelago* (1974). The editor of the paper was fired the day after the account appeared (English translation in *Ararat*, Spring 1976). After Stalin's death Gourgen Mahari returned to Armenia (1954) and lived in Yerevan until his death. His last novel about Van and the loss of W Armenia, *Ayrvogh Aygestanner* (Burning orchards, 1966), aroused one of the most violent polemics in contemporary Armenian experience. Rejected by the academics and accused of treason by the 'nationalists', it is Mahari's masterpiece, and undoubtedly one of the best Armenian novels altogether. His language and style are rich and highly individual; he intertwines the tragic and the humorous in warm lyricism.   VN

MAIORESCU, Titu (1840–1917), was the most influential Roumanian literary critic of the 19th century. After primary school in his native Wallachia he attended German-language schools in Braşov in Transylvania and in Vienna. 1858 he studied philosophy at Berlin and 1859 took a doctorate at Giessen. 1861 he took a degree in letters at Paris. 1863 he became 'rector' of the University of Iaşi in Moldavia. 1874 he was appointed Minister of Education and moved to Bucharest. 1910–12 he was Prime Minister and Foreign Minister. 1863 he founded the literary society *Junimea* (Youth) whose journal, *Convorbiri literare* (Literary discussions), set the agenda for a continually recurring debate concerning the direction of Roumanian culture. In his studies *O Cercetare Critică asupra Poeziei Române de la 1867* (A critical examination of Roumanian poetry in 1867) and *In Contra Direcţiei de Astăzi in Cultura Română* (Against today's direction in Roumanian culture, 1868) he advocated verse based on the oral tradition and denounced foreign, particularly French, influence on Roumanian literature. As Minister of Education he introduced his ideas into the secondary-school curriculum and they left their mark on a whole generation. His fear of submergence by foreign influences led in the opening years of the 20th century to the creation of reviews stressing the importance of national and peasant traditions.   DJD

MAJEROVÁ, Marie (i.e. M. Bartošová, 1882–1967), Czech novelist, born into a working-class family, after leaving school worked as a maid in Budapest and a typist in Prague; she lived in Vienna with her first husband, a Social Democrat journalist; then she studied in Paris, was active in the Social Democratic Party and 1921 joined the newly founded Communist Party. She was linked with NEUMANN's periodical *Nový kult* (New cult), and her first short-story collection *Povídky z pekla* (Stories from hell, 1907) was influenced by anarchism. Her first novel, *Panenství* (Virginity, 1907), the story of a working girl resisting social and economic pressure, was innovatory for its feminism and its treatment of female psychology. In her novel *Náměstí republiky* (Place de la République, 1914, severely rev. 1947) she portrayed a group of anarchists from many lands living in Paris: the main character is a caricature of the autocratic, lecherous anarchist leader Jean Grave. The theme of her *Nej-krásnější svĕt* (The most beautiful world, 1923), a country girl's path to Communism, was the same as that of OLBRACHT's *Anna proletářka*. *Siréna* (Factory siren, 1935, rev. 1947), set in a mining area, is a chronicle of economic and social changes over four generations, while in her better-structured short novel *Havířská balada* (Ballad of a miner, 1938) she concentrates on the story of an individual struggling against the world. Majerová used the technique of 'simultaneous' composition in her utopian novel *Přehrada* (The dam, 1932): set in the future and concentrated into a single day, it concerns the sabotage of a dam as a means of overthrowing the capitalist state. Majerová had a passionate love of life, an understanding of the human heart, a talent for seeing poetry in ordinary things, and a sense of humour, but she did great harm to her works when she rewrote them to satisfy the exigences of Socialist Realism.

●*Ballad of a Miner* (Prague, 1960).   KB

MAKRIYANNIS (i.e. Yannis Triandafillos, 1797–1864), Greek author of a volume of memoirs, not published until 1907, which constitute a unique testimony to both the events they record and the spoken language of their period, was a prominent figure in the War of Independence. He distinguished himself in several battles and attained the rank of general. In the aftermath of the war, feeling the need to record his own experience of it and his views on the conduct of the campaigns, he forced himself to acquire sufficient basic literacy to pen his account. He

seems to have written the first half of the memoirs, covering the events of his childhood and youth and the war itself, fairly rapidly. From 1828, when Capodistrias arrived as president-elect of the newly independent state, to 1840 the memoirs were continued in diary form, written up at frequent intervals. 1840, fearing that his house might be searched by the Security Police, he entrusted the MS to a friend who hid it on Tinos, where it remained for the next four years. During this period Makriyannis was involved in the conspiracies leading to the coup d'état of September 1843, when King Otho was forced to grant the country a constitution. Makriyannis then retrieved his MS and wrote up his account of the period 1840–4 using notes which he claims to have hidden in the ground. 1844–51 he reverted to the practice of writing up the text periodically, but 1850–1, thinking that it might be appropriate to think of publication, he composed a prologue and epilogue. 1851, however, he was put under house arrest, charged with treason, tried and imprisoned. It was clearly impossible for him to consider publication in the period from his release in 1854 to the dethronement of Otho (1862), and in the remaining two years of his life his state of health did not allow him to try to have the work published. In the memoirs Makriyannis is clearly anxious to justify his own life as a soldier and political activist, to criticise the conduct of those who he thought had betrayed the ideals of the revolution, both during the war and after it, and to promote his own view of the ethical and patriotic values necessary to the new Greece. It is not a simple descriptive document, however unschooled its writer, but a piece of persuasive polemic of considerable literary interest.

●H. Lidderdale, *Makriyannis: The Memoirs of General Makriyannis 1797–1864* (Oxford, 1966). CFR

MAKSIMOVIĆ, Desanka (b. 1898), Serbian poet, was born in Rabrovica, near Valjevo. She studied in Belgrade and Paris, and was a schoolmistress for many years. She has spent most of her life in Belgrade, where she is now considered as the doyenne of Serbian poets. Maksimović started writing early and since 1924 has published numerous collections. Her most notable verse, however, came later in her life, *Tražim pomilovanje* (I seek mercy, 1964), *Nemam više vremena* (I have no more time, 1973) and *Pamtiću sve* (I shall remember everything, 1988). Her poems manifest pure lyricism, immediacy, subdued sincerity of emotion, simplicity, and closeness to Nature, from which she derives most of her metaphors.

●*Poems* (Toronto, 1976); *Poems from Norway* [*Pesme iz Norveške*, 1976] (Belgrade, 1984). VDM

MALCZEWSKI, Antoni (1793–1826), Polish poet, initially pursued a military rather than literary career, distinguishing himself as an officer in the army of the Duchy of Warsaw that fought in Napoleon's campaigns. 1816 he left the army and spent the next five years travelling across W Europe. Back in Poland, beset by financial and personal problems, he completed his tale in verse, *Maria*, which appeared in 1825. Malczewski is an *auctor unius libri*, but the one long poem he left is a major work. Despite its obvious Byronic and Scottian inspirations, *Maria* is a brilliant study in Romantic melancholy and misanthropy, which uses the symbolic potential of the Ukrainian landscape to bring into

relief the inevitably tragic quality of human existence. StB

MALESKI, Vlado (1919–84), Macedonian prose writer, attended primary school in Albania, secondary school in Bulgaria and, 1939, went to Belgrade where he started reading law, but left because of the war. He was on the editorial boards of such literary journals as *Nov den* (New day) and *Razgledi* (Views); he also served as a diplomat in the Lebanon, Ethiopia and Poland. Maleski began publishing in the 1950s with short stories mainly concerned with the changes in his life brought about by national revolution and with his intimate experiences. He is best known for his novel *Ona shto beshe nebo* (Which was heaven, 1958); its main themes are revolution and the meaning of 'humaneness'. In his tale about a partisan brigade, Maleski examines human psychology, not revolutionary 'heroism'. With the partisans, his revolution occurs as a change within the hearts of the individuals. He does not depict revolutionaries as monolithic characters experiencing no doubts about their actions; they appear as human beings who live through a crisis of faith and identity and function as the 'real' people who made the revolution. By using several narrators Maleski tries to assemble a multilateral picture of the meaning of revolution. The novel *Razboy* (Loom, 1969) depicts the war years in a small Macedonian town. To some extent, this novel adds to the prehistory of the characters of *Ona shto beshe nebo*. *Razboy* also constitutes an analysis of contemporary society and examines human psychology in times of turmoil and impending changes. SIK

MANGER, Itsik/ Itzik (1901–69), Yiddish poet, dramatist and novelist, born in Czernowitz 1901, made his literary début in 1921 in the journal *Kultur* (Culture, Czernowitz). 1928–38 he lived mostly in Warsaw. His first collection of poems, *Shtern afn dakh* (Stars on the roof, Bucharest, 1929), already displays the seeming incongruity between sophisticated narration and *faux-naïf* content that he employed with particular virtuosity in *Khumesh-lider* (Pentateuch songs, Warsaw, 1935) and *Megile-lider* (Songs from the Book of Esther, Warsaw, 1936), in both of which biblical figures are anachronistically portrayed to humorous effect as the narrator's contemporaries. These techniques represent both a development of features latent in PERETS's *Monish* and the application of modern scholarly investigations of 15th and 16th-century Yiddish literature. Comparable effects are achieved in his *Dos bukh fun gan-eydn* (The book of paradise, Warsaw, 1939) in which he relies on the complicity of the sophisticated reader to lend a note of ironic social criticism to a disingenuously terrestrial view of heaven. He also made skilful adaptations of GOLDFADN's plays for a modern audience. 1938 he moved to Paris and fled to London when the Germans invaded France. *Der shnayder-gezeln note manger zingt* (Songs of the tailor's apprentice, Note Manger, London, 1948) is a memorial for his brother who died in Uzbekistan during the war. He moved to New York in 1951 and finally made his home in Israel in 1967.

● *The Book of Paradise* (New York, 1965); *TYS*, pp. 438–46; *PBMYV*, pp. 561–95. *AMYL*, pp. 100–6, 174–6, 209–12, 282–5.

J. Hadda, *Michigan German Studies*, 3:2 (Ann Arbor, 1977), pp. 1–12; Liptzin (1972), pp. 359–65.   HD

MANI-LEYB (i.e. Mani-Leyb Brahinski, 1884–1953), Yiddish poet, was born in Nezhin in the Ukraine. A childhood of poverty was followed by imprisonment for left-wing political activities. In danger of being arrested a second time, he fled to England in 1904, where he contributed his first poem to the London weekly *Di naye tsayt* (The new times). The following year he moved on to New York, where, discouraged by the failure of the 1905 Russian Revolution, he abandoned politics and became a working-class aesthete and a founder of the movement Di Yunge (The Young Ones). Inspired by the Russian and French Symbolists and by Yiddish folk-song, Mani-Leyb rejected the *engagé* poetry of his predecessors and contributed Impressionist lyrics to the newly founded journal *Di yugnt* (Youth, New York, 1907–8), from which the name of the movement was derived. The second issue of another of their organs, *Literatur, a zamlbukh* (Literature, a miscellany, New York, 1910), opened with his 'Toybnshtile' (Silent as doves) whose delicate melancholy is evoked by deft synaesthetic images. He continued to write neo-Romantic mood-poems in traditional stanzas characterised by their purity of language. They were collected as: *Baladn* (Ballads, New York, 1918), *Vunder iber vunder* (Wonder upon wonder, New York, 1930) and the posthumous, two-volume *Lider un baladn* (Songs and ballads, New York, 1955). The paradoxical nature of the movement was well expressed in another oft-cited poem, 'Ikh bin . . .' (I am . . .), first published in the journal *Di tsukunft* (The future, New York, 1932), in which he gives expression to the two sides of his personality, his life as an immigrant cobbler and his Romantic sensibility.

•*TYP*, pp. 87–96; *AMYL*, pp. 272–5; *PBMYV*, pp. 123–43.

R. Wisse, *Little Love in Big Manhattan* (Cambridge, Mass., 1988).   HD

MANNER, Eeva-Liisa (b. 1921), Finnish poet and playwright, was one of the first and most versatile exponents of Modernism in Finnish. After secondary education, she worked in business before devoting herself wholly to her own literary work and translation. The recurrent themes in Manner's work are loneliness and people's inability to understand each other; they are expressed through the conflict between 'magical order' and 'logical disorder'. Her treatment of these questions was shaped by a pantheist monism, visionary and later increasingly influenced by Oriental philosophy. Critics see in the structuring of her poetry an affinity with music, particularly J. S. Bach. The influence of Eliot and Hesse is apparent in *Tämä matka* (This journey, 1956), the work which marked the advent of Modernism in Finland and which provides the key to much of her later poetry. Her starting-point is man's alienation from Nature with which she seeks an idiosyncratic union. Her treatment of this subject ranges from microscopic detail to cosmic generalisations. The plays *Toukokuun lumi* (May snow, 1966) and *Poltettu oranssi* (Burnt orange, 1968) are less uncompromsing. Influenced by Freud, both concern the psychological development of an adolescent girl. The first examines the effects of lack of love, the second life in an oppressive family. Although the main themes of *Tämä matka* recur in various forms in her later works, a greater preoccupation with public af-fairs becomes apparent. Vietnam and Czechoslovakia appear in her poems of the 1960s. Andalusia, a favourite location, functions in her poems *Fahrenheit 121* (1968) and *Varokaa, voittajat* (Victors, beware, 1972) as a symbol for human warmth in the midst of cold reality.

•*Snow in May* (New York, 1973); R. Dauenhauer and P. Binham (Eds), *Snow in May. An Anthology of Finnish Writing 1945–1972* (London, 1978), pp. 110–20; H. Lomas (Ed.), *Contemporary Finnish Poets*, (Newcastle, 1991), pp. 47–59.

J. Ahokas, 'Eeva-Liisa Manner: Dropping from Reality into Life', *Books Abroad* (1973), pp. 60–5; K. Sala, 'Eeva-Liisa Manner: A Literary Portrait' in Dauenhauer and Binham (Eds), *Snow in May*, pp. 58–9.   MAB

MÁRAI, Sándor (1900–89), Hungarian novelist, short-story writer, essayist, playwright and poet, whose original name was Grosschmid, was born into the German (Saxon) bourgeoisie of Upper Hungary (now Slovakia). He went to school in his native Eperjes (Prešov) and Budapest. His first book, a collection of verse, was published in 1918. Having studied law in Budapest, he left Hungary in 1919 and became a journalist in Germany. 1923–8 he lived in Paris and became acquainted with the leaders of the international Avant-garde. After his return to Hungary (1928), he made a career as a highly successful novelist. In his journalism he harshly criticised Hitler's Germany. Since he continued to represent the values of 'bourgeois' liberalism after 1945, he was forced to leave Hungary by the Communists in 1948. In 1957 he became a US citizen. Because of poor health and growing isolation, he committed suicide in California. Although he was painfully aware of the conflict between the anarchism of the artist and the standards of his own class, he presented the legacy of the middle classes as the most valuable tradition of his country and was critical of the Populist interpretation of nationhood. His verse is of less value, but his autobiographical works and best novels are major achievements. Following KOSZTO-LÁNYI's precepts, he became one of the finest prose stylists in Hungarian. His early works, written under the influence of German Expressionism, have more historical than aesthetic value. *Egy polgár vallomásai* (The confessions of a *citoyen*, 1934–5) is not only an important social document of the values of the assimilated bourgeoisie but also an impressive vision of the social stability of central Europe before WWI. *Szindbád hazamegy* (Sindbad returns home, 1940) has a close-knit structure and several semantic strata: on the one hand, it is a novel about the writer KRÚDY and pre-capitalist Hungary; on the other, it is a self-portrait of Márai disguised in the form of a pastiche, anticipating the Postmodern cult of imitation. Although Márai became less prolific in his later years, he continued to publish significant works to the end of his life. As an essayist he never ceased to insist on the necessity of rationalism, but as a writer of narrative fiction he presented irreconcilable attitudes that make judgement impossible. *Ítélet Canudosban* (Judgement in Canudos, 1970), a novel about Latin America, concerns the endless battle between fanatics who reject civilisation and the representatives of the legacy of the Enlightenment. MSz-M

MARCINKEVIČIUS, Justinas (b. 1930), Lithuanian poet and playwright, 1954 graduated in Lithuanian language and literature at Vilnius, then worked in the editorial offices of literary journals. 1959–65 he occupied high posts in the Lithuanian Writers' Union. Together with MAČIULIS AND BRAZDŽIONIS, Marcinkevičius is a poet who has become a symbol of the nation's sufferings, integrity and hopes in times of extreme misfortune. The coming of the Soviet régime, the abominations socialism perpetrated in the countryside, the radical industrialisation and collectivisation it imposed on the people, relentless Communist propaganda – Marcinkevičius saw and understood it all and nevertheless tried to preserve the truth in the Lithuanian soul by rendering it poetically eloquent in his verse so that it would ring in the people's minds. His readers responded to Marcinkevičius's efforts, and he has become one of the most popular poets and public figures of today. The numerous collections of Marcinkevičius's poetry do not exhibit any overt hostility to the régime; if anything, he sometimes appears to be trying to make some of its aspects acceptable; he has, for instance, said kind things about Lenin in his unbuttoned overcoat, speaking to the people with great inspiration. What Marcinkevičius does most of the time, however, is to cast an emotional glow around simple objects and places in an agrarian life, and thus make this life a sanctuary worthy of deep human commitment, even if only in memory. His poetic language is highly imaginative, full of emotionally compelling images, and smooth rhythm and diction. He does not, however, seriously experiment with any new poetic forms. The best of Marcinkevičius's verse is collected in *Eilėraščiai, mažosios poemos*

(Lyrical and short narrative poems, 1975). His dramatic trilogy in verse, *Mindaugas* (1968), *Katedra* (The cathedral, 1971) and *Mažvydas* (1977), presents a broad panorama of Lithuanian history that looks closely at those historical figures that left a lasting mark on Lithuania's future and on the character of her people.   RŠ

MARINKOVIĆ, Ranko (b. 1913), Croatian novelist and playwright, born on the island of Vis, studied in Zagreb, worked at the Croatian National Theatre, and the Academy of Dramatic Art in Zagreb. His first short stories, published just before WWII, are satirical observations on small-town life, mostly in Dalmatia. His first play, *Albatros* (1939), displays an intuitive understanding of the theatre as a medium. Since WWII he has continued to write short stories, evoking the atmosphere of Dalmatian communities with black humour: *Proze* (Stories, 1948); *Ruke* (Hands, 1953) which won much critical acclaim. He has also written plays, of which the best known is *Glorija* (Gloria, 1955), a tragicomedy in which a circus dancer is asked by a monk to play the Virgin Mary in a tableau in church to attract a larger congregation; the novel *Kiklop* (The Cyclops, 1965) concerns the bewildered alienation of an intellectual in an urban setting on the eve of WWII, and the fate of modern man, his uncertainties and fear in the face of encroaching totalitarianism. The novel's most striking quality is its burlesque style, a feature of all Marinković's work. The title of his most recent novel, *Zajednička kupka* (Shared dip, 1980), described as an 'anti-novel', may be seen as a metaphor for the quagmire which human beings have made of the world.

●'Gloria', in B. Mikasinovich (Ed.),

Five Modern Yugoslav Plays (New York, 1977), pp. 147–266; 'The Hands', *BC Review*, London, 10 (1970), pp. 4–10; 'Politeia or the Inspector's Intrigues: Vaudeville', *The Bridge*, 55 (1978), pp. 17–32.

B. Donat, 'From Individual to Mythical Experience', *The Bridge*, 3–4 (1966), pp. 89–92.   ECH

MARKISH, Perets/ Peretz (1895–1952), Yiddish poet and novelist, born in Polonnoe, Volhynia, after being wounded in WWI participated together with BERGLSON, DER NISTER, Leyb Kvitko (1890–1952) and Dovid Hofshteyn (1889–1952), in the extraordinary burst of creativity that took place in Kiev amid the turmoil of the Civil War. He contributed to the innovative journal *Eygns* (Our own, Kiev, 1918, 1920) and brought out his first collection of poetry, *Shveln* (Thresholds, Kiev, 1919), which established him as one of the foremost Yiddish poets in the country. Following several waves of pogroms in the Ukraine he left the USSR and settled in Warsaw where he published a lament for the victims of the massacres entitled *Di kupe* (The heap, 1921), a gaunt cycle of poems, subverting traditional liturgical forms to indict heaven with images of carnage and putrefaction. *Di kupe* thus takes its place in a tradition of responses to anti-Semitism that includes 17th-century *lider* (songs) and Ḥayim Naḥman Bialik's famous Hebrew poem on the Kishinëv pogrom of 1903. Together with Y.-Y. ZINGER and Oyzer Varshavski (1898–1944) he edited the exuberantly Expressionist and provocative *Khalyastre* (The gang, vol. 1, Warsaw, 1922; vol. 2, Paris, 1924). During the mid-1920s he contributed to a range of émigré journals and to *Shtrom* (Current, Moscow), the organ of the 'Fellow-Travelling' writers in the USSR. In 1926, at the height of the NEP era of literary pluralism, he returned to Russia where the régime appeared to be offering unparalleled opportunities to Yiddish culture. However, he soon found himself coming under attack in the Proletarian journals and especially by Moyshe Litvakov (1875–1938). The novel, *Dor-oys, dor-ayn* (Generation after generation, vol. 1, Kharkov, 1929) which traces the advent of revolutionary thinking in the *shtetl*, was arraigned for putative Jewish chauvinism. None the less, Markish retained underlying confidence in Stalin and the régime until the time of the Ribbentrop-Molotov Pact. 1939 he was awarded the Order of Lenin. The war years brought greater freedom of expression and 1941–8 he was active in the Anti-Fascist Committee and worked on his monumental verse epic *Milkhome* (War, Moscow, 1948) which laments the sufferings of the 'Holocaust' and celebrates *inter alia* Hirsh Glik (1922–44), the poet of the Vilna (Vilnius) ghetto. By the time *Milkhome* was published hopes for the future for Yiddish culture in the Soviet Union had been dashed. Itsik Fefer (1900–52) felt called upon to castigate the supposed Zionism of *Milkhome*, which did not save him from being arrested at the same time as Markish and virtually all the significant Yiddish writers in 1948–9. Markish was shot in August 1952 together with those who had not already died in prison. The novel which he had completed immediately before being arrested, *Trot fun doyres* (March of generations, Moscow, 1967), finally appeared some time after his 'rehabilitation'.

●*TYP*, pp. 180–5; *PBMYV*, pp. 345–77.

Esther Markish, *The Long Return* (New York, 1978); D.G. Roskies, *Against the Apocalypse, Responses to Catastrophe in Modern Jewish Culture* (Cambridge, Mass., 1984); S. Wolitz, 'A Yiddish Modernist Dirge, *Di kupe* of Perets Markish', *Modern Jewish Studies, Annual VI = Yiddish*, 6:4 (New York, 1987), pp. 56–72.   HD

MARULIĆ, Marko (1450–1524), Croatian poet, theologian and scholar, represents the transition from medieval to Renaissance literature. He embodies the three strands of Croatian culture, out of which its mature achievements have grown: the medieval Glagolitic/Church Slavonic tradition, Latin scholarship, and Western, notably Italian, influences. Marulić was born into an old patrician family in Split where he attended the Latin school, going on to study in Padua. He worked for a time as a lawyer and judge in Split, before devoting himself to writing and studying archaeology and painting. His substantial Latin moralistic works, *De institutione bene vivendi* (1506), *Evangelistarium* (1516), *De humilitate et gloria Christi* (1519), *Dialogus de laudibus Herculis* (1524) were widely translated. His long Latin poem *Davidias*, found in 1954, has been described as his most ambitious and best work. Marulić also wrote short moralistic and satirical works in the vernacular for the enlightenment of his fellow citizens. Such works were based on popular medieval genres, for example the dispute between Lent and Carnival (*Poklad i korizma*). He was spurred to write his longer and artistically more serious Croatian works particularly by awareness that many women in convents, including his sister, had no knowledge of Latin and hence nothing to read. His most important Croatian work is the narrative poem *Judita* (Judith, 1521), an ambitious work, composed at a time when the vernacular was hardly established as a literary language and drawing on several dialects. His other narrative poem in Croatian, *Historija od Suzane čiste* (The story of chaste Suzanna), is simpler and less interesting. *Judita* is a successful balance of colourful set-piece scenes, psychological detail, movement and drama; the character of Holofernes is particularly well drawn. There is undoubtedly an allegorical dimension to *Judita*: in the context of the proximity of the Ottomans to Split during Marulić's lifetime, the poem may be read as a call to the Christian powers to resist their advance. Such an interpretation is justified by some of his other, shorter vernacular poems, notably the *Molitva suprotiva Turkom* (Prayer against the Turks) which became a symbol of patriotic sentiment incorporated into the works of later Dalmatian writers, and also by the *Epistola ad Adrianum VI* (1522), an appeal to the Pope to organise a campaign against the Ottomans.

● 'To the Virgin Mary', *The Bridge*, 25 (1971), p. 21; 'Letter to Pope Adrian VI', *BC Review*, 13 (1977), pp. 10–12; Extract from *Judita* in T. Butler (Ed.), *Monumenta Serbocroatica* (Ann Arbor, 1980), p. 229–36.

M. Usmiani, 'Marko Marulić (1450–1524)', *Harvard Slavic Studies*, 3 (1957), pp. 1–48; G. Gutsche, 'Classical Antiquity in Marulić's *Judita' SEEJ*, 19 (1975), pp. 310–21; E. D. Goy, 'Marko Marulić: An Early 16th-century View of East-West Conflict', *BC Review*, 13 (1977), pp. 3–12.　　　ECH

MASING, Uku (i.e. Hugo-Albert Masing, 1909–85), Estonian poet, theologian and student of the Orient, read theology at Tartu and continued his studies (1926–30) at Tübingen and Berlin; 1933 he began teaching at Tartu University. He started his literary career with the Arbujad (Logomancers) group, but in contrast to this group's Neoclassical terseness, he tended towards figurative, symbolistically polysemic, verse, where synctactic complexity blended with Masing's encyclopaedic knowledge (e.g. astronomical, botanical, ethnographical) and interest in Oriental civilisations, as in *Neemed Vihmade lahte* (Tongues into the Gulf of Rains, 1935). In contrast to the urgent Europeanness of the Young Estonians (*Noor-Eesti*), Masing uniquely coined an expressly Oriental conception of Estonian cultural identity. He also broke paths for the Oriental into Estonian literary consciousness with his translations (say of Tagore) and his academic work. After WWII Masing's possibilities of publication were severely limited, and his works appeared mainly abroad – *Džunglilaulud* (Songs of the jungle, 1965), *Udu Toonela jõelt* (Mist from Lethe, 1974), *Aerutades hurtsikumeistriga* (Pulling with the master, 1983) and *Kirsipuu varjus* (In the shade of the cherry tree, 1985). Masing earned official recognition as an artist only after his death. His collection *Ehatuule maa* (Zephyr land, 1985) appeared in Tallinn.

● Selections in W. K. Matthews (Ed.), *An Anthology of Modern Estonian Poetry* (Gainsville, 1953) and in *Contemporary East European Poetry* (Ann Arbor, 1983).　　　VM

MATESSIS, Antonios (1794–1875), Greek dramatist, friend and associate of SOLOMOS, began by writing poetry in Italian, but was inspired by the War of Independence to try writing in Greek. A firmly convinced demoticist, he contributed to the language debate in the same period when SOLOMOS was writing his *Dialogos*. His own poetry consists largely of light lyrics in Classical tone, a little satirical verse and one or two slightly more profound poems on personal themes. He also translated Gray and Foscolo. But his lasting contribution to Greek literature is the five-act play Ο Βασιλικός (The basil plant, 1859), written in 1830 and performed in his native Zakynthos in 1832. It is set in Zakynthos a century earlier, but the clash of conservative and progressive social ideas which it represents through a clash of generations is equally appropriate to the time of writing. At the same time Matessis gives a closely observed account of the Zantiot caste system. The play is the earliest, and one of the most effective, of Greek social dramas, combining intellectual debate, psychological verisimilitude and dramatic interest.   CFR

MATOŠ, Antun Gustav (1873–1914), Croatian writer, went to Belgrade in 1894 to avoid conscription into the Austro-Hungarian Army, and spent several years travelling in Europe. He returned to Zagreb 1908 where he became the central figure in cultural life until his death. He brought with him a thorough knowledge of W European, particularly French, literature, and a determination to apply its standards to his own milieu through his critical writings. A charismatic figure who earned the nickname 'rabbi', Matoš was an important stimulus to others. This period in the cultural life of both Serbs and Croats, commonly referred to as 'Modernism' and characterised by a general sense of having definitely joined the mainstream of contemporary European culture, was a time when literary critics in both Belgrade and Zagreb had exceptional authority. Matoš's literary contribution was considerable: he produced a substantial collection of short stories, remarkable for their blend of realistic and fantastic elements, travel sketches, essays and verse. A striking feature of all Matoš's writing is the blurring of distinctions between genres, a fashionable approach of the day: his critical writings are impressionistic rather than analytical and his travel sketches highly subjective. The positive contribution of this approach is an emphasis on style, which had a beneficial effect on writers he influenced. That he contributed to the greater maturity of Croatian literature in his lifetime may be seen in the fact that younger writers rejected his authority by the time of his death.

● 'At Saint Stjepan's' in A. Kadić (Ed.), *Contemporary Croatian Literature* (The Hague, 1960), p. 31; 'The Neighbour' in B. H. Clark and M. Lieber (Eds), *Great Short Stories of the World* (New York, 1925), pp. 824–30; 'A Sonnet' in *AMYP*, p. 92.   ECH

MATRËNGA, Lekë (i.e. Luca Matranga, 1567–1619), the earliest known Arbëresh (Italo-Albanian) writer, was born in Piana degli Albanesi in Sicily, and after finishing his studies in Rome, returned to Sicily and engaged in pastoral duties in his native village. Matrënga translated from the Latin a catechism which, after BUZUKU's missal, is the oldest monument of the Albanian language. It is the first complete work in Tosk, S dialect, and contains the first specimen of verse written in Albanian. Its title is *E mbsueme e krështerë* (Christian doctrine, 1592).

● M. La Piana, *Il catechismo albanese di*

*Luca Matranga (1592) da un manoscritto
Vaticano* (Grottaferrata, 1912);
M. Sciambra, *La 'Dottrina cristiana'
albanese di Luca Matranga.
Riproduzione, trascrizione e commento
del Codice Baberini Latino 3454.*
(Vatican City, 1964).   ShM

MAVILIS, Lorentsos (1860–1912),
Greek poet, belonged to an aristocratic Corfiot family and was
brought up on that island. Typically
of well-to-do Ionian islanders, Italian
was his first language and he learnt
Greek in school. 1875 he went to
Athens to study literature, but soon
left the university, disillusioned by
the teaching. 1878–89 he attended
various German universities, using
his time as an opportunity to read
European literature and to learn
thoroughly French, German,
English and Italian. In Germany he
read Kant, Fichte and Schopenhauer
and was much influenced by them.
He spent 1892–4 back in Corfu, but
found the intellectual atmosphere of
the island provincial and threw himself into various social and political
activities, culminating in the formation (with THEOTOKIS) of a volunteer
brigade to fight in Crete in 1896, and
further action in Epirus in 1897.
Disenchanted with the nationalist
movement after the failure of the
1897 war he returned to Corfu and
remained there until 1912, living
alone with his unmarried older sister
on their small private income. 1911
he was elected MP for Corfu. 1912 he
volunteered, despite his age, for
service in the Greco-Turkish War
and was killed in combat. In Corfu he
was closely connected with the other
intellectuals of his day, and later
mixed in politically and linguistically
liberal Athenian literary circles. In
theory and in practice he was a keen
demoticist. His work consists of 58

sonnets, published individually
1886–1912 but collected only posthumously. The thematic range of his
sonnets is wide: he wrote lyrical,
patriotic, philosophical and even satirical poems. But they have in common a close attention to technique
and expression and a melancholy,
even pessimistic, tone.

                                     CFR

MAŽURANIĆ, Ivan (1814–90),
Croatian poet and statesman, born in
N Dalmatia, educated in Rijeka
(Fiume) and Zagreb, and in Hungary, served as a civil servant in
Karlovac until 1848. Under police
supervision in the years of Neo-
absolutism, afterwards Mažuranić
was made Procurator General for
Croatia and Slavonia (1850–60). He
became the first Croatian Chancellor
(1861–6) and then the first Croat and
non-noble to be appointed to the post
of governor (*Ban*) (1873–80). He
contributed much to making Croatia
a modern state, introducing numerous reforms in education, the administration and justice. At the end of
his term of office, he devoted himself
to astronomy, mathematics and philosophy. Mažuranić's writing had
two main stimuli: a desire to forge
links between modern Croatian literature and Classical culture, and a
concern with the legacy of his own
culture as opposed to W European
models. One of his finest achievements, which brings together these
two aims, was the composition of
two canti to complete GUNDULIĆ's
unfinished epic, *Osman*. This under-
taking was so successful that Mažuranić's additions are barely distingu-
ishable from the original. Mažuranić
is best known for his own narrative
Smrt Smail-age Čengića (The death
of Smail-Aga Čengić, 1846). The
form of this work owes much to

Serbo-Croat oral-tradition poetry, which Mažuranić knew well. *Smrt* describes the downfall of a local Ottoman administrator in Herzegovina. Based on an historical figure, but altered to suit Mažuranić's aim, Smail-Aga is portrayed as a Classical tragic hero who challenges Fate by going too far in exercising his power. Divine retribution takes the form of an anonymous band from the mountains of Montenegro (a symbol of tough, noble independence), shielded on their march through the night by Nature and given Communion at dawn by a priest whose church is the natural world, before descending on Smail-Aga's camp to carry out the will of God.

●*The Death of Smail Aga* (London, 1925).

E. D. Goy, 'The Tragic Element in "Smrt Smail-age Čengića"', *SEER*, 44 (1966), pp. 327–36; I. Slamnig, 'Ivan Mažuranić', *The Bridge*, 17 (1969), pp. 35–9; C. Ward, 'The Image of the Turk in Mažuranić's *Smrt Smail-Age Čengića*', *Balkanistica*, 2 (1975), pp. 31–42.   ECH

MEDENIS, Jānis (1903–61), Latvian poet, failed to complete his university studies. 1927–37 he was the editorial secretary of the dictionary of the Latvian language. In spring 1945, he tried to cross the Baltic in a fishing boat to take refuge in Sweden, but the vessel was captured by the Soviets. Medenis was held in various gaols until the end of the 1940s, when he was deported to the Kolyma forced-labour camp in N Siberia. 1955, after an amnesty, the poet was permitted to return, but camp life had already broken his health: he had to be brought from the train on a stretcher and immediately taken to hospital. His collections, *Torņi pamalē* (Towers on the horizon, 1926), *Tecila* (The whetstone, 1933), *Varenība* (Mightiness, 1936), and *Teiksmu raksti* (Symbols of legendary tales, 1942), are lyrical statements full of virility and passion. Drawn from his own personal experiences and demonstrating a judicious use of satire, the poems revive dramatic events from the time of the 1905 Revolution. Medenis's style is reminiscent of Verhaeren's. His stanza-structure is founded on the metre of the folk-song. Medenis's name was banned from the press from 1945 until the Thaw. 1958 a collection, *Dienu krāšņums* (The splendour of days), was published, consisting mainly of Medenis's pre-Soviet works, which were now officially acknowledged as 'the property of the entire nation'. Another collection, *Ugunis naktī* (Flames in the night), appeared in 1961. Though recognised and even accepted into the ranks of the Soviet Latvian Writers' Union, Medenis remained a typical 'émigré in his own country', the reflection of which can be seen in a number of his poems which he managed to send his brother who lived as a refugee in the West. These purely lyrical poems, in which melancholy and longing for his far-off homeland and kinsfolk are manifestly the profoundest emotions of the poet, were published in the London Latvian émigré journal *Ceļa Zīmes* (Signposts, no. 40) in 1961). These 'unpublished' poems, most of which he wrote at the same time as his 'acceptable' poems, belong to the small known body of Latvian literature written 'for the desk drawer'. The majority of his 'underground' poems was written either in prison in Latvia in the late 1940s, or in the labour camp in Kolyma, where the poet suffered a stroke from which he never completely recovered.   EB

MEKULI, Esad (b. 1916), Albanian poet from Kosovo, considered as the founder of modern Yugoslav Albanian poetry, born in Plavë in Montenegro and, after secondary schooling in Pejë, studied veterinary medicine at Belgrade. He was editor of the Kosovo Albanian daily, *Rilindja* (Rebirth), and of the literary journal, *Jeta e re* (New life). His first collection, *Për ty* (For you, 1955), was dedicated to Kosovo. Subsequently, he published *Avsha ada, vjersha nga ishulli* (A.a., verse from an island, 1971) *Vjersha* (Verse, 1973); *Glasovi vremena* (The voices of the times, 1974), a selection of his Albanian poetry with the author's own Serbo-Croat translation; *Midis dashurisë dhe urrejtjes* (Between love and hatred, 1981); and *Brigjet* (The hills, 1981). He has also published translations of 19th-century Montenegrin poetry.   ShM

MELISSANTHI (i.e. Ivi Skandhalaki, née Kouyia, 1910–90), Greek poet, was educated at the French Institute and the German School in Athens. After studying drama, music and dance she taught French until her marriage to the politician and writer Yannis Skandhalakis in 1935. She published her first poems, Φωνές εντόμων (Insect voices) 1930, but it was her second collection, Προφητείες (Prophecies, 1931), that first won her critical acclaim. The inspiration for her prewar poetry was religious: her metaphysical sensibilities were heightened by an attack of TB from which she had to recuperate for eighteen months in a Swiss sanatorium. Many of the titles of her collections (let alone of individual poems) reveal this affiliation, e.g. Φλεγόμενη βάτος (Burning bush, 1935), Γυρισμός του ασώτου (Return of the prodigal, 1936). Numer-

ous collections followed in the postwar period. Her work of 1974–82 has been collected under the title Τα Νέα Ποιήματα (The new poems), and her collected works appeared (1986) under the title Οδοιπορικό (Cost of the journey). Her work is fundamentally philosophical in character. Gradually she has moved from a search for the presence of God in herself and the world around her to something closer to an Existentialist apprehension of the world. Rather than being burdened with a sense of original sin, mankind is endowed with a sense of its own pointlessness and consequent total responsibility for itself. The vision is not entirely negative. She expresses a belief in the power of human love to create at least temporary meaning out of the appalling tensions from which life is built.
● K. Friar (Ed.), *Modern Greek Poetry* (Athens, 1982), pp. 223–32.   CFR

MENART, Janez (b. 1929), Slovene poet and translator, after graduating in Slavonic studies and comparative literature worked in film and television, and later in a publishing house. He was one of the contributors to *Pesmi štirih* (Songs of the four, 1953), which represented a break with the simplistic attitudes of immediate postwar poetry and reestablished the claims of the subjective lyric. He won popularity with his own collections: *Časopisni stihi* (Journalistic verses, 1960) and *Semafori mladosti* (Youth's traffic lights, 1963). Apart from his lyrics, which have a tone of irony and sarcasm, he has written narrative verse, for example *Srednjeveške balade* (Medieval ballads, 1974). His style combines romantic imagery and colloquial speech.
● Translations in: *AMYP*; *SPT*; *Parnassus*, 1957, 1965.   HL

MENDELE MOYKHER SFORIM (i.e. Sholem Yankev Abramovitsh, c. 1835–1917), Yiddish and Hebrew writer, dubbed the 'grandfather' of Yiddish literature by SHOLEM ALEYKHEM, was born into a respected family near Minsk, but after the death of his father spent many months wandering between the *shtetlakh* of the Pale of Settlement in the company of a tramp (the model for his Fishke) until befriended by GOTLOBER and it was in the manner of the latter that he began his literary career as a Maskilic satirist. Before long his first-hand acquaintance with the sufferings of the Jewish masses gave his work increasing human sympathy and artistic complexity. The serialisation of his *Dos kleyne mentshele* (The little man, in *Kol mevaser* [The herald], Odessa, 1864) marked a turning-point in the history of Yiddish literature. By assuming the persona of a simple book peddler, the *moykher sforim* that became his pseudonym, he was able to develop a deceptively rambling, discursive voice, employing a *skaz* type of narration reminiscent of Gogol''s *Vechera na khutore bliz Dikańki* (Evenings in the farm near D.) that bridged the gap between the pre-Realist novel and the Modernist concern for the unconscious and enabled him to ironise the confrontation between popular culture and the modern world. There followed a series of elegantly ironic works including *Dos vintshfingerl* (The wishing-ring, Warsaw, 1865); *Di klyatshe, oder tsar baley khayim* (The nag, or the protection of animals, Vilnius, 1873), an allegory that portrays the Jewish nation as a prince transformed into a broken, maltreated nag; *Kitser masoes binyomin hashlishi* (A summary of the travels of Benjamin III, Vilnius, 1878), a satire inspired by both Benjamin of Tudela and Cervantes in which Mendele incorporates Romantic descriptions of the beauty of the Ukrainian landscape; and *Fishke der krumer* (F. the lame, Odessa, 1888), as well as a number of plays. The 1890 demise of SHOLEM ALEYKHEM's Folksbiblyotek deprived Mendele of an important outlet for his Yiddish works. He now turned to recasting his works in Hebrew translation, simultaneously extending the expressive capacities of modern Hebrew. For most of the rest of his life he was revising his existing works in Yiddish and Hebrew versions. The final versions of *Dos kleyne mentshele* and *Fishke der krumer* did not appear until 1907. Shortly before his death he was writing his memoirs. The fact that Mendele was born in Byelorussia but spent most of his life in Odessa gave him the opportunity to contribute significantly to the shaping of a literary standard from the disparate E dialects.

●*The Travels and Adventures of Benjamin the Third* (New York, 1949); *Fishke the Lame* (New York, 1960); *TYS*, pp. 97–111; *SOYN*, pp. 249–358. S. Dubnov in *WWT*, 2, pp. 519–27; Liptzin (1963), pp. 20–33; Madison, pp. 33–60; Miron, passim. HD

MERI, Lennart (b. 1929), Estonian writer, got his basic education in Paris and Berlin, where his Shakespeare-translator father, Georg Meri (1900–83), was a diplomat. Meri obtained his degree in history at Tartu in 1953; 1953–5 he was chief literary adviser at the Vanemuine Theatre and, later, worked with Estonian Broadcasting and Tallinnfilm. 1990–92 he was Estonian Minister of Foreign Affairs. Meri's literary work is intimately linked with his frequent travels to Soviet Central Asia, the Yakut Autonomous Republic, Kamchatka and Chukotka. In Meri's work the travelogue fuses with an original interpretation of historical and ethnographical material, and gradually forms itself in an inventive essay form which combines travel-writing with historiography. The main theme of his writing is the prehistory of the Finno-Ugric peoples and the other non-Russian inhabitants of Siberia. The clearest evidence of that is to be found in *Virmaliste väraval* (At the gates of the Aureola, 1974), *Hõbevalge* (Silvern white, 1976), and *Hõbevalgem* (Silvern whiter, 1984); in the last Meri placed Ultima Thule in Estonia.   VM

MERI, Veijo (b. 1928), Finnish novelist, playwright and poet, is an ironical commentator on post WWII Finnish society. Born into an army family he spent much of his early life in barracks. After university studies at Helsinki he worked as a publisher's editor before devoting himself wholly to his writing. Meri looks at life from below. He recreates the world through the eyes of ordinary people, exploring human behaviour in irrational situations. Meri heightens the sense of irrationality by the frequent interpolation in his narrative of rambling, grotesque anecdotes. The effect is often a black humour reminiscent of Gogol´, Kafka or HAŠEK. He emphasises the absurd by setting many of his works against the background of the 1939–40 and 1941–4 Finnish wars against the USSR. The grand designs of politicians and generals contrast absurdly with the soldiers' experience. For the latter, chaos prevails; boredom is the main feature of war; rumour and gossip are the sole sources of information, as in the novels *Manillaköysi*

(The manila rope, 1957) and *Sujut* (Quits, 1961), and the play *Sotamies Jokisen vihkiloma* (Private J.'s marriage leave, 1965). Various other illustrations of irrational behaviour in response to nonsensical situations are linked to army life, e.g. *Irralliset* (The rootless, 1959), *Everstin kuljettaja* (The colonel's driver, 1966) and *Kersantin poika* (The sergeant's son, 1971), while in *Vuoden 1918 tapahtumat* (The events of 1918, 1960) the context is the 1918 Civil War, and in *Suku*, (The family, 1968) family machinations.

●*The Manila Rope* (New York, 1967); *Private Jokinen's Marriage Leave* (New York, 1973).

V. Meri, 'The memoirs of a jobbing writer', *Books from Finland* (1989), pp. 229–31.   MAB

MÉSZÖLY, Miklós (b. 1921), Hungarian short-story writer, novelist, essayist, playwright and poet, was educated in his native town and at the Pázmány University in Budapest. He finished his PhD in law and started writing short stories. Sent to fight on the Russian Front in WWII, he became a prisoner of war. After his return from the USSR, he worked as an editor in Szekszárd. When Communist dictatorship started in Hungary in 1948, he had serious difficulties earning a living. After 1956 he was allowed to publish but was often attacked for his pessimism. Keeping the impulse of experiment and innovation alive in the darkest years of Communism, he made a consistent and sustained contribution to Hungarian prose. His earlier works are marked by an interest in the fantastic and the parabolic, whereas his later phase is characterised by an interweaving of autobiography and fiction. The title story of *Jelentés öt egérről* (Report on five mice, 1967), written in 1958, is a grotesque parable about cruelty. In the novel *Az atléta halála* (The death of an athlete, 1966), life is viewed from the perspective of death; in *Saulus* (1968) the death of Jesus makes the main character examine his values and lose his identity; and in *Film* (1976) history appears as an endless process of deaths caused by political terror. In one of his finest works, the short novel *Megbocsátás* (Forgiveness, 1984), life is presented as a mosaic painted with vivid clarity.   MSz-M

MICKIEWICZ, Adam (1798–1855), Polish Romantic poet, universally regarded as the national bard, born in Novogrudok or in the nearby village of Zaosie and educated in Vilnius, inherited the traditions of the Grand Duchy of Lithuania and was often inspired by local Byelorussian folklore. Detained and tried by the Russian authorities for his participation in the clandestine student movement (1824), he was eventually exiled to central Russia. When released, Mickiewicz visited Germany, Switzerland, Italy and eventually settled in Paris. 1840–4 he lectured on Slavonic literature at the Collège de France. 1849 he founded *La Tribune des peuples*, a republican newspaper, and during the Crimean War went to Constantinople to encourage the foundation of Polish, Cossack and Jewish troops in support of an anti-Russian alliance. While on this mission he suddenly died of cholera and was later buried at Wawel Castle in Cracow (1890). Mickiewicz's earliest poems reflect his Classical education. The same tradition can also be traced in the first two volumes of his poems (1822–3), regarded as the fountainhead of Polish Romanticism. Both *Ballady i romanse* (Ballads and romances, 1822) and parts 2 and 4 of *Dziady* (Forefathers' eve, 1823) demonstrate interests in folklore and spiritual communion with the dead, while proclaiming the superiority of feelings over pure intellect. In *Sonety krymskie* (Crimean sonnets, 1826) the compact form and pithy descriptions express the emotions of a pilgrim admiring Oriental exoticism and coming face to face with God in the wilderness. *Konrad Wallenrod* (1828), a narrative poem in Byronic style (Mickiewicz had translated *The Giaour*), introduces a Promethean hero who sacrifices his personal happiness and, in some ways, also his moral integrity to save his country. Part 3 of *Dziady* (1832), together with the two preceding parts, represents the pre-eminent achievement of Polish Romantic theatre. Rooted in the Byelorussian ritual of 'forefathers' eve', the drama is a monumental morality play where the struggle between good and evil encompasses not only its Promethean hero Konrad, but also Polish-Russian relations and, indeed, the world as a whole. A vision of a future saviour or messiah coexists with the idea of Poland as the 'Christ of nations'. The theatrical appeal of the group scenes, the powerful imagery and the unusual blend of the supernatural and the real assure the drama a unique status. *Pan Tadeusz* (1834) represents a conscious attempt to create a modern epic and combines various literary genres: the Homeric epic, the heroicomic, comedy and the Scottian novel. The way common events are transformed into poetry demonstrates the author's consciousness of a gap between illusion and reality (Goethe's *Dichtung und Wahrheit*), which often leads to unexpected counterpoint. The poem's personal dimension, namely Mickiewicz's nostalgia for his lost homeland and corresponding descriptions of the Lithuanian landscape and customs, is ultimately overshadowed by its patriotic content – an optimistic vision of a national regeneration during the Napoleonic Wars. After *Pan Tadeusz* Mickiewicz composed in verse but few outstanding lyrical poems. The most important of his late works are his French lectures on Slavonic literature (published in Paris as *Les Slaves*, 1849), in which the poet discloses his views on the special mission of the Slavs in the future of Europe. Mickiewicz's writings have exerted an enduring influence on Polish literature and on the national psyche.

●*Poems* (New York, 1944); *Forefathers* (London, 1968); *Konrad Wallenrod and Other Writings* (Westport, Conn., 1975); *Pan Tadeusz* (London, 1930, 1964; New York, 1962).
W. Weintraub, *The Poetry of A. Mickiewicz* (The Hague, 1954); D. Welsh, *Adam Mickiewicz* (New York, 1966); W. Lednicki (Ed.), *A. Mickiewicz in World Literature* (Berkeley, 1956).   SE

MIĘDZYRZECKI, Artur (b. 1922), Polish poet, fiction writer, essayist, and translator, published his first book of poems 1943 in Jerusalem while serving in the Polish Army, in whose ranks he then fought in the Italian campaign. After the war he studied journalism in Paris and 1950 returned to Poland. 1990 he was elected president of the Polish chapter of PEN. His numerous volumes of verse reveal Międzyrzecki as one of the most creative representatives of the powerful trend of 'ironic moralism' in Polish poetry, focusing (particularly over the 1970s and 1980s) on the theme of culture's struggle or survival under despotic régimes.

●Selected poems in S. Barańczak and C. Cavanagh (Eds.), *Polish Poetry of the Last Two Decades of Communist Rule: Spoiling Cannibals' Fun* (Evanston, Ill., 1991).   StB

MIELEŽ, Ivan (1921–76), Byelorussian novelist and playwright, was born into a poor peasant family in Polessia and first began writing when in hospital during WWII, publishing his first story in 1944. His first novel, *Minski napramak* (In the direction of Minsk, 1950–2), was better than most war novels of the time, and the postwar stories and plays are never less than competent, but Mielež's masterpiece was undoubtedly the three-part *Paleskaja chronika* (Polessian chronicle). The first novel of this lyrical epic, *Ludzi na bałocie* (People of the marsh, 1961), created a sensation on its first appearance, being an encyclopaedic yet psychologically convincing and philosophically subtle depiction of the peasants in Mielež's native region during the pre-collectivisation period. The sequel, *Podych navalnicy* (Breath of the storm, 1964–5), continues the same story with equal dynamism, whilst only the third part, *Zaviei, śnieżań* (Blizzards, snowfalls, 1976), perhaps unfinished, drops slightly below the earlier level. Mielež's tragic chronicle has been compared with Sholokhov's *Quiet Flows the Don* in scope, epic breadth and rich characterisation.

●*People of the Marsh* (Moscow, 1979).
                                                                           ABMcM

MIGJENI (i.e. Millosh Gjergj Nikolla, 1911–38), Albanian poet and short-story writer, was born in Shkodër, studied at the Serbian school in his native town and at an Orthodox seminary in Monastir. On his return to Albania, he gave up the idea of becoming a priest and became a village schoolmaster, working in

Vrakë, Shkodër and Pukë (1933–7) and began to write verse and short stories. Having contracted tuberculosis, then endemic in Albania, he went for treatment to Turin. After some time in a sanatorium there, he was transferred to the Waldensian Hospital in Torre Pelice, where he died. Migjeni was one of the first Albanian poets to break with the Romantic tradition, which had lasted exactly a century from DE RADA's publication in 1836 of the 'Songs of Milosao'. His prose and poetry manifest a strong social ethic, not pity for the poor but outrage and revolt against injustice and oppression. Powerful realism and satire on contemporary Albanian society under King Zog are evident in his work, which vividly portrays Albanian social reality. Migjeni published his first writings in 1934 in the periodicals *Illyria* and *Bota e re* (New world). His volume of poetry, *Vargjet e lira* (Free verse), went to press in 1936, but was immediately confiscated by the authorities; a second printing of it did appear in 1944. Migjeni left most of his prose writing in manuscript; it was posthumously published in the collection *Tregime nga qyteti i Veriut* (Stories from the town of the North, 1954).

● *Selected Albanian Songs and Sketches* (Tirana, 1962).

A. Pipa, *Albanian Literature. Social Perspectives* (Munich, 1978), pp. 126–63.   ShM

MIHAILOVSKI, Stoyan (1856–1927), Bulgarian writer, the son of the scholar, translator and writer Nikola Mihailovski (1816–92), spent a year at the Constantinople Imperial College (1872), read law in France (1875–83), simultaneously spending some time in Bulgaria working in a law firm and as a journalist. 1883–92

he was a civil servant and then took a post teaching French at the Sofia High School. He was three times elected MP (1886–7, 1894–6, 1903–8), but always resigned from his positions after scandals concerning his anti-establishment attitudes. His public behaviour and literary works gained him the reputation of an explosive, whimsical, but uncompromising character. He lost his teaching post 1905, after attacks on the monarchy, and became a journalist writing for the Church press. His collection of verse, *Dnes chuk, utre nakovalnya* (A hammer today, an anvil tomorrow, 1905), constituted his rejection of accusations levelled against him for having betrayed himself in asking for a state pension on losing his teaching post; it expresses his sense of himself as a prophet not without honour, save in his own country. After 1910 his name began to fade and critics barely ever mentioned him. He was completely forgotten by the time he died but his obituaries renewed critical interest. Mihailovski was strongly influenced by the French *poètes maudits*, but he was no mere imitator. Although he wrote semi-Decadent contemplative, almost philosophical verse, apophthegms, 'metapolitical contemplations' and religious meditations, he is remembered most for his satirical verse (e.g. on the political and social order, on Bulgarian 'Asiaticness' or uneducatedness). He was the founder of satire in Bulgarian literature and became known as the Bulgarian Juvenal. Nevertheless, his greatest contribution was his pessimistic verse of ideas, *Poema na zloto* (The epic of evil, 1889), which uses the myth of the Fall as its basis and speaks out against moral relativism, which he sees as originating in Eden. The heterogeneous *Filosoficheski i satiricheski soneti* (Philosophical and satirical sonnets, 1895) consist mainly of allegorical poems; e.g. we have a picture of Gutenberg in hell for having invented a method for the faster propagation of evil, or of an eagle feeding its young with the particularly scrumptious meat of a rationalist scientist. The themes of Mihailovski's verse were new to Bulgarian literature as was his use of colloquial to vulgar language to express philosophical ideas. His *Kniga za balgarskiya narod* (A book for the Bulgarian people, 1897), which shows the influence of Hugo, uses word-play and aphoristic irony to satirise life and society under Ferdinand I (reigned 1887–1918).

●G. Stadtmüller, 'Stojan Michajlovski, Kämpfer, Dichter, Grubler' in *Stimmen aus dem Südosten* (1942), pp. 111–16.

SIK

MIHALIĆ, Slavko (b. 1928), Croatian poet, born in Karlovac, worked as a technical draughtsman and journalist before studying at Zagreb. From his youth, Mihalić has maintained an active interest in painting and music. 1954 he published his first slim volume of poems, *Komorna muzika* (Chamber music), introducing a voice of rare authority into Croatian verse. In every one of his carefully worked poems Mihalić is concerned with fundamental questions of existence in the modern world – a world of fear, isolation and vain longing for communication.

●V. D. Mihailovich (Ed.), *Contemporary Yugoslav Poetry* (Iowa City, 1977), pp. 98–107; *Atlantis* (New York, 1983); *Black Apples* (Toronto, 1989).   ECH

MIHÁLIK, Vojtech (b. 1926), Slovak poet, born the son of a bricklayer greatly glorified in his works, read Slovak and philosophy at Bratislava (1945–9); as a student he published his disciplined intimate verse with strong R. Catholic elements, *Anjeli* (Angels, 1947), but he soon became a Communist and his wrestle with his religious past is evident throughout his works. By 1954 he had joined the cultural *apparat*, which he did not leave until 1989. The technical skill and the imagery of *Spievajúce srdce* (Singing heart, 1952) redeems the agitprop nature of this passionate cycle in praise of heroic work and Soviet science, which will make pineapples and oranges grow in Slovakia. *Vzbúrený Jób* (Rebellious Job, 1960) argues the case for atheism and satirises intellectuals; the sensitive *Trpky* (Pains, 1963) marks a turn away from political verse, here to consideration of the suffering of woman, in *Appassionata* (1964) to lost or spurned love, in *Útek za Orfeom* (Running after Orpheus, 1965) to the art of writing verse and to modern culture's tendency to vulgarisation. *Rekviem* (Requiem, 1968), in which Dubček becomes Christ, expresses despair at the Warsaw Pact intervention (1968). In the 1970s and 1980s Mihálik was a leading 'normaliser' and scourge of young writers.

RBP

MIKES,   Kelemen   (1690–1761), Transylvanian (Hungarian) writer and translator, left the Jesuit college at Kolozsvár (Cluj) at the age of 17 to become page to Prince Ferenc RÁKÓCZI II. He accompanied his master into exile in France and Turkey, steadily rising to the position of majordomo. He witnessed the prince's death in 1735, still hoping to return home, but he never did; after 1758 he was the sole survivor of RÁKÓCZI's large entourage. Mikes's reputation depends solely on *Törökországi levelek* (Letters from Turkey, written 1718–58, first publ. 1794). The volume contains 207 letters to a fictitious aunt in the style of Mme de Sévigné; some are personal, others anecdotal or culled from news-items that reached the exiles in Rodostó (Tekirdağ). Writing occupied much of Mikes's tedious years of exile. He translated several devotional works from French; these all remained in manuscript until the late 20th century. He also compiled and translated a selection of Mme de Gomez's popular tales, *Les Journées amusantes* (1722–31), transferring the scene of action to Transylvania and modifying the text accordingly. This volume, *Mulatságos napok* (Days of pleasure), was written in 1745 and eventually published in Budapest (1879). Mikes, whose education was broken off before he could acquire the stylistic niceties of Hungarian Baroque, wrote simply and concisely in elegant prose which is still eminently readable. All his writing reveals him as a sensitive and intelligent soul with a vein of gentle humour and mild sarcasm; he lays bare his joys and, more frequent, sorrows, his interests and his hopes and fears. His prose stands comparison with that of his contemporary FALUDI; both represent the best of post-Baroque prose-writing in 18th-century Hungarian.

•Extracts in T. Klaniczay (Ed.), *Old Hungarian Literary Reader* (Budapest, 1985); L. Hopp (Ed.), *Mikes Kelemen összes művei* (Budapest, 1966–74). D. Mervyn Jones, *Five Hungarian Writers* (Oxford, 1966) (also includes translations). GFC

MIKSZÁTH, Kálmán (1847–1910), Hungarian short-story writer, novelist and publicist, was born to parents from the lesser nobility. Mikszáth attended grammar school in Rimaszombat in 1857–62 and the similar Lutheran institution in Selmecbánya 1863–6. Although he studied law at Pest 1866–9, he never took his examinations. 1870 he became a counsellor to the magistrate of his native Nógrád County. Soon after his marriage in 1873 he resigned from his post and decided to earn his living by writing. Because of his financial difficulties, he had to divorce his wife in 1876, but remarried her in 1882, when his career as a journalist and novelist was established. He was an MP 1887–9 and again from 1892 to the end of his life. He died of pneumonia within two weeks of the national celebration of the 40th anniversary of his literary career. His art is rooted in the oral culture of the peasantry and the landed gentry. Most of his novels are episodic, but his best stories have great atmospheric beauty. He had a fine ear for stylistic nuances and a well-developed sense of humour. His best works concern Upper Hungary populated by Hungarians speaking the *palóc* dialect and by Slovaks. The tone of his works is often elegiac, and the characters portrayed live in harmony with Nature. The interrelating of scenery and consciousness is the most important characteristic of the long stories of *Tót atyafiak* (Slovak yokels, 1881), whereas the much shorter pieces of *A jó palócok* (The good *palóc* people, 1882) evince ballad-like fragmentation. He created successful works when his text consisted essentially of an anecdote, as in the short novel *A gavallérok* (The cavaliers, 1897), but he was unable to construct works based on larger conceptions. *A Noszty fiú esete Tóth Marival* (The case of Feri N. and Mari T., 1908), originally published in weekly instalments, consists of a series of anecdotes. He was often tempted to follow the example of

JÓKAI in relying on Romantic clichés, but had a greater sense of ambiguity and more psychological depth than his predecessor. Count Pongrácz, in *Beszterce ostroma* (The siege of Bystrica, 1895), represents the anachronistic, feudal illusions of the Hungarian aristocracy, and yet he is above the petty utilitarianism of the more advanced world that surrounds him. In a similar way, Pál Görgey, in *A fekete város* (The black city, 1910), is despotism incarnate, but his violent emotions and tormented soul make him a fascinating personality, in contrast to the impersonal Puritanism and lack of imagination characteristic of the bourgeoisie of Lőcse, the city which opposes his despotism.

●*A Strange Marriage* [*Különös házasság*] (Budapest, 1966); *St Peter's Umbrella* [*Szent Péter esernyője*] (London, 1966); *The Siege of Besztcrce* (Budapest, 1982). S. C. Scheer, *Kálmán Mikszáth* (Boston, 1977).   MSz-M

MILČINSKI, Fran (1867–1932), Slovene humorous writer of novels and short stories and sketches, son of a Czech tax collector, entered the legal service after studies in Vienna. He spent many years as a judge concerned with juvenile offenders. Under the pseudonym of Fridolin Zolna he published more than 200 humorous sketches on cultural, social and political themes. His best work is the novel *Ptički brez gnezda* (Birds without a nest, 1917) which describes the life of neglected suburban youths who run away from home. His novel *Gospodična Mici* (Miss M., 1916) is a satire on the selfishness of those who see fostering as an easy way of making money.   HL

MILEV, Geo (i.e. Georgi Kasabov, 1895–1925), Bulgarian poet, critic and translator, came from a cultured family, read Romance philology, initially at Sofia, then at Leipzig (1912–14), where he wrote his dissertation on Dehmel. 1914 he was in London to study English literature, where he met Verhaeren. On his return to Germany he was arrested on suspicion of spying for the UK. 1916 he was called up and went to the Front where he lost an eye. He spent 1918–19 in Germany and became involved with the Expressionist journal *Aktion*. In Bulgaria (1919–21) he defended Symbolism and Expressionism, but the political events of 1922–3 (see FURNADZHIEV) resulted in his left-wing, anti-individualist orientation, and he proclaimed that 'literature should serve the people'. As a result of his long Expressionist poem *Septemvri* (September, 1927), he was arrested and tried, and his journal *Plamǎk* (Flame) was banned. Milev was convicted of 'anti-government activities'; the police murdered him in prison. Milev's *Septemvri* was written under the slight influence of Blok. His perception of a people's 'revolution' is focused on the rejection of everything which burdens man in the form of 'bloody coincidence' (Fate), or 'unknown dark forces' gathered in a 'black fiction called God'. The work expresses the anger and the horror of man faced with a Fate imposed on him by a myth-ruled society. The main element of Milev's ideology is mythoclasm, where 'God' is the greatest evil left over from myths. His theomachy also concerns the 'gods' of society. Milev was an incisive critic and sensitive translator.

●*Septemvri* (Sofia, 1961).   SIK

MILJKOVIĆ, Branko (1934–61), Serbian poet, was born in Niš. He studied literature at Belgrade, where he spent most of his life until his suicide in Zagreb. Because of his death and of his powerful poetic statement, he has become a legend that seems still to be growing. Miljković published several books of verse in rapid succession: *Uzalud je budim* (In vain I wake her, 1957), *Smrću protiv smrti* (Death against death, 1959), *Poreklo nade* (Origins of hope, 1960), *Vatra i ništa* (Fire and nothing, 1960) and *Krv koja svetli* (Blood that shines, 1961). Influenced by French and Russian Symbolists, as well as by the intellectual Surrealism of Bonnefoy, Miljković wrote pessimistic, rebellious poetry, preoccupied with the theme of death. VDM

MIŁOSZ, Czesław (b. 1911), Polish poet, fiction writer, essayist and translator, a towering presence in contemporary Polish literature, was born in Szetejnie in the Lithuanian provinces. 1921 he went to Vilnius (Wilno) to study first in a local grammar school and then, from 1929 on, at the King Stefan Batory University. 1930 he published his first poem in a student journal, and a year later cofounded a group of poets called Zagary (Charred wood). 1931 he made his first trip to Paris, where he met his distant relation, the French Symbolist poet of Lithuanian descent, Oscar V. de la Milosz. Poetry of social protest, with catastrophist undertones, resounded in Miłosz's first book, a long poem published in 1933. 1934 he graduated and spent the next year on a grant in Paris. Back in Poland, he found a job as an editor in the Vilnius office of Polish Radio. 1936 his second, mature, book of verse *Trzy zimy* (Three winters) appeared to critical acclaim. At the same time, his allegedly leftist sympathies cost him his job. He moved to Warsaw, where he found shelter in the more liberal central office of Polish Radio. With the outbreak of war, he escaped from Warsaw to Vilnius, and was soon afterwards captured by the Soviets. A few months later he returned clandestinely to Warsaw, where he stayed until 1944, earning his living with odd jobs while also contributing to underground publications. Under Communist rule, he worked for a while as an editor, then joined the diplomatic service. As cultural attaché, he spent the next five years in the USA and France. Meanwhile, in 1945, his extensive collection of mostly wartime poems, *Ocalenie* (Rescue), appeared; it was to be his only book published officially in People's Poland until 1980. At the end of 1950 Miłosz was summoned to Warsaw and on his arrival his passport was withdrawn. He finally obtained another exit visa and, while in Paris in the beginning of 1951, decided to seek political asylum. The next decade, which he spent in France, was difficult. His only literary successes in those years were his politically charged prose, such as his widely discussed essay *Zniewolony umysł* (The captive mind, 1953) or his novel *Zdobycie władzy* (The seizure of power, 1953). Yet his French decade was not an idle period for his poetry. It was then that he wrote his long poem *Traktat poetycki* (Treatise on poetry, 1957) as well as a number of short lyrics. However, his poetic achievements began to multiply with his 1961 move to California, where he became Professor of Slavic Literatures at Berkeley. He won the Nobel Prize for Literature in 1980. Apart from being an active witness to modern history, a moralist and a visionary, Miłosz is first and foremost a magnificent artist of language, one of those poets whose verbal art is bold, perspicacious and versatile

enough to address all human experience.

●*Collected Poems, 1931–1987* (New
York, 1988); *The Captive Mind* (New
York, 1953); *Native Realm: A Search
for Self-Definition* (Garden City, NY,
1968); *The Land of Ulro* (New York,
1984).

A. Fiut, *The Eternal Moment*
(Berkeley, 1989); D. Davie, *Czesław
Miłosz and the Insufficiency of Lyric*
(Knoxville, Tenn., 1986); E.
Czarnecka and A. Fiut,
Conversations with Czesław Miłosz
(San Diego, 1987); L. Nathan and
A. Quinn, *The Poet's Work. An
Introduction to Czesław Miłosz*
(Cambridge, Mass., 1991).   StB

MINÁČ, Vladimír (b. 1922), Slovak
novelist and essayist, read Slovak and
German at Bratislava (1940–4), took
part in the Slovak National Uprising,
was captured and, December 1944,
sent to Mauthausen, and then to
Dachau. Since the end of WWII he
has had various posts in Communist
cultural and political institutions. He
retained his Communist views after
November 1989. His conception of
the Slovaks as a nation of builders
expressed in the essays *Dúchanie do
pahrieb* (Blowing into the embers,
1970) had a profound impact on
writers of the 1970s and 1980s. His
mythopoeic trilogy on the Uprising
and the arrival of socialism in Slovakia, *Dlhý čas čakania* (The long time
of waiting, 1958), *Živí a mŕtvi* (The
quick and the dead, 1959) and *Zvony
zvonia na deň* (The bells ring out for
day, 1961), is schematic and moralising, though, in the first two parts,
characters are carefully differentiated; the grossness of the distortion
of political reality in the third part
vitiates style and characterisation.

●L. Richter, 'Zur Rezeption von
Vladimír Mináč' Prosa in der DDR',
Zeitschrift für Slawistik, 26 (1981), pp.
834–43; R. B. Pynsent (Ed.), *Modern
Slovak Prose: Fiction Since 1954*
(London, 1990).   RBP

MINATTI, Ivan (b. 1924), Slovene
poet, broke off his medical studies in
Ljubljana, 1944, to join the partisans.
After the war he graduated in Slavonic studies and started to work as
editor in a publishing house. Melancholy and an elegiac mood are the
hallmarks of his verse as the poet
meditates on Time and the world in *S
poti* (From the road, 1947), *Pa bo
pomlad prišla* (The spring will come,
1955) and *Nekoga moraš imeti rad*
(You must love somebody, 1963).

●*AMYP; SPT*.   HL

MINKOV, Svetoslav (1902–66),
Bulgarian prose writer, came from an
officer's family and was sent to an
Austrian military academy (1917–
18); then he read philosophy at Sofia
and economics at Munich. He did not
complete his studies because of his
preoccupation with literature. He
worked as a bank clerk, as a diplomat
in Tokyo, and later earned his living
as journalist and editor. He was a
great admirer and translator of
writers like Hoffmann, Meyrink and
Poe, and began with three collections
of 'Diabolist' short stories (1922–7),
where hostile supernatural forces rule
man's life. In *Igra na senkite* (The
shadows' game, 1928) and *Kăshtata
pri posledniya fener* (The house by
the last street-light, 1930), the supernatural is employed for comic effect
and represents man's tendency to be
trapped by his own fantasies.
Minkov, who never ceased to employ
his knowledge of the 'occult' and
'mysterious', later used it to satisfy
his taste for unusual, often fantastic,
situations and to maintain his disregard for verisimilitude of plot. In his
Avtomati (Automata, 1932) and *Da*

mata s rentgenovite ochi (The lady with the X-ray eyes, 1934), the 'mysterious' is used to create grotesque images of reality; reality, on its side, is grotesque because of man's belief in 'technological progress' which now plays the role of the evil force in human life by creating disastrous illusions. For Minkov, America tends to be the symbol of the nonsensicality of technological civilisation. He employs wild 'scientific hypotheses' and 'discoveries' to parody the promised 'achievements' of the future. He remains a dystopian in his later work.

•*The Lady with the X-ray Eyes* (Sofia, 1965). SIK

MIRIVILIS, Stratis (i.e. Efstratios Stamatopoulos, 1890–1969), Greek novelist, was educated on his native Lesbos, and 1910 took a teaching job there. 1911 he started reading law at Athens, but volunteered for army service in the Balkan Wars and was wounded in the Battle of Kilkis (1913). 1911–22 he made regular contributions to the Lesbos press, sending accounts from the Front. At the same time he began writing fiction, publishing his first volume of stories in 1915. 1922 after the collapse of the Greek Army in the Asia Minor Disaster, he returned to Mytilene to continue his writing. His first major work, Ζωή εν Τάφω (Life in the tomb, 1924), is a war novel in the style of Barbusse and Dorgelès. Mirivilis's intention was to satirise the inadequacies of the military leadership, to reveal the horrors to which the men in the trenches were exposed, and to promote general humanitarian principles. The original edition is raw and direct, but subsequent editions were heavily revised and expanded to introduce a more reflective and philosophical tone. 1930 he moved to Athens, where he remained until his death, first as editor of various liberal newspapers, then working for Greek Radio, and eventually employed in the parliamentary library. His second major novel, Η Δασκάλα με τα χρύσα μάτια (The schoolmistress with the golden eyes, 1933), continues to reflect his war experiences but includes broader psychological and social themes. It was followed at regular intervals by collections of stories and lyrical prose pieces. His last major novel, Η Παναγιά η Γοργόνα (The mermaid madonna, 1949), still dwells on the themes of love, Nature and the details of life on Lesbos which inform his post-1930 works. In the post-WWII period he lost his radio job for political reasons but continued as librarian until 1955. He was elected to the Academy of Athens at his seventh attempt in 1958. Mirivilis is a good example of the virtues and shortcomings of the Greek novel in the 1930s and 1940s. 'Life in the tomb' is by its nature episodic. The later novels reveal how far Mirivilis's talents are really those of the short-story writer. He handles both lyrical and satirical material effectively, and continues the traditions of the ethographic novelists in presenting detailed pictures of the lives of ordinary people in rural communities. But he lacks the skill to bind the different elements of his fiction together into a coherent whole. His most effective later work is the novella Ο Βασίλης ο Αρβανίτης (Vasilis the Albanian, included in Το Γαλάζιο Βιβλίο [The blue book] in 1939 and published separately in 1944), which achieves its coherence through its fairy-tale elements.

•*Life in the Tomb* (Hanover, NH, 1977). CFR

MITKO, Thimi (1820–90), Albanian folklorist, born in Korçë of a family with patriotic traditions, left Albania in 1850, going first to Athens, then Plovdiv, and then Vienna; after 1859 he settled in Egypt where he spent the rest of his life. Mitko collected Albanian folklore material and collaborated with all the main figures of the Albanian national movement. His collection of Albanian folklore was published in Greek script under the Greek title *Alvaniki melissa* (The Albanian bee, 1878). This first collection of Albanian folklore was meant not only for the Albanian public, but also to provide Europe with information about Albanian folklore. Mitko also wrote poetry and numerous articles in European periodicals in support of the Albanian cause.   ShM

MJEDA, Ndre (1866–1937), Albanian poet and scholar of the late Revival, was born in Shkodër where he received a Jesuit education and was ordained. After studies in Spain (1879–82 at the Porta Coeli college in Valencia), Croatia (1882–7 at the Jesuit college and the Gregorian university in Kraljevica) and Poland (1891–5 at the Gregorian theological faculty in Cracow), he took a doctorate in philosophy and theology. He was appointed lecturer of philosophy and philology at the Gregorian university in Kraljevica where he worked until 1898 when, for reasons still unclear, he was expelled from the Jesuit order after a political conflict. While abroad he began writing Albanian verse, among which *Vaji i Bylbilit* (The nightingale morn, 1887) expresses nostalgia for the homeland. 1901 he founded the Agimi (Dawn) cultural society, which encouraged the use of Albanian for literature. 1902 he participated in the Congress of Orientalists in Hamburg. He also participated in the 1908 Monastir Congress, known as the Congress of the Albanian Alphabet, at which his Agimi alphabet lost to FISHTA's Bashkimi alphabet. 1920–4 he was an MP but withdrew from politics after the defeat of the June Revolution and the rise of King Zog's dictatorship. From 1930 onwards he taught Albanian language and literature at the Jesuit college in Shkodër. Mjeda's poetry, in particular the collection *Juvenalia* (1917), shows the influence of the oral tradition, nationalist ideology and late 19th-century Italian poets. *Lissus* (1921) and *Shkodra* (1940) deal with the past of these two Albanian cities.   ShM

MŇAČKO, Ladislav (b. 1915), Slovak novelist, trained as a pharmacist, was imprisoned in a concentration camp in WWII, and then worked as a reporter. His main work is the novel *Smrt' sa volá Engelchen* (Death is called E., 1959), which constituted an attempt to demythologise the battles between the Slovak partisans and SS units, but also dealt for the first time with the social, moral and existential questions arising from the 1944 Slovak National Uprising. After publishing his *Oneskorené reportáže* (Belated reportage, 1963) in order to reveal the truth about the persecution in the 1950s and 'to document my own guilt in these events', he depicted the Stalinist era in the novel *Ako chutí moc* (The taste of power, 1967), the life story of a high-ranking Communist official. Mňačko then defected to Israel, returning briefly in 1968 but emigrating once more in the same year.

●*Death is Called Engelchen* (Prague, 1961); *The Seventh Night* (New York, 1969); *The Taste of Power* (New York, 1967).

S. L. Auer, *Ladislav Mňačko. Eine Bibliographie* (Munich, 1989).   KB

MOCHNACKI, Maurycy (c. 1803–34), Polish literary critic and historian, as a radical politician, played an active role in the November Uprising, also distinguishing himself in battle. After the Uprising he settled and eventually died in France. Mochnacki's major critical work, *O literaturze polskiej w wieku dziewiętnastym* (Polish literature in the nineteenth century, 1839), is based on F. W. Schelling's philosophy of Nature, which he elaborates into his own views on the role of literature in shaping national consciousness. *Powstanie narodu polskiego w r. 1830 i 1831* (The Uprising of the Polish nation in 1830 and 1831, 1834) provides a factual and well-narrated account of events together with a defence of military dictatorship and informative remarks on the roles of Russia and Poland in E Europe.   SE

MÓRICZ, Zsigmond (1879–1942), Hungarian novelist, short-story writer, essayist, playwright and poet, was born into a peasant family. He went to school in Debrecen 1891–3, in Sárospatak 1894–6, and in Kisujszállás 1896–8. 1899 he entered the College of the Reformed Church in Debrecen to study theology but transferred to law after six months. At the same time he started working as a journalist. The following year he moved to Budapest, where he studied law for some time, and then pursued philosophy, theology, linguistics and literary history at the university. Having given up his plan to become a teacher, he worked in the Ministry of Culture and later in the Office of Statistics. 1902 he became a member of the editorial staff of *Az Ujság*, a liberal daily. 1903–8 he toured villages to collect folk-songs and tales. Recognition came to him in 1908 on the publication of the short story 'Hét krajcár' (Seven kreutzer) in *Nyugat* (West), the journal of the new generation. 1909 he became a close friend of ADY. During WWI he was sent to the Front as a correspondent. *Szegény emberek* (Poor folk, 1916) is a short novel about the destructive influence of the war on the human psyche. 1918 he firmly supported the land-reform introduced by the revolution. 1929 he became one of the editors of *Nyugat* but in 1933 he resigned and 1939 assumed the editorship of *Kelet népe* (The people of the East), one of the journals of the Populists. His early short stories and novels are Naturalist; the characters are determined by their environment and their biological features. After WWI and the fall of the Commune, he returned to the tradition of 19th-century Realism. In his later years his portrayal of peasant life exerted a profound influence on the Populist movement. Among his Naturalist works the best is *Az Isten háta mögött* (Behind God's back, 1911). Its heroine is the young wife of a teacher. Intellectually and emotionally she is above the provincialism of the town she lives in, but she cannot escape its suffocating atmosphere. Her attempted suicide is in harmony with the irony of the novel. *Légy jó mindhalálig* (Be faithful unto death, 1921) is autobiographical. On the surface, it concerns the sufferings of a small boy; on a deeper level, it indirectly expresses the bitterness caused by the attacks levelled at Móricz for his involvement in the revolutions of 1918–19. His best novel, *Tündérkert* (A garden of fairies, 1922), inspired by the Realist novels of KEMÉNY and written in the spirit of post-revolutionary conservatism, concerns Transylvania in the 17th century. The visionary Gábor Báthory is replaced by the pragmatic Gábor Bethlen as leader of Transylvania, and this change is portrayed as inevitable. The dramatic structure of his best short story, *Barbárok* (Barbarians, 1931), owes much to folk ballads, and his full-length *A boldog ember* (A happy man, 1935), the life-story of a peasant, based on interviews, has similarities with the sociographical non-fiction of ILLYÉS and other Populists.

● *The Torch* (New York, 1931); *Be Faithful unto Death* (Budapest, 1962).

MSz-M

MORSZTYN, Jan Andrzej (1621–93), Polish poet, son of a rich landowner, was educated in W Europe and 1648 started his long and colourful career as a courtier, diplomat and politician. A consistent supporter of the pro-French political orientation, 1683 he fell out of favour with the Austrian-inclined King Jan III Sobieski and, accused of high treason, had to escape to France where he spent the last decade of his life. Within Polish poetry of the 17th century, the 'Western European', more polished and cosmopolitan variety of the Baroque coexisted with the more common native variety known as the 'Sarmatian Baroque'. Sociologically, the 'Western' manner was demarcated by the cultural horizons of a royal or aristocratic court, and the 'Sarmatian' by those of the gentry's manors. Generically, the court poets preferred brief lyric or epigrammatic forms, whereas the 'Sarmatian' authors cultivated, beside those, the more extensive genres, ranging from the lengthy satire to the long historical epic. In all these respects, Morsztyn, who can be compared to the English Cavalier Poets, appears a characteristic, and brilliant, exponent of the 'Western' brand of the Polish Baroque. His poems, clearly modelled on Marino and Góngora, are dominated by wit and, as a rule, based on the conceit. Written mostly to entertain the author's friends (significantly, Morsztyn's two collections were published only posthumously), they express uninhibitedly his libertine outlook. Despite their being essentially light verse, Morsztyn's poems are not devoid of metaphysical depth. While mostly devoted to exploring 'worldly happiness', they focus on its inherent paradoxes. In particular, the paradoxes of love are illuminated here with a wide range of striking conceits, in which frivolity quite often yields to existential anxiety. At the same time, the complex interplay of symmetries and contrasts makes many of Morsztyn's brief poems masterpieces of construction. Besides writing original poetry, he also excelled as a translator, particularly in his Polish version of Corneille's *Le Cid*.

● Selected poems in B. Carpenter (Ed.), *Monumenta Polonica* (Ann Arbor, 1989).

StB

MORSZTYN, Zbigniew (1627?–89), one of the several Polish poets of the 17th century with the same surname, was a distant relation of J. A. MORSZTYN, but the outlooks and poetics of these two differed significantly. Z. Morsztyn was born into a family whose members traditionally belonged to the radical Protestant sect of the Arians; he was educated in Arian schools and remained a faithful believer even after 1660 when Arianism was banned in Poland. Throughout his life, he maintained strong ties with the Radziwiłł family, fighting under Prince Janusz Radziwiłł's command in a few wars and serving later as one of Prince Bogusław Radziwiłł's trusted courtiers. As a poet, his main achievement is a series of emblems and other poems of a devotional or metaphysical nature, included in his extensive collection *Muza domowa* (The domestic muse, publ. only 1954).

●Selected poems in B. Carpenter (Ed.), *Monumenta Polonica* (Ann Arbor, 1989).   StB

MOVSES KHORENATSI

(390–450) has become one of the most controversial figures of Armenian literature. Treated with reverence as *patmahayr* (Father of history) or *k'ert'oghahayr* (Father of poetry), in modern times many scholars have questioned his authenticity. The sometimes not very profitable criticism of Movses Khorenatsi has revolved around three questions: (i) what is the date of his History? (ii) what were his sources? (iii) is he honest and reliable? Critics have challenged the notion that he was a 5th-century author and have moved him into the 6th, 7th, 8th and even 9th centuries. All the biographical information we possess about Movses comes from his *Patmut'iwn Hayots* (History of the Armenians) and some brief references in contemporary or later writers. He states that he was a pupil of St Sahak the Patriarch (348–438) and St Mesrop Mashtots (355–439), who sent him to study abroad after the Council of Ephesus (431). He did a grand tour of Rome, Athens, Edessa, Alexandria and the Holy Land. The deaths of SS Sahak and Mashtots brought him back to Armenia. He wrote his History at the request of Sahak Bagratuni in 482. It comprises three books, and attempts to trace Armenian history from its origins to shortly after the death of Mesrop

Mashtots (439): I.K 'Genealogy of Greater Armenia', II. 'The Intermediate Period in the History of Our Ancestors', and III. 'The Conclusion [of the History] of Our Fatherland'. Movses has used literary sources and material collected orally. He describes these ancient stories and legends as 'song', 'tale' or 'fable'. From among other sources he used Eusebius, Pseudo-Callisthenes, Josephus and Socrates' (d. after 439) *Ecclesiastical History* and *Teaching of the Apostle Addai*. He was widely read in history, theology, philosophy and rhetoric. Movses's understanding of historiography is expressed in his dictum 'there is no true history without chronology'. To achieve this he integrates the information he gathers from other sources into his own framework. Movses Khorenatsi made the first attempt at bridging the gap between the oral and written tradition concerning the birth of the Armenian people.

●*Movsisi Khorenatswoy Patmut'iwn Hayots* (History of the Armenians), ed. M. Abeghyan and S. Yarut'iwnean (Tiflis, 1913, reprinted 1990 with the inclusion of variant readings of manuscripts found since 1913); *History of the Armenians*, translation and commentary on the literary sources by R. W. Thomson (Cambridge, Mass., 1978); see review, V. Nersessian, *The Journal of Ecclesiastical History*, vol. 30, no. 4 (October 1979), pp. 479–80.   VN

MROŻEK, Sławomir (b. 1930),

Polish dramatist and short-story writer, educated in Cracow, worked there as a cartoonist and journalist. He left Poland for Italy in 1963, lived in France 1968–89, and currently lives in Mexico. Mrożek's popularity derives mainly from his plays, although the short stories are equally remarkable. Witty and entertaining, particularly in his earlier works, Mrożek demonstrates a penetrating insight into 20th-century problems. Initially concerned with totalitarian systems and Polish national stereotypes, he later embraced more universal problems, including those of the W. His grotesque brand of reality is based on startling juxtapositions of normality and abnormality, authenticity and fiction, tradition and modernity, submission and brutality. His world is ruled by violence and intimidation, where puppet human beings ignore their own lofty rhetoric and meekly surrender their dignity and freedom when threatened by primitive strongmen. Mrożek also displays sensitivity to verbal cliché and mental stereotypes, exposing the spiritual vacuum which lies behind them. His first play, *Policja* (The police, 1958), suggests the relativity of historical progress by cynically reducing it to mere role reversal. *Męczeństwo Piotra Oheya* (The martyrdom of Peter Ohey, 1959) depicts a quiet family man whose mediocre existence has been shaken up by the presence of a tiger in his bathroom. In *Striptease* (1961) two suave civil servants cravenly follow absurd orders given by a disembodied hand. *Zabawa* (The party, 1962) presents a situation where the overwhelming inclination to have one's desires fulfilled forces their imagined reification. Mrożek's best-known play, *Tango* (1964), is a drama of the educated and refined who submissively yield to the rule of a pragmatic brute. The later plays are more sombre. One of the best, *Emigranci* (Emigrés, 1974), consists solely of a dialogue between two frustrated expatriates who both hate and need each other. In his more recent plays Mrożek attempts to portray more complex characters and searches for new means of expression (*Garbus* [Hunchback, 1975]; *Alfa*, 1984; *Portret* [Portrait, 1987]). Mrożek's short stories, at first conventionally satirical, subsequently became absurd and grotesque like his plays (*Słoń* [The elephant, 1957]). In time his stories have become more complex, sometimes parabolic and poetical. The finest of these, *Moniza Clavier* (1967), shows an expatriate Pole confronted with Western society.

●*Six Plays* (New York, 1967); *Three Plays* (New York, 1972); *The Elephant* (New York, 1965).

A. Pohl, *Zurück zur Form* (Munich, 1969).   SE

MRŠTÍK, Vilém (1863–1912), Czech essayist, critic, novelist and dramatist, intended to become a painter, studied law for a year, earned a precarious living as a journalist in Prague, went to live with his brother Alois (1861–1925) in Moravia, and committed suicide. He adhered to the principles of Russian Realism both as critic and author; in his semi-autobiographical novel *Santa Lucia* (1893) a poor Moravian student, dying in a Prague hospital, relives his brief existence in Prague where he had come with great hopes only to find misery, debauchery, suffering and death. Together with his brother, Mrštík wrote the tragedy *Maryša* (1895), where a strong-minded village woman is married against her will to an elderly widower for pecuniary reasons; refusing to give up her lover, she poisons her husband. The play, following those of PREISSOVÁ and JIRÁSEK, marked the advent of Naturalism on the Czech stage. KB

MUCHA, Jiří (1915–91), Czech novelist and journalist, son of the art nouveau artist Alphonse Mucha

(1860–1939), read art history, medicine and Oriental studies at Prague. 1939 he joined the French Army, and after the fall of France, went to London where he became an RAF officer and war correspondent. Back in Prague, he was arrested 1951, sentenced to six years, but amnestied 1955. He spent the rest of his life writing, making films and travelling. He was a writer who believed in the supremacy of experience over imagination. *Spálená setba* (Scorched crop, 1948) is partly a love story about a repulsive young bourgeois and a selfless working-class girl, and partly a psychological anaysis of ex-soldiers. In the selfish narrator-hero we see the germ of the amoral hedonism which guides the main characters of Mucha's later novels. The labour-camp diary novel *Studené slunce* (Cold sun, 1968) opposes culture (memories of childhood, youth and war, in Europe, Africa and Asia) to unculture (the socialist prison system). The narrator-author's anti-spiritualism dominates: 'Everything that is good and beautiful in the world was created by man'; 'man is the meaning of all knowledge'. Such views become more radical in his callous cosmopolitan paean to the female crotch, *Lloydova hlava* (Lloyd's head, 1987).

●*Scorched Crop* (London, 1949); *Living and Partly Living* [*Studené slunce*] (London, 1967). RBP

MURN, Josip (pseud. Aleksandrov, 1879–1901), Slovene poet, a virtual orphan, spent his childhood in the care of strangers. After the Ljubljana earthquake of 1895 he moved with his landlady into an erstwhile sugar factory, where he died of consumption, contracted 1898 during his stay in Vienna as a student of law. The main themes of his poetry are a yearning for happiness, resignation, melancholy, foreboding. Unlike his friend KETTE, he wrote little love poetry. Much of his verse takes the form of reflective impressions of Nature or country life. His so-called 'rustic' poems present an estranged and lonely townsman's view of peasant life; influences seen here are Slovene folk poetry, Burns, Kol´tsov and elements of contemporary Decadence and Symbolism. Murn's poems were published posthumously with an introduction by Ivan Prijatelj: *Pesmi in romance* (Poems and romances, 1903).

●Translations in: *AMYP*; *Parnassus*. HL

MUSARAJ, Shefqet (1914–86), Albanian prose writer, poet and journalist, was born into a peasant family in the village of Matogjin, near Vlorë. During WWII he took part in the resistance movement, writing articles, poetry and satire for the clandestine Communist press under the pseudonym Buburicka and after the war worked as a journalist. Musaraj's best-known work is the satirical poem *Epopeja e Ballit Kombëtar* (The epic of the National Front, 1944) about the conservative nationalists who were seeking power during the war. His most important works in prose are *Isha unë Çobo Rapushi* (It was me, Ç.R., 1960) and the novels *Para agimit* (Before the dawn, 1965–6) and *Belxhiku që këndon vënçe* (The Belgian rifle singing at its leisure, 1979), which mostly deal with the war. ShM

MUTAFCHIEVA, Vera (b. 1919), Bulgarian prose writer, began as an academic historian of the Balkans. She is best known for her historical fiction which takes its themes from Bulgarian medieval history and the Ottoman period. She transgresses the limits of nationalistic historiography and seeks to show the political and psychological reasons underlying historical events. In her work she often uses evidence taken from little-known or deliberately ignored documents; she combines scholarship with her own interpretation of the development of civilisation and regards the rise and fall of kingdoms as dependent on the cultural and historical awareness of nations. Mutafchieva is concerned with the psychological analysis of historical characters and with the role of the individual in historical events. Her novel *Sluchayat Jem* (The case of J., 1968) explores, on the basis of the fate of Jem Sultan (1461–95), the collision of Western and Eastern culture and the impact of political interests on the individual's destiny. Her best-known novel, *Letopis na smutnoto vreme* (Chronicle of the troubled times, 1964–5), concerns developments in the Ottoman Empire of the second half of the 18th century when Bulgarian aspirations to independence came to life; Mutafchieva points out the important role of the spiritual leader and believes a true leader comes with the promise of cultural revival and represents culture, not force. Accordingly, in her depiction, violence is a manifestation of the moral and cultural decay of the Empire rather than the reason for the Bulgarian uprising. She does not diminish the horror of violence but maintains that it alone could not cause the consolidation of people. Even more terrible violence came with the Turkish invasion (*Poslednite Shishmanovtsi* [The last Shishmans, 1969]), but the Bulgarians could not consolidate to defend their kingdom because of a lack of awareness of a cultural mission.   SIK

MUTAFOV, Chavdar (1889–1954),

Bulgarian prose writer and critic, studied civil engineering (1908–14), and architecture (1922–5) at Munich; he was a leading member of Strelets (Sagittarius) literary circle (see DALCHEV) and edited the circle's two journals, *Iztok* (East) and *Strelets*; his critical articles played the role of manifestos of the 'new art'. He attacked Symbolism for its static contemplative nature and proclaimed that artistic élitism could no longer be tolerated; the technological era with its numerous means for the 'multiplication of art' (art reproductions, gramophone records, the wireless, the cinema) excluded the 'absolute' of art and the 'absolute' of the artist's personality; it was an era of mass consumption of art through the medium of technology. His 'new aesthetics' comprised an entirely urban environment depicted in a Futurist manner, rejected traditional descriptiveness and psychology, rejected 'folkloristic thinking', and reflected a cosmopolitan outlook alien to contemporary Bulgarian literature. Most of Mutafov's short stories in *Tehnicheski razkazi* (Technological stories, 1940) epitomise these views; 'Radioto' (The wireless, 1932) is a polemic with the defenders of 'pure art'; in the vast 'space' of sounds created by wireless waves, Mozart's 'multiplied' music flies over the 'vulgar chaos' produced by the 'belching of the Algerians'; Caruso's voice enchants millions by its 'non-material existence'; the vulgar nature of the 'metal box' does not prevent millions from dreaming of experiencing harmony. In 'Pianoto' (The piano, 1920) the old piano, an emblem of élitist art, 'stylises its own death'. Stories like 'Zveroukrotitelyat' (The tamer, 1921) deal with 'modern' man's intimate world; love in this story consists of a strange encounter: the Stranger tells the Woman about everything which attracts and separates them and for his argument he enlists popular literary and philosophical views about woman; he confuses these ideas with his own mental background. In *Marionetki* (Puppets, 1920), an ironic series of 'entertainments', written in a style based on Cubism and Futurism in the plastic arts, Mutafov's characters lack any individuality and personify 'types' (e.g. the Dandy, the Dilettante, the Lady, the Gentleman); they are drawn as literary clichés which parody, e.g., Romantic, Symbolist, Decadent types. The frame of the 'entertainments' is another cliché: life as a stage, as theatre, human beings as puppets. The whole environment embodies the 'modern world' where links between the psyche and reality are broken; the lack of immediate perception is derived from layers of ideas (and roles) adopted by man; the 'decorative' depiction of the urban environment merely represents a deformed vision. Nature and her attributes are presented in a mock-Decadent manner, always artificial but derived from man's prevailing inability to perceive immediately. Love and beauty are experiences more as the internal aesthetic contemplation of archetypes than as individual emotion; the sex drive is also a biological archetype and that archetypal nature conflicts with assumed 'individualist' roles and produces more individual feelings than the 'roles'. Mutafov is, however, profoundly sceptical about the individual, regards him merely as a representative of collective experience.

SIK

MYKOLAITIS-PUTINAS, Vincas (1893–1967), Lithuanian poet, playwright and novelist, literary historian and critic, was attracted to R. Catholicism and nationalism, the two closely connected forces that shaped the minds of Lithuanian intelligentsia of his time, and entered the priesthood in 1915. Later in life, however, he found that the spiritual strictures of religious life were incompatible with the restless strivings of his own turbulent soul and he abandoned the priesthood in 1935, perceiving his decision as a choice made between the calling of a priest and that of a poet. Putinas's experiences of this difficult process are transmitted in his novel *Altorių šešėly* (In the shadow of the altars, 1933) to the main character, Liudas Vasaris, whose constant self-analysis gives psychological issues the dominant role in the text. In his early verse, Putinas manifests the influence of the 19th-century Russian contemplative poets Afanasii Fet and Fyodor Tyutchev; later he adopts something of the world-view of the Russian Symbolists, particularly their vague existential longings as embodied in abstractly conceived symbolic entities, such as the 'Stella Maris' in one of Putinas's poems. In his later poetry, the dominant theme is a constant dichotomy between grand gestures of revolt against an abstract, distant idea of God and tender allegiance to the Christ of Lithuanian wayside crosses whose divinity encompasses the humble soul of the peasant. This conflict is also transmitted as a struggle between idealistic visions and loyalty to the 'beautiful, sinful earth'. Putinas's plays are cast in a similar thematic mould. The Soviet system, firmly established in Lithuania after 1944, demanded works of Socialist Realism from Putinas as from the rest. In response Putinas wrote a novel called

Sukilėliai (The insurgents), about the 1863 Polish-Lithuanian revolt against Russia, from a pro-Russian perspective; however, he never finished it. Putinas's activity as a literary scholar resulted in two books, *Naujoji*

lietuvių literatūra (The new Lithuanian literature, 1936) and *Literatūros etiudai* (Literary sketches, 1937). In both, historical criticism blends with efforts towards more formal, technical analysis. RŠ

N

NADIRADZE, K'olau (1895–1991), Georgian Symbolist poet, was the last surviving member of the *tsisper-q'ants'lebi* (Blue horns). 1916 he was known as 'the troublemaker': his early Kutaisi poetry (*Baldakhini*, [The baldaquin, 1920]) was indebted to Emile Verhaeren (then well known in the Russian Empire) for its horrific cityscapes, despite the discrepancy between London's slums and Kutaisi's sleepy boulevards: it had social as well as aesthetic import. The same hopeless horror imbues Nadiradze's Golgothan visions of Georgia: just before independence he called it 'Idiot homeland, burdened with a thankless task, Aged, oppressed and tormented'. When independent Georgia was taken over by Soviet Russia, in verses that lay unpublished until 1989 he denounced the betrayal as a calvary organised by Judas. Nevertheless, because he had a language suited to political polemic, and because he was capable of producing Verlainean landscape-and-mood poems with no obvious political defects, he adapted to Communist requirements far less traumatically than did other 'Blue horns'. He subtly dealt with the tragedy befalling poetry through the past, e.g. by lamenting the murder of I. CH'AVCH'AVADZE in 1907: *ts'it-s'amuridan saguramomde ek'liani da p'atara gzaa ... ts'its'amuridan saguramomde didi mtebi da udziro tsaa* (From Ts'its'amuri to Saguramo is a thorny little path, From Ts'its'amuri to Saguramo are big mountains and a bottomless sky', 1936; Saguramo was CH'AVCH'AVADZE's home, and Ts'its'amuri the nearby site of his assassination). Nevertheless, in the purge of 1937 Nadiradze (and S. K'LDIASHVILI) were saved only by chance: their NKVD interrogator was himself arrested and the files mislaid. In postwar years Nadiradze became a silver poet and prose writer of patriotic contemplation and mood painting. Only in his nineties did he regain the freedom of his twenties and publish what he had suppressed.   DR

NAŁKOWSKA, Zofia (1884–1954), Polish novelist, the daughter of a renowned scholar and publicist, worked in various organisations and actively supported Communist rule in postwar Poland. Her earliest, Modernistic novels reflect an anti-social individualism and focus on the singularity of women's minds. The interwar period brought about a shift towards social criteria and traditional realism (*Granica* [Boundary line, 1935]). Very different is *Niecierpliwi* (The impatient, 1939), experimental in form and concerned with universal aspects of human life. The collection of short stories *Medaliony* (Medallions, 1946) describes the German genocide, as reported by eye-witnesses interviewed by the author. She has left a fascinating diary, covering almost the whole of her life (*Dzienniki*, 1975-). SE

NARUSZEWICZ, Adam (1733–96), Polish poet, historian and translator, scion of an impoverished magnate family, 1748 entered the Jesuit Order and after its dissolution in 1773 pursued a career as a lay priest to become a bishop in 1788. He was one of the closest collaborators of the last King of Poland, Stanisław II August, in his attempts at political reform and at remodelling Polish culture in the spirit of the Age of Enlightenment. 1771–7 Naruszewicz served as editor of *Zabawy Przyjemne i Pożyteczne* (Pleasant and useful pastimes), the organ of reform-minded writers. As a poet, he contributed to the renewal of interest in Classical genres such as the ode, the satire or the pastoral, although his style remains under the influence of the Baroque.

•Selected poems in B. Carpenter (Ed.), *Monumenta Polonica* (Ann Arbor, 1989). StB

NASTASIJEVIĆ, Momčilo (1894–1938), Serbian playwright, prose writer and poet, was a native of Gornji Milanovac. He attended the University of Belgrade, became a secondary-school master and spent his entire life teaching in Belgrade. Nastasijević's opus is not large: a play, *Medjuluško blago* (Treasure of Medjulug, 1927); a book of short stories, *Iz tamnog vilajeta* (From a dark province, 1927); and three collections of verse, *Pet lirskih krugova* (Five lyric cycles, 1932), *Pesme* (Poems, 1938) and *Sedam lirskih krugova* (Seven lyric cycles, 1962). He developed his own idiom, using laconic, precise, sometimes cryptic turns of phrase, which are difficult to penetrate, and yet aptly express his peculiar, almost mystical, outlook. He has become an influential force among present-day Serbian poets. VDM

NAZOR, Vladimir (1876–1949), Croatian poet and prose writer, born on the island of Brač, studied natural sciences and worked as a schoolmaster. He spent most of WWII with the partisans, publishing his experiences in his journal, *S partizanima* (With the partisans, 1945), which has distinct literary qualities in addition to its value as documentary prose. Nazor's work is rooted in his native soil, finding its inspiration as much in past as in contemporary experience, as is suggested by the title of his first published volume, *Slavenske legende* (Slav legends, 1900). This broad inspiration makes for a rich thematic range in Nazor's poetry, which includes anything from intimate verse to descriptions of the Croatian kings to the disillusion following WWI. Nazor was also drawn to narrative forms, expressing this tendency in a series of prose works of uneven quality. The best of these is his collection of stories, *Istarske priče* (Istrian tales, 1913), dominated by the figure of the legendary benevolent giant, Veli Jože, the personification of national resistance to foreign domination.

•Translations of selected stories in *SEER*, 25 (1946), pp. 191–2; 26 (1946), pp. 526–33; *The Bridge*, 50 (1976), pp. 47–9.

A. Kadić, 'Vladimir Nazor', *Journal of Croatian Studies*, 17 (1976), pp. 64–72. ECH

NECHUI-LEVYTS´KYI, Ivan (1838–1918), Ukrainian novelist of the Realist school, son of a priest and educated at a seminary, became a schoolteacher. His novels deal with problems in the lives of both the peasantry and the intelligentsia. The peasant world is depicted in *Mykola Dzheria* (1878) and *Kaidasheva simia* (Kaidash's family, 1879) and that of a peasant girl working in a factory in *Burlachka* (Vagabond woman, 1880). The efforts of the young Ukrainian intelligentsia are the subject of *Khmary* (Clouds, 1874) and *Nad Chornym morem* (On the Black Sea, 1890). He also wrote fictional and scholarly historical works. In *Ukrainstvo na literaturnykh pozvakh z Moskovshchnoiu* (Ukrainians in a literary dispute with Moscow, 1891) he pleaded for the divergence of Ukrainian from Russian literature. Concerning the Ukrainian literary language he was a conservative, romantic purist.

•*Mikola Dzherya: A Long Story* (Kiev, 1985).   GSNL

NĚMCOVÁ, Božena (1820–62), Czech writer, born in the German environment of Vienna, was brought up by her grandmother in Bohemia. She received only elementary education and, at 17, married a minor civil servant 15 years her senior. When he was moved to Prague (1842), she came into contact with the leading Czech literary figures. She soon moved again, to W Bohemia, but now both her and her husband's political views held him back in his career and he asked to be posted to Hungary, hoping for promotion there. However interested she was in things Slovak, she decided not to go there with him, and lived in Prague with her children. She supported herself and her children almost entirely with her literary work. She published some verse, a large number of adaptations of folk-tales, and lively short stories, mainly concerned with the lot of country women. The novel *Pohorská vesnice* (Mountain village, 1856) describes an ideal noble landlord who introduces new farming methods to the peasants; she manifests her old interest in the place of religious and folk festivals in village life. What is new for her here is the large number of carefully delineated male characters. Němcová's chief work is *Babička* (The grandmother, 1855), the framework narration of which is a year of rural life, where the author gives detailed accounts of folk customs, and where an ideal orderly world is represented by the cycle of festivals and seasons. The eponymous heroine is the mother of a manorial official's germanised wife and she brings up her grandchildren as good, devout Czechs. She is wisdom incarnate, advises the local duchess and wan young countess as well as villagers. The real action of the novel is restricted to interpolated tales, where foreigners disrupt natural, orderly Czech life. One of these tales, of a girl raped or seduced by a Hungarian soldier, becoming pregnant and going mad, is told with such grace and compassion that it has continued to inspire Czech writers.

•*Granny. Scenes from Country Life* (Prague, 1962); *The Shepherd and the Dragon. Fairy Tales* (New York, 1930). M. Součková, *The Czech Romantics* (The Hague, 1958); C. Bryner, 'Božena Němcová and Jane Austen' in *International Congress of Slavists. Canadian Papers* (Vancouver, 1968); A. R. Durkin, 'Two Instances of Prose Pastoral. Němcová and Aksakov' in *International Congress of Slavists. American Contributions* (Columbus, Ohio, 1983).   RBP

NĚMEC, Ludvík (b. 1957), Czech novelist, worked as a newspaper journalist, then as a tourist guide, then in Czechoslovak Radio, where he remained into the 1990s. After the superficial, somewhat melodramatic and slightly satirical *Nejhlasitější srdce ve městě* (The loudest heart in town, 1978), he published the mature study of socialist youth, *Hra na slepo* (Playing blind, 1982). The novel's disintegrated form represents the mental and moral disintegration of the main character, the chess-playing Oto Repus (i.e. Super Oto, but also Orpheus). This alienated young man only rarely sees his fellows as anything but something to manipulate like chess-men, and chess itself becomes a self-contained system of communication. *Hra na slepo* is also a study in obsession. *Průvodce povětřím a tmou* (Guide through air and darkness, 1988) is little more than jolly social and political satire, and the socially and politically critical *Negativ* (The negative, 1989) has an optimistic ending which suggests establishment schematicality.   RBP

NÉMETH, László (1901–75), Hungarian essayist, novelist, playwright and poet, the son of a geography and history teacher, started writing plays, verse and short stories at an early age. After he finished his secondary school in Budapest, he studied at the Medical University (degree 1923). Although he worked as a school medical officer until 1942, he also made a literary career. 1925 he won a competition of the journal *Nyugat* (West) with a short story. 1932 he founded the periodical *Tanú* (Witness), which he wrote entirely himself until it ceased in 1936. Joining the Populist movement, he contributed to *Válasz* and *Kelet Népe* (People of the East). 1945–50 he worked as a private tutor, and 1949–53 he was silenced for political reasons, and turned to translating. From 1954 he was allowed to publish his original works. In the late 1920s Németh was an independent critic who held reser-

vations about both the spokesmen of urban modernisation and those who believed in the values of traditional rural life. He found himself alone with his views, as he stated in *Ember és szerep* (Man and his role, 1934), a confessional work. Taking the idea of national character from SZÉCHENYI, about whom he published a book-length essay in 1942 and a play in 1946, he reached the conclusion that Hungarians could develop their own culture only through organic evolution. Regarding the development of the Hungarian bourgeoisie as inorganic, he joined the Populist movement. The starting-point of his long pamphlet *Kisebbségben* (In minority, 1939) is that the intelligentsia cannot do its job unless it emerges gradually from the masses. This argument provoked BABITS and the liberals, who attacked Németh for considering the assimilation of foreigners as Hungarians superficial. Similar criticism was levelled at him later, when he wrote a comedy about his trip to the Soviet Union (1958). While in the 1930s he was a shrewd critic of Stalinism, in *Utazás* (A journey, 1962) he suggested a compromise between Hungarians and the Soviet authorities. Despite the controversial, eclectic and inconsistent nature of his ideas, his essays exerted a powerful influence on the Hungarian public. While most of his fiction and plays simply illustrate his principles, some of his novels have considerable aesthetic value. Among these, *Iszony* (Revulsion, 1947) may be the best organised. Its heroine is forced into an unwanted marriage by her father, whom she idolises. The interest of this psychologically analytical novel is bound up with the manipulation of narratorial point of view. In a crucial scene the husband tries to approach his wife, but she fights back, and he dies. Since the story is told by the heroine, neither she nor the reader can be sure of the cause of the husband's death.

●*Revulsion* (London, 1965); *Guilt* (Budapest, 1966). MSz-M

NERIS, Salomėja (i.e. S. Bačinskaitė-Bučienė, 1904–45), Lithuanian poet, graduated from Kaunas and taught at grammar schools in several towns. At first an adherent of the Lithuanian R. Catholic ideology, Neris changed her views in the 1930s and joined the leftist 'Third Front' group of writers. During the war Neris withdrew to the Soviet Union and died soon after returning home. By inclination, Neris was a dreamer and an idealist, always attracted by the intimate and the emotional in the works of her favourite Romantics, Schiller, Heine, MICKIEWICZ, and by Rilke, and the Russian Symbolist-Acmeists Anna Akhmatova and Alexander Blok. Something in the essence of such writers, their emotional glow, shines through Neris's own intensely personal meditative lyrics and gives them a magnetic charm. Her verse has a lilting melodiousness, and her haunting sound and image repetitions come at just the right moment to create the greatest emotional impact. The overall effect is augmented by her emotional urgency, as it were, to 'enter the souls' of natural objects, flowers, trees, to make them the embodiments of her own sweet or bitter sorrow, or of her thirst for love. For the sake of these precious feelings Neris defied the constricting norms of society by engaging in love affairs which scandalised her acquaintances and, later, by choosing demonstratively the leftist-socialist position against the stale, mindless world of the bourgeoisie. Unfortunately, she hardly ever noticed that in her anger she was serving the Soviet propaganda machine and vitiating her own poetry. The long poem *Bolševiko kelias* (The path of the Bolshevik) is particularly striking for its juxtapositions of tender lyricism with harsh, wooden Stalin-worshiping rhetoric. Her main collections are *Pėdos smėly* (Footprints in the sand, 1931), *Diemedžiu žydėsiu* (I will bloom like the wormwood, 1938) and *Dainuok, širdie, gyvenimą* (Sing to life, my heart, 1943). RŠ

NERSĒS IV KLAYETS'I, known as **SHNORHALI** (the Graceful) (1102–73), Armenian churchman, theologian, diplomat, poet and musician, was the greatest literary figure of the 'Silver Age' of the 12th century. Nersēs Shnorhali, whose epithet was given to brilliant students of the monastery school of the Karmir Vank' (Red Monastery), was born in the fortress of Dzovk' to Prince Apirat Pahlavuni, and was the great-grandson of Grigor Magistros (990–1059). The fortress was situated in the province of Tlouk, part of the demesnes of Prince Vasil, Shnorhali's brother, which eventually became part of the Cilician kingdom (1090–1375). Shnorhali received his education at the monastic school, under the guidance of Bishop Step'annos Manouk. He was ordained priest and then bishop by his elder brother Grigor III Pahlavuni (1093–1166). 1141 he participated in the Church Council in Antioch. April 1166 Catholicos Grigor Pahlavuni appointed Nersēs *coadjator catholicos* and he conducted the administrative duties of the See until his death. Shnorhali's literary career extended for half a century from 1121. The relative security of the

Cilician Armenian kingdom gave new impetus to Armenian cultural activities and ushered in the so-called 'Silver Age'. He wrote poems, commentaries, anthems, hymns, theological treatises and encyclicals. Shnorhali's writings have been preserved almost intact. His first major work, *Vipasanut'iwn* (A rhythmic narrative of Armenian history), composed in 1121, is a work of 1590 octosyllabic lines in 'Homeric' style which tells his people's history from the Creation to 1120. Based on MOVSES KHORENATSI's 'History of the Armenians', the poem has two sections. The first covers the period up to 439–40, the deaths of SS Sahak and Mesrob. The second narrates the history of the Pahlavuni dynasty, beginning with Prince Vaska Holom (d. 1020) to 1120. In this he breaks new ground, for never before had national history been told in poetic form. His great-grandfather, Grigor Magistros, with his versified history of the Bible, had served him as a model. However, Shnorhali has gone further in choosing a secular subject. 25 years later Shnorhali produced his first masterpiece, *Oghb Edesioy* (Lamentation on the fall of Edessa). This poem of 2,096 rhymed octosyllabics records the fall of Edessa following the attack of Imad ed-Din Zengi, the Emir of Mosul, on 23 December 1144. The poem tells the story of the destruction of one of the oldest Christian centres. The city is personified as a widow who has lost her son. She first recalls her glorious past and Christian traditions and then, resting on the ruins, laments her present fate and invites the five ancient patriarchates, Jerusalem, Rome, Antioch, Constantinople and Alexandria, to lament her fate. Then she turns to Armenia, and in a long excursus the poet describes the past glories of the ancient Armenian capitals of Vagharshapat and Ani, contrasting them with their present sad state: 'But I invite also thee, O thou eastern city Ani, For thou too, in times past, A gracious bride, went under veil, Pleasing to those nearby, Desirable to those afar'. On becoming bishop Nersēs Shnorhali created his longest poem (2,000 lines), *Yisus Vordi* (Jesus, only-begotten son, 1152). Its lengthy full title, employing terms like 'spiritual', 'tragedy', 'lament' and 'conversation with God', reveals the multi-faceted nature of the work. In rhyming couplets, the poem summarises pertinent sections of the OT and NT, the suffering of the saints, the Second Coming, and the Last Judgement. In his own words, Jesus the Son presents the history of mankind and its future. In contrast to GRIGOR NAREKATSI's tragic image of man, Shnorhali in a serene and lucid manner uses biblical events as motives for prayers, sometimes highly mystical and sometimes down to earth. The poem displays the author's piety, compassion and moral courage. Among Shnorhali's other poems, *Ban Hawatoy* (Rhythmic exposition of the Christian faith), composed in 1151, explains the true faith (against the Chalcedonians); *Atenabanut'iw* (Oration) and *T'ught Endhanrakan* (Encyclical) were composed in 1166, soon after his elevation to the Catholicate of All the Armenians in which, like a good shepherd, he leads his nation out of suffering into a happier life on Earth and in heaven. Brief but important is *Hawatov Khostovanim* (In faith I confess) – a creed and a prayer – in twenty-four lines, intended to be recited individually at one-hour intervals day and night. One of the most remarkable aspects of Nersēs Shnorhali's career was his unremitting endeavours to recover the unity of the Armenian and Byzantine Churches. Letters were exchanged between the Emperor Manuel I Comnenus (1143–80), and Patriarch Michael III (1170–8) and Nersēs Shnorhali, including the doctrinal treatise, the 'Definition of the Faith of the Armenian Church'. Nersēs Shnorhali used his literary talents to achieve his religious, moral and social goals. His literary work marks the transition from the purely religious (GRIGOR NAREKATSI) to secular poetry, which reached its zenith with the works of Yovhannes Erznkatsi (1240–93), Frik (1234–1315) and Khatchatur *vardapet* Ketcharetsi (1260–1331).

●*Jesus, Son Only Begotten of the Father* (New York, 1947); *Jésus fils du Père*, introd., trans. and notes by I. Kechichian (Paris, 1973); V. Nersessian, 'Leben und Werk des Hl. Nerses Clajensis mit dem Beinamen Schnorhali' in Heyer (Ed.), *Die Kirche Armeniens* (Stuttgart, 1978), pp. 59–69; J. St Martin, *Notice sur Nerses Klaietsi, auteur du poème élégiaque sur la prise d'Edesse* (Paris, 1828).   VN

NERUDA, Jan (1834–91), Czech poet and prose writer, the son of a former soldier running a small grocer's shop, qualified as a teacher but was prevented from finishing his university studies by poverty and spent his whole life in journalism. He brought his journalism into play in his short-story writing. His novella *Trhani* (Scum, 1871), about navvies employed in building railways, was undoubtedly inspired by Bret Harte but manifests more compassion and social awareness than its American counterpart. In his *Povídky malostranské* (Tales from the Lesser Town,

1878) Neruda introduces typical or eccentric figures from the Prague quarter where he was born. He uses a method alternating the tone of narration from serious to humorous, addressing himself to each individual reader and curbing a foible for nostalgia by irony. The shortest of these stories ('U tří lilií' [At the sign of the three lilies]) in which the narrator recounts his encounter during a stormy night with a nymphomaniac who even immediately after her mother's death cannot overcome her obsession, prompted the Chilean poet to assume the *nom de plume*, Pablo Neruda. Although these stories are his best-known prose work, Neruda's *Arabesky* (Arabesques, 1864) and *Různí lidé* (Various people, 1871), with clever anecdote-like plots recounted in succinct style with something like black humour, show a more skilful writer. Neruda's reportage from his voyages in Europe and the Middle East introduced a new mode of narration, used later by ČAPEK. No less important was the impact of his verse. His *Hřbitovní kvítí* (Cemetery flowers, 1857), impressions and reflections brought about by the concept of cemetery, reveal a poet who is profoundly dissatisfied with Czech reality and the state of the world but has no clear idea of what he wants. In *Knihy veršů* (Books of verse, 1867) Neruda speaks as a radical cosmopolitan, hating the upper classes and contemptuous of the petty bourgeoisie, yet attached to his nation, although it repels him. The narrative poems of *Balady a romance* (Ballads and romances, 1883) are an attempt at objective verse; Neruda, an agnostic, looks for consolation to the simple faith of his mother, and maternal love becomes the symbol of the highest ideal of humanity for the lonely and ailing poet. His most intimate collection is *Prosté motivy* (Simple motifs, 1883), telling the story of his four unhappy loves with discipline and irony. The posthumously published *Zpěvy páteční* (Good Friday songs, 1896), exuding the heavy pathos of Baroque hymns, is the verse of a poet who began by storming literature as a cosmopolitan rebel and finds his final refuge in a mystical conception of his nation.

•*Tales of the Little Quarter* (Melbourne, 1957).   KB

NEUMANN, Stanislav Kostka (1875–1947), Czech poet, novelist and publicist, son of a lawyer and member of the Vienna Reichsrat, did not finish his secondary schooling and educated himself mainly during fourteen months as a political prisoner. In his early collection *Jsem apoštol Nového Žití* (I am the apostle of the New Life, 1896), a mixture of sensual lyricism and rhetoric, he aims to 'épater les bourgeois' rather than seriously protest against society. In *Satanova sláva mezi námi* (Satan's glory amongst us, 1897), influenced by Nietzsche and PRZYBYSZEWSKI, he extols pagan hedonism and sexual mysticism. For some time he preached Decadence and anarchism in his literary journal *Nový kult* (New cult, 1897–1904) and, abandoning his former individualism, envisioned a regenerated brotherly society in *Sen o zástupu zoufajících* (A dream of despairing crowds, 1903), reminiscent of SOVA in its free verse. *České zpěvy* (Czech songs, 1910), which is close to DYK in its nationalism and exhortations to activity, signalled Neumann's departure from his 'satanic' past, and his subsequent *Kniha lesů, vod a strání* (Book of forests, waters and slopes, 1914),

written in a Rousseauesque mood, was a Vitalist paean to Nature. After WWI during which he served in Albania, Neumann turned from Nature to technological civilisation in *Nové zpěvy* (New songs, 1918), celebrating the age of machines and human labour; the collection introduced Futurism to Czech poetry and influenced younger poets. Subsequently Neumann took an active part in the foundation of the Czechoslovak Communist Party, became the secretary of Proletkult, edited several Communist papers and wrote tendentious, rhetorical verse, e.g. *Rudé zpěvy* (Red songs, 1923). His only non-political collection after WWI was *Láska* (Love, 1933), a collection of salacious elegiac poems written in regular rhymed verse.   KB

NEZVAL, Vítězslav (1900–58), Czech poet, novelist and dramatist, son of a village schoolmaster, studied philosophy without graduating and devoted himself entirely to literature; 1945–51 he was in charge of the Film Department at the Ministry of Information. For a short period he was a member of the Devětsil but weary of the conception of art as propaganda he became with SEIFERT a leading exponent of Poetism launched by Karel Teige (1900–51). Poetism, borrowing some elements from Futurism, Dadaism and Surrealism, was intended to become 'a way of life, practising modernised epicurism in anti-Romantic poetry of Sunday afternoons, excursions, brightly lit cafés, intoxicating drinks, teeming boulevards and spa promenades as well as of silence, night and calm'. Nezval put the theory into practice in *Podivuhodný kouzelník* (Amazing magician, written in 1922) which recounts the metamorphoses of a magician of the imagination. The poem, a firework display of fancy and whimsical metaphors, was innovatory in the Czech context as it opened the way for the expression of personal enjoyment of life, playfulness and uninhibited transmission of the unconscious. Later Nezval adopted themes which he considered more spiritual: night, death and liberation from despair by creative work as in *Edison* (1927), but in the mid-1930s he founded a Surrealist group to which Breton and Eluard paid flattering homage and 1935 Breton delivered his important lecture on the political position of the movement in Prague. Nezval published Surrealist novels like *Dolce far niente* (1931), *Pan Marat* (Mr M., 1932) and *Jak vejce vejci* (As two peas, 1933). But after the French Surrealists' condemnation of Stalin he left the group and renounced Surrealism soon after publishing his most Surrealist poetry in *Absolutní hrobař* (The absolute grave-digger, 1937). Now Nezval treated his favourite themes – reminiscences of childhood, enchantment with Prague, love for his country, erotic experience – with a more direct approach to reality. After the war, as a régime poet, Nezval obliged with odes on peace, Stalin, President Gottwald and other praiseworthy subjects but towards the end of his life he turned to personal lyric, e.g. in a nostalgic confessional *Nedokončená* (Unfinished, 1960). He was prolific; he published about 25 volumes of poetry, some 10 plays (original and adaptations), 10 novels and several travel books and during the interwar period he dominated the Czech literary scene. His output was uneven but he holds an important place in modern Czech poetry for his imagination, unlimited *joie de vivre*, a facility for free association, and a mastery of rhythm and rhyme. KB

NIEMCEWICZ, Julian Ursyn- (1758–1841), Polish poet, playwright, fiction writer and memoirist, born into a noble family of average means, 1788 entered the world of politics as a Sejm deputy and political writer. He took part in the popular uprising of 1794 as a personal secretary to Tadeusz Kościuszko. Wounded and taken prisoner in the insurrection's final battle, he spent two years in a St Petersburg prison. After his release, he joined Kościuszko in leaving for America in 1796. Nine years later, he returned to Warsaw and to political activity; respected widely as a moral authority, he advocated staunch resistance against foreign oppressors yet condemned political terrorism. He was among the leaders of the November Uprising in 1830, and following its defeat he spent his last years as an exile in Paris. Niemcewicz's long life coincided with a period of dramatic change in Poland's political situation, from attempts at peaceful reform to instances of desperate armed struggle, and a period of equally revolutionary transformations in Polish literature, from the early phase of the Enlightenment to mature Romanticism. Accordingly, his own work went through many stages and often helped introduce new genres and styles to the Polish audience. Among his most innovative and influential works are the political comedy *Powrót posł* (Return of the deputy, 1791), a series of patriotic ballads *Śpiewy historyczne* (Historical songs, 1816) and three novels. Today's audience appreciates Niemcewicz first and foremost as an engaging memoirist.

•One poem in B. Carpenter (Ed.), *Monumenta Polonica* (Ann Arbor, 1989);

Under Their Vine and Fig Tree. Travels Through America in 1797–1805 . . . (Newark, NJ, 1965).   StB

NJEGOŠ, Petar Petrović (1813–51), Serbian poet, was born in Njeguš. His uncle, the ruler of Montenegro, arranged for Njegoš's private tutoring. One of his tutors, a poet Sima Milutinović Sarajlija (1791–1847), instilled in his young pupil a love for folk poetry. Njegoš entered monastic life, and when his uncle died he inherited the throne and was consecrated Bishop of Montenegro in St Petersburg in 1833. He was a good ruler, given his country's backward conditions and isolation, and the incessant skirmishes with the Turks. Njegoš instituted many reforms, united the Montenegrin tribes, and kept the Turks at bay, for which purposes he often travelled abroad. He died of tuberculosis. His tomb on the highest peak of Mt Lovčen has become a national shrine. Despite his irregular schooling, Njegoš was well versed in foreign literature, read Pushkin, Hugo, Lamartine, Dante and Milton, and was able to incorporate their ideas in his poems and epic dramas. He also wrote poems in imitation of the folk epic, in which he exhorted his people to persevere in their struggle for freedom and survival. He used variations on the same theme in his chief works, the epic dramas in verse, *Luča mikrokozma* (The ray of the microcosm, 1845), *Gorski vijenac* (The mountain wreath, 1847) and *Lažni car Šćepan Mali* (Tsar Š. the Small, the impostor, 1851). The first is a philosophical epic about the Fall, resembling Milton's *Paradise Lost*, in which man, together with Satan, rebels against God but is defeated and punished. While the body suffers, however, the soul preserves man's link with God and immortality. The

work's profound thought and lyrical beauty make it in the eyes of many Njegoš's most accomplished work. Others believe that *Gorski vijenac* is the best not only of his but of all works in Serbian literature. It is a drama based on historical events at the beginning of the 18th century as the Montenegrins decide to exterminate the Muslim converts in their midst. The historical framework allows Njegoš to develop his thinking about human existence, about the struggle between good and evil, and man's relationship to God, his country and his countrymen. Above all, Njegoš glorifies heroism as the most exalting virtue in man's service to his fellows. The poet's thought is supported by a lofty poetic style, laconic expression, and proverb-like turns of phrase. The third, weaker, drama is also based on historical fact, an impostor who claimed to be the missing Russian tsar and who rules Montenegro successfully, albeit briefly.

•*The Ray of Microcosm* (Munich, 1953; Cambridge Mass., 1957); *The Mountain Wreath* (Belgrade, 1930; Ervine, 1986; as *Mountain Laurel*, Ottawa, 1985).

M. Djilas, *Njegoš Poet-Prince-Bishop* (New York, 1966); Ž. R. Prvulović, *Religious Philosophy of Prince-Bishop Njegoš of Montenegro* (Birmingham, 1984).   VDM

NOLI, Fan Stilian (1882–1965), politician, religious leader (founder of the first Albanian Autocephalous Orthodox Church), writer and translator, was born in the Albanian village of Ibrik Tepe (Qytezë) S of Adrianople (Edirne). He attended the Greek secondary school in Adrianople until 1910, moving then to Constantinople and Athens. 1903–6 he lived in Egypt where he was in contact with leaders of the Albanian community there. 1906 he emigrated to the USA, soon becoming a leading figure of the Albanian community, editing Albanian newspapers, holding services in Albanian and founding the Panalbanian Federation Vatra (The hearth). 1912, after having graduated from Harvard, he returned to Albania and took part in the Congress of Trieste in 1913. 1915 he went back to the USA and 1919 was appointed Bishop of the Albanian Orthodox Church in the USA. He headed an Albanian delegation to Geneva where he succeeded in having his country admitted to the League of Nations in 1920. From Geneva he returned to Albania, representing the Vatra Federation in parliament there. 1922 he became foreign minister, and 1924 Prime Minister of Albania, leading a short-lived democratic government, which was overthrown by Zogist forces. He went back into exile in America, where he died. Noli started his literary career with a drama, *Israilitë dhe Filistinë* (Israelites and Philistines, 1907), writing at the same time for various newspapers. He was also a noted historian, publishing *Historia e Skënderbeut* (History of Scanderbeg, 1921) and *Beethoven and the French Revolution* (1947). His poetry was first published as *Albumi* (The album, 1948). In addition, Noli is the author of a number of religious works.

●*George Castrioti Scanderbeg* (New York, 1947).

A. Pipa, 'Fan Noli as a National and International Albanian Figure' in *Südost-Forschungen*, 43 (1984), pp. 241–70.   ShM

NORWID, Cyprian Kamil (1821–83), Polish poet, playwright, fiction writer, essayist, graphic artist, painter and sculptor, orphaned early, spent his childhood and adolescence in Warsaw. He published his first verse in 1840; his early poetry, typical in its expression of the young generation's despondency after the defeat of the November Uprising, was favourably received by critics and readers. 1842 Norwid, who had begun to study painting in Warsaw, decided to continue his studies abroad and left for Germany and Italy. While in Berlin in 1846, he was arrested by the Prussian authorities on a trumped-up political charge and spent a month in prison. After his release and a lengthy stay in Rome, he settled in Paris 1849. His émigré status, together with the experience of the 'Spring of Nations', increased his productivity: by the end of 1852 he had written a number of important works, including the poetic treatise on art, *Promethidion* (1851). Lack of favourable responses, near destitution, and unreciprocated love for an aristocratic lady led him to move to America. He arrived in New York 1853 and stayed there for more than a year, trying in vain to earn his living as a graphic artist and sculptor. By the end of 1854 he was back in Paris. His increasingly innovative ideas and idiosyncratic style, often labelled 'obscure' and 'incomprehensible', led from that point on to his gradual alienation from the milieu of Polish émigré intellectuals in Paris. The appearance 1863 of the one volume of his selected writings that he published in his lifetime was largely ignored by critics and the public. Nevertheless, during the 1850s and 1860s Norwid wrote his most important works, including long poems and treatises in verse, several plays, numerous pieces of narrative, essayistic or lyrical prose, and – finally – his crowning achievement, the collection of 100 lyrical poems titled

Vade-mecum. Completed by 1866, *Vade-mecum* could not find any publisher and remained in manuscript until 1903. 1877 Norwid's hopeless financial situation forced him to move to a poorhouse near Paris where he died. Forgotten and isolated in his lifetime and rediscovered a few decades after his death, by the end of the 1930s he was already regarded as the spiritual begetter of modern Polish poetry. His philosophy and art, developed both under the influence of and as a polemic with Polish Romanticism, replaced the prevalent nationalist messianism with an original concept of human universalism, in which modern man was viewed primarily as the heir to all the great civilisations of the past. From this perspective, Norwid was able to deal in a novel, thought-provoking way with the most complex problems of 19th-century history, politics and culture. Although he moved freely among various genres and forms, he was most successful in his brief lyric poems, distinguished by their highly intellectual content, ambiguous irony, irregular rhythm, semantic condensation, and dialogic structure. His *Vade-mecum*, in particular, may be said to have opened a new age in the history of Polish poetry.

●*Poezje/Poems* (Cracow, 1986).

G. Gömöri, *Cyprian Norwid* (New York, 1974).   StB

NOVAK, Slobodan (b. 1924), Croatian prose writer, born in Split, spent his childhood on the island of Rab, which plays a central part in his work, and was educated in Split, Rijeka (Fiume) and Zagreb where he worked in a publishing house until his retirement. Novak made his first impact with his short novel *Izgubljeni zavičaj* (Lost homeland, 1954), greeted as a lyrical evocation of childhood and of the restorative power of landscape. One of its central images is the identification of the Island of childhood with impotence and loss, and the Mainland of maturity with an inevitable set of obstacles. Novak's most important work is his novel *Mirisi, zlato i tamjan* (Gold, frankincense and myrrh, 1968), a first-person narrative of the experience of being trapped on the Island, caring for the aged, former landowner, Madonna. The narrator gradually comes to appreciate the true nature of the Old Order which Madonna represents: its intellectual freedom. The theme of the lost innocence of childhood is bound up here with the specific loss of illusion of the narrator's generation: the betrayal of expectations aroused by the rhetoric of revolution. The novel manifests an engaging generalised self-irony and treats humorously a group of idiosyncratic islanders. Novak's central theme is developed also in his other major work, the trilogy of short stories, *Izvanbrodski dnevnik* (Off-ship diary, 1988).

●'Mother Antonia the Prioress' in A. Stipčević (Ed.), *An Anthology of Yugoslav Short Stories* (New Delhi, 1969); *Twisted Space* (Zagreb, 1969); *Gold, Frankincense and Myrrh* (Zagreb and London, 1990).

C. Hawkesworth, 'The Allegorical Significance of *Mirisi, zlato i tamjan*', *Annali dell'Istituto Universitario Orientale*, 18 (1975), pp. 109–27.   ECH

NOVAK, Vjenceslav (1859–1905), Croatian prose writer, educated in Zagreb, served as a teacher in his native Senj (1879–84), studied at the Prague Conservatory (1884–7) and taught music at the Zagreb teachers' training college. He lived in great poverty, struggling to support a large family, and died of TB. He was a prolific writer in various genres, beginning to write poetry as a student before moving on to short stories, novels and plays. He tried his hand at various styles before settling for the Realist prose for which he is best known. His subject matter ranges from his native Senj and the N Dalmatian coast to contemporary life in the city. Novak was the first writer to bring into Croatian literature the life of the proletariat. His perspective is that of a Christian and a socialist, of a philanthropist who finds the egoism and corruption of the bourgeoisie incomprehensible: some of his memorable portraits have autobiographical features, notably that of the artist lost in a petty bourgeois environment in *Dva svijeta* (Two worlds, 1901). Novak tended to typify social phenomena in portraits of individuals. His best novel is *Posljednji Stipančići* (The last of the S., 1899).

•Extract from 'The Last of the Stipančići', *IYL*, pp. 329–31. ECH

NOVOMESKÝ, Ladislav (1904–76), Slovak poet and publicist, son of a tailor, went to grammar school in Budapest, then teachers' training college in Bratislava, briefly studied philosophy at university and then worked as a journalist in the Communist press in Bratislava and Prague. One of the leading members of the DAV group promulgating a Marxist-Leninist conception of literature, he was active in the Communist movement between the wars and took part in the organisation of the Slovak National Uprising, 1944; 1952 he was imprisoned as a 'bourgeois nationalist'; he was rehabilitated in 1962. Inspired by WOLKER, NEZVAL and later by Yesenin, Novomeský's verse combines elements of Poetism, e.g. free association, inventive imagery, playfulness and spontaneity of rhythm with factual asides, and it expresses social and political awareness in a somewhat despondent and even sentimental way without the bluntness and militancy of other Proletarian Poets. The prevailing mood of most of his collections from *Nedel'a* (Sunday, 1927) and *Romboid* (Rhomboid, 1932) onwards is that of a sensitive poet reminiscing about his childhood and adolescence, his friends, his travels and the countryside. Although some of the poems allude to contemporary events like strikes or the Spanish Civil War, they implicitly doubt the social function of the poet; this turns into pessimism and resignation in *Svätý za dedinou* (A saint outside a village, 1939) which refers to a saint who, realising he cannot help his country by miracles, turns into a statue. In *Vila Tereza* (1963) Novomeský pays tribute to the freedom of expression shown at the meetings of avant-garde writers hosted by the head of the Soviet mission in Prague, Antonov-Ovseenko, during the 1920s; in *Stamodtial' a iné* (From over there and other poems, 1964) Novomeský recalls his imprisonment and affirms that in spite of all the injustice suffered by him he retains his Communist convictions. KB

NOWAK, Tadeusz (1930–91), Polish poet and fiction writer, born into a peasant family, made his literary début in 1948. After graduating from Cracow University in 1954, he worked as an editor in Cracow until 1977, after which he lived in Warsaw. Nowak's poetry and his (highly lyrical) fiction form an artistically innovative personal record of the experience of the transition from traditional small-village to modern-city life. His mythopoeic imagination blends elements of both incompatible realities to suggest that the speaker has a disturbed spiritual identity. In his best poems, particularly those collected under the heading 'psalms' (beginning with the volume *Psalmy*, 1971), he reaches far beyond social observation and ultimately becomes a profound religious and metaphysical poet.

●Selected poems in S. Barańczak and C. Cavanagh (Eds), *Polish Poetry of the Last Two Decades of Communist Rule: Spoiling Cannibals' Fun* (Evanston, Ill., 1991).   StB

NOWAKOWSKI, Marek (b. 1935), Polish short-story writer, has been firmly associated with Warsaw where he was born and educated. He was among the most active and outspoken dissident writers of the 1970s and 1980s. He achieved recognition with his graphic descriptions of the Warsaw underworld (*Benek Kwieciarz*, 1961), but his later stories aim for a much broader account of the disintegration of Polish society and its moral decline under Communism (*Wesele raz jeszcze* [The wedding revisited, 1974]), as well as political involvement (*Raport o stanie wojennym* (A report on martial law, 1982–3]).

●*The Canary and Other Tales of Martial Law* (London, 1983).   SE

NUŠIĆ, Branislav (1864–1938), Serbian dramatist and fiction writer, was a native of Belgrade. After studying law at the university there, he served in diplomatic posts in several Balkan cities. He took part in WWI, in which he lost his only son. Later, he became interested in theatre life and remained active in Serbian theatres as an administrator and author. Nušić began to write drama when he was 19. During his long productive life he wrote scores of comedies, tragedies, historical dramas, and one-acters. He

was most successful in his comedies. From his first, *Narodni poslanik* (A member of parliament, 1883), to his last, *Pokojnik* (The deceased, 1937), he was the best comedy-writer of Serbian theatre. The secret of his success lies in his uncanny ability to combine the genuinely comic elements in daily life with sharp, though benevolent, satire on the morals and politics of his country. He depicted, for example, corruption among primitive politicians (*Narodni poslanik*), the usurpation of power by provincial authorities (*Sumnjivo lice* [A suspect, 1888]), moral hypocrisy (*Ožalošćena porodica* [The bereaved family, 1934]), and intellectual dishonesty (*Dr* [A PhD, 1936]). In his satire and social criticism, he hit his targets without bitterness or ill-will.

●*The Bereaved Family* (Novi Sad, 1983); *The Cabinet Minister's Wife* [*Gospođa ministarka*, 1929] (Novi Sad, 1984).   VDM

NYKA-NILIŪNAS, Alfonsas (i.e. Alfonsas Čipkus, b. 1919), Lithuanian poet, critic and translator, studied Romance languages and philosophy at Kaunas and Vilnius. 1946–9 he lived in Freiburg im Breisgau and taught French in an art college. In the USA from 1949, he worked as a manual labourer for a number of years, until he joined the staff of the Library of Congress. His poetry confronts the reader with notions that might belong equally well to the lexicon of a grand Romantic poet or an Existentialist philosopher. His first collection of verse, *Praradimo simfonijos* (Symphonies of dispossession, 1946), is dominated by such concepts as Time, Journey, Eldorado, Theology, History, Fatherland or God. His images comprise a tightly interwoven mass of ideas, emotions and allusions derived from all aspects of human culture. In the earlier collections, these images are grand, tragic and profound. In his world, trees are tall and severe; they 'thrash about in fury, drowning in passionate sorrow', his stars are angrily frozen in the endless, dark void; nights resonate like a huge double-bass; the fields are a boundless scream, and the poet stands alone on a 'pitilessly frigid Christmas evening', with God freezing to death in his blood. Later, in such collections as *Orfėjaus medis* (The tree of Orpheus, 1954) and *Balandžio vigilijos* (The vigils of April, 1957), the grand gestures diminish, become more subtle, and the imagery develops into a complex set of cross-references to the world's music, poetry, thought, and particularly, painting and mythology. Niliūnas is one of the most erudite Lithuanian poets. Yet the basic emotional dynamic remains the same: a constant yearning for space, distance, for Eldorado, a vision of beauty and truth. Opposed to this is an unyielding home-sickness, or rather, desire to return to inner worlds and to the images that populated them in his childhood dreams. Finally, in his last collection to date, *Žiemos teologija* (Theology of winter, 1985), Niliūnas becomes in the full sense a universal poet, because the entire history of humanity is now the source for both his thoughts and images. He also becomes a philosopher, totally devoted to grasping the human meaning of things; he calls this effort his theology.   RŠ

O

OBRADOVIĆ, Dositej (1740–1811), Serbian writer and educator, was born in Čakovo, Vojvodina. He began his adult life as a monk but left the monastery and embarked on a life of wandering throughout Europe, acquiring education. In Serbia he became Minister of Education, founded schools, including what would become the University of Belgrade, the National Museum, and other cultural institutions. He was the most learned man in Serbia in his time, and laid the foundations of her cultural and educational revival. Most of Dositej's writings are didactic, in accordance with his own desire for enlightenment. In this vein he wrote, for example, *Sovjeti zdravago razuma* (Counsels of common sense, 1784) and *Basne* (Fables, 1788), for which he used Aesop and La Fontaine as models. His most important work is his autobiography, *Život i priključenija Dimitrija Obradovića* (The life and adventures of Dimitrije Obradović, 1788). Although Dositej's works are primarily adaptations from foreign literature, they were instrumental in reviving Serbian literature and paving the way for KARADŽIĆ's linguistic reforms.

●*The Life and Adventures of Dimitrije Obradović, Who as a Monk Was Given the Name Dositej* (Berkeley, 1953).
N. M. Čurčić, *The Ethics of Reason in the Philosophical System of Dositej Obradović* (London, 1976). VDM

OLBRACHT, Ivan (i.e. Kamil Zeman, 1882–1952), Czech prose writer, son of the novelist Antal Stašek (1843–1931), read law at Berlin, then history and geography at Prague; he gave up his studies to become a left-wing journalist, and was a founder member of the Czechoslovak CP; he was twice imprisoned for political activities and was expelled from the CP in 1929, but after WWII became a member of the Central Committee (1945). Little of his original writing betrays his politics except *Anna proletářka* (A. the proletarian, 1928) where the maid Anna is initiated into socialism and sex by a fine young worker, and *Zrcadlo zamřížované* (Mirror with grating, 1932), his dull philosophising account of his first incarceration. *Žalář nejtemnější* (The darkest prison, 1916), loosely based on a tale by DYK, examined the psychology of jealousy and power in a loner, Schopenhauerian blind official. *Podivné přátelství herce Jesenia* (The strange friendship of the actor Jesenius, 1919) is an analytical study of the conflict between art and life and shows a man's development from passivity to activity. Olbracht's masterpiece is *Nikola Šuhaj loupežník* (N.S. the robber, 1933), a straightforward, mythopoeic prose ballad about a Sub-Carpathian bandit sung in praise of the 'natural man'. The collection of three stories, *Golet v údolí* (G. in the valley, 1937), concerns the life of Ḥasidic Jews in the Sub-Carpathian Ukraine and the conflict between security in tradition and insecurity in new ideas (e.g. Zionism), between the spiritual and the new mechanised world with its positivist view of Genesis and the nature of the heavens.

●*Nikola Šuhaj, Robber* (Prague, 1954); *The Bitter and the Sweet* [*Golet v údolí*] (New York, 1967).

W. E. Harkins, 'The Art of Olbracht's Novel *Nikola Šuhaj*' in M. Rechcígl (Ed.), *Czechoslovakia Past and Present* (The Hague, 1968), pp. 993–1,001; F. C. Weiskopf, 'Der Schöpfer von "Anna, dem Proletariermädchen" und "Nikola Šuhaj, dem Räuber" ', *Aufbau*, 9 (1953), pp. 181–3; J. Opelík, 'Olbrachts reife Schaffensperiode sub specie seiner Übersetzungen aus Th. Mann und L. Feuchtwanger', *ZfS*, 12 (1967), pp. 20–37.   RBP

ORBELIANI, Grigol (1804–83), Georgian Romantic poet, had close family ties to Georgian and Russian Romanticism: BARATASHVILI was his nephew, he fell in love with Griboedov's widow, Nino Ch'avch'avadze. He spent the first half of his adulthood as an officer in Russia. Only later was he, for political reasons, allowed back to Georgia. Like A. CH'AVCH'AVADZE, he was that extraordinary oxymoron, a Romantic general; as a poet, his Romanticism was watered down by his skill in traditional lyric composition. In the 1880s he played a leading role in establishing a standard text for RUSTAVELI's 'The knight in the panther's skin'. His best work is a poem he worked on between 1827 and 1870, *Sadghegrdzelo anu omis shemdeg ghame lkhini, Erevnis siakhloves* (Toast, or A night-feast after war near Yerevan), a nostalgic memory of military glory. He has been translated into Russian by a greater poet than himself, Zabolotsky.   DR

ORBELIANI, Sulkhan-Saba (1658–1725), the father of the Georgian 'Enlightenment', was virtually all his life uncle and tutor to VAKHT'ANG VI, first regent, then King of Kartli. Sulkhan was born a member of the royal Orbeliani family, when they, like the kings of Kartli, were under Persian suzerainty. At the end of the 17th century he divorced his second wife and became a monk (taking the name of Saba). His rise came with VAKHT'ANG'S in 1703, although Sulkhan-Saba was exiled ten years later for refusing to convert to Islam. (He had converted to R. Catholicism in 1710.) Later he played a leading part in the futile embassies sent by Georgian kings to Louis XIV of France and Pope Clement in Rome, soliciting Western help in exchange for concessions. Twelve years before his protégé King VAKHT'ANG, he died in exile. Despite his hardships he effectively laid the foundations for standardising the modern Georgian language and for resurrecting secular literature. His knowledge of E and W languages and traditions made him a Renaissance man. His most enduring work is *Ts'igni sibrdzne-sitsruisa* (The book of wisdom and lies), a collection of about 150 fables, some Georgian, some Eastern, arranged in a complex narrative, ostensibly a discussion between courtiers and a king with the clear intention of being a moral education for an enlightened monarch. The concision, wit and subtle transitions from story to story have made the work, however, a classic for children and adults to this day. Printed in 1720 on VAKHT'ANG's presses, it completed the belated emergence of Georgia into the post-Gutenberg era. Just as important is Sulkhan-Saba's dictionary (*sit' q'visk'ona*) of the Georgian language (compiled 1687–1716), not just because it is the first modern monolingual (and only unexpurgated) dictionary in Georgian, but because its depth and breadth prevent it from becoming redundant. Its influence was crucial for the poets of the next generation, Davit GURAMISHVILI and BESIK'I. Quite apart from stimulating others to write and publish, Orbeliani wrote religious works, collated and edited many manuscripts to prepare medieval works for publication. 1713–16 he also recorded his *Mogzauroba evrop'ashi* (Travels in Europe: only the second half is extant); it is, however, more concerned with the traveller's state of mind than the sights he saw.

•I. Abuladze (Ed.), Sulkhan-Saba Orbeliani, *Tkhzulebani*, 4 vols. (Tbilisi, 1959–66); *The Book of Wisdom and Lies* (London, 1894); *A Book of Wisdom and Lies* (London, 1982).
D. M. Lang, ' "Wisdom and Lies": Variations on a Georgian Literary Theme', *Bulletin of SOAS*, 18 (1956), pp. 436–48.   DR

ORBELIANI, Vakht'ang (1802–90), Georgian poet, was born of royal blood, sentenced to death for leading the 1832 conspiracy, reprieved and became an army officer. Like the work of many Georgian Romantics, his poetry was fixed on earlier models and preoccupied with the destruction of the Georgian state in the 18th century. His rank of general was as important as his literary talent for ensuring the prestige of Goethe and Hugo in Georgian. The 1894 edition of his collected works (Tbilisi) has not been superseded.   DR

ORTEN, Jiří (i.e. J. Ohrenstein, 1918–41), Czech poet, came from a Jewish family of drapers, studied at the Prague Drama Academy, but 1939 was expelled for reasons of race, worked briefly in various occupations, died after being accidentally run over by a German military ambulance. Orten associated with the group around BEDNÁŘ, URBÁNEK and I. BLATNÝ, and published four volumes of verse, *Čítanka jaro* (Primer spring, 1939), *Cesta k mrazu* (The road to frost, 1940), *Jeremiášův pláč* (The lamentation of Jeremiah, 1941) and *Ohnice* (Charlock, 1941); the fifth, *Elegie*, appeared posthumously 1946. Because of the race laws he wrote under the names Karel Jílek and Jiří Jakub. In his first collection he attempted to overcome his innate tragic sense of life and his feeling of isolation by a humble acceptance of everyday existence, tender love for his mother, loyalty to his friends and his beloved and nostalgia for his early youth. In his later verse he was gradually overcoming fear, his perception of life's absurdity and scepticism by seeking a refuge in less temporal values. His disciplined, melodious verse expresses his own plight, but also that of man in the great nightfall of the world. This is also revealed in his moving, reflective *Deníky* (Diaries, 1958).   KB

ORZESZKOWA, Eliza (1841–1910), Polish novelist, spent most of her life in Grodno (Byelorussia), working for Warsaw newspapers. Orzeszkowa typifies the social commitment of the Polish Positivists and, particularly in her early works, was a great campaigner. In *Marta* (1873) she advocates improved education for women and condemns 'sexist' job discrimination. *Meir Ezofowicz*

(1878), representing a more mature Realism, describes conflicts within a traditional Jewish community. *Dziurdziowie* (The Dziurdzias, 1885) is an ambitious attempt to portray the minds of superstitious, illiterate Byelorussian peasants. Her best-known work, *Nad Niemnem* (On the banks of the Niemen, 1888), is a remarkably 'well-made novel', realising the ideals of logical structure, dramatic plot and neutral omniscience. Its broad image of country life conveys an unequivocal message of encouragement for labour and national unity. *Cham* (The poor, 1888) glorifies the dignity and Christian compassion of a simple fisherman confronted with his wife's urban permissiveness and lack of principles. Orzeszkowa's late works encompass metaphysical anxiety (*Ad Astra*, 1904) and personal recollections of the 1863 Uprising (*Gloria victis*, 1910). Despite her occasionally obtrusive didacticism Orzeszkowa belongs among the classics of traditional Polish fiction and exerted an influence on numerous modern novelists.

●*Meir Ezofowicz* (New York, 1888).

SE

OTČENÁŠEK, Jan (1924–79), Czech novelist, was from his matriculation to 1952 a worker; then he joined the literary *apparat* and from 1959 was a freelance writer. His two chief works are *Občan Brych* (Citizen B., 1955) and *Romeo, Julie a tma* (R., Juliet and the darkness, 1958). The first, an *Erziehungsroman*, was the earliest Czech Socialist Realist novel to describe the mind of an intellectual faced with the new socialist reality, though Brych is barely a 'positive hero'. It depicts the beginning of the 'terror', but the police are frightfully nice chaps; non-Communists are weak-spined or traitors or corrupt, even criminal. Right-minded unselfish people will in the end see that joining in the building of socialism is the decent thing to do by one's country, and perhaps by all mankind. In contrast, *Romeo, Julie a tma* is an apotheosis of the self, and of the self's ultimate realisation, love. As a story about the love of an adolescent Czech for a Jewish girl, it is one of the first Czech works under socialism seriously to treat the German persecution of the Jews, a major theme of 1960s Czech literature.

●*Romeo and Juliet and the Darkness* (Prague, 1960).   RBP

P

PAISII OF HILENDAR (c. 1722–c. 73), Bulgarian writer, lived and worked from 1745 at the Hilendar Monastery on Mount Athos, and then, from 1762, in the Zograf Monastery; he travelled occasionally to Bulgaria, Austria and, possibly, Jerusalem. While at Hilendar, Paisii began working on his *Istoriya slavenobolgarskaya* (History of Bulgarian Slavs, completed 1762; first publ., Lublin, 1885), which played a significant role in the creation of Bulgarian national awareness. Paisii's work is compilatory, and is thus linked with the DAMASKINI. His main sources for Bulgarian history were Mauro Orbini's (d. 1614), *Il Regno degli Slavi* (1601) and Cesare Baronio's (1538–1607) *Annales ecclesiastici* (1588–1607), whole sections of which Paisii incorporated in his History. Paying great attention to pre-Christian times, Paisii emphasises the existence of strong Bulgarian monarchies, of Christian saints, and attacks those who allowed themselves to be hellenised and did not use their native language. 'Know your own nation and language' is Paisii's message, based on the glorification of the Bulgarian past. His 'cultural gesture' in providing Bulgarians with 'history' is considered to have instigated the National Revival. His text was distributed throughout 'Bulgaria' by patriots such as the priest Sofronii Vrachanski (1739–1813), whose own activities make him the most important figure after Paisii in the initial period of the Revival.

●R. Picchio, 'Gli Annali del Baronio-Scarga e la Storia di Paisij Hilendarski', *Ricerche slavistiche*, III (1954), pp. 212–33; R. Picchio, 'La Istorija slavenobolgarskaja sullo sfondo linguistico-culturale della slavia ortodossa', *Ricerche slavistiche*, VI (1958), pp. 103–18; A. Cronia, *Il 'Regno degli Slavi' di M. Orbini e la 'Istorija slavenobolgarskaja' del monaco Paisii* (Rome, 1940).   SIK

PALAMAS, Kostis (1859–1943), Greek poet and journalist, orphaned 1865, was sent with one of his brothers to live with the family of his austere schoolmaster uncle Dimitrios in Missolonghi, where he was educated. 1875 he registered to read law at Athens but immediately began to devote himself almost exclusively to literature. At first attracted to the rhetorical Romanticism (in *katharevousa*) of Achilles Paraschos (1838–95) and the heroic 'folk poetry' of VALAORITIS, Palamas soon fell under the influence of more revolutionary spirits, notably Nikos Kambas (1857–1927) and DROSINIS. Intermittently, 1879–82, Palamas had to return to Missolonghi for financial reasons. Thereafter almost all his life was spent in Athens. From 1882 he launched himself into a career as a journalist, as parliamentary correspondent for Μη χάνεσαι (untranslatable joke referring to favourite saying by contemporary politician), while regularly contributing poems and articles to a range of periodicals. His first collection of poetry, Τα Τραγούδια της Πατρίδος μου (Songs of my country, 1886), his epico-lyric Υμνός της Αθήνας (Hymn to Athena, 1889), and Τα Μάτια της Ψυχής μου (The eyes of my soul, 1890) show his experimentation with Greek popular, folk and other traditional material, his desire to rework Classical themes, and his gradual move towards what can loosely be called a Parnassian poetics. These works established him both as leader of the demoticist movement and as a poet with strong patriotic attachments. His role as spokesman of the demoticists was further strengthened by his publication of his short story of village life, Θάνατος Παλλικαριού (Death of a brave lad, 1891), and by his polemical critical articles published in the context of the uproar caused by PSIHARIS's 'My journey'. But it was only with the sonnet cycle Πατρίδες (Homelands, 1895) and the collection Ιάμβοι και ανάπαιστοι (Iambs and anapaests, 1897) that Palamas began to find his own poetic identity, an identity marked by a subtle use of symbolism, an instinctive ear for poetic music, and a tight control of metrical and linguistic effect. 1897 his financial position was made more secure by his appointment as secretary to the University of Athens, a post he was to hold for thirty years. In the wake of the disastrous military campaign of the same year, the need for a new political vision encouraged Palamas to look beyond personal lyricism (the 'lyricism of the I' as he later termed it in *My Poetios*) and national consciousness ('the lyricism of the We') to broader metaphysical and ethical issues ('the lyricism of the All'). The works of the next decade represent his major achievements. Ασάλευτη Ζωή (Life immovable, 1904) includes three extended symbolic works, Αλυσίδες (Chains), Η Φοινικιά (The palm tree) and Ο Ασκραίος (The Ascrean), in which the problems of personal, political and artistic freedom and development are concurrently explored. This visionary trilogy served as a prelude to Ο Δωδεκάλογος του Γύφτου (The twelve books of the Gipsy, 1907), a poem in twelve canti in which the Orphic theme of destruction and rebirth, coupled with the Nietzschean concept of the superman, forms the intellectual background to an exploration of the nature of Greekness and the role of the artist in its revitalisation. Using the technique of lyrical juxtaposition (the linking of material by imagery and music rather than narrative logic) the poet moves skilfully between different levels of symbolism – personal, political and metaphysical – and through a dazzling range of stanza shapes and metrical effects. Η Φλογέρα του βασιλιά (The king's flute, 1910), which aspires more openly to be a nationalist epic, shows similar technical expertise, but the subject matter is of more limited interest. From this point on, Palamas reverted to writing shorter lyrics on slighter themes: e.g. Οι καϋμοί της Λιμνοθάλασσας (The sorrows of the lagoon, 1912) contains a series of nostalgic reveries about the Missolonghi of his childhood. The many collections which followed – the last was Οι Νύχτες του Φημίου (The nights of Phimios, 1935) – seem only to repeat the themes and manner of his earlier work, though some of them contain pleasant lyric poems. When he died, his packed funeral became an occasion for occupied Greece, in honouring him, to make a symbolic act of resistance. Palamas's achievement as poet and critic cannot be underestimated. He introduced the relatively unsophisticated Greek reading public to a vast range of recent W European thought and literary forms, and his own synthesis of aspects of Romanticism, Parnassism and Symbolism shifted the level of literary aspiration and achievement among the demoticists to a startlingly higher plane within the space of fifteen years (1895–1910). If Greece has a 'national poet' it is not the crypto-Italian SOLOMOS, as is sometimes claimed, but Palamas.

•*The Twelve Words of the Gipsy* (London, 1974); *The King's Flute* [bilingual edition] (Athens, 1982). R. Fletcher, Kostis Palamas: a Great Modern Greek Poet (Athens, 1984).

CFR

PAPADIAMANDIS, Alexandros, (1851–1911), Greek novelist, born Skiathos, whose family's financial difficulties led to a very broken education, was partly self-taught. At age 12–16 much of his time was spent exploring the island, which was to be the main source of his literary inspiration. He went to Mount Athos at the invitation of a friend who had become a monk, and there acquired a profound knowledge of Church ritual and Byzantine psalmody. Deciding against taking vows, he went to Athens to finish his schooling and start a university course. He kept himself by journalism for a while but was eventually prevented by further financial difficulties from taking a degree. He eked out a living in the capital by his writing until 1908 when, his health undermined by poverty and drink, he returned to his native Skiathos. His major work comprises a short historical novel, Χρήστος Μηλιόνης (Christos Milionis, 1885), and about 170 stories and sketches, of which some 30 are set in Athens and the rest in Skiathos. The narrative and descriptive passages are written in a simple *katharevousa* with demotic dialogue. His works appeared in periodicals and were collected into book form only after his death. His stories exhibit sharply drawn characterisation, careful observation of the daily activities of life, and vivid descriptions of the natural environment and folk traditions. Though particularly sensitive to the difficulties of the poor, the problems faced by village women, the socially debilitating effect of large-scale emigration and of the absence of the menfolk at sea, he was deeply conservative on social, political and religious issues, regarding the introduction of Western ideas and manners as a process corrupting Greek society. At the heart of much of his work is an obsession with the nature and meaning of evil: salvation for his characters is only to be found in a stoical endurance, coupled with self-sacrifice and faith. His masterpiece, Η Φόνισσα (The murderess, 1903), raises issues of the nature of madness and moral responsibility. His narrative technique is interesting: narratorial interventions are largely confined to matters of factual information; the psychology of his characters is left to grow out of the action, and there is much use of changing point of view, sometimes in a complex cinematic way.

•*The Murderess* (London and Athens, 1977); *Tales from a Greek Island* (Baltimore, 1987).   CFR

PÁRAL, Vladimír (b. 1932), Czech novelist, read chemical engineering at Pardubice, and when he finished his studies (1954), worked in various chemicals plants, mainly in N Bohemia, until 1967. Since then he has been a freelance writer, except for 1972–9 when he worked as a publisher's editor. After the uneven comic love novel *Šest pekelných nocí* (Six nights of hell, 1964), he wrote a series of three concise, witty, thoughtful experimental novels satirising socialist consumerism, human beings trying to escape boredom through sex which leads to further boredom, in one case death, food and sex fetishism, the emotional aridity of modern society: *Veletrh splněných přání* (Trade-fair of fulfilled desires, 1964), *Soukromá vichřice* (Private gale, 1966) and *Katapult* (Catapult, 1967). His masterpiece is the subsequent *Milenci & vrazi* (Lovers and killers, 1969), a Vicoesque picture of the struggle between socialist barbarianism and *embourgeoisé* socialist civilisation, where God looks on helplessly at consumer man's destructive erotic and material greed. *Profesionální žena* (A professional woman, 1971) is a parody sadomasochist fairy tale where a skivvy (named Sonia after Dostoevski's prostitute) becomes a careerist. *Radost až do rána* (Joy until morn, 1975) sarcastically satirises the 'real-socialist' ideal of bourgeois inactivity and synchronised sex in tower-blocks. At this time, however, Páral's underlying message, society's need for true, altruistic, even mystical love, starts to come to the surface, his satire to sag into sentimentalisation or ineffectual grotesque; e.g. in *Mladý muž a Bílá velryba* (The young man and Moby Dick, 1973) and in would-be science-fiction

novels like *Pokušení A–ZZ* (The A–ZZ of temptation, 1982). The dystopian *Země žen* (World of women, 1987) aroused much discussion because of its anti-totalitarian theme, but it is schematic. Most of his novels since 1975, with the exception of the angry *Generální zázrak* (General miracle, 1977), manifest a gradual increase of overt political satire. His last work written under socialism, *Dekameron 2000 aneb Láska v Praze* (Decameron 2000, or Love in Prague, 1990), contains a great deal of political satire, but the bulk of the vacuous novel consists of a series of farcical erotic episodes.

●*Catapult* (New York, 1989); *The Career Woman* [*Profesionální žena*] (New York, 1992).

W. E. Harkins and P. I. Trensky (Eds), *Czech Literature Since 1956. A Symposium* (New York, 1980); H. Kunstmann, *Tschechische Erzählkunst im 20. Jahrhundert* (Cologne, Vienna, 1974).   RBP

PARNICKI, Teodor (1908–88), Polish novelist, born in Berlin and raised in Russia, spent most of his life outside Poland, including a lengthy stay in Mexico City. The most sophisticated and intellectually accomplished Polish writer of historical fiction, he developed a narrative technique based on the search for the hidden truth about his characters and the unknown forces behind historical processes. Parnicki painstakingly strives for final answers through shifting points of view and temporal perspectives, baffling discussions and 'documentary' evidence. His interests focus on the interrelations between various cultures in the course of the centuries, the role of outstanding individuals and the possibility of historical veracity. Parnicki's novels about the Ancient world include *Ko-*

niec 'Zgody Narodów' (The end of the 'Covenant of Nations', 1955), set in the Hellenistic state of Bactria, and *Słowo i ciało* (The word and the flesh, 1959), chiefly located in Alexandria but extending as far as China. His novels about medieval Poland also contain evocative pictures of Italy, France, Germany and Muslim Spain (*Srebrne orły* (Silver eagles, 1944]). *Nowa baśń* (A new fairy tale, 1962–70) is a six-volume cycle of novels covering the last thousand years in the history of the Old and the New Worlds.   SE

PARUN, Vesna (b. 1922), Croatian poet, born in N Dalmatia, attended school in Split and university in Zagreb, where she lives as a freelance writer. She published her first poems before WWII, but her first important volume, *Zore i vihori* (Dawns and gales), appeared in 1947. These fresh, often sensual, formally perfect lyric poems were attacked by the critical establishment as 'decadent', but her strong poetic voice, together with that of her contemporary, Jure Kaštelan (b. 1919), made an important contribution to expanding the range of lyric verse in the first postwar years. Parun's ease of composition has not always served her well, but her collection *Crna maslina* (Black olive tree, 1955) is a little masterpiece of concentrated expression.

●Translations of selected poems: Ante Kadić, *Contemporary Croatian Literature* (The Hague, 1960), pp. 79–80; *The Bridge*, 19–20 (1970); *Journal of Croatian Studies*, 20 (1979), pp. 76–9.   ECH

PASEK, Jan Chryzostom (c. 1636–1700 or 1701), author of the finest memoirs in Old Polish literature, educated in a Jesuit college, fought in numerous wars in the mid-17th century. A violent, boister-

ous noble, Pasek was eventually banished from Poland but died shortly before the implementation of the ban. His *Pamiętniki* (Memoirs) were published by Count Edward Raczyński (1786–1845) in 1836. Divided into two parts, they describe Pasek's wartime experiences (1656–66) and his life as a citizen and farmer (1667–88). Their artistic attributes greatly exceed those of simple documentation. Pasek selected those facts which best suited his narrative and occasionally 'adjusted' them to make the story more interesting. His traditionalist, frequently obscurantist, views and the unrestrained spirit of a pugnacious, wayward squire make him typically representative of the 'Sarmatian' Polish nobility.

●C. S. Leach (Ed.), *Memoirs of the Polish Baroque* (Berkeley, 1976).   SE

PAVČEK, Tone (b. 1928), Slovene poet and translator, after law studies in Ljubljana, worked as a newspaper journalist, then in broadcasting; he now works in a publishing house. He is a contributor to *Pesmi štirih* (Poems of the four, 1953), one of the postwar generation who abandoned Socialist Realism for subjective lyrics. In meditative verse he reflects on man's fate and his place in time and space. He is also a writer of lively children's poetry and a translator. Among his collections are *Sanje živijo dalje* (Dreams live on, 1958) and *Poganske hvalnice* (Heathen songs of praise, 1976).

●*Parnassus*; *Literary Review* II (1967); *SPT*.   HL

PAVIĆ, Milorad (b. 1929), Serbian fiction writer and poet, is a native of Belgrade, where he studied literature. He teaches Serbian literature at the university there. Pavić started out as a poet (1967) and short-story writer (1973), and from the beginning he was a meditative and erudite author, striving to merge fantasy and reality in an impeccable, controlled style. He has developed these talents in his most successful works, the novels *Hazarski rečnik* (Dictionary of the Khazars, 1984), and *Predeo slikan čajem* (Landscape painted in tea, 1988). Again playfully fusing reality and fantasy, erasing the borderlines between the present, past and future in a complex world, he tries to unravel the enigma of existence. The mysterious disappearance of the Khazars in the Middle Ages lends itself to Pavić's method of dealing with the problems and dilemmas of the present by resurrecting the world of the distant past. *Hazarski rečnik* proffers mystery, crime stories, historical essays, dream interpretations, and musing on life, death and the truth, all narrated in a modern idiom. Pavić attempts a similar task in *Predeo slikan čajem*, set in a contemporary ambience, but recounted in a no less fantastic and playful fashion. Both works are technically brilliant, employ a pure, almost lyrical language, and show unusual sensitivity to the demands of the late 20th-century intellect.

•*Dictionary of the Khazars* (New York and London, 1988); *Landscape Painted with Tea* (New York, 1990).   VDM

PAVLOVIĆ, Miodrag (b. 1928), Serbian poet, essayist, playwright and short-story writer, was born in Novi Sad, but his family ties are with Belgrade. He studied medicine at Belgrade, practised for a while, but then devoted his life to literature as a writer and as a publisher's editor. Pavlović made a decisive impact on Serbian literature with his first collection of verse, *87 pesama* (87 poems, 1952), ushering in, together with POPA, a new Modernist era in Ser-

bian, and Yugoslav, poetry. His emphasis on controlling emotion in poetry was modelled on Anglo-Saxon poets, especially T. S. Eliot. While his early poems reflect the horror and despair of urban life in the wake of WWII, his subsequent collections move in two divergent directions – inwards and back to the Slav and Serbian past, either in prehistory or in Ancient Greece or in Byzantine times. An erudite, intellectual poet of universal themes, he concentrates on the bleak, tragic aspects of life and the anxieties of modern man. At the same time, he finds hope in the solidarity of humanity and in a constant search for the purpose of existence. He exerts a considerable influence on younger poets. He has written incisive essays of literary criticism and is well known for his anthologies of Serbian literary and oral-tradition verse.

•*The Conqueror of Constantinople* (New York, 1976); *Singing in the Whirlpool* (Toronto, 1983); *The Slavs beneath Parnassus* (London, 1985).

VDM

PAVLOVSKI, Bozhin (b. 1942), Macedonian prose writer, read literature at Skopje and then worked as a journalist, film-critic and director of a publishing house. Pavlovski's main preoccupation is the lot of the individual in the waves of modern migration. This is based on the migration which was for centuries part of Macedonian village life; Pavlovski's starting-point is the local problem where 'profit-seeking' makes people leave their homes, but he uses the local problem to write about the universal problem of exiles; his conception of eternal wandering as the essential ingredient of human existence is well-nigh Romantic, but for him this wandering is the opposite of a search for the 'ideal'. His characters are exiles, even at home. In his first novel, *Igra so lyubov* (Playing with love, 1964), everyone is preoccupied with the problem of whether to remain in the plains or to travel away; he describes their restlessness making them feel restricted so that for them travelling becomes the pursuit of a dream. In his collection of short stories *Fantasti* (The dreamers, 1967) some of the characters are identical with those of *Igra*. This time, however, their preoccupation, indeed obsession, is returning rather than going away. In the novel *Miladin od Kina* (M. from China, 1967–8) the problem is internalised: his 'wandering souls' now meet in a town; they are lost in the miasmic labyrinth of town life and live deformed by their yearning to return. In the novel *West Aust. Prokletstavata na diasporata* (W. A. The curse of the diaspora, 1977) exile is depicted on the basis of the life of Macedonian émigrés on Philip Island, Western Australia, but it also becomes a radical human situation. Pressure is put on his characters to leave Macedonia and then they are lost in a world which lacks integrity and is dominated by alienation. Their drama begins at home, where they feel alien; in their new environment, apart from the harsh life they have to live, they witness moral misery and resist assimilation for fear of losing their humanity. There is exile, but no exit. Pavlovski is concerned with human unhappiness, with people dying in the bitterness of exile; for him, what can make life rich and meaningful is human understanding, but the roots of misunderstanding and intolerance are too deep. The whole of mankind appears to be driven to constant 'migration', from one misfortune to another, greater.

The novel *Tsrveniot hipokrit* (The Red hypocrite, 1985) describes another kind of exile, a Communist who has not lost his revolutionary passion or faith in his society and who is pure before society, but far from pure in his own conscience; he is split between the social ideals he lives for and his personal disillusion.

●A. Bosquet, 'Espagne, Brésil et Macédoine', *Magasine littéraire*, 1 (1980); H. Lotman, 'The Vision of Hell', *Publishers' Weekly*, 27.9.1980; L. Curzi, 'Vagabonds de métal', *L'Humanité*, 15.11.1979.   SIK

PAVLOVSKI, Radovan (b. 1937), Macedonian poet, read law and literature at Skopje but left because of poor health, then worked as a journalist; he became a freelance writer outside Macedonia, near Zagreb. 1966 he published his *Manifesto* concerning the new image of poetry. He wrote his first collection, *Susha, svadba i selitbi* (Drought, wedding and moving house, 1961), in his parents' native village, Zhelezna Reka; he spent his royalties for this on a trip to the European and African Mediterranean countries. 1979 he went to England and then to Czechoslovakia to study Czech; he spent part of 1981 in Paris; 1982 he went to live in Belgrade and did not settle in Skopje until 1985. Pavlovski is best known as a poet, but he also writes essays, short stories and travel impressions; he also paints and draws. A recurring theme in Pavlovski's verse is Zhelezna Reka. The bliss of childhood dominates *Susha, svadba i selitbi*; Nature is part of the harmony of living which is disturbed in his second collection, *Korabiya* (Ship, 1964). Motifs of 'exile' and parting (with innocent natural harmony, childhood, a nostalgically perceived 'past'), of a 'flood' which separates man from 'home', memory, of a 'ford' to cross that 'flood', are constants in Pavlovski's verse. His main concern is a striving for the restoration of a primal unity of perception; his world grows from a small 'village of harmony' up into a vast, almost cosmic, space where the knowledge of all things dwells; man becomes soul and spirit, ascending to heaven and, like Orpheus, descending to the dark labyrinths of the underworld. The poet sets himself up against the absurdity of existence (*Sunce za koje zmije ne zna* [The sun about which the serpent does not know, 1972]), for he dreams and wanders and, while dreaming, he 'wakes' others. His metaphor for man or the world is 'grain' (*Zrna* [Grains, 1975]), which symbolises the constant cycle of 'death' and 'resurrection' and resembles the Ancient myths of season deities and could be an image of the fruits of the soil and terrestrial life or of the human fate, or of poetry or the soul. The 'underworld' through which man goes on his quest for wisdom and harmony is symbolised by labyrinths or by chthonic creatures like the mole. He also regards man in his relation to the native land and its spirit; in the collection *Pir* (Feast, 1973), which concerns Antiquity, Macedonia is soaked in the spirit of Hellas; *Tsarstvoto Samuilovo* (The kingdom of Samuel, 1981) evokes a past of humiliation and pain which still haunts modern man. Pavlovski's poetic language has a biblical tone, although his imagery is of his own creation.

•*Free Song from Iron River* (Canberra, 1983); *Road to the Mountains* (Canberra, 1985). SIK

PAWLIKOWSKA-JASNORZEW-SKA, Maria (1891–1945), Polish poet and playwright, daughter of the painter Wojciech Kossak (1857–1942), was well educated at home and lived all her life to 1939 in an artistic and literary milieu. At the outbreak of WWII she went to Paris and then London, to join her husband who served as an RAF officer. She remained in England until her death. Pawlikowska-Jasnorzewska is the most outstanding woman poet to emerge in Poland in the first half of the 20th century. She published her first book in 1922, but it was her third, a collection of epigrammatical love poems, *Pocałunki* (Kisses, 1926), that established her reputation as an innovative poet of the erotic. Love is both viewed in the context of modern reality and spoken of in the language of modern times while never trivialised or stripped of its mystery. Pawlikowska comes close to the popular Skamander poets in the use of the contemporary colloquial idiom, and she owes to avant-garde poets the idea of metaphoric concision based on the paradoxical principle 'the fewer words, the more meanings'. This idea finds its most striking realisations in the lyrical miniatures from *Pocałunki*; poetic discipline remains Pawlikowska's hallmark also in her later career, including the nostalgic and catastrophist poems written in exile. StB

P'AWSTOS BUZAND (425–86), Armenian historian, is considered the author of *Patmut'iwn Hayots* (History of Armenia, earliest manuscript 1599), a major source for the study of early Christian Armenian society. The History is composed of four 'books', or rather *dprut'iwnk* (registers). These books cover the period of the later Arsacid Arshakuni dynasty in Armenia, from the reign of Khosrov II (ch. III) Kotak (c. 330–8) to that of Arshak II (ch. IV)

(378–86) or roughly to the partition of Greater Armenia between Byzantium and Sasanian Iran in 387. Chapter VI deals with the decadence of the Armenian kingdom after the partition, in a series of brief episcopal biographies, which some consider later interpolations. The dominant themes of the History, apart from the Persian War, are the opposition between the Church and the Arsacid kings, towards whom the author displays hostility. The narrative is interrupted, however, by episodes dealing with specific noble families and their quarrels, the lives of saints and ascetics, and so on. The position of most 19th and early 20th-century scholars was that P'awstos's History had originally been written in Greek by a Greek or a hellenised Armenian in the 4th century and been translated into Armenian a century later. Other scholars have observed some elements of syriacisms in the Armenian text; consequently they opted for a Syriac or partly Syriac original, and argued for double authorship, one a Syrian and the other a Greek. By the close of the 19th century, the analyses of the History showed that the quotations in P'awstos were drawn from the Armenian version of the Bible and other 5th-century texts, and concluded that the History had originally been composed in Armenian, probably in the 470s. The name Buzandaran has been explained as being a derivation from the Parthian *bozand* (a reciter of epic poems), followed by the suffix *aran* (denoting place). Taking this with the term *patmut'iwnk'* (tales or histories) the authentic title is 'Epic Tales' or 'Epic Histories'. It is a compilation dating from the late 5th century, and consequently one of the earliest native accounts of Armenian history. It was first printed, Constantinople, 1730.
●There is no critical edition, but the most reliable is K'. Patkanian (Ed.), *P'awstosi Buzandac'woy Patmut'iwn hayots* (St Petersburg, 1883); a facsimile reproduction of the 1883 St Petersburg ed. with an introduction by N. G. Garsoïan (New York, 1984); N. G. Garsoïan, *The Epic Histories attributed to P'awstos Buzand (Buzandaran Patmut'iwnk')* (Cambridge, Mass., 1989).

VN

PÁZMÁNY, Péter (1570–1637), Hungarian theologian, was the leading figure in the Hungarian Counter-Reformation. A convert to R. Catholicism, he entered the Jesuit Order in 1587; after studying in Cracow, Vienna and Rome and teaching in Graz, he returned to Hungary to battle with the Protestants. He became Archbishop of Esztergom in 1616 and 1635 founded the Jesuit university of Nagyszombat (Trnava) which, transferred to Buda by Maria Theresa, became the present University of Budapest. Pázmány was a prolific writer in both Latin and Hungarian. His main polemical works, *Felelet* (Reply, 1603) and *Öt szép levél* (Five fine letters, 1609), were followed by a monumental summary of R. Catholic doctrine, *Isteni igazságra vezérlő kaklauz* (Guide to divine Truth, 1613). His aids to worship include a fine translation of Thomas à Kempis's *De imitatione Christi* (1604) and *Keresztyén imádságos könyv* (Christian prayer-book, 1606). His collection of sermons (*Prédikátziók*, 1636) represents the finest example of the genre in Hungarian literature. Pázmány was a skilled debater, a powerful preacher and a consummate stylist, whose blend of immense erudition and knowledge of Hungarian life and customs gives his work a unique flavour. He is rightly regarded as the creator of the Hungarian literary language.

●Excerpts in T. Klaniczay (Ed.), *Old Hungarian Literary Reader* (Budapest, 1985); *Pázmány Péter összes munkái* (Magyar sorozat) (Budapest, 1894–1905); *Pázmány Petri Cardinalis opera omnia* (Series Latina) (Budapest, 1894–1904). GFC

PEIPER, Tadeusz (1891–1969), Polish poet, playwright, fiction writer and critic, dubbed 'the pope of the Avant-garde', in the early 1920s created a consistent literary programme, one adopted and propounded by poets who formed with him the Constructivist group popularly called the Cracow Avant-garde. On the pages of *Zwrotnica* (The switch), the group's programmatic periodical (1922–3 and 1926–7), Peiper published most of his articles and manifestoes, later collected in *Nowe usta* (New mouth, 1925) and *Tędy* (This way, 1930). As opposed to the anarchic Futurists, with whom he had collaborated at an early stage of his career, he based his mature programme on 'rigour', order and discipline. The poem should reproduce the structural characteristics of modern reality in its technological, architectural and social dimensions, and should first and foremost follow the principles of inner organisation and economy. As a consequence, it was not the isolated word (as in Futurist poetry), but the sentence that Peiper considered the fundamental unit of poetic utterance; and among the figures of speech based on syntactic connections, the most 'economic' was metaphor: the device able to produce the most meaning from the fewest words. This set of premisses allowed Peiper to develop an elaborate aesthetic system, from his own theory of verse to the notion of the modern poet as 'craftsman'. Peiper's own poems, in the 1920s more often than not dismissed by critics as mere illustrations of his theories, began to be appreciated only towards the end of his life, when, suffering from mental illness, he was voluntarily living in complete isolation and no longer taking part in literary polemics.

●B. Carpenter, *The Poetic Avant-garde in Poland, 1918–1939* (Seattle, 1983). StB

PEKIĆ, Borislav (1930–92), Serbian novelist and playwright, was a native of Podgorica, Montenegro. He went to secondary school in Belgrade and spent many years in London. He then lived as a freelance writer in Belgrade. A prolific author, Pekić published novels and plays, beginning with the novel *Vreme čuda* (A time of miracles, 1965), which brought him instant recognition. His second novel, *Hodočašće Arsenija Radovana* (Pilgrimage of Arsenije Radovan, 1969), was equally well received, as was his multi-volume *Zlatno runo* (The Golden Fleece, 1978–81). The themes of his plays, like his novels, are intellectual. Pekić's erudite works are broad canvases depicting modern man's efforts to orientate himself in events that are frequently out of his control.

●*The Time of Miracles. A Legend* (New York, 1976); *The Houses of Belgrade* (New York, 1978). VDM

PEKKANEN, Toivo (1902–57), Finnish prose writer and playwright, portrayed provincial urban life in the interwar period. The son of a labourer, he left school at the age of 12. He combined his writing with a job as a metal worker until 1932, when he began to devote himself wholly to literature. Pekkanen's insights into the life and aspirations of the urban working classes, detailed, realistic and presented without any sense of class antagonism, assisted the process of national reconciliation in the two decades following the 1918 Civil War. His main concern was with marginal social characters who through education, hard work, guile or business acumen found themselves no longer part of the society into which they had been born nor naturally at ease in their new circumstances. *Tehtaan varjossa* (In the factory's shadow, 1932), an autobiographical *Bildungsroman*, introduces the key themes running through most of Pekkanen's plays and novels. In ways reminiscent of D. H. Lawrence, the author chronicles the protagonist's self-education and the conflicts that arise at work, in politics and in love as his values and aspirations diverge from those of his peers. The theme is developed in *Isänmaan ranta* (The fatherland's shore, 1937), where the context is a strike. Its sequel, *Ne menneet vuodet* (Those past years, 1940), which gives a panoramic view of social unrest in Finland of the 1930s, ends with the outbreak of war against the USSR. The analytic realism of these works is tempered by the introduction of Kafkaesque fantasy and touches of mysticism in those works which probe more deeply into erotic, moral and intellectual questions. In his play *Demoni* (The demon, 1939), hubris is punished; the working-class wife who becomes a successful businesswoman apparently sells her soul to an unknown demonic force in the play *Rakkaus ja raha* (Love and money, 1937), while in the novel *Musta hurmio* (Black ecstasy, 1939) illicit love brings about, through the medium of a romantic tramp, death and disaster

for all those involved. After the war, Pekkanen embarked on a series of synoptic social historical novels about the town of Kotka of which three parts appeared before his death.
● *My Childhood* (Milwaukee, London, 1966); I. Väänäen-Jensen, K. B. Vähamäki (Eds), *Finnish Short Stories* (New York Mills, 1982), pp. 116–26.

MAB

PERETS, Yitskhok-Leybush/ Isaac Leib Peretz (1851–1915), was born in Zamość and came to be regarded as one of the three major classical writers of Yiddish literature, together with MENDELE MOYKHER SFORIM and SHOLEM ALEYKHEM. Although some eight years older than the latter, Perets came later to Yiddish literature, after writing in Hebrew and Polish. He was influenced by Polish neo-Romantic and Symbolist writers and developed an individual voice that came closer to the narrative techniques of contemporary W European literature. Following the pogroms of the early 1880s, his attitudes became more nationalistic and more favourable to Yiddish. In *Monish*, a mock-epic poem he contributed to SHOLEM ALEYKHEM'S Folksbiblyotek in 1888, Perets succeeds in extending the expressive range of Yiddish to encompass finer nuances of individual feeling. 1890, after the collapse of his legal career, he was commissioned to conduct an ethnographic survey of the Jewish settlements of the Tomaszów Lubelski region. The official results were never published, but his impressions were reflected in *Bilder fun a provintsrayze* (Impressions of a provincial journey, Warsaw, 1894) and proved to be an inspiration for much of his subsequent literary career, especially in the stories collected as *Khsidish* (Hasidic tales, Warsaw, 1908) and

Folkstimlekhe geshikhten (Folk-tales, Warsaw, 1909). Perets was the first modern Yiddish writer to draw directly on the rich folklore resources of the Galician *shtetl*. The Hasidic material is viewed obliquely from the standpoint of a secular literary intellect and becomes the vehicle for an elegiac contemplation of traditional Jewish values. Among Perets's dramatic works special mention should be made of the dream-play *Bay nakht afn altn mark* (At night in the old market place, Warsaw, 1907) which consists of a plotless and almost Expressionistic vision of existential contradictions in a wide spectrum of Jewish life. Perets played an important moderating role as deputy-chairman at the Yiddish Conference which assembled at Czernowitz in 1908 to promote the status of the language and its culture. He is also remembered for the inspiration he gave to many younger writers who congregated at his home on Warsaw's Ulica Ceglana. Among them were David Pinski (1872–1959), Avrom Reyzn (1876–1953), ASH, Perets Hirshbeyn (1880–1948), Yehoyesh (1872–1927) and many others who were later to achieve fame on both sides of the Atlantic. His concern for social justice and the lot of the common people found practical expression in his participation in illegal Socialist activities for which, together with Mordkhe Spektor (1858–1925), he suffered three months' imprisonment in 1899. Later on, however, in an article entitled 'Hofenung un shrek' (Hope and fear) which appeared 1908 in the Warsaw daily *Der veg* (The way), he voiced apprehension concerning the dogmatic rigidity on literary questions being increasingly manifested by some of the younger writers who were later to play an important role in the development of Yiddish literature in the USSR.

●*The I.L. Peretz Reader*, ed. R. Wisse (New York, 1990); *TYS*, pp. 118–48, 205–46; *VFY*, pp. 19–31; *GWJF* vol. 1, pp. 60–104, 114–22; vol. 2, pp. 18–24 *PBMYV*, pp. 51–81.

A. Novershtern, *Prooftexts*, 12:1 (Baltimore, 1992), pp. 71–90; R. Wisse, *I.L. Peretz and the Making of Modern Jewish Culture* (Seattle, 1991).   HD

PERONE, Lluka (i.e. Luca Perrone, b. 1920), Arbëresh (Italo-Albanian) poet and folklorist from Eianina near Castrovillari in Calabria, studied French and law and now teaches French language and literature. He has written several collections of verse: *Lule shkëmbi* (Rock flowers, 1969), *Hjea e ariut* (The shadow of the bear, 1969) and *Vjershe lirije* (Freedom's verse, 1971). He has also published a bilingual collection of Arbëresh tales and fables entitled *Novellistica italo-albanese* (1967).

                                        ShM

PETŐFI, Sándor (1823–49), Hungarian poet, prose writer and playwright, was born with the family name of Petrovics. His father was Serbian, and his mother Slovak. His schooling was frequently interrupted because of the ups and downs of his father's business activity. He went to Piarist and Lutheran grammar schools in Pest, and then 1835–8 to the Lutheran grammar school in Aszód. 1838 he entered the Lutheran lyceum in Selmecbánya. The following year he ran away and began a long period of wandering, which started with his joining the army. 1841, however, he was discharged on account of poor health. For a short time he studied in the Pápa grammar school, where he met JÓKAI. 1842 his poem 'A borozó' (The wine-bibber) was published. He worked as a wandering actor until VÖRÖSMARTY helped him publish a volume of verse in 1844. This book was an immediate success, and he became assistant editor of *Pesti Divatlap* (Pest fashion magazine). 1845 he resigned and began to live on earnings from his writing. Soon he decided to participate in political life, establishing a circle of radicals. 15 March 1848 he was one of the leaders of the revolution which broke out in Pest. In September he entered military service as a captain. Later he served as a major under the Polish General Bem in Transylvania. He died in a battle against the Russian Army. Not all his works represented an anti-Romantic Populist reaction; his most influential poems made the earlier style of Hungarian verse look extravagant, morally and aesthetically. As a result of economic and social reforms, a new bourgeoisie emerged in the 1840s that wished to see its own everyday life reflected in the arts. Liberals wanted to make the country aware of the conditions of peasant life, and they found support from Petőfi. His descriptive poems, from 'Az alföld' (The plains, 1844) to 'A puszta, télen' (The puszta, in winter, 1848) and 'Kis-Kunság' (1848), represented a radical transformation in the self-image of the Hungarians. In these works the peasantry of the lowlands is presented as the most significant element of the nation. The longer epic poem *János vitéz* (J. the hero, 1844), based on fairy tales, suggests that national culture should be based on folklore, and it implicitly calls for the abolition of serfdom. Petőfi was a republican, inspired by the French Revolution. 'Egy gondolat bánt engemet' (One thought torments me, 1846) is a prophecy of the triumph of liberty in the entire world; 'Az itélet'

(The judgement, 1847) predicts a radical social change, and 'A tizenkilencedik század költői' (The poets of the 19th century, 1847) has been interpreted by some as a socialist vision of universal equality. In 1848 he wished to be elected as deputy for his native lowlands, but was rejected by the people. His disappointment is reflected in the verse tale *Az apostol* (The apostle, 1848). The verse he composed during the revolution was a running commentary on the events.

●*Selections from the Poems of A. Petőfi* (Philadelphia, 1887) *The Apostle* (Budapest, 1961).

E. Molnár Basa, *Sándor Petőfi* (Boston, 1980). MSz-M

PETRESCU, Cezar (1892–1961), Roumanian novelist, son of a Moldavian agronomist, studied law at Bucharest and remained there to work as a journalist. 1920 he moved to Cluj in Transylvania and a year later founded the review *Gîndirea* (Thought) which attracted many of the prominent writers of the period; he remained editor until 1925. Thereafter he devoted himself to the novel. After WWII he aligned himself with the cultural precepts of the Communist régime and was made a member of the Roumanian Academy in 1955. Petrescu set out to write 'a chronicle of the 20th century' in which he aimed at portraying the evolution of all strata of Roumanian society. Behind his novels lies a determining Fate born of a conjunction of historical, geographical and socio-political factors. 1932 he declared that all his characters 'seemed predestined to a monotonous decline' and that the age was marked by 'a psychology of failure'. His principal themes are the consequences of *déracinement* (*Calea Victoriei* [Victory Road, 1929]), the perfidious effects of industrialisation (*Comoara regelui Dromichet* [The treasure of King D., 1931]), and the inability of social groups to communicate (*Întunecare* [Gathering clouds, 1927]) and *Carlton* (1942). Varied in style, his novels represent a comprehensive picture of Roumanian society during the first half of the „20th century.   DJD

PETROCZY, Kata Szidónia (1664–1708), Hungarian poet and translator, was educated in Poland and returned to marry the Transylvanian Lőrinc Pekry, an army officer whose military career was as straightforward as his political manoeuvring was devious. He was also flirtatious, but his wife remained faithful through all his tergiversations and bore him eleven children. She derived comfort from translating German Lutheran devotional works and confided her sorrows to a booklet of 49 intensely personal lyric poems of rare beauty. These were discovered only two centuries later. Kata Petrőczy was an accomplished poet. She wrote fluently in various metres, both Classical and Hungarian. Her language reveals her indebtedness to BALASSI and Protestant hymnals, but her emotions are profound.   GFC

PETROV, Ivailo (i.e. Prodan Kyuchukov, b. 1923), Bulgarian prose writer, lived in his native village until 1944, when he joined up and fought with the Allies; then he read law at Sofia and later worked as an editor for various literary journals and publishing houses. Petrov began in the 1960s with short stories, fragmentary lyrical impressions which followed the de-epicising tendency of contemporary Bulgarian prose. His novel *Predi da se rodya i sled tova* (Before and after I was born, 1968) is an ironic autobiography focused on self-re-evaluation. His major work,

the novel *Haika za văltsi* (Wolf-hunt, 1986), concerns collectivisation, which becomes a metaphor for the principles on which Bulgarian socialist society was founded. The novel contains the life-stories of seven people from one village. Petrov depicts prewar village life dominated by a somewhat ritualistic and mythical approach to work and Nature; human life is perceived through events arising out of the cycle of birth, reproduction and death. Petrov uses the harmony of this life as the focus through which to regard the Communist take-over and collectivisation. For him, these events caused people's alienation from each other and destroyed the community spirit; the new 'collective' was established by means of fear, hatred and humiliation; it was a creation of fanatics and 'theoreticians with no understanding of 'human soul'. Petrov regards social revolutions with profound scepticism because of their moral relativism which originates in a 'paradox of faith' which in turn leads to a belief in the 'sacralisation' of violence. One of the characters, who spends a lot of his time reading the Bible, discovers this moral relativism when, forced to hand over his land to the cooperative and blackmailed by the Party secretary who refuses to provide a certificate to allow his son to continue his university studies, he has a vision which puts him in a situation resembling that of Abraham: 'God' offers him the chance of sacrificing one of his sons and retaining his land for his other sons and his grandsons; he realises, however, that sacrifice is something one could demand only of oneself. Later he lives by the example of biblical innocent sufferers and believes, in a somewhat Tolstoyan manner, in not repaying evil with violence and awaits 'justice'; he tries to rid himself of his hatred for the Party secretary, who humiliates him for years and destroys his family even after the land has been given to the cooperative, but, in the end, when one of his sons dies as a result of the secretary's persecution, he kills the secretary, aware now that man should serve truth, not 'God', and himself take revenge for injustice, though he must give it its real name: murder.

SIK

PETROVIĆ, Rastko (1898–1949), Serbian poet and fiction writer, was born into a distinguished family in Belgrade. He took part in the exodus of the Serbian Army through Albania in WWI. After the war, he studied law in Paris and entered the diplomatic corps and served in various locations between the wars. WWII found him at the Yugoslav embassy in Washington. After the war he declined to return to his country and died of sunstroke in Washington. In 1986 his remains were taken to Belgrade, since he had been officially recognised. Petrović gained instant fame on publishing his first poems during and shortly after WWI. Together with CRNJANSKI, he became a leading proponent of Modernism in Serbian poetry. His first collection, *Otkrovenje* (Revelation, 1922), lived up to its title by creating a scandal because of his irreverence for tradition, and it helped establish him as a force in Serbian poetry. His verse was experimental, impulsive and anti-conventional, attempting to penetrate prenatal states and to create myths to represent true reality. Later he turned to other genres, notably novels, and had great success with *Burleska gospodina Peruna, boga groma* (A burlesque of Lord Perun,

god of thunder, 1921) and *Dan šesti* (The sixth day, written in 1933 and 1938, but published in 1961). He also wrote evocative travel journals, *Afrika* (A., 1930) and *Ljudi govore* (The people speak, 1931), the latter in the form of fictitious dialogues with Spanish fishermen.

VDM

PIDMOHYLNYI,   Valerian (1901–37), Ukrainian novelist, was in the 1920s a member of the apolitical group of writers *Lanka* (The link). He began his career as a writer of stories with a psychological interest. His reputation as a novelist rests on *Misto* (The city, 1930) and *Nevelychka drama* (A little touch of drama, 1930). Both deal with urban life and both have Existentialist overtones. Pidmohylnyi was also a translator of French literature, which in turn influenced him (Maupassant). Although there was nothing counter-revolutionary or nationalist in his work, he was arrested and later executed in a camp.

•*A Little Touch of Drama* (Littleton, 1972).

GSNL

PILINSZKY, János (1921–81), Hungarian poet, essayist, playwright, translator and novelist, came from a middle-class family of noble origin, and completed his secondary and university education in Budapest. His first poems appeared in 1940. 1944 he was called up for military service, and the experiences he met with as a soldier had a profound impact on him. 1946–8 he was one of the editors of *Újhold* (New moon). After this journal of young writers with liberal views was banned by the Communists, he worked as a copy editor and proof-reader. In the Stalinist period he was not allowed to publish. In 1957 he joined the staff of the R. Catholic weekly *Új Ember* (New man). Although Pilinszky was not a Jew, he identified himself with the victims of the 'Holocaust'. The style of his first collection, *Trapéz és korlát* (Trapeze and parallel bars, 1946), represents a continuity with those poems by JÓZSEF which insist on the tragic nature of human existence. In his next creative phase, in the apocalyptic poems written in the early 1950s and collected in *Harmadnapon* (On the third day, 1959), the 'Holocaust' is interpreted in Christian terms, although the promise of redemption is still uncertain. Most of the pieces in *Nagyvárosi ikonok* (Icons in a city, 1970), *Szálkák* (Splinters, 1972), *Végkifejlet* (Dénouement, 1974) and *Kráter* (Crater, 1976) are of epigrammatic brevity and contain an explicit religious message. In this final stage he drew inspiration from Simone Weil. Pilinszky was one of the least prolific of Hungarian poets. His *Négysoros* (Quatrain, 1956), in which the death of Christ is placed in the context of 20th-century existence, is a fine example of his economy of poetic style. *Apokrif* (Apocryphon, 1956), a long poem inspired by the Book of Revelation, in which the vision of the Last Judgement, the fates of the Prodigal Son and Christ are juxtaposed in an attempt to explain suffering, is one of the greatest lyric poems in Hungarian. At its best, Pilinszky's language has extraordinary tension and calls for constant reinterpretation.

•*Selected poems* (Manchester, 1976); *Crater* (London, 1976).   MSz-M

PODBEVŠEK, Anton (1898–1981), Slovene poet and journalist, one of the most radical Slovene Avant-gardists, promoted Futurism and Expressionism. His chief themes were war, the split personality of postwar man and the menace of inhuman technology. His collection *Člověk z bombami* (Man with bombs), ready for publication in 1920, came out in 1925. He rejected traditional features of poetry in order to reflect better 'the chaos of the time'.

•Translations in *Parnassus*.   HL

z PODĚBRAD, Hynek (Ignatius of Poděbrady,   1452–92),   Czech diplomat, statesman, poet and prose writer, Duke of Münsterberg, son of King George of Poděbrady, married Catherine of Saxony; he also earned fame in jousting, toping and dancing. 1473 he left the Calixtines to join the Roman Church to free himself from the papal interdict placed on his father; then he joined the court of Matthias Corvinus in Buda, whom he accompanied to Italy for his marriage to Beatrice of Aragon. He rebelled against Matthias in 1488. He died, impoverished, of tabes at his father's castle in Poděbrady. He is best known for the erotic *Májový sen* (May dream, 1470s); although he uses some of the conventions of the courtly love lyric, the author's attitude to love is entirely carnal; the praise of 'honour' is sarcastic, since it is declaimed by a lusting adulteress. Most of the poem is a dream consisting of a seduction; the dreamer wakes up with a jerk, giving the dog under his bed a terrible fright, and he finds he is embracing his pillow. *Veršové o milovníku* (Verses on a lover, 1470s) is less titillating but rhetorically more sophisticated; it is an ironically hyperbolic dialogue-poem about a pining young man and an over-cuddlesome lady pretending to desire to console him. The rollicking poem *O ženitbě* (On marriage, c. 1480) jokes about cuckolds, bossy wives, ready-fisted husbands and the delights of remaining a bachelor. Hynek also wrote lively allegorical poems and some deftly translated (via German) Boccaccio novelle; his own attempt at such a novella is cumbersome and coarse. More important is his original allegorical story *O Štěstí* (On Fortune, late 1480s), the first work in Czech literature where a town represents a microcosm; it is also remarkable for its characterisation and skilful linguistic differentiation between narration and direct speech. At the beginning the narrator is an optimist, at the end a pessimist, though that pessimism is alleviated by the comic scene of the knightly hero's death. The lively *Ctnost, rytíř a Moudrost* (Virtue, the knight and Wisdom, late 1480s), the most Renaissance of all Hynek's works, demonstrates the author's capacity for psychological analysis and his sensitivity to linguistic registers.

●Z. Tichá (Ed.), *Veršované skladby Neuberskéko sborníku* (Prague, 1960); Z. Tichá (Ed.), *Spisování slavného frejíře* (Prague, 1980). RBP

PODRIMJA, Ali (b. 1942), Albanian poet from Kosovo, born in Gjakovë, where he went to school, read Albanian at Belgrade. He has written for major Kosovo newspapers and journals and has been editor in the Rilindja publishing house in Prishtinë. Podrimja's verse, dedicated to the common people and their fates, is rich in imagery. Among his collections are *Thirrje* (The call, 1961), *Dhimbë e bukur* (Sweet pain, 1967), *Lili dhe lirija jonë* (The lily and our liberty, 1968), *Folja* (The verb, 1973) and *Drejtpeshimi* (Balance, 1981). ShM

POLIĆ KAMOV, Janko (1886–1910), Croatian poet, playwright and short-story writer, while still at secondary school in Zagreb imprisoned for participating in demonstrations against the rule of Ban Khuen-Hédeváry, left home to join a troupe of wandering actors and worked for a time as a travelling salesman. Suffering from TB since 1906, 1910 he went to Spain, where he died. Kamov's work has a rebellious, adolescent tone. Deliberately provocative, it is strikingly modern for its time, given the prevailing genteel Parnassism cultivated by the dominant literary critic, MATOŠ. The first line of Kamov's first collection of verse, *Psovka* (Curse, 1910), sets the tone: 'I shall rape you, innocent paper...'. The majority of Kamov's works contain clear autobiographical elements, including his Expressionist novel *Isušena kaljuža* (Dried ditch, 1957), the portrait of the inner development of an artist, his rejection of society and ultimate rejection of himself. Kamov's stories are evocations of intense emotional experience.

●C. Hawkesworth, 'Three Stories by Janko Polić Kamov' in C. Hawkesworth and B. Johnson (Eds), *South Slav Perspectives* (London and Kruševac, 1990), pp. 88–98. ECH

POLITIS, Kosmas (i.e. Paris Taveloudis, 1888–1974), Greek novelist, whose family moved to Smyrna in 1890 after a financial disaster, worked 1905–22 in various banks in the city. After the Asia Minor Disaster (1922), he fled with his family to Paris, then London. Eventually he settled in Athens, working for the Ionian Bank. His first novel, Το Λεμονοδάσος (The lemon grove, 1930), deals with adolescent love, also one of the subjects of his fourth and best-known novel, *Eroica* (1938). 1942 he lost his job and was plunged into severe financial difficulties. 1944–5 he briefly joined the Communist Party, and 1951 helped to found the EDA (Democratic Union of the Left), standing unsuccessfully as a parliamentary candidate in the subsequent elections. After WWII he had to live on what he could make from translating. His last major novel, Στου Χατζηφράγκου (At Hadjifrangou's, 1963), reflects his changed social preoccupations, but with its evocation of the lost world of Smyrna takes his career full circle. The novels of Politis combine psychological studies with evocations of social life and ambience. Above all a lyrical writer, he was influential in introducing Modernist techniques into Greek fiction. Given that his works were first published in serialised form, they are strikingly well crafted. In *Eroica* particularly, the matter of the novel, a study of a group of adolescents brought face to face for the first time with the problems of love and death, is of less importance than the manner of telling it. The interplay of lyricism and irony, the musical and literary references and the use of symbolism are the focus of the novel, for which its themes are only the occasion.

CFR

POPA, Vasko (1922–91), Serbian poet, was born in the Vojvodina, of Roumanian parents. He studied at Vienna, Bucharest and Belgrade, was involved on the Communist side in WWII, and afterwards occupied senior positions in the arts. From the age of thirty, he devoted himself primarily to writing verse. Popa entered literature at the beginning of the 1950s when, together with PAVLOVIĆ, he was the most successful in liberating Serbian verse from the pernicious dictates of Socialist Realism, ushering in a new modernising phase in poetry. His oeuvre is fairly small, only eight slender volumes of poems, but the quantity of his output is more than offset by its quality. He patiently chisels out his brief poems in a series of preconceived cycles, and he remains remarkably faithful throughout to his initial plan. His poetry manifests a predilection for objects, for the specific rather than generalities, and for the concrete rather than the abstract; he uses objects as symbols of his own concepts and attitudes. His language is deceptively simple, his verse terse and crisp, his metaphors related to the myths of Serbian folklore. His first collection, *Kora* (Crust, 1953), is considered a turning-point in contemporary Serbian poetry.

●*Selected Poems* (Harmondsworth, 1969); *Collected Poems 1943–1976* (New York, 1978); *Homage to the Lame Wolf* (Oberlin, Ohio, 1979 and 1987).

R. Alexander, *The Structure of Vasko Popa's Poetry* (Los Angeles, 1986). VDM

POPOVIĆ, Jovan Sterija (1806–56), Serbian playwright and poet, was born in Vršac, Vojvodina. He became a lawyer and 1840 went to Serbia, where he was a college professor, a school administrator and a theatre organiser. He also helped Serbia organise its school system. 1848 he returned to Vršac in deteriorating health and spent his last years withdrawn from public view and in a state of profound pessimism. Sterija wrote some decent poetry and forgettable novels, but his main contribution is to drama, especially comedy. He is the founder of Serbian drama. His most successful plays are *Laža i paralaža* (Liar of all liars, 1830), *Kir-Janja* (1837), *Zla žena* (An evil woman, 1838), *Pokondirena tikva* (Upstart, 1838) and *Beograd nekad i sad* (Belgrade then and now, 1853). Sterija's treatment of the foibles and vices of his middle-class characters, such as greed, falsehood and pseudo-patriotism, is couched in robust humour and eloquent satire. Although borrowed from foreign writers, especially Molière, his motifs and characters have a genuine indigenous colour and verve.

•*Liar of All Liars* (Novi Sad, 1987).

VDM

PORADECI, Lasgush (i.e. Lazar Gusho, 1899–1985), one of the greatest Albanian poets of the 20th century, born in Pogradec on Lake Ohrid, studied at the Roumanian school in Monastir, the French college in Athens, the Academy of Fine Arts in Bucharest, and finally at the University of Graz. From 1936 on, he was for many years a schoolteacher in Tirana and, after the war, did important translations of Burns, Pushkin, Lermontov, Mayakovsky, Goethe, Heine and Brecht. His poems were collected in two volumes, *Vallja e yjeve* (The dance of the stars, 1933) and *Ylli i zemrës* (The star of the heart, 1937). Poradeci's verse is influenced by Albanian folk-songs and Roumanian poetry, EMINESCU in particular. There is also an undeniable affinity between Lasgush and N. FRASHËRI. His verse shows aesthetic sensitivity and elements of pantheistic mysticism. Poradeci together with NOLI opened the way to a new generation of writers and men of letters known as the Generation of the 1930s.

ShM

PORUKS, Jānis (1871–1911), Latvian writer, after studying music and composition in Dresden, returned to Riga to live in shabbily furnished rooms where he wrote penetrating essays on Nietzsche and the compositions of Richard Strauss. In his last years he became more and more a prey to despair. He died in a sanatorium. Poruks's literary activity, which is closely linked with attitudes inspired by Nietzsche, spanned the years 1895–1905. He was the first to introduce psychologically analytical story-writing into Latvian literature. *Sirdis tarp sirdīm* (Heart among hearts, 1900) proclaims man's moral renewal in response to capitalist greed. His poetry of resignation begins Romantic and ends Symbolist.

EB

POSTOLI, Foqion (1889–1927), Albanian novelist and playwright, went to school in his native Korçë and later emigrated to the USA, where he became secretary of the Vatra Federation and worked on the Boston newspaper *Dielli* (The sun), where his writings were first published, e.g. his novels *Për mbrojtjen e atdheut* (For the defence of the homeland, 1919) and *Lulja e kujtimit* (The flower of remembrance, 1922). He is also remembered for his drama *Detyra e mëmës* (The mother's duty, 1925).

ShM

POTOCKI, Jan (1761–1815), Polish traveller and novelist who wrote in French, the descendant of a powerful aristocratic family, spent a great deal of his life abroad. Potocki published reports of his extensive journeys to North Africa and Asia. He is best known for his novel *Manuscrit trouvé à Saragosse* (written 1803–15), which was published only in part during his lifetime (1804–14). The Polish translation by Edmund Chojecki (1822–99) (*Rękopis znaleziony w Saragossie*, 1847) is the sole surviving record of the complete text. The novel is a framework narrative on multiple levels and combines Gothic tales and picaresque romance with the philosophy of the Enlightenment.

•*New Decameron* (New York, 1966).

'Jean Potocki et "Le manuscrit trouvé à Saragosse" '. *Actes du colloque . . .*

(Warsaw, 1975); J. Roudant, 'Les demeures dans le roman noir', *Critique*, 15 (1959), pp. 713–36; Z. Markiewicz, 'L'Espagne dans "Le Manuscrit trouvé à Saragosse" ' in *Actes du 4e Congrès national de la Société française de littérature comparée* (Paris, 1961).   SE

POTOCKI, Wacław (1621–96), Polish poet, born into a landowning family of Protestants (the so-called Arians or Polish Brethren), spent all his life as a provincial squire, taking part in public life occasionally but mostly residing in his manor house. In the seclusion of his estate he wrote a large amount of verse, including the epic *Wojna chocimska* (War of Chocim, 1670) and two extensive collections of short poems, *Moralia* (1688) and *Ogród . . .* (A garden . . ., publ. only in 1907). His writing – as a rule, moralistic, didactic or satirical – is characteristic of the 'Sarmatian', domestic and provincial, variety of Polish Baroque.

•Selected poems in B. Carpenter (Ed.), *Monumenta Polonica* (Ann Arbor, 1989).   StB

POTRČ, Ivan (b. 1913), Slovene novelist and playwright, after prewar imprisonment and wartime internment for left-wing activities, joined the partisans in 1943; after the war he worked first as a journalist and later in publishing. Before WWII he wrote a short novel, *Sin* (The son, 1937), showing the physical and mental development in harsh conditions of a peasant boy from childhood to maturity, and the first part of his drama trilogy *Krefli*. *Krefli* (1953), social realist in style but honest and free of ideological elements, presents the prewar, wartime and postwar crises of a peasant family. Most successful of his novels, *Na kmetih* (On the land, 1954) is the tale, related by a young convict in a racy vernacular with numerous regionalisms, of his desire for his own farm leading to seduction and murder.

•*The Land of the Flesh* [*Na kmetih*] (London, 1969).   HL

PREDA, Marin (1922–80), was one of the few Roumanian novelists who successfully portrayed social transformation in post-WWII Roumania. Born into a peasant family in the S of the country, he completed his formal education at the age of 19 and joined the staff of a major Bucharest newspaper. His first book was a collection of short stories (1948), but he attracted critical and public attention with his novel *Morometii* (The Morometes, 1955), which broke the mould of Socialist Realist stereotypes by introducing one of the most convincing characters of postwar Roumanian literature, the peasant farmer, Ilie Moromete. Set in the interwar years the novel centres on Ilie's relationship with his family and the village community. Scornful of change, indifferent to innovation, Ilie is the champion of the established order, one validated by time. The imprint of time can be found in the juxtaposition of memory and personal experience in the first-person narrative of *Marele Singuratic* (The great figure of loneliness, 1972). *Intrusul* (The intruder, 1968) gives an exceptionally realistic portrayal of a young man unable to adapt to the new morality of contemporary urban society which has corrupted traditional values. *Cel mai iubit dintre pămînteni* (The most beloved of the Earth-dwellers, 1980) is politically one of the most notable novels of the Communist period in Roumania. This testimony of the first 15 years of Communist power (that is, of the pre-Ceaușescu period) not only challenges some principles of 'Marxist' theory, such as the collecti-

visation of agriculture and the na-
tionalisation of all means of production, but also attacks the subversion
of the law for political ends and the
abuses committed by the *securitate*.
Perversion of values is once again a
major theme and is ascribed to the
'troglodytes' of the Party and the
security apparatus who lent their collective name to what Preda's hero,
and many Roumanians, call *era ticǎ-
loşilor*, 'the era of the villains'.   DJD

PREFÁT z VLKANOVA, Oldřich
(1523–65), born into a Prague patrician family, studied astronomy and
mathematics and, as a maker of scientific instruments, travelled in Europe
and the Middle East. In his *Cesta z
Prahy do Benátek a odtud potom po
moři až do Palestiny* (A journey from
Prague to Venice and then by sea to
Palestine, 1563) he describes his
travel experiences from 1546. He had
read both Latin and Czech travel
books including that of KABÁTNÍK
but relied mainly on his own experience and judgement. A meticulous
observer, interested in astronomy,
geography, the natural sciences and
history, he described and interpreted
phenomena in a rational, critical
manner. His travel book is not only
the well-documented work of a scholar but also an amusing account of the
skilful narrator, reporting dramatically the misfortunes of his expedition, for example a fight with pirates
or a storm at sea.   KB

PREGELJ, Ivan (1883–1960),
Slovene R. Catholic novelist, playwright and poet, abandoned the
seminary in Ljubljana, 1904, to take
up Slavonic and Germanic studies in
Vienna, taking his doctorate in 1908.
He worked as a grammar-school
teacher in Idrija, Kranj and Ljubljana. His historical novels are chiefly
concerned with his own region of

Tolmin: *Tolminci* (People of Tolmin,
1927), first published as a serial (1915–
16) under the title *Tlačani*
(The serfs), is a story of feudal oppression and peasant resistance: *Otroci
sonca* (Children of the sun, 1927), an
idyllic tale of family life with a
romantic appreciation of the joys of
Nature; *Plebanus Joannes* (Father J.,
1925), the psychological portrait of a
Renaissance man in conflict with
external enemies and his own
corporality; and *Zgodbe zdravnika
Muznika* (Tales of Dr Muznik, 1923,
1929).   HL

PREISSOVÁ, Gabriela (1862–
1946), Czech dramatist and prose
writer, after studies in Prague and
marriage, spent several years in Moravian Slovakia and Slovenia where
she became familiar with the mentality and customs of the people. Her
importance lies in her plays which
were the first to break away from the
Romantic and neo-Classical moulds
of Czech drama. She skilfully used
folklore elements and dialect and
touched on ethical and social problems, but the Realism of her drama is
restricted to the mode of expression;
the themes belong to Romanticism.
In her *Gazdina roba* (The farmer's
woman, 1890), Mánek, the son of a
rich farmer, loves the poor and head-
strong Eva, who refuses him because
she has been slighted by his mother.
When her consequent marriage fails
she and Mánek, now also married,
become lovers again. They leave as
seasonal harvesters for Austria where
they live as man and wife. But when
they are prevented from being divorced from their spouses, Eva,
driven by despair and guilt, drowns
herself in the Danube. In Preissová's
second drama *Její pastorkyňa* (Her
step-daughter, 1891), the orphan
Jenufa is brought up by her aunt

Kostelnička who is highly respected in the village for her piety and high morality. Jenufa is loved by two half-brothers Štefa and Laca, but prefers Štefa and the jealous Laca slashes her face. The disfigured Jenufa is rejected by Štefa although he made her pregnant and Laca refuses to marry her because she has a child. When the child is born in secret, Kostelnička drowns it to preserve both Jenufa's honour and her own. She goes to prison and Jenufa, determined to start a new life, marries Laca. Leoš Janáček used the drama for the libretto for his opera *Jenufa*. Both Preissová's dramas opened the way for the Realism of the MRŠTÍKS and JIRÁSEK.   KB

PRERADOVIĆ, Petar (1818–72), Croatian poet, served as an officer in the Austrian Army, taking an active part in several campaigns, attaining the rank of general. Writing first in German, he later became an admirer of the Illyrian Movement, began to write in Croatian and became the most popular poet of the Croatian National Revival. He is seen as the main codifier of the language of 19th-century Croatian poetry. He was immediately recognised by VRAZ as exceptionally talented. He published only two volumes of verse: *Prvenci* (First poems, 1846) and *Nove pjesme* (New poems, 1851). He translated Czech, French, German, Italian, Polish and Russian Romantic poets, introducing many themes from these traditions into his work. At his best, Preradović is fluent and fresh, excelling in simple, but accomplished, love poetry.

● 'To Slavdom', *IYL*, pp. 299–303; Three poems, *The Bridge*, 50 (1976), pp 35–6.   ECH

PREŠEREN, France (1800–49), Slovene poet, was the first to demonstrate the full literary potential of the Slovene language, with a corpus of verse of the highest quality in all genres: lyric, epic, elegiac, reflective, narrative, satirical, epigrammatic. After education in Ljubljana (1813–21) he studied philosophy and law in Vienna (degree in law 1828). He spent most of his working life as an articled clerk in the offices of a Ljubljana lawyer. By the time he eventually obtained permission to open his own practice in the small town of Kranj, 1846, he was a sick man and broken in spirit. His early poems, published in the *Illyrisches Blatt*, a German-language periodical, and the literary 'almanac', *Kranjska čbelica* (The Carniolan bee, 1830–4 and 1848), include verse warning haughty young beauties of their bleak future: *Dekletom* (To young girls, 1827), *Turjaška Rozamunda* (R. of Turjak, 1830), *Povodni mož* (The watersprite, 1830). The theme of unhappy, unrequited love persists through *Sonetni venec* (A garland of sonnets, 1834), a Petrarchan masterpiece dedicated to a wealthy heiress, Julije, who eventually married a German, up to *Krst pri Savici* (Baptism by the Savica waterfall, 1836), his epic describing the pagan Slovenes' last stand and the fate of the sole survivor, Čertomir, converted by his beloved but denied wedded happiness because she had taken a vow of celibacy. He produced some of his best work during a period complicated by unrequitted love and saddened by the premature loss of his close associates ČOP, KORYTKO, and Andrej Smole (1800–40). He met unhappiness and disappointment with stoicism and resignation.

● W. K. Matthews and A. Slodnjak (Eds), *Selection of Poems by France Prešeren* (Oxford, 1954; London, 1969).

H. R. Cooper Jr, *France Prešeren* (Boston, 1981); J. Lavrin, 'France Prešeren, 1800–1849', *SEER*, 33 (1955), pp. 304–26.   HL

PREVELAKIS, Pandelis (1909–86), Greek novelist, playwright, poet and critic, in the late 1930s went to Paris to extend his education, travelled widely in Europe and was deeply disturbed by the crisis of intellectual and social values which he found. So he returned to Greece to look for a solution in the Cretan past. 1939–74 he lectured on the History of Art in the School of Fine Arts in Athens, but this did not hinder a prolific literary output. His personal crisis is reflected in three collections of intimate verse published 1939–45, in the lament for the passing of the traditional way of life which is embodied in his first novel, Το χρονικό μιας πολιτείας (The tale of a town, 1938) and in the autobiographical second trilogy (1959–66) which starts with his best-known novel Ο Ήλιος του Θανάτου (The sun of death). The pattern of his own intellectual development he identified in El Greco, on whom he wrote his doctoral dissertation and later published two studies, seeing him as heir to an Ancient culture who came into contact with Western values, rejected them, and later learnt to combine the two. The reasons for his choice of the Cretan past are not hard to find. Crete was not liberated from the Turks until 1912, and he had an uncle who had been killed in adolescence in the defence of the Arkadi monastery (1866). This created in Prevelakis an obsession with the vanishing (if not mythical) heroic world of Cretan patriotism in which the physical landscape and identity of ethical and religious principles combined to unify the community. His second

novel is a chronicle of the 1866 Uprising, Παντέρμη Κρήτη (Wretched Crete, 1945). His trilogy Ο Κρητικός (The Cretan, 1948–50) covers the post-Uprising period, concentrating on the life of Venizelos, the political hero who will emerge from the masses to lead his people to freedom. His play Το Ηφαίστειο (The forge, 1962) dramatises the Arkadi story. And as late as 1973 he writes a long poem, Ο Νέος Ερωτόκριτος (The new Erotocritos), which defines itself, by its very title, with reference to the great Cretan romance of KORNAROS. All his oeuvre needs to be seen against this background. At the same time his works are not narrowly Greek. He is concerned with general questions of personal and national identity and individual and public freedom, as is clear from his last novel, Η αντίστροφη μέτρηση (The countdown, 1974), which explores the inherent inability of intellectuals to affect political history.

●*The Sun of Death* (London 1965); *The Tale of a Town* (London and Athens, 1976.)   CFR

PREŽIHOV, Voranc (i.e. Lovro Kuhar, 1893–1950), Slovene novelist, a self-taught writer of humble social origins, resembles Jack London and Maxim Gorki in his social awareness and working-class sympathies. His first success was with short stories depicting suffering, degradation, love and hatred among the Carinthian peasantry: *Samorastniki* (The wild ones, 1940). His first novel, *Požganica* (Scorched earth, 1939), described the fight for a free Carinthia and the revolutionary events of 1918–20. *Doberdob* (1940), 'the war novel of the Slovene people', was based on the author's own experiences at the Italian Front in WWI.

Jamnica (1945) is a monumental picture of life in a Carinthian village between 1921 and 1930. His last book was a collection of youthful reminiscences entitled *Solzice* (Lilies of the valley, 1949). He also left an account of his progress as Comintern agent through Europe and its gaols, *Borba na tujih tleh* (Fight on foreign soil, 1946).

● 'The birdman' in *IYL* and in B. Lenski (Ed.), *Death of a Simple Giant and Other Modern Yugoslav Stories* (Toronto, 1965).   HL

PRUS, Bolesław (i.e. Aleksander Głowacki, 1847–1912), the most accomplished Polish novelist of the 19th century, born into an impoverished noble family in the Lublin province, was forced to abandon his studies at Warsaw College (Szkoła Główna) and became self-taught. Prus supported himself by contributing articles and comic sketches to newspapers. As a journalist he was well known for his reports on current affairs within the Polish kingdom, published throughout his life as the 'Weekly chronicles'. His rather uneventful existence was almost exclusively confined to Warsaw, which figures prominently in his fiction. Prus was the most consistent follower of the 'organic theory' advocated by the Polish Positivists and modelled on the philosophy of J. S. Mill and Spencer. He believed in communal welfare based on economic and scientific progress and cooperation between all social groups. Consequently, he was hostile to everything disruptive to this evolutionary process, including national uprisings. Prus was a self-conscious novelist who treated writing with considerable deliberation. Admiring science and social commitment, and being a Realist in principle,

he was nevertheless fascinated by Romantic individualism, mystery, irrational powers and was, at a later stage, concerned with the role of Providence. Prus's earliest comic and satirical stories were rapidly supplanted by less didactic works of a broader conception. His short stories and novelle demonstrate a singular combination of humour and sadness, compassion and narrative distance, mystery and everyday detail. His emotional engagement, particularly in the case of children's suffering, has often been compared with that of Dickens. His first important novel, *Placówka* (The outpost, 1886), close to French Naturalism in its narrative structure, portrays the stubborn resistance of a Polish peasant to German settlers seeking to buy his land. Prus's finest novel, *Lalka* (The doll, 1890), with its uncharacteristic open ending and innovative strategy of narration, combines a panoramic view of Polish society with a love story of recurring illusion and disillusion, complemented by broader concerns for the future of modern civilisation. *Emancypantki* (Emancipated women, 1894) embodies Prus's vision of the ideal, compassionate woman, while criticising the contemporary feminist movement in which he saw only egoism, vulgarity and an absence of genuine feelings. *Faraon* (Pharaoh, 1897), set in Ancient Egypt and incorporating much mystery and adventure, portrays the state mechanism in action and poses questions about the nature of historical progress.

● *Outpost* (London, 1921); *The Doll* (New York, 1972); *The Pharoah and the Priest* (Boston, 1902).   SE

PRZYBOŚ, Julian (1901–70), Polish poet and essayist, born into a peasant family, graduated from university in

Cracow in 1923. Between the wars, he supported himself by teaching in provincial secondary schools while publishing his poems (five collections 1925–38) and participating in the activities of the poetic Avant-garde. He soon emerged as the leading poet within the group popularly called the Cracow Avant-garde, and a polemicist second only to the group's chief theorist, PEIPER. After 1945, he held a variety of positions, a diplomat in Switzerland (1947–51), a university head librarian, an editor of literary journals. Simultaneously, he continued to publish collections of poems and essays. Much younger than PEIPER, Przyboś started out in the shadow of his more theoretically minded and experienced colleague; he was heavily indebted to his ideas. At the same time, he soon turned out to be a more accomplished poet than PEIPER. After a brief period of superficial fascination with technological modernity, Przyboś found a more authentic voice in his third volume, *Z ponad* (From above, 1930). In this and ensuing collections, he broadened the thematic scope and temporal perspective of his poems while perfecting his characteristic technique of verbal condensation through metaphor and ellipsis. Throughout the postwar decades, Przyboś, unquestionably the most prominent living member of the 1920s Avant-garde, continued to grow as a poet and to play an active, sometimes galvanising, role in literary debates. He enjoyed the respect and admiration of younger poets and critics, although in the late 1950s the first attacks against his over-optimistic rationalism and restrictive aesthetics indicated the beginning of the end of the long-lasting domination of the Cracow Avant-garde's literary programme.

●Selected poems in C. Milosz, *Polish Postwar Poetry* (Berkeley, 1983). B. Carpenter, *The Poetic Avant-garde in Poland, 1918–1939* (Seattle, 1983). StB

PRZYBYSZEWSKA, Stanisława (1901–35), Polish playwright, illegitimate daughter of the writer PRZYBYSZEWSKI, led an isolated life, persecuted for her connections with the CP. Her vivid interest in the French Revolution was reflected in *Sprawa Dantona* (The Danton affair), published posthumously by Bolesław Taborski (b. 1927) in *Dramaty* (Dramas, 1975) and loosely adapted for cinema by Andrzej Wajda in his film *Danton* (1982). The play represents the universal conflict between the 'good genius' (Robespierre), fighting for the moral re-education of the human race, and the 'evil genius' (Danton), concerned solely with power and sensual pleasure.

●J. Kosicka and D. Gerould, *S. Przybyszewska. A Life of Solitude* (London, 1986). SE

PRZYBYSZEWSKI, Stanisław (1868–1927), Polish author who also wrote in German, as one of Berlin's bohemians, became acquainted in his youth with such artists as Strindberg, Dehmel and Munch. Following his move to Cracow he edited the influential Modernist magazine *Życie* (Life, 1898–1900). Much later he collaborated with the Expressionist journal *Zdrój* (Source, 1917–18). Przybyszewski's Berlin period, during which he wrote in German, was the most creative and innovative of his whole career. His prose-poems, plays, novels and essays were later rendered into Polish with somewhat questionable results. His influential theory of the 'naked soul', introduced in *Totenmesse* (1893) and later restated in Polish in *Confiteor* (1899) and other works, combined the notions of the subconscious and the libido with the metaphysical concept of the inner self as a transcendental reality constituting the core of human existence. His artistic output hardly matched the pioneering importance of his theories, which in many ways prefigured Expressionism.

●*The Snow* (New York, 1920); *Homo Sapiens* (New York, 1970).

M. Herman, *Un Sataniste polonais, S. Przybyszewski. De 1868 à 1900* (Paris, 1939); M. Schluchter, *S. Przybyszewski und seine deutschsprachigen Prosawerke 1892–1899* (Ludwigsburg, 1969).   SE

PSIHARIS (i.e. Ioannis Psiharis, 1854–1929), Greek scholar and novelist, was born in Odessa and had a cosmopolitan upbringing, moving first to Constantinople, then Paris, Marseilles (where his grandmother lived), Palermo (where his father was Greek consul-general) and back to Paris, all by the age of 12. He was accustomed to speak French at home and was fluent in Italian by the age of 9. 1868–70 he attended the Lycée Buonaparte in Paris, but had private lessons in Modern Greek. He then went to Bonn for a short time to study law, but returned to literary studies in Paris 1877–81, and began to mix in the highest intellectual circles there. In particular he became friendly with Taine and Renan, and married Renan's daughter Noémie in 1882. His first works were scholarly – *Essai de phonétique néo-grecque* (1884), *Essai de grammaire historique néo-grecque* (1885) – as befitted a man who was to teach Modern Greek 1885–1904 at the Ecole des Hautes Etudes and from 1904 onwards at the Ecole des Langues Orientales Vivantes. He first visited Greece in 1886, and for all the strength of his patriotism and the importance of his contri-

bution to Greek culture at the end of the 19th century, he remained a French citizen, rooted in French intellectual values, until his death. Besides his scholarly works Psiharis wrote novels in both French and Greek – T'Ονειρο του Γιαννίρη (Yianniris's dream, 1897), Ζωή κι αγάπη στη μοναξιά (Life and love in solitude, 1904), Τα Δυό Αδέρφια (The two brothers, 1910–11), Αγνή (Agni, 1912–13) – and a collection of short stories, Στον ίσκιο του πλατάνου (In the shade of the plane tree, 1911). His fiction has been wrongly judged by the standards of the ethographical Realism prevailing in Greece at the time he was writing. In fact it belongs firmly in the context of the hybrid *psychologiste*, Symbolist and didactic French fiction of the late 1880s and 1890s. It contains complex reflections on the role of the writer and makes frequent reference to other works of art, notably in 'Life and love in solitude' which uses *Robinson Crusoe* as its base, and in 'Agni' which centres on a musician and uses detailed musical references and quotations in the text. Unfortunately the potential intellectual interest of his fiction is not matched by effective literary language or a talent for the creation of plot and character. Psiharis's major contribution to Greek literature lies not in his fiction but in the strange hybrid work To Ταξίδι μου (My journey) – a mixture of autobiography, novel and academic treatise – which burst upon the Greek intellectual scene in 1888, and was undoubtedly the single most influential Greek work of the period 1880–1930. 'My journey' is in both form and content an impassioned defence of the case for basing written Greek on an extreme form of demotic (i.e. spoken) Greek. As such it had a powerful impact on the linguistic debate of the 1890s, but its very extremism led to an even greater polarisation of views than had existed before. It is also an intensely nationalistic document, designed to appeal to the expansionist patriotic fervour of the period. As such it exacerbated the tendency of supporters of demotic and *katharevousa* to vie with one another for the patriotic label.

● *Moóo*, 28 (1988) is devoted entirely to articles on Psiharis based on the Cambridge Centenary Symposium.

CFR

PULKAVA z RADENÍNA, Přibík (d. 1380), Czech court historian, 'rector' of a Latin college in Prague, was commissioned to write a chronicle of Bohemia in Latin by the Emperor Charles IV, who supplied him with many older Czech and foreign chronicles and documents from the state archives and collaborated with him in the preparatory work. The chronicle begins with the tower of Babel and ends with the death of Charles's mother Elizabeth in 1330. It exists in four versions, the last of which Pulkava translated into Czech. Although he boasts in the introduction that he has omitted all conjecture and only written what was true and well documented, his chronicle is unreliable and verbose; the Czech version, written in clumsy language, is an often inaccurate translation of the original. Nevertheless because of Charles's participation it was very popular; the Latin version survives in seventeen and the Czech in fourteen MSS.

KB

PUMPURS, Andrejs (1841–1902), Latvian poet, son of a farm-hand, as a land surveyor, wandered all over Latvia, and later lived in Moscow and Sevastopol. 1876 he fought among the Cossacks for the liberation of Serbia. He travelled a great deal as a soldier, once even to China. Besides Auseklis (1850–79) he was the most important Romantic. His masterpiece, the verse epic *Lāčplēsis* (Bear-slayer, 1888), was the result of twenty years' work. According to its subtitle 'folk epic compiled from legends of the people', its immediate model was the Estonian *Kalevipoeg* (see KREUTZWALD). In accordance with the fashion of Romanticism it was meant to substitute for the non-existent national epos. The action occurs in the 13th century, and the hero, Lāčplēsis, is the symbol of the Latvian nation. He fights against the Black Knight, representative of the German oppressors, and symbolises the nation's yearning for freedom.

EB

PUŠČA, Jazep (i.e. Iosif Płaščynski, 1902–64), Byelorussian poet, described the russification and imposition of Communism in his country with bold and cutting wit. Born in the Minsk region, he worked as a teacher and studied at Leningrad before being exiled 1930–58. Pušča's most striking poems were written in the late 1920s and include the satirical cycles *Listy da sabaki* (Letters to a dog, 1927) and *Pierad skupym abličcam času* (Before the miserly face of time, 1929), and the narrative poem *Sady viatroŭ* (Gardens of the winds, 1929), as well as a robust rebuttal of Party interference in literature, *Cień konsula* (Shadow of the consul, 1928). Not all Pušča's poems were political, but it was in satire that he found his most distinctive voice.

● A. Adamovich, *Opposition to Sovietization in Byelorussian Literature 1917–1957* (New York, 1958). ABMcM

Q

Q'AZBEGI, Aleksandre (1848–93), Georgian prose writer, was born to the rich feudal lord of Khevi (around Mt Kazbek), General Mikeil Q'azbeg-Chopik'ashvili. The influence of his nurse aroused his creative interests; the death of his father plunged him into poverty. A student of agriculture in Moscow, he led a dissipated youth, distinguished only for his solo sword-dancing. Illness, poverty, Tolstoy's preaching and radical ideas drove him to extraordinary actions: he returned home in 1879 and spent seven years as a transhumant shepherd in the Caucasus. Few sheep could have had such an aristocratic shepherd: Q'azbegi recorded this period in a fascinating ethnographical document, *Namts' q' esaris mogonebani* (Memoirs of a former shepherd, 1882–3). He insisted that the native peoples – Circassians, Chechens, Georgians – of the high Caucasus had the secrets of the good life. Ruined once more by trading in recruits for the Russian Army, disliked by his kith and kin, Q'azbegi sold his sheep and descended to Tbilisi as a writer. His passion for the theatre produced a score of plays adapted from French and Russian sources, but only his dancing was applauded. The publication of his ethnographical study *Mokheveebi da mati tskhovreba* (The Khevi people and their way of life,

1880) was a breakthrough. 1880–5 he wrote all his important prose for journals (mainly *Droeba*, [The times]) at a frenetic pace, finishing a story while its first part was being printed. In 1881 he achieved fame with *Elguja*, a short novel with a fictional hero (Elguja) of the very real 1804 mountain peoples' rebellion against the Russians. The plot is laden with ethnographical and historical material, melodramatic to a fault, with *Sturm und Drang* extremes of love and defiance and a Romantic exaltation of the primitive over the civilised. When Q'azbegi had Elguja killed by the Russians, the typesetters protested and the novelist had to prolong his hero's existence. The popularity of Q'azbegi's tragic stories among the Tbilisi middle classes brought him neither wealth nor critical acclaim, except from the veteran Grigol ORBELIANI, who rightly acknowledged *Elguja* as the first truly popular modern Georgian novel. (*Elguja* was banned as a book.) Of Q'azbegi's other stories from the past of the wild Khevi, the most enduring is *Khevisber Gocha* (Gocha, the chief [commander and priest] of the Khevi [valley], 1885). What VAZHA PSHAVELA did for the Khevsurs and Pshavs, Q'azbegi did for their neighbours, the Khevi tribes: he invested their culture – Hellenic pagan, shamanistic, only a

veneer of crusaders' Christianity –
with universal tragic force. The 17th-
century Khevisberi Gocha has to kill
his son Onise for being so carried
away by a moment of love that he lets
the enemy through in the battle
against the feudal lords, but the community's imperative is too much for
Gocha and he goes mad. Madness
interrupted Q'azbegi's career too. In
1885 he took to solitude and drink
and spent his last three years in a
psychiatric asylum, where he died, in
the same year and of the same disease
as Maupassant, to whom he is, at his
best, comparable. In 1927 (*Mnatobi*,
5,7/8) his niece, Sopio Tarkhnishvili,
argued strongly (and plausibly) that
Aleksandre Q'azbegi's five-year prodigious output came from purloining
the unpublished works of his cousin,
Dimit'ri, who had died of pneumonia
in 1880.   DR

R

RADAUSKAS, Henrikas (1910–70), Lithuanian poet and translator, studied literature at Kaunas, worked as announcer at the Klaipėda radio station and later with the book-publishing commission of the Lithuanian Ministry of Education. He fled to Germany in 1944, and in 1949 to the USA where he first worked in a factory and then in the Library of Congress. One striking feature of Radauskas's work is his imaginative use of interaction between feeling and form. He shapes the free flow of intense, vibrant feelings into verse of severe perfection, measuring with precision the semantic potential of each word, each sound pattern, every relationship between intonational stress and metre. The thrust of feeling is so intense in Radauskas that to control it he needs to devise increasingly complex forms sustaining their precision and balance and, most important to him, preserving an illusion of simplicity. The world of emotions in Radauskas's poetry revolves around the central fact of death. His images, whatever their subjects, mostly function as encodings of our confrontation with death. For example, he compares the writing of poetry with a hunter's effort to shoot down an eagle with his arrow, 'wounding instead the old, enormous sun And flooding all the twilight with its blood'. Thus it is through the presence of death that we perceive both the act of creation and its result, the image of a beautiful evening. Eternity itself is presented in the image of lotus-eaters grown old and feeble but who can never die, for in that land there is no time. Nevertheless, a dark, tragic view of things takes up only one segment of Radauskas's emotional world. He also manifests a disposition to humour, irony, and to games with words amidst a classical serenity that seems to have come from studying death and finding it of but little import in the pleasures of the cultivated mind. It happens in Radauskas that death, instead of being a grand presence of dark dignity, becomes a petty force destroying inconsequential things until it becomes faintly ridiculous. In one poem he speaks of little apples torn down in a storm and 'screaming horribly' as they die. Radauskas's poetry abounds with erudite associations, but he hardly ever locates any of his poems in any specific place or time. This lends him an air of aloofness as much from history as from daily concerns so that some readers resentfully call him a 'hermetic' poet. Radauskas has published four collections of increasingly high quality, all except the first written in exile: *Fontanas* (The fountain, 1935), *Strėlė danguje* (Arrow in the sky, 1950),

Žiemos daina (The winter song, 1955) and *Žaibai ir vėjai* (Winds and lightnings, 1965). He translated Thomas Mann, Stefan Zweig, Verlaine and Akhmatova.

●R. Šilbajoris, 'The Arts as Images in the Poetry of Henrikas Radauskas', *Baltic Literature and Linguistics* (Columbus, 1973), pp. 29–35.   RŠ

RADIČEVIĆ, Branko (1824–53), Serbian poet, was a native of Srem, Vojvodina. He studied law and medicine at Vienna, but died of TB before he was able to complete his studies. By that time he had already published his first volume, announcing a new era in Serbian poetry. The historical significance of Radičević's verse is augmented by its high artistic quality; essentially it constitutes the birth of modern Serbian poetry. He was among the first to write in the language of ordinary people, imitating folk-songs and supporting the language reform of Vuk KARADŽIĆ. His youthful ebullience, pristine lyricism, and the expression of the simple joys of life make him one of the most popular among Serbian poets.   VDM

RADICHKOV, Yordan (b. 1929), Bulgarian prose writer and playwright, was a newspaper correspondent, then, after 1952, worked in Sofia as an editor for various journals and as a literary adviser for the film industry. After the fall of Zhivkov's régime in 1989, he supported the former Communist Party (re-named Socialist), and 1990 became a Socialist MP, but 1992 resigned. Radichkov is the most prolific contemporary Bulgarian writer; his fame came with his short-story collection *Svirepo nastroenie* (A ferocious mood, 1965), although he had begun publishing in 1959. He employs folklore and literary conventions in mythoclastic narratives which ridicule automatic thinking. His characters are partly replicas of characters in the most popular Bulgarian mythopoeic literary works and are placed in a typically folksy environment; they 'live' in Radichkov's imaginary village Cherkaski; both characters and 'village' parody the whole paradigm of the familiar 'national universe' created by literature. While other writers concentrated on describing the external changes of village life and the 'new peasant mentality' under Communism, or indulged in ideological interpretations, Radichkov is concerned with the effects of 'modern times' and ironises all talk of 'change'. In his almost Absurdist stories Bulgarian peasants personify basic principles of healthy human thinking which cannot be changed and triumph over ideology. He employs a similar approach when writing about the 'anti-Fascist struggle' in his *Baruten bukvar* (Gunpowder primer, 1969), where common sense drives people, not ideology; he was the first writer to remove pathos from the depiction of WWII and to replace it with ironising compassion. His works on contemporary themes, the stories (*Kozheniyat păpesh* (The leather melon, 1969], *Skalni risunki* [Cave paintings, 1970]) and the novels (*Vsichki i nikoy* [All and none, 1975] and *Prashka* [The sling, 1977]), constitute grotesque evocations of the moral paralysis of society and the restraints imposed on man by myths and erroneous thinking, by false desires, ambition and resignation; the hidden opposition is the free individual, who may be only a product of dreams. Radichkov's plays, especially *Opit za letene* (An attempt at flying, 1979), set up inner freedom expressed either as an oneiric return to naive mythological thinking or as external eccentric action, as the highest value. Logical absurdity and the fantastic, usually derived from the folk tradition, are vital to Radichkov's works. His sophisticated style is based on concatenations of metaphor based on metonymy. He is the most original verbal artist in Bulgarian prose since WWII.   SIK

RADNÓTI, Miklós (1909–44), Hungarian poet, translator, essayist and short-story writer, was overshadowed by death from the very beginning. His mother died giving birth to him and his stillborn twin brother, and he lost his father at the age of 12. He studied at commercial academy and spent 1927–8 in Czechoslovakia, studying textile manufacturing. Having done his matriculation at a grammar school, he read French and Hungarian at Szeged. The professor who impressed him most was the R. Catholic writer Sándor Sík (1889–1963). His first volume of verse appeared in 1931. In the same year he visited Paris, where he came into contact with the French Communist Party. 1934 he obtained a doctorate in the humanities and married. Because of his Jewish origins, he was summoned for forced labour after the German occupation of Hungary in May 1944. In the autumn of the same year his group was marched from Yugoslavia through Hungary towards Austria. Since he was unable to keep up, he was shot by the retreating Germans in W Hungary. His body was not recovered until 1947. At the beginning of his brief career he wrote erotic poems which are of no great aesthetic value. He translated the works of Apollinaire and La Fontaine, and his own work was affected by two conflicting trends: the Avant-garde and Neo-

classicism. The second of these influences proved decisive. His most vivid poems are a series of eclogues and *Razglednicák* (Postcards, 1944), poems that were found in his coat pocket, after the exhumation of his body from a mass grave. His best volume is *Tajtékos ég* (Foamy sky, 1946), a moving document of the 'Holocaust'.

● *Clouded Sky* (New York, 1972); *Travel March* (Manchester, 1979); *The Complete Poetry* (Ann Arbor, 1980).

MSz-M

RADYSERB-WJELA, Jan (also: **WJELA,** Jan; **WEHLE** or **WEHLA,** Johann, 1822–1907), Sorbian story-writer, poet and folklorist, born the son of Handrij Wojak, a quarryman, in Židow (Seidau), a Sorbian suburb of Bautzen, adopted his father's nickname Wjela as his surname. He later added the *nom de plume* Radyserb (from *rady Serb*, 'gladly a Sorb'). At the age of 13 he began work as a cowherd, but friends made it possible for him to attend a teachers' seminary in Bautzen, where he qualified in 1842. From 1844 he was a teacher at Bórk (Burg), just outside Bautzen. 1852 he returned to his birthplace Židow and remained there as a teacher until his retirement in 1889. He participated in the foundation of the learned society Maćica Serbska in 1847 and collaborated with Jan Bartko (1821–1900) in publishing the weekly *Serbski Nowinkar* (Sorbian Messenger) from March to August 1848. Radyserb-Wjela's first collection of stories, *Pójdančka k wubudźenju a k polěpšenju wutroby za Serbow* (Stories to rouse and improve the heart for Sorbs, 1847), reveals his wish to edify his countrymen and to appeal to the humblest of them. He pursued these aims in eight further volumes of prose fiction. His subjects are often historical, as in *Nadpad pola Bukec 1758* (The attack at Hochkirch 1758, 1852), a tale from the Seven Years' War; *Křiž a połměsac abo Turkojo před Winom w lěće 1683* (The cross and the crescent or the Turks outside Vienna in 1683, 1883); and *Bitwa pola Budyšina 1813* (The Battle of Bautzen 1813, 1891). In *Jan Manja abo Hdźe statok mój?* (Jan Manja or Where is my home?, 1889) the hero is a Sorb who travels to America, makes his fortune, and returns to play his part in the Sorbian national movement. Radyserb-Wjela is also the author of hundreds of narrative poems and ballads which have their roots in the Sorbian oral tradition. His output in verse, in addition, includes fables, epigrams and lyric poems. He was an assiduous collector of folklore and published collections of thousands of sayings, proverbs, riddles, and rare words which had escaped the lexicographers.   GCS

RAFFI (i.e. Hakob Melik-Hakobyan, 1835–88), Armenian novelist, born in a small village in the province of Salmast in Persian Armenia, was in 1852 sent to Tiflis (Tbilisi) where he attended the Russian grammar school. 1856 he returned to his birthplace to look after his father's business. 1857–8 he undertook a long journey into Turkish Armenia and Persia where he met Mkrtitch Khrimian (later Catholicos of All Armenians, 1892–1907). On his return to Persia, Raffi wrote his novel *Harem* (1874), which so provoked the Persians that he had to leave the country and go to Russia. He settled in Tiflis, where he spent the rest of his life collaborating with Armenian intellectuals, in particular with Grigor Artsruni (1845–92), the editor of

Mshak (Labourer) – a periodical which helped to shape the mentality of the younger generation, and in whose pages he published his first works. Like ABOVYAN, Raffi aimed at uniting the Armenians of Persia, Turkey and Russia in a common struggle against foreign domination. A gentle, soft-spoken man, he became pugnacious when the subject was politics. He was convinced that words, action and, if necessary, force had to be used to combat tyranny. 'Patriotism and nationalism', he writes, 'are holy duties for every individual and the war for the freedom and defence of the fatherland is a holy war.' He wrote a group of novels vaguely outlining a plan of action for the political salvation of Armenia: *Jalaleddin* (1878), *Khent'ê* (The madman, 1881), *Kaydser* (Sparks, 1883–7) and *Khatcagoghi Hishatakaranê* (The memoirs of the cross-stealer, 1882–3). *Khent'ê* epitomises Raffi's dreams of a future independent Armenia. In its interweaving of battle scenes with everyday scenarios *Khent'ê* often reminds one of *War and Peace*. The war around which *Khent'ê* revolves is the Russo-Turkish War of 1877–8. During the 1870s secret societies dedicated to liberating Armenians from the Turks became active in Van, Erzerum and Kara-Kilisseh. With the outbreak of the war between the Turks and Russians, hopes arose among the members of these societies that the time for liberation had come. Most disturbing to Raffi is the enemy within, members of the Armenian community who help the Turks subject the Armenians. The monumental *Kaydser* is Raffi's most impressive effort to understand Turkish Armenia. It is also the novel in which Raffi makes the fullest use of autobiography, incorporating his vivid memories of the inadequate education he received as a child in a Persian village, his notes on his Turkish journey of 1857, and much of his reading of Armenian mythology and history. *Kaydser* pictures the sickness of Turkish Armenia and, also, indicates remedies for the sickness. What Raffi emphasises most as the source of the Armenian sickness is the Armenian Church, which he sees as having succeeded in preventing the libertarian spirit of the OT and NT by fostering superstition, the passive acceptance of persecution and of an inadequate education, untouched by the advances of modern science. *Davit' Bek* (1882) investigates and fictionally recreates the Armenian past. *Davit' Bek*: 'God knows that this nation deserves to have its throat cut, and I would do it myself if I could hate her, and yet I love her . . . I love this skeleton – this poisoned body, contaminated as it is with a thousand diseases, and breathing death-diseases that she has contracted from the lovers she has exchanged.' The last novel before Raffi died of TB, *Samvel* (Samuel, 1886), deals with events in the latter half of the 4th century when two empires, the Persian and the Byzantine, are in conflict, and Armenia is a bone of contention between them. Raffi's novel centres on Shapouh's (the Persian King of Kings) attempt to make Armenia his vassal through the manipulation of two Armenian princes, Samvel's maternal uncle, Merouzhan, whom Shapouh intends to crown king, and Vahan Mamikonian, Samvel's father who is made the commander of the Armenian forces. Like Scott, Raffi returns to his country's past to enable his readers to feel national historical continuity.

● 'Raffi: The Armenian National Writer', *Contemporary Review* (August 1916), pp. 3–8.   VN

RAICHEV, Georgi (1882–1947), Bulgarian writer, attended a grammar school at Stara Zagora but did not finish his schooling because he was so preoccupied with reading and writing. He was working as a minor civil servant in Stara Zagora when an unhappy love drove him to Sofia (1908). Initially supported by LILIEV and other writers, he found another post as a civil servant and continued writing. 1909–13 he attended lectures in philosophy and literature at Sofia. His war experience as a conscript in the Balkan Wars and WWI led to his losing faith in human spirituality and goodness and he developed extreme views about the bestiality of man. Raichev belongs to the generation which removed literature from its previous folklore and village framework and set its action in an urban environment. His novels *Tsaritsa Neranza* (Queen N., written 1910, publ. 1920) and *Ecce Homo* (unpublished), influenced by Hamsun and PRZYBYSZEWSKI, verge on Decadence, but lack originality. They contain some of the hallmarks of his later work: the power of instinct, woman as enemy, an interest in the unconscious and in psychological abnormalities. One exception in his early work is the novella *Mănichăk svyat* (Small world, 1919), in which his favourite theme of the tragic battle between the sexes receives a new treatment: love originates in the need for warmth and intimacy and is not simply a manifestation of a 'biological law'. In the 1920s Raichev wrote a series of 'Diabolist' pieces (*Razkazi* [Short stories, 1923]), expressing his views on human nature strongly influenced by his favourite PRZYBYSZEWSKI, by Artsibashev's *Sanin*, and Strindberg. His characters are not ruled by mystical evil forces (which is the case in MINKOV's 'Diabolist' stories), but by an evil which forms the essence of human nature (cf. ŠLEJHAR). His depiction of the pathological and bestial in man is unique in Bulgarian literature: personality is described as mere sexuality; there is no harmony in the hallucinatory world of his characters; violence, physical or psychological, appears to be the only means of human communication. In this period Raichev was so disgusted by man that he proclaimed it nonsense to learn foreign languages or to be educated since 'man has never left the path of the beast'. Many of his stories resemble Dostoevski's explorations of the 'dark side' of human nature, but lacked the Russian's belief in the illuminating effect of 'beauty' and in the 'resurrection' of goodness. His novella *Grechovna povest* (Sinful tale, 1923) is a masterpiece of psychological horror where love (as a manifestation of omnipotent instinct) results in monstrous violence. It has a village setting, which is an exception; otherwise his Diabolist horror tales concern the sick mentality of the modern city (cf. MUTAFOV) and the psyche damaged by war. Raichev's short stories concerning war destroy the myth of the 'good Bulgarian soldier' created by patriotic literature and describe him as the worst kind of animal. His novel *Pesenta na gorata* (The song of the forest, 1928), however, represented an absolutely new attitude to man and love; the root of all evil is clearly ascribed not to human nature as such but to the abnormalities of urban existence; when his characters return to Nature (the forest), their love is

purified. His legend in verse, *Elenovo tsarstvo* (The realm of the stags, 1929), concerns the redemption of tribal guilt sacrifice; his stylisation (which has no links with folklore) has as its main character Princess Algara (an epitome of virginity), who redeems her tribe from a curse through sacrificing her love for the sake of the tribe; the suspicions of her husband, however, cause her death. Algara embodies spirituality which is the opposite of an emblem of Raichev's other work: the bull in the short story *Karachakal* (1930) which embodies primal, hypnotic sexual energy. SIK

RAINIS, Jānis (i.e. J. Pliekšāns, 1865–1929), Latvian poet, playwright and translator, was the child of an estate manager, went to the German grammar school in Riga, and 1884–88 was a law student in St Petersburg. He sent ethnographic articles to the Riga paper *Dienas Lapa* (Daily gazette), the first publication of the national movement. A young man of socialist persuasion, he published, with Pēteris Stučka (1865–1932), a collection of satires, *Mazie dunduri* (Little horse-flies, 1888). After graduating from university Rainis practised law at country courts. 1891–95, he was editor-in-chief of the *Dienas Lapa*, a paper which not only stood for Latvian independence but also became the first Latvian propagator of Marxist ideas. 1897 Rainis was arrested, and in prison he translated Goethe's *Faust*. In the same year he was exiled to the province of Viatka where he was confined until 1903. In the wave of repression that followed the 1905 Revolution he escaped abroad. Rainis and his wife ASPAZIJA lived in Switzerland. In exile, he wrote his major works. Returning to the new Republic of Latvia in 1920, he held several prominent positions in the government, including that of Minister of Education, and in the Social Democratic Party. He was instrumental in founding the Riga Art Theatre in 1920 and directed the Latvian National Theatre 1921–5. Though belonging to New Current and a Social Democrat, Rainis was also heir to the National Awakening. His work – as much as that of ADY, KRLEŽA, or Blok – forms a part of a type of Symbolism which, in its ideas, has several points of contact with Marxist social criticism. Rainis's plays, especially, also exploit elements of Latvian folklore. In his works, particularly those written after the war, one can also see the influence of Expressionism. With the first two collections, *Tālas noskaņas zilā vakarā* (Distant moods in a blue evening, 1903) and *Vētras sēja* (Sowing the storm, 1905), which established his pre-eminence as a lyric poet, Rainis proved himself an exquisite technician with a fastidious sense of form and diction. He used an abbreviated sonnet form, nine lines in iambic pentameters (the 'Rainis stanza'). In his next three volumes, *Jaunais spēks* (New strength, 1906), *Klusā grāmata* (The silent book – banned by the censors, 1909, republished, 1910 as *Vēja nestas lapas* – Leaves driven by the wind), and *Tie, kas neaizmirst* (Those who do not forget, 1911), we find fiery verse striving to strengthen the national spirit of his compatriots who had taken part in the abortive 1905 revolt against Tsarist autocracy. In the allegorical *Ave, sol!* (1910), Rainis extols the forces of light and wisdom symbolised by the sun. Into his most intellectual collection, *Gals un sākums* (End and beginning, 1912), the poet projects his own spiritual and social crisis and that of

his nation; that is meant to indicate the underlying restlessness of all civilisation. One solution he recommends is the acceptance of perpetual changeability – a theme which often appeared in his dramas. Latvia's independence in 1918 was greeted by Rainis with two volumes, *Sveika, brīvā Latvija!* (I salute you, free Latvia!, 1919) and *Daugava* (1919). His postwar poetry abounds in the bitterness of old age and solitude as well as faith in love: *Addio, bella!* (1920), *Sudrabota gaisma*, (Silvery light, 1922, *Mēness meitiņa* (The moon's daughter, 1925). Most of Rainis's fifteen dramas espoused national causes and drew heavily on Latvian history and folklore. In them he appealed to universal human emotions. He who tramples others humiliates himself – this is the central theme of Rainis's plays. His *Uguns un nakts* (Fire and night, 1907) is built around the popular legend of the Latvian epic hero, the Bearslayer. *Pūt, vējiņi!* (Blow, winds, 1913), described by the author as a 'consequence of the atmosphere of exile and reflections on its psychology', follows the highly stylised trochaic tetrameters of folk-songs. Sombre mysticism and numerous elusive symbols and allegories characterise his *Spēlēju, dancoju* (I played, I danced, 1919). This fairy play in verse, abounding in demons, witches and hobgoblins, is perhaps Rainis's most original drama. *Jāzeps un viņa brāļi* (Joseph and his brothers, 1919) is, however, usually considered Rainis's greatest drama because of the striking psychological treatment of its characters. Though based on the Bible, it has little in common with the biblical story and nothing at all with Thomas Mann's *Joseph und seine Brüder*. *Ilja Muromietis* (1922), is a dramatisation of Russian *byliny*. Here, the hero Ilja of Murom turns into stone because he fails to understand the law of 'dialectical movement'. The subject of *Rīgas ragana* (The witch from Riga, 1928) concerns the taking of Riga by Peter the Great in 1710. The entire play, based on historical fact and folk legends, is a symbolic warning of Russian aggression. The prose tragedy *Mīla stiprāka par nāvi* (Love is more powerful than death, 1927) is devoted to the legend of Maija Greif of Turaida which had inspired several works of literature since 1848, by both Latvian and Baltic German writers.

●R. Ekmanis, 'Religion and Poetry: Jānis Rainis', *Canadian Slavic Studies*, 1970, pp. 108–12; A. Gāters, 'Jānis Rainis: Sein Leben und sein Werk', *Baltische Hefte*, 19 (1973) pp. 84–152.

EB

RAINOV, Nikolai (1889–1954), Bulgarian Symbolist prose writer, poet, painter and art historian, was from his early teens educated in an Orthodox seminary; he was then a novice at a monastery, but soon became involved with Theosophical circles (1905), came into conflict with the ecclesiastical authorities and decided not to continue his theological studies. 1908 he went to Sofia University to read philosophy, but ran out of money and had to work for his living in the provinces. At the time he was in close contact with the Theosophical Society and Freemasons, was studying comparative religion, philosophy and esoteric doctrines, learning ancient languages and reading Old Bulgarian APOCRYPHA, legends and tales from the oral tradition, lives of saints and Oriental literature. 1910 he enrolled at the Academy of Art in Sofia; he participated in the Balkan Wars (1912 as a

medical orderly, 1915 as a war correspondent). 1914 he went on a long journey to Egypt, Syria, Palestine, Asia Minor, and then the Greek islands and Italy. 1922–7 he was the chief librarian of the Plovdiv Library, but spent 1925–7 in Paris. 1927 he was given a chair in the History of Art at the Sofia Academy and remained at this post until 1950, when he was expelled by the Communists on 'ideological' grounds. Rainov published his first book, *Bogomilski legendi* (Bogomil legends, 1912), as 'Anonym'; it concerns the Dualist philosophy of the Bogomils as presented in their Creation legends; it also interprets biblical figures, e.g. Cain, Moses, Melchizedek, in the spirit of Bogomilism. The pursuit of transcendental truth, of a mystical Absolute, is the main theme of the book; it owes its effect to a style which comprises an original combination of biblical linguistic stylisation with esoteric imagery, parables and Baroque ornamentation. The book also included *Kniga na zagadkite* (Book of enigmas), a series of miniature parables in Oriental style which carries in the form of 'riddles' modern ideas (e.g. about woman or 'the meaning of life') combined with Ancient mystical knowledge. Rainov became enormously popular in 1918, when he brought out five most inspired works, issued the second edition of *Bogomilski legendi* under his own name and published *Kniga na zagadkite* as a separate book. His *Videniya i săzertsaniya iz drevna Bălgariya* (Visions and meditations from ancient Bulgaria) and *Kniga na tsarete* (Book of the kings) make Old Bulgarian history into spiritual history; Rainov uses legends and chronicles as stylisations aiming to 'remove the reader from the contemporary world', to enable him to contemplate 'eternal values and meanings' cleansed of 'earthly illusions'. He doubts history 'created by the sword' and depicts it as something arising out of base illusions. His 'dream ballads' *Ochite na Arabiya* (The eyes of Arabia) and *Slanchevi prikazki* (Sun tales) are Symbolist prose which interprets the idea of life as a dream in an Oriental environment. The desert appears simultaneously as a symbol of life, dream, woman and love; Rainov distinguishes between 'love' as a biological archetype and 'love' as eternal spiritual force; the overcoming of 'love-passion' is regarded in the spirit of Kierkegaard's overcoming of the 'aesthetic' man, of the 'soul' which for Rainov belongs to the world of the senses; the 'spirit' which leads out of the Desert, out of the cobwebs of illusion, is linked to spiritual love, a quality achieved by ordeal; woman is an instrument of the ordeal. These views are to be found in all Rainov's works, including his most hermetic work, *Gradăt. Poema na taynite* (The city. A poem of the secrets), constructed as a cycle of incarnations of 'soul' and 'spirit' through the signs of the zodiac in their esoteric meaning. His novel about Christ, *Mezhdu pustinyata i zhivota* (Between the wilderness and life, 1919), caused Rainov's excommunication from the Orthodox Church. His Messiah reminds one of Zarathustra and epitomises rebellion against all conventions; his self-hatred and hatred for men as they are form the basis of the highest spiritual love. Rainov published more than 70 works (including a 12-volume history of the plastic arts). SIK

RAKIĆ, Milan (1876–1938), Serbian poet, was a native of Belgrade. After studying law at Belgrade and Paris, he entered the diplomatic service, in which he worked in various capitals until his retirement for health reasons in 1933. He spent his last years in complete seclusion. Rakić wrote about sixty poems and published only three slim volumes, 1903, 1912, and 1924. Like DUČIĆ, he fell, and remained, under the influence of French Symbolists and French literature in general, particularly Baudelaire. He wrote mainly erotic and philosophical verse. The chief component of his outlook is pessimism, a Decadent spirit acquired in Paris but distilled through his sensitive perception of reality. The overriding theme of his finely chiselled poems is the inevitable transience of all things. His love poems express his pessimism most clearly, predicting the failure of sincerely felt happiness even before it begins. In philosophically tinged poems he is resigned to the misery of existence as expressed in man's inability to enjoy his experiences and to halt the passage of time amid decay and approaching death. This pessimism is somewhat muted in his patriotic poems highlighting his countrymen's enthusiasm for fighting on the eve of WWI.

•J. Mousset, *Milan Rakitch* (Paris, 1939). VDM

RÁKÓCZI, Ferenc II (1676–1735), Prince of Transylvania, is known chiefly as the leader of the Hungarian War of Independence (1704–11), but he was also a prolific writer and publicist. He initiated the first newspaper in Hungary, the Latin *Mercurius Hungaricus*, later *Mercurius Veridicus* (1705–10), to inform public opinion at home and wrote his Manifesto (*Recrudescunt : ..*, 1704) and other pamphlets for consumption abroad, all in the cause of his rebellion.

His importance as a writer rests on two works written in exile. His *Mémoires sur la guerre en Hongrie* (written 1716 and published at The Hague in 1739) were aimed at French public opinion to obtain support for his cause. Rákóczi's style here is straightforward and persuasive, as befits his purpose. His *Confessiones*, written in Latin 1716–19, is an autobiography modelled on St Augustine's work. Like Miklós BETHLEN he combines a lively and often dramatic account of his life with self-analysis and meditations. Although the two works differ in both language and style, they complement each other: the *Confessiones* omit the war described in the *Mémoires*. The posthumous *Testament politique et moral du Prince Rákóczi* (The Hague, 1751) contains his reflections on the Christian ruler, primarily addressed to his sons. Rákóczi demonstrates the depth of Latin culture in Hungary. He writes fluently and expressively, using an extensive vocabulary, interweaving it with biblical phrases and expressions that show his knowledge of the Vulgate.

•Excerpt from the *Confessiones* in T. Klaniczay (Ed.), *Old Hungarian Literary Reader* (Budapest, 1985); *Principis Francisci II. Rákóczi Confessiones et Aspirationes Principis Christiani* (Budapest, 1876).   GFC

RANGAVIS, Alexandros Rizos (1809–92), Greek poet and novelist, was born in Constantinople, of an aristocratic Phanariot family related to the SOUTSOS family. He attended military academy in Munich on a scholarship from Ludwig of Bavaria, and returned to Greece as an officer in the Greek Army. Later he became Professor of Archaeology at Athens (1844), Foreign Minister (1866) and ambassador, first in Washington,

then in Berlin (1867–87). Despite a full professional life he produced a substantial body of writing. Heavily influenced by the German Romantics, he was also initially inspired by Greek folk traditions, as his long poem Δήμος και Ελένη (Dimos and Elena, 1837) shows. In general his works of the 1830s are in a modified demotic, as can be seen from his Διάφορα ποιμήατα (Various poems, 1837), a collection including a verse drama and a short story. Thereafter his language became consistently more archaising, so that his historical novel Ο Αυθέντης του Μορέως (The lord of the Morea, 1850), though its themes and plot structure are effective, is easier to read in translation than in the original. His later verse, e.g. Διονύσου πλους (The voyage of Dionysos, 1864), a narrative poem on a mythological theme, reflects a shift to the frigid neo-Classicism of theme and style which had become fashionable. He was one of the few writers of his generation to have reacted favourably to the new writing of the 1880s.

CFR

RATSIN, Kosta (pseud. Neven Peyko, 1908–43), Macedonian poet, a member of the Sofia Macedonian Literary Circle and one of the founders of Macedonian as a literary language, left school in 1922 to work with his potter father; 1926 he began writing for the left-wing newspaper *Organizovan radnik* (Organised worker) and the following year he began writing verse in Serbo-Croat. 1934 he became a member of the Macedonian district committee of the Yugoslav CP and edited its periodical, *Iskra* (Spark), which led to his arrest in the same year and sentencing to five years' hard labour, but he was released towards the end of 1935, and the following year published his first piece of writing in Macedonian, 'Do eden rabotnik' (To one worker). In the late 1930s he became interested in the Bogomils and wrote about the movement. 1942 the Bulgarian occupying forces arrested him, tortured him, but after a few months released him to internment in what was the Bulgarian part of Macedonia (Pirin Macedonia); he was released in 1943 and joined the partisans in W Macedonia. His best-known work is the collection *Beli mugri* (White dawns, 1939), a work of lyrical social criticism, tinged with sentimentality; the poet looks forward to the dawn of social and national freedom.

●*White Dawns* (Skopje, 1974).   SIK

REBREANU, Liviu (1885–1944), Roumanian novelist, was the eldest of thirteen children born to a village schoolmaster and his wife in N Transylvania. He attended Roumanian and Hungarian schools before entering the Ludoviceum military academy in Budapest in 1903. He served for a year in the Austro-Hungarian Army in 1907 but had to resign following financial irregularities. He then worked as a notary in a small town close to his birthplace where he began to write short stories. 1909 he moved to Bucharest where he found employment as a journalist. His first volume of short stories was published 1912 and subsequent collections appeared 1916 and 1919. A number of the stories, such as 'Răfuiala' (Getting even) and 'Iţic Ştrul, dezertor' (I. S., deserter), share themes developed in his major novels. During the interwar period he founded several short-lived literary reviews, became president of the Society of Roumanian Writers and, 1939, was elected to the Roumanian Academy. Rebreanu expressed his artistic credo in an article published in 1924: 'Art, like the divine creation, becomes the most wonderful mystery. By creating living people with their own lives, the writer approaches the mystery of eternity. It is not beauty, a human invention, which is of interest in art, but the pulsation of life.' Often his perspective on life seems bleak, offers no illusions about the prospects of improvement. His first novel, *Ion* (1920), is striking for the cold detachment with which the author allows the land-hungry young peasant Ion to satisfy his greed for gain at any cost. Ion is completely dominated by primitive egotism, fuelled by a desire to advance his social status. At the level of personal relationships the author breaks free from the mould in which the Transylvanian village is presented in earlier Roumanian literature as a place of bucolic stability, upheld by a ritual cycle of custom, and by the acceptance of a social hierarchy spanning the landless labourer, the landowning peasant, the schoolteacher, and the priest. *Ion* challenges these assumptions, first by showing how the hero's quest for land threatens the social status quo, and secondly by depicting the harshness of life on the land. Absent from the novel is the nostalgia for the village evident in the work of uprooted Roumanian Transylvanian writers disillusioned with urban life. The reader's sense of inevitability about Ion's premature death in a duel is matched by a similar feeling concerning the hero's destiny in *Pădurea spînzuraţilor* (The forest of the hanged, 1922), which is based on the fate of the author's brother Emil, hanged for attempted desertion from the Austro-Hungarian Army in 1917 when faced with fighting fellow Roumanians. The novel follows the crisis of conscience of a soldier in whom the bond of national brotherhood proves stronger than his sense of duty to the state. The protagonist, Apostol Bologa, is a citizen of the State and the State demands discipline and devotion; yet his sense of belonging to a people or nation derives from an instinctive love and in displaying that love he discovers his own self. Bologa's dilemma can be seen in terms of a dialectic between the real and the ideal, the real being his sense of obligation to the State or to a society, and the unreal being a natural attachment to the nation or community. *The Uprising* (1932) conveys the social pressures leading to the peasant revolt of 1907 and is memorable for its depiction of a restless Roumanian society which, in memorable crowd scenes, explodes into violence.

●*The Uprising* [*Răscoala*] (London, 1964); *Ion* (London, 1965); *The Forest of the Hanged* (London, 1967).   DJD

REJ OF **NAGŁOWICE, Mikołaj** (1505–69), Polish poet, prose writer and translator, traditionally called 'the father of Polish literature', was indeed the first major author in the early Renaissance, an epoch of either Latin or bilingual authors, to choose Polish as the sole language of his literary expression. A country squire with almost no formal education, he was self-taught (he learnt Latin by himself, too) and was well versed in the arts. His use of the vernacular was a deliberate choice, symptomatic of the awakening of a sense of national identity at this stage of the Renaissance. The vast oeuvre of Rej mainly consists of didactic, descriptive or satiric works ranging from enormous treatises or dialogues in verse or prose (such as those collected in his *Zwierciadło* [A mirror, 1568]) to relatively brief epigrams. He felt at home in

different genres, and frequently drew from other, particularly Latin, authors, adapting, modernising and enlivening their works rather than merely translating them; thus, his play *Żywot Józefa* (The life of Joseph, 1545) is a creative adaptation of a medieval mystery play, and his *Kupiec* (The merchant, 1549) is a rewritten medieval morality play. As a writer, Rej lacks subtlety and artistic balance; his strengths are his passion for the particulars of life, resulting in colourful descriptions, and his robust style.

●Selected poems in B. Carpenter (Ed.), *Monumenta Polonica* (Ann Arbor, 1989).   StB

REYMONT, Władysław Stanisław (1867–1925), Polish novelist, the son of a village organist, trained as a tailor, subsequently joined a touring actors' company and later supervised railway workers. From 1893 he was able to support himself by writing and frequently travelled abroad. 1918–20 he twice visited the United States, soliciting aid for independent Poland. He was awarded the Nobel Prize for Literature in 1924. Reymont's singular life experiences are reflected in his fiction, appreciated more for its realistic observation than intellectual content. Initially he published short stories about peasants, ranging from Naturalist, impassive descriptions of their struggle for survival to idealised portrayals of their dignity and religiousness. The novel *Ziemia obiecana* (The promised land, 1889), depicting the new textile centre Łódź, reflects Reymont's anxiety about urban corruption, allegedly acceptable to Germans and Jews but alien to the rural purity of the Polish mind. The panoramic cross-section of the city's population contains shocking portrayals of human greed and bestiality, shown against a background of demonic factories and the garish mansions of businessmen. Reymont's best-known novel, *Chłopi* (The peasants, 1904–9), attracted international recognition. Intended as an epic of country life, it blends realistic details and a Naturalist approach to human character with high style, deployed in lofty descriptions of farming, religious festivals and dignified ploughmen whose toils verge on ritual. The annual cycle of the seasons, beginning with autumn, divides the novel into four parts within which changing Nature is paralleled by corresponding stages in the cultivation of land and Church festivals. Interrelations between the sacred and the profane universalise Reymont's world into an image of the human condition, where death is part of Nature and God is present throughout everyday existence.

●*The Promised Land* (London, 1927); *The Peasants* (New York, 1924–5). J. R. Krzyżanowski, *Wladislaw S. Reymont* (New York, 1972); F. L. Schoell, *'Les Paysans' de Ladislas Reymont* (Paris, 1925).   SE

ŘEZÁČ, Václav (i.e. V. Voňavka, 1901–56), Czech novelist, son of a cabman, studied at commercial academy, worked at the State Statistical Office and later as a journalist; from 1949 he was the director of the Writers' Union publishing house. His novels written 1940–4, in which he analyses mental states and their manifestations in well-nigh psychotic individuals against the background of a society without moral values, represent, together with the novels of HOSTOVSKÝ, the chief works of Czech analytical prose. The passive embittered anti-hero of *Černé světlo* (Black light, 1940) tries to assert

himself by villainy; the egoistic old man in *Svědek* (The witness, 1942) discovers and incites the base instincts of his neighbours. Only the lonely, timid third-rate scribbler in *Rozhraní* (Borderline, 1944), who is struggling to compose a serious novel, achieves self-confidence by identifying himself with the successful actor whom he constructs for his novel. After the establishment of the Communist régime Řezáč turned to Socialist Realism, to praise of economic and social change in *Nástup* (Taking over, 1957) and the struggle of the Party with those who wanted to renew the capitalist order in *Bitva* (The battle, 1956).

●*Dark Corner* [*Černé světlo*] (Prague, 1963); *If the Mirror Breaks* [*Rozhraní*] (Philadelphia, 1959).   KB

RIMAY, János (c. 1570–1631), Hungarian poet, witnessed BALASSI's death and was his literary executor. He conscientiously adopted his master's themes and technique, but he was neither a serving soldier nor a passionate lover like him. His verse is characterised by a stoic acceptance of the state of the world as it is, with war and inflation raging. *Laus mediocritatis*, the title of one of his lyric verses, may be regarded as his main theme, and it is no surprise that he corresponded with the Dutch stoic Justus Lipsius. Rimay was a virtuoso poet with an enviable mastery of form and metre. His mannered style laid the foundations of Hungarian Baroque verse.

Selections in T. Klaniczay (Ed.), *Old Hungarian Literary Reader* (Budapest, 1985); *Rimay János összes művei* (Ed. S. Eckhardt) (Budapest, 1955).   GFC

RISTIKIVI, Karl (1912–77), Estonian prose writer, 1936–42 studied at the Mathematics and Natural Sciences Department of Tartu University.

He deserted from the German Army and fled to Finland; from 1944 he lived in Sweden, where he worked as an archivist in the Geography Institute of Uppsala University, then as a health-insurance clerk in Stockholm. He became one of the central figures of Estonian literature abroad. Following his 'Tallinn trilogy', *Tuli ja raud* (Fire and iron, 1938), *Võõras majas* (In a strange house, 1940) and *Rohtaed* (The garden, 1942), which traced the social atmosphere of Estonia from the end of the 19th century to the 1930s on the basis of characters from various classes, Ristikivi covered the events of 1939–40 in reflective novels written in exile. The planned trilogy, which began with *Kõik, mis kunagi oli* (Everything that once was, 1946) and *Ei juhtunud midagi* (Nothing has happened, 1947), remained unfinished as a result of the welter of exile literature on the subject, and Ristikivi concluded it indirectly with his Kafkaesque modular-prose portrait of the émigré psyche, *Hingede öö* (All Souls' night, 1953). In the 1960s he turned to the historical novel. The colourful style of his depictions of the Middle Ages and Renaissance combine adventure story and picturesque elements with those of a chronicle; he creates panoramas of the transformations of values and human beings seeking their place in their age: e.g. *Põlev lipp* (Flaming banner, 1961), *Surma ratsanikud* (Riders of death, 1963) and *Nõiduse õpilane* (The sorcery apprentice, 1967). The direct comparison and contrasting of past and present, which was evident in the historical utopia *Imede saar* (Miracle island, 1964), was often, in the last period of Ristikivi's writing, projected into a complex narrative which fused historical prose with contemporary social novel: *Õilsad südamed* (Noble hearts, 1970) and *Lohe hambad* (Dragon teeth, 1970).   VM

RITSOS, Yannis (b. 1909), Greek poet, was brought up in Monemvasia. His father's financial ruin in 1922, coming on top of the deaths of his mother and an elder brother from TB in 1921, set the seal of misery on his adolescence. 1925 he moved to Athens in search of work, but 1926 he too contracted TB and was in and out of sanatoria for the next eleven years. During the German occupation and the Civil War he enrolled in EAM (the left-wing resistance movement). Consequently, 1948 he was arrested and exiled for four years on the islands of Lemnos, Makronisos and Ayios Efstratios. The collection Αγρύπνια (Vigil, 1954) contains many poems reflecting his harrowing experiences from 1941 to 1952; it incorporates 'Romiosini', a tribute to the defeated left-wing resistance fighters and through them to all those past, present and future who had fought and would fight for Greece's freedom. Drawing its material from history, legend and folk-song, the poem is a defiant call for a socialist future. 1953–67 he concentrated on writing, but after the military coup he was arrested again, detained in various camps and eventually exiled to Samos. He became seriously ill and was only allowed to return to Athens after widespread European protests at the treatment accorded him. Γραφή των τυφλών (Scripture of the blind, 1979) reflects his experiences of this period. His work has received much international recognition, including the Lenin Prize (1977). His poetry is marked by a duality of the personal and political throughout, but both are approached via the emotions rather than the intellect. His first collections, Τρακτέρ (Tractor, 1934), Πυραμίδες (Pyramids, 1935) and Επιτάφιος (Burial Hymn, 1936), are notable for their social revolutionary content. The first two are still marked by a lyrical pessimism influenced by the work of KARIOTA-KIS, but Επιτάφιος, the lament of a mother for her son killed in a demonstration of unemployed tobacco workers, adds a new element derived from folk-song. The collections of the 1930s show considerable formal experiment, inaugurating in particular an important strand in his later style, the discursive, highly personal poem in which mood and musical flow control the development of the poem rather than theme or predetermined architecture. In Σημειώσεις στα περιθώρια του χρόνου (Notes in the margins of time, 1938–41) he revealed for the first time a need to express himself in a completely different form, the laconic, concrete, often symbolic, short poem in which opposing values and emotions, discordant objects and events are abruptly juxtaposed. Thereafter he moves unpredictably between the two styles, neither relating to a particular area of his thematic interests. Apart from those already named his major collections include Η σονάτα του σεληνόφωτος (The Moonlight Sonata, 1956), the three volumes of Μαρτυρίες (Testimonies, 1963, 1966, 1967) and Διάδρομος και σκάλα (Corridor and stairs, 1973).

•*Scripture of the Blind* (Columbus, Ohio, 1979); *Yannis Ritsos: Selected Poems 1938–1988* (New York, 1989).

CFR

ROBAKIDZE, Grigol (1884–1962), Georgian poet, novelist and dramatist, was literally and figur-atively entranced at the age of 7 by Goethe's 'Erlkönig'. He studied in Germany and returned to Georgia in 1908. In April 1911 he stunned the grand old man of letters, Ak'ak'i TS'ERETELI, with his lecture on Nietzsche; his poise and seniority made him in 1916 the effective leader of the Symbolist *tsisperq'ants'lebi* (Blue horns) group. His heroic stance was modelled on poets such as Bryusov and Gumilev (the Russian Rimbaud, but born in Georgia) and on Wagnerian myth. He attributed to the mountain tribes, such as the Khevsurs, and their legendary ancestors, such as Mindia, a primeval tragic heroism, but his verse developed along lines of European clarity. His personality allowed him to dominate post-revolutionary literary politics; he interpreted Lenin and Trotsky as elemental forces beyond morality or negation. His early prose, such as *Gvelis p'erangi* (The snake-skin shirt, 1926), portrays a British hero (Archibald MacAsh [*sic*]) discovering in a journey across ancient Persian sites his true Georgian self and accepting a primitive heroic destiny. The absurdity of plot and characterisation is mitigated by the intensity of Robakidze's aspirations. His dramatic work, such as his third play *Lamara* (1925–30), (after the unsuccessful *Londa* and *Malshtremi* [The maelstrom, 1923] also owes much to Gumilev's post-Symbolist drama, in which legendary heroes meet their deaths from bearers of an inferior civilisation. *Lamara*, however, in the extraordinary production by the autocratic director of the Rustaveli Theatre, Sandro Akhmet'eli, who despised most Georgian writers, was triumphant at the 1930 Moscow Olympiad of Drama. Two Khevsur twins, the poet-seer Mindia and the warrior Torghva, fall in love with an enemy girl, Lamara, who cannot tell them apart and marries the warrior by mistake. She dies and Mindia is inconsolable. Following up VAZHA PSHAVELA's *Gvelis mch'ameli*, Robakidze created a paean to the primitive, Nature-worshipping world of his tribesmen: the play triumphed because of, or despite, its total indifference to Soviet values. Its success was the first general acknowledgement by Russians of Georgian literature's worth. Robakidze and his wife were allowed by Orjonik'idze, Stalin's most trusted henchman at the time, to travel abroad (although Beria's GRU managed to prevent Akhmet'eli's Rustaveli Theatre from following and marked Akhmet'eli down for death). *Gvelis p'erangi* was published in Germany (1928) with an introduction by Stefan Zweig; knowing his fate at the hands of Beria, Robakidze defected to Germany, where he wrote in German several novels set in Georgia: of particular interest is *Die gemordete Seele* (The murdered soul, 1933) for its 'horoscope' of Stalin, a devastating, not entirely second-hand psychopathological study, in the context of an heroic self-portrait of the author as an anti-Bolshevik Svan with a belief in blood and sperm. *Die Hüter des Graals* (The guardians of the Grail, 1937) deals with Georgian resistance to the GRU. Robakidze won notoriety with an essay, *Adolf Hitler von einem fremden Dichter gesehen*. 1945 he fled to Geneva, where he reverted to Georgian: philosophical essays and a fragment of a novel, *Palest'ra* (Palaestra, a wrestling school), a view of 'Europe through an alien eye' dedicated to Zweig. Robakidze's defection was Beria's pretext for killing

his friends: Akhmet'eli, JAVAKHISHVILI, T'itsian T'ABIDZE. Yet *Lamara* was performed even in 1937, though with no mention of its author or first director; Robakidze's name was unspeakable in Georgia until 1987. Demonic, pretentious, often inspired and convincing, his poetic prose and drama have survived the 50 years' silence.

●N. Sombart, *Jugend in Berlin* (Frankfurt on Main, 1986), pp. 141–53; L. Magarotto, 'Nietzsche's Influence on the Early Work of Grigol Robakidze' in *Annali di Cà Foscari*, Venice, 1989, 3, pp. 97–109.   DR

ROIDIS, Emmanuel (1836–1904), Greek essayist, novelist and critic, whose family went to Genoa in 1841, returned to his native Syros alone in 1849 and went to school there. 1855–6 he studied literature and philosophy in Berlin. 1857–9 he worked in the offices of his maternal uncle's trading company in Braila, Roumania. From 1859 onwards he settled more permanently in Athens, and began his literary career by publishing translations from Chateaubriand. From the 1860s onwards he contributed to newspapers inside and outside Greece. His most important work of fiction, Η Πάπισσα Ιωάννα (Pope Joan), appeared in 1866. The only classic written in *katharevousa*, it uses the forged medieval tale of the female pope as the basis for a humorous, indeed satirical, look at all kinds of moral and religious issues. 1873 Roidis suffered severe financial difficulties, obliging him to devote more time to journalism and commercial translation. None the less he shows, from 1877 onwards, an increasingly liberal linguistic view on contemporary Greek writing and criticism. 1880 he was put in charge of the National Library. His other major work, Τα Είδωλα (Idols, 1893), is a collection of essays vigorously promoting various liberal intellectual causes.   CFR

ROSA, Václav Jan (c. 1620–89), Czech poet and philologist, doctor of laws and philosophy, after practising as a lawyer was appointed Counsellor of the Court of Appeals. His *Discursus Lypirona, to jest smutného kavalíra, de amore aneb o lásce* (Discursus of Lypiron, i.e. of a sad cavalier, de amore or on love, 1651) is an allegory comprising 24 songs with the total of 3,258 lines, introduced and connected by prose. The hero abandoned on an island dreams of a maiden who gives him a golden apple which changes into a ball of thread. Following the thread he arrives in a town where he sees a lady resembling the maiden, falls desperately in love and wants to kill himself. Fidelity and Fickleness try to dissuade him; Courage urges him on, but finally Venus discovers the name of the lady and orders Cupid to kindle love in her heart; the melancholy gallant identifies himself with his hero and decides to approach her. The work, exploiting the medieval dispute and combining echoes of late medieval erotic poetry with fashionable gallant verse, is outstanding for its rich vocabulary and metaphors. Equally accomplished is Rosa's spiritual poetry *Pastýřské rozmlouvání o narození Páně* (The shepherds' discourse on the Lord's birth, 1672), composed in quantitative verse. Rosa includes it in his *Čechořečnost seu Grammatica languae bohemicae*, 1672, where he proves himself a staunch defender of the Czech language, a purist and an indefatigable inventor of neologisms.
                                        KB

RÓŻEWICZ, Tadeusz (b. 1921), Polish poet, playwright, fiction writer and essayist, whose formative experience was WWII, worked as a manual labourer before joining 1943 a Home Army guerrilla unit. After the war, he read art history at Cracow. 1949 he settled in Gliwice, and since 1968 he has lived in Wrocław (formerly Breslau). Różewicz did not have to wait long for recognition: his first verse collection, *Niepokój* (Anxiety, 1947), was a sensation. What attracted the critics' attention was not so much its unflinching depiction of the brutality of war as its distinctly new diction, tone and style. Spoken, as it were, by an 'anonymous voice', the voice of an average witness to unspeakable horror, the poems' force derived from the straightforwardness of the testimony, stripped of the traditional features of poetic utterance. In his prolific production since *Niepokój*, Różewicz has remained faithful to this stylistic principle, while significantly broadening his themes and narrative perspective; since the early 1960s, his poems, in particular the long collage-poems, have focused on the ills of modern civilisation, and they have moved freely between the past and the present. Różewicz's first and arguably best-known play, *Kartoteka* (The card index), was staged in 1960. Of the numerous plays he has subsequently written, almost all are variations on the model first presented in *Kartoteka*, that of an open-ended dramatic construction with deliberately indefinable identities of characters. Drama of this kind exposes the fundamental doubt underlying Różewicz's work: whether the individual can attain a personal identity at all in a world devoid of values.

●*Selected Poems* (Harmondsworth, 1976); *Conversation with the Prince and other Poems* (London, 1982); *The Card*

Index and Other Plays (New York, 1969).   StB

RUMMO, Paul-Eerik (b. 1942), Estonian poet and dramatist; son of the poet Paul Rummo (1901–65), after reading, 1959–65, Estonian at Tartu, spent some time as literary adviser at the Vanemuine Theatre and the Tallinn Repertory Theatre; then he was a freelance writer. He worked in the *apparat* of the Writers' Union and, since 1989, a leading Liberal Democrat, has worked in the cabinet office of the Estonian Republic. His first work was the verse collection *Ankruhiivaja* (The anchor-weigher, 1962), and the further collection *Tule ikka mu rõõmude juurde* (Keep coming to my joys, 1964) became the unofficial manifesto of the younger generation. Rummo's lyric verse expressed most clearly of all the vitalism of his generation, which conceived of youth as elemental enchantment with a world whose horizons it could expand. But by the collection *Lumevalgus ... lumepimedus* (Snow light ... snow darkness, 1966) he is expressing an increasing consciousness of tragedy as an inevitable aspect of human existence. (His collected verse appeared as *Luulet 1960–1967* [Poetry 1960–7, 1968]). In these poems one sees signs of Rummo's later departure from richly metaphorical verse to the raw text. He would not agree to the censoring editor's corrections to the openly provocative *Saatja aadress* (Return address, which did not appear in full until 1989) and Rummo remained demonstratively silent for some years. A collection of his later verse, with a substantial selection from *Saatja aadress*, appeared under the title *Ajapinde ajab* (Agnails of time, 1985). Among the fruits of Rummo's work in theatre is the Absurdist

drama, the 'philosophical fairy tale', *Tuhkatriinumäng* (Cinderella play, 1969).

●*Cinderellagame* in *Confrontations with Tyranny. Six Baltic Plays* (S. Illinois, 1977), pp. 265–322. One poem in *Cross-Cultural Review Chapbook*, 16 (New York, 1981).

M. Valgemäe, 'Introduction to *Cinderellagame*' in *Confrontations with Tyranny*; M. Valgemäe, 'The Cinderella Skirmish. A Personal Chronicle', *Baltic Forum* 2, 1 (Spring 1985), pp. 70–87. VM

RUNEBERG, Johan Ludvig (1804–77), Finland-Swedish poet, short-story writer and playwright, was the first major Finnish literary figure. The son of a merchant-navy captain, after completing his studies at Helsinki University he combined university lecturing with teaching in the newly founded Helsinki grammar school and editing a newspaper. 1837 he left Helsinki to teach Classics at Porvoo grammar school. 1857 he retired to devote himself wholly to his writing. Like his contemporary LÖNNROT, Runeberg was educated in the Classical tradition and played a central role in the shaping of a Finnish national identity. Runeberg's main ideas were shaped by a blend of pantheism and Christianity, a devotion to Classical form and harmony, and the belief that only in Nature was man in his proper place. Central to his philosophy was the supreme importance of social stability and the view that man reaches perfection through a hierarchy of social unions in each of which he surrenders part of his own freedom for the greater good of the whole: family – community – nation – civilisation. Love plays a critical role in his earlier works. His own writings of the 1830s and 1840s created a gallery of characters perceived by successive generations as typically Finnish, providing stereotypes for imitation and, later, rejection. His Swedish translations of KARADŽIĆ's collections of Serbian lyric and epic folk poetry were to influence not only the style and content of his own lyric poetry, e.g. *Dikter* (Poems, 3 vols, 1830–43), but also the growing interest in Finnish ORAL POETRY. Cast in hexameters, the rhapsodic *Elgskyttarne* (The elk hunters, 1832) presents an idealised view of a nevertheless realistically described harmonious backwoods peasant society in which each person knows his place and in which everyone, including the beggars, is cared for. The elk hunt becomes the metaphorical backdrop for courtship. In *Hanna* (1836) and *Julqvällen* (Christmas Eve, 1841) the setting shifts to the Biedermeier homes of a pastor and an officer. The themes of love and self-sacrifice and social harmony are common to both. Man's behaviour in war recurs throughout Runeberg's work. It was present in *Elgskyttarne*, triggers the action in *Julqvällen* and is central to *Fänrik Ståls sägner* (The songs of Ensign Stål, 1848–60). Ever since their publication, the *Stål* collections (especially the first volume), set for the most part against the background of the 1808–9 Swedish-Russian War, have served as a powerful assertion of Finnish nationalism. Their message is, however, more complex. Not all the poems refer to a specific enemy, while others praise Russian bravery in the war, suggesting a universal statement about the duties of nationhood. In two later works, Runeberg uses tragic heroes from the Norse and Classical past to illustrate the retribution that will be brought on those who challenge the established order: the hero of *Kung Fjalar* (King F.,

1844) loses his son and daughter, while the usurper king in *Kungarne på Salamis* (The kings of S., 1863) kills his own son.

●*The Tales of Ensign Stål* (Helsinki, 1952); *King Fialar* (London, 1912).
T. Wretö, *J. L. Runeberg* (Boston, 1980); K. Laitinen, 'J. L. Runeberg: Time for Reappraisal', *Books from Finland* (1977), pp. 121–3; K. Nilsson, 'J. L. Runeberg as a Modern Writer', *Scandinavian Studies* (1986), pp. 1–9.

MAB

RUNNEL, Hando (b. 1938), Estonian poet and essayist, after matriculation, worked in a *kolkhoz* in the Paide district and gained his agricultural-college qualifications by correspondence course. 1966–71 he was on the editorial board of the literary magazine *Looming* and then he went freelance. 1989–90 he was deputy editor of the revived journal *Akadeemia*. His first two collections were *Maa lapsed* (Children of the earth, 1965) and *Laulud tüdrukuga* (Songs with a girl, 1967). From the very beginning, Runnel stood apart from his, formally, more aggressive contemporaries; he acquired his own special reserve as an authentic voice of the rural, a voice which approached the idea of national differentness. The simplicity of Runnel's poetic approach was rendered more profound by *Avalikud laulud* (Public songs, 1970) and *Lauluraamat* (Song-book, 1972) which frequently shared features in common with the 'rationalism' of the younger generation of the 1970s. The uncompromising stand of Runnel as citizen and poet (see *Punaste õhtute purpur* [The purple of crimson evenings, 1982]) actually predestined him to the role of the unofficial spokesman of the 1988 'Singing Revolution'. Many of Runnel's texts from the collection

Laulud eestiaegsetele meestele (Songs for the lads of Estonia's times, 1988), while in themselves attempts at the *lied*, became part of popular culture and, thus, a component of political rallies. His political stance is also clearly expressed in his publicist work, *Isamaavajadus* (The country's need, 1991).   VM

RUSTAVELI (RUSTVELI), Shota (?1166–?), the author of *Vepkhist' q'aosani* (The knight in the panther's skin), the greatest classic of Georgian secular literature, is believed to have been born in SW Georgia. He may have been the treasurer, even friend (and perhaps a distant relation) of Queen Tamar (reigned 1184–1213), under whom medieval Georgia enjoyed a flourishing, if brief, renascence. (He has also been identified as a feudal lord, Shota III of Hereti.) A portrait found this century in Jerusalem is alleged to be of Rustaveli: he may have undertaken a mission or pilgrimage to Palestine around 1192. Few poets of his stature have left so little proof of their existence. Apart from folk traditions, virtually all the evidence for his identity and personality has to be drawn from his sole extant work (though Rustaveli has been credited with an anonymous eulogy of Queen Tamar's reign): the 1,666 stanzas (each consisting of four sixteen-syllable rhyming lines) of *Vepkhist' q'aosani*. Stylistic analysis suggests that the prologue which introduces the poet and his ideas is by a different hand from the body of the text; there are many interpolations by an anonymous 'rhymester' of inferior or contradictory verse into the main text, perhaps to fill lacunae in the manuscripts. A canonical edition is problematic: the first extant manuscripts date almost four centuries after the likely time of composition;

the poem's first publication was King VAKHT'ANG VI's 1712 edition. The 1988 Academy edition, twenty years in the making, based on the 'symphonic' principles of Giorgi TS'ERETELI, is the best that can be envisaged. It is an extravagant tale of the search by the desperate Prince T'ariel (the knight in the panther's skin) for his captive betrothed, the Princess Nest'an-Darejan, and of the devoted self-sacrifice of his friend Avtandil, who also acts for love of Queen Tinatin. The story involves much combat against human and superhuman forces, and is very peripatetic: it is set in a hyperbolic Arabia, Persia, India and fantastic or demonic kingdoms; the characters' names suggest Persian influence. Clearly, Rustaveli was familiar with the Persian narrative tradition, e.g. Firdausi, who first had a knight in a panther skin (Rostom, *Shah-Nameh*). There are very many similarities in plot, characterisation, aphorism and metaphor to Georgian ROMANCES of the early 12th century, to the *Amiran-Darejaniani* with its Promethean hero fighting demons, and to the *Visramiani* (a Georgian version of Fakhruddin Gurgan's Persian *Vis-o-Ramin*), with its star-crossed lovers. But there is no reason to think Rustaveli's poem a translation of a lost Persian original. The poet's philosophy curiously avoids Christianity – Christ, the Trinity, the saints are never mentioned, although St Paul is cited – yet Rustaveli mocks Islam. Oaths are made to Zoroastrian and pagan formulae. Aphorisms and reflections shape the stanza structure, yet it is difficult to form a coherent picture of Rustaveli's mind: sometimes a neo-Platonist, sometimes baroque in his extravagant expostulations, he varies from extreme idealism to worldly scepticism. Often the pocm is a celebration of feudalism, courtly love and altruism, sometimes of common sense and worldly love; Rustaveli can be bloodthirsty in his descriptions of combat and yet humorous or sentimental. The optimistic conclusion with the triumph of love and friendship gives the work overtones of a political eulogy of contemporary Georgia. Even though its eccentricities (comparable with Spenser's *The Faerie Queen*) make it more a national than an international masterpiece, Rustaveli's poem is for Georgians what Dante's *Divine Comedy* is for Italians. Its aphorisms have become idioms; Georgian folklore and literature both quote the work. Its complex narrative structure and virtuoso rhyming suggest that it stands at the climax of a literary tradition, most of whose monuments have been lost. Verse translation into English has been too unimpressive to be mentionable, but Rustaveli's poetic technique loses less in heavily inflected languages: notable are the Russian version by Nutsubidze and recent Finnish translation (via the English) by Linnus.

●A. Baramidze (chief. ed.), *Vepkhist' q'aosani* (Tbilisi, 1988). Translations: M. S. Wardrop, *The Man in the Panther's Skin* (London, 1912, repr. 1966); K. Vivian, *The Knight in the Panther Skin* (London, 1977); R. H. Stevenson, *The Lord of the Panther-skin* (Albany, NY, 1977). C. M. Bowra, 'Rustaveli' in *Inspiration and Poetry* (London, 1955); W. Boeder, 'Stanza Structure and Cohesion in Rustaveli' in *Proceedings of the Turku Rustaveli Conference*, Studia Orientalia, forthcoming.   DR

RVAČOVSKÝ z RVAČOVA, Vavřinec Leander (1525–after 1590), Czech prose writer, Utraquist priest, composed the moralising allegory *Masopust* (Carnival, 1580) to warn young people against the licentious revelry occurring during carnival. The work begins with an accusation of the Devil for introducing the Saturnalia and Bacchanalia which had become the source of carnival festivities. After the explanation of Carnival's origin and power follows the most original part of the work. It introduces twelve sons of Carnival who personify various vices which befall people who succumb to Carnival's power. Their character and behaviour are illustrated by cautionary tales taken from the traditional collections of *exempla* as well as other sources. The story then returns to Carnival who in his pride decides to open legal proceedings against good Mr Quadragesima, i.e. Lent, who curtails his power. But he loses his case, is executed and buried. The work shows considerable erudition, great biblical knowledge, familiarity with history and astronomy as well as theology and court protocol. It presents a realistic picture of the debauchery of 16th-century life in outspoken, even drastic, language.   KB

RYL´S´KYI, Maksym (1895–1964), Ukrainian poet and translator, was a member of the Neoclassicist group. His first collection of verse appeared before the Revolution. In the 1920s, which marked the peak of his poetic achievement, he published *Pid osinnimy zoriamy* (Under the autumn stars, 1918), *Synia dalechin* (Sky-blue distance, 1922) and *Trynadtsiata vesna* (The thirteenth spring, 1925). His poems are rich in imagery and classical in form. In the early 1930s Ryl´s´kyi was briefly arrested and later released. As a result, he became a follower of the Party line, although occasionally during WWII he produced valuable work – – the long poem *Zhaha* (Yearning, 1943). After Stalin's death Ryl's'kyi sometimes returned to his earlier purely lyrical verse – in *Holosiivska osin* (The autumn of Holosiiv, 1959). Some of his poems (*Mandrivka v molodist* [Journey into youth, 1941–4]) had to be rewritten after sharp criticism. He did masterful translations from Polish and Russian poetry, and Shakespeare. In the early 1960s he defended young poets' right to detach themselves from Socialist Realism.

•*Selected Poetry* (Kiev, 1980).   GSNL

RYMKIEWICZ, Jarosław Marek (b. 1935), Polish poet, playwright, fiction writer, essayist, translator and critic, chief advocate of Classicism in Polish literature of the late 1950s–70, presented his programme in his original poetry and his translations (called by him 'imitations') and in a number of essay-manifestos (collected as *Czym jest klasycyzm* [The essence of Classicism, 1967]). During the 1970s–80s, however, his poetry has acquired a neo-Romantic vision and style. Since 1977 he has published four book-length semi-fictional essays on the chief figures of Polish Romanticism. In the 1980s he also issued two widely discussed novels, one dealing with Polish life under martial law and the other with the fate of Polish Jews. StB

RZEWUSKI, Henryk (1791–1866), Polish novelist, descended from a rich and very conservative family, represents traditional R. Catholicism, rooted in the philosophy of de Maistre, and a conciliatory attitude towards Russian rule. His *Pamiątki Pana Seweryna Soplicy . . .* (The memoirs of Mr Seweryn Soplica, 1839–41) imitates spoken tales (Polish *gawęda*) as narrated by a common nobleman of the 18th century and, by virtue of its imaginative reconstruction of bygone times, initiated a new literary genre in Polish literature. The novel *Listopad* (November, 1845–6) portrays the period of King Stanisław Poniatowski (latter half of the 18th century) and praises the virtues of rural traditionalism as opposed to cosmopolitan urban culture.   SE

S

SAARIKOSKI, Pentti (1937–83), Finnish poet, essayist and translator, was one of the greatest Finnish Modernists of the mid-twentieth century. Born into a middle-class family, well educated in the Classics, he abandoned his university studies at Helsinki to devote himself to a literary career. The formal rigour of the Classical tradition is apparent throughout his work. Saarikoski brought to Finnish poetry a new simplicity and a clarity of language and image through the use of everyday speech. His work was strongly influenced by Pound and by the experience of translating Joyce, Henry Miller and J. D. Salinger. An exuberant left-wing, often Stalinist, concern with public affairs, interspersed with personal sentiments, characterises his early poetry, *Runoja* (Poems, 1958), *Mitä tapahtuu todella* (What really happens, 1962) and *Kuljen missä kuljen* (I go where I go, 1965). In the late 1960s he travelled widely, producing a series of satirical but highly egocentric epistolary accounts: *Aika Prahassa* (The time in Prague, 1967), *Kirje vaimolleni* (Letter to my wife, 1968) and *Katselen Stalinin pään yli ulos* (I look out over Stalin's head, 1969). In the last years of his life, after settling in Sweden, his work regained its former capacity for innovation and incisive perception when he developed several Classical themes and forms in his trilogy, *Tanssilattia vuorella* (The dance floor on the mountain, 1977), *Tanssiinkutsu* (Invitation to the dance, 1980) and *Hämärän tanssit* (Dusk dances, 1983). Four key images dominate the trilogy: the Minotaur at the centre of the labyrinth, the snake, the dance floor, and the rowan tree. The poems convey Saarikoski's 'anguished experience of loss, perhaps of promise, certainly of friends, who still live with him as ghosts' (Lomas).

●*Helsinki* (Helsinki, 1965); R. Dauenhauer, P. Binham (Eds), *Snow in May. An Anthology of Finnish Writing 1945–1972* (Rutherford NJ, London, 1978), pp. 160–71; H. Lomas (Ed.), *Contemporary Finnish Poets* (Newcastle, 1991), pp. 176–210.

K. Simonsuuri, 'Myth and Material in the Poetry of Pentti Saarikoski since 1958', *World Literature Today* (Winter 1980), pp. 41–6; V. B. Leitch, 'The Post-modern Poetry of Pentti Saarikoski', *Scandinavian Review* (1982) 4 pp. 61–74; Lomas, pp. 36–41.

MAB

SADOVEANU, Mikhail (1880–1961), Roumanian novelist, son of a lawyer, was educated in his native Moldavia, had his first sketch published in 1897, and 1904 moved to Bucharest where four books of his appeared in that year: *Povestiri* (Stories), *Şoimii* (The hawks), *Dureri înăbuşite* (Suppressed pains) and

Crişma lui moş Precu (Old man P.'s bar). He soon became an inspector in the Ministry of Education, was director of the National Theatre 1910–19, and then moved to Iaşi to continue his writing. A string of novels followed evoking the history and landscape of his native land which were a great success with the public and critics alike: *Hanu Ancuţei* (Ancuţa's inn, 1928), *Baltagul* (The hatchet, 1930), *Zodia Cancerului* (The sign of Cancer, 1929), *Creanga de aur* (The golden bough, 1933), which owes only its title to Frazer's work, and *Fraţii Jderi* (The J. brothers, 1935–43). Elected MP in 1926 and president of the Senate in 1930–1, Sadoveanu aligned himself with the Communists after WWII and was appointed vice-president of the Grand National Assembly. His political affiliation was compounded by his recruitment to the methods of Socialist Realism. *Mitrea Cocor* (1949) is the story of an orphan who realises his ambition of working on a collective farm after the Communist takeover. Sadoveanu excels as a storyteller. He combines realistic portrayal of his peasant characters with high adventure and displays a powerful historical imagination based on solid learning. His descriptions and dialogue are enriched with the savour of local Moldavian dialect. *Baltagul* is the most enduring of his stories. As one critic observed, it raises the tale of a peasant woman's search for her murdered husband and his murderers to the dignity of a Classical tragedy. Sadoveanu describes with a simple directness the lives of the Carpathian shepherds and the narrative has the compulsive power of an accomplished detective story as it draws the reader along the trail followed by the widow and her young son.

●*Mitrea Cocor* (London, 1953); *The Hatchet* (London, 1965).   DJD

SAHLIKIS, Stefanos (c. 1331–c. 1391), Greek poet, the son of a wealthy family, appears to have led a misspent youth, wasting his family fortune and ending up in gaol. Eventually he managed to use his aristocratic connections to get himself appointed lawyer. Life and literature are closely connected in his case in that much of what is known about him derives from his poems, the Γϱάφαι καὶ στίχοι καὶ εϱμηνεῖαι (Writings and verses and interpretations), although there is sketchy documentary evidence for aspects of his story. One section of his writings (in 15-syllable verse) is couched as an admonition to Francesco, the son of a friend, not to follow his bad example. The other, the 'Strange narrative', is an 'autobiography' but rather in the sense that Villon's *Testament* is. His poetry contains a great deal about contemporary life, both in the country and the town, and a very colourful picture of the underworld, centring on taverns and brothels. The satirical portrait of the whores and the reproduction of their conversations is particularly striking.

●G. Wagner, *Carmina Graeca Medii Aevi* (Leipzig, 1874).   CFR

ŠANTIĆ, Aleksa (1868–1924), Serbian poet, was born in Mostar, Herzegovina. He attended commercial academies in Trieste and Ljubljana and then returned to his native city, where he was active in the cultural life of the Serbian community and edited literary journals. Šantić's early poems imitate NJEGOŠ, JOVANOVIĆ ZMAJ, JAKŠIĆ and ILIĆ. Later he developed his own style in erotic, patriotic and social poems, all of which are imbued with profound emotion, compassion and lyricism. Some of these poems were set to music and remain popular. Šantić also wrote two plays in verse. VDM

SANTORI, Françesk Anton (1819–94), Arbëresh (Italo-Albanian) poet and playwright, born in Santa Caterina in Cosenza of a poor peasant family, studied theology and passed most of his life in a monastery. Santori wrote much but he could publish only a few of his works. Among these are: a collection of lyric verse, *Il canzoniere albanese* (The Albanian song collection, c. 1845); the poems, *Valle e haresë së madhe* (Dance of great joy, 1848), published in DE RADA's periodical *L'Albanese d'Italia*, *Il prigioniere politico* (The political prisoner, 1850) containing Albanian and Italian verse; and the play *Emira* (E.) which appeared in part in DE RADA's journal *Fiamuri i Arbërit* (1886–87) and is the first original Albanian drama. Santori is the author also of an unfinished novel, *Sofia Kominiate*, adaptations of more than 100 Aesop fables, and of an Albanian grammar written in verse.

•F. Altimari, *Un saggio inedito di F. A. Santori sulla lingua albanese e i suoi alfabeti* (Cosenza, 1982). ShM

SARBIEWSKI, Maciej Kazimierz (1595–1640), Polish poet and literary theorist writing in Latin, a Jesuit since 1612, taught poetics and rhetoric in various Jesuit schools and at Vilnius Academy; he also lectured in Rome where he had an admirer in Pope Urban VIII. After 1635, he served as a court preacher to King Władysław IV (reigned 1632–48). Dubbed the 'Christian Horace', Sarbiewski was one of the most famous Latin poets of 17th-century Europe. His poetry was characteristic of the Jesuit cultural strategy aimed at combining the Classical heritage with Christian doctrine; as a result, his odes and epodes, while formally imitating Horace, contain typically Baroque conceits and images. Among his theoretical works, the treatise *De perfecta poesi* proved particularly influential. StB

SAYAT-NOVA (1712–95), like most Tbilisi Armenians, knew Georgian; as an *ashugh* (minstrel) he was uniquely polyglot. The Georgian poems of his *Davt'ar* (Collection) are lost, but about 30 (with distortions) survived in manuscript. Most were first published by GRISHASHVILI in 1918. Some are youthful (c. 1750), but at least two autobiographical lyrics, *She sats'q'alo chemo tavo*, 'O my poor self,' and *Samartali miq' av*, 'Do me justice', were written just before he took holy orders in 1768. Apart from four didactic poems, the rest are all songs of ardent love. Too passionate for conventional court *ashugh* lyrics, they may have been addressed to T'alita, a Catholic married woman. They are musical and ingenious – if clichéd – and may have stimulated BESIK'I's verse, but the Georgian consensus is that Sayat-Nova was a greater poet in Armenian, Azeri and Farsi. DR

SCHIRO DI MAGGIO, Giuseppe (i.e. Xhusepe Skiro di Maxho, b. 1944), Arbëresh (Italo-Albanian) poet and translator from Piana degli Albanesi in Sicily, studied literature and is now a teacher. Among his verse collections are *Nëpër udhat e parrajsit shoipëtarë e t'arbëreshë* (On the roads of Albanian and Arbëresh paradise, 1974), *Trima të rinj arbëreshë apo arësyeja e gjëravet* (New Arbëresh heroes or the origin of things, 1976) and *Gjuha e bukës* (The language of bread, 1981). He has also translated Leopardi. ShM

SCHULZ, Bruno (1892–1942), Polish short-story writer and artist, the son of middle-class Jewish parents from Drogobych (Galicia), studied architecture in Lwów (Lemberg) and painting in Vienna. His lonely life as a teacher in Drogobych was disrupted by the German invasion in 1939. Detention in the local ghetto was followed by death. Schulz is one of the most important representatives of Polish avant-garde fiction. With much in common with Expressionism and often compared with Kafka, he developed his own narrative technique. Unlike Kafka, he foregrounded his lyrical self against the subjective images of a reality founded on a specific conception of naming and of the role of words. In the short essay *Mityzacja rzeczywistości* (The mythologisation of reality, 1936) Schulz maintains that the poet defamiliarises words, restores their original meanings and thus regenerates primordial myths. Apart from a handful of critical essays on Polish and foreign writers, Schulz published only two books: *Sklepy cynamonowe* (Cinnamon stores, 1933) and *Sanatorium pod klepsydrą* (Sanatorium under the sign of the hourglass, 1936). They constitute two cycles of short stories, the former being more coherent and novelistic due to the continuity of its characters. Schulz's world is composed of elements taken from his environment, the trivial details of everyday reality, but transformed through his creative vision and inventive language into dreams, poetic wonders and mythological grandeur. It is a dynamic world of metamorphoses, filled with mutated shapes, and of the surreal, where pure fantasy enters bleak urban dwellings. His is also a syncretic world, where poetic creativity stemming from mythopoeic words is contrasted with the gruesome commercialism of the 'Street of Crocodiles', typified by monochrome photographs in dreary business brochures. The final triumph of clowns over a dreamer (the father) in the closing episode of *Sklepy cynamonowe* exemplifies this incompatibility. Schulz's striking drawings reflect in particular his masochistic obsession with sexually domineering women.

● *The Street of Crocodiles* (New York, 1963); *Sanatorium under the Sign of the Hourglass* (New York, 1978).

E. Goślicka-Baur, *Die Prosa von B. Schulz* (Berne, 1975); J. Ficowski (Ed.), *The Drawings of B. Schulz* (Evanston, Ill., 1990).   SE

SEFERIS, George (i.e. Yoryos Seferiadis, 1900–71), Greek poet and essayist, was born in Smyrna, but his family moved to Athens in 1914, when the position of the Greek community in Asia Minor deteriorated. 1918 Seferis went to Paris to study law, and remained there until 1924, perfecting his French, learning English and becoming acquainted with modern literature. The Asia Minor Disaster (1922) and the destruction of Smyrna left him with a sense of rootlessness which permeates his poetry. His subsequent career in the diplomatic service, with its constant changes of post, did little to counter that sense: he was successively in London, Albania, South Africa, Egypt (with the Greek Government in Exile) and only returned to Greece in 1944. His postwar career then took him to Turkey, London again, the Middle East, to the UN in New York and finally back to London for the third time, now as ambassador (1957–62). In this sensitive diplomatic post Seferis played a significant role in the negotiations which led to

Cypriot independence. 1963 he received the Nobel Prize for Literature. He retired to Greece during the military dictatorship. His last public act, an uncharacteristic one, was political: 1969 he issued a statement to the foreign press in which he openly condemned the Junta. Seferis's first published collection of poetry, Στροφή (Turning point, 1931), and his second, Η Στέρνα (The cistern, 1932), contain poems written in fairly traditional forms, and showing the influence of the French Symbolists. His discovery of T. S. Eliot in 1931 helped him to develop further, both in verse technique and in poetic manner. His first major work, the poem-cycle Μυθιστόρημα (Mythistorema), in 24 short sections, reminiscent of the books of a Homeric epic, came out in 1935, the year in which he helped found the influential Modernist periodical Τα Νέα Ρραμματα (New writing). His works of 1936 included his translation of Eliot's *The Waste Land*, the introduction to which marked Seferis's entry upon a substantial career as essayist and critic. The most significant of his poems of the late 1930s appeared under the title Ημερολόγιο καταστρώματος Α' (Logbook 1) in 1940, and the poems of exile in South Africa during the war were collected as 'Logbook 2' in 1944. Then, in 1946, Seferis wrote another extended poem, Κίχλη (Thrush), probably his most significant individual work. Thereafter his major work is the third 'Logbook' (1955), containing poems inspired by visits to Cyprus. He wrote one novel, Εξι νύχτες στην Ακρόπολι (Six nights on the Acropolis), on which he worked in the 1920s and again in the 1950s but which was only published, in more or less finished form, post-humously (1974). In his poetry Seferis explores the plight of modern man, but in a fundamentally Greek context. The timeless landscape of the Aegean, the myths of antiquity, references to different periods of history all mix with the artefacts and events of the modern world and with frequent and complex literary allusion, forming a pessimistic comment on human nature and the purpose and achievements of life. The essence of his poetry is fixed from *Mythistorema* onwards, but the postwar poetry is richer in its political and metaphysical implications.

•*Collected Poems 1942–1955* (bilingual ed.) (London, 1969).

R. Beaton, *George Seferis* (Bristol, 1991). CFR

ŠEGEDIN, Petar (b. 1909), Croatian prose writer, born on the island of Korčula, educated in Dubrovnik and Zagreb, has spent most of his life living in Zagreb as a freelance writer. His first novel, *Djeca božja* (Children of God, 1946), concerns his native village, the mentality of the villagers, particularly the children, and the influence of the R. Catholic Church. The modern, stream-of-consciousness approach of the work and its measured, expressive language guaranteed Šegedin a central place in contemporary Croatian literature, confirmed by his later works: his collections of short stories published in the 1960s, *Orfej u maloj bašti* (Orpheus in a small garden, 1964), *Sveti vrag* (Holy devil, 1966), *Tišina* (Silence, 1982), his novel *Vjetar* (Wind, 1986), and several volumes of essays. He has also been active in the programme of Croatian democratisation in the late 1960s and early 1970s, as may be seen in his *Svi smo mi odgovorni* (We are all responsible, 1971).

•'His Window' in A. Stipčević (Ed.), *An Anthology of Yugoslav Short Stories* (New Delhi, 1969), pp. 126–39; 'Holy devil', *The Bridge* (1970), pp. 123–31; 'The Marriage of Figaro' in *IYL*, pp. 474–90.   ECH

SEIFERT, Jaroslav (1901–86), Czech poet, left grammar school before doing his matriculation and immediately started his literary career. 1929 he was expelled from the CP; for a brief period at the end of the 1960s he was head of the Writers' Union, signed Charter 77 and, 1984, became the first Czech writer to win the Nobel Prize for Literature. His first work of Proletarian Poetry, *Město v slzách* (City in tears, 1921), is a vigorous tendentious collection of spontaneous revolutionary songs; the poet enthusiast sees himself as a prophet besinging the glorious future that awaits the poor and downtrodden. With *Na vlnách TSF* (On the wireless waves, 1925) Seifert expresses modern life as poetry and poetry as life; the poet is a clown (see the typographical experimentation) talking about love and the whole beloved world which surrounds that love. Much of the collection consists in jolly visual or verbal jokes. His post-WWII verse manifests over-sentimentalisation (*Maminka* [Mummy, 1954]), facile nostalgic impressionism (*Koncert na ostrově* [Island concert, 1965]), slightly self-ironic confessional nostalgia (*Morový sloup* [The plague column, 1977]) and a sometimes mawkish, almost childish, gratitude to life (*Deštník z Piccadilly* [Umbrella from Piccadilly, 1979] and *Býti básníkem* [Being a poet, 1983]); the last two also show Seifert as something of a peace-freak. His autobiographical sketches, *Všecky krásy světa* (All the beauties of the world, 1981), while containing useful information about acquaintances, predominantly consists in musing about women, particularly their bodies.

•*The Selected Poetry of Jaroslav Seifert*, ed. G. Gibian (New York, 1986); *The Plague Column* (London, 1979); *An Umbrella from Piccadilly* (London, 1983).

W. E. Harkins, 'On Jaroslav Seifert's *Morový sloup*' in *Cross Currents. A Yearbook of Central European Culture*, 3 (Ann Arbor, 1984), pp. 131–5; A. French, *The Poets of Prague. Czech Poetry Between the Wars* (London, 1969); A Brousek, 'Jaroslav Seifert' in W. Kasack (Ed.), *Zur tschechischen Literatur 1945–1985* (Berlin, 1990), pp. 63–80.   RBP

SELIMOVIĆ, Meša (1910–82), Serbian fiction writer, was a native of Tuzla, Bosnia. He was a teacher at his hometown secondary school. In WWII he fought with the partisans. He died in Belgrade. His first book, a novel *Tišine* (Silences, 1950), was followed by several collections of short stories and other novels, of which *Derviš i smrt* (Dervish and death, 1966), *Tvrdjava* (Fortress, 1970) and *Ostrvo* (The island, 1974) are the most accomplished. They manifest incisive psychological analysis and concentrate on extreme mental and social states like war, the lust for power, greed and injustice.

•*The Island* (Toronto, 1983).   VDM

SELIŠKAR, Tone (1897–1969), Slovene poet and prose writer, journalist and translator, published his first collection of verse, *Trbovlje*, in 1923; this was verse of social protest against the harsh life of coalminers, Expressionist, with difficult imagery, in *vers libre*. He later reverted to a simpler style, as in the cycle *Iz dnevnika komisarja za ljudsko štetje* (From the journal of a census officer), which appeared in his second collection, *Pesmi pričakovanja* (Poems of expectation, 1937).

•*AMYP*; *Parnassus*. HL

ŠENOA, August (1838–81), Croatian prose writer, born in Zagreb into a family of Czech origin, studied law at Prague but devoted most of his time to literature and politics. He lived in Vienna for some years, but returned to Zagreb in 1866, entering government service and eventually becoming a senator. 1874–81 he edited the most important Croatian literary journal, *Vijenac* (The wreath), making it a vehicle for serious critical comment. He first wrote short stories of everyday urban and village life, and short sketches, published as *Zagrebulje* (Zagreb sketches, 1866–7). These contained the germ of his historical novels, the first extended prose works in Croatian literature, manifesting a blend of Romantic themes and treatment, and a methodical approach more readily associated with later Realist prose. His first novel, *Zlatarevo zlato* (The goldsmith's gold, 1871), describes the struggle of the people of Zagreb for justice as they are subjected, collectively and individually, to violent abuse by an aristocrat, with whose son the goldsmith's daughter (the 'gold' of the title) is in love. The main characters are oversimply described; the strength of the work lies in the depiction of daily life in Zagreb in the late 16th century. It remains immensely popular with a wide reading public. The same is true of Šenoa's other, best-known, novel, *Seljačka buna* (The peasant revolt, 1877), a vivid account of the origins, progress and ultimate defeat of the revolt of 1573. His other historical novels are *Čuvaj se senjske ruke* (Beware the hand of Senj, 1875), set in Senj,

Dalmatia, the centre of piracy and brigandage; and *Diogenes* (1878), depicting 18th-century Croatian society in a way that invites parallels with Šenoa's own day and has led it to be seen as the most 'contemporary' of his novels. While the longer novels remain the most popular of Šenoa's works, his novella *Prosjak Luka* (L. the beggar, 1879) is generally considered his masterpiece. The main character is one of the most complex in his whole oeuvre. It has been said that Šenoa's outstanding contribution to Croatian literature lies not so much in any one of his prolific works, but in their sum. One of his main achievements was the creation of a reading public by writing in a style that would have wide popular appeal. In his critical essays, he expresses his impatience with the general provision of imported reading material available in his day, pale descriptions of events that could have happened anywhere, and his energetic conviction that for a nation's literature to have meaning it must be rooted in the specific events of that nation's history.

•*The Peasant Rebellion* (abridged) (Zagreb, 1973); 'The Cobbler and the Devil', *The Bridge*, 50 (1976), pp. 37–41.

ECH

SĘP SZARZYŃSKI, Mikołaj (1550?–81), the most intriguing of all Polish authors of the 16th century, a fully-fledged Baroque poet who lived in the Renaissance and long before the emergence of the Baroque proper in Polish literature, was born into a noble family and sent to study in Wittenberg and Leipzig; this is interpreted as an indication that he was a Protestant in his youth. Back home, he spent the rest of his brief life in his family estates near Lwów and

Przemyśl. Only a small fraction of Sęp Szarzyński's work has been preserved in the form of his posthumous collection of poems, mostly sonnets, songs and paraphrases of the Psalms, published by his brother in 1601 as *Rytmy abo Wiersze polskie* (Polish rhythms or verses). His sequence of six sonnets, in particular, shows him as a profound metaphysical poet. Preoccupied with the world's instability and transitoriness, fearful of the randomness of Fortune's decrees and man's freedom of choice, he reveals an acute sense of man's solitude in the universe. The individual soul, naturally weak and constantly tempted to sin, can find solace only in hoping for God's grace – this, however, works in a manner beyond human comprehension. The only behaviour worthy of the pious soul is incessant struggle, Christian heroism. The paradoxes of Sęp's philosophy and theology find a consistent reflection in his complex style, where tortuous syntax, violent enjambments and oxymoronic imagery portray a mind torn by spiritual torment. His ascetic religiousness and the exacting nature of his philosophy and poetics could hardly be adopted by the later poets, and so his collection sank into oblivion; it was rediscovered only in the 20th century.

•Selected poems in B. Carpenter (Ed.), *Monumenta Polonica* (Ann Arbor, 1989).
R. Sokoloski, *The Poetry of Sęp-Szarzyński* (Wiesbaden, 1990).   StB

SEREMBE, Zef (i.e. Giuseppe S., 1843–1901), Arbëresh (Italo-Albanian) Romantic poet, one of the most original lyric poets in Albanian literature, was born in Stringari (San Cosmo Albanese) in Cosenza and though of a poor family, travelled widely throughout Italy and France trying to win support for the Albanian cause. He studied at the San Adriano College where he was taught by DE RADA. 1875 he sailed for Brazil, from where he soon returned to Europe disappointed and dejected. On his way home, he lost most of his manuscripts (poetry, dramas and a translation of the Psalms). Those of his poems that survived were published by his grandson Cosmo Serembe. Towards the end of his life, he emigrated again to S. America, managing this time to start a new life in Buenos Aires, but a few years later, mentally exhausted, he died in São Paolo. His verse is pessimistic but often also idealistic, and patriotic in inspiration. In his lifetime, some of his early poems appeared in journals and in the bilingual collection *Poesie italiane e canti originali tradotti dall' Albanese* (Italian poetry and original songs translated from the Albanian, Cosenza, 1883). Othr verse was published as *Vjersha* (Verse, 1926). ShM

SHANOUR, Shahan (1903–74), Armenian novelist, like many Armenian intellectuals in Istanbul, emigrated to France in 1923 and settled in Paris, where he worked in a bookshop, as a freelance retoucher of photographs and then as a studio photographer. This experience furnished him with the background for his autobiographical masterpiece. He read literature at the University of Paris 1928–32. He fell ill in 1931 and, apart from some forty years he spent in various hospitals in France, he resided mainly in a cheap attic room in a Paris hotel. He started writing in French from the time he settled in France under the pseudonym of Armen Lubin. The first published work under that name appeared in 1939 in *NRF*, with stories based on hospital life. These were later included in his only volume of French prose, *Transfert nocturne* (1955). He gained fame in French mainly as a poet, e.g. *Le Passager clandestin* (1946), *Sainte Patience* (1951), *Les hautes Terrasses* (1957) and *Feux contre feux* (1968). Shanour's literary output in Armenian consisted of his autobiographical novel, *Nahanj aṙants ergi* (Retreat without song, 1929), which bore the subtitle, 'An illustrated history of Armenians'. In the 1920s, Armenian writers in France tried to reassess Armenian· literature and to incorporate contemporary literary trends in their own writing. They formed a group called Menk' (We) in the early 1930s and had their own magazine. They felt that Armenians had become lethargic and were trammelled up in superstition and tradition, so that there was an urgent need for a renewal. It was in that mood that he produced his novel concerning half a dozen Armenian boys, mainly from Constantinople, stranded in Paris, who retreat from their Armenianness and become assimilated. Predatory Parisian females charm one Armenian boy in one direction and lead another in another. Some married. Others kept mistresses. Armenian girls with unseeded wombs wait and wilt. Fewer and fewer letters are sent to their parents back home. Shanour's main target is GRIGOR NAREKATSI and his book of elegies. It is, we are told, the most immoral, unhealthy, poisonous book, a work that had debilitated the Armenians as a nation. The Armenians remain defeated in trying to emulate GRIGOR's miserable, maimed soul. 'We are Orientals and we believe in what is called Fate – what is written on our foreheads. Some of it is inscribed in Indian ink; the rest is jotted down with pencil

and then there are smudges of dust. It is up to us to change this at last.' Shanour's attack on his people arises from his deep love for them.   VN

SHANSHIASHVILI, Sandro (i.e. Aleksandre Sh., 1888–1979), Georgian poet, was noted for his drama in verse and prose. In 1908 revolutionary fervour landed him in prison: he began writing long poems based on Greek and Semitic legends of Colchis. Travels to Berlin and Zürich (1911–12) brought the influence of Symbolist narrative poetry. He showed a gift for dramatic verse and sensitive translation in his adaptation of Edmond Rostand's *La Princesse lointaine* (1919). Twenty years of his lyrics are gathered in *Gavlili shara* (The high road I have travelled, 1925): his best poems, even the shortest, either tell a story, e.g. the charming *Shveli da monadire* (Roe-deer and hunter, 1909), or idealise a woman. By the 1920s Shanshiashvili longed for the heroic: 'I sing of chivalry to fire the timid' (*Genesis*, 1922). At last, in 1930, he achieved heroic notoriety throughout the USSR with *Anzor*, his adaptation of 'Armoured Train 14–69', a Russian Civil War play by Vsevolod Ivanov. The action was transferred to Dagestan, the White Army deleted, and the Chechen hero Anzor Cherbizh became an idealised heroic tribesman. The original end, in which a Chinese revolutionary lies down on the railway line to stop the armoured train, is replaced by a *lezginka* danced by Zaira, whose choice of partner decides the victim of the train. Ivanov's bleak Siberian realities give way to a rich, legendary Caucasian world of song and dance. Sandro Akhmet'eli, director of the Rustaveli theatre, collaborated in this transformation of a classic of Socialist Realism into a Wagnerian spectacle, very like ROBAKIDZE's *Lamara*. The 'left', including the Futurist poet Simon CHIKOVANI, attacked *Anzor* for trivialising the Revolution. Despite his willingness to praise Stalin as early as 1931 ('Were I to compare you to a titanic oak . . .'), association with Akhmet'eli and ROBAKIDZE was to endanger Shanshiashvili in the purges of 1937. He was accused of failing to denounce others; he even tried to speak up for the doomed P'aolo IASHVILI, but expiated these sins by writing a 'Song to Lavrent'i Beria'. His later dramas draw factually on the catastrophes of 18th-century Georgia (*K'rts'anisis gmirebi* [The heroes of K'rts'anisi, 1942]; *Imeretis ghameebi* [Imeretian nights, 1945]) or return to a fantasised Civil War (*Okt'ombris zeimi* [October triumph, 1944]).   DR

SHEVCHENKO, Taras (1814–61), Ukraine's greatest poet, was born a serf. His freedom was purchased in 1838 and he enrolled as a student in the St Petersburg Academy of Fine Arts. At that time he also began to write poetry, and 1840 published his first collection, *Kobzar* (The minstrel). His long poem *Haidamaky* (The Haidamaks, 1841) was attacked by Visarion Belinski, who considered writing in Ukrainian a fruitless pursuit. 1843–4 Shevchenko made extended trips to Ukraine and wrote many of his political poems attacking the Tsarist system and the Tsar himself (the poem 'Son', Dream). His poems, collected in a notebook *Try lita* (Three years, 1843–5), were not for publication but circulated among his friends. 1845–7 he lived in Ukraine, and he joined the Kiev secret Brotherhood of SS Cyril and Methodius headed by Mykola Kostomarov (1817–85), espousing a

Christian Utopia and pleading for Ukraine to become a free member of a Slav federation. 1847 Shevchenko was arrested along with other 'brethren' and after a short trial in St Petersburg was sentenced to serve as a soldier in a remote corner of the Empire for the rest of his life. During his exile he continued to paint and to write. He also wrote short stories and a journal in Russian. After the death of Nicholas I, Shevchenko was pardoned and returned, in 1858, to St Petersburg. He wrote two splendid long poems, 'Neofity' (The neophytes, 1857) and 'Maria' (1859), as well as some exquisite short lyrics. He died in St Petersburg. His early works were often Romantic ballads and historical poems, glorifying Ukraine's past. A sharp critic of tsardom, Shevchenko also often castigated his countrymen for their servility and lack of national pride. The very structure of his poems is mythopoeic. In Ukraine there exists a veritable cult of Shevchenko as both poet and prophet.

●*The Poetical Works of Taras Shevchenko* (Toronto, 1964); *Selected Poems* (Jersey City, 1945); *Song out of Darkness* (London, 1961).
P. Zaitsev, *Taras Shevchenko: A Life* (Toronto, 1988); G. Luckyj (Ed.), *Shevchenko and the Critics* (Toronto, 1980); G. Grabowicz, *The Poet as Mythmaker* (Cambridge, Mass., 1982).
                                        GSNL

SHEVCHUK, Valerii (b. 1939), is the leading contemporary novelist in Ukraine. He is the author of *Naberezhna 12* (12 The Esplanade, 1968), with its Existentialist overtones, and *Vechir sviatoi oseni* (A blessed autumn evening, 1969). During the 1970s Shevchuk concentrated on translating Ukrainian medieval and Baroque texts into modern Ukrainian. 1979 he published a collection of short stories, *Kryk pivnia na svitanku* (Cockcrow at dawn), and a novel, *Na poli smyrennomu* (On a submissive field), in which he ventured into the supernatural. A great mythological prose achievement was *Dim na hori* (The house on the hill, 1983). Then, 1986, he published the accomplished historical novel *Try lystky za viknom* (Three leaves outside the window). 'He seeks an alternative to authority itself; an escape from the world's structures, the baroque ideal most frequently invoked . . . might well serve as an emblem of his work as a whole' (Marko Pavlyshyn, 1991). Shevchuk is committed to writing cycles of historical novels in order, in his own words, 'to find the history of human souls'. His narrators are philosophers who try to rationalise the irrational flow of history. His heroes are exceptional people whose life stories have a similar meaning whatever the century. The evocation of the past to understand the present is a distinguishing feature of contemporary Ukrainian prose (Pavlo Zahrebelny [b. 1924]) and poetry (KOSTENKO).

● 'The Cobbler' and 'My Father Decided to Plant Orchards' in G. and M. Luckyj (Eds), *Modern Ukrainian Short Stories* (Littleton, Col. 1973).

M. Pavlyshyn, 'Mythological, Religious and Philosophical Topoi in the Prose of Valerii Shevchuk', *Slavic Review* (Winter 1991), pp. 905–14.   GSNL

SHKRELI, Azem (b. 1938), Albanian poet and prose writer from Kosovo, was born in Shkrel near Pejë and studied Albanian at Prishtinë, was president of the Writers' Union, a theatre director in Prishtinë, and head of the 'Kosovo Film' studios. Both his prose and his highly expressive poetry deal with life in the Rugova mountains and the conflict between traditional ways of life and modern society. Among his major publications are the collections of verse *Engjujt e rrugëve* (The angels of the roads, 1963), *E di një fjalë prej guri* (I know a word of stone, 1969), *Pagëzimi i fjalës* (The baptism of speech, 1981), the short-story collection *Sytë e Evës* (Eve's eyes, 1965), the novels *Karvani i bardhë* (The white caravan, 1960) and *Lotët e maleve* (The mountain tears, 1974); and the drama *Varri i qyqes* (The cuckoo's grave, 1983).   ShM

SHKRELI, Ymer (b. 1945), Albanian writer from the Rugova region near Pejë, attended school and university in Prishtinë. He is among the most prolific of Kosovo writers, with prose works for adults and children. He has also written plays and filmscripts. Among his publications are the collections of verse *Ditari i Hajnit* (Heine's diary, 1971) and *Balcanica* (1980), the novels *Njeriu në bisht* (The squatter, 1975) and *Pikëpjekja* (The meeting, 1982), the short stories *Bima e dreqit* (The devil's plant, 1981) and the play *Triologji ilire* (Illyrian trilogy, 1977).   ShM

SHOLEM ALEYKHEM/ Shalom/ Sholom Aleichem (i.e. Sholem Rabinovitsh, 1859–1916), regarded as one of the three major classical writers of Yiddish literature, together with MENDELE MOYKHER SFORIM and PERETS, was born in Pereyaslav in the Ukraine. By canonising MENDELE as the 'grandfather' of Yiddish literature and castigating the facile pulp-fiction of Shomer (1849–1905), he brought aesthetic criteria to bear on Yiddish literature and became the first to see himself as occupying a position within a literary tradition. With a fortune inherited from his father-in-law, Sholem Aleykhem was able to promote his vision of Yiddish writing capable of standing comparison with other literature in his lavishly produced 'Di yidishe folksbiblyotek' (The popular Jewish library, vols 1 and 2, Kiev, 1888–9) in which *inter alia* he published works by MENDELE, LINETSKI and PERETS as well as early versions of his own novels, 'Stempenyu' and 'Yosele solovey'. These are both restrained, sad love stories in which self-fulfilment is sacrificed to traditional concepts of chastity and in which Sholem Aleykhem was not entirely successful in reconciling form and content. The Folksbiblyotek-project was abandoned in 1890 when Sholem Aleykhem lost his fortune on the stock exchange. Lacking suitable, regular outlets for Yiddish works, he turned for a while to writing in Russian. It was during this period, inspired largely by Gogol''s *skaz*-monologues, that Sholem Aleykhem found the style most suited to his genius. 1892 he began the serialisation of his epistolary satire *Menakhem-mendl*, and 1894 he initiated the most successful and famous of his *feuilleton* series, *Tevye der milkhiker* (Tevye, the milkman). In both these series, which he continued to produce almost up to the time of his death, he created personae whose voices enabled him to express his ironic view of a traditional society in crisis. In *Ayznban-geshikhten* (Railway stories), which appeared 1902–11, Sholem Aleykhem skilfully exploited a situational framework of fleeting encounters to paint a picaresque composite picture of the precarious economic circumstances of Jews attempting to make a living in the Pale of Settlement. Most of his fiction, which also included the stor-

ies he wrote for Jewish holidays and his many children's stories, appeared in the first instance as *feuilletons* in various papers, being collected in book form usually at a much later date. In later life Sholem Aleykhem returned to the novel. In *Motl peysi dem khazns* (M. Peysi the cantor's son, serialised 1907–16), he succeeded in combining a continuous narrative with the distancing voice of a narrator, in this case that of an 8-year-old boy who perceives only the opportunities for childish adventure as his widowed mother is turned out of her home and the family emigrates to the USA. On several occasions Sholem Aleykhem tried writing for the stage, but without great success. Generally speaking dramatisations of his stories by other hands achieved lasting fame, most notably the Tevye-stories which eventually became the musical, *Fiddler on the Roof*. Sholem Aleykhem was at work on his lightly fictionalised autobiography, *Funem yarid* (From the fair), at the time of his death. In his multifarious works, which constitute a Jewish *comédie*, portraying the transition from the old order of traditional life to modern times, there runs the theme of unrealisable aspiration, followed by catastrophe and renewed hope, epitomising courage in adversity and survival against all odds both in the Old World and the New.

●*The Best of Sholom Aleichem* (New York, 1982[2]); *Marienbad* (New York, 1982); *From the Fair, the Autobiography of Sholem Aleichem* (New York, 1985); *Tevye the Milkman and the Railroad Stories* (New York, 1987).
S. Gittelman, *Sholom Aleichem* (The Hague, 1974); M. Samuel, *The World of Sholom Aleichem* (London, 1973[2]); M. Waife-Goldberg, *My Father Sholom Aleichem* (London, 1968).   HD

SHOPOV, Atso (b. 1923), Macedonian poet and translator, read philosophy at Skopje; 1947 he became a publisher's editor while also editing literary journals such as *Nov den* (New day), *Idnina* (Future) or *Savremenost* (Today); he became director of a publishing house; he has also worked as a diplomat. 1967 he was accepted as one of the first members of the Macedonian Academy of Arts and Sciences. Shopov's early verse, published in the 1940s, comprises an apotheosis of national revolution and the building of Socialism (*Pesme* [Songs, 1945]) and *Nashim rukama* (With our own hands, 1950). His verse became more personal in his collections *Stihovi za makata i radosta* (Poems on torment and joy, 1953) and *Sley se so tishinata* (Fuse with the silence, 1955), concerned with such themes as loss, grief, parting, resignation, tiredness with life. The prevailing mood in these collections is melancholy arising out of the awareness of misfortune as the inevitable lot of man; 'silence' (introverted self-questioning), 'white sorrow' and 'white dream' (compassion, love, beauty) possess a liberating power. Self-questioning and the quest for self-definition and for the meaning of art become his main themes in *Vetrot nosi ubavo vreme* (The wind brings nice weather, 1958), *Nebidnina* (A dream that never comes true, 1963) and *Gledach vo pepelta* (The ember gazer, 1970). Love receives particular attention in *Nebidnina* where in the cycle 'Molitvi na moeto telo' (The prayers of my body) Shopov perceives love as the life-force through which knowledge and understanding of life, beauty and death are obtained. Some of his verse is sensualist and Shopov also writes as a hedonist (e.g. his 'African motifs' in *Pesen na crnata*

zhena [The song of the black woman, 1975]), although his poetic meditations are imbued with bitterness. SIK

SIAMANT'O (i.e. Atom Eartcanian, 1878–1915), Armenian writer, born in Akn, near Kharberd, was educated in Constaninople and at the Sorbonne (1897–1900). He travelled widely in France, England and the US. The change in the political scene in his native land brought him back in 1908 (Second Ottoman Constitution). After the Adana massacres of 1909, Siamant'o arrived 1910 in Boston, and spent a year there as editor of *Hayrenik'* (Homeland), urging Armenians to go back to their homeland because of the apparent dawn of the new era. He himself returned soon and was one of the first to lose his life in 1915. His works appeared in five books: *Diwtsaznoren* (Triumphantly, 1901), *Hogevark'i ew yoysi jaher* (Torches of despair and hope, 1907), *Karmir lourer barekames* (Bloody news from my friend, 1909), written under the impact of the massacres of Adana, *Hayreni hrawer* (Call of the earth, 1910), and *Sourb Mesrob* (St Mesrob, 1913). The last is his masterpiece, marking the 1,500th anniversary of the creation of the Armenian alphabet. Siamant'o weeps over the destruction of his homeland and the suffering of his people, especially during 1890–1909. His verse is pessimistic. 'Human justice – I spit in your face', he writes, and calls on the Armenians to rebel like the heroes of the past, and so to be confident in achieving victory. Siamant'o describes in a poem the climate in which he lived thus: 'What a cursed, what a blood-soaked country, wherein even the core of the sun appears bleak and bloody, like a dagger-stabbed eye.'

●Selections in *Anthology of Armenian Poetry*, trans. and ed. by D. D.

Hovanessian and M. Margossian (New York, 1978); *Armenian Poetry Old and New*, compiled and trans. with an introd. by A. Tolegian (Detroit, 1979); *An Anthology of Western Armenian Literature*, ed. J. Etmekjian (Delmar, NY, 1980).
T. Cross (Ed.), *Lost Voices of World War I* (London, 1988), pp. 377–9.   VN

SIENKIEWICZ, Henryk (1846–1916), popular Polish novelist, born into an impoverished noble family, initially earned his living from journalism. As a correspondent for Warsaw's *Gazeta Polska* he spent two years in the USA (1876–8). His admiration for the democratic structure of American society and fascination with the 'Old West' were reflected in *Listy z podróży do Ameryki* (Letters from a journey to America, 1876–8). Having achieved great popularity in the 1880s, Sienkiewicz played a major role in public life. He frequently travelled around Europe and visited Africa. 1905 he became the first Pole to be awarded the Nobel Prize for Literature. Sienkiewicz's literary career began with short stories, committed to the social programme of the Polish Positivists and to patriotic sentiments. In the 1880s he abandoned Positivism and turned his attention to the historical novel, which led to his phenomenal success. His declared intention was to boost the morale of Polish society by glorying its heroic past, although in fact he gained attention through his well-narrated adventures, graphic descriptions of events and simple, vivid characters. Sienkiewicz's approach to history and novelistic technique recalls Dumas Père. The foundations of Sienkiewicz's reputation were built on his trilogy: *Ogniem i mieczem* (With fire and sword, 1884), *Potop* (The deluge, 1886) and *Pan Wołodyjowski* (Mr W. 1888). Their appealing descriptions of wars waged by 17th-century Poland against the Cossacks, Swedes and Turks are blended with stereotypical love stories, where the recurring pattern of abduction, duels and recapture displays the form's various possibilities. Sienkiewicz's contemporary novel *Bez dogmatu* (Without dogma, 1891) was intended as an attack on overrefined intellectual scepticism and defended simple religious faith, but its main value stems from its pointed description of fin-de-siècle Decadence and aristocratic idleness. *Quo vadis?* (1896) earned Sienkiewicz international recognition, due more to its vivid episodes of Roman life than the pallid depictions of Christianity whose final triumph it was intended to portray. *Krzyżacy* (The Teutonic Knights, 1900) reconstructs everyday life in medieval Poland and the Poles' struggle against Germanic conquest. Despite frequent criticisms of his intellectual shortcomings, Sienkiewicz continues to be appreciated as a first-rate storyteller.
●*The Deluge* (New York, 1991); *Quo vadis?* (London, 1960); *Selected Tales* (Miami, 1975); *With Fire and Sword* (New York, 1991).
W. Lednicki, *Henryk Sienkiewicz. A Retrospective Synthesis* (The Hague, 1960); M. Giergielewicz, *Henryk Sienkiewicz* (New York, 1968).   SE

SIKELIANOS, Angelos (1884–1951), Greek poet and dramatist, started 1901 to read law at Athens, but, like many other literary figures, soon dropped out, joining the Νέα Σκηνή (New stage) theatre group (formed by Constantine Christomanos [1867–1911]), as did his sisters Penelope and Helen. Penelope later married Raymond Duncan, brother of the dancer Isadora, who was to introduce Sikelianos to theatre groups in Paris. His first poems appeared in the periodical *Dionysos* in 1902. 1906 he went to America with Eva Palmer, and married her 1907 in Maine. 1909 he published his first poem-cycle, Αλαφροίσκιωτος, and thereafter produced poems at a regular rate. 1911–12 he travelled to France and Italy, meeting Rodin. He returned to Athens before the outbreak of the Balkan Wars and served in N Greece. 1914–15 he became a close friend of KAZANTZAKIS, touring Athos and various Classical and Byzantine sites with him. 1924 Sikelianos and his wife began the unsuccessful attempt, which was to occupy their energies for a decade, to organise an International Delphic Centre and a Delphic University. 1926–7 the project crystallised into a Delphic Festival, with theatre, dance, concerts, an athletic competition and an arts-and-crafts exhibition: another such was held in 1930. 1931 Sikelianos was in Paris, where he met various French writers and intellectuals including Valéry. In the same year he began research into the Eleusinian Mysteries. 1932, inspired by the revivals of Classical tragedy at the Delphic Festival, he wrote his first original play, Ο Διθυραμβος του ρόδου (The dithyramb of the rose), which was performed in Athens the following year. Thereafter he completed four more verse tragedies, principally on mythological and religious themes. 1933 his wife returned to the USA, having run through her private funds, and 1938 she was joined by the couple's only child. She stayed in America until after her husband's death. During the late 1930s Sikelianos became disillu-

sioned with the Delphic project, which was clearly doomed to failure. His finances were precarious, his difficulties worsening during the Occupation, and he withdrew into increasing isolation, although he re-married in 1940. 1946–7 he collected his poetry into the three volumes of the Λυρικός βίος (Lyrical life). He died, having been accidentally poisoned by his maid. Sikelianos's work is a blend of lyrical celebration of life and mystical contemplation of its meaning, expressed through complex symbolism in which the physical presence of Greece and its cultural manifestations of all periods play an essential part. The task of the poet is to attempt to restore the unity between the tangible natural world and the hidden metaphysical world which it represents. In Αλαφροίσκιωτος, the joyful but also mystical response of the young poet to Nature is expressed as a personal outpouring which compels the reader's sympathy by its sheer intensity. At times, in the poetry of the 1920s and 1930s, in particular, the assumption of the privileged role of the seer turns the subjective voice of the poems into something more didactic and intrusive. The poems of his last years combine the subjective and the narrative in a way which is more accessible to the modern reader.

●K. Friar (Ed.), *Modern Greek Poetry* (Athens, 1982), pp. 66–76.   CFR

ŠIKULA, Vincent (b. 1936), Slovak prose writer, studied at the Bratislava conservatory and then was a schoolmaster, before beginning (1967) to earn his living as a literary editor. Šikula is a naivist writer mainly concerned with the workings of the minds of apparently simple countryfolk. In *S Rozarkou* (With Rozarka,

1966) the narrator adopts the role of a folk story-teller to recount the experiences of a man who tries to look after his mentally retarded sister. *S Rozarkou* is a study in the insecure frontier between the real and the imagined. The trilogy about the National Uprising, *Majstri* (The master carpenters, 1976–9), is Šikula's masterpiece. A colourful, gently ironic patchwork of the sublime and the ridiculous, the macabre and the earthy, it questions national mythologies. Like the trilogy, *Vlha* (The golden oriole, 1978) treats a woman whose lot it is to wait and suffer; the gentle irony here on politics and human frailty also stimulates a questioning of conventions. That same irony is used in the rhapsodic *Vojak* (A soldier, 1981), but here the poor, jolly, life-affirming veteran, whose main concern is enjoyment of his multiple identity, is at the end hanged by the Germans in a piece of arbitrary violence; irony suddenly becomes pathos. The short stories of *Heroické etudy pre kone* (Etudes héroiques for horses, 1987) take up many themes the reader knows from his earlier works and are in themselves repetitious; they contain just too much quaintness.

●R. B.Pynsent, *Conceptions of Enemy. Three Essays on Czech and Slovak Literature* (Cambridge, 1988); R. B. Pynsent (Ed.), *Modern Slovak Prose: Fiction Since 1954* (London, 1990). RBP

SILLANPÄÄ, Frans Eemil (1888–1964), Finnish prose writer, was a portrayer of Finnish social life between the two world wars. After leaving secondary school, he studied biology intending to qualify in medicine. 1913 he abandoned this in order to devote himself to his writing. 1939 he was awarded the Nobel Prize for Literature. The main focus of his work is the changes wrought on rural life by the 1918 Civil War, modernisation and the encroachment of urban values. Influenced by the monistic nature philosophy of Haeckel and Ostwald, the central theme in all Sillanpää's writing is man as part of the totality of Nature. Rather than seeing Nature through human eyes, he sees man as if through Nature's eyes, subject to the same cycle of birth, reproduction and death. He did not regard man as more or less important than any other part of Nature, nor did he regard one person's life as intrinsically more important than another's. For him each life was of infinite interest. Sillanpää developed this idea in a series of novels and short stories about the lives of the inhabitants of his home region, the farming area of Hämeenkryö (his characters often appear in more than one work). A device employed in two novels was to start at the moment of the main character's death and to recount his or her life history. *Hurskas kurjuus* (Pious misery, 1919) sketches the social history of the landless farmhands in late 19th and early 20th-century Finland through the life history of a failed revolutionary, executed for a crime he did not commit in the 1918 Civil War. A young woman's death from TB in *Nuorena nukkunut* (Died young, 1931) provides the starting-point of the story of the last member of a once rich family. Sillanpää also developed his theme of biological determinism by concentrating on one aspect of the life cycle, particularly reproduction, in a variety of contexts. *Hiltu ja Ragnar* (H. and R., 1923) follows the daughter of the executed revolutionary into domestic service in the city where she becomes pregnant by her employer's son. The social impossibility of marriage leads to her suicide.

Miehen tie (A man's way, 1932), a *Bildungsroman*, describes the life of a young man forced into an unhappy marriage, widowed, who finally, defying convention, marries his first love. The latent violence and brooding lust, always present in Sillanpää's depictions of country life, erupt in *Ihmiset suviyössä* (People in a summer night, 1934), a snapshot of events in one village during the course of a single short summer night.

●*Meek Heritage* (London, New York, 1938; Helsinki, 1971); *Fallen Asleep while Young* (Dunwoody, 1974); *People in the Summer Night* (Madison, 1966).
L. Viljanen, 'Sillanpää', *Scandinavian Review* (1940), pp. 49–53; G. Kinneavy, 'Sillanpää', *Scandinavica* (1981), pp. 205–12.   MAB

ŠIMIĆ, Antun Branko (1898–1925), Croatian poet, educated in his native Bosnia and Herzegovina, settled in Zagreb where he lived as a professional writer. He achieved a remarkable amount in his brief life, beginning to publish periodicals in Zagreb while still at school, and later editing several literary journals. He followed current trends in European literature and endeavoured in his critical essays to apply demanding standards to contemporary Croatian writing. In his verse Šimić was one of the representatives of Expressionism in Croatian literature, seeking to free poetic expression of all superfluous rhetorical elements, aiming at maximum clarity. His collection *Preobraženja* (Transformations, 1920) gives form to these aims, Šimić's free verse is robust and severe, dealing with basic themes – love, death, illness, hunger, poverty, eternity – in primary colours.

●Translations of selected poems in *IYL*, pp. 386–7; *The Bridge* (1980), pp. 47–51.   ECH

SINOPOULOS, Takis (1917–81), Greek poet, grew up in a rural area of the Peloponnese. 1935 he enrolled in the medical school of the University of Athens. 1941 he was drafted into the army and served in an army hospital in Loutraki in the Gulf of Corinth, where he had to deal with casualties of the Italian campaign. This, and subsequent service during the Civil War with units involved in guerrilla warfare, was to have a great effect on his later writing. Having completed his medical degree in 1943–4, he embarked on a career as a pathologist in 1949, holding a government post but also setting up his own private practice. His first collection of poems, Μεταίχμιο (Midpoint, 1951), contains visions, dreams and nightmares, full of darkness and destruction, fire and blood, in a way which indicates how deeply his experience of war had affected him. The same world-view, in which sensuality and death are the key factors, and a poetic manner rooted in Eliot's *The Waste Land* and SEFERIS's *Mythistorema*, recurs in all his collections of the 1950s. Ασματα I–XI (Songs I–XI, 1953), Μεταίχμιο Β (Midpoint 2, 1957), Ελένη (Helen, 1957) and Η Νύχτα και η Αντίστιξη (The night and the counterpoint) (1959), with the exception of his Surrealist Η Γνωριμία με τον Μαξ (Acquaintance with Max, 1956), a poem written to free himself from writer's block and to rid himself of his deeper obsessions (it achieved the former but not the latter). In the figure of Max, Sinopoulos created an idealised magical creator, a modern healer of souls. The optimism of the poem was, however, a mirage. The next collection in which Sinopoulos created 'characters' in this way, Το Ασματης Ιωάννας και του

Κωνσταντίνου ('The Song of Ioanna and Constantinos, 1961), returns to the theme of the individual shut into his or her own individuality, lonely and unable to communicate. At this point there was a break in Sinopoulos's writing career. He produced a volume of prose poems-cum-aphorisms on the nature of poetry, Η Ποίηση της Ποίησης (The poetry of poetry, 1964), acted as poetry critic for various periodicals and produced a radio programme on poetry (1966–7). When he does publish again, his thematic range and general poetic style are relatively unchanged, but his work has become more politically focused; he has synthesised the theme of writing itself with his critique of the nature of life, and he has brought together the techniques of his surreal narrative style with the mirages and obsessions of his shorter lyrics. Νεκρόδειπνος (Death feast, 1972) and Το χρονικό (The chronicle, 1975), both heavily influenced by the experience of the dictatorship of 1967–74, thus bring together all the strands of his previous work.

●*Landscape of Death: The Selected Poems of Takis Sinopoulos* (Columbus, Ohio, 1979).   CFR

SKARGA, Piotr (1536–1612), Polish preacher, was a member of the Jesuit Order and served as a royal preacher at the court of Sigismund III Vasa (reigned 1587–1632). As one of the main supporters of the Counter-Reformation he was greatly responsible for the decline of religious tolerance in Poland. Skarga's popularity among his contemporaries was secured by his *Żywoty świętych* (Lives of the Saints, 1579), but his posthumous fame stems from *Kazania Sejmowe* (Sermons to the Sejm, 1597), where he passionately de-

nounced the anarchy of the nobility and presented inspired images of the country's possible downfall. Accordingly, in the 19th century Skarga attained the status of a national prophet.

●A. Berga, *Un Prédicateur de la cour de Pologne sous Sigismond III, Pierre Skarga* (Paris, 1916).   SE

SKARYNA, Franćišak (c. 1490–c. 1551), Byelorussian Bible translator, was also a poet, engraver, publisher and one of the first printers in the non-Czech Slav world. Born into a merchant's family in Połack, he studied in Cracow where he may have received a doctorate in liberal arts, and it is possible that he visited Copenhagen, Breslau, Moscow and Wittenberg before being awarded a doctorate in medicine at Padua, 1512. He lived in both Prague and Vilna, and 1535 finally settled in Prague where he ended his days as Royal Gardener to the King of Bohemia. On 6 August 1517 Skaryna published in Prague his first edition, *Psaltyr'* (Book of Psalms), which was followed over the next two and a half years by twenty-two books of the BIBLE (*Bivlija ruska*), translated (mainly from the Vulgate and the Czech Bible published in Venice in 1506) into a language which was basically Church Slavonic (though with an admixture of vernacular elements), but with original prefaces and postscripts in Byelorussian. The latter vary greatly in content but are often elegant and always lucid 'for the better instruction of the common people', though they sometimes also achieve exegetical profundity. Only two examples of Skaryna's Vilna printing survive (others were almost certainly lost and may have been confiscated): *Małaja podorožnaja knižica* (Liber viaticus, 1522) and

Apostol (Acts of the Apostles, 1525). His four original poems are important as the first examples of their kind in Byelorussia. Skaryna was a pioneer in several fields and a true son of the Renaissance.

●A reprint of Skaryna's Bible has been publ. (Minsk, 1990–91).

Arnold McMillin, 'Francis Skaryna's Biblical Prefaces and their Place in Early Byelorussian Literature', *Journal of Byelorussian Studies*, VI, 1 (1988), pp. 3–11.   ABMcM

ŠKĖMA, Antanas (1911–61), Lithuanian playwright, novelist and author of short stories, born in Łódź, returned to Lithuania in 1921 and studied medicine, then law, at the University of Kaunas. In 1935, Škėma became an actor and later director with the Lithuanian State Theatre. After spending the immediately postwar years in Germany, he went to the USA in 1949 and earned his living as a lift-boy, writing prose and plays in his spare time. Škėma's work reflects the confluence of three general factors: postwar malaise and despair in Europe, articulated in several varieties of Existentialist thought, exile itself with its sensations of alienation and dispossession, and elements in Škėma's own personality and experience that drove him to take up a bitter, ironic, at times slightly theatrical stance towards life. In such a framework, Škėma's only novel, *Balta drobulė* (White shroud, 1958), his short stories, particularly in the *Šventoji Inga* (Saint I., 1952) cycle, and his plays *Pabudimas* (The awakening, 1956), *Žvakidė* (The candleholder, 1957), and *Kalėdų vaizdelis* (The Christmas skit, 1961) are all focused on death, or rather, on the often cruel, nightmarish processes by which human beings come to understand that the moment of death is the most significant reality. Lithuania's traumatic experiences connected with the Soviet occupation and subsequent genocide give Škėma ample material to make his point in his plays and stories. Curiously, there are no real villains in Škėma, but only anguished people who dimly perceive themselves as actors playing out the dark designs of a blind and pitiless Fate. Only in his last play, *Ataraxia* (posth., 1970), about a Lithuanian Jew, Izaokas, who tortured Gluosnis during the Soviet occupation while the latter, in turn, killed Izaokas when the Germans came, do both players manage to conspire against their destiny in the person of a mental-hospital supervisor guarding them in some indefinite netherworld. They suddenly turn and kill him with the same trench spade Gluosnis had once used on Izaokas. In *Balta drobulė*, the main character, Garšva, is a modern-day Sisyphus moving his lift up and then down again through all the storeys filled with desperate humanity and through the layers of his own reminiscences of childhood, war, death, lost love, and dreams that somehow become warped into nightmares. In the end, he goes insane and lives on very happily in this condition.

●R. Šilbajoris, 'The Tragedy of Creative Consciousness: Literary Heritage of Antanas Škėma', *Lituanus*, 4 (1966), pp. 5–23.   RŠ

ŠKVORECKÝ, Josef (b. 1924), Czech novelist and publicist, read English and philosophy at Prague, and on finishing his studies (1949) became a schoolmaster. 1956–63 he worked in publishing, and then went freelance. He left Czechoslovakia after the Soviet occupation and eventually began teaching Anglo-American literature at Toronto. 1971–91 his wife and he ran the main émigré publishing house, 68 Publishers. Perhaps only with the brief novel *Legenda Emöke* (The E. legend, 1963), a tale of failed love and the conflict between the spiritual and socialism, did Škvorecký aspire to mainstream mimetic literature. His first novel, *Zbabělci* (The cowards, 1958), was a landmark. The cowards of the title are all Czechs except the Communists, and yet this novel marks the true beginning of the post-Stalinist Thaw in Czech literature. Dominated by the postpubertal lucubrations of the Waverley-like narrator, the novel demythologises the Czech 'revolution' against the Germans in 1945. The short stories, *Sedmiramenný svícen* (The menorah, 1964), are important for the author's determinedly antisentimental approach to the wartime persecution of the Jews in Bohemia. *Tankový prapor* (The tank battalion, 1971) is a comic series of episodes from life in the People's Army which has no lasting value. *Mirákl* (The miracle, 1972), while conceptually and stylistically chaotic, evokes with skilful irony the horrors of the Stalinist terror and presents the first balanced view of the 1968 'Prague Spring' in Czech literature. *Příběh inženýra lidských duší* (The story of an engineer of human souls, 1977) shows Škvorecký losing grip of the Czech language (however much he satirises émigré Czech in the novel); Danny, the girl-crazed boy of *Zbabělci*, now suffers from manic erotic vulgarity. The author's self-indulgent authoritarian attitude comes out in his narrator's literary-critical divagations. Škvorecký is an accomplished recounter of comic anecdotes, but a novelist of no profundity.

●*The Cowards* (London, 1970); *The Miracle Game* (London, 1991); *The Engineer of Human Souls* (London, 1985).

J. Kalish, *Josef Škvorecký. A Checklist* (Toronto, 1986); S. Solecki, *Prague Blues. The Fiction of Josef Škvorecký* (Toronto, 1990); P. I. Trensky, *The Fiction of Josef Škvorecký* (Basingstoke, 1991). RBP

SLÁDEK, Josef Václav (1845–1912), Czech poet, son of a village bricklayer, studied science and languages at Prague, spent two years in the USA as a teacher, navvy and journalist and, after his return, taught English at commercial academy; during the last ten years of his life he was seriously ill. Although, 1877–98, he edited the monthly *Lumír* which provided the platform for the cosmopolitan programme of VRCHLICKÝ, Sládek was steeped in the national tradition. His *Básně* (Poems, 1875) and *Jiskry na moři* (Sparks on the sea, 1879) contain elegies on the premature death of his wife, impressions from his American sojourn, compassionate dirges on the persecuted Indians and melancholy thoughts on the Czech national and social situation. The gloom lifts in *Světlou stopou* (On the bright path, 1881) and *Na prahu ráje* (On the threshold of paradise, 1883), singing of his love for his second wife and children, confessing loyalty to his country and admiration for his mother tongue, whilst in *Selské písně a české znělky* (Peasant songs and Czech sonnets, 1890) he identifies himself with the peasant and his view of life and affirms his faith in a better future for his nation. His last collections, *V zimním slunci* (In the winter sun, 1897) and *Za soumraku* (In the twilight, 1907), are marked by resignation, meditations on death and God. Sládek's language is concise; he puts emphasis on rhythm and melody and many of his poems were set to music. Although with ERBEN and ČELAKOVSKÝ he represents the spirit and style of folk-poetry, together with VRCHLICKÝ he did more than anybody else to spread the knowledge of English culture in Bohemia by his translations, in particular of Burns with whom he had much in common in his original poetry. The task of his life was the translation of all Shakespeare's works; he finished 33 plays and his versions, in spite of occasional prudery, still retain their poetic impact. KB

SLÁDKOVIČ, Andrej (i.e. Ondrej Braxatoris, 1820–72), Slovak Romantic poet, was taught by ŠTÚR at the Pressburg Lyceum, then went to university in Halle. He spent most of his life as a country parson. His chief works are *Marína* (1846) and *Detvan* (The Detva lad, 1853). The former, 291 ten-line stanzas, is a complex paean to love, youth and Slovak Nature; love is a religion and the source of all goodness and beauty in the world. Overtly following KOLLÁR, Sládkovič closely links love for a woman with love for one's country (Marína's red lips and white teeth represent the narrator's national colours). He educates his readers with cosmopolitan topographical and literary allusions. *Detvan*, an introduction and 250 ten-line stanzas, tells the story of a Slovak lad who shoots a royal falcon that is threatening the life of a hare, but because of his courage in then seeking out the king, Matthias Corvinus, he is rewarded by being made a member of the élite Black Guard. The style is similar to that of *Marína*, but the call to Slovak national pride is more strongly expressed. RBP

SLAMNIG, Ivan (b. 1930), Croatian poet, prose writer and essayist, born in central Dalmatia, studied at Zagreb where he spent his working life teaching comparative literature, acquiring a fluent knowledge of the major European languages and a wide understanding of both Classical and modern literature. One of the most original voices of his generation, coming from a background where two dialects meet to Zagreb, dominated by a third, Slamnig is fascinated by language and his poems are often virtuoso games, exploring the limits of language. In addition to seven volumes of poetry, Slamnig has published two collections of short stories and a novel, *Bolja polovica hrabrosti* (The better part of valour, 1972).

●Selected poems in *NWY*, pp. 139–42; V. D. Mihailovich (Ed.), *Contemporary Yugoslav Poetry* (Iowa City, 1977), pp. 129–33. ECH

SLAVEIKOV, Pencho (1866–1912), Bulgarian poet, was the son of the National Revival writer Petko Slaveikov (1827–95), a man who contributed to the development of the Bulgarian literary language. Because of the unsettled life of the family, Pencho Slaveikov was educated at home, then at schools until 1884, when he was disabled by an injury for three years; he remained a semi-invalid and his health was poor for the rest of his life. He initially regarded sickness as a 'punishment', but later as a sign of 'chosenness'. He was fascinated by Turgenev's *The Living Corpse* because of the victory of 'soul' over body. 1892–8 he read philosophy, aesthetics and literature at Leipzig. On returning to Bulgaria, he became a teacher, then deputy director of the National Library; 1909–11 he was director; he ran the National Theatre (1908–9), but was dismissed because of his attacks on the government. 1911 he went into voluntary exile accompanied by the poet Mara Belcheva (1868–1937), with whom Slaveikov had been close since 1903. After wandering about Switzerland, they went to Italy where Slaveikov died. Slaveikov began writing his first, callow, verse in 1888. 1892 he joined the literary magazine *Misăl* (Thought) and is thus linked with the dawn of Bulgarian Modernism. He became an established poet with the publication of his *Epicheski pesni* (Epic songs, 1896–8), where he blends Bulgarian folk motifs with universal themes, like art, beauty, genius; the work is imbued with the thought of Nietzsche, Schopenhauer, Ibsen and Kierkegaard, as well as of Slaveikov's teachers, the aestheticians Johannes Volkelt and Wilhelm Wundt. Slaveikov assumed the role of a cultural messiah; his 'Modernism' meant a modification of the literary model created during the National Revival, dominated by the 'national ideal' and national collectivism. Slaveikov proclaimed the importance of the individual, which led to a new perception of his nation's destiny. Death was no longer just part of the natural cycle (and no longer symbolised heroism in the national fight), but the supreme knowledge 'in God', and was anticipated with existential anxiety. Slaveikov's incomplete poem *Kărvava pesen* (Song of blood, 1911–13), on which he worked from 1893 until his death, also expressed his ambition to alter the understanding of Bulgaria and was inspired by MICKIEWICZ's *Pan Tadeusz*. His most individual work, *Na ostrova na blazhenite* (The isle of the blessed, 1910), is an anthology of verse by authors who never existed; each sample of their works is 'translated' by Slaveikov and accompanied by a literary portrait of the 'author'. Behind the odd names, such as Ivo Dolya or Bojko Razdyala (Slaveikov could not stand the Slavonic ending -ov), one could often recognise contemporary Bulgarian writers, but they are also incarnations of Slaveikov himself. However critical or ironical, the work still expresses Slaveikov's dream of a more spiritual Bulgarian culture.

●P. Slaveikoff and E. Dillon, *The Shade of the Balkans* (London, 1904).
E. Damiani, *Il più europeo dei poeti bulgari P. Slavejkov* (Rome, 1940); R. Picchio, 'L'occidentalismo conservatore di Penco Slavejkov', *Ricerche slavistiche*, 1 (1952), pp. 124–43.   SIK

ŠLEJHAR, Josef Karel (1864–1914), Czech prose writer, began reading chemistry at Prague in 1881, but did not finish his studies; after working briefly in a sugar refinery, he became a farmer, but personal and financial problems forced him to leave farming and take up teaching in a commercial academy. Šlejhar is a misanthropic anti-materialist, a writer with a mystical belief in love and beauty who sees little but violence, greed, hatred and cruelty around him. His weaknesses are a tendency to didacticism and sentimentalisation, and his strengths lie in the evocation of horror, and of compassion with the weak. His writing blends the Naturalist and the Symbolist. In *Kuře melancholik* (The melancholy chicken, 1889) the power of evil, generally identified with Fate, is the prime mover of this story of a persecuted boy and his only friend, a persecuted chicken. *Povídka z výčepu* (Bar story, 1908) is similar: a crippled boy with a hamster friend. *Zátiší* (Still-lifes, 1898) consists of three stories concerned with the transcendental, but mostly representing the cruelty of humankind and of Nature. *Vraždění* (Murdering, 1910) is a more precisely elaborated version of the same thing; here the imminent evil within makes people perpetrate violence; the village where the action is set is a microcosm of the world of 'progress', and the six pages Šlejhar spends depicting the slaughter of a goat epitomises the mentality of those who run the 'modern' world. Šlejhar's most important work is the long experimental novel *Peklo* (Hell, 1905). The action consists in one day in a chemical engineer's life, and the narrative, which has strong elements of the stream of consciousness, describes the man's preoccupations: one concerning his many visual and olfactory experiences during his inspection tour of the factory, the other concerning his love for one of the workers, a beautiful country girl, as yet untainted by factory hell. She is an object of period erotic mysticism, and that idealism is not sullied, for, at the end of the novel, when they copulate, the factory goes up in flames. RBP

SLOBODA, Rudolf (b. 1938), Slovak novelist, after one year's study at Bratislava (1957-8), worked as a miner, builder's labourer and, after military service, a foundry worker; since 1965 he has sometimes been employed as a literary editor, sometimes worked freelance. He is a highly regarded novelist, but that is because he has lively ideas, not because he is an accomplished verbal artist. His works lack balance. *Hudba* (Music, 1977) is an oversimplified idyll, but also a serious study in teenage psychology. He can write slow-moving Socialist Realism, brimful of optimism and didacticism,

like his account of life in a drying-out unit, *Stratený raj* (Paradise lost, 1983); in contrast to that he has novels showing the human warmth of a sexually frustrated murderess who can eventually endure only being alone, *Uršuľa* (1987) and *Rubato* (1990), the latter of which has a strong feminist element. Sloboda's greatest achievement is the highly literary *Rozum* (Reason, 1982), a series of episodes from the narrator's life, with interpolated tales, the complete outline of a film-script and brief essays on art and life. The Surrealist film-script provides the story to the novel and its idea – that film may be more capable of communicating fully than ordinary human contact.

●R. B. Pynsent (Ed.), *Modern Slovak Prose: Fiction Since 1954* (London, 1990). RBP

SŁONIMSKI, Antoni (1895–1976), Polish poet, playwright, fiction writer, essayist and critic, one of the five founders of the Skamander group (1920), was born in Warsaw and lived there until 1939, when the outbreak of war forced him to escape to Paris and then to London. He stayed in London after the war, but returned to Poland in 1951. 1956–9 he was chairman of the Polish Writers' Union. Throughout his career, Słonimski reached a large readership and exerted a strong influence on Polish minds. His poetry, however, had a relatively small part in this. During the 1930s, and again the 1960s–70s, his poems, though undoubtedly popular, were overshadowed by his widely read *feuilletons*. He was an accomplished master of this genre, which under his pen became a hybrid combining elements of literary essay, political column, and lampoon. Before 1939, his popularity was also due to his vitriolic theatrical reviews, comedies in the Shavian manner, and science-fiction novels with some of the flavour of H. G. Wells. In all these genres, poetry included, he is a tireless defender of common sense and civil liberties, always the first to ridicule totalitarian and chauvinist follies. In Communist Poland, his intransigent stance exposed him more than once to the ill-will of the régime, while the public considered him, especially towards the end of his life, a living symbol of the best traditions of the liberal intelligentsia.

●Selected poems in C. Milosz, *Postwar Polish Poetry* (Berkeley, 1983).   StB

SŁOWACKI, Juliusz (1809–49), Polish poet, playwright and epistolographer, traditionally considered one of the three national 'bards' beside MICKIEWICZ and KRASIŃSKI, was a bitter rival of the former and a close friend of the latter, although towards the end of his life his political evolution made him an opponent of KRASIŃSKI's. Son of a literature teacher at the lycée in Krzemieniec who died in 1814, Słowacki was brought up by his mother who was to remain his closest confidante and the addressee of his splendid letters for the rest of his life. In 1818 she married a professor of the University of Wilno (Vilnius) and the family moved to that city. Słowacki completed his education at the University of Wilno and in 1829 left for Warsaw to work for the Ministry of Finances. At this point he had already been writing poetry for four years; with the outbreak of the November Uprising in 1830, his patriotic poems brought him sudden popularity. In March 1831, entrusted with a diplomatic mission by the leadership of the Uprising, he left via Dresden for Paris and London; the mission accomplished, he stayed for a while

in Paris, then settled for the next three years in Geneva. In 1832 two volumes of his *Poezje* (Poems), containing his early work, came out to almost no response except a critical remark from MICKIEWICZ. In Switzerland, however, Słowacki found his authentic voice as a poet. The third volume of *Poezje* (1833) and the poetic drama *Kordian* (1834) put him in the forefront of Polish Romantic literature. In 1836 he embarked on a long journey through Greece, Egypt and Palestine, and on his way back to Paris he spent over a year in Florence. These experiences prompted him to write a number of poems in which the ever-present theme of Poland's tragedy was reflected upon from new perspectives. During the last decade of his life, spent almost entirely in Paris, Słowacki wrote with feverish speed. This period produced first his virtuoso 'poem of digressions' *Beniowski* (1841), major plays (e.g. *Balladyna* [1839], *Lilla Weneda* [1840], *Fantazy* [1866]) and numerous important poems. In 1842 the poet met the mystical thinker Andrzej Towiański (1799–1878) and joined his circle for a while, but their ways soon parted. Słowacki eventually developed his own philosophical system, presented by him in a poetic treatise *Genezis z Ducha* (Genesis from the spirit, 1844) and in an immense mytho-historical epic *Król-Duch* (King Spirit, written 1845–9). These two works together with two more plays and a verse polemic with KRASIŃSKI form the core of the so-called 'mystical period' of Słowacki's career. It ended with his death from TB. Słowacki's voluminous oeuvre spans a great many genres, from lyric verse to poetic dramas, to tales in verse and visionary epics. His plays are a crucial factor in the evolution of

Polish Romantic poetry as well as theatre. Written mostly in verse, they experiment with both versification and dramatic construction; their settings are variously realistic, historical, legendary, oneiric or symbolic. In his poems, Słowacki felt equally at home in epic description and lyric confession, in complex stanza patterns and in biblical prose. His significance lies not only in his matchless technical virtuosity but also in that in his last phase he was an early forerunner of modern trends in poetry, including Symbolism.

●Selected poems in J. Peterkiewicz and B. Singer, *Five Centuries of Polish Poetry* (London, 1960); *Anhelli* (London, 1930); *Balladyna* (Cambridge Springs, 1960); 'Fantazy' in H. B. Segel (Ed.), *Polish Romantic Drama* (Ithaca and London, 1977).
S. Treugutt, *J. Słowacki – Romantic Poet* (Warsaw, 1959); M. Kridl, *The Lyric Poems of J. Słowacki* (The Hague, 1959); J. Bourilly, *La Jeunesse de Jules Słowacki (1809–1833)* (Paris, 1960).   StB

SMREK, Ján (i.e. J. Čietek, 1898–1982), Slovak poet and publicist, studied at the teachers' college and at the Protestant theological faculty, worked as a journalist and editor in the Slovak publishing house in Prague. 1931 he founded the literary monthly *Elán*, which became the home of most young Slovak writers and which he edited. His first collection, *Odsúdený k večitej žízni* (Condemned to everlasting thirst, 1925), was influenced by BŘEZINA and KRASKO, but his second book, *Cválajúce dni* (Galloping days, 1925), celebrating life, youth and love, made him the main exponent of Vitalism in Slovak poetry. 'In my happiness, in my intoxication, I love all that I do not detest – cities, rivers, women, all the marvels of the world, all its beauties, my own people and all foreign races . . .' Unflinching optimism and unbridled eroticism expressed in simple language remained the hallmark of his subsequent collections, like *Božské uzly* (Divine knots, 1929) and *Iba oči* (Nothing but eyes, 1933), and woman remained his inspiration in *Básnik a žena* (Poet and a woman, first four canti, 1923, epilogue, 1934), a story of meetings with his lady admirer during the four seasons of the year. In Smrek's verse written during WWII and immediately after, published in *Hostina* (The feast, 1944) and *Studňa* (The well, 1945), the former carefree mood gave way to anguish caused by the misery of war. His poems contained encoded indictments of its perpetrators and eventually open condemnation of the aggressors and celebration of the Slovak insurgents and the Red Army. In his collection *Obraz sveta* (The picture of the world, 1948), however, Smrek returned to his prewar Vitalism.   KB

SÖDERGRAN, Edith (1892–1923), Finland-Swedish poet, was the first and the most important Expressionist in Finland. Born in St Petersburg of middle-class parents and educated in the German school, she contracted TB in 1907 and was treated in sanatoria in Finland and Switzerland. Impoverished by the Russian Revolution, she spent her last years supporting herself by her writing and translation. Her unusual background had brought her into greater contact than most Finnish poets of her time with the intellectual life of Russia and central Europe. Her first volume, *Dikter* (Poems, 1916), is striking for the stark simplicity of its language and the directness of its sensuality. In *Septemberlyran* (September lyre,

1918), published in the aftermath of the Civil War, Södergran is bolder in her idiom. Her growing preoccupation with Nietzsche shows itself in the more forceful projection of her own personality. Her themes become increasingly mystical with *Rosenaltaret* (The rose altar, 1919), which concludes with a sensualist reworking of the Ariadne myth. This collection marked a turning-point in her life. *Framtidens skugga* (Shadow of the future, 1920) reveals a poignant longing for her home, a fascination with sexual fantasies, and a growing fear of death. The posthumous *Landet som icke är* (The land that is not, 1925) comprises poems from her last years. As her life drew to a close and the indignity of her illness became more oppressive, she abandoned her Nietzschean attitudes and turned to Rudolf Steiner's anthroposophy and Christianity.

●David McDuff (Ed.), *Complete Poems* (Newcastle, 1984).
G. C. Schoolfield, *Edith Södergran: Modernist Poet in Finland* (Westport, 1984); W. G. Jones and M. A. Branch (Eds), *Edith Södergran: Nine Essays* (London, 1992); McDuff, 'Introduction' to *Complete Poems*.   MAB

SOLANO, Francesco (i.e. Dushko Vetmo, b. 1914), Arbëresh (Italo-Albanian) poet, prose writer and scholar, born in Frascineto in Calabria of a family of Çamëria origin and moved in 1934 to Buenos Aires where he studied theology and foreign languages and later worked as a teacher and priest. He returned to Italy and taught Albanian at the University of Cosenza. Solano has written in a wide variety of genres. Among his publications are *Bubuqe t'egra* (Wild buds, 1946), *Tregimet e Lëronit* (Ploughing tales, 1975) and *Te praku* (At the threshold, 1977). He is the author of the textbook *Manuale di lingua albanese* (Albanian language manual, 1972).   ShM

ŠOLJAN, Antun (b. 1932), Croatian poet, novelist, playwright, critic and translator, born in Belgrade, studied in Zagreb, where he has lived all his life as a writer. The basic theme of his poetry is the search of the contemporary urban intellectual for his 'lost identity'. In his works he combines modern colloquial urban speech with archaic references to older literary texts. His prose is preoccupied with the problems of the Cold War generation. His first important novel, *Izdajice* (Traitors, 1961), introduced a new, analytical, controlled style. Šoljan's 'traitors' are outsiders incapable of inclusion in the world around them. *Kratki izlet* (Brief excursion, 1965) describes an allegorical quest for medieval frescoes in the myth-filled landscape of Istria, in which the main character is finally left alone, to contemplate the meaninglessness of existence. *Luka* (The harbour, 1974) is a satirical description of the building of a harbour, an enterprise doomed to failure from the outset. *Drugi ljudi na mjesecu* (The second men on the moon, 1978) returns to the subject matter and artistic procedure of Šoljan's first important novel.

●'Galileo's Ascension', *The Bridge*, 10 (1968), pp. 56–75; translations of selected poems, *The Bridge*, 19–20 (1970), pp. 70–5; V. D. Mihailovich (Ed.), *Contemporary Yugoslav Poetry* (Iowa City, 1977), pp. 134–40.   ECH

SOLOMOS, Dionysios (1798–1857), considered by many the 'national poet' of Greece, was the illegitimate son (later legitimised) of Count Nikolaos Solomos, whose title he inherited. He spoke Greek with his mother but was educated in Italian.

At ten he was taken by his tutor to Italy, where he remained until 1818, first at school, then studying law at Pavia. He returned to his native Zakynthos, where he lived for ten years. 1828 he settled in Corfu, living there until his death. The private income which accompanied his inheritance relieved him of the need to work at anything but his writing. Accordingly his was a life in which public events outweighed private pressures. Above all he was affected by the War of Independence. He celebrated the early Greek successes in the Ύμνος εις την Ελευθερίαν (Hymn to liberty, 1823, from which the Greek national anthem is taken) and the second siege of Missolonghi formed the subject of the three drafts of Οι Ελεύθεροι Πολιορκημένοι (The free besieged, 1829, 1833–4, 1844–9). Culturally he was influenced by Romanticism in general, and Italian poetry in particular. Hence the importance he gives to themes of liberty, Nature, spirituality, chastity and the contemplation of beauty. Hence, also, his belief in the constant polishing of his poems, a factor which led to the unfinished or fragmentary state of many of them. Solomos's career as a poet falls into two periods, before and after 1828. His first work, 33 sonnets in Italian, appeared in 1822 as *Rime improvvisate*. His early poems in Greek – light lyrics and poems on the deaths of real or fictitious characters – were largely exercises in various metres. His first two major poems, the 'Hymn to liberty' and Εις το θάνατο του Λορδ Μπάιρον (Ode on the death of Lord Byron, 1824) both show signs of continued technical and linguistic experiment. At the same period he was writing his Διάλογος (Dialogue, 1824) in support of the literary use of spoken Greek, together with a number of light satires in Italian and highly dialectal Greek. The poetry of his Corfiot period is far more sophisticated in both form and content. By 1829 his poems reveal a new concern with Romantic metaphysics, and soon after this he sought to strengthen the philosophical basis of his writing through a serious study of German thinkers, particularly Schiller. The great works of the second periods are Ο Κρητικός (The Cretan, 1833–4), 'The free besieged' and Ο Πόρφυρας (The shark, 1847–9). His method of composition was curious. He liked to formulate the idea of a poem independently. This he would write down in Italian prose, then gradually transform his material, through a number of drafts, into Greek verse. This method reflects his belief that the attempt to capture an idea in language is an attempt to translate the metaphysical into the physical, necessitating the polishing and repolishing of metre, word, structure and metrical effect.

●P. Mackridge, *Dionysios Solomos* (Bristol, 1989).   CFR

SORESCU, Marin (b. 1936), Roumanian poet and dramatist, is one of the most original voices of contemporary Roumanian literature. The son of farm workers, he graduated from Iaşi University in 1960 and obtained an editorial post on the literary weekly *Luceafărul* (Lucifer/Venus) in Bucharest. His first work was a book of verse parodies and pastiches, *Singur printre poeţi* (Alone among the poets, 1964). His first major volume of *Poeme* (1965) with its rich vein of irony and humour brought him immediate success. His subsequent volumes in the same mould secured him a uniquely large audience, particularly among the young, among Roumanian contemporary poets. Sorescu's status as one of the leading writers of his generation was confirmed by his writing for the theatre, much of which fell victim to Ceaușescu's censors because of its political allusiveness. *Iona* (Jonah, 1968) was one such casualty. The biblical tale becomes a metaphor for freedom. Jonah cuts himself out of the belly of the whale only to find that it had been swallowed by a larger one, and so the fisherman's predicament is repeated, leading to the suggestion that the universe is itself such a confined space. Jonah is able to overcome this plight only by taking his own life. We may also see Jonah as a prisoner of convention whose escape by suicide did not suit Ceaușescu's cultural dictate that writers should 'echo the people's welfare and man's happiness'. After a six-week run in 1969 it was staged only once in Roumania during Ceaușescu's lifetime, in 1982, by a group of Latin American drama students. *A treija Țeapă* (The third stake, 1978) had a similar fate. Its portrayal of the complex Vlad the Impaler's cruelty and indifference to the daily life of his subjects proved too uncomfortable for the censors and it was staged only for a brief run in the provinces in 1979 and for a two-week season in Bucharest in 1988. Yet Vlad is not an Ubuesque monster; he arouses compassion and in so doing makes the spectator question whether his or her own sense of values has become distorted. Sorescu's verse is largely anecdotal in character and confronts human reality with irony. His approach is exemplified by epigrammatic caricatures of love or death. The inspiration is everyday life, the tone prosaic, the mood ironic. Workaday experience is translated into mockery of the human condition, including that of the poet himself. His verse parables convey truths in a commonplace vocabulary which render them universally accessible. Often the poems' premisses are destroyed by paradoxical 'punch-lines', unexpected syllogisms that challenge conventional views.

●*The Thirst of the Salt Mountain. Three plays by Marin Sorescu* (London, 1985); *Vlad Dracula the Impaler. A Play by Marin Sorescu* (London, 1987); *Selected Poems 1965–1973* (Newcastle, 1983); *The Youth of Don Quixote* (Dublin, 1987).   DJD

ŠOTOLA, Jiří (1924–89), Czech writer, read drama production at the Prague Academy of Dramatic Arts and, on finishing (1951), started studying philosophy and aesthetics at Prague University; meanwhile he worked as an actor and producer in provincial theatres (1949–52). 1954–64 he edited various literary periodicals; 1964–7 he was in the literary *apparat*, and then he went freelance. He was banned after the Soviet occupation, but recanted in 1975 and so continued to publish. He first made his mark as a 'poet of everyday life', and *Venuše z Mélu* (Venus de Milo, 1959) is typical of that mode: the dominant mood is melancholy; the eponymous beautiful, white, naked woman who is the collection's theme represents hope and the female principle. An example of the second, slightly ironic, phase of Šotola's verse is *Co a jak* (What and how, 1964), which expresses the doubt that life has any meaning at all; it is anti-messianic. His plays of the 1970s and 1980s tend to be bland comedies where empty quirkiness is set up as humour, e.g. *Cesta Karla IV. do Francie a zpět* (Charles IV's journey to France and back, 1979) or

Možná je na střeše kůň (Perhaps there is a horse on the roof, 1980). Šotola's most important works are his first three novels, all of which were generally understood as metaphors or allegories. The psychological analytical *Tovaryšstvo Ježíšovo* (The Society of Jesus, 1969) describes with ironic skill how the Jesuits wore down nobles, the common people, but also honourable members of the Order itself, so that the whole country comes to believe that ends justify means when they are To the Greater Glory of God. The pseudo-documentary, picaresque *Kuře na rožni* (K./Chicken on the spit, 1976) is set in the Napoleonic Wars, another period of chaos. Its main figure, Matěj Kuře, is an outcast artist, a puppeteer; his and the other characters' main concerns (not the nobles') are food and shelter. When the Czech populace are ordered to use various weeds instead of flour and vegetables, they first laugh at the régime, but then submit. The novel studies arbitrary persecution. The narrator of the third novel, *Svatý na mostě* (The saint on the bridge, 1978), is another 'ordinary man', a 1970s railwayman with a passion for Czech history and an intimate knowledge of recent events in Czechoslovakia. The main figure, however, is the 14th-century St John Nepomucene and the main theme, the relativity, manipulation and troublesomeness of truth – one of the themes of *Kuře*. Nepomucene is a Party careerist.

●Heinrich Kunstmann, *Tschechische Erzählkunst im 20. Jahrhundert* (Cologne, Vienna, 1974); W. Schamschula, 'The Contemporary Czech Historical Novel and Its Political Inspiration' in E. Bristol (Ed.), *World Congress for Soviet and East European Studies. East European Literature* (Berkeley, 1982), pp. 57–86.   RBP

SOUTSOS, Panayotis (1806–68), Greek poet, dramatist and novelist, was born in Constantinople, of an aristocratic Phanariot family. His younger brother Alexander (1803–63) was a competent but facile writer of satirical political verse influenced by Béranger. The brothers were educated on Chios and later in Paris. Panayotis's first poetic works, Ποιήσεις (Poems, 1831) and Η Κιθάρα (The lyre, 1835), and an epistolary novel Λεάνδρος (Leander, 1834) represent a significant proportion of his literary production. Like Lamartine, his later poems (and more particularly his plays) show a loss of the lyrical instinct which was his chief gift. Of all his works, it is for the long poem Ο Οδοιπόρος (The wayfarer, included in the Poems of 1831) that he is chiefly remembered. It tells of two lovers separated by Fate. The hero had abandoned his betrothed, Ralou, placing love for his country above personal commitment. At the end of the war he learns of her death and decides to work off his grief by journeying far and wide. Ralou, meanwhile, is alive, and divided between undying love for the hero and thirst for revenge. They meet at Mount Athos, where Ralou poses as a ghost, causing her beloved to commit suicide, whereupon she in turn dies. This Gothic farrago shows genuine lyric qualities mixed with Romantic cliché and rhetoric. It is interesting to compare the first edition, which is linguistically quite fresh and lively in parts, with the process of archaising to which the poem is subjected in the editions of 1842, 1851 and 1864. It is a short practical demonstration of what went wrong with the language of poetry in the hands of the 'purifiers' over those three decades. CFR

SOVA, Antonín (1864–1928), Czech poet and prose writer, son of a schoolteacher and choirmaster, too poor to finish his law studies, worked in the editorial offices of an encyclopaedia and eventually as the Director of the Prague Municipal Library. His first verse was of an impressionist who comprehended reality as a lyrical drama. He later turned to contemporary social problems and, like MACHAR, criticised bourgeois society but his criticism was milder and his irony subdued. Sova's collection *Soucit i vzdor* (Compassion and defiance, 1894) expressed a reaction of a sensitive artist rather than the conscious revolt of an opponent of the social order, but his *Zlomená duše* (Broken soul, 1896) in which he dismissed all contemporary Czech literary and political trends voiced the antisocial protest of the young generation. In his *Vybouřené smutky* (Calmed griefs, 1897) Sova envisaged a better life on a higher plane and in *Ještě jednou se vrátíme* (We shall return once more, 1900) he presented a vision of a utopian future for humanity as a new kingdom built entirely by spiritual effort. Sova, a poet of delicate shades of emotional conflicts, was at his best when expressing his own inner states through the medium of Nature.

●K. David, 'Vltava Diverted: The Czech crisis in A. Sova's "The River"', *East European Politics and Societies*, 6 (1992), 2, pp. 170–90.   KB

SPAHIU, Xhevahir (b. 1945), Albanian poet, born in Skrapar, S Albania, studied at the University of Tirana and afterwards took up a career as journalist, working for various newspapers and literary periodicals. Spahiu's poetry lays emphasis on the close connection between art and reality and is concerned with the Albanian past and present and with the poet's role in society. Among his publications are the verse collection *Mëngjes sirenash* (Siren morning, 1970), *Vdekje perëndive* (Death of the gods, 1977), *Agime shqiptare* (Albanian dawns, 1981) and the collection of essays *Dver dhe zemra të hapura* (Open doors and hearts, 1977).   ShM

SPASSE, Sterjo (1914–89), Albanian prose writer, was born into a poor peasant family in Gollomboç on Lake Prespa, where he took his first schooling. 1932 he matriculated in Elbasan and after working for a period as a teacher, studied in Italy. After the war he continued his studies in Tirana and at the Gorki Institute in Moscow. Spasse had a considerable impact on the development of modern Albanian prose. His first work, the novel *Pse?* (Why?, 1935), a typical nihilistic work of prewar Albanian literature, portrays the dilemma of a young intellectual in a backward rural society, based largely on Spasse's experiences as a village schoolmaster. His later novels, *Afërdita* (1944) and *Afërdita përsëri në fshat* (A. in the countryside again, 1955), are similar in theme but viewed from a more consciously social perspective. His novel *Ata nuk ishin vetëm* (They were not alone, 1952) describes the first awakening of Marxist class consciousness among the prewar Albanian peasantry. His other novels include *Zgjimi* (The awakening, 1974); *Pishtarë* (Torches, 1975), *Ja vdekje, ja liri* (Liberty or death, 1978) and *Kryengritësit* (The rebels, 1983), which deal with the Revival period leading to the Albanian independence. Spasse is also the author of several collections of short stories and translations.   ShM

ŠRÁMEK, Fráňa (1877–1952),

Czech poet, novelist and dramatist, whose early near anarchist and anti-militarist poetry was inspired by his aversion to philistinism and to WWI, in which he took part, but its rebelliousness was stimulated less by hatred of bourgeois society than by personal unease caused by conflict between sensuality and spirituality, showed in *Splav* (The weir, 1916) and *Básně* (Poems, 1926) that his conflict had been pacified by the promotion of eros as the most positive expression of life and the means of liberation of the individual. His most typical novels, *Stříbrný vítr* (The silver wind, 1910), which depicts sexual awakening, and *Tělo* (The body, 1919), in which the heroine opposes war by putting into practice the motto 'make love not war', have meagre plots and moods instead of psychology. Šrámek's early plays, e.g. *Léto* (The summer, 1915) introduce sensual young people in revolt against puritanism and the banality of petty bourgeois existence. In his later plays, e.g. *Měsíc nad řekou* (The moonlight over the river, 1922), the young rebel against their nostalgic elders, but eventually compromise and sink into banality and despair.

KB

SRUOGA, Balys (1896–1947), was a Lithuanian poet, playwright, memoir-writer and literary critic. The Symbolist elements in his verse would place him as a poet from the beginning of the 20th century, but he also witnessed all the horrors of WWII and continued through them all to speak, when he could, with the voice of the artist, as well as that of the scholar. Sruoga studied literature at Moscow but returned to Lithuania after independence in 1919, and worked for the Lithuanian press. He took his PhD in Slavonic studies and theatre at Munich, and then taught at the Universities of Kaunas and, later, Vilnius. Sruoga published three volumes of lyrics and several narrative poems. Some, like *Deivė iš ežero* (Goddess from the lake, 1919), are romantic in mood and deal with mythological subjects; others, for example, *Miestas* (The city, 1922), play with irony and humour in portraying the grotesqueries of a modern metropolis. His lyrics convey a troubled, searching spirit building sets of symbols in an attempt to discern a pattern of meaning in the universe. Yet, they also manifest enthusiasm for life, articulated in images resembling those to be found in Lithuanian folk-songs. Sruoga's main contribution may well be to verse drama. His *Milžino paunksmė* (The shade of the giant, 1932), written to commemorate the death of Grand Duke Vytautas (1430), retains a pensive, philosophical aloofness from the petty squabbles of mediocre individuals gathered around the dying ruler. The philosopher's mantle is worn by Jogaila (Jagiełło), Vytautas's cousin and the King of Poland who himself is close to death. Other plays, *Baisioji naktis* (The terrible night, 1935), *Algirdas Izborske* (A. at Izborsk, 1938) and *Kazimieras Sapiega* (Casimir Sapieha, 1947), also deal with historical topics. Sruoga's last work, a set of memoirs called *Deivų miškas* (The forest of the gods, posth., 1957), is an eloquent, at times sardonic, at times bitter, commentary on the author's period in the Stutthof concentration camp where Sruoga was sent by the Germans in 1943, together with other Lithuanian intellectuals.

RŠ

STAFF, Leopold (1878–1957), Polish poet, playwright and translator, whose life spans three very different periods of literary history (the turn-of-the-century period of Young Poland, the two interwar decades, and the first decade under Communist rule), remained in each of these among the most respected Polish poets. He was the most thoroughly Classicist of Polish 20th-century poets, but his individual brand of Classicism stemmed from many seemingly incompatible sources, e.g. Nietzsche on the one hand and Francis of Assisi on the other. His strongly Nietzschean first collection, *Sny o potędze* (Dreams of power, 1901), cast him as the chief opponent of Young Poland's tendency to Decadence and morbid pessimism. In the ensuing decades, his poetry grew aesthetically more harmonious and philosophically more Franciscan in its serene acceptance of the ways of the world. This double tendency can be best illustrated by his two interwar volumes, *Wysokie drzewa* (Tall trees, 1932) and *Barwa miodu* (The colour of honey, 1936). Finally, one of the greatest surprises of the postwar years was the seemingly sudden 'rejuvenation' of Staff in his last two volumes, the legendary *Wiklina* (Osiers, 1954) and its continuation, *Dziewięć muz* (Nine Muses, 1958). In these, Staff turned to the free verse and austere style of much younger poets like RÓŻEWICZ, and he did so with impressive results.

● *An Empty Room* (Newcastle upon Tyne, 1983).   StB

STĂNESCU, Nichita (1933–83), Roumanian poet, born into a well-off family in Ploieşti, graduated from Bucharest University in 1957 and began work as an editorial assistant. Through his sixteen volumes of verse, the first of which appeared in 1960, Stănescu established himself as the most innovative of the postwar generation of Roumanian poets. In keeping with Roumania's lively tradition of literary experiment, he challenges our conventional view of the world, inviting us to consider new perspectives, and each perspective is itself complex. As Stănescu asks: 'Since man has a perspective on the leaf, why shouldn't the leaf have a perspective on man?' Logic is turned on its head as Nature observes man, as plants assume human features. His search for a new reality, for a new 'purity of existence', is conducted in *Sensul iubirii* (The sense of love, 1960) and *O viziune a sentimentelor* (A vision of feelings, 1964). It is continued in *Dreptul la timp* (The right to time, 1965) which introduces his notion that only the future is important because only the future is true; the past is falsified, and what is present soon becomes past. The poet's language becomes more abstract in *11 elegii* (11 elegies, 1966), where Stănescu pursues his search in a dialectical form (one of the elegies is dedicated to Hegel). The essence of language itself becomes the object of his scrutiny as the poet attempts to isolate form from content. Discovering whether words can exist solely as form or content is an experiment which the poet shares with the reader and during its course the musicality of the verse entrances the reader into meditation. This aspiration to an absolute language, one which, in the poet's view, does not need to communicate, only to identify, leads him to *Necuvintele* (Non-words, 1969) and his subsequent volumes. The word is only a vehicle for speech. True poetry is only vision, feeling, a transparent glimpse of an absolute which does not require the vehicle of speech. The poet's mutilation of words and his irreverence for grammar seem to drive home the point, expressed in the last of the *Elegii*, that 'everything is so simple that it becomes unintelligible'.

•*The Still Unborn About the Dead* (London, 1975); *Bas-Relief with Heroes* (Memphis, Tenn., 1988). DJD

STANKOVIĆ, Borisav (1876–1927), Serbian fiction writer and dramatist, was a native of Vranje, S Serbia. He studied law at Belgrade, spent WWI in prison and afterwards served in the Ministry of Education until his death. Stanković is best known for a *mélodrame*, *Koštana* (1902) and a novel, *Nečista krv* (Tainted blood, 1910). He wrote one other play (*Tašana*, 1927) and three collections of short stories. In all his works he depicts the conflict between life before and after liberation from the Turks. His vigorous characters are driven by passion and beset by an inability to adapt to new ways.

•*Sophka [Nečista krv]* (London, 1932); *Koštana* (Novi Sad, 1984). VDM

STEFANYK, Vassyl´ (1871–1936), Ukrainian short-story writer, son of a peasant, studied medicine in Cracow where he made contact with the Polish writers' group Młoda Polska (Young Poland). 1899 his first collection of Expressionist short stories about peasant life, *Synia knyzhechka* (Little blue book), was published. It was followed by *Kaminny khrest* (The stone cross, 1900), *Doroha* (The road, 1901) and *Moie slovo* (My word, 1905). Written in the Pokuttia dialect, his stories manifest an austere, laconic style. In Soviet Ukrainian literary criticism he was unjustly regarded as a Realist. Stefanyk departed radically from earlier populist and Realist portrayals of the peasants. Soon after 1900 he abandoned literary activity, returning to it in 1916. His earliest work, however, remained unsurpassed.

•*The Stone Cross* (Toronto, 1971); *Maple Leaves and Other Stories* (Kiev, 1988).

D. Struk, *A Study of Vasyl´ Stefanyk: The Pain at the Heart of Existence* (Littleton, Col. 1973) (contains some translations). GSNL

STEMPEL, Kito Fryco (i.e. Christian Friedrich S., 1787–1867), Lower Sorbian poet, born in Parcow (Groß Partwitz), the son of a Lutheran pastor, after attending the Bautzen grammar school, studied theology at the University of Leipzig 1807–10. He first worked as a private tutor, then became pastor of Malin (Greifenhain), where he served 1812–23. 1823–64 he was senior pastor of Lubnjow (Lübbenau), where he remained in retirement until his death. His masterpiece, *Te tśi rychłe tšubały: zuk, głos a rěc* (The three lively trumpets: sound, voice, and speech, first complete edition 1963), written between 1859 and 1863, consists of 522 syllabic sestine representing the world as an acoustic phenomenon. He is also the author of several smaller original poems, as well as metrical translations of Phaedrus and Theocritus. GCS

STEMPOWSKI, Jerzy (1893/94–1969), Polish essayist and literary critic, born into the gentry, was educated in Poland and abroad. During WWII he settled permanently in Switzerland. In the postwar period he regularly collaborated with the Paris émigré monthly *Kultura*. As an outstanding representative of Polish essay writing, he took a wide interest in modern culture whilst taking full advantage of his Classical schooling. The main body of his literary output, collected in *Eseje dla Kassandry* (Essays for Cassandra, 1961) and *Od Berdyczowa do Rzymu* (From Berdichev to Rome, 1971), concerns the future of European society. Alarmed by the mechanisation of modern life, the supremacy of group interests over individuals and the excessive influence of non-European, culturally inferior powers, he compared the status quo with the fall of Greek civilisation. He was nevertheless convinced of the possibility of regeneration. Frequently critical of avant-garde trends, Stempowski belongs among the most important representatives of Classicism in modern Polish culture.   SE

STËRMILLI, Haki (1895–1953), Albanian prose writer and dramatist, was born in Dibër, now in Macedonia. 1920–4 he joined the Albanian democratic movement, becoming one of the leaders of the Bashkimi (Union) Society. After the fall of the democratic government of 1924, Stërmilli went into exile. 1930 the Yugoslav authorities extradited him to Albania and King Zog's régime sentenced him to five years in prison. During WWII, he participated in the resistance movement. Among his writings are the drama, *Dibranja e mjerueme* (The Dibër woman in distress, 1923) and *Dashuni e besnikri* (Love and fidelity, 1923) in which the struggle of the Dibër people against Serbian rule is described. 1935 he published *Burgu* (Prison), an account of his years in prison, but the most widely read of his works is his novel in diary form, *Sikur t'isha djalë* (If I were a boy, 1936), dedicated to the struggles of a young girl named Dija (Knowledge) for emancipation in an oppressive patriarchal society. He is also the author of *Shtigjet e lirisë* (The paths of freedom, 1967) and *Kalorësi i Skënderbeut* (The knight of Scanderbeg, 1967).   ShM

ŠTÍTNÝ ZE ŠTÍTNÉHO, Tomáš (c. 1333–c. 1405), Czech writer of religious and moral works, member of the impoverished lower nobility, studied at Prague University but gave up his studies, returned to his estate in S Bohemia and, 1381, leased out his land and lived in Prague. His tracts, usually composed in the form of a conversation between a father and his children, are intended to provide concise explanations of religious matters. They are not abstract theological essays but exegeses of Church teachings accompanied by Štítný's views on the relationship between the nobility and the common people, and between family and servants. Rebuked by the Church authorities for writing as a layman about theology, and for his use of Czech, Štítný responded that he felt it was his duty to his children and those without a knowledge of Latin. As a translator Štítný was an eclectic interested in ethics rather than metaphysics. He accepted the teachings of the Church in matters theological as well as secular and aimed solely at the moral regeneration of man and society and the consistent implementation of Christian principles in private and public life. Štítný's main works are *Knížky šestery o obecných věcech křest'anských* (Six books on general Christian matters, 1374), which he revised and enlarged several times, the more philosophically demanding *Řeči besední* (Talks, c. 1385) expounding his views on God, angels, Adam and Eve, man and the world, and *Řeči nedělní a sváteční* (Talks for Sundays and Holy Days, c. 1392), a collection of sermons on the prescribed lessons. As the first Czech prose writer dealing with themes normally treated in Latin, Štítný enriched the vocabulary of Czech with specialised terms and contributed to its syntactic development. He was an accomplished stylist with great feeling for the rhythm of the narration and together with the author of *Tkadleček* (see DISPUTE) established a standard for artistry in prose not equalled before KOMENSKÝ.   KB

STODOLA, Ivan (1887–1977), Slovak dramatist, after studying medicine in Berlin and Budapest worked as a consultant, and eventually as a functionary in the health administration. His comedies *Náš pan minister* (Our minister, 1926), *Čaj u pana senátora* (Tea with the senator, 1929) and *Jožka Púčik a jeho kariéra* (J.P. and his career, 1931) satirise unscrupulous bourgeois politicians and their sycophants in postwar democracy, whilst his *Cigánča* (A Gipsy, 1933) attacks racial prejudice. Stodola enlarged his field in *Bankinghouse Khuwich and co.* (1935), where he attacks American rapacity and other infamies real or imagined by tracing the fortunes of various families of Slovak immigrants to the USA. During the WWII Slovak State, Stodola mocked its corrupt establishment in the allegorical farce *Mravci a svrčkovia* (The ants and the crickets, 1943). Stodola's fresh, mischievous comedies overshadow his serious conventional dramas, such as the melodramatic *Bačova žena* (The head shepherd's wife, 1928), about a woman who remarries after being wrongly informed of her husband's death, the mythologising pseudo-historical *Svätopluk* (1931), *Marina Havranová* (1941) and *Básnik a smrt'* (The poet and Death, 1946), which celebrates the partisans of the Slovak National Uprising (1944).   KB

STRITAR, Josip (pseuds: Boris Miran, Peter Samotar, 1836–1923), Slovene novelist, poet and literary critic, after grammar school in Ljubljana studied Classics in Vienna and thereafter worked as a tutor in rich Austrian families, travelling widely in Europe. From 1874 until retirement a grammar-school teacher in Vienna, he returned to Slovenia shortly before his death. Pessimistic notes occur in his early verse and are fully expressed in his essays on PREŠEREN and his poetry (published as an introduction to the 1866 edition), where this life is characterised as a vale of tears, since reality can never satisfy our ideals or yearnings. Stritar is chiefly notable for his critical writings, polemics against the conservatives and the overrated talents of Jovan Kosecki (1798–1884), for his work as editor of the literary periodical *Zvon* (Vienna, 1870 and 1876–80 after a closure brought about by conservative critics) and for his satirical *Dunajski soneti* (Viennese sonnets, 1872). His novels were largely adaptations of foreign models.   HL

ŠTÚR, Ľudovít (1815–56), Slovak philologist, critic and poet, studied theology at Halle and was greatly influenced by the philosophy and aesthetics of Hegel. As a lecturer in Czech at the Lutheran lyceum in Pressburg, he took a leading part in the movement for Slovak cultural and political self-determination. More than any other writer from the 'subject nations' of the Habsburg Monarchy, Štúr made the language question a political one. He contributed decisively to the codification of the Slovak literary language based on the dialect of Central Slovakia and wrote a treatise on its theoretical basis as well as its grammar. He also founded the Slovak paper *Slovenskje národňje noviny* (Slovak national news) with a literary supplement *Orol tatránski* (The Tatra eagle), which became a platform for a group of Slovak Romantic writers. Whilst his lyric verse was personal and elegiac, his epic poems were intended to arouse awareness of national identity amongst the Slovaks by reminding them of their role in the history of Hungary. Štúr was active as a politician as a member of the Hungarian Diet and defended his radical views at the Prague Slav Congress (1848). He also organised a Slovak revolutionary force which initially fought on the side of the Hungarian anti-Habsburg rebellion in 1848–9, but subsequently turned against it. When after her victory over the Hungarians Vienna abrogated the promise of Slovak autonomy, Štúr retired from public life.   KB

SUDRABKALNS, Jānis (i.e. Arvīds Peine, 1894–1975), Latvian poet and journalist, in the interwar years proved himself a man of refined taste and Western outlook. In his earliest poems, *Spārnotā armāda* (The winged armada, 1920), he gave indications of great lyrical gifts in describing the contemporary middle-class atmosphere of convention and hypocrisy. He published, under the pseudonym Olivereto, two playful books of avant-garde verse, *Trubadūrs uz ēzeça* (Troubadour on the back of a donkey, 1921) and *Džentlmens ceriņu frakā* (Gentleman in lilac-coloured tails, 1924). He belonged to those 'bourgeois humanist' poets who lived in the intellectual ghetto of their literary cafés. Sudrabkalns, however, had no Communist leanings, and his books were in blatant opposition to Soviet writing. Nevertheless, he renounced his 'bourgeois past' completely in the name of the new faith and became one of the first Latvian disciples of Stalin. Sudrabkalns joined the *apparat* and was appointed as literary editor of the daily, *Padomju Latvija*, to which he

contributed almost weekly combative articles. At the same time Sudrabkalns expressed his feelings and hinted that perhaps the interests of the Party and historical determinism had reduced him to a hack. His poems changed into jingles about the friendship of nations and Soviet freedom.   EB

SUITS, Gustav (1883–1956), Estonian poet and literary critic, went, after a semester at Tartu, to study comparative literature, aesthetics and Finnish at Helsinki (1905–10), where he did not lose contact with Estonian intellectual life. He organised the cultural movement Young Estonia (Noor Eesti). 1910–17 he worked as a university librarian and secondary-school master. 1917 he joined the Estonian Revolutionary Socialist Party and became a member of its Central Committee. After a stay in Finland, he began teaching at Tartu (1924, reader; 1933, professor). 1924 Suits was founder and chairman of the Academic Literary Society and, 1944, he went into exile in Finland, then Sweden. Suits was a founding father of modern Estonian literature (the creation of Young Estonia, publishing its anthologies, managing its publishing house, propagating LIIV's work), above all on account of his own poetry. Suits's first collection, *Elu tuli* (The fire of life, 1905) demonstrates the younger generation's desire to be in contact with contemporaneous European cultural trends. The disturbing rhythm of Suits's innovative stanza-system and acoustically rich organisation of free verse came to express artistic and social revolt. It is true that Suits's verse later abandoned romantic exaltation and the heroisation of the poet's *Ich* (*Tuulemaa* [Land of the winds, 1913], *Kõik on kokku unenägu* [Everything is only a dream, 1922]), but it retained its emphasis on the sovereign independence of artistic creation demonstrating aesthetic form. Suits concluded his verse work in exile with *Tuli ja tuul* (Fire and wind, 1950), which constitutes an aging poet's retrospective on his own life. Representative of Suits's literary-critical works are *Noor-Eesti nõlvakult* (From the meadows of Young Estonia, 1931) and *Eesti kirjanduslugu I* (History of Estonian literature, I, 1953).

●*Flames on the Wind* (London, 1953).
O. A. Webermann, 'Gustav Suits', *Commentationes Baltici*, VI/VII (1959), pp. 424–32.   VM

SULEJMANI, Hivzi (1912–75), Albanian prose writer, playwright and poet from Kosovo, born in Mitrovicë, went to school in Skopje and then studied electrical engineering at Belgrade. After WWII he held various posts in the Kosovo regional administration and retired 1963. Among Sulejmani's publications are the short-story collections *Era dhe kolona* (The wind and the column, 1965) and *Ëndrra e korbit* (The raven's dream, 1968), the autobiographical novel *Njerëzit* (The men, 1966) *Poezi, drama* (Poetry, drama, 1981).   ShM

SUTSKEVER, **Avrom**/Abraham Sutzkever (b. 1913), undoubtedly the most significant of living Yiddish poets, born in Smorgonie in the Vilna guberniya (now Smorgon', Byelorussia), fled with his parents during WWI to Siberia. After the death of his father in 1920 he returned to Poland with his widowed mother and settled in Vilna (Vilnius) where he studied literary theory at the university, though he gained much of his education by wide, independent reading in the Strashun Library. He

also studied under Max Weinreich at the YIVO Institute at Vilna which, following its foundation in 1925, had become the foremost centre of Yiddish scholarship. In the 1930s, together with Hirsh Glik (1922–44), Khayim Grade (1910–82), Shmerl Katsherginski (1908–54) and Doniel Tsharni (1888–1959), he was a member of the avant-garde group of poets known as Yung-vilne who published their miscellanies as *Bleter* (Leaves, Kaunas, 1938) and *Naye bleter* (New leaves, Kaunas, 1939). After a literary début in 1927 with Hebrew verse, Sutskever published his first Yiddish poems in *Vokhnshrift far literatur* (Weekly literary journal, Warsaw) and *Vilner tog* (Vilnius daily). His first collection of lyric verse, *Lider* (Songs, Warsaw, 1937), brought him widespread recognition; and he then contributed poems to the New York journal *In zikh* (In oneself). Sutskever was working in a radio station at the time of the 1941 German occupation of Vilna and was active in the ghetto resistance movement. Poems written in the ghetto and in the forests of Byelorussia, where he fought with the partisans, appeared in *Di festung* (The fortress, New York, 1945). Returning to Vilna after the liberation, he helped Katsherginski retrieve YIVO materials which the latter had been able to conceal from the Nazis. Sutskever testified at the Nuremberg trials in 1945 and 1946. Via Łódź he moved to Paris and settled in Israel 1947 where he published his long poem *Geheymshtot* (Secret city, Tel Aviv, 1948) in which he records life in the sewers of Vilna, the partisans' dreams of a better future and his own responsibility as the surviving poet to commemorate the past. Since 1955 he has been the editor of *Di goldene keyt*

(The golden chain), a literary and political journal which continues to appear in Tel Aviv.

•*Siberia* (London, 1961); *Burnt Pearls, Ghetto Poems* (Oakville, Ont., 1981); *The Fiddle Rose, Poems 1970–1972* (Detroit, 1990); *Selected Poetry and Prose* (Berkeley, 1991).
J. Leftwich, *Abraham Sutzkever, Partisan Poet* (London, New York, 1971); D. G. Roskies, *Against the Apocalypse, Responses to Catastrophe in Modern Jewish Culture* (Cambridge, Mass., London), pp. 225–57.   HD

SVAJAK, Kazimir (i.e. Kanstancin Stapovič, 1890–1926), Byelorussian spiritual poet and dramatist, studied at the Vilna R. Catholic Seminary and began publishing his verse in the weekly journal *Biełarus* (1913–15). His literary legacy includes three plays, a brochure on the evils of alcohol, and a posthumously published book of memoirs, *Dzieja majoj myśli, serca i voli* (The history of my thought, heart and will, 1930) as well as a collection of verse and prose miniatures, *Maja lira* (My lyre, 1924), which contains some of the most effective spiritual and patriotic poetry in all Byelorussian literature. No formal perfectionist, he had a strong sense of style, but his poems are mainly remarkable for their patent sincerity, concision of expression and depth of feeling.
•A. McMillin, 'Early 20th-Century Byelorussian Spiritual Poetry' in R. Lachmann *et al.* (Eds), *'Tgolí chole Mêstro.' Gedenkschrift für Reinhold Olesch* (Cologne, 1990), pp. 535–46.
                                                    ABMcM

ŠVANTNER, František (1912–50), Slovak prose writer, a schoolmaster, is the main exponent of the Lyrical Prose school. The theme of both his novella *Malka* (1942) and his novel *Nevesta hôl* (The mountain bride, 1946), set in the rugged landscape of the Slovak mountains, is the mysterious participation of Nature in the life of human beings. The 'mountain bride', Zuna, is impervious to human feelings; she lives in unity with the primeval world impenetrable to those whom she bewitches and she pays for her encounters with them with her life. Although Švantner's view of Nature is somewhat reminiscent of that of Giono, it is more extreme. It combines pantheism with the anthropomorphism of folk myths, and individual characters behave under the spell of dark, even demonic, forces. The strongest point of Švantner's prose lies in the narration which reduces the epic element to a minimum. By exploiting the poetic potential of the language, he conjures up an atmosphere of disquieting dreams. Švantner turned to Realism in the unfinished *roman-fleuve*, *Život bez konca* (Life without end, 1956), a critical picture of Slovak society in the years 1894–1934.
•'Malka' in *An Anthology of Slovak Literature* (Riverside, Calif., 1976). KB

SVĚTLÁ, Karolína (i.e. Johanna Mužáková, 1830–99), prolific Czech prose writer from the German Prague patriciate, married a dryasdust patriotic schoolmaster (from whose birthplace she took her pseudonym), and her later great love was NERUDA; she became involved in the women's movement and co-founded the Women's Work Society (1871); 1875 she went almost entirely blind and for the rest of her life dictated her works to a niece. Her novels and short stories concerning the National Revival, and, later, 1848, are conventional, even formulaic, but do show her as an accomplished story-teller. In her village prose, however, she often manifests considerable skill in characterisation. Her most read novel, *Kříž u potoka* (The cross by the brook, 1868), concerns a bright village girl's taming of a wild man from the gentry. The racily written work sometimes suffers from over-sentimentalisation and didacticism. Světlá's most important work is *Vesnický román* (A village novel, 1868), where three women mould a perfect man: his wife (pagan materialism), his beloved (pure emotion, Nature, Protestantism) and his mother (reason, severe Catholicism); he loses wife and beloved; his mother wins; he becomes the most respected man for miles around and dies a psychological wreck. Světlá tries to conceal this irony by showing how socially useful the man's bigoted mother is.

• *Maria Felicia* (Chicago, 1898).

Antonín Měšt'an, *Geschichte der tschechischen Literatur im 19. und 20. Jahrhundert* (Cologne, Vienna, 1984).

RBP

SVETOKRIŠKI, Janez (monastic name of Tobija Lionelli, 1647–1714), Slovene Capuchin monk, popular preacher, author of Baroque sermons of great wit and charm, son of a Venetian noble and a Slovene mother, also of noble family, joined the Capuchin Order c. 1660, served as priest, preacher and monastic superior in Trieste, Ljubljana, Novo Mesto and Gorica. His sermons in Slovene were so popular that he had to preach in the open in summer. At the request of his colleagues he published 1691–1707 five large volumes of sermons: *Sanctum promptuarium*.

HL

SZCZEPAŃSKI, Jan Józef (b. 1919), Polish novelist, served in the army in September 1939 and later in the underground forces. Since the war he has had links with the R. Catholic weekly *Tygodnik Powszechny* (Weekly for all). As chairman

of the Polish Writers' Union, he fought courageously against its abolition by the Jaruzelski government (1981–3) and subsequently described the experience in his book *Kadencja* (Tenure, 1988). Szczepański is best known for his war fiction, for example, *Polska Jesień* (The Polish autumn, 1955) and the collection of short stories *Buty* (Boots, 1956), where he combined documentary accuracy with a great sensitivity to moral problems. Szczepański's more recent books have an essayistic and autobiographical character, reflecting the writer's extensive overseas travels (*Rafa* [Reef, 1974]).

SE

SZÉCHENYI, Count István (1791–1860), Hungarian prose writer, was the son of the rich Count Ferenc Széchényi (name usually spelt thus) who was a prominent representative of the Hungarian Enlightenment and founded the Hungarian National Library in 1803. Having distinguished himself as a soldier in the Napoleonic Wars, Széchenyi travelled extensively in W Europe. 1825 he offered one year's income from his estates towards the expenses of establishing an Academy of Sciences in Pest. He exerted a decisive influence on Hungarian social, political and economic renewal. Although he disagreed with Kossuth's plan to separate Hungary from Austria, he accepted a post in the revolutionary cabinet of 1848. His inability to prevent the suppression of the Hungarian revolution, which he had foreseen from the very beginning, caused his mental breakdown in September 1848, after which he moved to an institution near Vienna. When the Hungarians were defeated by the Russian Army and neo-absolutism was introduced, he decided to attack Vienna in writings published anonymously in London. Harassed by the secret police, he took his own life on Easter Sunday, 1860. Széchenyi was the most important Hungarian essayist of the first half of the 19th century. His diary, written mainly in German and published in six volumes 1931–9, is the *journal intime* of a highly self-contradictory character, one of the great Romantic 'confessions'. His lyric poems are few in number and are mainly of historical interest, but the books and articles he wrote in Hungarian show him to be a brilliant stylist. *Hitel* (Credit, 1830), the first important book he published with the aim of introducing social reforms in Hungary, shows his double allegiance. The thesis that the criterion of social good is the happiness of the greatest number of people and the programme asking for a market economy, capitalist enterprise, and unlimited property would suggest an acceptance of Bentham's ideas, but his insistence on the spiritual independence of the individual represents a departure from the principles of utilitarianism. He explored the ontological implications of his Romantic liberalism in *Világ* (Light, 1831), and summarised his political programme in *Stádium* (The state of affairs, 1833). In *Hunnia*, written between 1831 and 1835 but not published until 1858, he outlined a relativist definition of culture and insisted that the survival of even the smallest and most primitive nation is of utmost importance for mankind. This principle led him to publish a satirical pamphlet in German, *Ein Blick* (A look, 1859), attacking the oppression of one nation by another.

●G. Barany, *Stephen Széchenyi and the Awakening of Hungarian Nationalism* (Princeton, 1968); R. Porter and M. Teich (Eds), *Romanticism in National Context* (Cambridge, 1988).   MSz-M

SZENCI MOLNÁR, Albert (1574–1634), Hungarian scholar and poet, spent most of his life outside Turkish-occupied Hungary translating and publishing for the Calvinist cause. His works include a revision of the Vizsoly BIBLE (Hanau, 1605), and translations of Calvin's *Institutions* (Hanau, 1624) and the Heidelberg Catechism (Heidelberg, 1607). He compiled a Latin-Hungarian/Hungarian-Latin dictionary (*Dictionarium latino-ungaricum et ungaro-latinum*, Nuremberg, 1604) and a grammar of Hungarian in Latin (*Novae grammaticae ungaricae ... libri duo*, Hanau, 1610). His greatest literary achievement was the translation into Hungarian verse of the Geneva Psalter (*Psalterium ungaricum*, Herborn, 1607). Unlike his contemporaries, he adapted his verse to fit the melodies of the original and succeeded magnificently; his versions are both fluent and poetic, and the best of them appear in all standard anthologies as well as in modern hymnals. His preface to the Psalter is the earliest essay on Hungarian prosody, in which he was one of the foremost innovators.

●Translation of the *Preface* in T. Klaniczay (ed.), *Old Hungarian Literary Reader* (Budapest, 1985); B. Stoll (Ed.), *Szenci Molnár Albert költői művei* (Budapest, 1971).   GFC

SZKHÁROSI HORVÁT, András (16th century), Hungarian poet, was a Franciscan friar who became a vigorous protagonist of Lutheranism and pastor, 1542–9, in the village of Tállya, NE Hungary. His ten surviving lengthy poems are virtual sermons in verse; they reveal him as a passionate and irascible advocate of reform, castigating all and sundry, from R. Catholic priests to princes, merchants to millers, who oppress the poor. His paraphrase of the curse in Deuteronomy 28 is the most terrifying poem in Hungarian. Szkhárosi Horvát's verse is carefully constructed to produce the maximum rhetorical effect; his OT vocabulary is spiced with his own sarcastic humour. He is a competent poet, using a variety of metres and stanza-forms, all to suggest that hell is never far away.

●Excerpts in T. Klaniczay (Ed.), *Old Hungarian Literary Reader* (Budapest, 1985); A. Szilády (Ed.), *Régi magyar költők tára*, vol. II (Budapest, 1880), pp. 159–230.   GFC

SZTÁRAI, Mihály (?–c. 1575), Hungarian poet and playwright, studied in Padua, entered the Franciscan Order and then adopted Lutheranism. He became a passionate proselytiser in Turkish-occupied S Hungary 1544–64 and organised a flourishing church there. Temperamental and quarrelsome, he then moved north and disappeared after losing the Lutheran superintendency in Pápa to BORNEMISZA, who declares that Sztárai was 'overwhelmed sometimes by wrath and sometimes by wine'. Sztárai was among the first Hungarian poets to adapt and versify Psalms to suit the contemporary situation. He also wrote poetic versions of biblical tales and a lengthy poem on the death of Cranmer (1560), identifying himself with the martyr. Often involved in public disputes with R. Catholics, he dramatised two of these in his *Comoedia lepidissima de matrimonio sacerdotum* (1550), only a fragment of which has survived, and *Comoedia lepidissima de sacerdotio* (1559), both in Hungarian. Sztárai was an innovator in that he altered his style to suit his audience. While his verse and metrical Psalms possess an ecclesiastical solemnity,

his plays are written in a rustic idiom for a largely illiterate public. His Psalms, which appeared in numerous hymnals, bear the stamp of a fine lyric poet.

●A. Szilády (Ed.), *Régi magyar költők tára*, vol. II (Budapest, 1880), pp. 317–24 and vol. V (Budapest, 1886), pp. 73–262; T. Kardos (Ed.), *Régi magyar drámai emlékek*, vol. I (Budapest, 1960), pp. 581–614.   GFC

SZYMBORSKA, Wisława (b. 1923), Polish poet, essayist and translator, the most outstanding woman poet of post-1945 Poland, was born in the small town of Bnin but since 1931 has lived continuously in Cracow. She made her literary début in 1945; the planned publication of her first collection in 1948 was halted for political reasons, and the book, *Dlatego żyjemy* (That's what we live for), came out only in 1952, followed by *Pytania zadawane sobie* (Questions put to myself, 1954). The second collection shows her as a poet of intellectual and moral anguish. This is increasingly true of her subsequent volumes: *Wołanie do Yeti* (Calling out to the Yeti, 1957), *Sól* (Salt, 1962), *Sto pociech* (A hundred laughs, 1967), *Wszelki wypadek* (There but for the grace, 1972), *Wielka liczba* (A great number, 1976) and *Ludzie na moście* (The people on a bridge, 1986). She has also published essays and translations from French poetry. Szymborska's characteristic creative method consists of starting with a deceptively simple observation to end up with a poem structured as a highly complex ironic conceit. Her own brand of 'ironic moralism' seldom touches on overtly political issues yet it treats the most crucial problems civilisation faces, first and foremost the problem of the irresoluble contradiction between the needs of the individual and the demands of collectivist and utopian ideologies. Szymborska incessantly defends the right to an individual position in spite of the terror of the collective. Each of her poems undertakes in its own way the same task of defending individual uniqueness from imposed uniformity, randomness from determinism, the concreteness of existence from the abstract anonymity of time, the exception from the rule, the right to doubt from the blind self-assurance of utopias.

•*People on a Bridge* (London, 1990); *Sounds, Feelings, Thoughts: Seventy Poems* (Princeton, 1981); selected poems in S. Barańczak and C. Cavanagh (Eds), *Polish Poetry of the Last Two Decades of Communist Rule: Spoiling Cannibals' Fun* (Evanston, Ill., 1991).
M. G. Levine, *Contemporary Polish Poetry, 1925–1975* (Boston, 1981); S. Barańczak, *Breathing Under Water* (Cambridge, Mass., 1990).   StB

SZYMONOWIC, Szymon (pseud. Simon Simonides, 1558–1629), Polish poet and playwright, writing in Polish and Latin, born into a burgher family in Lwów, studied liberal arts at Cracow Academy and abroad before coming under the patronage of Chancellor J. Zamoyski. Early in his career, Szymonowic wrote in Latin (among other works, a Classical tragedy, *Castus Joseph* [1587]). 1614 marks the publication of his most important work written in Polish, *Sielanki* (Pastorals). This sequence of 20 pastorals, variously mythical or realistic, set in Arcadia or contemporary Poland, exerted a powerful influence on the ensuing development of Polish pastoral poetry. It is considered the last great work of Polish Renaissance literature.

•Selected pastorals in B. Carpenter (Ed.), *Monumenta Polonica* (Ann Arbor, 1989).   StB

T

T'ABIDZE, Galak't'ion (1892–1959), Georgian poet, author of over a thousand lyrics, was a cousin and virtually neighbour of T'itsian T'ABIDZE but a totally autonomous poet. His first book, *Crâne aux fleurs artistiques* (1919), was heavily influenced by French Symbolists, especially Verlaine, but showed a totally new talent for making Georgian a subtly sonorous, almost onomatopoeic medium for conveying mood. By the 1920s his themes of isolation, lovelessness and nightmarish premonitions had made certain lyrics ('Usiq'varulod', [Without love]; 'Me da ghame', [I and the night]; 'Kari hkris', [The wind blows]) as widely known as nursery rhymes: he was accorded the rare honour of being known simply as Galak't'ion. He was at his greatest and most cryptic in the mid-1920s in poems such as 'Sasaplaoni' (Graveyards), where 'the row of centuries is counted by a mummy'. His rhythmic virtuosity was diverted to write intoxicatingly revolutionary poems which won him acceptance from the Party without his ever making a coherent act of submission. By luck, he was spared the political manoeuvres and purges of the Georgian Union of Writers in the 1930s, but in 1937 the judicial murder of his wife, née Okujava, plunged him into relentless alcoholism and clinical depression.

Occasional remissions produced extraordinarily ingenious, almost fugue-like poems, e.g. the 80-line paean to the church of Nik'orts'minda (1947), or painful suicidal elegies, such as 'Midikhar . . . ise migakvs ts'valeba' (You're going . . . you carry your distress', 1956). In true Mallarméan fashion, 'Las du triste hôpital, et de l'encens fétide', he jumped to his death from the window of a psychiatric hospital. His archive of about 100,000 items in the Literary Museum, Tbilisi, still awaits full investigation.

●D. Rayfield, *Galaktion Tabidze: Ten Poems* (Tbilisi, 1975).   DR

T'ABIDZE, T'itsian (1895–1937), Georgian Symbolist poet, was born into a priest's family in Shuamta on the River Rioni; like other 'Blue horns' (*tsisperq' ants' lebi*) poets and Mayakovsky, he was educated in Kutaisi. He was an intimate of IASH-VILI and together they were spellbound by European Decadence. He studied at Moscow 1913–17, and was heavily influenced by Blok's poetry, Wilde and the Belgian Symbolists combined with his evocations of the malarial marshes of the River Rioni and his memories of his family's ecclesiastical forebears. This unlikely synthesis made T'abidze's first lyrics highly original. His early 'Blue horns' poetry of 1915–16 is obsessed with ominous Chaldean sorcery.

Like Georgian poets before him, he aimed to fuse East and West: 'I put Hafiz's roses in Prudhomme's vase, Baudelaire's poisonous flowers in Besik'i's garden.' In the independence period (1918–21) poems such as 'Birnamis t'q'e' (Birnam Wood), 'Mghvdeli da malaria k'uboshi' (Priest and malaria in coffin) equal Picasso paintings: they infuse pathos with the surreal. Under Soviet rule T'itsian switched to more conventional modes: he adopted the Yesenin cult of the doomed country lad (*Me q'achaghebma momk'les Aragvze*, [Robbers have killed me on the Aragvi, 1926]) and took up Pasternak's celebration of Nature as poetic creation (*Leksi-mets'q'eri* [Poem-avalanche, 1927]). It was no wonder that Pasternak treated him as a second Rilke. Moving cadences from Georgian folklore and the heroic resignation of VAZHA PSHAVELA infuse T'itsian's 1920s lyrics. Inspiration falters after 1926 and dies with Mayakovsky in 1930. Despite a physical resemblance to Tiberius, T'itsian abandoned his Decadent manner: he became a compliant *apparatchik*, expelling fellow writers from the Union, anxiously celebrating Stalin's industrialisation. Like IASHVILI, he was favoured, then doomed, by Beria. Unwilling to 'confess' in 'courts' held by the praesidium of the Georgian Union of Writers, he was denounced for loyalty to his mentor, the defector ROBAKIDZE: he was arrested in October 1937 and killed after prolonged torture. Unlike IASHVILI, he anticipated his fate in his last lyrics: 'The poet's throat, slashed from ear to ear, Will live in the atom of verse.'

●D. Rayfield, 'Georgian Poetry: Titsian and Galaktion Tabidze', *Modern Poetry in Translation*, 1974, pp. 11–13.

Boris Pasternak, *Letters to Georgian Friends* (London, 1975); T. Nikol'skaya, 'Russian Imazhinists in Tbilisi', in Ellendea & Carl Proffer, (Eds), *The Ardis Anthology of Russian Futurism* (Ann Arbor, 1980), pp. 295–326; D. Rayfield, 'Pasternak and the Georgians', *Irish Slavonic Studies*, III (1982), pp. 39–46, and 'Unicorns and Gazelles: Pasternak, Rilke and the Georgian Poets', *Forum for Modern Language Studies*, xxvi (1990), 4, pp. 370–81.   DR

TACHTSIS, Kostas (1927–88), Greek prose writer and poet, brought up in Athens by his grandmother after his parents' separation, began studying law but dropped out (1947). In the years after his military service he showed no interest in a career or stable lifestyle, finding it difficult as a homosexual and transvestite to fit into conservative postwar Greek society. At this period he began publishing poems in private editions, and mixing in the avant-garde poetic circles of the capital. 1954–64 he moved around the world, returning periodically to Athens: his travels took him to England, Germany, Austria, Africa, Australia and the USA. During his first stay in Australia (1957–9) he began writing his masterpiece, Το τρίτο στεφάνι (The third wedding), which was privately published in 1962, selling precisely ten copies. It was only under the Junta that the novel became, mysteriously, a cult book among political detainees, leading to its reissue and instant public success in 1972. Two years later he brought out a volume of autobiographical short stories, Τα ρεστα (Small change), and in 1979 a collection of occasional pieces entitled Η γιαγιά μου Αθήνα και άλλα κείμενα (My grandmother Athens and other texts). He was murdered in 1988. His reputation rests on only two works, but they are both outstanding. His poetry had revealed a sharp eye for the power of everyday detail. His prose harnessed this talent to evocative effect. 'The third wedding' uses its two female narrators to uncover the values of the Greek middle classes in the first half of the 20th century in a way which is psychologically veracious, outstandingly funny and persuasively satirical. The stories of 'Small change' constitute fragments of confessional self-exploration while interrelating in broader preoccupations with his novel. In both works the power of the family and its relation to the personal and sexual development of the individual offer a microcosm of the problems of the individual in contemporary Greek society.

●*The Third Wedding Wreath* (Athens, 1985). CFR

TAMMSAARE, A. H. (i.e. Anton Hansen, 1878–1940), Estonian prose writer, dramatist and essayist, was the son of a farmer, the name of whose house provided him with his *nom de plume*. After his matriculation (1903), he worked as a journalist in Tallinn. After the defeat of the 1905 Revolution, he went to Tartu University to read law, but TB prevented him from completing his studies. 1912–13 he took a cure amongst Estonian settlers in the Caucasus and, after that, lived mainly with his brother in Koitjärve, until 1918, when he fled the war to Tallinn. An outsider to social and political life, he devoted himself there only to literature; he did not even take part in the 1936 ceremony unveiling a monument to himself in Järva-Madise, or in the official celebration of his sixtieth birthday. At the beginning of his literary career, Tammsaare was close to the artistic conception of Russian 'Realism' (*Raha-auk* [Trea-

sure trove, 1907]), but simultaneously, in connection with the aesthetic programme of Young Estonia, he tried his hand at psychologising, impressionistic prose, e.g. *Pikad sammud* (Strides, 1908) and *Noored hinged* (Young souls, 1909). These two lines intersect in his novel, *Kõrboja peremees* (Husbandman for K., 1922), in which a reappraisal of the rural theme, in the manner of Scandinavian neo-Romanticism, becomes a starting-point for a polysemic parable concerning the present and future of the nation. The pentalogy *Tõde ja õigus* (Truth and justice, 1926–33) forms the apex of Tammsaare's endeavours at some synthesis; it is an epic comprising the development of Estonia from the 1870s to the 1920s, behind whose backdrop is concealed a tract on humanity's 'search for truth', a tract ingeniously constructed on a game with paradoxes. A sense of paradox in language and action is also manifest in Tammsaare's erotic novels, *Elu ja armastus* (Life and love, 1934) and *Ma armastasin sakslast* (I loved a German woman, 1935). The mock-fairy-tale, grotesque novel *Põrgupõhja uus Vanapagan* (A new devil from Hell, 1939) constitutes a bitter conclusion to Tammsaare's work, reflecting the social and political crisis of the late 1930s. His plays had a certain impact at the time – *Juudit* (Judith, 1921) and *Kuningal on külm* (The king is cold, 1936).

●*Miniatures* (Tallinn, 1977); *The Misadventures of the New Satan* (Moscow, 1978); one story in H. Puhvel (Ed.), *Estonian Short Stories* (Tallinn, 1981).

E. Siirak, *A. H. Tammsaare in Estonian Literature* (Tallinn, 1978). VM

TANK, Maksim (i.e. Jaŭhien Skurko, b. 1912), Byelorussian poet, born in

W Byelorussia (E Poland), was one of many writers to be imprisoned for his Communist beliefs; nevertheless, his prison poems, though powerful, are far from dominant in his work. Beginning to write in 1931, he produced three remarkable verse collections before WWII: *Na etapach* (Staging posts, 1936) displays a dazzling range of subgenres, metres and themes, occasionally complex to the point of obscurity; *Žuravinavy ćviet* (Cranberry blossom, 1938) is notable for its evocative associative imagery; the best of the three, *Pad mačtaj* (Beneath the mast, 1938), contains much allegory, but with more classical restraint than hitherto; as before, the themes range from Nature, love and philosophy to politics, the latter often treated with venomous satire. Two of Tank's longer poems depict life under alien rule: *Narač* (Lake N., 1937) in the form of a rhapsodic allegory and, more realistically, *Kalinoŭski* (1938); also important is the sophisticated folk stylisation *Skaz pra Viala* (The tale of Vial, 1937). Though an establishment figure in the Soviet period, Tank succeeded in maintaining his poetic inventiveness and freshness of vision.

●'Maxim Tank's Poetry', *Soviet Literature* (1966), no. 10, pp. 129–35; *Red Lilies of the Valley* (Minsk, 1986).

ABMcM

TATARKA, Dominik (1913–89), Slovak prose writer, became a symbol for Slovaks in the 1970s and 1980s because he was the only highly regarded Slovak literary figure to join Charter 77. He read Slovak and French at Prague and the Sorbonne, was a schoolmaster during WWII, after which he became a Communist journalist. His literary career was wayward, even opportunistic. The ironically lyrical and escapist pastiche *Panna Zázračnica* (The miraculous maiden, 1944) concerns a young woman who becomes muse to Bratislava artists, though her existence provides self-delusion rather than inspiration to the artists. *Farská republika* (The parish republic, 1948) is a sophisticated Socialist Realist novel depicting the development of the Slovak puppet state from the beginning of WWII to the Soviet liberation; *Prvý a druhý úder* (The first and second blow, 1950) is crass Stalinist sentimentalising, melodramatic fiction about a partisan who becomes a builder of socialist bridges. In *Démon súhlasu* (The demon of conformity, 1963) Tatarka makes fun of Socialist Realism. Then in his 'dissident' works, like *Písačky* (Jottings, 1984) or *Navrávačky* (Tapings, 1988), he pursues egocentric sensualism and nostalgic folksy didacticism.

●R. B. Pynsent (Ed.), *Modern Slovak Prose. Fiction Since 1954* (London, 1990).

RBP

TAVČAR, Ivan (1851–1923), Slovene prose writer, son of a small farmer, attended grammar school in Ljubljana and studied law in Vienna. After working as a legal assistant in Ljubljana and Kranj he opened his own independent practice in 1884 remaining in Ljubljana till his death, and becoming mayor of the city, 1911–21. He led an active political life, as an anticlerical, antisocialist liberal. Towards the end, he withdrew from public life. He began writing while still a student, proving himself a born story-teller. His first tales were concerned with unrequited love; his early novels of peasant and manorial life were Romantic in spirit: *Ivan Slavelj* (1876), in which a poor boy, the author personified, becomes a medical man, and marries into the manorial class. *Mrtva srca* (Dead hearts, 1884) is a pessimistic and satirical portrayal of bourgeois and manorial life.   HL

TCHARENTS, Eghishe (1897–1937), Armenian poet, born in Kars, conceived during the massacres of 1896, a witness and chronicler of the 1915 Genocide, a volunteer in the battalion to help liberate his 'blue-eyed fatherland', a devout believer and participant in the 1917 October Revolution, was himself eventually devoured by another terror, the Stalinist purges. Tcharents's early poems glorified the fresh breath that the Revolution was meant to generate and reflected the changes raging around him. He had proclaimed his credo to be: 'If you want your song to be heard, then be the breath of your age.' At 18 (1915) he had witnessed the devastation of his own country and the Genocide of his people; he could not have been indifferent. His two long poems, *Danteakan Aŕaspel* (Danteesque legend, 1916) and *Aboghnerê ghelagarvats* (Frenzied masses, 1919), brought him instant recognition. In the chaotic days of 1919, the republic's Minister of Culture and the country's leading literary critic, Nikol Aghbalyan, lectured on the new poet, which was an event in itself. 1920–30 Tcharents published several volumes of verse, two novels and a book of memoirs. Since he was director of the State Press, major new writers had their first works published through his encouragement and initiative. Tcharents's last work, *Girk' Tcanaparhi* (The book of the road, 1934), is a patriotic canvas glittering with metaphors; the reader is drawn into their vertiginous whirl as the poet's vibrant voice sometimes laments and sometimes glorifies the past. Along with this volume, Tcharents's last poems written between

1934 and his death, first published in 1983, represent a complete departure from his early revolutionary work. In them Tcharents develops further the thematic shift begun in *Girk' Tcanaparhi*; while the style may sometimes appear diffuse, the briskness and lucidity of the poet's voice are unmistakably Tcharentsian. The symbolism is far less oblique, to the point of seeming over-obvious. If there was ever any doubt about his patriotism, it was put to rest by his long poem 'In Memory of N.S.', that first appeared in *Grakan T'ert* in 1967. In it Tcharents audaciously reaffirms the indestructibility of the Armenian spirit. A comparable mood also obtains in his novel *Erkir Nayiri* (The land of N.), written in 1922, long before his persecution had gathered momentum. Though satirical, it is an agonising re-creation of the 1918 fall of the fortress of Kars. His hopes of seeing Kars liberated were dashed by successive treaties in 1921 between the USSR and Turkey, treaties that formalised the annexation of Armenian provinces. He was a devout Communist, having seen the rise of the 'red dawn' as the liberation of his homeland; but when that did not materialise, he felt deceived; his disillusion and grief found immediate expression in the work he produced from 1933 to his death. Tcharents wrote his last poem on a table-napkin on the night of 27 September 1937, two months before his death. It is a short poem dedicated to Avetik' Isahakyan (1875–1957), a thought triggered by Isahakyan's epic poem *Abu-Lala-Mahari* (Abul Ala Maarri, 1911), and is the last heart-searing tribute Tcharents paid to the culture he loved and enriched. Tcharents's life ended in a prison in Yerevan. We know nothing about the circumstances nor whether he even has a grave.

•Selection in *Anthology of Armenian Poetry* trans. and ed. by Dian Der Hovanessian and Marzbed Margossian (New York, 1978).
'The Life and Work of Eghishe Tcharents', *Ararat*, vol. XXVI, 4 (Autumn 1985), pp. 14–61.   VN

TEIMURAZ I (1589–1663), King of Kakhetia (E Georgia) for the first third of the 17th century (under Persian suzerainty), was also King of Kartli 1634–48 and died in exile at Astarabad. (His life was described in verse by King ARCHIL of Imeretia and Kartli in the 15th 'response' of his *Comparison*.) Son of the ruthless King Davit I of Kakhetia and of one of the last Georgian martyrs, Queen St Ketevan (both of them, however, *literati*), he was educated in Persia under Shah Abbas's tutelage. He had such a universal knowledge of Persian and Georgian literature that he thought himself superior to RUS-TAVELI. Few poets or kings had such a traumatic life. For most of his reign feudal lords or neighbouring kings forced him into Turkish, Persian, Imeretian or Russian exile; his mother was martyred in 1624 for refusing to accept Islam; in 1610 his first wife died; his sons Aleckandre, Levan and Davit perished at the hands of the Persians; his daughter Darejan – the Georgian Cleopatra – had a catastrophic life: she was to be speared to death in 1660. (Even Teimuraz's grandsons had tragic fates.) His sole success in a last humiliating exile was to take holy orders (at the age of 70) and refuse Islam. Spectacular political failure was compensated by singlehanded poetic success: the Georgian cultural renascence recognised Teimuraz I as its progenitor. (Nihilist critics disagree:

Ant'on Purtseladze [1839–1913] wrote [1911], 'Teimuraz added poetry to banqueting, luxury and hunting, and preferred it to all these. He imagined, like Nero with his music, poetry and acting, that no poet had ever equalled him and sat for days on end at his ugly, mindless verses and wrecked his life thereby. One is amazed . . . that, the victim of a thousand tragic, lamentable events, . . . was not once struck by a worthwhile, heartfelt idea.') Teimuraz I's first creative period was 1629–34, when he was secure on his throne; he then adapted from the Persian the romances of *Leila and Mejnun, Josef and Zuleika*. The second period, 1649–56, was at the court of his brother-in-law, Aleksandre III of Imeretia: poetry was therapy – 'Tears flowed mercilessly like the Nile from my eyes. To overcome I wrote from time to time, I threw my heart into it. I spent many days and nights, By sitting plunged in thought, I salvaged my heart, The wheel turned back, it was fate that wept for me' (the introduction to his version of the Persian *Shamiparvaniani* [Candle and ash]). His original verse includes *Gazap-khul-shemodgomis keba* (Praise of spring and autumn), more elegy than eulogy; in a number of odes to beauty *Majama* (here: Anthology) he expresses Persian ascetic and aesthetic ideals of mystical union with the divine, as well as Christian resignation and repentance. For all his virtuosity in rhyme, Teimuraz I's personal pessimism imbues everything: 'The accursed world has made me regret my days with utter bitterness, It has given me no sleep, nor has it ever said a tender word to me. The world has not exhausted its treachery on me, It has given me mortal poison to drink . . . It has given me a shroud for a skin...' Teimuraz's most painful poem, however, is probably his first (c. 1630): 80 lines of *Ts'igni da ts'ameba Ketevan dedoplisa* (The book and passion of Queen K.), describing the capture of his mother Ketevan and of his sons, Aleksandre and Levan, by Shah Abbas, after the Shah had laid waste to Kakhetia. After five years the Shah removed Ketevan's grandsons from Shiraz and ordered her to be converted or killed. She endured appalling torture: Teimuraz spares his readers nothing of the eye-witness accounts. His ability to describe horrors, albeit in the medieval hagiographical genre, is proof that whatever Georgia lost in the king, it gained in the poet.   DR

TEIMURAZ II (1700–62), King of Kakhetia 1731–44, then of Kartli until his death (in Astrakhan, after a visit to Tsaritsa Elizaveta of Russia), despite his political successes in uniting central and eastern Georgia and keeping the peace with the Persian sovereign, was constantly at war or on guard. His cultural activities were a continuation of the europeanising work of the Tbilisi Catholicos Ant'on I. As well as translating the *Timsariani* (Sinbad, 1737) from Persian, he composed (on horseback) a verse *Dghis da ghamis gabaaseba, anu Sark'e tkmulta* (Dispute between day and night, or mirror of sayings, 1738). *Khilta keba* (Praise of fruit, date unknown) – a description of 38 fruits – and a number of ingenious acrostics show that Teimuraz II lacked originality, depth or artistry, but had exemplary motives.

•D. M. Lang, *The Last Years of the Georgian Monarchy* (New York, 1957).
DR

T'EK'EYAN, Vahan (1878–1945), Armenian poet, born in Constantinople, in the Ortakoy district which had been, since 1840, inhabited by rich Armenians and the intellectual élite, attended various Armenian schools in his native city. 1894 he was obliged to leave school and go to work as a clerk for Armenian commercial firms, and for the next fourteen years he lived and worked in London, Marseilles, Amsterdam and Egypt. 1892, when a schoolboy, he published his first poems in two Constantinople newspapers, *Hayrenik'* and *Tsaghik*. After the Genocide of 1915, he lived in Bulgaria and Greece, then Paris, and finally, Cairo, where he died. He was the homeless Armenian poet par excellence. His first volume of poems, *Hoger* (Cares, 1901), was published in Paris; it is a collection of 36 lyrical poems and 28 prose-poems. Much of it is adolescent verse, for which he himself wrote the epitaph: 'Here I seal up my sated youth, Here stops my pursuit of shadows.' *Hrashali yarut'iwn* (Miraculous resurrection, 1914) was published in Constantinople, on the eve of WWI and the Genocide. It contains 107 poems written over 13 years, and is a rich, if uneven, collection. Passionate religious feelings and fervent nationalism mark many of these poems, while others deal with love and disappointment. He published his *Kes Gisher mintcev arshaloys* (From midnight to dawn, 1918) in Paris; this includes some of his most powerful poems, expressing the poet's agony over the national tragedy he had witnessed. *Ser* (Love, 1933) is considered his masterpiece. His postwar preoccupations, hopes and sorrows find expression here: the appearance and disappearance of the little Armenian Republic, the problem of orphans, and uncertainty about the future are his inspiration.   VN

TEMESVÁRI,   Pelbart   (c.

1440–1504), Hungarian Franciscan scholar and writer, studied in Cracow and taught in Buda. All his published works provided practical and simple material for use among the ordinary people by his fellow preachers. His *Stellarium Coronae Mariae Virginis* (1498) and *Sermones Pomerii* (1499) were widely used in Europe and republished from Venice to Paris; they formed the basis of sermons in the vernacular and were translated in whole or part into various languages, including Hungarian. His *Aureum Rosarium Theologiae* (1503–8) is a vast theological encyclopaedia, of which his pupil Ozsvát Laskai completed the final volume. In a Humanist age, Temesvári was no Humanist, but clung to Scholasticism. Nevertheless his encyclopaedic knowledge of both secular and sacred themes, from local anecdotes to legends, made him one of the most important sources of European tales and fables, as La Fontaine admits. In Hungary, his work lies behind much of 16th-century literary activity, and was used by Czech Counter-Reformation writers.

GFC

TETMAJER, Kazimierz Przerwa (1865–1940), Polish poet, fiction writer and playwright, based initially in Cracow, and Zakopane in his beloved Tatra Mountains, moved to Warsaw after WWI. The period of his literary prominence, however, was confined to the two decades before 1914, during which he published seven volumes of his *Poezje* (Poems) and most of his fiction; c. 1925 mental illness put an end to his creativity. Tetmajer was most important during the turn-of-the-century Young Poland movement, to whose success he greatly contributed. Inspired by Schopenhauer and Hindu philosophy, in his first three verse volumes (1891, 1894, 1898) he laid down the norm of lyrical expression for the contemporary Decadent mood. In fiction, his greatest achievement is a sequence of short stories about Tatra mountaineers, *Na Skalnym Podhalu* (In Upper Podhale, 1903–10).   StB

THEOTOKAS, Yoryos (1905–66), Greek prose writer and dramatist, was born in Constantinople. After the Asia Minor Disaster (1922) he fled with his family to Athens where he read law (degree 1926). He lived in Paris 1927–8, making visits to London. 1928–9 he wrote Ελεύθερο Πνεύμα (Free spirit), which he published under the pseudonym of Orestes Diyenis, offering it as an intellectual manifesto for the 1930s. In it he criticised the fact that the idea of a Greater Greece was the only ideal which the Greeks had pursued since the War of Independence, and the language question the only problem which they had seriously confronted. In place of these outmoded preoccupations, he preached a new intellectual freedom and creative rebellion designed to bring Greece truly into the 20th century. 1931 he began to practise law in Athens, and published his first purely creative work, Ωρες αργίας (Hours of idleness). 1935 he helped to found the influential Modernist periodical Τα Νέα Γράμματα (New writing). His first novel, Αργώ (Argo, 1936), translated the anxieties and intellectual conflicts of the urban younger generation into a fictional context. 1937–8 he produced short stories and a novella in quick succession, showing a shift towards a balance between psychological focus and social analysis which characterises Λεωνής (Leonis, 1940), a novel built on nostalgia for the lost world of

Constantinople but showing, in the hero, the need for a whole generation to come to terms with the implications of that loss of its past. WWII and its aftermath in Greece had a significant effect on Theotokas. He turned from prose to the more public medium of theatre, experimenting with historical plays and folk drama as vehicles for his intellectual preoccupations. Twice he served as director of the National Theatre (1945–6 and 1950–2) and was later instrumental in the founding of the National Theatre of Northern Greece (1961). At the same time his last major novel, Ασθενείς και Οδοιπόροι (Sick and wayfarers, 2 vols, 1950 and 1964), deals with the onset of the war, the effects of occupation, famine, resistance and Civil War, and with the vulnerability and guilt of human beings caught in the consequent moral and physical upheavals. Throughout the 1950s and 1960s he continued to publish essays on contemporary social and intellectual issues. He died, remembered not so much as a creative writer (his imaginative works are in general aesthetically unsatisfactory), but as a stimulating thinker who never hesitated to plunge himself into contemporary debate.

●T. Doulis, *George Theotokas* (New York, 1975). CFR

THEOTOKIS, Konstandinos (1872–1923), Greek prose writer, poet and translator, studied literature, philosophy, mathematics, medicine and chemistry in Paris, without taking a degree. He was a polyglot, who spoke the major European languages, and read Latin, Sanscrit and Old Persian. He returned to his native Corfu for a while, adding his weight to the demoticist movement and becoming friendly with the poet MAVILIS. They fought together in Crete in 1896 and both took part in the disastrous campaign against Turkey in N Greece in 1897. 1898 Theotokis went to Graz, and in 1907 to Munich, to follow university courses. During this period he became familiar with German socialist thought and espoused the aims of the socialist movement. On his return to Greece he worked to promote democracy and social justice, but after financial ruin in 1917 he divided his time between paid work and writing. He died, his health undermined by TB. Theotokis never got over the death from meningitis of his only daughter, aged 5, in 1900. Neither nationalist ideals nor the pursuit of a society freed from the constraints of capital ever disguised the resulting pessimism of his underlying world-view. He helped to orientate contemporary prose towards social psychological fiction of a Realist kind. Much of his work is a form of didactic Naturalism which has not born the test of time well, e.g. Οι Σκλάβοι στα δεσμά τους (Slaves in their chains, 1922), an attack on the idle rich. His best works preach less and are more psychologically developed, notably Ο Κατάδικος (The condemned man, 1919) and Η ζωη και ο θάνατος Καραβέλα (The life and death of Karavela, 1922). CFR

TINÓDI, Sebestyén (c. 1505–56), Hungarian poet, was a wandering minstrel whose talent enabled him to publish his songs. Nothing is known of his early life, but he was well educated. He entered the service of the powerful Transdanubian landowner Bálint Török as a soldier, but after losing three fingers from his left hand in battle served as a clerk until his master was captured by the Turks when Buda was occupied in 1541.

Thereafter Tinódi led a peripatetic life witnessing battles and seeking patronage. Tamás Nádasdy, the Palatine, recommended his ennoblement in 1553; 1554 he published a selection of his verse and melodies in *Cronica* (Chronicle, 1554). His aim was to provide a record of the struggle against the Turks. He also versified biblical and Classical stories. Tinódi was a fiercely patriotic and precise chronicler with a journalist's eye for detail and a predilection for reeling off lists of names, presumably expecting due reward for this publicity. His energy compensates somewhat for his mediocre poetic skill. But he was an accomplished musical composer and performer, styling himself 'lutenista' as well as 'literator'; the popularity of his verse owed much to his original and attractive melodies, some of which still survive in modern hymnals.

Selections in T. Klaniczay (Ed.), *Old Hungarian Literary Reader* (Budapest, 1985); W. Kirkconnell (Ed.), *Hungarian Helicon* (Calgary, 1985).   GFC

TODOROV, Petko (1879–1916), Bulgarian prose writer and playwright, the son of a rich landowner and politician, was educated in Tărnovo where his interest in politics led to an admiration of socialist ideas; he published his first collection of socialist verse at the age of 15, *Draski* (Sketches, 1894). He was sent to Toulouse to complete his secondary education (1896); back in Bulgaria he got into trouble because of his socialism and went to Berne (1898) to read law but left for Berlin and Leipzig where he read literature (1899–1904), and wrote a thesis on Slav cultural relations, *Za otnoshenieto na slavyanite kăm bălgarskata literatura* (On the attitude of the Slavs to Bulgarian literature, 1944). As a student, he

came under the influence of German philosophy and of modern aestheticism; in Bulgaria he associated with the circle around the *Misăl* (Thought) literary journal, who shared many of his ideas, and became a devoted disciple of SLAVEIKOV. His most creative period followed and, up to 1910, he published four plays and his best-known work, the lyrical-prose *Idilii (Idylls,* 1908). During this period he was for some time employed at the National Library in Sofia but, when he discovered he had TB, he left for Italy and then Switzerland, where he died. Todorov was the first author of lyrical prose in Bulgaria; his 'idylls' preserve the genre's traditional association with the bucolic through the stylisation and aesthetisation of folklore; Todorov perhaps derived the idea from the idylls of Johannes Schlaf whom he knew through his contacts with the German literary circle Die Kommenden. His idylls marked the beginning of Modernism in Bulgarian prose and transformed the attitude to the oral tradition typical of the Realist rustic prose of the 1880s and 1890s. Todorov's spiritualisation of folklore consisted in introducing individualist, even existentialist, motifs into the framework of rustic life; his characters are split between the 'divine' and the mundane life of the collective, and experience well-nigh Decadent disillusion, involving a sense of being both chosen and cursed. In his examination of the situation of the spiritual 'outsider' or 'wanderer' he approaches the problems of the 'modern era' (e.g. the artist's self-consciousness, the 'sin' of neglecting marriage and domestic responsibility, the problem of 'choice' faced by the individual, and the necessity of self-definition, redemption from 'sin'). Typical oral-tradition images like the 'Sun' come to personify the new artist-hero divided between he spiritual task to which he feels called and the desire for ordinariness. The Christ myth is interpreted analogously, and in his idylls concerning Christ, Todorov makes Him an emblematic self-doubting individualist who experiences Kierkegaard's 'stages' of development from aesthetic to religious (the influence of SLAVEIKOV, who was the first to introduce Kierkegaard's ideas to Bulgaria). Apart from idylls where folk stylisation makes individualist problems almost 'invisible', Todorov has pieces like 'Kamăni' (Stones, 1909), 'Plennikăt na Kalipso' (K.'s prisoner, 1907), 'Kasandra' (Cassandra, 1906) or 'Guslareva maika' (The rebec-player's mother, 1901), where he employs complex structures based on reminiscence, the interweaving of time-levels and elements of the stream of consciousness. Todorov's plays, such as *Samodiva* (The wood-nymph, 1931), *Strahil strashen hajdutin* (S., the terrible bandit, 1932) and *Parvite* (The first ones, 1934), laid the foundations of the modern Bulgarian drama.   SIK

TOPOL, Josef (b. 1935), Czech dramatist, went straight into theatre life after his matriculation (1953), when he became part-time reader for a prominent Prague theatre; 1954–9 he read dramaturgy and drama at the Academy of Performing Arts. From 1967 till its closure in 1972 he was in charge of a leading 'small theatre'; he worked as a proof-reader, but after signing Charter 77 became a builder's labourer until he fell seriously ill in the early 1980s. He began with a verse historical drama, *Půlnoční vítr* (North wind, 1956), an elegantly simple play about love. If it has any

burden, it is that cowardice and a disrespect for women in matters erotic engenders evil. With his next play, *Jejich den* (Their day, 1962), Topol turns to contemporary life. It is a play of despair at the present political situation; some hope remains in young people and the old values which bring them together with their grandparents' generation. Its light-heartedness is overshadowed by death and the moral decrepitude of Communist careerists. The technically and politically complex *Konec masopustu* (End of the carnival, 1963) uses elements of 'Absurdism' and of the Baroque, on the surface to criticise collectivisation, in fact to discuss relativist notions of truth and guilt. A slapstick village drama turns into something close to tragedy. *Kočka na kolejích* (Pussy on the rails, 1965) depicts an apparently frustrating seven-year-old erotic relationship, where the man, Véna, is not convinced that love is enough. It presents an image of social inertia. Évi serves, gives, while Véna is simply restless, changing, Cain rather than the Abel of his saintly namesake (Wenceslas). Linguistic tension is supplied by the contrast between their working-class language and intellectuals' conversation. The lively, ironic, even sardonic, *Slavík k večeři* (Nightingale for dinner, 1967) concentrates on the power of unreality, the lack of distinction between nightmare and living, and on the reality of physical and psychological bullying. *Hodina lásky* (Hour of love, 1968), like *Kočka*, concerns a crisis in an erotic relationship. Topol skilfully manipulates time, so that the man's and woman's past and present together are juxtaposed in acted-out dialogue, all of which is overlooked or overheard by the Aunt as Fate and Time. *Hlasy ptáků* (The voices of birds, 1988) is an ironic, but insubstantial, variation on *King Lear* which comments on moral compromise and the victory of materialist values under socialism. Written in 1976, the two-act *Sbohem, Sokrate* (Farewell, Socrates, 1990) in the first act concerns youth, love and affection, in the second, stale or vulgar marital or pseudo-marital relationships. Again, bullying, betrayal and death are motifs.

●P. I. Trensky, *Czech Drama Since World War II* (White Plains, NY, 1978); M. Goetz-Stankiewicz, *The Silenced Theatre. Czech Playwrights Without a Stage* (Toronto, 1979).   RBP

T'OT'OVENTS, Vahan (1893–1938), Armenian prose writer, born in Mezre, Kharpers province, W Armenia, attended secondary school in Kharpert. His first book appeared in 1908. 1909 he went to America, where he worked in a shop, mastered English and French, and studied literature, history and philosophy at the University of Wisconsin. 1915 he went to the Caucasus as a volunteer to defend his country. He edited a newspaper in Tiflis (Tbilisi) 1917–18, wrote numerous articles, a novel and literary studies. 1920 he returned to America but 1922 he was back in E Armenia, by this time known as Soviet Armenia, where he devoted all his time to writing. His most famous work, *Kyank'ê hin Hromeakan tcanaparhi Vra* (Life on the Old Roman Road, 1933), is a lyrical narrative which deals with the author's reminiscences of life in W Armenia, marked by considerable imagination and an idealised evocation of Nature. *Bats kapuyt dsaghikner* (The pale blue flowers, 1935), *Hovnat'an ordi Eremiayi* (Jonathan, son of Jeremiah, 1934), *Erku gerezmanner* (The two graves) and *Yeldiz*, for example,

manifest an affection for man and Nature. T'ot'ovents had intended writing a long novel about the history of the Armenians and their resurgence from the ashes of 1915, but he did not live to achieve this aim because, together with some 300 other Armenian intellectuals, he died a victim of the Stalin purges. He did, however, write a fragment on this theme, entitled in English translation. 'Tell me, Bella', in which he and his companion Setrak return to Armenia from America as volunteers and on revisiting Setrak's home-town find it deserted except for the handful who had fled to the mountains and caves during the massacres. In *Dsirani Dsar* (The apricot tree) T'ot'ovents describes metaphorically the murder of childhood and innocence at the hands of a senseless, cruel world. More than that, however, this work shows how the experience of this innocence and the memory of its beauty, the longing for the Lost Eden, live for ever in the human heart and, above all, in the work of art.

●*Tell me, Bella* (London, 1972); *Scenes from an Armenian Childhood*, with a foreword by the translator, M. Kudian (London, 1980).   VN

TOVAČOVSKÝ z CIMBURKA, Ctibor (c. 1437–94), one of the leading Utraquists in Moravia, the Chief Judge at the Moravian Crown Court and Governor of Moravia for twenty-five years, supported King George of Poděbrady (1420–71) against the revolt of R. Catholic noblemen and vanquished their army in 1467. In the same year he wrote *Hádání Pravdy a Lži o kněžské zboží a panování jich* (The dispute of Truth and Untruth concerning the property and rule of the clergy, printed 1539) and dedicated it to the King. It is primarily a religious-philosophical and political work intended to prove that the theological, social and political order of the Utraquist Church is the work of God; it denounces those in the R. Catholic hierarchy who oppose the King and advises him to remain firm. It is presented in the form of a report on a court case between the plaintiff Truth, personifying Utraquism, and Untruth, defending R. Catholicism; it is loosely based on the novel *Belial*, adapted into Czech at the beginning of the 15th century. The court sits in Antioch because Untruth has no access to Rome but the case is conducted according to the procedure of the Moravian court. Tovačovský was not an educated man and his work does not display erudition, but he shows great knowledge of the Bible and animates the narrative with popular fables and proverbs. The liveliest passages are those depicting the entry of Untruth and describing the character and appearance of her sisters who accompany her. The descriptions reveal the author's idiosyncrasies: Wrath is a countess from Babylon, Avarice a lady from Denmark, Hatred a woman from Austria, Laziness comes from Poland and Pride is a princess from Rome. After the trial the Chancellor, St John the Evangelist, announces the verdict: Untruth and her sisters are cursed; God will punish them, and Truth is authorised to pursue her rights even by armed force.   KB

TRAYANOV, Teodor (1882–1945), Bulgarian poet, read mathematics and physics at Sofia and Vienna; he worked as a diplomat in Austria and Germany (until 1921), where he came into close contact with writers like Hofmannsthal, Rilke and George. 1914, together with a Bulgarian composer, he designed a pantomime on motifs from Oscar Wilde for the Vienna Volksoper. From 1923 he devoted himself entirely to literature. He was one of the editors of the Symbolist journal *Hyperion* (1922–31), together with the main theorist of Bulgarian Symbolism, the critic Ivan Radoslavov (1880–1969). After the Communist take-over he was arrested as an 'ideological enemy' and beaten to death by the police. Trayanov was the most consistently Symbolist Bulgarian poet; he was inspired by writers like Novalis, Dehmel and George. His *Regina mortua* (1909) is the first entirely Symbolist collection in Bulgarian literature (even if there are strong Symbolist elements in YAVOROV). It is dominated by death and the perception of life as a dream; for the poet, life is already 'behind' him, he faces only the Chimera, night and death. His melancholic verse reflects all kinds of dying and loss (e.g. dying emotions, the dying flame of life, dying 'light' and 'day', the loss of the beloved, Decadently expressed in autumn symbolism) out of which an aloneness comparable to death arises; his crystalline, icy aloneness is wrapped in night and walks among funeral flowers and neo-Romantic black lakes whose 'dead waters' reflect 'dead stars'. In his second collection, *Himni i baladi* (Anthems and ballads, 1911), the motif of wandering is transformed; he is a 'pilgrim in black', an emblem of the creative spirit who rejects the material world and the flesh and for whom 'death' means the 'death' of the material and the liberation of the 'pure spirit', who is no longer a pathless sufferer, but has some higher, secret mission. WWI led him to write about Bulgarian history, *Bălgarski baladi* (Bulgarian ballads, 1921), but he did not abandon his abstractionist pose and warned that the ballads were not connected with the war, but expressed the 'beauty and eternal forms of the Bulgarian spirit'; for him, extreme individualism leads to a 'crystallisation' of the 'national spirit' and this is the way to 'universalism'; Symbolism provides the means for an expression of the 'mystique of the soil and the sacredness of blood'; it creates the superreality of superindividualism. Creation of this 'superreality' is the true task of the poet, who has to eliminate existing realities and to seek a universal path for the progress of the human spirit. Thus his *Panteon* (Pantheon, 1934) is an attempt to universalise the 'national genius' (genius of the race), to blend the philosophical and artistic traditions of the West and East (the Slavs), and to create new ethical imperatives; his vision of a new European culture (also influenced by Nietzsche's Superman), like the 19th-century French idea of 'salvation from the Slavs', supposes the Slavs would contribute by overcoming Western scepticism; the poet is seen as man at his greatest, embodying harmony by following the invisible, universal spiritual path of mankind. *Panteon*, to a great extent, expresses Trayanov's view concerning the 'end of the romantic-heroical period of the nation' embodied in the works of BOTEV, VAZOV, SLAVEIKOV, YAVOROV and his own; what he achieves in this collection and in *Bǎlgarski baladi* is a radical symbolist modification of the problem of the 'nation'.

C. Ognjanoff, *Bulgarien* (Nuremberg, 1967), pp. 362–9.   SIK

TREMBECKI, Stanisław (1739?–1812), Polish poet, born into a noble family of moderate means, squandered his inheritance but was saved from destitution by Stanisław II August (reigned 1764–95), the last King of Poland, who made him his chamberlain and court poet. Trembecki soon became one of the most popular poets of the Polish Age of Enlightenment, not so much thanks to his official (mostly panegyric) court poetry as to his libertine satirical poems and Epicurean erotic or Anacreontic verse. After the King's death, he lived at the court of, among other magnates, Szczęsny Potocki, whose famous garden in Tulczyn provided Trembecki with the subject matter for his descriptive poem *Sofiówka* (Sophia's garden, 1806). The fable is another genre in which he excelled. A neo-Classicist, Trembecki transcends neo-Classicist stylistic norms with his lively, dynamic, sensuous language, sometimes (particularly in his fables) bordering on the colloquial. Since he never bothered to collect his casually written poems, the body of his work has not yet been fully established by literary historians.

•Selected poems in B. Carpenter (Ed.), *Monumenta Polonica* (Ann Arbor, 1989).

C. Backvis, *Un grand Poète polonais du XVIIIe siècle: S. Trembecki* (Paris, 1937).   StB

TRUBAR, Primož (1508–86), Slovene Protestant reformer, translator of the Scriptures, 'father of the Slovene literary language', was the most eminent figure of the Slovene Reformation, author of 22 books in Slovene and two in German. His translations included all of the NT and the Psalter. Much of his life was spent in exile in Germany, where 1561 he set up an institution for the publication of Lutheran books in Slovene and Croat. His works include: *Catechismus*, 1550, the first

Slovene printed book; *Abecedarij* (An ABC, 1550); *Cerkovna ordninga* (Church rule-book, 1564); *Ta celi psalter Davidov* (David's Psalter, complete, 1566); *Ta celi novi testament* (The NT, complete, 1582); *Hišna postila* ([Luther's] Household postil, 1596).   HL

TS'ERETELI, Ak'ak'i (1840–1915), born near Sachkhere in W Georgia, is one of the three Georgian writers of the late 19th century so renowned that they are known by their Christian names. His family had been leading noblemen at the court of the last Imeretian kings and had survived the collapse of the kingdom only to live in rural isolation, a decay which fired Ak'ak'i's indignation (despite his affection for his parents) for a lifetime. Ak'ak'i went to school in Kutaisi, and after abandoning service in the Russian Army and an unfortunate marriage, returned to Georgia as a *tergdaleuli*, 'one who had drunk from the River Terek', i.e. absorbed Russian and European culture. In Tbilisi, however, because of his dour individualist views, he had an uphill struggle with new literary circles. His poetry, melodious and simple, long on sentiment if short on originality (the Czech Václav Černý called it 'Heine without the irony'), attracted critical praise – 'exemplary', his *Saidumlo barati* (Secret letter) of 1860 was called – and won wide popularity, especially when set to music. Songs such as 'Sulik'o' (1895) are extremely well known to this day. Longer poems, such as the historical *Tornik'e Eristavi* (1884), despite their familiar, didactic aim of exhorting his contemporaries to live up to the heroism of their forefathers, showed a talent for graphic and dramatic narrative, which put Ak'ak'i above his fellow writers. His non-fictional

writing, like that of Ilia CH'AVCH'AVADZE, gave him the status of a civic and political luminary. From 1868 to 1900, Ak'ak'i wrote a steady stream of short stories, some historical, some fabulous, some reminiscent of Turgenev's *Sportsman's Sketches* in the author's guiding role and narrative competence, condemnation of decaying gentry and sympathy for the oppressed peasantry. His most enduring prose – and one of the best prose narratives in Georgian literature – is the autobiographical *Chemi tavgadasavali* (The story of my life, 1894–1909), which is a classic portrait of a rural genteel childhood and a mid-nineteenth-century grammar school in the Russian Empire. Its profound insights into the formation and inheritance of character peter out: he is tantalisingly reticent about his entry into and discord with the Georgian intelligentsia. Ak'ak'i Ts'ereteli's death was rightly perceived as the end of the classic, Realist and national-liberal school of Georgian culture.

•D. M. Lang, *Modern History of Georgia* (London, 1962).   DR

TS'ERETELI, Giorgi (1842–1900), Georgian prose writer, a contemporary, namesake and distant relative of Ak'ak'i TS'ERETELI, despite his versatility (he was an amateur archaeologist and naturalist), is chiefly known for his prose works, often autobiographical, which offer a painstaking record of country life as the great reforms of the Russian Empire destroyed the old relationships of peasant and master. At the age of 21 Giorgi Ts'ereteli had declared his mission: 'The writer is the sympathiser of society's torment and pleasure . . . he must show it the means he thinks best to get rid of its defects.' *Chemi tskhovrebis q'vavili* (A flower of my life, 1872) sees rural disintegration through the eyes of a young boy; the chronicle is continued for the 1860s in *K'ik'olik'i, Chik'olik'i da K'udabzik'a* (K'ik'olik'i, Chik'olik'i and K'udabzik'a, 1867–73). Novels such as *Gulk'ani* (Gulk'an, 1868) won Giorgi Ts'ereteli a popularity later eclipsed by more flamboyant Realists.   DR

TSIRKAS (Stratis; i.e. Yannis Hadziandros, 1911–80), Greek novelist and poet, was born in Cairo. At 16 he was already publishing translations of poetry (Heine, Musset) and short stories in periodicals. 1929–39 he worked in cotton factories in Upper Egypt, first as accountant, then as manager. 1939 he became the director of the Halkousi Foundation in Alexandria, a post he held until 1963, when he moved to Athens. During the 1930s his anti-British feelings and pro-Communist leanings were consolidated, and from 1935 he took an active public part in left-wing cultural and political activities. Initially he continued to write poetry, publishing two volumes, Φελλάχοι (Fellahin, 1937) and Το Λυρικό Ταξίδι (The lyric journey, 1938) and receiving critical attention in the pages of Τα Νέα Γράμματα (New writing). After WWII he produced three collections of short stories which more or less conform to the requirements of Socialist Realism. But these early works are all essentially an apprenticeship for his trilogy Ακυβέρνητες Πολιτείες (Cities adrift). The three novels Η Λέσχη (The club, 1961), Αριάγνη (Ariadne, 1962) and Η Νυχτερίδα (The bat, 1965), explain in political terms, and seek to justify in moral terms, what happened during the 1944 attempt (in which Tsirkas was closely involved) to get the Greek Government in Exile and the Greek troops in Egypt to back the left-wing resistance movement in Greece proper. The literary technique of the novels, and particularly of 'The club', with its multiple points of view and kaleidoscopic chronology, is much more sophisticated than that of the stories. He attempted to repeat the formula with a trilogy on life under the Junta, the first and only volume of which, Η χαμένη Άνοιξη (The lost spring), appeared in 1976. The novel was not a success, and ill-health prevented him from completing the trilogy. Apart from 'Cities adrift', he is remembered for his literary criticism, in particular for Ο Καβάφης και η εποχή του (Cavafy and his times, 1958), a powerful but tendentious attempt to politicise CA-VAFY, whom Tsirkas had interviewed at some length when only 19.

•*Drifting Cities* (New York, 1974). CFR

TUGLAS, Friedebert (i.e. – up to 1923 – F. Mihkelson, 1886–1971), Estonian prose writer, went to secondary school in Tartu and, after the quelling of the 1905 Revolution, in which he took part, was imprisoned. 1906–17 he was in Finnish exile and in Paris. April 1917 he returned to Estonia, edited three literary periodicals and became the first president of the Union of Estonian Writers and first editor-in-chief of the journal *Looming* (Creation, 1923–6). 1946 he was made a corresponding fellow of the Estonian Academy of Sciences and given the title National Artist, but, soon afterwards, he lost that title and was expelled from the Writers' Union, having been condemned for 'bourgeois nationalism' and 'decadence'. His title and membership were returned in the mid 1950s. Tuglas was among the leading writers of Young Estonia and the interwar grouping, Siuru. In his early work, *engagé* social realism is combined with a neo-Romantic hero-cult and dreamy rebelliousness: see the short-story collections *Kahekesi* (In a pair, 1908) and *Liivakell* (Hour-glasses, 1913). Tuglas fulfilled the contemporaneous conception of 'modern' prose-writing (a style expressing *névrosité*, impressionist sensibility, musicality and, on the other hand, rationality and irony) most clearly with his novel *Felix Ormusson* (1915). He expressed himself best, however, in the novella. In his novelle, he employs strong elements of fantastic, mythical and symbolic writing; in this he laid the foundations of modern Estonian prose. Towards the end of the 1930s he turned to his childhood as a source of inspiration in his novel *Väike Illimar* (Little I., 1937). Tuglas was a particularly important literary critic and essayist. ●Selections in E. H. Harris (ed.), *Literature in Estonia* (London, 1943); *Riders in the Sky* (Tallinn, 1982); *Popi and Huhuu* (Tallinn, 1986).   VM

TUSAP, Srbuhi (1841–1901), was an Armenian poet and novelist, the first Armenian feminist and woman writer, literary *salon* hostess, member of the influential group of writers known as the 'Renascence Generation'. Her works were very important in the 19th century, and her three novels, scores of poems and articles all underscore the fundamental feminist principles: a woman's right to be educated, her right to work and her right freely to choose her personal circumstances. Tusap was born in Constantinople, when the Ottoman Empire had launched the Tanzimat Reform which was meant to catapult the century into a new age, and the Armenian world had already embarked on its own literary and social renascence. She was brought up in a

French milieu, knew Italian, Greek, French and was steeped in the works of, for example, George Sand and Victor Hugo. At 22, she met the Armenian Romantic poet Mkrtitch Peshikt'ashlian (1828–68), who became her Armenian tutor. 1871 she married her music teacher Paul Tusap. During the 1880s she emerged as writer, social activist, and public speaker. 1880 she published a brief work on the importance of Modern Armenian at a time when much of the Armenian literary world was debating the use of the contemporary vernacular. 1881 her article on women's rights appeared in *Terciman-i-efkyar*, and was reprinted in the *Arevelyan Mamoul*. During the 1880s she also appeared in the Constantinople and Smyrna press, mostly on feminist issues. The first of her novels, *Mayda* (1883), influenced by such as Rousseau, Goethe and Sand, was the first written by a woman in Armenian and the first to champion women's rights. Epistolary in form, it centres on the correspondence between two women, Sira and Mayda. Mayda, young and beautiful, has been widowed and left with a daughter, whom she adores. Sira writes letters of consolation and encouragement to her. Mayda meets Dikran and they fall in love. Through the interference of the jealous Herikeh, Dikran is driven to marry another woman in Paris. When he is widowed, he and Mayda are again united, but Mayda soon dies. The plot is marred by melodrama and contrivedness, but the plot is secondary to the theories it promotes, namely, that women are slaves and need to liberate themselves through education, meaningful work, the securing of freedom of choice. The novel caused a storm in all quarters. The best-known attacks came from Grigor ZOHRAB and Hakob Paronian (1843–91). ZOHRAB attacked it for what he saw as its insidious blow to the fabric of Armenian family life. Paronian had no objection to its philosophy but criticised its literary ineptitude and sentimentality. In her second novel, *Siranoush* (1885), the eponymous heroine falls into an arranged marriage and is mistreated by a jealous, philandering husband. She is also the victim of her greedy father who chooses a rich husband over Yervand, the man she loves. Her third novel, *Arak'sya kam Varjouhin* (A. or the teacher, 1887), concerns a young schoolmistress, whose sweetheart, Nersess, is stolen by a richer woman. Tusap's daughter, Dorine, contracted TB in 1889 and died 1890, which so shattered her that she never wrote again.   VN

TUWIM, Julian (1894–1953), Polish poet and translator, born in the industrial city of Łódź, 1916–18 studied law and philosophy at Warsaw. There he made his début in a student periodical and met LECHOŃ and SŁONIMSKI; joined later by WIERZYŃSKI and IWASZKIEWICZ, the five young poets were to gain fame as the Skamander group; Tuwim was soon to be recognised as the most talented among them. He published his first collection, *Czyhanie na Boga* (Stalking God), in 1918. Within the next five years he produced three more volumes of verse, all marked by their violent rejection of the Decadent mood and Symbolist style of the preceding epoch: Vitalist praise of life, the urban setting, a democratic approach to society, colloquial language, and dynamic, sensual imagery. This youthful, energetic optimism gradually vanishes in his later volumes. Tuwim's most accomplished collections, *Rzecz czarnoleska* (The Czarnolas speech, 1929), *Biblia cygańska* (The Gipsy Bible, 1933) and *Treść gorejąca* (Fiery essence, 1936), are preoccupied with existential anxiety, catastrophist forebodings, and irresoluble paradoxes of language, while stylistically they approach Classicist clarity and discipline. His poetic virtuosity and catastrophist pessimism reached their peak in the long poem 'Bal w Operze' (Ball at the Opera), an explosive political satire written in 1936 but for censorship reasons published in its entirety only ten years later, in People's Poland. Meanwhile with the outbreak of war Tuwim escaped to the West, first to France, then, via Brazil, to New York, where he settled in 1942. During the war he feuded with almost all his former friends who were disturbed by his blindly pro-Soviet attitude and wholesale condemnation of prewar Poland. Tuwim's illusions about the goodwill of the Communist régime made him return to Poland in 1946. He was welcomed and rewarded with privileges and honours, but he turned out to be almost unable to write. The only significant work he published after the war was his book-length neo-Romantic 'poem of digressions' *Kwiaty polskie* (Polish flowers, 1949); this flawed yet brilliant work had been written, however, in Brazil and New York, and Tuwim never managed to complete it. He died suddenly as a result of a heart attack. Tuwim was one of the most gifted masters of poetic language in the entire history of Polish literature.

StB

TWARDOWSKI OF SKRZYPNA, Samuel (1600?–61), Polish poet and translator, a characteristic representative of the 'Sarmatian' (as opposed to the 'Western-influenced') variety of Polish Baroque, led the life of an average Polish nobleman of the 17th century: he attended a Jesuit school, fought in numerous wars, was in the service of a powerful magnate, and spent his last years in the provinces as a gentleman-farmer. His work manifests the 'Sarmatian' taste for the historical epic but it also includes a relative novelty, fiction in verse. The former is best represented by his long epic on the mid-century wars with Cossacks and Swedes, *Wojna domowa*... (A civil war, 1651–60); the latter found its incarnation in Twardowski's 'romances', such as his charming pastoral *Dafnis*... (1638) or the more extensive tale of love and adventure, *Nadobna Paskwalina* (Lovely P., 1655).   StB

TYCHYNA, Pavlo (1891–1967), Ukrainian Symbolist poet, whose collection *Soniashni kliarnety* (The sunny clarinets, 1918) was acclaimed as the finest poetry of the Revolution. Apart from purely lyrical verse, it contained striking poems about the fratricidal, tempestuous years of the national revolution. At that time Tychyna did not yet support the Bolsheviks, and his philosophy was pantheistic. His later collections, *Pluh* (The plough, 1920), *Zamist sonetiv i oktav* (Instead of sonnets and octaves, 1920) and *Viter z Ukrainy* (Wind from Ukraine, 1924), confirmed his position as the leading poet of Ukraine. Gradually, however, under the pressure of Communist Party controls, he embraced the new doctrine of Socialist Realism. The first signs of this were visible in the collection *Chernihiv* (1931). By 1934 Tychyna had proclaimed himself a true believer in *Partiia vede* (The Party is leading). From then on he wrote at Stalin's behest, only occasionally showing his earlier poetic power (in the poem *Pokhoron druha* [The funeral of a friend, 1942]). His long philosophical poem *Skovoroda* remained unfinished (an incomplete version was published in 1971). His earlier works, partly banned under Stalinism, have recently been republished.

● *Selected Poetry* (Kiev, 1987); some Tychyna poems in Z. Honcharuk (Ed.), *Anthology of Soviet Ukrainian Poetry* (Kiev, 1982) and G. Andrusyhen and W. Kirkconnell (Eds), *The Ukrainian Poets, 1189–1962* (Toronto, 1963).
G. Grabowicz, 'Continuity and Discontinuity in the Poetry of Pavlo Tychyna' in E. Bristol (Ed.), *East European Literature* (Berkeley, 1982).
                                        GSNL

TYL, Josef Kajetán (1808–56), Czech dramatist and prose writer, taught at school by KLICPERA, was an itinerant actor (German), but then ran Czech theatre productions in Prague and edited several periodicals; for ten years he worked as a clerk for the Austrian War Office. Among his most successful plays are the social study *Paličova dcera* (The arsonist's daughter, 1847), the political historical *drame à thèse, Kutnohorští havíři* (The Kuttenberg miners, 1848), the patriotic fairy-tale comedy *Strakonický dudák* (Strakonice piper, perf. 1847, publ. 1858), the grand historical drama expressing various aspects of nationalist ideology, *Jan Hus* (1849), and the musical farce *Fidlovačka* (Urban folk festival, perf. 1834, publ. 1877), whence the Czech national anthem is derived. Tyl's historical novels and short stories like *Alchemista* (1837) or *Rozina Ruthardova* (1844) suffer from oversimplified psychology and melodrama. His social short stories, like 'Ze života chudých' (From the life of the poor, 1845) or 'S poctivostí nezahyneš' (Saving honour, 1846), however, present vivid, dignified, unsentimental depictions of working-class life.

●P. Brock and H. G. Skilling (Eds), *The Czech Renascence of the Nineteenth Century* (Toronto, 1970).

RBP

U

UGREŠIĆ, Dubravka (b. 1949), Croatian prose writer, engaged in research into Russian avant-garde literature. She has published four volumes of prose: a collection of sketches concerned with the nature of writing, *Poza za prozu* (A pose for prose, 1978); a short novel, *Štefica Cvek u raljama života* (Š.C. in the jaws of life, 1981); a collection of parodies, *Život je bajka* (Life is a fairy tale, 1983); and the spoof detective novel *Forsiranje romana-reke* (Forcing the *roman-fleuve*, 1988). Ugrešić is one of the freshest voices in contemporary Croatian literature, the humour of whose works contains an underlying sadness which has caused her to be compared to one of her own favourite writers, HRABAL.
•Translations of 3 prose pieces, *The Bridge*, 50 (1976), p. 100; *Fording the Stream of Consciousness* (London, 1991); *In the Jaws of Life* (London, 1992).
C. Hawkesworth, 'Dubravka Ugrešić', *SEER*, 68 (1990), pp. 436–46.   ECH

UJEVIĆ, Augustin-Tin (1891–1955), Croatian poet, born in Dalmatia, attended secondary school in Split and graduated from Zagreb University. He lived for several years in Paris, then in Belgrade, Sarajevo, Split and Zagreb, where he finally settled in 1940. A bohemian figure, he attracted devotees to his café tables. The strongest poetic voice in Croatian literature between the wars, Ujević went through several phases of development. His contribution to the influential anthology *Hrvatska mlada lirika* (New Croatian lyric poetry, 1914) introduced a new tone, breaking with writers' subjugation to critics and calling for a new independence of expression. His first volume of poems, *Lelek sebra* (The lament of the serf, 1920), expresses defeat in the face of merciless Fate, taking its essential tone from 'Svakidašnja jadikovka' (Everyday lament), a poem included in all anthologies of S Slav verse. The whole volume is marked by bewilderment in the face of 'the mystery of things', and a vain search for answers to the fundamental questions preoccupying modern man. Ujević characterises the language of his second volume, *Kolajna* (Necklace, 1926), as 'black with depth', telling himself to 'step along the path of delusion, dead Ujević'. It expresses the end of delusion, the muffled cry of a man 'crushed by the weight of the sky'. After these two volumes Ujević broadens his range and adapts the free-verse form, exploring the philosophical ideas of various cultures. His eclectic, erudite essays manifest an individual poetic style: *Skalpel kaosa* (The scalpel of chaos, 1938).
•Translations of selected poems in

AMYP, pp. 99–102; *IYP*, pp. 417–18.

                                              ECH

UJKO, Vorea (i.e. Domenico Bellizzi, b. 1918), one of the best-known Arbëresh (Italo-Albanian) poets, was born in Frascineto, Cosenza, where he teaches modern literature. Ujko's verse has been published in Italy, Albania and Kosovo. Among his works are the collections *Zgjimet e gjakut* (The awakening of the blood, 1973), *Kosovë* (Kosovo, 1973), *Ankthi* (Anguish, 1979) and *Këngë arbëreshe* (Arbëresh songs, 1982). ShM

UKRAINKA, Lessya (i.e. Laryssa Kosach, 1871–1913), Modernist Ukrainian poet, wrote in her early collections, *Na krylakh pisen* (On wings of songs, 1892) and *Dumy i mrii* (Thoughts and dreams, 1899), lyric patriotic verse. Later, at the turn of the century, she wrote poetic dramas on biblical and historical themes: *Cassandra* (1907), *Boiarynia* (Noblewoman, 1910); the latter was banned in the Soviet Ukraine for its anti-Russian views. In her plays antiquity and Christianity are often the sources of dramatic conflict. The Don Juan theme was given original treatment in *Kaminny hospodar* (The stone host, 1912). Her masterpiece is the dramatic poem *Lisova pisnia* (A forest song, 1912), based on Ukrainian folk motifs. Her main themes are universal: service to society and the pursuit of individual and national freedom.

●P. Cundy (Ed.), *Spirit of Flame* (New York, 1950).

C. Bida, *Lesya Ukrainka; Life and Work* contains some translations (Toronto, 1968).   GSNL

UNDER, Marie (1883–1980), Estonian poet, daughter of a teacher, had a German schooling, worked as a governess, cashier, and later clerk in the offices of the newspaper *Teataja*; on marrying, she followed her husband to Russia. On her return (1906) she began gradually to escape from her disintegrating marriage into literature and the friendship of young Tallinn writers; she was divorced in 1917. In 1924 she married the poet Artur Adson (1889–1977), with whom she emigrated to Sweden in 1944. Under, a founder of modern Estonian lyric verse and one of the leaders of the Siuru group, made her début with a collection of sensual verse, *Sonetid* (Sonnets, 1917), whose spontaneity and passion aroused something of a scandal. In Under's verse an excited joy in life expressed with a stylisation typical of the Fin de siècle and set against a background of middle-class interiors and gardens (*Eelõitseng* [Budding, 1918]; *Sinine puri* [Blue sail, 1918]) was gradually imbued with an awareness of the 'tragedy' of human existence (*Verivalla* [A flowing of blood, 1920]) which turned Under's attention to German Expressionism and which drew her to an attempt at modernising the ballad form (*Õnnevarjutus* [The eclipse of happiness, 1929]). The synthesis of these two poles led to her plain lyric verse of the 1930s and 1940s, e.g. *Lageda taeva all* (Under the open sky, 1930) or *Kivi südamelt* (A stone from my heart, 1935). The death of her mother and the tragedy of her homeland fused into a single dramatic picture in the poems of *Mureliku suuga* (With careworn lips, 1942). The work she wrote in exile was closely concerned with the contemporary fate of Estonia, e.g. the collection *Sädemed tuhas* (Sparks in the ashes, 1954).

●*Child of Man* (London, 1955).

K. Vogelberg, 'Marie Under' in C. Hawkesworth (Ed.), *Writers from Eastern Europe* (London, 1991), p. 36.

                                              VM

UNT, Mati (b. 1944), Estonian prose writer and dramatist, read journalism at Tartu (1962–7); till 1971 he was literary adviser at the Vanemuine Theatre, after that at the Theatre of Youth, in Tallinn. After the anti-illusive analyses of erotic relationships, *Elu võimalikkusest kosmoses* (On the possibility of life in the cosmos, 1967) and the novel from theatre life, *Via regia* (1975), Unt's artistic register broadened markedly towards the grotesque, to ingenious play with literary styles and to parody; he became the mouthpiece of his generation's rebellious discontent. This development prepared the way for his ironic anti-novel *Sügisball* (Autumn ball, 1979), which concerns the self-contained fates of the inhabitants of a Tallinn high-rise estate. In drama, Unt's development moves from topical mythological allegories like *Phaeton, päikese poeg* (Phaeton, son of the Sun, 1971) to plays like *Peaproov* (Dress rehearsal, 1985), which ironically measure the ideals of the past against the scepticism of today. Sometimes his dramatic texts were published together with prose works, e.g. his *Räägivad ja vaikivad* (They speak; they are silent, 1986).

•*The Autumn Ball* (Tallinn, 1985). Individual works in E. Mallene's anthologies, *The Play* (Tallinn, 1984) and *The Sailor's Guardian* (Tallinn, 1984).
K. Vogelberg, 'Mati Unt' in C. Hawkesworth (Ed.), *Writers from Eastern Europe* (London, 1991), p. 36.
                                                          VM

UPĪTS, Andrejs (1877–1970), Latvian writer, son of a tenant-farmer, employed as a teacher for ten years, from 1908 onwards made his living by writing. Because of his political views he was put in prison for a short time in 1920. 1940 he joined the Communist Party, a few weeks after the Red Army marched into Latvia. Although some of his earlier writings protested loudly against the subordination of artistic work to narrow-minded utilitarianism, he became one of the most unquestioning propagators of the Party's official demands. Most of his critical pieces were not intended to improve the qualities of literature but to drive 'bourgeois' elements out of Latvian letters. His truckling was richly rewarded. In later years he expressed it thus: 'The year 1940 and Soviet rule opened a fresh path ... from a prohibited and silenced writer I became a representative of the Supreme Soviet and later the Chairman of its Praesidium.' Upīts did not mention that to the last days of Latvia's independence he had been one of the principal beneficiaries of government funds set aside for writers. Soon he became chairman of the Latvian Writers' Union and the editor-in-chief of its official organ, *Karogs*. Because he engaged in such activities as delivering inflammatory speeches, signing political manifestos, serving on committees, and marching in parades, Upīts had no time to write new works and the state publishing house came out with eleven of his earlier volumes, works which had been published when he claimed to have been 'prohibited' and 'silenced'. His long novels were extolled as philosophical documents of Latvian history and for their positive approach to life and their concept of the people as the repository of the nation's vitality. Like Gorki's works in Russian literature, Upīts's novels were said to have formed a bridge between pre-Soviet and Soviet Latvian literature. Strangely enough, unlike in his polemical articles, in his works of fiction during the new phase he abstained from any glorification of the Soviet régime and did not write a single work about Soviet rule in the country. Upīts was a prolific writer. As a Realist, he may be compared in many respects to Maksim Gorki and Theodore Dreiser. In his novels we find gloomy unrelieved Naturalism; his style is often ponderous and crude, and he likes to employ realistic detail for the sake of sheer weight. Among his novels, of importance is his trilogy presenting the life of a Latvian peasant family from the end of the 19th century until the Revolution of 1905–7, *Jauni avoti* (New sources, 1909), *Zīdā tiklā* (In a silk net, 1912) and *Ziemeļa vējš* (Northern wind, 1921). Later he supplemented it with *Jaņa Robežnieka pārnākšana* (The return of Jan Robežnieks, 1932) and *Jaņa Robežnieka nāve* (Jan Robežnieks's death, 1933). In these two books he chronicles the family's history since 1918. In his best stories he attacks philistine morals: *Mazas komēdijas* (Little comedies, 1909–10). He also wrote successful comedies like *Peldētāja Zuzanna* (The bathing Susanna, 1922), historical plays and an historical prose tetralogy: *Laikmetu griežos* (At the turn of centuries, 1937–40), a Latvian literary history and a four-volume history of world literature.   EB

URBAN, Milo (1904–82), Slovak novelist, could not finish grammar school because of his forester father's death (1920), and later poverty prevented his finishing forestry college. Apart from one year, from 1926 till the end of WWII he worked for right-wing periodicals; 1940–5 he was editor-in-chief of the main Fascist daily, *Gardista*. Just before the end of the war, he escaped to Austria, was briefly interned by the Americans, returned to Slovakia in 1947 and was put on trial and condemned to a public reprimand. His chief work was *Živý bič* (Living scourge, 1927), a monumental chronicle of life in a Slovak village during WWI. Its characters are representative of types and classes in whom mental and physical violence is unleashed by the war's depriving human beings of their normal rituals and mental situations. On the other hand, it depicts the necessity of violence for social and political reform. Life at the Front enters directly only in the Expressionist memories of the main character of the novel's second part, Adam Hlavaj; indirectly, it enters in the return of invalid soldiers. Another chronicle novel, *Zhasnuté svetlá* (Extinguished lights, 1958), concerns events leading to the creation of the puppet Slovak State. Here, Adam Hlavaj begins as a Fascist journalist and ends a Communist activist. Urban's interpretation of history is stated at the start: 'Capitalism in its death agony was bringing its bitter fruit.'   RBP

URBÁNEK, Zdeněk (b. 1917), Czech novelist, son of a farmer, after commercial academy in Prague, was an editor in a publishing house; during WWII he worked on his father's farm, then after the war in the Ministry of Information and the state film company and after being prohibited from publishing his own works, devoted himself to translation. A friend of BEDNÁŘ, he endorsed his views in the essay *Člověk v mladé poezii* (Man in new poetry, 1940), expressing the same existential anxiety and disbelief in ideologies and advocating the same quest for the unchanging in the 'individual'. Urbánek's predilection for minute descriptions of the psychological states of outsiders, together with his endeavours to bring about their rebirth in a new faith in God, is apparent in his early 'dreams, studies and stories', *Úžeh tmou* (Sunstruck by darkness, 1940). This came to full fruition in his *Příběh bledého Dominika* (Pale Dominik, 1941), the story of a pure-hearted student, aggrieved by his human condition, persecuted by philistines, an enemy to himself, tortured by anxiety, on which, however, he depends, and vainly seeking faith. The narration was original in its use of similes to reveal the characters' moods and emotions, e.g. 'snow falling as calm and tender as the sudden opening of thousands of children's eyes'. Urbánek turned away from this method in his more realistic *Cestou za Quijotem* (On the road to Quixote, 1949), which portrays Cervantes as a man dragged into adventure unwillingly, and abandoned it completely in his semi-autobiographical short stories *Stavitelé světa* (The creators of the world, 1989).   KB

UROSHEVICH, Vlada (b. 1934), Macedonian poet, prose writer and critic, went to Skopje University and worked on the editorial boards of various periodicals (e.g. *Razgledi* [Views]), which he edited for a long period) and as an arts producer for Skopje TV. In his work Uroshevich drifted away from national and local problems and became a leader of a group of cosmopolitan writers. His first collections, *Eden drug grad* (Another town, 1959) and *Nevidelitsa* (The unseen, 1962), manifest Surrealist influences. In *Eden drug grad* the poet has a vision of a double world, and that vision is based on associative metamorphoses of what his senses transmit to him. His world looks like a Chagall picture and, in *Nevidelitsa*, there are poems about Bosch, Breughel and Chagall,

where he expresses admiration for their poetics of the fantastic. The 'invisible' world is sensed through dreams and through the associative contemplation of gestures, smells and colours in *Zvezdena tereziya* (Cusps, 1973). Dreaming is the theme of collections like *Nurkachko zvono* (Diving bell, 1975) or *Sonuvachot i praznotata* (The dreamer and the emptiness, 1979). His 'picture-poems' resemble naivist paintings and their mischievous absurdity. The image of his dreamer who 'flies' with 'no thought of return' and 'forgets all his relations', challenges the Macedonian topos of 'departures' and 'returns', where *Heimat* is of greater importance than anything else. His dreamer does not suffer the claustrophobia of others. Occasionally he dreams of the 'real' world; his dreamworld then crumbles and he feels claustrophobia, e.g. in 'Zhestoki peizazhi' (Cruel landscapes, *Sonuvachot i praznotata*) glimpses of that world suggest its elimination of privacy ('the illumination of marriage-beds with search-lights') or its cruelty ('tanks on a meadow with strawberries'). Uroshevich has written two collections of tales which verge on the fantastic, *Znatsi* (Sighs, 1969) and *Nochniyot paiton* (Night phaeton, 1972). His novel *Vkusot na praskite* (The taste of peaches, 1965) is a love story where love, Fate and Death are inseparable. For Uroshevich, man has no choice either in love or in death, which are ruled by Fate, an unknown and unknowable force. Fate brings together a young man and a girl; falling immediately in love with her, the young man dreams of her face drawn on some old coins and begins to search for those coins, but dies in an earthquake trying to save the girl's life. She tries to learn more about him and meets another young man in his native town who, she believes, is his reincarnation. A mad inventor, whom everyone in the novel meets at different times, believes that there is a 'hidden energy' which, re-embodied through the centuries, is attracted by the similarities of its objects. Finally, the coins with the girl's face on them are found by an archaeologist, but she and her reincarnated lover never learn that. The atmosphere and the structure of the novel suggest the predetermined-ness of all meetings and emotions and that all men can do is to submit to the whisperings of some mysterious voice.

●'The Tailor's Dummy' in *The Big Horse and Other Stories of Modern Macedonia* (Columbia, 1974), pp. 191–8.   SIK

V

VĀCIETIS, Ojārs (1933–83), leading Latvian poet of the Thaw following Stalinism, became known as the Latvian Yevtushenko. His verse often expresses the new generation's repudiation of the past and the urgent if vague search for a better future, e.g. *Elpa* (Breath, 1966). Modern history is chaotic, undirected, aimless and, indeed, often tragic in exposing the desultoriness of a drifting era. In his collections *Aiz simtās slāpes* (In the wake of a hundred desires, 1969) and *Melnās ogas* (Black berries, 1971) Vācietis celebrates humanity and individualism and expresses an almost Pasternakian appeal against materialism and the mechanisation of man. EB

VACULÍK, Ludvík (b. 1926), Czech novelist and columnist, son of a carpenter, after elementary schooling worked for the Bat'a shoe company (1941–6) while simultaneously studying at commercial academy; 1946–50 he studied at the Communist-run College of Politics and Sociology. He was then a tutor in a workers' hostel and, after military service (1953), began his career as a publisher's and periodical editor which he combined from 1959 with work in Czechoslovak Radio. He was expelled from the CP in 1967, banned after the Soviet occupation and became a tireless organiser of *samizdat* publication. His first novel,

Rušný dům (The bustling house, 1963), is a semi-autobiographical Communist idyll. If his second novel, *Sekyra* (The axe, 1966), has a hero, it is the narrator's rather stupid, kind-hearted Communist carpenter father, who becomes very unpopular by so keenly collectivising and who eventually volunteers for an experimental brain operation to support the wonders of Soviet science. This novel about the failure of Stalinism consists mainly in memories and is written in a sophisticated lyrical style which combines Moravian dialect with cultivated modern Czech and urban colloquialisms. The humour and the use of authorial intrusions approach the Sternean. *Morčata* (The guinea-pigs, 1977) is a satirical fairy-tale which deals with unseen authority and comically evokes either paranoia or the state of oppression. *Český snář* (Czech dreambook, 1983) is so ruthlessly honest an account of 'dissident' life that it is an anti-novel. If the police leave one no privacy, one must display one's most private thoughts and actions, however base, to the whole world. Vaculík's skill as a columnist may be seen in the 1967–8 *feuilletons*, *Stará dáma se baví* (An old lady enjoying herself, 1990), which traces the development of Vaculík's attitude to socialism from disillusion to contempt.

• *The Axe* (London, 1973); *The Guinea Pigs* (New York, 1973).

A. French, *Czech Writers and Politics, 1945–1969* (Boulder, Col., 1982); K. Mercks, 'The Semantic Gesture in the Guinea Pigs' in *Vozmi na radost´. To Honour Jeanne von der Eng-Liedmeier* (Amsterdam, 1980), pp. 309–22; R. B. Pynsent, 'Ludvík Vaculík' in C. Hawkesworth (Ed.), *Writers from Eastern Europe* (London, 1991), pp. 28–9.   RBP

VAJANSKÝ, Svetozár Hurban (1847–1916), Slovak poet, novelist and critic, was a lawyer, but, after serving in the Austro-Hungarian Army during the occupation of Bosnia in 1878, he took up journalism in the service of the Slovak national cause. He became an ardent Slavophile holding the Slav East to be the only pure and vital force in Europe and believing in the messianic mission of Tsarist Russia to liberate the Slavs. His book of lyrical verse, *Tatry a more* (The Tatras and the sea, 1879), though not free of Romantic clichés, was nevertheless innovative for its militant nationalism as well as its use of varied verse forms imitating German and English poetry. In his novels *Suchá ratolest'* (The dead branch, 1884), *Koreň a výhonky* (The root and the shoots, 1895) and *Kotlín* (1901) Vajanský wished to paint a complete picture of contemporary life but he neglected social problems.
                                    KB

VAJDA, János (1827–97), Hungarian poet, prose writer and playwright, son of a forester, studied in Székesfehérvár and Pest. His first poems were published in the periodical *Életképek* (Genre pictures) in 1844. 1845–6 he was an actor in a wandering troupe, and later he worked as a tutor, apprentice farm manager, and official in an agricultu-ral association. Because of his involvement in the revolution of 1848–9, he was enlisted for military service in 1850. 1853 he decided to earn his living solely by writing. He edited and wrote for various periodicals. His political attitude was far from consistent. In his long pamphlets *Önbírálat* (Self-criticism, 1862) and *Polgárosodás* (Bourgeois civilisation, 1860) his target was Hungarian nationalism. Expressing contempt for the provincialism of the nobility, he helped pave the way for the *Ausgleich*. After 1867, however, he became one of the most violent critics of the agreement. His inconsistencies alienated him from many of his contemporaries, but his nonconformity made him influential at the beginning of the 20th century. His Romantic cult of the subjectivist sublime is often at odds with his interest in determinism. Still, the historical significance of his works cannot be questioned. Introducing a highly personal form of love poetry and topics from urban life, he marked a transition from the post-Romantic style of ARANY to the Symbolism of ADY. In *A virrasztók* (The vigil-keepers, 1857), an allegorical poem, he mourns the apparently lifeless body of the nation during neo-absolutism, thus reminding his readers of 1849. His early cycles, inspired by his unhappy love, *Sirámok* (Laments, 1854), *A szerelem átka* (The curse of love, 1855) and *Gina emléke* (The memory of Gina, 1856), are uneven. His finest lyric verse was written after 1870. *A vaáli erdőben* (In the forest of Vaál, 1875) is an expression of an irresistible nostalgia for the idyllic, and in *Húsz év múlva* (After twenty years, 1876) unrequited love is turned into a symbol of the impossibility of existential fulfilment.   MSz-M

VAKHT'ANG VI (1675–1737), King of Kartli (ineffectively reigning 1716–24), was one of the first modern Georgian writers. He was well educated by Sulkhan-Saba ORBELIANI; appointed regent by the Shah of Persia in 1703 and king in 1709, he followed his uncle, Giorgi XI, in seeking Russian help to escape Iranian vassalage, installed his brother as patriarch, collated chronicles and laws, introduced printing presses and modern sciences, and personally edited RUSTAVELI's work for printing. He was forced to accept Islam in 1716 and was kept hostage in Iran, where he translated from Persian and began writing lyrics in Georgian. Like other Georgian kings (ARCHIL, TEIMURAZ I), he wrote a *Majama* (here: Anthology) of poems on love, as well as elegies on his own tribulations: 'Grief has enslaved me, sadness has become my medicine, I always use melancholy as ink, I make my heart its pen.' Even his Christian poetry has the sensuousness of the Song of Solomon: 'The lips of immortality are steeped in sugar.' After 5 troubled years in Tbilisi, betrayed by fellow Georgians, by Iranians, Turks and Russians, he and his enlightened court of 1,200 emigrated to Moscow, where they had at least freedom to compose and publish. Vakht'ang VI died in Astrakhan, a broken man, but an exemplary 18th-century philosopher-king.
●D. M. Lang, *The Last Years of the Georgian Monarchy* (New York, 1957).
                                        DR

VALAORITIS,   Aristotelis (1824–79), Greek poet, educated on Corfu, then in Geneva, studied law in Paris and Pisa (1844–8). 1847 he was involved in anti-Austrian revolutionary activity in N Italy which revealed his liberal political leanings. 1848 he returned to Corfu and became a leading figure in Ionian Islands politics, eventually representing Corfu in Athens, after union with Greece in 1864. Although he was publishing verse as early as 1847, his first significant collection, Μνημοσύνη (Mnemosyne), appeared in 1857. It includes most of his best-known lyric poems, e.g. 'Thanasis Vayias', 'Kitsos and the hawk', 'Funeral ode', and 'Dimos and his rifle'. Later he turned to long narrative poems, Φροσύνη (Frosini, 1859), Αθανάσιος Διάκος (Athanasios Diakos, 1866) and Φωτεινός (Fotinos, unfinished, publ. posthumously). He sought his material in the War of Independence and the struggles of the *klephts* and *armatoles* in the pre-revolutionary period. Both his language and material are heavily influenced by folksongs but he also shows the influence of the ideals and rhetoric of French Romanticism. His poems are a curious mixture of idealised heroism, Gothic supernatural and Greek folk elements. He prefaced many of them with comments on their sources and significance. *Fotinos* (1891) is the most significant of his works for the modern reader. The subject derives, exceptionally, from earlier history – a rising of the Greek inhabitants of his native Lefkas against Frankish rulers in the 14th century. Despite its heroic subject the focus of the poem is psychological, and its language, though still perceptibly Romantic, is lyrical and dramatic by turns, without resort to the earlier clichés of rhetoric.   CFR

VALTON, Arvo (i.e. A. Vallikivi, b. 1935), Estonian prose writer, studied at the Tallinn Polytechnic and after his degree (1959) worked as an engineer in Maardu and Tallinn and did an external degree in scriptwriting at the Moscow All-Union State Cinematographical Institute (degree 1967), and since 1975 he has worked for Tallinnfilm. His first collections of stories, *Veider soov* (A strange wish, 1963) and *Rataste vahel* (Under the wheels, 1966), concentrated on an intimate picture of the everyday life of the 'ordinary man', whose concealed paradoxes Valton points up in gentle, lyrical tones. From this he moved to modular grotesque tales which attempt to state truths about humankind by means of clinical descriptions of eccentrics, for example in *Kaheksa jaapanlannat* (Eight Japanese girls, 1968), *Sõnumitooja* (The messenger, 1972) or *Pööriöö külaskäik* (Visit at the solstice, 1974). He attempted to transfer the principles of his grotesque short stories to more expansive prose with *Muinasjutt Grandi leidmisest* (Fairy tale about finding Grand, 1976), a tenebrose journey through the Kafkaesque labyrinth of a vast factory. Valton exploited his gift for putting essentially philosophical problems into literary form in his historical novel set in the Mongol Empire, *Tee lõppmatuse teise otsa* (The path to the other end of infinity, 1978). For the most part, however, even in his longer works, Valton tries to find an appropriate experimental form, plays with literary genres, whether it be a matter of a travel journal as in *Arvid Silberi maailmareis* (A. Silber's journey round the world, 1984), or of mythology as in the cycle of would-be fables, which he published under his real name, *Põhjanaela paine* (The compulsion of the Pole Star, 1981). Apart from the miniatures and aphorisms of *Meentused eikuhugi* (Reminders nowhere, 1987) and *Kiirustav kahetsus* (Hasty regrets, 1989), Valton wrote the lengthy novel *Masendus ja lootus* (Depression and hope, 1989), treating the mass deportations of Estonian smallholders after WWII.

●Individual pieces in H. Puhvel (Ed.), *Estonian Short Stories* (Tallinn, 1981); E. Mallene (Ed.), *The Play*; E. Mallene (Ed.), *The Sailor's Guardian* (Tallinn, 1984).   VM

VALVASOR, Janez Vajkard, (1641–93), historian and geographer of Slovenia, born in Ljubljana of a noble family from Bergamo, was educated by the Jesuits in Ljubljana and later in Germany. He took part in wars against the Turks under Count Nikolaj Zrinski (ZRÍNYI). He travelled widely in Germany, Italy, N Africa, France and Switzerland, observing Nature and national character, and collecting books, drawings and sculptures. 1679 he began to publish his work. He was made a member of the Royal Society for his monograph on Lake Cerkno. 1689 he published his greatest work, the monumental account with maps and engravings of the province of Carniola, *Die Ehre des Herzogthums Crain* (The glory of the Duchy of Carniola).   HL

VÁMOŠ, Gejza (1901–56), Slovak prose writer, was something of an outsider in literature and life; he was the son of a Hungarian Jewish railway official, and he read medicine at Prague and London. He practised as a doctor in Prague and Piešťany, but, fearing persecution, left Slovakia for China in 1929; then he worked as a doctor among the poor in Brazil, where he died. The collection of short stories, often ironic monologues, *Editino očko* (Edita's eye, 1925), manifests the main subjects of his writings: human beings' nastiness to each other, their fundamental inconstancy, the sexualisation and materialisation of life in a world of prejudice and superficiality. His despairing scepticism often verges on cynicism. The satirical novel *Atomy Boha* (Atoms of God, 1928) depicts a world ruled by gonococci. A keen young doctor in a VD clinic experiments on himself with disastrous results, and his girlfriend, having been raped by an infected degenerate, ends in his clinic, and, finally, both commit suicide. Sex and VD are the caprice of a cold, almost vindictive, puppeteer God, for whom medical science provides jolly entertainment. The novel is perhaps the most significant product of Expressionism in Slovak literature. Vámoš's popular episodical novel *Jazdecká legenda* (Cavalry legend, 1932) is a predictable prose farce whose satire is directed mainly at army officers. The novel *Odlomená haluz* (Broken branch, 1934) is a critical study of Slovak Jewish life since WWI. RBP

VANČURA, Vladislav (1891–1942), Czech writer, qualified as a doctor at Prague (1921), but practised for only a few years, soon to devote himself to writing. He was a member of the CP from its founding (1921), was expelled in 1929, and after the German occupation worked underground for the Communists. He was arrested by the Gestapo and, a few days later, shot by firing squad. He was not a political writer, and when he introduced left-wing politics into his sophisticated, lyrical novels, he did so out of a sense of duty, and such passages are written in a simple style in discord with his normal accomplished blend of archaisms, poeticisms, colloquialisms, slang and rhythmical, cultivated intellectual Czech. His first novel, *Pekař Jan Markoul* (The baker, J.M., 1924), is a down-to-earth prose ballad in high style about a man who is too good for this world, a modern myth about a tradesman who becomes a proletarian. The eponymous hero has something of Don Quixote and something of a Christian martyr; his independence derives from his optimism and his humility before Fate. The magisterial, ironic, *Pole orná a válečná* (Fields for plough and sword, 1925) is a symbolic description of the bloody dissolution of the Habsburg Monarchy in WWI. It depicts a society with no bourgeoisie except a vile Jewish publican. The main character is the degenerate foundling, Řeka, who ends ceremonially interred as the Unknown Warrior. The only positive character is the brave, whoring, noble, Ervín, who has extraordinary compassion for the men he commands; worthy of a hero's death, he dies of dysentery. In contrast, his next novel, his most popular, *Rozmarné léto* (Capricious summer, 1926), is an idyll. In language which sometimes approaches the liturgical, he satirises with immense affection petty bourgeois life. Simultaneously, it constitutes an apotheosis of poetry and the poet. *Marketa Lazarová* (1931) is an epic hymn of praise to health, strength, vitality. The narrator is a bardic high-priest chanting the stories of two bands of robber-barons and their routing by the king's troops. The more conventional *Útěk do Budína* (Escape to Buda, 1932) concerns love and social change in the Czechoslovak First Republic; the novel's dominant mood is wistful optimism.

●*The End of the Old Times* [*Konec starých časů*, 1934] (Prague, 1965).
L. Doležel, *Narrative Modes in Czech Literature* (Toronto, 1973); W. Giusti, 'Un prosatore cèco contemporaneo

Vladislav Vančura', *Rivista di Letterature Slave*, 5 (1930), pp. 253–63.

RBP

VAPTSAROV, Nikola (1909–42), Bulgarian poet, was born into the family of a Macedonian patriot friend of YAVOROV; Vaptsarov went to the Varna Maritime Academy (1926–32), where his sensitivity to social injustice was augmented by the influence of Communist ideas. After the Academy he became a manual labourer and was active in Communist cells. 1940 he was arrested because of his involvement in seeking public support for the signing of a treaty with the USSR. After his release he became a leader of Communist guerrilla resistance and, 1942, was again arrested; he was tried, condemned and shot. Under the Communists he became an emblem of proletarian martyrdom and unshakable faith. As a writer, he was fascinated by YAVOROV, BOTEV and Gorki, had a special affection for the theatre and wrote one play, *Vălnata, koyato buchi* (The thundering wave, written 1935, publ. 1957), which shows the influence of Ibsen. He associated with left-wing writers like Georgi Karaslavov (1904–84) and Hristo Radevski (b. 1903), and after 1936 was involved with editing literary journals. His only collection, *Motorni pesni* (Engine songs), was published in 1940. All his work reflects his idea of a 'new aesthetics' which has its roots in some of MILEV's views: the treatment of 'low' themes in literature, the delyricising of verse. For Vaptsarov that meant the introduction into literature of socialist class consciousness among the deprived, a replacement of 'empty poetic chimeras' by the dream of a new, just society. The hero of his verse is the deprived class with whom the poet identifies himself. His 'new romanticism' is the class struggle and the dream of a future liberation of man (e.g. 'singing engines' as an emblem of that liberation). Vaptsarov registers, in Marxian terms, the deprived classes' alienation from life, history and art. His social awareness results in a dream of a humane world; the most important element of the dream is 'faith'. This faith is a humanist replacement of Christian faith; Christian images, as in, e.g., Czech Proletarian Poets, like 'miracle', 'resurrection', 'last judgement', constitute the vehicles of a social 'catharsis' achieved through a revolution. He understands revolution as the historical mission of the masses, who replace the traditional Bulgarian hero propagated by BOTEV's verse; in this he is also influenced by the poet Hristo Smirnenski's (1898–1923) romantically coloured visions of a mass proletarian rising. In Vaptsarov's verse revolution is de-heroised in a strict Marxist-Leninist manner, since revolution is an historical necessity, not an ideal; the ideal is contained in the dream of the future; there are no heroes; the life of the individual is meaningless.

●*Poems* (Sofia, 1955).   SIK

VARIBOBA, Jul (i.e. Giulio Varibova, 1724–c. 88), Arbëresh (Italo-Albanian) poet, one of the most original 18th-century Arbëresh authors, was born in Mbusat (San Giorgio Albanese) in Cosenza, and was one of the first students of the Italo-Albanian College of San Benedetto Ullano. After having worked for a time as a teacher and priest in his native village, he went to Rome where he passed the last years of his life. It was in Rome that he published a volume of poetry entitled *Ghiella e Shën Mëriis Virghiër* (Life of the

Virgin Mary, 1762), which contains a long narrative poem in two parts and a number of short poems. Variboba's narrative poem deals mainly with the Nativity, with the poet's native Calabria as its background. Some of the verse clearly resembles Arbëresh folk-songs and dances. Variboba's poetry is at its freshest when describing the scenery and customs of Calabria; his narrative poem is one of the first works of artistic value in Arbëresh literature, indeed Albanian literature as a whole.

●G. Ferrari, *Giulio Variboba e la sua opera poetica albanese* (Bari, 1963); M. Lambertz, 'Giulio Variboba', *Zeitschrift für vergleichende Sprachforschung* 74 (1956), pp. 47–224. ShM

VARNALIS, Kostas (1884–1974), was born in Burgas (Pirgos), educated in Plovdiv (Philippopolis), then left Bulgaria to read literature at Athens. Qualified as a teacher in 1908, taught in Bulgaria and Greece until 1925, when he was dismissed because of his left-wing views. During 1919 he studied literature, philosophy and sociology at the Sorbonne. His early poetry (1904–19), heavily influenced by the French Decadents, is intimate, erotic and highly crafted. Το φως που καίει (The light which burns, 1922), a mixture of prose and poetry, showed a radical move towards political commitment. 1923 he published a powerful Marxist interpretation of SOLOMOS. The new direction of his work was confirmed by a second long poem, Οι Σκλάβοι πολιορκημένοι (The enslaved besieged, 1927 – the title echoes SOLOMOS's 'Free besieged') which expresses its rejection of accepted social and moral ideas in a mixture of satire and lyricism. In the late 1920s he became a journalist and translator. His commitment is at its most hec-

toring and negative in such prose works as Η αληθινή απολογία του Σωκράτη (The true apology of Socrates, 1931) and Το ημερολόγιο της Πηνελόπης (The diary of Penelope, 1947). 1958 he received the Lenin Prize. Towards the end of his life he devoted himself principally to translation again.

●K. Friar (Ed.), *Modern Greek Poetry* (Athens, 1982), pp. 60–5. CFR

VAROUJAN, Daniel (i.e. D. Tcough'earian, 1884–1915), Armenian poet, born in a small village near Sebastia, had 'barely begun to read his breviary at the village school' when he was taken to Constantinople (1896) during the massacres of the Armenians, where, searching for his father, 'in the horror of blood, I found him in prison falsely accused'. 1902 he went to Venice to the Mourad Raphaelian school, where he discovered the ideas of Rousseau and Tolstoy. Then he went to the University of Ghent to read political science and sociology (1905–8). 1912 he returned to Constantinople, where in 1914 he founded and edited the literary annual *Navasard*. In a letter to a friend, Varoujan describes his own development: 'Two environments have had a great influence on my artistic maturation: Venice with her Titian and the Low Counties with their Van Dyck. It was the vivid colours of the former and the barbaric realism of the latter that sharpened my senses.' Varoujan's collection *Sarsurner* (Tremors, 1906) is a celebration of life and glorification of love; his second work, the monumental *Tseghin Sirtě* (The heart of the race, 1910), consisting of three cycles, constitutes a crystallisation of the grief, the blood and the tears of a relentlessly persecuted people. Varoujan's most famous work, however, is *Het'anos Erger* (Pagan songs, 1912), where Varoujan expresses his universality, his urbanity and his love of 'pagan beauty'; it is a sharp rebuke to the conservative bourgeois Armenian community of Constantinople. 1912–15 he wrote the collection *Hatsin Ergĕ* (Songs of bread, 1921), where the poet exalts and affirms the tormented and the tormenting life of the ruthlessly exploited common man, the poor landless peasant. Life is a hot-house wherein, like an exotic perishable plant, our human dignity and our charity are revitalised and preserved quietly, as if fermenting for the humanisation of posterity.

●T. Cross (Ed.), *The Lost Voices of World War I* (London, 1988), pp. 373–6.

VN

VASA, Pashko (i.e. Vaso Pasha, Vasa Pasha Shkodrani or Wassa Effendi 1825–92), Albanian statesman, scholar, prose writer and poet, after school in his native Shkodër, served as a secretary at the British consulate there. 1849 he took part in the Venetian uprising against the Austrians and had therefore to flee to Turkey, where he occupied high office in the Ottoman administration. 1879 he acquired the title of Pasha and 1883 became Governor of the Lebanon. Despite his functions, he never forgot his homeland and took an active part in the organisation of the Albanian national movement. Vasa is the author of *La verité sur l'Albanie et les Albanais* (1878) in which he informs the Western reader about the plight of his people. To make the Albanian language better known he published a *Grammaire albanaise à l'usage de ceux qui desirent apprendre cette langue sans l'aide d'un maître* (Albanian grammar for those wishing to learn this language without the aid of a

teacher, London, 1887). He also wrote a volume of verse in Italian entitled *Rose e spine* (Roses and thorns, 1878) and, under the pseudonym Albanus Albano, a novel in French, *Bardha de Temal, scènes de la vie albanaise* (1890) and several historical publications in Western languages, but he is better known in Albania for his poem *Moj Shqypni, e mjera Shqypni!* (Oh Albania, poor Albania, 1880).

●A. Khair, *Wassa Pacha (1883–1892), le moutaçarrifat du Mont* (Beirut, 1973).

ShM

VASILIKOS, Vasilis (b. 1933), Greek prose writer, whose family, on the outbreak of WWII, moved to Thessaloniki (Salonica), where eventually he was to return to study law at the university. After military service as an interpreter and a brief period in Athens, he went to New York at the end of the 1950s to study television directing at the RCA School. His first novella, Διήγηση του Ιάσονα (Story of Jason), appeared in 1953. He returned to Greece at the end of 1960, and the following year published his trilogy of novelle Το πηγάδι (The well), Το φύλλο (The leaf) and Το αγγέλιασμα (The announcement). At the same period he began working as a regular contributor to the periodical Ταχυδρόμος (Postman) and as assistant director and scriptwriter for various films at home and abroad. In 1966 he published his documentary novel *Z* on the Lambrakis affair (the politically motivated assassination of a left-wing member of parliament). Under the Junta (1967–74) he went into voluntary exile in W Europe. On his return he worked for the papers Ελευθεροτυπία (Free press) and Τα Νέα (The news). 1981, with the rise of PASOK (The Greek Socialist

Party) to power, he was given a senior post in television, a position from which he resigned in 1985. His prolific production of stories and novelle in the 1960s and 1970s was rewarded with the Mediterranean Prize at Palermo in 1978. His most recent novel, Ελικόπτερο (Helicopter), appeared in 1985. From the outset his work is characterised by its anti-heroes, the ambiguity of the values of the world in which they move, the imprecision of place and time, the use of symbols and allegory, all of which impose an active process of interpretation on the reader. The growth of his left-wing commitment, though for a period it seemed to lead to a simplification of both his ideas and forms, has eventually proved compatible with his previously established literary persona.

●Z (London, 1968).   CFR

VAZHA PSHAVELA ('A lad from Pshavia', i.e. Luk'a Razik'ashvili, 1861–1915), was the greatest of all Georgia's poets. The Razik'ashvilis were leading tribesmen of the wild mountain communes of Pshavia. Vazha's father was a priest, although pagan traditions had reasserted themselves in Pshavia. With a cantankerous father and poetically effusive mother, Vazha and his brothers were all creative individualists: Nik'o Razik'ashvili (1866–1927) was a poet known as Bachana, Tedo (1869–1922) was an ethnologist and collector of folk poetry. Vazha was given a rough education in the Kakhetian centre of Telavi, and then in Tbilisi and Gori, ending as a schoolteacher. Poverty forced him to abandon university studies at St Petersburg. He remained a hunter and a boxer all his life, but had an extraordinary memory for poetry, spoken or written. By 1886 he had

married (the one happy year in his life) and he returned to his native Chargali. His first 'burst' of poetry, 1885–90, culminated in the epic poem 'Gogotur and Apshina', and his bitterest narrative poem, 'Aluda Ketelauri' (1888), which introduces the theme of conflict between individual morality (Aluda prays for the soul of the Ingush he has killed) and the commune's imperative (they expel him for sacrilege). From the start, his poetry combined the native folklore and dialect of Pshavia and the high Caucasian frontierlands of Khevsureti with European literary traditions and literary Georgian. He evolved a harsh, laconic language, tempered with hypnotic incantation, which took little heed of the standardised narrative style evolved in metropolitan literary circles; his poetry was built on a core of Hellenic tragedy which was still alive in the folklore of the Pshavs and Khevsurs. His native steely pessimism evolved under the influence of Goethe, the Bible and Shakespeare into a complex, articulate vision of idealistic man battling indifferent Nature. Vazha would not harness his work to furthering the Georgian national struggle; the Tbilisi literary establishment, except for Ilia CH'AVCH'AVADZE, dismissed him. Vazha was no mean ethnologist and collector of folk poetry: he is one of the few poets to succeed in making literature out of folk poetry. Poems such as *Aluda Ketelauri* fed back into folk culture and were as likely to be heard from a shepherd as read in print. Aluda's isolation reflects Vazha's own loneliness. Horror at the outside world, whether mountain blood feuds or the political oppression of the Russian Empire, was fed by personal tragedy: his poetry becomes more and more intransigent. 1890 he lost an eye from anthrax; 1902 his wife died in pregnancy. (Vazha remarried 1904.) While he lived like an impoverished peasant, his poetry reached a zenith with *St'umar-masp'indzeli* (Host and guest, 1893), where the clash of laws of blood feud and of hospitality drive the hero and heroine to isolation and death, and *Gvelis mch'ameli* (The snake-eater, 1901), a Georgian *Faust* whose hero, Mindia, is developed from folk myth into an archetype of the poet-shaman unable to coexist with family or community. Later Vazha had success with poetic prose and drama, but his influence on Symbolists as well as Realists stems from his longer poems and from such profoundly despairing lyrics as 'Ias utxarit t'urpasa, Mova da shegch'ams ch'iao' (Tell the lovely violet, Worms will come and eat you, 1903). Vazha died of pleurisy on a visit to Tbilisi, just as his colossal stature achieved recognition. In the 1930s–40s four major Russian poets translated Vazha; Pasternak's translation of 'The snake-eater' affects his own work, such as *Dr Zhivago*.

● *Three Poems (Aluda Ketelauri, Host and Guest, The Snake Eater)* (Tbilisi, 1981); *Aluda Ketelauri*, in *Modern Poetry in Translation*, 1983, pp. 116–32. L. Magarotto, 'La poesia epica di Važa-Pšavela' in *Georgica*, I (Rome), 1985, pp. 7–47.   DR

VAZOV, Ivan (1850–1921), Bulgarian writer and translator, the son of a rich merchant, received an exceptionally good education for his day. He failed to follow his father in the family business; when sent to Roumania to finish his merchant's apprenticeship, he went to live among the exiles planning the liberation of Bulgaria and became involved with revolutionary activities. Pat-riotism inspires the whole of his work. After the Russo-Turkish War of 1877–78, Vazov worked as a court official, then, 1880, went to live in Plovdiv. He became the chairman of the Plovdiv Learned Society (1881) and established the first Bulgarian scholarly journal, *Zora* (Dawn, 1885). 1886 he had to emigrate to Russia on account of his publicly proclaimed Russophilia. 1889 he returned, settled in Sofia, founded and edited various journals, became Minister of Education, but was pleased to leave the post after the fall of the government. He lived through the political and social crises of the post-Liberation period, the Balkan Wars and WWI. In his later work he satirises the Bulgarian society that had abandoned the spiritual ideals of the National Revival and was indulging in commercialism and political power-struggles. Vazov, regarded as the patriarch of Bulgarian culture, remains the most prolific Bulgarian writer; to some extent he was the architect of new Bulgarian literature. Amongst other things, he was the first serious Bulgarian playwright. His best-known work is the novel *Pod igoto* (Under the yoke, 1888), concerning the 1876 April Uprising, a novel widely understood as patriotic, but containing one of the most precise, if somewhat ironical, analyses of the spirit of the National Revival. His mythopoeic cycle of poems, *Epopeya na zabravenite* (Epopee of the forgotten, 1881–1884), creates a pantheon of figures in the Revival; Vazov compares them with the saints and martyrs and the heroes of the greatest events in the history of the world. Another prose work, *Chichovtsi* (Old chaps, 1884), gives a sometimes humorous picture of pre-war Bulgarian society; his portraits of original types here become part of the literary myth of a 'national character', and later became themselves the object of reinterpretations (e.g. RADICHKOV). His novel *Nemili-nedragi* (Outcasts, 1883), concerning the ideals of Bulgarian exiles in Roumania and their fate after the Liberation, is both an apology for and an ironisation of the myth of national heroism during the Revival and is among the first expressions of Vazov's post-Liberation social criticism. Vazov's verse has a predominantly patriotic mood which converts, e.g., the beauty of Nature into an apotheosis of the Bulgarian historico-geographical space. His patriotism becomes chauvinist in some of his verse written during the Balkan Wars. Vazov, however, also wrote meditative verse where Nature simply arouses the poet's wonder at the beauty of Creation and where, instead of the national 'bard', he is a poet expressing his own subjectivity. In his travel journals, e.g. *Velikata rilska pustinya* (The great Rila wilderness, 1892), Nature provides the source of philosophical contemplation.

•*Under the Yoke* (London, 1894; Sofia, 1960); *Selected Stories* (Sofia, 1967).

P. Christophodroph, *Ivan Vazov, la formation d'un écrivain bulgare* (Paris, 1938); T. Pavlov, *The Social Roots of Vazov's Work* (Sofia, 1950).   SIK

VENEZIS, Ilias (1904–77), Greek prose writer, was born in Aïvali (Turkey), and 1914 his family fled to Mytilene to escape Turkish persecution during WWI. He went to school there 1914–18. After the Armistice his family returned to Aïvali, and Venezis completed his education there in 1921. The Asia Minor Disaster of 1922 led to his family's 'permanent expulsion', along with the rest of the Greek population, from Anatolia. Venezis was arrested after his family's expulsion in 1922, imprisoned, then endured the slavery of the labour battalions which the Turkish authorities dispatched into E Turkey. His experiences are graphically recorded in his best-known novel, Το Νούμερο *31328* (Number 31328, 1931). In November 1923 he was released and allowed to join his family in Athens. His first published work, a volume of stories named after its title story 'Μανώλης Λέκας' (Manolis Lekas), appeared in 1928, but his reputation rests on 'Number 31328' and on two other novels which also embody his nostalgia for the 'paradise lost' of Anatolia, Γαλήνη (Calm, 1939) and Αιόλικη Γη (Beyond the Aegean, 1943), in which there is a curious mixture of ethographical realism, symbolism and lyricism. His later works include the play Μπλοκ C (Block C, 1945) and Εξοδος (Exodus, 1950), both of which are responses to the German occupation, but he never succeeded in renewing his literary manner, and the elements of melodrama, didacticism and symbolism seem to grow more artificial and heavy-handed as his career progresses.

•A. and H. Karanikas, *Elias Venezis* (New York, 1969).   CFR

VEQILHARXHI, Naum (1797–1846), first ideologist of the Albanian National Revival and inventor of an Albanian alphabet, was born in the village of Vithkuq in the Korçë region. His family emigrated to Roumania, where 1821 he took part in the Wallachian uprising against the Turks. Later he worked as a lawyer in Braila on the Danube and died in Constantinople having been poisoned by Greek Orthodox fanatics. Veqilharxhi was the first to formulate the ideals and objectives of the Albanian national movement in a pamphlet, pointing out the backwardness and misery of the Albanians during the long centuries of Turkish rule. He stressed in particular the need of a new Albanian alphabet as a means of overcoming the situation and uniting the country. 1844 he published his 32-letter alphabet, on which he had already begun working in 1824–5, in his *Evëtar shqip* (Albanian orthography). In 1845 a second, augmented, edition was published.   ShM

VETRANOVIĆ, Mavro (1482–1576), Croatian poet and playwright, a member of the Benedictine Order which he joined in Italy in 1507, lived in Monte Cassino until 1522. He returned to his native Dubrovnik as an abbot. A man of great learning, he was one of the most prolific writers of his day: masquerades, lyric and satirical verse, epic poems, eclogues and religious drama. His most important works are two long narrative poems, *Remeta* (The hermit), describing the poet's life on the isolated island of St Andreja; *Pelegrin* (The pilgrim), an unfinished religious-fantastic epic; *Orfeo*, a mythological drama; and *Posvetilište Abramovo* (Abraham's sacrifice), a religious drama.

•Translations of poems in *The Bridge* 25, 1971, pp. 56–9 and T. Butler (Ed.), *Monumenta Serbocroatica*, (Ann Arbor, 1980), pp. 190–3.   ECH

VIDRIĆ, Vladimir (1875–1909), Croatian poet, born and educated in Zagreb, studied law in Prague, Zagreb and Vienna, and worked in a barrister's office in Zagreb. He published just one volume of 25 short poems, *Pjesme* (Poems, 1907) and another ten poems were found after his death. Essentially visual in its starting-point, Vidrić's verse excels in suggestive detail. A typical poem will exploit the connotations of a chosen setting – a patrician villa in Roman Herculaneum, a Classical Greek landscape where sunlight through trees conjures up wood nymphs, or an archetypal character – a Jewish merchant in Palestine or a Jesuit in Spain – to convey an atmosphere with minimal elaboration. Then, in a few carefully selected strokes, the poem tells a story with the communicative potential of a piece of narrative prose. His work has been likened to splinters of ancient Classical vases which convey a more concentrated impression precisely because of their fragmentary nature. Vidrić would recite his poems in company, apparently improvising nonchalantly. In fact, these carefully wrought miniatures are the result of painstaking application.

•'A Landscape' in A. Kadić (Ed.), *Contemporary Croatian Literature* (The Hague, 1960), p. 25.

E. D. Goy, 'The Poetry of Vladimir Vidrić', *Annali dell'Istituto Universitario Orientale*, 19 (1976), pp. 137–61.

          ECH

VIIDING, Juhan (b. 1948), Estonian poet and actor, son of the poet from the Arbujad (Logomancers) group, Paul Viiding (1904–62), studied acting at the Tallinn State Conservatory, 1968–72, since then has belonged to the Tallinn Repertory Theatre, and is now one of Estonia's leading actors. The main characteristics of Viiding's verse are actorly autostylisation as a melancholic clown and vivacious games with literature and literariness. With this verse he became the most prominent poet of the 1970s generation and, with the help of dramatisations of his poetry, which was sometimes set to music, he gained a wide readership. When he started, he published under the pseudonym Jüri Üdi, which he occasionally used in a literal English translation, George Marrow. His work first appeared in book form as 'Aastalaat' (The fair) in a volume containing works of three other authors, Jõel Sang (b. 1950), Toomas Liiv (b. 1946) and Johnny B. Isotamm (b. 1939), *Närvitrükk* (Neuropress, 1971); his own first book appeared in the same year, *Detsember* (December). Viiding's poetic talent gradually crystallises from *Käekäik* (Curriculum vitae, 1973) and *Selges eesti keeles* (Understandable, in Estonian, 1974) to *Armastuskirjad* (Love letters, 1975); he arrives at an individual fusion of the grotesque with the tragic, pathos with clowning, experimentation with banality, high art with feigned dilettantism. The very title of the first book Viiding published under his own name, the extensive 'selected verse', *Ma olin Jüri Üdi* (I was J.Ü., 1978), constituted an ostentatious removal of his literary mask and signalled a gradual withdrawal from the clownish pose; that is evident in *Elulootus* (ambiguous title: either Life's hopes, or An absence of biography, 1980) and *Tänan ja palun* (Thank you and please, 1983).   VM

VIKELAS, Dimitrios (1835–1908), Greek prose writer and poet, as a boy travelled widely; at 17 he went to London to work for his uncle's corn-merchant company, eventually became a partner and stayed in England until 1872, when he went to Paris. There he involved himself in the plans to revitalise the Olympic Games, and was partly responsible for the first games (Athens, 1896). Thereafter he stayed in Athens, and threw himself into various educational projects, setting up museums, libraries, and training for the blind. His early liter-

ary efforts were in moderate Romantic verse, but, like all *katharevousa* poetry of the period, its language makes it unacceptable to the modern reader. However, he made an important contribution to the development of the Modern Greek short story and novella, with Λουκης Λάρας (Loukis Laras, 1879) and Διηγήματα (Stories, 1887). 1850–80 was a dead period in Greek literature in general. 'Loukis Laras' tells the story of an old man who escapes with his family from the destruction of Chios during the War of Independence. It thus couples the Realist observation typical of ethographia with an heroic subject. In general Vikelas's stories have realistic plots in Greek settings, and a didactic element designed to show the virtues of the hero. His work offered an efficacious model for the writers of the 'Generation of 1880'.   CFR

VILARAS, Ioannis (1771–1823), Greek scholar and poet, was brought up in Janina, studied medicine at Padua and returned to Janina as court physician to Ali Pasha and personal physician to his son Veli, whom he accompanied on his military expeditions in the Peloponnese and Thessaly. When the Sultan's armies laid siege to Janina in 1820, Vilaras fled, along with the great majority of the Greek population, and took refuge in the Zagora district of Thessaly, where he died in poverty. The only work by Vilaras published during his lifetime was his Ρωμέικη Γλώσσα (Greek language), a short essay on the orthographical system of Greek, an exposition of his own linguistic theories and the application of his principles in a selection of examples of poetry and two pieces of prose translation. Vilaras bases his theory and practice exclusively on the contemporary spoken language and shows himself prepared for a radical break with the past in his proposed spelling reforms. The six poems used in illustration belong to the same general thematic and stylistic areas as the poems of CHRISTOPOULOS, though the language is more vivid and the verse more highly wrought. Vilaras re-introduces the 15-syllable couplets dear to Cretan Renaissance poetry, a metre which he will later use for his translation of the pseudo-Homeric βατραχομυομαχία (Battle of frogs and mice), published in the first edition of his complete poetry, in Corfu in 1827. This posthumous 'complete works' adds, in particular, a body of satirical work which shows both keen observation and a cultured familiarity with the tradition of the character sketch.

CFR

VILDE, Eduard (1865–1933), Estonian prose writer and dramatist, failed to complete his schooling partly because he was a bad learner and partly because he came into conflict with his teachers; nevertheless his first literary endeavours were such that he was able to make a career as a writer and journalist in Tallinn and Riga. His elopement, marriage and almost immediate estrangement from his wife took him to Berlin (1890–2). 1896–7 he lived in Moscow and, after returning to Estonia, he worked as a journalist in Narva and Tallinn. Because of his involvement in the 1905 Revolution he had to live in exile in the West until 1917. After a triumphal return he became active in political life as a Social Democrat and briefly worked as literary adviser at the Vanemuine Theatre. 1919–20 he was a diplomat in the Estonian legations in Copenhagen and Berlin. For the rest of his life he was a freelance writer in Tallinn. Inspired by his work as a journalist and by Western literary models, particularly German Realist prose, Vilde gradually moved away from producing time-serving light reading and began to observe the social mechanisms determining human fates, urban and rural (*Külmale maale* [Into a cold region, 1896]). He was always interested in topical themes, e.g. the life of the proletariat in the novel *Raudsed käed* (Hands of iron, periodical form 1898, book 1910) or the woman question. His concern for the realia of social milieux enabled Vilde to overcome the traditional romanticising approach of historical fiction in the trilogy, *Mahtra sõda* (War in M., 1902), *Kui Anija mehed Tallinna käisivad* (When the men of A. went to Tallinn, 1903) and *Prohvet Maltsvet* (The prophet M., 1906–8), a raw picture of the mid-19th-century peasant rebellion. The social-critical emphasis of Vilde's work is less intense in the psychologically profound, almost intimate novel, *Mäeküla piimamees* (The dairy man from M., 1916).

●*Milkman of the Manor* [*Mäeküla piimamees*] (Tallinn, 1976); some shorter prose in the anthology *25 Stories from the Soviet Republics* (Moscow, 1958).   VM

VILIKOVSKÝ, Pavel (b. 1941), Slovak fiction writer, briefly studied film directing in Prague, but then read Slovak and English at Bratislava (degree 1965), and since he was an undergraduate (1964) has worked as a publisher's or periodical editor. The essentially intimate short stories, *Citová výchova v marci* (Sentimental education in March, 1965), records of people and happenings come across while travelling, have as their background a mainly rural society, where man is largely in harmony with Na-

ture; the style here owes much to the Lyrical Prose school. The next book he was allowed to publish, *Prvá veta spánku* (First movement of sleep, 1983), a somewhat playful psychological study of types of perception, begins with sexual violence where his first book had ended with it. His third work, *Večne je zelený . . .* (Ever green is the . . ., 1989), is his most accomplished; it is a sidesplitting satire on totalitarianism, 'spy mania', Slovaks and nationalism, whose narrator is being interrogated supported over a bath of sulphuric acid only by a spike of ice stuck up his anus; the ice is gradually melting. The brief novel *Kôň na poschodí, slepec vo Vrábl'och* (A horse upstairs, a blindman in Vrable, 1989) analyses another extreme, a man driven to suffocating his demented mother; it also constitutes an ironic study in the nature of identity. *Eskalácia citu* (The escalation of emotion, 1989) contains some stories from *Citová výchova*; the other, lyrical, stories concern mortality, political opportunism, crass Socialist Realist writing, violence and guilt, but their main theme is human physicality – and the narrator creates a sarcastic tension between himself and his reader by obliterating the possibility of the spiritual. The main part of the epistolary *Slovenský Casanova* (A Slovak C., 1991) satirises Party-functionary salacity, promiscuity, arrogance, opportunism, jargon-boundness and fear of Party bosses. Vilikovský's humour ranges from the aggressive to the clownish, and beneath his grotesque or macabre, sometimes even sentimental, writing lies a concern with human solitude, alienation, in amoral socialist society.
RBP

VIRZA, Edvards (i.e. E. Lieknis, 1883–1940), was a Latvian poet, whose principal teachers were the French poets of the Renaissance and Verhaeren. His *Straumēni* (The Straumēni manor house, 1933) describes an old Zemgale farm and its people during the four seasons of the year, blending in equal proportions the biblical patriarchal spirit with the life wisdom of the ancient Latvians. Virza earned the position of 'Latvian state poet'. Shortly before his death he wrote *Baigā Vasara* (The ominous summer, 1940). In this 'catastrophist' poem he prophesied the coming of an 'iron age', when 'horror will loom from behind every bush'. Virza was the acknowledged teacher of many young poets.
EB

VISNAPUU, Henrik (1890–1951), Estonian poet, qualified as an elementary-school teacher in 1907 and taught at various village schools until 1912, when he moved to Tartu where he gave Estonian lessons at the preparatory school of the girls' grammar school; he matriculated externally in 1916 and then started reading philosophy at Tartu, but his studies were interrupted by the war with Russia, in which he served as a war correspondent. 1935–7 he worked as cultural adviser in the State Propaganda Office and 1937–40 was editor-in-chief of the periodical *Varamu* (Storehouse). 1944 he fled Estonia and until 1949, when he went to the USA, lived in the Geislingen refugee camp. Visnapuu was one of the most important poets of the Siuru group. In his work he combined elements of, particularly Russian, Symbolism (emphasis on a musical stylisation of verse, his interest in Theosophy and Buddhism) and of Cubofuturism (emphasis on the expressive value of the word and on the aesthetic colouring of the 'metalogical' sound). He sought new rhythms for his verse, rhythms which had no place in the Estonian literary tradition, but which opened a path to expressing modern experience in a wide range of conflicting emotional levels both in intimate verse like *Amores* (1917), *Jumalaga, Ene!* (Farewell, E., 1918) or *Käoorvik* (The meadow violet, 1920), and in verse reflecting topical problems like *Talihari* (The peak of winter, 1920), *Maariamaa laulud* (Songs of the Virgin Mary's land, 1927) and *Päike ja jõgi* (The sun and the river, 1932). Visnapuu attempts, by means of a series of joyous rural landscapes and oppressive symbols of the fate of his nation, to create a new form of patriotic lyric. That type of writing continues in his exile verse, *Esivanemate hauad* (Ancestors' graves, 1946) and *Mare Balticum* (1948).

●*A Selection of Poems* (London, 1958); two poems in E. H. Harris, *Literature in Estonia* (London, 1943).   VM

VIZYINOS, Gregorios (1849–96), Greek prose writer and poet, born in Vizyi, in E Thrace, after experiencing poverty as a youth in Constantinople and in Cyprus, was enabled by the financial help of a rich Greek living abroad to study in Athens, then in Germany. 1874–82 he studied philosophy and psychology, taking his doctorate at Leipzig in 1881. He went to Paris where he got to know VIKELAS; they both began by publishing collections of *katharevousa* poetry, but Vizyinos's collection Ατθιδες αύραι (Breezes of Athis, 1883) is a set of short verse tales. VIKELAS then pushed Vizyinos towards his own preferred genre, the short story, and the six tales for which the latter is known were written 1881–5 and published in the periodical *Estia*. 1884 he became a lecturer at the University of Athens, having submitted a thesis on the aesthetics of Plotinus. He also wrote essays on psychology and education. 1892 he became mentally ill. Seen as one of the initiators of *ethographia* because of the rural settings and the socially simple characters his stories contain, Vizyinos is in fact much more interesting than that, in that his studies in psychology and philosophy lead him to present reality as a problem. Each of his stories is based on an apparent contradiction which leaves a mystery to be solved. Thus in 'The only journey of his life' the adolescent narrator has to learn to recognise the distance between the wonderful tales of travel and adventure told to him by his grandfather and the limits of his grandfather's actual experience. Yet, when his grandfather dies at the end of the story it is only in terms of the language of the old man's fairy tales that the boy can cope with the reality of death: the reader questions whether the old man's tales offer a 'reality' any less important for the boy than day-to-day experience. The other stories continue this pattern of contrasting different perceptions and understandings of people and events, leaving the reader in doubt as to their relative validity, e.g. in 'Who was my brother's murderer?' each of the main characters copes with, and can only cope with, a particular knowledge and interpretation of the events concerned.

●R. Beaton (Ed.), *The Greek Novel A.D. 1–1985* (London, 1988), pp. 11–22.

CFR

VODNIK, Anton (1901–65) was the most important of Slovene R. Catholic Expressionist poets. His lyrics represent an ascetic alienation from material existence and an escape from reality and social conflict into the world of the religious visionary and of mystic eroticism. He freely employs similes from the liturgy and the Scriptures. Among his collections are *Žalostne roke* (Sorrowful hands, 1922), *Skozi vrtove* (Through the gardens, 1941), *Zlati krogi* (Golden rings, 1952), *Glas tišine* (The voice of silence, 1959) and *Sončni mlini* (Mills of the sun, 1964).

●*AMYP; Slovene Poets of Today*, 1965; *Parnassus*, 1957, 1965.   HL

VODNIK, Valentin (1758–1819), Slovene poet, educator, translator, lexicographer and journalist, after grammar-school education in Ljubljana, entered the Franciscan Order and completed his theological studies in 1782. 1793 he met the Slovene Maecenas, Baron Žiga Zois (1747–1819), who arranged his transfer to Ljubljana, where he became a grammar-school teacher in the following year. For patriotic reasons he collaborated fully with the French authorities during the Napoleonic period (1809–13) as grammar-school head and inspector of schools. With the restoration of Austrian power he had to retire. He began to write verse as a contributor to *Pisanice* (Trifles), and later included some of this early verse in *Zadovoljni Kranjec* (The happy highlander, 1781). He edited and himself contributed to *Velika pratika* (The great almanac, 1795–7) and its successor, *Mala pratika* (The small almanac, 1798–1806). 1797–1800 he edited *Ljubljanske novice* (Ljubljana news), the first Slovene newspaper, which came out twice weekly till mid-1798 and thereafter once a week. He published his *Pesme za pokušino* (Trial verses) in 1806 and *Pesmi za brambovce* (Soldier songs) in 1809, a translation of the Austrian patriot Heinrich Joseph von Collin's *Wehrmannslieder*. He wrote a Slovene grammar for primary schools, translated a French grammar and compiled an extensive German-Slovene-Italian dictionary which remained in manuscript.   HL

VODUŠEK, Božo (1905–78), Slovene poet and essayist, studied at Ljubljana Romance languages, 1924–8, and law, 1926–33. His legal career was interrupted by WWII in which he joined the partisans. After the war he worked as editor of *Ljudski pravnik* (The people's lawyer), 1946–9, later as a freelance writer, and from 1953 onwards at the Slovene Language Institute. He published a psychological study of CANKAR (1937) and a collection of poems, *Odčarani svet* (Disenchanted world, 1939).

●Selected poems in *AMYP*; *Parnassus*, 1957, 1965.   HL

VOJNOVIĆ, Ivo (1857–1929), Croatian playwright and poet, born in Dubrovnik, studied law and worked at the Croatian National Theatre in Zagreb. His first published work was a short novel, *Geranium*, which appeared in the journal *Vijenac* (Wreath), 1880. This was followed by a collection of novelle, *Perom i olovkom* (With pen and pencil, 1884). But it was after the publication of an unfinished novel, *Ksanta* (Xantha, 1887), that Vojnović turned definitively to drama and to the subject matter that he treated in his best-known work: the history and legends of his native Dubrovnik. His play *Ekvinocij* (Equinox, 1895) concerns social inequality and the resentment of the poor in Dubrovnik; it is written in the local dialect characteristic of Vojnović's best work, *Dubrovačka trilogija* (Dubrovnik trilogy, 1903). The trilogy describes three stages in the downfall of Dubrovnik as an independent republic. The first part, *Allons enfants*, deals with the entry of Napoleon's army under General Marmont into the city which had retained its independence throughout the centuries of notional allegiance to successive overlords. *Suton* (Twilight) and *Na taraci* (On the terrace) are concerned with the social transformation of Dubrovnik as the old nobility tries to resist the inevitable encroachment of new forces rendering them impotent and irrelevant. The play's subject matter dictates their melancholy tone, which verges at times on the sentimental, but they succeed in evoking an atmosphere of dignity and nostalgia which remains fresh today. Vojnović's work contributed much to the advancement of drama in Croatia, which had remained somewhat amateur in the 19th century.

● *A Trilogy of Dubrovnik* (Boston, 1951).

S. Venzelides, 'The Plays of Ivo Vojnović', *SEER*, 8 (1929), pp. 368–74; D. Suvin, 'Vojnović's Dramaturgy and Its European Context', *Canadian Review of Comparative Literature*, 2 (1975), pp. 10–34.   ECH

VÖRÖSMARTY, Mihály (1800–55), Hungarian poet, playwright and prose writer, came from a family of noble origin but of no property. After studying at Cistercian grammar school in Székesfehérvár and Piarist school in Pest, 1811–17, he had to support his studies of the humanities at the University of Pest as a private tutor. 1824 he passed his law exams. 1828–32 he edited the journal *Tudományos Gyűjtemény* (Scholarly review). After March 1848 he became involved in political activities. When the revolution was crushed, he was forced into hiding. He was unquestionably the finest poet of Hungarian Romanticism. Although the public expected him to compose epic and dramatic works, his greatest poems are visionary, apocalyptic lyric verse in which he proves a highly original creator of metaphors and syntax. *Zalán futása* (The flight of Zalán, 1825), the work that first brought him fame, is a verse epos about the Hungarians who settled in the Danube Basin at the end of the 9th century. It became an important source of national consciousness. Historically less significant but artistically more successful are the much shorter *Tündérvölgy* (A valley of fairies, 1826) and the fragmentary poem *A Délsziget* (An island of the south, 1826), testifying to the poet's interest in the fantastic. *Magyarvár* (The fortress of the Hungarians, 1830), another epic fragment, is an attempt to re-create Hungarian pagan traditions. Like most Romantics, Vörösmarty was attracted to the Middle Ages, but as a liberal he viewed feudalism as self-destructive. *A két szomszédvár* (Two neighbouring fortresses, 1831) is a powerful interpretation of the family feuds which dominated medieval Hungary. Among his plays *Salamon* (Solomon, 1827), *A bujdosók* (The fugitives, 1830) and *Czillei és a Hunyadiak* (C. and the Hunyadis, 1844) are dramatisations of incidents from Hungarian history, inspired by Shakespeare, whose *Julius Caesar* and *King Lear* he translated. His most original play, *Csongor és Tünde* (Cs. and T., 1828–31), however, is a dramatic fairy tale which sets out to interpret the history of mankind. Although he approved of the ideology of the Enlightenment, as the epigram 'A Guttenberg-albumba' (For the Guttenberg album, 1840) demonstrates, he was sceptical about human progress. The Night's monologue, marking the climax of *Csongor*, is a frightening vision of the darkness surrounding existence. *A Rom* (The ruin, 1830) is a verse parable about a destructive God, and *Gondolatok a könyvtárban* (Thoughts in a library, 1844) is a long meditation on the moral implications of knowledge. In the 1830s and 1840s Hungarian liberals identified themselves with those Poles who were struggling to liberate their country. This explains why the vision of history is as tragic in *Az emberek* (Mankind, 1846) as in *Előszó* (Preface, 1850), the two most important poems composed by Vörösmarty. The first was inspired by the Polish, the second by the Hungarian 'tragedy', but neither refers to any specific historical event. In *Az emberek* history is presented as circular; in *Előszó* it is given cosmic dimensions. Although Vörösmarty was an active supporter of the revolution of 1848–9, his pessimism was not the consequence of its outcome. Even 'Szózat' (Appeal, 1836), which became something like a second national anthem after it was set to music by Béni Egressy (1814–51) in 1843, contains a vision of the death of the Hungarian nation. Among his major poems on history, *A vén cigány* (The old Gipsy, 1854) is the only one offering some hope, in the final stanzas.

•D. Mervyn Jones, *Five Hungarian Writers* (Oxford, 1966); R. Porter and M. Teich (Eds), *Romanticism in National Context* (Cambridge, 1988); F. Garber (Ed.), *Romantic Irony* (Budapest, 1988). MSz-M

VOVCHOK, Marko (i.e. Maria Vilinska Markovych, 1834–1907), Ukrainian prose writer of Polish-Russian descent, learned Ukrainian from her husband. In 1857 P. KULISH published her *Narodni opovidannia* (Folk tales) which realistically depicted the life of the peasants under serfdom. Turgenev edited a Russian translation of these stories. In the early 1860s she lived in Paris, where her Ukrainian story *Maroussia* (1871) gained much acclaim when it was adapted into French. She was also a minor writer in Russian, the author of several novels on feminist themes. Her lifelong interest in Ukrainian folklore as well as in world literature helped her to refine her narrative prose. Liberal and radical Russian intellectuals (Herzen, Dobroliubov, Chernyshevsky, Pisarev) welcomed her stories as a protest against serfdom. Her short novel *Instytutka* (Boarding-school girl, 1860) was regarded as a masterpiece by FRANKO.

•*Marusia: A Maid of Ukraine* (New York, 1890); *Ukrainian Folk Stories* (Saskatoon, 1983); *After Finishing School* (Kiev, 1983). GSNL

VRATISLAV z MITROVIC, Václav (1576–1635), the son of a minor nobleman, was educated by the Jesuits and at 15 took part in a diplomatic mission sent by the Emperor Rudolph II to the Turkish Sultan. Together with the whole mission Vratislav was imprisoned in Constantinople, forced to work on the galleys and returned home only four years later after repeated payments of ransom by his relations. During the revolt of the Estates in 1618 he was exiled, but was appointed Chief Justice and Privy Counsellor after the victory of Ferdinand II. In his *Příhody* (Adventures, written 1599, publ. 1777) Vratislav recalls what he lived through without self-pity and with unusual impartiality towards the Turks. He is impressed by their military might, art of fortification, hot baths, well-organised network of caravanserais, their hospitality, religious devotion and pious behaviour in their mosques and by the splendid ceremonial at the Sultan's court, but is critical of their avarice. Vratislav shows his talent as a congenial narrator when, without sentimentality and often with black humour, he relates the daily life of the captives chained to each other and subjected to mental and physical torture. Although he wrote his book some four years after his return and added much geographical and historical information derived from other books, the description of the adventures themselves is typical of an adolescent: unaffected, almost naive.

• *Adventures of Baron Wenceslas Wratislav of Mitrowitz* (London, 1862).

KB

VRAZ, Stanko (i.e. Jacob Frass, 1810–51), Croatian poet and literary critic, born a Slovene, studied philosophy in Graz, where he met Ljudevit Gaj (1809–72), the Croat leader of the Illyrian Movement. The ideas of his pan-South-Slav movement appealed to Vraz so much that he moved definitively to Zagreb and devoted himself to Croatian literature. Vraz considered that the main task of the Illyrians was to create as quickly as possible a proper 'Illyrian' literature. He founded and edited the most important literary journal of the period, *Kolo* (Round-dance). Vraz helped to establish Zagreb as a cultural centre, particularly in his discriminating literary-critical work. He contributed some subtle lyric verse to the Croatian National Revival and is considered to be the founder of modern Croatian literary criticism.

• Two poems in *IYL*.   ECH

VRCHLICKÝ, Jaroslav (i.e. Emil Frída, 1853–1912), Czech writer and translator, the son of a tradesman, after a short period at a seminary studied philosophy and Romance languages, worked as a private tutor

in Italy, was appointed Professor of Comparative Literature at Prague in 1898 and member of the Upper House of the Austrian parliament in 1901; struck down by dementia in 1908, he died after four years of pitiable existence. He was the originator of a cosmopolitan movement, part-positivist and part-sceptic, and together with MÁCHA exercised an enormous influence on modern Czech poetry. He went through medievalist, neo-Classical and Romantic phases and his verse was moulded by Parnassism, Impressionism and, later, Symbolism. His intimate lyric verse in *Sny o štěstí* (Dreams of happiness, 1876), *Eklogy a písně* (Eclogues and songs, 1880), *Pouti k Eldoradu* (A pilgrimage to Eldorado, 1882), and many other collections celebrated the glory of love, the beauty of woman, the mystery of Nature, the splendours of life and the supreme role of art; but subsequently this sensual ecstasy was shattered by disillusion and mistrust in *Okna v bouři* (Windows in the storm, 1894), and finally, in *Meč Damoklův* (The sword of Damocles, 1913), his verse attained purity and tranquillity cleansed of its earlier rhetoric. His reflective lyrics were inspired by almost any external stimulus; beginning with pessimism he later came nearer to a belief in an evolving civilisation, but ended in scepticism and stoic resignation; most of his reflective verse, e.g. *Sfinx* (1883), *Dědictví Tantalovo* (The heritage of Tantalus, 1888), *Hlasy v poušti* (Voices in the wilderness, 1890) or *Život a smrt* (Life and death, 1892), reveals a disquieting undertone of doubt about the sense of human endeavour. A large part of Vrchlický's poetic work is formed by the fragments of the epopee of humanity he conceived after the example of Hugo. Humanity, as Vrchlický sees it, is groping towards something transcending material reality, but it is uncertain whether it progresses. As a dramatist, Vrchlický produced at least two *chefs-d'oeuvre*, both in verse, the trilogy *Hippodamie* (1st part, 1889; 2nd and 3rd parts, 1891), a tragedy of fate in the modern sense of the term, and *Bar Kochba* (1897), presenting the leader of the Jewish revolt against the Romans as the victim of his own moral corruption. Vrchlický's role in modern Czech literature cannot be overrated; he published 84 vols of original poetry, 31 dramas and comedies, 10 libretti, 5 vols of short stories, one novel, 13 vols of literary criticism, and translations of some 4,265 poems by 472 authors from 18 different literatures. He forced Czech literature to turn towards France, England and Italy, enriched the poetic language, established a highly personal mode of expression, introduced new forms, and was the first Czech poet to fight for the right of the writer to express himself freely with disregard for national, political, religious or moral considerations.

●A. Jensen, *Jaroslav Vrchlický. Etude littéraire* (Stockholm, 1894); M. Součková, *The Parnassian Jaroslav Vrchlický* (The Hague, 1964).   KB

VRETO, Jani (1822–1900), publicist of the Albanian National Revival, like many of his contemporaries, studied at the Zosimea secondary school in Ioannina, where he first began to take an interest in his native language. At this time he wrote a poem on Scanderbeg in Greek script and collected Albanian folklore. In Constantinople he came into contact with leading figures of the Revival movement and became a member of various Albanian committees and cul-tural societies. Vreto is the author of some of the first Albanian school textbooks, for example *Mirëvetija* (Ethics, 1886) and *Numeratoreja* (Arithmetic, 1886). He transliterated and published KYÇYKU's *Erveheja*.

ShM

VYNNYCHENKO, Volodymyr (1880–1951), Ukrainian novelist and playwright of the Modernist era, was throughout his life politically active and a member of the Ukrainian government during the brief spell of independence, 1918–19. In his works he looked at the seamier side of life and depicted it in a Naturalistic fashion. Psychological and moral problems fascinated him. He preached the amoral philosophy of 'honesty with oneself' (title of one of his works). His best novel is the ironic, satirical *Zapysky kyrpatoho Mefistofelia* (Notes of a pug-nosed Mephistopheles, 1917). The best of his plays were *Chorna pantera i bily medvid* (The black panther and the white bear, 1911) and *Brekhnia* (A lie, 1910). His Wellsian utopian novel, *Soniashna mashyna* (The sun machine, 1921–4), was particularly popular with readers. After 1919 he emigrated to W Europe, where he continued writing philosophical novels (e.g. *Nova zapovid* [The new commandment, 1948]). He is also the author of the powerful political pamphlet *Slovo za toboya, Staline* (Now you speak, Stalin, 1950). He died in France.

●B. Rubchak (Ed.), *Studies in Ukrainian Literature* (New York, 1984–5).   GSNL

VYSKOČIL, Ivan (b. 1929), Czech fiction writer and dramatist, studied acting and production at the Academy of Performing Arts and, on finishing (1952), read philosophy, education theory and clinical and criminal psychology at Prague (degree, 1957). While still a student (1950–7) he worked part-time in reform schools and taught psychology. From 1957 he directed, acted in and wrote for Prague 'small theatres'. After the Soviet occupation he could not publish, but was able to perform. None of his plays has so far appeared in book form. His first prose collection, *Vždyť přece létat je snadné* (After all, it's easy to fly, 1963), is a series of tightly knit sketches set in Utopia or Dystopia. The inhabitants of these spaces are eccentrics, sufferers from hallucinosis, and megalomaniacs. The main vehicles for Vyskočil's humour are slapstick, satire and word-play. *Malé hry . . . Maléry* (Little games . . . gaffes, 1967) constitutes a series of episodes combining political satire with horror story and fairy tale. The episode 'Návštěva' (The visit) contains the idea which eventually produced HAVEL's *Zahradní slavnost*. The world of *Malé hry* is 'Absurd', and the ordinary individual actively helps the authorities make it so. The book's theme is externally imposed and self-imposed roles and identities, and the characters in these fluctuant episodes are both manipulated and manipulating. *Malý Alenáš* (1990) is, as the title suggests (= 'Little Alenáš' or 'Small, but ours [Czech]'), a text relying almost entirely on word-play. It concerns identity and the boundary between dream and reality.

RBP

W

WAT, Aleksander (1900–67), Polish poet, fiction writer, essayist and translator, as a precocious 19-year-old student of philosophy at Warsaw, co-founded the Polish Futurist movement and published his first book, a long Dadaist poem in prose. For the next few years Wat remained in the orbit of the Futurist movement. By the mid-1920s, however, he had stopped writing verse and, after the publication of his collection of short stories *Bezrobotny Lucyfer* (Lucifer unemployed, 1927), abandoned creative writing altogether. This lapse into silence coincided with his espousal of Communism. Although never a Party member, he served as editor-in-chief of a Communist literary monthly. This record did not save him when, after the outbreak of war in 1939, he found himself a refugee in Lwów, soon to be taken by the Soviets. In January 1940 he was arrested by Stalin's secret police. Separated from his wife and son, he spent two years in Soviet prisons; in one of them he converted to R. Catholicism. Released in 1942 he was exiled with his family to Kazakhstan where they lived until their repatriation in April 1946. In Stalinist Poland, Wat was mistrusted because of his reluctance to support the régime's policies. After a public castigation by his fellow writers in 1953, he suffered a stroke; its conse-quence was the incurable neurological disorder that was to plague Wat for the rest of his life. In the wake of the Thaw of 1956, his first book in 30 years, *Wiersze* (Poems, 1957), came out; 1959 he was allowed to go to the West to seek a cure. He lived with his family mostly in S France, Italy and Paris, writing new poems and essays. 1963 he accepted an invitation from the University of California at Berkeley, where by 1965 he had recorded his 'conversation' with MIŁOSZ, published later as his 'spoken memoir', *Mój wiek* (My century). All Wat's most important books were published only posthumously: his collected poems, *Ciemne świecidło* (The dark source of light), came out in 1968, and *Mój wiek* in 1977. During the 1980s many of the essays and notes that had remained in manuscript were edited and published. This body of work shows Wat as an incomparable analyst of the evil underlying totalitarianism and the individual's responsibility for it. As a poet, in his late period he was able to offer a consistent tragic vision of human fate torn between the extremes of suffering and salvation.

●*With the Skin: Selected Poems* (New York, 1989); *My Century: The Odyssey of a Polish Intellectual* (Berkeley, 1988); *Lucifer Unemployed* (Evanston, Ill., 1990).

B. Carpenter, *The Poetic Avant-garde*

in Poland, 1918–1939 (Seattle, 1983);
S. Barańczak, 'Four Walls of Pain: The
Late Poetry of A. Wat', *SEEJ*, 2 (1989),
pp. 173–89.   StB

WAŻYK, Adam (1905–82), Polish
poet, fiction writer, essayist and
translator, born in Warsaw, was recognised very early as one of the most
original voices among poets of the
interwar Avant-garde and was a leading proponent of Cubism in Polish
poetry. His first two collections, *Se-
mafory* (Signals) and *Oczy i usta*
(Eyes and lips), came out to critical
acclaim in 1934 and 1926. Soon after
that, he turned to fiction, and only
back to poetry during the war, which
he spent in the USSR. This time,
however, he emerged as a representative of Socialist Realism in its
Classicist variety, which he continued to propound after his repatriation, until the unexpected 1955 publication of his controversial 'Poemat
dla dorosłych' (A poem for adults), a
sweeping condemnation of the moral
and political failure of People's Poland. In the following years he returned to his old Cubist techniques,
combining them with more topical
concerns in such collections as
Wagon (The railway carriage, 1963)
or *Zdarzenia* (Occurrences, 1977).
He also published an autobiographical novel, several collections of essays, and numerous translations from
Latin, French and Russian.
●Selected poems in C. Milosz, *Postwar
Polish Poetry* (Berkeley, 1983);
S. Barańczak and C. Cavanagh (Eds),
*Polish Poetry of the Last Two Decades
of Communist Rule: Spoiling Cannibals'
Fun* (Evanston, Ill., 1991).   StB

WEINER, Richard (1884–1937),
Czech poet and prose writer, a research chemist, worked in Germany
and Switzerland, fought on the S
Front and then worked in Paris as a
journalist. His early poetry, *Pták*
(The bird, 1914), is that of a timid,
oversensitive individual but his war
experiences changed his perception
and attitudes. He sees the world as a
senseless maze of vice and torment;
thus burdened, all man can achieve is
to be aware of his own absurdity in an
absurd universe. The poet must be an
indifferent witness negating his individuality. In *Rozcestí* (Crossroad,
1918) and *Mnoho nocí* (Many nights,
1926) Weiner constructs icy verse
that approaches reality with an extreme destructive logic. Applying
this approach to the unconscious, he
develops a highly individual brand of
Surrealism exposing the unconscious
as a frightening source of utter loneliness. His stories *Lítice* (The fury,
1916), *Škleb* (Grin, 1919) and
Lazebník (The baths man, 1929) equ-
ate the ideal with the concrete, hallu-
cination with reality, life with death.
Weiner is one of the most complex
Czech writers both in his ideas and
his style, which exploits lexical and
syntactic deformations. His prose
had an impact on that of Josef Čapek
(1887–1945) and VANČURA.   KB

WEÖRES, Sándor (1913–89), Hungarian poet, translator, playwright
and essayist, was born into a family
of noble origin, and studied in the
grammar schools of Szombathely,
Győr and Sopron. He was recognised
as a promising poet at the age of 14,
and was awarded prizes for both his
first and his second volumes (1934
and 1935). At the University of Pécs,
a stronghold of *Geistesgeschichte*, he
studied law, geography, history, philosophy and aesthetics, obtaining a
doctorate in philosophy. 1937 he
visited the Far East. 1941–50 he
worked in libraries in Pécs,
Székesfehérvár and Budapest. 1947
he married the poet Amy Károlyi (b.

1909), with whom he went to Italy. In the Stalinist period he was allowed to publish only children's verse, fairy tales, and translations. After 1956 he gradually returned to literary life. His work is voluminous and varied. Believing that verse should be recited, he drew inspiration from oral culture and focused on language games and the imitation of such musical forms as the fugue, toccata or waltz. Anticipating Postmodernism, he not only wrote a great number of poems in the forms and styles of the distant past, but also continued the experimental tradition of the Avant-garde. By the use of different stylistic masks and of textual fragments found in non-poetic contexts, he undermined the Romantic conception of poetic individualism and originality. After WWII he was asked by Zoltán Kodály to write words for short melodies used in musical instruction. This gave him the inspiration to compose one-line poems. In the same period he tried to revive the genre of the verse epic, relying both on Classical Antiquity and on the oral tradition of the Far East. One of his best volumes, *Medúza* (Medusa, 1944), contains 'Dalok Naconxypan-ból' (Songs from Naconxypan), a poem in 20 stanzas, inspired by the imaginary world created by the early 20th-century painter Lajos Gulácsy. The heavy emphasis on the independence of imagery in this work is somewhat reminiscent of the style of the Surrealists. Among his later works *Psyché* (1972) is a collection of poems by a fictitious poetess of partly aristocratic, partly Gipsy origin, who lived at the beginning of the 19th century. The style in this case is imitative of the poetic idiom used by the barely known Hungarian poets who lived and worked in the decades following 1800. His anthology *Három veréb hat szemmel* (Three sparrows with six eyes, 1977) is a collection of forgotten pieces, compiled with the aim of changing the institutionalised canon of Hungarian verse.

●*Selected Poems* (Harmondsworth, 1970); *If All the World Were a Blackbird* (Aberdeen, 1985); *Eternal Moment* (London, 1988).   MSz-M

WIERZYŃSKI,   Kazimierz (1894–1969), Polish poet, fiction writer and essayist, born into the family of a station-master in Drohobycz, studied at Cracow and Vienna for a while before the outbreak of WWI. Drafted into the Austrian Army, he was taken prisoner by the Russians and spent two years in a POW camp. 1918 he escaped and arrived in Warsaw where he met the four poets with whom he was to form the Skamander group in 1920. After the Polish-Soviet war in which he took part as a war correspondent, he settled in Warsaw and devoted himself to writing. When WWII began, he escaped to France and then to the USA. A staunch opponent of the Communist régime, he was never to return to Poland, living first in New York and New England, then moving to Italy and the UK for the last years of his life. Wierzyński's first collection, *Wiosna i wino* (Spring and wine, 1919), was a spectacular success. The euphoric exultation of these youthfully energetic lyrics provided the readers with a much needed antidote to the martyr-like or Decadent moods of the Romantic and neo-Romantic generations. The poet continued in a similar vein with his next collection, but in the mid-1920s his poetry started exploring more complex issues of Nature and history, and in his volumes from the 1930s he has become a catastrophist. This outlook, however, was still trapped in traditional stylistic conventions. That is even more striking in Wierzyński's wartime poetry written in exile: its patriotic theme and popular aim resulted in an anachronistic, 19th-century form. The poet's awareness of being in this blind alley led to a prolonged crisis of creativity. 1949, when he had re-examined his aesthetic positions and resumed writing, marks the beginning of his second life as a poet: the six collections of verse he published after 1950 dispose of the conventional verse structure and excessive rhetoric of his earlier poetry, introducing instead a modern, personal, colloquial and flexible style.

•Selected poems in C. Milosz (Ed.), *Postwar Polish Poetry* (Berkeley, 1983) and in A. Busza and B. Czaykowski (Eds), *Gathering Time* (Mission, BC, 1983); *Selected Poems* (New York, 1969).   StB

WIRPSZA, Witold (1918–85), Polish poet, playwright, fiction writer, essayist and translator, published several Socialist Realist collections 1949–56, but it was only in the 1960s that he emerged as an innovative writer and original literary theorist. His collection of essays *Gra znaczeń* (Interplay of meanings, 1965), a manifesto for an anti-utilitarian attitude to writing, provoked heated debate. Although Wirpsza advocated the idea of literature freed from social commitment, he did not shun political writing himself: his book-length German essay, *Pole, wer bist du?* (Who Are You, Pole?, 1971), earned him repeated attacks from Poland's official media. From 1969 until his death he lived in exile in W Berlin.

•Selected poems in S. Barańczak and C. Cavanagh (Eds), *Polish Poetry of the Last Two Decades of Communist Rule: Spoiling Cannibals' Fun* (Evanston, Ill., 1991).   StB

WITKIEWICZ, Stanisław Ignacy (pseud. Witkacy, 1885–1939), Polish writer and painter, was the only son of an art critic and artist. A prodigy, he began to write and draw as a child. 1914 he visited Australia with Bronisław Malinowski (1884–1942). On his return to Europe he served in the Russian Army and witnessed the 1917 Revolution. 1918 he returned to Poland and lived in Warsaw and the mountain resort of Zakopane. He committed suicide the day after the Red Army invaded E Poland. Lacking any systematic education, he developed varied talents. Initially a painter close in style to German Expressionism, he subsequently launched Polish avant-garde drama, published two novels and eventually devoted himself to philosophy. Regarded as an eccentric, he was little respected by his contemporaries. Associated with the Cracow Avant-garde, he introduced his own theory of 'pure art', first in painting (1919) and then in the theatre (1923). Defying the Polish tradition of national commitment, he advocated an art concerned with transcendental emotions. He rejected mimetic realism and illustrative symbolism in favour of purely formal relations. He maintained that modern drama should replace traditional action with oneiric associations, while language would constrain its communicative function in favour of formalistic relationships between sounds, images and meanings. Whether or not he strictly followed his own principles is a matter of controversy. Regarded as a precursor of the Theatre of the Absurd, he wrote black comedies about a dehumanised world peopled by dummies and threatened by automatisation that would annihilate individualism. His heroes attempt to escape into artificial, self-constructed worlds of narcotics, masochism, perverse eroticism and philosophical contemplation: *Oni* (They, 1920), *Kurka wodna* (The water hen, 1921). Some of them fight mechanisation with political despotism, which offers illusory freedom of self-expression to a chosen few: *Gyubal Wahazar* (1921), *Mątwa* (The cuttlefish, 1922). By nature resistant to mechanisation, artists find themselves estranged and lost in an everlasting search for 'pure form': *Wariat i zakonnica* (The madman and the nun, 1923), *Sonata Belzebuba* (The Beelzebub sonata, 1925). His premonitions of the decline of modern culture are reflected in *Matka* (Mother, 1924) and his most admired play, *Szewcy* (The shoemakers, 1931–4), where the twin threats of Fascist dictatorship and socialist revolution are apprehended. The disintegration of Western culture, decadence, barbaric invasion or automatic egalitarianism in the wake of social revolutions comprise the core of the two novels *Pożegnanie jesieni* (Farewell to autumn, 1927) and *Nienasycenie* (Insatiability, 1930). Their pastiche of various styles and the blend of high and low genres approximate the Postmodern experience.

●*The Madman and the Nun and other Plays* (Seattle and London, 1968); *Belzebub Sonata: Plays, Essays, Documents* (New York, 1980); *Insatiability* (Urbana, Ill., 1977). D. Gerould, *Witkacy* (Seattle, 1981); A. van Crugten, *S. I. Witkiewicz. Aux sources d'un théâtre nouveau* (Lausanne, 1971).   SE

WOLKER, Jiří (1900–24), Czech writer whose verse was a cult from his death into the 1960s, was a keen Boy Scout who became a Communist. He contracted TB in 1922; his well-heeled parents sent him to a sanatorium in 1923, but to no avail. He published two collections of verse. In the first, *Host do domu* (The blessing of guests, 1921), the pacifist author's wish to change the world is not politicised; his longing for complete social harmony is essentially based on Christianity; his compassion with the working classes is sentimental, and his evident sensualism is usually smothered by social concern. In the lyrical *Host do domu* he expresses sympathy for the whole of mankind, but in the predominantly narrative *Těžká hodina* (Pains of labour, 1922) that sympathy is concentrated on the proletariat. This mawkish verse on workers as sufferers or potential messiahs fails to be as Marxist as he would wish. He manifests fatalism rather than determinism, folksiness rather than street-wise bluntness; near-pauper young people have enough money to pay rent for a room and to go to an abortionist. Only class hatred is transmitted, with something of the crassness of a Leninist. One of his *Tři hry* (Three plays, 1922), *Nejvyšší obět'* (The greatest sacrifice), is a schematic, melodramatic, linguistically flat play about an illegal Communist cell's assassination plot. The main message of the play is that intellectual Communists are unreliable.

●A French, *The Poets of Prague. Czech Poetry Between the Wars* (London, 1969); A. French, 'Wolker and Nezval' in M. Rechcígl (Ed.), *Czechoslovakia Past and Present* (The Hague, 1968), pp. 983–92.   RBP

WOROSZYLSKI, Wiktor (b. 1927),

Polish poet, fiction writer, biographer, essayist, translator, and author of children's literature, in the late 1940s and early 1950s one of the most vocal supporters of the new political order among young Polish writers, was cured by his experiences in the 1956 Hungarian Uprising, which he covered as a war correspondent. He soon became a leading representative of political dissent in Polish literature. A participant in numerous protest actions, he was also a co-founder and editor of the first uncensored literary periodical in Poland, *Zapis* (Record, 1977–81). He was arrested and interned for a year in the wake of the imposition of martial law in 1981. His poetry and fiction often focus on the issue of the individual's potential for resisting the course of history.

•Selected poems in S. Barańczak and C. Cavanagh (Eds), *Polish Poetry of the Last Two Decades of Communist Rule: Spoiling Cannibals' Fun* (Evanston, Ill., 1991).   StB

WYKA, Kazimierz (1910–75), Polish scholar and literary critic, was a professor at Cracow University (1948–75) and director of the Institute of Literary Research in Warsaw (1953–70). His critical oeuvre covers modern literature and Romanticism. It includes postwar fiction (*Pogranicze powieści* [On the borderline of the novel, 1948]) and poetry (*Rzecz wyobraźni* [A matter of imagination, 1959]), the Młoda Polska (Young Poland) period (*Modernizm polski* [Polish Modernism, 1959]) and numerous studies of authors (e.g. FREDRO, SŁOWACKI, NORWID, ŻEROMSKI, RÓŻEWICZ) and works (e.g. MICKIEWICZ's *Pan Tadeusz*, 1963). Wyka also wrote about film and painting. His imaginative, wide-ranging approach to literary problems exerted a considerable influence on younger critics and academies. SE

WYSPIAŃSKI, Stanisław (1869–1907), Polish poet, painter, dramatist and theatre reformer, spent most of his life in his native Cracow. Wyspiański was closely associated with the city's cultural life and much affected by its history and art. During his visits to Paris (1890–4) he became acquainted with French painting and theatre. Initially he was predominantly active in the fine arts, producing portraits, landscapes and drawings in an Art Nouveau manner. He also designed typography, furniture, stained-glass and decorations for Cracow churches. Wyspiański's interest in the theatre, dominant during his later career, had its roots in Polish Romantic drama and Wagner's operas. He developed the idea of 'monumental theatre', using numerous actors and cumulating diverse stage effects. His study on *Hamlet* (1905) contains general remarks which pioneered interest in the theatre as a category distinct from literature because of its extra-verbal effects. His drama includes plays in verse based on Greek mythology, Polish history and contemporary events. Their techniques encompass those of Ancient tragedy, Romantic drama and Symbolism. He maintained the patriotic commitment of the Romantics, but his modern 'intellectual dramas' seek out truth by unmasking human role-playing. *Warszawianka* (Varsovienne, 1898), a one-acter about the November Uprising, contains his first attack on the enactment of a 'patriotic theatre' in real life. Its stage innovations encompass the roles of music and pantomime. *Klątwa* (The curse, 1899), set in a contemporary Galician village afflicted by drought, represents a blend of Greek-style tragedy and a modern approach to Fate, guilt and responsibility. Tragedy generated by self-deception found its finest expression in *Wesele* (The wedding, 1901), Wyspiański's most popular play. Based on an authentic event, it portrays in partly realistic and partly symbolic terms the dangers of artistic illusion and national mythology. The rapid succession of dialogues and events at the wedding-party is subsequently elevated by the appearance of phantom guests representing the human characters' hidden fears and desires. The combination of the commonplace with the poetic produces visions unsurpassed in Polish literature. Accusations against the deceptive power of art over the Polish mind, present in *Wesele*, are continued in *Wyzwolenie* (Deliverance, 1903), Wyspiański's most avant-garde and complex play. This play within a play is a plotless poetic drama which blurs the demarcations between stage rehearsals, national symbols and external political reality. *Akropolis* (1904) is another experimental play or dramatic poem, conceived as an imaginary animation of works of art in Wawel Cathedral. *Noc listopadowa* (November night, 1904) portrays the first hours of the November Uprising, following Polish Romantic drama in its loose, disjointed form. It brings to life the statues of the Greek gods in a Warsaw park in order to enhance the events represented and to lend them a more general dimension by drawing an analogy with the Eleusinian myth of rebirth. *Sędziowie* (The judges, 1907) elevates a common crime, actually committed in Galicia, into a universal tragedy where only the death of an innocent secures genuine justice. Wyspiański's theatre anticipated 20th-century drama in Poland. His assessment of Polish society has influenced modern writers (ANDRZEJEWSKI, MROŻEK) and film makers (Wajda).

•*The Wedding* (Ann Arbor, 1900).

T. Terlecki, *Stanisław Wyspiański* (Boston, 1983); C. Backvis, *Le Dramaturge S. Wyspiański* (Paris, 1952).

SE

X

XENOPOULOS, Grigorios (1867–1951), Greek prose writer and dramatist, was born in Constantinople, brought up on Zakynthos, moved to Athens at 16, enrolled in the School of Physics and Mathematics at Athens but soon devoted himself entirely to literature. He had a busy career as a journalist on various Athenian periodicals and newspapers 1890–1951, and founded the main Greek literary periodical Νέα Εστία (New hearth and home), editing it 1927–33. As a critic he was influential: he was responsible, for example, for first drawing attention in Athens to the work of CAVAFY. 1931 he was elected to the Academy of Athens. The end of his life was clouded by the destruction of his library and personal papers in the December Uprising of 1944. His writing includes an enormous body of stories, novels and plays. He started as an ethographical novelist, and many of his early works are set in his native Zakynthos, e.g. Ο κόκκινος βράχος (The red rock, 1905). But his importance lies in the fact that he went beyond the limits of previous ethography, and that he attracted a wider reading public. His major novels are the social trilogy Πλούσιοι και φτωχοί (Rich and poor, 1919), Τίμιοι και άτιμοι (Honourable and dishonourable, 1921) and Τυχεροί και άτυχοι (Fortunate and unfortunate, 1924). As a novelist he acknowledges the influence of Balzac, Daudet, Zola and Dickens. His plays dominated Greek theatre for twenty years. They represented the introduction of the principles of the well-made play, coupled with the influence of Ibsen, to the Greek stage. His work can be divided into three groups: psychological analytical, ideological and philosophical. Representative works are Το μυστικό της κομτέσσας Βαλεραίνας (The secret of Countess Valeraina, 1904), Στέλλα Βιολάντη (Stella Violanti, 1909) and Το ανθρώπινο (The human factor, 1922). CFR

XOXA, Jakov (1923–79), Albanian novelist, was born in Fier and read French at Sofia. 1952 he returned to Albania and worked as journalist, university teacher and professional writer. Xoxa is the author of two widely read novels situated in his Myzeqe area. The first, *Lumi i vdekur* (The dead river, 1965), portrays the exploitation of the peasantry in this backward, swampy region of prewar Albania. His second novel, *Juga e bardhë* (The white south, 1971), deals with the collectivisation of agriculture in the same region after the war. His later works include the novel *Lulja e kripës* (The salt flower, 1981), *Novela I* (Short stories I, 1949) and *Novela II* (Short stories II, 1958). ShM

Y

YANEVSKI, Slavko (b. 1920), Macedonian poet and prose writer, studied at a technical college; then he was on the editorial board of literary journals and worked in publishing houses. He is the author of the first Macedonian novel, *Selo zad sedumte yaseni* (The village beyond the seven ashes, 1953), which concerns the Socialist 'reconstruction' of a Macedonian village. His subsequent novels (*Dve Marii* [The two Marys, 1956], *Mesechar* [The sleepwalker, 1958], *I bol i bes* [Pain and rage, 1969]), although set in various environments and telling different stories (e.g. *Dve Marii* is a love story, *Mesechar* is the story of an ex-priest who rejects the community's conventions, *I bol i bes* is a guerrilla-war story), are all concerned with Yanevski's main theme: the fates of individuals who cut themselves off from the community. The individual, if living in his own world, is regarded by him as a man with no 'roots'; the individual dreamer's rebellion against the community's conventions is narcissistic and sterile; the removal of old conventions could be brought about only by those who possess true values, i.e. union with the community. Yanevski's interest in human community (as a cultural or national entity) forms the basis of his most accomplished work, a series of six novels where he employs his own mythical interpretation of Macedonian history (*Tvrdoglavi* [The stubborn ones, 1965], followed in 1984 by the trilogy, *Mirakuli na grozomorata* [The miracles of horror], *Chakaiki chumata* [Waiting for the plague] and *Kucheshko razpyatie* [The dog's crucifix], then, *Devet kerubinovi vekovi* [Nine cherubim centuries, 1988] and *Rulet so sedum broevi* [Seven-figure roulette, 1989]). The first book in this mythopoeic panorama of Macedonian life, *Tvrdoglavi*, set in 1835, describes the trip of a group of villagers from one village, Kukulino, to another, Lesnovo. Their journey is a metaphor; their path leads through a series of horrors and epitomises Macedonian history. What they meet is a mythically metamorphosed Macedonian 'universe': a mixture of historical events (e.g. Turkish rule, war, violence), historical figures (e.g. St KLIMENT of OHRID, historical anti-Turkish heroes), regional legends and folk rituals, a picture that as a whole represents despair. The journey becomes a walk through an inferno of blood, unheard-of diseases, apocalyptic monsters, visions of the worst of the violence in the violent history of Macedonia, a series of moral and physical horrors; they are confronted with the whole mythic world of the Macedonian mind; except for the villagers, the 'stubborn ones', everyone appears to have abandoned that path, 'man and serpent', even death, so that the suffering becomes eternal. 'The stubborn ones' emblemise 'national character', which is the national curse. Walking along the path becomes a search for and a campaign against Fate, which Yanevski considers the peculiar tragedy of his people. The oral tradition suffuses the language, ideas, sensitivity, ethics, cosmogony of the work. There are no individual characters, only the collective consciousness of the people. The novel's perception of national fate as 'graves, graves and graves again', of a nation of 'martyrs and widows' whose stars are 'frozen drops of their sorrow', its cult of heroes, its funereal lamentation over births, its rejoicing in death as salvation from torment, its intense imagination, are also typical for the subsequent volumes of the series. Moreover, they make up a paradigm of Balkan literary self-perception; Yanevski may be said to have presented what Stephen Runciman called 'the tragic and mysterious Balkan microcosm'. Yanevski is also an accomplished poet whose verse is likewise concerned with Balkan and Macedonian history and mentality (e.g. *Evangeliye po Itar Peyo* [Gospel of Clever Peyo, 1966] and *Kainavelia* [Cains and Abels, 1968]).

●'Pain and Rage by Slavko Yanevski' in M. Yovanovski (Ed.), *The Macedonian Novel* (Skopje, n.d.).   SIK

YAVOROV, Peyo (i.e. P. Kracholov, 1878–1914), Bulgarian poet and playwright, rumoured to have a bedouin Christian Arab for a grandfather, began work at 16 as a telegraph operator. He moved from town to town until 1900, felt buried alive in the provinces and sought relief in 'Bacchus and Venus' and in writing verse. He published some of it in *Misăl* where SLAVEIKOV invented his pseudonym and, 1899, the poem 'Kaliopa' made his fame; literary friends helped him to move to Sofia, where he soon gave up his 'killing' job at the telegraph office and became editor of the Macedonian insurgents' newspaper, then, 1902, joined a Macedonian guerrilla group. 1903, when the leader of the Macedonian organisation was killed and the Ilinden Uprising suppressed, Yavorov ceased his guerrilla activity and had a nervous breakdown. Later he wrote two memoirs, *Hajdushki kopneniya* (Bandit yearnings, 1909), and *Gotse Delchev* (1904), a portrait of the killed Macedonian leader. 1904 he was employed at the National Library in Sofia; 1906–7 he was sent to France; 1908 he became artistic director of the National Theatre where he was the first to create pronunciation norms for actors. 1910 he attended in France the death-bed of his beloved Mina (TODOROV's sister), whom he could not marry and rarely had the chance to meet since her family thought him a low-class womaniser who had no future. Mina's innocent beauty inspired the most subtle tones of Yavorov's verse while Lora (niece of KARAVELOV, daughter of a former prime minister), whom he married in 1912, embodied the fatal woman in his life. Her possessive love for him and her jealousy led her to shoot herself in front of him (1913); minutes later Yavorov attempted suicide but only blinded himself. His last year was a nightmare; he was blind, had no money, was accused of murdering Lora and faced trial; his friends, with a few exceptions, were abandoning him; at the end he took poison and shot himself to ensure his death.

Yavorov was a stranger to any environment; a poet among bandits, a bandit among poets, someone for ever separated from the rest, and from 'life', by an 'icy wall'. His early verse, published in *Stihotvoreniya* (Poems, 1901), contains social motifs, mainly based on harsh village life, echoes Revivalist emotions and, apart from vivid poems like 'Kaliopa', is coloured by the same dramatic intensity of perception which later appears, internalised, in his individualist verse. His collections, *Bezsănitsi* (Insomnias, 1907) and *Podir senkite na oblatsite* (Following the clouds' shadows, 1910), introduced into Bulgarian literature the themes of metaphysical anxiety, the horror, but also the ecstasy, of aloneness and death, the perception of life as timeless torment where the divided self is endlessly falling into an abyss of incarnations. Yavorov's images of the beloved and love – angelical, spiritual, and demonic, carnal ('burning flesh and weightless ghost') – reflect the ambivalent qualities of the *anima* and are closely linked to other feminine images: 'song', 'death', 'soul', 'night'. E.g. the 'mother' is perceived with love but also called 'the merciless one who gave me life'. There is some proto-Symbolist verse in *Bezsănitsi*; it is blended with the Romantic, the Decadent and with his intense personal dramaticism. In his plays (e.g. *V polite na Vitosha* [In the foothills of the V., 1911]), Yavorov externalises the personae of his internal drama with the help of autobiographical material (the story of his and Mina's love). His inventive poetic language created a new era for Bulgarian verse.

●G. Stadtmüller, 'Pejo Jaworow' in *Stimmen aus dem Südosten* (1940/1), pp. 86–90, 104–8; E. Daminai, *Un poeta delle tenebre. P. K. Javorov* (Rome, 1940); P. Poggioli, 'Il poeta bulgaro Pejo K. Javorov', *Rivista di letterature slave*, III, fasc. 4–5–6 (1928), pp. 317–37. SIK

YAZOVA, Yana (i.e. Lyuba Gancheva, 1912–74), Bulgarian poet and novelist, began writing when still at school; she read Slavonic studies at Sofia. 1931 she published her first collection of verse. An outstandingly beautiful woman, she led the life of a cosmopolitan intellectual spending most of her time travelling in the Orient and Europe. She was banned from publishing after the Communist take-over. 1944 also put an end to her public life and her travelling. She supported herself by gradually selling off the artefacts she had brought back from her travels. She was murdered in her flat and almost all her papers and library disappeared; what remained was auctioned. The authorities maintained silence about the circumstances of her death. Later some of Yazova's manuscripts appeared in the Central State Archives. Not until 1987 was the first part of Yazova's historical trilogy *Balkani* (Balkans) published. Based on her own scholarly research, the trilogy, *Levski* (1987), *Benkovski* (1988) and *Shipka* (1989), is her most accomplished work. It concerns the Bulgarians' struggle against the Turks during the second half of the 19th century and ends with the 1877–8 Russo-Turkish War. The trilogy's main value lies in its examination of the spiritual source of all freedom. Yazova's conception of self-sacrifice and martyrdom augments the perception of the National Revival established by the writings of authors like VAZOV, BOTEV, SLAVEIKOV. Her aphoristic diary, containing her contemplations of socialist reality, written 1963–9, *Zlatni iskri na skrăbta*

(Golden sparks of sorrow), has yet to be published.   SIK

YESSAYAN, Zabel (1878–1943), Armenian prose writer, born in Scutari, a suburb of Constantinople, at the age of 17 published a short piece in a literary magazine. While studying literature at the Sorbonne, she wrote articles and stories regularly in French literary magazines like *Mercure de France*, *L'Humanité nouvelle*, and *La grande France* – and the Armenian periodicals *Anahit*, *Masis* and *Arevelyan Mamoul*. 1908 she returned to Constantinople after the declaration of the new constitution by the Young Turks. During the next six years she was the most active Armenian literary and public figure in Constantinople. Soon after the massacre of Cilicia (1909) she was sent there to distribute food and clothing to the needy and to help the sick. Based on what she had seen and heard, Yessayan wrote *Averaknerun mej* (Among the ruins, 1911). The book is not just impressionistic reportage; it is a work of immense passion. After the publication of this book, she was propelled into an even more fulgent limelight. The Young Turks ranked her with ZOHRAB, SIAMANT'O and VAROUJAN by placing her name, the only female writer, on their list of Armenian intellectuals to be liquidated. In April 1915 she slipped across the border into Bulgaria, then, 1918, she went to Cairo, then to Paris as a member of the Armenian delegation at the Peace Conference. 1927 she visited Soviet Armenia and published her impressions in *Promet'eos azatagrvats* (Prometheus unchained, 1928), which was no more than a propaganda piece, and it appealed to the authorities in Yerevan. Unheeding of numerous warnings by her friends

and admirers, 1933 she settled in Soviet Armenia and became a Soviet citizen. She lectured at the university and published numerous articles on literature apart from her creative works. In *Silihtarhi Partezner* (The gardens of Silihader, 1936), an account of her childhood and adolescence, she recalls the beauty of her native district of Scutari. For this Yessayan was accused of fostering nostalgia; analogous criticisms were levelled against BAKOUNTS, T'OT'OVENTS and Mkrtitch Armen (1907–72). In *Krake Shapik* (Shirt of fire, 1936), she dwells on the gloomy aspect of life in her birthplace. In the same year she completed a longer novel called *Barpa Khatchik* (Uncle K., 1966), which was as close to a piece of Proletarian prose as any written by a confirmed Communist and yet aesthetically effective, indicating that she had made the 'new ideas' part of her being. Only two chapters were published before she was completely silenced. 1937 Yessayan was banished from Yerevan with BAKOUNTS, T'OT'OVENTS, Armen, MAHARI and some 200 other intellectuals. She was charged with being a 'counter-revolutionary-nationalistic criminal who wished to blanket our beloved fatherland with black clouds'. She died in exile. Yessayan has left an impressive legacy. *Spasman srahin mej* (The waiting room, 1903) is a short novel written soon after the Dreyfus affair, composed in French and then translated into Armenian. It was serialised in the Armenian literary journal *Tsaghik* 1903. Like Zola, Yessayan trusts in the artistic impact of the sordid to create an aversion towards the ugly in the readers and thus to make them appreciate beauty all the more. Yessayan's satirical novel

Keghts Hantaŕner (Phony geniuses, 1910) ridicules the author Diran Cherakian (Indra, 1875–1921). About herself as a young girl on the verge of becoming a writer, she spoke of her insatiable appetite for living and her need to express the desires and tensions within her. In the Fin de siècle, divorce was not easily obtained in Constantinople, and she must have thought hard before securing her freedom from the marital yoke. As a result of her broodings we have two short novels concerning unhappily married women. In *Anjkut'yan zhamer* (Hours of agony, 1911) Arousiak despises her weakling husband and wishes him dead – as, at the time, nothing else but his death could set her free. She finally induces him to commit suicide. Adrine, the protagonist of *Verjin Bazhakê* (The last cup, periodical form 1917, book 1924), also hates her husband Mikayel, who was rigid in matters of outward respectability, while she abhors conventional restrictions and favours the extravagant. Adrine has been carrying on an affair with a married man and finally is caught. She wants her husband to be 'moved by blind passion' and to beat her so that she might regain her senses and become obedient. 'But once more he did not find a way to my heart', laments Adrine. Then 'death provided a wonderful outlet', she says after he dies. VN

YOVKOV, Yordan (1880–1937), Bulgarian prose writer, read law at Sofia but left when he ran out of money and worked as a teacher in Dobrudzha for 11 years, then was appointed a press attaché at the embassy in Bucharest (1920–5), and then dragoman on the Roumanian-Bulgarian frontier; 1927 he became a mere translator at the Foreign Ministry.

The most accomplished of Yovkov's literary works are his short-story collections, published 1917–36. He also wrote plays, some of them based on his own stories. The passion of his life was Dobrudzha, with its endless paths, vast fields and deep sky and its silent, contemplative inhabitants. Yovkov's approach to depicting life owes much to his idealised vision of this region; in his stories reality is elevated and aestheticised. They usually have a rural setting; they concern man close to an animated Nature. In Nature originate the two mystical forces which embody natural moral law and dominate Yovkov's world: beauty and love. In the interwar period when many Bulgarian writers maintained profound philosophical scepticism and regarded man as the worst kind of beast, especially after the brutalities of WWI, Yovkov provided a counterbalance through his apotheosis of the vital spirituality of man; he is, however, influenced by the prevalent contemporary mistrust of social institutions. He turned to Nature for a model of morality and in his stories the only sin is a sin against Nature. Love and beauty are perceived as the very essence of life; they comprise a supernal morality because they preserve life; Yovkov's characters who follow the call of beauty and love come into conflict with the social order and are judged to be sinners and criminals and are punished. In the short story 'Albena' (1915), however, society's punishment is felt to be unjust because the cause of the crime is Albena's beauty and her love for a man who is her natural match, unlike her ugly husband. In many of the stories, those who sin against Nature, beauty and love receive their punishment not from society but from Nature; in 'Indzhe' (1918), a bandit-terrorist leader is a man of extreme cruelty, but something of his potential goodness is revealed when he falls in love with the beautiful Pauna; they marry and she rides with him; one day, however, he strikes their new-born son with a scimitar; years later Indzhe is converted from being a scourge of the people to their protector against the Turks; one day, he meets a hunchback whom he chases for fun, but who shoots him; he learns that the hunchback is the son whom he had struck with a scimitar. For Yovkov work on the soil purifies man; outsiders and those who fail to remain close to the soil and Nature often embody hostile, destructive forces and introduce evil into the natural, village world; e.g. in *Vecheri v Antimovskiya han* (Evenings in the Antimovo inn, 1928), the inn symbolises alienation from the soil and work and at the end is burned to ashes. Yovkov's moralising view of the soil and work is apparent in works like *Zhetvaryat* (The harvester, 1920), a utopia of purification and moral resurrection through work. Although the tendency to moralisation vanishes in his later work (*Posledna radost* [Last joy, 1926] or *Ako mozheha da govoryat* [If they could speak, 1936]), and he concentrates more on internal beauty, the cycle 'sin-resurrection-redemption' is typical for the majority of his stories. Even in his near-pacifist depictions of war he writes of the beauty of collective effort and the collective energy with which soldiers go to fight like peasants going to till the fields (e.g. 'Beliyat eskadron' [The white squadron, 1916], *Zemlyatsi* [Countrymen, 1915]).

●*Short Stories* (Sofia, 1965); *Stara Planina Legends. The Inn at Antimovo* (London, 1990).
C. Moser, 'The Visionary Realism of Jordan Jovkov', *Slavic and East European Journal*, 1, XI (1967), pp. 44–58.   SIK

Z

ZAGAJEWSKI, Adam (b. 1945), Polish poet, fiction writer and essayist, born in Lwów, graduated from Cracow University (where he read philosophy and psychology) and taught philosophy for a while before deciding to devote himself entirely to writing. With the publication of his collection *Komunikat* (Announcement) in 1972, he emerged as a leading representative of the 'Generation of 68'. He has since then published six more books of poems, three novels, and five collections of essays including the widely debated *Świat nie przedstawiony* (The world unrepresented, 1974, with Julian Kornhauser [b. 1946]) and *Solidarność i samotność* (Solidarity and solitude, 1985). Since 1982 he has lived in France.

●*Tremor: Selected Poems* (New York, 1985); *Solidarity, Solitude* (New York, 1990).

S. Birkerts, *The Electric Life* (New York, 1989). StB

ZAJC, Dane (b. 1929), Slovene poet and playwright, had a grammar-school education in Ljubljana and now works as a librarian. In his poetry, e.g. *Požgana trava* (Burnt grass, 1958), *Jezik iz zemje* (The tongue of earth, 1961), *Ubijavci kač* (Snake-killers, 1969), *Rožengrunter* (1975) and *Zarotitve* (Conspiracies, 1985), there is a complete shift from revolutionary romanticism and the programmatic verse which reflected the brief Soviet influence in Slovene literature. His plays include *Otroka reke* (The children of the river, 1963) and *Potohodec* (The pathwalker, 1969).

●Translations in: *Le Livre slovène* (1982), 1/2; *IYL*; *MPT*. HL

ZAPOLSKA, Gabriela (i.e. G. Korwin-Piotrowska, 1857–1921), Polish playwright and novelist, born into a prosperous noble family, chose an acting career, performing without much success in Poland and in Paris. She later ran her own drama school in Cracow and a touring company in Lwów (Lemberg). Zapolska achieved great popularity as the author of well-made Naturalist plays in which she denounced middle-class hypocrisy, stressed human selfishness and defied existing taboos on sexual matters. Marital infidelity is portrayed in *Żabusia* (My darling, 1897) and *Ich czworo* (The four of them, 1907). *Moralność pani Dulskiej* (Mrs Dulska's morality, 1906), Zapolska's most respected play, illustrates the duplicity of moral standards reduced to the observance of appearances. *Panna Maliczewska* (Miss M., 1910) describes a young actress whose career relies on the patronage of promiscuous males. In her novels Zapolska portrayed the drab lives of civil servants and artists (*Sezonowa miłość* [Seasonal Romance, 1905]), house maids (*Kaśka Kariatyda* [Kaśka the caryatid, 1888]) and prostitutes (*O czym się nie mówi* [What is not spoken of, 1909]).   SE

ZARYAN, Kostan (1885–1969), Armenian writer, son of a prosperous general in the Russian Army in Shemakh, former capital of Azerbaidjan, attended the Russian grammar school in Baku. 1895 he was sent to the college of St Germain in Asnières, near Paris, where he promptly fell in love with 'a blue-eyed slender beauty', a Russian dancer at the Folies Bergères. He continued his studies in Belgium and took a doctorate in literature and philosophy from the University of Brussels. During this period, in addition to meeting Lenin in Geneva, Zaryan also met and befriended such as Apollinaire, Picasso, Plekhanov, Ungaretti, Céline, Eluard and Verhaeren. Heeding the advice of the last, Zaryan studied classical and Modern Armenian with the Mekhitarists on San Lazaro in Venice (1910–13), where he also published the Italian verse originally written in French, *Three Songs* (1916), one of which, 'La Primavera' (Armenian text, 1931), was set to music by Ottorino Respighi and first performed in 1923. Next we find him in Constantinople, where, 1914, he co-founded the literary journal *Mehian*. The so-called 'Mehian Writers', like their contemporaries in W Europe, defied the establishment by fighting against ossified artistic traditions. (Most of the 'Mehian Writers' were murdered by the Turks in the Genocide of 1915.) Zaryan was one of the few to survive by escaping to Bulgaria, and then to Italy, where he established himself in Rome. 1920 he returned to Constantinople, where, together with T'EK'EYAN, Hakob Oshakan (1883–1948), and a number

of other survivors of the Genocide, he founded another literary journal, *Barjravank'* (Monastery on a hill). At this time he also published a second book of poems, *Ōreri psakê* (The crown of days, 1922). Following the establishment of Soviet rule in Armenia, Zaryan returned and for the next three years taught comparative literature at Yerevan. Disappointed with the régime, in 1925 he again went abroad and led a nomadic existence between Paris, Rome, Florence and Corfu. While in New York, he taught Armenian culture at Columbia (1944–6), and founded the English-language *Armenian Quarterly* (1946). 1952–4 he taught history of art at the American University of Beirut. 1961 he returned to Armenia, where he worked at the TCHARENTS Museum of Literature and Art. An edited edition of his novel *Navé leṙan Vray* (The ship on the mountain), originally published in Boston in 1943, appeared in Yerevan in 1963. He died in Yerevan. The genre in which Zaryan excelled was the diary-form with long autobiographical divagations, reminiscences and impressions, e.g. *Antsordê ev ir Chamban* (The traveller and his road, 1926–8), *Arevmutk'* (West, 1928–9), *K'aghak'ner* (Cities, 1930), *Bankoopê ew mamut'i oskornerê* (Bancoop and the bones of the mammoth, 1931–4), and *Erkirner ev astuadsner* (The island and a man, 1955), all of which were published in the émigré monthly, *Hayrenik'*, Boston. In Soviet Armenian literature Zaryan's fame rests on the narrative poem *Tatragomi harsê* (The bride of Tetrachoma, Yerevan, 1965, originally publ. in Boston, 1930) and the novel *Navé leṙan Vray*. His Armenian prose, which is an amalgam of the elegant W Armenian and the rough E

Armenian vernaculars, creates unexplored harmonies and rhythms. It is masculine, powerful prose, which, however, never loses a certain feminine poetic charm.

•*The Traveller and His Road* (New York, 1981); *Bancoop and the Bones of the Mammoth* (selection) (New York, 1982).   VN

ZEJLER, Handrij (SEILER, Andreas, 1804–72), poet, was the leading Sorbian writer of the Romantic period and the father of modern Sorbian literature. Though of humble origin (his father was a well-sinker), he managed to attend the Bautzen grammar school and to read theology at Leipzig. His native village of Słona Boršć (Salzenforst), about four miles NE of Bautzen, had a partly R. Catholic, but mainly Lutheran population, and its spirit of religious tolerance moulded his character for life. 1835 he moved out of Saxony to the remote Prussian village of Łaz (Lohsa) and remained there as Lutheran pastor for the rest of his life. He was the founder of the Upper Sorbian newspaper *Tydźenska Nowina* (Weekly news), which first appeared in 1842, and chairman of the committee that founded the learned society Maćica Serbska in 1845. Zejler stands at the beginning of the Sorbian National Awakening. While still at school he began to collect folk-songs and to write his own poetry, much of which is in the folk-song style. He celebrates friendship, love, Nature, and the daily occupations of Sorbian peasants. Collaboration with the Sorbian composer Korla Awgust Kocor (1822–1904) resulted in a cycle of poems, set to music, entitled *Serbski kwas* (A Sorbian wedding), which was first performed in 1847. Zejler's masterpiece is the cycle *Počasy* (The seasons),

inspired by James Thomson's work of the same name. Only two of the projected five parts were completed and these were first published in 1847 and 1851. All known fragments of the other three parts appeared in the collected works in 1883. The poems embody the peasant's unsentimental view of Nature and found great favour with the common people. Zejler always aimed to be accessible to the simplest reader and it was in simplicity that he achieved his greatest successes. A didactic strain is apparent in some two hundred verse fables, mainly written 1847–50. Sixty of them were published in *Serbske basnje* (Sorbian fables, 1855). As in Sorbian folk-tales, animals appear in semi-human guise and are used to expose human failings. Zejler's collected works were published by Ernst Muka (1854–1932) in four volumes, 1883–91.

•G. Stone, *The Smallest Slavonic Nation. The Sorbs of Lusatia* (London, 1972), pp. 51–60.   GCS

ŻELEŃSKI, Tadeusz (pseud. Boy, 1874–1941), Polish literary critic and translator, educated as a physician, soon devoted himself solely to literature. Before WWI he contributed songs and witty, often ribald, poems to the 'Green Balloon', a literary cabaret in Cracow. His subsequent career as a translator of French writers, from the *Chanson de Roland* to Proust, produced over a hundred volumes of classic texts, widely appreciated for their rich and ingenious Polish idioms, well adjusted to various literary periods and individual styles. As an author of theatrical reviews and literary essays Boy demonstrated much common sense, respect for traditional realism, and a provocative attitude towards national 'sacred cows'. Żeleński's narrative talents are illustrated by his recollections of the Cracow of his youth. SE

ŻEROMSKI, Stefan (1864–1925), Polish novelist, born near Kielce into an impoverished noble family, experienced forced russification as a schoolboy. Afterwards he worked first as a private tutor, then as a librarian in Rapperswil (Switzerland) and Warsaw. He spent most of his life in Warsaw and in the holiday resorts of Zakopane and Nałęczów. He also travelled and lived abroad, particularly in Paris and Italy. Regarded by his contemporaries as the national conscience and Poland's last 'bard', Żeromski exerted a powerful influence on the intelligentsia, shaping its views on moral, social and political issues. An heir to Romanticism, Positivism and Naturalism, he represents diverse ideas and techniques: Promethean individualism coexists with the cult of science and technology, a moral sense of duty with the biological understanding of human nature. Correspondingly, narrative impassivity is interwoven with effusive lyricism and flamboyant style, initially admired but later denounced. A writer of profound commitment, Żeromski avoided simple didacticism by dialogically confronting different ideas. Żeromski's earliest short stories and novelle (1895–8) attracted some attention, but his popularity gained momentum with the publication of *Ludzie bezdomni* (Homeless people, 1900). The hero, torn between an ascetic sense of duty and a natural inclination to sensuality, introduces the characteristic pattern of Żeromski's approach to moral dilemmas. His historical novel *Popioły* (Ashes, 1904) combines dramatic love scenes with a polyphonic assessment of the Napoleonic Wars and their impact on Poland.

Żeromski's notorious novel *Dzieje grzechu* (The story of sin, 1908) and his political drama *Róża* (The rose, 1909) stirred up public opinion and provoked ruthless attacks. At this time the author had lost his faith in political parties and sought remedy in utopian solutions. His own social programme was based on moral principles, whereas he regarded revolutions as brutal and destructive. Another historical novel, *Wierna rzeka* (The faithful river, 1913), describes the loneliness of the insurgents of 1863 in the simple form of an old tale. Żeromski's initial optimism following Polish independence was short-lived as the new free Poland fell short of his expectations. His disillusion is reflected in *Przedwiośnie* (Before the spring, 1924), his most controversial and most denounced novel, where the Romantic myth of social justice confronts sombre reality. Żeromski also published prose poetry and plays; the finest is *Uciekła mi przepióreczka...* (A quail escaped me, 1924).

•*Ashes* (New York, 1928); *The Faithful River* (London, 1943).

I. Kwiatkowska-Siemieńska, *S. Żeromski. La nature dans son expérience et sa pensée* (Paris, 1964).   SE

ZEROV, Mykola (1890–1937), Ukrainian poet, translator and literary critic, as the unofficial leader of the Neoclassicist group of poets, published an anthology of translations of Latin poetry (1920) and a collection of poems *Kamena* (Camena, 1924). Most of his best poetry was published posthumously in W Europe: *Sonnetarium* (1948), *Catalepton* (1952), *Corollarium* (1958). 'The hard form of Classicism', writes George Shevelov 1944, 'was a refuge from the poet's feeling of disillusionment, loneliness, the world's illusoriness, man's meanness and loss of faith . . . and brutal and dirty reality of his day.' Nevertheless, Zerov remained a master of the Classical form and of the sonnet. A professor of literature at Kiev University, Zerov also published *Nove ukrainske pysmenstvo* (New Ukrainian literature, 1924) and a collection of scholarly essays, *Do dzherel* (The sources, 1926), the title of which became a rallying cry for many Ukrainian intellectuals. Arrested in 1934, he was exiled to the Solovky Islands, where he was executed. Before his death he completed a translation of Virgil's *Aeneid*.

●Some of Zerov's poems appeared in English translation in G. Andrusyhen and W. Kirkconnell (Eds), *The Ukrainian Poets 1189–1962* (Toronto, 1963).
'Modern Ukrainian Literature', *Ukrainian Review*, Winter 1987. GSNL

ZEYER, Julius (1841–1901), Czech writer from a German-speaking family, spent almost as much of his life outside Bohemia as in the country for which he bore a passionate love. He failed his matriculation and so could not go to university, but became one of the best-educated men of the times. He travelled in the Russian Empire, the Near East, N Africa, Italy, Spain, Germany and, most of all, France. He was a dilettante in the finest sense of the word and opened as many new vistas for Czech literature as his friend, then enemy, VRCHLICKÝ. His works are set all over Eurasia and N Africa and at all periods from biblical times to the present. His main interest was beauty and combined with that, mysticism, and esoteric thinking from French materialist spiritism, to medieval Catholicism, Buddhism and Ancient Egyptian religion. Apart from his earliest, rather conventional, short

stories and his intimate lyric verse, everything he wrote manifested his mystical interests, and most of his works were what he called 'renovated pictures', imaginative reworkings of Ancient, medieval and Oriental literature. In these highly original works he made creative poetic use of his erudition as well as his gifts as a story-teller. He was often condemned for 'plagiarism' or 'Jewish sensualism' or 'unmanliness'. And yet few 19th-century Czech writers had such a lasting impact on major later writers and no Czech writer except MÁCHA elicited as many works of literary criticism, up to the socialist period, during which he was not exactly ignored by critics, but became a cult figure in the intellectual underground. He made his most immediate impact with his few semi-autobiographical works, *Jan Maria Plojhar* (1891), *Dům 'U tonoucí hvězdy'* (The house the sign of the sinking star, 1897) and *Troje paměti Víta Choráze* (Three memoirs of Vít Choráz, 1905). His mentality and his language were completely uncluttered by the Czech peasant tradition, and even his melancholy was altruistic.

●R. B. Pynsent, *Julius Zeyer. The Path to Decadence* (The Hague, 1973). RBP

ZIEDONIS, Imants (b. 1933), Latvian writer, son of a fisherman, has been a village teacher, librarian and later attended the Gorki Institute in Moscow. He attempts to reawaken in concise stanzas and bold and even far-fetched metaphors, the basic feelings of his people, to interpret their desires and hopes, and to stir their conscience, especially those of his younger compatriots. Ziedonis is an impulsive, impatient and even angry poet, as is demonstrated by the titles of his collections: *Sirds dinamīts* (The heart's dynamite, 1963, *Es ieeju sevī* (Delve into myself, 1968), *Caurvējš* (Draft, 1975). Some of his poems narrate a subject in a traditional way, attacking the object of his criticism head on, using simple images. Others project a montage of conflicting images and allusions without any narrative line. Although not always free of Party propagandistic appeals in his verse, he asserts the right to personal freedom and attempts to resurrect 'truth' and to challenge indirectly the role of the authorities. Perhaps clearer than elsewhere, that is reflected in his *Kurzemīte I–II* (Dear Kurland, 1970–4), a penetrating first-person account of a summer journey through the literary, cultural, historical and geographic landscape of Kurland. Besides giving many verbal snapshots of the countryside and people encountered, in a witty, erudite and often amusing way he discusses topics ranging from his native language to the Latvian cultural heritage, from ecology to old rural churches and other historical monuments. Though well within the prevailing ideological limits, at times this work reads like a journalist's chronicle of social horrors, especially those pages where Ziedonis expresses his anger at the abuse of the soil, the inhumanity and incompetence of the bureaucracy, the spiritual callousness, corruption and stupidity of various managers and chairmen, and the indifference of *kolkhoz* peasants. His *Epifānijas I–III* (Epiphanies, 1971–8) are poems in rhythmic prose which expose to us the personality of an original moralist in contemporary literature. Ziedonis knows how to talk to children. Upon opening his books children enter a wonderful world under the guidance of a clever, loving magician. Such works are

Lāču pasaka (The bear tale, 1976) and *Krāsainas pasakas* (The colourful fairy tales, 1973). Believing in the brightness of children, Ziedonis almost attains the level of his epiphany genre, teaching his young readers to avoid indifference and passivity. Ziedonis has also written film scripts, plays and critical essays.   EB

ZINGER, Yisroel-Yeshue/ Israel Joshua Singer (1893–1944), Yiddish novelist and playwright born in Biłgoraj in the Lublin guberniya, the brother of Yitskhok BASHEVIS and of Ester Kraytman (1891–1954), made his literary début in Warsaw during WWI, following which he moved to Kiev and contributed to the Soviet journals. He was encouraged by BERGLSON, but the doctrinaire Proletarian writer Moyshe Litvakov (1875–1938) rejected Zinger's *Perl* (Pearls) with the result that he returned to Warsaw and published the story in the Expressionist journal *Ringen* (Links). After publishing a Symbolist drama, *Erd-vey* (Earth-pains, Warsaw, 1922), dealing with the War, the Revolution and the ensuing pogroms, he joined forces with Perets MARKISH to edit the first volume of the provocatively avantgarde journal *Khalyastre* (The gang, Warsaw, 1922). Influenced both by the Futurism of Mayakovsky and the Expressionism of Werfel and Else Lasker-Schüler, they sought to participate in the Modernist movement and to respond to the anguish and chaos of the postwar world with universal images of apocalyptic pessimism. *Perl*, meanwhile, came to the attention of Abraham Cahan, editor of the New York daily *Forverts* (Forward), who printed it in his paper and made Zinger his Warsaw correspondent. There followed a period of material prosperity and prolific journalism during which he travelled for the paper, continued to write for the theatre, wrote the novel *Shtol un ayzn* (Steel and iron, Vilnius, 1927) and together with Meylekh Ravitsh (1893–1976) and Alter Katsizne (1885–1941) edited the prestigious Warsaw weekly, *Literarishe bleter* (Literary pages). After coming under attack in a number of journals, Zinger swore to forsake literature, but again Cahan came to his rescue. In New York his novel *Yoshe kalb*, which portrays aspects of life at the Ḥasidic courts of Galicia in the second half of the 19th century, was serialised in *Forverts* and was staged in a dramatised version by Moris Shvarts's New York Art Theatre. In 1933, after the death of his eldest son, Yankev, Zinger moved to New York and there he wrote the novels on which his fame largely hangs, *Di brider ashkenazi* (The brothers Ashkenazi, Warsaw, 1936), a family saga set against the background of Jewish participation in the development of the Łódź textile industry, *Khaver nakhmen* (East of Eden, New York, 1938) and *Di mishpokhe karnovski* (The Karnovski family), a novel dealing with the recrudescence of racism in Nazi Germany. Zinger died of a heart attack while still at the height of his powers as a major social novelist. It is instructive to compare his posthumously published memoirs, *Fun a velt vos iz nishto mer* (Of a world that is no more, New York, 1946), with the autobiographical writings of both his sister, Ester, and his brother, BASHEVIS, which portray essentially the same environment from differing perspectives.

• *Yoshe Kalb* (New York, 1988²); *Of a World that Is No More* (New York, 1970; *The Brothers Ashkenazi* (New York, 1980; London, 1983); *TYS*, pp. 350–85.

C. Sinclair, *The Brothers Singer* (London, New York, 1983); S. A. Slotnick, *German Quarterly*, 54 (1981), pp. 33–43.　　　　HD

ZĪVERTS, Mārtiņš (b. 1903), Latvian playwright, author of more than forty plays, worked first as a journalist, then as dramatic adviser in a theatre. He fled to Sweden in 1944. Ever since his first play, *Katakombas* (Catacombs, 1926), Zīverts had been an untiring experimenter in both the form and the matter of modern drama. In his best plays, *Vara* (Power, 1936) and *Minchauzena precības* (The marriage of Münchhausen, 1941), he is particularly interested in the building-up of a play towards one 'great scene' in which everything is resolved. In his late dramas, e.g. *Kāds kura nav* (Someone who does not exist, 1954), there are echoes of the ideas of the Existentialists.　　　　EB

ZLOBEC, Ciril (b. 1925), Slovene poet, journalist, translator, novelist and essayist, was expelled from the 4th year of grammar school in Koper for nationalist attitudes, joined the partisans in 1943, and after the war completed grammar school and university studies in Slavonic languages in Ljubljana. He worked as journalist, co-editor of *Beseda* and, from 1968, editor of *Sodobnosti*. After the war he published poems in numerous periodicals and, 1953, together with fellow spirits, contributed to *Pesmi štirih* (Poems of the four, 1953), which reestablished personal lyric poetry after the self-congratulatory verse of the immediate postwar period. He has been and remains active in political and cultural life. Among his collections of poems are *Pobeglo otroštvo* (Lost childhood, 1957), *Ljubezen* (Love, 1958), *Najina oaza* (Our oasis, 1964) and

Nove pesmi (New poems, 1985). He has written the novels *Moška leta nasega otroštva* (The manly years of our childhood, 1962) and *Moj brat svetnik* (My brother the saint, 1970).
•Translations in: *Parnassus*; *IYL*. HL

ŽMICHOWSKA, Narcyza (1819–76), Polish novelist, worked as a teacher and was active in patriotic organisations. Her *Poganka* (The heathen woman, 1846) belongs among the finest achievements of Polish Romantic fiction. Its lyrical form and parabolic structure represent the illusory character of Romantic love, rooted in the imagination and detached from reality. The heroine, a *femme fatale*, transpires as the complete opposite of the wishful preconceptions of her hapless lover. Žmichowska's other outstanding work, *Czy to powieść?* (Is this a novel?, 1877), presents a psychological portrait of a woman of the author's own generation.   SE

ZOHRAB, Krikor (1861–1915), Armenian prose writer, was the foremost personality among the 761 Armenian intellectuals 'sent into exile', i.e. murdered, by the Turks in 1915. He is known as the founder of the Realist short story in W Armenian literature. The Russo-Turkish War of 1877–8 and its aftermath, the Congress of Berlin, raised hopes among the Armenians that the Great Powers would prevail on Turkey to treat them on an equal basis with all others. Zohrab did not believe any changes would occur to better the lot of the Armenians, and his editorials and political reviews in *Lragir* (Newspaper) and *Erkragound* (The universe) castigated those who did. He was a brilliant orator and lawyer who, as an MP, was concerned with national, social, economic and educational problems. In the

many short stories and novelle published during his life time, *Anhetatsats seround me* (A disappearing generation, 1887), *Khghtcmtank'i Jayner* (Voices of conscience, 1909), *Keank'e intcpes vor e* (Life as it is, 1911) and *Lour tsaver* (Silent griefs, 1911), he skilfully analyses the complexities of urban life. His commitment to the Armenian cause was firm and uncompromising. Under the pseudonym Marcel L'eart, he printed in Paris *La Question arménienne à la lumiére des documents* (1913) in which he foresees the approaching catastrophe: 'If, in the new war, Turkey and Germany become allies', he writes, 'the fate of the Armenians in Turkey will be in mortal peril.' In his last letter he writes, 'We are struggling against the conception which states that right belongs to the mighty.' On 20 May 1915, Zohrab was arrested on the road from Aleppo; he was set upon by a marauding band, who having killed him, crushed his head between two massive stones.
•T. Cross (Ed.), *The Lost Voices of World War I* (London, 1988), pp. 368–72; 'The Storm' and 'Ayinga' in *Ararat*, XVII, 4 (Autumn 1976), pp. 27–43; *Voice of Conscience* (New York, 1983).
H. Gertmenian, 'Krikor Zohrab' and H. Kelikian, 'Krikor Zohrab. The Complete Armenian', *Ararat*, XVII, 4, pp. 27–30, 31–6.   VN

ZORANIĆ, Petar (1508–before 1569), Croatian writer (little is known about his life or early works), wrote *Planine* (The mountains, 1569), the first secular prose work in Croatian, which earned him his place in literary history. Modelled on Sannazaro's *Arcadia*, it aims to celebrate the surroundings of Zoranić's native Zadar by giving landmarks a legendary history in the manner of Classical texts (notably Ovid's *Metamorphoses*). It contains many references to Classical and Italian literature. The writer's starting-point is the neglect of his country and its language by his fellow countrymen. The work is given shape by being presented as an allegory in the Petrarchan mode: the narrator (Zoran), suffering from the prerequisite 'pangs of love', sets out on a journey to find a cure. Along the way groups of shepherds outdo one another in their pastoral prowess at singing songs of love, adorned with acrostics and other Petrarchan devices. Zoran makes a Danteesque journey to the underworld and eventually to the 'Garden of Glory' where the literary languages of the world are celebrated and Croatian is beginning to earn a place. The pagan nature of the work is transformed, as is the case with so many works of early Croatian literature, by a vision of the Truth: St Jerome, who came to be seen as the patron saint of the Croatian language in the course of the Middle Ages, descends from a cloud to bless his sons and encourage them on the path of righteousness. ECH

ZRÍNYI, Miklós (1620–64), Hungarian poet and essayist. The Zrínyi family, whose vast estates were continually threatened by the Turks, were doughty fighters and Miklós maintained this tradition. Educated in Vienna and Italy under the direction of his guardian PÁZMÁNY, he was the author of the finest epic in Old Hungarian literature, generally known as *Szigeti veszedelem* (The peril of Sziget), but originally entitled *Adriai tengernek Syrenaia . . .* (Siren of the Adriatic Sea . . ., 1651). It recounts the story of his great-grandfather's heroic defiance of the Turks at the siege of Szigetvár (1566) and its

aim is to urge Hungarians to expel the Turks once and for all, a theme pursued in Zrínyi's prose works too, most passionately in *Az török áfium ellen való orvosság* (Remedy against Turkish opium, written 1660–1, publ. 1705). He also wrote on military leadership and the monarchy. His few lyric poems include a fine elegy on the death of his young son. Zrínyi's skill as an epic poet is evident in his management of material that had to be historically accurate – the Hungarians failed, the Turks won – yet reveal the losers in a heroic light. This he achieved with his knowledge of Homer, Virgil and Tasso: the huge Turkish forces are riven by dissension, while the Hungarians are united and after their final battle are borne to heaven by angels. Zrínyi excels at detailed description and has the eye of a film-director. His prosody has long been compared unfavourably with that of his contemporary GYÖNGYÖSI, but this is unfair; his metre is based on four stressed syllables per line of varied length and not the Hungarian alexandrine. This gives his verse a rugged quality that suits its theme.

•Excerpts in T. Klaniczay (Ed.), *Old Hungarian Literary Reader* (Budapest, 1985) and W. Kirkconnell (Ed.), *Hungarian Helicon* (Calgary, 1985). D. Mervyn Jones, *Five Hungarian Writers* (Oxford, 1966). GFC

ZUPAN, Vitomil (1914–87), Slovene novelist and playwright, much travelled before WWII as a casual labourer, was interned by the Italians in 1942 and joined the partisans in autumn 1943. For some time after the war he worked for Radio Ljubljana; 1947 he became a freelance writer, was imprisoned 1948–54, then completed civil engineering studies in Ljubljana, 1958. His novel *Menuet* *za kitaro* (Minuet for guitar, 1975) is a highly personal and irreverent reminiscence of the partisan war; *Igra z hudičevim repom* (Playing with the Devil's tail, 1978) is a Strindbergian picture of married life; and *Komedija človeškega tkiva* (A comedy of human tissue, 1980) a confessional novel in the manner of Henry Miller. His plays show great variety of style from the Socialist Realism of *Rojstvo v nevihti* (Birth in the storm, 1945) to the sentimental 'humanism' of *Ladja brez imena* (Ship without a name, 1972) or the neo-Naturalism of *Bele raketa letijo na Amsterdam* (White rockets in flight for Amsterdam, 1973).

•*Minuet for Guitar* (Ljubljana, 1988).

HL

ŽUPANČIČ, Oton (1878–1949), Slovene poet, playwright and translator, attended grammar schools in Novo Mesto and Ljubljana, where he became an associate of CANKAR, KETTE and MURN in a students' secret literary society called the Zadruga. Together these four constituted the Slovene Modernist movement (Mod-erna). Student days in Vienna (1896–1902) and travels abroad, including a visit to Paris in 1905, greatly widened his literary horizons. *Čaša opojnosti* (A cup of rapture, 1899), his first published collection, contained echoes of folk poetry, European Romanticism and even Decadence (Verlaine). *Čez plan* (Over the plain, 1904) included a cycle of poems dedicated to MURN, some love poems, his first patriotic verse, and ballads and romances on folk themes. *Samogovori* (Soliloquies, 1908) sounded notes of pessimism, doubt, concern for his homeland and the fate of his people, which found noble expression in the poem 'Duma' (Meditation). His last collection, *Zimzelen pod snegom* (Periwinkle beneath the snow, 1945), contains wartime and postwar poems, including the patriotically defiant 'Veš, poet, svoj dolg?' (Poet, do you know your duty?, 1941). His work for stage includes the historical tragedy *Veronika Deseniška* (1924).

•*A Selection of Poems* (Ljubljana, 1967); AMYP: IYL.

HL

Anonymous, collective and oral-tradition texts

THE BIBLE

ALBANIAN The translation of religious literature in Albanian has a long tradition, beginning with BUZUKU and other authors of the Middle Ages, but a translation of the NT into Albanian appeared for the first time in 1827. It was translated by Vangjel Meksi (d. c.1823), the doctor of Ali Pasha Tepelena. Robert Pinkerton, representative of the British and Foreign Bible Society in Constantinople, reports in 1819 that Meksi had also written a grammar of the Albanian language in Albanian and a translation of a religious work of abbé Claude Fleury, both of them lost. Meksi finished his translation of the NT for the British and Foreign Bible Society in 1821. He never lived, however, to see the publication of his work, which was undertaken by Grigor Gjirokastriti, Bishop of Euboea and later Archbishop of Athens. The Gospel of St Matthew was published in Albanian in 1824 and the NT as a whole in a bilingual Greek-Albanian edition in 1827. A new edition of the NT in both the N and S dialects (1872–9), was published again by the British and Foreign Bible Society, translated this time by KRISTOFORIDHI.   ShM

ARMENIAN After Greek and Aramaic translations of the OT, came the Syriac translation of the NT, and afterwards translations of the whole Bible into Latin, Coptic, Gothic, Ethiopian, and then Armenian. The Armenians call the Bible *Astuatsashuntch matean*, 'the Breath of God', in accordance with II Timothy 3: 16. Armenia was the first state to accept Christianity as 'the established' religion, some time between 278 and 313. According to the testimony of AGAT'ANGEĹOS, who was secretary to Trdat III, King of Armenia (c. 284–314), the founder of Armenian Christianity was Gregory the Illuminator (c. 257–331). Armenian historical sources attribute the foundation of Armenian literature, including translations of the Scriptures, to St Mesrob Mashtots (c. 355–439), and to the Catholicos Sahak Partev (c. 350–439). With encouragement from King Vŕamshapouh (c. 395–415), Mesrob founded, c. 406, an Armenian alphabet and gathered around him a group of enthusiastic collaborators called 'the Translators' who initiated a programme of translations from the Greek and Syriac. The first translation of the Bible, partly from Syriac and partly from Greek, was made between 406 and some time prior to the third Ecumenical Council, 431. With the help of two of his pupils, Hovhan Ekeghetsi and Hovsep

462

Paghnatsi, Mesrob began the translation of the Bible with Proverbs, which starts with the exhortation 'to know wisdom and instruction, to perceive the words of understanding'. In reference to the books translated KORIWN states, 'whence by the hands of two colleagues, suddenly, in an instant, Moses, the Law-giver, together with the order of the Prophets, energetic Paul with the entire phalanx of the Apostles, with Christ's world-sustaining Gospel became Armenian speaking' and informs us that 'completing the twenty-two famous books [i.e. the Hebrew Canon] he also translated the NT into Armenian'. The origin of the Canon comprising twenty-two books in Armenia rests on the influence of the Syriac *Peshitta* version, which enjoyed considerable authority in the regions under Persian jurisdiction. The second phase of translations into Armenian falls in the period after the Council of Ephesus, when the pupils of Mesrob, KORIWN and Łewond returned from Byzantium with the canons of the Councils of Nicea and Ephesus and authoritative Greek versions of the Scriptures. On this basis Sahak Partev and the Bishop of Koghb, EZNIK KOGHBATSI, revised the Armenian translation of Mesrob and his disciples. Thus, by the middle of the 5th cent. the Armenian Church had a revised and completed text of the Scriptures, which has survived unchanged, albeit with minor contaminations. With the exception of the Vulgate, more manuscripts of the classical Armenian version have survived than of any other ancient version. Rhodes lists over 1,244 MSS of the NT, the oldest dated 887. Among noteworthy features of the Armenian version of the Bible was the inclusion of certain books that elsewhere came to be regarded as apocryphal. The OT included the History of Joseph and Asenath and the Testament of the Twelve Patriarchs, and the NT included the Epistles of the Corinthians to Paul and a Third Epistle of Paul to the Corinthians. The Armenian Bible was first printed 1666 Amsterdam by the Armenian Orthodox priest Voskan of Yerevan. It is based on a MS copied for the Armenian King He-t'um II of the Cilician kingdom in 1295. This was reprinted in Constantinople in 1705. The NT was published in Venice in 1789, the entire Bible in 1805. The text of this edition reproduces, in the main, a Venice Mekhitarist Monastery MS dated 1319, with variant readings from eight other MSS of the entire Bible, 30 of the Gospels, 14 of the Acts and 4 lectionaries. The first modern vernacular translation of the complete Bible was made in 1858 by the American Bible Society and the British and Foreign Bible Society.

●A facsimile reproduction of the 1805 Venetian edition, with an introduction by Claude Cox (Delmar, NY, 1984). B. M. Metzger, *The Early Versions of the New Testament: Their Origin, Transmission and Limitations* (Oxford, 1977), pp. 153–81; F. C. Conybeare, 'Armenian version of the Old Testament' in Hastings (Ed.), *A Dictionary of the Bible* (Edinburgh, 1906), vol. I, pp. 151–4; F. Rhodes, *An Annotated List of Armenian New Testament Manuscripts* (Tokyo, 1959).

VN

BULGARIAN The oldest extant translations of parts of the Bible into Bulgarian are the *Asemanievo evangelie* (Codex Assemanianus, Glagolitic MS; the text is closest to the 9th-century translation of Cyril and Methodius), the *Zografsko* *evangelie* (Zograf Gospel, Cyrillic) and the *Mariinsko evangelie* (Marian Gospel, Glagolitic), all from the end of the 10th or the beginning of the 11th century, and the 11th-century *Savina kniga* (Gospel Book of Sava), *Sinaiski psaltir* (Psalterium Sinaiticum, Glagolitic), and *Eninski apostol* (Codex Eninensis, Cyrillic, an anthology of passages from the Epistles). Numerous Gospels, Psalters and 'Apostols' (containing the Acts and the Epistles) exist from subsequent centuries. During the 10th–15th centuries the texts underwent significant changes: three Slavonic redactions in which Greek words and terms were gradually replaced by Bulgarian, other lexical and exegetical changes were made as a result of comparison with different Greek redactions. The Glagolitic part of the Rheims Gospel, copied in Bohemia in 1395 from a far older original, contains part of the OT. The redaction of the Gospels accepted at the Tărnovo School (perhaps the work of Bulgarian scholars on Mount Athos) became standard in the 1370s and was translated into Roumanian, Russian and Serbian during subsequent centuries. This redaction forms the basis of the standard Orthodox Gospel texts. The first translation into modern Bulgarian was concluded by Petar Sapunov (1800–72), who published the NT, 1828; a translation of the NT was done by Neofit Bozveli (1785–1848) and published in 1840 (6 editions up to 1859). 1859–71 the complete Bible was translated by two American missionaries with Konstantin Fotinov (1790–1858) and Petko R. Slaveikov (1827–95), and published in Constantinople in 1871. This translation is still used, together with the standard translation of the Bulgarian Holy Synod (1925, rev. ed. 1985).

●J. Vajs and J. Kurz, *Evangeliarium Assemani. Codex Vaticanus 3. Slavicus glag.* (Prague, 1929–55).
M. Weingart, 'Zum altkirchenslavischen Apostolus', *Slavia* 1 (1922–3); V. Vondrak, 'Über das gegenseitige Verhältnis der älteren Evangelientexte', *Altslavenische Studien* (Vienna, 1890).

SIK

BYELORUSSIAN By far the most significant Bible translations into Byelorussian were made by SKARYNA in the early 16th century. The twenty-two books were embellished with original commentaries and engravings and remain one of the country's greatest cultural monuments. SKARYNA's *Bivliia ruska* (1517–19, 1525) was followed by the translation of parts of the NT by Vasil Ciapinski (c. 1540–?1603). His versions of Matthew, Mark and part of Luke (published at his estate Ciapinka in the Čašniki region between 1570 and 1580) are clearly influenced by SKARYNA's Vilna typography, but their eloquently nationalistic prefaces and exegetical commentaries have a strongly polemical and publicist slant. The decline of Byelorussian culture over the next two and a half centuries under Polish and then Russian domination all but killed the literary language and put a stop to translating activity. Renewed attempts to promote the use of Byelorussian in church began in the mid-19th century, but the major modern biblical translations were made for the British and Foreign Bible Society under the leadership of Anton Łuckievič (1884–1946) during the 1920s, and a full Byelorussian version of the NT appeared in 1931. This publication prompted further activity by, amongst others, Vincent

Hadleŭski (1888–1942), though none has surpassed Łuckievič's work, which was revised for a new edition in 1948 and is still widely used, despite more recent translations.

●G. Picarda, 'The Heavenly Fire: a Study of the Origins of the Byelorussian New Testament and Psalms (1931)', *Božym šlacham*, 1–2 (143–4) (1975), pp. 9–24; M. Altbauer, 'Studies in the Vocabulary of the Byelorussian Translations of the Bible', *Journal of Byelorussian Studies*, II, 4 (1972), pp. 359–68.

CROATIAN Extracts of the Bible in the vernacular were known in Croatia in the 14th century, but the first complete translation of the NT was carried out by Stjepan Istranin Konzul and Antun Dalmatin, 1560–3, in both the Glagolitic and Cyrillic alphabets. The first translation of the entire Bible was done in 1821 by a Slavonic Franciscan, Petar Katančić (1750–1825): *Sveto Pismo Starog Zakona* (Holy Scripture of the OT, 2 vols), and *Sveto Pismo Novog Zakona* (Holy Scripture of the NT, 4 vols). In this edition, the Vulgate and the Croat texts were printed in parallel.   ECH

CZECH The oldest extant translations of parts of the Bible into Czech are the 'Glossed' and Wittenberg Psalters, from the end of the 13th and beginning of the 14th centuries, and some fragments of the Gospels from the 1330s or 1340s. The first complete translation (from the Vulgate), the Dresden Bible, was concluded, by perhaps ten scholars, in the 1370s. In 1914 this Bible was sent to Louvain for photographing and was destroyed in the German bombardment of the city; copies and photostats of large parts of it have, however, survived, as have later redactions of the Dresden Bible, particularly the Litoměřice-

Třeboň Bible (1411–14) and the Olomouc Bible (1417). The latter is important for its 'improvements' where the copyist has adapted phrases to more popular literary fashions, for example, introduced a synonym pair where the Dresden text has one word. A completely new translation was made by 1420, the Padeřov Bible, and a later redaction appeared in two incunabula, the Prague Bible (1488) and the Kuttenberg Bible (1498). The first translation to pay attention to the original languages was the Bohemian Brethren's so-called Kralice Bible (*Bible Kralická*, 1579–88), on whose editorial board were two converted Jews to help with the Hebrew. The NT was a revised version of Jan Blahoslav's (1523–71) translation (1564). The Kralice Bible remained the standard translation into the 1970s, although during the Counter-Reformation a new R. Catholic translation was done by Matěj Václav Šteyer (1630–92), Jiří Konstanc (1607–73) and Jan Barner (1643–1708), the St Wenceslas Bible (*Svatováclavská bible*, 1677–1715). Now a new ecumenical translation is used by all confessions.

●J. Vintr, *Die älteste tschechische Psalterübersetzung* (Vienna, 1986); J. Vintr, *Die ältesten tschechischen Evangeliare. Edition, Text und Sprachanalyse* (Munich, 1977); V. Kyas (Ed.), *Staročeská bible drážd'anská a olomoucká* (Prague, 1981–8). J. B. Souček, 'Die tschechischen Bibelübersetzungen', *Die Bibel in der Welt*, 6 (1963), pp. 1–22.   RBP

ESTONIAN The superintendent-general of Livonia, Johann Fischer (1633–1705), was the man who, towards the end of the 17th century, inspired serious interest in the translation of religious literature into Estonian. In 1686 a translation into S Estonian of the NT was published in 500 copies in Riga (*Meie Issanda Jesusse Kristusse Wastne Testament*), the translators probably being Andreas Virginius (1640–1701) and Adrianus Virginius (1663–1706). The latter also started work, with the aid of Johann Hornung (1660–1715), on a N Estonian version. The Bible Conferences held in 1686 and 1687 were intended to settle the conflict with the Tallinn consistory which the translating and publishing endeavours of Riga had aroused (indeed, even the Riga translation of the NT was withdrawn), but no compromise version was published, and the N Estonian translation of 1705 remained unpublished. After the end of the Northern War Heinrich Gutslef (1680–1747) was instrumental in producing a N Estonian version which was published in 1715 in an edition of 400 copies. Although in 1727 a new edition of the S Estonian version was published in 10,000 copies, the initiative in this work now moved to Tallinn (2nd ed. of N Estonian version, 1729). In 1731 the Tallinn consistory established a commission for a complete translation of the Bible, whose members were Gutslef, H. C. Wrede and Artur Thor Helle (1683–1748); the last became the leading spirit of the enterprise. The complete translation (*Piibli Raamat*) appeared in 1739.

●K. G. Sonntag, *Versuch einer Geschichte der lettischen und esthnischen Bibel-Übersetzungen* (Riga, 1817); G. O. F. Westling, 'Vorarbeiten zu der esthnischen Übersetzung des Neuen Testaments 1715', *Mittheilungen und Nachrichten für die evangelische Kirche in Russland* (1893), pp. 453–74.   VM

FINNISH Parts of the R. Catholic liturgy were performed in Finnish before the Reformation. The Reformation was formally accepted in Finland in 1527 following the Diet of Västerås, and the translation of the Bible into Finnish was begun by Mikael Agricola (c. 1510–57) while studying under Luther in Wittenberg in the 1530s. After his return to Finland in 1539, as 'rector' of the Turku Cathedral School and later as bishop, he published a Finnish prayer book (1544), and Finnish translations of the NT (1548), the Psalter (1551) and fragments of the OT (1551–2). A committee set up in 1602 continued Agricola's work and under the editorship of Eskil Petraeus (1593–1657) published a translation of the whole Bible (*Coco Pyhä Ramattu Suomexi*) in 1642. Although several attempts were made to retranslate the Bible in the 19th century, the Agricola-Petraeus translation remained the sole authorised version of the Bible until the 1930s. The Finnish of the Bible, based on the spoken SW dialect, played an important role in shaping the modern literary language.

●A. F. Puukko, *Raamattumme* (Helsinki, 1946); K. Laitinen, 'The birth of a literature' in K. Laitinen (Ed.), *The Book in Finland 1488–1988* (Helsinki, 1988), pp. 2–11.   MAB

GEORGIAN Translations from the Bible into Georgian date from soon after the conversion of the Georgians and the evolution of their alphabet, no later than the end of the 5th century. The earliest Gospel texts extant are the 'Khanmet'i' and 'Haemet'i' (so called because they use the archaic Georgian pronominal prefix 'kh', later 'h'), followed by the substantial Adysh MS of 897. The revisions produced by Georgian monks on Mount Athos brought both the Bible and Georgian syntax closer to Byzantine Greek norms. The Oshki MS version of the OT (dated 978 and preserved on Mount Athos) is virtually complete. Much of its wording is used in the Mtskheta MS of the late 17th century, currently being published. In 1710 Sulkhan-Saba ORBELIANI, the father of the Georgian Enlightenment, collated and corrected earlier versions, principally the 12th-century Gelati MS, and, at the instigation of King VAKHTANG VI of Kartli, began printing them in 1710 in Tbilisi. The first complete printed version (Moscow, 1743), filling in gaps by crude translation from Church Slavonic, evolved these heterogenous versions into what has until now been the standard liturgical text. From a scholarly point of view, these versions are defective; there is little direct translation from the Hebrew, and there is evidence of retranslation from Armenian, Syriac and Latin. Despite the work of scholars such as Blake, Birdsall, A. and M. Shanidze, an enormous amount of textological and historical research is still called for to determine the sources and sequence of Georgian versions of the Bible. With the end of Soviet rule a new wave of translation by competent scholars has been undertaken. The 1990 version commissioned and printed by the Georgian Orthodox Church and serialised in formerly Communist publications (Mnatobi, Tbilisi, 1990–1) is an impressive, accurate rendering that reconciles traditional phrasing with modern literary Georgian usage. Further revision is planned before the Church will allow it to supersede the magnificent, if flawed and occasionally unintelligible, medieval texts still in use.

•E. Dochanashvili (Ed.), *Mtskheturi*

khelnats'eri vol. 1–5 (Tbilisi, 1981–6); J. Molitor, 'Das Adysh-Tetraevangelium neu übersetzt', *Oriens Christianus* 38 (1954), p. 19; R. P. Blake, M. Brière, *The Old Georgian Versions of the Prophets* (with Latin translation), *Patrologia orientalis*, 29–30 (Paris, 1961–3). R. P. Blake, 'Ancient Georgian Versions of the Old Testament', *Harvard Theological Review*, 19, 1926, pp. 271–97; M. V. Songulashvili, 'The Georgian Bible', *The Bible Translator*, 41, 1 (1990), pp. 131–4.   DR

MODERN GREEK The question of translating, adapting or paraphrasing the Bible into spoken Greek seems only to have become an issue in the period after the fall of Constantinople, although the problem of making religious texts accessible to an illiterate population, especially one containing a significant number of people whose mother tongue was not Greek, became tangible in the last two hundred years of the Byzantine Empire – hence the large quantities of religious, patristic and ascetic texts in simplified Greek preserved in the monastic libraries of Greek Anatolia. The first more precisely biblical texts tend to come from Greeks in areas of Italian occupation or of the Diaspora. At the end of the 15th century a Cretan lawyer, Yoryos Houmnos (fl. late 15th cent.), produced a paraphrase of Genesis and Exodus in decapentasyllabic couplets, though he was probably relying on much earlier paraphrases rather than working directly from the biblical text. Similarly in 1536 a Corfiot, Ioannikos Kartanos (c. 1500–c.1550), published Το Ανθος και Αναγκαίον (The Flower and Essence of the OT and NT) in Venice. The work contained substantial passages of translation (including many from the books of the Apocrypha which were popular with the Greeks), together with commentaries and other didactic material. The work of both Houmnos and Kartanos is clearly designed to keep religion accessible to the people in Italian-occupied or Italophone territories. (We can see the echo of this kind of work in the fact that Liverios Kolettis [c. 1685–1738/9], one of the contributors to the Ανθη Ευλαβείας [a collection of sonnets and longer poems produced by a group of schoolboys in Venice in 1708], collaborated on an edition of a translation of the NT.) Later in the 16th century, however, the activities of R. Catholic and Protestant missionaries in translating the NT for the purposes of proselytising more widely in Greek communities complicate the picture. The Orthodox Church condemned such translations as impious, arguing that they created a breach between contemporary Greeks and the religion of their ancestors, and that therefore the preservation of the language of the Bible was an integral part of the preservation of Greek national characteristics. Henceforth the educational function, religious politics and patriotic implications of translation were all entangled. The first major contribution resulted from the activities of Kirillos Loukaris (1572–1638), three times Patriarch of Constantinople 1620–38 (when he was executed by the Turks), an enlightened intellectual who had close links with Western Protestants. Loukaris encouraged the translation produced between 1622 and the 1630s by Maximos of Gallipoli (d. 1633) in collaboration with Antoine Leger. The translation was published in Genoa in 1638, at the expense of the Dutch government, with a preface in demotic by Loukaris, stressing the import-

ance of such translations for the Christian instruction of ordinary people, and citing the positive achievements of biblical translation into Western languages. Other translations were done at a similar period, e.g. one by Athanasios Patelaros and another by Mitrofanis Kritopoulos (c. 1589–1639), a friend and protégé of Loukaris, but it was Maximos's text which was to have a lasting influence – when Seraphim of Mytilene (fl. 18th cent.) produced a new translation; in 1703 he published it as a revision of that of Maximos. In 1710 a genuine revised version of Maximos's text appeared in Halle, under the supervision of Anastasios Michail (c. 1680–1725), a member of the Royal Society of Prussia, later influential in Orthodox circles in St Petersburg. This version in turn was the basis of the 1810 re-edition published in London by the British and Foreign Bible Society as part of the renewed missionary campaign by Protestant churches in Greece 1805–20. Hostility to Maximos's translation continued throughout this period, initiated by Meletios Sirigos (1590–1664). The educational argument for translation is turned on its head in a work published in Nuremberg in 1714 by Alexandros Helladios (?–?), on the current state of the Greek Church, arguing that to replace the original text by a modern translation was to condemn the Greek people to ignorance and barbarism, since the Greek of the original was relatively simple and read daily in every household. After the War of Independence, the political significance of biblical translation was, if anything, intensified. Neofitos Vamvas (1770–1855), initially a protégé of KORAËS, produced a translation of the four Gospels and the Acts of the Apostles into simplified Greek, which was condemned by the Synod and roundly criticised by conservative intellectuals, such as Konstantinos Oikonomos (1780–1857). The last great controversy was caused by the translations of the Gospels by Alexander Pallis (1851–1935) in 1901, at the height of the struggle between supporters of *katharevousa* and demotic for the right to be thought of as 'true' nationalists and patriots. Conservative elements in the university deliberately fomented student discord leading to the infamous Gospel riots (Evangelika).

●F. H. Marshall (Ed.), *Old Testament Legends, from a Greek Poem on Genesis and Exodus by Georgios Choumnos* (Cambridge, 1925).   CFR

HUNGARIAN Parts of the Bible were translated by the Hussites in the 15th century and are preserved in three contemporary codices. But the Reformation and the development of printing instigated a flood of translations during the 16th century. Gábor Pesti's Four Gospels (Vienna, 1536) were soon superseded by János Sylvester's (c. 1504–55) complete New Testament (Sárvár, 1541). Gáspár HELTAI, aided by other Lutheran pastors in Transylvania, planned a complete translation; he published the NT (Kolozsvár [Cluj], 1562) and several further books, but the venture ended with his death in 1574. The task was taken up by the Calvinist Gáspár Károlyi (c. 1539–91), who edited, helped to translate and annotated the complete Bible (Vizsoly, 1590). This version has influenced Hungarian language and literature more than any other book. Károlyi, who translated from Hebrew and Greek, prided himself on his use of 'pure Hungarian words and phrases',

and the basic text, though revised from time to time, still preserves the ruggedness and strength of the original. Some 300 editions were recorded up to 1940. The R. Catholic Bible, translated from the Vulgate by the Jesuit György Káldi (1572–1634), appeared first in Vienna in 1626. Though commended for its elegant style, it never achieved the popularity of the Vizsoly Bible; substantially revised by Béla Tárkányi (1821–86) in 1865, it became the standard Catholic Bible. Modern translations appeared in Budapest in 1973 (R. Catholic) and 1975 (Protestant).

●I. Nemeskürty, *Magyar bibliafordítások* (Budapest, 1990).   GFC

LATVIAN The first translation of the Bible into Latvian was made by the German clergyman Ernst Glück (1652–1705). Since, however, this translation was submitted to an editorial commission, it became more or less a collective work. The NT was printed in 1685 and the OT in 1689. Although the translation contains a considerable number of germanisms, it greatly promoted the development of the Latvian literary language.   EB

LITHUANIAN The first biblical texts in Lithuanian are to be found in the first Lithuanian printed text, the Lutheran pastor, Martynas Mažvydas's (?–1563), Catechism (1547). The first complete translation of the Bible was done 1575–90 by another Protestant priest, Jonas Bretkūnas (1536–1602), on the basis of Luther's German version. In R. Catholic Lithuania (Lithuania Major) the first biblical texts appeared in Mikalojus Daukša's (1676–1747), *Postilla Catholica* in Vilnius. The Protestant translation by Samuel Chylinski (1634–68) was not accepted by the Vilnius Protestant Community and so was never published in full. A NT translated by the Protestant Samuel Bitner (c. 1632–1710) was published in 1701. Then in 1727 a group of Protestant pastors published a complete Bible that was frequently republished, with revisions and additions. A R. Catholic NT was done by Bishop J. A. Giedratis in 1816. The best translation of the complete Bible was, however, the scholarly Archbishop Juozapas Skvireckas's (1873–1959), which was published 1911–35 and remains the standard Lithuanian version. RŠ

MACEDONIAN Macedonians generally used the Church Slavonic, Bulgarian or Serbian Bible. The United Bible Societies published a Macedonian NT (London, 1976), which was, notably, printed in Ljubljana. The Macedonian Orthodox Church regards itself as the true inheritor of the Bulgarian Church. KLIMENT OF OHRID (St Clement of Ochrida) as his agname informs us was active in today's Macedonia, and one may consider that the history of Bulgarian translations of the Bible (qv) is the same as the history of the Macedonian. SIK

POLISH The first translation (OT only) was completed in the middle of the 15th century for queen Sofia (*Biblia królowej Zofii*, The Bible of Queen Sofia), the fourth wife of Władysław II Jagiełło (reigned 1386–1434), and was based on a Czech Bible. It is commonly thought that the NT, particularly the Gospels, was also translated in the 15th century, but only fragments remain. A genuine breakthrough occurred in the 16th century with the Reformation, which brought a Polish version of the NT (by S. Murzynowski, done 1551–2). This was followed by two full translations of the Scriptures: R.

Catholic (Vulgate version by J. Leopolita, 1561) and Protestant (*Biblia brzeska* [The Brest Bible, 1563]). The late 16th century produced the finest of the Old Polish texts in the form of Jakub Wujek's translation. (NT in 1593, complete Bible in 1599). The unique value of this work derives from Wujek's profound knowledge of Hebrew, Greek and Latin, and his masterly command of Polish idiom. Although the final version was eventually spoiled by amendments introduced by a Jesuit commission, Wujek's Bible became the most popular and influential translation of the Scriptures and retains much of its literary value to this day. The Protestant response, known as *Biblia gdańska* (The Gdańsk Bible, 1632), gained recognition in non-R. Catholic circles. New translations continued to be published into the 20th century, particularly after WWII. They include *Biblia tysiąclecia* (The Millennial Bible, 1965) and the *Pallotinum* edition in 12 volumes (since 1958). MIŁOSZ has translated the Book of Job (*Księga Hioba*, 1980). It is not unlikely that Polish translations of the Psalms were already in circulation in the 13th century. The earliest extant manuscript dates from the turn of the 14th century (*Psałterz floriański*, St Florian Psalter) and its beautifully illuminated pages contain three parallel texts: Latin, Polish and German. Two subsequent translations originated in the late 15th or early 16th century: *Psałterz puławski* (The Puławy Psalter) and *Psałterz krakowski* (The Cracow Psalter). In the 16th century the Psalms were rendered into Polish by two outstanding poets, REJ and KOCHANOWSKI. The latter's *Psałterz Dawidów* (Psalms of David, 1579) is universally regarded as a masterpiece. KARPIŃSKI's translation of 1786 proved rather unsuccessful. Prominent poets who have recently attempted the task include STAFF and MIŁOSZ (*Księga Psalmów*, The Book of Psalms, 1979). The best modern editions of early versions include: *Biblia królowej Zofii*, ed. L. Bernacki (Cracow, 1930); *Psałterz floriański*, ed. L. Bernacki (Lwów, 1939); *Psałterz puławski*, ed. S. Słoński (Warsaw, 1916).

•D. A. Frick, *Polish Sacred Philosophy in the Reformation and the Counter-Reformation: Chapters in the History of the Controversies (1551–1632)* (Berkeley and Los Angeles, 1989).   SE

ROUMANIAN The first printed scriptural text in Roumanian appeared in Transylvania under the influence of the Reformation and is a Gospels printed in a parallel Slavonic and Roumanian Cyrillic text by Filip Moldoveanul (Philip the Moldavian, c.1500–c.1558) at Sibiu 1547–54. In 1582 the opening two books of the OT were printed by Şerban Coresi at Orăştie in Transylvania, based on HELTAI's Hungarian version. In 1648 the first NT was printed on the initiative of the Roumanian Orthodox Metropolitan of Transylvania, Simion Ştefan (?–1656), at Alba Iulia. The first complete translation of the Bible was commissioned by Prince Şerban Cantacuzino of Wallachia and printed at Bucharest in 1688. The basis for the text was a MS translation of the OT, made by Nicolae Milescu (1636–1708) 1661–4, while the NT books were translated by the brothers Radu (c.1655–c.1725) and Şerban Greceanu (?–c. 1710), and by Metropolitan Germanos Locros of Nyssa (?–1687), a former teacher at the Greek Academy in Constantinople, who was resident in Bucharest

at the time. A new, more fluent, translation was printed at Blaj in Transylvania in 1795. The paucity of copies of both these Bibles persuaded the British and Foreign Bible Society to support an initiative of the St Petersburg Bible Society, founded by two Scotsmen in 1812, to make the Bible available to Roumanians in Bessarabia which, 1812–1918, was under Russian control. In 1817 the NT was printed at St Petersburg and distributed not only throughout Bessarabia, but also in the neighbouring Roumanian principalities of Moldavia and Wallachia. In 1819 a complete edition of the Bible followed. The British and Foreign Bible Society produced a Roumanian Bible in Latin type in Pest in 1873 and in 1874 it was reprinted at Iaşi in Moldavia. The first translation into the modern orthography of standard Roumanian was made by Gala Galaction (1879–1961) and Vasile Radu (Bucharest, 1938).   DJD

SERBIAN Before 1847, the Serbs used the Church Slavonic translation of the Bible. In 1820 KARADŽIĆ translated the NT from the Church Slavonic, Russian and German versions, but it was not sanctioned by the Church because it was not done from the original and the translator was not a theologian. It was published in 1847 in Vienna by the British and Foreign Bible Society. Since then it has been republished regularly and many revisions have been made. There have been other translations since. KARADŽIĆ's translation is easy to understand because it has retained the clarity of the contemporary language of the people. For this reason, it played a significant role in his reform of the literary language, his argument being that, if the Bible could be translated into 'the language of the shepherds', that language could certainly be used for other purposes. The OT was translated by Djuro Daničić (1825–82), a linguist and KARADŽIĆ's chief ally in the reform movement, and published, together with the NT, in Budapest by the British and Foreign Bible Society in 1865. VDM

SLOVAK Generally, until the 19th century Slovaks used the Czech Bible. To be sure, a MS translation of the Bible into the W Slovak dialect (probably done 1756–9 [attributed to Romualdus Hadbávny (1714–80)]) did exist, but it was not important for the creation of a Slovak literary language. Jur Palkovič (1763–1835) spent thirty years translating the Bible into BERNOLÁK's version of Slovak, but the fruits of his work were published only a few years before the first successful codification of literary Slovak. Thus, his translation (1829–32) had little impact. The first translation of the NT into standard Slovak was published by the British and Foreign Bible Society (London, 1884). Ján Lajčiak (1875–1918) failed to complete his translation (Psalms, 1904; NT, 1912). The first complete translation was published by the R. Catholic St Adalbert Society in Trnava (editors: Ján Donoval [1864–1920], Andrej Hlinka [1864–1938] and Martin Kollár [1853–1919]) between 1913 and 1926. The same society published the first translation from the original languages: New Testament, 1947; Old Testament, 1955.

•K. Gabris, 'The Translation of the Bible into Slovak', *Bible Translator*, 11 (1960), pp. 145–52. RBP

SLOVENE The first translations of the Scriptures known on Slovene soil were those of the Apostles to the Slavs, Cyril and Methodius, who were welcomed by Kocel´, Prince of Pannonia, early in the second half of the 9th century; marked similarities with the Slovene vocabulary in some recensions justified their 19th-century title of 'Altslowenisch, Palaeoslovenicus', especially during a period when Slovene scholars were preeminent in Slavonic philology (Kopitar [1780–1844], Miklosich [1813–81]). The first Slovene vernacular translation was made by a Protestant reformer, DALMATIN (1584), a richly illustrated large-print folio subsidised by the Austrian Estates and smuggled into Slovenia in barrels. Dalmatin's text, purged of some germanisms, provided extracts from the Gospels and Epistles first published by Tomaž Hren (1560–1630), Bishop of Ljubljana (*Evangelia inu Lystuvi*, Graz, 1613), and frequently reissued thereafter. The first Bible translation made by the R. Catholic clergy was that of Jurij Japelj (1744–1807), who in collaboration with Blaž Kumerdej (1728–1805) first published the NT in two parts (1784 and 1786) and the Pentateuch in two parts (1791); he himself translated a third part containing Joshua, Judges and Ruth (1796); when the whole Bible had been finished by other collaborators, the Slovene Jansenists thought of producing a completely new version based on the original Hebrew and Greek; work was started but the project failed. Japelj's translation largely followed DALMATIN, but improved his vocabulary, syntax and word order. HL

SORBIAN A complete NT was translated into Lower Sorbian by a certain Miklawuš Jakubica who completed his task in 1548. The manuscript survives (in Berlin), but it was never printed until it appeared in a scholarly edition in 1967. Jakubica was the pastor of a Sorbian parish in the vicinity of Žarow (Sorau), now in Poland, and his translation is in the dialect of this region. An anonymous Lower Sorbian translation of the Psalter made in the second half of the 16th century also remained in manuscript (a scholarly edition was published in 1928). Seven penitential Psalms (nos 6, 32, 38, 51, 102, 130 and 143) were published in an Upper Sorbian translation by Gregorius Martini (c. 1575–1632) in Bautzen in 1627. An Upper Sorbian version of the Gospels of SS Matthew and Mark, the work of Michał Frencel (1628–1706), Lutheran pastor in Budestecy (Postwitz), was printed in Bautzen in 1670. This was followed in 1706 by Frencel's translation of the whole NT, published in Zittau. The complete Upper Sorbian Bible, incorporating Frencel's work, was translated by Jan Běmar (1671–1742), Matej Jokuš (1668–1735), Jan Langa (1669–1727), and Jan Wawer (1672–1728). It was published in Bautzen in 1728. The translators worked mainly from Luther's German version, but made use also of the original Hebrew and the Czech, Polish and Slovene Bibles. The 11th edition appeared in 1905. Portions of the Bible for R. Catholics (translated from the Vulgate) in the Upper Sorbian dialect of Kulow (Wittichenau) were published by Jurij Hawštyn Swětlik (or Swótlik) (1650–1729) in his *Swjate Sćenja* . . . (Holy Gospels . . ., 1690), but his translation of the whole Bible (completed in 1711) has remained in manuscript. R. Catholics remained without a printed version of either Testament until 1896, when the NT, translated by Jurij Łusčanski (1839–1905) and Michał Hórnik (1833–94), appeared in Bautzen. A new R. Catholic version of the NT, translated by a committee, was printed in Bautzen in 1966; it was followed in 1973 and 1976 by a R. Catholic translation of the OT in two volumes. The first printed NT in Lower Sorbian was produced in 1709 in Korjeń (Kahren), SE of Cottbus, by Johann Gottlieb Fabricius (1681–1741), who compiled the text from an earlier anonymous version, though the titlepage attributes the translation to him. It is apparent that the translator used not only Luther's version but also the Greek. New editions were printed in the 18th and 19th centuries, the most recent being in 1895. The Lower Sorbian OT, translated by Jan Bjedrich Fryco (1747–1819), was first published in Cottbus in 1796. In 1824 the two Testaments were published under one cover, but the NT in this volume had been printed in 1822 and the general title 'Bible' was not used. The complete Bible in Lower Sorbian has been printed only once – in Halle 1868.   GCS

UKRAINIAN The oldest translations of the Holy Scriptures in Ukraine were Church Slavonic (*Ostromir Gospel*, 1056–7; *Ostrih Bible*, 1581). In the 16th century parts of the Bible were translated into the vernacular – the *Peresopnytsia Gospel*, 1556–61; the *Krekhiv Apostol*, 1560. Attempts to translate the Bible into standard Ukrainian date from the 19th century. The Gospels and the Acts were translated by Pylyp Morachevsky (1806–79) in 1862. These were banned by the synod of the Russian Orthodox Church and remained unpublished till 1906. Hence, other Ukrainian translations of the Bible had to be printed outside the Russian Empire: the NT, translated by P. KULISH and Ivan Puliui (1845–1918) in Vienna, 1871. The complete Bible, translated by P. KULISH, I. Puliui and NECHUI-LEVY-TS´KYI, appeared under the imprint of the British and Foreign Bible Society, Vienna, 1903. A new translation, by Ivan Ohienko, was published in the West in 1962. Another complete translation of the Bible in the 1960s was by I. Khomenko, Rome, 1963. After being proscribed for decades by the Soviet government the Gospels appeared in Ukrainian in a new translation by Les Heramsychuk in nos 3, 5, 7, 9, 1990 of the Soviet Ukrainian journal *Vitchyzna*. They are linguistically the most accomplished.

●T. Halushchynsky, 'De Ucrainis Sanctae Scripturae Versionibus', *Bohoslovia* (Lwów [Lemberg], 1925).

GSNL

YIDDISH The translation and adaptation of the Hebrew Scriptures dominated the early history of Yiddish literature. Interlinear and marginal glosses go back to the 12th century. The earliest independent MS texts in Yiddish were discovered in the Cairo Genizah and are now housed in Cambridge. They date from 1382 and include rhymed tales based on a number of biblical sources. The first direct translation into Yiddish to which a definite date may be assigned is a 1490 anonymous MS version of the Psalms. A Hebrew-Yiddish glossary and brief biblical concordance, the *Seyfer shel reb anshl* (Book of Rabbi Anshl, Cracow, 1534), is the first book known to have been printed in Yiddish. Printed Pentateuchs were first published in Constance and Augsburg, 1544; a *Taytsh khumesh* (Cremona, 1560) is a Pentateuch accompanied by the appointed portions of the Prophets and the *Megilot*, together with extracts from the 11th-century commentator Rashi. One of the best examples of the 16th-century

biblical epics is the *Shmuel-bukh* (Samuel book, Augsburg, 1544) which was probably composed in the 15th century. Its anonymous author rendered the story of the Prophet Samuel, King Saul and, above all, King David into *Nibelungenlied* stanzas. The biblical material is embellished with legends drawn from the *Talmud* and from midrashic (i.e. homiletic) sources and is filled with realistically depicted battle scenes, heroic deeds narrated with an element of suspense and humour, all centred on the somewhat idealised image of King David. ELYE BOKHER's translation of the Psalms, *Tilim* (Venice, 1545), was the first to be printed and achieved great popularity. Of all the various forms of Yiddish biblical literature the most popular was the *Tsenerene* ('Go forth, [oh, daughters of Zion,] and behold . . .', Lublin, c. 1595), a paraphrase of the Pentateuch with other appointed portions by Yankev ben Yitskhok Ashkenazi (c. 1550–1623) who appeals to his predominantly female readership by embellishing the narrative with legends and parables drawn from midrashic material. Subsequently the *Tsenerene* went through over 200 editions and has remained constantly in print to this day. Though the 16th century had seen numerous rhymed and adapted versions of parts of the Bible, it was not until 1678–9 that Yekusyel ben Yitskhok Blits and Yoysef ben Aleksander Vitsnhoyzn, in fierce competition with each other, produced translations of the entire Hebrew Scriptures in Amsterdam. Under the influence of Luther and the Dutch *Staatenvertaling*, they kept closely to the Hebrew text, but also moved away from word-for-word glossing. Menakhem-Mendl Lefin's (1749–1826) translation of the Book of Proverbs (Tarnopol, 1814) and of Ecclesiastes (Odessa, 1873) are remarkable for having been the first to attempt to bring the diction closer to spoken E Yiddish. Numerous other modern authors including MENDELE MOYKHER SFORIM and PERETS have attempted the translation of one or more biblical books. The translation of the entire Scriptures (*Tanakh*, New York, 1926–36), to which Yehoyesh (1872–1927) devoted the latter part of his life, has become the standard modern version. From 1540 onwards numerous partial and complete translations of the NT have been made, either by or with the aid of Jewish converts. Though the readership has been negligible, the quality of the translations has sometimes been high.

●W. Staerk and A. Leitzman, *Die jüdisch-deutschen Bibelübersetzungen von den Anfängen bis zum Ausgang des 18. Jahrhunderts* (Frankfurt on Main, 1923); M. Waxman, *History of Jewish Literature*, vol. 2 (New York, 1960^2), pp. 625–39; I. Zinberg, *History of Jewish Literature*, vol. 7 (1975), pp. 29–48, 87–139.   HD

APOCRYPHA

BULGARIAN In the late 9th and early 10th centuries a number of apocryphal (pseudepigraphical) works from Greek were translated into Bulgarian (Church Slavonic). In the 10th century the number of apocrypha grew with new translations, compilations and original compositions. Although for the most part dependent on Byzantine apocrypha, the genre became one of the most important strands in Old Bulgarian literature. Most of the Bulgarian apocrypha translations were widely diffused in the Slav Orthodox world. Some of these texts are preserved in late Slavonic manuscripts and betray a complex series of redactions. The 1973 so-called *Izbornik* (Index) gives epitomes of 25 apocrypha circulating in Bulgaria in the 9th–10th centuries. Over the next two centuries the number of translated or adapted or original apocrypha had grown to at least 120. Following the traditional categorisation of the pseudepigraphical works in Jewish and Christian literature, the Bulgarian apocrypha may be classified thus: translations of OT pseudepigrapha (e.g. Apocalypses, 'historical' and legendary expansions of the OT [e.g. the Creation legend]) and NT pseudepigrapha (e.g. apocryphal Gospels, Acts, Apocalypses, *vitae*) as well as original apocryphal works (e.g. 'historical', heterodox and heretical). Some scholars add apocryphal prayers (some of these are to Christian saints, to Christ or Mary, but others contain no Christian element and originate in heathen beliefs); epistles (e.g. *Poslanie na Pilat do tsar Tiberii* [Epistle of Pilate to the Emperor Tiberius]; *exempla* (e.g. *Zavet Simeonov za zavistta* [The testament of Simeon concerning envy]); books of divination (concerning different methods of divination, e.g. *Grămnik, Lunnik, Kolednik, Trepetnik, Sănovnik* which are based on observations of natural phenomena, or on phenomena linked with the human body or mind); disputes (e.g. *Razumnik* where knowledge is given in a form of questions and answers). Among OT Bulgarian apocrypha are pseudepigrapha like *Otkrovenie Varuhovo*

(The Apocalypse of Baruch [3 Baruch]), *Zaveti na dvanaisette patriarsi* (The testaments of the Twelve Patriarchs), *Videnie Isaevo* (The vision of Isaiah); NT apocrypha include, e.g. *Părvoevangelie na Yakov* (The Protogospel of Jacob), *Nikodemovo evangelie* (The Gospel of Nicodemus), *Tomino evangelie*, also called *Detstvo Isusovo* (The Gospel of Thomas/The childhood of Jesus), *Otkrovenie Pavlovo* (The Apocalypse of Paul). Particularly important is the group of three OT pseudepigrapha extant only in Slavonic, first translated and circulated in Bulgaria: *Kniga za svetite taini Enohovi* (The book of the secrets of Enoch [2 Enoch]); the *Otkrovenie Avraamovo* (Apocalypse of Abraham) and *Stălbata na Yakov* (The ladder of Jacob). Original Bulgarian apocrypha include new versions of older apocrypha, motifs like *Legenda za krăstnoto dărvo* (The legend of the Rood-Tree) by Jeremiah the Priest (10th century), or adaptations of older apocryphal material for the creation of legendary 'history' like the so-called *Bălgarski apokrifen letopis* (Bulgarian apocryphal annals, 12th cent.) or the Thessalonian legend of the Baptism of the Bulgarians (*Solunska legenda* [Salonica legend]). Some early translations of apocrypha most probably contributed to the elaboration of the doctrine of the Bogomil heresy which later spread to central and W Europe and had a considerable impact through related heretical teachings such as Catharism. It is not clear, however, whether certain Dualist elements which are to be found in Bogomil doctrine were transmitted through such apocrypha. Only one authentic Bogomil apocryphon has survived, in Latin: the so-called 'Secret book of the Bogomils' or *Interrogatio Johanis* or *Liber secretum*, from the 12th and 14th centuries. Some Bulgarian apocrypha might have been copied or partly edited by Bogomils (e.g. *Tiveriadsko more* [The Sea of Tiberias] or *Prenie na Hristos s Dyavola* [The dispute of Christ with the Devil]).

●J. H. Charlesworth (Ed.), *The Old Testament Pseudepigrapha* (New York, 1983–85); W. Schneemelcher, *New Testament Apocrypha*, 2 vols (Cambridge and Louisville, 1991–2); C. Tischendorf, *Apocalipses apocryphae* (2nd ed., Heidelberg, 1966 A. Santos Otero, *Die handschriftliche Überlieferung der altslavischen Apokryphen* (Berlin and New York, 1978–81).   SIK

CZECH – Judas In its action the verse legend of Judas, a fragment known as *Legenda o Jidášovi* (c. 1306), largely corresponds to the story told in the *Legenda aurea*, and includes the Aesopian fable of the snake overtaken by winter. The Czech version is linguistically inventive, rich in imagery, and introduces some psychology: it also has a patriotic reference to the recent dying out of the Přemyslide dynasty (1306); Judas is compared with Wenceslas III's assassin, who the author imagines belonged to that 'treacherous tribe', the Germans. Like the PILATE legend, the text shows some minor similarities of phrase and technique to the verse ALEXANDER ROMANCE.

●J. Cejnar (Ed.), *Nejstarší české veršované legendy* (Prague 1964). Translation in W. Schamschula (Ed.), *An Anthology of Czech Literature. 1st Period* (Frankfurt on Main, 1991), pp. 92–100.   RBP

Pilate The verse legend of Pontius Pilate, a fragment known as *Legenda o Pilátovi* (c. 1306), appears to be loosely based on a Latin poem, *De vita Pilati*, which has the same Mainz setting. It recounts only Pilate's conception: King [Atus] of Mainz goes out hunting; the detail the author goes into, together with his approach to Atus, suggests that he might be a nobleman. Atus copulates with a girl called Pila, and using the art of astrology learns of the role that the offspring of this union, Pilatus, will play on Good Friday. The use of a moralising apostrophe to the reader and two couplets almost identical to couplets in the Czech verse ALEXANDER ROMANCE testify to the popularity of the romance rather than to identity of authorship, as has been suggested.

•J. Cejnar (Ed.), *Nejstarší české veršované legendy* (Prague, 1964). Translation in W. Schamschula (Ed.), *An Anthology of Czech Literature. 1st Period* (Frankfurt on Main, 1991), pp. 87–90.   RBP

POLISH In comparison with neighbouring Russia, Polish apocrypha are not abundant and their subject is usually restricted to the lives of Jesus and the Virgin Mary. The most important medieval work, *Rozmyślania przemyskie* (The Przemyśl meditations), dates from the 15th century. It is based on various Latin and Polish sources and combines apocryphal motifs with Gospel texts. The anonymous compiler (translator?) portrays the childhood and youth of the Virgin Mary and the life of Christ, interpolating learned and didactic comments into the story. Another contemporary text, *Rozmyślania dominikańskie* (Dominican meditations), discovered in 1958, was compiled by a monk and describes the Passion. The same subject appeared also in *Sprawa chędoga o męce Pana Chrystusowej* (The true story of Christ's Passion), known from a copy of 1544 but thought to be much older (14th century). Apocryphal literature in Poland achieved its peak in Baltazar Opeć's (late 15th and early 16th centuries) *Żywot Pana Jezu Krysta* (The Life of Our Lord Jesus Christ, 1522). With over forty editions, the book was in circulation until the mid-19th century. It closely follows the *Meditationes vitae Christi* ascribed to St Bonaventura and includes 28 prayers to Christ and 21 hymns. Apocryphal motifs are also present in sermons, Christmas carols, Passion songs and vernacular plays. The most notable in the last group is *Historya o chwalebnym Zmartwychwstaniu Pańskim* (The history of the glorious Resurrection, c. 1580).

•Among the best modern editions of medieval manuscripts are: *Rozmyślania o żywocie Pana Jezusa tzw. przemyskie*, ed. by S. Vrtel-Wierczyński (Warsaw, 1922, phototype); *Rozmyślania dominikańskie*, ed. by K. Górski and W. Kuraszkiewicz (Wrocław, 1965); *Sprawa chędoga*, ed. by S. Vrtel-Wierczyński (Poznań, 1933).   SE

HAGIOGRAPHY

GEORGIAN Possibly the earliest surviving Georgian literary text is hagiographic: *Tsamebay ts'midisa Shushanik'isi dedoplisay* (The passion of Queen St Shushanik', c. 480?) attributed to Iak'ob Tsurt'aveli. The dating is questionable, for the manuscript shows 7th-century linguistic and intertextual features. Some incidents are only found in a 10th-century Armenian version. Iak'ob describes, with many dramatic nuances and few hagiographical clichés, the Armenian Shushanik''s six-year torments after she refuses to follow the conversion to Zoroastrianism of Varsken (her husband, an Iranian viceroy [*pitiakhsh*] in Georgia). Her martrydom was a recent event: Iak'ob was Shushanik''s faithful chaplain, and his moving, twenty-page, often first-person memoir conveys personal pain and admiration for a victim as much of marital breakdown as of religious imperatives. It may be a fragment of Iak'ob's lost writings.

After the anonymous *Evst'ati mtskhetelis ts'ameba* (The passion of Evst'at of Mtskheta, 6th century), the next major work of Georgian hagiography is Ioane Sabanisdze's *Abos ts'ameba* (The passion of Abo, c. 790). Abo was an attaché to Nerse, the Arab viceroy in Tbilisi. He had himself baptised and for apostasy was martyred (beheaded, burnt and his ashes thrown into the River Mt'k'vari) by the Amir in Tbilisi. Ioane's hagiography is a stylised life with good descriptive material, e.g. on Abkhazia, and strong national-Christian propaganda. Abo, like Shushanik', was a foreigner repudiating the religion of Georgia's overlords: an unexpected, but cogent, example to Georgians wavering under infidel yokes.

The bulk of Georgian hagiography lies in collections, such as the *Mravaltavi* (The Many Chapters, full recension by 1000), which owe much to collation and translation by expatriate monastic scholars in Jerusalem, Mt Athos, Anatolia or Sinai. Some works, such as the *Moktsevay Kartlisay* (The conversion of Kartli), which deals with the missionary work of St

Nino (also dealt with in the CHRONICLES of Mroveli), are better classified as history. Others, especially those written on Georgian soil, such as the influential work of Grigol Khandzteli (758–861), can no longer be identified, except for excerpts in his biography by Giorgi Merchule. From the tenth century, lives (*Tskhovreba*) of the Fathers predominate over *Ts'ameba* (Passions). Basil Zarzmeli (920) wrote a life of his uncle, St Serap'ion Zarzmeli (fl. 830–900), the founder of the Zarzma monastery in Samtskhe (S Georgia); it exists in an 11th-century version: its use of archival sources makes it recognisable as a modern biography.

The most substantial patristical work is Giorgi Merchule's *Shromay da moghwats'ebay ghirsad tskhovrebisay ts'midisa da net'arisa mamis chwenisa Grigolisi Arkimandrit'isay, Khandztis da Shat'berdisa aghmashénebelisay . . .* (The work and achievement of the worthy life of the blessed saint, our father Grigol the Archimandrite, builder of Khandzta and Shat'berdi, 958–966). Though incomplete, it is political and historical as well as hagiographic: Giorgi Merchule widened the range of literary Georgian narrative to cover intimate detail, rhetorical pleas and historiosophy. Apart from hymns, collected c. 980 by Mikel Modrek'ili, this life of Grigol Khandzteli is Merchule's only extant work. For the life of St Nino in *Moktseva kartlisay* (The conversion of Georgia), see CHRONICLES.

Georgian religious literature was crowned by the massive hymnographic collection (texts and neumes) of 978–88 of Mikel Modrek'ili's (Modrek'ili = lit. 'bent', also, 'the hermit'), who explained: 'With the help of God's great goodness, I,

Mikel the Hermit, the wretched man of a very idle life, swallowed by the upsets of the world and weighed down by the manifold weight of sins, have worked ... and collected the hymns to the Holy Resurrection, which I found in Georgian, by masters Greek and Georgian, complete for all purposes, in accord with the rites of the Church.'

From 915 to 1235, between the Arab and Mongol occupations, a body of religious writing – homilies, apocrypha, philosophy – was accumulated by Georgian scholars: among the greatest are Leont'i Mroveli and Eprem Mtsire (both c. 1060). Even their translations are valuable, for many Greek, Armenian and Syriac originals have been lost. Some original Georgian religious writers and their works of great repute are known by name only (for instance Ioane Shavteli fl. 1120s and perhaps the *Abdulmesia* now dated 13th century). Between 1620 and 1800 hagiographical literature was reproduced or versified; for the last original 'Passion', see TEIMURAZ I.

●R. Tavaradze (Ed.), *Dzveli kartuli motkhroba*, (Tbilisi, 1979). Translations into Latin: P. Peeters, *Histoires monastiques géorgiennes*, Analecta Bollandiana, XXXI, XXXVII, 1923. M. Tarchnishvili, *Geschichte der kirchlichen georgischen Literatur* (Vatican, 1955); D. M. Lang, *Lives and Legends of the Georgian Saints* (London, 1956); C. Toumanoff, *Studies in Christian Caucasian History* (Georgetown, 1963); J. N. Birdsall, 'Evangelienbezüge im georgischen Martyrium der hl. Schuschaniki', *Georgica* (Jena), 4, 1981, pp. 20–3.   DR

BYZANTINE GREEK Hagiography constitutes an important branch of Byzantine religious literature up to the 11th century, and was subject to occasional bursts of activity thereafter, particularly in the late 13th century. The earliest saint's life is Athanasius's *Life of St Antony* (4th century), which seems to have provided a model for the more seriously biographical form of hagiography, which preserves contemporary testimony. The best examples of this sort of saint's life can be found in the work of writers such as Cyril of Scythopolis (c. 520–560: lives of Sabbas, Euthymius, John the Hesychast and Cyriac) and Leontios of Neapolis ([d. c. 650], lives of John the Almsgiver and Symeon of Edessa). Such works contain valuable historical information, particularly of a sociological kind. However, 'biographical' saints' lives are in a minority. The literary antecedents of hagiography include not only Ancient biography but also Hellenistic romance and Hellenistic and Middle Eastern popular literature, with their traditions of myth and legend. It is easy to identify in the lives thematic and presentational motifs such as the saint's freedom from ordinary needs and his possession of extraordinary powers (see, for example, the lives of St Symeon the Younger and of Nikon Metanoitis), which, while they may derive from such theologically impeccable sources as the Gospels, are part of the rhetoric of the genre rather than factual elements. The language of the lives ranges from near-vernacular to austerely Classical. Many of them were reworked in the 11th century, e.g. by Symeon Metaphrastes, and made not only more rhetorical in style but more didactic in content (and less factual). The main functions of the bulk of hagiographical texts seem to have been liturgical. They were collected into volumes containing, for example, lives of saints for each day of the year.

•*Acta sanctorum*, started 1642, supplemented annually since 1882 by Analecta Bollandiana. P. van den Ven (Ed.), *La Vie ancienne de S. Syméon Stylite le Jeune* (Brussels 1962).
S. Hackel (Ed.), *The Byzantine Saint* (Univ. of Birmingham Fourteenth Spring Symposium of Byzantine Studies) (Birmingham, 1981). CFR

ST CATHERINE OF ALEXANDRIA – Czech The 3,519-line high-style verse legend of St Catherine, known as *Život svaté Kateřiny* (1360s), is the most sophisticated, imaginative work of Czech poetry from the 14th century. It was composed by an unknown Moravian on the basis of the most popular version, *Tradunt annales historiae*, and an account of Catherine's conversion and marriage to Christ, *Fuit in insula Cypri*. Where *Tradunt* concentrates on Catherine's dispute with the heathen sages, our author reduces that to a minimum, and greatly expands what is in *Fuit*. The fast-moving legend concentrates on Catherine's visions of the BVM and Christ, the description of a heavenly palace and the scourging of Catherine. Catherine is a chivalrous figure, wise, rich and beautiful and the golden-locked chivalrous Christ's wooing of her linguistically follows the courtly code. The description of the heavenly palace resembles pictures of exotic luxury dwellings in romances. And the scourging is a fine example of mystic eroticism, verging on sado-masochism, where the colours of Catherine's bruises, weals and gashes are interpreted according to courtly symbolism. Still it remains a picture of perfect Christian devotion. Stylistically, it is highly accomplished: intricate enjambment, complex images, neologisms.

•J. Hrabák, A. Škarka and V. Vážný (Eds), *Dvě legendy z doby Karlovy* (Prague, 1959). Extract trans. in W. Schamschula (Ed.), *An Anthology of Czech Literature. 1st Period* (Frankfurt on Main, 1991), pp. 103–16.
G. M. Cummings, *The Language of the Old Czech 'Legenda o svaté Kateřině'* (Munich, 1975); R. B. Pynsent, 'The Baroque Continuum in Czech Literature', *SEER*, 62 (1984), pp. 321–43; A. Thomas, *The Czech Chivalric Romances Vévoda Arnošt and Lavryn in their Literary Context* (Göppingen, 1989). RBP

Hungarian Prose versions of this popular legend appear in 16th-century codices from 1519 onwards. But the most complete account, in the Dominican Érsekújvár Codex of 1530–1, is in verse. The poem of 4,064 lines is divided into three sections: nativity, conversion and suffering. No single Latin source has been discovered. The unknown translator had an admirable command of Hungarian prosody; the lines flow as naturally as good folk poetry, and the narrative is enlivened with spirited dialogue.

•C. Horváth (Ed.), *Régi magyar költők tára*, vol. I. (2nd ed., Budapest, 1922). GFC

ST MARGARET OF HUNGARY – Hungarian Of the main saints of the House of Árpád, Margaret (1242–71) is the best known. The daughter of King Béla IV, she spent most of her ascetic life in the Dominican convent on the island in the Danube now named after her. The original Latin legend was written by her spiritual director Marcellus shortly after her death. To this description of her life were added an account of her miracles and depositions of witnesses taken in 1276 for the process of beatification. She was canonised in 1943. The complete Latin text was faithfully translated into Hungarian, probably during the early 14th century; the version copied by the Dominican nun Lea Ráskai in 1510 was the earliest to appear in print (*Vita S. Elisabethae viduae nec non B. Margaretae virginis*, 1770) and gained wide popularity. The legend of Margaret has inspired many poets, including ADY, and novels, of which Gárdonyi's (1863–1922) *Isten rabjai* (Prisoners of God, 1908) is best-known.

•Volf György (Ed.), *Nyelvenléktár*, vol. VIII (Budapest, 1879).   GFC

ST PROCOPIUS – Czech The lively 1,084-line, low-style verse legend of St Procopius, known as *Legenda o svatém Prokopu* (1350s), is based on the so-called *Vita sancti Procopii major*, which had been composed a decade or so before. This source has fundamentally the same ideological content as the Czech: a positive attitude to the poor, patriotism, praise for the Church Slavonic Mass. Nevertheless the Czech author changes the emphasis, particularly in his account of the fulfilling of Procopius's prophecy concerning the expulsion of the Slavonic monks from Sázava; he ends the work with the monks' return instead of continuing, like the *Vita major*, with a long account of the saint's posthumous miracles. The author deliberately perverts history by having Procopius appear, not as the aristocrat he was, but as a rugged Czech peasant, whose muscular arms wield his staff to great effect against Germans and devils. The expression of xenophobic patriotism is similar to that of 'DALIMIL' though the *Legenda* author's hatred is directed mainly at German monks, and foreign merchants and minstrels who come to swindle the Czechs. The legend is racily narrated in almost colloquial language.

•J. Hrabák, A. Škarka and V. Vážný (Eds), *Dvě legendy z doby Karlovy* (Prague, 1959).
V. Vondrák, *Zur Würdigung der altslowanischen Wenzelslegende und der Legende vom heiligen Prokop* (Prague, 1892).   RBP

ORAL POETRY

FINNISH After the publication of LÖNNROT's *Kalevala* (1835, 1849) the collection of traditional Finnish oral poetry in the so-called *Kalevala* metre (non-strophic trochaic tetrameters) acquired a national urgency. The material deposited in the archive of the Finnish Literature Society (Helsinki) today numbers some 86,800 poems, songs, spells, riddles and proverbs comprising more than two million lines and embracing epic, lyric, incantations, festive poetry, cradle songs, and occasional verse. Archives in Estonia and the Karelian Republic also have large holdings of *Kalevala*-metre poetry. Similarity of themes, motifs and topoi suggest a common origin of at least 2,000 years ago. Analysis of variants and their distribution indicates later influence from Scandinavian and Slavonic sources. The tradition, which died out in Finland after the Reformation, survived longest in Russian Orthodox Karelia and Ingria where W European culture scarcely penetrated. Although in more recent times singers composed new poems in performance, the characteristic fixity of *Kalevala*-metre poetry suggests a primary function as the oral accompaniment to ritual. The *Kalevala* was the first of many artistic works to draw on oral poetry. Traditional poetry was a rich source of inspiration for artists, musicians and painters during the fin-de-siècle neo-Romantic period and there have been several revivals of interest since then. In the late 19th century, the scholarly study of Finnish oral poetry soon embraced the whole of oral culture and led to the creation of the influential Finnish school of folklore research.

●J. Hautala, *Finnish Folklore Research 1828–1918* (Helsinki, 1969); M. Kuusi, K. Bosley and M. A. Branch (Eds), *Finnish Folk Poetry: Epic* (Helsinki, London, Montreal, 1977); L. Honko, S. Timonen, M. Branch and K. Bosley (Eds), *The Great Bear. A Thematic Anthology of Oral Poetry in the Finno-Ugrian Languages* (Helsinki, 1992).   MAB

GEORGIAN Georgia's folk poetry is, next to its polyphonic folk-music, its culture's richest asset. Collected only from the middle of the last century, it was alive until WWI destroyed its ethnic basis. Its core is the mythological and heroic songs of the mountain tribes (above all, Khevsurs, Tush, Pshav), sharing much with other indigenous Caucasian cultures (Circassian, Chechen etc.), with a Hellenic pantheon of gods and a grim view of life bounded by *shaveti* ('the black land' of hell). Although Christianised in the 5th century, the mountain tribes reverted to pagan beliefs after the Georgian unitary state crumbled, and thus wove Christian, Muslim and pagan into a rich folk-culture. Heroic songs probably stem from funeral laments, *khmit nat'irali* ('vocal weeping'), in which a dead hero recounts his fate in the first person through a reciter (*mtkmeli*). Pre-Christian gods are confused with post-Christian warriors: on the one hand 'Khogay's Mindia was dying, The sun went red, faded. The sky thundered, the earth rumbled . . .'; on the other, 'Mindia killed twelve, Stopped, threw down his sword. The heathen dogs didn't hesitate, They felled the dead man with a salvo.' Historical songs confuse the real Queen Tamar with a goddess of rain and dew. Much of the imagery – of snakes, cats, golden chains, oaks – is also found in Indo-European and Asiatic mythopoeia, but the Georgian heroic epic (or debris of epic) is especially grim: 'Death said, "I shall pour an army of chosen men into Elysium (*suleti*)." ' Apart from memorial function (women mourners were often the folk poets), folk poetry sustained the dead, offering them *shendoba* (grace or forgiveness) to parallel the food left on the graves: 'Those who have nobody to mention them sit with their backs to the table.' The supernatural plays a lesser role, however, in Georgian than in neighbouring folk poetry: only Torghva with his invincible 'floating armour', or the werewolf-like *gveleshap'i* of Acharian songs brings in an aura of magic. The influence of chivalry, so strong in Persian as in W European romance, is strikingly absent from the Georgian hero, who rarely bothers to rescue heroines. In later times, folk poetry had political overtones: it argued against tribal disunity; or it justified the bandit (e.g. *Arsenas leksi*, 'The Poem of Arsena', who is known by the term once used for knight, *k'ai q'ma*, 'brave young man'). Heroic folk poetry resisted the overlord, Turk or Russian: 'Why don't they give you, the killer of

Q'ara-Namaz, a medal? If a stinking Russian had killed him, They'd have made him an officer.' Similar poetry in the same metre (8 syllable, ABAB rhymes) celebrates tragic hunters (the best known is *Leksi vepxvisa da moq'-misa*, 'The poem of the youth and the panther', which ends with the youth's mother visiting the panther's for mutual consolation). The last Khevsur poems were about their swordsmen attacking German machine-gunners in 1915, but as the folk poet said, 'Here the whole Arkhot'i valley died.' Warriors gave way to shepherds and recent folk poetry is self-deprecating: 'I do not long for the valley, Nor to sleep and lie with beautiful women. I prefer the red-eyed maiden ewe And tugging at her forelock.'

Western Georgia, with its richer musical tradition, has much more lyrical folk poetry, with more love songs, lullabies, ritual and agricultural texts. Overall, the Georgian folk tradition has been penetrated by 'sunken' literature of medieval times, not only by indigenous Caucasian stories, such as the Nart epic or Amirani myth (see ROMANCE), but by a wealth of Greek and Oriental fable, which has created a rich genre of *zghap'ari* (fairy tale). Folk poetry, far more laconic and elliptic than the rhetorical and exuberant written culture, has in its turn enriched literature, particularly the poetry of VAZHA PSHAVELA and his successors. Georgian hymns, it can be argued, not only took their polyphony from folk music, but transferred their imagery of the Cross as the vine, the Virgin as the newly planted poplar, from pagan folk poetry.

•D. Rayfield, 'Georgian Poetry' [introduction and transl.], in K. Bosley (Ed.), *The Elek Book of Oriental Verse* (London, 1979), pp. 182–90.

G. Charachidze, *Le Système religieux de la Géorgie païenne* (Paris, 1968); D. Rayfield, 'The Heroic Ethos in Georgian and Russian Folk Poetry', *SEER*, LVI (1978), 4, pp. 505–21; 'The Soldier's Lament: Folk Poetry in the Russian Empire 1914–1917', *SEER*, 66 (1988), 1, pp. 66–90.   DR

GREEK The impetus to record and preserve Greek oral poetry seems to have derived in part from early 19th-century Philhellenism, in part from the Romantic interest in folk lyric as a phenomenon. As early as 1815 Goethe was commenting favourably on Greek folk-songs translated by Baron von Haxthausen. Claude Fauriel, in 1824, published the first substantial collection of such poems, and in his preface put forward the argument which was to find favour with the nationalist aspirations of the Greeks themselves, that is, the importance of the character and customs of the contemporary Greeks as descendants of their illustrious Ancient forebears. The first major Greek collections appeared in Corfu, and were both produced by members of the circle of SOLOMOS: Antonios Manousos (1829–1903) and Spiridon Zambelios (1815–81). In the second half of the century a large number of collections of songs from specific regions appeared. Then in 1860 the publication of a proper scholarly edition by the German Alexander Passow began to put the study of the material on a more academic footing. It was, however, Nikolaos Politis (1852–1921) who, as part of his scheme to establish *laografia* (folk studies) as a formal science, started to collect and collate the material already published, to establish a taxonomy of folk-songs and to comment on them. Politis was motivated by a deep commitment to Greek nationalism, which led him to stress historical continuity and cultural roots at the expense of a broader view of the place of Greek folk-songs in Balkan culture generally. Although there was reaction as early as 1929 against the highly literary way in which Politis treated the establishing of the 'original' text of the songs, many of his patriotic assumptions have only been questioned very recently. The songs have traditionally been divided into four groups. The first, historical songs, can be subdivided into (a) songs which refer to specific events (e.g. the fall of Constantinople); (b) Akritic songs, which derive from the life and legends of frontiersmen in the 8th–11th century Byzantine Empire; and (c) Klephtic songs, which deal with the adventurers of the 18th and early 19th-century Klephts (in origin: bandits) and *armatoli* (in origin: local militia recruited to suppress the bandits) – the two terms became synonymous as indicating bands of young heroes who constituted a resistance movement against the Turks. The second group, Παραλογές, contains narrative songs of a magical nature: fairy tales, of a sort. The third group contains domestic songs: lullabies, wedding songs and laments. With these can be grouped songs of exile. The last group contains love songs. These groups may serve to disguise, to some extent, the thematic and stylistic overlap between different types of song. Fatalism, the figure of Death, birds which speak, the cycle of the seasons, the qualities to be praised in men and women remain the same, as do stylised images based in Nature, verbal formulae, and structural uses of repetition and balance. 15-syllable metre is also a constant feature. At the same time different types of song, especially in regional variation, are invaluable sources of information on the customs and values of rural Greece over a long period. The importance of the folk-songs in the development of 19th-century demotic poetry cannot be overemphasised. The poets of the Ionian Islands, particularly SOLOMOS and VALAORITIS, studied their language carefully, and they were an equally important linguistic model for the poets of the 1880s.

●N. Watts, *The Greek Folk Songs* (Bristol, 1988).   CFR

THE EPIC

CHRONICLE OF THE MOREA

(Greek) Χρονικό του Μορέως is a poem in over 9,000 15-syllable lines, written c. 1300, recounting the conquest of the Peloponnese by the French knights, and the founding and subsequent history of the principality of the Morea (the medieval name for the Peloponnese). Though the poem is in Greek, its author's sympathies are entirely Frankish. It begins with an account of the Fourth Crusade and the capture of Constantinople which, in outline, concurs with the account in the French chronicle of Villehardouin. The major section of the poem is devoted to the reigns of the first three princes of the Morea, Guillaume de Champlitte (1205–9), Geoffroy I de Villehardouin (1210–18) and Geoffroy II (1218–45), and to that of the chronicler's hero, Guillaume de Villehardouin (1245–78). The narrative stops around 1292.

The poem is a mixture of historical document, legend and epic. The events are interspersed with descriptions of feudal manners and details of popular life which would not be out of place in a chivalric romance, and there is a plentiful use of rhetorically crafted direct speech to give colour to the characterisation. Versions of the Chronicle are also preserved in French, Italian and Aragonese, but the Greek version seems independent of the others. The language of the surviving MSS is not consistent and contains large numbers of loan-words.

•J. Schmitt, *The Chronicle of the Morea* (London, 1904).   CFR

DIYENIS AKRITIS (Greek) This heroic narrative in 15-syllable verse was rediscovered in 1869. There are six extant MSS, of which two, known as E and G (see editions, below), are thought to be the best witnesses. The oldest piece of extended writing in a form of Modern Greek, its physical setting is the frontier between the Christian (i.e. Byzantine) and Muslim worlds. Its temporal setting reflects conditions existing at different periods between the 9th and beginning of the 11th centuries. It is constructed on the same loose bipartite structure as the early Western epics. The first part (about one third of the poem) contains the story of Diyenis's parents and the birth of the hero. This section is in essence an epic of Christianisation, and its themes and values are similar to those of the *chansons de geste*. The second part tells of the hero's childhood, later exploits and early death, and is closer to the conventions of romance. The sources seem to have been in part oral (traditional narratives of life on the Eastern frontier), in part religious (references to the OT and use of standard hagiographic motifs), in part literary. Elements of love rhetoric and formal description derive from the traditions of the Hellenistic romance: Diyenis seems in some respects modelled on the hero of the ALEXANDER ROMANCE. There is also some (superficial) reference to Homer. The poem was probably constructed from orally transmitted material by a writer attempting to create a consciously literary structure. The latest theory of the date, place and purpose of composition is that it was written in Constantinople at a period after the disastrous defeat of the Byzantines by the Seljüks at Manzikert in 1071, as a deliberate attempt to preserve, nostalgically, the traditions of the lost Anatolian lands, and to assert patriotically the superiority of that lost culture. Consciously or not, the poet contrives, by blending the traditions of the violent world of the frontier with the moral values of the romance, to suggest a movement from primitive machismo to a more sophisticated world in which heroic deeds are justified by the love of a woman.

•(E) D. Ricks, *Byzantine Heroic Poetry* (Bristol, 1990) (contains introduction, text and translation); (G)
J. Mavrogordato, *Digenis Akrites*, edited with an introduction, translation and commentary (Oxford, 1956).
R. Beaton, *The Medieval Greek Romance* (Cambridge, 1989), pp. 27–48.   CFR

THE SASUN CYCLE (Armenian) The Armenian epic narrative known under various titles, *Sasna p'ahlevanner* (Sasun's strongmen), *Sasna tun* (The house of Sasun), *Sasuntsi Davit* (David of Sasun) or *Mheri Duṙ* (Mher's door), *Sasna dsṙer* (Daredevils of Sasun), had a long period of gestation and reached its present form probably in the 12th century; parts of the work, however, go back to biblical times. It was first discovered and transcribed by Bishop Garegin Srvanjtean (1840–92) in 1873 and published a year later in the dialect of Mushin Constantinople as *Grots u brots ew Sasuntsi Davit' kam Mheri dur*. The second variant transcribed by Manouk Abeghyan was published as *Davit' ev Mher* (David and M.) in 1889. By 1980 over 160 variants had been recorded and transcribed, of which 70 have been published. Manouk Abeghyan and K. Melik'-Ohanjanyan collected and published 50 of these variants in three scholarly volumes (Yerevan, 1936, 1944, 1941) under the general title *Sasna Tsrer*. In 1939, on the occasion of the 'thousandth anniversary' of the epic, variants were collated in a popular edition under the title *Sasuntsi Davit* (David of Sasun). As the texts are in various dialects, which present many difficulties to the modern reader, the story was reworded and a fairly uniform style comprehensible to E Armenians was adopted. Most of the variants are in W Armenian dialects; Sasun itself is in W Armenia (E Turkey today). The entire cycle consists of four 'branches' which tell the story of four generations of heroes of royal descent, Sanasar and Baghdasar, Mher the Elder, David of Sasun, and Mher the Younger. The central idea is that the Armenian experience can be meaningful in an heroic environment only if the charisma of the clan is preserved, free from contamination or dispersal among enemies. Clan charisma should be seen in the context of displaced myth: their genetically transmitted charisma gives the Sasun heroes their superhuman strength. The experience of the Sasun heroes is displaced myth, but Armenian historical experience merges with the mythic in the person of Mher the Younger: heirless, he cannot transmit the clan charisma to subsequent generations, and so the charisma is set apart from history. But immortal, he preserves the charisma in himself and offers hope of a return to an heroic age, and thus the heroism continues to exist on the edge of history. The theme of the epic, as of the people it portrays, is freedom, freedom as the national goal, the Armenian dream. The Armenian 'daredevils' fiercely resist any encroachment on their freedom; in Sasun the archvillain is the tax collector, who represents the King, and the King is not satisfied with gold and silver; he must also have beautiful maidens. By refusing to pay taxes the Sasunians assert their independence and their dignity as free men. The heroes who defeat kings, Sanasar, David, and the two Mhers, have no desire for a royal crown, are content to live as peasants. They fight victorious wars, but do not covet the possessions of other peoples, and they fight only when attacked, when the 'enemy is fully awake' and are never aggressive towards women and children. It is a genuine popular epic. When the sword of Sasun strikes, it strikes for freedom, freedom for all.

●Leon Surmelian, *Daredevils of Sassoun: The Armenian National Epic* (London, 1964); A. K. Shalian (Ed. and trans.), *David of Sassoun. The Armenian Epic in Four Cycles* (Ohio, 1964).
E. R. Anderson, 'The Armenian Sasun Cycle: Folk Epic Structure and Theme', *REA*, XIII (1978–9), pp. 175–86;
E. Gulbenkian, 'The Attitude to War in "The Epic of Sasun" ', *Folklore*, 95 (1984), p. xxx; Chake Der Melkonian-

Minassian, *Epopée populaire arménienne David de Sasoun: Etude critique.* (Montreal, 1972), 'The Sacred World of Sasna Tsrer: Steps Toward an Understanding', *Journal of the Society for Armenian Studies*, 2 (1985–6), pp. 107–39.   VN

THE CHRONICLE

GEORGIAN The fundamental chronicles of Georgia, its historiography, have an origin which parallels Georgia's hagiography: Georgia's prehistory and paganism end at the same time, traditionally 337. *Moktsevay Kartlisay* (The conversion of Georgia, before 973, the date of the Shat'berdi codex) was written shortly after the split between the Armenian and Georgian Churches to establish a politically correct chronicle of Georgia's Christianisation. The account of the conversion, the *Moktsevay Kartlisay* proper, is the first and shorter half of a document which is largely devoted to a life of St Nino. 'The conversion' itself and its variant manuscripts differ on Nino's dates of arrival and death, anything between 310–24 and 358–73; the work is collective and the authors and scribes unknown. It has great value for its description of the pagan pantheon and its use of lost Greek and Georgian written sources, but must be treated as fiction, not just as history. Some of 'The conversion' is incorporated into Georgia's fundamental chronicles, known as *Kartlis tskhovreba* (The life of Kartli); their basic materials are probably mid-11th century (though some source materials may be very archaic) and include Leont'i ᴍroveli's *Tskhovreba kartvelta mepeta* (The life of the Georgian kings, c. 1066), ᴊuansher's *Tskhovreba da mokalakoba Vakht'ang Gorgaslisa* (The life and public activity of V. Gorgasali, c. 1080), an anonymous life of ᴅᴀᴠɪᴛ ᴀɢʜᴍᴀsʜᴇɴᴇʙᴇʟɪ (King Davit IV) and Sumbat Davitisdze's *Tskhovreba da uts'q'eba Bagrat'onianta* (The lives of and known facts about the Bagrationis). The section of 'The life of Kartli' by the author known as 'the Annalist' (*zhamta aghmts'ereli*) is a unique account of Georgia under Mongolian rule. 'The life of Kartli' was expanded with the years, until the collapse of Georgia as a unitary state in the mid-15th century, resulting in collations such as the 'Queen Mariam' chronicle. It was updated in the 17th century with only skeletal lists of events. In the 1710s King ᴠᴀᴋʜᴛ'ᴀɴɢ ᴠɪ set up a commission which edited and standardised the whole chronicle. A large part of Vakhusht'i Bagrat'ioni's (1696–1757; illegitimate son of ᴠᴀᴋʜᴛ'ᴀɴɢ ᴠɪ) massive historical, geographical, cartographical and ethnographic *Aghts'era sameposa Sakartvelosa* (Description of the Georgian kingdom, 1745) was a rigorous critical revision of 'The life of Kartli', to which he added a totally new version of history since the 15th century. Davit Bagrat'ioni (1767–1819) also relied on 'The life of Kartli' for much of his Russian-language 'History of Georgia'; he had recorded in Georgian the period from the 18th century to 1819.

The Georgian renascence was characterised by versification of the chronicles' material, with little revision of content. The *Shah-Navaziani*, c. 1665, a life, largely in verse, of Vakht'ang V (Shah Navaz), is attributed to a georgianised Armenian, Peshangi Pashvibert'q'adze (or Mkhitarishvili). For the fine RUSTAVELIan poem *Teimuraziani* (Life of TEIMURAZ I, before 1663), see King ARCHIL. The verse *Didmouraviani* (Life of the Great Governor [Giorgi Saak'adze], c. 1685) by Ioseb Tbileli (d. 1688), Bishop of Tbilisi, ends in a jeremiad on inhumanity (but does not mention Saak'adze's death). The flaws of the Georgian chronicles are their virtues: they are often the historian's sole source of information for a period whose documentation was destroyed by the Mongols and Persians. See also

Kings ARCHIL, TEIMURAZ I, TEIMU-RAZ II, VAKHT'ANG VI, Prince IOANE BAGRAT'IONI, Davit GURAMISHVILI.
●S. Q'aukhchishvili (Ed.), *Kartlis tskhovreba, Vakhusht'is Aghts'era . . .*, 4 vols (Tbilisi, 1973). Transl. into English: K. Vivian, *The Georgian Chronicle: The Period of Giorgi Lasha* (Amsterdam, 1991), French: F. Brosset, *Histoire de la Géorgie depuis l'Antiquité jusqu'au XIXᵉ siècle* (St Petersburg, 1856).
R. Baramidze, 'Die Anfänge der georgischen Literatur', *Georgica* (Jena), 10, 1987, pp. 39–43; W. E. D. Allen, *A History of the Georgian People* (London, 1932).   DR

LYRIC VERSE
(MEDIEVAL AND EARLY MODERN)

CZECH Old Czech lyric poems, of which about a hundred have survived, can be only roughly divided into the religious and secular, for the borderline is not always clear. Numerically, the two types are represented almost equally. The earliest complete text is the song *Hospodine pomiluj ny* (Lord, have mercy on us), probably composed in the second half of the 10th century when the Slavonic liturgy existed in Bohemia side by side with the Latin; according to tradition it was composed by St Adalbert (c. 957–97). The first two or three stanzas of the song *Svatý Václave* (St Wenceslas) date probably from the end of the 12th century while *Ostrovská píseň* (The song of Ostrov), showing some connections with Latin poetry both in form and theological speculation, appears first in a MS from the end of the 13th century. Much more sophisticated is *Kunhutina modlitba* (see DEVOTIONAL VERSE) preserved in a MS from the beginning of the

14th century; from then on religious verse flourished without interruption and had a decisive influence on the formation of Polish religious poetry. The greater part of secular lyric verse consists of love poems amongst which the most accomplished are those manifesting features of the courtly-love code. There are some German, French, Italian and even Provençal elements, e.g. the idea of erotic service as the relationship of a vassal to his suzerain, the use of the masculine form lord for the lady, her anonymity, the figures of the gossip and guard, the identification of love with suffering and, finally, the fusing of courtly convention with the Marian Cult. But in spite of this the Czech love lyric does not reproduce the courtly model in its traditional form and in some cases introduces apparent oral-tradition elements and irony. It may be presumed that the conventional features of the courtly-love lyric, by then obsolete, were combined with those of the contemporary German love lyric. With the exception of *Závišova píseň* (The song of Záviš, c. 1410), which is somewhat dependent on Frauenlob, the authors are anonymous and precise dating is impossible. A different type of erotic verse is constituted by obscene student songs describing the sexual act with inventive graphic metaphors. Satirical verse is also of student origin, mocking peasants, women and Hussite zealots, as are the witty and usually obscene begging songs. Reflective poems, with the usual themes of death, the fear of God and the depravity of the world, are, naturally, written in a higher style.

●Ten poems translated in A. French (Ed.), *Czech Poetry*, vol. I (Ann Arbor, Mich., 1973); ten poems in W. Schamschula (Ed.), *An Anthology of Czech Literature. 1st Period* (Frankfurt on Main, 1991).   KB

VIRÁGÉNEK **(Hungarian)** *Virágének*, 'Flower-song', is the name given to a type of anonymous love lyric that flourished in Hungary from the 16th to the 18th century. In it the beloved, female or male, is addressed as 'flower' or given the name of a particular flower; birds are also used in this way. Condemned by the Churches as immoral, such songs were passed on either orally or in manuscript and consequently display countless variants. They began to appear in print in the late 18th century in chapbooks. They vary in length, metre and content. Some are refined Baroque confessions of love by poets versed in the Classics while others are bawdy soldiers' songs. By the 18th century the influence of Italian dance-rhythms becomes obvious; later, German sentimental love lyric also colours it. The style was perpetuated by imitators of PETŐFI in the 19th century.

●B. Stoll (Ed.), *Virágénekek és mulatónóták, XVII–XVIII. század* (Budapest, 1956).   GFC

POLISH Since Poland adopted Christianity in its Western version in 966, Latin served as the language of the educated, and therefore also the language of most written texts, for at least three centuries. One has to assume that, regardless of lack of written evidence, an oral tradition in the vernacular existed at this early stage. This is indirectly corroborated by the fact that the first recorded poem in Polish is the sophisticated 'Bogurodzica' (Mother of God), a hymn from the 13th century preserved in a 15th-century manuscript; it consists of two stanzas with a highly complex verse structure and use of parallelism; such refined literary products are unlikely to have emerged in a cultural void. What has been preserved from the late medieval period (14th–15th centuries) consists mostly of poems elaborating religious topics. These beginnings of devotional poetry in the vernacular are usually adaptations from the Latin. In this period there are no artistically convincing examples of narrative verse; on the other hand, the devotional lyric is represented by quite accomplished poems such as Lent songs, Easter hymns, Christmas carols or hymns to the Virgin Mary. Some of these poems are innovative. The planctus 'Żale Matki Boskiej pod Krzyżem' (Lament of the Mother of God at the foot of the Cross, c. 1450), for instance, forsakes the allegorical commonplaces of its epoch for an individualised point of view and emotional intensity. 'Pieśń o Męce Pańskiej' (Passion song) is an early attempt at syllabic regularity, with its 13-syllable line with a caesura after the 7th syllable. As a rule, however, the verse structure of Polish medieval poetry was based on a loose system of relative syllabism, with uneven lines comporting with grammatical clauses and approximate rhymes. Polish secular poetry of the Middle Ages was far less abundant than its devotional counterpart. Several works or fragments are extant, written for various purposes and with varying artistic results. Some of these poems were supposed to serve as mnemonic devices; others, like a fragment known as 'A satire on lazy peasants', represented the didactic and satirical modes; there are a few timid explorations of the erotic as well. The most interesting secular poem of the period is the 15th-century 'Rozmowa Mistrza ze Śmiercią' (Conversation of a master with Death, also known as *De morte prologus*). A variation on the *memento mori* theme, it strikes the reader with its vivid, if slightly macabre, imagery and humour.

●Selected poems in B. Carpenter (Ed.), *Monumenta Polonica* (Ann Arbor, 1989).   StB

DEVOTIONAL LYRIC

CUNIGUNDA'S PRAYER

(Czech) The late 13th-century eucharistic poem known as 'Kunhuta's/Cunigunda's prayer' (*Kunhutina modlitba*) is the first piece of vital religious philosophy to be expressed in Czech. It may be slightly influenced by Thomas Aquinas's *Lauda, Sion, Salvatorem*. In octosyllabic monorhyming quatrains, it explains the doctrine concerning the Communion Bread. After an apostrophe to Christ and a thanksgiving for the gift of the Sacrament, stanzas 7–22 give an explication in imaginative, clear images of the Eucharist and the doctrine of Transubstantiation. It is a mystical poem of exquisite acoustic qualities and is technically flawless.

●H. Kunstmann (Ed.), *Denkmäler der alttschechischen Literatur von ihren Anfängen bis zur Hussitenbewegung* (Berlin, 1955). Translation in W. Schamschula (Ed.), *An Anthology of Czech Literature. 1st Period* (Frankfurt on Main, 1991), pp. 63–8.   RBP

NARRATIVE AND POLITICAL VERSE

BAD FORTUNE AND GOOD FORTUNE

(Greek) Λόγος Παρηγορητικός περί Δυστυχίας και Ευτυχίας (Consolation concerning Bad Fortune and Good Fortune), an allegorical poem, is preserved in two MSS, the older of which has been dated to the period 1354–74. It is a narrative of 756 lines, beginning with a prologue which promises a moral tale. The main narrative is in the first person. The anonymous speaker sets out to find the Castle of Bad Fortune from which all his troubles emanate. The personified figure of Time is initially unhelpful, but eventually persuades the Queen of Bad Fortune to grant the unfortunate man a signed and sealed charter releasing him from her service, and to send him to her sister, the beautiful Queen of Good Fortune. The text displays the conventions of the contemporary romances: allegorical castles, beautiful heroines and extended passages of elaborate description.   CFR

KURUC SONGS (Hungarian)
This name is given in Hungarian to a very large corpus of mainly anonymous verse written and circulated during the rebellions of Imre Thököly and Ferenc RÁKÓCZI II from the late 17th century to the early 18th century. The rebel forces were known as *kuruc* and the imperial troops as *labanc*. The term is a misnomer, for both sides wrote these songs; they appear in Hungarian, Latin, German and slovacised Czech, and there is also a Roumanian-Hungarian macaronic example. They are political in content, often describing battles and eulogising leaders; they also pour scorn on the enemy and lament the fate of those forced into exile. The authors include known poets such as István Koháry (1649–1731) and MIKES; others, like Erzsébet Révay (dates unknown), are known only for their few poems in this genre. They represent a wide stylistic range; some are clearly the work of well-educated authors, so that elegiac couplets and sapphics are found alongside the traditional Hungarian alexandrine and rustic dance-rhythms. Their vocabulary varies accordingly.   The *Rákóczi-nóta* (Rákóczi song, before 1735), by an unknown but skilled poet, became the most popular 18th-century verse; banned by the Austrians and circulated in manuscript, it was virtually a national anthem and was sung during subsequent revolutions.

●Selection in T. Klaniczay (Ed.), *Old Hungarian Literary Reader* (Budapest, 1985) and W. Kirkconnell (Ed.), *Hungarian Helicon* (Calgary, 1985).
                                        GFC

THE ROMANCE

GEORGIAN ROMANCE By the 11th century translations of Greek romance (e.g. Pseudo-Callisthenes) and Persian romance, such as Firdausi's *Shah-Nemeh*, existed in Georgian, although from that time they are known only by quotations. The *Balavariani* (The story of Balahvar and Iodasaph [Barlam and Josaphat]) is believed to derive from a Christian, perhaps Syriac, version of the Arabic 'Book of Bilauhar and Budasaf'. (Originally it was an Indian Life of Buddha.) The 1956 discovery of a Jerusalem manuscript c. 1070 has made the Georgian version of this Indian romance, adapted for hagiographical purposes, a missing link between the Oriental and Greek worlds. (The *Balavariani* spawned new versions in Georgian, the last being an 18th-century versification recently discovered in a yew tree in Rach'a.) The first relatively original Georgian romance, however, is *Amiran-Darejaniani* (The story of Amiran and Darejan, c. 1150), attributed to Mose Khoneli: it was composed in twelve prose sections (*k'arebi*, 'gates'), whose order is often transposed in manuscripts. It begins with an introduction in which King Absalom is haunted by a portrait of unnamed heroes and seeks out the last survivor depicted, Savarsamidze, who then becomes one of the main narrators of the romance. Thus the painting of Amiran son of Darejan and his titanic exploits is expanded into a nest of tales. Each section, or 'gate', is an episode told to King Absalom about Amiran and his followers Savarsamidze, Nosar and Badri on their elaborate and violent missions. Amiran is last seen, 120 years old, defeating a hero half his age. The story's universality, a non-Muslim ambience and many heroes' Georgian names presuppose *Amiran-Darejaniani* to be no translation. Nicolas Marr, more plausibly, believed the work to be adapted from Persian folklore or a lost Persian text. To judge by its influence on RUSTAVELI, it dates from the mid-12th century. More than any other medieval work, it seeped into mountain folklore among the Khevsurs and also into Svan (the archaic cousin of Georgian), as fairy tale or legend. Over the five following centuries *Amiran-Darejaniani* was versified several times in the style of RUSTAVELI's 'The knight in the panther's skin'.

Fakhruddin Gurgan's 1048 Persian version (8,000 lines) of the lost Sassanid story tale of 'Vis-o-Ramin', or 'Vis and Ramin', gave rise to the Georgian *Visramiani*, its first translation, by an unknown hand, in the mid-12th century. The sensual passion of the original (an E *Tristan und Isolde* with a plot based on incest, internecine feuds, exile and unity in death) is maintained in the Georgian. The work was immensely popular and, shorn of the taboo themes, elements of its plot seep into RUSTAVELI's 'The knight in the panther's skin'. It was versified by King ARCHIL, but more prudish Georgian versifiers disapproved of the romance: an anonymous verse of 1769 warns, 'Any man who believes in God, let him not look at the *Visramiani*. It will darken his daylight, he will see its faults in hell.'

For the zenith of Georgian romance, the *Vepkhist'q'aosani* (The knight in the panther's skin), see RUSTAVELI. From the same time, the end of the 12th century, we have a collection of eleven odes and one elegy (possibly by one author) praising, often deifying Tamar, *Tamariani*. It is attributed to a poet from the Khevi area in the high Caucasus, known only as Chakhrukhadze (speculatively identified with RUSTAVELI), and their twenty-syllable metre is called *chakhrukhauli*. The *Tamariani*'s popularity is implied by the number of imitations. Another eulogy in this metre may also be attributed to the shadowy Chakhrukhadze: a text once known by the cryptonym *Abdulmesia* ('Slave of the Messiah') and dated 1210–12, it borrows from the NT, the liturgy, hagiography and chronicles to praise both King DAVIT IV)'the Builder') and his great-granddaughter Tamar.

Following Queen Tamar's death, the Georgian classical romance fell into decline. RUSTAVELI's techniques and attitudes persisted, but the level of invention fell to imitating the *Shah-Nameh* or forging sequels to RUSTAVELI. (King ARCHIL of Imeretia [c. 1670] names at least one of the pseudo-Rustavelis as the bibliophile Nanucha or Manuchar Tsitsishvili [before 1620–58].) In the 16th and 17th centuries T'ariel and Avtandil die, leave testaments, and their children grow up into new pairs of lovers. The last story, attributed to Kaikhosro Omanishvili-Choloq'ashvili c. 1620, forms a poem almost as long as RUSTAVELI's: the *Omainiani* (The story of Omain). Omain is a *Wunderkind*, even greater than his grandfather T'ariel, while his quests and adventures cover similar ground to his maternal grandfather Avtandil's. Such derivative romances persisted until the 19th century (see also RUSUDANIANI) the last being the *Dilariani* (The story of King Dilar the Mighty) by P'et're Laradze (1770–1837). Laradze's claims that he had merely restored the lost *Dilariani* by Sargis Tmogveli (fl. 1180s) are unconvincing. Laradze's brilliant military career (which included retrieving King TEIMURAZ II from Persia) led to the loss of most of his manuscripts: in exile in Russia, where he died, he could only reconstruct part of his *Dilariani*'s 2,000 stanzas before they were borrowed, misappropriated and lost by the infamous IOANE BAGRAT'IONI. The *Dilariani* is also a much underestimated pastiche of *Amiran-Darejaniani*: Laradze had a more tenuous relationship to Tmogveli and other sources than Tennyson had to Malory. Falsification was as essential to the Georgian 18th-century 'renascence' as to the Czech Revival: links had to be forged to a lost medieval glory.

●D. M. Lang, *The Balavariani* (London, 1966); R. H. Stevenson, *Amiran-Darejaniani* (Oxford, 1958); O. Wardrop, *Visramiani* (London, 1914). M. Tarchnishvili, *Geschichte der kirchlichen georgischen Literatur*, (Vatican, 1955). P. Dronke, 'Georgia' in *Medieval Latin & the Rise of the European Love Lyric*, vol 1 (Oxford, 1968).   DR

ACHILLES (Greek) Διήγησις του Αχιλλέως (The tale of Achilles) is preserved in three versions, the fullest of which (approx. 1,760 lines) is a Naples MS dated to the third quarter of the 15th century. This appears to contain the substance of the original poem, although the ending seems to have been lost. The romance takes little from the Classical legends of Achilles. It opens with an invocation to the power of Eros, continues with

tales of the prowess of the hero as child and adolescent, and then focuses on an incident in which he besieges a castle, falls in love with the daughter of the defeated king, abducts her and marries her. After six years' happiness, the girl falls ill and dies, and the romance closes on the hero's grief. Some of the motifs and their handling are reminiscent of DIYENIS AKRITIS, but the roughly equipollent three thematic sections (war, love, synthesis of war and love) present a more sophisticated structure.

●D. Hesseling (Ed.), *L'Achilléide byzantine, avec une introduction, des observations et un index* (Amsterdam, 1919).   CFR

ALEXANDER ROMANCE – Armenian The translation of Pseudo-Callisthenes is the first secular work rendered into Armenian and scholars support the widely held hypothesis that it was translated into Armenian by MOVSES KHORENATSI, who in his 'History of the Armenians' freely borrows from it, adapting phrases, descriptions, and whole episodes. The Armenian version is of prime importance in the reconstruction of the original text, as it appears to be an extraordinarily accurate rendering of the oldest MS tradition. Since, however, the oldest surviving Armenian MS of Pseudo-Callisthenes dates from c. 14th century, it is natural that the epic had undergone changes. The essentially pagan spirit of the Alexander text contributed to the desire among the monastic scribes to produce new redactions. From this point the development of the romance in Armenian literature has two distinct phases. In the first phase (5th to 13th centuries) there was a deliberate intent among Armenian poets to Christianise the story. Khatchatur *vardapet* Ketcharetsi (1260–1331), in his Colophon that follows the translation, describes the text as 'unseemly', 'baseless', 'pagan writings'. He states that the pagan writings were 'lacking in unity' and that although the text before him was still 'unskilful' and faulty, by 'editing and correcting it in a poetic fashion' he had 'cleared a straight' path through the material. So Ketcharetsi, followed by Grigoris Aght'amartsi (1480–1544) and Zak'aria Gnunetsi (1500–76), set about writing epigrammatic poems of their own (over 400 verses in total) after each section of the romance. Alexander's deeds are likened to those of Christ and try to portray Alexander as a prototype of Christ. Eighteen events in the life of Christ are matched with events in the life of Alexander, and the BVM doubles with Olympias. Because there were no such romances and legends relating to the Armenian heroes and kings, the popularity of the romance was substantial, but there was also a need to comply with the scholastic thinking of the period. At the end of their poems the authors attach notices in which they plead forgiveness for their 'audacity in writing such a comparison'.

●R. Raabe, *Istoria Alek'sandrou: Die armenische Übersetzung der sagenhaften Alexander Biographie (P-C) auf ihre mutmassliche Grundlage zurückgeführt* (Leipzig, 1896); *The Romance of Alexander the Great by Ps. Callisthenes*, trans. from the Armenian version with an introduction by A. M. Wolohojian (New York, 1969).   VN

Bulgarian In the 5th century Pseudo-Callisthenes began to circulate in Byzantium and became the source of translations into Bulgarian in the 10th century. The earliest Bulgarian version of the Alexander Romance introduced changes to Pseudo-Callisthenes, e.g., inserted episodes and data from Hamartolos's 9th-century *Chronicle of the World*. Later versions incorporated material from other historical writings, motifs from APOCRYPHA and Christian legends; exotic descriptions are also hyperbolised. The most popular extant text of the Bulgarian Romance is from the 15th century (most probably translated from a Serbian redaction based on earlier Bulgarian and Russian versions). The narration maintains a close relationship to the narrative technique of the Ancient Greek 'novel'. Alexander does appear as a Christian hero, but his fate suggests the influence of Ancient Greek ideas (e.g. his life is related with a strong emphasis on the power of Fate). The Bulgarian Alexander Romance demonstrates a cultural approach different from those Slavonic versions based on Latin sources and coloured by the culture of the Western Church. The Romance was popular in Bulgaria in the 19th century, from which period date two late translations (1810 and 1816), and its 1844 publication was followed by many chapbook editions. Because of the absence of a domestic literature, translations of texts like the Alexander Romance provided Bulgarians with their first secular reading-matter and thus contributed to the creation of original literature in Bulgaria.

●V. Jagić, 'Život Aleksandra Velikoga po textu recenzije bugarske', *Starine*, V, 1873.   SIK

Czech (a) The *Alexandreida* (c. 1290) is an unknown petty noble's adaptation mainly of Gautier de Châtillon's *Alexandreis* (c. 1184); it also betrays the possible influence of Wolfram von Eschenbach. It survives in several 14th-century fragments and in this incomplete state has 3,450 lines in octosyllabic couplets. The author employs a wide vocabulary and imaginative rhymes; it is one of the most sophisticated high-style works in Old Czech literature. The author transmits his own Christian petty-noble morality in tercets, some of them adaptations of biblical sayings or *Disticha Catonis*, but many of them his own. He disapproves of the changing social order, where low-born are acquiring posts in the administration, and where the Czech aristocracy, including the king, are adopting German language and manners. Alexander is depicted as a Christian king, noble and wise in all his doings until he is overcome by pride and love of luxury, whereupon the 'Saracen' Darius appears more noble than the Christian. The author's drastic battle scenes and his concern for the suffering of the peasantry during war have led critics to suggest he might have taken part in King Přemysl Otakar II's crusade against the heathen Prussians. Furthermore, because the poem is to a degree a political tract, it has also been posited that Philip is Přemysl Otakar, Olympias, his wife Cunigunda, and Alexander, his son Wenceslas II; Alexander himself has been compared with Přemysl Otakar and Darius with Rudolph of Habsburg. The author localises his text by allusions to contemporary Bohemian politics, by posting Czech soldiers in Alexander's army and by his agricultural imagery.

(b) The only localisation in the prose *Kronika o Alexandru Velikém* (late 14th century) consists in the inclusion of Moravia among Alexander's domains. This work is a slightly abbreviated translation of the 11th-century *Liber Alexandri Magni regis Macedonie de Preliis*, a version of Leo of Naples's *Nativitas et Victoria Alexandri Magni* (c. 951–69). The Old Czech version survived as a work of printed popular literature into the 19th century. Unlike the *Alexandreida*, the *Kronika* was aimed at a 14th-century burgher audience, to whom the fantastic elements appealed. The esoteric imagery surrounding the semi-divine Alexander made this text together with the contemporary Asenath legend (*Asenech*) one of the first vernacular stimuli to an interest in Ancient Egypt in Bohemia. From a literary historical point of view, the *Kronika* is most important for its remarkably lucid style.

●(a) V. Vázný (Ed.), *Staročeská Alexandreida* (Prague, 1963); V. Jeinek (Ed.), *Translation and Edition of the Old Czech Alexandreis* (St Louis, 1952). H. H. Bielfeldt, *Die Quellen der alttschechischen Alexandreis*, Berlin, 1951; 'Neue Studien zur alttschechischen Alexandreis', *Zeitschrift für Slavistik*, 4, 1959, pp. 184–98.
(b) J. Kolár (Ed.), *Próza českého středověku* (Prague, 1983); S. Harrison Thomson, '*Kronika o Alexandru Velikém*: A Czech Prose Translation of the *Historia de Preliis*', *Speculum*, 3, 1928, pp. 204–17.   RBP

Hungarian (a) Though elements of the Alexander Romance are found in the 15th century, the first known complete version appeared in 1548 in the verse *Historia Alexandri Magni* attributed to ILOSVAI. The author declares his source to have been Quintus Curtius, and he recounts Alexander's life from his father's death to his own death by poison. Although the poem has no other purpose than to amuse, ILOSVAI adds his own comments on the inconstancy of Fate and the lot of the over-ambitious. The popularity of this *széphistória* (see this section), which was reprinted four times in the 16th century and frequently after that, depends more on the rapid changes of scene than on the quality of the verse.

(b) Gáspár HELTAI published the first extant complete prose version of the *Historia de Proeliis* of Leo of Naples at Kolozsvár in 1573. The unknown translator of *Nagy Sándornak históriája* (The story of Alexander the Great) followed his source closely, but abbreviated the long account of Alexander's Indian expedition and omitted some of the natural curiosities to create a more compact and unified story. It is a fluent and colourful tale.

(c) By far the most popular prose version was by János Haller (1626–1697), a Transylvanian nobleman who spent four years in prison 1678–82 and there amused himself by translating an 'ancient Latin book'. This contained three histories, of Alexander the Great, the Romans (the *Gesta Romanorum*) and the Trojan War, and was allegedly published at Strasbourg in 1494. Haller was a competent translator with a lucid style, and his book, *Hármas Istoria* (Triple story, 1695), was to become one of the most widely read volumes in Hungary.   GFC

Roumanian The Romance came to the Roumanians via the Serbs. In most Roumanian versions it is a text of c. 30,000 words which preserves much of the historical account of Alexander's exploits by Pseudo-Callisthenes. Alexander is presented, however, as a Christian king and in some versions the text has been localised to include references to the origins of the Roumanians. The first translation is thought to have been made during the 16th century as the earliest surviving text in Roumanian is a MS copy made in 1620 in Transylvania. In 1794 the first printed text appeared in Sibiu in Transylvania and thereafter the Romance was reprinted on a regular basis until the 1920s, being one of the best-known works amongst peasant communities. The Romance inspired icon painters, left its mark in oral literature where Alexander appears in Christmas carols and his horse carries the bridegroom in wedding songs, and lives on in the popular Christian names Darie and Ruxanda.

•Standard text in D. Simonescu and I. Chitimia (Eds), *Cărţile Populare in Literatura Românească*, vol. 1 (Bucharest, 1963), pp. 3–85.   DJD

Serbian The origins of the so-called *Srpska Aleksandrida* have not been established with any certainty. For some time it was thought to be a 14th- or 15th-century adaptation of Pseudo-Callisthenes, but now it is generally believed to have come from a 13th-century Dalmatian Glagolitic translation of Latin and Italian adaptations. The Serbian Cyrillic version later found its way into Russian and other E European literature. In the Middle Ages it was the most popular 'book' in Serbia and continued to influence the oral tradition and Serbian writers into the 18th century.   VDM

BRUNCVÍK (Czech) *Kronika o Bruncvíkovi* (Chronicle of Bruncvík, late 14th century) is an heraldic tale about the eponymous Czech prince's acquisition of the lion in the Bohemian coat of arms, based loosely on the German saga of Heinrich der Löwe, with the use of other sources (e.g. *Herzog Ernst*, the Sinbad stories). In this story of the son of STILLFRIED seeking adventure 'for the glory of his nation', elements of the fantastic prevail. Czech greatness is demonstrated by his successful encounters with Europe (an enigmatic mermaid who foreshadows Mélusine), the monstrous Olibrius's beautiful daughter, Africa, who is a prisoner of the basilisk, Arabia. The romance is important for its realistic psychology and for its esoteric use of numerals and symbolic beasts.

•J. Kolár and M. Nedvědová (Eds), *Próza českého středověku* (Prague, 1983).

W. Baumann, *Die Sagen von Heinrich dem Löwen bei den Slaven* (Munich, 1975); W. Baumann, *Der frühe Roman. Untersuchungen deutscher und slavischer Texte* (Frankfurt on Main, 1977); W. Baumann, 'Der tschechische Bruncvík und die Melusinensage', *Wiener slavistisches Jahrbuch*, 19–20 (1974–5), pp. 7–11.   RBP

KALLIMACHOS AND CHRISORROI (Greek) Τα κατά Καλλίμαχον και Χρυσορρόην Ερωτικόν Διήγημα,

probably written by Andronikos Palaeologos, nephew of Michael VIII, between 1310 and 1340, is a poem of 2,607 lines, surviving in a single early 16th-century MS. The themes and settings of this romance are particularly fairy-tale-like. A king sends his three sons out into the world to discover which is the worthiest to succeed him. The youngest, Kallimachos, leads his brothers up a mountain to a castle defended by live snakes and dragons, but the older brothers leave after giving him a magic ring. He duly enters the castle and rescues a beautiful princess, Chrisorroi, from the ogre who is holding her prisoner. Hardly have the lovers been united before the king of a neighbouring country arrives and abducts the princess, leaving Kallimachos for dead outside the castle.

But the death is an enchantment which his brothers break. He duly penetrates the palace of his new rival in disguise, and attempts to rescue Chrisorroi yet again. All seems lost when the lovers are found sleeping together in the royal gardens, but, as often happens in the Greek romances, it is the heroine who saves the day. Chrisorroi persuades the king that she is already married to Kallimachos, and the happy pair are freed to return to the ogre's den. This is a skilfully told romance. The language has a noticeable proportion of learned forms on a demotic base, and there are long and quite complex sentences running across the groups of fifteen-syllable lines. The sorts of rhetorical devices common to the learned romances of the 12th century – formal description, a courtroom speech, various conventions of love rhetoric – are made to serve the story rather than ornamentally developed for their own sake. Parallels of incident and repetitions of imagery are used both to strengthen and to vary the standard bipartite nature of the plot (a first section leading to the union of the lovers, a second providing obstacles which divide them but are overcome). An epigram by the court poet Manuel Philes discussing what seems to be this romance offers a reading of the text as a moral allegory. Though difficult for the modern reader to accept, such an interpretation offers interesting testimony to the attitudes of contemporaries to this type of material.

•M. Pichard *Le Roman de Callimaque et Chrysorrhoé* [critical text and translation] (Paris, 1956).

R. Beaton, *The Medieval Greek Romance* (Cambridge, 1989).   CFR

LIVISTROS AND RODAMNI (Greek) This Greek romance,

loosely datable to the period 1310–50, is preserved in five highly divergent versions. It is thought that the original version cannot have been exactly like any of them. The fullest version, a MS in the Vatican, has evidently been extensively reworked by a scribe or redactor. The three oldest MSS have gaps and transpositions which make nonsense of the story. It is a romance unique among the Greek vernacular texts in that it tells two stories in parallel, those of Livistros and of his friend and confidant Klitovos. In the main plot Eros, King of Love, reveals to Livistros in a dream that he is to marry Rodamni, daughter of King Chrysos of Argyrokastron (King Gold of Silver Castle). Livistros duly sets off on a journey to find this castle, and the plot proceeds, full of the customary allegory and magic, rhetorical descriptions and tournaments. There are also unusually long sections reporting the contents of love letters, messages and songs. The subplot is of less importance, though well integrated. The narrative organisation of the romance is skilful, as is its use of imagery, but it is a less imaginative work than KALLIMACHOS AND CHRYSORROI.

●J. A. Lambert, *Le Roman de Libistros et Rhodamné* (Amsterdam, 1935).
R. Beaton, *The Medieval Greek Romance* (Cambridge, 1989).   CFR

RUSUDANIANI (Georgian) Rusudaniani (The story of Queen Rusudan), a Georgian fairy-tale prose epic, by an unidentified author, composed c. 1640, is one of the most important works heralding the Georgian renascence. Its frame story is original and reflects Georgian realities in the 13th century under the Mongols: Queen Rusudan, like her historical namesake, has to endure isolation and anguish while her husband Manuchar seeks confirmation of his throne from a pagan ruler. While she waits, her twelve brothers console her with fairy tales: these, as the author hints, are derived, and parallels can be found in folklore and both Occidental and Oriental literature. The *Rusudaniani*, however, turns these tales into a coherent text not only because of the frame-story, but because of a didactic, Christian continuum, counselling patience and faith, the last two tales anticipating the happy return of the king. The *Rusudaniani* employs Georgian folk motifs and has in return enriched Georgian folk-tales. It was a popular manuscript. In 1732 at King VAKHT'ANG VI's behest, the second fairy tale, 'The tale of King Jimshed', was expertly (if archaically) versified in RUSTAVELIAN metre by Mamuk'a BARATASHVILI. As Mamuk'a Baratashvili avowed, this was a daring attempt to raise the *Rusudaniani* to the level of Shota RUSTAVELI: 'Shota sits on his steed, this horseman nobly prances. Many copied him and mounted their own trained horses. They have left this world, they give us instructions. I don't know what they have done, I have tried to share their lot.'   DR

STILLFRIED (Czech) *Kronika o Štilfrídovi* (Chronicle of Stillfried, early or mid-14th century) is the earliest, briefest and most courtly Czech prose romance. It is an heraldic tale about a prince riding out to earn the eagle for the Bohemian coat of arms. The probable sources are German sagas. Štilfríd finds the King of Naples sorely harried by the King of England 'or Mesopotamia', and undertakes a *Zwölfkampf* and proves Czech greatness by defeating most of the world (England, Mesopotamia,

Poland, Hungary, Abyssinia, Saxony, Louvain etc), including the great *Nibelungenlied* hero, Siegfried. The formulaic structure of the main part of the work, the *Zwölfkampf*, together with the fact that this part is scattered with rhyming couplets, suggests that there was an earlier Czech verse version of the romance.
●J. Kolár and M. Nedvědová (Eds), *Próza českého středověku* (Prague, 1983). Translation in W. Schamschula (Ed.), *An Anthology of Czech Literature. 1st Period* (Frankfurt on Main, 1991), pp. 221–42.
W. Baumann, *Der frühe Roman. Untersuchungen deutscher und slavischer Texte* (Frankfurt on Main, 1977); A. Schmaus, 'Zur Entstehungsgeschichte der alttschechischen Stilfrid', *WSJ* 3 (1953), pp. 28–36; C. Lacouteux, 'Herzog Ernst v 2164 ff – Das böhmische Volksbuch von Stillfried und Bruncvig und die morgenländischen Alexandersagen', *Zeitschrift für deutsches Altertum und deutsche Literatur* 109 (1980), pp. 247–51.   RBP

TANDAREIS AND FLORDIBEL

(Czech) The Czech rhymed romance *Tandariáš a Floribella* (2nd half 14th century) is based on the work by the Austrian poet Der Pleier (fl. 1250–80). A beautiful orphan maiden, Floribella, who has arrived at the court of King Arthur, and Tandariáš, who has been assigned to serve her as her gentleman-in-waiting, fall in love and elope. When the knights sent to capture Tandariáš are vanquished by him, Arthur agrees to judge the lovers but first Tandariáš must prove his valour. After many adventures he is pardoned and the lovers are united. Although the plot remains basically the same as in Pleier, the anonymous Czech poet presents the theme of true love conquering all difficulties as a universal idea not restricted by the courtly code. He narrates the adventures in a matter-of-fact way, depicts the characters as late 14th-century individuals, puts stress on their psychology, and turns Tandariáš into a liberator of oppressed peoples and a fighter against the heathen oppression of Christians.
●K. Brusak, 'Some notes on "Tandariáš and Floribella" ' in R. Auty, L. R. Lewitter and A. P. Vlasto (Eds), *Gorski vijenac* (Cambridge, 1970).   KB

TRISTAN (Czech) Three sections of the 8,931-line Czech *Tristram (a Izalda)* (last third 14th century) were based on Eilhart von Oberge's version (2nd half 12th century), one section on Gottfried von Strassburg's version (c. 1200) and one on Heinrich von Freiberg's (c. 1290). A most unusual form of compilation has, then, been employed, especially since only two Czech authors can be seen by their styles to have been involved. The first composed the first third of the text; the livelier second author, the rest. The irregularity of the octosyllabic couplets brings it even closer to prose than 'DALIMIL'. The philosophising and static descriptions of the German texts are reduced to a minimum (a major exception is Izalda's canoodling with her dog), whereas dynamic descriptions are often greatly extended (the scene where a spurt of mud penetrates Izalda Weisshand's groin) or added (the two Izaldas quarrelling like washerwomen over Tristram's corpse). The Czech authors also fairly consistently attempt to regenerate stock phrases and epithets. They also occasionally localise events (e.g. Mark is warring against a Slav king) and introduce Czech proverbs (e.g. on women's long hair and short wit).
●U. Bamborschke (Ed.), *Das*

altčechische Tristan-Epos, 2 vols (Wiesbaden, 1968–9); Z. Tichá (Ed.), *Tristram a Izalda* (Prague, 1980). A. Thomas, *The Czech Chivalric Romances Vévoda Arnošt and Lavryn in their Literary Context* (Göppingen, 1989). RBP

TROY BOOK (Greek) Διήγησις γεναμένη εν Τροία (The tale of Troy) was probably the last of the original (i.e. not translated or adapted) medieval Greek romances to be written. It derives substantially from Konstandinos Manasses's Σύνοψις ιστορική (Synopsis of history, written 1143–52) and shows a wide range of influences from other literature of the period. A poem of 1,166 lines, preserved in a single 16th-century MS, the bulk of it is devoted to the story of Paris, who is duly converted into a hero of romance. He suffers shipwreck, disguises himself (as a monk), distinguishes himself by courtly bearing and feats of arms, gains access to Helen's castle and heart. The union of the lovers is duly thwarted and overthrown by the expedition of the Greeks.
●R. Beaton, *The Medieval Greek Romance* (Cambridge, 1989). CFR

VELTHANDROS AND CHRISANTZA (Greek) Διήγησις εξαίρετος Βελθάνδρος του ρωμαίου (Velthandros and Chrisantza) was probably written soon after KALLIMACHOS AND CHRISOROI and is preserved in only one MS, totalling 1,348 lines. The world in which the action takes place is in some respects loosely identifiable with the political geography of Anatolia in the 13th century, but the hero's travels are essentially fantastic. Prince Velthandros, having quarrelled with his father, leaves home to seek his fortune. In the rich and strange castle of Eros the King he finds inscriptions prophesying that he will fall in love with Chrisantza, daughter of the King of Antioch. After various adventures he duly seduces Chrisantza and elopes with her from her father's castle. Surviving a harrowing journey back to Velthandros's homeland, the couple are duly married and proclaimed king and queen. It is a particularly well-constructed romance, its two parts achieving balance through both similar and contrastive motifs. The first half of the poem, with its magical castle of Eros and a highly 'Freudian' dream sequence in which Velthandros has to give a wand to whichever of forty princesses he wishes to marry, affords plentiful opportunity for extended rhetorical descriptions of places and people. The second half, which thematically offers a mirror-image of the first, is superficially more realistic.
●R. Beaton, *The Medieval Greek Romance* (Cambridge, 1989). CFR

THE DISPUTE

CONTENTIO SATRAPAE ET SCHOLARIS (Czech) The 490-line work known as *Podkoní a žák* (The groom and the student, end 14th century) is a verse parody of a disputation. It is probably loosely based on a Bohemian-Latin poem comparing the miserable lives of students and courtiers, *Videant qui nutriunt*. It was first printed c. 1498. The student author describes through a well-characterised burgher narrator the argument between a groom from court and a student in a pub; both are very poor and have no chance of a better life, but they try to out-argue each other on the material benefits of their callings. The groom has the first and last words, and the argument ends in a brawl. Written in a lively, matter-of-fact style, it gives a vivid picture of contemporary urban life.

●J. Hrabák (Ed.), *Staročeské satiry Hradeckého rukopisu a Smilovy Školy* (Prague, 1962).   RBP

HÁDÁNÍ PRAHY S KUTNOU HOROU (Czech) This anonymous poem (Dispute of Prague with Kuttenberg) of more than 3,000 lines is a Hussite propaganda work written c. 1420 at the time of the battles between the crusaders of the Emperor Sigismund and the Hussite armies. In a dispute conducted before Christ, the two warring camps are represented by Prague, whose university sided with the Hussites, and by Kutná Hora (Kuttenberg), a royal mining town that remained Papist. The author who from the outset is partial to Prague presents her as a beautiful virtuous young woman, while Kutná Hora is a hunchbacked hag. Kutná Hora expresses the religious, social and political views of the Roman Church and of the Council of Constance, which condemned HUS. These are contested and refuted by Prague who continually has the upper hand and finally victory. The work was intended for an educated public and the author of the poem, which is written in conventional octosyllabic couplets, was well versed both in the technique of the dispute and in religious literature. He tries to show Prague as the more skilful orator and enlivens her speech with puns and other devices but his means of expression are repetitive.   KB

SPÓR DUŠE S TĚLEM (Czech) The theme of The dispute of the Soul with the Body is treated in three Czech poems composed c. 1330; two of these follow the Latin original, *Visio Philiberti*, but the longest and most accomplished is independent of it. The fundamental difference lies in the fact that the dispute does not take place after death. The body is probably that of a boisterous young man, boasts of its strength, reason, good looks and riches, and urges its owner to lead a wanton life. When Death suddenly comes, devils carry the Soul away but the Czech author continues even further. The Soul, which the devils place on a scale, turns in anguish to the Virgin Mary who intercedes with Jesus to set up a court of four judges, Truth, Peace, Justice and Mercy. The devils insist on their right but although the conclusion is missing from the MS, one presumes that after a plea from Peace, Christ pardons the Soul. The poem, outstanding for its imaginative plot, its sophisticated use of the language and metaphor and its inventive and complicated rhyming, foreshadows the style of *Život svaté Kateřiny* (see HAGIOGRAPHY) and *Závišova píseň* (see LYRIC VERSE).   KB

TKADLEČEK (Czech) The unknown author of the lengthy dispute or contemplative discourse, *Tkadleček* (The little weaver, i.e. *textor*, i.e. writer, c. 1407), appears to have used the same source as Johannes von Tepl in his *Der Ackermann aus Böhmen* (1400). The German work comprises a widowed ploughman's argument with Death, the Czech, the knightly Ludvík Tkadleček's with Misfortune. Tkadleček has been abandoned by his beloved, Adlička. In the dispute Tkladleček might represent Feeling (or the ego) and Misfortune, Reason (or the superego); the disputants are equally educated, however; both use large numbers of quotations, mainly from Aristotle, to support their arguments. (Most quotations are derived from Burley or Valerius Maximus.) Of the 16 chapters Tkadleček has the first and Misfortune the last; the author appears to be more on the side of slightly mischievous and paternalistic Reason than of melancholy, slightly hysterical Feeling. The work's subject is love; both disputants use courtly terminology and Misfortune has a lengthy didactic passage on the courtly code; on the whole, however, he mocks the courtly. Indeed the fair Adlička herself, for all her courtly manners and for all the noble qualities Tkadleček endows her with, appears to be a flighty wench. *Tkadleček* is lexically innovative and syntactically complex, but elegant. As a Czech prose stylist the author has no match before KOMENSKÝ.

●F. Šimek (Ed.), *Tkadleček. Hádka milence s Neštěstím* (Prague, 1974).

A. Hrubý, *Der 'Ackermann' und seine Vorlage* (Munich, 1971).   RBP

VÁCLAV, HAVEL A TÁBOR

(Czech) This anonymous poem (V., H. and T) of 1,185 lines is a satire written from the R. Catholic standpoint in 1424 during the Hussite Wars. In his introduction the author summarises the current situation. In addition to those who remained true to Rome, the supremacy of the Pope and the heritage of St Wenceslas, there are two heretical groups. One is composed of those who merely follow the teaching of HUS, whilst the other consists of the militant Hussites, the Táborites who are murderers, arsonists and plunderers. Apart from all these there remain those who sway between changing sympathies according to their greed for material gain. The three disputants, Václav representing the R. Catholics, Havel the waverers, and Tábor the militant Hussites, meet on a Friday in a burnt-out church. Tábor has brought some pork; the greedy Havel hesitates to eat meat on a Friday but is willing to accept it. Václav scolds him, however; since they are in a church, albeit ruined, they should pray there and not picnic. In the tripartite dispute that ensues, Václav defends the unity of the Church and reproaches the Táborites for the confiscation of ecclesiastical property, the murders of priests, monks and nuns, the destruction of churches and the burning of books. Tábor asserts that they are acting in accordance with the will of God – if God were against their killing, burning and plundering they would be prevented from doing so. Havel, on the other hand, remains noncommital. Tábor becomes enraged and threatens the others with his club, but the dispute ends peacefully. Since Václav cannot persuade either of them, he advises Havel not to succumb to heresy and warns Tábor that he will repent in Hell. The author, although a R. Catholic, avoids proselytising and allows the characters to express their convictions without distortion. He writes in a vivid style peppered with humour and breaks the conventional norm by using lines with a varying number of syllables which causes his verse to approach rhymed prose. KB

MEDIEVAL DRAMA

HRA VESELÉ MAGDALENY **(Merry Magdalene) (Czech)** The Czech Magdalene play (1350s) depicts Mary as a jolly pleasure-seeker who enjoys making love, especially with priests and students, but also likes going for walks to pick flowers. Only a few lines at the end are spent on her conversion by Martha; the only sign that she is truly converted is that she gives herself a slap, but that is no doubt because what we have is only a fragment. In the prelude the royal Lucifer assembles three folksy devils, the aggressive Beelzebub from the upper classes, the cosmopolitan Satan from the merchant class, and the lower-class Bēřit.

• J. Hrakák (Ed.), *Staročeské drama* (Prague, 1951). Translation in W. Schamschula (Ed.), *An Anthology of Czech Literature. 1st Period* (Frankfurt on Main, 1991), pp. 159–64.

RBP

MASTIČKÁŘ **(Unguentarius) (Czech)** *Mastičkář* (c. 1340), which survives in two versions, is a raucous Easter farce about the quack who sells the ointment to embalm Christ's body to the Three Marys. The quack, Severin, who may be a German, has a Czech assistant, but hires a Venetian Jewish assistant, Rubín, who provides much of the comedy. For all its low elements (e.g. Rubín's grabbing a woman by her genitalia, the parody of the Resurrection where Severin resurrects the spoilt Jewish boy, Izák, by pouring faeces into his anus), its scatological and sexual jokes, it is a highly literary work many of whose jokes would have been understood only by its student actors (e.g. parody of courtly literature or citation of the *Disticha Catonis*). It makes fun of most layers of society: the nobility, clerics, students, merchants, prostitutes, hawkers.

• J. F. Veltrusky, *A Sacred Farce from Mediaeval Bohemia. Mastičkář* (Ann Arbor, 1985) (includes both Czech versions with English translation); W. Baumann, 'Der alttschechische Mastičkář als selbstständiges Mercator-spiel', *ZfSlPh* 38 (1975) pp. 178–86; W. Schamschula, 'The Place of the Old Czech Mastičkář – Fragments within the Central European Easter Plays' in *International Congress of Slavists. American Contributions*, vol. 2, (Columbus, Ohio, 1978), pp. 678–90.

RBP

SATIRES AND FABLIAUX

DESATERO KÁZANIE BOŽIE **(Czech)** The 1,158-line *Desatero kázanie božie* (God's Ten Commandments, 1360s) is a verse sermon on the Decalogue, where the worldly clerical author spends much more time on the seven (according to the Augustinian division) sins against human beings than the three against God. For each Commandment the author gives three types of transgression. The longest section concerns 'Thou shalt not commit adultery' (in Czech: 'fornication'), where in the third category, procuresses, the author has a lively version of a *Gesta Romanorum* story which does not exist in the Old Czech version of that work. The satire condemns the hedonism of all society.

•J. Hrabák (Ed.), *Staročeské satiry Hradeckého rukopisu a Smilovy školy* (Prague, 1962). W. Schamschula (Ed.), *An Anthology of Czech Literature. 1st Period* (Frankfurt on Main, 1991), pp. 142–8 (extract).   RBP

PRODROMIKA   (Greek)

Φτωχοπροδρομικά is a group of four poems written at the court of the Comneni c. mid-12th century, and attributed to the court poet and savant Theodore Prodromos (c. 1100–c. 1170). All four poems are built around the 'voice' of a narrating character, each a different 'poor Prodromos'. The first poem is the complaint of the narrator about his poverty and his nagging wife, designed to touch his patron for funds. The second bewails the problems of being the father of 13 children. The third is a classic satire on high-living monks (the narrator having metamorphosed himself into a newly arrived monk, Hilarion Ptochoprodromos). The fourth is an equally classic lament by a poor intellectual, contrasting his misery with the lives of craftsmen and merchants in contemporary Byzantium. It is arguable that there are elements in the four major Prodromic poems that are consonant with such learned works by the historical Prodromos as his romance *Rodanthe and Dosikles*, his group of Lucianic satires (including the 'Sale of lives of poets and politicians' and his Κατόμυομαχία (Battle of cat and mice). The use of popular Greek by a court intellectual is surprising, but there are metrical grounds for regarding the attribution of at least one poem in demotic to Prodromos, and so it cannot be argued that the linguistic argument is foolproof. The elements of parody, role-creation and 'variation on a theme' which characterise the poems show significant literary skill.

•R. Beaton, 'The Rhetoric of Poverty: The Lives and Opinions of Theodore Prodromos', *Byzantine and Modern Greek Studies*, 11 (1987), pp. 1–28. CFR

RADA   ZHOVADILÝCH...

(Czech) *Rada zhovadilých zvieřat a ptactva k člověku* (The counsel of base animals and birds to man), a didactic work, inspired by Dubravius's (c. 1486–1553) *Theriobulia* which is a Latin version of the poem by FLAŠKA, by Physiologus and Aesop's fables, was certainly written by several authors, but the main contributor and compiler was probably the printer and publisher Jan Mantuan Fencl who printed it in Pilsen in 1528. A prose introduction, explaining that even if animals cannot speak they can advise man by their actions, is followed by poems in which not only common quadrupeds, birds and insects but also legendary beasts like the phoenix and unicorn describe their qualities and advise man either to emulate or avoid their behaviour; each poem ends with man's reaction. The prose promyth of each poem contains much zoological, moral and theological erudition, but the verse is written in a vivid, linguistically inventive, witty, ironic style. Some advice is practical, other moral, such as that of the elephant exhorting man to bow before God as he bends his knees before men. Many speeches express sharp criticism of human character and habits and the work presents a vivid picture of contemporary society.   KB

TRADESMEN (Czech) The cycle

of seven verse satirical pictures or fabliaux known as *O řemeslnících a konšelích* (Of tradesmen and aldermen, 1360s) concerns dishonest shoemakers, aldermen (mainly as corrupt magistrates), blacksmiths, maltsters, barber-surgeons, butchers and bakers. The liveliest are those concerning blacksmiths and barber-surgeons. The former are attacked for supplying burglars with skeleton-keys and for being careless as farriers – the narrator asks what the smith would feel like if he had a nail knocked into his foot. Barbers are threatened with a punch in the face for shaving with a blunt razor and with their teeth being knocked out for missing a vein while letting blood. ●J. Hrabák (Ed.), *Staročeské satiry Hradeckého rukopisu a Smilovy školy* (Prague, 1962). The maltsters and blacksmiths are included in a translation in W. Schamschula (Ed.), *An Anthology of Czech Literature. 1st Period* (Frankfurt on Main, 1991), pp. 149–53.

RBP

POPULAR LITERATURE (EARLY MODERN)

POLISH Popular literature, including *Spielmannsepik*, 'historical songs' and *exempla*, emerged in the 16th century when various texts were translated or freely adapted into Polish prose and verse. Polish romances have been divided into six groups: (1) religious (see APOCRYPHA), (2) ribald, (3) pseudo-historical, (4) didactic, (5) chivalric, (6) 'Humanist'. The ribald romance features popular heroes and its unrefined humour is often based on clever wordplay. The three most representative texts relate the adventures of popular characters: Aesop (*Żywot Ezopa Fryga* [The life of Aesop the Phrygian] by BIERNAT OF LUBLIN, 1510), Marchołt-Marculphus (*Rozmowy, które miał król Salomon mądry z Marchołtem grubym a sprosnym*, Conversations between wise King Solomon and the coarse and bawdy Marcolf, by Jan z Koszyczek, 1521), and Till Eulenspiegel (*Sowizrzał*, c. 1530–40). As elsewhere in Europe, pseudo-historical romances include the tales of Alexander the Great (1510) and the Trojan War (1563). Descriptions of contemporary events are rare (*Historia prawdziwa ... książęcia finlandzkiego Jana ...*, The true story of the Finnish Prince Jan, by Marcin Kromer [c. 1512–89], 1570). Didacticism dominates the collection of forty anecdotes, fables and parables selected and translated from the *Gesta Romanorum* and published as *Historie rozmanite z rzymskich i z innych dziejów wybrane ...* (Diverse stories selected from the history of Rome and other countries, 1543). Chivalric adventures, sometimes related to Arthurian legends, appear in the stories of Mélusine (1569), Magelona (c. 1565–87), Emperor Otto (1569) and Fortunatus (c. 1570). 'Humanist' romances are limited to rather inconsequential adaptations of the *Decameron*. In the 17th century adventure was inextricably linked with love in the Baroque adaptations of Italian, French and Spanish courtly narratives (e.g. w. POTOCKI's *Judyta*, 1652, *Syloret*, c. 1680, and *Argenida*, 1697). TWARDOWSKI unsuccessfully attempted to impose didacticism on sensuality in *Nadobna Pasqualina ...* (The fair Pasqualina, 1665). The development of didacticism at the end of the 17th century was carried on into the next century by Elżbieta Drużbacka (c. 1695–1765).

SE

DAMASKINI (Bulgarian) The Bulgarian popular-literary form, *damaskin*, derives from a Greek work of popular exegetical sermons by Damaskinos Studites (d. 1577), *Thesauros* (Treasury, first printed, Venice, 1558), first translated into Bulgarian towards the end of the 16th century. The term *damaskini* soon came, however, to be applied not only to tracts signed by the Greek, but to translations and adaptations of sermons from other sources. Furthermore, in time, the narrative element of the Bulgarian versions was emphasised. Some *damaskini* included translations and adaptations of Old Bulgarian texts and oral-tradition accounts of miracles, e.g. those by the Rila priest Josif Bradati (c. 1695–c. 1757). By the 17th century *damaskini* were predominantly hagiographic, moralistic and apocalyptic and were essentially written in New Bulgarian. They continued to be composed throughout the 18th century, by which time the codices began to look something like encyclopaedias-cum-manuals, and included historically important APOCRYPHA. The *damaskini* constitute the only non-liturgical link between Old Bulgarian literature and the literature of the National Revival (see PAISII).

•L. Miletich, 'Svistovski damaskin', *Bălgarski starini*, 7, 1923.

R. Gyllin, *The Genesis of the Modern Bulgarian Literary Language* (Stockholm, 1991). SIK

SZÉPHISTÓRIA (Hungarian) *Széphistória*, 'Fair story', is the collective term in Hungarian for secular narrative verse that became popular in the late 16th century and flourished during the following two centuries. Its early appearance in print was a result of censorship: Protestant printers, forbidden to publish theological works, turned to popular literature. Such poems include Classical and biblical tales, romances and historical and mythical anecdotes; they were composed solely as a source of amusement and as such frequently condemned by the Churches. Many are derived from Boccaccio and Petrarch; some relate local and contemporary incidents. Their authors are usually unknown, but some display dazzling virtuosity; *Euryalus and Lucretia* (1577) has been ascribed to BALASSI; GERGEI's *Argirus* and the anonymous tale of *Szilágyi and Hajmási* (1560) are further fine examples of the genre. While most preserve a moralistic tone, some are purely comic (*Béla király és Bankó leánya* [King Béla and Bankó's daughter, 1570]). The metre most often found in these poems is the so-called Hungarian alexandrine, a 12-syllable line with a caesura after the sixth syllable. Stanzas consist of four rhymed lines. This metre attracts bad poets as surely as the English iambic pentameter. These poems preserved their popularity until they were overtaken by translated prose-tales in the 18th century. They were still published by provincial printers to the end of the 19th century. GFC

Brief histories of East European literature, alphabetically arranged according to language

ALBANIAN

The first reference to the existence of writing in Albanian is to be found in the work of the French Bishop of Antivari, Gullielmus Adae (i.e. Brocardus Monacus), *Dictionarium ad patagium faciendum* (1332), in which we learn that Albanian is written in the Latin alphabet. Another witness is that of the Albanian scholar Marin BARLETI, who, in *De obsidione Scodrensi* (1504), speaks of certain chronicles or annals, written in the vernacular. The works of Barleti and of the other 15th–16th century Albanian Humanists, though in Latin, are considered to mark the beginnings of Albanian literature.

In the 16th and 17th centuries, under Ottoman rule, a large number of writers emerged in Albania. Though of liturgical character, the works of the representatives of this literature like BUZUKU, the author of the first Albanian book (1555), had learnt the techniques of *belles lettres*. In the 18th century, a new literary movement developed among the Muslim population of Albanian. The most valuable part of this literature constitutes the first secular poetry in Albanian.

The period from the 1830s to the proclamation of independence, 28 November 1912, is the period of National Revival. Its first centre was in S Italy among the Arbëresh (Italo-Albanian) communities, which had preserved their language and customs intact. Having escaped from the Ottomans, they were able to become acquainted with the ideas of the Enlightenment and the French Revolution.

DE RADA was at the head of the architects of Albanian Revival literature and culture in the Arbëresh lands. But it was in Albania itself that the new national literature was born. No one made a greater contribution to this cultural movement than N. FRASHËRI, the true founder of an Albanian 'national literature', and he inspired numerous writers and thinkers. The literary ideology of Frashëri and De Rada, and other literary Awakeners was followed and developed by ÇAJUPI, MJEDA and FISHTA.

1912–44 produced writings known as the Literature of Independence. The proclamation of Independence took place in November 1912; a democratic government was formed, led by NOLI, in 1924; King Zog's rule lasted 1924–39 and, finally, Albania was occupied by Italy and Germany (1939–44). The literature of this period came under the strong influence of three poets, NOLI, PORADECI and MIGJENI.

After the liberation and the Communist take-over, Socialist Realism became the official artistic method in Albanian literature. Thus only the writers who had participated in the war of liberation or had embraced Socialist Realism were declared real writers; other writers of the prewar period were forced to cease literary activity. This harsh official stand held back the development of Albanian literature; nevertheless one cannot deny completely the existence of serious literature over the five decades of socialism. The literature of the 1950s and early 1960s was enthusiastic, didactic and moralising, and produced few serious works. In the 1960s, new writers appeared, among them the three best-known poets of contemporary Albanian literature, AGOLLI, KADARE and ARAPI. 1960s Albanian literature tried to detach itself from conformism. Poetry and prose were renovated with new means of expression, though, as a whole, literature remained highly politicised. The writers of the 1970s tried to develop the literary achievements of the 1960s, while the writers of the 1980s, for the first time for many years, tried to liberate themselves from official dictates and censorship. By now they have managed to create their own trend.

•S. E. Mann, *Albanian Literature. An Outline of Prose, Poetry and Drama* (London, 1955); M. Lambertz, *Albanisches Lesebuch* (Leipzig, 1948); S. Skendi, *Albanian and South Slavic Oral Epic Poetry* (Philadelphia, 1954); G. Petrotta, *Svolgimento storico della cultura e letteratura albanese* (Palermo, 1950); G. Gradilione, *Studi di letteratura albanese* (Roma, 1960); A. Pipa, *Albanian Literature: Social Perspectives* (Munich, 1978); N. Resuli, *Albanian Literature* (Boston, MA, 1987); K. Bihiku, *A History of Albanian Literature* (Tirana, 1980); A. Zotos, *Anthologie de la prose albanaise. Presentée par . . .* (Paris, 1984); R. Elsie, *Dictionary of Albanian Literature* (New York, 1986); A. Pipa, *Contemporary Albanian Literature* (New York, 1991); R. Elsie, 'Albanian Literature in English Translation: a Short Survey', *SEER*, 70 (1992), 2, pp. 249–57. ShM

ARMENIAN

By the edict of King Trdat, Armenia converted to Christianity at the end of the 3rd (287 or 289) or the beginning of the 4th century (313). The streams of Christian influence – the 'Greek' from the NW and the 'Syrian' from the SW – infiltrated Armenia and coexisted all through the 4th century with old pagan institutions and traditions. The orientation of Armenia towards the West was irrevocable after the acceptance of Christianity. To preserve the Christian tradition the ancient pagan conception of the world was imperceptibly transformed into one which was both Christian and Western. Political relations with Sasanian Iran degenerated rapidly and culminated in the partition of the Armenian kingdom between Byzantium and Sasanian Iran in 387. To counterbalance political losses and to combat the gradual process of 'iranisation', and to minimise the influence of both Greek and Syrian Christianity on the young Armenian Church, the Catholicos St Sahak Partev (350–439) and St Mesrop Mashtots (355–439) invented the Armenian alphabet in 406; this laid the foundation for Armenian 'national literature'. What little ancient poetry had survived was transcribed in the work of later writers. The 5th-century Armenian historian MOVSES KHORENATSI (390–450) in his *Patmut'iwn Hayots* (History of the Armenians) uses various terms to describe the ancient oral stories which he utilised to build the histories of his heroes: *zroyts* (story), *gusanakan* (bard, minstrel), *nuag p'andran* (song on the lyre), *erg* (song), *vep* (tales, epics). These unwritten sources, in verse and prose, provide the material for his legends of 'Hayk and Bel', 'Ara the Beautiful and Semiramis', 'Tigranes and Azhdahak', 'Artashes and Artawazd'. P'AWSTOS BUZAND's (425–86) 'Epic histories' are based on the oral tradition in which whole cycles of legends were used to write the series of episodes – Khosrov and Trdat, Khosrov and Vatche, Tiran, Arshak, Pap, Vasak and Mushegh, Manuel Mamikonian. Much early and medieval Armenian literature consists of translations, an activity which began, as F. Finck has stated, as a 'conscious programme of transplantation of culture'. This 'programme' begins with the translation of the BIBLE, followed by liturgical, patristic, exegetic, apologetic, ecclesiastical historiographical, hagiographical works and works on canon law – i.e. the creation of sources to satisfy the immediate needs of the Armenian Church.

The 'Graecophil' School translations from Syriac and Greek, made principally 450–720, comprised works of the Church Fathers, e.g. Athanasius of Alexandria (c. 297–c. 373), Basil of Caesarea (c. 330–79), Gregory of Nazanzus (329–89), Eusebius of Caesarea (c. 260–c. 340), Ephraim the Syrian (c. 306–73), John Chrysostom (c. 347–407), Cyril of Alexandria (d. 444). Two observations should be made in regard to these. First, some of these translations have preserved texts of Greek and Syriac writers the originals of which are lost. Such works include the first part of the *Chronicle* of Eusebius, the *Commentaries on the Benediction of Moses* by Hippolytus, the *Refutation of the Definition of the Council of Chalcedon* by Timothy Aelurus, *The Demonstration of Apostolic Preaching* and the fourth and fifth books of *Adversus Haereses* by St Irenaeus of Lyons. Second, in addition to the purely religious works, the translations comprise secular works like the ALEXANDER ROMANCE, the *Grammar* of Dionysius of Thrax, treatises by Philo Judaeus, and numerous philosophical writings, in particular those of the neo-Platonic school such as Porphyry, Probus and Diodochus.

The passage from translations to the creation of original religious and historical works was so rapid that the phenomenon has continued to exercise specialists. The religious and intellectual effect of the literary activities of the 5th century resulted in the formation of a 'national' literature and art which combined the Oriental spirit, the Christian mentality, 'ethnic' sensibility, and the culture of the West, producing a 'national' culture which was both Eastern and Western. The *sharakan* (religious poems), which constituted a genre that was one of the major developments in Armenian poetry, were written by Mesrop Mashtots and their elegant form influenced generations of Armenian poets. Original religious and historical works, as well as hagiographic texts, homilies and hymns were produced. KORIWN, EZNIK, AGAT'ANGEĹOS, EGHISHE, Ghazar P'arp'etsi (437–500) and MOVSES KHORENATSI dominated in the field of historiography. Historiography continued to occupy a leading place in the literary production of subsequent centuries, e.g., Sébeos (600–62), Ghewond *vardapet* (730–88), Step'anos Asoghik (935–1015), T'ovma Ardsruni (840–906) and Yovhannes Draskhanakertsi (850–929).

After a lapse of more than three centuries the Armenian monarchy was restored in 885/6; this lasted until the period of the Seljük invasions of Armenia in 1048, followed by the fall of Ani in 1064, and the total subjugation of Armenia by the Seljüks in 1071. History apart, the works of this period are almost entirely religious writings, hagiography, homilies and commentaries on the Scriptures or on the liturgy. Following in the footsteps of Komitas Catholicos (560–628) and Sahakadught (675–736), poetry attained eloquence in GRIGOR NAREKATSI whose 'Book of lamentations', containing 95 mystical meditations, focuses on the inner man. His style was the strongest single influence on the Armenian poets that followed. Under his direct influence the 10th century saw an enormous upsurge of interest in both religious and secular poetry. Grigor Magistros (990–1059), continuing the elegiac trend, composed his 1,016-line religious-didactic poem, *Aṙ Manutche* (To M., 1045), a résumé of the Bible, beginning with Adam and ending with the Second Coming. He was the first to use rhyme throughout a work. It was no literary masterpiece, but by means of his erudition, his pedagogical ideas, and his expansion of the intellectual horizons of his time, he helped to give new direction to Armenian literature. Two centuries later another religious figure, NERSĒS IV KLAYETS'I, abandoned the use of classical Armenian and wrote poetry that was to have a significant influence on the trend towards secular lyrics.

In the 13th century a new phase in Armenian literature began, marked by the rise of Middle Armenian. Secular poetry was now written in Middle Armenian, which had been long dead as a spoken language and remained in use only among historians and religious authors. After abandoning religious themes, poets treated the 'real' world, to discuss the chances for human happiness, to consider love and woman, and the theme of the rose and the nightingale became dominant. Mkhit'ar Gosh's (1140–1213) *Datastanagirk* (Book of laws, 1184) and *Aṙakk'* (190 riddles) expanded the realm of secular literature. Poets of talent like Frik (1234–1315), Khatchatur Ketcharetsi (1260–1331), Kostandin Erznkatsi (1250–1314/28), Hovhannes T'lkurantsi (1320–1400), Arak'el Siunetsi (1350–1431) and Grigoris Aght'amartsi (1480–1544) wrote secular verse and returned only in isolated instances to the themes of supplication and sin, absolution and redemption. For example, forsaking heaven, Erznkatsi glorifies the sun as the creator of all that is good and beautiful; he and other poets who sense the conflict between spiritual purity and bodily desires resolve the issue, sometimes uneasily, in favour of love. Indeed, T'lkurantsi seeks immortality through love, while Aght'amartsi declares that his beloved can work more wonders than 'the mighty Cross'.

In spite of the disastrous consequences of wars, the 15th to 17th centuries marked a period of transition. In a number of schools, scholars and scribes preserved the received tradition by recopying old manuscripts. Historians and poets alike decried oppression and yearned for deliverance from Muslim domination. The spread of secular poems put traditional religious poetry, which was now jejune and lacking its former spontaneity, into a secondary position. Nahapet K'ouchak (d. 1592) in the over 500 *hayrenner* (quatrains) attributed to him wrote in fine, frank sensuous imagery not unlike that of the Songs of Songs. Naghash Hovnat'an (17th–18th century) was the most prominent poet of the age; his verse is rich in eroticism and satire and abounds in songs in praise of wine and merry-making. However, SAYAT-NOVA is the most enduringly popular. By common consent the quintessential troubadour, many of his poems are still sung by Armenians everywhere. His work abounds in songs of love – often unrequited love. He uses a wide range of poetic devices and an easy, frequent scattering of words from the languages of neighbouring countries. His handling of Persian, Georgian, Kurdish, Azeri, and Turkish words and phrases is so deft that their appearance in his poems seems quite natural and imparts a distinctive folk quality.

Armenian printing began in 1512 in Venice; Mkhitar Sebastatsi (1676–1749) founded the Mekhitarist Congregation in Venice 1717 and in Vienna 1811. Historic Armenia was divided between Russia and Turkey. The declaration of the T'anzimat, the reform decree of 1839, played an important part in freeing the Armenian spirit within Constantinople, in a period which culminated with the 'National Constitution' of the Armenian community of the Ottoman Empire (1860; ratified by the Turkish government 1863). The Mekhitarist Congregations in Venice and Vienna acted as relay-stations for the transmission to the Armenian population of the Ottoman Empire of European Romanticism, political liberalism and neo-Classicism. The works of such pre-Romantics as Young, Gessner, Fénelon or Bernardin de Saint-Pierre were translated into classical Armenian and helped shape the literary taste of the Armenians. The guiding spirits were Ghevond Alishan (1820–1904) in the West and ABOVYAN in the east. Alishan, in his poetry, championed the struggle for liberation from Turkey; ABOVYAN, in his novel *Verk'Hayastani* (Wounds of Armenia, 1840), laid the foundation for a modern Armenian literature and a modernised vernacular.

By the mid-19th century, poetry had emerged as Armenia's dominant literary form, and it was through their poetry that writers of both E and W Armenia voiced the people's fears, and their desire for freedom. Among these new poets were Mik'ayel Nalbandian (1829–66) and Petros Durian (1851–72). At the end of the Russo-Turkish War of 1877–78, the Turkish government imposed a tight censorship on all literary activities, followed by massacres in 1896; the Romantic era came to an end. Writers turned to the novel and short story, vignettes that sketched the ironies and frustrations of the times with chilling realism. The major Realists are Hakob Baronian (1843–91), ZOHRAB, Arp'iar Arp'iarian (1851–1908), R. Zardarian (1874–1915), YESSAYAN and Ervand Otian (1869–1926). The major non-Realists were Zapel Asadour (1863–1934, pseud. Sipil), the prominent feminist writer, and the mystic poet Diran Tcherakian ('Indra', 1875–1921). The one real Romantic voice left belonged to the poet Misak Medsarents (1886–1908). He was influenced by the sensuousness of Keats's poetry and the forms of Shelley, and produced some of the most musical poems in Armenian literature. C. 1872, just as W Armenian literature was entering a long period of stagnation, the E literary scene was taken over by a major novelist, RAFFI. Though under the influence of Dumas, Hugo, Sue, Scott, Tolstoy and Turgenev, he wrote in typically 'national' style. Very soon, his long historical novels dominated literature and soon fired the popular imagination and made him one of the most potent spiritual godfathers of the Armenian revolution. In 1908, when the Young Turks deposed the Sultan and formed a new government, their constitution promised equality and liberty to all minorities. A euphoric optimism spread among the Armenians.

From the last decade of the 19th century, until the massacres of 1915, poetry in both E and W Armenia was vigorous. Original and highly talented poets published their first volumes mainly during the first fifteen years of the 20th century: SIAMANT'O, VAROUJAN, Vahan Teryan (1885–1920), Misak Medsarents, Ruben Sevak (1885–1915) and TCHARENTS. Medsarents and Teryan remained in an imaginary, dream-like world, fitting for the second half of the 19th century: SIAMANT'O and VAROUJAN reached for Symbolism and T'ek'eyan continued to bear the imprint of Baudelaire.

The Armenian massacres of 1915 and the socio-political troubles of pre-Soviet Armenia (1918–20) slowed down the normal evolution of Armenian thought. The Russian Proletkult made its appearance in Armenia in 1922. In this connection, the 'Declaration of the Three', written by TCHARENTS, Gevorg Arshak Abov (1897–1965) and Azat Vshtuni (1894–1958) is important. Derenik Demirjian (1877–1956), Hovhannes T'umanyan (1869–1923), and Avetik Isahakyan (1875–57) managed to adapt and continue their literary careers. The period 1920–37 proved to be the most fertile in creative minds in the whole history of E Armenian letters. Most managed to reconcile the demands of the Proletarian aesthetics with their own nationalist temperament. The most accomplished work was that of BAKOUNTS whose sure sense of epic form and style was unmatched in E Armenian letters. Others include MAHARI, the imaginative and incisive poet and novelist, Teryan, the poet of tender despair, and T'OT'OVENTS, the delicate, sensitive story-teller. Pre-revolutionary literature appeared trite and parochial by comparison. The intellectual climate of this period was charged with polemics. Noisiest among these writers was the poet TCHARENTS, who perceived revolutionary socialism to be the only road to salvation for a small country, and much of his poetry from that period is a call to his countrymen to participate in the new life. But as time passed, his poetry became increasingly nostalgic and lyrical. 'The poet of the Revolution . . . the last poet', he calls himself, suggesting perhaps that the era of revolutionary idealism had died. Revolutionary fervour had indeed disappeared by the mid-1930s. The purges of 1937 finished it for ever. Most writers perished in prisons or labour camps, charged with nationalist and anti-revolutionary activities.

With the 1915 Turkish massacre of the Armenian population, and the establishment of Kemal Atatürk's régime in 1920, the curtain fell on four centuries of Armenian cultural presence in the Ottoman capital. W Armenian belonged to history. The modern Armenian diaspora had come into existence. Those handful who survived formed a sort of Transition Generation – T'EK'EYAN, Levon Shant (1869–1951), ZARYAN, Hakob Oshakan (1883–1948) and SHANOUR went on to produce some of their most sensitive works, identifying themselves with the destiny of their nation, searching desperately for a new identity and for respect.

●H. Thorossian, Histoire de la littérature arménienne dès ses origines jusqu'à nos jours (Paris, 1951); V. Inglisian, 'Die armenische Litteratur' in G. Deeters (Ed.), Handbuch der Orientalistik, vol. VIII (Leyden, 1963); J. Etmekjian, French Influence on the Western Armenian Renaissance (New York, 1964); A. Baliozian, 'Armenian Literature' in his The Armenians: Their History and Culture, (New York, 1980), pp. 43–133. J. Eetmekjian, History of Armenian Literature: Fifth to Thirteenth Centuries (New York, 1985).   VN

BULGARIAN

Bulgarian literature came into being with King Boris I (reigned 852–89) who accepted Christianity from Byzantium. The first Bulgarian liturgical works, lives of saints and chronicles were translations from the Greek. When original work began to appear, it was heavily influenced by Byzantine Greek literature. Nevertheless, indigenous heathen beliefs also found their way into literary production, mainly in the form of glosses to translations of Greek texts (see APOCRYPHA). The beginnings of Bulgarian literature are linked with the missionary activities of Cyril (826/7–69) and Methodius (815–85) to whom the first translations of the Scriptures are ascribed and also the authorship of the Cyrillic alphabet. Two alphabets were in use in Bulgaria until the end of the 12th century (the Glagolitic, probably based on N Semitic or Caucasian, and the Cyrillic, based on the Greek) and the Glagolitic is generally regarded as the older; scholarly opinion is divided over which alphabet Cyril designed. Cyril and Methodius went to Great Moravia (862) and there, together with a number of disciples, they began translating liturgical texts and Scripture. They used a Slavonic dialect which became the liturgical language of the Eastern (Orthodox) Slavs (Old Church Slavonic); its closeness to the language used in early Bulgarian literature (Old Bulgarian) creates some confusion, but generally, the two terms are interchangeable.

In 885, after the death of Methodius, their disciples were expelled from Great Moravia and most of them went to the Bulgarian Empire where, supported by Boris I, they established two cultural centres, in Ochrida (see KLIMENT OF OHRID) and in the capital of the Empire, Preslav (see KONSTANTIN OF PRESLAV). The two centres served as seminaries; their literary production consisted mainly of translations. Under King Simeon (reigned 893–927), who was educated in Constantinople and had worked for years at the Preslav literary school, the so-called Golden Age of literature began; it lasted until 1018, when the Empire fell under Byzantine rule. Meanwhile, in the mid-10th century, the Dualist Bogomil heresy emerged; many nobles and clerics became its adherents, which weakened Christian dogma and evoked strong reactions from strict churchmen (e.g. Cosmas the Priest [fl. 2nd half 10th cent.] who wrote his *Beseda protiv novopoyavilata se eres na bogomilite* [A treatise against the newly-arisen Bogomil heresy, late 10th cent.]) and gave rise to translations of Byzantine anti-heretical texts. Byzantium ruled Bulgaria until 1186; numerous translations were done, mostly APOCRYPHA and hagiographic works.

After 1186 for nearly two centuries Bulgaria was in such a state of military turmoil that literary production comprised for the most part only hagiographic works and panegyrics of rulers and saints. In the 14th century royal patronage of culture revived literature. The Tărnovo School was founded and it produced translations (theological works, sermons, chronicles, *vitae*, liturgical texts, treatises) and original works where important changes in hagiography took place, mainly through the influence of Hesychast teachings (see EVTIMII OF TĂRNOVO). The power-struggles in the Bulgarian Empire after 1370 and the Turkish invasion (1393–6) confined literary life to monasteries (e.g. Rila) where chronicles were composed and older texts copied. From the end of the 16th century DAMASKINI constituted the main genre. In the 17th and 18th centuries an independent R. Catholic Bulgarian literature appeared, mostly written in Latin script, but sometimes in Cyrillic. Nearly all this literature was religious. One of the most prominent Bulgarian Baroque figures was Filip Stanislavov (1600s–74) whose collection of Bulgarian prayers, including apocryphal texts, known as *Abagar* was published in Cyrillic in Rome, 1651.

A limited cultural revival began after PAISII OF HILENDAR wrote his patriotic 'History', mainly because of its impact on the priest, Sofronii Vrachanski (1739–1813), who began spreading PAISII's ideas, and who wrote the first autobiography in Bulgarian literature, *Zhitie i stradaniya greshnago Sofroniya* (The life and sufferings of Sofronii the sinner, 1804), and a collection of sermons and homilies, *Kiriakodromion, sirech Nedelnik* (K., or postil, 1806). Petăr Beron (1800–71), who studied in Heidelberg and Munich and lived in Germany, England and France, became the first Bulgarian Enlightenment *littérateur*; he wrote in Latin, Greek, French and German, more than 20 academic works, but his fame rests on his *Riben bukvar* (Fish primer, 1824), which is the first Bulgarian school textbook and contains prayers for children, parables, fables and tales. The periodical press, which was founded outside Bulgaria (*Lyubo-slovie* [The literature lover], Smyrna, 1842), printed the first modern Bulgarian verse.

Not before Petko Slaveikov (1827–95), however, did modern Bulgarian literature have an accomplished writer. In 1860 the first Bulgarian novel appeared, *Neshtastna familia* (The unfortunate family) by Vasil Drumev (1840/2–1901), and in the 1860s the first theatre performances began; the first Bulgarian play was Dobri Voinikov's (1833–78) *Raina Knyaginya* (Princess R., 1866), but the same author's *Krivorazbranata tsivilizatsiya* (The misunderstood civilisation, 1871) was the first play of literary value and it is still performed today.

19th-century Bulgarian literature, dominated by the 'national idea', was one of the main instruments of the National Revival. Georgi Rakovski (1821–67), revolutionary, scholar and writer, formulated the ideology of the National Revival and the strategy of revolution; his long poem *Gorski patnik* (Forest wayfarer, 1857) set an example for literature linked with national 'awakening'. Works of writers like BOTEV, KARAVELOV or VAZOV were devoted to the national cause; they not only reflected Revivalist ideas, but to a large extent created them. Lexicography and collections of oral-tradition songs, tales and legends also boosted national awareness.

1880–1930 is the most fruitful period in modern Bulgarian literature. Realist writing of the pre-WWI period varied from village prose to psychologically analytical prose concerning urban life. Neo-Romantic fiction was represented by TODOROV whose 'Idylls' marked the beginning of Modernist prose in Bulgarian literature. In verse, writers like SLAVEIKOV and YAVOROV went further than prose writers in 'catching up' with W European movements like Symbolism and Decadence. Although much Modernist writing was published in periodicals before WWI. Modernist literature in book form began seriously to flourish after WWI. This included not only Decadent, Symbolist and Naturalist writing, but also, e.g., the Diabolist trend (based on a Poeësque conception of 'mystery and imagination'). Expressionism was particularly strong in verse, but in MUTAFOV's prose it is combined with Futurism. At the beginning of the 1920s left-wing writing became particularly strong, e.g. Georgi Karaslavov (1904–84) or Hristo Smirnenski (1898–1923). Some of the most original writers of this period, e.g. YOVKOV and RAINOV, cannot be placed in any definite literary trend. After WWII and the advent of Communism, the development of Bulgarian literature was suffocated by the cheap feather-bed of Socialist Realism. With rare exceptions like RADICHKOV, until the 1970s the socialist elimination of individual identity blocked the development of innovative writing in Bulgaria. In the 1970s and 1980s, though writers tended to keep to socialist themes, their interpretations rejected Socialist Realist models. Among the more inventive poets were the philosophical Nikolai Kănchev (b. 1937), Stefan Tsanev (b. 1936) and the sarcastic Konstantin Pavlov (b. 1933), and among prose writers Emilian Stanev (1907–79) and Viktor Paskov (b. 1952). The most accomplished dramatists were RADICHKOV, Stefan Tsanev and Stanislav Stratiev (b. 1941).

●E. Riggs (Ed.), *Popular Bulgarian Songs and Proverbs* (New York, 1863–4); P. Danchev (Ed.), *Bulgarian Short Stories* (Sofia, 1960); [no editor], *In the Fields. Bulgarian Short Stories* (Sofia, 1957); R. Pridham and J. Norris (Eds), *The Peach Thief and Other Bulgarian Stories* (London, 1968); P. Tempest (Ed.), *Anthology of Bulgarian Poetry* (Sofia, 1980).

C. A. Manning and R. Smal-Stocki, *The History of Modern Bulgarian Literature* (New York, 1960); C. A. Moser, *A History of Bulgarian Literature 865–1944* (The Hague, 1972); G. Hateau, *Panorama de la littérature bulgare contemporaine* (Paris, 1937); L. Salvini, *La letteratura bulgara 1878–1912* (Rome, 1936); C. Obreschkoff, *Das bulgarische Volkslied* (Berne, 1937); V. Pinto, *Bulgarian Prose and Verse* (London, 1957).   SIK

BYELORUSSIAN (BELARUSIAN)

Byelorussian literature shared its origins with Russian and Ukrainian in the 11th–14th centuries when the common literary language was Church Slavonic. Amongst the earliest monuments to appear on ethnically Byelorussian territory were the *vitae* of St Euphrosyne of Połack (12th century) and Abram of Smalensk (c. 1240); the pilgrimage literature of this period was uninteresting compared with the eloquent homiletic writing of Clement of Smalensk (d. after 1164) and, particularly, St Cyril of Turaŭ (c. 1130–c. 1182), but the major figure in ecclesiastical literature was also the last, SKARYNA. Chronicles were written in Byelorussian, but towards the end of the 16th century memoir literature came to the fore, notably in the *Dzionnik* (Memoirs) of Fiodar Jeŭłašeŭski (1546–1604), the *Dopisy* (Reports) of Fiłon Kmita-Čarabylski (1530–87) and the *Barkułabaŭski letapis* (The Barkułabava chronicle, 1562–1608), with, somewhat later, the *Dyaryuš* (Diary, 1645) of the polemicist Afanasii Filipovič (c. 1597–1648). Most other literature of the time was highly sectarian and of no literary interest, though two lively political satires have survived: *Pramova Mialeški* (The speech of Mialeška, c. 1630) and *List da Abuchoviča* (Letter to Abuchovič, 1655). After SKARYNA's verse prayers, the main lyric subgenre from the late 16th century was that of armorial epigrams, laborious 13-syllable panegyrics, of which the main practitioners were Andrej Rymša (?1550–?99), Łukaš and Kuźma (d. 1606)

Mamonič (fl. last quarter of 16th century). One outstanding poem, however, was the (probably collective) *Lamient* (Lament, 1620) on the death of Abbot Laoncii Karpovič (1580–1620). Simiaon Połacki (1629–80), best known for his Russian verse, also wrote in Byelorussian during his early years, between 1648 and 1664.

Byelorussia in the 18th century was almost entirely polonised (the process had gathered pace after the Union of Lublin in 1569) and only one major Byelorussian work (albeit macaronic) was written: *Kamiedyja* (A comedy, 1787) by Kaetan Maraševuski (fl. end 18th century), based on the tradition of school dramas and their interludes. Drama was further developed in the 19th century by DUNIN-MARCINKIEVIČ, who in his three plays combined the traditions of 18th-century Polish Sentimentalism with satirical Realism, thereby laying elementary foundations for later Byelorussian drama. He also helped to revive Byelorussian poetry through his ethnographically rich, often humorous, verse narratives. Ethnography had, in fact, been the starting-point for several early 19th-century writers like Jan Barščeŭski (1794–1851), Jan Čačot (1796–1847) and Radvan Rypinski (1811–1900); outside this pattern lies the first known poem since Byelorussia was incorporated into the Russian Empire at the start of the 19th century, 'Zahraj, zahraj, chłopča mały . . .' ('Play, then, play . . . , 1828) by the peasant poet, Paŭluk Bahrym (1831–91). Two anonymous verse burlesques circulated widely in this period: a pastiche, *Enieida navyvarat* (The *Aeneid* inside out, c. 1820), and *Taras na Parnasie* (Taras on Parnassus, c. 1840), satirising contemporary Russian and Polish literature. In terms of literary quality they at least match contemporary works of known authorship.

The various bans and confiscations that had plagued Byelorussian literature were slightly reduced towards the end of the 19th century when several socially minded poets appeared: Janka Łucyna (pen-name of Ivan Niesłuchoŭski, 1851–97), Adam Hurynovič (1864–94) and, above all, BAHUŠEVIČ, sometimes called the 'father of modern Byelorussian literature' who promoted social reform and national consciousness. Greater freedom came in 1905, and a major event was the founding of the newspaper *Naša niva* (1906–15), which was to provide a vital focus and stimulus for all national aspirations: in the first three years of its existence the paper published 950 contributions from nearly 500 different villages and towns. Amongst them were the first works of several writers who were to become national classics, notably KUPAŁA, KOŁAS and BAHDANOVIČ. KUPAŁA's neo-Romantic poetry struck a unique chord at a time of transformation and crisis, as did his play *Paŭlinka*, the cornerstone of modern Byelorussian drama; KOŁAS wrote fine prose, but above all created the first major verse epics in the language; BAHDANOVIČ brought the W European cultural heritage to his literature, thereby irreversibly raising its level of sophistication. Hardly less significant were the exiled poet HARUN, and BIADULA, impressionist short-story writer and poet, who later became a novelist.

The Russian Revolution of 1917 coincided with the development of the Byelorussian novel by, in addition to BIADULA, HARECKI and Ciška Hartny (i.e. Żmicier Żyłounovič, 1887–1937). After the short-lived Byelorussian National Republic in 1918, the 1920s was an age of enthusiasm, with, at first, an official policy of byelorussification and vigorous literary groups, most notably Maładniak (1923–8) and Uzvyšša (1926–31). Poets like Michaś Čarot (i.e. Michaś

Kudzielka, 1896–1938) and Michajła Hramyka (1885–1969) attacked the past with vigour, whilst others like DUBOŬKA and PUŠČA attempted to resist Communist conformism and repression. Stalin's purges (1936–9) removed many Byelorussian writers. In any case, little of interest was written from the early 1930s until the Thaw, apart from the analytical psychological novels of ČORNY, and some poetry in W Byelorussia (E Poland), the best of which was by TANK. W and Soviet Byelorussia were united at the end of WWII, but another decade was to pass before Byelorussian creative writing really revived.

In the late 1950s some excellent poets appeared including Nił Hilevič (b. 1931) and Ryhor Baradulin (b. 1935), with preservation of the Byelorussian language as a recurrent theme; drama failed to develop, but prose flourished as never before. BRYL is the doyen of short-story writers, whilst MIELEŽ created a prose epic comparable in scope to KOŁAS's verse masterpieces. Also outstanding are the war novels of BYKAŬ, the historical works of KARATKIEVIČ and the country prose of Ivan Ptašnikaŭ (b. 1932). Amongst other interesting contemporary prose writers are Viktar Karamazaŭ (b. 1934), Barys Sačanka (b. 1936). Aleś Žuk (b. 1947) and, especially, Michas Stralcoŭ (b. 1937), who all continue to develop the tradition of psychological realism in which Byelorussia is now one of the leading literatures of the former Soviet Union. Outside Byelorussia the only writers of any stature are in America the poet Natalla Arsieńnieva (b. 1903) and in Poland the prose miniaturist Sakrat Janovič (b. 1936).

●Anthologies: V. Rich, *Like Water, Like Fire: An Anthology of Byelorussian Poetry from 1828 to the Present Day* (London, 1971); N. Voŭk-Levanovič, *Colours of the Native Country. Stories by Byelorussian Writers* (Minsk, 1972); *Byelorussian Folk Tales* (Moscow, 1983); *Soviet Literature*, 1983, no. 3, devoted to the literature and arts of Soviet Byelorussia; E. Moroz (Ed.), *Home Fires: Stories of Writers from Byelorussia* (Moscow, 1986).
A. B. McMillin, *A History of Byelorussian Literature from Its Origins to the Present Day* (Giessen, 1977); E. F. Karskij, *Die weissrussische Volkspoesie und Literaturgeschichte* (Berlin, 1930).   ABMcM

CROATIAN

The Croats were one of the Slav tribes to settle on the territory of ancient Illyricum, where they organised a state in the 7th century, and were converted to Christianity during the 9th. With the arrival of the Hungarians, Pannonia joined Dalmatian Croatia, becoming a fully independent state in the 9th century and a kingdom in the first quarter of the 10th. Following a political crisis, the Croatian crown passed to King Koloman of Hungary, proclaimed ruler of Hungary and Croatia under the Crown of St Stephen in 1102. Croatia remained allied or subservient to Hungary until the end of the Habsburg Monarchy.

The first vernacular Croatian texts date from the 9th-century mission of Cyril and Methodius who introduced the Glagolitic alphabet. The oldest surviving Glagolitic text is the Baška tablet from the island of Krk (c. 1100). Glagolitic was used in all aspects of public life which ensured continuity with other Slav cultures rooted in the Byzantine Slavonic tradition. The earliest Glagolitic genres were those current in the Christian literature of early medieval Europe, e.g. homilies, apocrypha, hagiography. There were also secular stories translated from Greek. In the late Middle Ages we find traces of translations, via Venice, of French legends, the TROY BOOK and the ALEXANDER ROMANCE, and anthologies of wise sayings, notably *Disticha Catonis*. During the 15th century came increasingly elaborate verse legends of the saints and popular imitations of Italian miracle plays.

The transformation of Croatian culture came at the turn of the 15th and 16th centuries, when the growth of commerce in the coastal towns provided the conditions for Renaissance influence. The Dalmatian towns and islands had fallen from Byzantine to Venetian control (the last in 1480), with the exception of the republic of Ragusa (Dubrovnik) which was able to buy its virtual autonomy as vassal to successive overlords. The croaticised core of town-dwellers formed a patrician class ready to respond to cultural stimuli from Italy.

The first poets of the 16th century made the final transition from devotional to secular writing, epitomised by the work of MARULIĆ. In this century, while writers followed trends in Italy, producing numerous translations, there was a conscious sense of a Croatian tradition: the first lyric poems were modelled on the indigenous oral tradition. In other genres, writers exploited social similarities to develop local versions of Italian models. Examples are the works of the 16th-century dramatist DRŽIĆ, and the 17th-century poet GUNDULIĆ. In the second half of the 17th century the literature of Dubrovnik declined sharply, with the city's decreasing prosperity and the devastation caused by the earthquake of 1667. The main focus of Croatian literature now moved northwards.

Conditions for cultural activity in the Croatian lands other than Dubrovnik and Venetian Dalmatia were unfavourable. On the one hand the whole population, particularly of Slavonia, was depleted by constant fighting, and many old families died out. The Military Zone established as a buffer against the Ottomans was settled largely by foreign families with no roots in the Croatian lands and the administrators in Inner Croatia tended also to be foreign, thus creating a predominantly German-speaking middle class. In the prevailing conditions of constant fear of Turkish attack the Renaissance and the Reformation found little echo. It was only with the Counter-Reformation and the activity of the Franciscans and the Jesuits that the situation began to change. With the growth of education that they stimulated, Zagreb was gradually able to emerge as a cultural centre. The most important figures in Croatian literature of the 18th century were didactic writers, two of them Franciscans from the coast, Filip Grabovac (1697–1749) and KAČIĆ-MIOŠIĆ, and the third a Slavonian, Matija Reljković (1732–98), whose education, like that of many of his countrymen, was gained in W Europe in the Seven Years' War.

The main issue dominating Croatian culture in the first half of the 19th century was language: resistance to German and Hungarian domination, and the need to codify the vernacular as the standard literary language. The reform of the language was carried out by Ljudevit Gaj (1809–72). Within the framework of his Illyrian Movement there were echoes of European Romanticism, and the Revival of Croatian literature was finally established with the work of the poet MAŽURANIĆ. The most important figure of the 19th century was ŠENOA, who

played a vital role in the formation of a reading public. In the second half of the
century prose emerged as the dominant genre, reflecting European trends, the
most important writers being KOVAČIĆ and v. NOVAK.

The beginning of the 20th century saw a return to poetry, stimulated by the
main exponent of Croatian Modernism, MATOŠ, a convinced 'European'. The
interwar period was dominated by avant-garde writers, at first under the
influence of central European Expressionism, notably the poet ŠIMIĆ and the
early KRLEŽA, then by socially committed writing and work of R. Catholic
orientation. The outstanding poet of the period was UJEVIĆ. KRLEŽA was
influential in the first years after WWII in ensuring that Socialist Realism did not
take root. The writers around the journal *Krugovi* (Circles) established the
freedom to exploit foreign models, notably the Soviet Avant-garde, French
Existentialism and T. S. Eliot. The 1970s were marked by POSTMODERNIST trends.
The 1980s saw a new interest in the historical novel and the emergence of
consciously feminist prose.

●F. Trgogranić, *Storia della Letteratura Croata (secolo XV–XIX)* (Rome, 1953); A.
Barac, *A History of Yugoslav Literature* (Belgrade, 1955); S. Lukić, *Contemporary
Yugoslav Literature* (Urbana, 1972).   ECH

CZECH

The 'Czechs' settled in Bohemia in the 6th century and the fact that the
Christianisation of Bohemia was begun by Irish and 'German' monks before the
Greek 'Apostles of the Slavs', Cyril and Methodius, reached Moravia has had a
lasting impact on Czech literary culture. The earliest surviving complete Czech
text, the kyrie, 'Hopodine, pomiluj ny' (Lord, have mercy upon us), shows the
influence of the Slavonic liturgy in two words, but demonstrates that in the 10th
century Bohemia is already in the Western sphere of influence. Several other
hymns survive before Czech becomes firmly established as the medium of
literature in the 13th century. Latin legends of SS Ludmila, Wenceslas and
Adalbert and the artistically sophisticated *Chronica Boëmorum* of Cosmas
Pragensis (?1045–1125) manifest an awareness of a separate Czech identity. The
last forty years of the 13th century produced two works of high literary culture,
the DEVOTIONAL LYRIC 'Cunigunda's Prayer' and the *Alexandreida* (see
ALEXANDER ROMANCE).

During the 14th century Czech literature blossomed in all genres, verse and
prose legends, chronicles, satires, verse and prose romances, secular and
devotional lyric, *exempla*, drama, theological and philosophical works; the first
complete Czech translation of the BIBLE is from the 1370s. This century also saw
the first lexicographical works, the Latin verse dictionaries of the Czech
language compiled by Master Claretus de Solentia (Bartoloměj z Chlumce, d. c.
1379) and his collaborators.

Czech theological writing reached its zenith in the works of HUS and those
inspired by the Church Reform movement which centred on him and then, after
his burning at the stake, his writings. The most original writer to arise from this
movement was CHELČICKÝ. The movement and the wars which accompanied it
produced lively polemical writing, epic disputes and balladic satires, as well as

original hymns. It also produced the first works on military strategy in Czech. Hussitism, however, was fundamentally detrimental to Czech literary culture. The Renaissance period, which may be said to date from around the 1470s in Bohemia, compared with the previous and subsequent period, produced little of lasting value. Nevertheless, the translations and adaptations of Eastern and Western fabliaux, jests, traditional tales (such as *Mélusine*, *Faustus* or *Fortunatus*), works of scholarship (including herbals and, most important, alchemical works) and legends laid new foundations for a popular literature, which, having gone through only insignificant, politically inspired, changes, remained alive well into the 19th century. Some serious attempts at Humanist writing in Czech were made by such as Viktorin Kornel ze Všehrd (c. 1460– 1520). HÁJEK's chronicle (1541) was to shape Czech historiography until the National Revival, and literature till the end of the 19th century. Highly original travel literature was produced, usually accounts of journeys to the Holy Land. Czech vernacular drama of the period was uninventive, but the end of the Renaissance saw original, witty, satirical and didactic verse works by such as DAČICKÝ and RVAČOVSKÝ.

KOMENSKÝ (Comenius), though he straddles the Renaissance and Baroque (Counter-Reformation) periods, remained firmly rooted in Renaissance Humanism, however Baroque the style of his first main work. In the Baroque most work of any profundity was written in Latin (for example, the historiography and patriotic tracts of Bohuslav Balbín [1621–68]), but religion-inspired lyric (especially BRIDEL) and secular verse (especially ROSA) showed considerable originality; Rosa's purist Latin grammar and style-manual (1672) had a considerable influence on National Revival lexicography.

The Czech National Revival began under two chief impulses, the Emperor Joseph II's introduction of German as the language of instruction into secondary schools, and the national (racial) theories of the German Enlightenment. The Revival was initially dominated by scholars like Josef Dobrovský (1753–1829), and the leadership of scholars persisted right up to 1848: Pavel Josef Šafařík (a Slovak, 1795–1861), JUNGMANN, ERBEN, and the founder of modern Czech historiography, František Palacký (1798–1876). The Revival tended to be backward-looking, and so, first, historical dramas, epics and prose, and influential forged medieval manuscripts and, second, works harking back to the oral tradition, in which it was believed that the 'national soul' could be found, were predominant. A few writers, however, did concentrate on universal themes, and predominant among them was MÁCHA. After 1848, though initially Romantic writing prevailed, Czech literature gradually moved towards Realism. The most influential group of writers in the 1860s and 1870s were the Poetic Realist Máj school, led by NERUDA, SVĚTLÁ and Vítězslav Hálek (1835–74). In the 1870s, however, serious Czech literature began to divide more or less clearly into two streams, nationalist or neo-Revivalist writers like ČECH and JIRÁSEK, and Cosmopolitans like VRCHLICKÝ and ZEYER. In the 1890s, when Czech writers no longer felt any need to defend 'Czechness', these two streams became more radical. Young 1890s writers, instead of being neo-Revivalists, turned to political writing and Realism (e.g MACHAR, SOVA, F. V. Krejčí [1867–1941], F. X. Šalda [1867–1937]) and, instead of being Cosmopolitans, turned to Decadence and Symbolism (e.g. BŘEZINA, HLAVÁČEK, Arnošt Procházka [1869–1925]).

The Czech Decadence was probably the most thoroughgoing of all European Decadences. After the turn of the century, Czech literature went through the same main fashions as most continental literature, Expressionism, Vitalism, Proletarian Poetry and Surrealism. One movement they call their own, Poetism, a trend which combines Futurism and Surrealism with limited, usually playful, social *engagement* (see NEZVAL). Although Russian Socialist Realism had had an impact before 1939, after WWII this mode of literature began to be the (largely imposed) main force in Czech literature, until the end of the 1950s. In the 1960s literature concentrated on the self, on the experience of Stalinism, and on the Jews' fate during WWII. The notional split after c. 1970 between literature published in state-run publishing houses, that produced in *samizdat* and that published abroad by writers in exile is largely spurious. Apart from in the works of Party establishment and émigré hacks, the modes of the 1960s continued. Towards the end of the 1970s, and even more strongly, the mid-1980s, a more inventive literature began to appear.

•Still the best history of Czech literature in a Western language is H. Jelínek's *Histoire de la littérature tchèque* (Paris, 1930–5). A survey of literature from the Revival to 1939 is to be found in R. Pynsent, *Czech Prose and Verse* (London, 1979). For prose from the turn of the century to the 1960s: H. Kunstmann, *Tschechische Erzählkunst im 20. Jahrhundert* (Cologne, 1974).　　　　　　　　　　　RBP

ESTONIAN

Estonian literature did not come into being until the 19th century, and did not really attain maturity until the 20th. Its background was an extensive oral tradition, and early attempts at literary expression in Estonian were linked primarily with practical religious and educational needs. Aesthetically superior to the first secular occasional verse in Estonian in the 17th century (Reiner Brocman [1609–47]) was the anonymous elegy on the destruction of Tartu in the Northern War, 'Oh, my wretched city of Tartu' (1708). This work, apparently written by a native Estonian (Käsu Hans (?–1715?]) was an exception that proved the rule that for centuries Estonian literature was written by outsiders for Estonian readers thanks to the work of German intellectuals. After it had become secular it was almost entirely limited to works of popular instruction and educational works (Peter A. F. von Mannteuffel [1768–1842]). Kristjan Jaak Peterson's (1801–22) attempts at odes modelled on Klopstock and the pre-Romantics, where the author tried to blend the art of his models with the domestic oral tradition to create artistically authentic verse in Estonian, were condemned to virtual oblivion; a collection of his verse, diary entries and letters did not appear until 1922.

The foundations of a new attitude to language and nation began to be laid at the end of the 1830s by patriotic men of letters linked with the Estonian Learned Society in Tartu. Friedrich R. Faehlmann's (1798–1850) interest in Estonian folklore and mythology, which was not quite free of a desire for mystification, inspired KREUTZWALD to create on the model of the Finnish *Kalevala* (see LÖNNROT) an artificial 'national epos', the *Kalevipoeg*. Patriotic poetry began to be written under the influence of German verse (KREUTZWALD, KOIDULA), and the Vanemuine theatrical society in Tartu laid the foundations for Estonian national drama (KOIDULA, Juhan Kunder [1852–88]). The development of an Estonian periodical press, e.g. *Perno Postimees* (1857–86), *Eesti Postimees* (1864–80) or *Sakala* (1878–82), gradually provided an even wider audience for the activities of the patriotic intelligentsia. From the 1890s onwards, quasi-mimetic prose and the romanticising glorification of the past in historical prose (Eduard Bornhöhe [1862–1923]) were replaced by social realism in prose (VILDE) and an interest in the sources of social conflict in drama (KITZBERG). LIIV's work, permeated as it was by his own wretched lot, constituted the first break from the old conventions of Estonian lyric verse.

The 1905 foundation of the Young Estonia (Noor Eesti) movement with its accentuation of Europeanness formed the basis for a modern literature in verse (SUITS) and prose (TUGLAS). Their programme also influenced older writers (VILDE) and writers who remained outside the movement (the imaginative Symbolist, Ernst Enno [1875–1934]). A decade later, the writers of the Siuru group (GAILIT, Johannes Semper [1892–1970], UNDER, VISNAPUU) followed Young Estonia's aesthetic programme.

The creation of an independent Estonian republic aided the maturation of a national literature. August Jakobson (1904–63) modified elements of French Naturalism to create his panoramic visions of Estonian life, and August Mälk (1900–87) sought the roots of true Estonianness in idealised pictures of the tough inhabitants of the seaboard. Oskar Luts (1887–1953) continued to exploit the prototype of colourful folk story-telling which he had created before WWI, while GAILIT's writing was affiliated to Scandinavian neo-Romanticism. The novels of TAMMSAARE were a grand attempt at a synthesis of the *Moderne* with 19th-century East European Realism, particularly in his pentalogy. The aestheticism of Young Estonia and the Siuru group had its counterpart in social critical poetry concentrating on life in the raw (August Alle [1890–1952], Johannes Barbarus [i.e. Vares, 1890–1946], Jaan Kärner [1891–1958], Juhan Sütiste [1899–1945]) and in the Tartu group of poets, Arbujad (Logomancers) (ALVER, MASING, KANGRO, Kersti Merilaas [1913–86], August Sang [1914–69], Paul Viiding [1904–62]), whose works manifest a conception of art as a spiritual search for the absolute. One of the literary periodicals founded between the wars, *Looming* (Creation), is still published.

The Red Army's occupation of Estonia and her incorporation into the USSR as a Soviet Republic (1940), the subsequent German occupation (1941), and then her reincorporation into the USSR (1944) were a profound shock for literary life. A large number of writers went into exile, and Lund became an important literary centre with its own publishing house, Eesti Kirjanike Kooperatiiv. Among those who went into exile were Artur Adson (1889–1977), GAILIT, Ivar Grünthal (b. 1924), KANGRO, Raimond Kolk (b. 1924), Ilmar Laaban (b. 1921), Kalyu Lepik (b. 1920), RISTIKIVI, SUITS, UNDER and VISNAPUU. Meanwhile domestic literature was forcedly sovietised, adapted to Soviet literary models; the panoramic social novel (Aadu Hint [b. 1910]) and *kolkhoz* prose (Hans Leberecht [1900–60]) were favoured, like naive lyric verse expressing social utopianism and euphoria (Juhan Smuul [1922–71], D. Vaarandi) and drama of stereotyped class conflict (Jakobson). Not until the end of the 1950s did the domestic literary scene begin to show signs of life – a distaste for the imposed literary canon and for the normative interpretation of history led to the emergence of short contemplative prose works (for example, Smuul's lyrical travel journal, *Jäine raamat* [Antarctica, ahoy!]) and to ostentatiously subjective verse which returned 'freedom' to poetry (which, among other things, meant the rehabilitation of free verse). This new verse was the product of the Boxed Generation (so called because their first books were produced boxed together with those of other members of the generation): KAPLINSKI, LUIK, RUMMO. Novelists tried to find new ways of approaching their material (A. Beekman), but, in the 1960s, the way was led by the more adaptable novella and the 'little novel' concentrating on a given problem, which replaced the grand-scale epic by carefully contrived formal and semantic structures (KROSS, Rein Saluri [b. 1939], Mats Traat [b. 1936], UNT, Enn Vetemaa [b. 1936]). Dramas tend to the modular and employ the techniques of the Western Theatre of the Absurd (RUMMO). Since the 1970s verse has been dominated by sober, unsentimental writing (Andres Ehin [b. 1940], J. B. Isotamm [b. 1939], Jaak Jõerütt [b. 1947], VIIDING); the greatest achievements in prose are to be found in the works of the philosophical grotesque by VALTON and in KROSS's historical novels. LUIK has expressed the experience of the Boxed Generation in her reflective memoirs of her own childhood, *Seitsmes rahukevad* (Seventh year of peace). The 1988 'Singing Revolution' revived literary themes which had been taboo for decades and a strong publicist note (as in the song poetry of RUNNEL) and independence (1990) means that domestic and exile literature can merge.

●E. H. Harris, *Literature in Estonia* (London, 1947); H. Jänes, *Geschichte der estnischen Literatur* (Stockholm, 1965); O. Loorits, *Estnische Volksdichtung und Mythologie* (Tartu, 1932); A. Oras and B. Kangro, *Estonian Literature in Exile* (Lund, 1967); A. Mägi, *Estonian Literature* (Stockholm, 1968); E. Nirk, *Estonian Literature* (2nd ed., Tallinn, 1970).   VM

FINNISH

Finnish literature is written in Finnish and Swedish. Still today writers draw inspiration from the ORAL POETRY tradition. Although Finns published poetry in Finnish and Swedish in the 17th and 18th centuries, a literary culture as such only begins in the 19th century as an essential component of cultural and, later, political nationalism. A sense of the past complete with a golden age, and poetic landscapes inhabited by a gallery of 'typical' national characters, was created principally by RUNEBERG and LÖNNROT in the first half of the 19th century. The neo-Hegelian statesman Johan Snellman (1801–81), who steered Finland on a course that would lead to greater autonomy in her own affairs, placed great importance on the development of a Finnish-language literature in preparing the people for nationhood. The development of the national image during this time owes much to Zachris Topelius's (1818–98) historical tales, August Oksanen's (1826–89) didactic poetry and Theodolinda Hahnsson's (1839–1919) uplifting social stories. KIVI, the outstanding writer of the period, introduced a degree of realism that some of his contemporaries found distasteful but which posterity has recognised. The Realism of the 1880s came to Finland principally from Norwegian and French sources but found original development in the work of

CANTH, AHO and Arvid Järnefelt (1861–1932). The 1890s marked the beginning of a remarkable flowering in the Finnish arts. Known as neo-Romanticism and lasting into the 1910s, it was a Finnish adaptation of art nouveau, heavily influenced by German *Jugendstil* and Symbolism. The Fin de siècle brought major political problems: from within, bitter conflict between the younger and older generations of Finns, and from without, russification. Thus neo-Romanticism became synonymous with the national cause and a powerful political allegory is present in the work of several authors. The outstanding authors of this period were the prose writers AHO, LINNANKOSKI, Volter Kilpi (1874–1939), Teuvo Pakkala (1862–1925), Karl Tavaststjerna (1860–98) and the poets LEINO and the Symbolist Otto Manninen (1872–1950). The early years of the 20th century saw a growth of interest in the social and regional novel, an essential part of the nation-building process. A contributory factor was the rise of socialism and the growing divisions in Finnish society, culminating in the 1918 Civil War between the 'Reds' and the 'Whites' and ending in the defeat of the 'Reds'. Important social writing from this period includes the works of Iemari Kianto (1874–1970), who placed much of his work in NE Finland, Maila Talvio (1871–1951) and Maria Jotuni (1880–1943), a powerful writer on the cause of women. The Civil War and its aftermath are prominent in LEHTONEN's and SILLANPÄÄ's work, the latter tending to concentrate on rural life, the former on the city, and Runar Schildt (1888–1925). The conditions of the rural and urban poor, and militarism are often the subjects of the ironical writings of working-class life by Pentti Haanpää (1905–55) which shook the establishment and made it difficult for him to find publishers. PEKKANEN's writing, less passionate but realist, found a more receptive readership. During the interwar years poets such as V. A. Koskenniemi (1885–1962) tended to write on Classical themes, Uuno Kailas (1901–33) and Kaarlo Sarkia (1902–45) preferred traditional styles, while Aaro Hellaakoski (1893–1952) and P. Mustapää (1899–1973) are concerned in different ways with man's relationship to Nature and belief. Expressionism reached Finland through SÖDERGRAN, although her greatness was not immediately recognised. Elmer Diktonius (1896–1961), apart from writing about the Civil War, was also a bold experimenter in Finland-Swedish poetry. A number of writers on the right, who came together in the mid-1920s in the *Tulenkantajat* (Torchbearers) group, looked towards central and S Europe for inspiration, introducing the symbol and metaphor of the machine age to Finnish writing. Towards the end of the 1930s, a group of left-wing writers formed the *Kiila* (Wedge) group, united by politics and social criticism, e.g. Elvi Sinervo (1912–86), Viljo Kajava (b. 1909) and Arvo Turtiainen (1904–80). The 1939–40 and 1941–4 wars against the USSR, Finland's subsequent relations with that country, neutrality, economic growth and urbanisation, and adjustment to a changing Europe are among the factors that have shaped postwar Finnish cultural life. Once again the social and regional novel played an important role. Poetry has been the medium of self-examination and, often, of political commitment. Closely following literary developments in the West and adopting Western styles and subgenres, prose writers and poets have produced a lively, thematically rich literature which has often been central to political debate and social change. Several authors use the war years as the starting-point for their social portraits. LINNA's war novel set in train a national reappraisal of the war and events that led up to it. Paavo Rintala (b. 1930), MERI and Antti Tuuri (b. 1944) are among those who have also probed the same theme in addition to their novels on wider social themes. Mika Waltari (1908–79) bridged the pre- and postwar years, turning from novels about life in interwar Finland, especially city life, to historical novels, often allegorical. Modernisation has produced a crop of novels about the problems of the rural poor, emigration, the experiences of the first generation of city-dwellers and their children, and key political events. Interesting works on these subjects have been written again by Rintala and Tuuri, and by several others including Eeva Kilpi (b. 1928), Eeva Joenpelto (b. 1921), Hannu Salama (b. 1936), Antti Hyry (b. 1931) and Alpo Ruuth (b. 1943). The work of postwar Finland-Swedish writers follows a similar pattern, although, not surprisingly, they show a particular interest, sometimes ironical, in the question of their own cultural distinctiveness. Of particular interest in this respect are Märta Tikkanen (b. 1935), Henrik Tikkanen (1924–84), and Christer Kihlman (b. 1930). Almost immediately after the war the young generation of Finnish poets turned to Modernism. Katri Vala (1901–44) and MANNER were the first, followed soon afterwards by Helvi Juvonen (1919–59), Tuomas Anhava (b. 1927), Pentti Holoppa (b. 1927) and Lassi Nummi (b. 1928). HAAVIKKO and SAARIKOSKI dominated the post-WWII period. Powerfully influenced by Western currents of thought, they have been innovators in style, form, language and subject matter. Their work, which embraces most of the developments in Finnish poetry, has been fundamental to the development of Finnish in the late 20th century.

•Anthologies: R. Dauenhauer and P. Binham (Eds), *Snow in May. An Anthology of Finnish Writing 1945–1972* (London, 1978); H. Lomas (Ed.), *Territorial Song. Contemporary Writing from Finland* (London, 1981); D. McDuff (Ed.), *Ice Around Our Lips. Finland-Swedish Poetry* (Newcastle, 1989).
J. Ahokas, *A History of Finnish Literature* (Bloomington, 1973).   MAB

GEORGIAN

Christianity, literacy and literature were all established in Georgia by the 5th century. Literature was at first overwhelmingly religious: lives of saints, liturgical texts, chronicles. Much, but not all, was translated – from Greek, Syriac, Armenian, Arabic. The literary language, while unrelated to Indo-European or Semitic languages, showed ample resources – Georgian has a lexical wealth out of all proportion to the number of its speakers – and translation from Greek helped to develop the complex syntax of sophisticated argument. Arab invasions of the 9th century destroyed much of what Byzantine and Caucasian culture had achieved; only in the early 11th century, when the next wave of invaders, the Seljük Turks, had receded, did Georgia establish real sovereignty in a new Byzantine cultural framework. 1072–1225 was a golden age, under effective rulers with a strong interest in literature as well as power. Most of the great chroniclers and poets who created a secular literature, culminating in RUSTAVELI's 'The knight in the panther's skin', lived under DAVIT the Builder (1073–1125) and Queen Tamar (1184–1213). Georgian in RUSTAVELI's time probably had as many speakers and readers as English in Shakespeare's. But uncertainties of identity, chronology, the slow changes in the language, the destruction of so many manuscripts make all information on medieval texts speculative: RUSTAVELI cannot even be proven to have existed; a chronicler such as Leont'i Mroveli could have existed anywhere between the 7th and 11th centuries; we cannot be certain even that the *Amiran-Darejaniani* (see ROMANCE) is an original text. Modern systematic evaluations are, however, overcoming the tendency of native literary historians to exaggerate antiquity and authenticity.

The Mongols in the 13th century dealt Georgian literature a fatal blow. The kingdom effectively lost its sovereignty; its unity was soon shattered into three: W Georgia, Imeretia, under Ottoman domination, while the central province of Kartli (a term often applied to all Georgia) and eastern Georgia, Kakhetia, fell under ruthless Iranian rule. Literature was dormant until the start of the 17th century, when wise kings, such as TEIMURAZ I, made a contact with the West that was reciprocated by Italian monks. New political ambitions and long periods of exile gave Georgia's aristocracy motivation and scope for reconstituting the debris of medieval culture and adding to it what they had learnt from Persian overlords and R. Catholic missionaries. The 18th-century Georgian renascence was halting, but favoured by the compatibility of the modern and the medieval language, by the introduction of the printing press and by the appearance of Renaissance men, such as the didact and lexicographer S.-S. ORBELIANI or the reckless hedonist poet Besarion Gabashvili (BESIK'I). When the Georgian states finally collapsed into Russian annexation, the enforced 'resettlement' of the royal blood in Russia paradoxically diverted the country's élite into literature. Few dynasties can have had as many writers as the Bagrations. Russian Romantics and Realists fed Georgians on European genres and attitudes; the 19th century has a copious, if derivative, literature. It may seem small beer if compared with a major European literature of the time, but it had a preparatory role, like small animals decaying into a coral reef on which a rich organic life will be built. That flourishing came at the end of the 19th century with VAZHA PSHAVELA, a poet of unquestionably universal stature; early 20th-century prose and poetry under Symbolist and Futurist auspices achieved real originality with figures such as ROBAKIDZE, GAMSAKHURDIA, JAVAKHISHVILI, the T'ABIDZE cousins. But the invasion of independent Georgia in 1921 was followed in 1923–4 by Sergo Orjonik'idze's bloody massacre of gentry and intellectuals. Others were deported to the Arctic in 1927 by a fundamentalist Communist régime; the pathological cruelty of Stalin's henchman Lavrent'i Beria exterminated most important survivors, so that 1931–7 was comparable with 1225–35 in making a literary desert. Poetry and prose have been published ever since, but only the breakdown of Soviet rule in 1989 has given hopes of a resurrection.

Every Georgian writer and unattributable text of temporary or permanent importance or curiosity has been included in this *Companion*, apart from those living writers whose full profile has yet to be clear, and writers who would only be published and read under a modern totalitarian régime. Because of its wealth and relevance to written culture, we have an entry on Georgian folk poetry. Medieval literature, where so many authors are anonymous, has been largely dealt with crudely divided into genres (chronicle, hagiography, romance), with cross-referencing of names of known authors. In consulting entries, readers should be aware that the genres overlap, and that writers until 1750 are conventionally listed under their Christian name followed by a sobriquet derived by the adjectival suffix -*eli* from their place of origin, or a patronym. Only in the 18th century did Georgian writers acquire surnames.

(I have used a simple form for transliterating Georgian: an apostrophe after the consonants *ch*, *k*, *p*, *q*, *t*, *ts* indicates that the consonant is 'ejective', i.e. that is is pronounced with no aspiration and the glottis closed.)

●G. Deeters, 'Georgische Literatur' in *Handbuch der Orientalistik, Abt. I, Bd.7, Armenisch und kaukasische Sprachen* (Leiden, Cologne, 1963), pp 129–55; K. Salia, *La littérature géorgienne*, Bedi Kartlisa 17–26 (Paris, 1964–9), id., trans. by Katharine Vivian in *History of the Georgian Nation* (Salia, Paris, 1983); H. Fähnrich, *Die georgische Literatur* (Tbilisi, 1981).

DR

BYZANTINE AND MODERN GREEK

It is impossible to determine at what point Byzantine literature ceases to be an extension of antiquity and becomes distinctively Modern Greek. To the last, historians, orators and poets reproduced the language and literary forms of their forebears. Even the hagiographical tradition had its roots in ancient biography, panegyric and romance, and by the 10th century it was thought proper to rewrite the simpler early 'Lives' in a more literary (i.e. Classical) form of language and style. Only in hymnography was a distinctively modern genre – the *kontakion* – developed early, under the influence of the Syriac-speaking sector of the Church. The greatest composer of *kontakia* was Romanos the Melode (first half of the 6th century). A further form, the *kanon* – a sequence of separate odes – developed between the early 8th century and the end of the 11th, when the ecclesiastical authorities forbade the introduction of new hymns into the liturgy.

In general, it was at the court of the Comneni, in the mid-12th century, that a sense of literary renascence can first be found in Byzantium, though paradoxically the language and literary art of this period are particularly archaising. After 1204 the exposure of Byzantium to the West as a result of the Fourth Crusade and the occupation of Greek-speaking lands by Frankish overlords is accompanied by a growth of literature written in more popular forms and in a language more closely related to the contemporary spoken idiom. In particular, romances and allegorical narratives abound.

For 150 years after the final fall of Constantinople (1453) the survival of Modern Greek culture was largely confined, beyond folk poetry, to those places (mostly islands) which remained in Frankish hands, notably Crete and Cyprus. In Crete particularly the late 16th and early 17th centuries saw a substantial and distinctive renascence. In Turkish-occupied Greece the Church, initially relatively quiescent, began to play a more overt intellectual role towards the end of the 16th century, seeking to develop a religious humanism which would shore up its dual aim of promoting nationalism and Orthodoxy. With the fall of Crete to the Turks in 1669 the forms of cultural survival fragmented further. The émigré community in Venice, and the Greeks of the Ionian Islands with whom they were in contact (and whither many Cretans had fled), drew increasingly on the intellectual traditions of Italy. At the same time the Patriarchate and leading Greeks of Constantinople (known as Phanariots) extended their own conservative version of Greek culture in Turkish-occupied territories. In due course the changing economic position of Greeks in the Turkish Empire after the treaty of Kutchuk Kainardji (1774) led to the development of a middle class unexpectedly open to Western Enlightenment ideas.

Throughout the period 1453–1770 Greek literature in the Italian-speaking areas was based on spoken Greek (demotic). In Turkish-occupied areas the emphasis was on sustaining linguistic continuity with Byzantium, and the language favoured was consequently archaising. Towards the end of the 18th century, however, the issue of the form of language used in writing became overt, closely connected with warring philosophies of education and national identity. The idealisation of Greek antiquity by Western Philhellenes in the run-up to the Greek War of Independence (1821–30) unfortunately lent weight to the conservative faction. As a result, the cultural divisions of pre-independence Greece are carried over into the 19th century. The official language of the new kingdom is an artificial 'purified' form, *katharevousa*, which will provide a stumbling block to the spread of education in Greece until demotic is at last permanently recognised as the official language in 1974.

1830–80 the Greek Romantics – the so-called Old School of Athens – and their neo-Classical rivals, mesmerised by Western intellectual influences and hamstrung by the unnatural and unstable language form in which they were obliged to write, produced little of interest. Meanwhile the *real* Greek Romantics were the writers of the Ionian Islands, who continued the demotic tradition of their forebears. Only with the 'Generation of 1880' (sometimes also referred to as the 'New School of Athens') and the growth of a new kind of nationalism at the end of the 19th century did spoken Greek establish itself throughout Greece as the natural basis for the language of poetry, and it was not until after the Balkan Wars and their aftermath (1911–22) that prose fiction broke definitively with *katharevousa*. The catalyst in both processes was the ethographic movement, inspired by the folklore studies of N. G. Politis, which focused the attention of writers on rural life, manners, customs and values as the basis for a nationalist literary realism. Ethographia was in turn closely associated with the Megali Idea (the Great Idea), the dream of restoring to Greece the geographical limits of the Byzantine Empire. This ideal was destroyed only by the ignominious defeat of the Greek army by the Turks in the Asia Minor Disaster of 1922 and the consequent permanent elimination of Greek culture from Anatolia, a theme which haunts much of the literature of the 1920s and 1930s.

The history of 20th-century Greek literature begins in a sense, then, in 1922. Since 1880 writers had been busily absorbing and re-interpreting in a Greek context the traditions of 19th-century Western writing and thought (particularly French and German), so that curious and original blends of Romanticism, Realism and Symbolism, and influences as diverse as those of Hugo and Nietzsche, will appear in a single text. Having hurriedly digested 150 years of European culture in a third of that time, by the 'Generation of the '30s' Greece was ready to open itself to contemporary outside influences and desperate to find a new identity in the post-Megali Idea era. The strengths of Greek writing before WWII still lay principally in poetry, where fruitful Modernist and Surrealist influences were easily absorbed. In prose the dominant mode was still a modified ethography, though quite different approaches to fiction could already be found in the works of individuals such as POLITIS, AXIOTI and the 'School of Thessaloniki'. Unfortunately the political instability of Greece between the wars, the horrors of the German occupation and the fratricidal experience of the subsequent Civil War destabilised the development of Greek culture yet again. Greece 1950–67 was a highly politicised society, yet one in which cautious self-censorship prevented the development of the kind of politically aware literature which the French enjoyed at the same period. Such literature had to be provided by the substantial number of left-wing intellectuals living in enforced exile. Paradoxically, it was the period of military government 1967–74 which led eventually to the opening up of cultural and social values and to a greater freedom in the manner in which these values are explored in literature.   CFR

HUNGARIAN

The history of literature in Hungary began in the 11th century with the arrival of Christian missionaries. Whatever traditions the Hungarians brought into the Danube Basin where they settled in the 9th century were submerged beneath Latin culture. Latin remained the ecclesiastical language till the Reformation and the official language of state until 1844. Hungarian gradually replaced Latin as the literary language from the Reformation onwards. Literature in Hungary followed a course familiar in W Europe, but its history is fragmented; wars and invasions, fire and vandalism have totally destroyed much that is known to have existed.

The earliest Latin literary products were mainly ecclesiastical. The canonisation of medieval Hungarian kings produced some colourful legends. Chronicles, notably the 12th-century *Gesta Ungarorum* by an anonymous notary and Simon Kézai's (fl. 13th century) *Gesta Hunnorum et Hungarorum*, proved fertile sources for fiction and sometimes equally fictitious historical writing after their publication in the 18th century. A fine example of narrative verse is the poignant *Planctus destructionis regni Hungariae per Tartaros*, by a monk who witnessed the Mongol invasion of 1241–2. Fragments of medieval Hungarian have survived; these include a brief but effective funeral oration (c. 1200) and the Lament of Mary (before 1300), a paraphrase of a Latin planctus that displays remarkable poetic skill.

Until the 16th century, Hungarian scholars studied mainly at Italian universities, and it is from Italy that Renaissance and Humanist culture spread to Hungary. This reached its zenith during the reign of Matthias Corvinus (1458–90), who employed Italian scholars at his court. This period produced, paradoxically, the greatest Hungarian Humanist poet, JANUS PANNONIUS, and the most renowned anti-Humanist theologian, Pelbart TEMESVÁRI. Meanwhile Hungarian translations of hymns and other liturgical texts revealed some striking talent, from the sombre rhythmic prose of the Dance of Death (copied 1510) to the radiant verse of the 'Master of the Ten-lined Stanza', whose virtuoso paraphrases of hymns (copied 1506 and 1510) reveal an artistry unsurpassed until the appearance of BALASSI.

The 16th century witnessed the invasion of the Turks, who occupied central Hungary for 160 years, the arrival of printing, the Reformation and the institutionalisation of censorship, a concatenation of events that certainly promoted literature in Hungarian but also ensured that writing and printing took to the countryside and remained isolated occupations for two centuries in a land effectively divided into three separate provinces. The Reformation, whether Lutheran, Calvinist or Unitarian, had no urban base and printing was largely confined to villages, except for the Calvinist press in Debrecen and HELTAI's establishment in Kolozsvár (now Cluj). The need for hymns and metrical psalms stimulated verse-writing in Hungarian. Some was of high quality, like SZENCI MOLNÁR's Psalter and the few hymns by women poets. But the supreme lyric poet of the age was BALASSI, the passion, originality and metrical ingenuity of whose verse set a style that was often imitated but never surpassed. Popular verse, in the form of the lyrical *virágének* (see LYRIC VERSE) and the narrative *széphistória* (see ROMANCE), spread rapidly. Prose developed through BIBLE translations and polemical sermons, many of which were printed; they frequently included anecdotes, a favourite form in Hungarian literature till the 20th century. Drama, nurtured in the medieval Church, flourished only in Church schools, some of which built their own theatres. Initially only biblical and Classical scenes were performed, but in later centuries contemporary dramatists like Racine and Holberg figured in their repertoire.

The 17th century was dominated by three writers, PÁZMÁNY, GYÖNGYÖSI and ZRÍNYI. Pázmány's polished prose and Gyöngyösi's meticulous prosody provided norms for the future, while Zrínyi wrote the most spectacular Hungarian epic. After Pázmány, ecclesiastical literature ceased to dominate the scene; entertainment, provided by narrative and lyric verse, became paramount. Numerous poets supplied this need, often evading censorship by circulating their works in manuscript. Some versified historical events, some, writing in captivity, lamented their fate and others wrote stoical lyric for a war-weary age. Political verse appeared in the *kuruc* (see POLITICAL VERSE) poetry of rebellion. Imaginative prose was rare; Haller's version of the ALEXANDER ROMANCE and other tales is the only known example. Scholarly writing, however, flourished in Transylvania, where Cartesian ideas took root, imported by Protestant scholars who after the Counter-Reformation were compelled to study abroad, mainly in Holland and England. Transylvania was also the centre of memoir-writing, a genre that began in Hungary in the 16th century and still continues to thrive, providing much of the most original Hungarian writing. The finest contemporary examples, those of Miklós BETHLEN and Ferenc RÁKÓCZI II, were written in the early 18th century.

With the retreat of the Turks and the end of rebellions, the Peace of Szatmár (1711) heralded a period of stability and reconstruction. The literary scene changed perceptibly. The novel, usually translated from German or French, ousted narrative verse; over 100 'romances' are listed before 1800, many of them disguised as moralistic works to placate the censors. New developments occurred in lyric verse. AMADE's rhythmical invention and FALUDI's experiments with form and language marked a sharp break with tradition. Readers grew in number, as indicated by the popularity of Kata BETHLEN and the sale of cheap and often uncensored literature at markets. Meanwhile the products of the

French Enlightenment began to trickle into Hungary, alarming the Austrian authorities to whom reading spelt sedition. The stage was set for the birth of 'national' literature, but that required a midwife and the end of writing in isolation.

Although the Hungarian Enlightenment is often associated with the influence of the French *philosophes*, there was also an organic and gradual evolution made possible by such antecedents as the Cartesianism of Count Miklós BETHLEN, whose *Emlékiratok* (Mémoires) were written 1708–10, the Jansenism of Ferenc RÁKÓCZI II or the Pietism of Countess Kata BETHLEN, whose *Életének maga által való rövid leírása* (A brief account of her own life) is the self-portrait of a passionate and tortured Protestant woman. It is somewhat misleading to associate the the beginning of the new period with the activity of György Bessenyei (?1747–1811), despite his central role in the last decades of the 18th century. He himself acknowledged his indebtedness to Baron Lőrinc Orczy (1718–89), who was well versed in the French ideas and composed poems inspired by his reading of Voltaire. There were also other noblemen who found their own way to the new ideology. Count János Lázár (1703–72) studied with Christian Wolff and translated Voltaire into Latin; Count János Fekete (1741–1803) corresponded with Voltaire and wrote anti-religious poetry in French, and Count József Teleki (1738–96) visited Rousseau. The decisive change from the world-view of the Baroque to that of the Enlightenment occurred in the mid-1760s. Joseph II was made co-regent by his mother in 1765 and Bessenyei became the empress's bodyguard in the same year. Although Bessenyei was to cultivate a wide range of genres, his plays and poems have more historical than aesthetic value and are certainly less significant than his essays, in which he anticipated later trends. *Magyarság* (To be Hungarian, 1778) prepared the way for the language reform, and *Egy magyar társaság iránt való jámbor szándék* (A modest proposal about a Hungarian Society, 1790) contained suggestions for the institutionalisation of science and scholarship.

The death of Joseph II in 1790 was a heavy blow to all the Hungarian writers who tried to replace religion by science as the basis of culture. In 1794 the Hungarian Jacobins were arrested. Among them was KAZINCZY, the central figure of the second generation of the Hungarian Enlightenment, who, after his release in 1801, organised a large-scale language reform. József Kármán (1769–95), the author of *Fanni hagyományai* (The posthumous papers of Fanni, 1795), a supporter of 'liberal' values and the autonomy of the individual, invented a language for the expression of mental states, thereby becoming a forerunner of the interior monologue; whereas László Ungvárnémeti Tóth (1788–1820), a materialist, wrote Classicist verse in the tradition of Pindar and Anacreon. The two major lyric poets of the turn of the century, CSOKONAI and BERZSENYI, made the transition from the Baroque and Classicism to a cult of sensibility which prepared the way for Romanticism.

Although KATONA wrote an historical tragedy of lasting value, the major genres of the Hungarian Romantics were confessional prose and the lyric, as represented by SZÉCHENYI, the reformist statesman who was a self-tormenting analyst in his diary, and VÖRÖSMARTY, a poet of apocalyptic visions. By the 1840s the liberals wished to change the status of the peasantry. Their political campaign coincided with the rise of Populism, which emerged as a reaction against Romanticism, especially in the poetry of PETŐFI. When the Hungarian revolution was crushed in 1849, disillusion coincided with the growing influence of Positivism. *Az ember tragédiája* (The tragedy of man, written 1859–60), a lyrical drama by MADÁCH, is a vast dialogue between Romantic liberalism and Positivist determinism. The whole career of ARANY, the greatest poet of the post-1849 decades, could be characterised as a life-long struggle with these two ideologies. While the superficial technical devices of Romantic fiction survived in the popular novels of JÓKAI, the dilemma of free will and determinism helped KEMÉNY in his attempt to combine the Romantic techniques of portraying consciousness with the Realistic treatment of time and space.

After ARANY made the transition from Romanticism to Symbolism and KEMÉNY developed the psychologically analytical novel, the last decades of the 19th century saw a decline in artistic quality. The representative genre of this period of transition was the short story, cultivated by such writers as MIKSZÁTH and István Petelei (1852–1910), who succeeded in combining interior monologue with a symbolic treatment of Nature. The new era did not start until the publication of *Nyugat* (West), the most important literary periodical of the new century, at the end of 1907. The most important representatives of the new generation, the poets ADY, BABITS and KOSZTOLÁNYI and the novelist KRÚDY discarded scientism and functionalism, and were attracted to Symbolism, *Secession*, psychoanalysis and other trends representing a reaction against Positivism. With the publication of *A Tett* (Action), the first avant-garde periodical, in 1915, Hungarian Expressionism began. Its most lasting achievement, the free verse of KASSÁK, led to a radical change in the concept of the poetic.

One of the consequences of WWI was that the belief in progress entered a crisis. Aesthetic modernity seemed to disintegrate soon after it was established. The political conservatism of the 1920s accompanied a cult of Neoclassicism and a second wave of Populism, a movement which found a predecessor in the novelist MÓRICZ and an influential ideologue in the essayist, novelist and playwright NÉMETH. Folklore was raised to the status of high art, and nonfiction became a canonised genre. Relatively few poets tried to continue experimentation. Lőrinc Szabó (1900–57) and JÓZSEF created a poetry of ontological implications, relying on the legacy of the Avant-garde. Although their example was followed in the 1930s and 1940s by such younger poets as WEÖRES and PILINSZKY, after 1948 their generation was silenced by Communism.

While the second generation of Populist poets succeeded in reviving epic verse – *A szarvassá változott fiú kiáltozása a titkok kapujából* (The boy changed into a stag clamours at the gate of secrets, 1955) by Ferenc Juhász (b. 1928) is based on an old legend – the eclectic style called Socialist Realism did not produce any significant achievement, and the come-back of 'bourgeois' culture was slow. *Iskola a határon* (School at the frontier, 1959), a parabolic novel about the autonomy of the individual, by Géza Ottlik (1912–90), bridged the gap between KOSZTOLÁNYI's fiction and the innovative novels of the generation that emerged in the 1970s. The techniques of Western literature have often been significantly transformed by the Hungarian writers of recent decades: the descriptive devices of the French *nouveau roman* are placed in the context of parabolic writing in the

fiction of MÉSZÖLY and in *A látogató* (The case worker, 1969), a novel by
György Konrád (b. 1933); the imitation of Thomas Mann's style goes together
with a political message about the decline of Communism in *Emlékiratok
könyve* (A book of memoirs, 1986), by Péter Nádas (b. 1942); and the language
games of Postmodernism are combined with an insistence on Christian values in
Bevezetés a szépirodalomba (An introduction to literature, 1986), by Péter
ESTERHÁZY. The last two of these works may be regarded as the most significant
achievements of Hungarian literature in the final years of Communism, before
the reintroduction of multi-party democracy in 1990.

●F. Riedl, *A History of Hungarian Literature* (London, 1906) M. C. Ives,
Enlightenment and National Revival (Ann Arbor, 1979); T. Klaniczay (Ed.), *A
History of Hungarian Literature* (Budapest, 1982); L. Czigány, *The Oxford History of
Hungarian Literature* (Oxford, rev. ed. 1988); A. Tezla, *An Introductory
Bibliography to the Study of Hungarian Literature* (Cambridge, Mass., 1964); A.
Tezla, *Hungarian Authors. A Bibliographical Handbook* (Cambridge, Mass., 1970).

GFC/MSz-M

LATVIAN

The tribes constituting the ancestors of the Latvian people have never been
united into a single state. The reason for that, beside geographic division, was
that by the end of the 13th century Danish and German priests and knights had
conquered the area, which was divided up by the Livonian Order of Knights and
the Episcopates of Riga and Kurland. In the course of the Livonian War (1558–
83) Russia, seeking seaways, had also declared her claim, but failed to occupy the
Latvian territories, which belonged first to Poland, then, from 1629 on until the
Northern War, to Sweden. Meanwhile the German Reformation had been
replaced by the Counter-Reformation aspirations of Polish R. Catholicism, and,
once again, by the Reformation of the Protestant Swedes. Russia succeeded in
seizing some Latvian territories only during the Northern War (1700–21), then
all of them in 1795, during the third partitioning of Poland. (Because of
privileges accorded to the German landowners, the so-called black barons, the
German spirit continued to prevail even under Russian domination.) Such a
history meant that Latvian literature had been confined to folklore for nearly
two centuries. Its leading genre was the *daina*, a folk-song consisting in four
lines. The oldest extant Latvian texts date from the first half of the 16th century.
The first known book, a translation of the Catechism, was printed in 1585.
Georgius Mancelius's (1593–1654) *Lettische Postille* (1654) became the oldest
monument of artistic prose. Christophorus Fuereccerus's (1615–85) translations
of German hymns and several of his original writings make him the first poet.
Janis Reiters (1632?–95?) was the first author of Latvian descent.

Secular literature only began to develop in the second half of the 18th century
when German priests were trying to keep their communities under their
influence. Their most outstanding representative was Gotthardus Fridericus
Stenders (1714–96), otherwise called Old Stenders. He was of Dutch origin, a
rationalist and pietist. Although he defended the social status quo (serfdom) and
his talent was limited, he left his mark on the second half of the 18th century.
Stenders's works manifest a didactic spirit and a purpose – to serve as a useful

pastime. His verses or 'ditties' resemble sentimental rustic songs.

The avowed aim of writers committed to principles similar to those of Stenders, Indrikis Neredzīgais (Blind Indrikis 1783–1828), Ansis Leitāns (1815–74) and, to a certain degree, even Jānis Rugens (1817–76), had been to push into the background the extraordinarily rich folk poetry. The first to stand up for national art was G. Merkelis (1769–1850) who wrote exclusively in German. A certain momentum was given to the evolution of vernacular literature by the Latvian Literary Society, founded in 1827 by German intellectuals. They had issued an 'almanac' urging the collection of *dainas*. A similar role was played by the first Latvian newspaper, *Latviešu Avīzes*, published from 1822. All the same, the National Awakening received real stimulus only in the 1850s, by the movement of the so-called Young Latvians; Latvian literature essentially dates from that time. After the abolition of serfdom in the western and central parts of the country, in 1817–19, Latgale (E Latvia) followed suit; growing economic unity made national unification possible. As one of the most important conditions of this trend there had begun the formation of a uniform literary language based on the Central Latvian dialect. Above all through a rich tradition of literary translations but also due to the efforts of linguist-journalists such as Krišjānis Valdemārs (1825–91) and BARONS, and in the poetry of ALUNANS, the first professional Latvian poet, and the first personality of real importance, Auseklis (1850–79), who stood on the borderline between Sentimentalism and Romanticism. To withstand increasing Russian pressure the Latvian language reformers turned to folk poetry to stir up national consciousness. It is not surprising, then, that the most prominent work of Latvian Romanticism, PUMPURS's folk epos *Lāčplēsis* (Bear-slayer, 1888) took its main character, conflicts and style from folklore. National aspirations had been helped by the first 'progressive' newspaper, *Pēterburgas Avīzes* (1862–5) and the Latvian theatre in Riga, which opened in 1868 under the directorship of Ādolfs Alunāns (1848–1912). Prose had also taken shape in the 1870s following the Realist manner. The first novel was written by the KAUDZĪTE brothers, in 1879; prose reached high standards in the stories of Jēkabs Apsīšu (1858–1929) and the satirical writings of Pērsietis (1862–1901). Their achievements were, as it were, crowned by the literary activity of BLAUMANIS.

One of the most productive periods began in the 1880s and 1890s. The intelligentsia gathering in the Jaunā Strāva (New Current) movement put the absence of tradition and national backwardness to their own use by implanting the most up-to-date Russian and Western ideas in Latvian literature. Thus the authors publishing in the paper *Dienas Lapa* were by 1890 familiar with the literature of Marxism and French Symbolism. Subsequently, Naturalism and neo-Romanticism were added to their knowledge. The latter was mainly represented by Andries Niedra (1871–1942). The New Current had groups in Dorpat (today's Tartu), Riga, Moscow and St Petersburg. *Dienas Lapa* had as its editors the Marxist publicist Pēteris Stučka (1865–1932) and RAINIS. The movement included, among others, PORUKS and ASPAZIJA; it linked, for the first time, the issue of national liberation with the struggle against exploitation, and the creation of 'modern' personality with the principle of the free state.

1897 the Tsarist authorities destroyed New Current; the majority of its members were put in prison or forced into exile or underground. Yet the continuity of Latvian literature remained. The turn of the century saw the formation of Symbolism which has, right up to the present day, embodied the basic aesthetic norms of Latvian poetry. In prose, Realism and Naturalism had been established in the same period. The greatest master of Naturalism was UPĪTS; its other prominent representatives were Ernests Birznieks-Upītis (1871–1960) and Anna Brigadere (1861–1933). In Symbolism two interplaying branches may be distinguished, frequently in the work of the same author. The first was revolutionary, especially strong at the time of the Revolution of 1905. Its most outstanding representatives were, besides RAINIS, Vilis Plūdonis (1874–1940) and Kārlis Skalbe (1879–1945). The second branch tended more towards Decadence. Literary criticism developed, mainly in the columns of W European and American newspapers. Light reading and literature for children and young people also began to be written.

In contrast to the socially concerned literature Impressionist-Symbolist writers grouped around the periodical *Dzelme* (Depth). They tended to look to French and Russian poetry: Kārlis Jēkabsons (1879–1946), Jānis Akurāters (1876–1937), Kārlis Krūza (1884–1960). Out of this circle grew the poetry of VIRZA, and his follower MEDENIS, as well as the short-story writing of Ēriks Ādamsons (1907–46). The prose of Jānis Jaunsudrabiņš (1877–1962) may be compared with that of Knut Hamsun. The principle of *l'art pour l'art* had been advocated by Viktors Eglītis (1877–1945), the melancholic, almost mystical, leader of the Latvian Decadent and Symbolist school.

During WWI and the ephemeral Latvian Soviet Republic was born a revolutionary literature, mainly poetry; a strong current of Proletarian literature was developed. Following the establishment of an independent Latvia in 1918, numerous representatives of this current emigrated to the USSR. Some fifty Latvian Communist literary figures died in the late 1930s in the Soviet Union. The beginning of the 1920s saw the rise of the Avant-garde in Andrejs Kurčijs's (1884–1959) Expressionism (here called Activism). As elsewhere in Eastern Europe, it soon turned into Constructivism, centred on the periodical *Trauksme* (Alarm). It included the writers Pēteris Ķikuts (1907–43), ČAKS and Jānis Grots (1901–69). The 1930s also brought noticeable changes into Latvian literature: the euphoria over the attainment of independence had passed; the economic crisis and the presidential seizure of power in 1934 set the 'catastrophist' mood of writers. The encouraging words from the second generation of Proletarian writers, appearing at the end of the 1920s, proved untimely and ineffective. In this period works of merit were produced mainly in prose and drama.

Soviet annexation shattered Latvian literature. Approximately sixty to seventy per cent of the Latvian writers who had stood at the centre of literary affairs between 1918 and 1940 fled westwards before the advancing Soviet Army. A literature of emigration was organised around two periodicals: *Jaunā Gaita* (The new path) published from 1955 in Canada and *Ceļa Zīmes* (Signposts), published from 1957 in London.

Domestic literature lost 15–20 years. During the first Soviet year only two established Latvian literary figures, SUDRABKALNS and UPĪTS, and one partially recognised author, the novelist Vilis Lācis (1903–66), became the Kremlin's tools for propaganda. Later, though, the Stalinist terror destroyed all values. The first sign of resuscitation was the appearance of the poem *Nepabeigtā dzeisma* (The unfinished song) by Harijs Heislers (b. 1926) in December 1956. The author, who had returned after many years of Arctic exile, tells the reader of his own fate, a fate which befell tens of thousands in the Baltic States. Heislers's poem was one of the first works of literature in the entire Soviet Union to deal with the theme of banishment to Siberia. It is difficult to distinguish trends in the literature that developed from the 1960s, for the authors were compelled to struggle for the mere right to speak against the Soviet régime. In poetry the names of BELŠEVICA, Imants Auziņš (b. 1937), ČAKLAIS, Vitauts Lūdens (b. 1937) Jānis Peters (b. 1939), VĀCIETIS and ZIEDONIS are the most important; among prose writers Albert Bels (b. 1938), Zigmunds Skujiņš (b. 1926), Regīna Ezera (b. 1930) and Visvaldis Eglons-Lāms (b. 1923) are significant. Of the playwrights Lelde Stumbre (b. 1952) seems the most promising.

The regaining of Latvian independence at the end of the 1980s made it possible to cease the artificial division of exile and domestic Latvian literature.

•*Anthologies*: A. Baumanis (Ed.), *Latvian Poetry* (Augsburg, 1946); W. K. Matthews (Ed.), *A Century of Latvian Poetry* (London, 1957); W. K. Matthews, *Tricolor Sun: Latvian Lyrics in English Versions* (Cambridge, 1936); A. Rubulis, *Latvian Literature* (Toronto, 1964); *Windows: Latvian Poems Translated by Ruth Speirs* (Reading, 1972); A. Straumanis (Ed.), *Baltic Drama* (Prospect Heights, 1981).

J. Andrups and V. Kalve, *Latvian Literature* (Stockholm, 1954); G. v. Wilpert-I. Ivask (Eds), *World Literature since 1945* (New York, 1973); R. Ekmanis, *Latvian Literature under the Soviets 1940–1975* (Belmont, Calif., 1978); G. S. N. Luckyj, *Discordant Voices: The Non-Russian Soviet Literatures 1953–1975* (Oakville, 1975); I. Ivask, 'Baltic Literature in Exile: The Balance of a Quarter Century' in A. Ziedonis, J. Puuvel, R. Šilbajoris and M. Valgemäe (Eds), *Baltic Literature and Linguistics* (Columbus, 1973); A. Rubulis, *Baltic Literature: Survey of Finnish, Estonian, Latvian and Lithuanian Literatures* (Notre Dame, London, 1970). EB

LITHUANIAN

The first significant works of Lithuanian literature appeared in the 18th and mid-19th centuries, but they remained isolated pieces, lacking an adequate reading public. An educated Lithuanian readership developed only by the end of the 19th century, under the stimulus of Romantic nationalism that swept across Central and Eastern Europe.

The beginning of the 20th century brought influences of Russian and French Symbolism, German Expressionism and, later, Russian and Italian Futurism to Lithuanian literature, particularly poetry. In order to build up a national cultural identity, some poets tried to blend their adapted world outlook with the imagery and diction of Lithuanian folk-songs, in the process creating a 'folkloristic Symbolism' that had nothing at all to do with the national heritage. Prose works of the time showed influences of self-preoccupied, romantic Scandinavian writers like Knut Hamsun. This trend towards introspection produced psychologically analytical writing, especially in the novelistic genre, in the work of MYKOLAITIS-PUTINAS.

Ideological influences from the Soviet Union stimulated the leftist 'Third Front' movement in literature. Its most original poet, NERIS, fused politics with personal emotions. Within this movement, Petras Cvirka (1909–47) wrote novels satirising the bourgeoisie.

In opposition to the leftists, Lithuanian poetry of the 1930s was dominated by R. Catholic ideology combined with rhetorical patriotism in the work of BRAZDŽIONIS, and the intense individualism of AISTIS, who sought a blend of Modernist European style with a subjectivist contemplation of art, love and the fatherland.

After 1944, writers were subjected to the dictates of Socialist Realism, and writers in exile were confronted with a variety of challenges from the Western world. The periodical *Literatūros lankai* (Literary folios, published in Argentina, 1952–9) brought together the younger generation abroad. Kazys Bradūnas (b. 1917), a poet devoted to the mystique of the native soil, was at the centre of this group. Other basic aims were to strive for a poetry of thought as well as of beauty, and to open up Lithuanian culture to more Western influences.

The most prominent playwrights, Algirdas Landsbergis (b. 1924), ŠKĖMA and Kostas Ostrauskas (b. 1926), reflected their condition as exiles in plays about efforts to sustain human dignity in the face of tyranny. The scene of their plays is Lithuania under Soviet occupation, but Ostrauskas expands his settings to other times and places, thus raising his plays to a higher level of abstraction, which allows him to introduce elements of Existentialist philosophy.

The poetry written abroad also focuses for the most part on the trauma of exile and dispossession. This is particularly striking in the work of Algimantas Mackus (1932–64) who tests all human values against the ultimate finality of death. The only poet largely free of this exile syndrome was RADAUSKAS, the most intellectual and arguably the best Lithuanian poet of all time, who stands by himself in a highly complex, sophisticated, artistic world dedicated to the achievement of itself alone.

Socialist Realism in Lithuania was first challenged soon after the 1956 Thaw by a number of writers then in their twenties and thirties. The poet and playwright MARCINKEVIČIUS is thought by some to be the leading artist in this generation, although Judita Vaičiūnaitė (b. 1937), a poet of urban romanticism, and Sigitas Geda (b. 1934) who mixes earthy realism with an ancient mythological ambience, possess artistic talent comparable with that of MARCINKEVIČIUS.

Some prose writers extended the challenge to Socialist Realist conformity beyond the confines of art as such and into the realm of the basic tenets and activities of Soviet socialism, such as the forced collectivisation of agriculture. Other novelists, playwrights and poets augmented and elaborated this fundamental challenge to the Soviet régime, indeed, to its very right to continue its rule in Lithuania. Many also became concerned with the environment, with the quality of urban life, and with the presence of Soviet troops on Lithuanian soil.

•J. Mauclère, *Panorama de la littérature lithuanienne contemporaine* (Paris, 1938); V. Jungfer, *Litauen: Antlitz eines Volkes* (Kaunas, 1948); A. Landsbergis and C. Mills (Eds), *The Green Oak* (New York, 1962); A. Rubulis, *Baltic Literature* (Indiana, 1970), pp. 163–212; R. Šilbajoris, *Perfection of Exile: Fourteen Contemporary Lithuanian Writers* (Oklahoma, 1970); R. Šilbajoris, 'Lithuanian Literature' in I. Ivask and G. von Wilpert (Eds), *World Literature Since 1945* (New York, 1973), pp. 456–61; A. Ziedonis, *et al.* (Eds), *Baltic Literature and Linguistics* (Columbus, Ohio, 1973); R. Šilbajoris, Foreword to J. Zdanys (Ed.), *Selected Postwar Lithuanian Poetry*

(Chicago, 1978), pp. 7–12; R. Šilbajoris, Introduction to A. Skrupskelis (Ed.),
Lithuanian Writers in the West: An Anthology (Chicago, 1979); R. Šilbajoris,
Introduction to L. Dovydėnas, *The Brothers Domeika* (Boston, 1976); A. Straumanis,
Baltic Drama: A Handbook and Bibliography (New York, 1981), pp. 381–560.   RŠ

MACEDONIAN

Slav Macedonia (part of which today lies in Bulgaria) has only existed as a state
since 1944 and declared itself independent of the rest of one-time Yugoslavia in
1992. From the late 14th century to the beginning of the 20th century it was
under the Turks. Then, in the Balkan Wars, it was first occupied by Bulgaria
(1912), then Serbia (1913), and the Greeks also fought for it (1925). In interwar
Yugoslavia it was part of Serbia. Now it is a state of two million inhabitants, 25
per cent of whom are Albanians.

The problem of what constitutes Macedonian literature is academically more
complex than the problem of what constitutes Slovak literature, for Macedonian
was not officially recognised as a literary language until 1944, when Macedonia
was given republican status by Tito. On the other hand, Macedonians are
entirely justified in considering much of what is called Old Bulgarian and even
Middle Bulgarian as their literary heritage – just as the Ukrainians and Russians
share the same medieval literature. The real problem comes in the 19th and early
20th centuries, i.e. with writers who use specifically Macedonian elements in
their form of Bulgarian. Bulgarians and Macedonians alike consider, for
example, Grigor Pärlichev (1830–93) or Konstantin Miladinov (1830–62) as
belonging to their respective literatures. At the beginning of the 20th century
Krste P. Misirkov (1874–1926) published a programmatic work, *Za
makedonskite raboti* (On Macedonian matters, 1903), which laid the
foundations for the development of a Macedonian literary language. It was
written in the Prilep-Bitola dialect, on the basis of which that literary language
was later codified. 1937–41 two writers in particular established the Macedonian
literary language in their works, RATSIN and Kole Nedelkovski (1912–41); the
latter avoided arrest by the Bulgarian authorities by committing suicide.

In 1944 Macedonian began to be used in the mass media, theatre and schools.
As with any young literature (see Slovak, but also Estonian and Latvian) and
indeed literature that went through a National Revival (see late 18th and early
19th-century Czech, late 19th-century Bulgarian), lyric verse was the dominant
genre (see KONESKI and SHOPOV). Initially also the short story was the only
prose form and the first Macedonian novel was published by YANEVSKI in 1953.
For obvious reasons, most early Macedonian literature dealt with the war,
partisans, socialist construction, and had a strong patriotic flavour. Soon,
however, more intimate lyric verse became widespread and its mood was
melancholic (e.g. KONESKI); indeed, in some cases it expressed even resignation
and apathy. In the mid-1950s, as in other socialist literatures, writers began to
break away from Realism and find a path to Modernism. In the 1960s the verse of
authors from the younger generation (the dissident Bogumil Gyuzel [b. 1939],
UROSHEVICH and Radovan PAVLOVSKI) showed how untopical Realism had
become. The novel developed quickly at the hands of such as Georgi Abadzhiev

(1910–63), Simon Drakul (b. 1930), Yordan Leov (b. 1920); after the 1960s the scope of the Macedonian novel ranges from CHINGO's dream-lands and UROSHEVICH's naivism to the mythopoeic epics of YANEVSKI or the eccentrically complex narrative technique of Yovan Pavlovski (b. 1937) in his macabre *Sok od prostata* (Prostatic gland juice, 1991). Macedonian drama is weak, however many one-acters Leov wrote. Not until CHASHULE did accomplished drama begin to be written and this author has become the 'grand old man' of Macedonian literature. Nevertheless, the recent work of Goran Stefanovski (b. 1952), mainly Postmodernist interpretations of historical themes, and especially his play *Chernata dupka* (The black hole, 1987) concerning the unofficial civil war in Yugoslavia during the 1970s and 1980s, has now set higher standards for Macedonian drama.

•M. Bronisch (Ed.), *Moderne makedonische Lyrik* (Tübingen, Basle, 1978); E. Osers (Ed.), *Contemporary Macedonian Poetry* (London, 1991); M. Holton and G. Reid, *Reading the Ashes* (Pittsburgh, 1977); M. Holton, *The Big House and Other Stories* (Columbia, Missouri, 1974); S. Mahapatra (Ed.), *Longing for the South* (New Delhi, 1981); A. L. Armaout (Ed.), *Modern Macedonian Poetry in Yugoslavia* (Cairo, 1983).

V. Pinto, 'Dawn-Courtship in Bulgarian and Macedonian Folk Poetry', *SEER*, 34 (1955), pp. 200–20; V. Mihailovich, *A. Comprehensive Bibiography of Yugoslav Literature in English, 1593–1980* (Columbus, Ohio, 1984); M. Yovanovski (Ed.), *The Macedonian Novel* (Skopje, n.d.); B. Vishinski (Ed.), *Tradition in Macedonian Literature* (Skopje, 1974).   SIK

POLISH

In its beginnings, literature in Poland was largely confined to Latin, the language of W Christianity and of the written word. The earliest known literary text in the vernacular, the hymn 'Bogurodzica' (Mother of God), dates from the 13th century. Medieval literature in Polish was chiefly devotional: as opposed to numerous biblical translations, APOCRYPHA, hagiographies, and religious songs, lay themes and genres were still underrepresented.

Western Humanism began to spread into Poland at the end of the 15th century. Its coincidence with the rapid progress of the Reformation produced an impressive amount of religious literature. 1508 marks the appearance of the first book printed entirely in Polish. A number of excellent Latin poets revived Classical culture, while a plebeian variety of Humanism emerged in the Polish work of BIERNAT OF LUBLIN. The first major figure of the Renaissance was REJ, who wrote in Polish as a matter of principle. The Golden Age in Polish culture reached its peak in the second half of the century, represented by the greatest Polish poet before Romanticism, KOCHANOWSKI, and prose writers GÓRNICKI, Stanisław Orzechowski (1513–66) and SKARGA. The author of descriptive poems, Sebastian F. Klonowic (1545–1602), and the author of pastorals, SZYMONOWIC, are characteristic of the last phase of the Renaissance in poetry. Curiously, the brilliant metaphysical poet SĘP SZARZYŃSKI, who died young even before KOCHANOWSKI, was a fully-fledged Baroque author *avant la lettre*.

Beginning with the 17th century, Polish literature, prompted by the advance of the Counter-Reformation, entered the long epoch of the Baroque, which soon developed into two different stylistic manners – the urbane and cosmopolitan Baroque based on Western models and the parochial and conservative 'Sarmatian Baroque'. The former found its chief representatives in poets' connected to royal or aristocratic courts, e.g. Jan A. MORSZTYN; the latter was typical of provincial nobility, producing, like Wacław POTOCKI or TWARDOWSKI, immense historical epics or tales in verse, or, like PASEK, excelling in vivid memoir prose.

The richness of Polish Baroque literature diminished c. 1700; the first half of the 18th century, the 'Saxon night', was a period of stale conventions and stagnation. This changed abruptly with the beginning of the reign of the last king of Poland, Stanisław August (reigned 1765–95). Under his auspices, the Polish Age of Enlightenment, though brief, brought about profound changes in literature and theatre. Western, particularly French, influences led to the rebirth of a lucid style and a rationalistic spirit. In poetry, Classical genres were revived by gifted authors like NARUSZEWICZ, KRASICKI and TREMBECKI. KRASICKI, the most versatile writer among them, was also the author of the first modern Polish novel (1776). Sentimentalism surfaced in the lyrical songs of KNIAŹNIN and KARPIŃSKI. NIEMCEWICZ and Franciszek Zabłocki (1752–1821) were the most outstanding comedy writers.

The final Partition of Poland (1795) enhanced rather than diminished the value of 'national literature'. In particular, Polish Romanticism, after a brief phase of mostly emulating Western models, assumed a highly original shape in the wake of the defeat of the Uprising of 1830–1. After that, the greatest Polish Romantics worked abroad as émigrés, and most of their works revealed their preoccupation with the national struggle. MICKIEWICZ was both the pathfinder and the central figure of the Romantic movement. His early poetry set a standard of Romantic sensibility and his works written in the West – in particular, his poetic drama *Dziady, cz. 3* (Forefathers' eve, Pt 3) and his epic *Pan Tadeusz* – secured him his unquestioned status as the spiritual leader of the nation. His younger rival, SŁOWACKI, a virtuoso of poetic language, left behind an extensive lyric, epic and dramatic oeuvre. KRASIŃSKI, the most perspicacious mind among the three great 'bards', was the author of two penetrating political plays. Finally, NORWID, a poet misunderstood and forgotten by his contemporaries, eventually turned out to have been the greatest literary figure of the second half of the century; his *Vade-mecum*, published many years after his death, is a milestone in Polish literature.

While the great émigrés worked, mostly in Paris, on their poetry, numerous Poland-based authors contributed to the growth of fiction and drama. KRASZEWSKI wrote several hundred novels of various kinds. FREDRO remains unsurpassed as a comedy writer.

After the failure of another Uprising in 1863–4, there followed in Poland the epoch of Positivism, with its concentration on economic, social and cultural issues rather than armed struggle. In literature, Realism reigned and the novel became the most popular genre. Contemporary fiction found its best examples in the novels of PRUS and ORZESZKOWA and the short stories by KONOPNICKA; the historical novel gained enormous popularity in SIENKIEWICZ.

Reaction against Positivism and Realism came towards the end of the century. The new literary movement called Young Poland (and also Modernism or neo-Romanticism) included trends as different as Symbolism in the poetry of TETMAJER, KASPROWICZ, STAFF or the most original among them, LEŚMIAN, and Naturalism blended with Symbolism in the novels of ŻEROMSKI and REYMONT and the mixture of Symbolic and pre-Expressionist traits in BERENT. WYSPIAŃSKI revived the Romantic drama and enriched it with his modern theatrical vision.

In reborn Poland, 1918–39, literature's evolution reflected the transition from the initial euphoria to the dark premonitions of a world catastrophe. Poets of the popular Skamander group, such as TUWIM, as well as poets of the Avant-garde, such as CZECHOWICZ, evolved, as a rule, into catastrophists by the end of the 1930s. This mood, however, did not preclude intensive artistic experimentation in poetry, drama and fiction. WITKIEWICZ in his plays and novels, GOMBROWICZ in his novel *Ferdydurke*, and SCHULZ in his short stories offered modern literature dazzling new perspectives.

The immense cultural losses caused by WWII and the spiritual devastation put into effect by Communist rule never managed seriously to threaten Polish literature. In Poland itself as well as in the diaspora, the last half-century has abounded in works of great significance, to mention but the poetry of MIŁOSZ, BIAŁOSZEWSKI, HERBERT or SZYMBORSKA, the plays of RÓŻEWICZ or MROŻEK, the novels of GOMBROWICZ or KONWICKI, and the essays of WAT, STEMPOWSKI or HERLING-GRUDZIŃSKI.   StB

ROUMANIAN

The earliest text in Roumanian to have been dated is a letter of 1521, while a Lutheran Catechism of 1544 from Sibiu is the first printed book. However, the oral tradition upon which the literature draws is probably much older. Contact with the Slavs S of the Danube in the 14th century resulted in the first durable cultural links and via them, in a Slavonic garb, the Roumanians received from Byzantium its religion, art, legal system, literature and, with revisions, its alphabet. Roumanian culture was thus initially an off-shoot of Byzantine culture and the language of literary culture was Church Slavonic. It remained so until the 17th century. Early literature in Roumanian consisted in the gradual translation from Church Slavonic of the Bible, of liturgical works, of hagiography, and of Byzantine theologians such as John Climacus. Between 1557 and 1583 Deacon Coresi (c. 1510–83), with Lutheran and Calvinist patronage, printed at Braşov (Kronstadt) in Transylvania, a series of liturgical works in Roumanian, but Orthodox conservatism in the Roumanian-ruled principalities of Moldavia and Wallachia delayed the appearance there of the first book entirely in Roumanian until 1640. This collection of homilies, and a subsequent one printed three years later at Iaşi, marks a noted advance in fluency of expression. Nevertheless, literature in Roumanian remained until the early 19th century almost totally confined to the printing of religious books, and printing in Moldavia and Wallachia was exclusively in the hands of the Orthodox prelates. The Reformation made virtually no impact in these two principalities and the

Roumanians there did not experience the revival of Classical culture until the late 18th century. Only then did a handful of educated people have access to it through translation from Greek and French. Although Moldavian chroniclers of the 17th century such as Grigore Ureche (c. 1590–1647) and Miron Costin (1633–91) were able, through their privileged positions as sons of boyars, to enjoy an education in Poland and to incorporate some of the fruits of Classical historiography in their own writings, their works remained in manuscript and were known only to a few of their fellow countrymen.

Only in the 18th century did a secular culture, independent of the Church, begin to emerge amongst the Roumanians in Transylvania. The creation of the Roumanian Uniate (Greek Catholic) Church in 1700 made Western centres of R. Catholic learning accessible to a small number of Roumanians and produced the leading figures in the Şcoala Ardeleană (Transylvanian School). This educated elite brought their fellow countrymen into contact with the Enlightenment and at the same time stimulated the development of a national consciousness by publishing studies which emphasised the Roman origins of the Roumanian people. In Moldavia and Wallachia the establishment of Phanariot rule in the second decade of the 18th century introduced a century of Greek cultural influence which further delayed the development of a vernacular secular culture until the impact of the Transylvanian School made itself felt in the early years of the 19th century. Roumanian-language schools were started in Bucharest and Iaşi and the movement towards cultural autonomy continued after the end of Phanariot rule in 1821 with the foundation of theatres and other institutions. A literature in Roumanian, at first heavily dependent on French Romantic models, made its appearance in the 1830s, its publication facilitated by the acquisition of private presses and the creation of literary journals. A major contribution to poetry and drama was made by ALECSANDRI, who was among the first to use oral literature as an inspiration and who almost single-handed created a theatre repertoire. Within thirty years verse was to reach some of its greatest heights in the hands of EMINESCU, who crafted an exquisite literary language from archaisms, neologisms and dialect. EMINESCU was supported in his studies abroad by MAIORESCU, whose literary circle Junimea (Youth), founded in 1863, and its journal Convorbiri literare (Literary discussions) set the agenda for a debate that has continued to dominate Roumanian culture. The fear of submergence by foreign influences, expressed by MAIORESCU in his studies, led in the opening years of the 20th century to the creation of reviews stressing the importance of national and peasant traditions. The most notable of these were Sămănătorul (The sower) and Viaţa românească (Roumanian life).

During the interwar period the review Gîndirea (Thought) promoted the role of the Orthodox Church as guardian of tradition and national cohesion while at the same time figures such as Urmuz (i.e. Demetru Demetrescu Buzău, 1883–1923) and Ilarie Voronca (1903–46) experimented in their verse with the fragmentation of language. This period, the most fertile in Roumanian literature, saw the affirmation of the poets BARBU, ARGHEZI, BLAGA and the novelists REBREANU and PETRESCU. The Communist dogmatism of the immediate postwar years stifled any literature not written in the spirit of Socialist Realism but an ideological thaw designed to harness younger talents to the Party allowed both the emergence of poets such as BLANDIANA and STĂNESCU and the reappearance of others of an older generation who had written 'for the desk-drawer', among them DOINAŞ. Ceauşescu's 'mini cultural revolution' of July 1971 constituted a return to the method of Socialist Realism but several writers, in particular PREDA and BUZURA, abetted by the censors, ignored it and addressed social problems, in particular the perversion of traditional values by Communist rule. In a country which produced cars and oil but where there were petrol shortages, and which announced record grain harvests but where people were suffering from malnutrition, it is not surprising that a sense of the absurd should recur in literature and that the most widely read poet of the 1980s was SORESCU.

The overthrow of Ceauşescu and the removal of censorship placed writers in a new situation. They were faced by two considerations. The reading public now had access to rich, diverse mass media. If in the past literature had no competition from newspapers or from television, and even assumed part of the media's functions, after 1989 that is no longer the case. Disciplines like history, sociology and political science, which were deliberately emasculated under Ceauşescu, now developed and reconquered a part of the ground lost to the novel. The public no longer had to read PREDA's *Delirul* (Delirium, 1975) to discover who Roumania's pro-German wartime leader Marshal Antonescu was, or BUZURA's *Refugii* (Places of refuge, 1984) to learn about the miners' strike of 1977. Furthermore, an 'aesopian' language characterised a major part of the literature of the Communist era. Novels developed numerous allusive formulas, e.g. the parable. Poetry had recourse to a sophisticated symbolism stemming from the same strategy of circumlocution and insinuation. The intertextual or ludic were means of denying censors access to the main message. In the literature composed after the revolution reality no longer needs to be encoded in this way; but the absurd and the comic will remain part of the heritage of Roumanian literature.

●Anthologies: R. MacGregor-Hastie (Ed.), *Anthology of Contemporary Rumanian Poetry* (London, 1969); O. Manning (Ed.), *Romanian Short Stories* (Oxford, 1971); A. Deletant and B. Walker (Eds), *An Anthology of Contemporary Romanian Poetry* (London, 1984); A. Deletant and B. Walker (Eds), *Silent Voices. An Anthology of Contemporary Romanian Women Poets* (London, 1986).
D. Popovici, *La Littérature roumaine à l'époque des lumières* (Sibiu, 1945); E. D. Tappe, *Roumanian Prose and Verse* (London, 1956); H. Juin, *Introduction à la poésie roumaine* (Paris, 1961); J. Steinberg (Ed.), *Introduction to Rumanian Literature* (New York, 1966); D. Deletant, 'Literature and Society in Romania since 1948' in G. Hosking and G. F. Cushing (Eds), *Perspectives on Literature and Society in Eastern and Western Europe* (London, 1989).   DJD

SERBIAN

The beginnings of Serbian literature coincide with the introduction of Christianity in the 9th century. The first works were written by monks in the Serbian recension of Church Slavonic for the needs of the Church. The first preserved written document, the ornamented *Miroslav's Gospel*, is from the 12th century. In the medieval period, among many Church-related works the biographies of state and Church rulers stand out as literary accomplishments. The towering figure in the Old Serbian literature was St Sava (1175–1235), generally considered to be the father of Serbian education and literature. Then came the centuries of Turkish occupation, during which little literature was written or has survived. The only literature that existed unhindered was oral epic poetry, folk-songs, folk-tales, and other oral forms. This very large body of epic poems, folk-songs and tales were collected and published in the 19th century.

The hiatus lasted until thousands of Serbs migrated to the N province of the Vojvodina and revived Serbian cultural activity in the 18th century. Writers wrote again mostly Church-related works, using a hybrid language between Church Slavonic and Russian, so-called 'Slavonic-Serbian'. When the uprisings against the Turks in Serbia proper resulted in the establishment of a new state, literature came back to life. The two most deserving writers in this revival are OBRADOVIĆ and KARADŽIĆ. The former, inspired by the ideas of the Enlightenment and Rationalism, wrote many didactic works in order to educate his countrymen. KARADŽIĆ reformed the literary language by using the vernacular of his time; he also composed the first Serbian grammar, compiled the first dictionary, and published collections of oral-tradition works. With the works of NJEGOŠ and RADIČEVIĆ, among others, a modern period in Serbian literature was ushered in.

The middle of the 19th century marks the beginning of Romanticism, during which NJEGOŠ and RADIČEVIĆ played a leading role, especially NJEGOŠ with his epic drama *Gorski vijenac* (The mountain wreath, 1847), still considered to be the best work in Serbian literature. Other notable Romantics are JAKŠIĆ, JOVANOVIĆ ZMAJ and KOSTIĆ. Poetry was the dominant genre in this period, although drama was abundantly represented. The themes centred on Serbian history and folklore, often treated emotionally and with patriotic fervour.

By the 1860s, Realism had begun gradually to replace Romanticism. The changing social and political conditions in Serbia caused writers to switch their emphasis to everyday life and topical problems. Since most of the writers came from the provinces, a new genre developed – a realistic 'village story', using an ethnological and socially conscious approach. The leading writers in this period were Jakov Ignjatović (1822–89), LAZAREVIĆ, Simo Matavulj (1852–1902), Stevan Sremac (1855–1906) and Janko Veselinović (1862–1905).

Towards the end of the century new approaches began to be perceptible. In poetry, ILIĆ freed Serbian poetry from its Romantic tradition. After the turn of the century, DUČIĆ and RAKIĆ, influenced by French Symbolists, completely modernised Serbian poetry, opening it up to foreign influences. This process continued between the wars, as CRNJANSKI and PETROVIĆ wrote in the spirit of Expressionism and a number of leftist writers created their own branch of Surrealism. In general, the interwar period showed much activity but not much literature of lasting value.

Serbian literature reached its highest peak after WWII, not only with the novels of ANDRIĆ but also with a number of writers of outstanding achievement, such as POPA, KIŠ and PAVIĆ. There are many accomplished writers, an abundance of works of lasting value in all genres, and a great variety of approaches to literature. For the first time in its history Serbian literature has truly joined world literature.

•Anthologies: *IYL*; *Contemporary Yugoslav Poetry* (Iowa City, 1977); *An Anthology of Medieval Serbian Literature in English* (Columbus, Ohio, 1978); *Monumenta Serbocroatica* (Ann Arbor, 1980); *Serbian Poetry from the Beginnings to the Present* (New Haven, 1988).

A. Kadić, *Contemporary Serbian Literature* (The Hague, 1964); A. Barac, *A History of Yugoslav Literature* (Ann Arbor, 1973); T. Eekman, *Thirty Years of Yugoslav Literature 1945–1975* (Ann Arbor, 1978); S. Koljević, *The Epic in the Making* (Oxford, 1980); V. D. Mihailovich, *A Comprehensive Bibliography of Yugoslav Literature in English* (Columbus, Ohio, 1984, 1988 and 1992).   VDM

SLOVAK

In 20th-century Slovakia it has become a convention to state that the beginnings of Slovak literature lie in the Church Slavonic literature composed by Greeks on the territory of what is now Slovakia and in Old Czech literature. Furthermore, it has become normal to treat anything written in Czech, Latin or even Hungarian on Slovak territory, and anything written by Czech writers of 'Slovak' provenance, as part of Slovak literature. That is academically untenable. The Slovaks are a group of Slavs who inhabit, roughly speaking, what was Upper Hungary. How closely they are ethnically linked to the Czechs is debatable. Certainly, however, from the Hussite Reformation and the spread of the Czech BIBLE to Slovak territory (early 15th century) to the mid-19th century Czech was the language the vast majority of Slovaks employed, if they wished to write in the vernacular.

It has been argued that Hugolin Gavlovič's (1712–87) voluminous and tedious version of *Disticha Catonis* (not published in full until the 1980s) is the first work in conscious Slovak, but the language is no less slovacised Czech than the 'historical songs' and rebel songs of the previous century. BAJZA's two-part novel is the first work in something one can call Slovak. The first work in BERNOLÁK's unsuccessful codification of Slovak (based on W Slovak and thus still close to Czech) is Juraj Fándly's (1750–1811) anticlerical dialogue (1789), and the only writer of lasting value to write in BERNOLÁK Slovak was HOLLÝ. Slovak writers still wrote predominantly in Czech until 1844, when the first works were published in ŠTÚR's version of literary Slovak.

Slovak literature was born of Romanticism and Romanticism remained the fundamental mode of Slovak writing into the 1870s, perhaps 1880s. This National Awakening quickly took a military turn in 1848–9, when the Slovaks rose against the Magyars and thus became the one 'revolutionary' pro-Habsburg force in the period. The Russian intervention in Hungary to help the Habsburgs encouraged Slovak panslav feelings (see KOLLÁR), and thus subsequently made the efforts of Slovak nationalist intellectuals increasingly difficult. The Magyars tended to label any Slovak literary or cultural endeavour 'panslav'. After the *Ausgleich*, the creation of Austria-Hungary, the Magyars became even more set against Slovak institutions, closed the Slovak grammar schools the nationalists had recently set up and, more important, abolished the centre of Slovak cultural activity, the Matica slovenská. In this period the mainstream of Slovak literature, represented, e.g., by Jonáš Záborský (1812–76) or Ján Palárik (1822–70), concentrated on social themes. The chief writers to appear to struggle positively against magyarisation, to try to find solutions to the Slovak national cultural situation, were VAJANSKÝ and the Magyar, Pál Országh (i.e. HVIEZDOSLAV.) At the same time original Realist prose writing influenced by trends in Russian and Western literature issued from the pens of such as KUKUČÍN, Jozef Gregor-Tajovský (1874–1940), and Timrava (i.e. Božena Slančíková, 1867–1951).

The main turning-point in Slovak literature, the time when it achieves a degree of self-assuredness, and (excepting the Romantic KRÁL') a simple, specifically Slovak manner of expression, is in the fresh intimate verse of KRASKO and JESENSKÝ. After WWI, poets like Vladimír Roy (1885–1936), Martin Rázus (1888–1937), LUKÁČ and SMREK represented Modernism; prose writers like VÁMOŠ and the almost Socialist Realist, Fraňo Král' (1903–55), introduced elements of Expressionism, while others, like URBAN and CÍGER HRONSKÝ, treated rural Slovakia in a non-nationalist, rural mythopoeic manner. The next development in verse followed on from Czech Proletarian Poetry and Poetism in writers of the Communist DAV group (mainly NOVOMESKÝ, Daniel Okáli [1903–89] and Ján Poničan [1902–78]). More or less simultaneously Slovak Surrealism arose (see FÁBRY). In prose, that was accompanied by the Lyrical Prose school (see CHROBÁK, FIGULI, ŠVANTNER), which dominated Slovak literature from the late 1930s to the brief flowering of Socialist Realism.

The Slovaks broke away from Socialist Realism sooner than the Czechs (see BEDNÁR) and from the 1960s onwards developed a lively, sometimes eccentric, tradition in verse, (e.g. Miroslav Válek [born 1927], Marián Kováčik [b. 1940] or Tat'jana Lehenová [b. 1961]) and prose (for example, JOHANIDES, BALLEK, VILIKOVSKÝ or Dušan Mitana [b. 1946]). Slovak writing of this period is largely independent, though, e.g., the techniques of the *nouveau roman*, the thought of Existentialism and, sometimes, a new version of prewar patriotic Ruralism, have had some impact.

●A. Mráz, *Die Literatur der Slovaken* (Berlin, 1942); L. Richter, *Slowakische Literatur. Entwicklungstrends vom Vormärz bis zur Gegenwart* (Berlin, 1979).   RBP

SLOVENE

Before the Magyar incursion into the Hungarian plain and the Bavarian expansion, the breakdown of Avar rule in central Europe had apparently left the Slovenes in control of extensive territories between 'Moravia' and 'Croatia'; these included Pannonia (W Hungary), Carinthia and Styria. We can presume the introduction of the Latin script and the Christian religion into the area by Irish monks in the late 8th century, well before the mission of SS Cyril and Methodius (862–85) gave the Slavs their first translations of the Scriptures. The monuments of pre-Reformation literacy are few.

The 10th-century Freising Texts comprise three penitential prayers; 14th and 15th-century manuscripts, recording the most common prayers (Our Father, Hail Mary, the Apostles' Creed) and some legal formulas, merely serve to prove the continuing existence of the vernacular.

The Reformation period (1550–95) begins with the first Slovene printed book, a catechism by TRUBAR, 'father' of the Slovene literary language, and ends with his posthumous version of Luther's postil. Most important of 56 publications were DALAMATIN's Bible and BOHORIČ's grammar in Latin of the Slovene language. The Counter-Reformation and Baroque period (1595–1768) gave rise to little publishing activity, yet not entire stagnation. Tomaž Hren (1560–1630), Bishop of Ljubljana (Laibach), brought out in 1613 3,000 copies of a lectionary for Sundays and feast days, entitled *Evangelia inu lystuvi* (Gospels and Epistles), using the text of DALMATIN's Protestant Bible but partially purging it of loan-words. Homiletic literature flourished with the publication of the Baroque sermons of the Capuchin monks, SVETOKRIŠKI and Rogerij of Ljubljana (1667–1728). VALVASOR produced in German his laudatory account of Slovenia, *Die Ehre des Herzogthums Crain* (The glory of the Duchy of Carniola, 1868). Among works that remained unpublished are the compendious Slovene-Latin-German dictionary and accompanying Slovene version of KOMENSKÝ's *Orbis sensualium pictus* by the Capuchin monk Hipolit of Novo Mesto (1667–1722).

The Enlightenment and Revival period (1768–1848) had as its key figure in the early part of the period the Augustinian monk Marko Pohlin (1735–1801), author of numerous works including *Kraynska grammatika* (Carniolan grammar, 1768), a dictionary of Slovene, German and Latin, an etymological dictionary and a bibliography of Slovene literature. An anthology of homespun secular verse, *Pisanice* (1779, 1780, 1781), emanated from his circle. A new translation of the BIBLE appeared (1784–1802). A particularly active and fruitful group gathered around Baron Žiga Zois (1747–1819), a rich landowner and ironmaster, thanks to whose encouragement Slovenia acquired in Anton Tomaž Linhart (1756–95) her first historian and dramatist, in VODNIK her first poet and journalist and in Jernej Kopitar (1780–1844) her first modern grammarian and comparative philologist. The early part of the second, Romantic, period of the Revival was marred by the so-called War of the Alphabets between traditional-ists and innovators who accepted Franc Metelko's (1789–1860) phonetically worthy but graphically bizarre concoction, which supplemented the standard Latin alphabet with new variants and Cyrillic characters. The innovators were defeated largely by the effective polemics of ČOP. Poetry of mature quality began to appear in the anthologies *Krajnska čbelica* (The Carniolan bee, 1830–4, 1848), to which the chief contributors were Miha Kastelic (1796–1868), the editor, and PREŠEREN. The latter's poetic talents enabled him to handle with elegance the most 'difficult' forms. The dignity conferred on Slovene by his oeuvre averted any danger of cultural subservience to the Illyrian Movement, which envisaged a 'Highland laddie' role for the Slovene language.

The period between Romanticism and Realism (1848–99) is important for the development of narrative prose. Popular early themes are taken from folklore, praising love of liberty and resistance to foreign influence (Janez Trdina [1830–1905], Matija Valvajec [1831–97]). JENKO and Fran Erjavec (1834–87) wrote tales of village life. LEVSTIK brought the rewriting of the folk-tale to artistic perfection with his *Martin Krpan*, laid the foundations of literary criticism and indicated lines of development for future prose. His most notable successor, JURČIČ, progressed from an historical novelist to a realistic portrayer of Slovene life. STRITAR produced in *Zorin* (1870) and *Gospod Mirodolski* (Mr M., 1876) novels modelled on Goethe's *Werther* and Goldsmith's *Vicar of Wakefield*. KERSNIK introduced the light-hearted *feuilleton* and developed Realist tendencies in his novels of provincial society. TAVČAR combined Realist and Romantic elements in his historical novels. The most original collections of verse to appear in the period were the lyric poems of JENKO and GREGORČIČ, STRITAR's satirical and polemical *Dunajski soneti* (Viennese sonnets, 1872) and the ballads, romances and epic poems of AŠKERC.

The period of Slovene Modernism and Expressionism (1899–1930) was a period of considerable achievements in lyric verse with the work of KETTE, MURN and ŽUPANČIČ, in prose and drama with the short novels and plays of CANKAR. Contemporary with but not of the Modernist school were the humourist MILČINSKI and the two novelists and playwrights, FINŽGAR and KRAIGHER. The most notable Expressionist poets are PODBEVŠEK, an Avant-gardist with Futurist leanings, the Proletarian Poet SELIŠKAR, the free-thinkers KOSOVEL and JARC, the R. Catholics Anton VODNIK and VODUŠEK in the 1920s, with KOCBEK and BALANTIČ as later representatives of the school. Expressionist elements are evident in the historical novels of PREGELJ and the drama of GRUM.

While the post-revolutionary role of Soviet Socialist Realism was to extol the virtues of the new society and its heroes, the task of Slovene social realism (1930–48) was to publicise the grievances of the rural or urban poor, particularly outside Yugoslavia (Carinthia: PREŽIHOV; Italy: BEVK, KOSMAČ) and in the regions (Gorica: BEVK; Prekmurje: KRANJEC; Tolmin: KOSMAČ). The trend was represented in poetry by SELIŠKAR, Mile Klopčič (b. 1905), GRUDEN and Ivo Brnčič (1912–43). Prose writers dealing mainly with peasant life include PREŽIHOV, KRANJEC, Anton Ingolič (b. 1907). The best work of KOSMAČ and POTRČ belongs to the postwar period. Social realism in the theatre was represented by Ferdo Kozak (1894–1957), Brnčič and POTRČ. Among the works inspired by the partisan struggle against the occupying forces most notable are the poems of BOR and DESTOVNIK and the diaries and poems of KOCBEK.

The influence of Socialist Realism, strong in the immediate postwar years, began to wane with the growing exposure to W European literary trends. In the 1950s late Expressionism and Symbolism were evident in the poetry of KOCBEK, Cene Vipotnik (1914–72) and Jože Udovič (b. 1912), the prose of Alojz Rebula (b. 1924) and Andrej Hieng (b. 1925). In the 1960s Existentialism affected the poetry of ZAJC, Gregor Strniša (b. 1930) and Veno Taufer (b. 1933), and the prose and drama of Dominik Smole (b. 1929), Peter Božič (b. 1932) and Primož Kozak (1929–81); towards the end of the 1960s new avant-garde techniques emerge in the poetry of Tomaž Šalamun (b. 1941) and the prose of Rudi Šeligo (b. 1935).

Slovene is rich in lyric and narrative folk poetry, some of this involving historical figures from the 15th century. Noteworthy themes are 'Lepa Vida' (The fair Vida), a symbol of restless yearning which has inspired a number of authors, and 'Rošlin and Verjanek', a Slovene Hamlet. The first collections are made by KORYTKO, a Polish dissident exiled in Ljubljana (Laibach), who enshrined the Slovene claim for cultural independence in his title, 'Slav songs of the Slovene nation', and Stanko Vraz (1810–51), a Styrian Slovene supporter of Croatian Illyrianism, who made no such claim.

●Articles and translations in: *Le Livre slovène* (Ljubljana, 1963-); *Slovene Studies,*

Journal of the Society for Slovene Studies (Columbia University, New York, 1979) – also
as *Papers in Slovene Studies* (1975–8).
Translations in *AMSL*; *AMYP*; *IYL*; *MPT*; *NWY*; *Parnassus*, 1957, 1965); E. W.
Underwood (Ed.), *The Slav Anthology* (Portland, Maine, 1931); I. Zorman (Ed.),
Slovene Poetry (Cleveland, 1922); *SPT*; S. Koljević (Ed.), *Yugoslav Short Stories*
(Oxford, 1966); I. Zorman, *Pesmi* (Cleveland, Ohio, 1922).
Other secondary literature: J. Pogačnik, 'Twentieth-Century Slovene Literature' in *Le
Livre slovène*, 1989, no. 1. Bibliography of translations from Slovene up to 1969 in *Le
Livre slovène*, 1971, special number; also 1970–4; 1975, nos 3–4.   HL

SORBIAN

The earliest surviving works of literature in Sorbian are 16th-century translations from German made in response to the demands of the Reformation for the
Word of God to be made accessible in the language of the people. The oldest
original composition is an Upper Sorbian poem by Jurij Ludovici (1619–73) in
praise of Michał Frencel (1628–1706), printed in Frencel's Upper Sorbian
translation of the Gospels of St Matthew and St Mark (1670). There is also a
collection of ten poems written between 1684 and 1701 by members and friends
of the Frencel family on various family occasions. An original Lower Sorbian
poem, signed with the undeciphered initials T.K., was written to celebrate the
opening of a new school in Frankfurt on the Oder in 1694 and was published that
year. 18th-century Sorbian literature consists mainly of occasional poetry,
sermons and hymns. Of particular note is the work of Michał Hilbjenc (1758–
1816), Handrij Ruška (1755–1810) and Jurij Mjeń (1727–85) in Upper Sorbian,
and of Pomagajbog Kristalub Fryco (1744–1815) in Lower Sorbian.

Secular literature expanded dramatically in the first half of the 19th century
owing to the influence of Romanticism and the growth of national consciousness. New features included closer links with the literatures of the other Slavs,
especially the Czechs, preoccupation with the national theme, and an interest
in the oral tradition. The first collections of folk-songs had been made in the
18th century, but the main thrust came only now with the appearance of two
volumes of *Volkslieder der Wenden in der Ober- und Nieder-Lausitz*,
published in Grimma in 1841 and 1843 by Leopold Haupt and J. E. Smoler
(Schmaler, 1816–84). The language of literature was also changed by the
rejection of German borrowings and their replacement with new elements from
Czech. The leading representatives of Romanticism are ZEJLER and RADYSERB-
WJELA, but a key role was also played by Jan Ernst Smoler, who, as editor and
publisher, prepared the soil in which literature could flourish. In the middle of
the century various periodicals sprang up, including *Tydźenska Nowina*
(Weekly news), *Łužičan* (The Lusatian) and *Lipa Serbska* (The Sorbian lime).
The latter two were amalgamated in 1882 as *Łužica* (Lusatia), a mainly literary
monthly. The Maćica Serbska, a learned society founded in 1845, had its own
journal, the *Časopis Maćicy Serbskeje* (from 1848), which published not only
learned but also literary works. The literary scene was always dominated by
Upper Sorbian writers, but the journals occasionally carried contributions in
Lower Sorbian. The only Lower Sorbian periodical was the weekly

Bramborski serbski casnik (Brandenburg Sorbian newspaper), in which the literary element was small.

Throughout the 19th century and well into the 20th, verse always prevailed over prose. Upper Sorbian literature was led by BART-ĆIŠINSKI and the first discussion on Sorbian versification was conducted between him and Křesćan Bohuwěr Pful in *Łužica* in 1883. The leading Lower Sorbian poet at this time was KOSYK. However, in Upper Sorbian literature at least, the importance of prose was growing. The most interesting prose writers in the 1920s and 1930s were Jakub Lorenc-Zalěski (1874–1939) and Romuald Domaška (1869–1945). Writing for the theatre was also on the increase, though theatrical performances were still entirely the work of amateurs.

There is a blank space in Sorbian literary history between the banning of Sorbian publications by the Nazis in 1937 and the appearance in 1952 of BRĚZAN's *Kak stara Jančowa z wyšnosću wojowaše* (How old Mrs Janč fought with the authorities). This was the beginning of Socialist Realism. The Sorbs were now given unprecedented opportunities to develop their literature, so long as they respected certain ideological limits. *Łužica* (suppressed in 1937) was revived as *Rozhlad* (Survey) in 1950. The establishment of the Domowina (Homeland) publishing house in 1958 made possible the publication of hundreds of Sorbian books with state subsidies. The novel, a genre unknown to Sorbian literature before 1937, made its entry in the form of Kurt Krjeńc's (1907–78) *Jan. Roman pytaceho člowjeka* (Jan. A novel of a searching man, 1955), to be followed by BRĚZAN's trilogy and further prose works of substance by Marja Kubašec (1890–1976), KOCH and others. At the same time, the state-supported, professional Sorbian theatre blossomed, while the poets, led by LORENC, demonstrated the vitality of Sorbian verse. There were, of course, qualms about the political compliance induced by state subsidies and the air was cleared when the German Democratic Republic gave up the ghost in 1990.

●Robert Elsie (Ed.), *An Anthology of Sorbian Poetry from the Sixteenth Century to the Present Day* (London, Boston, 1990).

G. Stone, *The Smallest Slavonic Nation. The Sorbs of Lusatia* (London, 1972), pp. 41–89.

GCS

UKRAINIAN

Even before the Christianisation of Kievan Rus´ (988), service books were being translated into Church Slavonic from W and S Slavic sources. During the reign of Volodymyr ([Vladimir] 978–1015) and especially that of his son Yaroslav (1019–54) much was done to spread literature translated from Byzantine sources. The oldest extant book is the *Ostromir Gospel* (1056–57) (see BIBLE), though there were many other liturgical and devotional books, translations of the lives of the saints and of sermons. Some apocrypha also circulated in Ukraine and historical works (*The Jewish Wars* of Josephus) were translated in Kiev. Much of this literature was didactic in nature, but there were also some romances and adventure stories (e.g. a version of the ALEXANDER ROMANCE).

The original literature of Kievan Rus´, written in Church Slavonic, developed slowly, based on Byzantine models, and reached its zenith in the period from the

11th to the 13th centuries. The style of this literature has been described as both simple and monumental. Perhaps the most scholarly achievement of this era is the so-called *Tale of Bygone Years*, an 11th-century chronicle by Nestor (?–1113) and several other authors, a devoutly Christian work of profound Kievan patriotism. Church oratory found its best expression in the patriotic *Slovo* of Metropolitan Hilarion, written between 1037 and 1050.

Although the old epos of the 11th century has not been preserved in Kiev, remnants of it have survived in N Russian *byliny* cycles. An epic work of great literary accomplishment, which has been preserved in a 16th-century manuscript, is the *Slovo o polku Ihorevi* (The tale of Ihor's/Igor's campaign). Sometimes incorrectly described as a political pamphlet, it excels as poetry, and has fine lyrical moments. Certainly, the intention of the author was to plead for unity among the princes and for the defence of his native land. It deals with an historical event – the unsuccessful expedition of Prince Ihor (Igor) Sviatoslavych against the Polovtsians in 1185. The ending – Ihor's escape from captivity and his return home – has an intensely dramatic quality. It is rich in symbolism and hyperbole. Many images connect the work to Ukrainian folklore. Attempts to question the authenticity of *Slovo* and to dismiss it as an 18th-century forgery have proved unsuccessful.

Among the extant original prose works, mention should be made of *Pouchenie* (Instruction) by Vladimir Monomakh (1053–1125), a description of the journey to Palestine by 'Daniel', and the juridical text of *Rus´ka Pravda* (Rus´ Law). Chronicle writing continued throughout the 13th century and later.

The decay of Kievan Rus´ and its break-up into various principalities led to the incorporation in the 14th century of most Rus´ territories into the Lithuanian-Polish Commonwealth. Culture declined. Although earlier works were re-copied, there were no outstanding writers in Ukraine at that time and only in the 16th century did new influences from the W European Renaissance reawaken literary life. Although these influences were weak, they generally diminished the Church's hold on literature. The printing of the Ostrih BIBLE in 1581 was a great scholarly achievement. The Ostrih academy was a centre of learning which also produced some important polemical literature. The most prominent polemical works were the anonymous *Perestoroha* (Warning, 1605) and the writings of Hypatius Potii (1541–1613). The most prominent Ukrainian polemicist was Ivan Vyshensky (d. 1625), a monk on Mount Athos. His language was rich and colourful, and ideologically, he was an ascetic Orthodox Christian, fiercely anti-Catholic.

The 16th century witnessed the birth of the Ukrainian folk epos – the *dumy*. These were lyrical epic songs, chanted to the accompaniment of a *kobza*, *bandura* or *lira*. Thematically they constitute two cycles: songs about Tatar and Turkish captivity and military expeditions, and songs about the Polish-Ukrainian wars. The heroes of these oral works were the Cossacks. In form, the *dumy* were akin to funeral laments. They survived into the 20th century.

Ukrainian literature achieved its flowering during the 17th and 18th centuries. The content of literary works was inclined to be more secular and the form tended to elaborate adornment. Much syllabic verse was written on both spiritual and secular themes. The short story and drama also made their appearance. The latter appeared under the influence of the Polish theatre, especially 'school theatre'. Pamva Berynda (d. 1632), Dmytro Tuptalo (1651–1709), Ioaniki Volkovych (dates unknown) and later Teofan Prokopovych (1681–1736) and Iuri Konysky (1718–95) were among the authors of the period. Comic plays, known as *intermedia*, were written, akin to the later plays of the Ukrainian folk puppet theatre, *vertep*. Sermons and theological treatises (Lazar Baranovych [1620–93], Antonii Radyvylivsky [d. 1688]) were also popular.

Historical works occupied a special place in Ukrainian Baroque literature. Among these were, above all, the so-called 'Cossack chronicles' by 'Samovydets', Hryhorii Hrabianka (d. 1737) and Samiilo Velychko (1670–1728); these chronicles were dedicated primarily to the Cossack wars of liberation against the Poles 1648–56 and expressed national pride. They are full of anecdotal and invented detail and they glorify the Cossack leaders, above all hetman Bohdan Khmelnytsky.

Hryhorii Skovoroda (1722–94) wrote philosophical treatises, dialogues and sermons. Educated at the Kiev academy and abroad, he is the best-known Ukrainian philosopher – the 'Ukrainian Socrates'. He also left a cycle of verse, *Sad bozhestvennykh pesnei* (An orchard of divine songs, 1753–85), and the Kharkiv (Kharkov) fables (1760s). His poetic works manifest lyricism and reflect his philosophy – the search for spiritual happiness; sometimes he was moved by natural beauty and influenced by folk poetry. Some of his works became popular songs. The fables were written in prose in the tradition of Aesop and La Fontaine.

Historical consciousness, which first came to the surface in the 18th century, continued to inspire Ukrainian writers. An undated work, *Istoriia Rusov* (History of the Russes) by an unknown author, published in 1846, circulated in manuscript form early in the 19th century. It is a romanticised history of the Cossacks. The father of modern Ukrainian literature, KOTLIAREVSKYI, was also attracted to Cossack history. Writing in what was close to the vernacular language, he published, in 1798, the first parts of his *Eneida* (*Aeneid*), a travesty of Virgil's poem. KOTLIAREVSKYI transcended the heroicomic structure of his neo-Classicist genre and, using a wealth of ethnographic material, depicted the heroic, patriotic Cossacks in highly individual poetic language. The prose of the neo-Classical period was represented by Hryhorii Kvitka-Osnovianenko (1778–1848). His short stories, in the sentimental tradition, are didactic, but display a good knowledge of folklore and ethnography. In his moralistic stories ('Marusia', 1833; 'Serdeshna Oksana' [Unfortunate O., 1841]) slight Romantic elements are discernible. Kvitka, like most Ukrainian writers in the early 19th century, also wrote in Russian.

Ukrainian literature did not truly blossom until Romanticism, which came late to Ukraine but its seed fell on fertile ground. The earliest Ukrainian Romantic literature arose in the so-called Kharkov (Kharkiv) School of the 1820s–30s. Its members were the scholars Izmail Sreznevskyi (1812–80) and Mykola Kostomarov (1817–85) and the poets Levko Borovykovskyi (1806–89) and Amvrosii Metlynskyi (1814–70). They wrote ballads and imitated folk and historical songs. In W Ukraine, under Austrian rule, there was the so-called 'Ruthenian Trinity', Markian Shashkevych (1811–43), Ivan Vahylevych (1811–66) and Yakiv Holovatskyi (1814–88) who in 1837 published an anthology in the Romantic tradition, *Rusalka Dnistrovaia* (The Dniester nymph).

Kiev became the centre of the Ukrainian Romantic movement in the 1840s. The leader was the poet SHEVCHENKO, regarded as the greatest Ukrainian poet of all time. His collection of poems, *Kobzar* (The minstrel, 1840), marked a new era in Ukrainian literature. SHEVCHENKO wrote other, fiercely patriotic, poems, not for publication, in the 1840s. He was arrested in 1847 and spent 10 years in exile. After his return to St Petersburg in 1857 he wrote some outstanding religious verse. His poems were sometimes akin to folk-songs, but they could also be philosophical, lyrical, and occasionally satirical. He immensely enriched the Ukrainian poetic language and secured the sense of national identity. SHEVCHENKO's friend was Panteleimon KULISH, a poet and translator, who wrote the first modern Ukrainian novel, *Chorna rada* (The Black Council, 1857). He also translated the BIBLE and many of Shakespeare's plays. It was he who discovered another talented prose writer, VOVCHOK, the author of a collection of short stories in Realist vein, *Narodni opovidannia* (Folk-tales, 1857).

The second half of the 19th century was dominated by Realism. Writers wrote a great deal about the life of the peasants. The development of literature was seriously hampered after the 1863 official circular forbidding the use of Ukrainian which, in 1876, led to a complete ban on Ukrainian publications in the Russian Empire, a condition which lasted till 1905. Most of the Ukrainian works written in the East were published in Galicia, which was under Austria-Hungary. Among the Ukrainian Realists the poets Stepan Rudanskyi (1834–73), Osyp Yurii Fedkovych (1834–88), Leonid Hlibov (1827–93) and a belated Romanic, Yakiv Shchoholiv (1824–98), have their place in literary history. Prose was represented by Anatol Svydnytskyi (1834–71), NECHUI-LEVYTS´KYI, Panas Myrnyi (1849–1920) and Borys Hrinchenko (1863–1910). The last was the author of the first comprehensive dictionary of the modern Ukrainian language (1902–9). In drama, Mykhailo Starytskyi (1840–1904) and Ivan Tobilevych (1845–1907) wrote many plays, based on folklore and history, for the popular 'ethnographic' theatre.

A giant literary figure who straddled the centuries and both Realist and Modernist trends is the Galician FRANKO. His prose is essentially in the Realist tradition, but some of his poetry – *Ziviale lystia* (Withered leaves, 1896) – leans towards the Modernist. The turn of the century witnessed the appearance of works concerned more with aesthetic values and W European influences than with traditional Realism and populism. In W Ukraine this new trend was espoused by a literary group Moloda Muza (The young muse) and in the East by writers gathered around the magazine *Ukrainska khata* (Ukrainian home, 1909–14). Outstanding representatives of Modernism in E Ukraine were UKRAINKA with her innovative poetic dramas, Oleksander Oles´ (1878–1944), a neo-Romantic poet, and KOTSIUBYN´SKYI, the author of impressionistic novels and short stories. In W Ukraine STEFANYK was a master of the Expressionist short story, and Olha Kobylianska (1865–1942) wrote novels with feminist overtones and both sentimental and realistic short stories. A very popular writer, author of novels and plays, was VYNNYCHENKO.

The 1917 Revolution became a war for national liberation in Ukraine. The establishment of the short-lived Ukrainian People's Republic (1918–19) had a strong influence on cultural life. One result was that some writers, after the Bolsheviks came to power, emigrated to the West (Oles´, VYNNYCHENKO).

The 1920s witnessed a literary renascence in Soviet Ukraine because of the relatively liberal cultural and economic policy of the Communist Party. Several literary groups sprang up – *Hart* (Tempering), *Pluh* (Plough) *Lanka* (Link) and VAPLITE (Free Academy of Proletarian Literature). Futurists (Mykhail Semenko [1892–1938]) and the Neoclassicists (ZEROV) were also active. 1925–8 a 'Literary Discussion' was held on the present and future of Ukrainian literature. The instigator was KHVYĿOVYI, a charismatic personality and talented prose writer, who later committed suicide. The leading poets of that era were TYCHYNA, RYĽS′KYI, BAZHAN, ZEROV, Volodymyr Sosiura (1898–1965) and Yevhen Pluzhnyk (1898–1936). Prose was represented by KHVYĿOVYI, Yurii Ianovskyi (1902–54) and PIDMOHYLNYI. An outstanding playwright was KULISH. With the coming to power of Joseph Stalin the Party changed its policy and began a massive purge of writers and intellectuals accused on trumped-up charges of Ukrainian nationalism. It is estimated that over 300 writers perished in the Gulag or were shot. No literature could sustain such blood-letting. Those writers who survived the purge had to join the Writers' Union and follow the dictates of Socialist Realism which denied artistic freedom. Thus, the period of Socialist Realism (1930–60) was virtually empty of works of literary merit. Hundreds of poems and works of prose extolled the building of socialism, the collectivisation of agriculture (during the period of a huge man-made famine in Ukraine's villages) and the emergence of the 'new Soviet man'. They are a fit subject of study for a sociologist, not a literary historian. Among Socialist Realists who showed some literary talent were the poet and novelist Leonid Pervomaiskyi (1908–73), the poet Andrii Malyshko (1912–70) and the dramatists KORNIYCHUK and Ivan Kocherha (1885–1952). TYCHYNA, RYĽS′KYI and BAZHAN, who escaped the purges, became faithful followers of the Party line.

The 1960s brought some relaxation of Party controls and a new creative vigour. This was heralded by the publication, in 1957, of a lyrical autobio-graphical novel *Zacharovana Desna.* (The enchanted D.) by the film producer Oleksander Dovzhenko (1894–1956). He also left a revealing war diary, first published in full in 1990. A younger generation of poets, called *shestydesiatnyky* (the Sixtiesers) came to the fore: Vasyl Symonenko (1935–63), DRACH, KOSTENKO and the short-story writer Yevhen Hutsalo (b. 1937). They rediscovered the function of poetry and an unprogrammatic prose. At about the same time some writers, in *samizdat* editions, defended human rights and national aspirations. Some promising young poets (Ihor Kalynets [b. 1939]) were arrested. A poet of great originality, Vassyl′ Stus (1938–85) died in a camp. Fortunately, after a wave of terror in the 1970s, a return to Stalinism proved impossible. Socialist Realism slowly disintegrated (HONCHAR's novel *Sobor* [The cathedral, 1968]) and during Brezhnev's 'era of stagnation' innovative writers appeared (Hryhir Tiutiunnyk [1931–80], Pavlo Zahrebelnyi [b. 1924], Volodymyr Drozd [b. 1939], SHEVCHUK).

Mikhail Gorbachev's greatest contribution to literature was *glasnost*. In Ukraine, after 1985, this led to the full rehabilitation and republication of writers destroyed in the purges. The political turmoil of 1989–91 was not conducive to literary creation. Many writers forsook writing for political activity. For example, DRACH became the leader of RUKH, a democratic nationalist movement. Yet the new freedom also spawned many new poets and stimulated literary scholarship now free from political strictures.

Mention must be made of Ukrainian literature produced outside the borders of what was Soviet Ukraine. This, primarily, includes writers in W Ukraine (under Poland 1919–39) and in exile. Among them were two outstanding poets – the Lwów Imagist Bohdan Ihor Antonych (1909–37) and the émigré Yevhen Malaniuk (1897–1968) who lived in Warsaw and Prague, the haven of many Ukrainian writers. A Realist novelist was Ulas Samchuk (1905–88). Another corner in Europe where for some time (1960–70) Ukrainian literature flourished was E Slovakia. Immediately after WWII many Ukrainian writers found themselves as refugees in DP camps in W Europe where they organised the MUR (Ukrainian Artistic Movement). Later most of them emigrated to N America, where they continued writing. Some young poets in the USA formed the New York Group.

Independent Ukraine, which finally emerged in 1991, recognised all past and present writers in exile and the diaspora as part of the Ukrainian patrimony. Today their works are being published in Kiev.

●D. Čyževskyj, *A History of Ukrainian Literature (From the 11th to the End of the 19th Century)* (Littleton, Calif., 1975); G. Grabowicz, *Toward a History of Ukrainian Literature* (Cambridge, Mass., 1981); G. Luckyj, *Ukrainian Literature in the Twentieth Century: A Reader's Guide* (Toronto, 1992); B. Rubchak (Ed.), *Studies in Ukrainian Literature* (New York [*Annals of the Ukrainian Academy in the U.S.* XVI], 1984–5).

GSNL

YIDDISH

Though in the 19th and 20th centuries Yiddish literature flourished primarily in E Europe, its roots lie in Germany and Italy. The language itself originated in the 10th century as the result of the migration into Bavaria of Jews coming mostly from Italy and the Balkans. From the outset their complex linguistic heritage and distinct settlement and migrational patterns (in addition to the use of the Hebrew alphabet) differentiated the Middle High German they adopted vis-à-vis the speech of the ambient population. The exodus of the majority of Ashkenazi Jews into E Europe that took place from the 13th century onwards and the fact that New High German was subsequently standardised on Central German norms reinforced the divergence between the two languages. Yiddish glosses are found in Hebrew MSS from the 12th century. A complete Yiddish sentence inscribed in a Hebrew prayer-book has survived from 1272. The earliest substantial texts (1382) were discovered in the Cairo Genizah. The early literature is primarily devotional in character. Translations and paraphrases of the BIBLE predominate. In N Italy, however, which absorbed significant numbers of Ashkenazi immigrants between the 14th and 17th centuries, conditions favoured cultural exchange and led to the brief burgeoning of a sophisticated secular literature whose preeminent exponent was ELYE BOKHER, the author of the famous *Bove-bukh* (Bevis-book, Venice, 1541). The liberating spirit of the Italian Renaissance is similarly evident in the anonymous *Pariz un viene* (Paris and Vienna, Verona,

1594) and *Ku-bukh* (Cow-book, Verona, 1595). North of the Alps the avowed aim of authors and publishers was not infrequently to wean readers from licentious tales like the *Ku-bukh* with more edifying material such as *Eyn sheyn mayse-bukh* (A beautiful story-book, Basle, 1602). In the 17th century Holland also became a Yiddish-speaking centre. In Amsterdam the first complete translations of the Hebrew Scriptures were made under the influence of Luther and the Dutch *Staatenvertaling* and the first Yiddish newspaper appeared in 1686. The century of conflict between the Haskalah and Ḥasidism that began in the 1770s revitalised the development of Yiddish literature. On the one hand the pietistic enthusiasm generated by Ḥasidism liberated the imagination and paved the way for the quasi-Romantic tales of Rabbi Nakhmen (1772–1811). On the other hand the Haskalah, which had grown from the German *Aufklärung* and had brought about the demise of Yiddish in Germany, had the paradoxical effect of stimulating Yiddish writing in E Europe, since in a Slav environment it was only through the medium of Yiddish that it was possible for the Haskalah to accomplish its educative mission. A series of Maskilic writers subjected Ḥasidism to scathing satire, among them Menakhem-Mendl Lefin (1749–1826), who was the first to employ the contemporary E Yiddish language, ETINGER and GOTLOBER. Modern Yiddish literature came of age when the artistic resources developed by the Maskilim became an end in themselves in the works of MENDELE MOYKHER SFORIM. The pogroms that followed the assassination of Alexander II brought about a transformation of Jewish sensibility and an increasing need for alternatives to dependence on an obsolete religious culture on the one hand and facile assimilationism on the other. SHOLEM ALEYKHEM and PERETS created an autonomous Yiddish literature that aspired to match the highest standards in 'European' writing. After WWI, during which these three classical writers all died, a new generation of writers sprang up, not only in the USSR and Poland but also among the millions of Jews who had sought refuge in the USA. In Kiev, Minsk, Warsaw, Vilnius, New York and other centres Modernist movements reacted to the latest developments in Russian, German, French and English literature. Despite the severe constraints of Soviet cultural directives, BERGLSON, DER NISTER, Moyshe Kulbak (1896–1940) and MARKISH succeeded in creating masterpieces of Yiddish prose and poetry before falling victim to Stalin. Uri-Tsvi Grinberg (1894–1981), SUTSKEVER, Y.-Y. ZINGER and his younger brother, BASHEVIS produced varied, often startlingly innovative work in Poland before migrating to the USA or Israel, while in New York the poets of the Introspectivist school, such as LEYELES and GLATSHTEYN, while employing Yiddish as their medium, made a major contribution to modern American literature. After the 'Holocaust' the predominant sentiments reflected in the work of the surviving authors were grief for the destruction of a language and its culture.

●K. Shmeruk, in *Encyclopaedia Judaica*, vol. 16 (Jerusalem, 1971), cols 798–833; B. Harshav, *The Meaning of Yiddish* (Berkeley, Los Angeles, Oxford, 1990); Zinberg, *History of Jewish Literature*, vols 7–12 (Cincinnati, New York, 1975–8); Madison; Miron; Liptzin (1963, 1970, 1972); Wiener; A. Abramovitch, *Yiddish Literature in English Translation, Books Published 1945–67* (New York, 1968[2]); *Yiddish Literature in English Translation, List of Books in Print* (New York, 1976).

Note: The transcription of Yiddish is a vexed question. The practice adopted here is to apply throughout the romanisation-system recommended by the Yidisher Visnshaftlekher Institut or YIVO Institute for Jewish Research (New York). This is the system with the widest currency in academic publications and gives an unambiguous representation of the standard pronunciation. However, in the case of authors' names, where non-standard spellings have become established, they are also cited at the head of each article and appropriately cross-referenced in the index. For a more detailed discussion of the issues involved see: L. Prager, *Yiddish Literary and Linguistic Periodicals and Miscellanies, A Selective Annotated Bibliography* (Darby, Penn., Haifa, 1982), pp. 21–4.　　　　　　　　　　　　　　　　　　　　　　　　　　HD

Index A: Listed authors according to language

Albanian
Agolli, Dritëro (born 1931)
Arapi, Fatos (born 1930)
Asdreni (1872–1947)
Bardhi, Frang (1606–43)
Barleti, Marin (c.1450–c.1512)
Bogdani, Pjetër (c.1625–89)
Budi, Pjetër (1566–1623)
Bulka, Nonda (1906–72)
Buzuku, Gjon (16th century)
Çajupi, Andon Zako (1866–1930)
Dara, Gavril, the Younger (1826–85)
De Rada, Jeronim (1814–1903)
Fishta, Gjergj (1871–1940)
Frakulla, Nezim (c.1680–1760)
Frashëri, Naim (1846–1900)
Frashëri, Sami (1850–1904)
Gjata, Fatmir (1922–90)
Grameno, Mihal (1872–1931)
Gurakuqi, Luigi (1879–1925)
Gurra, Milto Sotir (1884–1972)
Hoxha, Enver (1908–85)
Hoxhi, Koto (1824–95)
Jakova, Kolë (born 1916)
Jubani, Zef (1818–80)
Kadare, Ismail (born 1936)
Kamberi, Hasan Zyko (18th–19th century)
Kandreva, Karmel (1931–82)
Kelmendi, Ramiz (born 1930)
Koliqi, Ernest (1903–75)
Konica, Faik (1875–1942)
Krasniqi, Mark (born 1920)
Kristoforidhi, Konstandin Nelko (1827–95)
Kullurioti, Anastas (1822–87)
Kuteli, Mitrush (1907–67)
Kyçyku, Muhamet (1784–1844)
Lako, Natasha (born 1948)
Lera, Nasi (born 1944)
Matrenga, Lekë (1567–1619)

Mekuli, Esad (born 1916)
Migjeni (1911–38)
Mitko, Thimi (1820–90)
Mjeda, Ndre (1866–1937)
Musaraj, Shefqet (1914–86)
Noli, Fan Stilian (1882–1965)
Perone, Lluka (born 1920)
Podrimja, Ali (born 1942)
Poradeci, Lasgush (1899–1985)
Postoli, Foqion (1889–1927)
Santori, Françesk Anton (1819–94)
Schiro di Maggio, Giuseppe (born 1944)
Serembe, Zef (1843–1901)
Shkreli, Azem (born 1938)
Shkreli, Ymer (born 1945)
Solano, Francesco (born 1914)
Spahiu, Xhevahir (born 1945)
Spasse, Sterjo (1914–89)
Stërmilli, Haki (1895–1953)
Sulejmani, Hivzi (1912–75)
Ujko, Vorea (born 1918)
Variboba, Jul (1724–c.88)
Vasa, Pashko (1825–92)
Veqilharxhi, Naum (1797–1846)
Vreto, Jani (1822–1900)
Xoxa, Jakov (1923–79)

Armenian
Abovyan, Khatchatour (1809–?48)
Agat'angełos (5th century?)
Bakounts, Ak'sel (1899–1936)
Dzerents (1822–88)
Eghishe, Vardapet (c.410–70/75)
Eznik Koghbatsi (c.390–455)
Grigor Narekatsi (915–1003)
Koriwn, Vardapet (4th–5th centuries)
Mahari, Gourgen (1903–69)
Movses Khorenatsi (390–450)
Nersēs IV Klayets'i, Shnorhali (1102–73)

Bulgarian

Byelorussian

Croatian (including Dalmatian)

Ujević, Augustin-Tin (1891–1955)
Vetranović, Mavro (1482–1576)
Vidrić, Vladimir (1875–1909)
Vojnović, Ivo (1857–1929)
Vraz, Stanko (1810–51)
Zoranić, Petar (1508–before 1569)

Czech

Arbes, Jakub (1840–1914)
Bednář, Kamil (1912–72)
Benešová, Božena (1873–1936)
Bezruč, Petr (1867–1958)
Blatný, Ivan (1919–90)
Blatný, Lev (1894–1930)
Bozděch, Emanuel (1841–c.90)
Březina, Otokar (1868–1929)
Bridel, Bedřich (1619–80)
Čapek, Karel (1890–1938)
Čapek Chod, Karel Matěj (1860–1927)
Čech, Svatopluk (1846–1908)
Čelakovský, František Ladislav (1799–
   1852)
Chelčický, Petr (c.1390–c.1460)
Dačický z Heslova, Mikuláš (1555–1629)
'Dalimil', (? – soon after 1314)
Deml, Jakub (1878–1961)
Drda, Jan (1915–70)
Durych, Jaroslav (1886–1962)
Dušek, Václav (born 1944)
Dyk, Viktor (1877–1931)
Erben, Karel Jaromír (1811–70)
Flaška z Pardubic a Rychmburku, Smil
   (1340s–1403)
Fried, Jiří (born 1923)
Fuks, Ladislav (born 1923)
Hájek z Libočan, Václav (died 1553)
Halas, František (1901–49)
Hašek, Jaroslav (1883–1923)
Havel, Václav (born 1936)
Havlíček Borovsky, Karel (1821–56)
Herrmann, Ignát (1854–1935)
Hilbert, Jaroslav (1871–1936)
Hlaváček, Karel (1874–98)
Hodrová, Daniela (born 1946)
Holan, Vladimír (1905–80)
Holub, Miroslav (born 1923)
Hora, Josef (1891–1945)
Hostovský, Egon (1908–73)
Hrabal, Bohumil (born 1914)
Jelínek, Ivan (born 1909)
Jirásek, Alois (1851–1930)
Jungmann, Josef (1773–1847)

Kabátník, Martin (died 1503)
Karásek ze Lvovic, Jiří (1871–1951)
Klicpera, Václav Kliment (1792–1859)
Klíma, Ladislav (1878–1928)
Kohout, Pavel (born 1928)
Kollár, Jan (1793–1852)
Komenský, Jan Amos (1592–1670)
Kundera, Milan (born 1929)
Langer, František (1888–1965)
Lomnický z Budče, Šimon (1552–?1623)
Mácha, Karel Hynek (1810–36)
Machar, Josef Svatopluk (1864–1942)
Majerová, Marie (1882–1967)
Mrštík, Vilém (1863–1912)
Mucha, Jiří (1915–91)
Němcová, Božena (1820–62)
Němec, Ludvík (born 1957)
Neruda, Jan (1834–91)
Neumann, Stanislav Kostka (1875–1947)
Nezval, Vítězslav (1900–58)
Olbracht, Ivan (1882–1952)
Orten, Jiří (1918–41)
Otčenášek, Jan (1924–79)
Páral, Vladimír (born 1932)
z Poděbrad, Hynek (1452–92)
Prefát z Vlkanova, Oldřich (1523–65)
Preissová, Gabriela (1862–1946)
Pulkava z Radenína, Přibík (died 1380)
Řezáč, Václav (1901–56)
Rosa, Václav Jan (c.1620–89)
Rvačovský z Rvačova, Vavřinec Leander
   (1525–after 1590)
Seifert, Jaroslav (1901–86)
Škvorecký, Josef (born 1924)
Sládek, Josef Václav (1845–1912)
Šlejhar, Josef Karel (1864–1914)
Šotola, Jiří (1924–89)
Sova, Antonín (1864–1928)
Šrámek, Fráňa (1877–1952)
Štítný ze Štítného, Tomáš (c.1333–
   c.1405)
Světlá, Karolína (1830–99)
Topol, Josef (born 1935)
Tovačovský z Cimburka, Ctibor
   (c.1437–94)
Tyl, Josef Kajetán (1808–56)
Urbánek, Zdeněk (born 1917)
Vaculík, Ludvík (born 1926)
Vančura, Vladislav (1891–1942)
Vratislav z Mitrovic, Václav (1576–1635)
Vrchlický, Jaroslav (1853–1912)
Vyskočil, Ivan (born 1929)
Weiner, Richard (1884–1937)

Hungarian

Roumanian

Serbian

Stritar, Josip (1836–1923)
Svetokriški, Janez (1647–1714)
Tavčar, Ivan (1851–1923)
Trubar, Primož (1508–86)
Valvasor, Janez Vajkard (1641–93)
Vodnik, Anton (1901–65)
Vodnik, Valentin (1758–1819)
Vodušek, Božo (1905–78)
Zajc, Dane (born 1929)
Zlobec, Ciril (born 1925)
Zupan, Vitomil (1914–87)
Župančič, Oton (1878–1949)

Sorbian
Bart-Ćišinski, Jakub (1856–1909)
Brězan, Jurij (born 1916)
Dyrlich, Benedikt (born 1950)
Koch, Jurij (born 1936)
Kosyk, Mato (1853–1940)
Lorenc, Kito (born 1938)
Radyserb-Wjela, Jan (1822–1907)
Stempel, Kito Fryco (1787–1867)
Zejler, Handrij (1804–72)

Ukrainian
Bazhan, Mykola (1904–83)
Drach, Ivan (born 1936)
Franko, Ivan (1856–1916)
Honchar, Oles (born 1918)
Khvyl´ovyi, Mykola (1893–1933)
Korniychuk, Oleksander (1905–72)
Kostenko, Lina (born 1930)
Kotliarevskyi, Ivan (1769–1838)
Kotsiubyn´skyi, Mykhailo (1864–1913)
Kulish, Mykola (1892–1937)
Kulish, Panteleimon (1819–97)
Nechui-Levyts´kyi, Ivan (1838–1918)
Pidmohylny, Valerian (1901–37)
Ryl´s´kyi, Maksym (1895–1964)
Shevchenko, Taras (1814–61)
Shevchuk, Valerii (born 1939)

Stefanyk, Vassyl (1871–1936)
Tychyna, Pavlo (1891–1967)
Ukrainka, Lesya (1871–1913)
Vovchok, Marko (1834–1907)
Vynnychenko, Volodymyr (1880–1951)
Zerov, Mykola (1890–1937)

Yiddish
An-ski [Shloyme Zaynv Rapoport]
   (1863–1920)
Ash, Sholem (1880–1957)
Bashevis, Yitskhok [Yitskhok Bashevis
   Zinger] (1904–91)
Berglson, Dovid (1884–1952)
Der Nister [Pinkhes Kahanovitsh]
   (1884–1950)
Dik, Yitskhok Meyer (1814–93)
Elye Bokher [Levita] (1468/9–1549)
Etinger, Shloyme (1803–56)
Glatshteyn, Yankev (1896–1971)
Glikl, Haml (1645–1724)
Goldfadn, Avrom (1840–1908)
Gordin, Yankev (1853–1909)
Gotlober, Avrom-Ber (1811–99)
Halpern, Moyshe-Leyb (1886–1932)
Leyeles/Glants-Leyeles, Arn [Arn
   Glants] (1889–1966)
Leyvik, H. [Leyvik Halpern] (1886–
   1962)
Linetski, Yitskhok-Yoyl (1839–1915)
Manger, Itsik (1901–69)
Mani-Leyb [Mani-Leyb Brahinski]
   (1884–1953)
Markish, Perets (1895–1952)
Mendele Moykher Sforim [Sholem
   Yankev Abramovitsh] (1835–1917)
Perets, Yitkokh-Leyb (1851–1915)
Sholem Aleykhem [Sholem Rabinovitsh]
   (1859–1916)
Sutskever, Avrom (born 1913)
Zinger, Yisroel-Yeshue (1893–1944)

Index B: Anonymous, collective and oral-tradition works

Index C: General Index, including cross-references

Note: References to names of nationalities and countries/linguistic areas are normally listed only for articles which do not concern writers of the given nationality. Names in SMALL CAPITALS *indicate that the writer has his or her own entry in the Companion.*